Literary Exile
in the
Twentieth Century

Literary Exile in the Twentieth Century

AN ANALYSIS AND BIOGRAPHICAL DICTIONARY

Edited by
Martin Tucker

Greenwood Press

NEW YORK • WESTPORT, CONNECTICUT • LONDON

Library of Congress Cataloging-in-Publication Data

Literary exile in the twentieth century : an analysis and biographical
  dictionary / edited by Martin Tucker.
     p.   cm.
  Includes bibliographical references (p.   ).
  ISBN 0-313-23870-7 (lib. bdg. : alk. paper)
    1. Authors, Exiled—20th century—Biography—Dictionaries. 2. Literature,
Modern—20th century—History and criticism. 3. Exiles' writings—
History and criticism.   I. Tucker, Martin.
PN495.L43 1991
809'.8920694—dc20   89-25920

British Library Cataloguing in Publication Data is available.

Library of Congress Catalog Card Number: 89-25920
ISBN: 0-313-23870-7

First published in 1991

Greenwood Press, 88 Post Road West, Westport, CT 06881
An imprint of Greenwood Publishing Group, Inc.

Printed in the United States of America

∞™

The paper used in this book complies with the
Permanent Paper Standard issued by the National
Information Standards Organization (Z39.48-1984).

10 9 8 7 6 5 4 3 2 1

Copyright Acknowledgments

Grateful acknowledgment is given for permission to publish:

Excerpts from the Introduction by Salman Rushdie to *On Writing and Politics 1967–1983* by Gunter
Grass, copyright © 1984 by Hermann Luchterhand Verlag GmbH & Co., English translation copyright
© 1985 by Harcourt Brace Jovanovich, Inc., reprinted by permission of Harcourt Brace Jovanovich,
Inc.

From KNOCKING ON THE DOOR by Alan Paton. Copyright © 1975 Alan Paton. Reprinted with
permission of Charles Scribner's Sons, an imprint of Macmillan Publishing Company.

Excerpts from MANICHEAN AESTHETICS: THE POLITICS OF LITERATURE IN COLONIAL
AFRICA by JanMohamed (Amherst: University of Massachusetts Press, 1983), copyright © 1983
by The University of Massachusetts Press.

Contents

Preface

This encyclopedia is an attempt to provide both a general survey of the field of literary exile and detailed analytic entries on representative writers of exile from different parts of the world. It includes writers who have suffered the experience of banishment, deportation, voluntary departure (with varying degrees of hope and/or expectation of return), flight from possible imprisonment, harassment or torture, or flight from incarceration for reasons of expression of belief, and, in a few selected cases, writers who reflect a profound state of psychic exile that permeates their consciousness and brings to their work a characteristic tenor or recognizable portrait of attributes that may be distinguished as part of the gallery of literary exilic behavior. With nine exceptions, this encyclopedia does not contain entries on writers who have not yet left their native lands even though they may have suffered the pain and afflictions of imprisonment for the crime of writing the way they write and/or censorship of their work. Such writers, sometimes called dissidents, subversives, or revolutionaries, or in some bureaucratic ledgers notated as criminals, are not included here for reasons, unhappily, of space. A separate volume, or volumes, of this history would be needed to record this variant condition of repression and the writers' fight against its bureaucratic fevers. The few exceptions included in this volume, most centered in Italy during the Fascist/World War II period, represent an exile for those writers transported from one area of their native land (north or south) to another who experience a distinct feeling of banishment—akin to that of Dante or Ovid—to the strange wilderness of foreign custom. The exception of the Italian examples may be seen in a comparison with the more invidious condition of Soviet Russia at various periods of its history: Siberia is not a new country but hovers in the writer's consciousness as the ground of ice on which an artist skates his individual figure and which can claim him with a slip of his glittering blade.

The wilderness of Siberia, in spirit if not also in literal summary, is a part of the Soviet homeland as much as the thronging onion bells of Moscow or the wide boulevards marbleized above Leningrad's Neva River. As in parallel countries in the West, in Africa, in South America, and in Asia, exile to Siberia becomes not a strange confinement but a familiar room in a soundly locked house for those who refuse to change their vowels.

Originally this study was to be a comprehensive survey of modern writers in exile—that is, of those writers who suffered the experience of exile and its corresponding impact on their work. Writers who returned to their native lands were still considered part of this world in exile, following the assumption that exile does not disappear with geography: memory persists in the psychic sphere. Comprehensive, as used today, indicates fullness, completeness. It soon became apparent that a comprehensive study would prove, literally, too voluminous for viability in the academic and critical world. Although a Germanic scholar of the old school might, after a lifetime, be able to put a figure on the number of writers in exile around the world and to produce an encyclopedia of their work and critical sources on them, the wait seemed a heavy price to pay for a crop that was maturing in the awareness of its observers. The resulting compendium, completed over a period of some seven years, is a representative survey of the modern writer in exile, with some 550 entries. Even given this compromise of approach, some omissions will inevitably be discovered for which the editor apologizes.

Full entries have been provided for those writers whose work has received both wide acceptance and high critical evaluation. The length of these full entries—many written by esteemed critics in specialized fields—varies not so much out of judgment of literary stature as out of the need to reflect a balance of exilic forms and types. The primary editorial decision to reflect the variety of exile in the modern age is the key factor for length of representation. Some entries—notably the ones on Samuel Beckett, Joseph Conrad, Thomas Mann, Czeslaw Miłosz, Robert Musil, Joseph Roth, I. B. Singer, and Elie Wiesel— are unusually long because they deal in depth with the issues of the writer's milieu as well as with his biography and work. Other significant writers involved in these same milieus are treated more briefly (compare, for example, I. J. Singer and Walter Benjamin). Cross-references are provided to these and other exemplary cases to suggest further related study. Particularly in cases of writers who have suffered exile as a result of the Holocaust, the length of entries varies: Hannah Arendt is covered in depth; other writers are treated more cursorily; still others are only listed. Names of writers in entries followed by asterisks denote that full entries have been devoted to those writers elsewhere in this work.

In order to provide *perspective* on *kinds* of exile without judgment on the *kind*, several full entries of minor writers may be found that explore a special kind of exile. The reader will also find ''group'' entries summarizing an exile endemic to a whole society or group within a larger frame (e.g., Iranian Writers in Exile, Gay and Lesbian Writers, Armenian Writers, Holocaust Writers). In some cases writers surveyed in these group entries do not receive individual entry attention, although their stature may entitle them to such a distinction. In sum, not every entry is cast in the same mold, since each life and work surveyed is variegated in historic time and circumstance of exile and personal being.

Three giants of modern literature in English prove how difficult it is to find a coherence of definition of exile. I am thinking of Henry James, T. S. Eliot, and W. H. Auden. Two of these writers left their native land and became naturalized British citizens; the other deserted England for American naturalization. Eliot and James have never been viewed as exiles; rarely have they been considered immigrant or emigrant writers. Yet they forsook one land for another, with the difference that they seemed to have no agony or qualms about their decision. In the case of James and Eliot, they seemed to the manner born of England, not made or remade by experience. Their decisions are parallel to Eliot's reminder that he was born "middle-aged." In a similar fashion Eliot and James were born English and simply changed their identity papers as confirmation of the fact. (James, it may be argued, did experience some anguish over his disaffiliation; at least he never forsook ambiguous Americans in his cast of characters.) Auden's case is different. His departure from England in 1939 was both accidental and deliberate, and still remains of questionable intent. In the years after his arrival in the United States he became such a familiar figure as poetry reader, lecturer, and literary statesman that he loomed above national consignment. Auden did write poetry and prose about psychic loneliness, and it may be argued that the journey of overcoming—whether it be the obstacle/burden of physical pain or spiritual anomie—was the centerpoint of his being as poet and visionary. Yet Auden never felt such loss as a term of exile. His way of traveling "without maps" brought him above boundaries of geography; his world was beyond even internationalism: he wrote out of a sui generis view that was timeless in expression and of its time in character. For these reasons, James, Eliot, and Auden are listed in the alphabetical entries, but the focus in such entries is on biography and bibliography.

Two exceptions to the general rule of one-writer-one-entry are those of Samuel Beckett and Else Lasker-Schüler. Beckett is given extensive treatment in this work because he is, in the view of the editor, the outstanding specimen of modern exile in its psychic essence. It may be argued that others can claim this fame. Certainly Beckett's first master, James Joyce (for whom Beckett was an amanuensis in Beckett's young manhood), may in some critics' eyes deserve the crown (or thorns). The editor chose Beckett as the most exceptional (or, paradoxically, characteristic) figure of the modern era because Joyce's experience as swimmer in the stream of literary awakening is more role model than colleague, whereas Beckett, with his double voluntary exile from his native land and from his first tongue, and in his later work almost another voluntary exile from language itself, becomes an exemplary figure of the isolate commentator. Else Lasker-Schüler, a relatively unsung heroine these days, also receives two entries because of widely differing critical views of her work and her poses of artistry.

Readers may also notice that addenda are provided by the editor for several writers whose later works appeared after the original entry on them was completed by a distinguished specialist. In one case, James Joyce's last work *Finnegans Wake*, which this editor sees as an exemplar fini of self-exile, is given special treatment in addition to the comprehensive consideration of Joyce's exile by the critic Katherine Hill-Miller.

Generally, emphasis is given to work from the author's exile period and after, if he or she has returned to the home country. However, reference is made to the writer's corpus and to nonexilic work whenever relevant to an understanding of the writer's sentence of exile. In general, titles of works are given in English, particularly if the work was written in an alphabet different from the Latin or Germanic. In general, the date of publication is given for the first and/or original version of the work and for both if the dates of the first edition and the original-language versions differ. The date of publication for the first English edition is usually supplied. If no English-language edition has appeared, the original-language title is usually given with a translated title in parentheses. When a title in parentheses is italicized, it signifies publication in English; when it appears unitalicized, it signifies merely the English translation of the original-language title. Place of publication is assumed to be the United States unless otherwise noted. In a few cases, the city and/or state location in the United States is given of difficult-to-find small presses or foreign-language publishing houses.

Additional titles are listed at the end of each entry. This unit entitled "Selected Titles" lists *only* works not discussed in the entry proper; it does not duplicate reference to works already listed. Following the selected titles (of additional work by the author) is a bibliographic unit of critical source material on the writer. This reference list is entitled "Consult." It includes English-language critical sources wherever possible, and on occasion criticism by the writer's colleagues in his or her native language (in translation) and by foreigners (in translation).

All unsigned entries and commentary are the work of the editor, who bears responsibility for them. Unsigned updates or addenda to a signed entry are also the work of the editor, and any interpretation offered in such material is that of the editor. Some entries written by the editor are occasionally signed. Such a procedure is used whenever there may be possible confusion about the author of the entry, as in the cowritten entries.

In ending this preface, I should like to emphasize what I and the many distinguished contributors began with as the focal point of our journey to knowledge and awareness of exile. In essence, this study is an exploration of the varieties of exilic experience. The parameters of such experience are fluid and must, by nature, remain so. But certain guideposts, more in the form of questions and questing insight, provide markers of direction. The distinctions between exile, expatriatism, émigré, emigration-immigration, and social outlawry are clear in outline and in analytic terminology; they are rarely absolute in the experience of them. The presence of the exilic spirit may be detected by any number of emotional and psychic characteristics; its absence may be felt (if absence is recognized as a force of presence) either in a successful assimilation in which conception of alien distinctions no longer procreates or in a consciousness of distinctions within units, a compound of identities in which divisive complexes no longer are to be gleaned. The most singular definition of exile, then, is that it is a plurality of referents.

Perhaps we may end with a series of minor questions. Is the term *writer in exile* to be applied only to a writer who has died in a state of exile or who is living in such a state when the reference to him or her is made? Similarly, as if this were a Beckettoquiz, how long does one have to be in exile to be in exile? Can the American Indian or native American writer be said to be in a state of exile since he can rarely publish in his original language? Do expatriates truly belong in the same place, the same book, as the exile who has suffered so much more greatly and deeply? Is someone like Hans Koning (originally Hans Koningsberger) an exile, or a double exile? Koning left Holland to become an underground fighter in World War II; he departed for the United States after the war and became an American citizen. After 1968 he roamed the world in a kind of wandering protest against America's involvement in the Vietnam War. His sense of alienation, his emotional dislocation, and his constant shuffling of physical and emotional residences signify an abiding *exilism*, though never has he been forced into any banishment from the promised land of his intellectual construct. To take another example from the expatriate unfolding: how is the viewer to view Anthony Kerrigan, an American citizen now returned to the United States and an ardent supporter of its democratic procedures, but for many years a defiant protester of American foreign policy toward Cuba and Vietnam, and a strong supporter of petitionary condemnation of the then-current State Department policy? Kerrigan has said he is more in tune with the different drumming of the "outsider" than with any other grouping. Or Jerzy Kosinski, now also an American citizen and a writer who no longer draws on his experiences of exile in writing his novels? Kosinski is a satirist of American manners, but no longer from the point of view of a foreign observer. He writes as part of the family of writer-satirists zeroing in on their familiar targets. Even given the allowance of expatriation into the field of exile, should writers who left their country when they were still children, or before they begin professional writing careers, be considered in this volume? Should such writers properly be in a separate inclusion of immigrant authors? Among such World War II–Holocaust writers who only became writers later may be placed George Steiner, John Simon, Walter Abish, and Lore Segal. In this volume entries are made for Abish, Segal, and Steiner, who constitute a form of exilic identity; an entry is also provided that facilitated the project. Among the many students I thank are Harriet Greenbaum (in the early stages of the project), Francesco Cesari and Marinia Galinakis. Institutions were helpful and provided inestimable for John Simon, even though he has lived in the United States for most of his life. Such a range of examples shows the variety and complexity from which exile begins and moves and begins anew.

In dealing with this wide range and variety of exilic experience I do not wish to equate the experience of exile that victims of genocide and/or political torture have known to those of lesser forms of horror, nor do I wish to trivialize exile into a blanket expression covering alienation and all its angsts. All pain is pain—the knowledge of its many and constituent streams makes for clearer distinction and for the possibility of healing the wounds stirring from such knowledge.

Finally I should like to express my gratitude and acknowledgment to the many people and institutions who have made the completion of this project possible. First I should like to thank my publisher, Robert Hagelstein, who, from the start of this project, showed unwavering faith in its completion in spite of many delays, and my diligent, supportive editors, Marilyn Brownstein and Lynn Flint, who made many profoundly useful suggestions. Three colleagues who not only wrote entries but conferred with me at various stages of the project, Clara Györgyey, Edmund Miller, and Paul Schlueter, were instrumental in finding some of our other distinguished specialist-contributors. I wish to thank Jan Culik for providing additional information on Arnost Lustig and Anthony Kerrigan for information on several Cuban writers in exile, and *Index on Censorship* for information on Nizar Qabbani. Other colleagues who gave support and suggestion include Marek Kadzierski, Helmut Pfanner, Don Shojai, Elizabeth Paterson, D. H. Melhem, Henrik Eger, Christine Friedlander, Jeanne Welcher Kleinfield, Cynthia Newby Luce, Suzanne Jill Levine, Richard Bjornson, and Lee Mhatre. Graduate students often provided clerical assistance that facilitated the project. Among the many students I thank are Harriet Greenbaum (in the early stages of the project), Francesco Cesari and Marinia Galinakis. Institutions were helpful and provided inestimable services, among them The New York Public Library, New York University, Long Island University, PEN American Center, PEN International, the Writers in Exile chapter of PEN in the United States, and the British Museum. Finally I should like to express my gratitude to the C. W. Post (Long Island University) Research Committee, which provided concrete support in the form of released time grants.

Many scholars who made this book possible through their published work and findings are listed in the General Bibliography at the end of this work. I thank all of them for their inspiration and knowledge.

Introduction

Because the awareness of exile has recently grown to such an extent—witnessed by the many studies of it published in the past fifty years and by university courses specifically centered on the definition and experience of exile—the term has become a generalized one. Exile as a concept and as an experience is never vague, but it is a complex of emotional reactions and residues of feelings. Its complex nature, based on a simple fact of rejection or isolation, has caused sympathetic observers and speculative commentators to apply its characteristics in varying ways and means. It is best, at this point, to go beyond the beginning to define terms.

Exile is not a new phenomenon: it is as old as the first home one has left in the prime of consciousness. Its growing incidence, and the psychic states attendant upon the awareness of the loss it renders, is, however, a contemporary phenomenon. Exile, or the consciousness of it, has become a dominant part of the modern age and in some cases has acted as a nurturing stimulus to creative expression of its impact.

Historically, exile has always been awesome, drawing on mythic sources to sustain its power, whether those powers stem from religious, psychological, geographic, political, or social and communal pressures. By its nature exile posits the awareness of loss. In this volume psychic loss as exemplified in works of literature generated either by forced or voluntary physical separation is considered the basic content of exile. But as in all vital content, the experience of it is rendered in different forms and produced by different agents in different fashion. Exile is invidious, but the stages of its mutabilities are protean.

In the past the use of the word *exile* was generally restricted to the incidence of forced physical separation, to a decree of banishment by an external force, whether that force were governmental, churchly, communal, or authoritarian in some other guise. A form of expulsion associated with national, communal, and religious roots, the term rarely has been applied to such mundane expulsions as those from a school, fraternal group, or community organization. The feelings generated by expulsion—those of separation, isolation, alienation, loss, confusion, desire to rejoin the group or its converse, unrelenting rancor against the expelling body—are similar, and they delineate what some commentators call the exilic behavorial response. It is assumed that loss of one's country or religion or family is of a profounder nature than loss of one's school or club, but in a psychological perspective and context the matter is debatable. That which makes one feel exiled is the form and shape of exile; its affect is its own demonstration of the fact of an incontrovertible feeling. In this study, exile is viewed as the experience of rejection from one's native land; all other incidences of exile as they spring from this loss of literal land may follow, but inclusion in these pages demands the loss or rejection of country as a primary, native consideration. Thus, internal exiles and dissidents and writers in prison for their ideas—all forms of another body of exile, which some critics put under the umbrella term *internal exile* —are not listed here. If the internal exile in turn becomes a victim banished from his native land, he or she is included in this survey. On a few occasions, when the banishment is to another part of the country or geographic area that is *different* in feel and culture from the lost land, the act is recorded in these pages as one of exile.

This study, however, treats more than the literal exile. Exile, even by denotative signification, covers in its blanket sweep the voluntary exile, that is, one who chooses to absent himself from his country and often in consequence his home and family. The word, which comes from the Latin root *to jump*, carries with it the notion of flight, as one must jump from somewhere, and the *where* in a jump must come from above in order for descent to be made. Both in the classical and in Joyce's modern version, the figure of Daedalus is an exilic one, who must fly by the nets that constrain him from wandering, as well as through the nets of wandering to home; both the Greek Daedalus (and his son Icarus) and the Joycean Dedalus must jump into flight in order to conclude their period of exile.

Daedalus is but one example of exile; in the classical version he is motivated into it by a whimsical emperor who wants his crafty mazeman by his side, but the crafty inventor in his turn finds escape through flight. An earlier Egyptian example of exile may be found in the legend of Osiris and Isis. When the king Osiris was assassinated by his brother, the assassin ordered that the coffin bearing his brother's body be taken beyond the country's borders; even death in this tale is put out to exile. After the discovery that the jewelled coffin bearing Osiris's body had been brought back to his native land by Osiris's loyal wife, Isis, and hidden in a swamp, the brotherly assassin went mad with rage and cut his brother's dead body into fourteen parts. Such is the power of allegial presence; such is the desire to disperse and thus exile any presence of a powerful memory.

Other examples abound from the classical past: Sappho on Lesbos, Ariadne on Naxos, Oedipus on Colonnus; from Roman history: Ovid and Seneca banished by their emperors; from the medieval and Renaissance periods: Dante, who wrote his masterpiece in exile, and Shakespeare, whose works exhibit a context of exile's enduring presence. Compare, for example, the most tender banishment, that of Romeo, but also the bitter spite of Timon, who spits on his countrymen; Coriolanus, who rejects the Rome that has rejected him; Antony, who gives up a world of honor for bondage in Egypt in the arms of Cleopatra; the Moor Othello, yearning for his native land even as he performs his yeoman service for the Venetian Republic; and most profoundly, Lear, banished from castle, family, and all in which he has vainly believed before he becomes a new citizen unto himself again, shorn of everything but his awakening and longed-for death.

Conceivably the sense of wandering, nostalgia, yearning for its own sake that would produce oxymorons of pleasurable pain began at the end of the eighteenth century when reason was discovered to be less than visionary and a rational worldview insufficient to meet the demands of a sensuous soul. *Weltschmerz*, however, is not a German prerogative, and its coinage is a period piece; its phenomenal appearance in the nineteenth century, along with the rooted veils of the Romantic movement, bears intense witness to the exilic contagion that spread over Europe in that century.

Some observers see as the primal exile that of the expulsion of Adam and Eve from the Garden, or in its psychological parallel, that of the child wrenched from the womb of utter self-centeredness. The theme and position of exile dominate religion and religious lore—Moses and the flight from Egypt to the Promised Land; Jesus and the exile to martyrdom as the son of God; Muhammed and the Hegira to Mecca; Buddha and Tao on their pilgrimages to vision.

In this study such concepts of extranational exile as those mentioned above are surveyed in the personal experiences of writers who have departed their country because of religious, social, communal, sexual, political, and personal pressures. Some of these flights into exile have been voluntary, if by voluntary is meant that no specific authoritarian force or decree was employed in the isolate action of exit. Voluntary exit is, however, as much a form of exile as an involuntary move, if what follows it is the pattern of exilic behavior. Thus an expatriate may be viewed as a variant form of exile, if what drives him from his native land to a foreign one is a sense of aloneness, psychic separation, and the despair of nonbelonging. Expatriation is of course a happier state than exile; for the expatriate, if nothing else, is a willing exile who can take his baggage of home supplies with him; he does not have to take flight at a moment's notice, and he can return at whatever point he wishes, unlike the banished victim of exile who must wait for a new order in his land.

What both the exile and the expatriate feel in common is this apprehension of being cast out from their group. Though expatriates do not wander like the exile Cain with the brand of memory goading them, they are never at home till they travel beyond their home communities. The expatriate has been included in this survey as a representative example of the modern phenomenon of the choice of a foreign land over one's own. That choice represents, if not literal exile, the evidence of psychological exile and separation from community.

Literary terms have their semester of fashion as do any other quotients of living language. In the twentieth century, the image of the suitcase is intimately associated with the modern refugee—once the suitcase has been taken away, or the refugee no longer worries where his suitcase sits, he is transformed from a refugee into some other being; he acquires a new name, whether for the better or the worse. An exile then may also be defined as a refugee without a suitcase, one who has found a place after much wandering, and one who begins the equally tortuous routes of wandering through memory and yearning.

One critic, Leszek Kolakowski (in the *Times Literary Supplement*, October 11, 1985), separates the refugee from the exile in terms of personal action. The refugee is one who flees (suitcase or no) to a new border; the exile is one whom his group expels or banishes. In Kolakowski's view the exile is acted upon, while the refugee, shabby as his material condition may be, has engaged in a heroic retreat from the tyranny of the majority and keeps as an option a later battle with his oppressors. Kolakowski places the exile in such a mode of transport as physical deportation or banishment, while the refugee is a fugitive who has made good his escape from persecution and a possible death sentence from his enemies. He is in effect living in self-exile.

Kolakowski sees in the distinction not so much an operating terminology as a means of insight into psychological states and conditions of being. The refugee may harbor guilt for having fled and survived, while those left behind, or those who chose on their own to remain, may have suffered imprisonment or death. Conversely, the exile, if he or she survives, may feel freed from all lingering responsibility to his or her national and local state, and for his or her physical and psychological state, having borne the consequences meted to him or her. The exile in such a case becomes a stoic creature accepting the tragedy of history.

Distinction must also be made between exile and émigré, émigré and emigrant. One is an active choice, the other is a passive reaction, though decision and action are taken in the tension of reaction. Émigré activity follows a flight by choice, a decision taken on to avoid a feared harm or wrong and/or an expulsion by decree of the sociopolitical unit, whether it be a group of people, a religious community, or a local/national government. An émigré, in this scheme, flees to avoid harassment, torture, imprisonment, or worse apprehensions; the method of operation is a matter of varying circumstance and opportunity. An exile, by contrast, is more passive; choice is determined by a decree of banishment from a group above. Continuing this scheme, the emigrant is one who leaves not out of fear but out of the apprehension of a larger, better opportunity elsewhere. Yet, while each distinction is clear in the abstract of definition, every concrete case is murky in its peculiarities. Exclusivity of label, in effect, includes profound deviations from the exclusivity of the label; the exilic complex is never a simple sentence of biography. For example, émigrés and exiles arrive in a foreign land as a result of the same circumstances and attitudes; they feel the same pangs of loss. Even emigrants, who consciously and without ostensible fear of physical harm have chosen to leave, suffer the guilt of the survivor; they sometimes desire to return to that land they thought they had put into a past tense. Again, it is more pertinent to refer to each case, circumstance by circumstance, in order to understand and to draw configurations of the exilic complex.

Paul Tabori, in his pioneering study *The Anatomy of Exile* (London, 1972), a book now sadly out of print, lists several terms that together make up the exilic experience but singly represent different aspects of it. These differences are subtle, sometimes protean, but always *felt*. It is essential to keep such differences in mind when reading the various entries on individual writers in this book, but it is impossible to label a writer definitively by these intellectual categories, simply because a writer's work reflects many moving experiences—that is, the writer's material is transmitted by his or her *being* into a *been* that subsumes differences before they are analyzed. Few of us are pure in any case (although we can be "purified" in case studies for analytic purposes). Our experiences reveal an amalgam of virtues and ideals, decadence and failures, and occasionally premeditated crimes against personhood and community. The reader in using this study will find that a writer's exilic experience is described in biographic/historic terms and his or her work examined in literary/critical ones; on further study the student may discover that distinguishing referents can be applied to the writer so that his or her uniqueness can be summed up by a specialized term. The decision of the editor to use such terms sparingly in the biocritical entries is based on a simple precept: it is better to be reportorial in commentary before approaching critical encapsulation.

Yet the dangers of such an approach are also apparent. Exile, defined as national allegial loss or psychic-centered void, is so broad a concept that a whole age can be swallowed in it without the distinctions (the teeth) that aid understanding (digestion). To avoid enveloping fumes of critical haze, the following flags have been set up as markers for communities of exile.

Political. Writers who have been forced to leave or who have fled their native land to avoid feared arrest and/or harassment by ruling local or national authorities. Among the state conflicts of the twentieth century that have resulted in political exile of writers are the rise of Hitler in Germany and later the German military action in Europe; the Spanish Civil War; the change of national boundaries after World War I; World War II; the Russian Revolutions of 1905 and 1917; the military dictatorships of Latin America, whether on the Right or Left; the Socialist Revolutions in China and the ensuing Cultural Revolution in the four decades since the 1950s; Red Scares in the United States and Canada following World War I and during the era of Senator Joseph McCarthy's anticommunist campaign in the 1950s; the repressive regimes in East and West Europe; the abuse in many areas of the world of individual rights and political persuasions; the Armenian Genocide, in which some 2,000,000 people of one faith were slaughtered or starved; and the revolutions in Iran, Cuba, Kenya,

Iraq, and elsewhere, which both freed and later imprisoned outspoken, independent critics.

Religious. Writers who have been forced to leave, or who have fled before their feared arrest, harassment, and/or ostracism because of conflicts in their religious beliefs with those of their local and national community. Among such conflicts are the Holocaust, with its record of extermination of 6,000,000 Jews; persecution in socialist and communist revolutionary states in which atheism is proclaimed as the national and single religion; civil war, in Africa and Ireland over religious beliefs; Iran, where a zealous and theocratic state punishes non-believers in fundamental Islam; and Israeli and Arab wars of hatred and the ensuing stones of the heart.

Cultural. Writers who have left their country because they desired a freer state of being, whether in politics, religious observance, or social and/or sexual mores. Generally, this work lists expatriates as examples of this kind of exile. The American expatriate movement in Paris in the post–World War I decade is seen as a form of voluntary cultural exile. (The expatriates would probably say they gained a new culture rather than lost an old one, since they did not view their departure from their country as any significantly cultural sacrifice.) Under this rubric would also be found colonial writers who chose to emigrate to the large metropolis, to the supposed center or dominant focal place of culture. Frantz Fanon's concept of the colonial victim manipulated by imperialistic forces, and his struggle for freedom from its cultural yoke, serves as an example of cultural exile both for the colonized writer who takes flight to the imperial center and for the writer who moves into another domain. Among these colonial writers are Katherine Mansfield, V. S. Naipaul, Sam Selvon, Ngugi wa Thiong'o, Randolph Stow, Doris Lessing, and Jean Rhys.

Personal/Social. Writers who have chosen separation from their social groups or communities for a number of reasons other than the specific ones listed here. What distinguishes them is their sense of isolation.

Sexual. Writers who have left their country for greater freedom in their sexual expression and/or for a sense of acceptance in a less hostile world. Some of these writers have felt more like exiles in their home communities than in their adopted land. Most of these writers have not been banished or expelled and possibly not even harassed for their sexual behavior or for their writings, but they consider themselves nevertheless victims of repressive milieus. Many of these writers have also felt alienated from their social communities in political, cultural, and economic matters as well. See the group entry ''Gay and Lesbian Writers in Exile'' as well as individual entries on Gore Vidal, Frederick Rolfe (Baron Corvo), Robin Maugham, and Alfred Chester, among others.

Legal and Criminal. Some writers have chosen exile and/or emigration for reason of tax abatement, finance, or flight from criminal prosecution. Although such writers are not exiles in that they have not fled or left their country for any reason beyond the mundanely personal one of saving money or ameliorating their financial or legal situations, they often suffer the consequences of exile.

Their works bear the stamp of loneliness and yearning for a return home, or they are a broad, often satirical, canvas of memories and observations. Those writers who have fled their country either as criminals or as fugitives from criminal prosecution bear the burden of a home lost to them with a heavy reparation as the condition of return. Among such writers may be mentioned Eldridge Cleaver and Louis-Ferdinand Céline.

It should be emphasized again that these "markers" are guideposts and directional signals for clarification in a complex of observations. No one category may be fully satisfactory for an encapsulation of a writer's work in exile; religious persecution in Hitlerite Germany, for example, was a political event as well as an antireligious act. Indeed all religious persecution is political in consequence, if not also in origin, and all cultural harassment is equally an abuse of political freedom, as no culture exists in a societal vacuum. Lists of writers are provided under each of the above categories in the appendices at the end of this book, but individual entries of specific writers should be studied for a less terminal understanding of categorical exile.

Unfortunately, the most virulent form of exile in the modern period is the obvious one—forced emigration because of political, religious, and communal harassment. The diasporas continue in modern times; once started, the stones of the heart they induce cannot be rolled back but must in some way be shattered into the powder of transcendent adaptation. The reverberations of the Jewish exile from the Holy Land thousands of years ago continue, both in the current loyalty to a Zionist state and in the awareness of Jewish people in various countries of their differentness from the majority of their community; in the black experience, both in return-to-Africa movements and in the striving for more viable worlds and landscapes of different and equal crops of human activity and responsibility; in the Holocaust, with its afflictions of the knowledge of horror and evil, which lie dormant but tensed for awakening in the capacious breasts of humans; in the revolutions in the name of greater religious or social good that have displaced hundreds of thousands, in some cases millions, of nonbelievers in those later adherences that evolve from the newly established systems of revolutionary activity. In the twentieth century the list is frighteningly fulsome.

Although other centuries have played host to persecution and exile, it is apparent that exile is more than a passing current in the modern era: it is one of its most dominant literary fortresses and a stasis of the time. The critic Terry Eagleton has asserted that among the eight major writers of the first half of the twentieth century, only one, D. H. Lawrence, is a nonémigré. (See Eagleton's book *Exiles and Emigres: Studies in Modern Literature*, 1970.) Eagleton's point may be strengthened by my assertion that D. H. Lawrence is a preeminent example of an exile, a wanderer whose roots were in no land but that of his visionary world of pantisocracy and who traveled, restlessly, for thirty years after World War I to find a place he could call home. Lawrence chose Taos, New Mexico, with its mix of ancient North American and Renaissance Spanish culture as his "favorite" place; his ashes are buried there, brought by his widow

Frieda. The exile thus came home to a foreign place more natural to his nature than the England that lay behind his novels, short stories, and plays.

Exile may also be perceived as a concomitant of the Western postempirical age, with its cause rooted in a political system rather than in such aberrations of history as the Holocaust and the Armenian genocide. The critic Andrew Gurr posits that exile is integral to empire, and that the colonized victim who becomes a writer exploits his empirical servitude and imposed menial status into a nurturing material of literary exploitation and substance. Gurr's thesis of exile as a constructive force for the colonized writer may be compared to Edmund Wilson's earlier premise (in turn indebted to Sigmund Freud) that the artist works from a wound that shoots its own arrows of artistic strength and stimulation. Gurr proposes the consideration that the colonized writer, growing up in a place distant from the metropolis of the empire, or its ruling center, makes a conscious, and subconscious, decision to flee from his origins and to build a new home on foreign shores. The colonized writer is already a victim of alienation; in his new surroundings in the metropolis he gains strength from his memory of what he has fled, and he uses material of early life for the substance of his work. The pattern is suggestive of that of James Joyce, who, adopting the creed of silence, exile, and cunning, wandered through Europe but never forsook the land of his birth and in the process immortalized Ireland, the Catholic church, and his family in every one of his fictions. The colonized writer's pattern, then, is that of flight at an early age, reconstruction during the next decade of his origins through revision of memory, followed by an artistic flowering. By their reliance on concrete details of memory of home, these writers are saved from the self-pity, isolation, and alienation an impersonal and often amorphous metropolitan society imposes on its inhabitants.

The most significant ironies in Gurr's thesis are that the artist, if he is successful in his constructs—that is, if he achieves the creations of his vision—will emerge without any home or history. For in creating his own myths about his native land he will have rendered the historical constructs of them anachronistic. This pattern again is similar to the one Joyce exemplifies—Joyce's Ireland is not a reportorial land naturalistically described, but a modernist communion with Celtic myth and history filtered through the unique Joycean vat of ironic glories and comic quiddities. Not merely for literary declaration did Joyce parallel Ireland with Homer's Greece, but for a deeper rationale—the need of the psychic exile to make contact with a cosmology and an era that would return him to his local place in a universality of time, and in the process transform history into both legend and a new period literature.

The converse of the exile who refuses repatriation is the one who returns to the homeland he has left earlier. He returns to the rocks and sturdy trees of his origin to find he no longer bears the same spacial relationship to those physical manifestations he has sheltered in his dreams during his long years of exile; he no longer is a perennial season, becoming green again each spring like the trees in their appointed (for him preappointed) places. Such a return is at least as unbearably painful as the concomitant knowledge that time passes all human things into a great wash of record. For such a writer-observer, the knowledge of such experience is likely to lead again to the preference of memory over revisitation. The harbor of memory eliminates the inconveniences of new sailings, protecting berth-rights from trauma. In some exilic works, the shelter of dream visions overcomes historical realities, but the dreams are of an imposed past overwhelming the tension of a personal and future mood. Such dreams represent an allegiance to shadows that will not dim their lights.

Such exiles, full of the certitude of uncertainty, construct order over the chaos they feel by re-creating in their literary renderings a world turned static; their memorialized perspective provides a reassuring system of time's notation for their traumatized dynamic. This operation of activity cuts reality down to the size of entropy in a long run of time, but in the immediacy of therapy it realizes a profundity of vitality. Judgment on whether the look-back opens the course into the future, or whether such gleanings are the symptoms of cantankerous despair, lies with each individual reader. One reader will find in Vladimir Nabokov or in James Joyce a linguistic wordplay that dramatizes the profound game of freedom and represents a player's fight against a world armed with clubs that smash niceties of language in their uniform regulations. Others will see in Nabokov's and Joyce's work a profusion of puns, anagrams, and eccentricities of extraordinary variety and craft but without much redeeming social grace or communal utility.

Judgment of the work of literary exiles may thus be seen as inextricably connected with the persona of these works, if by persona is meant the totality of the writer's content, form, style, personal vision, and intimate baggage of technique by which the gift of personality is made. All writers of course use their experience in some way as the premise of their art and as a conclusion to the transmutation of it. What lies, or tells the truth, in the middle of it is the alchemy that changes their biographical experience into something universally new and by so doing creates a felt experience for readers and viewers coming into contact with it. By its nature art is both a birth and a reconstruction of existent material; it is a new body flying in space traveled for the first time every time it is traveled by the high flyer, the Daedalus-like reader who becomes one with the Daedalus creator. What is new if literature is to be made anew is the material presentation of the writer, but the material itself has been present and available since consciousness began. What happens when the fabric is—or fabrics are—suddenly, violently or irremediably torn away becomes the matter of exile. The reader will have noticed the use of dualisms in the previous sentence; this awareness of duality for anyone pursuing the quest of the meaning of exile becomes endemic, since an exile immediately has two selves. He is from *there*, but he is *here* now. Where then is he at base? Once having left a place, he has literally reshaped it by a wrenching of its steady habitual appointments. Even if he goes back to the original place, it cannot be the same. For indeed he has changed, by the fact and means of leaving. And if the place has literally stayed the same, then it has atrophied by remaining unchanged and thus decaying, while other constants have moved and replenished their shape. James Joyce knew this fact of time, this irreversible presence facing every exile's choice of departure and return. He could not go back to Dublin because to do so would destroy his memory of it, his grasp of the truth of its *place* which he was stealing into his art. Only by distance was he able to come home. Only by separation was he able to stay a true Catholic in the capital sense of the word, and only by using the confines of a relatively small world capital was he able to remain catholic in his range of material.

Joyce's transplantation and his protective devices to keep the seeds of his plant and flowering art warm are one way of dealing with exile. Joyce chose exile—or rather he recognized its nature, which a less discerning eye, the conventional citizen of Dublin, avoided through the eager aid of their willing ignorance. Other writers have chosen or been forced to accept other ways of transplanting themselves and thus their creativity, and other methods of keeping alive their roots in an alien land. I. B. Singer came to the United States because he had to flee his native land or suffer the deadly horrors of the Holocaust. He chose never to desert his native language—but which was his native language? Polish, the language of the country in which he was born? Yiddish, the international language of the group by which he achieves his profoundest identity? or English, specifically the version of the English language spoken by Jews in the United States, a land in which Singer has lived for more than forty years. For Singer, the choice has been Yiddish, from first to last, with only an occasional aside in English. For Singer, his style, his view, his meaning has been *Yiddishkeit*, the sheltering community (and possibly ghetto) of Jewishness, the sense of or rather attempt at making sense of a world gone awry. Singer's transplantation may be seen in his current living habits—is he an exile in Miami from New York? The question, deceptively comic at first (one hopes), is ironic because it is the root question in any discussion of exile. In deciding how to identify a person's *place*—that is, the spirit of the place of a person—the observer is deciding how to place him in the context of profoundest identity. There is a second step to this process, and that is the process of transcending exile, of integrating past into present, of discovering that roots have grown anew without severance of old vines. The critic and scholar Asher Milbauer has written on this phenomenon of transcendence of exile, using three literary exiles—Joseph Conrad, Vladimir Nabokov, and Isaac Bashevis Singer—to justify his assertion. Milbauer's analyses illuminate the pattern by which literary exiles go beyond their past into a future that does not deny the validity of the past while assigning it a less dominant territory than its former hegemony. I would suggest in addition that transcendence works in a multitude of ways: for some, the bridges of memory become routes to another path of life; for others, transcendence burns its own bridges of memory, creating a new life without seeds to till anew; for still others, transcendence loses its power because belief in it may be or become less potent than the routine of hopeless habit. In sum, there is a point for some writers at which memory refuses to seed its distinctive parochial boundaries and demands a recognition of isolate identity. Thus the exiled writer achieves again another instance of duality—he has a new identity, a new tradition of which he is a part, a tradition that has helped to shape him but allows him distance as well.

Language, which makes possible a writer and whose "foreignness" makes possible the destruction of that same writer, is another measure of both psychic, rooted exile and literal exile. Indeed, language may be the ultimate measure of psychic exile, for the exilic sense of separation springs from the fall of communication between foreign writer and local/national community. When a writer's language is not comprehended, he is as isolated spiritually as he is physically in an alien land. When he begins to understand the foreign tongue of the land in which he resides, his exile is lessened, for the intelligible world has joined him to a new confederacy. When a writer begins to write in the adopted language of his new country, he may well be stating that he has reached the end of his exile, that he is now associating himself with a new identity, a *word* no longer foreign to him. In this sense, a writer transcends exile once he adopts the home of a new language. Joseph Conrad and Nabokov exemplify this moment of literary conversion, while, representing an alternative view, I. B. Singer has steadfastly refused to divorce himself from Yiddish. In Conrad's case the issue is layered in the fact that Conrad did not write for publication, with rare exceptions, in any language but English; at the earliest stage of his literary career, he chose English as his medium. Although Conrad did not change his literary language in midstream, he did arrive at English as a third linguistic way. His background was Polish, and he spoke fluent French before he chose English as his writer's voice. Conrad's pattern represents the reverse of the usual exilic experience; his was an act of selfmotivated declaration rather than a practical reaction to circumstance. Nabokov's case differs from Conrad's in that he began the composition of his novel *The Real Life of Sebastian Knight* in 1939 in English, fully conscious of forsaking one language (in which he had achieved public distinction) for another. It is pertinent that in *Sebastian Knight* Nabokov explores the question of identity and puts his protagonist through a series of unveilings that allows the character to clothe himself in the new trappings of an emigrant. At the same time Nabokov continued his Russian literary studies and translated work from the Russian into English.

Yet while language is a measure of the distance spanned in the circles of isolation and community, it is a fluid measure. Many writers do not simply exchange languages. More often they become bilingual or trilingual and write in a language that suits their particular context. It may be argued that such a stance proves the validity of the proposed thesis of language as a measure of exile and the isolation erased from it as on a palimpsest of new allegiance. For if a writer retains his native language and learns no other while living in a new land, he is likely to become one kind of exile and remain one kind of foreigner; if he adopts a new language he is likely to become a naturalized citizen of his adopted language-country, though his naturalness with it will come in questing stages; if he learns many languages and uses each in his planned turn of events, then he is more likely to become another kind of exile, perhaps a transcendent of it if he integrates his employment of languages into a unified personal vision rather than a dichotomous, partite set of specific goals. Examples may clarify the issue, although they cannot resolve it: Joyce knew many languages but chose to write in only one; Stefan Heym writes alternately in two, English and German, and lives in one state of Germany which until 1989 banned his work while the other state of Germany read it eagerly; Joseph Brodsky has written in two languages and seems determined to employ English as his language from this point on; Thomas Mann, although he lived for a long time in the United States and expressed his gratitude to his place of haven (even when he departed from it in fear of what he conceived as its political hysteria), did not forsake the German language and relied on translators to spread the word in his fictions; Samuel Beckett, an Irishman resident in France, wrote in French for many years and only later in life wrote in English (a reverse from his earlier habit of writing first in English and then translating into French); Ngugi wa Thiong'o and Chinua Achebe, who once wrote in English and who now write in their African languages (Kikuyu and Ibo), either before or after writing their creations in English, in their attempts to reach and educate a local audience and to reach and educate in a different way the Western and Eastern worlds; and Jerzy Kosinski, who writes only in English, having made a conscious choice to identify himself with the new society he chose to enter a generation ago.

Life is never a losing matter, even in the gain of loss and sorrow. Accretion of experience is what shapes our present and future and makes possible our understanding of the past. In this sense memory is a revisionist movement, forcing us to see yesterday in present light. The duality of perspective is shared by others besides the exile, but the impact of the lensing experience may provide a greater illumination to the exile's consciousness than to others.

Exile is a living tissue that grows in stages and degrees. We are exiled from the womb in the psychological apparatus of growing up. We have been exiled from the Garden of Eden. We leave things behind and cannot go back to them at many moments in our lives, and there are moments we cannot revisit; moments pass even when we are silent and hold our breaths in the fierce wish to hug a moment forever to our breasts. Such examples are universal and common to mankind, but rarely studied as exile. The more usual forms have been mentioned earlier: the historical, the political, the religious, the social and cultural, the sexual. Exile has been studied as a time capsule—a hurtling from the space of time as well as from the land.

I believe that now, at the end of the twentieth century, exile may be seen as one of the most deeply rooted characteristics of the modern era. Exile, which by definition makes one feel always the other, has become a widely traveled terrain of our times. It represents one of the modern era's significant communities of experience.

Martin Tucker

Group Entries

AMERICAN EXPATRIATES IN EUROPE, 1900–1990. American expatriates of the 1920s constitute a cultural phenomenon unmatched in the history of the United States. The majority of these expatriates lived abroad for a rationalized purpose—to discover a liberating aesthetic vision not available in what they perceived as a constraining home society, and to do so more cheaply than in their home state. Often their activities were less than reasoned, and, on occasion, some of these writers indulged in unreasonable flights of fancy. The mystique of their flights—both physical and imaginative—continues to exert a powerful appeal on succeeding generations of American writers, intellectuals and students.

Among American expatriates of the 1920s–30s decade are Djuna Barnes*, Natalie Barney*, John Peale Bishop*, Kay Boyle*, Louis Bromfield*, Bob Brown*, Louise Bryant*, Robert Coates*, Malcolm Cowley*, Caresse Crosby*, Harry Crosby*, Countee Cullen*, e. e. cummings*, H. D. (Hilda Doolittle)*, John Dos Passos*, F. Scott Fitzgerald*, Janet Flanner*, Ernest Hemingway*, Archibald MacLeish, Claude McKay*, Henry Miller*, Anais Nin*, Ezra Pound*, Gertrude Stein*, Virgil Thomson, and Glenway Westcott. Later expatriates (and earlier writers such as T. S. Eliot*, Henry Furst*, Henry James*, and John Reed*) were drawn to foreign shores for much the same reasons as the fabled artists of the 1920s era, although in Reed's case, politics played more of a part than esthetics or glamor. Such later expatriates include Raymond Andrews, James Baldwin*, Elizabeth Bishop*, Paul Blackburn, Jane (Auer) Bowles*, Paul Bowles*, Barbara Chase-Riboud*, Alfred Chester*, Robert Creeley, J. P. Donleavy*, Russell Hoban*, Langston Hughes*, Anthony Kerrigan*, Ring Lardner, Jr.*, John Howard Lawson*, Archibald MacLeish, David Plante*, Sylvia Plath, Katherine Anne Porter, Ned Rorem*, Clancy Sigal*, Susan Sontag*, Anne Stevenson, Paul Theroux*, and Gore Vidal*.

Consult: William G. Bailey, comp., *Americans in Paris, 1900–1930: A Selected, Annotated Bibliography* (1989).

ANGOLAN AND MOZAMBIQUE WRITERS. Many Angolan and Mozambique writers suffered some form of coerced residence in Portugal or in underground activities in their own lands as a result of their covert or overt fight for independence from the colonialist Portuguese Empire. Although these writers technically are neither exiles nor émigrés since Angola and Mozambique were part of the Portuguese Empire, they were forcibly moved or fled out of fear of harassment or incarceration to lands not their primary choice. Below are listed some of those writers, most of whom returned to newly independent Angola and Mozambique to serve either in government roles or as writers and colleagues in a cultural-nationalist expressiveness. Most of these writers wrote in Portuguese, although the language they use is at times infused with African oral traditional forms and lexical techniques. Negritude—the cry for Africanness, or the "being of African-ness" in Jean-Paul Sartre's phrase—dominates most of their work since poetry was a willing tool for social, communal expression, both as an ancient tradition and as a twentieth-century rebellion against European denigration of African values.

Angola. Costa Andrade, born 1936, Lepi, Huambo; Arlindo Barbeitos, born 1940, Angola; Viriato da Cruz, born 1928, Porto Amboim; Antonio Jacinto, born 1924, Luanda; Agostinho Neto, born September 17, 1926, Kaxikane Village, Catete District, near Luanda; Luandino Vieira, born 1935 in Portugal, grew up in Angola.

Mozambique. José Craveirinha, born May 28, 1922, Maputo; Noémia de Sousa, born September 20, 1927, Maputo; Marcelino Dos Santos, born 1929, near Lumbo (published under pseudonyms of Kalungano, Micai, Bébé, and Lilinho); Jorge Rebelo, born 1940, Maputo.

Consult: Donald Burness, ed. *Critical Perspectives on Lusophone Literature* (1981); Frank Mkalawile Chipasula, ed., *When My Brothers Come Home: Poems from Central and Southern Africa* (1985); Hans M. Zell et al., *A New Reader's Guide to Africa*, 2nd ed. (1983).

ARMENIAN WRITERS IN EXILE. Since the beginning of the Mongol invasions across the Armenian homeland, a literature of displacement, a genre known as *ashoughagan*, a category of poetry that may be called the songs of the wandering minstrel or the lyric/epic tale of the displaced, has been characteristic of Armenian literature.

Armenia's geography, its plateau-land between East and West, made it a natural highway that contributed to its downfall as Mongol and Ottoman Turks swept westward. Uprooting of population, and exile for the Armenians, began in the twelfth century and was capped in the twentieth by the final "solution of the Armenians," the first genocide of the present century, reports of which gave Adolf Hitler the idea of annihilation of the Jewish minorities in Europe.

Although Armenia's land has diminished, and its population was decimated by more than 75 percent in 1915, the language, a member of the Indo-European family, has become the "home of the Armenian," in the words of poet Moushek Ishkhan (born 1913, and orphaned in the 1915 genocide). Ishkhan was brought up in Beirut, Lebanon, where he taught and wrote until his death in August 1990. In Ishkhan's words:

The Armenian language is the home
and haven where the wanderer can own
roof and wall and nourishment.
He can enter to find love and pride,
locking the hyena and the storm outside.
For centuries its architects have toiled
to give its ceilings height.
How many peasants working
day and night have kept,
lamps lit, ovens hot.
Always rejuvenated, always old, it lasts
century to century on the path

where every Armenian can find it when he's lost
in the wilderness of his future or his past.

During the Middle Ages, poets such as Frik, who lived between the thirteenth
and fourteenth centuries, wrote not only love poetry but poetry of protest against
the conditions of their countrymen. Another early Armenian troubador whose
songs of love, protest, and wandering are still sung was Sayat Nova of Tiflis,
who wrote in Armenian, Georgian, Azerbaijani, and Persian; he was killed by
Persian invaders. In the nineteenth century Armenians who wished to write free
from censorship by the Turks were obliged to travel to Venice or Vienna. There
they found Armenian cultural centers and presses operated by the Mekhitarist
priests. Ghevont Alishan, born in Istanbul in 1820, was one of those who
remained in Venice to teach and to influence his students, many of whom became
writers. These students were responsible for a renaissance in Armenian literature,
which reached a zenith when Turkish censorship became lax because of a Western
presence in Istanbul just before 1915. In Eastern Armenia, which by then was
under the Russian Czar, other writers were exiled for writing anything that
appeared incendiary or political to the Russian censors. Mikael Nalbandian
(1829–1866) and Raphael Badgamian (1830–1892) both suffered an exile's fate.
Raffi (1837–1888), who was born in former Armenian territory in northern Persia
and was educated in Tiflis, began to write historical novels after his 1858 travels
through Turkish Armenia; he saw so much suffering that he dedicated himself
to revitalizing Armenian culture and historic pride among his countrymen.

The 1915 genocide removed all the major poets of Western Armenia except
Vahan Tekeyan,* as well as the readership of such literature. Those who lived
in the eastern regions of Armenia enjoyed a brief period of freedom (1918–
1920), but after 1920 these writers were displaced by the Sovietization of the
small Armenian land into a provincial Soviet republic. Today a very small portion
of Armenia remains as a Soviet republic; the rest of the country, annexed after
1919 by Turkey, has remained under Turkish rule. Joseph Stalin ceded Ngorney
Karabagh to the Azerbaijani Turks in the 1920s–1930s, and other regions to
Georgia of the USSR.

The 1915 exiles reached various lands: Avedik Issahakian (1875–1957), a
major poet of the eastern area, went to Italy, then France, eventually returning
to Soviet Armenia. Gostan Zarian (1885–1969) made his way to the United
States and France; his writing, always complex and multidimensional, became
cosmopolitan and multilingual. Novelist and patriot Avedis Aharonian (1866–
1948), who served as president of the National Assembly of independent Armenia, settled in France. Among the writers who also eventually arrived in
France were Aharon Dadourian and Puzand Topalian, both strongly influenced
by the French surrealists, as well as the poets Harout Gosdantian and Nighoghos
Srafian and novelist Shahan Shanour. Shanour continued writing his prose in
Armenian, but wrote his poetry in French. Yeghivart (Jerusalem), Ishkhan,
Andranik Zarougian, and Vahe-Vahian, orphaned children of the genocide, grew

up in Syria, Jerusalem, and Beirut, and were published there by Armenian periodicals and presses. Zarougian, known for his acid wit as the author of the novel *Men Without Childhood*, a novel of his own orphan days, edited the literary biweekly *Nayiri* in Beirut until 1985, when he moved to Paris; he died in 1989. Nishan Beshigtashlayan, the satirist and humorist-poet, lived in Cairo, Egypt. Novelist Hagop Oshagan and critic-anthologist Arshag Chobanian, who had spent much of his life gathering the stories of the oral epic "David of Sassoun," made the Paris of the 1920s a literary center for exiled Armenians. Later, Shavarsh Missakian began publishing *Hratch* as a vehicle for many of these talents. In Boston, Massachusetts, critic and editor of *Hairenik Daily,* Rouben Tarbinyan, developed a literary monthly to publish another stellar group: Gostan Zarian, short story writer Hamasdegh, the best exponent of village life (pseudonym of H. Galenian, U.S., 1895–1966), Aram Haigaz, and Roupen Der Minassian. In New York, exiled writers Hagop Asadourian, Aram Haigaz, and Benjamin Nourigian were published in *Nor Gir* (New Letters). A younger generation of writers—Vahe Oshagan (son of the major literary critic Hagop Oshagan), Krikor Bledian, Zulal Kazanjian, Zareh Melkonian, Vehanoush Tekayan, Jacques Hagopian, all born to exiled parents and who settled in Beirut—are now expatriates themselves, forced out of Beirut by the civil war there. Many of these poets, also influenced by French surrealists and European absurdists, now live and write in France or the United States.

The best known of the satirists who survived the genocide was Yervant Odian, who went to Egypt. Armenian literature has a long tradition of satire, both gentle and sharp, in theater and essay. Today, aside from the Soviet Union's *Vozni* (Porcupine), edited by humorist Aramais Sahagian, one of the best-loved wits is Gisavor (Khosrov Nersessian), who writes a weekly humorous essay or story in *Hairenik*, continuing a traditional column started in the late 1940s by Jirair Missakian. Nersessian was born in 1917 to exiled parents in Greece. Kourken Mekhitarian, writer-essayist-editor, came from Cairo, Egypt, another center of Armenian exiles, to edit *Hairenik* in the 1950s until his death. Hrach Yervant edited *Baikar* from his home base in Watertown, New York; and Antranig Antreassian, a survivor and chronicler of the genocide, who is also a short story writer and novelist based in California, succeeded him. Another group forced out of Iran includes novelist Hagop Karabents (Jack Karapetian, in English). Today, again, exiled Armenians are moving out of the historic Armenian regions of Karabagh because of mistreatment by the ruling Azerbaijani Turks, and the tradition of exiled Armenian writers, unfortunately, continues.

One of the leading prose writers in Yerevan today is Zori Balayan from Karabah; the prominent poet Vahakn Davtian has also recorded his childhood memories of a home lost to Turkey, when Young Turks went on a latter-day rampage in 1922–1924.

The sacred mountain Ararat, a symbol of lost lands of Armenia, rises in the mists across the border in Turkey, "always in sight, always out of reach, like a great love," in the words of poet Gevorg Emin. Mount Ararat and the "cranes" flying from home are two recurring metaphors for exile in Armenian writing. The image of cranes reaches back as far as the medieval period when Nahabed Koutchag wrote these lines:

Groung (Crane)

Where do you come from, crane?
I ache to hear your call
to know you come from home.
Have you any news at all?

I bless your wings, your eyes.
My heart is torn in two.
The exile's soul all sighs
waiting for shreds of news.

The only major Western Armenian poet to escape the genocide was Vahan Tekeyan (1878–1945), who by chance was not in Istanbul that April of the terrible time. Tekeyan spent his life in service to his native land, writing painstakingly honed sonnets that have earned him a reputation as a visionary comparable to the apocalyptic poets John Milton, Percy Bysshe Shelley, and Friedrich Schiller. His poems search for the affirmation and redemption that are the cathartic reward of tragedy. Ironically, his most frequently quoted work is a bitter sonnet, written in 1917, ''We Shall Say to God'':

Should it happen we do not endure
this uneven fight and drained
of strength and agonized
we fall on death's door not to rise
and the great crime ends
with the last Armenian eyes
closing without seeing a victorious day
let us swear that when we find
God in his paradise offering comfort
to make amends for our pain,
let us swear that we will refuse
saying No, send us to hell again.
We choose hell. You made us know it well.
Keep your paradise for the Turk.

Selected Titles: *Anthology of Armenian Poetry*, ed. Diana Der Hovanessian and M. Margossian (1978). See also Gevorg Emin, *For You on New Year's Day* (1987); (Medieval Armenian poems), *Come Sit Beside Me and Listen to Kouchag* (1985); Vahan Tekeyan, *Sacred Wrath* (1983) All translations are by D.D.H.

Consult: Michael J. Arlen, *Passage to Ararat* (1975); Arra Avakian, ''Armenian Poetry,'' *Princeton Encyclopedia of Poetry and Poetics* (1974); V. Brussov, ''The Poetry of Armenia,'' *Armenian Review* 1 (1948); Sirarpie Der Necessian, *The Armenians* (1970);

H. Thorossian, *Histoire de la littérature arménienne* (1951); Christopher Walker, *Armenia, Survival of a Nation* (1980).

DIANA DER HOVANESSIAN

AUSTRALIAN/NEW ZEALAND EXPATRIATE POETS AND WRITERS. A significant number of Australian and New Zealand poets have emigrated to England to justify special attention as an expatriate grouping. Though most of these poets work in a manner distinct from one another, they also show common patterns as artists leaving a colonial land for a metropolitan center. Their work reflects both spurning of the parochial, native country and adjustment to a larger, liberating, and demanding "foreign" empirical center. Among these poets are Peter Porter and Peter Conrad from Australia; Fleur Adcock, John Gallas, Kevin Ireland, C. K. Stead, Vincent O'Sullivan, and Ian Wedde from New Zealand. Of the work of New Zealand poets Adcock, Wedde, O'Sullivan and Ireland, critic Lachlan Mackinnon, in *Times Literary Supplement*, May 26-June 1, 1989 wrote: "For Fleur Adcock, the choice of traditional form is a homecoming; for Ian Wedde, Vincent O'Sullivan, and Kevin Ireland the opposite choice appears as a spurning of the ex-colonial power, a preference for new and open country. A formal option taken is a political stand made—of which no one can be more than C. K. Stead, author of *The New Poetic*."

Selected Titles: Fleur Adcock, *Meeting the Comet* (Newcastle upon Tyne, 1989); John Gallas, *Practical Anarchy* (Manchester, 1989); Peter Porter, *Collected Poems* (1983); C. K. Stead, *Between* (Auckland, N. Z., 1989); see also *The Penguin Book of Contemporary New Zealand Poetry* (Auckland, 1990 [includes work by Adcock, and other expatriates, among them, Eric Beach, Alan Brunton, and Nigel Roberts]).

BRITAIN AS A CENTER FOR GERMAN-LANGUAGE WRITERS IN EXILE (1930–). During the 1930s London, like other European capitals, became a battleground for contending ideologies of the Right and the Left and, despite its ancient liberal traditions, sometimes proved less attractive for German writers in exile than Paris, Amsterdam, or Stockholm. Until the Czech crisis of 1938, the official voice of Nazi Germany was heard in the debate: authors like Hans Grimm or the less militant Rudolf Binding could lecture in England and display the "gentlemanly" face of fascism. Refugees were handicapped by the absence of a German-language newspaper. The weekly *Die Zeitung* (1941–45), printed under the auspices of the Ministry of Information, was intended more for consumption overseas than to supply the needs of émigrés. *German Life and Letters*, founded by L. A. Willoughby in 1937, provided an occasional forum for humanists. Encouragement also came from a broad spectrum of public opinion, ranging from the Bloomsbury Circle, pacifists like Aldous Huxley, the Quakers, Catholics like Arnold Lunn, and publishers such as Gollancz and Secker. The influential Left Book Club, launched by Victor Gollancz in 1928, disseminated some German writings in translation (e.g., Paul Frölich's life of Rosa Luxemburg). When Fredrick Warburg joined Martin Secker in 1936, he

continued to favor German authors, including Thomas Mann,* Lion Feuchtwanger,* Arnold Zweig,* and Hermann Rauschning. Another opportunity for
refugees, during and after World War II, was offered by the German Service of
the British Broadcasting Corporation, the most distinguished contributor being
Alfred Kerr (1867–1948), the leading German drama critic. Another valued
member of the service was Carl Brinitzer (1907–74).

The vicissitudes and activities of many German-language writers can be traced
through the documentation of the German PEN Club in Exile (1933–48), which,
after opposing the official German delegation at the Ragusa conference of 1937
(chaired by H. G. Wells), had established its secretariat in London. Its first
secretary was Rudolf Olden (1885–1940), a former editor of the *Berliner Tageblatt*; founding members included Georg Bernhard, Bernard von Brentano, Lion
Feuchtwanger,* Emil Ludwig,* Klaus Mann,* Heinrich Mann,* Ernst Toller,*
Peter de Mendelssohn, and Arnold Zweig*. Not all members were domiciled in
Britain, which was often a staging post for residence elsewhere. Thus Ernst Reu-
ter, author of a celebrated appeal to Thomas Mann and later mayor of Berlin,
passed through London before settling in Turkey. As Hitler menaced first Austria,
then Czechoslovakia, Olden and publicists like Gilbert Murray and J. B. Priestley
sought to assist the new waves of refugees. After Olden's tragic death (the boat
bringing him to America was torpedoed), the PEN Club in Exile continued to
function under the direction of Robert Neumann (head of the Austrian section),
Friedrich Burschell, Alfred Kerr, and Richard Friedenthal. World War II, while
bringing fresh stimuli, also brought further restrictions. The passing of an era was
symbolized in September 1939 when Stefan Zweig* spoke the laudation at the
funeral of Sigmund Freud* in London.

Zweig was to become a notable casualty; but many émigrés, overcoming all
handicaps, successfully established themselves in Britain. Richard Friedenthal
and Peter de Mendelssohn ably exploited the rising demand for well-researched
biographies. Eminent Germanists like S. S. Prawer and Erich Heller found ha-
vens in universities. British publishing, too, was to be well served by the founders
of such distinguished firms as Deutsch and Weidenfeld; even the format of
Penguin paperbacks owed much to the typographer Hans Schmöller. Some new-
comers bestrode with equal mastery not only two languages but more than one
discipline. Thus Erna Pinner and Fred Uhlman combined successful careers as
painters, book illustrators, and writers. F. B. Steiner lectured at Oxford on social
anthropology but also made his mark as a poet. Others who gave plangent
expression in their verse to the pangs of exile were Felix Braun and Max Herr-
mann-Neisse, whose *Flüchtlings Klage* (*The Fugitive's Complaint*) typifies the
lament of the enforced vagrant. A younger generation, who had left their homelands as children or young adults, found it easier to adapt to an Anglo-Saxon
environment while still enjoying the enhanced vision springing from bilingual-
ism. A conspicuous example is Michael Hamburger (b. 1924 in Berlin), a poet
in his own right who has become a leading translator and interpreter of Friedrich
Hölderlin. Cross-fertilization in this and other fields (e.g., Ernst Gombrich on art

and Pevsner on architecture) has, since the 1950s, brought increasing benefit to Britain and Germany alike within an emergent European cultural framework.

Select Bibliography: N. Bentwich, *They Found Refuge: An Account of British Jewry's Work for the Victims of Nazi Oppression* (London, 1956); M. Berghahn, *German-Jewish Refugees in England* (London, 1984); *Der deutsche PEN club im Exil, 1933–48* (Frankfurt, 1980) (this exhibition catalog, though primarily in German, contains some documentation in English on the London scene); T. R. Fyvel, *No Ease in Zion* (London, 1938); Michael Hamburger, *Zwischen den Sprachen* (Frankfurt, 1966; Between the Tongues, essays and poems); B. Heilig, *Men Crucified* (London, 1941); R. Olden, *The History of Liberty in Germany* (London, 1946); F. B. Steiner, *Unruhe ohne Uhr* (Darmstadt, 1954, posthumously published poems); A. Stevens, *The Dispossessed: German Refugees in Britain* (London, 1975); Paul Tabori, *The Anatomy of Exile* (London, 1972); F. Uhlman, *Reunion*, with an introduction by Arthur Koestler (London, 1977); J.M. Ritchie, *German Literature under National Socialism* (Totowa, N, J., 1983).

CEDRIC HENTSCHEL

EXPATRIATES. Expatriatism is a voluntary and transient form of exile. On occasion an expatriate becomes an exile when his government deprives him of his citizenship or disbars him from reentry to his native land; on occasion an expatriate opts for migrant status or permanent residence in a new land. Expatriate movements well known in the twentieth century include the American cultural migration to Europe in the 1920s (mostly Paris and the French Riviera) and the Latin American intellectual Grand Tour, which can last anywhere from one year to twenty years or more. Expatriate writers are listed by geographical category in the Categorical Exile Index. An asterisk preceding the name indicates a more detailed entry in the alphabetical list of writers in this volume.

Generally those who choose a temporary stay in a foreign land for economic reasons or for formal education are not included in this expatriate list, since the motivating factor for departure is less voluntary than urgent and/or life-threatening. Such writers—for example, Camara Laye,* Léopold Sédar Senghor,* Buchi Emecheta,* and others—are given full entries whether one wishes to call them expatriates, emigrants, exiles, or sojourners in a foreign land.

FRANCOPHONE AFRICAN WRITERS IN EXILE. Many African writers from former colonies in the French Empire went to France for their education or moved there for periods of time for career or economic or personal reasons. Many of these writers returned to their newly independent countries. Some of these writers were unwilling journeyers, forced into a certain direction by reasons beyond their desired circumstances; others were voluntary migrants or students seeking tools by which to return and enrich their countries. Those writers experiencing this kind of displacement who are treated in this study include Francis Bébey, Mongo Beti, Cheik Hamidou Kane, Ferdinand Oyono, and Tchicaya U Tam'si.

GAY AND LESBIAN WRITERS IN EXILE. In Mikhail Kuzmin's *Wings* (1906), the first postclassical novel by a gay male writer to focus openly and exclusively on a homosexual subject, one of the central characters, Larion Dimitrievich Stroop, holds a regular private salon for other St. Petersburg homosexuals. At one of these, Stroop voices an acute insight into society's oppression of homosexuals that foreshadows the gay liberation movement that would develop later in the twentieth century, a remark that in its prescience may seem startling to readers unfamiliar with homosexual literature and history. Dismissing a society that "would bind the idea of beauty to the beauty of a woman seen through the eyes of a man" and that maintains a "slavish attachment . . . to the getting of heirs, to seed," Stroop promises his assembled fellows that instead "Somewhere lies our ancient kingdom, full of sunlight and freedom, of beautiful and courageous people, and thither we sail, my argonauts, over many a sea, through mist and darkness. And in things yet unheard we shall descry ancient roots, in glittering visions yet unseen we shall know our own dear land!"[1]

In homosexual experience under oppression, this resistance to society's enforced heterosexual norms and assumptions has often taken the form of a quite literal "sailing"/exiling to other lands in search of greater social freedom and of a more appropriate culture that might to some extent already honor and incorporate the kind of distinctive features of gay identity emphasized by Kuzmin here (e.g., attraction between "sames" rather than "differents," the organizing of adulthood around such peer attachments rather than around an obligatory biological procreation). The twentieth century is the age in which, at present, an abundant exiling among homosexual/bisexual writers can be seen most clearly, with exile defined to include both lifetime residence away from native country and shorter but significant periods of expatriation. The twentieth century has certainly contained a number of scandals and mass political developments that particularly targeted homosexuals for persecution and that helped spark several of the flights into exile to be mentioned here—e.g., the Oscar Wilde trials and imprisonment of 1895–97, the rise of fascism and Nazism in Spain and Germany in the 1930s, McCarthyism in America in the 1940s and 1950s. The seventy modern gay, lesbian, and bisexual literary exiles documented below are indeed a striking number, a distribution among writers that seems far to outstrip what is presumed the proportion of homosexuals in the population at large.

One should be cautious, however, about viewing the twentieth century as a uniquely "banishing" era for homosexuals. A clear pattern that emerges from the information below is a relatively steady stream of gay exiling through all of the specific historical episodes just mentioned, an exiling that does not decisively break until the rise of the contemporary gay liberation movement in the 1960s and 1970s. This pattern implies that exile among homosexuals is primarily a function of the more deeply embedded and pervasive structures of gay oppression than of any one specific menacing event. And since gay oppression is obviously not a uniquely modern phenomenon, it further suggests that this notable mass of twentieth-century homosexual exiling is not so much the consequence of an unprecedented homophobia in the modern era as of several distinctly modern developments that made such exiling easier to accomplish and/or to identify— e.g., the relatively greater ease of travel, the increased social frankness about homosexuality, and the increased biographical information available about more writers. In fact, research into precontemporary homosexuality points to a continuing trend toward exile in Western gay/bisexual artists' lives from at least the mid 1700s—compare Johann Joachim Winckelmann and William Beckford in the eighteenth century and, in the nineteenth, Lord Byron, August Platen, Paul Verlaine, Arthur Rimbaud, Karl Heinrich Ulrichs, John Addington Symonds, and Henry James*—and additional historical research into gay/lesbian experience may uncover yet more instances of gay exile from those and earlier ages. This finding, too, suggests that, despite the formidable number of writers covered below, the twentieth century should not be seen as a uniquely exiling period for homosexuals.

The twentieth century began auspiciously negatively for Western homosexuals, with the death in Paris in November 1900 of the age's most famous male homosexual exile, Oscar Wilde (1854–1900). After his release in 1897 from his maximum, two-year sentence at hard labor for "gross indecency between males" (as male homosexual acts were then denoted in British law), Wilde fled to the Continent, often traveling under the name "Sebastian Melmoth" (based in part on the title character of the popular nineteenth-century gothic novel, *Melmoth the Wanderer*), a pseudonym manifestly depicting his journeying as an enforced exile. The pioneering American homosexual-emancipation writer Edward I. Prime-Stevenson (1869–1942) emigrated to Europe in 1901 and lived there for the rest of his life. Under the pseudonym "Xavier Mayne," he published a novelistic defense of homosexuality called *Imre: A Memorandum* in 1906 and a historical study of the subject, *The Intersexes*, in 1908 (both were issued in Naples). The constant traveling abroad that the novelist Ronald Firbank (1886–1926) began in 1902 was ostensibly for reasons of health, but seems also to have stemmed from his extreme discomfort as a homosexual at home. Firbank died on one of these journeys, in Rome, and is buried there under a headstone that describes him as "entered into rest . . . far away from his country."[2] The decision that H. H. Munro, better known as Saki (1870–1916), made to serve abroad as a foreign correspondent for the London *Morning Post* from 1902 to 1908 may have had something to do with the same sexual uneasiness as Firbank's. When, at the relatively advanced age of forty-three, Munro enlisted in the army at the outbreak of World War I (he was killed in battle on November 14, 1916), there were sarcastic rumors among his literary colleagues that his reason was the greater sexual opportunity he imagined in the all-male environment.

The British novelist Norman Douglas* (1868–1952), whose witty *South Wind* (1917) has much homosexual innuendo, moved to Capri in 1904 after his divorce, remaining there until 1910. He returned in 1916 and remained abroad, chiefly in Florence, for twenty-four years; after World War II Douglas returned to Capri and lived there until his death. The eccentric British writer Frederick Rolfe*

(1860–1913), better known by his pseudonym Baron Corvo and familiar chiefly for his autobiographical fantasy *Hadrian the Seventh* (1907), left London for Venice in 1908. At first regarding the trip as only a holiday, a respite from his continuous wandering within England and Scotland, Rolfe found a happiness in Venice he had never known before and remained there for the rest of his life, composing while there his masterpiece, the homosexual roman à clef *The Desire and Pursuit of the Whole* (posthumously published, 1934). Carl Van Vechten (1880–1964), whose novels of the 1920s like *The Blind Bow-Boy* (1923) contain veiled representations of his experience of homosexuality, first lived in Paris from 1908 to 1910 as a correspondent for the *New York Times*. One of his express reasons for his second trip there in 1913 was to meet Gertrude Stein,* and though Van Vechten was chiefly based in New York for the rest of his life, he maintained a close relationship with Stein and her expatriate homosexual circle from then on and became her literary executor after her death. The homosexual Colombian poet Miguel Angel Osorio Benitez (1883–1942), better known by his pseudonym Porfirio Barba Jacob, began what would be a pattern of continuous wandering in 1908. Though he resided in Mexico more than anywhere else during the remainder of his life (his last four years were spent there), Barba Jacob also lived at different times in Honduras, Guatemala, Haiti, Cuba, Peru, and Texas.

T. E. Lawrence* spent considerable voluntary time in the Middle East before the World War I exploits in Arabia that made him famous, and it seems that one reason was the freer opportunity to express his homosexuality that he sensed there. Lawrence was away from England entirely from 1910 through 1918, and it was on an archaeological dig in Carchemish that he met Sheik Ahmed a Dahoum, the man to whom the love poem–dedication to *Seven Pillars of Wisdom* (1926) is written ("I loved you, . . . I drew these tides of men into my hands / . . . that your eyes might be shining for me").[3] Lawrence's living under an assumed name as an enlistee in the RAF (Royal Air Force) for the last thirteen years of his life could also be thought of as a kind of "internal exile." The American painter and poet Marsden Hartley (1877–1943) began what would be an extended series of expatriations with his first trip to Europe in 1912, remaining until 1915 and then returning in 1921 for what he planned to be the rest of his life. In 1929 Hartley was forced to return by the Depression, but he did not settle permanently back in the United States until 1937. Hartley's famous series of Berlin abstractions in 1914–15 was inspired by the death in the war of his lover, the German soldier Karl von Freyburg, and Hartley's first book of poems was published abroad, in Paris, in 1923. The "adopted" American philosopher and writer George Santayana* (1863–1952), whose 1894 *Sonnets and Other Verses* contains several male-male love poems and whose *The Last Puritan* (1935) is sometimes marked by strong homosexual feeling, resigned from the Harvard faculty in 1912 and returned to Europe to live for the rest of his life, finally settling permanently in Rome in 1925. Though E. M. Forster (1879–1970) is usually not associated with exile, the three major trips abroad that he took as an adult all had homosexual bases or liberating homosexual dimensions for him. For example, Forster's first visit to India in 1912–13 was significantly motivated by his desire to see Syed Ross Masood, with whom he had fallen in love in 1906 when he served as his tutor, and during his stay in Alexandria from 1915 to 1919, as a World War I Red Cross "searcher," Forster met the homosexual poet C. P. Cavafy* and had his first consummated homosexual affair.

A striking number of expatriate lesbian writers gravitated to Paris at the start of the century and then again after World War I; all eventually came to meet, know, and support each other. The American Natalie Barney* (1876–1972) is remembered now less for her own works than for the writings she inspired (she is the original for the character Valerie Seymour in Radclyffe Hall's *The Well of Loneliness*) and for her salon on the rue Jacob that became a famous meeting place for writers and other artists, many of them gay and lesbian. Barney lived in Paris on and off from 1894 and settled permanently there in 1902, after the death of her father left her independently wealthy. Another heiress who settled in Paris upon reaching her majority was the Anglo-American poet Pauline Tarn (1871–1909), better known by the name she adopted when she began writing, Renée Vivien. Vivien lived with Barney from 1898 to 1900 and during the same years bought a villa on Lesbos as part of her determined commitment to a frankly lesbian subject matter. As a sign of their thoroughgoing expatriation, both Barney and Vivien wrote in French rather than in their native English. Perhaps the most famous lesbian expatriate of this period is Gertrude Stein (1877–1946), who set up house in Paris in 1903, first with her brother Leo and then, from 1909 on, with her lover Alice B. Toklas. Stein and Toklas's evenings in the rue de Fleurus became, like Natalie Barney's salon, legendary meeting places for expatriate and French artists, many of them, again, gay. Stein returned to the United States only once in her lifetime, for a triumphant lecture tour in 1934 after the surprising popular success of *The Autobiography of Alice B. Toklas*. The American-born bookseller, publisher, and memoirist Sylvia Beach (1887–1962) settled permanently in Paris in 1916, after several shorter, earlier stays abroad. Beach established her famous English-language bookstore and lending-library Shakespeare and Company, chiefly remembered now for its 1922 publication of the first complete edition of Joyce's *Ulysses*, across the street from her lover Adrienne Monnier's French-language bookshop. It was in France that Vita Sackville-West (1892–1962) planned to live permanently with Violet Trefusis after their projected escape from their marriages in 1920. The story of their failed elopement is told in the extended autobiographical fragment that Sackville-West left unpublished at her death and that appeared for the first time in her son Nigel Nicholson's memoir of his parents, *Portrait of a Marriage* (1973).

The bisexual American poet H. D.* (Hilda Doolittle, 1886–1961), who had been living abroad since 1911, moved to Switzerland in 1922 with the British lesbian writer Bryher (b. Winifred Ellerman, 1894–1983). Though H. D. still had occasional affairs with men (she had married Richard Aldington in 1913 and had once been engaged to Ezra Pound*), she retained a fundamental, lifelong association with Bryher, and, except for a return to England for the World War

II period, H. D. and Bryher remained based in Switzerland for the rest of their lives. The American author Djuna Barnes* (1892–1982) arrived in Paris in the early 1920s, and France remained her base until her return to the United States in 1940. Barnes produced her most important work while abroad, including her *Ladies Almanack* (1928), an affectionately satirical portrait of Natalie Barney and her lesbian circle, and *Nightwood* (1936), with its central lesbian and gay male characters. Janet Flanner* (1892–1978), who under the pen-name of "Gênet" was to write the *New Yorker*'s "Letter from Paris" from 1925 to 1975, settled in Paris in 1922 with her journalist lover Solita Solano. Except for residence in the United States during World War II, Flanner was based in Paris until 1975, when she returned to New York with her later lover, Natalia Murray. Margaret Anderson (1886–1973), the editor and memoirist best remembered for founding the influential *Little Review* in Chicago in 1914, moved to France in 1923 with the two women who were her major relationships, the editor-writer Jane Heap and the singer Georgette Leblanc (she remained with Leblanc until the latter's death in 1941). Except for returns to the United States during World War II and the year of 1955, Anderson lived in France for the rest of her life.

France was also a magnet for several expatriate gay and bisexual male writers after World War I. Born in Paris and raised there for the first ten years of his life, W. Somerset Maugham* (1874–1965) returned to the Continent in his student years, choosing to study in Heidelberg in 1890. After service in the British ambulance corps and as an intelligence agent during World War I, Maugham began a pattern of constant traveling away from England, finally settling in 1927 in the villa at Cape Ferret in the south of France that would be his home for the rest of his life. Robert McAlmon (1896–1956), the American writer-publisher whose works like *Distinguished Air (Grim Fairy Tales)* (1925) reflect his experience of homosexuality, moved to Paris in the spring of 1921 after his marriage of convenience to the lesbian Bryher. With the exception of a total of three years' travel to the United States and Mexico, Europe—and chiefly France—remained McAlmon's home from the early 1920s until he returned permanently to America in 1946. Paris was one of the several places that the wandering Langston Hughes* (1902–67) sampled during his early years. Hughes lived a bohemian expatriate existence there for most of 1924 and enjoyed some briefer visits in the 1930s (among the other places Hughes journeyed to before finally settling in Harlem in 1941 were West Africa, Italy, Cuba, Haiti, the Soviet Union, Mexico, and Spain). The American novelist Glenway Wescott (1901–87) and his lover Monroe Wheeler (1900–1988), the typographical designer and book publisher, moved to France in 1925, after two extended European visits in the earlier 1920s. They remained there for eight years, chiefly in Villefrance-sur-Mer in the south, during which time Wescott produced most of his major work. Their return to the United States in 1933 was largely prompted by concern about the rise of Hitler, which Wescott chronicled in his 1932 nonfiction book about Germany, *Fear and Trembling*.

The homosexual Peruvian poet César Moro (1903–56), whose given name was Alfredo Quispez Asín, went to Paris in 1925. He remained for eight years, assimilating French culture so deeply that he wrote his most vigorous poetry in French thereafter and earned his living as a French instructor when he returned to Lima. Later Moro expatriated for another, longer, period—to Mexico from 1938 to 1948—then returned to Lima again and lived there until his death. The black American poet Countee Cullen* (1903–46) went to Paris on a Guggenheim fellowship in 1928, remaining for two years and then returning each summer until World War II. As his poem "To France" indicates, Cullen saw France as a kind of spiritual home (like Moro, he earned his living as a French teacher after his return), and, though Cullen's attitude certainly reflected his experience as a racial outsider in the United States, it may have had something to do with his feelings as a sexual outsider as well. The American composer and writer Paul Bowles* (b. 1910) first went abroad at the end of the 1920s and lived chiefly in Europe from 1930 to 1934, studying music with Aaron Copland in Berlin and Virgil Thompson in Paris. After several years back in the United States, where he married the writer Jane Auer (see below) in 1938, Bowles returned abroad after World War II and settled in Morocco, which Gertrude Stein had first suggested as a place of expatriation to him and where he still lives and writes. The American writer-editor Charles Henri Ford (b. 1910), whose novel *The Young and Evil* (1933, coauthored with Parker Tyler) is one of the frankest earlier twentieth-century representations of homosexuality, moved to Paris in 1931 and lived there intermittently until 1934; then he returned to the United States with his lover, the Russian painter Pavel Tchelitchew (whom he had met at Gertrude Stein's). The two men remained in America for eighteen years, then moved to Italy in 1952, for the last five years of Tchelitchew's life; since the early 1960s Ford has divided his time among Nepal, Crete, and the United States.

A new post–World War I development was the number of expatriate gay and bisexual male writers who clustered in central Europe, chiefly in Germany. As reflected in Christopher Isherwood's frank remark from his autobiography that "Berlin meant Boys," Germany in the 1920s and early 1930s had a reputation for many kinds of daring expressiveness, including a relatively greater freedom for homosexuals.[4] The American poet and dance critic Edwin Denby (1903–83) began a twelve-year stay in Europe in 1923, five of which were spent in Vienna (1923–28) and five throughout Germany (1928–33). Denby returned to Europe in 1948, on a Guggenheim fellowship that turned into a four-year stay, this time chiefly around the Mediterranean. Of course, the expatriate male homosexual group most associated with Germany in this period is W. H. Auden,* Christopher Isherwood,* Stephen Spender, and their circle. Auden (1907–73) was the first of this group to go to Berlin, on a supported year abroad his parents gave him after his graduation from Oxford in 1928. Of his compatriots who gathered in Germany, Auden was to stay there the shortest time, returning to England in a year. After another period of repeated traveling in the later 1930s (to Iceland, Spain, and China in 1936, 1937, and 1938), in 1939 Auden expatriated to the

United States and settled in New York; he became an American citizen in 1946. Auden did not sever his ties with Europe completely—he began returning for part of each year in the later 1940s, and in 1972 moved back to England, accepting an honorary fellowship at his Oxford college. He died in Vienna in the following year, near the Austrian summer home he had owned since 1957. Isherwood (1904–86) first went to Berlin on a visit to Auden in 1929. The years he spent teaching English there, from 1930 to 1933, became the basis for his famous *Berlin Stories*, and after a year back in England, Isherwood spent 1934 through 1937 moving among several European cities with his German lover Heinz, in what was ultimately a futile attempt to help Heinz escape conscription into the German army. After his 1938 trip to China with Auden, Isherwood emigrated to the United States with Auden in 1939, becoming an American citizen in the same year, 1946. Unlike Auden, however, Isherwood ultimately moved to California and, in addition, remained based entirely in America for the rest of his life.

Stephen Spender (b. 1909) followed Isherwood to Berlin in 1930, after a summer visit to Hamburg in the previous year ("Now I shall begin to live," he wrote in his journal at that time).[5] In a pattern perhaps mirroring the private sexual split he reveals in his autobiography, *World Within World*, Spender divided each year between Germany and London from 1930 to 1933 and between Vienna and London until 1936, when he again made England his chief base. Then, from 1947 through the 1960s, Spender again divided his time almost equally between two countries, this time England and the United States. Another member of this circle who sojourned to the same places was the poet John Lehmann (b. 1907), whose homosexuality can clearly be inferred from his autobiography and who ultimately became best known as an editor and publisher. Lehmann first went to Berlin at the urging of Spender, whom he had met in 1930, and spent considerable time in Germany and Austria until late in the decade. The poet and journalist Brian Howard (1905–58), who had been one of the older aesthetes at Oxford during Auden's undergraduate years, lived chiefly abroad during the 1930s, mostly in Germany. In 1949 Howard expatriated permanently, carrying his reputation for dissoluteness with him as he wandered among France, Italy, and Spain. He committed suicide in France in 1958, four days after his lover's accidental death.

Other gay male writers of the period expatriated to diverse countries. Sir Harold Acton (b. 1904), perhaps best known for his *Memoirs of an Aesthete* (vol. 1, 1948; vol. 2, 1970) and as the figure upon whom Evelyn Waugh is said to have based the character of Anthony Blanche in *Brideshead Revisited*, was another older Oxford decadent during Auden's time. Acton lived in China from 1932 to 1939 and after World War II settled permanently in Italy (where he had been born), chiefly in Naples. Born in London but brought back to Australia as an infant, the Nobel Prize–winning novelist Patrick White (1912–90) felt himself an alien when he came home in 1930 after education at a British public school. White returned to England in 1932 for what he thought would be a permanent exile, graduating from Cambridge in 1935 and then moving to London to write. In a contrast to the dominant pattern described in this essay, it was White's achievement of a happy homosexual relationship—with Manoly Lascaris, a Greek whom he met during his wartime service in Egypt—that enabled him to return home to Australia after World War II, where he and Lascaris lived from then on. Klaus Mann* (1906–49), Thomas Mann's eldest son, went into exile with his lesbian sister Erika Mann* shortly after Hitler's rise to the German chancellorship in January 1933. During the next three years Klaus Mann lived in France, Switzerland, and the Netherlands (staying for periods with Isherwood and Heinz in Amsterdam), finally emigrating to the United States with Erika in September 1936. After service with the U.S. Army in World War II, Mann spent his remaining years back in Europe, trying, and failing, to achieve a reconciliation with his native Germany and finally committing suicide in France in 1949. Thomas Mann* (1875–1955), whose homosexual feelings are implied in works like *Death in Venice* (1912) but are made much clearer in letters and diaries published later, was on a lecture tour outside Germany when Klaus and Erika fled. At their warning, he decided not to return, settling first near Zurich, then from 1938 to 1952 in the United States (where he became an American citizen in 1944), finally returning to Switzerland for the last three years of his life.

For six years between 1937 and 1946, the American poet Robert Friend (b. 1913) taught English in Puerto Rico and Panama, which he experienced as freer environments for his homosexuality. Friend has lived permanently away from the United States since 1948, first in France and Germany and since 1951 in Israel, where he emigrated when the House Un-American Activities Committee seemed about to revoke his passport and where he recently retired from the faculty of Hebrew University in Jerusalem. The Spanish poet Luis Cernuda* (1902–63), who published a number of daring gay poems in his lifetime, left Spain permanently in 1938, near the end of the civil war. Cernuda lived in Britain for nine years and then in the United States for five (where he taught at Mount Holyoke College), finally settling in 1952 in Mexico, where he lived until his death. The American novelist Frederick Prokosch (b. 1908), whose homosexuality is clearly suggested in recent works like *The Missolonghi Manuscript* (1968) and his memoir *Voices* (1983), started living chiefly in Europe in 1938, after several earlier periods of study and travel abroad. After wartime service in the United States and Stockholm, Prokosch lived in Italy from 1946 to 1953 and then, after a brief return to America, went back to Europe for good in 1954; he now lives and writes in France. The Greek poet and scholar Demetrios Capetanakis (1912–44) went to England in 1939, on a research project to Cambridge to study the life of Thomas Gray, whose homosexuality he recognized. Soon becoming a regular part of John Lehmann's London circle, Capetanakis remained in England during the German occupation of Greece and wrote several revealing male-male love poems in English during those years; he died suddenly in London in 1944, from leukemia.

Among lesbian writers in the post–World War II period, there was a smaller number of exiles, and nothing like the concentrated group in Paris earlier in the century. Jane Bowles* (1917–73), who, as mentioned, married the homosexual composer-writer Paul Bowles in 1938 and whose works like *Two Serious Ladies* (1943) reflect her fundamental attraction to other women, led a wandering existence in Central America, Mexico, and Europe before World War II and, after some years in Paris and Ceylon after the war, finally settled in Morocco with her husband in 1952. Marguerite Yourcenar* (1903–87), who in 1981 became the first woman elected to the French Academy, lived for forty years with another woman, her translator Grace Frick, but wrote about male rather than female homosexuals in her work (e.g., *Alexis*, 1929; *Memoirs of Hadrian*, 1951; *The Abyss*, 1968). Yourcenar traveled widely in the earlier 1930s and planned to expatriate permanently to Greece, but came to the United States in 1939 at the outbreak of World War II at the invitation of Grace Frick and lived there for the rest of her life, chiefly on Mount Desert Island off the coast of Maine; Yourcenar became a U.S. citizen in 1947. Mary Renault (1905–83), who was born Mary Challans, also had a lifelong relationship with another woman but focused on male rather than female homosexuality in her work, in the series of historical novels for which she is best known and in her 1953 *The Charioteer*. Unlike Yourcenar, Renault did deal with lesbians in some earlier work—for example, her 1944 *The Friendly Young Ladies*. After extensive travel immediately after World War II, Renault expatriated to South Africa in 1949 and lived there with her female lover until her death. The American poet Elizabeth Bishop (1911–79) also had an extended relationship with another woman, but never dealt explicitly with homosexuality of any kind in her work. Bishop settled in Brazil in 1951 and was based there for twenty years, until her Brazilian lover's death; she moved back to the United States in 1974 (to Boston, where she had begun to teach at Harvard in 1972), remaining there until her death. The novelist Jane Rule (b. 1931), whose work is frankly lesbian (e.g., her 1964 *Desert of the Heart*, filmed in 1986 as *Desert Hearts*), was born, raised, and educated in the United States, but has lived in British Columbia since 1958 and writes now as a Canadian author. The American poet Marilyn Hacker (b. 1942), whose subject lately has been exclusively lesbian, lived in London in the first half of the 1970s and, though now based back in New York, regularly spends part of each year in France.

A similar number of gay/bisexual male writers expatriated after World War II as in the era between the wars, but in patterns that are usually more periodic or episodic. Though no one international event precipitated all these acts of exile, for the American expatriates one factor was certainly the McCarthy period of the late 1940s and early 1950s, when homosexuals, among other "subversives," were hounded. Robin Maugham* (1916–81), the novelist-travel writer and Somerset Maugham's nephew, was an almost-constant traveler, living more outside England than in it for almost thirty years after the war (his longest residence in one place was on the Spanish island of Ibiza for ten years starting in the 1960s). Maugham's autobiography, *Escape from the Shadows* (1972), is his frankest statement of his homosexuality. Tennessee Williams (1914–83) moved about obsessively, both inside and outside the United States. His first extended foreign stay was a period in Mexico in 1945; this was followed by almost yearlong trips in 1948 and 1949 to Europe and North Africa (where he visited Paul and Jane Bowles), and in 1953 Williams decided to summer abroad each year from then on. After publishing two books in the earlier 1940s in America and serving in France and England during the war, the homosexual American poet Dunstan Thompson (1918–75) settled in England in 1947, where he lived, in Norfolk, for the rest of his life. Gore Vidal* (b. 1925) served in the U.S. Army from 1943 to 1946, and in 1947 began what would be a pattern of periodic expatriation, with trips to Guatemala in that year and in 1949, and a 1948 tour of Europe in between (where he made pilgrimages to several older gay male authors—e.g., George Santayana,* André Gide, E. M. Forster). After living chiefly in the United States in the 1950s, Vidal resumed extended visits abroad in 1963 and lived chiefly in Italy from 1967 to 1976. Though based now more in the United States than anywhere else, Vidal was named an honorary citizen of Ravello in 1983.

James Baldwin* (1924–87) went to Paris in 1948 in what was decidedly a self-conscious exile, one that then could only safely be described in racial terms but that also had a definite homosexual basis (the title of Baldwin's 1962 novel *Another Country* clearly reflects the importance that living abroad had for him, even though the book's action takes place chiefly in the United States). Baldwin returned to America in 1957 and was active in the civil rights movement through the 1960s. After that France became Baldwin's permanent residence (he died at his home in St. Paul de Vence), though he made so many extended return visits to the United States in the 1970s and 1980s that he called himself a commuter rather than an expatriate. After the notoriety of *Other Voices, Other Rooms* (1948) associated him definitively with homosexuality, Truman Capote (1924–84) lived entirely in Europe until the later 1950s, and he maintained a home in Switzerland after his return to the United States at that time. The American composer and memoirist Ned Rorem (b. 1923) first went abroad in 1949, for what became an eight-year stay in France and Morocco. His 1966 *Paris Diary* covering that period was, at its time, one of the frankest revelations of homosexuality by an American. Though based back in the United States from the late 1950s on, Rorem has continued to visit Europe for extended periods since then. William S. Burroughs* (b. 1914) lived almost entirely outside the United States from 1949 to 1974, at first because of conflicts with the law and his addiction to drugs (of which he was finally cured in 1959). From 1949 to 1952 Burroughs lived chiefly in Mexico and South America, from 1953 to 1958 in Tangier (where he wrote most of what became *Naked Lunch* and the trilogy *The Soft Machine*, *The Ticket That Exploded*, and *Nova Express*), from 1958 to 1964 in Paris, and from 1965 to 1974 in London; Burroughs has been based back in the United States since the mid 1970s. The American painter and writer Tobias Schneebaum (b. 1921), whose homosexuality figures in his *Keep the River on Your Right*

(1969), *Wild Man* (1979), and *Where the Spirits Dwell* (1988), began a pattern of repeated traveling in 1949 and lived in a variety of foreign countries for a total of fourteen years between then and the early 1980s. Schneebaum's journeying has ranged from Mexico and Peru, to Greece and Italy, to Ethiopia, Somalia, and the Sudan, to Turkey, the Philippines, and New Guinea.

John Horne Burns (1916–53), the American novelist whose 1947 *The Gallery* contained a daring, extended gay episode and was hailed as one of the most important novels to have come out of World War II, moved to Europe at the end of the 1940s and died of a stroke at the age of thirty-six in Livorno, where he had been living with his Italian lover. The Anglo-Indian novelist and travel writer Aubrey Menen (1912–89), who alludes to his homosexuality in his autobiographical *The Space within the Heart* (1970) and implies it strongly in his 1974 novel about William Beckford, *Fonthill*, settled in Rome in the late 1940s, after work in journalism and the theater in England in the later 1930s and service in India during World War II. Alfred Chester* (1928–71), the American novelist and short story writer in whose work homosexuality is often a subject, first expatriated in 1951, living in Paris until 1959. He went abroad again in 1963, spending two years in Morocco, then from 1965 to 1970 moved back and forth among New York, Morocco, Paris, and London; in 1970 Chester moved to Israel and died there in the following year. The American poet Allen Ginsberg (b. 1926) has often led a wandering life. Beginning with a year's visit to the Yucatan in 1953, and with some later extended trips (e.g., a year's traveling in Tangier, Spain, Italy, Vienna, Munich, and Paris in 1957–58 and a journey through France, Morocco, Greece, Israel, India, Vietnam, and Japan from 1961 to 1963), Ginsberg often lived abroad, until settling back in New York in the mid 1970s. The American poet Harold Norse (b. 1916), who has written openly about his homosexuality throughout his career, expatriated to Europe in 1953 after the publication of his first book. He lived in Italy, Greece, and Morocco until 1968, when he returned to settle in the San Francisco area. The British-born poet Thom Gunn (b. 1929), whose homosexuality has become increasingly plain in his work, left England in 1954 for the United States, where, except for a year back in London in the mid 1960s, he has lived ever since. Gunn's initial reasons for leaving were both personal and professional—an involvement with an American man and the award of a creative writing fellowship at Stanford—and he has made his home in San Francisco since 1960.

The American poet John Ashbery (b. 1927), whose homosexuality is often obscured in his work, lived in Paris for almost the entire decade between 1955 and 1965, working for about half that period as an art critic for the Paris *Herald Tribune*, *Art News*, and *Art International*; he has been based in New York since the later 1960s. The Argentine-born novelist Manuel Puig* (1932–90), whose well-known *Kiss of the Spider Woman* (1976; English, 1979) is the clearest revelation of his homosexuality, lived chiefly outside Argentina after 1956—in London, Rome, Stockholm, Paris, and New York from 1956 to 1967, then back in New York in 1973 for almost a decade, and finally in Brazil. David Malouf (b. 1934), the Australian novelist and poet in whose work homosexuality has been a recurring motif, left Australia in 1958 and spent ten years teaching in England and traveling on the Continent. After another ten years back in Australia, he moved to Italy to live and write in the late 1970s and has only just recently returned to live in Sydney. The American poet James Merrill (b. 1926), whose homosexuality is expressed most directly in his recent trilogy—*The Book of Ephraim* (1976), *Mirabell's Book of Numbers* (1978), and *Scripts for the Pageant* (1980)—has been living for half of each year in Athens since 1959. The poet and classicist Daryl Hine (b. 1936), whose recent verse narratives, *Academic Festival Overtures* (1985) and *In and Out* (1989), are his frankest homosexual statements, was born in British Columbia and went to college in Canada, but came to the United States in 1962 for graduate study and has lived and taught there ever since. David Plante* (b. 1940), the American novelist in whose work homosexuality has become an increasingly central theme (e.g., his recent *The Catholic*, 1986), has been living in England since 1966, though since 1979 he has spent part of each year back in the United States, as a writer-in-residence at the University of Tulsa.

As this survey indicates, permanent or periodic exile from native country has been a strikingly visible phenomenon among gay, lesbian, and bisexual writers in the twentieth century, in a proportion that seems far to outstrip what is presumed to be the distribution of homosexuals in the population at large. A decisive break in that pattern of exiling does occur, however, but not until the emergence of the contemporary gay liberation movement, with its symbolic beginning in the 1969 Stonewall riots in New York City and its rapid expansion throughout the West in the 1970s. Through the rise and fall of specific oppressive historical episodes for homosexuals (e.g., the Oscar Wilde scandal, Nazism in Europe, American McCarthyism), twentieth-century gay literary exile remained relatively steady and abundant until the 1960s and 1970s; of the sizable group of post–World War II gay/lesbian literary expatriates mentioned here, only three—Hacker, Malouf, and Plante—can be said to be chiefly or exclusively post-Stonewall writers. Optimistic predictions should not necessarily be drawn from the recent marked decline in gay literary exiling, however. As mentioned, the steady earlier stream traced here suggests that exile among homosexuals is primarily a function of the more deeply embedded and pervasive structures of gay oppression than of any one specific menacing event; consequently, any social and political developments that threaten to stifle, halt, or reverse the general gay liberation movement could spark another round of large-scale exile among homosexuals. For example, such recent developments in the United States as the Supreme Court's upholding of the Georgia sodomy law against homosexuals in 1986 and the 1988 election of the Bush-Quayle ticket with its right-wing campaign themes could imperil the gay movement there and create a whole new generation of American gay literary exiles in the late twentieth century.

Notes

1. Mikhail Kuzmin, *Selected Prose and Poetry*, ed. and trans. by Michael Green (Ann Arbor: Ardis, 1980), pp. 32–33.

2. Quoted in Miriam J. Benkovitz, *Ronald Firbank* (New York: Knopf, 1969), p. 294.

3. T. E. Lawrence, *Seven Pillars of Wisdom* (New York: Penguin, 1976), p. 9.

4. Christopher Isherwood, *Christopher and His Kind, 1929–1939* (New York: Farrar, Straus & Giroux, 1976), p. 2.

5. Stephen Spender, *World Within World* (New York: Harcourt Brace, 1951), p. 95.

JOSEPH CADY

HOLLYWOOD TEN. *See* John Howard Lawson* and Dalton Trumbo*.

HOLOCAUST WRITING. Holocaust writing is the name given to that period in history (1932–45) in which writers observed and recorded the horrors of Nazi Germany's racist policy aimed at the extermination of the Jewish people in Europe, and during which time more than 6 million European Jews perished under direct orders of German political leaders. The name assigned to this period of horrors in which man treated his fellow man with a contempt and sadism never before witnessed on so massive a scale is redolent of the crematoriums in Nazi German concentration camps into which Jews were flung after their death as a result of showers of poison gas, torture, brutality, and a determined Nazi regimen of starvation and slave labor. Most Holocaust literature takes as its aim the "witnessing" of these horrors as a means of forbidding the loss of its memory. In exploring the distinctions of Holocaust literature, Alvin H. Rosenfeld, in his study *A Double Dying: Reflections on Holocaust Literature* (Bloomington, Ind., 1988, c. 1980), lists the following questions for study:

Who are its significant authors? What are its major themes, styles, and genres? Have we yet learned sufficiently well how to read it so as begin to distinguish between its "good" and "bad" books, its most authentic or spurious and exploitative strains of expression? Can Holocaust literature be "literary" in the common and accepted senses of that term? Can it afford *not* to be literary? In what ways does it seem, almost unavoidably, to be a religious literature . . . ? What is to be gained from reading Holocaust literature, which is bound to be distressing and frequently more than distressing, or what is to be lost from avoiding it? (p. 5)

Rosenfeld's systematic study indicates many of the levels of complexity in what is seemingly an awesome phenomenon of the literature of a particular genocide. His commentary suggests and explores the difficulty of refacing and reviewing in fiction, poetry, and drama the incidents of the Holocaust and of attempting to play "witness" to them in a never-to-be-forgotten record. His commentary echoes other writers on the Holocaust caught in the terrible dilemma of "witnessing" and possibly exploiting the experience of regraving the images of that Hellish period.

Many Holocaust writers attempted to flee from Nazi Germany and the lands it conquered—Austria, Poland, Czechoslovakia, France, Italy, Hungary, and Yugoslavia—but were too late in their hindsight of perception. Many writers refused to leave Germany or its conquered territories out of a stubborn belief that what they were witnessing was a transient nightmare that a new day of reason would disperse. Such visionaries perished of their own accord with their own natures, noble in their dedication to an obliterated nobility of man. A few Jews escaped the horrors; many of these people were writers and intellectuals who began a new wandering as outcasts and refugees. Their exile sometimes resulted in a new home in the United States, England, Australia, New Zealand, South America, and elsewhere; others were to die of exhaustion and the vengeance of their memory, a memory that would not permit them the energy of a new pursuing dream.

It is important to distinguish Holocaust writers, those observers who suffered persecution and/or exile, from Holocaust writings, those works dealing with the period of the Holocaust and its effect on human existence. Listed below are Holocaust writers; some are treated with individual entries in this volume. Holocaust literature, which includes work by non-Jews, may be studied in various critical works and in academic institutions as a specialized area of literature. One of the perplexing problems of Holocaust writing and Holocaust writers is that some writers began their careers in the rendering of their real and/or associational experience of the Holocaust—among them Jerzy Kosinski* and Andre Schwarz-Bart—but then turned to other areas for the subject, content and vision of their work. Are such writers to be considered Holocaust writers if only the first part of their writing lives was the Holocaust? As survivors unlike Elie Wiesel,* who continues with each novel to "witness" the testing Holocaust of his experiences, are they to be considered Holocaust writers or simply writers?

Holocaust Writers: Ilse Aichinger, Yehuda Amichai,* A. Anatoli (Kuznetsov),* Aharon Appelfeld,* Hannah Arendt,* Hanoch Bartov, Giorgio Bassani, Jurek Becker,* Dan Ben-Amotz, Bruno Bettelheim, Tadeusz Borowski, Rachmil Bryks, Elias Canetti,* Paul Celan,* Elie Cohen, Hana Demetz,* Viktor Frankl, Saul Friedlander, Ladislav Fuks, Romain Gary, Yehoshua Gilboa, Chaim Grade,* Kitty Hart, Eva Heyman, Yorum Kaniuk, Chaim Kaplan, Josef Katz, Yitzhak Katznelson, Ka-Tzetnik 135633 (Yehiel De Nur), Gerda Weissman Klein, Janusz Korizak, Jerzy Kosinski,* Abba Kovner, Isabella Leitner, Carlo Levi,* Primo Levi,* Jakov Lind,* Arnost Lustig,* Curzio Malaparte, Janos Pilininszky, Mikos Radnoti, Tadeusz Rozewicz, Yitskhov Rudashevski, Nelly Sachs,* Andre Schwarz-Bart, Lore Segal,* Hannah Senesh, Isaac Bashevis Singer,* Israel Joshua Singer,* Manès Sperber,* George Steiner,* Simone Weil,* Elie Wiesel,* Simon Wiesenthal, Michael Zylberberg, Krystana Zywulska.

Consult: Edward Alexander, *The Resonance of Dust: Essays on Holocaust Literature and Jewish Fate* (1979); Robert Alter, *After the Tradition* (1969); Lucy Davidowitz, *The War against the Jews 1933–1945* (1975); *Dimensions of the Holocaust: Lectures at Northwestern University* (Elie Wiesel, Lucy Davidowitz, Dorothy Rabinowitz, Robert McAfee Brown, 1977); Terrence Des Pres, *The Survivor: An Anatomy of Life in the Death Camps* (1976); Israel Gutman, ed., *Encyclopedia of the Holocaust*, 4 vols. (1990); Raul Hillberg, *The Destruction of the European Jews* (1961); Laurence L. Langer, *The Holocaust and the Literary Imagination* (1975); Charles S. Maier, *The Unmasterable Past: History, Holocaust, and German National Unity* (1989); A. Mintz, *Hurban: Response to Catastrophe in Hebrew Literature* (1985); Alvin H. Rosenfeld, *A Double Dying: Reflections on Holocaust Literature* (1988); David Rosenberg, ed., *Testimony: Contem-*

porary Writers Make the Holocaust Personal (1990); Byron L. Serwin and Susan G. Ament, eds., *Encountering the Holocaust: An Interdisciplinary Survey* (1979); Yuri Suhl, ed., *They Fought Back: The Story of the Jewish Resistance in Nazi Europe* (1967); A. J. Yuter, *The Holocaust in Hebrew Literature: From Genocide to Rebirth* (1984); Susan Zuccotti, *The Italians and the Holocaust: Persecution, Rescue and Survival* (London, 1987). See also *Guide to Jewish History under Nazi Impact*, ed. Jacob Robinson and Philip Friedman (1960), and annual volumes published by Yad Vashem (Jerusalem) and YIVO (New York).

HUNGARIAN WRITERS IN EXILE. (*See also* individual entries on Sándor András, George Faludy, Julius Háy, Arthur Koestler, György Lukács, Sàndor Márai, Ferenc Molnár, Paul Tabori, Lajos Zilahy)

BAKUCZ, József. Born January 2, 1929, in Debrecen; residing in Burlington, Vermont. Avant-garde Hungarian poet and critic; published in French, English, and Hungarian.

BARÁNSZKY-JÓB, László. Born September 8, 1930, in Budapest; residing in New York City; Hungarian poet, critic, and art historian; published in French, English, and Hungarian.

CSIKY, Ágnes-Mária. Born December 23, 1918, in Budapest; residing in Colon, West Germany. Hungarian poet, playwright, and essayist; published in German and Hungarian.

DEDINSZKY, Erika. Born January 26, 1942, in Budapest; residing in Hilversum, Holland. Hungarian poet, translator, critic, and essayist; published in Dutch, English, and Hungarian.

DÉNES, Tibor. Born July 15, 1907, in Nagyvárad, Rumania, then part of the Austro-Hungarian Empire. Died March 17, 1983, in Lugano, Switzerland. Hungarian novelist, critic, essayist, dramaturge, and journalist; published in German, French, Italian, English, and Hungarian.

ENCZI, Endre. Born 1903 in Budapest; died 1974 in Paris, France. Hungarian novelist, essayist, and editor. Published in French and Hungarian. In Paris he was the editor-in-chief of the most influential literary periodical of exiled writers after the 1956 revolution.

FÁY, Ferenc. Born June 20, 1921, in Pécel; died July 6, 1981, in Toronto, Canada. Hungarian poet; published in French, English, and Hungarian.

FERDINANDY, György. Born October 11, 1935, in Budapest; residing in Cayey, Puerto Rico. Hungarian novelist, critic, and essayist; published in French, Spanish, English, and Hungarian.

FORRAI, Eszter. Born February 26, 1938, in Budapest; residing in Paris. Hungarian poet; published in French and Hungarian.

GÖMÖRI, György. Born April 3, 1934, in Budapest; residing in Cambridge, England. Hungarian poet, critic, translator, and essayist; published in English, Hungarian, and Polish.

HALÁSZ, Péter. Born April 10, 1922, in Budapest; residing in Munich, West Germany. Hungarian novelist, journalist, and critic; published in German, English, and Hungarian.

HORVÁTH, Elemér. Born April 15, 1933, in Csorna; residing in Mahopac, New York. Hungarian poet; published in English and Hungarian.

KABDEBÓ, Tamás. Born February 5, 1934, in Budapest; residing in Maynooth, Ireland. Hungarian novelist, translator, and essayist; published in English, Welsh, and Hungarian.

KEMENES-GÉFIN, Làszló. Born October 16, 1937, in Szombathely; residing in Montreal, Canada. Hungarian poet and essayist; published in French, English, and Hungarian.

KIBÉDI VARGA, Áron. Born February 4, 1930, in Szeged; residing in Amsterdam, Holland. Hungarian poet, critic, translator, and essayist; published in English, Dutch, and Hungarian.

MAJOR-ZALA, Lajos. Born January 1, 1930, in Kerkateskánd; residing in Pensier, Switzerland. Hungarian poet and essayist; published in French, German, and Hungarian.

MAKKAI, Ádám. Born December 16, 1935, in Budapest; residing in Lake Bluff, Illinois. Hungarian poet, linguist, translator, and essayist; published in Russian, French, German, English, and Hungarian.

MÉRAY, Tibor. Born April 6, 1924, in Budapest; residing in Paris. Hungarian journalist, novelist, essayist, and scriptwriter; published in French, English, and Hungarian. Editor of the most influential, Paris-based literary periodical in Hungarian where most of the exiled writers contributed their manuscripts.

MONOSZLOY, Dezsö. Born December 28, 1923, in Budapest; residing in Vienna, Austria. Hungarian novelist, playwright, poet, journalist, critic, and essayist. Published in German, French, English, and Hungarian. Since 1962 he has been editor-in-chief of the *Gazette Littéraire* (Irodalmi Ujság), the most important Hungarian literary periodical outside Hungary.

NAGY, Pál. Born August 23, 1936, in Salgótarján; residing in Paris. Avant-garde Hungarian poet, printer, critic, and essayist; published in French and Hungarian.

NYIRÖ, József. Born April 13, 1889, in Székelyzsombor, Rumania, then part of the Austro-Hungarian Empire; died in 1953 in Madrid, Spain. Hungarian novelist and essayist; published in German, Spanish, and Hungarian.

PÁLÓCZY-HORVÁTH, György. Born in 1908 in Budapest; died in London, England. Hungarian novelist, journalist, critic, editor, and essayist; published in German, French, English, and Hungarian.

PAPP, Tibor. Born April 2, 1936, in Tokaj; residing in Paris. Avant-garde Hungarian poet, printer, and essayist; published in French and Hungarian.

SAÁRY, Éva. Born November 28, 1929, in Balatonkenese; residing in Lugano, Switzerland. Hungarian journalist, poet, painter, and essayist; published in German, Italian, and Hungarian.

SZTÁRAY, Zoltán. Born June 20, 1918, in Magyarcsacholy; residing in San Bernardino, California. Hungarian journalist, critic, and essayist; published in English and Hungarian.

TARDOS, Tibor. Born January 20, 1918, in Berettyóújfalu; residing in Paris. Hungarian novelist and essayist; published in French, German, and Hungarian.

THINSZ, Géza. Born June 9, 1934, in Budapest; residing in Stockholm, Sweden. Hungarian poet, translator, and essayist; published in Swedish and Hungarian.

TOLLAS, Tibor. Born December 21, 1920, in Nagybarca; residing in Munich, West Germany. Hungarian poet, editor, publisher, and essayist; published in German, French, Spanish, English, and Hungarian.

TÜZ, Tamás. Born April 18, 1916, in Gyor; residing in Toronto, Canada. Hungarian poet; published in English and Hungarian.

VAJDA, Albert. Born in 1918; residing in Sarasota, Florida. Hungarian novelist, journalist, humorist, and essayist; published in German, French, English, and Hungarian.

VITÉZ, György. Born April 10, 1933, in Budapest; residing in Montreal, Canada. Hungarian poet and essayist; published in French, English, and Hungarian.

ZEND, Róbert. Born December 2, 1929, in Budapest; died June 27, 1985, in Toronto, Canada. Hungarian poet, cartoonist, translator, journalist, and essayist; published in English and Hungarian.

CLARA GYORGYEY

IRANIAN WRITERS IN EXILE. Over the past century, exiled Iranian writers have contributed substantially not only to their nation's literature but also to its major social and political changes. Indeed, both of the nation's revolutions— the Constitutional and the one of 1979—were inspired, if not directly led, by prominent figures who lived and wrote outside the country.

During the period of struggle for national independence, which began with the Tobacco Protest of 1890–92 and culminated in the Constitutional Revolution of 1905–11, the most influential writers were those who wrote for progressive journals in Turkey, Egypt, India, and England, where there were established Iranian intellectual communities. Of these the most important community was in Istanbul, where a circle of outstanding poets and journalists worked on the newspaper *Akhtar* (Star), founded in 1875. Two other notable newspapers were *Habl al-Matin* (The Firm Chord), founded in Calcutta in 1893, and *Soraya* (The Pleiades), founded in Cairo in 1898. Among the writers, the most important politically was the utopian pan-Islamist and principal architect of the Constitutional Movement, Jamal al-Din Afghani (1839–97), who spent much of his life abroad, in India, Afghanistan (where he assumed his surname), Arabia, Egypt, and later Europe and Istanbul. Also prominent were Mirza Malkum Khan (1833– 1908), who settled first in Istanbul then in London, where in 1890 he founded the influential prerevolutionary newspaper *Qanun* (Law), to which Afghani contributed, and Abdol Rahim Talibof (1855–1910), who lived in Russia and whose *Ways of the Charitable* (Cairo, 1905) was one of the major prose works of the period. All three men died in exile: Afghani in Istanbul, Malkum Khan in London, and Talibof in Baku. In contrast, one of the nation's leading journalists, satirist Ali Akbar Dehkhoda (1879–1956), fled to Europe temporarily to escape imprisonment, returning to Iran in 1908 to resume an active literary and political career. During this period, too, the first novel in Persian was published abroad by yet another writer who lived long in exile, Haj Zaynal Abedin Maraghehi (1837–1910): this was *The Travel Diary of Ibrahim Beg*, which appeared in three volumes printed separately in Cairo (vol. 1, 1903), Calcutta (vol. 2, 1905), and Istanbul (vol. 3, 1909).

With the passage of the Constitution of 1906, which turned the country into a parliamentary monarchy, there followed, according to historian Nikki R. Keddie, four "relatively free periods" in modern Iranian history: 1906–11, 1918–21, 1941–53, and 1978–80.[1] During each of these periods of relative freedom at home, there was a corresponding lack of need for writers, intellectuals, and political activists to seek exile. At the same time, for those who did, during the ensuing intervals, exile became more or less a permanent condition, especially for those who had sought refuge in the Soviet Union and Eastern Europe. In any case, it was during the long intervals between the "relatively free periods" that exile communities grew in Europe and later also in America.

1912–21: The Post-Constitutional Period

During World War I, the first major European community of Iranian exiles was established in Berlin. Here a group of democrats opposed both to the reactionary Qajar regime and to the British and Russian presence in Iran, founded, with the aid of the German government, the Kaviani Press, which in 1916 started publishing the innovative and progressive journal *Kaveh*. Under the editorship of Hasan Taqizadeh (1877–1969), who later returned to Iran to become a member of government and head of the Progressive Party, *Kaveh* was first a purely political journal, then from 1920 on turned to literature, thereby becoming, as one scholar put it, "one of the important focal points of the Persian literary renaissance."[2] Among *Kaveh*'s foremost contributors was Mohammad Ali Jamalzadeh (b. 1895), who had left Iran in boyhood and whose literary classic, *Once Upon a Time*, published by the Kaviani Press in 1921, was the first collection of Persian short stories. Thus, the originators in Persian of both the novel and the modern short story were writers who had chosen to live in permanent exile.

1921–41: The Period of Reza Shah

Following the rise in 1921 of the military leader Reza Khan, who in 1925 became Reza Shah Pahlavi, there gradually set in another period of repression, especially for those politicized writers who were opposed to his dictatorial rule. In 1922 the Marxist poet Abol Qasem Lahuti (1887–1957) fled to Russia, where he spent the rest of his life in exile and published his *Divan*, or collected works, in Moscow in 1946. Although Lahuti was generally admired as an accomplished as well as a revolutionary poet, his reputation diminished with his stay in Russia, where he was more widely read than in his own country. Another poet Mohammad Reza Eshqi (1893–1924), who failed to escape, was murdered. Also critical of Reza Shah was the controversial and eclectic man of letters Ali Dashti (1896–1981), who, after several bouts in prison, went to Russia on the tenth anniversary of the Russian Revolution, then traveled in Europe, subsequently returning somewhat tempered to enter the Majlis, or parliament, and later to rise in government service.

During the twenties, too, a growing number of Iran's future writers left the country to study in Europe, mainly in Germany, France, and Switzerland. In Germany, following the temporary closure of *Kaveh* owing to lack of funding, there appeared several other Iranian journals, the two most notable being *Iranshahr* (Iran City), founded in 1922 and from the literary standpoint the successor of *Kaveh*, and the monthly *Farangistan* (Europe), both of which were published in Berlin.

In 1931, following the passage of legislation in Iran outlawing communism, there was another round of repression in the country, causing the outspoken revolutionary poet and journalist Mohammad Farrokhi Yazdi (1899–1939) to flee first to Russia then to Berlin, where he wrote for the socialist Iranian newspaper *Paykar* (Struggle). Another such paper, *Setareye Sorkh* (Red Star), was put out in Leipzig. Yazdi later returned to Iran, on the assurance that he would be left free, only to be arrested and to die in prison under mysterious circumstances. Meanwhile, in 1937 there occurred the wholesale arrest and imprisonment of the largest group of intellectuals with leftist leanings. This group, which came to be known as "The Fifty-Three People," was headed by the socialist writer and teacher Taqi Erani (1902–40), who died in prison, and included the future founding members of the Communist Tudeh Party, among them the major writer and novelist Bozorg Alavi (b. 1904). Also in 1937 the nation's foremost literary artist, Sadegh Hedayat (1902–51), spent a brief and unhappy period of voluntary exile in India, where he published in Bombay (owing to censorship at home) what is still, perhaps, the most celebrated Iranian novel, *The Blind Owl*. Another edition was subsequently published in Tehran in 1941, after the fall of Reza Shah.

1941–79: The Reign of Mohammad Reza Shah Pahlavi

With the Allied Occupation of Iran in 1941 and the resultant abdication of Reza Shah—who himself died in exile in Johannesburg three years later—there followed the longest period of relative freedom in the country's recent history: twelve years. During this stretch, of all the notable Iranian writers only two remained living abroad: the poet Lahuti in Moscow and the prose writer Jamalzadeh in Geneva. In early January of 1951, however, Hedayat unaccountably left Iran again, this time for Paris, the city of his youth, where, on April 9, he committed suicide. This event, along with his burial in Père Lachaise cemetery, augured a turning point: whereas before, Paris had been an intellectual rather than a political haven for Iranians abroad, henceforward it was to become increasingly the principal center of dissident activity. In terms of political as well as cultural importance, Berlin was giving way to Paris.

This shift occurred particularly after the CIA-sponsored coup d'état of 1953, which brought down the government of Mohammad Mossadegh and restored the regime of Mohammad Reza Shah Pahlavi. Once again there were widespread arrests and executions, along with the dissolution of leftist and liberal political organizations, including the outlawed Tudeh Party. Alavi, who at the time had been in Europe to receive the gold medal in literature at the World Peace Council in Prague, opted to stay abroad rather than to return home to face reimprisonment. Thereafter he lived in East Berlin—for the next generation his country's most prominent literary dissident in exile—teaching Persian at Humboldt University and writing scholarly works in German and fiction in Persian, mainly for *Kaveh*, which had been revived in Munich, where it continues to be published.[3] Another Marxist writer who abandoned the country to avoid imprisonment was poet and satirist Mohammad Ali Afrashteh (1908–59), who went in 1954 to Russia then to Bulgaria, where he wrote for a number of Bulgarian-Turkish publications under the pseudonym Hasan Sharif, and where he also wrote a collection of short stories, *The Nose of the Shah*, which was published posthumously in Sophia in 1963. During their exile, the works of both these writers were banned in Iran.

Significantly, however, over the next two decades, most of the nation's leading writers continued living and writing in the homeland, despite political restrictions and censorship. Among them were the major novelist Sadegh Chubak (b. 1914) and former Tudeh Party members Mohammad Etemadzadeh (aka Behazin, b. 1915) and poet Nima Yushij (1895–1960), as well as a younger generation of literary artists, including prose writers Jalal Al Ahmad (1923–69), Simin Daneshvar (b. 1921), Ali Mohammad Afghani (b. 1925), Gholam Hosein Saedi (1935–85), and Samad Behrangi (1939–68), and poets Ahmad Shamlu (b. 1925), Nader Naderpur (b. 1929), and Forough Farrokhzad (1935–67), few of whom had left the country except for brief excursions. This was the period which, in essence, reaped the literary harvest of the dozen "relatively free" years of 1941–53.

Meanwhile, in 1963 the country went through another round of political turmoil, largely as a result of the widespread opposition to the Shah's forceful implementation of his land and social reform programs known as the White Revolution. This led to the exile of three key figures who were to play prominent roles in the next revolution. Of these the most important, politically, was the Ayatollah Ruhollah Khomeini (1902–89), who was exiled first to Turkey, then to Najaf, Iraq, where he set up his headquarters in opposition to the Shah's regime and wrote his blueprint for the one to follow, *Islamic Government* (Najaf, 1970), before moving on to Paris in 1978 for the final stage of the revolutionary takeover. Also important politically were two theorists who studied in Paris: Ali Shariati (1933–77), whose later writings made him, in the words of one historian, "the main intellectual, even the Fanon, of the Islamic Revolution,"[4] and Abol Hasan Bani-Sadr (b. 1933), who, like Khomeini, was out of the country from 1963 to 1979, and who was later to become Iran's first elected president. Whereas Shariati wrote most of his works after returning to Iran in 1964, Bani-Sadr wrote his in Paris. After a period of imprisonment and internal exile in 1974–76, Shariati again left Iran for Europe, where he died in London.

Also relevant but in another category—that of emigrants rather than exiles—a small number of disaffected writers came to America, during the fifties and early sixties, ostensibly to study. Among these was the promising novelist Taghi

Modarressi (b. 1934), who, after completing his medical training, settled in Baltimore (with his wife, American novelist Anne Tyler) as a child psychiatrist at the University of Maryland School of Medicine. Having written both of his early novels in Persian, Modarressi wrote his third, *The Book of Absent People* (1986), in English. Other westernized Iranians who likewise emigrated to America and write in English are F. M. Esfandiary (b. 1930), Donné Raffat (b. 1938), and Nahid Rachlin (b. 1941).

As for the Iranian writers who stayed home and wrote in Persian, matters became increasingly difficult during the seventies, especially for those who were actively involved with the Iranian Writers Association in denouncing government repression and censorship. One such member was poet and art critic Khosrow Golesorkhi (1941–74), who was executed. Other members were variously imprisoned. These included poet, critic, and novelist Reza Baraheni (b. 1935), who came to America in 1974 and again in 1977–78; poet Ahmad Shamlu, who in 1976 spent a year in Princeton, New Jersey, reviving the journal *Iranshahr*, which was published first in Washington, D.C., then in London; and playwright, screenwriter, and novelist Gholam Hosein Saedi, who, following his imprisonment, spent several months in America in 1978. Of these writers, perhaps the one best known to Americans was Reza Baraheni, who, during his exile, wrote in English and published *The Crowned Cannibals* (1977), a graphic exposé of repression under the Pahlavis.[5]

1979–Present: The Iranian Revolution and After

With the Iranian Revolution of 1979, the Shah was overthrown and removed from the country—like his father, to die in exile in 1980—and literally all the writers who had left Iran for political reasons were free to return, including the one of longest standing, Bozorg Alavi. By the following year, however, the Shiite fundamentalists had taken over the revolution, replacing the secular Constitution of 1906 with the religious one of 1980, which turned the country into an Islamic republic under the rule of Ayatollah Khomeini. From this point on, writers opposed to the Islamic regime had, essentially, three options: to remain silent; to voice their views and risk imprisonment (as did Baraheni) or execution (as did poet Said Soltanpur in 1980); or to seek refuge abroad. A substantial number chose the last alternative. After two trips to Iran, Alavi returned in 1980 to permanent exile in East Berlin, where he continues writing. Novelist Sadegh Chubak left for America to settle in Berkeley, California, where he is currently working on his memoirs. Poets Ibrahim Golestan (b. 1922), Ibrahim Khoi (b. 1938), and Hasan Fakhrai (aka Golchin) settled in London. The greatest number of writers, however, went to Paris, which continues to be the major center of Iranian exile activity. Residing here is the leading poet in exile, Nader Naderpur, who in 1982 published his collection of verse *False Morning*, expressing his response to the revolution. Another poet living in Paris is Nemat Mirzadeh (aka M. Azarm, b. 1938). Also in 1982 Gholam Hosein Saedi escaped Iran via Pakistan and arrived in the city to reestablish *Alefba*

(Alphabet), a major cultural journal that had been discontinued in Tehran. Saedi was at work on several other projects, including a film on the Iranian Revolution, when he died in Paris in November 1985. About this Parisian community of Iranian exiles, novelist Esmail Fassih (b. 1935) has written a novel, *Sorraya in a Coma*, published in Tehran in 1984 and in an English version in London in 1985.

Politically, too, as before the revolution, Paris remains a hive of anti-Iranian government activity. Published here are journals such as the Mojaheddin's *Enqel-abe Eslami* (Islamic Revolution), which first supported then rejected exiled former President Bani-Sadr's views on Iranian politics, and the National Resistance Movement's *Nahzat* (Resurgence), organ of the followers of the Shah's last prime minister, Shahpur Bakhtiar. Elsewhere there are other news journals, ranging from the Tudeh party's *Nameye Mardom* (The Peoples' Newsletter), published in Sweden, to the conservative *Iran Times*, a bilingual weekly published in Washington, D.C. Notable also are several other journals with international circulations: *Ruzgare Now* (New Era), founded in Paris in 1982; the satirical weekly *Asqar Aqa* (Mr. Asqar, the equivalent of *Punch*), founded in London in 1979 and also published in Newport Beach, California; the literary monthly *Par* (Quill), centered in Arlington, Virginia, and published in Washington, D.C.; and two other publications brought out in southern California: the monthly *Mellate Bidar* (Awakened Nation), founded in Los Angeles in 1982, and the literary digest *Rahavard* (Souvenir), published in Beverly Hills and consisting mostly of translations from Western literature into Persian for the Farsi-reading exile community. Finally, issued in London as of July 1988, is the new monthly review of Iranian affairs, *Zendehbad* (Long Live!), published in English by former *Tehran Journal* British journalist James Underwood, which extends the concept of exile literature to include the contributions of those foreigners who have found in Iran a home away from their home of origin.

Overall, since the Iranian Revolution, the number of Iranian exiles has been estimated at two million. Although this figure is only general, it does reflect the vast increase in the segment of the nation's literate populace living abroad in either temporary or permanent exile; which increase, in turn, provides the broadest base in history for continuing Iranian exile activity.

Notes

1. Nikki R. Keddie, *Roots of Revolution* (New Haven, Conn.: Yale University Press, 1981), p. 196.

2. Věra Kubíčková, "Persian Literature of the Twentieth Century," in *History of Iranian Literature*, ed. Jan Rypka (Dordrecht, Holland: D. Reidel, 1968), p. 368.

3. For an account of Alavi's life in exile, along with a translation of his prison stories, see Donné Raffat's *Prison Papers of Bozorg Alavi* (Syracuse, N.Y.: Syracuse University Press, 1985).

4. Ervand Abrahamian, *Iran Between Two Revolutions* (Princeton, N.J.: Princeton University Press, 1982), p. 466.

5. A concise assessment of Baraheni's stay and writings in America is given in Michael Hillmann's article, "Reza Baraheni: A Case Study of Politics and the Writer in Iran, 1953–1977," *Literature East and West* 20, nos. 1–4 (January-December 1976): 304–11.
DONALD SHOJAI

IRISH MODERNISTS. Brian Coffey: Born June 8, 1905, Dublin, Ireland. Denis Devlin: Born April 15, 1908, Greenock, Scotland; died August 21, 1959, Dublin, Ireland. Thomas MacGreevy: Born October 26, 1893, Tarbert, County Kerry, Ireland; died March 16, 1967, Dublin, Ireland.

Being an Irish poet in the 1920s and 1930s was no easy task. Many poets like James Stephens, Austin Clark, and F. P. Higgins spent their whole life reacting sometimes to, other times against, W. B. Yeats; no matter what their direction, Yeats's enormous Anglo-Irish revival resonates in their work. If the revival was not enough, between 1928 and 1940 over 12,000 books and 140 periodicals were suppressed as a result of the passage of the Censorship of Publications Act (1928). Some poets chose to leave Ireland as a way of bypassing this stifling atmosphere. Four of these poets, Coffey, Devlin, MacGreevy, and a more famous Dubliner, Samuel Beckett,* met in Paris in the years between 1928 and 1934. To say that they were all poets in exile would be misleading, although all spent a majority of their creative life outside Ireland. They left for various reasons, not least among them the search for a less provincial environment in which being a poet was not conditioned on being an Irish nationalist.

The four are referred to as a literary entity by various names, "the thirties generation," "Irish modernists," even the misleading "members of the Joyce circle." In Paris, these men were joined by something more solid than the need to seek out companionship among their compatriots. They were joined by a philosophy, a vision of Ireland (which is reflected in their work) distinct from that held by the Anglo-Irish literary milieu of Dublin (Devlin's *Lough Derg and Other Poems*, 1946; Coffey's *The Heavenly Foreigner*, 1967). They went abroad to search for an Ireland whose literary heritage reached back into European-Catholic tradition rather than British Protestantism. MacGreevy could be speaking for all of them when he wrote: "Through the English language, English cultural values dominated in Ireland, which since the Famine, had all but lost its own language, and in which it was difficult to be anything but an English provincial." Provincial they are not.

The four often promoted each other's work and careers. Beckett wrote reviews of MacGreevy's *Poems* (1934—the only book of poetry to be published during his lifetime) and of Devlin's *Intercessions* (1937). Coffey, after Devlin's death, edited his *Collected Poems* (1964), and MacGreevy introduced Coffey to T. S. Eliot,* who published several of Coffey's literary and philosophical reviews in the *Criterion*.

However, the work of these men remains obscure and is studied little, both in and outside Ireland. It is perhaps that they are difficult poets, combining in their poetry a knowledge (and a corresponding knowledge exacted of their readers) of classical and modern literature, history, art, and religion. To categorize these writers as a generation or a school would be a gross simplification, yet all their writing is informed by a knowledge, and an understanding, that poetry need be more than lyrical or free verse; that is to say, it needs to be informed by a culture, rooted in history through understanding of great literary and philosophical traditions. It was this search backwards, into the traditions, cultures, and languages of Europe, that launched their writing forward into the heart of the modernist movement, and onto a plane concurrent with trends in European literature. Yet it was this very process of exploration and innovation, mixing a private anger with public protest, that has relegated them to the peripheries of modern Irish poetry—they do not fit neatly into post-Yeatsian academic discourse.

Selected Titles: Brian Coffey: *Selected Poems* (1971). Denis Devlin: *Intercessions* (1937); *Selected Poems* (1963); *The Heavenly Foreigner* (1967); *Collected Poems* (1989). Thomas MacGreevy: *Richard Aldington: An Englishman* (1931); *T. S. Eliot: A Study* (1931); *J. B. Yeats: An Appreciation and an Interpretation* (1945); *Collected Poems* (1971).

Translations: Coffey, of *Dice Thrown Never Will Annul Chance* by S. Mallarmé. Devlin, of *Exile and Other Poems* by St. John Perse (1949).

Consult: For Brian Coffey: James Mays, "Passivity and Openness in Two Poems by Brian Coffey," *Irish University Review* (Spring 1983); *Irish University Review* (Autumn 1975), special issue devoted to Brian Coffey.

For Denis Devlin: Stan Smith, "Precarious Guest: The Poetry of Denis Devlin," *Irish University Review* (Spring 1978); Dillon Johnston, "Devlin's Poetry: Love in Abeyance," *Concerning Poetry* (Fall 1981).

For Thomas MacGreevy: Susan Schreibman, *Collected Poems of Thomas MacGreevy: An Annotated Edition* (Dublin, 1991).

SUSAN SCHREIBMAN

ROMANIAN WRITERS IN EXILE. Among the many writers and intellectuals in exile who celebrated the overthrow in 1989 of Communist Party absolutism in Romania were Sorin Alexandrescu, editor of the exile publication, *The International Journal of Romanian Studies*, published in Amsterdam, and a professor of Romanian Literature at the University of Amsterdam; Matei Calinescu, the scholar-critic in exile in the United States; Nina Cassian*; Andrei Codrescu*; Mircea Eliade*; Eugène Ionesco*; Mircea Iorgulescu, whose most recent work *Eseu despre lumea lui Caragiale*, an allegorical satire of the Nicolai Ceauşescu regime, was published a few months after he went into exile in September 1989 in Paris; Norman Manea*; Dorin Tudoran*; and Virgil Nemoianu, Professor of English and Comparative Literature at Catholic University in Washington, D.C. Those writers and intellectuals who elected to remain in Romania during the brutal Joseph Stalin-inspired era and its successive periods of rigidity and seeming thaw were celebrated as heroes of an intellectual ferment that had grown despite the corrupt and autocratic administration of Nicolae Ceauşescu. Among the writers who returned in 1989 and 1990 to record the historic turn of events were Andrei Codrescu and Sorin Alexandrescu.

RUSSIAN/SOVIET WRITERS IN EXILE. Three waves of emigration and exile are generally considered to characterize Russian/Soviet literary movements in the twentieth century: the first wave occurred during or after the Russian Revolution of 1917 and until the consolidation of the Stalinist Reign of Terror; the second wave turns from the Stalinist period through the Cold War of the 1950s and until the "thaw" of the Khrushchev era; the third wave has been taking place since the 1970s and reflects both a more liberal Soviet policy and at the same time a defiant "refusenik" stance inimical to the morality of commitment to Communist Party goals. Among writers generally placed in these categories, all of whom are given individual entries in this study, are:

First Wave: Leonid Andreyev, Konstantin Balmont, Nikolai Berdyaev, Ivan Bunin, Ilya Ehrenburg, Zinaida Hippius, Boris Khazahnov, Vladislav Khodasevich, Konstantin Korovin, Voranc Prezihov, Alexei Remizov, Marina Tsvataeva.

Second Wave: Vadim Andreyev, Lev Kopelev, Victor Serge, Yevgenii Zamayatin.

Third wave: Nizametdin Achmetov, Vassily Aksyonov, Sergei Dovlatov, Juri Druzhnikov, Ivan Elagin, Michael Heifetz, Mark A. Popovsky, Gregory Svirsky, Vladimir Voinovich, Vasily Yanovsky, Igor Yefimov, Zinovy Zinik, Alexander Zinoviev.

One of the significant genres or modes that appeared with the second wave of literary Soviet emigration was the Stalinist novel, which followed upon the freewheeling experimentalism of the first years of the Soviet revolution. The Stalinist regime dictated artistic performance as well as social behavior, and the novel of this period became one in which the class struggle took on the air and tone of an epic work. Instead of an individual engaging in a mighty struggle against monstrous, gigantic enemies, the hero of the Stalinist novel became a worker chastening his pride through his role in the service of the community. In effect, the young hero found his faith in the service of socialism and of the communist state; his passage to goodness, or his virtue in action, became that of a worker in solidarity with other workers in the struggle to achieve a classless society. As the Stalinist dictatorship waned, the Stalinist novel disappeared, and a new kind of experimentalism took place. What may be observed in this third wave of emigré literature is an increasing turn to personal concerns and matters of self. The "I" became as important in the literature of the 1970 and 1980 decades in Russian exile literature as the success-oriented persona in the territory of Western yuppiedom during the same period. The reaction to the Stalinist novel thus cohered into an atmosphere in which commitment to social programs were regarded with suspicion even before the programs were examined. While courageous rebels—like Joseph Brodsky, Irina Ratushinskaya, Andrei Sakharov, Andrei Sinyavsky, and Aleksandr Solzhenitsyn—resisted the easy convenience of evasion of social comment, a host of other writers in the third wave of émigré/ exile literature reflected an active indifference to problems of state. Their reflection may be seen in their collegial techniques of exaggeration and fancy, a shaping of contemporary history through a barbed satire and a wilful collection of anachronistic futuristic settings. Among writers who employ these techniques in a predominant manner are Vassily Aksyonov, Sergei Dovlatov, Juri Druzhnikov, Vladimir Voinovich, Alexander Zinoviev, and Zinovy Zinik.

THE SPANISH GENERATION OF 1927. In 1927 when a group of young Spanish poets celebrated Luis de Góngora's tercentenary in Sevilla, they were just entering a great period when they would write some of the finest poetry of the modern era; they could not have known that in ten years they would be scattered by the Spanish Civil War; that Jorge Guillén,* Pedro Salinas,* Rafael Alberti,* Luis Cernuda,* Emilio Prados, Léon Felipe, and Manuel Altologuirre would live their later lives in exile; that Federico García Lorca would be killed by Falangists in Granada in 1936; and that young Miguel Hernández would die in Franco's prisons in 1942. Of the major figures, only Gerardo Diego, Vincente Aleixandre, and Dámaso Alonso would remain in Spain.

The period from 1920 to 1936 was a new Golden Age in Spanish letters. The masters of the Generation of 1998—Miguel de Unamuno,* Antonio Machado,* and Juan Ramón Jiménez*—were still alive, writing their great later works, and ready to act as significant influences on the development of the younger poets. These younger poets, meanwhile, were responding to diverse stimuli: native folk traditions, the Spanish classics, and the most recent experiments—*Creacionismo*, Dada, surrealism. They were engaged in a conversation that included Pablo Picasso, Salvador Dali, Luis Buñuel, Pablo Neruda,* and César Vallejo.* Jorge Guillén recalls the mutual support, the friendship, and the rich dialogue. In this atmosphere, with Jiménez as their mentor, they wrote their early poems emphasizing technical mastery and cultivation of the image, but by the end of the 1920s they had left these concerns behind. The major works of the pre-exile period stress the relationships between self and world and self and others.

Reacting to personal crises, Alberti in *Sobre los ángeles* (1927–28) and Lorca in *Poeta en Nueva York* (1929–30) focus on a sense of loss and severance from others. The poems explore emotional and spiritual exile by using the techniques of the grotesque in order to reveal a gap between language and experience and a fundamental absence, an exile that begins with birth and is reiterated by later aesthetic and personal estrangements. Alberti examines exile from a disintegrating paradise, perhaps the childhood paradise of his first poems. Lorca, traveling in New York in 1929 and finding himself alienated from a large urban culture and a foreign language, indicts the exile of blacks in Harlem and tests the possibility of a regenerative force, an otherness found in the irrational and the body itself. Cernuda, Prados, and Altologuirre are mainly concerned with isolation. Aleixandre in *Espadas como labios* (1931–32) and *La destrucción o el amor* (1932–33) continues the exploration of the gap between language and experience by means of the grotesque, but his goal seems to be immersion of the self in the world.

Meanwhile Salinas in *La voz a ti debida* (1933) and *Razón del amor* (1936) and Guillén in *Cántico* (1928 and 1936) affirm the possibility of dialogue with the other and the world. Although for Salinas the beloved may be elusive or absent, the *tu* is essential, given with the self. Severance and exile would be phases of the dialogue but not the final word. Guillén, perhaps more than any other modern poet, begins with the given world where self and other are fundamentally inseparable; he is, for Willis Barnstone, "a secular mystic." Exile in an ontological or spiritual sense would be an illusion. While Alberti, Lorca, and Aleixandre critique late Romantic notions of a unified poetic voice, Salinas and Guillén redefine its very ground, and all five seem to be conversing with Antonio Machado, who explored throughout his career, but especially in his late work *Cancionero apócrifo* and *Juan de Mairena*, the temporality of the poetic voice and the experience of inner exile. Machado's awareness of fundamental severance as evidence for the necessary other opens up a new site for poetry and leads to Schelerian and Heideggerian themes. Neruda and Vallejo should also be considered as major members of this conversation.

In the 1930s, Alberti committed himself to communism and a poetry of the people. Lorca turned to drama and wrote his great plays (*Bodas de sangre* [1933], *Yerma* [1934], and *La casa de Bernarda Alba* [1936]), while as a director he brought the Spanish classics to the small towns of Spain and to Latin America. Lorca's plays reveal his sensitivity to the conflicts and oppressive forces in the Andalusian psyche and in Spanish society while continuing his pursuit of otherness in the irrational and on the earth. When the Civil War began in July 1936, Lorca, at the height of his artistic powers, was writing still another play. He rejected flight and returned to Granada. On August 19 he was executed. In September Guillén was arrested in Pamplona, but he escaped execution and in 1938 went into exile in the United States, where Salinas had already gone on a visiting lectureship at the outbreak of the war. Alberti joined Prados, Altologuirre, Cernuda, and Felipe in support of the Republic, and they all left before the final defeat. Of the older masters, Unamuno died in 1936, Machado died in 1939 having just crossed the border as a refugee at Collioure, and Jiménez followed the younger poets into exile. Those who remained behind, like Aleixandre, whose health failed, thus forcing him to stay, would experience inner exile, cut off from the other members of their generation and from the vitality of pre–Civil War Spain.

After 1936, all the poets of the Generation of 1927 were compelled to face the horrors of the Civil War, World War II, the Holocaust, and Hiroshima, as well as their personal experience of exile, and it can be argued that this period posed the supreme test for their poetry, confirming their earlier suspicions about loss and severance and/or providing a new opportunity for affirmation. Much of the later work is reflective, nostalgic, and elegiac, and the death of Lorca is a major recurrent theme. Alberti, who fled to Paris, and then to Buenos Aires (his home for the next twenty-five years), before moving to Rome, maintained his political commitments and resumed his first love, painting, while continuing to write voluminously, including such major postwar works as *A la pintura* (1948), *Retornos de lo vivo lejano* (1952), and the autobiographical *La arboleda perdida* (1942 and 1959), the last two especially haunted by what Alberti had lost in Spain and the past. For decades, Alberti suffered "unbearable nostalgia" (introduction to *Pleamar*, 1944). Cernuda, Prados, Altologuirre, and Felipe all found exile difficult and eventually made their homes in Mexico, returning to their native language. Cernuda was perhaps the most affected by his encounters with other languages, particularly German and English, and he completed important translations of Friedrich Hölderlin. He also wrote some of his finest works in exile, especially *En las horas contadas* (1956), *Desolación de la quimera* (1962), and the prose *Ocnos* (1963), which express nostalgia for a lost perfection, whether aesthetic ideal or childhood paradise. Guillén and Salinas both settled in the United States and taught, Guillén mainly at Wellesley, Salinas at Wellesley and Johns Hopkins. In *Clamor* (1957, 1960, 1963), Guillén confronts midcentury history and the death of his first wife but still affirms his earlier vision. *Cántico, Clamor,* and *Homenaje* (1967) form a single work, *Aire nuestro* (1968), one of the major poetic achievements in any language in this century. As for his own experience of exile, Guillén said in 1968: "I have never been able to consider myself completely exiled. I am always in this home country called the planet earth" (Claude Couffon, interview with Jorge Guillén in Paris, 1963, cited in I. Ivask, Introductory essay in *The Impulse Toward Form*, pp. vii-viii). His close friend Salinas, after three years in Puerto Rico, finished *El contemplado* (1946), a serene, even mystical work, then *Todo más claro y otros poemas* (1949) and the novel *La bomba increíble* (1950), both concerned with social issues, especially the threat of nuclear destruction, and *Confianza*, published posthumously (1955), which offers a final affirmation.

Those who have survived the longest have enjoyed recognition worldwide, especially Aleixandre, who was awarded the Nobel Prize in 1977 for a lifework affirming the unity of humankind and world (the culmination being *En un vasto dominio*, 1962). Some eventually returned to Spain, at least briefly, and Altologuirre died there after a car accident in Burgos in 1959. Some of course never returned. Guillén, along with others, diagnosed the major ill of exile as the loss of one's native language, and there was also the loss of the vital prewar conversation and community, not to mention the fact that their books were often censored or banned by Franco's government. Yet all these poets continued to write major works in the lands of their exile, and now these works have finally returned to Spain, signaling the end of a critical period of exile, not only of these poets, but of artists, intellectuals, and thousands of others who fled Franco's victory and repeated what so many earlier generations had experienced in Spanish history, including the Jews, the Moors, and Ruy Díaz de Vivar.

Consult: Willis Barnstone, "The Greeks, San Juan, and Guillén," in *Luminous Reality: The Poetry of Jorge Guillén*, ed. Ivar Ivask (1971); Jorge Guillén, *Language and Poetry:*

Some Poets of Spain (1961); Paul Ilie, *The Surrealist Mode in Spanish Literature: An Interpretation of Basic Trends from Post-Romanticism to the Spanish Vanguard* (1968); G. B. Morris, *A Generation of Spanish Poets: 1920–1936* (1971).

MICHAEL MANLEY

TURKISH LITERATURE OF EXILE. Exile has been an enduring theme of Turkish literature for at least one thousand years. Among the earliest specimens of verse is a quatrain that laments defeat and exile:

We have lost the Yen-chi-san mountain
The beauty of our women was wrested from us
We have abandoned the valleys of Chi-li-yen
Nowadays our cattle can find no pastureland

In *The Book of Dede Korkut*, a series of twelve tales that constitute the Turkish national epic, there are poignant episodes about heroes who languish because of separation from their loved ones, from their tribes and homeland.

During the Ottoman centuries (fourteenth to twentieth), the classical poetry written by and for the urban establishment and the folk poetry composed by minstrels in the countryside made a sense of exile and longing a recurrent theme. Especially the mystics expressed the anguish of having fallen apart from the Godhead and from the divine and the human beloved as a leitmotif. It can be said that exile constituted the terra firma of Ottoman poetry.

In the twentieth century many major Turkish writers, like their Ottoman predecessors who were banished to some far corners of the the empire or who sought political asylum in Europe, have been sent into exile or found haven abroad. At the turn of the century, the leading satirist Eshref, after lambasting Sultan Abdul Hamid II's repressive regime, escaped to Egypt where he lived for five years. Another satirist, Neyzen Tevfik, also took refuge in Egypt. Abdul Hamid's ruthless despotism led a group of major literary figures, including the renowned poet Tevfik Fikret and his friends Cenab Shehabeddin, Mehmet Rauf, Hüseyin Cahit, and others, to make elaborate plans to emigrate to New Zealand where they hoped to create their own commune and live free from harassment and oppression, but they did not leave Turkey.

After the creation of the Turkish Republic in 1923, several major writers who had remained loyal to the ancien régime or had a falling out with Mustafa Kemal Pasha (later Atatürk), the hero of the national liberation struggle and the first president of the Republic, were forced to go into exile. These included Riza Tevfik, a poet and prolific prose writer; Halide Edib, the leading woman novelist who published many books in England and the United States while in exile (including a critically acclaimed novel entitled *The Clown and His Daughter*, 1932); her second husband Dr. Adnan (Adivar), who became a writer during their fifteen-year exile; and Refik Halit (Karay), one of Turkey's most popular novelists whose books include a novel entitled *Sürgün* (Exile) based upon his fifteen years of banishment abroad.

Cevat Shakir, who gained fame under the pen-name Halikarnas Balikcisi (The Fisherman of Halicarnassus) was sentenced to three years of "internal exile" for a "short story inciting the public to oppose the War of Independence." He was in banishment at the Aegean town of Bodrum (ancient Halicarnassus) for a year and a half, after which he was pardoned; he chose to remain in Bodrum for more than two decades.

Mehmet Akif Ersoy, the patriotic poet revered as the author of the words of the Turkish national anthem, chose a ten-year self-exile in Egypt to be away from Mustafa Kemal Atatürk's secularist reforms which he, as a devout Moslem committed to the ideals of the Pan-Islamist ideology, violently opposed.

The most renowned Turkish exile in and outside Turkey is the widely influential communist poet Nazim Hikmet.*

Other writers living in self-exile because of political reasons include Abidin Dino (short story writer, playwright, essayist, and painter) and his wife Güzin Dino (critic and literary historian); the late Fahri Erdinc (fiction writer who had escaped to Bulgaria in the late 1940s); Demir Özlü (novelist and short story writer); and the poets Ataol Behramoglu and Tekin Sonmez. Two of the most prominent writers of Turkey, Mahmut Makal and Fakir Baykurt (both of them have been extensively translated into Western languages), chose, in the early 1980s, to live in West Germany to avoid possible harassment by the authorities for political reasons, but they are able to visit Turkey.

Many Turkish writers have become longtime residents of other countries by choice, not as a result of political constraints. Neoclassical poet Yusuf Mardin, after working in London, Bonn, and Washington as Turkey's press counsellor, retired in Surrey, England. Many writers have opted for residence abroad for professional work or as a result of marriage. These include the prominent translator of Turkish literature into English, Nermin Menemencioglu; the award-winning short story writer and poet Feyyaz Kayacan; Mrs. Nilüfer Mizanoglu Reddy (English translator of Turkish women writers); the internationally famous photographer Lütfü Özkök, who writes poetry and translates; Engin Coskun (essayist and translator); poet-translator Abdullah Riza Ergüven; poet Turhan Doyran; literary historian and critic Adnan Binyazar; poet Seyfullah Bascillar, who is among the finest of his generation; and poets Ilyas Halil, Mrs. Tulin Erbas, Tahsin Yigit, Ozkan Mert, Nihat Ziyalan, Ozgur Savasci, Mevlut Ceylan, and others. To this list must be added the late poet and short story writer Fethi Savasci; the novelists Dursun Akcam and Yusuf Ziya Bahadinli, the poets Ilhan Sonuc and Sitki Salih Gor and essayist-poet-editor Kemaleddin Senocak. One of Turkey's best neoclassical poets, Nevzat Yalcin, taught English in West Germany (now retired, he continues to live in West Germany).

At least a million and a half Turks live in West Germany, where a new generation of German writers of Turkish origin is growing up. This generation includes younger authors who write in Turkish rather than in German. Among them Aras Ören has become very popular. Güney Dal and Habib Bektas are also well known. Zafer Senocak, who has published several books of poems in

German, has been receiving considerable critical praise. One of the most successful Turkish writers in West Germany is Yuksel Pazarkaya, who does original work (poetry, fiction, essays, radio plays, and translations) in both German and Turkish.

Two novelists in France, Ibrahim Necmi Gürmen and Nedim Gürsel, have attracted wide attention for their works in French.

No Turkish novelist writing in English since Halide Edib in the 1930s and Irfan Orga in the 1950s has emerged except Erje Ayden, who briefly attracted attention in the United States in the 1960s. The woman novelist Guneli Gun has published two works in English. In poetry the Cypriot Turkish poet Taner Baybars, who writes exclusively in English, has won an estimable success. His compatriot, Osman Turkay, has also published his poems in English. Cengiz Dagci, a Crimean Turk who has published ten novels, settled in London after World War II.

In the late 1980s, several exiles, some of whom had been stripped of their citizenship, were able to return to Turkey. These included Ataol Behramoglu and Demir Özlü, but by 1990 it had not been possible for the poet Nihat Behram to return.

The second half of the 1980s witnessed the emergence of numerous "exile" literary periodicals published by groups of Turkish writers living in France, West Germany, Holland, and other countries. All of them are in Turkish and feature poems, short stories, articles, and translations by writers living in Turkey and abroad. *Anka*, published by Ataol Behramoglu in France, is the only one of them that includes writing or translations in French.

"Exile literature," particularly as a result of the psychological problems of the massive numbers of Turkish workers in Western Europe, has become a branch of modern Turkish literature. This new genre, however, has yet to produce a major work. Most of the Turkish writers abroad, whether they have left Turkey because of political persecution or for employment, seem to write about their homeland, for a Turkish audience, out of Turkish tradition or in keeping with modes fashionable back home. Very few of them achieve any level of interaction with the literature of the country in which they take up residence—and only a handful ever try to write in their new language. In that negative sense, they flounder in desperate exile.

TALAT SAIT HALMAN

TWO GERMANYS. With the division of Germany into two Germanys at the close of World War II, German writers found themselves faced with the choice of one political allegiance against another, no matter what their views of cultural unity. The problem of the two Germanys was a political one, kept continually so by power politics, rather than by a cultural divide. In the Cold War of the 1950s and the two following decades, many German writers defected from East to West or West to East, making their move on grounds of humanitarian terminology and/or sociopolitical language. Since politics invariably proves transient as well as unsettling, some of these same writers redefected to their original or newly renewed status in succeeding years. In the 1980s decade, changes of identity abated, largely because German writers became less confrontational with their once-polarized counterparts. Culturally, economically, and socially the mood in both Germanys became one of compromise, and the idea of one Germany as a cultural frame was increasingly defended. However, as late as the autumn of 1989, writers in both Germanys agreed that the political reality of one Germany depended on a reaching greater than the grasp of cultural cohesiveness. In December 1989, an extraordinary series of events occurred that reflected a new political spirit and altered the governments and economies of Eastern Europe and the two Germanys. The changes began with the exodus into West Germany of thousands of East Germans on vacation in Hungary and Czechoslovakia. In the ensuing weeks, the surge of refugees proved insurmountable at the East German borders, and the GDR government capitulated to the demands for free travel without conditions. Hundreds of thousands joined the exodus into West Berlin, some staying in the sector permanently. The GDR government collapsed, and the ruling Communist Party saw its monopoly of office vanish. Ernst Honecker, the head of the government, was confined to a hospital bed; on his release he was indicted on charges of political malfeasance. Under the succeeding interim government of Hans Modrow, human rights restrictions and economic bans were lifted. The Berlin Wall, the symbolic reality of the separation of the two Germanys, was opened to allow an unprecedented migration into West Germany. Some petty bourgeois entrepreneurs chipped away at the wall to cart off blocks of it for sale in Paris, London, and New York.

Prognosticators and analysts of the German scene suggest that reunification of Germany may become a reality by the end of 1991, a premise made more likely by the national elections in East Germany on March 18, 1990, in which conservative candidates backed by West German Chancellor Helmut Kohl's Christian Democratic Party largely defeated opposition candidates. Although the GDR Christian Democratic Party did not win a majority and was obliged to form a coalition government, the significance of their plurality indicated a strong desire on the part of East German voters for a united Germany in the near future, since such a unification is one of the major planks of the GDR Christian Democrats.

With the reunification of Germany will come new problems of identity rather than a simple dissolution of moral guilt and schizoid partisanship. While political division is likely to become a matter of history, problems of variant economic and social emphases, and controversies of idea-mongering politics on all sides, have already surfaced in different areas of the still two Germanies and are likely to continue to cause unsettling pain and angry provocations.

Those writers who moved into exile from one divide of Germany to another, and those who remained, will become the historians of the phenomenon of the 1990s. Among the writers of the two Germanys who have exiled themselves or been forced into exile one or more times are the following, all of whom have individual entries: Johannes R. Becher, Jurek Becker, Wolf Biermann, Bertolt Brecht, Hilde Domin, Martin Gregor-Dellin, Hans Habe, Peter Hacks, Stephan

Hermlin, Stefan Heym, Peter Huchel, Uwe Johnson, Gunter Kunert, Reiner Kunze, Monica Maron, Jochem Ziem, Gerald K. Zschorsch, Arnold Zweig, and Gerhard Zwerenz. Reference to these writers' states of citizenship, allegiance, and residence is made by use of the following place-names, all of which have been used without discrimination: I. Federal Republic of Germany; West Germany, FRG; II. German Democratic Republic; East Germany; GDR; DDR (Deutsches Demokratik Republik).

YIDDISH WRITERS. Yiddish writers departed from Eastern Europe, in the main, during the early and later parts of the twentieth century because of political persecution and cultural bias against their language and culture. When there was no apparent bias of political or social exclusion, there was a slant of haughty ignorance that placed Yiddish beyond the pale of worldly cultures.

Yiddish began as a folk culture in Germany in the late Middle Ages but flowered most strongly in Poland and Russia during the nineteenth and twentieth centuries and served both as exile and buffer against an imperial rule that was at best tolerant.

Unlike many Jewish writers who, in their stance of liberated cosmopolitanism and rational universality, wrote in their national language, Yiddish writers by choice accepted a form of cultural separatism. The German Jewish writer who wrote (and thought) in German saw himself as both German and Jewish, perhaps German first; the Yiddish writer, by his commitment of language, accepted the contemporary ghetto of cultural nationalism and a corresponding pride in his identity or religious/racial roots. Today, with a strong revival of Yiddish as a literary tradition that can rank on its own merits and does not represent a subsidiary of achievement, the Yiddish writer more rarely exhibits an inferiority mired in a pale recognition. In the early part of the twentieth century, however, "to be Yiddish" was to be "refrocked" in garments that proclaimed sorrow and exile, and to engage in self-mockery and the exuberance of a cosmic dance as a way of engaging a forgiving God.

Most Yiddish writers who left Europe before the Holocaust emigrated to the United States and Canada; a few journeyed to Palestine and stayed on to see the land become Israel. It is difficult to classify such writers as either exiles or refugees; the usual term has been *emigrant* or *immigrant*. If one distinguishes between voluntary leave-taking and involuntary flight, Yiddish writers before the Holocaust were more volunteers of a dream than desperate people in fear of their lives. Yet racist pogroms existed in czarist Russia, and suppression of a native culture, whether in actual decree or in degrees of silence and cunning prohibition, made the Yiddish writer feel his plight keenly. Many such Yiddish writers were faced with the choice of starting a new life as wanderers in a new land or remaining in a familiar envelope in which their roots had been sealed off. Some Yiddish writers remained in Russia, continuing their Yiddish tradition, until the Revolution of 1917, when after a brief outpouring of mutual support among the revolutionaries and ethnic minorities, they, too, largely departed in disappointment of their hopes. With the coming of the Holocaust, the invasion of the Soviet Union by Germany, and continued prejudice against Yiddish and ethnic expression in a socialist order of allegiance, the Yiddish writer found greater and greater barriers to his existence. Many such writers emigrated to Israel, where they are a distinct component of the Israeli people (many Yiddish writers speak and write Hebrew, but not all) and in the United States, particularly New York, where Yiddish literature is again flourishing. In the 1988–89 New York theatrical season, at least four plays, either with a Yiddish theme or presented in Yiddish, were staged on and off Broadway.

Yiddish writers who left their national land in the modern era and thus suffered a form of exile are S. Y. Agnon,* Sholem Aleichem, Ghayim Nachman Bialik,* Jacob Glatstein,* Chaim Grade,* Uri Zvi Greenburg,* Moyshe Leyb Halpern,* Isaac Leib Peretz,* David Pinski,* Avrom Reisen, and Morris Winchevsky.*

Consult: Irving Howe and Eliezer Greenberg, eds., *A Treasury of Yiddish Poetry* (1969); Aaron Kramer, ed., *A Century of Yiddish Poetry* (1989); Howard Schwartz, ed., *Voices within the Ark* (1980); Ruth Whitman, ed., *Modern Yiddish Poetry* (1966).

WRITERS IN EXILE —

A ———————————————————————

ABBASI, Talat (also known as Talat Jafri). Born on September 10, 1942, in Lucknow, India; she came to the United States in 1977, and lives in New York City. Abbasi's family moved to Karachi, Pakistan, when India was partitioned in 1947. She attended St. Joseph's Convent School there, and went on to study at the London School of Economics from 1963 to 1966, after an interlude of philosophy and literature at Kinnaird College of Punjab University from 1959 to 1962. Abbasi was married in 1969; divorced in 1986. She has two children, a boy (b. 1970) and a girl (b. 1972). The boy was born with a severe developmental disability, and it was in order to seek treatment for him that she and her husband moved to the United States in 1977. Her son is in residential care in New York. She does not consider herself a religious or political exile, although she admits that she will probably not move back to Pakistan, which she regularly visits. She has published eight short stories, the earlier ones under her married name, Talat Jafri.

Her favorite author is Anton Chekhov. Her stories tend to focus on a moral issue and often question the roles which society assigns to women. "Proper Shoes" is Abbasi's only story to have a male protagonist, a little boy who learns that charity is better than selfishness. Her longest and most disturbing work is "Simple Questions" (*Feminist Studies* 13, no. 1 [Spring 1987]:83–92), which questions the assumptions of the patriarchal, dowry-driven society of poor Pakistani women. Living outside of Pakistan has given Abbasi the distance that she needs to retell the stories of her home culture.

No studies of Abbasi have yet been published.

JUDITH M. BRUGGER

ABISH, Walter. Born December 24, 1931, in Vienna, Austria; he lives in New York City. Abish does not consider himself an exile writer since he left Austria when he was six years old. He received his first schooling in France and studied in private English schools in Shanghai, to which his Jewish family had fled with the fall of France. Abish has lived in Israel, and served in the Israeli army. He married a Jewish-American girl working on a kibbutz there, the sculptor Cecille Abish. He came to the United States with his American wife in the late 1950s to work as a city planner (the area of his educational specialty), and became an American citizen in 1960.

Abish believes English is his native tongue since he has written only in English. His work bears the mark of exilic experience both in its experimentation of authorial distancing from narrative material and in its subject content of isolate protagonists and weary world-travelers. His best-known work, the novel *How German It Is* (1980), explores the anxiety of modern postwar Germany in its splintered geographic and spiritual states.

Selected Titles: Fiction: *Alphabetical Africa* (1974); *Minds Meet* (1975); *In the Future Perfect* (1977). Poetry: *Duel Site* (1970).

Consult: Jerome Klinkowitz, *The Self-Apparent Word: Fiction as Language/Language as Fiction* (1984); John Updike, "Through a Continent Darkly," in *Picked-Up Pieces* (1975).

ABRAHAMS, Peter (Henri). Born March 19, 1919, in Vrededorp, a slum area of Johannesburg, South Africa; he lives in Jamaica, West Indies. Abrahams's mother was a Cape Colored and his father an Ethiopian who died when Abrahams was five years old; Abrahams's family was broken up and he was sent to live with his aunt and uncle in Elsenburg, a village in the Transvaal. He returned when he was eight years old to live with his mother, brother, and sister in Johannesburg. At nine, he began working in a tinsmith's shop; a year later, as he tells it in *Tell Freedom* (London, 1954), a "short-sighted Jewish girl" read him passages from "Othello" from Charles Lamb's *Tales from Shakespeare*, and thus began Abrahams's love of English literature. He immersed himself in John Keats, William Shakespeare, and Francis Turner Palgrave's *Golden Treasury* (of poems), and the rich world of literature became as real to him as the poverty of his daily life. He attended school sporadically, working as a dishwasher, office boy, messenger, and porter to earn money to live on; he enrolled at St. Peter's College, but stayed there briefly. Already his main interest was in writing, and in "telling freedom" to his reader-listeners. He traveled through South Africa in 1935, and went to sea in 1939, working at various times as a steward, cabin boy, and stoker on the same freighter that roamed the world from the Orient to London. He left ship to settle in England in 1941. He began his writing in England, drawing on his African experiences as his content. (Like another foreign seaman who came to English shores, Joseph Conrad,* Abrahams did not engage any English locales except in his late novel, *A Wreath for Udomo* [1956]). In 1952 he returned to Africa as a correspondent for the London *Observer*, working on stories about Kenya and South Africa. Abrahams's work until 1957 is centered on South Africa and on either direct or felt experience with South African prejudice and triumph over suffering with one exception, *A Wreath for Udomo*; this novel is set in a West African country and England, and describes the rise and fall of an ambitious, liberal politician who started out with a grand vision and who fell, out of hubris, from the heights to which his dreams had led him. Some critics regard this atypical novel for Abrahams as his finest fiction, and see in it a veiled character study of Kwame Nkrumah, the first president of a newly independent Ghana. Significantly, Abrahams's mine of central interest shifted after *Udomo* from South Africa to other climes. In 1957 he went to Jamaica on invitation of the government to draw an official report on the British West Indies. He published his travel book, *Jamaica: An Island Mosaic*, in 1957; that same year he moved to Jamaica with his family permanently. In Jamaica, Abrahams has worked as editor of the *West Indian Economist*, as an official of the daily radio network West Indian News, and as a television and radio commentator. In 1964 he resigned from many of these posts to return to writing, but his output has been slim in the past twenty-five years. His emigration to Jamaica seems to have satisfied his creative spirit, and he apparently feels he has made his individual voice heard: the rest is sharing in social commentary with his people on daily and public events.

Abrahams is unquestionably one of South Africa's pioneering black writers. His novel *Mine Boy* (London, 1946) was the first novel by a black South African to appear anywhere since 1930; political repression of government had smothered literary incentive and spiritual expression as well in longer fiction, though black writers' short stories and poems were published in local outlets during those years. Abrahams's first published prose work was the short story collection *Dark Testament* (London, 1942).

The theme of the revolution of thought, the beginning of forgiveness by both black and white, distinguishes the work of Abrahams and several writers, black and white, of his generation. In their work temporary political and social defeat is secondary to man's eternal spiritual resistance to isolation by color. The rationale for this belief is neither intellectual nor sentimental; it is spiritual. Hate contracts and dries up the inherent powers of man; love expands them into a sea of potentially glorious experience. Abrahams treats the problem of adjustment in his novels in two characteristic ways. One is to bring a native into the big city, in search of the things white people possess, and to show his descent into crime and violence before he comes to that measure of understanding which obliterates resentment and envy. The other manner is to treat the relationship between white and black on levels in which each alternately becomes master and servant. The Jew, in this mode, is used as a symbolic brother of the black African; each is a pariah, and thus each is in understanding of the other. In *The Path of Thunder* (1948), possibly his best novel, Abrahams utilizes both these thematic manners as well as treats the matter of miscegenation, whose spirit is everywhere felt and whispered about in the racially paranoid state of South Africa. As the novel opens, a brilliant Cape Colored young man, Lanny, returns to his home village after seventeen years in Cape Town, where he has reaped a university education. He has rejected the city, where the road to personal success is easier and more lucrative, for the small town, where he will take a job teaching in night school. As he steps off the train, he is assailed and beaten by two Boer farmers who object instinctively to his clean, well-dressed appearance. When they have finished beating and insulting him, Lanny lifts his suitcases and trudges down the long road to his mother's house. In Lanny's visionary world, color makes no difference, but he resists the love he feels for a young white woman until he comes to the realization that he has been rejecting their union because of *her* color. The young Jewish observer in the novel, Isaac, describes their surrender to their feelings in this way: "To Swartz [Lanny], Sarle Villier is a girl. He is not conscious of her colour. For days, he tried to keep the fact that she was white firmly fixed in his mind. Today, in front of my eyes, she swept it aside, for she's not conscious of his colour. Yes, in front of my very eyes she swept race and colour and nationality away as though it were a filthy little cobweb. They were just a man and a woman.'' (p. 163). Miscegenation thus becomes in Abrahams's novels a painful but inevitable evolution in South Africa.

In spite of his experiences, or perhaps because of the texture of his suffering, Abrahams's work is filled with a sense of urgent compassion for all those afflicted by and with the germs of racial and group prejudice. His autobiography, *Tell Freedom*, which has gone through innumerable printings, stands, along with Alan Paton's *Cry the Beloved Country* (London, 1948), as a testament to the belief that humanity has longer staying power than violence and legalized repression. Abrahams's triumphant victims remain imbued with hope that man's humane spirit will prove unconquerable, even in the stockyards of bullish tyranny.

Abrahams's earliest work was *A Blackman Speaks of Freedom*, a collection of poems, in 1940. He published a book of essays, *The Quiet Voice*, as well as his novel *This Island, Now* in 1966. Unlike his previous novels, *This Island, Now*, is set on a Caribbean island, but like his South Africa, it is a land in which racial tension simmers, and in which a white minority holds the reins on a black underclass majority.

Selected Titles: *Song of the City* (London, 1946); *Wild Conquest* (1950); *Return to Goli* (London, 1953); *A Night of Their Own* (London, 1965).

Consult: Kolawole Ogungbesan, *The Writings of Peter Abrahams* (London, 1979); Martin Tucker, *Africa in Modern Literature* (1967); Michael Wade, *Peter Abrahams* (London, 1972).

ACHMETOV, Nizametdin (also spelled Akhmetov). Born 1947 in Kunashak, Chelyabinsk Region, USSR; he lives in Hamburg, Federal Republic of Germany. Achmetov, a Bashkir, was imprisoned when he was eighteen years old supposedly for subversive nationalist goals. He developed his writing skills and poetic vision while in prison; he served three successive terms in hard-labor penal camps and part of the time in solitary confinement. After serving more than twenty years of prison time, he was released from Chelyabinsk OPH in June 1987. He chose Hamburg as his place of exile and has been in residence there, with time off for various visits to different countries. When he appeared at the International PEN Conference in Cambridge, England, in April 1988, he aroused compassion among his writer-colleagues by his plea for love through forgiveness rather than hatred issuing from anger as a worldly reaction to his personal fate. That theme—love and forgiveness and the concert of new beginnings—pervades Achmetov's corpus. Although Achmetov's poems are highly regarded, little of his work has been published in English. A volume of his poems was issued by Fischler Verlag in 1987.

   Consult: Jean Blot, "Report," *PEN International* 34, no. 1 (1984): 52–54; English Centre *PEN*, Autumn 1988, pp. 28–29.

ACZEL, Tamas. Born December 16, 1921, in Budapest; he now lives in Amherst, Massachusetts, where he is professor of English at the University of Massachusetts. Aczel's first collection of poems, *Ének a hajón* (A Song on the Ship, 1941), showed a young poet of sensitivity and linguistic power but without any particular political inclination, even though Aczel was already a Social Democrat and his first poems had appeared in the daily newspaper of the Hungarian Social Democratic party. After the war he joined the Communist party, and together with a number of poets and writers of his generation, became one of its literary flag-bearers. His first postwar collection of poems *Éberség, hüség* (Vigilance and Faith, 1948), won the Kossuth Prize for Literature in 1949; his first novel, *A szabadság árnyékában* (In the Shadow of Liberty, 1948), was awarded the Stalin Prize for Literature in 1952. Together with his second novel, *Vihar és napsütés* (Storm and Sunshine, 1950, the second part of a planned but never finished trilogy), these works were severely criticized by official organs of the Hungarian government for failing to achieve the artistic/political mastery of "socialist realism" and for failing to overcome the writer's bourgeois upbringing. During the period between 1953 and 1956, Aczel became one of the leaders of the literary and political opposition to the Stalinist regime, and a friend and associate of Imre Nagy, the prime minister of the Revolutionary Government of 1956.

   Aczel left Hungary in November 1956, after the second Russian intervention and the arrest of Imre Nagy and his friends. It was in exile that his literary talent, almost destroyed by the oppressive climate of Stalinism, regained its scope and power. He became bilingual. His poetry, in Hungarian (published in the Paris-based *Irodalmi Ujság* [Literary Gazette], of which he was, until 1964, editor), broke with traditional modes and rhythms of realistic poetry and instead evolved into a series (some of the works are poetic cycles) that showed both abstraction and precision in forms and ideas that tended now to the metaphysical rather than the political. In *Revolt of the Mind* (1959, with Tibor Méray), considered by many a classic evocation of intellectual history, he gave an extensive account of prerevolutionary intellectual ferment in Hungary as well as of the transformation of young communist intellectuals. In his first novel written in exile, *The Ice Age* (1965), he worked within the framework of traditional realism, but signs of a more experimental, more exuberant style and attitude can be seen. *The Ice Age* is a remarkably incisive work that evokes the sting of Hungary's slavery during Stalinist years of terror.

In *Illuminations* (1981) Aczel's powers came to full fruition. Written in English with ironies that some consider Nabokovian, the novel is concerned with exile—both the physical exile of its hero and the metaphysical exile of man from the Garden of Eden. The novel shows life in the Iron Curtain under a comic lens, creating in the blind protagonist a Tiresias-like figure whose battle with the torments of his mind and of the impinging world give him the status of a contemporary hero, a man burdened with guilt for the state of the world and for his own state. *Illuminations* is a virtuoso comic novel in the European modernist tradition of dark expressionist humor overlaying moral concern.

Aczel's newest novel, *The Hunt*, appeared in 1989.

CLARA GYORGYEY

ADAMOVICH, Gregory V. Born 1894, Russia. Adamovich was a follower of the Acmeist school in Russia; he became an emigre in 1923. He is reputed to be the real-life figure on whom Vladimir Nabokov based the character Christopher Mortus in *The Gift*. Although he remained in self-imposed exile the rest of his life, Adamovich publicly praised Stalin for his World War II leadership. He published a study of French culture, *L'Autre Patrie*, in 1947.

Selected Titles: *Oblaka* (Russia, 1916); *Chistilische* (Russia, 1922); *Na Zapade* (Paris, 1939); *Edinistvo* (Paris, 1967).

Consult: Nina Berberova, *The Italics Are Mine* (1969).

ADAMS, Perseus (Peter Robert Charles Adams). Born 1933, South Africa; he lives in London. Adams journeyed through Africa, Europe, and the Far East for many years before settling down in London, where he now teaches. He considers his stay in England a self-imposed exile, and his travels and distance from his homeland a necessary stimulus to his poetic art.

Selected Titles: *The Land At My Door* (1965); *A Single Leaf of the Baobab* (1966); *Grass for the Unicorn* (1975).

ADORNO, Theodor W[iesengrund]. Born September 11, 1903, in Frankfurt, Germany; died August 6, 1969, in Visp, Switzerland. Adorno was forced into exile in 1938 when he could no longer ignore the persecutorial tyranny of the National Socialist party. He came to New York, where he rejoined forces with his Marxist colleagues who had formed the Institut für Sozialforschung (Institute for Social Research) at the University of Frankfurt and who had been forced out of Germany because of their radical beliefs, intellectual outspokenness, and/or Jewish origins. Adorno participated in lectures at the New School for Social Research in New York, where his ideas had preceded him through the intercession of colleagues and disciples who had fled from Nazism earlier than he. The New School's graduate faculty and its program had been started by the school's president, Dr. Alvin Johnson, in 1933 as a "University in Exile," a means by which intellectuals fleeing from Nazism could start a new life in the United States. When Adorno moved to Los Angeles in 1941, he took the Institute for Social Research with him, but many of his colleagues stayed on in New York and at the New School (among them Henry Pachter, Max Ascoli, and Horace Kallen), providing a rigorous interdisciplinary approach to historic events. Music, as well as analytic expression of philosophy and literature, was one of Adorno's abiding concerns, stretching back to his early study with Alban Berg in 1925, and in Los Angeles Adorno gave advice to Thomas Mann* on the musical references and passages in Mann's *Doktor Faustus*. Several of Adorno's musicological works were published late in his life or posthumously; among them are *Philosophie der neuen Musik* (Frankfurt, 1949; *Philosophy of Modern Music*, 1973); *Versuch uber Wagner* (1952; *In Search of Wagner*, London, 1981); *Einleitung in die Musiksoziologie: 12 theoretische Vorlesungen* (Hamburg, 1962; *Introduction to the Sociology of Music*, 1976); *Impromptus. Zweite Folge neu gedruckter musikalischer Aufsatze* (Frankfurt, 1968, Impromptus); and *Mahler* (F.R.G., 1960, rev. 1963). In general, Adorno's published work appeared largely after his return to Germany in 1949, though he had been writing "notes" all his life.

Adorno's aesthetic theories are expressed most cogently in *Negative Dialektic* (Frankfurt, 1966; *Negative Dialectics*, 1973), though he made it a point of philosophic and linguistic honor to require concentrated effort for accessibility to his ideas. He believed, as expressed in *Negative Dialectics*, that the artist had to escape from the nets of the "culture industry" that threaten to trap him in jargon and fashionable styles of expression. It was the artist's duty to reject the popular mode, Adorno proclaimed, since such a mode was a convenience of system that justified moral value by the largest number of common denominators of accessibility. Such a value system, putting quantity (the mass of people) over quality (the purity of the artist's dedication to his vision), was anathema to Adorno. He proposed instead that the artist remain committed to his difference from the norms of the "culture industry." By so doing, the artist reaffirmed his commitment to the highest value of art, that of providing vision for his readers. Adorno proclaimed that the triumph of his proposed dialectic lay in the eternal dialogue between artist and community, a dialogue whose values were to be seen in the acts of progress to understanding rather than the completion of any shibboleths of easy form.

Adorno's dialogue, or dialectic, is *negative* in that its goal is one of immediate failure as a spur to continued movement toward the goal of understanding. The artist, by definition in Adorno's argument, is always ahead of his time and remote from it; at the same time, he or she must find a link to it, otherwise the artist's contribution is of no socially redeeming value. Curiously, in Adorno's terms of reference based on his Marxist and other philosophic stores of erudition, the artist is not a man or woman of the people but one who must protect himself against the exploitive, corrupt demands of the folk of his land. Adorno, however, shows his Marxist bias in positing that the artist's responsibility is linked to society and that failure to strive for connection—by the paradoxical means of intellectual distance—depletes an artist's value. It is quite possible that behind Adorno's cautionary vision lay his portrait of the National Socialist leader Adolf Hitler, who had perverted the artist's moral calling into a propaganda weapon of the fascist state.

Adorno's period in exile removed him from the familiar physical surroundings of his German university setting, but it did not significantly alter his intellectual approaches and views. Indeed, his philosophy and aesthetics show little dependence on physical texture. Their import lies in the philosopher-artist-intellectual keeping his or her society at a distance while he or she embroiders on the intellectual screen the various forms and shapes that provide a model for the artist's society to sketch. At the same time Adorno makes it patent that once the artist becomes a direct and/or political leader, using the easy routes of jargon and cliché, he or she has forsaken art for formula. The path of the artist becomes in Adorno's portrait a tortuous maze in which the artist must keep a balance between the irresponsibility of alteration by the social fabric, on one side of the scale, and the irresponsibility of adoption of the dress of social fashion, on the other.

In the late 1950s and early 1960s Adorno became embroiled in an intellectual controversy on positivism and the value of the dialectic. Associating himself with ideas paralleled in Max Weber's and Edmund Husserl's disquisitions, Adorno argued that the separation between fact and judgment is an arbitrary one, and thus a false dichotomy, but that the distinction is a necessary one made viable through recourse to recognized standards. In *Der Positivismusstreit in der deutschenSoziologie* (Neuwied, F.R.G., 1969; *The Positivist Dispute in German Sociology*, London, 1976), Adorno wrote that only in art is the world of truth possible, since art is the "beautiful illusion" that cannot lie. Earlier, in his *Negative Dialectics*, Adorno had written that "in illusion there is a promise of freedom from illusion."

One of Adorno's critics, Rudiger Bubner, in *Modern German Philosophy* (1981), has written of Adorno's *Asthetische Theorie* (F.R.G., 1970; *Aesthetic Theory*, 1983):

Adorno by no means wishes simply to extend to art a philosophy which is fundamentally certain of what it is about. He seeks rather to rediscover in art the totally uncertain subject-matter of philosophy. The fluctuating definition of the task of philosophy, which moves to and fro indecisively between the criticism of ideological illusion and the autonomy of theory, is surprisingly reflected in the phenomena of art, which also do not allow themselves to be tied down. They give the impression of autonomy and yet they are merely illusion. They wish to say something to us which is worth understanding and yet they do not stand up to any theoretical analysis. In sounding out these effects Adorno the connoisseur displays all the mastery of sensitive reflection of which he was capable. I believe that in *Asthetische Theorie*, which frequently crosses the boundaries between literary criticism, musicology and history of art, his true legacy is to be found. (p. 182).

Selected Titles: *Konstruktion des Asthetischen* (1933; rev. 1962, 1966; *Kierkegaard: Construction of the Aesthetic*, ed. Robert Hullot-Kentor, 1989); *Jargon der Eigentlichkeit: zur deutshen Ideologie* (1964; *The Jargon of Authenticity*, 1973); with Mark Horkheimer, *Dialektic der Auflarung* [originally *Philosophische Fragmente*, written 1944] (Holland, 1947; *Dialectic of Enlightenment*, 1972; repr. 1982); *Minima Moralia: Reflexionen aus dem beschadigten Leben* (F.R.G., 1951; *Reflections from a Damaged Life*, London, 1974, 1978); *Prismen* (F.R.G., 1955; *Prisms*, 1967); *Zur Metakritick der Erkenntnistheorie, Studien uber Husserl und die phanomenologischen Antinomien* (F.R.G., 1956; *Against Epistemology: a metacritique: Studies in Husserl and the Phenomenological Antinomies*, 1982); *Noten zur Literatur*, 4 vols. (Frankfurt, 1958–74); *Philosophische Terminologie*, 2 vols. (F.R.G., 1973–74); *Gessammelte Schriften*, 20 vols. (Frankfurt, 1970–continuing); see also *Theodor W. Adorno: eine Auswahl*, ed. Rolf Tiedemann (Frankfurt, 1971, Selected Works).

Consult: S. Buck-Morss, *The Origin of Negative Dialectics* (1977); Frederic Jameson, *Late Marxism: Adorno or the Persistence of the Dialectic* (1990); M. Jay, *The Dialectical Imagination: A History of the Frankfurt School and the Institute of Social Research 1923–1950* (1973); G. Rose, *The Melancholy Science: An Introduction to the Thought of Theodor W. Adorno* (1978).

AGNON, S. Y. (pseudonym of Shmuel Yosef Czaczkes). Born July 17, 1888, in Buczacz, Galicia, Austro-Hungarian Empire; died February 17, 1970, in Jerusalem. Agnon spent eleven years in exile in Germany, between 1913 and 1924, when he became stranded there by the outbreak of World War I and by his hesitancy to return to a Palestine ravaged by Arab raids on Jewish settlements. It was not an exile characterized by poverty or neglect of attention; Agnon had achieved wide recognition for his work in the short story and the novel, and he was frequently in the company of prominent Jewish intellectuals in Berlin, among them Max Buber and Gershom Scholem. Yet Agnon felt estranged from his homeland, Palestine, or what he called The Land, for what informed his sense of being was his consciousness of being a Jew. It is, however, just as accurate to say that Agnon's German experience was only one of his experiences of exile, and that his whole life was the experience of exile until he resolved this sore of ambiguity into a sense of "wholeness." The resolution of his many conflicts of allegiance may be seen in his posthumously published novel, *Shira* (1971), while the profound struggle to understand his sense of alienation and ambivalence can be seen in all his work from his juvenile poetry to his mature fiction, which earned him the Nobel Prize in 1966 (he shared the prize with the poet Nelly Sachs*).

Agnon studied Jewish lore privately with his father and took instruction in Talmudic studies with Rabbi S. Y. Shtark at the local synagogue school. He achieved early success with his poems, written both in Hebrew and Yiddish, and he was an editor of a Yiddish weekly by the time he was eighteen. In 1907 he made his first trip to Palestine, disembarking at Jaffa and later becoming a staff member of the Land of Israel Council. He took his pen name from his first Jaffa-based story, "Agunot," written in Hebrew and published in 1908. (*Agunot* is the plural of *aguna*, a woman deserted by her husband but in Jewish law still bound to him until *he* divorces her.) From this point on, he wrote in Hebrew, with occasional forays into Yiddish and German.

Agnon's sojourn in Palestine proved fruitful. His novel *Vehaya He'Akov Le Misha* (And the Crooked Shall Be Made Straight), published in 1912 a year after Agnon had moved to Jerusalem, attracted wide attention, and Agnon believed he had found both a Jewish recognition and a world following. Characteristic of him was the need, usually expressed after the trauma of some important loss, to experience a fusion (or refusion) of his identities and roots. In leaving Galicia, his birthplace, for Palestine, he was hoping to gain a deeper identity. In deciding to travel to Germany in 1913, he was hoping to integrate Jewish-German philosophy with Semitic history and Zionism-socialism. The need for integration of the multifaceted forces in his world is a recognition of his awareness of the ambiguities that pervaded his sensibilities; he was never at rest with his questions of identity till the final few years of his life. His German experience proved fruitful as well for Agnon, for he met and married Esther Marx in 1920. In 1924 his library of rare books and manuscripts and the manuscript of his unfinished novel were destroyed by fire. The loss probably decided Agnon to return to Jerusalem to invigorate his roots. In a bitter parallel, his newly acquired library of valuable books and papers was destroyed in 1929, this time by Arab marauders. In what may well be a parallel psychic response, Agnon returned to Galicia after the loss, in an attempt to restore his sense of identity and to regain his first "home."

Agnon's life and work exemplifies the prism of the exilic complex. As a Jew he yearned, from his earliest training and his religious traditions, to return to The Land from which his ancestors had been exiled thousands of years before by their Babylonian captors. In his first nineteen years in Galicia, he was an outsider, a Jew writing in Hebrew and Yiddish, and the quest for the Promised Land stimulated his most profound feelings. In his second stage of development, he lived in Palestine, and here, as an emigrant, he experienced an identity with his community. He associated with settlers who had come to Palestine before the second (socialist) *Aliyah* (from 1908 to 1913) as well as with his friends in the more recent Zionist-inspired wave of immigration. From 1913 to 1924 he was in literal exile, since he was unable to return or fearful of returning to his Land beset by Arab pillaging and terrorism. In his final return to Jerusalem in 1921, he seems to have made peace with his battles of identity and to have become a "whole" person. One of his critics, Harold Fisch, sees the two points of significance in Agnon's life as his birthplace, Buczacz, and his adopted city, Jerusalem, and suggests that the movement from Buczacz to Jerusalem is "a movement from the confusion and frustration of exile to the wholeness and ease of redemption." However, Fisch qualifies his "scheme of metaphysical geography" by admitting that Agnon yearned for the peace of Buczacz when he lived amid the riots in Jerusalem in the 1920s and 1930s. Perhaps it is more accurate to say that Agnon's dreamplace of peace is a quest that attains its meaning in philosophic journey rather than destination of actual place. In his style and his choice of content, Agnon also exhibits a movement from divisions of ambiguity to a wholeness of philosophic calm. He writes of both the Yiddish peasant and the Hebrew scholar, of simple piety and excruciating intellectual niceties. His style ranges from the clearing of a field of penetrating images to the density of a construct of Talmudic probings.

Selected Titles: "Agunot" (1908) is available in English in *Congress Bi-weekly* 33, no. 14 (1966); *BiLevav Yamin* (1935; *In the Heart of the Seas*, 1948); *Oreah Nata Lalun* (1935; *A Guest for the Night*, 1968); *Ad Henna* (1952, Till Here; Eng. *Two Tales*, 1966).

Consult: Arnold J. Band, *Nostalgia and Nightmare: A Study in the Fiction of S. Y. Agnon* (1968, contains bibliography); Baruch Hochman, *The Fiction of S. Y. Agnon* (1970); Harold Fisch, *S. Y. Agnon* (1975).

AI Qing (also spelled Ai Ch'ing; pseudonym of Jiang Haincheng). Born 1910 February 17, 1910, in Iwu, Chin-hua County, Chekiang Province, China; he lives in Beijing. Son of a landowner, Ai Qing studied medicine briefly, then, against the wishes of his parents, went to Paris in 1929, where he made his living by painting porcelains. His ambition turned from painting to poetry as he read the French Symbolists and other modern Western poets, including Walt Whitman and Vladimir Mayakovsky. Returning to China in 1932, he became active in progressive Chinese literary circles. He was arrested in July of 1932 by police of the French Concession for harboring "dangerous ideas." Many of his best-known poems were written while he was in prison.

In 1941 he went to Yanan, capital of the area held then by the Chinese Communist party, and soon espoused Mao Zedong's principle that literature must serve the revolution by portraying people and their revolutionary leaders in a favorable light. While serving as editor-in-chief of *Poetry* he became China's best-known poet. During the 1950s he also served as associate editor of *People's Literature*. In 1957 the Party prosecuted him as a Rightist; for twenty years he was kept isolated, mainly in Singkiang. Although he was not prevented from writing poetry, all the poems he wrote during this period have been lost.

Ai Qing returned to Beijing in 1975 and began to publish poems again in 1978 after the fall of the Gang of Four. In 1979 he became the vice-chairman of the Chinese Writers Association. When Bei Dao and other young poets began publishing their New Poetry in the late 1970s, Ai Qing joined the well-known elderly poets Tsang k'o-chia and Yuan Shui-p'ai in publicly denouncing the alleged obscurantism and antisocialism of the Misty Poets. His own reputation has suffered, however, since the "Misties"—so-called because of the alleged ambiguity in their work expressing personal feelings of melancholy and despair— gained enthusiastic public following.

Selected Titles: *Hsiang t'ai-yang* (1938); *Shih lun* (1940); *Huo-pa* (1940); *K'uang-yeh* (1940); *Ch'un-t'ien* (1956).

Translations: *Selected Poetry of Ai Qing* (1982).
Consult: J. C. Lin, *Modern Chinese Poetry: An Introduction* (1972).

                                                                                        EDWARD A. MORIN

AISTIS, Jonas (pseudonym of Jonas Aleksandričius). Born July 7, 1904, in Kampiskes near Kaunas, Lithuania; died June 13, 1973, in Washington, D.C. Aistis's family name was Aleksandravičius. In his early publications he used the name of Kossu-Aleksandravičius and Kuosa Aleksandriškis, but in 1952 he changed his name, legally, to his new pen name Aistis. He studied Lithuanian literature at the University of Kaunas and philology at the University of Grenoble, France, where he received his doctorate in 1944. He was coeditor of an independent avant-garde literary magazine *Piūvis* (1929–30, The Cross-Section). After the publication of four volumes of poetry—*Eilérašciai* (1932, Poems); *Imago Mortis* (1933); *Intymios giesmés* (1935, Intimate Songs); and *Užgese chimeros akys* (1937, The Burnt-Out Eyes of the Chimera)—he was recognized as a foremost Lithuanian poet. Aistis was influenced by futurism, but his poetry is also close to French surrealism and early existentialism. He drew inspiration from Lithuanian folklore, Catholic tradition, and major works of world literature as well. Most of his early poems express a profoundly pessimistic worldview colored by a presentiment of World War II and Lithuania's defeat and occupation. During the Sovietization of Lithuania in 1940, Aistis, who was studying in France, chose to remain abroad. He emigrated to the United States in 1946, taught at a high school in Connecticut, worked at Radio Free Europe, and from 1958 to his death, was employed at the Library of Congress. While living in exile he published several volumes of poetry, among them *Nemuno ilgesys* (1947, The Longing for the Nemunas); *Sesuo buitis* (1951, My Sister Life—the title borrowed from Boris Pasternak, one of the poets who influenced Aistis), and *Kristaliniam karste* (1957, In the Crystal Coffin). In general these books fail to achieve the same level as Aistis's prewar poems, but his *Poezija* (1961, Collected Poems) establishes him as one of the leading figures in modern Lithuanian letters. Aistis is also the author of three volumes of essays: *Dievai ir smūtkeliai* (1935, Gods and Wayside Shrines); *Apie laika ir žmones* (1953, On Time and People); and *Milfordo gatves elegijos* (1969, Milford Street Elegies). As an essayist, Aistis is sophisticated and caustic. His last book of essays stirred controversy in émigré circles because of its pronounced nationalistic stance.

   Selected Titles: *Poezija* (1940); *Pilnatis* (1948).
   Consult: Rimvydas Silbajoris, *Perfection of Exile: 14 Contemporary Lithuanian Writers* (1970).

                                                                                        TOMAS VENCLOVA

AKSYONOV, Vassily Pavlovich (also spelled Aksenov). Born August 20, 1932, in Kazan, USSR; he lives in Washington, D.C. Aksyonov's mother (Eugenia Ginsburg) and father were both arrested in 1937 during the Stalinist purges. Aksyonov's mother later wrote her memoirs of the eighteen-year prison period,

Krutoy marshrut (2 vols., 1967, 1979; *Journey into the Whirlwind*, 1967; *Within the Whirlwind*, 1981), a work which brought her world attention. In 1956 Aksyonov graduated from the Leningrad Medical Institute and practiced medicine until he decided in 1960 to become a full-time writer. His first two novels, *Kollegi* (1960; *Colleagues*, 1962) and *Zvyozdmy bilet* (1961; *A Starry Ticket*, 1962), were immediate successes in their portrait of young intellectuals throwing off the restrictions of rigid Stalinist regulations. Aksyonov's early work, particularly *Zatovareunaya bochkotara* (1968, An Excess Stock of Barrels) is filled with a bright enthusiasm for words and for the dazzling effects of experimental literary media; he showed the influence of contemporary American and European writers as well as Russian masters. One critic of Russian literature, Edward J. Brown, calls Aksyonov's style of this period a "carnivalization" of language, an assimilation of creative uniqueness and common, vital phraseology. Brown attributes Aksyonov's style to the influence of Mikhail Bakhtin and Bakhtin's theories of literature as described in Bakhtin's book on Rabelais. Such a "carnivalization" suggests a vibrant indulgence in linguistic play and a sense of pleasure in trampling on guidelines imposed by Social Realism. During this period Aksyonov also published *Kruglie sukti non-stop 1976* (*Open 24 Hours a Day*) in the Soviet journal *Novy Mir* (*New World*) in 1976. Also translated as *Non-Stop Round the Clock*, the satirical account of Aksyonov's tenure as a visiting professor at the University of California in Los Angeles increased his audience with the young, and made him a favorite of the cultural establishment as well. Aksyonov paints a carnivalistic view of the American academic system; the world he presents is one in which everyone runs at a dizzying pace in a circus-like atmosphere in their professional and home lives.

Aksyonov published two novellas, *Zolotaya naska zhelezha* (Our Golden Bit of Rail) and *Crimea Island*, in 1980. *Crimea Island* is another satire drawing on Aksyonov's knowledge/opinion of life in California in which a mythical island becomes an independent capitalist democracy; its proximity to the USSR places it in political jeopardy. Using these premises, Aksyonov pokes fun at the fast-lane amoralities of American/California life and the slow trodding of human aspirations in the Soviet Union.

In 1980, with the publication of his satirical novel, *The Burn*, a mock-portrait of contemporary Soviet life, Aksyonov suffered a fall from bureaucratic grace. His participation in the 1979 American publication of *Metropol*, a collection of banned Soviet writings, and the adverse reception of *The Burn*, led to his expulsion from the Writers Union and from the editorial board of the periodical *Yunost*. He emigrated to the United States in the summer of 1980 and settled in Washington, D.C., after traveling through the country for some months.

Aksyonov continues to write satires of Soviet life, drawing on past experiences as well as present exilic ones. He writes in a style that may be said to possess the sharp bite of a tongue-in-cheek wit. A recent work, *In Search of Melancholy Baby* (1987), is, as described in the preface, the "story of my emigration, alienation, and acceptance of a new home." Although it is largely a nonfiction narrative, it includes a story, "Sketches for a Novel to Be." *Newsweek* magazine, in its May 1, 1989, issue, described the expatriate Soviet novelist's witty memoir of his experiences in the United States as "unique in attempting a pointillist panorama of national diversity." The work represents his second look at America, following *Non-Stop Round the Clock*.

At the International PEN Congress in New York in January 1986, Aksyonov utilized one of his native country's literary masters, Nikolai Gogol, to compare the difference between modern alienation and nineteenth-century exile. Gogol, in exile from his native land for eighteen years, could always return to it without fear of physical harassment; it was Gogol who could not stand to face the bureaucratic slush and slug-faces of his government inspectors. The reverse, Aksyonov countered, applies to the modern scene; it is the government inspectors who cannot bear to face the exile or émigré writer's contempt of bureaucratic stupidity. In discussing his own case, Aksyonov stated that while a writer may physically escape from his native land, he can never escape from its language. What he takes with him in his flight outward is the imagination spawned by his history, and that history is inevitably tied both to the country from which he is alienated and to the ambivalent loss and love he feels for his native land. Aksyonov characterized such a condition as a writer's "gills" and "lungs." He must learn to dive, hold his breath, swim and at some point breathe free and break the waves surrounding him. Surprisingly, Aksyonov said, he found Washington, D.C., the area in the United States most closely approximating the place where he could use both his "gills" and "lungs"—that is, for him, Washington, D.C., provided a nurturing nexus of American nostalgia. "We missed the European eclecticism of Moscow and Leningrad. Roaming about the U.S. during the first year of my American life, I didn't realize that I was looking for urban eclecticism. When we ran into it in Washington, we decided to settle there for good. It took five years before American nostalgia ceased to be alien—foreign to me," Aksyonov declared.

In 1989 Aksyonov published a new novel, *Say Cheese!* Like Zinovy Zinik,* a Russian exile living in London, Aksyonov peoples his new book with young, foolish cynics, creatures who cut the wires of everybody's dreams, including their own bursts of personal illumination. These young people stand in contrast to the prior generation, creatures who were crafty cynics striving after power with an open ruthlessness for material gain. The new generation of Russian intellectuals exploits its cynicism to challenge power as a corruptor of humanity and, in the fervency of their social indifference and moral resistance to power brokerage, to render bureaucratic power uselessly weak.

Aksyonov has also written plays, a few of which have been produced in the USSR and published in English translation outside the Soviet Union.

In August 1990, by order of Mikhail Gorbachev, full Soviet citizenship was restored to Aksyonov, who had been stripped of his Soviet citizenship in 1966.

Selected Titles: *Poiski zhanra* (1978, Search of the Genre); *Your Mother* (1965) in *Performing Arts Journal* 2, no. 1 (Spring 1977).

Translations: *Faith in the Word* (1977); *The Steel Bird and Other Stories* (1979); *Quest for an Island* (1988).
Consult: Edward J. Brown, *Russian Literature Since the Revolution* (1982); Max Hayward and E. L. Crowley, eds., *Soviet Literature in the Sixties* (1964); H. B. Segel, *Twentieth-Century Russian Drama* (1979).

ALAVI, Bozorg. *See* Iranian Writers in Exile

ALBERTI, Rafael. Born December 16, 1902, in El Puerto de Santa María, Spain; he returned to Spain in 1977. Alberti has made exile a major theme of his work and has lived through a series of exiles that have taken him from the Old World to the New and back again to Rome, the original home of his great-grandparents, and finally to Spain after Franco's death. At first a painter, Alberti turned to poetry in the 1920s, and only after a long exile from his first love did he resume painting while in Argentina. He has since pursued both arts, allowing them to engage in a dialogue in search of an uncertain paradise.

Alberti's early books revealed his mastery of the Spanish tradition from the *Cancionero* to the Baroque and placed him with Federico García Lorca at the forefront of the Generation of 1927. The title of his first book, the prize-winning *Marinero en tierra* (1924), suggests exile, and the poems, however exuberant their surface, express nostalgia for a childhood paradise, the sea, which survives only in memory. By 1929 Alberti was entering his artistic maturity. *Cal y canto*, while a brilliant formal display, satirizes late Romantic poetic concerns; it parodies *Marinero en tierra* and tests the possibilities of a new aesthetic, affirming the power of the imagination, but *Sobre los ángeles*, one of the great works of twentieth-century poetry, questions the foundation of Alberti's art. Severed from a disintegrating paradise and lost in a world where body and soul are exiled from each other, the speaker of these poems faces a gap between self and others and between language and experience, an absence haunted by often hostile angels; in the end only one angel with amputated wings survives. The sense of loss in all these books reflects Alberti's early experiences: his family's economic decline; his years at a Jesuit *colegio* where he was a day student and an outsider, his only escape the sea near Cádiz; his expulsion from the *colegio*; and his family's move to Madrid where a landlocked and disillusioned Alberti took up painting until serious illness and his self-doubts led to a crisis and to his first poems. By the end of the 1920s a friend's suicide and an ambiguous love betrayal were additional factors precipitating a second crisis, and after exploring the trauma in *Sobre los ángeles, Sermones y moradas*, and *Yo era un tonto y lo que he visto me ha hecho dos tontos* (1929–30), Alberti seemed to have exhausted his art.

After his marriage to María Teresa León, Alberti found a new direction through political commitment. While traveling on several continents and working as poet, playwright, director, and editor, he pursued the project of a collective paradise in history rather than a personal one in memory; he also wrote his great elegy for Ignacio Sánchez Mejías (*"Verte y no verte,"* 1934). After 1936 all of Alberti's hopes were tested severely by the Spanish Civil War; he and María Teresa devoted themselves to the Republic, at times risking their lives, and Alberti's poems of the war years express their initial optimism followed by increasing doubt and the inevitable recognition of failure (*Capital de la gloria*, 1938). They fled to Paris in 1939, finding asylum with Pablo Neruda.* In his autobiography, *La arboleda perdida*, Alberti remembers seeing the "starvation," "persecution," and exile of his people. With the fall of France, Alberti and María Teresa fled to Buenos Aires, where their daughter, Aitana, was born in 1941, and for the next twenty-five years they made Argentina their home.

In exile Alberti examined his loss of homeland, his separation from friends, and his experience as a refugee in Paris (*Vida bilingüe*, 1939–40) and as an expatriate in Argentina (*Entre el clavel y la espada*, 1941, and *Pleamar*, 1944). Anger, bitterness, oppressive images of the Civil War, and despair when Franco survived World War II had to be faced along with life on a new continent. The poems of the 1940s test various escapes, ranging from erotic diversion to spiritual contemplation, but Alberti's final answer to exile is memory, and his mode is elegiac. His major postwar collections, *A la pintura* (1948) and *Retornos de lo vivo lejano* (1952), along with his resumption of painting, can be seen as related attempts to recover his own past and find in the order of art the possibility of restoring a lost world, not only the sea near Cádiz but the whole of Spain. While Alberti's "unbearable nostalgia" recurs in later volumes like *Baladas y canciones de Paraná* (1953–54) and the autobiographical *La arboleda perdida* (1959), the power of memory is consistently reaffirmed.

Maintaining his political commitments and his dedication to his art, Alberti has continued to write and draw in Rome and more recently in Spain (he returned in April, 1977). Works like *Roma, peligro para caminantes* (1968) increasingly express resignation. After a lifetime of rich and varied production, as diverse as his friend Pablo Picasso's, Alberti is recognized as one of the great modern poets of exile in the Western world.

Translations: *Selected Poems* (1966); *Concerning the Angels* (London, 1967); *The Owl's Insomnia: Poems* (1973); *The Lost Grove* (1976).

Consult: Judith Nantell, *Rafael Alberti's Poetry of the Thirties: The Poet's Public Voice* (1986); Peter Wesseling, *Revolution and Tradition: The Poetry of Rafael Alberti* (Valencia, Spain, 1981).

MICHAEL MANLEY

ALDANOV, Mark. Born 1886, Russia; he died 1957, United States. Aldanov emigrated to the U.S. via France in 1942; a political exile from the USSR, he had lived in Paris from 1919 until the Nazi invasion. He is best known as a historical novelist, though he also published a philosophical fiction, *Ul'mskaya noch* (1953, The Night of Ulm), in which he posits chance as the leading factor in historic determinism; he published his memoirs in 1954.

Selected Titles: *Istoki* (1950, The Sources); *Samoubiystvo* (1958, Suicide); *Povest'o smerti* (1952–53, A Story About Death).

Consult: Ivar Ivask, *World Literature Since 1945* (1973).

ALEGRIA, Claribel. Born May 12, 1924, in Esteli, Nicaragua; she lives in Managua, Nicaragua. Although Alegria was born in Nicaragua, she considers herself Salvadorean: she was only nine months old when her parents moved to Santa Ana, El Salvador. Her father was a political refugee who fled his country because of his ties with Augusto César Sandino, the leader of the uprising against the U.S. occupation of Nicaragua in the 1930s. In 1943 Alegria came to the United States to study at George Washington University, where she earned a B.A. There she met the writer Darwin J. Flakoll, whom she married and later collaborated with on many projects, including *Nicaragua, la revolucion: una cronica politica 1885–1979* (1984), an account of the Sandinista revolution that pays particular attention to the events between 1960 and 1979, and *Cenizas de Izalco* (1966; *Ashes of Izalco*, 1989), a novel set in Santa Ana at the time of the 1932 massacre. Flakoll has also translated a collection of Alegria's poetry, *Woman of the River* (1989), and *Louisa in Realityland* (1987), a fictionalized self-portrait in poetry and prose that is a nostalgic, yet ambiguous account of Alegria's attachment to Santa Ana, and a testimony of one woman's witness to the persecution of her people.

After Alegria's graduation from the university, she and Flakoll lived in the United States. They also spent several years in residence in Latin America, first in Mexico (in 1951), then in Uruguay and Argentina. In 1962 they moved to Paris, and four years later settled in Deya, Mallorca, where they were to live for many years before moving to Managua, Nicaragua, in 1980 after a brief visit to El Salvador.

Alegria is best known as a poet. She began publishing her poems in 1948, and to date has published ten collections. Her early books, including *Anillo de silencio* (1948), *Vigilias* (1953), and *Hyuesped de mi tiemp* (1961), are lyrical poems that treat of death, journeying, and identity. With the publication of *Via Unica* (1965) and *Aprendizaje* (1940), Alegria's poetry became more openly political. Subsequent collections, including *Pagare a cobrar* (1973), *Sobrevivio* (1978), and *Suma y sigue* (1981), continue to make strong political statements about Central America. Outside of Latin America, Alegria is probably the most well known woman poet writing today, and is one of the most respected of all contemporary Central American writers. In 1978 she received the prestigious Casa de las Americas poetry award for her book *Sobrevivio*, and in 1982 a collection of her poems, translated by Carolyn Forché, was published in a bilingual edition under the title *Flowers from the Volcano*. *Luisa in Reality* was published in 1987, and *Woman of the River* in 1989 in a bilingual edition.

Consult: Carolyn Forché, "Interview with Claribel Alegria," *Index on Censorship*, April 1984; George Yudice, "Letras de emergenica: Claribel Alegria," *Revista Iber-oamericana*, July-December 1985.

SUSAN SCHREIBMAN

ALESHKOVSKY, Yuz. Born 1929 in Siberia, USSR; he lives in Middletown, Connecticut. Aleshkovsky was sent to a prison camp early in his youth because of the exhibition he made of his "anti-social" views; he wrote poems about his camp experiences and drew on his knowledge of criminals and their wardens for his fictional portraits. His work circulated in *samizdat* (underground) fashion during the 1970s and appeared in print in the West in the 1980s, after Aleshkovsky left the Soviet Union in 1979. He has published children's books as well as adult novels. A translation of one of his novels, under the title *Kangaroo*, was issued in 1986 in the United States (the work was first published in a Russian-language edition in Western Europe in 1981). Aleshkovsky has taught Russian literature at Wesleyan University in Connecticut.

In a panel discussion at a Writers in Exile conference at Boston University on May 7 and 8, 1982, Aleshkovsky made the following remarks: "Having escaped from Dracula, from the Soviet regime, I suddenly began to encounter its closest blood relatives in the amazingly beautiful expanses of the New and the Old Worlds. Trembling with horror and loathing, I see *Sovieticus draculat* in the talentless specimens of mass culture that truly ravage the human spirit, in the obtuseness and blindness of independent politicians surrendering one after another the bastions of freedom to world totalitarianism, not without any resistance, but without any special pressures from it . . . . I think that one of the greatest ironies in history is that the peoples of the Soviet Empire, having long ago overcome the seduction of evil at the cost of unimaginable sacrifices, watch in horror as the West, as the entire free world, heads in the direction from which they have come, at least morally—toward the epicenter of seductive evil, where the free creative spirit of man resides behind heavy bars. Are not the sympathies toward Communism of millions of French and Italians tragicomic?" (*Partisan Review*, pp. 509, 511).

Aleshkovsky has not changed his views in print on the current rapprochement between East and West. Having known the rigors of prison life, and having learned the defenses of the subject criminal, Aleshkovsky is not easily swayed by notions of benevolent change. His fiction, like his life, has been a hard one, and he has survived through wariness, a condition he is unlikely to give up without sustained assurances of a new beginning.

Aleshkovsky's most recent work in English, *The Hand, or The Confession of an Executioner* (1990; it was published in the original Russian version at the author's expense in 1980) is a fictional reconstruction of an unreconstructed angry man, a victim of Communist zealots in the early days of the Soviet regime: the man's father was killed for resisting collectivization and he himself, as a member of a youth group, was beaten and wounded to such an extent that his testicles were frozen and he lost his sexual drive and potency. The protagonist seeks revenge against his torturers and tormentors, but he does not doubt the system; he remains a functioning member of the new society and through his role as a KGB agent he is able to wreak revenge on those who had played their part in his family tragedy. This protagonist, Bashov, who earned his sobriquet from Joseph Stalin when the agent stopped a rabid dog from attacking the Great Leader, has his agenda: the novel takes place when he has scored off all but the last of his list of tormentors and is about to have that remaining offender legally executed. Before the execution Bashov torments this man who had been an agent of Bashov's misery by making him listen to Bashov's tales of condign justice. Within these tales are found stern and unrelenting diatribes equating Soviet rule with the tyranny that issues out of violence and treachery: no thaw in Aleshkovsky's attitude can be gleaned from the views he held during the 1970s and earlier. Written at least a decade before its publication, the novel has been overtaken by the historic events in eastern Europe in the past three years, and it suffers from a rigidity of view: it becomes a period piece, an instance of data whose relevance is rooted in historic fact but also limited to it. Aleshkovsky refuses any fresh interpretation of the contemporary scene that has followed his experience of terror and repression, and in so refusing to make accommodation with new history—that is, to recognize the facts of current events—his passion for redressing the injustices of the past becomes a shrill voice of exile in time as well as in place of refuge.

Selected Title: *Nikolai Nikolayevich* (1970).

Consult: Joseph Brodsky, Introduction in *The Hand* by Aleshkovsky; Edward J. Brown, *Russian Literature Since the Revolution* (1963); "Writers in Exile: A Conference of Soviet and East European Dissidents," *Partisan Review* 50, no. 4 (1983).

ALLENDE, Isabel. Born 1942 in Lima, Peru, where her father, the Chilean diplomat Tomás Allende, was stationed. She now lives in Marin County, California. Allende's parents were divorced when she was three years old; she returned with her mother to Santiago, Chile, where she grew up with her maternal grandparents, who later became the inspiration for her first novel, *La Casa de los Espíritus* (1982; *The House of the Spirits*, 1985). Her grandfather, Agustín Llona, ruled the household with an iron hand, banning radios and other modern implements. When he found Allende in the kitchen with a maid listening to a soap opera, he smashed the radio with his silver cane. Allende was fond of her grandmother, a spiritualist after whom she was named, and watched séances taking place in their home. She stayed in her grandparents' house until her mother married another diplomat and the family began traveling again. Later Allende was separated from her mother while she attended private schools in Santiago, but she remained in close touch with her; they corresponded daily. She became a journalist when she graduated from school; she also wrote several unsuccessful plays. She married Michael Frías, an engineer, and became the mother of a daughter and son, now students in their twenties. She has since divorced Frías and married William Gordon, a San Francisco lawyer.

Allende greatly admired her uncle, President Salvador Allende. Two years after he died during the military takeover of 1973, she decided to leave Chile with her family and live in exile in Venezuela. In 1981, she was notified of her grandfather's death and started writing *The House of the Spirits*; once published, it quickly became a best-seller in Europe, Latin America (including Chile), and the United States. Essentially a family saga encompassing four generations, it is set is an unnamed South American country which can only be Chile, as a half-century of Chilean history is identifiable in it. Allende modeled her story and style on *One Hundred Years of Solitude*, also a four-generation family chronicle, by one of her mentor-writers, Gabriel García Márquez*. Allende thus takes her place in the tradition of Latin American magic realists. However, the novel's last chapters reveal a striking reversal of style and are a reminder that Allende began her writing career as a reporter. In these final chapters, political and social events are described in a starkly realistic technique.

Allende published a second novel in 1984, *De Amor y de Sombra* (Of Love and Shadow), which did not receive the critical acclaim of her first. Her third novel, *Eva Luna*, was published in 1988, and on January 8, 1990 she began work on a fourth. She has returned to Chile on visits.

Consult: Alexander Coleman, "Reconciliation among the Ruins," *New York Times Book Review*, May 12, 1985; Cecilia Eyzaguirre, "*Una semana con Isabel Allende*," *Paula* (Santiago, Chile), June 1986; Patricia Hart, *Narrative Magic in the Fiction of Isabel Allende* (1989); Ignacio Valente, "*La casa de los espiritus*," *El Mercurio* (Santiago, Chile), August 21, 1983.

VERONICA KIRTLAND

ALVARO, Corredo. Born 1896, in Santa Luca, Italy; died 1956, in Rome, Italy. Because of his quarrels with the Italian fascist government, Alvaro lived in exile in France and Germany during the 1920s. He traveled throughout Western Europe, the Middle East, and the USSR during this period. Although he returned to Italy, he had to live in hiding until the fall of Mussolini. His attitude to totalitarianism, whether on the Right or Left, may be seen in his novel *Man Is Strong* (1938), based on observations made during his trip to the USSR in 1934.

Alvaro lived a productive literary life in his native land after the end of World War II.

AMADO, Jorge. Born August 10, 1912, Ilhéus, Bahia, Brazil; he lives in Salvador, Bahia, and maintains a residence in Paris, France. Amado was born in northeastern Brazil and has lived in that region for most of his life; several of his early "cacao novels" are set in the region. His father, João Amado de Faria, carved plantations out of the jungle, and Amado was born on such a plantation. He attended a Jesuit secondary school in Bahia until he rebelled and left; he subsequently attended a school noted for enrolling youthful rebels. At sixteen he was working as a reporter and allied himself with other writers interested in modernism; the group, the "Academy of the Rebels," briefly published two little magazines.

After the group's dissolution in 1930, Amado studied law in Rio de Janeiro and began writing social-protest fiction, with his first novel, *O Pais do Carnaval* (Carnival Land), appearing in 1932 when he was twenty. In this and other early novels, including *Cacáu* (1933, Cacao), *Suor* (1934, Sweat), *Jubiabá* (1935), *Mar Morto* (1936, Dead Sea), and *Capitães da Areia* (1937, Beach Waifs), thinly disguised naturalistic propaganda pieces set on cacao-producing plantations or in city slums and focusing on the social conditions governing the lives of the impoverished workers, he consistently identified with radical political positions.

Imprisoned briefly in 1935 for his political activities, two years later he embarked on his first self-exile from Brazil, living in Mexico and the United States before returning to Brazil. By this time his works were available in such foreign languages as Russian and French, and he had won a major award from the Brazilian Academy of Letters. Again imprisoned, he went into exile once more, spending two years in Uruguay and Argentina, in 1941–43. In 1946 he was elected as a Communist deputy to the Brazilian congress, but after the party was outlawed, he went into exile in Europe from 1948 to 1952, living in Paris and in Czechoslovakia and traveling extensively throughout Europe and Asia. He subsequently returned to Brazil permanently, living first in Rio de Janeiro (where he edited a cultural journal from 1956 to 1958). He then moved to Salvador, capital of Bahia, where he continues to live and write. His work written during exile is generally considered uneven; evidently more than with most authors, Amado was most productive and creative on his own soil, though in recent years, with the coming of fame and public attention in Brazil, he now finds he writes best in hideaways and hotel rooms.

Amado's subsequent literary work has been more concerned with technique and style than with doctrinaire sociopolitical positions, though the same outrage at social injustice may be found in them. One of his best-known works, the epic *Terras do Sem Fim* (1943; *The Violent Land*, 1945; rev., 1965), also deals with the cacao-producing region but is relatively free of polemics; it is, as Carlos Fuentes* has noted, more Balzacian than Zolaesque. He received the Stalin Peace Prize in 1951 and has also been nominated for the Nobel Prize in Literature.

His first major work to achieve popularity in English-speaking nations was *Gabriela, Cravo e Canela* (1958; *Gabriela, Clove and Cinnamon*, 1962), and this and some of his subsequent novels—*A Morte e a Morte de Quincas Berro Dáqua* (1961; *The Two Deaths of Quincas Wateryell*, 1965), *Tenda dos Milagres* (1969; *Tent of Miracles*, 1971), for example—are noted for their warm characterization and humor. The female protagonists in *Gabriela* and such subsequent novels as *Dona Flor e Seus Dois Maridos* (1966; *Dona Flor and Her Two Husbands*, 1969) and *Tieta do Agreste* (1977; 1979) subtly combine Amado's social convictions with irony and caricature, leading some critics to compare him to Geoffrey Chaucer, Laurence Sterne, and John Steinbeck. His twenty-odd works have been translated throughout the world in some fifty languages, and some have become successful films and plays.

Selected Titles: *O Pais Do Carnaval* (1931, Carnival Country); *Suor* (1934, Sweat); *Jubiabá* (1935); *Mar Morto* (1936, Dead Sea); *Capitães da Areia* (1937, "Sand Captains" or beach bums); *ABC de Castro Alves* (1941, The ABC of Castro Alves, biography); *Terras Sem Fin* (1942, Violent Land); *O Cavaleiro da Esperance* (1942, Horseman of Hope [biography of Luis Carlos Pretes]); *Sao Jorge das Ilheus* (1944, St. George of Illeus); *Bahia and todos os Santos* (1945, Bahia and All Its Saints, literary tourist guide); *Seara Vermelha* (1946); *O Amor de Castro Alves* (1947); *O Mundo da Paz* (1950); *Os Subterraneos da Liberdade* (1954, Caves of Liberty); *A Morte e a morte de Quincas Berro d'Agua* (1959, The Two Deaths of Quincas Wateryell); *O Mundo da Paz* (1950);

Os Subterraneos da liberdade (1954, Caves of Liberty); *A Completa Verdade Sobre as Discutidas Aventuras do Comandante Vasco Moscoso de Aragao, Capitão de Longo Curso* (1961; *Home Is the Sailor*, 1964); *Os Pastores da Noite* (1964; *Shepherds of the Night*, 1967); *Tereza Batista Cansada de Guerra* (1973; *Tereza Batista, Home from the Wars*, 1975); *Farda, Fardão, Camisole de Dormir* (1986; *Pen, Sword, Camisole*, 1986); *O Amor do Soldado: Teatro* (1986); *Tocaia Grande* (1985; *Showdown*, 1988); *Capitaes da Areia* (1988; *Captains of the Sands*, 1988).

Consult: Fred P. Ellison, *Brazil's New Novel: Four Northeastern Masters* (Berkeley, 1954); Linda B. Hall, "Jorge Amado: Women, Love, and Possession," *Southwest Review* 68 (1983): 67–77; Linda Ledford-Miller, "A Question of Character: The Black Presence in Jorge Amado's *The Violent Land*," *Studies in Afro-Hispanic Literature* 2–3 (1978–79): 152–63; Nina M. Scott, "Humor and Society in the Frontier Novels of the Americas: Wister, Guiraldes, and Amado," in *Proceedings of the Tenth Congress of the International Comparative Literature Association*, vol. 3, ed. Anna Balakian et al. (New York, 1985), pp. 20–27.

PAUL SCHLUETER

AMALRIK, Andrei Alekseyvich. Born May 12, 1938, in Moscow. He died November 11, 1980, in an automobile accident near Guadalajara, Spain, while traveling to Madrid to take part in an international conference organized by dissident groups. Playwright, historian, and human rights advocate, Amalrik was perhaps the most fiercely independent and uncompromising of the social and political critics to emerge in the post-Stalinist Soviet Union. Rigid in his purely moral, apolitical defense of intellectual and artistic freedom, often at personal risk to himself and family, Amalrik suffered repeated harassment, imprisonment, and both internal and external exile in reprisal for his unbending idealism. Exhibiting early signs of nonconformity and unorthodox behavior, Amalrik was expelled from secondary school and first clashed with Soviet authorities while attending Moscow University. As a result of submitting a controversial dissertation advocating a publicly unacceptable viewpoint and then attempting to publish his work abroad, Amalrik was forced to forfeit both his degree and his pursuit of an academic career. Engaging in menial employment as a means to earn his livelihood, Amalrik surreptitiously began to write a series of experimental plays, later collected and published under the title *Nose! Nose? No-se! and Other Plays* (1973).

In the artistic tradition of Samuel Beckett* and Eugène Ionesco,* Amalrik recognized the theater as an effective vehicle to confront the linguistic and philosophical complacency, impoverishment, and disintegration within contemporary society, and specifically to apply this condition to the reality of the totalitarian state. Interestingly, although his plays possess the existential qualities associated with Jean-Paul Sartre and Albert Camus, Amalrik was unfamiliar with their work as he was with the body of literature referred to as "the theater of the absurd." Kept under constant surveillance by the KGB (State Security Committee), Amalrik was arrested in May 1965. During a search of his apartment, Amalrik's plays, illustrated by avant-garde artist Anatoly Zverev, were confiscated and Amalrik was charged with "disseminating" pornographic and anti-Soviet materials. Released, but then rearrested on the charge of social "parasitism," Amalrik was sentenced to two and a half years of forced labor on a collective farm in the Siberian village of Guryevka. While in exile, Amalrik began to chronicle the Kafkaesque experience of his arrest, trial, and internment.

Released after sixteen months, Amalrik returned to Moscow to live with his wife, the painter Gyusel Makudinova. Despite continued government harassment, Amalrik completed his autobiographical account entitled *Involuntary Journey to Siberia* (1970) as well as the historical essay *Will the Soviet Union Survive until 1984?* (1970). Based primarily on their publication abroad, Amalrik was arrested in May 1970, tried, and sentenced to three years imprisonment. Shortly before his scheduled release, Amalrik was resentenced to an additional three-year term, later commuted to two years in exile, despite both failing health and an international protest in his behalf. Released in 1976, Amalrik, with his wife, was permitted to leave the Soviet Union, first for the Netherlands, then the United States, and eventually France.

Unlike other dissidents either forced or coerced into exile in lieu of prison, Amalrik characteristically thrived in the West. In 1980, Amalrik completed *Notes of a Revolutionary* (1982), a remarkable descriptive history of his last ten years in Russia. There is only speculation as to the cultural and literary impact Amalrik could have generated but for his untimely death. It seems a tragic and perverse irony that Amalrik survived the horror of the Soviet labor camps only to perish in a senseless accident.

Selected Title: *Nose! Nose? No-se! and Other Plays* (1973).

Consult: Harold B. Segel, *Twentieth-Century Russian Drama: From Gorky to the Present* (1979).

STEVEN SERAFIN

AMICHAI, Yehuda. Born May 3, 1924, in Würzberg, Bavaria, Germany; he lives in Jerusalem, Israel. As a Jewish youth, Amichai fled Germany with his parents for Palestine in 1936. He became a student at Hebrew University three years later. During World War II he fought with the British Army; in 1948 he fought in the Israeli war for independence; he again served in the Israeli army in the 1956 conflict and in the Six-Day War in 1973. He settled in Jerusalem, where he has worked as a secondary school teacher for some years. Amichai's poetry has achieved world recognition, and he has read and lectured at universities throughout Europe and the United States.

Amichai's work, extremely popular in Israel, is rooted in the comedic disruptions of daily life, disruptions that, when transmuted by his love of human and animal life, evolve into profound conversations with the Lord of the Land. Amichai accepts sorrow with the wink of religious understanding; his universe, or the poet's breadth of vision and comprehension, stands on the shoulders of love. He turns and returns to love in his dialogue with God and with his fellow mortals: the memory of past love sustains him through his day. This high school teacher who served in three wars is a man of peace constantly on the lookout for difficult compromises. He shoulders his burdens of love both through memory and in spite of the memory of centuries of racial hatred.

Amichai writes in Hebrew. He has published more than ten volumes of poetry, two novels, several collections of stories, and plays. His first book appeared in 1955. Most of his work has been translated into English.

Selected Titles: Poems: *Shirim: 1948–1962* (1962; rev. ed., 1977, Poems 1948–1962); *Achshav baraash: Shirim 1963–1968* (1968, Now in the Noise: Poems 1963–1968). Novel: *Mi yitneni malon* (1971, Hotel in the Wilderness). Stories: *Baruach hanoraah hazot* (1961, In This Terrible Wind).

Translations: *Songs of Jerusalem and Myself* (1973); *Amen*, with introduction by Ted Hughes (1977); *Time* (1979); *Love Poems* (1981); *Great Tranquillity: Questions and Answers* (1983); *Travels* (1986; bilingual ed.); *Selected Poetry of Yehuda Amichai*, ed. Chana Bloch and Stephen Mitchell (1986); *The Early Books of Yehuda Amichai* (1989). Novel: *Not of This Time, Not of This Place* (1969; orig. pub. as *Lo meachshav, lo mikan*, Jerusalem, 1963).

Consult: Chana Bloch, Foreword to *Selected Poetry of Yehuda Amichai* (1986); Noam Flinker, "Jewish Tradition and the Individual Talent of Yehuda Amichai," *Denver Quarterly* 12, no. 2 (1977); Robert Friend, "Yehuda Amichai," in *The Modern Hebrew Poem Itself*, ed. Stanley Burnshaw (1965); Michael Hamburger, Introduction to Yehuda Amichai, *Selected Poems* (London, 1971).

ANDIIEVSKA, Emma. Born March 19, 1931, in Donetske, Ukraine; she lives in the Federal Republic of Germany. An émigré since 1943, Andiievska at first lived in Germany, where she completed her higher education, then in France and the United States, and now again in Germany. She has published twelve collections of verse: *Poeziii* (Poems, 1951), *Narodzhennia idola* (Birth of the Idol, 1958), *Ryba i rozmir* (Fish and Dimension, 1961), *Kuty opostin'* (Corners on Both Sides of the Wall, 1963), *Pervni* (Elements, 1964), *Bazar* (Bazaar, 1967), *Pisni bez tekstu* (Songs without a Text, 1968), *Nauka pro zemliu* (Science of the Earth, 1975); *Kavarnia* (Café, 1983); *Spokusy sviatoho Antoniia* (The Temptations of St. Anthony, 1985), *Vigiliii* (Vigils, 1987), *Arkhitekturni ansambli* (Architectural Ensembles, 1989); three collections of short prose: *Podorozh* (Journey, 1955), *Tyhry* (Tigers, 1962), and *Dzhalapita* (1962), and three novels: *Herostraty* (Herostrati, 1970), *Roman pro dobru liudynu* (Novel about a Good Person, 1973), and *Roman pro liuds'ke pryznachennia* (A Novel about Human Destiny, 1982).

The hermeticism of her poetry and the self-imposed and strict structural constraints of her prose do not lend themselves to easy comprehension. Andiievska's poetic world consists of surrealistic landscapes rooted in real descriptions of nature or works of art, which Andiievska views from various perspectives and to which she provides exquisite instrumentation.

Although only some of her poems reflect her inner views, Andiievska's novels provide her with the necessary canvas on which to paint her experiences as an émigré. She covers the whole gamut of experiences—political, social, aesthetic, marital, philosophical, and spiritual—but with great economy. The concept of "round time" (simultaneity of events) and a narrative that links episodes centered on different characters permit her to present the enormity of human life in *Roman pro liuds'ke pryznachennia*. While in *Roman pro dobru liudynu*, Andiievska limited herself to describing experiences in one displaced persons (DP) camp in Germany after World War II, in *Roman pro liuds'ke pryznachennia* she widens her sights to encompass the whole of the Ukrainian diaspora. Furthermore, *Good Person* is a study of the uprooted Ukrainians' rites of passage to a new life—a sort of purgatorial existence in the DP camps. The heroes of the novel are all fugitives from Stalin's terror (Andiievska's term is *m'iasorubka* —meatgrinder), and the episodes are anchored in the reality of camp life amid flashbacks to earlier Ukrainian life. In *Destiny* Andiievska's thematic scope is broadened to include not only the life of émigrés in their respective new homelands but also the life of their children born since World War II. Andiievska moves freely in time from one decade to another and mixes various episodes from the destinies of her characters to produce not only a superb work of fiction but also a chronicle of the collective experiences of Ukrainians in the diaspora.

Consult: *Encyclopedia of Ukraine*, vol. 1 (Toronto, 1984); Danylo Husar Struk, "Andiyevs'ka's Concept of Round Time," *Canadian Slavonic Papers* 27, no. 1 (March 1985).

DANYLO HUSAR STRUK

ANDRÁS, Sándor. Born March 27, 1934, in Budapest, Hungary; he lives in Silver Springs, Maryland. András left Hungary after the 1956 uprising. He worked in factories and at the British Broadcasting Company offices in London, and then moved to the United States. He has published two volumes of poems, *Oasis on the Run* (1970) and *Sayings* (1982), and a study of Heinrich Heine, *The Exile of God*. He is coeditor of the Hungarian journal in exile, *Arkanum*, and a regular contributor to the American journal *World Literature Today* (formerly *Books Abroad*). András teaches German literature at Howard University in Washington. He writes in Hungarian and English.

ANDREWS, Raymond. Born 1934, in Morgan County, Georgia; he lives in Georgia. Andrews left Georgia to join the U.S. Air Force. Returning to civilian life, he opted for study at Michigan State University, then moved to New York City in 1958. He lived there and in Europe, alternately, for twenty-seven years before returning to his home state. He is the author of four novels, the first three set in his native northeast Georgia.

Selected Titles: *Appalachee Red* (1978); *Rosiebelle Lee Wildcat Tennessee* (1980); *Baby Sweet's* (1983).

ANDREYEV, Leonid (also spelled Andreev). Born August 21, 1871, in Orel, Russia; died September 21, 1919, in Neuvola, Finland. Andreyev's first exile from his native land occurred in 1905 when he fled to Germany after his arrest for political activities. Andreyev accepted an invitation to visit Maxim Gorky* in Capri, a visit that lifted Andreyev's depressed psychological state but resulted in a quarrel with the older, famous writer. Andreyev returned to Russia in 1907 and built himself a mansion in the Finnish territory. When Finland achieved independence in 1917 and its border with the USSR was sealed in 1918, Andreyev became an exile of circumstance. Because of his antipathy to Bolshevism, he remained in Finland during the last two years of his life. His was a bitter end as he loved his country but hated both its czarist past and its contemporary Bolshevik regime.

Andreyev wrote little of importance in his exile years.

Selected Title: *Leonid Andreyev: Photographs by a Russian Writer*, ed. Richard Davies, with preface by Olga Carlisle (1989).

Consult: Olga Carlisle, *Voices in the Snow* (1962); J. M. Newcombe, *Leonid Andreyev* (1972); J. B. Woodward, *Leonid Andreyev: A Study* (1969).

ANDREYEV, Vadim. Born December 25, 1902 (Old Style), January 7, 1903 (New Style), in Moscow, Russia; died May 1976, in Geneva, Switzerland. The elder son of Aleksandra Veligorskaya and Leonid Andreyev,* one of Russia's most successful story writers and dramatists at the turn of the century, Andreyev grew up in a household in which Maxim Gorky,* who thought of himself as Andreyev's godfather, was for several years a frequent visitor. Andreyev was educated at home and at schools in St. Petersburg/Petrograd and Helsinki, where his first published verse appeared in 1919. His poetic vocation began early, and was markedly influenced by Aleksandr Blok.

After his father's death in 1919, Andreyev fought in the Russian Civil War, taking part in a brief quixotic campaign in the Caucasus directed both against the Whites and Reds. By way of Constantinople and Bulgaria, Andreyev reached Berlin in 1922 and resumed his education under a Whittimore Foundation scholarship. This period of his life is described in his *Story of a Journey* and *Return to Life*, published in the Soviet Union in 1966 and 1969. Andreyev moved to Paris in 1924, where he became an associate of several Russian literary groups and enjoyed the friendship of Marina Tsvetaeva,* Boris Poplavsky,* and Alexei Remizov.* He married Olga Chernova, one of three daughters of a well-known socialist-revolutionary family, in 1927.

From 1924 onwards Andreyev's poetry was published in leading émigré journals in Berlin, Prague, and Paris; *Russkie Zapiski* (Russian Annals) also brought out his first major work in prose, *Childhood* (originally called *The Story of My Father*), in 1938. Andreyev issued three books of poems in 1924, 1928, and 1932, and participated in several collective publications of works by young poets. (Vladimir Nabokov* reviewed one of Andreyev's early books of poetry; his favorable commentary is extant in a copy in the Hoover Institution library at Stanford University, California.)

During World War II Andreyev worked for the French Resistance and later described his experiences in his novel *Wild Field*, published in the Soviet Union in 1965. He became a Soviet citizen after World War II and worked in the publishing division of the United Nations in New York and Geneva. At this time he published in the journal *Novoselye* (New Home, published in New York) and issued a fourth book of poems in 1950. During the Khrushchev era, Andreyev and his wife made several trips to the Soviet Union. His autobiographical works *Childhood, Wild Field, Story of a Journey*, and *Return to Life* were published in the USSR in rapid succession in journals and as books from 1963 to 1974; translations appeared in Bulgarian, Czech, French, Hungarian, Polish, and Romanian. The Leningrad journal *Zvezda* (The Star) brought out a selection of his poems in 1971. To be published in the land of his birth was Andreyev's fondest wish, but when the repressive Brezhnev era set in, he forsook caution and became active in his support of Moscow dissidents, particularly the case of Aleksandr Solzhenitsyn.* In 1965 Andreyev brought out to the West the manuscript of Solzhenitsyn's *The First Circle*.

A selection of Andreyev's poems, *Na rubezhe* (On the Border) was published in Paris by YMCA-Press in 1977; several of his poems appeared in *Avrora* in 1978 and *Zvezda* in 1983.

Consult: Yurii Terapiano, "Vadim Andreyev," *Sovremennik* (The Contemporary) (Toronto) 32 (1976). There are no known articles or appreciations in English.

OLGA CARLISLE and RICHARD DAVIES

ANDRIC, Ivo. Born October 10, 1892, in Dolac, near Travnik, Bosnia, a region now in Yugoslavia; died March 13, 1975, in Belgrade, Yugoslavia. Andric showed an extraordinary ability to distance himself from his own people when writing about them, yet all the cultural, ethnic, and religious influences of his native Bosnia are present as motifs in his work, written in Serbian. His education, including scholarly stays at Vienna, Krakow, and Graz, gave him a knowledge of other traditions and helped to shape his objectified view. Andric's literary abilities were noticed early in his career, as were his political concerns. *Ex Ponto* (1918, From the Sea [Latin]) and early collections of short stories, written while he was interned by Austria during World War I, demonstrated his belief in nationalism. After World War I, Andric was chosen for diplomatic service by the new state of Yugoslavia. Such reward again imposed exile from his native Bosnia. He served in Rome, Bucharest, Geneva, Madrid, and Berlin. Distant from his own people geographically, he remained close to them psychologically. When he was minister to Berlin, he made an impassioned but futile plea to forestall the German bombing of Belgrade.

Andric's intimate sympathy with Bosnia's people and landscape is evident in *Travinčkna Hronika* (Bosnian Story) and in his masterpiece, *Na Drina Cupria* (The Bridge on the Drina), both published in 1945. *The Bridge on the Drina* is a tapestry of political history, folktales, and hundreds of characters, none of whom persist throughout the work. The story begins in the town of Visegrad, Bosnia, in the early sixteenth century when the Grand Vezir Mehmed Pasha orders a great stone bridge erected across the Drina to facilitate trade rapidly developing between East and West. Using the bridge as a central focus in lieu of any single character, the novel progresses through the centuries until World War I, when the bridge is closed down. Andric demonstrates in the novel a special love for his Bosnia countrymen but also shows conflicting motives and base emotions operating in all ethnic groups. This distinction of literary objectivity that does not prevent a concurrent flow of emotional sympathy may also be seen in Andric's novel *Gospodjica* (1945; *The Woman from Sarajevo*, 1966).

Andric was awarded the Nobel Prize in 1961. Yugoslavia honored him with its State Prize for Life Work.

Selected Titles: *Prokleta avlija* (1954; The Devil's Yard, 1962); *Priča o verzirovom slonu* (1948; The Vizier's Elephant, 1962).

Consult: Thomas Eekman, *Thirty Years of Yugoslav Literature 1945–1975* (1978); Zelimir B. Juricic, *The Man and the Artist: Essays on Ivo Andric* (1986); John Simon, Afterword to *The Bridge on the Drina* (1967).

CHARLES KOVICH

APPELFELD, Aharon (also spelled Aron Apelfeld). Born in 1931, in Czernovitz, Bukovina (now part of the USSR); he lives in Jerusalem. Appelfeld was deported to a concentration camp when he was eight years old. He managed to escape and survive for three years in hiding in the Ukraine; later he was rescued by the Russian army, which he joined. At the end of World War II, he moved to Italy and in 1946 made his way to Palestine, where he stayed to become an Israeli citizen. He teaches Hebrew literature at Ben-Gurion University of the Negev.

Appelfeld's rendering of material is unique to his vision—generally he presents a double or myopic world in which people continue on their plateau of civilized habit even as the thunder of barbaric hordes is heard below them. In Appelfeld's fictional milieu a method of survival lies in the refusal to admit to knowledge of barbarism; such evasion leads to doom, but Appelfeld's characters at least live out their lives as they began them and without the vulgarity of armed resistance. Appelfeld's achievement is this profound portrait of sophisticated Jewish people torn between a world of elegant wisdom they have shaped and perfected and the Nazi brutes smashing their lives; his characters choose to continue on their old high roads until they are cut down by deportation and annihilation. This pattern of stoicism may be viewed both as heroism and foolhardiness; Appelfeld is probably suggesting that no explanation is possible either for the Holocaust or for the resistance of Jewish people to it. All one can do is record the events in wonder and grieve at the phenomenon: *Badenheim 1939*, his first novel translated into English (1980), is a brilliant recording of just such a history. In this novel set in an elegant spa, people continue with their mud baths and health programs, their sexual innuendos and imbroglios and their teenage children's problems, in the hope that what is not admitted will not have to be owned. In *To the Land of the Cattails* (1986) a mother and son leave their elegant town world to journey to the mother's native village in search of a lost world of identity, a world whose beckoning light will prove the mother's death but possibly also her son's transcendence of its sorrow. The story is quite likely Appelfeld's memorial to his mother, who perished at the hands of the Nazis when he was a young child.

Appelfeld's work is not pessimistic. In its stately prose and stoic pose it holds out hope for a change in the history of anti-Semitism and an understanding of the cataclysmic events of the Holocaust, perhaps even a forgiveness and a moving forward to a new history. *The Age of Wonders* (1981), *Tzili: The Story of a Life* (1983), and *The Retreat* (1984) suggest, however, ironically, that new fires can spring from ashes.

Appelfeld, the author of twenty novels, has been honored by the Israeli government (the Israel Prize) for his literary achievements. He won the Commonwealth Award in Literature in 1990. He writes in Hebrew.

Selected Titles: *The Immortal Bartfus* (1988); *For Every Sin* (1989); *The Healer* (1990).

ARENAS, Reinaldo (also spelled Reynaldo). Born July 16, 1943, in Holguín, Oriente Province, Cuba; he lives in New York. After working as an agricultural accountant in his home town, Arenas moved to Havana in 1962 to study city planning and literature at the University of Havana. He was employed at the Institute of Agrarian Reform and at the National Library before his arrest and incarceration in El Morro Prison from 1974 to 1976 for homosexuality; he was subsequently jailed several times on charges of homosexual offenses to Cuban society. Although Arenas had fought with Fidel Castro and his band of rebels in the early days of the revolution, he was unable to find publication in Cuba because of his sexual proclivities. Arenas sent his manuscripts abroad to Western Europe, Mexico, South America and the United States, where they were praised for their vitality of spirit and style. His most celebrated fictional work is his second novel, *El Mundo Alucinante* (Mexico City, 1969). It has been reprinted several times and has appeared in many language editions under varying titles. It won the Best Foreign Novel in France prize under the title *Le monde hallucinant*, was published under the title *Hallucinations* in London and New York in 1971, and was later reissued in paperback in New York under the title *The Peregrinations of Fray Servando*.

Arenas entered the United States as a member of the 1980 Mariel boatlift operation, an arrangement by which Fidel Castro sent thousands of Cuban political prisoners and convicted felons into exile in the United States. At the time Arenas was *persona non grata* to the Castro regime both as an irrepressible iconoclast and as an apologist for the untolerated cause of homosexuality. Acknowledging his debt to the circumstances of his peculiar road to freedom, Arenas founded a literary journal in 1983 to which he gave the name *Mariel*.

Arenas's work is a mix of buoyancy of style complemented by gravity of subject matter, a combination of respect for the sacred text of life and an irreverence for pomp and ritual. He mixes genres as well as obscures the lines between tragedy and comedy, fact and willing suspension of disbelief. In his prose fiction, poetry is utilized as fitting hyperbolic description and as intrusive commentary. Sequences and events jump from the probable to the ordinarily implausible as occurrences to be taken without grains of salt; Arenas demands an organic grace of madness from his readers. In *El Mundo Alcinante* he utilizes the voyage motif as a means of bestriding the world of obstructions to personal freedom by the sheer act of willed energy and naive idealism. His hero, Fray Servando Teresa de Mier, is based on a real Mexican priest who lived in the late eighteenth and early nineteenth centuries and who became a legend of vital nonconformism. Arenas's fictional protagonist is not inhibited by any blockades of circumstance; indeed he finds everything a challenge, like Don Quixote, to be grandly met if one keeps faith in one's vision. Arenas's portrait of Servando epitomizes his protagonists who regard what inhibit their paths as obstacles to be ridden from the world; their truth lies in the act of self-expression, even when they are shunned for that expression of self. In *El Mundo Alcinante* Arenas also utilizes all three personal viewpoints as narrative/thematic devices: the protagonist, Servando, speaks to the book's readers in the first person; the narrator of the book speaks to Servando in the second person, addressing him as if he were the object of an interview; and third person commentary is added by Arenas as a completion of perspective. Thus Arenas's use of viewpoint prevents any surety of pronoun reference, an authorial device of signifying thematic matter relating to the pomposity of authority.

Arenas, who has published seven novels to date, continues to write in Spanish; he rewrote his novel *Farewell to the Sea* (*Otra vez el mar*, Barcelona, 1982) twice from memory after his manuscripts were confiscated in Cuba. His works after exile are more measured in their craft and content that the works of his pre-exile period, but the spirit of originality and his idealistic non-conformity break through the surface of all his writing at some point. His newest work in English, *Old Rosa: A Novel in Two Stories* (1990), tells the story of a mother and her son each experiencing an epiphany before their individual deaths. In the case of the mother, Old Rosa, she sees her life before her as her house is burning in flames: a time of sexual repression as a result of her Catholic upbringing and a release from that pent-up energy into the hard and grinding work of a farm owner, and some limited happiness in fulfilling what she had decided was her course of life. When the Castro revolution succeeds, her elder son Armando forces her to sign over the farm to a revolutionary collective; in despair she sets fire to the house and to herself. (The novella, *La vieja Rosa*, was written in Havana in 1964 and first presented in its original Spanish version in a 1981 edition; the English title is "Old Rosa.") In the second novella, *Arturo, la estrella mas brilliant* —in the English version, "A Brilliant Star"—the son Arturo, Rosa's last-born child and her second son, relives the moment of his discovery of his mother's charred body and his own time as a convict in a labor camp for homosexuals. While attempting to escape, he is shot but before the final moment of death he flies through a cascade of vision and imagery that gives to him a finished and unending shape of his life. The novella, written in

1971 in Havana and first published in a Spanish edition in Madrid in 1984, is dedicated to Nelson Rodriguez Leyva, a short story and children's literature writer who was imprisoned in 1965 in Cuba in a forced labor camp for homosexuals. Rodriguez Leyva attempted to hijack a Cuban National Airlines plane to Florida in 1971 but was overpowered by Cuban soldiers, and later executed by a Cuban firing squad. Arenas's dedication is a tribute to his friend who at last felt free, perhaps for the only time in his entire short life when he held a grenade in his hands in a plane over his native island of homosexual concentration camps.

Selected Titles: *Celestino antes del alba* (Buenos Aires, 1968); *Le puits: roman* (Paris, 1973, translation from Spanish original); *El palacio de las blanquisimas mofetas* (Caracas, 1980; first published in French translation, Paris, 1975); *El Central* (Barcelona, 1981; *El Central*, 1983 [English title]); *Cantando en el pozo* (Madrid, 1982; *Singing from the Well*, 1987).

Consult: Oscar Ortiz Rodriguez, *Sobre narradores y heroes: a proposito de Arenas, Scorza y Adoum* (Caracas, Venezuela, 1980); Gladys Zaldivar, *Novelistica cubana de los anos 60* (Miami, 1977).

ARENDT, Erich. Born April 15, 1903, in Neuruppin, near Berlin, Germany; died September 25, 1984, in Wilhelmshorst, near Berlin, German Democratic Republic (East Germany). Arendt's mother was a washerwoman and his father the janitor of the local elementary school. Arendt studied progressive elementary education, a discipline he practiced from 1930 to 1933 in Berlin. He also took up painting and drawing, and began writing. His first poems were published in the expressionist vanguard journal *Der Sturm* (1926). Johannes R. Becher* through his membership in the KPD (1928) and in the *Bund proletarisch-revolutionärer Schrifsteller* (1928), urged him to write leftist propagandistic poetry. After several frustrating attempts at this mode, Arendt stopped writing. In March 1933 he fled to Switzerland because of his political allegiances and the Jewish origin of his wife, Katja Hayek, whom he had married in September 1930. In the summer of 1938 he entered Spain to participate in the Spanish Civil War as a war correspondent and to engage in pedagogical work among the 120 men of the 27th Catalonian Division "Carlos Marx" in Barcelona.

The encounter with nature and southern atmosphere led him back to poetry: Spanish and North African topics prevail in many of his poems. He would become even more inspired by his final country of exile, Colombia, South America, where the couple arrived in March 1942, after endless Odyssean adventures and mishaps, among them internment in Curaçao and Trinidad by the British. Two volumes of poetry reflect the experience of these two phases of his life: *Trug doch die Nacht den Albatros* (1951) and *Bergwindballade, Gedichte des spanischen Freiheitskampfes* (1952). He returned to Berlin, then part of the German Democratic Republic, in 1950.

Arendt's keen awareness and interest in visual arts found expression in the photographic work *Tropenland Kolumbien* (1954) and four more albums on the

Mediterranean region based on travels during the 1950s and 1960s, each with a foreword by and prepared in collaboration with Katja Hayek-Arendt.

In Bogotá the home of the Arendts became a meeting place for artists and intellectuals, and close friendships evolved with many of them, including Rafael Alberti* and Pablo Neruda.* During this time Arendt and Katja began translating Latin American and Spanish literature into German. Katja's previous philological studies and sensitivity for languages were a decisive factor in the high achievement of their renderings. She died in 1979.

As the critic Wolfgang Emmerich posits, Arendt's experience is an example whereby an exiled author "found" his language in alien surroundings by returning to his expressionist origins. Two themes recur in Arendt's work: human separation from nature (in the urban poems) and nature's perennial presence—a German poetic tradition—clad in a new language. This language is not descriptive of surface realities but achieves its meaning through expressionist techniques of fragmented syntax and philological, lexical experimentation. A net of recurring metaphors is the key to Arendt's progressively hermetic expression.

In the 1970s Arendt arrived at the limit of language as a means of communication and as a vehicle for rational thought. He brought to German poetry a new direction in his combination of expressionism and his love for Friedrich Hölderlin and German romanticism, but the hermeticism of his work denied him any popular appeal. While Arendt was highly honored in East Germany, his historical pessimism was not in accordance with official state ideology.

Selected Titles: *Tolú* (1956); *Über Asche und Zeit* (1957); *Gesang der sieben Inseln* (1957); *Flug-Oden* (1959); *Unter den Hufen des Windes* (1966); *Ägäis* (1967); *Aus fünf Jahreszeiten* (1968); *Feuerhalm* (1973); *Gedichte* (1976); *Memento und Bild* (1976); *Zeitsaum* (1978); *Starrend von Zeit und Helle* (1980); *Das zweifingrige Lachen* (1981); *Entgrenzen* (1981).

Consult: Renata von Hanffstengel, "Erich Arendt, ¿continuador del expresionismo alemán?," *Anuario de Letras Modernas* (Mexico, UNAM, 1985), pp. 11–23; Gregor Laschen and Manfred Schlösser, eds., *Der zerstückte Traum* (Berlin/Darmstadt, 1978); Inca Rumold, "Erich Arendt, a Poet between Continents: Federico García Lorca and Pablo Neruda in Arendt's Poetry," *Kulterelle Wechselbeziehungen im Exil* (Bonn, 1986), pp. 180–89; Suzanne Shipley Tolivier, *Exile and the Elemental in the Poetry of Erich Arendt* (Frankfurt, 1985). See also Archives in Utrecht, Holland, compiled by Gregor Laschen.

RENATA VON HANFFSTENGEL

ARENDT, Hannah. Born October 1906, in Hannover, Germany; died December 4, 1975, in New York City of a heart attack. Arendt was the only daughter of wealthy Jewish parents and grew up in Königsburg, East Prussia. She attended Marburg, Freiburg, and Heidelberg universities, and in each she studied under one of the major figures of contemporary German philosophy, Martin Heidegger, Edmund Husserl, and Karl Jaspers, respectively. At Marburg she became Heidegger's mistress, and the isolation and estrangement of her secret love for him became an early and lasting influence on her work. Though she described herself as a political scientist, and was often considered a metaphysician, she has been characterized as a storyteller; her work is filled with anecdotes and quotations used skillfully and instructively.

She began her biography of the late eighteenth-century Berlin salon hostess, *Rahel Varnhagen: The Life of a Jewess* (1958), soon after finishing her doctoral dissertation in 1929 but did not finish it until she was living in exile in Paris in 1938; she did not publish it until twenty years later in New York. It has been argued that this work above all was the book of her exile, and that its theme—the development of Rahel into "a self-conscious pariah"—was also the theme of Arendt's years in exile. Certainly, all her life, whether consciously or not, she remained an outsider, despite her later public recognition and academic prominence. Her exilic sense may be the culmination, however, of her philosophical perspective as much as her political orientation. She insisted toward the end of her life that thinkers are forced to withdraw from the public domain of politics and action to dwell in private recesses of the mind. She often quoted the older Cato to stress the paradoxical nature of thinking: "When I do nothing I am most active and when I'm all by myself, I am the least alone."

She left Germany in 1933, and after a brief stay in Prague settled in Paris where she did social work for Youth Aliyah, a Zionist organization helping refugees to emigrate to Palestine. In 1941 she and her second husband, Heinrich Blucher, were able to obtain emergency visas to come to New York. There she worked with various Jewish organizations for the next ten years and became an editor at Schocken Books. She also began her study *The Origins of Totalitarianism* (1951), which argued that anti-Semitism was part of a larger movement of political oppression and dehumanizing alienation that is a prevalent feature of post-Renaissance politics. Freedom is possible in her view only when it is based on a tradition of participation first established during the Periclean age of Athens and the Republican period of Rome. Otherwise private interests and the cult of personal power squelch opportunities for broad-based participation in affairs of state. She saw the American Revolution as a successful attempt to achieve such a sharing of power and responsibility, while the French Revolution stood for her as an archetypal perversion of the ideals of liberty, equality, and fraternity. These views are presented in her polemical book, *On Revolution* (1963).

Some of her best work is found in essays she wrote for a variety of journals. *Between Past and Future* (1961; rev. ed., 1968) contains commentary on authority, freedom, and education as well as one of her best pieces, "Truth and Politics." *Crises of the Republic* (1972) reveals her most disenchanted period of mind as she observed the civil rights movement, the antiwar movement, and the Watergate scandal. She is reputed to have told her friend Mary McCarthy that she thought of emigrating back to Europe "while there was still time." Her series of biographical appreciations in *Men in Dark Times* (1968) is perhaps the most accessible of all her works other than *Rahel Varnhagen*, and in it she sings the praises of her mother's idol, Rosa Luxemburg, and of Pope John XXIII,

Karl Jaspers, Isak Dinesen,* Hermann Broch, Walter Benjamin,* Bertold Brecht,* Waldeman Gurian, and Randall Jarrell.

In *The Jew as Pariah* (1978), a collection of pieces on Jewish themes that Arendt wrote between 1942 and 1966 (edited and introduced by Ron H. Feldman), Arendt speaks of the advantages and dangers of living on the borders of society and the meaning of such a continuous marginality for the sense of Jewish identity and destiny. She supported the Zionist cause and felt that with the formation of kibbutzim the ancient enmity between public and private realms would be resolved.

The Human Condition (1958), her first work to outline the public realm or *vita activa* thoroughly, explores the nature of action, labor, and work and shows how such forces are related to social and political arenas. Critical of Karl Marx's notion of alienation, she offers her own restatement of its causes. It was not until her posthumous *The Life of the Mind; Thinking and Willing*, 2 vols. (1978) that she contributed to the public a considered treatment of the private realm of *vite compliva*.

Her most controversial work was a series of articles she wrote while covering the Adolf Eichmann trial in Jerusalem for the *New Yorker*. Published as a book, *Eichmann in Jerusalem: A Report on the Banality of Evil* (1963) caused widespread resentment, for in it she claimed that Jewish leaders in Europe had not done enough, and even in some cases had done the wrong things during the Holocaust; she posited that they were in part responsible for the terrible death camps because of their cooperation with and nonresistance to Hitlerian policies. Eichmann was not just a madman, filled with hatred, but someone who had developed an extraordinary inability to think. He could calculate, but he could not think, for thinking is a moral activity that necessitates judgment. Though she never intended to diminish Eichmann's guilt, her views were severely attacked for encouraging such a possibility in others.

Arendt felt a particular sympathy to Walter Benjamin's views and edited a selection of his writings, *Illuminations* (1968). She held professorships at the University of Chicago and the New School for Social Research, among other distinguished positions and awards. Her life has been recounted in the biography by Elisabeth Young-Bruehl, *Hannah Arendt: For Love of the World* (1982), which contains a bibliography of her published work and some unpublished poetry.

Consult: Margaret Canovan, *The Political Thought of Hannah Arendt* (1974); Melvyn A. Hill, ed., *Hannah Arendt: The Recovery of the Public World* (1979); Gisela Kaplan and Clive Kessler, *Hannah Arendt: Thinking, Judging, Freedom* (1990); Bhikhu Parekh, *Hannah Arendt and The Search for a New Political Philosophy* (1981); Stephen J. Whitfield, *Into the Dark: Hannah Arendt and Totalitarianism* (1980).

CHRISTOPHER P. MOONEY

ARGUETA, Manlio. Born November 24, 1935, in San Miguel, El Salvador; he lives in San Jose, Costa Rica. Recipient of the Casa de las Americas Prize in 1977, one of the high literary distinctions in Latin America, Argueta is known for both his fiction and his poetry. His first novel, *Un Dia en la vida* (San Salvador, 1980; *One Day of Life*, 1983), is banned in his native country (though available in English and other languages) presumably because of its harsh and unflattering first-person portrait of Salvadoran peasant life as well as its tribute to the triumph of the Salvadoran peasant over man-made and natural adversities. Argueta has been arrested several times and expelled from his country four times. His novel *Cuzcatlan: Where the Southern Sea Beats* (1986; in English, 1987) is a re-creation of the essence of Salvadoran history through the portrait of a family from the hegemony of the death-dealing indigo-based economy to the fratricide of the modern era. The eponymous title is the aboriginal name of El Salvador, but the novel restricts its scope to the past two centuries. Similar in technique to the magic realism of Gabriel García Márquez,* Mario Vargas Llosa,* and other Latin American writers in its transcendence of historical time while holding onto chronological labels and guideposts in the same breadth, Argueta's novel depicts a country progressively assaulted by its citizens until the point in its present history when the entire family/country is at civil war. Yet the novel ends on a defiantly vital note: the rapacious, criminal soldier is sentenced to "go on living" (rather than to be executed) so that he may learn the meaning of his crimes and by that knowledge perhaps learn how to alter history. Argueta's compassion for his villains is plaintive, for his cry represents not only a reflection of physical pain but the anguish of an aware witness to the repetition of human failure in a seemingly inevitable pattern.

Selected Titles: *El valle de las hamacas* (1935, The Valley of the Hammocks [winner of the Miguel Asturias Prize]); *Capercita en la zona roja* (1977, Little Red Riding Hood in the Red Zone).

ARIAS, Arturo. Born in 1950 in Guatemala; he teaches at the Institute of Latin American Studies in Austin, Texas. Arias's second novel, *Iztan Na,* won the Casa de las Americas award in 1982. He has established a reputation for rendering the consequences of war in his native Guatemala in stark, expressionistic tones. Arias is also a scholarly critic who has published articles on Central American literature and politics, and is a film writer as well. He coscripted the 1986 Academy Award nominee film *El Norte.*

Selected Titles: *Despues de las bombas* (1979; *After the Bombs,* 1990); *Ideologias, literatura y sociedad durante la revolucion guatemalteca, 1944–1954* (Havana, 1979).

ARLEN, Michael. Born November 16, 1895, in Routschouk, Bulgaria; died June 25, 1956, in New York City. Arlen's sophisticated novels and dramas provided a world of wit and glamor for his readers. He left his native Bulgaria, where he was a member of the minority Armenian sect, for the worldly pleasures of London, Paris, and New York, and for triumphal successes there. Although he never suffered any ill effects of exile, he remained a psychically stateless person in the world of international manners by which he came to define himself.

His most famous novel is *The Green Hat* (1924), which became a celebrated Broadway success with Katherine Cornell as its star.

ARLEN, Michael J. Born December 9, 1930, in London, England; he lives in New York City. Son of Michael and Atalanta (Mercati) Arlen, Michael J. Arlen was raised in London and the south of France before coming to the United States in 1940. He attended St. Paul's School and Harvard College (class of 1952). He worked as a reporter for *Life* magazine; spent two years in the peacetime army working for *Stars and Stripes* in Germany and England; and has been a staff writer and television critic for the *New Yorker* since 1966. He married Ann Warner in 1957, a union that produced four children: Jennifer, Caroline, Elizabeth, and Sally; they were divorced in 1970. He married Alice Albright in 1972.

Exiles (1970) and *Passage to Ararat* (1975) establish Arlen as an important Armenian-American writer. In both books he explores various conditions of exile. In *Exiles*, he writes about his father, the famous novelist Michael Arlen (born Dikran Kouyoumdjian), and examines the father's enigmatic personality and the distance that existed between father and son. He reconstructs the histories of his parents (his Armenian father, raised in England but born in Bulgaria while his parents were fleeing the Turkish massacres of the Armenians; and his half-American, half-Greek mother, who was raised in Greece and France and whose father was a Greek count). In remembering his childhood in Europe and his growing-up in the elegant literary world of New York and at St. Paul's and Harvard, he allows the reader to see how his family's complex historical background stands behind the mute tensions of the family foreground. *Exiles* is a moving elegy that presents one version of an uprooted twentieth-century family.

Passage to Ararat may be seen as a sequel to *Exiles*. In continuing to search for his father's identity, Arlen finds the key in his father's Armenian heritage. As his quest for his father's identity becomes a search for his own, the idea of father and fatherland dovetail in a profound way. His search for self-definition leads him to uncover the tragic history of Armenia, in particular the genocide committed by the Turkish government in 1915, which took nearly two million Armenian lives. He dramatizes the value of understanding the past in order to achieve a humanized identity. He discusses the Armenian genocide as the first modern genocide, and his analysis of the impact of the Turkish denial of the genocide on Armenians in the diaspora provides a provocative piece of psychohistory and helps him understand his own father. The book unites in a poetic fashion autobiography, history, and sociology. In both his books, Arlen's ironic perspective lies in his willingness to face painful truths; his honesty enables him to be empathetic without sentimentality, while his compressed lyrical language provides a counterpoint of tender irony.

Selected Titles: *Living Room War* (1969), essays; *An American Verdict* (1973); *The View from Highway 1* (1976); *Thirty Seconds* (1980); *The Camera Age: Essays on Television* (1981); *Say Goodbye to Sam* (1984), novel.

Consult: Harry Keyishian, *Michael Arlen* (1975).

PETER BALAKIAN

ARMAH, Ayi Kwei. Born 1939 in Takoradi, Western Region, Ghana; he lives in Senegal and visits Ghana infrequently. Armah's parents were Fante. He attended Achimota College near Accra. In 1959 he came to the United States on a scholarship to Groton school in Connecticut. He received his degree in sociology from Harvard University, after which he moved to Algiers to work on the weekly *Révolution Africaine*. He returned to Ghana in 1966, where he taught English and also wrote scripts for Ghana television. On a grant from the Farfield Foundation he attended Columbia University in New York; he then moved to Paris to work on the journal *Jeune Afrique*. In 1968 he taught at the University of Massachusetts. He left there for Tanzania to teach in Dar es Salaam.

During his many travels Armah has continued his writing, but his recent work has not seen much publication in the West, possibly because Armah vowed in the 1970s to publish in Africa, thus keeping to his pledge to de-Westernize his consciousness. Armah's relative obscurity in the past decade is in marked contrast to his early career. His first novel, *The Beautyful Ones Are Not Yet Born* (Boston, 1968), was damned for its ''scatological'' emphases by the Ghanaian writer Christina Ama Ato Aidoo. Several critics, however, found in its imagery anchored to the dung of the earth an aesthetic and thematic triumph on Armah's part, while others praised the novel for its celebration of the common and commonsensical man in Ghana (The Man in Armah's allegorical text) and his survival in the face of venal corruption everywhere around him. Armah's second novel, *Fragments* (1970), showed his pervasive condemnation of postindependent Ghanaian life. The novel concerns a young scholar, a ''been-to'' (one who ''has been'' to the United States or England for study or professional reasons), who returns to a Ghana that finds him out of place there. The protagonist is ultimately committed to an institution by his mother, who sees in her son the seeds of anomie that constitute bewitchment. Armah is scoring both Western culture, which has tempted the brilliant young hero into an education that has unfitted him for a traditional, nonmechanized Africa, and the conservative tribal culture of Ghana unwilling to yield to change. Armah's work reflects the sense of displacement, a world in which no ground is safe from illusion and its corollary, disillusionment. In his third novel, *Why Are We So Blest?* (1972), Armah shows an anger that blasts out at the reader, an anger that attacks European culture as the villain in the rape of African customs. The narrative has autobiographical overtones in its use of one protagonist who has been to Harvard, another who works in Afrasia (Algeria) as a translator, and a third, a young American white woman who is sympathetic to black revolutionary causes. The novel also revels in explicit, violent sexual incident and language. Armah's tone in this novel startled and offended readers, and his departure from the United States around this time (with his white girlfriend, who became the model for the heroine in *Why Are We So Blest?*) was in some measure his ambivalent farewell to a country that he had once admired and that had recognized his talents. In his fourth and fifth novels, *Two Thousand Seasons* (Nairobi, 1973) and *The Healers* (Nairobi, 1978), Armah attempted a resolution of his conflicts, particularly as seen in the context of Frantz Fanon's colonial antitheses, by returning Africa to its mythic and historic glory before European domination. *Two Thousand Seasons* (one thousand years of imperial African glory) is almost an epic poem in its mythos, its soaring allusions, and its great sweeps of action. In *The Healers* Armah is searching for a medicine, imbibed through traditional African rites of the spirit, to place on the wounds inflicted by colonialism.

Armah, as an angry young man, scorched his countrymen in Ghana and his liberal audience in the United States because he wished to awaken them to the adulteration of African values by European colonial ones. He saw in postcolonial Africa an infection of Europeanization, an infection that persisted under the skin in spite of the surface departure of colonial structures. Under the influence of Fanon's call for real independence from the legacy of colonialism, Armah became a voice calling for secession from established, conventional European norms and a return to African values. He exemplified this call by changing his artistic venues from the city and its sophisticated ways to historic and mythic African fields and plains of common language and from Western-educated and -oriented protagonists to peasants with a dominant African consciousness. One of his important critics, Robert Fraser, describes the process in this manner: "His essential theme has been the process through which a nation may force its way back to a state of natural health after a prolonged period of spiritual infection. He is thus concerned with the salvation of the people in toto, the reformation of the public will, rather than the redemption of the private soul, or mind" (*The Novels of Ayi Kwei Armah*, p. xii). While some Marxist critics deny that Armah has achieved his goal, or even intended it, the critical consensus is that he has been attempting his own redemption through the purgation of those qualities he considers his Westernness.

Consult: Robert Fraser, *The Novels of Ayi Kwei Armah* (London, Ibadan, Nairobi, 1980); Neil Lazarus, *Resistance in Postcolonial African Fiction* (1990); Derele Wright, *Ayi Kwei's Africa: The Source of his Fiction* (Kent, England, 1989).

ARRABAL, Fernando. Born August 11, 1932, in Medilla, Spanish Morocco, grew up in Spain; he has lived in France since 1954. He began writing in Spanish but now writes primarily in French. Arrabal's work may be considered a classic example of the psychological struggle of a grievance-clad rebel fighting with oblique means of technique against a bewildered and condescending world. His novels, plays, films, and periodic interviews are reflections both naïve and self-conscious in their broadsides against the world that fostered the kind of childhood he was forced to endure. His vision indicts the whole of bourgeois society for its prejudicial hypocrisies.

Arrabal left Spain for exile in France soon after his twenty-first birthday; he has lived in Paris since 1955. He was the child of politically divided parents—his father was a left-wing anti-Franco sympathizer in the Spanish Civil War; his mother, pro-Franco, ultraconservative, and rigidly Catholic. When Arrabal was three years old, his father disappeared, having been arrested in the middle of the night by Franco forces. (Arrabal's father later escaped from captivity, but Arrabal never saw him again.) Arrabal's mother forbade any mention of the father and told her children that the father was dead.

Arrabal's exile is motivated both by political/religious reasons and by personal choice. He was unable to accept his mother's dominance or his sense of her betrayal (although he no longer believes his mother denounced his father to the Franco authorities, he has written that she did nothing to help the father in his distress following his arrest). His shock of betrayal may be seen in all his work, ranging from his first autobiographical novel *Baal Babylone* (1963), which recounts his childhood, to his latest published novel in English, *The Tower Struck by Lightning* (1988; originally published in Spanish, *La Tore Herida por el rayo*, 1983). *Baal Babylone* is the story, told in simple language, of a child growing up during the Spanish Civil War. The mother has denounced the father to the Franco police "for his own good," but the boy clings to his memory of an ennobled, sheltering father. The mother insists on the boy's allegiance to the conservative institutions of Spain; the boy refuses to surrender his memory of illusions—his mechanism for escape from the oppressive world everywhere around him. In a climactic scene he urinates in front of a convent.

In France Arrabal found a more congenial atmosphere, a sense of freedom that inspired him with bursts of creative energy. His output during these early years—from age twenty-one to forty—is impressive. His first novel was followed by successful forays in drama, the genre for which he is best known. His plays, unusual in their techniques, have been variously described as tragic farce, and as both absurd and ritualistic. Ritual is found in his work, particularly in his use of games as a device for stylized confrontation of ideas. In perhaps his most famous work, *L'Architecte et l'empereur d'Assyrie* (1967; *The Architect and the Emperor of Assyria*, 1969) Arrabal has the Emperor indulge in Act I in games of accusation against the Architect; the procedure is reversed in Act II, with the Architect airing his charges against the Emperor. Each of the titular characters represents different ways of life—the hierarchic, closed, exclusionary against the open, humble, and wide-ranging. Arrabal's statement on this perpetual war between conformity and rebellion in social intercourse may be seen as his view of world history.

Perhaps the most personal testament in his dramatic works may be found in his one-act play, *La bicyclette du condamné* (1958; produced in Paris, 1967; *The Bicycle of the Condemned*), in which a man is condemned to ride a bicycle and a pianist is condemned to play the piano (the protagonist is the same man, that is, interchangeable during the course of the play). Each of these protagonists now has the sanction to perform what he has always wished, yet for each such freedom becomes an unyielding sentence of commitment. Arrabal treats the circular effect of the caged wheel, the crescendo effect of repetitive piano music, as images both of chaos and freedom. Somewhere in the midst of the mindless action is a chamber pot, which may signify a lowly rainbow or the depths to which rainbows in modern times have fallen. In this work Arrabal may not clarify what he wants, but he is clear about the gulf that confronts man and forces him to a choice between the plateau and the abyss as a style of life. Arrabal denies, however, that he is an absurdist; he also claims never to have been influenced by Antonin Artaud,* with whose Theater of Cruelty some critics associate his work. Although Arrabal consistently employs sadomasochism in what he calls his human comedies (he also enjoys being identified with the Marquis de Sade as a revolutionary thinker), he asserts he is not a metaphysical writer and therefore has no links with the philosophy of absurdism. More accurately, his plays are rooted in his personal history and are statements about the wounds that families inflict on their members, wounds that can grow into social cancers.

Arrabal admits he uses the techniques of farce, but for a somber purpose—his farce is supposed to deepen into a view of the tragic consequences of farcical behavior. Arrabal himself prefers the term *panique* as a description of his work, and was associated with what is known as the "Panique" movement in artistic circles in Paris in 1962. For Arrabal, panic is not a cry of despair or helplessness but a reference to the great god Pan, to the force that allows man to taste everything with a sense of abandon. Arrabal uses the term ironically as well, for his "panique" men do not risk anything. They try all but do not commit themselves and thus do not have to struggle against the oppression of conformity.

In the 1970s Arrabal engaged in a new form for him, the cinema. Among his films are *Vive la muerte* (1974; A Scream from My Guts, which depicts the coming of age of a boy raised in a Catholic/Franco–dominated Spain); *J'irai comme un cheval fou* (1975, adapted from his play, *L'Architecte et l'empereur d'Assyrie*); and *Guernica* (1976, Guernica: Tree of Liberty). Arrabal's personal history and his obsession are evident in these works, as are the techniques found in his plays—farce, abrupt swings of mood, serious charges of social wrong, and psychological symbols. Arrabal's interest in the cinema has extended to acting as well. In 1981 he played in *The Great Chess Movie*, a documentary about the 1981 world championship match between Anatoly Karpov and Viktor Korchnoi. His love of chess, and its provocations for speculative movement, are evident in his newest novel, *The Tower Struck by Lightning* (1988), in which an Albanian Marxist puritan is pitted in a chess match against a Spanish worker who has few ideologies but much reliance on human intuition. The symbolic approaches to chess and the political and social allusions in the novel show that Arrabal is commenting on his society as well as probing the psychology of different individuals.

Arrabal's work has been attacked for its exploitation of brutal sexuality, for blasphemy, and for pornography. Arrabal denies all these charges, claiming his work is filled with love. In his plays he shows a consummation on stage of the love a man feels for a dead woman (*La communion solemnelle*); a man hanging himself in a maze of blankets on a clothesline (*Le labryinthe*), and a Christ who "steals, lies, is hypocritical, and makes love" in an automobile graveyard (*Le cimetière des voitures*). (See the interview with Bettina Knapp in *First Stage*, 1, no. 4 [Winter 1967–68].) Arrabal's defense of sexual exploitation is that he began writing when he was young, when, in his words, sex was all-important. His later work integrates the sexual into a larger, political statement, particularly in *Et ils passèrent des menottes aux fleurs* (1967; *And They Put Handcuffs on the Flowers*, 1969), which he directed in both Paris and New York. In this play, which is related to Arrabal's arrest and incarceration in a Spanish jail for writing an allegedly indecent inscription in a copy of one of his own novels, he allies himself again with his victimized father. Arrabal treats exile specifically in *Sur le fil, ou, La ballade du train fantôme* (1974, On the wire, or The Ballad of the Phantom Train), employing the motif of a ghost town in New Mexico that bears the proud name of Madrid; the allusion suggests both exile and survival.

Arrabal is characterized in the Introduction to *The Tower Struck by Lightning* (1989) by Anthony Kerrigan, his translator, in this manner: "He takes exception to almost everything. In his work as a whole he is as far outside the 'mainstream' as it is possible to be."

Selected Titles: *Bestialité érotique* (1969); *Une tortue nommé Dostoievski* (1969); *Lettre au Générale Franco* (1972); *Vole-moi un petit milliard* (1978); *Punk et Punk et Colégram* (1978); *Lettre aux militant communistes espagnols* (1978).

Translation: *The Red Madonna, or a Damsel for a Gorilla: A True Story* (1986).

Consult: T. Donahue, *The Theatre of Fernando Arrabal* (1980); Martin Esslin, *The Theatre of the Absurd* (1961); Bettina Knapp, "Interview with Arrabal," *First Stage* 1, no. 4 (Winter 1967–68).

ARSIENNIEVA, Natalia. Born November 20, 1903, in Baku, Azerbaijan, now part of the USSR. Arsiennieva was a student at Vilna University when she married an officer in the Polish army and returned with him to (ethnic) Poland in 1922. In 1940 she was deported by the Soviets to Kazakstan. Appeals from many Byelorussian and other writers led to a revocation of the order, and Arsiennieva spent the war years in Minsk under German occupation. At the end of the war she was put in a displaced persons camp, where she lived till her emigration to the United States in 1950.

Byelorussian nationalism is profoundly intertwined in her poetic expression as well as historical corollaries of diaspora and exile. In her work temporal defeat is turned into a celebration of religious endurance. She is considered one of the significant Byelorussian poets of the modern age by critics on both sides of the Polish and Russian borders that currently divide Byelorussia.

Consult: Jan Zaprudnik, *Encyclopedia of World Literature*, vol. 1 (1981).

ARTAUD, Antonin. Born September 4, 1896, in Marseilles, France; died March 4, 1948, in Paris. Artaud searched for an enclosing community of spirit in which meaningful ritualistic theater would replace complacent daily gesture. He believed he had found such a shaping force in the primitivism of Mexican deities and their structured rites; he wrote his perceptions into dramatic criticism and theory of theater. His own theater had collapsed earlier in Paris, but his new ideas proved equally unpopular. Drug problems began to affect his visions, and he entered a detoxification program in 1946. On his release Artaud left for Ireland but he suffered paranoid delusions there; on his return to France he was committed to a mental asylum, where he died. Artaud's theories of drama are hailed today as the legacy of a visionary thinker. While some critics see the Artaudian pattern as a separation from humanity in its cruelly clean lines of response, others see in the patterns a cry for communion with sustaining myth.

Artaud also wrote poetry, expressing feelings of isolation, paranoia, and withdrawal from a society he felt had rejected his offerings. Because of his quest for wholeness through Mexican gods and his incarceration in an Irish mental asylum, Artaud is included in this study as a variant of exile.

Selected Title: *Oeuvres complètes* (1984).

Consult: Susan Sontag, Introduction, *Antonin Artaud: Selected Writings* (1985).

ASCH, Sholem. Born January 1, 1880, in Kutno, Poland; died July 10, 1957, in London, England. Asch moved from his native small town to the metropolitan capital of Warsaw when he was nineteen years old to take up a career as a Hebrew teacher. He brought with him essays and memoiristic sketches, which began to appear in the Yiddish press in Warsaw. He also associated with another well-known Yiddish writer, H. L. Peretz, whose broad influence proved a stimulus to Asch. In 1909 Asch emigrated to the United States, where he became a naturalized citizen in 1920. He returned to Poland after World War I, but moved on to France and then back to the United States. He lived in England before he settled in Bat Yam, Israel, in 1954. He died in London while visiting his daughter there.

Asch may be viewed as part of the Jewish diaspora. He began his career as a portraiteur of the *shehtl*, the ghetto of the small-town Jew that was both community and exile to its residents. He traveled over the world and became a rich and famous writer, honored in many countries. He lived to see his works translated into many of the major languages of the world. At the end of his life Asch was a sophisticated writer who performed proudly, for his international audiences, his presentation of common and complex Jewish experiences.

ASTURIAS, Miguel Ángel. Born October 19, 1899, in Guatemala City, Guatemala; died June 9, 1974, in Madrid, Spain. Asturias's accomplishments in a number of genres, especially in telling Guatemala's story from its colonial past to its problematic current situation, were recognized by his receiving the Nobel Prize for literature in 1967. Asturias grew up under the dictatorship of Manuel

Estrada Cabrera, and when Asturias's father, a prominent attorney, joined the opposition to Estrada Cabrera, the family had to move from Guatemala City to the town of Salamá. The regime was toppled by Asturias and others in 1920. Asturias began medical studies in 1916 but switched to law after one year, and throughout his university years he was politically active. He received his degree in 1922 with a thesis denouncing the social injustice the Guatemalan Indians had received. His subsequent writings have continued to criticize social injustice throughout Latin America.

In order to escape Guatemala's continued repression by Estrada Cabrera's successor, José Maria Orellana, Asturias went to Paris in 1923 to study ethnology at the Sorbonne. His ten years in Paris led him to become a surrealist through the influence of André Breton,* and while there he wrote poetry and a major prose work, *Leyendes de Guatemala* (1930, Legends of Guatemala); this work, about Mayan life before Spanish colonialism, was praised by Paul Valéry. Hence from the start of his literary career, Asturias combined a sense of Mayan mysticism with a strong social conscience. His 1926 entry to a literary contest sponsored by a Guatemalan newspaper was refused, but the work, "Los mendigos politicos" (Political Beggars), became the germ of his most widely known work, *El Señor Presidente* (written in 1932). Asturias returned to Guatemala in 1933, founding a radio magazine and writing several volumes of poetry. Living under then-dictator Jorge Ubico Casteñada, who ruled till 1944, meant that he could not publish *El Señor Presidente* until 1946 (Eng. trans. *Mr. President*, 1963), after the democratic president of Guatemala, Juan Arévalo Martinez (who ruled from 1945 to 1951), took office.

Asturias received wide praise for his novel, combining as it did social protest with vivid pictures of grotesque political repressiveness and a hallucinatory style. It is a symbolic, surrealistic portrayal of an archetypal though shadowy Latin American dictator whose hellish world is filled with repulsive followers and many ordinary folk who suffer and endure. Asturias's experiments with novelistic structure and language have led to comparisons with Joseph Conrad* and William Faulkner (Asturias has been called the "Faulkner of Latin America"). "Magic realism," a term from German art criticism, was subsequently applied to Asturias and other writers, including Jorge Luis Borges and Gabriel García Márquez*; it implies a blend of the fantastic and the realistic, along with a strong sense of regionalism.

Asturias's friendship with Arévalo Martinez led to Asturias's diplomatic career, first as minister of culture in Mexico and then in several other Latin American nations. While posted in Argentina in 1948, he published a collection of poetry from 1918–48, *Sien de Alondra* (1949), and a play, *La Audiencia de los Confines* (1956). His greatest work, *Hombres de Maiz* (1949; *Men of Corn*, 1975), explores supernatural conceptions of life held by Guatemalan Indians, focusing on ancestral myths as inextricably mixed in with the Indians' hopeless living conditions. He also deals with Indian oppression in his epic trilogy, *Viento Fuerte* (1949; *The Cyclone*, 1967; *Strong Wind*, 1969), *El Papa Verde* (1954;

The Green Pope, 1971), and *Los Ojos de los Enterrados* (1960; *The Eyes of the Interred*, 1973). This trilogy focuses on the United Fruit Company's sordid incursions in Guatemalan affairs, including the corporation's eventual control over the government; a strike that restores some amount of freedom to the workers; and the end of the dictatorship.

In 1956 Asturias published *Weekend en Guatemala*, a group of eight stories dealing with the 1954 coup that again brought repression to Guatemala. *Mulata de Tal* (1963; *Mulata*, 1967) uses magic to describe conflicts between Indian deities and Roman Catholic priests. *Maladrón* (1969, Bad Thief) tells of the Spanish conquest of Latin America and the subsequent merger of Indian and Spanish cultures. In the same year he collaborated with Pablo Neruda* on *Comiendo en Hungria* (1969; *Sentimental Journey Around the Hungarian Cuisine*, 1969).

Asturias's versatile handling of various literary genres has led, especially with his fiction, to wide translation outside Latin America and even to theses and dissertations on his work. But his verse, indebted as it is to surrealism and other influences, is more local, centering as it does on Indian culture, nationalism, and family. In addition to nonsense verse, he has, along with other Guatemalan poets, created a kind of poetry combining both Latin American modernism and traditional Guatemalan values. His five plays, particularly *Solkuna* (1955, Sun-Moon), also contrast present-day Guatemala with its Indian past, but these are not well known outside Latin America.

After Castillo Armas exiled Asturias in 1954, he never again lived in Guatemala, not even after the dictator was assassinated in 1957, Asturias's subsequent exile in Argentina was ended by the military coup there in 1962. He thereafter lived in Italy, Switzerland, and, finally, in Paris, where he served as Guatemalan ambassador from 1966 to 1970. His extensive travels took him throughout Latin America, Europe, and the Soviet Union; he died on a lecture tour in Spain. He received the Lenin Peace Prize in 1966 and the Nobel Prize the year after. Unesco has sponsored a twenty-four–volume edition of his complete works.

Selected Titles: *Sociologia Guatemalteca: El Problema Social del Indio* (1923; *Guatemalan Sociology*, 1977); *Hombres de Maiz: El Mito Como Tiempo y Palabra* (1949; *Men of Maize*, 1988); *El Alhajadito* (1961; *The Bejeweled Boy*, 1971); *Rumania: Su Nueva Imagen* (1964); *Teatro* (1964); *Espejo de Lida Sal* (1967); *America, Fábula de Fábulas* (1972); *Viernes de Dolores* (1972).

Consult: Gordon Brotherston, *The Emergence of the Latin American Novel* (1977); Richard J. Callan, *Miguel Ángel Asturias* (1970); Ariel Dorfman, "Myth as Time and Word," *Review*, no. 15 (Fall 1975); Rita Guibert, *Seven Voices* (1973); Luis Harss and Barbara Dohmann, *Into the Mainstream* (1967); Carlos Meneses, *Miguel Ángel Asturias* (Madrid, 1975); *Papeles de Son Armadans* 62 (Palma de Mallorca, 1971), special Asturias issue.

PAUL SCHLUETER

AUB, Max. Born June 2, 1903, in Paris; died July 23, 1972, in Mexico City. Aub was the son of a well-to-do German businessman and his French wife. When he was eleven years old, the family moved to Valencia to escape the outbreak of World War I. Aub passed his *bachillerato* but instead of pursuing university studies chose to accompany his father on his business trips across Spain. His heritage is trilingual, but at the age of twenty-one he opted for Spanish citizenship, and all of his many works—poetry, novels, plays, literary criticism, and essays—are written in that language.

As a result of his many travels through his adopted land, Aub became that rare paradox: at once intensely Spanish, but also culturally very European. Under the influence of José Ortega y Gasset* (whom he later repudiated for having divorced Spaniards from reality), Aub began writing in 1925, publishing his *Teatro incompleto* in 1931. He was thirty-three when the Spanish Civil War broke out. A convinced socialist, he threw himself into the struggle as editor of the newspaper *Verdad*, and in 1938 worked closely with André Malraux on the film version of the latter's *L'Espoir*. After the Loyalist defeat, Aub escaped to Paris, the city of his birth, only to be denounced as a communist and sent to a series of concentration camps. Fortunately, because of a timely diplomatic intervention, he found refuge in Mexico in September 1942, where he spent the remaining thirty years of his life.

Not surprisingly, the majority of his later works, whatever the genre, deal with the Spanish experience. Aub visualizes the Spanish Civil War as a warning to all nations that remain indifferent to the suffering of others. His many novels, including the series *Campo cerrado* (1939), *Campo de sangre* (1945), *Campo abierto* (1951), and the later *Campo de moro* (1963), portray the agony of that conflict and emphasize the need for solidarity among all humans. In 1960 appeared his *La verdadera historia de la muerte de Francisco Franco*, the story of a bizarre but successful assassination plot that removed the Spanish dictator. Notwithstanding his jeu d'esprit at Franco's expense, Aub was allowed to visit his beloved Spain in 1970, only to find that the country of his imagination no longer corresponded with the tawdry reality. Disillusioned, he returned to Mexico, where he died two years later.

In addition to his novels, Aub was a prolific, if unsuccessful, playwright. His literary criticism, *Discurso de la novela española contemporánea*, has been well received. It is, however, as an impassioned chronicler of the Civil War that he will be remembered.

Selected Titles: *Cuentos mexicanos* (1959); *Hablo como hombre* (1967).

Consult: Ignacio Soldevila Durante, *La obra narrativa de Max Aub* (Madrid, 1973); Michael Ugarte, *Shifting Ground: Spanish Civil War Exile Literature* (1989).

DOUGLAS HILT

AUDEN, W. H. (Wystan Hugh). Born February 21, 1907, in York, England; died September 29, 1973, in Vienna, Austria. Auden achieved success early, publishing his first book of poems, *Poems* (1932), to great acclaim shortly after graduation from Oxford. From this time till he left England in 1939 he was a celebrated poet and verse dramatist of strong Freudian and Marxist views tempered by a daily compassion for human error and a glittering malice for human pretensions. He served as an ambulance driver for the Republicans in the Spanish

Civil War, and often traveled to Germany, where he experienced dismay at the growing specter of National Socialism there, particularly in the light of his own lasting admiration of nineteenth-century and Weimar Republic German culture. With Christopher Isherwood* he wrote several verse plays dealing with social issues (e.g., *The Dog Beneath the Skin*, 1935; *The Ascent of F6*, 1936), dramas that display his woe over the class system in England that denied free access to social progress for the majority of its inhabitants. (Significantly, Auden stopped writing plays once he left England.)

As early as 1936 Auden said he would have to leave England because its values were collapsing into a class war of selfish interest. In 1939, after a long period of doubt and despair over the choices facing him in a world turning barbaric on one side, and selfish, greedy, and morally corrupt on the other, he emigrated to the United States. Auden's move from his country at a time of national crisis occasioned much unfavorable comment and proved a traumatic experience from which he suffered for many years and which he justified in many ways and in many poems. His "New Year Letter," published in *The Double Man* and "September 1, 1939" are two works that deal directly with his feelings on the matter and that were fairly close in time to the event. In "New Year Letter" Auden makes the point that the contemporary artist is in effect an exile, suffering for his people the pain of divorce from joy in both its religious and its temporal affect. As sufferer, the artist becomes a kind of conscientious observer of his own culture and makes of his experience the material to be transmuted into art. In so doing the artist provides a community of consciousness whereby the citizenry is purged of its weight of exile and enabled to move on. Auden expressed, in an extraordinary lyric, "Musée des Beaux Arts," this ethos of suffering as a triumph rather than a defeat in human endeavor and survival.

Auden's Marxism was eclipsed by his return to the Anglo-Catholic faith after his remove to New York, although he never forsook the other great tenet of his youth, Freudianism. He utilized psychology in prolific renderings of ages and stages of anxiety, and of release from such anxiety through the balm of suffering grace. He became a much-traveled lecturer on American campuses, a sought-after reader on the poetry circuit, and a prolific literary journalist. In gratitude to his new country, he became a naturalized American citizen in 1946. In 1957 he began summering in a house in Austria, and after his retirement from lecturing and poetry reading, he moved there for the last years of his life.

Auden received the Pulitzer Prize, the National Book Award, the Bollingen Prize for Poetry, and the National Medal for Literature given by the National Book Committee in 1967.

Selected Titles: Poetry and Criticism: *The Collected Poetry of W. H. Auden* (1945); *The Age of Anxiety* (1947); *The Enchafèd Flood* (1950); *The Shield of Achilles* (1955); *Homage to Clio* (1960); *The Dyer's Hand, and Other Essays* (1962); *Collected Shorter Poems 1927–1957* (1966); *Collected Longer Poems* (1968); *Collected Poems*, ed. Edward Mendelson (London, 1976); *Selected Poems* (rev. ed. 1977); *Thank You, Fog. Last Poems*

(1974). Plays: with Christopher Isherwood: *The Dog Beneath the Skin* (1935); *The Ascent of F6* (1936); *Plays and Other Dramatic Writings by W. H. Auden and Christopher Isherwood*, ed. Edward Mendelson (1988).

Consult: B. C. Bloomfield and Edward Mendelson, *W. H. Auden: A Bibliography 1927–1969* (1972); Frederick Buell, *W. H. Auden as a Social Poet* (1973); Samuel Hynes, *The Auden Generation* (1976); Randall Jarrell, *The Third Book of Criticism* (1969); Lucy McDiarmid, *Auden's Apologies for Poetry* (1990); Edward Mendelson, *Early Auden* (1981); Charles Osborne, *W. H. Auden: The Life of a Poet* (1979); Monroe K. Spears, *The Poetry of W. H. Auden: The Disenchanted Island* (1963).

AUERBACH, Erich. Born November 9, 1892, in Berlin, Germany; died October 13, 1957, in Wallingford, Connecticut. In 1935 Auerbach lost his position at the University of Marburg, where he held the chair of Romance philology, because he was a Jew. He moved to Turkey in 1936, where he wrote his famous work, *Mimesis*, and where he taught at Istanbul State University. At the conclusion of World War II, he emigrated to the United States. He taught at several American universities, among them Pennsylvania State, Princeton, and Yale.

Mimesis is considered one of the seminal works in critical theory in the twentieth century in its use of European literary texts as palimpsest of reality. In turn the representations of reality made by the artist shape the way reality is concurrently perceived, and new cultural awareness takes shape from a progression of representations. Auerbach's achievement in drawing on explication of passages from Homer to Dante in *Mimesis* was to suggest that the various representations of reality are, if not progressive, at least triumphant in their sustaining humanistic vision. That he could perceive his vision of a greater and more benign world than the immediate Holocaust about him, and that he could persuade others of the substance of his vision, remains a testament to the power of his critical writing.

Selected Titles: *Dante als Dichter der iridischen Welt* (1929; *Dante, Poet of the Secular World*, 1961); *Mimesis: Dargestellte Wirklichkeit in der abendlandeschen Literatur* (1946; *Mimesis: The Representation of Reality in Western Literature*, 1953); *Introduction aux études de philologie romane* (1949; *Introduction to Romance Languages and Literatures*, 1961).

Consult: Francis Fergusson, "Two Perspectives on European Literature," *Hudson Review* 7 (1954–55); Harry Levin, "Two *Romanisten* in America: Spitzer and Auerbach," in *The Intellectual Migration*, ed. D. Fleming and B. Bailyn (1969).

AWOONOR, Kofi (born George Awoonor-Williams). Born March 13, 1935, near Keta in the Togo region of Ghana. His father was born in Sierra Leone and his mother in Togoland. Awoonor returned to Ghana in 1975. Awoonor received his secondary education in Achimota. After graduation from the University of Ghana, he studied vernacular poetry at the Institute of African Studies. He edited *Okyeame*, a literary journal, in the 1960s and served as an associate editor of *Transition* and as director of the Ghana Film Corporation. In the late 1960s Awoonor went to England for further study; he received a master's degree from the University of London in 1968, and in 1969 he came to the United States to speak at an International Poetry Festival in New York City. That appearance led to his selection as a visiting professor in African literature at the State University of New York in Stony Brook. Subsequently he became chair of the Department of Comparative Literature at Stony Brook. Although Awoonor was not in exile and could return to his country, personal and political reasons kept him abroad. His sense of sorrow, an empathetic response to the diaspora of African people, is reflected in all his writing: an aura of displacement, an erosion of native customs by imperial dominance, and a retreat into invidious but contained pain pervade his work. The mood may be seen most clearly in such early poems as "Rediscovery" and "The Weaver Bird" and in later poems such as "Poem, Fall '73," "Departure and Prospect," and "The Wayfarer Comes Home," and in his novel *This Earth, My Brother* (1971) and in his critical commentary on African literature, *The Breast of the Earth: A Survey of the History, Culture and Literature of Africa South of the Sahara* (1974).

Awoonor returned to Ghana in 1975 to teach at Cape Coast College and to be reunited with his wife and family after many years of separation. In December 1975, Awoonor was imprisoned on a charge of harboring a fugitive, a government official in flight from a coup. Awoonor claimed innocence in that he gave shelter to the man without any knowledge of the coup. The official stayed only one night in Awoonor's house, but Awoonor remained in jail for about a year in Ghana. During this time he wrote a collection of poems, later published as *The House by the Sea* (1978), which treat his prison experience and give expression to the yearning for a return to home and an end to division of spirit. Today Awoonor is an honored member of his country's government, having served as Ghana's ambassador to Brazil for several years, and, most recently, as ambassador to the United Nations.

Selected Titles: *Rediscovery and Other Poems* (Nigeria, 1964); *Night of My Blood* (1971); *Ride Me, Memory* (1973); *Until the Morning After: Collected Poems, 1963–1985* (1985).

Consult: Kofi Anyidoho, "Kofi Awoonor and the Ewe Tradition of Songs of Abuse (Italo)," and L. R. Early, "Kofi Awoonor's Poetry," both in *Ghanaian Literatures*, ed. Richard K. Priebe (1988); Albert S. Gerard, *European Language Writing in Sub-Saharan Africa*, 2 vols. (1986); Martin Tucker, "Kofi Awoonor's Prison," *Worldview* 22, no. 11 (November 1979).

AYALA, Francisco. Born March 16, 1906, in Granada, Spain; he returned to his native country in 1976 after thirty-seven years of exile.

During his year as a scholarship student in Germany in 1929, Ayala observed the Nazi rise to power; it made a lasting impression on him and was to remain, along with his knowledge of his own country's history, one of the key constituents in his awareness of social corruption. Ayala was a prolific writer and had published much fiction and nonfiction by the mid–1930s. In 1934 he was appointed to a professorship at the University of Madrid. In 1936 he was on a lecture tour in South America when the Spanish Civil War erupted. Offering his services to the Republican government, he was appointed secretary of the Spanish Republic's legation in Prague. When the Franco forces triumphed in 1939, Ayala went into exile, first to Buenos Aires, where he remained for ten years until he no longer felt at ease with the Peronist dictatorship. He moved to Puerto Rico in 1950; from 1958 until 1976 he taught Spanish literature at the university. He has taught at various universities in the United States, among them the University of Chicago, New York University (NYU), and City University of New York (CUNY). He visited Spain in 1960 and returned there permanently in 1976, after retiring from his professorial post at CUNY. In 1984 he was elected to the Spanish Royal Academy; in 1986 he was asked to become the first holder of the King Juan Carlos Chair at NYU. Both these honors, and many others (including the 1971 Premio de la Critica award for his novel *El jardin de las delicaces*) signified Ayala's triumphal return to this people and their homage to his vast achievements in the fields of fiction, belles-lettres, and criticism. Ayala has written four novels, nine collections of stories, many books of sociopolitical analysis, and a two-volume memoir, which was awarded a national prize in Spain in 1983.

As detailed by Carolyn Richmond in the introduction to her translation of Ayala's *Usurpers* (1987; *Los usurpadores,* 1949), Ayala's publishing history is replete with examples of censorship, banning, harassment, official silence, and the eventual triumph of an author's freedom of expression. His books were banned in Spain from 1930 to 1955. In that year censors allowed a limited edition of Ayala's collection of stories *A Monkey's Tale*, but refused permission for publication of his two novels *Muertes de perro* (1958, Dog's Death) and *El fondo del vaso* (1962, The Bottom of the Glass). Again in 1962, Ayala was disallowed publication of his new collection of stories, *El As de Bastos* (The Ace of Clubs); the volume was published in Buenos Aires in 1962. He was permitted, however, to have his short novel, *The Abduction*, appear in 1965. In 1968, *Dog's Death* was published in Spain, four years after it had appeared in an English translation under the title *Death as a Way of Life*. As late as 1969, and in spite of national and world homage, Ayala's *Complete Narrative Works* was denied publication in Spain because Ayala refused to submit to censors' demands for deletion of one work from the text; the complete edition was issued in Mexico that same year.

Ayala is widely respected both as a scholar and as a creative artist. His writings have tended to concentrate in one genre during one period of activity, then in another genre in a following period. In the 1930s he devoted himself to sociological studies and literary essays. In 1939 after a ten-year hiatus from fiction and one year after the killing of his father and brother by Franco forces, he composed the prose poem "Dialogue of the Dead: A Spanish Elegy"; this work was to become the thematic link between his two collections of stories published in 1949, *Usurpers* and *The Lamb's Head*. Although *Usurpers* appeared after *The Lamb's Head* in the same year, the stories in it were written earlier; they concern violence and corruption in past Spanish ages. The stories in *The Lamb's*

Head are all placed in the Civil War period and reflect Ayala's admonition against violence and corruption of power as an unfortunate tradition of his country, but a tradition more pronounced in the twentieth century than in earlier times. Carolyn Richmond says that Ayala viewed fanaticism as the "factor of paramount importance" in his "depiction of the human passions giving rise to violence" (Introduction, *Usurpers* [1987], p. xii). Through the guise of a fictitious critic interpreting Ayala's work in a mock-preface to the first edition of *Usurpers* (Ayala gives the leg-pulling critic the clue name F.[rancisco] De Paula A.[Yala] G. Duarte), Ayala commented on his own work in this manner: "The excesses of our era and the author's personal experiences justify his perceiving and underscoring what is demonic, deceptive, and vain in the eagerness to dominate, and his view that the health of the spirit resides in saintly resignation" (*Usurpers*, 1987 ed., p. 174).

B

BACHMANN, Ingebord. Born June 25, 1926, in Klagenfurt, Austria; she died October 17, 1973, in Rome, Italy. Bachmann's childhood was spent in Carinthia. After World War II she studied philosophy at the Universities of Innsbruck, Graz, and Vienna, where in 1950 she completed a doctoral dissertation. She worked in Austria until 1953, when, committing herself to full-time writing, she moved into several large cities, among them Munich, Zurich, and Berlin. She spent the year 1959–60 teaching poetry at the University of Frankfurt. During the last year of her life, she spent increasing time in Rome, where she died in a fire in her apartment.

Bachmann's work is filled with existential doubt and reflects constantly on a sense of loss of place. "Place" as a spiritual ground not apprehended can be particularly seen in her poetry. Bachmann is also highly admired as a prose fiction stylist.

Selected Titles: *Die gestundete Zeit* (1953, Borrowed Time); *Anrufung des Grossen Baren* (1956, The Great Bear Constellation); *Malina* (1971, Malina); *Werke*, 4 vols. (1978); *Thee Paths to the Lake* (1990).

Consult: B. Keith-Smith, ed., *Essays on Contemporary German Literature* (1966).

BALDWIN, James. Born August 2, 1924, in New York City; he died December 1, 1987, in St. Paul de Vence, France. Baldwin's experience has served as the primary source for his explorations of racial and literary exile. At the heart of his writing is a struggle to discover his relationship as a black man to the white world and as an artist to the cultural ethos of America. Born in Harlem to fundamentalist religious parents, Baldwin found himself in a world from which he desperately desired to escape, but a world that provided him with rich experience he would later transmute into art. To avoid the despair of poverty and hopelessness of ghetto life, Baldwin turned to religion, becoming at fourteen, like his father, a storefront evangelical preacher. During his subsequent years at DeWitt Clinton High School he became a passionate reader, discovering there his talent for writing, which soon superseded his work of religious ministry.

The year before his father's death in 1943 Baldwin exiled himself from Harlem by moving first to New Jersey and then to Greenwich Village, where he remained for five years. There he began his actual career as a writer. During those years he placed a few essays and stories in prominent intellectual periodicals (*Nation, New Leader, Commentary*, and *Partisan Review*). But he had become dissatisfied with his fiction and was beset by personal problems. Feeling displaced both racially and culturally in a country that favored straight hair and white skin, Baldwin opted for exile. In 1948 with the encouragement of Richard Wright,* he moved to Paris. For nine years, until he returned to the United States in 1957, Baldwin lived not only in Paris but in southern France and in Switzerland. Out of this experience came two essays: "Equal in Paris," which explores the life of the expatriate writer, and "Stranger in the Village," which explores the theme of estrangement.

During his years of self-imposed exile Baldwin completed and published some of his best work: *Go Tell It On the Mountain* (novel, 1953); *Notes of a Native Son* (essays, 1955); and *Giovanni's Room* (novel, 1956). This last book is the only full-length work in which Baldwin deals specifically and extensively with the subject of exile, though its central animus is the search for self and the forging of an identity. The novel centers around two expatriate bisexuals, one an American, the other an Italian, both of whom are living in Paris. The American, David, goes to France in part to find himself and in part to escape his demons: his father's drunken affairs with women, his recurring nightmares about his deceased mother, and his confused sexual identity. In Paris, however, David becomes sexually involved first with Hella, an apprentice painter and American expatriate who leaves him, and then with Giovanni, a bisexual Italian bartender. Ultimately David betrays Giovanni, who, driven to desperation, commits a murder for which he is executed. David is torn by guilt and remorse stemming both from his betrayal and from his inability to accept his sexual self, an inability that Baldwin intimates derives from puritanical American attitudes about love and sexuality.

Although *Giovanni's Room* is doubly exilic in being written abroad and in its concern with expatriates, it is not Baldwin's most forceful statement about either literary or cultural exile. This expression may be found in a series of short works, both fictional and factual, which cumulatively illustrate a spectrum of exilic conditions. In these works Baldwin explains why he left America, why he returned, and what difference his exile made for his life and work.

Four stories touch on different aspects of exile: "Previous Condition," "This Morning, This Evening, So Soon," "Come Out the Wilderness," and "Sonny's Blues." "Previous Condition" depicts the struggle of an aspiring artist, Peter, to cope with his double estrangement of being black and an artist in a society that has little use and respect for either. "This Morning, This Evening, So Soon" describes a black singer's escape from an oppressive childhood to seek fulfillment in Paris. By leaving America the protagonist attempts, unsuccessfully, to prevent his young son from experiencing the degradation he suffered as a boy in a prejudice-ridden land. In "Come Out the Wilderness" Baldwin explores the alienation of a character from her self. After a traumatic childhood experience in which the protagonist, Ruth, has been mistakenly judged guilty of fornication by her brother and her parents, she experiences a disintegration of self from which she never fully recovers. At the end of the story, having attempted to work through her irrational guilt, Ruth remains lonely, frustrated, and alienated, lost in the wilderness of her confused sexuality and selfhood.

Baldwin's frequently anthologized story "Sonny's Blues" reveals still another facet of estrangement: alienation from one's culture, illustrated by the breach in social values and cultural disposition between a young jazz musician, Sonny, and his older brother, the narrator, an algebra teacher in a middle-class community. The older brother cannot reconcile Sonny's jazz milieu with his own borgeois domesticity. Having escaped the Harlem ghetto, the narrator evades his responsibility for his younger brother (whose charge he inherits when their parents die) until he reads by chance in the daily paper that Sonny has been arrested on a narcotics charge. This event sets in motion a process through which the two brothers come to see each other and themselves more clearly, and ultimately to accept each other's right to live by the values he believes in. Baldwin makes clear, however, that it is the narrator, not Sonny, who has the greatest distance to travel in accepting the cultural values of his younger brother (and of his own past). By the end of the story the breach between the brothers is closed partly through the different suffering each experiences and partly through the agency of music, which Baldwin employs as a metaphor for communication. Ultimately, it is Sonny's ability to express himself through music that enables him to communicate the common suffering that he and his brother and members of their race share.

Taken together, these stories reveal the range of Baldwin's depiction of both literal and metaphoric exile: estrangement from one's self ("Come Out of the Wilderness"); estrangement from one's people ("Previous Condition"); alienation from one's country ("This Morning, This Evening, So Soon"); and alienation from family and culture ("Sonny's Blues"). Although Baldwin's fiction displays various types of exile, it is his essays that explore the significance of exile on personality. "Equal in Paris" reveals Baldwin's ambivalence about the America from which he exiled himself, particularly when on his way to a sojourn in a Parisian jail for becoming innocently involved in stealing bedsheets, he thinks of the home from which he had fled, a Harlem he had both hated and loved. Another essay, "Stranger in the Village," shows an equally strong sense of alienation overcoming Baldwin when, as the only black in a remote mountain village, he decides that by virtue of their European ancestry and their white skins, the provincial Swiss villagers among whom he is staying possess a cultural and historical relationship to the great artists of the Western World from which he is forever excluded. In still another essay, "Encounter on the Seine," Baldwin describes how the American Negro has endured an "utter alienation from his people and his past." Black Americans in Paris, he suggests, attempt to escape both their country and their blackness; in so doing, they suffer double deprivation.

More elaborate than these meditations on exile is Baldwin's essay "The Discovery of What It Means to be an American," which Baldwin, following Henry James,* calls a "complex fate." In this important document of self-disclosure, Baldwin acknowledges that he left the country because he doubted his ability to survive, as he put it, "the fury of the color problem" in the United States. He wanted to prevent himself from becoming "merely a Negro; or even, merely a Negro writer" and to see if, as he explained, "the specialness of my experience could be made to connect me with other people instead of dividing me from them." In this manner Baldwin acknowledges both the recovery of his past and the acceptance of his native culture. He achieved this reconciliation partly by listening to the music of the blues singer Bessie Smith. In the United States Baldwin had refused to listen to her sing as he had avoided watermelon and anything else he connected with stereotypical black behavior. In Europe, however, he released himself from such constraints. Although Baldwin found it necessary to leave his homeland, he found it equally necessary to return to it in spirit in order to achieve reintegration.

It was in exile that Baldwin discovered the central themes of his work and the subject matter that provoked his most ambitious achievements.

Selected Title: *The Price of the Ticket: Collected Nonfiction 1948–1985* (1989).

Consult: Kenneth Kinnamon, ed., *James Baldwin: A Collection of Critical Essays* (1974); Louis H. Pratt, *James Baldwin* (1978); Quincy Troupe, ed. *James Baldwin, The Legacy* (1989); W. J. Wetherby, *James Baldwin: Artist on Fire* (1989).

ROBERT DIYANNI

BALMONT, Konstantin Dmitrievich. Born July 15, 1864, in Gumnishchi, Russia; died 1943, in Paris, France. Balmont was expelled from Moscow University for his revolutionary activities. He became a voluntary political exile from 1905 to 1912, living in various places in Europe and writing abrasive attacks on the Russian army and the czarist monarchy. Balmont was equally critical of the October Revolution of 1917, which he witnessed, and he became both unpopular and ignored in the ferment that was sweeping Russia in the early days of the czarist overthrow. He emigrated again from Russia in 1920, sick and bitter. He spent the last years of his life a mentally ill man in a Russian old people's home near Paris.

His poems were published in an edition, *Stikhot Voreniia*, in Leningrad in 1969.

BARAHENI, Reza. *See* Iranian Writers in Exile

BARANCZAK, Stanislaw. Born November 13, 1946, in Poznan, Poland; he lives in the Boston area and teaches Polish literature at Harvard University. After graduation from Adam Mickiewicz University in 1969, Baranczak was hired to teach there; when he left Poland in March 1981, he held the rank of associate professor. Baranczak wrote in a letter to the editor of this volume:

My departure had been preceded by a long tug-of-war with the Polish authorities who for three years had repeatedly rejected my application for an exit visa. Since the mid-seventies I had been active in the rapidly emerging Polish human rights movement, in particular, as one of the co-founders of KOR (Committee for the Defence of Workers, later renamed Committee for Society's Self-Defence), and editor of underground publications like the uncensored literary quarterly *Zapis*. I had already published several books, but since the end of 1975, I had been blacklisted as a result of my signing certain letters of protest. My next books were published either abroad or by underground presses without the authorities' consent. This, combined with my activities in KOR and *Zapis*, led in 1977 to my disciplinary expulsion from Poznan's Adam Mickiewicz University.

In 1977, harassed by government surveillance, unemployed, and unable to publish even his translations of John Donne and George Herbert, Baranczak was invited to Harvard University as a guest lecturer. When Polish authorities refused him an exit visa, Harvard's Slavic Department chairman flew to Poland, interviewed Baranczak in Poznan, and awarded him a three-year contract. Baranczak was unable to accept the offer because his application for an exit visa was rejected eight times in spite of Harvard's intervention on his behalf through diplomatic channels. In August 1980 the Poznan chapter of Solidarity specifically demanded Baranczak's reinstatement at the university, and in 1981 Baranczak left Poland with his wife, two children, and "two suitcases." Baranczak wrote in his letter that

Our small baggage meant, to all intents and purposes, that we did not consider ourselves emigres then. Indeed, at this point, we tended to see our stay in America as a three, perhaps five-year affair. On the one hand, I was by no means sure of my tenure prospects; on the other, the political situation in Poland, precarious as it was, offered many reasons for generally optimistic expectations. In other words, I was hedging my bets, while by no means excluding the possibility of our return to Poland. These plans and hopes were, however, nullified on December 13, 1981, when martial law was imposed in Poland. Most of my Polish friends were arrested or interned. Obviously there was no point in returning. Instead, for the next couple of years, I tried frantically to help the cause of Solidarity in the West, inasmuch as I was able to do anything significant to this end while working full-time at Harvard. In between my classes I toured campuses all over the country and gave talks on Solidarity and Polish culture. I wrote a number of articles on Poland for American and West European periodicals. I helped establish a Polish literary quarterly in Paris, and took part in a number of other political/cultural activities.

In 1983 Baranczak received a letter from the Polish consulate in New York informing him that his and his family's passports, due to expire in March 1984, would not be renewed. Baranczak was ordered to return to Poland with his family by the end of 1983. Ignoring this directive, Baranczak applied for permanent residence in the United States; he expects to gain full citizenship by 1991. Baranczak's post at Adam Mickiewicz University was also canceled in 1984, but he received tenure at Harvard University a few months after his second firing from his alma mater.

Baranczak and his family have not visited Poland since 1981, even though

we miss our friends and family terribly. (Fortunately, some of them have been able to visit the United States.) The reason is simple: since the expiration of our Polish passports we have had no travel documents that are valid from the viewpoint of the Polish authorities. Hypothetically, I might apply for an appropriate Polish document and perhaps even obtain it. But there is no guarantee that after my arrival in Poland I would ever be allowed to return to the West. On the contrary, I am rather sure that even under the present circumstances of a relative political relaxation, the Polish authorities would still consider me a citizen who once disobeyed their order to come back, and therefore, since 1984, has resided in the West illegally. In order to visit my homeland more or less safely in the future, I would first have to become an American citizen while also renouncing my Polish citizenship, and then have a Polish visa stamped in my American passport. But then, I have no certainty that my application for a Polish visa will ever be approved.

On the subject of exile, Baranczak is eloquent and aware of its many webbing strands. On December 9, 1988, he wrote:

Do I consider myself an exile then? It depends on the term's definition. If an exile is someone forcibly expelled from his country, my answer is negative: it was my own wish back in 1978–1981 to leave Poland (not permanently, to be sure), while the regime's intent was indeed to prevent me from doing so. If an exile is someone cut off from his native culture and language, my answer is negative again: as a Polish scholar and poet, my true homeland is not so much any geographic area as precisely Polish culture and language, and these I can carry along in my brain. If an exile is someone who can never feel at home in his adopted country, I have no unequivocal answer: though I have a genuine love for America, it is true that I am not and will never be completely assimilated here—but then again, I'm most probably one of those types who never feel completely at home anywhere. If an exile is someone who would feel better in his native country, I have no unequivocal answer either: I'm simply not sure whether I would like to go back and whether I would be able to live in today's Poland at all. But if an exile is someone deprived of his fundamental freedom of choice of the place to stay, then I certainly do consider myself an exile. As long as I cannot return safely to my homeland— if only to check my reactions and come to the conclusion that I'd rather live outside it— I am not a free man. As long as I am effectively barred from this patch of land, my decision to stay elsewhere is not entirely my own.

Baranczak has published twenty-five books in Polish, including collections of his own poems, scholarly works, collections of essays, anthologies, and translations from English, American, and Russian poetry. His work has appeared in many journals in the United States. He has published three books in English: *A Fugitive from Utopia: The Poetry of Zbigniew Herbert* (1988); *Selected Poems: The Weight of the Body* (1989); and *Breathing Under Water and Other East European Essays* (1990).

There are at present no easily available studies of Baranczak's work.

BARKA, Wasyl (pseudonym of Wasyl Otcheret). Born July 16, 1908, in the village of Solonytsia, Ukraine; currently residing in Glen Spey, New York. Barka first worked as a secondary school teacher of mathematics and physics in the Poltava region of Ukraine. Circumstances forced him to move to the Caucausus in 1928, where he switched from the sciences to medieval literature. There he taught for several years and for a time served as curator of an art museum. In 1930 he published his first collection of poetry, *Shliakhy* (Pathways), for which he was branded a "class enemy." His next collection in 1932, *Tsekhy* (Guilds), met with more critical success as a result of its proletarian content, but rather than continue in the same vein, Barka stopped publishing during the years of Stalinist terror. He married in 1932; his son, Yuri, was born the following year. In the late 1930s he took several courses in literature at Moscow University and just prior to the war defended his dissertation on Dante's *Divine Comedy*. Drafted into the Soviet army, he was severely wounded in late 1942. He was captured by the Germans and in early 1943 was evacuated without his family to various German "Ostarbeiter" camps, where he again began writing poetry, literary essays, and his first novel, *Rai* (Paradise), which appeared in 1953. The near-death experience transformed Barka's mode of thinking: his works following this period are imbued with great religiosity as well as stylistic and verbal texture, qualities difficult to translate into English. He emigrated to the United States after the war, and worked first as a coal carter and then as a janitor in a hospital. He found work more suitable to his background at Prolog Publishers in New York, and later as editor of the Ukrainian section of Radio Liberty. He retired on account of illness to the Ukrainian settlement Verkhovyna in the Catskills, where he continues to write. His major collections of poetry include *Apostoly* (1946, Apostles); *Bilyi svit* (1947, White World); *Okean* (1957, 2nd expanded ed., 1979); *Lirnyk* (1968, The Lyre Player); and the monumental four-volume poem-novel *Svidok* (1981, The Witness). Major volumes of essays include *Vershnyk neba* (1956, Horseman of the Sky); *Pravda Kobzaria* (1961, The Truth of the Kobzar); *Khliborobs'kyi Orfei, abo kliarnetyzm* (1961, A Tillerman's Orpheus, or Clarinetism); and *Zemlia sadivnychykh* (1977, Land of the Orchard Keepers). Barka is best known for his novel on the Great Famine of 1933, *Zhovtyi kniaz* (1963; 2nd ed., 1968; The Yellow Prince). The Paris press greeted the French translation of this novel with considerable acclaim in 1981. Barka has also translated the Apocalypse for an edition of the Ukrainian Bible published in Rome. Currently he continues to write poetry and is reworking his novel *Rai* with a new title, *Dushi Edemitiv* (The Souls of the Edenites).

Translations: *Trojanden-Roman* (Rai) (Manheim, 1956); *Le Prince Jaune* (Zhovtyi kniaz) (Preface by Piotr Rawicz; Paris, 1981) (English translation forthcoming); "The Wanderer" in the journal *Modern Poetry in Translation*, 1983.

Consult: *Literaturna tvorchist' na chuzhyni: Vasyl' Barka* (Literary Works in Emigration: Wasyl Barka), in *Terem* (The Tower), no. 6 (May 1979). Also see the anthology *Koordynaty* (Coordinates), vol. 2 (New York: Suchasnist Publishers, 1969).

MICHAEL M. NAYDAN

BARKER, George. Born February 26, 1913, Loughton, England; he lives in England. Barker was a wandering sojourner in many places after his first volume of poems was published in 1933. He was visiting professor of English in Japan in 1939; he moved to the United States in 1940 to be poet-in-residence at the Universities of Wisconsin and Miami (Florida). At the end of World War II he lived in Italy as well as the United States before returning to England in 1964. His themes centered on quest, exile and spiritual odyssey, and he has remained an itinerant traveler for much of his life.

Selected Title: *Collected Poems* (1987).

Consult: Martha Fodaski, *George Barker* (1969); *Homage to George Barker on his Sixtieth Birthday*, ed. John Heath-Stubbs and Martin Green (1973).

BARNES, Djuna (pseudonym of Lydia Steptoe). Born June 12, 1892, in Cornwall on Hudson, New York; died June 18, 1982, in New York City. An art student at Pratt Institute in Brooklyn and the Art Students League in Manhattan, Barnes secured her first job as an illustrator and feature writer for *The Brooklyn Eagle*; she also wrote for other newspapers in New York City in her early years. She was married briefly (1917–19) to Courtney Lemon. She lived in London and Paris from 1928 until the beginning of World War II; during her expatriate period she became associated with James Joyce and T. S. Eliot, both of whom had a strong influence on her work. From the time of her return to her death she lived in seclusion in a small Greenwich Village flat on Patchin Place; her neighbors and friends included e.e. cummings, Marianne Moore and her publisher Roger Straus. Her major work, *Nightwood* (1936), has been reissued several times and is considered a classic work of alienation and psychic exile. Her other work includes her first book, *A Book*, which in its original form (1923) consisted of three one-act plays, twelve stories, eleven lyrical poems and several drawings; on republication in 1929, the volume contained three new stories and a new title, *A Night Among the Horses*. Barnes published little after the 1960s and was often in dire financial straits, yet she refused, proudly, to ask for charity; friends had to contribute to her support anonymously.

Barnes was one of the legendary figures of the 1920s–30s American expatriate movement in France.

Selected Titles: *The Book of Repulsive Women: 8 rhythms and 5 drawings* (1915, reissued 1948); *She Tells Her Daughter* (a one-act play), in *Smart Set* (1923); *Ladies Almanack* (1928, repr. 1972); *Ryder* (1928, repr. 1981); *The Antiphon: a Play* (1958); *Selected Works: Spillway, The Antiphon, Nightwood* (1962); *Greenwich Village As It Is*

(1978); *Creatures in an Alphabet* (1982, poetry); *Smoke, and Early Stories* (1982); *Interviews* [by D.J.] (1985).

Consult: Alyce Barry, ed., *Djuna Barnes* (1989); Andrew Field, *The Life and Times of Djuna Barnes* (1983, reissued as *Djuna: The Formidable Miss Barnes* [1985]); Robert Giroux, "The Most Famous Unknown in the World—Remembering Djuna Barnes," *New York Times Book Review*, December 1, 1985; Douglas Messerli, *Djuna Barnes: A Bibliography* (1975); James B. Scott, *Djuna Barnes* (1976).

BARNEY, Natalie. Born October 31, 1876, in Dayton, Ohio; died February 2, 1972, in Paris, France. Born of a wealthy family in the Midwest, Barney lived most of her creative life in France, where she drew attention to herself as a phenomenon as well as a writer. Adept with French, and enamored of what she perceived as the French temperament, she wrote principally in her second language. A self-acknowledged lesbian, Barney was flamboyant in her public pronouncements and appearances; her prose fiction, likewise, was candid and daring. She remained in Paris throughout World War I but fled to Italy when France fell to the Germans.

BARTON, Paulé. Born 1916 in Haiti; died 1974 in Costa Rica. Barton worked as a goatherd and wrote his stories largely for communal folk-telling. Drawing on his Creole heritage and Ananse tradition, he wrote several stories with spider-trickster rogue heroes; he also used his knowledge of goats as a buttress for his humor. The protagonists of Barton's stories are usually men who are dreamers and women who are doers; his philosophy seemed one of goodwilled fatalism, or as his friend and translator, Howard Norman, wrote in "Afternotes": "He used the language of 'waking dreams' by which I mean that the deeper tensions of existence were drawn forth and absorbed fully into the beauty of the language. The humor, poverty, shame and love of his characters is autobiographical."

Barton fled from Haiti with his family after being sent to prison by dictator Papa Doc Duvalier; he settled in Costa Rica.

Translation: *The Woe Shirt, Caribbean Folk Tales* (1980).

Consult: "Afternotes," *Sudden Fiction International*, ed. Robert Shapard and James Thomas (1989).

BAUM, Vicki. Born January 24, 1888 in Vienna, Austria; died August 29, 1960 in Hollywood, California. Baum was a respected popular novelist who came to the United States in 1931 for business with her publisher, Doubleday. In 1932 she came back with her family to the United States as a political refugee. She made her way to Hollywood, where she became part of the brilliant European exile colony in the movie capital.

Selected Title: *Es war alles ganz anders: Errinnerungen* (Berlin, West Germany, 1962; *It Was All Quite Different: The Memoirs*, 1964).

BEAVER, Harold. Born 1929, in Dessau, Germany; he lives in England. Beaver left Germany with his Jewish parents in 1934; the family lived first on the Isle of Wight and then settled in London in 1937. He earned a scholarship to Oxford University and graduated with honors before he was twenty-one. He then went to Harvard Business School but decided to concentrate on comparative literature. He has worked for Oxford University Press, written for the *Times Literary Supplement*, and published widely. He taught at a Quaker school in western Kenya in 1962, an experience that resulted in his first-published book, *The Confessions of Jotham Simiyu* (London, 1962).

BÉBEY, Francis. Born July 15, 1929, in Douala, Cameroon. Bébey studied at the Sorbonne and worked for UNESCO in Paris from 1961 to 1974. His early work reflects the conditions of imposed separation and longing for an African homeland. *See* Francophone African Writers in Exile.

Selected Titles: *Embarras & cie; nouvelles et poèmes* (Yaounde, Cameroun, 1968); *Le fils d'Agatha Moudio* (Yaounde, 1968); *Trois petits cireurs* (Yaounde, 1972); *Concert pour un vieux masque* (Paris, 1980).

Translations: *Agatha Moudio's Son* (London, 1971); *The Ashanti Doll* (1977); *King Albert of Effidi* (1981).

BECHER, Johannes R. Born May 22, 1891, in Munich, Germany; died October 11, 1958, in East Berlin. In his early years Becher was one of the leading expressionist poets in Germany. He voiced his strong opposition to World War I in such collections as *An Europa* (1916, To Europe). Drawn to left-wing politics, Becher joined the Independent Socialist party in 1917, the radical Spartacus League in 1918, and the newly founded German Communist party in 1919, and increasingly distanced himself from his expressionist past. In his poetry and the play *Arbeiter, Bauern, Soldaten* (1921, Workers, Peasants, Soldiers), he stressed the role of literature as a weapon in the class struggle. Such activist works as the collection *Der Leichnam auf dem Thron* (1925, The Corpse on the Throne) led to his arrest for treason, although the case was later dropped. In October 1928, Becher was one of the founders and then the first secretary of the League of Proletarian-Revolutionary Writers, whose journal *Die Linkskurve* (The Left Curve) he edited between 1929 and 1932.

As one of the leading communist writers in Germany, Becher fled from the Nazis after the Reichstag fire in 1933; by way of Austria, Czechoslovakia, and Switzerland, he reached France. At the end of 1935 he moved to the Soviet Union, where he spent the next ten years, mostly around Moscow. Exile was a difficult time for Becher. In a letter to the writer Hans Carossa in 1947, he confessed that these years were for him purgatory, if not hell. In exile Becher felt isolated (he spoke no Russian) and homesick, and he became aware for the first time of his strong love for Germany and its culture. In public, however, he stressed how important his exile in the Soviet Union was for his development as a writer and a human being. Throughout his exile, Becher was actively involved in promoting resistance to the Nazis among both communist and noncommunist exile groups, first as a member of the International Organization of Revolutionary Writers and, later, in 1943, as a member of the National Committee for a Free Germany. Becher was also editor-in-chief of the German edition of the journal *Internationale Literatur*. Despite his acute homesickness and his fear of becoming, like other exiles, a victim of the Stalinist purges, Becher wrote prolifically during his exile. He published over fifteen collections of poems in addition to essays, the novel *Abschied* (1940, Parting) and two plays, one of which, *Schlacht um Moskau* (Battle for Moscow), was written at the time of the battle and published in 1942 when he was in exile. In nearly all Becher's exile works, certain themes predominate. In many he writes to encourage resistance to the Nazis. In some of his poems he expresses longing for Germany. Through his lyrical evocations of the German landscape, he proclaims both the pain of exile and the hope that his homeland will soon be freed from Nazism. During his exile Becher also stressed the importance of Western classical tradition, particularly German literature, as a reminder to his German readers of their cultural heritage. Through this reminder he presented a model for a more humane Germany after the destruction of the Nazi regime. In other works, Becher praised aspects of life in the Soviet Union, including Stalin's policies.

Because of his important position in the Communist party and his adherence to the Party line, Becher was asked to take a leading role in shaping communist cultural policy for Germany after the war. He began shaping this policy in 1943, and until the end of his life much of his work focused on the spiritual recovery of Germany and its culture, issues that had preoccupied him in exile.

Becher was one of the first Soviet exiles to return to Berlin in May 1945. He took a leading role in cultural affairs, serving as president of the Cultural League for the Democratic Renewal of Germany and, later, in 1954 until his death, as the first minister of culture in East Germany. Despite his position as the state poet, Becher became the target of Party criticism for his support of cultural reforms, and he felt increasingly isolated at the end of his life. Becher's exile thus shaped both his works and his later role as a political figure in the GDR. It reinforced such earlier concerns as the need for peace and his belief in literature as a force for social renewal.

Selected Titles: *Der Glucksucher und die sieben Lasten* (1938, The Seeker of Happiness and the Seven Burdens); *Wiedergeburt* (1940, Rebirth); *Deutschland ruft* (1942, Germany Calls).

Consult: Eberhard Hilscher, "Johannes R. Bechers Exiljahre," *Weimarer Beiträge: Zeitschrift für deutsche Literaturgeschichte* 4 (GDR, 1958); Hans Dieter Schäfer, "Stilgeschichtlicher Ort und historische Zeit in Johannes R. Bechers Exildichtungen," *Die deutsche Exilliteratur 1939–1945*, ed. Manfred Durzak (Stuttgart, 1973); Alexander Stephan, "Johannes R. Becher and the Cultural Development of the GDR," *New German Critique* 1, no. 2 (Spring 1974).

JENNIFER E. MICHAELS

BECKER, Jurek. Born September 30, 1937, in Lodz, Poland; he lives in West Berlin, FRG. Becker was sequestered in the Jewish ghetto of Lodz after the German invasion of Poland and imprisoned in the concentration camps at Ravensbruck and Sachsenhausen during 1943 to 1945. He and his father moved to East Berlin at the end of World War II, where he learned German and completed his high school education. He served in the East German army, after which he studied philosophy at the university level; he was expelled from the university for heretical political beliefs.

Becker spent the 1977–78 academic year as a guest professor at Oberlin College, Ohio, and wrote *Schlaflose Tage* (1978, Sleepless Days) while in the United States. The book was greeted with such dismay by the East German government that Becker was refused reentry to East Germany. He has lived in West Berlin since 1978, where he writes novels, filmscripts, and television plays.

Selected Titles: *Jakob der Lugner* (Neuwied, 1971, c. 1969; *Jacob the Liar* (London, 1976; rev. 1990); *Der Boxer* (Rostock, 1976); *Schlaflose Tage* (Frankfurt, 1978); *Bronsteins Kinder* (Frankfurt, 1986; *Bronstein's Children*, 1988).

Consult: Lowell A. Bangerter, entry in *Encyclopedia of World Literature*, ed. Leonard Klein, vol. 1 (1981); E. Korn, "Hope Proffered," *Times Literary Supplement*, February 6, 1976.

BECKETT, Samuel (Barclay). Born April 13, 1906 (Good Friday), in Foxrock, near Dublin, into a relatively affluent Protestant family: his father, William Beckett, was a quantity surveyor and his mother, Mary (May) Roe Beckett, a former nurse; Beckett was the second son. He died December 22, 1989, in Paris, France. Beckett attended Portora Royal School in North Ireland and Trinity College, Dublin, from which he graduated in 1928. From 1928 to 1930 he lived in Paris, working as an exchange "lecteur" in English at École Normale Supérieure, and became one of James Joyce's* circle. In 1930 he began teaching French literature at Trinity College, but resigned a few weeks after receiving his M.A. in December 1931. During his *Wanderjahre* period from 1932 to 1937 he lived in Ireland, England, France, and traveled in Germany, finally deciding to settle in Paris in 1937. At the outbreak of World War II, while vacationing in Ireland, he promptly returned to France. He was active in the resistance network, and in 1942, having narrowly escaped arrest by the Gestapo, he fled to the Unoccupied Zone where he spent over two years in the small town of Roussillon. In 1945 he volunteered to work for an Irish Red Cross hospital in St. Lô, Normandy.

From 1945 Beckett resided predominantly in Paris. He came to fame with the Paris premiere of *Waiting for Godot* in 1953, and his reputation as a major avant-garde dramatist was his award of the Nobel Prize for Literature in 1969. Beckett's work has drawn numerous commentators, and his criticism has become, especially in English-speaking countries, a veritable academic industry. Beckett himself shrank from commenting on or "interpreting" his work.

For over six decades Beckett wrote in various genres: stories, novellas, novels, poetic-prose pieces, poems, plays for stage, radio, television, a film scenario, mimes, translations, and criticism, and directed his own works on stage and in the media. Until 1945 he wrote almost exclusively in English. "Dante

... Bruno. Vico ... Joyce'' (Paris, 1929), Beckett's debut in print, was his contribution to a collection of explanatory essays on Joyce's work in progress, *Finnegans Wake*. *Proust* (London, 1931) a personal interpretation of *À la recherche du temps perdu*. The two texts remain his most pronounced criticism, a discipline to which several reviews and essays from the 1930s and 1940s also belong. His first separately published creative work, *Whoroscope* (Paris, 1930), is a poem on René Descartes; his other poems were collected in the volume *Echo's Bones* (Paris, 1935). His major genre of this period is prose fiction: several short stories, some of them incorporated into his unpublished novel *Dream of Fair to Middling Women* which was subsequently rewritten into a collection of short stories, *More Pricks than Kicks* (London, 1934), and two novels, *Murphy* (London, 1938) and *Watt* (written 1941–1944, published in Paris, 1953). His early prose, with the idiosyncratic Belaqua (named after a figure in Dante's *Divine Comedy*) as the main character, is replete with high erudition, and distinctly autobiographical. This early prose work employs the techniques of realism to question the principles of realism and its values. *Murphy*, contains exquisite examples of philosophical parody and black humor while at the same time depicting the pathetic withdrawal of the lonely protagonist, an Irish exile in London from ''the big blooming buzzing confusion'' of the world of society into his mind's inner world. *Watt*, set in much more vague physical scenery, is a story of one inmate of a mental institution as told by another in an absurdly meticulous manner.

Beckett's texts from 1945 to 1957, written almost exclusively in French (most of them later translated into English by the author) mark a further step toward works in which the outer world is but a distant background to the protagonist's mental world. In his prose, usually first-person narrative, the characters (their despair relieved only by laughter) explore dark regions of human destitution and death, the attributes of existence which, to Beckett, illustrate human experience better than the appearing truths of science, philosophy, religion and popular ethics. The culmination of this phase is the trilogy of novels, *Molloy* (Paris, 1951; English, *Molloy/I*, Paris, 1955), *Malone meurt* (Paris, 1951; *Malone Dies*, 1956), and *L'innommable* (Paris, 1953; *The Unnamable*, 1958), in which he portrays human consciousness in search of the essential self. Plot, initially employed, becomes later merely a pretext for the main task of the narrators: to point at the deeper self that structures human experience.

En attendant Godot (Paris, 1952, *Waiting for Godot*, 1954), Beckett's first published play, marks a turning point in the history of drama. By making the dramatic core of the play the conventionally undramatic act of waiting and by not allowing the eponymous protagonist to appear onstage, Beckett proved that drama transcends conventional notions of plot, action, and simple referential relations between the world onstage and the world outside the theater. Onto this formal structuring he projected his existential preoccupations, and in tune with modern sensibility, he employed his unique humor to enhance the pathos and profundity of his statement on the human condition. In *Fin de partie* (Paris,

1957; *Endgame*, 1958), he further displayed the strategy so effective in *Godot*, that of inviting the audience to fill in the play's many enigmas while simultaneously frustrating any efforts at a definite interpretation. The ambiguity of Beckett's guises deepens the psychological realism of elementary human situations played in a context lacking specific social reference.

After 1958, Beckett's work underwent an evolution towards brevity, intensity, and a sense of concentration unparalleled in modern literature. In the late texts, written either in English or French and usually translated into the other language, he arrived at a unique idiom, striking in its austere beauty. Among the plays following *Fin de partie*, the radio drama *All That Fall* (1957) is a view of old age and, surprisingly, Old Ireland (this work is probably Beckett's most Irish work); *Krapp's Last Tape* (London, 1958) is a confrontation between a writer's present and past egos presented as a dialogue of an old man with an earlier-recorded tape of his views on life. Experimental as these two plays are, they seem conventional when placed beside *Happy Days* (1961), a two-act monologue of a heroine literally buried in a mound. The same may be said for Beckett's following works—*Play* (London, 1964), *Come and Go* (London, 1967), *Breath* (London, 1970), *Not I* (London, 1973), *That Time* and *Footfalls* (1976), *Ohio Impromptu* and *Rockaby* (1981), and several short pieces for television and broadcast media, all of which demand another interpretation than realism and representationalism. These texts mark Beckett's further step away from realistic poetics: the author not only obliterates the traditional distinctions of dramatis personae but challenges the view that an actor representing a human being is the principal agent onstage. Instead, Beckett posits a stage spectacle that unfolds in the interaction of visual and acoustic elements, to which the body of an actor is subject and as a result of which a story is generated, often in elaborate patterns. It is possible that in his later works Beckett had found the exterior dimension of mental space, a universe given to the only thing worthy of the artist's concern, namely, "the issueless predicament of existence."

Beckett's evolution in prose parallels that of his dramatic writing. The accentuated prose of *Comment c'est* (Paris, 1961; *How It Is*, 1964), set in a limitless expanse of mud, remains Beckett's last attempt at a novel. It was followed by "chamber" texts written chiefly in the 1960s and showing a reduction of the elements of outer reality in his work; by such reduction of the physical representation, the emphasis is placed on autonomous cerebral reality. Among such exemplary works are *Imagination morte imaginez* (Paris, 1965; *Imagination Dead Imagine*, London, 1965); *Le Dépeupleur* (Paris, 1970; *The Lost Ones*, 1972); *Bing* (Paris, 1966; *Ping*, London, 1967); *Sans* (Paris, 1969; *Lessness*, London, 1970). The elementary vision woven by the residues of individual memory and imagination become Beckett's thematic concern after *Sans*; "everyday" experience finds more access to his interest. Reduced to carefully selected images, his more recent work included uttered motives of love, compassion, suffering, and autobiographic reference; compare, for example, *Company* (1980).

Beckett lived outside Ireland for most of his adult life, and most of his works were written and published abroad. Although he was not forced to leave Ireland, nor was he subject to persecution in his native land, his exile is related to his attitude toward his country. He has never refrained from criticizing what he found provincial or pretentious about Ireland, or from deriding, with biting sarcasm, what he considered Irish idiosyncrasies. Correspondingly, Beckett and his work have been criticized by his Irish observers; in the 1930s his work was sometimes found indecent by national censors, and he was labeled "the atheist from Paris" by some Dublin newspapers. On his decision to return from neutral Ireland to Paris in 1939, he once commented: "I preferred France in war to Ireland in peace." His self-imposed exile, however, should be seen in the wider context of his view of human existence and the fate of the artist. Beckett's work heralds the universal exile that his characters so well impersonate: estrangement from nation, society, loved ones, and also from the individual past, the body, and the native language.

Beckett's view of the fate of artists is that all beings are in exile, and those who have left their country have no illusions about their condition. Literature is not a vehicle for the dissemination of social and/or political views; the artist should renounce any claim to description of the social sphere while moving on to the higher sphere of metaphysical reality.

Yet, while universal meanings are his concern, Beckett was never blind to acts of social injustice and political repression. Works such as *Rough for Radio II* (1976) or *What Where* (London, 1984), may be seen as having political content. *Catastrophe* (London, 1984) dedicated to the Czech dissident writer Vaclav Havel and first performed at the Avignon Festival in 1982, has been referred to frequently as a political play. To Beckett, it exposes political evil only insomuch as it is a part of universal evil.

Consult: Deirde Bair, *Samuel Beckett: A Biography* (1978); Ruby Cohn, *Just Play: Beckett's Theatre* (1980); Lawrence Harvey, *Samuel Beckett: Poet and Critic* (1970); James Knowlson and John Pilling, *Frescoes of the Skull: The Later Prose and Drama of Samuel Beckett* (1982).

MAREK KEDZIERSKI

II

For Beckett, exile was both a literal fact of life and a concept central to his art for more than half a century. After completing his course work at Trinity College, Dublin, he spent two years as an exchange lecturer at École Normale Supériere in Paris, where he became friends with the most celebrated literary exile of the time, his countryman James Joyce.* Beckett was immediately attracted to the experimental writing and cosmopolitan lifestyle of Joyce and his circle in France. From his teenage days, Beckett had been fascinated by the lives and work of exiles, most notably Dante, who had been banished from Florence for political reasons in 1302. Like Joyce, who had composed his saga of Dublin while in Trieste and Paris, Dante had written his majestic *Commedia* in exile, and that poem became a continual source of rich inspiration for Beckett.

All of young Beckett's early writing had something to do with the condition of exile. His first essay, "Dante . . . Bruno. Vico . . . Joyce" (1929), celebrated the book later to be called *Finnegans Wake* by linking it to the philosophical beliefs of iconoclasts and banished men. (Bruno, the sixteenth century Italian thinker, had been burned as a heretic; while Vico's early 18th century ideas about history were far ahead of his time.) Beckett's prize-winning poem, *Whoroscope* (1930), a bizarre monologue spoken by René Descartes, refers to the period when the great philosopher was living away from France at the court of Queen Christina of Sweden. Beckett's first collection of poetry, *Echo's Bones* (1935), takes its title and much of its imagery from Ovid's account of the beautiful nymph banished by Hera for having been infatuated with Narcissus. According to myth, Echo was forbidden to use her tongue except to repeat what was said to her, and she became so wasted away with longing that only her voice was left to her. From this image of an avid disembodied voice condemned to repeat words originating elsewhere, much of Beckett's major fiction was eventually to develop.

Through the early 1930's Beckett remained away from Ireland. He travelled about in Germany, stayed briefly in France and England, and expressed his disaffected mood at the time in the terse quatrain, "Gnome," as well as many other works. During this period, Beckett published (in addition to miscellaneous critical essays and reviews) a collection of stories, *More Pricks Than Kicks* (1934) and the novel, *Murphy* (1938). *Murphy* was his breakthrough book, a brilliant philosophical comedy about a zany, anti-intellectual intellectual who tries, by rocking bound and naked in a chair, to escape from the confusing contingency of the daily world into the sovereignty and freedom of his own mind, a mind that functions less like an instrument than a place. In one of the book's most memorable sequences, Murphy gets a job at the Magdalen Mental Mercyseat, an asylum where he quickly comes to feel closer to the inmates than to the doctors. Instead of perceiving the mentally ill as cut off from reality, Murphy sees as "sanctuary what the psychiatrists called exile," and he thinks of the patients "not as banished from a system of benefits but as escaped from a colossal fiasco."

The belief in separation as sanctuary rather than exile was confirmed in 1937 when Beckett interrupted his *Wanderjahre*, decided to settle in Paris, and soon afterwards began writing in French. In later years, when asked why he turned from English to French, Beckett gave many different answers, but a consistent theme runs through all of them. "It is easier," he told Nicholas Gessner in 1957, "to write without style in French." Some time later he explained to Herbert Blau that French appealed to him because it had "the right weakening effect," and he also observed to Richard Coe that he was afraid of English because "you couldn't help writing poetry in it." In 1962, responding more expansively to the same question, Beckett told Lawrence Harvey that "for him, an Irishman, French represented a form of weakness by comparison with his mother tongue. Besides, English because of its very richness holds out the temptation to rhetoric and virtuosity, which are merely words mirroring themselves complacently, Narcissus-like. The relative aestheticism of French seemed more appropriate to the expression of being, undeveloped, unsupported somewhere in the depths of the microcosm.'' And in 1968, he told his friend Ludovic Janvier: ''I took up writing again—in French—with the desire of impoverishing myself still further.''

Exiled being—''undeveloped, unsupported somewhere in the depths of the microcosm''—this was to be Beckett's subject for the rest of his writing life, and his distinctive signature as an artist the astonishing facility for inventing resonant new images to express a perception of being in a state of perpetual estrangement. At the heart of Beckett's vision is what he once described as ''existence by proxy,'' a deepseated intuition that ''being is so unlike what one is standing up,'' the consciousness of ''a presence, embryonic, undeveloped, of a self that might have been but never got born, an *être manqué*.'' Life, then, for Beckett is expiatory, and the atonement itself a needful, hopeless quest for some unconscious, preverbal, bedrock source of being.

But before Beckett was able to explore the subject of deficient or abortive being in his stories and plays, he experienced several shocks that confirmed his sense of alienation. Early on January 7, 1938, walking with friends on a Paris street, Beckett was approached by a neighborhood pimp named Prudent who asked for money. When Beckett refused the request, the pimp stabbed him above the heart, an assault that nearly ended his life. Weeks later, after having recuperated in a hospital, Beckett visited Prudent in prison and asked the man why he had knifed him. ''Je ne sais pas (I don't know),'' the attacker said, a startling confirmation of Beckett's belief that the essential facts of one's life are unknowable. Two years later, after the Germans invaded Poland and then France, Beckett joined the underground French Resistance to gather information about enemy troop movements. His cell was betrayed by an informer, but before the Gestapo arrived at his Paris apartment, Beckett fled with his friend Suzanne Deschevaux-Dumesnil (who later became his wife) to the village of Roussillon in the unoccupied south. There, in hiding, he wrote a darkly comic novel in English about an obscure figure named Watt, who works in the house of the mysterious Mr. Knott, and is progressively estranged from language and finally banished from his master's home. Although not published until 1953, *Watt* was the first of a series of novels that explored the conditions of anguished separation that had become one of Beckett's most passionate concerns.

When the war ended, Beckett returned to his Paris apartment and began what he later called ''the siege in the room,'' a period of extraordinary creativity during which he wrote *Molloy*, *Malone meurt*, *En attendant Godot*, *L'Innommable*, and other works in French (written between 1946 and 1952; published in France between 1951 and 1953; translated by Beckett and published in English between 1954 and 1958). For all their variousness, each of these works can be read as an imaginative response to a different form of severance and expulsion. In the first volume of what is now commonly called *The Trilogy*, the ancient and impoverished Molloy announces that he is in his mother's room trying to write an account of how he got there for some mysterious person who appears every week to pick up his pages. The epitome of worldly worn, disillusioned self-consciousness, Molloy tells a story that is by turns (and often at the same time) monstrous, lyrical, wildly humorous, violent, frenzied, and serene; and yet he never manages to tell us what he originally set out to relate. Trying to narrate an external journey, Molloy ends up talking more about what he calls "the within, all that inner space one never sees"; and yet even exploring those uncharted subterranean depths, he ends up far from the center, describing himself in a ditch, hearing still one more voice telling him "not to fret, that help was coming. Literally." "Molloy," he concludes, "could stay, where he happened to be." Molloy, like so many of Beckett's indefatigable protagonists, is a kind of haunted cartographer, trying to map previously uncharted (and perhaps unchartable) zones of being.

Molloy's counterpart in the second half of the novel is Jacques Moran, a characteristically middle-class private investigator sent out by his superiors to locate Molloy. After a ludicrous journey that duplicates much of the grotesque, fantastic, and zanily comic action of the first part of the narrative, Moran breaks down and is stripped of that which "has always protected me from all I was always condemned to be." In his anguish he is forced to recognize those parts of Molloy—the harsh primitivism and disillusioned sensitivity—that have been hidden elements in his own nature; and as a result, he too is separated from society and from his earlier self.

In *Malone Dies*, Malone (man alone) is confined to bed in a room of what may be a nursing home, where he struggles to write down a sequence of stories to pass the time until he dies. Here, the old man is set apart from his own death, trying fitfully to shape sardonic fictions that suit his demise. Even more exacerbated is the Unnamable, *literally* the voice of disembodied consciousness, who tries with defiant, panic-stricken single-mindedness to talk about his true self without recourse to the fictional surrogates (Murphy, Watt, Molloy, Moran, Malone, etc.) who had previously stood in for him. But he ultimately discovers that the embryonic presence, which might be his abortive self, can only be expressed in terms of stories about "others"—linguistic inventions he distrusts and tries to (but cannot) forswear. The last of these others is "the absentee," a figure who is *of* the silence, an elusive self forever resistant to detection in words. Yet, stammering "you must go on, I can't go on, I'll go on," the propulsive voice of the Unnamable heads into the silence.

When Beckett turned from fiction to writing for the theatre, ("as a relaxation," to escape from "the wildness and rulelessness of the novels"), he found equally graphic forms for his obsessive preoccupations. His most famous plays, *En attendant Godot* (1952, translated as *Waiting for Godot,* 1956) and *Fin de Partie* (1957, translated as *Endgame,* 1958), are tragicomedies about the dilemmas of separation and unfulfillable desire. In the first, two men, Vladimir and Estragon, pass the time on a country road while waiting for a mysterious, authoritarian figure named Godot, who never arrives. Although their plight is serious, they pass the time in ways that continually provoke laughter as well as fear and concern. A work of dazzling theatrical and poetic originality, *Waiting for Godot* blends humor and metaphysics (the circus and the seminar) to give balked aspiration an authentic tragi-comic voice. In *Endgame*, Hamm and Clov, master and servant, are exiled in a shelter-like room with no signs of life outside. Blind and paralyzed, the tormented Hamm cries out: "Here is my only elsewhere" as he longs for and is terrified of death. The title of Beckett's play is a term from chess, signifying the moments at the close of the match where most of the pieces have been eliminated, and the contest reduces itself to a few stylish moves, the end of which is clearly foreseen. On stage, near the armchair from which the stricken Hamm cannot move, are his parents, Nagg and Nell, encased in ashbins. Estranged from his servant, his parents, and himself, Hamm hungers to die, but—like Vladimir and Estragon—makes unforgettably stylish (and often explosively funny) linguistic moves while waiting for what does not happen.

By the end of the 1950s, Beckett had written most of the works on which his reputation as a major novelist and playwright would rest; and he had also brought his imaginative vision of exiled being into sharp and densely suggestive focus. In his invented world, to have been born is to have been banished into a state of forlorn separation from some glimpsed but never-to-be-achieved condition of original existential harmony. This condition remains a figment because it exists only as a mental product of the human consciousness of separation and expulsion itself. But in Beckett's finest work the permanently impoverished outcasts respond to their desolate situations with a resiliency, stylistic variety, philosophical provocation, and comic optimism that gives their destitution a kind of poetic beauty, even at times a sumptuousness.

In the 1960s and 1970s, the themes of *The Trilogy* and the two enormously influential plays were explored in increasingly stark and startling works. The exiled self was now both prison *and* sanctuary, the bizarre site of a persistently ironical kind of soul-making. People reduced to abortive minims never lose their faculty for analyzing their own deprivation and finding endless, often endearingly comic ways of bearing it. *Happy Days* (1961) dramatizes the predicament of a garrulous woman buried in the ground up to her waist and then to her neck. Separated from her husband, who crawls about behind the mound of earth that progressively swallows her, Winnie sings like a nightingale, and in her interment becomes every solitary woman and man whose body will be committed to the ground, but who is given no assurance of resurrection to eternal life. The novel *Comment c'est* (1961, translated as *How It Is*, 1964) is the unpunctuated, feverish, poetically structured narration of a primordial figure crawling on his belly through the mud, describing how life is while he waits for, then encounters, and is finally separated from another creature named Pim. The torment and victimization of exile has rarely been rendered in more disquieting (and yet—because of its lyrical murmur and structural symmetry—strangely consolatory) terms. After *Happy Days* and *How It Is*, Beckett wrote many short plays and prose texts that distilled and made even more vivid his theme of needful consciousness incarcerated in, and forced to sing of, its own separation. In *Play* (1963), a man, his wife, and his mistress are condemned to spend what may be eternity in separate urns tormented by a spotlight and forced to repeat their story. In *Not I* (1972), a garishly lighted mouth, eight feet above the stage, releases a torrent of words recounting the barren life of a woman she refuses to admit is herself. In the short novel, *Le Dépeupleur* (1970, translated as *The Lost Ones*, 1972), Beckett describes life inside a flattened cylinder fifty meters round and eighteen meters high. Two hundred and five naked bodies roam about searching in vain for something lost but indeterminate. At the end, darkness descends, the temperature rests near freezing and life comes to a stop.

Two of the last and most memorable of Beckett's works, the short autobiographical prose text *Company* (1980; London, 1981) and the fifteen-minute play *Rockaby* (1981) are late variations on the theme of solitary separation. In *Company*, a voice comes to a man on his back in the dark. Speaking in the second person, the voice tells of the man's past; speaking in the third person, the voice is that of the "cankerous other." And a fundamental Beckett dilemma is expressed in five short sentences: "Could he speak to and of whom the voice speaks there would be a first. But he cannot. He shall not. You cannot. You shall not." In the spectral *Rockaby*, an old woman in an elegant black dress rocks and converses with the recorded voice of her own memory, narrating the story of how she gave up the search for "another living soul," and sat down in the rocker in which her mother died, to try to rock herself into oblivion.

The desire and yet the inability ever to engage another self—whether it be a separate person or some longed-for part of one's own vestigial inner nature—remains to the end Beckett's essential subject. One way of describing his great accomplishment as a novelist and playwright is to say that more imaginatively than any writer of his time, he expressed (in a French and English poetic prose) the modern consciousness of the anguish and comedy of solitary banishment, the predicament of being exiled alone wherever one exists.

Selected Titles: *Collected Poems in English and French* (1977); *Collected Shorter Prose, 1945–1980; Ill Seen Ill Said* (1981); *Collected Shorter Plays* (1984); *Stirrings Still* (1989); *As the Story was Told: Uncollected and Late Prose* (London, 1990).

Consult: Beryl S. Fletcher and John Fletcher, *A Student's Guide to Samuel Beckett*, 2nd ed. (London, 1985); Lawrence Graver, *Waiting for Godot* (1989); Lawrence Graver and Raymond Federman, *Samuel Beckett: The Critical Heritage* (London and Boston, 1979); Lawrence Harvey, *Samuel Beckett: Poet and Critic* (Princeton, 1970); Linda Ben Zvi, *Samuel Beckett* (Boston, 1986).

LAWRENCE GRAVER

BEER-HOFFMANN, Richard. Born July 11, 1866, in Vienna, Austria; died September 26, 1945, in New York City. Beer-Hoffmann was raised in Brunn (now Brno, Czechoslovakia), and took a law degree at the University of Vienna in 1890. He was part of the "Young Vienna" informal association of writers—colleagues who met in cafés and salons to discuss aesthetic and intellectual matters. Members of the gilded circle included Arthur Schnitzler and Hugo von Hoffmannsthal. Beer-Hoffmann was also actively involved with Max Reinhardt in the director's productions of classic German theater, particularly the works of Goethe. He visited Palestine in 1936, drawn there by his recognition of his Jewish identity exacerbated by the anti-Semitism of Germany and Austria in the 1930s. After Germany annexed Austria he left in voluntary exile for Switzerland; he emigrated to the United States in 1939 and lived in New York until his death in 1945. During the last year of his life he became an American citizen and received the Distinguished Achievement Award of the (American) National Institute of Arts and Sciences.

Beer-Hoffmann is known for his achievements in several genres, though he was not a prolific writer in any form. He concentrated on poetry in his youth, wrote an experimental (for the time) novel, *Der Tod Georgs* (1900, The Death of George), and in midcareer turned to drama. Of his plays, probably the best-known is *Die Historie von Konig David* (The History of King David), an uncompleted series on the biblical hero.

During his exile period Beer-Hoffmann explored both the painful irony of a Jew's mission as a "chosen" leader and of the Jew's "difference" and outcast status in middle European society. Beer-Hoffmann also wrote a memoir, several odes, and laments after his wife's death in exile in Switzerland in 1939, collected in *Paula, ein Fragment* (1949, Paula, a Fragment). He wrote little after 1939— his book of poems, *Verse* (Verses), published in 1941, contains only twenty-four poems.

Selected Title: *Gesammelte Werke* (1963).

Consult: T. Berman, "Richard Beer-Hoffmann," *Jewish Quarterly* 14, no. 2 (1966); A. Werner, "Richard Beer-Hoffmann: Austrian Jew," *Judaism* 1 (1982); Harry Zohn, *Encyclopedia of World Literature*, vol. 1 (1981).

BEI Dao (pseudonym of Zhao Zhenkai). Born August 1949, in Peking, China. He is living in Stockholm. Bei is considered the finest of the underground poets who emerged during the 1970s to create an alternative literature that challenged the orthodoxy of the post–1949 period and that is often compared to twentieth-century modernist poetry in the West. The son of an administrative non–Communist party member and a doctor, he began life as part of the ruling class in China. He was in his last year in one of the elite secondary schools in Beijing when the Cultural Revolution began in 1965. Like many of his generation, he joined the Red Guards but soon became disillusioned with the factionalism and violence of the movement and the cynical manipulation of the youth by Chairman Mao. He gave up his political activities and began writing in the early 1970s. Other poets of the early 1970s were experimenting with new forms and imagery, and Bei joined them in a spirit of awakening to new frontiers of language and vision. In spite of his desire to be apolitical, his poetry was viewed as an act of defiance by the authorities.

Bei took part in the Tiananmen demonstrations of spring 1976, which preceded the death of Mao Zedong and the fall of the Gang of Four, and his most famous poem, "The Answer," is often characterized as a clear expression of his personal challenge to the political leadership. During the Democracy Wall movement of 1978–80, which pressed for further political change under the regime of Deng Xiaoping, Bei and fellow-poet Mang Ke founded an "unofficial" literary journal, *Today*; the journal was banned in 1980.

In the spring of 1989, Bei wrote an open letter to the government of China calling for the release of Wei Jingsheng and other political prisoners, many of whom had been imprisoned since the crackdown on the Democracy Wall movement in 1979–80. The letter was originally signed by thirty-three writers and intellectuals and eventually gained the support of thousands, both in and outside China. During the Tiananmen Square demonstrations of May and June 1989, his work was often cited by student leaders as a source of inspiration. He was a visiting scholar at the University of Oslo in Norway at the time and is now unable to return to China.

Bei was a visiting fellow of the Swedish Center of International PEN in Stockholm from January to September 1990. Together with fellow writers-in-exile Wan Zhi (Norway); Gao Xingjian, Lao Mu, and Su Xiaokang* (Paris); Duo Duo* and Zhao Yiheng (Britain); Li Tuo,* Qui Xiaolong, and Ah Cheng (United States); and Gu Cheng* and Yang Lian* (New Zealand), he is planning to republish *Today* to provide a forum for the large number of Chinese writers and intellectuals around the world. In a conference hosted by PEN American Center in New York in October 1989 Bei described the plight of Chinese writers: "Exile literature is a new phenomenon on the Chinese literary scene. Even though in the past hundred years there have been some noted literary works, as a whole it is a new phenomenon. I think every writer in exile is faced with a great personal test. The crisis comes from being caught between two cultures."

A collection of his poetry, *The August Sleepwalker*, and a book of short fiction, *Waves*, were published in the United States by New Directions in 1990.

ANDREA GAMBINO

BEI Ling (pseudonym of Huang Bei Ling); he lives in New York City. Bei was assigned to the Beijing Industrial Food and Brewery Company as punishment for his writing and his political activities. He had been a member of the editorial board of *China Human Rights* and a contributor to *Beijing Spring* and *Today*; all three were well-known Democracy Wall movement publications, until they ceased publication in 1980. Bei had been an activist for the democratic movement in China since the "April 5th movement" of 1976.

In 1988 Bei, Lao Mu, Xi Chuan, Zhang Zhen, and Chen Dongdong cofounded *Directions*, a poetry magazine that published one issue before it was closed by the government. During the later winter and spring of 1989, Bei helped organize an open letter to the Chinese government demanding the release of Wei Jingsheng, signed by 2,500 Chinese students and scholars in North America and Western Europe; he was a cosigner with Liu Xiaobo (now in prison), Hu Ping, and others of an open letter demanding the resignation of the Li Peng government, release of political prisoners, and wide-ranging political reforms. In May 1989 he was officially dismissed from his teaching post at Shenzhen University; in July he was blacklisted by the Chinese government.

Bei spent the spring 1990 semester at Brown University on a writing fellowship. He has been organizing a Center for Chinese Writers in Exile.

Selected Titles: *The Deceived* (Beijing, 1983, samizdat edition); *Wandering in March* (Beijing, 1985, samizdat edition); *One-hundred Love Poems*, ed. Bei Ling and Liu Zhanqiu (Guizhou, China, 1989); his poems may be found in translation in *Nimrod* 29, no. 2 (Spring-Summer 1986).

Consult: PEN American Center Factsheet Program, October 3, 1989.

BENEDETTI, Mario (also uses pseudonyms Damocles and Orlando Fino). Born September 14, 1920, in Paso de los Toros, Uruguay. Benedetti left Uruguay because of harassment as a result of proletarian views expressed in his writings. His subject in fiction has often been the lower middle class, people whose lives are filled with slow erosion of enthusiasm for any creed but routine and undemanding compromise. He is also an outspoken critic, usually of leftist persuasion, against Latin American tyranny. He is as well a significant literary critic (see his *Literatura uruguaya siglo XX* (1963, Uruguayan Literature in the Twentieth Century). He returned to Uruguay in 1985.

Selected Titles: *Ester mañana* (1949, This Morning); *Quién de nosotros Montevideonos* (1959, People of Montevideo); (1953, Who Among Us); *Gracias por el fuego* (1965, Thanks for the Light); *Cuentos* (1982); *El desexilio y otras conjeturas* (1984); *Antologia poética* (Madrid, 1984).

Consult: J. Brushwood, *The Spanish-American Novel: A Twentieth-Century Survey* (1975); J. M. Caballero Bonald, "Introduction," in *Antologia poética* (Benedetti); Eileen M. Zeitz, *La Critica, El Exilio y mas alla en las novelas de Mario Benedetti* (Montevideo, 1986).

BENJAMIN, Walter (pseudonyms Detlev Holz and K. A. Stampflinger). Born July 15, 1892, in Berlin. He committed suicide on September 26, 1940, at the Franco-Spanish border, Port Bou, Spain, while fleeing from the Gestapo. Benjamin, the son of a wealthy Jewish art dealer, studied philosophy at Freiburg, Berlin, and Munich. In 1917 he moved to Berne, Switzerland, where he completed his doctorate in 1919, but returned the following year to Berlin, where he lived until 1933. His first major work, *The Origin of German Tragic Drama* (*Ursprung des deutschen Trauerspeil*, 1928), was written to obtain a position at the University of Frankfurt. It was not accepted, and Benjamin devoted himself to criticism and letters. After extended trips to Spain, Italy, and France, he was forced to emigrate to Paris in 1933. There he became a member of the Institut für Sozialforschung, and he published several pieces in its journal, including one on Charles Baudelaire and his far-reaching essay "The Work of Art in the Age of Mechanical Reproduction" (*Das Kunstwerk im Zeitalter seiner technischen Reproduzierbarkeit*, 1936). Though Benjamin obtained a visa to come to the United States, the police chief at the border town of Port Bou, Spain, threatened to send back to France the group of refugees with whom he had fled; in despair he took his life.

Benjamin was a well-known figure among German-Jewish intellectuals, and he had close friendships, particularly with Gershom Scholem and Theodor Adorno.* Though he was drawn to Scholem's Jewish mysticism, he also was strongly influenced by Adorno's Marxism. He nonetheless remained fiercely independent of the Communist party, even after a visit to Moscow in 1926–27. He was one of the first to appreciate Bertold Brecht*, and his pieces on Brecht are invaluable, if difficult.

Benjamin was a Francophile, and his German translations of both Baudelaire and Proust are important; of all authors, Franz Kafka* most fascinated Benjamin. He spent much time with Brecht discussing Kafka and exploring the cross-fertilization of politics and literature. During his exile he published under the pseudonym Detlev Holz an annotated collection of German letters from 1783 to 1883, which chronicled the first flowering and wilting of German bourgeois culture (*Deutsche Menschen, Eine Folge von Briefe*, 1936).

Benjamin considered himself to be a philosophical critic of cultural events as well as an acute observer of modern social conventions. His approach to any topic is somewhat oblique and often autobiographical; some of his most interesting work is found in his autobiographical writings: *A Berlin Chronicle* (*Berliner Chronik*, 1970), *A Berlin Childhood in the Nineteenth Century* (*Berliner Kronik um Neuzehnhundert*, 1950), and "Moscow" (1927). Because most of his work has been published posthumously, Benjamin received late recognition, but he is now acknowledged as one of the most acute and original German writers of the twentieth century.

The most representative collections of his writings available in English are *Illuminations* (1968), edited by Hannah Arendt,* and *Reflections* (1978), edited by Peter Demetz. Both also contain notable appreciations. In addition, Gershom Scholem has written *Walter Benjamin—The Story of a Friendship* (1975), and Theodor Adorno has given his view in "A Portrait of Walter Benjamin," in *Prisms* (1967). The most complete edition of his writings is *Gesammelte Schriften* (1972–   ), edited by R. Tiedemann.

Consult: Terry Eagleton, *Walter Benjamin* (1985); J. Roberts, *Walter Benjamin* (1982); R. Wolin, *Walter Benjamin, An Aesthetic of Redemption* (1982). See also *The Correspondence of Walter Benjamin and Gershom Scholem: 1923–40*, ed. Gary Smith and Andre Lefevere (1989).

CHRISTOPHER P. MOONEY

BERBEROVA, Nina. Born 1901, in Russia; she lives in Princeton, New Jersey. Berberova is an outspoken impressionistic critic and historian of modern Russian literature who writes with the authority of personal experience. As a novelist and fiction writer, and as the wife of one of Russia's foremost modern poets, Vladislav Khodasevich,* she brings to her criticism and memoirs the intimate knowledge of her craft and the direct knowledge of working relationships with many of her country's exile and émigré writers. Her memoir *The Italics Are Mine*, published in translation in the United States in 1969, where Berberova has lived since 1948, emphasizes her personal insights and lively opinions. Although the book is called an autobiography, Berberova makes clear in her preface that the work is a series of reflections fired by sparks of recollections and is not intended as objective measure. Conversely, she argues, such a mode of recollection provides insight into the truth of the century she is recalling to her readers.

With her husband, Vladislav Khodasevich,Berberova left the Soviet Union in May 1923; cold, hungry, despairing of finding a way to live in a country besieged by civil strife, the couple emigrated first to Berlin and then to Paris. Berberova and Khodasevich were divorced in the late 1930s, and Berberova remarried; she never lost interest, however, in Khodasevich's work and person and attended to him in France during his painful death from a debilitating disease. In 1937 she and her second husband had moved to a country house after selling their Paris flat, and during the Nazi occupation of France she managed to survive outside the attention of the Gestapo. In contrast to her own situation, she saw many of her French and Russian-émigré friends rounded up and sent to concentration camps. After World War II she was forced to sell her house; she began writing articles for the Paris-based émigré journal *Russian Thought*, and in 1948 poured what few funds she had available into the publication of her new book, the first time she had engaged in self-publishing. (Berberova was largely unknown to the new generation of postwar French readers.) That same year she left France for the United States. In the 1950s she began writing criticism along with her fiction. She returned to France in the mid–1960s for a nostalgic visit only to realize that she could not recover the past. Undaunted by the discovery, as she writes in her memoir, she found satisfaction in what she had journeyed through, and where she had arrived as a human being.

Berberova's fiction has recently received new attention in translation: *The Accompanist* appeared in the United States in 1988 and *The Revolt* in England in 1989. Both works emphasize the warfare between self-discovery and self-deception, a battle fought not always openly but always with brilliant subterfuges of intellect and desire. In *The Revolt* the motif of a journey—in terms of a train ride and station, the recollection of the heroine's personal history, and the narrative sequence of events—is utilized as the heroine faces, or refuses to face, the manipulations of her reality.

Berberova continues to write in Russian and to see herself as an émigré in a welcoming but alien land. Rooted in the dramatic encounters of her youth with the history of the Russian Revolution and its intellectual promises and betrayals, her vision has grown deep but not traveled far from its shores of exile.

Selected Titles: Novels: *Poslednie i Pervye* (Paris, 1930, The First and the Last); *Bez Zakata* (Paris, 1938, Without Sunset); *Mys Bur* (*Novy Zhurnal*, 1959, The Cape of Storm). Stories: *Oblezgchenie Vchasti* (Paris, 1948, The Easing of Fate). Biography, Memoir, and Reportage: *Tchaikovsky* (Paris, 1937); *Borodin* (Paris, 1938); *Alexandre Blok et son temps* (Paris, 1948, Alexander Blok and His Time); *Delio V. A. Kravchenko* (Paris, 1950, The Kravchenko Lawsuit); *Zeleznaia zensina: raskay o zizni* (New York: Russika House, 1982); *Liudi i lozhi: russkie masony XX stoletiaa* (New York: Russika House, 1986); *Three Novels: The Resurrection of Mozart; The Waiter and the Slut; Astashev in Paris* (London, 1990 [all written during the 1930s and 1940s]). Staged Drama: *Madame* (Paris, 1938).

BERDYAEV, Nikolai Alexandrovich. Born March 19, 1874, in Lipky, a suburb of Kiev, Russia; died March 4, 1948, in Paris. Berdyaev was expelled in 1898 from the University of Kiev for his Marxist political activism. Rejecting his aristocratic family traditions, Berdyaev became further involved in radical activity, for which he was arrested in 1900 and sentenced to banishment in Vologda in northern Russia. During his exile he experienced a change of faith, and upon his release he went to Heidelberg, Germany, for study and contemplation. When he returned to Russia in 1905, he settled in St. Petersburg and became one of the prime movers in a new religious revival of Orthodox values. The movement spread among the Russian intelligentsia and gathered many literary adherents. Berdyaev lived mostly in Moscow during this time. When the Revolution occurred in 1917, he opposed the Bolshevik party in the power struggle for control of the government. He denounced communism from his desk at Moscow University; after several arrests he was exiled in 1922 as an ideological enemy of the new regime. He lived in Berlin from 1922 to 1924, where he organized a Religious-Philosophical Academy; later he moved the headquarters to Clamart near Paris (1924–28). His journal *Put*, which he edited in Paris from 1925 to 1940, achieved world renown; in it he portrayed Christianity as the last bulwark against communism in the battle for man's soul. He lived through the German occupation of Paris and refused all offers of return to the Soviet Union after World War II.

Selected Titles in Translation: *The Meaning of History* (1936); *The Destiny of Man* (1937).

Consult: Alexis Klimov, *Berdiaeff* (Paris, 1967); Donald A. Lourie, *Rebellious Prophet* (1960). For bibliography, see *Bibliographie des oeuvres de Nicolas Berdiaev*, compiled by Tamara Klépinine, with Introduction by Pierre Pascal (Paris, 1978).

BERGENGRUEN, Werner. Born September 16, 1892, in Riga, Latvia; died September 4, 1962, in Baden-Baden, West Germany. A conservative right-wing critic and convert to Roman Catholicism, Bergengruen angered the Nazi government by his aristocratic calls for a more tolerant social policy. His books were banned in the 1930s, and he fled into hiding in the Tyrols. A few months before the end of World War II, he was smuggled into Switzerland.

Selected Title: *Der letze Rittmeister* (1952; *The Last Captain of the Horse*, 1953); *Figur und Schatter* (1958, Figure and Shadow); *Herbstlichen Aufbruch* (1965, Autumn Departure).

Consult: Martin Seymour-Smith, *The New Guide to Modern World Literature* (1985).

BERNANOS, Georges. Born February 20, 1888, in Paris, France; died July 5, 1948, in Neuilly, France. Bernanos, who worked as a journalist for the right-wing periodical *Action française* between 1906 and 1913, was angered by his country's treatment of leftist and communist Catalans during the Spanish Civil War. Bernanos had lived on Majorca for some years in the mid–1930s, and his sympathies were with the oppressed poor rather than with any political ideology. He proclaimed his bitterness at France's insensitivity to the oppressed of the Spanish Civil War in his book *Les grands cimetières sous la lune* (1938, Diary of My Times), but the book's appearance, and message, did little to assuage the situation and led to Bernanos's increasing sense of isolation, shame, and dismay. Feeling separated from his countrymen, he left France in 1938 for Paraguay and later moved to Brazil, where he tried to live the life of a farmer. His best-known work, his second novel, *Journal d'un curé de campagne* (1936; *The Diary of a Country Priest*, 1937), is the record of a willing exile from the world of temporal power trying to plow a new land in which the verities of God's grace inhabit the scene. This novel, as well as his first one, *Sous le soleil de Satan*, treats the issue of man's duality, his battle between the opposing desires of the pursuit of grace and harmony, through the means of simple living, and the pursuit of power and wealth through corrupt and venal play. In leaving for South America Bernanos was in essence trying to live the life that he had envisioned in his fiction and that he conceived as the antidote to modern satanism. Bernanos returned to France in 1945, aware his efforts had not triumphed, and the pall of despair he had experienced earlier in his country greeted him even more strongly. He moved to Tunis, from where, feeling even more alone, he returned to France to die.

Bernanos's first novel, *Sous le soleil de Satan*, which catapulted him to fame, was published in 1926 when he was thirty-eight years old; it has recently been reissued in a revised and corrected edition. Bernanos published two other novels—*Nouvelle histoire de Mouchette* (1937; *Mouchette*, 1966) and *Monsieur Ouine* (1943; *The Open Mind*, 1949)—before turning in his last years to writing moral essays seeking a new spiritual awakening in humankind. All of his work explores man's struggle between good and evil, and the abiding moral courage or lack of it that distinguishes that struggle. Theological in its concerns with grace and corruption, his work is a passionate plea for God's forgiveness in the face of human duplicity and weakness.

Much of Bernanos's work has been published in posthumous scholarly editions with careful textual apparatus. Among these are *Lettres retrouvées 1904–1948*, ed. Jean-Loup Bernanos (Paris, 1983); *Sous le soleil de Satan, 1st edition conform au manuscrit original*, ed. René Guise and Pierre Gille (Paris, 1982); and *Sous le soleil de Satan: Extraits avec une notice sur la vie de Georges Bernanos, une étude sur la genèse de Sous le soleil de Satan, des notes, des questions, des documents critiques, des sujets de reflexion, et une note bibliographique par Michel Esteve* (Paris, 1973).

Selected Titles: *Lettre aux Anglais* (1942; *Plea for Liberty*, 1944); *Les enfants humilés* (1949; *Tradition of Freedom*, 1950); *La liberté pour quoi faire?* (Paris, 1972 [c. 1953]);

Oeuvres romanesques (1966); *La France contre les robots*, ed. Jean-Louis Bernanos (Paris, 1970); *Essais et ecrits de combat*, ed. Yves Bridel et al. (Paris, 1971); *La vocation spirituelle de la France*, ed. Jean-Louis Bernanos (Paris, 1975); *Les prédestinés*, ed. Jean-Louis Bernanos (Paris, 1983).

Consult: Jean-Loup Bernanos, *Georges Bernanos, à la merci des passants* (Paris, 1986); Gerda Blumenthal, *The Poetic Imagery of Georges Bernanos* (1965); Yves Rivard, *L'imaginaire et le quotidien, Essai sur les romans de Georges Bernanos* (1978). See also *Société des amis de Georges Bernanos Bulletin*, Paris.

BETI, Mongo (pseudonym of Alexandre Biyidi). Born 1932 in Mbalmayo, near Yaoundé, Cameroon; he lives in France. Beti obtained his *baccalauréat* in Yaoundé at age nineteen and then left the Cameroon in 1951 to study at Aix-en-Provence, France, and at the Sorbonne. He has lived in France since that time. He published his first novel, *Ville cruelle* (under the pseudonym Eza Boto), in 1954. He used a second pseudonym Mongo Beti, for his second novel, *Le pauvre Christ de Bomba* (Paris, 1956); the novel went out of print, possibly because of its offensiveness to the French colonial regime, but it was reprinted in 1971 (English translation in 1971). In 1957 Beti published *Mission terminée* (Mission Accomplished), which some critics consider his most important novel. In 1959 he visited the Cameroon before Independence ceremonies. As an outspoken critic of the new Ahidjo administration, Beti became persona non grata in his own country, and his books were banned in the Cameroon. Beti returned to France, where he later wrote a commentary on postindependent Cameroon, *Main basse sur le Cameroun* (1972). Ironically, this book was banned in France as well, and Beti had to pursue his case in court to have the ban lifted (he won his appeal in 1977). The ban may have been imposed because of diplomatic pressure from the Cameroonian government.

Beti published his fourth novel, *Le roi miraculé: Chronique des Essaazam* in 1960 (*King Lazarus*, 1960), before entering a long period of literary silence, which was not broken till 1974. Then, in quick succession, he published three novels: *Perpétue ou l'habitude de malheur* (1974; *Perpetua and the Habit of Unhappiness*, 1978); *Remember Reuben* (1974; *Remember Reuben*, London, 1979; 1980); and *La ruine presque cocasse à un polichinelle* (1979).

Beti considers all his work political in context. His most frequent narrative device is a young man fulfilling a social duty or a personal demand, and in the process embarking on a quest to self-knowledge. An outspoken critic of whatever offends him morally and politically, he has attacked the French colonial experience of history and the postindependence record in Africa. He also has attacked, sometimes without moderation, African writers who, in his estimation, play tunes that the Western audience likes to hear.

BIALIK, Ghayim Nachman (also spelled Chaim). Born 1873, in Radi, a village in the province of Volhynia, Russia. He died 1934, in Vienna. He is buried in Tel Aviv, Israel. Bialik's early years are typical of the Russian Jewish intellectual of his time. Born in a small village, he moved to the larger town of Zhitomir when he was five years old. At sixteen, he enrolled in a Talmudic academy. He taught Hebrew for a number of years in various towns in Russia. After the Russian Revolution, he felt pressured—because of his strong Orthodox beliefs—to leave the Soviet Union. He went first to Berlin; here he founded the publishing house Dvir, which specialized in the reprinting of classic Hebrew texts. In 1924 he emigrated to Tel Aviv, where he lived until his death except for trips abroad.

Bialik wrote his poems and stories both in Hebrew and Yiddish. His early poems evoke the cry in the wilderness of a Diaspora victim. Although Bialik was committed to Zionism, he draws more in his creative work on the pain of exile than on possible solutions to its dilemmas: weeping is more characteristic of his early work than exhortation to action. In his later life Bialik was a tireless participant in humanitarian programs and Zionist causes.

Selected Title: *Selected Poems* (1981, bilingual edition).

BIERMANN, Wolf. Born November 15, 1936, in Hamburg, Germany; he lives in West Germany. Under the exhilaration of his socialist ideals, Biermann left West Germany voluntarily in 1953 for residence in East Germany, where he studied mathematics, philosophy, and economics. He began a writing career in the German Democratic Republic (GDR) in the 1960s, but soon was harassed by GDR censors who objected to his critical commentary, particularly because of Biermann's immense popularity with East German Youth. From 1963 to 1965 he was allowed to tour both German states, East and West, where he championed social and political activism. In 1965 the GDR imposed a ban on his work; his books were taken from stores, and his plays were not allowed to be performed. Biermann secured permission to travel abroad, and knowing he would not be allowed to reenter the GDR, he left his second homeland in 1976 for reentry into West Germany.

The refusal of the East German government to allow Biermann to return home produced a storm of protest among East German writers and intellectuals, many of whom signed letters of appeal and engaged in demonstrations in support of Biermann's freedom of expression. As a result of their outspoken stand on the controversy surrounding the then-most popular poet-songwriter in East Germany, these writers and intellectuals were in turn ostracized and suffered harassment. Less than fifteen years later, with the crumbling of the Berlin Wall, Biermann returned to East Berlin to participate in a mammoth concert in celebration of German unity. In concert with German writers and musical/theatrical performers, both those who had been in exile and those who had remained behind, Biermann performed to thousands of spectators; the audience shouted their enthusiasm for the coming of a new state of Germany.

Selected Titles: *Fir meine* Genossen; *Hetzlieder Balladen, Gedichte* (Berlin, 1972, For My Comrades); *Verdrehte Welt—das seh' ich gerne* (Koln, 1982, Crazy World —I Like to See It).

BIN Xin. Born 1900 in Fujian Province, China. Bin Xin left for study at the University of Wisconsin in 1923, but returned to her country in 1926 to teach at several universities in Beijing. In 1946 she began teaching at Tokyo University and continued writing in Chinese. A council member of the Chinese Writers Association, she has published twenty-nine collections of poetry, prose, and short stories. Over ninety, she remains active as a writer, and her influence is acknowledged by younger writers in China. Although she has not been an exile in the conventional sense, her travels and her nostalgia for her native land have often resulted in exilic strains of lyric lament.

                                                                                          EDWARD MORIN

BISHOP, Elizabeth. Born February 8, 1911, in Boston, Massachusetts; died October 6, 1979, in Boston, Massachusetts. Bishop lived in Nova Scotia, Canada after her father died and her mother went insane; she returned to live with her paternal grandparents in Worcester, Massachusetts, when she was six years old. After her graduation from Vassar in 1934, she travelled through Europe and North Africa; in 1939 she settled in Key West, Florida, and began writing many of her famous poems in which travel and journey become the motif for initiation into self-awareness. She became ill on a trip to South America in 1951, and after her recovery, settled in Brazil for fifteen years (she lived with a faithful companion). She won the Pulitzer Prize for her volume of poems, *North and South: A Cold Spring* in 1955. In 1966 she came to the United States for three years as an invited guest at several universities; after a brief return to her Brazil residence, she came back to Massachusetts in 1969. She was poet-in-residence at Harvard University until her retirement there in 1977.

    Consult: David Kalstone, *Becoming a Poet: Elizabeth Bishop with Marianne Moore and Robert Lowell* (1990); Anne Stevenson, *Elizabeth Bishop* (1966). See also special issue *World Literature Today* 51, no. 1 (1977).

BISHOP, John Peale. Born 1892, West Virginia; died 1944. Bishop's first exposure to French culture came with his university education at Princeton. He served overseas in 1918 as a second lieutenant in the U.S Army. From 1922–24 he travelled through Italy, Austria, and France. After his return to New York in 1924, he was unable to find a publisher for his projected novel dealing with the return of literary expatriates. He left America again for Europe, where he lived in France from 1926 to 1933. In 1933 he settled in Cape Cod, Massachusetts.

    Selected Title: *Collected Poems*, ed. and with Introduction by Edmund Wilson (1948).

BISSOONDATH, Neil. Born 1955, in Trinidad. He lives in Toronto and is now a Canadian citizen. Bissoondath's mother Sati was the sister of V. S. Naipaul* and Shiva Naipaul.* Bissoondath's famous writing uncles encouraged him in his literary endeavors. After schooling in Trinidad, Bissoondath emigrated in 1973 to Toronto, where he attended York University and received a B.A. in

French in 1977. He says V. S. Naipaul advised him to emigrate to Canada when Bissoondath wrote that he wished to leave his place of birth. Naipaul felt, in Bissoondath's words in an interview, that "decaying England was no place to go looking for a future, that the States were simply too big. I would be swallowed up. So he suggested Canada as a good compromise."

Bissoondath's reason for leaving Trinidad, as reported in a Canadian newspaper, is that he saw no future for himself there. "I grew up with a feeling of not belonging, of wanting to leave Trinidad because I did not wish to be a doctor, lawyer, or businessman," the only career and professional choices open in his country. As an immigrant, he feels at home in Canada. In answer to the question "You have been living in Canada for sixteen years. Do you consider yourself an exile?," Bissoondath said, "I feel myself to be Canadian. I feel I belong here. In fact, it is the only label—'Canadian writer'—that I willingly accept. Canada is home. You know, it is a new feeling for me, this sense of home, of belonging, one for which I remain grateful." Bissoondath thus denies any sense of rootlessness in his current situation. Indeed he claims cosmopolitanism as his creed and condemns any kind of cultural ghetto or ethnic segregation.

Bissoondath's first book was a short story collection, *Digging Up the Mountains* (Toronto, 1986); many of the stories draw on his experience teaching English as a second language and French at a private language school. His first novel, *A Casual Brutality*, published in 1988 in Canada, England, and the United States (1989) to critical acclaim, deals with issues profoundly related to the immigrant and exile experience. The narrative concerns a young East Indian who emigrates to Canada, choosing to reside in Toronto; he acquires Canadian citizenship, yet is drawn back to the West Indies island of his birth for one final visit (the fictional name of the island is Casaquemada). Bissoondath claims the island location is a composite of the Caribbean rather than solely Trinidad, because he wishes to universalize his theme rather than write a portrait of contemporary Trinidad. "I wanted the freedom to create and invent, so the book, in a very large sense, is an amalgamation of post-colonial Caribbean history and ideas," he said in a published interview in August 1988. During the course of the novel's narrative, the hero, Raj, must come to terms with his sense of awakening identity and with a past that cannot be shaken off merely by naturalization papers.

Bissoondath and his immediate family—his father, brother, and sister—all live in Toronto. He has not visited Trinidad since 1984, when he returned for the funeral of his mother.

Consult: There are as yet no studies of Bissoondath.

BLASCO IBAÑEZ, Vicente. Born January 29, 1867, in Valencia, Spain; died January 28, 1928, in Menton, France. Because of feared arrest by the monarchist government for his political pronouncements in support of democratic movements within Spain, Blasco Ibañez fled into exile in 1890 to Paris. He returned in 1891 but fled again in 1896, this time to Italy; the cause of government action against him was his open alliance with the Cuban Independent movement. Blasco Ibañez returned to Spain in 1896 and was sentenced to a two-year prison term, but the sentence was commuted. His belief in a writer's participatory responsibilities led to his service in the Spanish Parliament through election to six terms in office.

As a writer Blasco Ibañez is second only to Miguel Cervantes in the number of translations of Spanish novelists in foreign languages. His early work, with its naturalistic detail of the Valencian milieu in which he grew up, is particularly admired by critics. As a spokesman for social justice he is revered in Spain as much as his fellow writer-exile, Émile Zola, is admired in France.

Selected Titles: *Cañas y barro* (1902, *Reeds and Muds*, 1928); *La catedral* (1903, *The Shadow of the Cathedral*, 1919); *Sangre y arena* (1908; *Blood and Sand*, 1919); *Los cuatro jinetes del apocalipsis* (1916; *The Four Horsemen of the Apocalypse*, 1918).

Consult: John Dos Passos, *Rosinante to the Road Again* (1922); A. Grove and E. C. Knowlton, Jr., *Vicente Blasco Ibanez* (1972).

BONASSO, Miguel. Born Buenos Aires, Argentina; he lives in exile in Mexico City. Bonasso's best-known work is the novel *Memories of Death*, an account of the reign of terror in the 1970s in Argentina, when opposition voices to the military dictatorship were stilled by imprisonment, torture, and death.

BORCHARDT, Rudolf. Born 1877, in Germany; died 1945 in Italy. Borchardt left Germany in 1933 before the racial laws against Jews were passed. A well-known critic and poet, who propagated and exemplified the tradition of the artist in isolation, he continued to believe that the ivory tower provided the means by which the artist could objectify his work. In 1945 trying to reach Switzerland he was arrested by Germans near the Brenner Pass; an unconfirmed report speculated that Borchardt was allowed to escape. In any case he reached Italy, only to die shortly thereafter.

BORGESE, Giuseppe. Born 1882, near Palermo, Sicily; died 1952, in Fiesole, Italy. As an act of conscience in protest against the fascist state of Italy, Borgese left his university post in Milan and emigrated to the United States in 1931. He taught modern literature at Smith College and the University of Chicago. In 1947 he returned to his university post at Milan.

Borgese was a highly respected dramatist, novelist, critic, and essayist. He continued to write in Italian during his exile period.

BOWLES, Jane Auer. Born February 22, 1917, in New York City; died May 4, 1973, in Malaga, Spain. Auer moved with her Jewish parents to Woodmere, Long Island, in 1927; when her father died in 1930, she and her mother moved back to New York. She married Paul Bowles in 1938; they lived for a time on Middagh Street in Brooklyn Heights, where they shared quarters with W. H. Auden*, Carson McCullers, Tennessee Williams, and Gypsy Rose Lee at various times. In 1948 she traveled to Morocco to join her husband in Tangier. She remained in Tangier for the rest of her life, with trips to Europe and back to the United States. She and (Paul) Bowles lived in separate quarters and led independent sexual lives but related to each other in a profoundly emotional supportive manner. She was institutionalized in a psychiatric hospital in Malaga, Spain, in 1968; she spent the following year in a clinic in Malaga run by Catholic nuns. She returned to Tangier in 1969 but left again in 1971 for the Malaga clinic as her medical condition worsened after a stroke. She died in the convent clinic there.

Although her literary output is small, a number of critics believe she is an important delineator of people who clothe themselves in fantasy for shelter against a tattered world. Her use of phantasmal mendacity as a buffer against unmannerly reality allied her, during her brief creative period, with the techniques and spirit of contemporary (American) Southern writing and exilic feeling. Bowles wrote fiction, drama, and poetry in which the central character was invariably a female victimized by her sensitivities.

Selected Titles: *Two Serious Ladies* ([Written 1941] 1943); *In the Summer House* (drama produced 1951 in New York); *Feminine Wiles* (1977); *Collected Works*, with introduction by Truman Capote (1978). See also *Out in the World: Selected Letters, 1935–1970*, ed. Millicent Dillon (1985).

Consult: Millicent Dillon, *A Little Original Sin: The Life and Work of Jane Bowles* (1981).

BOWLES, Paul. Born December 30, 1910, in New York City. He lives in Tangier, Morocco. Bowles has been living in Tangier since 1947, and his two most important works of fiction, *The Sheltering Sky* (1949), a first novel, and *The Delicate Prey and Other Stories* (1950), appeared soon after his self-imposed exile. Both the novel and the short fictions pursue the leitmotif that has dominated his imagination and entire career: the high price, mental and physical, paid by outsiders from "advanced" societies when attempting to penetrate or assimilate the harsh mores of a less evolved culture; almost all of Bowles's literature utilizes a North African setting for this implicit theme. Violence, often extreme, ensues, while existential fears intensify to a dangerous edge of imminent negation. This utilization of setting places Bowles in the American tradition of Edgar Allan Poe and, more recently, of Joyce Carol Oates. The pervasive Gothic element, however, has narrative roots in the cultural clashes illuminated by Joseph Conrad* and later post-Empire writers, where a sophisticated Westerner of uncertain selfhood is forced by an exotic, primitive environment into a psychic unmasking, by which experience his unconscious desires are exposed. At the heart of Bowles's obsession with anguished confrontations between a civilized sensibility and mysterious foreign locales is a tenacious identity crisis and its attendant despair. He has translated Jean-Paul Sartre's *No Exit* and shares the French writer's deep concern for the angst and alienation that awareness of an indifferent universe engenders. A similar situation prevails in Bowles's poetry, as evident in *Next to Nothing: Collected Poems 1926–1977* (1981), which projects a severe, anti-Romantic lyric stance that never raises self beyond the level of passive victimization.

Critical reactions to Bowles's work have varied sharply, including charges that he depends upon adolescent shock techniques for many of his climactic effects, though there is general agreement concerning the fluid grace of his dispassionate style. The last decade has witnessed a continuing effort to bring the bulk of his fiction and nonfiction—the latter includes, several travel books and numerous translations, largely from the Arabic—back into print, a movement suggesting a renewed interest in his oeuvre. Though not the products of a major talent, several stories and perhaps *The Sheltering Sky*, as well as his understatedly candid autobiography, *Without Stopping* (1972), remain significant contributions to American literary history.

Selected Titles: *Let It Come Down* (1952); *The Spider's House* (1955); *Their Heads Are Green* (1963, essays, repr. London, 1990); *Up Above the World* (1966); *Collected Stories 1939–1976* (1979); *Call at Corazon and Other Stories* (1988); *Two Years Beside the Strait: Tangier Journal* (1987–1989) (London, 1990).

Consult: Hans Bertens, *The Fiction of Paul Bowles: The Soul Is the Weariest Part of the Body* (1979); Richard F. Pattison, *A World Outside: The Fiction of Paul Bowles* (1987); Christopher Sawyer-Laucanno, *An Invisible Speaker: A Biography of Paul Bowles* (1989); Lawrence D. Steward, *Paul Bowles: The Illumination of North Africa* (1974).

EDWARD BUTSCHER

BOYCHUK, Bohdan. Born 1927 in the Western Ukraine, now part of the USSR; he lives in New York City. Boychuk emigrated to the United States in 1949, finishing his studies in New York City, where he still lives and works. He has published six volumes of poetry, which are included, together with previously unpublished works, in *Poems: Selected and Next to the Last* (1983). He has translated extensively into Ukrainian the works of Samuel Beckett,* Juan Ramón Jiménez,* e. e. cummings, Stanley Kunitz, and David Ignatow. Boychuk has also published *Two Dramas*, a volume of one-act plays, and the study *The Theater-Studio of J. Hirniak and O. Dobrovolska* (1975). He and Bohdan Rubchak are coeditors of a two-volume anthology of modern Ukrainian poetry, *Coordinates* (1969).

Critic and fellow-poet Wasil Barka* characterized Boychuk's work as having a ''severe and courageous lyrical structure and cadence, sharp contours, authentic expression of a unified state of soul.''

BOYLE, Kay. Born 1902, in St. Paul, Minnesota; she lives in Oakland, California. Boyle lived in Europe as a child and spent her summer vacations in France and her winter holidays at skiing resorts in Switzerland. When economic reversals hit her wealthy father's business dealings as a result of shifting World War I pressures and priorities, the family returned to the United States; Boyle grew up in New York, surrounded by the accoutrements of high social station.

When she was eighteen she married a Frenchman, Richard Brault, and returned to Paris in 1923 to meet his family. With her first husband she became the mother of two daughters born in Paris; after their divorce she married the expatriate American writer, Lawrence Vail, in 1931. The couple lived in Switzerland until the outbreak of World War II, when in 1941 they returned to the United States; their three daughters were born in Europe. Boyle's early fiction draws on her experiences of expatriatism. In her novel *My Next Bride*, written in 1934, she utilized the premise of a young American woman caught up in Paris in the fever of a dazzling utopian scheme and its charismatic leader. The heroine is rescued from her follies by another expatriate, one who has gone even further in his exilic journey than she, and who has realized the bittersweet triumph of self-imposed distancing. Boyle's first collection of stories, *Wedding Day*, was published in 1929 by Harry and Caresse Crosby's Paris-based firm, The Black Sun Press.

At the end of World War II, Boyle returned to Europe, where she wrote several essays on the state of Occupied Germany for *The New Yorker* magazine (she lived in Occupied Germany from 1946–1953). In 1963 she became a professor of English at San Francisco State University; she retired from the post in the 1980s after a long and active career as a teacher of creative writing. Boyle is known as a master short story writer, a provocative novelist and essayist, a poet, and an inspirational teacher; she was also an active fighter in causes in which she believed. She marched in many protests against American involvement in Vietnam in the 1970s and supported various civil rights movements.

Selected Titles: *Crazy Winter* (1938); *Collected Poems* (1962); *Fifty Stories* (1980).
Consult: Sandra Whipple Spanier, *Kay Boyle: Artist and Activist* (1986).

BRAITHWAITE, (Lawson) Edward. Born May 11, 1930, in Bridgetown, Barbados; he lives in Jamaica. Braithwaite left Barbados in 1950 to attend Cambridge University on an island scholarship, choosing history as his specialization and Pembroke as his college. He stayed an additional year after graduation in 1953 to earn a teacher's certificate. He left for Ghana in 1955, drawn there by his sense of African roots and that country's locus in the diaspora of his people and the colonial slave trade. Securing a job in the Ministry of Education, he stayed in Ghana for seven years (1955–62); he became a director of a children's theater there and wrote several plays, which have been collected in *Four Plays for Primary Schools* (London, 1964). He returned to the West Indies in 1962 as an extracurricular tutor in St. Lucia, and moved to the Mona, Jamaica, campus of the University of the West Indies, where in 1983 he was promoted to professor of social and cultural history.

Braithwaite's major writings—his volumes of poetry and critical essays—were published on his return to the West Indies. The theme of the African diaspora and exile, particularly the awareness of heritage of Africanness, was intensified by his sojourn in West Africa.

Braithwaite's major works are *The Arrivants: A New World Trilogy* (1973), published separately as *Rights of Passage* (1967), *Masks* (1968), and *Islands* (1969); *Other Exiles* (1975); *Black and Blues* (1976); *Mother Poem* (1977); and *Sun Poem* (1982). His publications include distinguished scholarly commentary: *The Folk Culture of Jamaican Slaves* (1969) and *The Development of Creole Society in Jamaica 1770–1820* (1971). His poetry draws on the history of the West Indian black man, and his exploiters and tyrants, whether colonial, tribal, economic, and/or military. His work is a cycle of memory that resonates with a proud cry of hope of regeneration. Employing archetypes as voices that link the black man through history, Braithwaite's cycle in *The Arrivants* ends with a return to roots; the suggestion is that the black man must acknowledge his mythic totality, which includes his African past, his West Indian present, and his painful colonial history.

Braithwaite's *Black and Blues*, which won the Cuban Casa de las Americas poetry prize in 1975, shows an urban, realistic emphasis. In these poems Braithwaite paid attention to the appeal of Rastafarian culture as a mythic triumph over adversity and colonial exploitation of the West Indian.

Mother Poem and *Sun Poem*, Braithwaite's later work, reveal an autobiographical direction in their devotion to his growing up and opening of consciousness, and to his awareness of his need to return to roots both in the West Indies and in Africa. This awareness of the exile's return to home is given mythical status in both volumes. In creating the imagery and allegorical frame of Adam (the hero, son and father and then grandfather) in the new island world, Braithwaite again suggests a cyclical view of history for the black man, and a hope that the wheel of transition is moving closer to the first state of natural paradise.

Braithwaite's work provided controversy in the 1970s when critics battled over his views of regeneration through a return to African mythos and symbology and a consequent rejection of Western literary and cultural referents of support for the black man. The controversy developed heat and division as Braithwaite and Derek Walcott* were used as code names (without, always, their permission or agreement) for two oppositional views: one (Braithwaite) favoring African exclusivity, the other (Walcott) suggesting a progressive amalgamation of Western traditions with African customs and culture. The controversy also drew into its net various argument on the applications, both historical and theoretical, of jazz and island/African music to black consciousness and cultural perspectives. The controversy has since simmered, and many critics now see both Braithwaite and Walcott as two complementary irons forging new depths of West Indian cultural history.

Selected Titles: *Roots* (1986); *Self* (1987).

BRANDYS, Kazimierz. Born 1916, Poland; he lives in the United States. Brandys left Poland in 1982 in the wake of the military crushing of the Solidarity movement and ensuing martial law. A well-established writer in his country, he had endured the Nazi occupation of Poland and had supported the succeeding

Communist government. In the 1950s he published several works of fiction critical of Stalinist policies in the immediate post-World War II era. *Rondo*, released in the United States in 1989, is the last work he wrote in Poland before his exile. A prescient satire, it concerns the protagonist's awakening from a sleep of deceptions and self-deceptiveness: "Rondo" is the name of a secret organization used as a cover for the imaginative (and sometimes real) pranks by the hero against the government and his community. The non-existent organization takes on a life of its own as government agents begin to believe in its workings, and the hero is forced to create a real "Rondo" in order to prevent his deception from being unmasked. "Rondo" thus becomes a reality through the faith of hard-liners in its presumed successes. What in previous years in Poland and Central Europe would have been a farce of mistaken identities in the manner of a Ferenc Molnár or a Witold Gombrowicz becomes in Brandys's contemporary version a grim tale of cold war tactics and morality. The irony of the tale is enhanced by its format: an epistolary recollection of the events forty years later, the letters serve as a further distancing of the narration so that the truth of observation becomes an amazement of unfounding, confounding revelations.

Brandys has also written two nonfiction works describing his life in Poland before and after his exile: *A Warsaw Diary 1979–1981* and *Paris/New York 1982–1984*.

Selected Titles: *Miasti nie pokanane* (1946, The Indomitable City, story of the Warsaw uprising); *Miedzy wojnami* (tetralogy, Between the Wars, 1948–51); *Obronoa Grenady* (1956, The Defense of Granada); *Matka Krolow* (1951, The Mother of the Krols); *A Question of Reality* (1977).

BRAZDŽIONIS, Bernardas. Born February 2, 1907, in Stebeikéliai, Eastern Lithuania. Brazdžionis studied Lithuanian language and literature at the University of Kaunas. As journalist, editor, and foremost as poet, he became, early in his life, one of the most famous contemporary Lithuanian literary figures. He was a member of the Lithuanian neo-Catholic movement, influenced by Jacques Maritain, Charles Péguy, Paul Claudel, and Georges Bernanos.* In his collections of poetry, especially *Krintančios žvaigždés* (1933, Falling Stars) and *Ženklai ir stebuklai* (1936, Omens and Miracles), Brazdžionis distinguished himself by his bold and modern treatment of biblical themes. His apocalyptic prophesies of war and totalitarianism were similar in spirit to the Polish Catastrophist poetry of Czesław Miłosz* and others. Under the pen name of Vyté Nemunélis, Brazdžionis won immense popularity as a writer of literature for children: in Lithuanian context, he is comparable to Lewis Carroll and A. A. Milne. Under the German occupation of 1941–44, Brazdžionis wrote patriotic and humanistic poetry, protesting against the Nazi atrocities. He left Lithuania in 1944, entered the United States in 1949, and settled in Los Angeles. During his exile period, he published several collections of poems: *Svetimi kalnai* (1945, Alien Mountains), *Šiaurés pašvaisté* (1947, Northern Lights), *Didžioji kryžkelé* (1953, The

Great Crossroads) and *Vidudienio sodai* (1961, Orchards of Noon). His *Poezijos pilnatis* (Collected Poems) appeared in 1970, and his collected poems for children in 1984. Brazdžionis's poetry written in exile is mainly nostalgic. It tries to help preserve Lithuanian identity in the diaspora. More often than not, Brazdžionis ironically complains of the insensitivity of the world to the Lithuanian plight. From an artistic point of view, his later poetry is inferior to his prewar achievement. A young generation of Lithuanian émigré writers has criticized him severely. Nevertheless, his best poems are highly individual, dramatic, and profoundly human, and in Lithuanian letters he deserves the name of a living classic.

Consult: R. Šilbajoris, *Perfection of Exile* (1970).

TOMAS VENCLOVA

BRECHT, Bertolt. Born February 10, 1898, in Augsburg, Germany; he died August 14, 1956, in East Berlin, German Democratic Republic. Defined by complexity as well as controversy, Brecht was an artist of extraordinary talent and unique creative vision. Acknowledged as one of the most influential figures in the contemporary theater, he amassed during his lifetime an extensive body of literature, both fiction and nonfiction, which earned him a position of international acclaim. Without question, however, Brecht is most widely recognized as a playwright and theatrical innovator, and his artistic legacy rests primarily with his impact on the development of political drama. Rejecting the traditional conventions of dramatic theater, Brecht envisioned in its place a "theater of alienation" and shaped his plays to create an aesthetic distance between the audience and the performance in order to heighten awareness and perception of social purpose. Anti-illusionistic by design, his revolutionary form of drama attempted at once to enlighten, to entertain, and of most importance, to enhance the future of humanity.

Early demonstrating an affinity to merge literature and politics, Brecht was already considered a promising poet when he completed his first mature play in 1918 during a period of revolutionary turmoil in his native Bavaria. Afterwards, following the death of his mother in 1920, Brecht left Augsburg for Munich, initiating his development as a dramatist with productions of *Trommeln in der Nacht* (1922, Drums in the Night), *Im Dickicht der Städte* (1923, In the Jungle of the Cities), and *Leben Eduards des Zweiten von England* (1924, Edward II). Determined to enhance his reputation while instinctively drawn to the climate of theatrical experimentation, Brecht eventually settled in Berlin, where he became affiliated with the famed Deutsches Theater, the artistic inspiration of Max Reinhardt. During this period, Brecht experienced a radical and virtually uncompromising transformation. Highly influenced by the experimental director Erwin Piscator, whose unorthodox staging techniques formulated in part his concept of "epic theater," Brecht simultaneously embraced the social and economic ideology of Marxism. In addition, now divorced from his first wife, he married the actress Helene Weigel, herself an avowed communist, who would become a pivotal figure in his life as well as an artistic collaborator in his work. It was at this point that Brecht fully recognized his potential as an artist and clearly formulated his concept of the theater as a vehicle to exercise his political expression and to evoke the necessity of change.

Beginning with the production of *Mann ist Mann* (1926, A Man's a Man), Brecht firmly established himself as a dramatist of merit as well as increasing popularity. His career was decisively solidified with the premiere in 1928 of his collaborative effort with Kurt Weill of *Die Dreigroschenoper* (The Threepenny Opera), followed by productions of *Aufstieg und Fall der Stadt Mahagonny* (1930, Rise and Fall of the City of Mahagonny), *Die Massnahme* (1930, The Measures Taken), and *Die Mutter* (1932, The Mother). Achieving critical as well as commercial success, Brecht seemed virtually assured of a productive future and prestigious position in German drama; ironically, his success was in sharp opposition to the concurrent rise of Nazism. Consequently, his individual recognition as an influential artist and communist sympathizer earned him deep resentment from the emerging power structure and increasing difficulty in producing his plays. As the political situation in Germany deteriorated and reprisal became apparent, Brecht prepared for the inevitability of his arrest. On February 28, 1933, following the burning of the Reichstag, he and his family fled Germany to Prague en route to refuge in Denmark. Undoubtedly conceived as a temporary solution to ensure his safety, his self-imposed exile would last for the duration of World War II.

Although separated from his homeland as well as his cultural heritage, Brecht was nevertheless adamant in his continual indictment of the Nazi regime, which together with his identification with the communist movement resulted in the loss of his German citizenship in 1935. In addition to his political activity during his exile, Brecht remained extremely productive as an author. He resided in Denmark for a period of six years and during that time completed *Die Rundköpfe und die Spitz-köpfe* (1931–34, Roundheads and Peakheads), *Furcht und Elend des Dritten Reiches* (1935–38, The Private Life of the Master Race), the first version of *Leben das Galilei* (1938–39, Galileo), and, perhaps of most significance, *Mutter Courage und ihre Kinder* (1939, Mother Courage and Her Children).

In 1939, anticipating Germany's invasion of Denmark, Brecht fled with his family first to Sweden and then to Finland, ostensibly in search of a haven from the encroachment of war. Aided in his plight by the support and generosity of friends, he finally in desperation with his family and collective entourage crossed the Soviet Union in order to emigrate to the United States. Arriving in California, he settled in Santa Monica, where he remained from 1941 to 1947. During this time he completed *Die Gesichte der Simone Machard* (1941–43, The Visions of Simone Machard) and *Der kaukasische Kreidekreis* (1944–45, The Caucasian Chalk Circle); reception to his work, however, was extremely limited. Reluctant to accept his unconventional theatricality and his rejection of traditional social patterns, American audiences were suspicious of Brecht as an artist as well as of his concept of theater. Attempting to write for the film industry, Brecht achieved only partial success with the script for *Hangman Also Die*, released in 1942. Ironically, while preparing a commercial production in New York of a revised version of *Galileo*, Brecht was called to testify before the House Un-American Activities Committee concerning his communist affiliations. Although exonerated of criminal charges, Brecht departed from the United States for Switzerland.

Arriving in Europe, Brecht encountered for the first time the harsh aftermath of war; his response was a new confirmation of his need to engage in political and theatrical activity. Establishing himself as both director and dramatist at the Zuricher Schauspielhaus, he simultaneously began to negotiate his return to Germany, now divided into East and West. Undoubtedly attempting to capitalize on his public renown, the government of East Germany enticed Brecht to East Berlin by providing him with his own theater and a generous subsidy for his work. In 1948, after a period of nearly sixteen years, Brecht returned to his homeland to resume his career and ultimately to realize his artistic vision. Insistent in his demand to create a vehicle for the production of his plays, Brecht, together with his wife, founded the Berliner Ensemble, which would become one of the leading acting companies in the postwar theater and the embodiment of his presentational form of drama. Although his theatrical reputation in Germany had suffered a severe depreciation during his exile, Brecht's association with the Berliner Ensemble restored his credibility as an artist. Having written his most vital drama without the means of effective physical staging, he would now fulfill the promise and purpose of his creativity. Most notably, with the production in 1954 of *Mother Courage* at the Théâtre des Nations in Paris, Brecht received the international recognition that would accentuate and define his career for the remainder of his life. Interestingly, although Brecht was markedly critical of the dramatic theater, his most significant contribution as a dramatist is generally cited as his capacity to create characters of universality and depth in their struggle for survival. Although less active as a dramatist in his final years, Brecht continued to devote himself to the management of the Berliner Ensemble while adeptly preserving the delicate balance in his relationship with the East German government. Criticized in part for his apparent political acquiescence, Brecht is generally credited with having maintained a firm allegiance to his Marxist ideology as well as an inherent belief in the theater as an extension of social commitment. Brecht remained the dominant presence and the creative visionary of the Berliner Ensemble until his death in 1956. He was survived by his wife who continued to manage the Berliner Ensemble as well as perform as an actress until her death in 1971.

Selected Titles: *Das Verhör des Lukullus* (1939, The Trial of Lucullus); *Der gute Mensch von Sezuan* (1939–40, The Good Woman of Setzuan); *Herr Puntila und sein Knecht Matti* (1940–41, Mr. Puntila and His Hired Man); *Der aufhaltsame Aufsteig des Arturo Ui* (1941, The Resistable Rise of Arturo Ui); *Schweyk im zweiten Weltkrieg* (1941–43, Schweyk in the Second World War). See also *Brecht Letters*, ed. John Willett and Ralph Manheim (1990); *Poems and Songs from the Plays*, ed. John Willett (1990).

Consult: Bruce Cook, *Brecht in Exile* (1982); Martin Esslin, *Brecht: The Man and His Work* (1961); Frederic Ewen, *Bertolt Brecht: His Life, His Art, and His Times* (1967); Ronald Hayman, *Brecht: A Biography* (1983); James K. Lyon, *Bertolt Brecht in America* (1980).

STEVEN SERAFIN

BRETON, André. Born February 18, 1896, in Tinchebray, France; died September 28, 1966, in Paris, France. The founder of surrealism and the supporter of Dadaism, Breton consistently called for a literature that denied the necessity of social engagement and/or rational explication. In one of his *manifestes* (manifestos), *Légitimate Défense* (Paris, 1926), Breton stated his opposition to any external control of the artist, whether by critical reason or through political ideology. Because of Breton's belief in the separation of the artist from the goals of the community, Jean-Paul Sartre called him a permanent exile.

Breton spent five years in exile in the United States, from 1941 to 1946. He left France because he feared arrest by the German Gestapo as an enemy of fascism and of any system denying free thought and expression. The American Committee for Aid of Intellectuals arranged his safe passage, and Peggy Guggenheim paid for the ship tickets for Breton and his wife and young daughter. He lived in a fifth-floor walk-up apartment in Greenwich Village, New York, in some poverty; adding to the misery of his exile was his inability to speak any language but French. In her study *André Breton* (Oxford University Press, 1971), the surrealist scholar-critic Anna Balakian writes, on first meeting him during this time, that she was "struck by the irrelevance of his personal situation with the premises of surrealism. Where was the freedom to dream, the nonslavery to life, the freedom of speech, the desire to transform life?" Instead, she saw "a powerful man trapped in a cage, muzzled by a language he could not speak, circumvented by a society he could not understand, caught in economic obligations to a wife and small child he did not have the means to support, reduced to a fearful reality that seemed forever to obliterate the possibility of the dream" (p. 173). In the following months Breton was hired by the Office of War Information for its Voice of America's "La Voix de l'Amérique en Guerre" section. He became a propagandist for the cause of democracy and Free France. As Balakian writes, "The man who had declared himself so forcefully and continuously against the role of propagandist, against direct involvement in government service, was obliged to take a job in which his function was to put, not his pen but his powerful, resonant voice and impeccable diction, to the service of propaganda" (p. 174).

While Breton's material circumstances improved, his emotional life worsened. His wife left him and took their daughter with her. Alone and miserable, Breton found solace in his writing; he was a frequent contributor to the avant-garde journal *View*, edited by Charles Henri Ford in New York. In 1943, Breton traveled to Reno, Nevada, to obtain a divorce. During his trip there and back to New York, he was inspired by the magnificence of the scenery of the American

West. He began recording his states of exaltation in the long poem, *"Les États Generaux"*; the work utilizes the long light of the Aurora Borealis, which had appeared for one moment in New York a few months earlier in 1943, as a symbol of illumination and triumph over the darkness of adversities and tyranny. The poem is a tribute to three defenders of liberty, two of them martyrs in their causes—the General Assembly that led to the French Revolution; the Albigensian heroine Esclaramonde de Foix; and the socialist journalist Delescluze, who was killed during the Commune riots in Paris in 1871. While the poem makes use of the images of the sun in its majesty over the American southwest and in the light of the Aurora Borealis, its main view is that of the spires of hope in New York City: the poem is Breton's epic testament to the city that made his survival possible.

In 1944 in a New York restaurant Breton met the final great love of his life, Elisa (who became his wife). Months later they traveled to the Canadian province of Gaspé, where Breton wrote one of his finest prose pieces, *Arcane 17*, combining in its tapestry of symbols, in Balakian's words, "the great forces of eroticism and political destiny, the commitment of the human will to love and the social need for fraternity" (page 177). In a continuing burst of creative energy, Breton wrote a short time later, in 1945, the third of his major poems of this period, *Ode à Charles Fourier*. *Fata Morgana*, written in 1940–41, was the first of his "epic poems"; *Les États Generaux* was the second; the third, *Ode à Charles Fourier*, was published in 1947 in the Parisian review *Fontaine* and later in translation in 1961. Breton's ode shows an expansion of the poet's views in its inclusion of not only dreams as an allowance of the freedom of automatic writing but also of visions of social and utopian concerns as exemplified in the work of the nineteenth century French philosopher and social critic Fourier. In the *Ode* Breton widens his universe to allow the entry of social issues into art, a gesture contrary in theory to the manifestos of pure and earlier Bretonian surrealism, but the supposed contradiction results in a unity of complementary opposites. The *Ode*, in fact, became Breton's triumphal return to the literary world of France, when the work was published in Paris in 1947. Balakian sums up the poem in this manner: "Whereas in his early works his interrogation of the mysteries is strictly related to his own personal identity, in the wiser, more adept human that he has become the questions are 'What are we?' 'When will we learn?' Personal salvation is not possible without group liberation; his destiny is intimately linked with that of all others, and the macrocosm of the human condition as a totality finds its correspondence in the vistas of enormous mountain chains, deep schisms, and unmeasurable values. Man no longer triumphs singlehanded over anything; that is why there are no more heroes" (page 200).

Breton encouraged many literary artists and movements through his journal *Littérature*, which he founded in 1919, and through his voice in such exile journals as *View* and *VVV*, published in New York during the World War II years. Along with Sartre, he promoted *négritude* in French intellectual circles; though the two writers disagreed on their definition of the writer's responsibilities, both recognized the achievement of African and Caribbean culture in world civilization. Breton, who with Pablo Picasso and other surrealists, had felt the excitement of their discovery of African art in the 1920s and 1930s, turned to West Indian culture in the 1940s, particularly after his trip to Haiti and Martinique in 1946; he became a lifelong friend and admirer of the poet Aimé Césaire*.

Selected Titles: *Nadja* (Paris, 1928; *Nadja*, 1960); *Qu'est-ce que le surréalisme?* (Brussels, 1934); *Position politique du surréalism* (Paris, 1935); *Jeunes cerisiers garantis contre les lièvres* (1946, *Young Cherry Trees Protected from Hares*, 1947, selected poems in translation); *Yves Tanguy* (1946); *Poemes* (Paris, 1948, collected poems including "Fata Morgana," "Les États generaux," and "Ode à Charles Fournier"); *Les Manifestes* (Paris, 1955); *Oeuvres complètes*, Tome 1, ed. Marguerite Bonnet (Paris, 1988).

Consult: Anna Balakian, *Literary Origins of Surrealism* (1947, reissued 1966); Clifford Browder, *André Breton, Arbiter of Surrealism* (Droz, Geneva, 1967); Salvador Dali, *Journal d'un Genie* (Paris, 1964); Wallace Fowlie, *Age of Surrealism* (1950); Julien Gracq, *André Breton* (Paris, 1948); Claude Mauriac, *André Breton* (Paris, 1949); Philippe Soupault, *Le Vrai André Breton* (Liege, 1966). See also Herbert Gershman, *A Bibliography of the Surrealist Revolution in France* (1969).

BREYTENBACH, Breyten. Born 1939 in Bonnievale, in the Western Cape, South Africa; he lives in Paris. Breytenbach was born in a rural community he has likened to a bucolic paradise on the surface but one diseased in its underside with racist evil. At age twenty he began his journey outward, traveling abroad for two years and then settling in Paris in 1962, where he began a first career in painting. With his marriage to a Vietnamese woman, Lien Yolande, he became subject to imprisonment in South Africa should he return there; his marriage was viewed in then-existent South African law as contravening the cohabitation ban between races in his country. In the following years Breytenbach's Paris apartment became a hub for dissidents and exiles from many countries venting their anguish and despair over their condition; Breytenbach also participated in many public demonstrations against apartheid. He petitioned the South African government for permission to visit his family, and finally in 1973 he was allowed to return, with his wife, for a visit of three months. During this visit his father suffered a heart attack, from which he recovered. In 1975 he returned to South Africa, in disguise and with false identity papers, in an attempt to mobilize support against apartheid and to organize militant groups to fight against apartheid. He was arrested as he was boarding the plane for his return flight; a nine-year prison sentence was imposed on him. In 1977 he was tried on new charges of involvement in a Soviet-submarine surveillance attempt on Cape Town; he was also accused of inciting to prison riot by attempting to smuggle his letters out of jail. After repeated world protests, Breytenbach was released from prison in 1982 and allowed to return to Paris. To date he has published more than twelve volumes of poetry and three of prose, one of them the widely noticed autobiography of the events leading to and occurring during his incarceration in South Africa.

Breytenbach is probably South Africa's most distinguished Afrikaans poet, though since his early years he has also tried his hand at writing in English and French and/or translating his Afrikaans work into these languages. His paintings have in addition earned him an international reputation. Some of his recent notoriety springs from his accounts of his extraliterary activities. An anguished Boer, not merely content to observe and lament the plight of the South African blacks and the demoralization of the South African whites, Breytenbach decided early on to join underground organizations in an attempt to bring the South African ruling classes to some acceptance of change. In his prison memoir, *The True Confessions of an Albino Terrorist* (London, 1984), Breytenbach explores his motives and assesses his several roles: as a member of the ruling class he abhors; as a white man who must take drastic action to bring justice to black South Africa; as a husband yearning for the love of his Vietnamese wife forbidden to visit him except a few times in the seven years of his imprisonment; as a writer, poet, painter, and creative spirit. His account of his agony treats in detail his own intentions, his sense of social justice, his view of world history, and his statement of social demands. His style is that of a poet—often he is unable to leave any moment alone without investing it with a content of motive. Uncompromising in his explorations, Breytenbach structures his book around the motif of an investigation: the interrogator is always present in Breytenbach's innermost cells. His references to "Mr. Investigator" and "Mr. Eye" are equivalents to a search for the core of his "I," the true skin of his identity. Breytenbach concludes that the modern South African Boer is a more damned prisoner of conscience than the black native he has shackled over the centuries.

Not all readers will join in complicity with Breytenbach's approach to the South African situation. In his zeal Breytenbach appropriates a righteousness that is impolitic, but two facts remain indisputable: (1) Breytenbach has earned his right to preach his integrity, having proved it; and (2) his evocation of the hell of prison and of the test of the human spirit that prison and exile from human companionship make (Breytenbach spent several years in solitary confinement) have rarely been written with such extraordinary clarity and with such strokes of poetry.

Breytenbach continues to write in Afrikaans, French, and English. He is a French citizen.

In a summary article on Breytenbach's poetry, the Africanist Gerald Moore wrote in *Ariel: A Review of International English Literature*:

Few modern poets display a texture of images as continuous and alive as Breytenbach's. Every line of his early poetry (1964–1977) is packed with the mingled pain and delight of his exiled existence in Paris, where the unfolding South African tragedy continued to lay its touch on him almost daily, denying his right to the private happiness which seemed within his grasp. The actual return to the Western Cape, recorded in *A Season in Paradise*, also oscillates between the same poles of feeling; the delight and the pain of rediscovery. The book's title is not merely ironical. Bonnievale, his birthplace, has all the paradisiacal potentialities, without the realization. (p. 6)

Moore also commented:

The poems which appeared in a flood during the years 1964–1976 are immediately remarkable for the fire and tenderness of their imagery. Breytenbach is a poet who creates entirely in the language of imagery and whose poems have no argument which can be detached from that language. He is not a narrative, confessional, or didactic poet, but a celebrator of intense moments of vision or experience. His moods range from typical evocations of love or landscape to wry self-mockery and deadly anger. He is also constantly aware of the immanence of death pervading every living moment . . . (p. 4)

Moore contends that the use of both color (a natural consequence of Breytenbach's apprenticeship as a painter and his Afrikaner awareness of the color bar impeding expression of his connubial love) and sexual imagery (seen especially in poems about his wife) dominates Breytenbach's poetry. His poetic work thus may be said to veer between the ecstasy inherent in natural sexuality and the intrusion of political brutality into that paradise. Moore sums up the rending vision to be found in Breytenbach's poetry in this manner:

Breytenbach's poetry is situated where a consuming anger becomes inescapable and all-embracing, refusing all private content, all marginal accommodations in the name of sanity or survival. Yet few poets so impress us with their capacity for joy, with their yearning for a time and a condition in which that joy could flower. The passion which surges through his love poems is creative and self-renewing. (p. 11)

Breytenbach reached his widest audience during the years he was in prison when his friends translated many of his poems into English and issued such work in a number of separate volumes. Among these are *Sinking Ship Blues* (1977), edited by André Brink; *And Death White as Words* (1978), edited by A. J. Coetzee, in which are included works from all previous volumes written by Breytenbach through 1976; *In Africa Even the Flies Are Happy*, (London, 1978), edited by Denis Hirson, which includes prison poems as well as earlier work from 1964 to 1977; and the English version of *A Season in Paradise* (1980).

Breytenbach has visited South Africa twice since his release from prison—the first time in 1986, when he was given the Rapport Prize, an important Afrikaans-language literary honor. In July 1989 he was allowed, with his wife, into the country for four days (he had gone to neighboring Zimbabwe as an invited speaker at an academic conference).

Breytenbach's new novel, *Memory of Snow and of Dust* (1989), continues his moral plunge into the expanse of exile. Difficult in its poetic style and allusion, the novel is structured in two parts. In the first, "Uteropia" (a coined word combining roots of uterus and utopia), the heroine, Meheret, writes letters in Paris to her unborn child. Meheret's lover, a South African colored who can "pass" for white, has returned to South Africa to do research on a movie about the life of an exiled South African writer. He becomes entrapped there on a murder charge, is found guilty, and sentenced to be hanged. The familiarity, at least in outline with Breytenbach's own journey to South Africa—and his arrest and imprisonment—is apparent; the long passages of revolutionary rhetoric about the etiology of dislocation serve as reminders of Breytenbach's intense concerns with the state of South Africa. Breytenbach shows his characteristic humor in his satiric leveling of pretensions of Boer society, but he suggests a sliver of hope in his conclusion: while the writer-protagonist dies, his child will be born in Paris, a child who one day will return to a different Africa. The novel thus becomes a fictional filling-out, and drawing-in, of Breytenbach's personal history. For some readers the depth of the exploration, through its poetic language, signifies a maturity in Breytenbach's development. For others, the constancy of his obsessions grows into a burden that while justifiable by the history of Breytenbach's sufferings, does not progress into a liberating illumination.

Selected Titles: *Mouroir: Mirrornotes of a Novel* (London, 1984); *End Papers: Articles, Essays, Letters of Faith, Workbook Notes* (London, 1986); *Shadowvoices: for choir and instrumental ensemble* (Amsterdam, 1987); *Judas Eye/Self-Portrait/Deathwatch* (London, 1988).

Consult: Gerald Marzorati, "True Confessions of an Exiled Afrikaner," *New York Times Sunday Magazine*, August 27, 1989; Gerald Moore, *Ariel: A Review of International English Literature* 16, no. 2 (April 1985).

BROCH, Hermann. Born November 1, 1886, in Vienna, Austria, died May 30, 1951, in New Haven, Connecticut, of a heart attack. Broch's father, an aggressive working-class owner of a spinning mill, married a lady of some wealth from a solid bourgeois family. Broch's mother proved vain and whimsical, sometimes leaving Broch alone when she went on periodic travels. Broch thus spent a lonely childhood, often deserted during his vacations in the small resort town of Baden, halfway between the residence of his parents in Vienna and the village of Teesdorf, where his father's factory was located.

Broch was caught in battles between his mother, who insisted Broch learn "social graces," and his father, who decreed that Broch, as his eldest son, was to become a spinner. Early in his life, Broch was used by his father as a troubleshooter to pacify objections when the father made questionable business deals. This exposure to cynicism and corruption may have led to Broch's lifelong passion for justice and salvation. Broch's mother fixation developed early, and is revealed in two exemplary incidents. When he was twenty-five, Broch signed a letter to his mother with the closure "*père de famille.*" At thirty-one, and married to a woman two years older than he, Broch addressed his wife in a poem as "mother."

Broch attended a college for textile technology in Mülhausen. After graduation, he was sent, as a gift, on a two-month tour of the United States, which took him from New York City into the South. He bought some cotton for his father's mills in Memphis and New Orleans. Shortly after his return, Broch met Franziska ("Fanny") von Rothermann, fell in love with her, and announced their coming marriage against the wishes of both families. He dressed like a dandy, converted for social, and not religious, reasons to Catholicism, and wrote, as a "game," one (the last) chapter of a questionable novel for which his fiancée and seven of her sisters and friends each wrote another. During the same time, as an obedient son of his father who was loyal to the Hapsburg monarchy, Broch became a reserve officer in the Austrian army. Only after he had made the grade of lieutenant and returned home from service did he marry Fanny in 1909.

Broch worked as director of the spinning mill in Teesdorf, living there without a regular salary. Financial quarrels took their toll in his relationships with his wife and with his father. In his growing isolation, Broch began a double life. During the day he ran the spinning mill; at night he pored over books. He enrolled in the University of Vienna, where he took classes in mathematics and philosophy. His most famous and influential teacher at this time was Ludwig Boltzmann, the follower of Ernst Mach at the University of Vienna. Boltzmann was a founder of modern statistical physics and, like Mach, a representative of formal mathematics.

Broch also visited Vienna's literary cafés, particularly the Café Central and Café Museum, where he was likely to meet Karl Kraus, Franz Blei, Alfred Polgar, Robert Musil,* and Franz Werfel.* He befriended painters like Albert Paris Gütersloh and Georg Kista; he read Otto Weininger. Later he read Arthur Schopenhauer and Immanuel Kant systematically along with biblical and church studies, and he began his study of Hebrew in order to read the *Sohar*.

He perceived that the period before the outbreak of World War I was the end of an the era; his prophetic sight triggered his first serious literary production, in 1913, a long poem composed of alternating verse and prose passages, ''Cantos.'' During World War I, he was in charge of a Red Cross convalescent home for wounded soldiers. In his capacity as a representative of the Austrian union of industrial producers after the war, he became involved in settlement of labor disputes and in an advisory role on the general unemployment crisis. Because of Broch's knowledge of technology and his social awareness, Teesdorf became the first village in Austria to utilize electrical power and to maintain a grocery co-op for workers. At this time he also began psychoanalytic treatment, and although it was not entirely successful and although he spoke of ''unsolved rests,'' he expressed gratitude to psychoanalysis for making it possible for him to write. Probably of no less help was his involvement with Eva von Allesch, a beautiful and highly intellectual woman who was at the center of a circle of artists. Broch rented an apartment for her in Vienna, and occasionally lived there with her.

His first serious philosophic publications appeared in the journal *Der Brenner* in 1913. His first story was written for the journal *Summa*, which was published by his friend Franz Blei; it was a parody of expressionism. In his later philosophic essays he confronted the ideas of Kant and Edmund Husserl with theories of early neopositivism. He planned to write a book on the theory of values, but the work was never produced. After several years of silence, in 1927, the same year in which he sold the family mills, and just one year before Austria suffered a severe economic crisis, he met Anja Herzog, a native of Romania, who combined tenderness with a kind of analytic salve for Broch. In her house he wrote his first great novel, *The Sleepwalker* trilogy. At the same time he resumed his studies at the University of Vienna, where he took classes in mathematics, philosophy, and psychology.

Broch reworked the first two volumes of the trilogy slightly, but he drastically changed the third volume. Motivated by aesthetic considerations and under the influence of James Joyce,* particularly the novel *Ulysses*, he created a portrait of his time at the same time he was communicating a plea to his readers for activism and change. His political consciousness, and his awareness of the dangers of fascism, pervade the trilogy.

Die Schlafwandler, published in three volumes (Zurich, 1931–32; *The Sleepwalkers*, 1932), does not take a particular stand on daily politics, but as a "polyhistorical novel" it suggests an overall view of the political, economic, social, and philosophical developments in Germany in three stages: 1888 ("Pasenov the Romanticist"); 1903 ("Esch the Anarchist"); and 1918 ("Huguenau the Realist"), and with it what Broch called the "decay of values." In this broad view in which total social breakdown appears to be exemplified in the advent of World War I, the dangers of fascism in particular and totalitarianism in general are seen as symptom and consequence of the decay of modern moral values. The novels Broch wrote were created out of no less an intention than to serve as an antidote for what he perceived as the profound sickness of his age. By analyzing the roots of this decay, Broch's novels were to provide cognition, and beyond this analytical cognition of evil would be found the foundation of universal compassion.

Thus Broch's characters have to come to terms with the irrational, which is misconceived in a limited romantic way by Joachim von Pasenov in the first part of the trilogy; in the second novel the irrational is misconceived in an even more dangerous and limited way by Esch in the strange dreamworld of his "sleepwalking"; in the third novel the irrational is practically not recognized by Huguenau as he sinks into hopeless nihilism.

After *Die Schlafwandler*, Broch's literary reputation was established. He lectured in Vienna's Volkshochschule Leopoldstadt and in the famous Kulturbund. He attended the "Blei-Kreis" in the Café Herrenhof once a week, a circle named after Broch's friend, the writer and critic Franz Blei. Besides Blei and himself, Robert Musil, Albert Paris Gütersloh, Ernst Schönwiese, and Ernst Polak-Schwenk (the husband of Franz Kafka's Milena) were members.

After hurriedly finishing an insignificant novel, *Die unbekannte Grosse* (Berlin, 1933; *The Unknown Quantity*, 1935), he began work on his second great novel, the so-called *Berg-Roman*. Broch's intensive wish to bring awareness of the era's political developments grew to such consciousness that he wrote his friend and publisher, Daniel Brody, that he was possessed by a burning ambition to intervene in the world. It seemed to Broch that a metaphysical obligation had announced itself to him. In *Berg-Roman* he tried to exemplify in a small Tyrolean village how the unleashing of mass hysteria leads to injustice, enslavement, and murder.

From 1935 to 1937 Broch lived alone in Mösern, a small Tyroleon Alpine village, and worked on *Berg-Roman*. In 1938 he worked on it in Alt-Aussee as Hitler was annexing Austria. Broch was arrested and incarcerated for three weeks in a local prison; he was released and allowed to go to Vienna. Realizing his jeopardy, he tried to secure a visa. He managed to get his passport returned from the Gestapo and to obtain a visa for England. According to a letter from his publisher Daniel Brody, many people vouched for Broch—among them, Willa and Edwin Muir (his British translators), James Joyce, Aldous Huxley, and Stephen Hudson. Broch flew to London on July 29, 1938. His efforts to obtain a Danish, French, or Swiss visa proved unsuccessful.

Broch stayed with Stephen Hudson in London, and later with the Muirs, only to leave two months later on board the *Statendam* for the United States, where he arrived October 10, 1938. He never returned to his homeland.

He stayed first in an apartment on Amsterdam Avenue in New York City, then for a short time with Henry S. Canby, editor of the *Saturday Review*, in a small village in Connecticut, and for three months at the artist colony Yaddo in Saratoga Springs, New York. From Yaddo he went to Princeton, where he lived for a month in Albert Einstein's house, while Einstein was on vacation. Then he rented an inexpensive room in Princeton, and finally through Einstein was introduced to the philosopher Erich von Kahler, who was an exile himself and a friend of Thomas Mann.* Broch moved to Kahler's house and stayed there from 1942 to 1949.

The experience of exile strengthened Broch's humanistic commitment. In *The Death of Virgil* he explored the quandary of whether it is permissible to devote one's life to the creation of literature in a time of totalitarian encroachment. In this work, an interior monologue covering the last eighteen hours of his life, Virgil asks himself whether he should burn the great work of his lifetime, the *Aeneid*, because it deals only with the cognition of life. In order to be a truly great work of art, it must include death. Three dreamlike figures arise from Virgil's unconscious in his fever visions to make him aware of the insufficient scope of his work. This lack of cognition coincides with neglected loves in his life: the figure of the young boy Lysanias, who stands for Virgil's own childhood and serves at the same time as a guide to the world of death; the figure of Plotia, his sweetheart whom he had left many years ago; and the figure of a slave, who symbolizes the compassionate love of social commitment, which Virgil has not experienced. Out of love for his friend, the emperor Augustus, Virgil is persuaded not to destroy his poem but to save it for posterity.

In contrast to reductionist and partial views by which totalitarianism perceives reality, Broch offered his view of the totality of the human condition. He presented the totality of the many intellectual streams and movements the Roman Empire was undergoing at a time of crisis and transition through the figure of Virgil, who, aware of his imminent death, is able to discover the totality of life in the last eighteen hours of his living/dying.

Broch shaped his novel by employing the pattern of a symphony. The novel's four parts correspond to the four movements of a symphony. They relate to each other in their motifs as well as in their formal qualities. As in the closed and unified structure of a symphony, the structure of the novel is reflected in its parts, and, as in a musical variation, the motifs unfold in recurrence. Finally, Broch uses narrative and the microcosmic view of Virgil to achieve a cosmogony. *The Death of Virgil* becomes then not merely a historical novel providing a parade of Roman history, but it summarizes in some way the basic ideas of the ancient world about life and art, and it suggests parallels with Broch's contemporary world.

Broch was planning to write a book on political theory, to be followed by a three-volume work on mass psychology. The three most significant concepts in his study were in the field of philosophy of history—with his theory of historical *Fehlsituationen* (failing situations); in the field of sociology—with his detailed theory of totalitarianism; and in the field of philosophy of law—with his notion of a "human right" as an "earthly absolute." Broch did not live to finish this work. His unfinished commentary on mass psychology was published posthumously. Consult Wolfgang Rothe, ed., *Hermann Broch: Massenpsychologie* (Zurich, 1959), and Paul Michael Lützeler, ed., *Hermann Broch: Massenwahntheorie* (Frankfurt am Main, 1979).

Broch accepted a post in residency at Saybrook College of Yale University in 1949. On rereading galleys of a collection of his stories, he decided to add new stories in order to turn the collection into a unified novel. Thus the novel *Die Schuldlosen* (The Guiltless) came into existence (1950). Its main concern is the guilt of passivity, or rather the lack of activity of people who do not fulfill their human duties when other human beings are being persecuted, enslaved, and/or murdered. At the same time the novel posits the paramount spiritual sin of any totalitarian state, namely, the reduction of the absolute and infinite to the finite, as well as the projection of the finite into the absolute and infinite.

Broch started to write the last and by far the most superior version of his *Berg-Roman* but finished only the first four chapters. He died of a heart attack in his apartment in New Haven. The novel was pieced together from its three versions by Felix Stossinger under the title *Der Versucher* (Zurich, 1953).

Broch's position as poet is less assured than his stature as novelist and thinker. Of his few attempts as playwright, only *Die Entsühnung* has achieved eminence; it was published for the first time in its radio-play version in 1961.

Exile forced Broch into his final, almost superhuman efforts of responsibility to friends and to theoretical studies of cognition in the philosophy of law and the philosophy of history, and to his pursuit of the understanding of value theory and mass psychology. Broch considered mass psychology the single most important area for a social thinker in modern times.

Selected Title in Translation: *The Spell* (1986).

Consult: Manfred Durzak, *Hermann Broch* (Reinback bei Hamburg, 1966); Paul Michael Lützeler, *Hermann Broch* (Frankfurt am Main, 1986).

JOSEPH P. STRELKA

BROD, Max. Born May 27, 1884, in Prague, Austria (now Czechoslovakia); died December 20, 1968, in Tel Aviv, Israel. Brod studied and practiced law in his native city, but his devotion to the arts led him to become music and drama critic of the *Prager Tageblatt*. A fervent Zionist, he was chosen in 1918 as Vice President of the National Council of Czech Jews. In 1939 he emigrated to Palestine, settling permanently in Tel Aviv, where he took charge of the Hebrew National Theater (Habimah). Remaining productive to the end of his life, Brod wrote novels, plays, biographies (Heinrich Heine, Franz Kafka), as well as religious and philosophical works. Also a musician, he composed a *Requiem Hebraicum* and translated libretti by Leoš Janáček and Gerhard Weinberger into German.

Brod won acclaim with his trilogy of biographical novels based on the careers of the astronomers Tycho Brahe and Galileo, and the Jewish leader Reubeni. On completing this tripartite "Struggle for Truth," Brod was awarded the Bialik Prize. His study of the German humanist Johannes Reuchlin is cast in a similar mold. He remains best known, however, for his advocacy on behalf of Franz Kafka,* a fellow-member of the Prague Circle, to which Franz Werfel had also belonged. Brod became the chronicler of the entire group, edited Kafka's posthumous works (having refused the author's request that they be destroyed), and established a Kafka Archive in Tel Aviv. His intensive preoccupation with Kafka throughout his own experiences as an expatriate, including the upheavals of World War II and the Arab-Israeli conflict, demonstrates suggestive links between alienation and the problems resulting from internal and external exile. Brod also became involved in the new, militant phase of Zionism, and in 1949 wrote a novel about the Israeli war of independence. His writings are noteworthy for their spirit of tolerance and concern for bridging the divisions between separate faiths.

Selected Titles: *Tycho Brahes Weg zu Gott* (1916; *The Redemption of Tycho Brahe*, 1928); *Reubeni, Fürst der Juden* (1925; *Reubeni, Prince of the Jews*, 1928); *Galilei in Gefangenschaft* (Winterthur, 1948); *Johannes Reuchlin und sein Kampf* (Stuttgart, 1965); *Unambo* (Zurich, 1949; *Unambo, a novel of the War in Israel*, 1952); *Heinrich Heine* (Vienna, 1934; *Heinrich Heine: The Artist in Revolt*, London, 1976); *Franz Kafka, eine Biographie* (1946, *Franz Kafka, a Biography*, 1947); *Franz Kafka, Tagebucher 1910–1923* (1948–49, ed. Max Brod; *The Diaries of Franz Kafka*, 1948–49); *Heidentum, Christentum Judentum*, 2 vols. (1921; *Paganism, Christianity, Judaism*, University of Alabama Press,1970); *Streitbares Leben* (1960, autobiography); *Der Prager Kreis* (1966, The Prague Circle).

Consult: H. Gold, ed., *Max Brod: Ein Gedenkbuch* (Tel Aviv, 1969); M. Pazi, *Max Brod: Werk und Persönlichkeit* (Bonn, 1970).

CEDRIC HENTSCHEL

BRODSKY, Joseph. Born May 24, 1940, in Leningrad, USSR; he lives in New York City. Brodsky first became known in the West when on November 29, 1963, the newspaper *Evening Leningrad* picked him out from the new intelligentsia for a frontal attack on "social parasitism." Arrested and brought to trial in early 1964, he had the support of prominent Russian cultural figures such as Dmitri Shostakovich and Anna Akhmatova, but it was his own words at the show trial that won him international renown. Hectored by the presiding judge about whence he presumed the authority to write poems, Brodsky, who was well-read in religious philosophy, classical studies, and metaphysical poetry, answered that some things came "from God." His pre-ordained conviction brought him a five-year sentence at hard labor, which took him to a remote village pitching manure and chopping firewood in the Archangelsk region of the northern USSR. Continued intercessions on his behalf mitigated that term to a year and a half, after which he returned to Leningrad. Brodsky made a minimal living over the next seven years as a translator, rendering work from the English, Polish, and Serbo-Croatian, but he was able to get only a handful of his own poems published in the Soviet Union. His work at this time already showed a preoccupation with the metaphysical themes of death and solitude, separation and betrayal, but always tinged with loyalties to affections he had known. He began one cycle called "The School Anthology," which was to be forty poems in honor of his grammar schoolmates. He completed a 1400-line poem featuring conversations between two invented characters, Gorbunov ("the hunchback") and Gorchakov ("the embittered"). No less than W. H. Auden* praised Brodsky's work from his Soviet period, citing the clear distinction and virtuosity of voice, craft, and theme in *Selected Poems*, his first book in English translation (1973). He had already been anthologized in English translation earlier, in Olga Carlisle's 1968 work, *Poets on Street Corners*. His first Russian-language book-length collection was published by Chekhov Press in New York in 1970, *A Halt in the Desert*, after the famous poem in it about the razing of a church in Leningrad. In 1972 while Brodsky was being prominently featured in another American anthology, Suzanne Massie's *The Living Mirror: Five Young Poets from Leningrad*, Soviet officials sent him into exile abroad.

Because of his friendship with Carl Proffer of the University of Michigan, Brodsky honored that institution's offer to make him poet-in-residence in Ann Arbor. He had turned down similar European offers for distinguished posts, but over the next few years, he traveled widely in Europe, briefly accepting a post at Cambridge University in England, before settling finally, in 1977, in New York.

Exile has suited Brodsky. In the Soviet Union, he has already proven his attachments to classical cultures and myth, and to a formalism associating his poems with the force of time more than any place. In a 1980 interview published in *Columbia: A Magazine of Poetry and Prose*, he said that "basically every country is just a continuation of space," and that "by being displaced you arrive at the ultimate privacy." Privacy, however, was not all that he wanted. He became a much-loved and venerated teacher, adding brief posts at Queens College and Smith College before settling finally to teaching every fall at Columbia, and every spring at Mount Holyoke, where he keeps a small country home in addition to his basement and courtyard apartment in Greenwich Village. To a whole generation of young American poets, he taught the merits of classical form and meter. He maintained a close association with fellow émigrés, and with friends still in the Soviet Union, playing instrumental roles in getting many of the best European poets of the century translated and published in the United States and in helping to free many of his former countrymen from Soviet labor camps.

Brodsky's esteem among his fellow American poets is shown by the quality of translations in his book of verse published in English, *A Part of Speech* (1980). This includes translations by Richard Wilbur, Derek Walcott,* and Anthony Hecht, among others. His work during exile has continued to show metaphysical themes and varying voices, from the lyrical radiance of his *Roman Elegies* to a 1980 poem expressing his reaction to the invasion of Afghanistan by his native country, and to many more works with something between despair and mockery regarding individual human suffering, solitude, and separation. His verse has remained noun-dense and syntactically flowing, complex, and formal.

The man who never attended college himself, much less high school—he dropped out of school at age fifteen—was awarded an honorary doctorate from Yale University in 1978. The American Academy and Institute of Arts and Letters made him a member in 1979. He was among the first recipients of the MacArthur Foundation's new "genius" fellowships that began in 1981. Perhaps his most telling award, as an émigré and a lover of his adoptive culture, came in 1987 when the National Book Critics Circle chose his collection of auto-biography and literary essays, *Less Than One*, as the finest work of criticism published in the United States the previous year. Brodsky had written almost all of those essays originally in English as his own tribute to the works of W. H. Auden,* George Orwell, and others to whom he relished his debts.

Brodsky was awarded the Nobel Prize for Literature in 1987. Two volumes have appeared since he became a Laureate: the collection of poems, *To Urania: Selected Poems 1965–1985* (1988) and *Marbles* (1989), a play in three acts. The play is written in Russian; Brodsky has written some of the poems in *To Urania* in Russian, some in English, and has himself translated some of the Russian poems into English.

Selected Titles: *End of the Beautiful Era* (in Russian, Ann Arbor, Michigan, 1977); *A Part of Speech* (in Russian, Ann Arbor, 1977); *Roman Elegies* (in Russian, New York, 1982; *Roman Elegies* published in English in *Vanity Fair*, December 1983); *Democracy* (play, produced in London, 1990, in English).

Consult: Sven Birkets, *Paris Review* (1982); Valentina Polukhina, *Joseph Brodsky: A Poet for Our Time* (1989).

PHILIP BALLA

BROMFIELD, Louis Brucker. Born December 27, 1896, in Mansfield, Ohio; died March 18, 1956 in Columbus, Ohio. Bromfield first went to France during World War I. He returned in 1925 and stayed on for 13 years. He wrote a defense of American expatriatism in his essay, "Expatriate—Vintage 1927," arguing that exposure to European culture enriched the appreciation of American con-sciousness and achievement. He returned to the United States in 1938. Among his many best-selling novels are *The Green Bay Tree* (1927); *Awake and Rehearse* (1929); *Night in Bombay* (1940). He published his memoir, *Malabar Farm*, in 1948. Bromfield won the Pulitzer Prize for *Early Autumn* in 1926.

BRUCKNER, Ferdinand (pseudonym of Theodor Tagger). Born August 26, 1891, in Sophia, Bulgaria; died December 5, 1958, in West Berlin. Bruckner was forced into exile in the United States during the Hitler period because his mother was Jewish. He had left his native Bulgaria to form a theater company in Berlin in 1921 after extensive stays in Paris, New York, Vienna, and Los Angeles. He left Berlin in 1933 as an act of conscience against Hitler's Jewish extermination program and moved to France, from which he fled when it fell to the Nazis in 1939. He returned to West Berlin after the war and played a prominent role in the renaissance of the German theater.

The interruption of Bruckner's career when he was at the height of his artistic growth and the resultant hardships in his emotional, financial, professional, and personal life exemplify the power of exile to dampen but not to still the creative spirit.

Consult: Otto Mann, "Exkurs über Ferdinand Bruckner," *Deutsche Literatur im 20 Jahrhundert* [34], vol. 1 (1961): 162–78.

BRUTUS, Dennis. Born November 28, 1924, in Salisbury, Rhodesia (now Zimbabwe), of South African parents; he teaches at Northwestern University in Evanston, Illinois. Brutus grew up in the township of Dowerville in Port Elizabeth. According to South African law, he is a "Coloured," one of mixed heritage. He graduated from the segregated Fort Hare University College, and taught English and Afrikaans for fourteen years on the high school level. He was fired from his job in 1962 and moved to Johannesburg, where he briefly attended Witwatersrand University (he also worked as a tea boy there). His campaign against racism in sports led to his arrest in 1963, later to a ban on his holding any political and social rallies and on publication of any of his writings. Brutus was on his way to an Olympic Sports Committee meeting in Germany when he was arrested by Portuguese police at the Mozambique border. He was turned over to South African Security Police for transfer to Johannesburg. Because both the Portuguese and South African police who arrested him were secret security forces, Brutus feared that he could disappear without a trace. He attempted to escape, but was shot in the leg, captured, and sentenced to penal servitude for eighteen months at the notorious Robben Island prison in South Africa. His first volume of poems, *Sirens, Knuckles and Boots* (1963), appeared while he was in prison.

His second volume of poems, *Letters to Martha and Other Poems from a South African Prison* (1968), is a rendering of his feelings while in prison and of the conditions he observed and suffered. Because of possible prison censorship Brutus disguised his poems as "letters." After his release in 1965, he was given one-way exit permits for himself and his wife and seven children. He left for England, where he lived for several years and then moved to the United States. He taught first at the University of California in Los Angeles, then at the University of Texas in Austin, then at the University of Pittsburgh, and has for some years been active at Northwestern University as teacher, organizer of African literary conferences, and activist against South African racism in literature and sports.

In 1982 the U.S State Department informed Brutus that it would not renew his residence permit. Brutus was vulnerable to deportation because he had never applied for permanent residence in the United States but had renewed his temporary visa each year since 1970. He appealed the decision, claiming that if he returned to Zimbabwe (he is technically a citizen of that country, although he left Rhodesia before it became independent and traveled with a British Commonwealth passport), his life would be in danger from South African sources. The U.S. State Department countered that Brutus could return to England, his first place of refuge: he would be in no danger there. Brutus protested that his livelihood and career in teaching would be put in jeopardy by such a move. Strong support from writers, intellectuals, civil rights groups, academic groups such as the African Studies Association and the African Literature Association, and the Freedom-to-Write Committee of American PEN, led to a reconsideration of the ruling. On September 7, 1983, Brutus was granted political asylum in the United States by an immigration judge in a Chicago courtroom. As poet in exile, Brutus remains defiant in his sworn fight against apartheid and for racial equality. His fight, which he regards as a necessarily abrasive one, is summed up in his self-characterization from *A Simple Lust* (1972): "I am an alien in Africa and everywhere."

In his youth Brutus was a great reader of nineteenth-century poetry, and he has said that images of knighthood, chivalry, and troubadors pervade his work. His early writing may be seen as a quest for the Holy Grail that would revitalize an erring-ailing South Africa. All of his poetry is redolent of pain, and his imagery, with its cross-references to dream visions and barbaric indignities, enforces the shock value of his work, much of which is now openly protest poetry. Yet, although Brutus has written some declamatory and clearly political poems, his style remains symbolistic and at times hermetic in its concision. His activities in the area of civil rights, his leadership in the fight against racism in sports, and his severity in international boycott campaigns against South Africa— Brutus was in the forefront of the successful movement to ban South African athletes from Olympic Games competition—constitute a profound source of his being and make him a visible figure in the press and at rallies and meetings around the United States involving African issues. Another ineradicable source of his being is his poetry, which, with the exception of occasional poetry, he tends to keep shorn of shibboleths. In a review in *Choice* magazine, Martin Tucker wrote of one of his volumes of poems, *Stubborn Hope*: "Brutus's poems have always had a spare quality: his line is clean and direct, its power coming from one image revealed in both traditional and nonconventional lights."

Selected Titles: *Poems from Algiers* (1970); *Thoughts from Abroad* (1970); *China Poems* (1975); *Strains* (1982) ed. Wayne Kamin and Chip Dameron; *Salutes and Censures* (1988).

Consult: Kenneth Goodwin, *Understanding African Poetry: A Study of Ten Poets* (London, 1982).

BRYANT, Louise (Anna Louisa Mohan Bryant Trullinger Reed Bullitt). Born December 5, 1885, in San Francisco; died January 6, 1936, in Sères, France. Though famous mainly as the wife of John Reed, Bryant was an important journalist for the Left, known especially for her reports on Bolshevik Russia and her support of socialism and feminism. She first published poetry, reviews, and articles in small socialist papers in Greenwich Village, attracting attention with *The Game: A Morality Play* (1916), produced by the Provincetown Players. Eventually she became a war correspondent for the Hearst organization.

Six Months in Red Russia: An Observer's Account of Russia before and during the Proletarian Dictatorship (1918) is an anecdotal account of Bryant's experiences during the Bolshevik Revolution, a sympathetic description both of those exiled by the revolution and of those exiles who came into power. After Reed's death, Bryant wrote *Mirrors of Moscow* (1923), a collection of portraits of the leaders of the Soviet Union in the early 1920s. Her last publications were a series of articles on Mussolini and Kemal Pasha of Turkey.

In 1923 Bryant gave up professional writing soon after marrying William C. Bullitt, but the marriage ended in divorce, and Bryant died in poverty after a long bout with alcoholism, drug abuse, and Dercum's disease.

Consult: Virginia Gardner, *"Friend and Lover": The Life of Louise Bryant* (1982), contains bibliography of works by and about Bryant.

JAMES C. MCDONALD

BUBER, Martin. Born February 8, 1878, in Vienna, Austria; died June 13, 1965, in Jerusalem, Israel. Buber's early life reflects a number of displacements. Born in Austria, he moved when he was three years old to his grandfather's house in Lwov, then the capital of the Austrian province Galicia and today part of the Soviet Ukraine. In a spot of land contiguous to the cultural/historical borders of Poland, Austria, and Russia, Buber studied in a Polish secondary school. As a youth he studied in many places—in universities in Vienna, Leipzig, Zurich, and Berlin (Buber's disciplines were philosophy and art history). He taught Jewish theology and ethics at the University of Frankfurt am Main before emigrating to Palestine in 1938. He taught social philosophy at Jerusalem's Hebrew University and in later life traveled widely for lecture tours. Teaching at the Jewish Theological Seminary in New York, the College of Jewish Studies in Los Angeles, and at Columbia and Princeton universities, he become a familiar figure to American students.

Buber is recognized as one of the significant philosophical writers and thinkers of the twentieth century. Much of the groundwork of his ideas grows from his sense of diaspora. Buber's major ethic is community, the relationship of two selves of humanity—the I and thou—and the necessary communication between them. For Buber the consciousness of place, if place is defined in the context of a *being*-ful experience, is paramount to the sanity of humankind.

Buber wrote in German all his life.

BUKOVSKY, Vladimir. Born 1942, in the USSR; he lives in France. Bukovsky achieved world renown for his autobiography, *I vogoraschchaetsya veter* (Paris, 1978; *To Build a Castle*, 1979), on human rights abuses in the Soviet Union.

A courageous spirit who withstood psychological harassment and mistreatment while in confinement, Bukovsky managed to hold onto his sanity in the face of 1960s–1970s-style Soviet medicine. After his release from detention—in part achieved by worldwide protests from Amnesty International, PEN International, and other groups—he was allowed to emigrate to France. His recent volume, *Pacifisty protiv mira* (Paris, 1982; Pacifists Against Peace), posits the unsettling thesis that disarmament activists weaken safeguards against the spread of the Soviet empire. Bukovsky's book appeared several years before the events of 1989–90, in which most of Eastern Europe shed the Soviet presence harbored there since the beginning of the post-World War II era.

BUNIN, Ivan Alexeyevitch. Born October 10, 1870, in Voronezh, Russia; died November 8, 1953, in Paris, France. Poet, prose writer, memoirist, essayist, critic, and translator, Bunin descended from an aristocratic but impoverished family. At sixteen, he left school but continued his education under the guidance of his elder brother. He traveled extensively in Russia, writing fiction and poetry while working as journalist, librarian, and statistician. He published his first poem in 1887; his first book of poems, contemplative and elegiac in tone, appeared in 1891. In 1893 Bunin's first story, "Derevensky eshiz" (Country Sketch) was published; at that time he was influenced by the moral philosophy of Leo Tolstoy. In 1901 Moscow Decadent Publishing House "Scorpio" printed a collection of his poems, *Defoliation* (Listopad), which reflected moods of tentativeness, illusion, and twilight. Bunin's stories, which appeared in such periodicals as *Russian Wealth, New Word*, and *North* proved nostalgic and melancholic as well, with regret at the passing of Russian aristocratic modes.

The stories carried a prophetic feel of approaching social change and a desire to prolong the present before it became "fanciful, obscure, incomprehensible neither by mind, nor by heart, of what is called 'the past' " (in *The Golden Fall*, Moscow, 1901). In 1903 in Moscow Bunin was awarded the Pushkin Prize for poetry and for his translations from English of Henry Wadsworth Longfellow's "The Song of Hiawatha" and Lord Byron's *Manfred*. In 1909 he was nominated for membership in the Russian Imperial Academy.

His realistic novelette *Derevnja* (1910; *The Village*, 1923) brought him wide popularity. His novelette *Suchodol* (1911; *The Dry Valley*, 1935), a chronicle of the fall of a gentry family Khrulyov and written in the manner of Ivan Turgenev, contains many autobiographical reminiscences. In 1911–12, Bunin wrote a series of "peasant stories" preceded by an epigraph by a Slavophile, Ivan Ajksakov; "The Ancient Russian did not yet pass away." Bunin's poems written during 1910–14 show evidence of folklore themes and motifs with an influence of aestheticism. Before and during World War I, Bunin traveled to Egypt, Palestine, Turkey, Greece, Italy, Ceylon, and elsewhere. The impressions that followed these wanderings are reflected in a new style for Bunin. His well-known story *"Gospodin iz San Frantsisko"* (1915; "The Gentlemen from San Francisco," 1923) demonstrates his skillful handling of details treating the themes of vanity and death, themes which will become prevalent, along with the power of love, in his new work. Although these themes are never the subject of overt speculation, their pervasive demands shape the structure and texture of Bunin's prose, as in the *Grammar of Love* (1915, trans. 1953) and the *Light Breathing* (1916, trans. 1933).

Although Bunin remained in Russia after the Bolshevik Revolution, he found himself increasingly at odds with the government and fled to the Balkans in February 1920, and later to France. He lived in exile for thirty-three years. During this time he wrote what many consider his best works of prose. He published a novella, *Mitina Lynbov* (1925, Mitya's Love), and the *Life of Arsenyeva*, an autobiographical novel consisting of two volumes, the *Well of Days* (1927–29) and *Lika* (1933). One critic wrote that Bunin "reached his full artistic flourishing only in emigration—he became rejuvenated, and steadier inwardly in his reactions to the Bolshevik revolution, refusing to consider himself defeated, turning from what is temporary and transient to that which escapes the boundaries of time and death."

Bunin considered himself a follower of Gustave Flaubert in prose and of the Parnassians in his poetry. He developed a rare equilibrium of form and content, image and logic in his writing. He fought against what he considered a hypertrophy of lyricism and sentimentality, being at the same time profoundly sensitive to the condition of suffering. His reputation as a stylist is based on the unique correspondence in his work between words and themes, feeling and thought. In spite of an inherent and prevalent tragic view, Bunin turned his prose into an acceptance of humanity by the transforming power of art. The union of sorrow and exaltation produced that interrogative, rapturous, mournful-joyful tone that allowed some critics to define his style as a "tragic major." His last prose work was *Tyomnye Aller* (1943; *The Dark Alleys*, 1946), a collection of thirty-eight love stories, in which love is presented as the "unexplainable divine and devilish phenomenon" (Bunin); Bunin considered it his best-written work, in the sense "of preciseness, verve, and literary artistry."

As memoirist and publicist, Bunin had a sober and merciless pen. His diary, *Cursed Days* (1925–26), and his *Memoirs and Portraits* (1951) contain sharp and ironic characterizations of contemporaries, providing valuable firsthand testimony in subjective chronicles of his times; the diary, additions to which were published posthumously in 1973, 1974, and 1977, also reflects his fierce opposition to Bolshevik policies. Bunin interpreted the Russian Revolution as an archetypal confrontation between Abel and Cain, and in his words, he could not forgive "the Russian Cain."

Bunin became a major influence on the "villagers"/Narodniki Populists (*dereventshikov*), a group of Socialist Realist writers who treated *kolkhos* village life in the Soviet Union, when his collection of stories about Russian peasant life, *The Village*, appeared in 1923.

Bunin received the Nobel Prize for Literature in 1933. In 1960 and after, some of Bunin's books were designated official Soviet literature.

Selected Title: *Sobranie sochinenu*, 9 vols., (Moscow, 1965–67, Works).

Consult: Victor Terras, *Handbook of Russian Literature* (1985); James B. Woodward, *Ivan Bunin: A Study of His Fiction* (1980).

ARKADY ROVNER

BURGESS, Anthony (pseudonym of John Anthony Burgess Wilson). Born February 25, 1917, in Manchester, England. He is a legal resident of Monte Carlo, Monaco, and travels extensively throughout the world. Raised as an Irish Catholic in a Protestant country, Burgess felt alienated in his English homeland. By the time he came to publish his first novel in 1956 at the age of thirty-nine, he had long since ceased practice of his Catholicism, although its doctrines have continued to influence his books. After service in the army (1940–44), he worked in various education posts in Birmingham, Preston, and Oxfordshire until low pay caused him to seek employment in the civil service in Malaya. During this self-imposed exile, Burgess published *Time for a Tiger* (1956), which was later included in a trilogy with *The Enemy in the Blanket* (1958) and *Beds in the East* (1959).

Moving to Borneo in 1957, Burgess wrote two more novels, *The Right to an Answer* and *Devil of a State*, before he was diagnosed as having a brain tumor and recalled to England in 1959. He has speculated that the diagnosis was false, an attempt to get him away from revolutionary friends among the natives. Moreover, the early novels were critical of colonialism and may have made the civil service uneasy. The hero of *Time for a Tiger*, accused of communist sympathies, loses his headmaster position. The second volume of the trilogy brings the hero up against antigovernment terrorists, and the final volume concludes with independence for the country. *Devil of a State* moves on various levels of rebellion: against paternal authority, against religious strictures, against the British Empire.

Having returned to England, Burgess, thinking he had but one year to live, wrote furiously in order to leave money for his ailing wife. The novels completed by 1960 were published under his own name and a pseudonym (Joseph Kell) at the insistence of the publisher, who decided no one author could generate sales for five novels in one year. *A Clockwork Orange*, Burgess's most famous novel, appeared in 1962, and its film version, directed by Stanley Kubrick, brought Burgess to international attention in 1971. Its hero lives in a kind of suspended decadence, neither totally present nor totally future. He is in the ultimate exile, at odds with a society that discovers a method to manipulate his evil. Finally, he is allowed to return to his own control, once the government understands that an individual's freedom to choose evil is more valuable than his being programmed to do good.

In 1968 Burgess decided to leave England. His wife, Llewella, having died, he married his mistress, Liliana Marcellari, and, with their four-year-old son, moved to Malta. England, he claimed, had become impossible to inhabit because of the high taxes required to support a welfare state. Forced to leave Malta for speaking out against the government, Burgess settled in Italy, first in Bracciano, then in Rome, Siena, Montalbuccio, Eze, and Callian. Between 1969 and 1973, he taught in the United States at Chapel Hill (University of North Carolina), Princeton, Columbia, and City College in New York. In 1975 Burgess and his family moved to Monte Carlo, Monaco, where he continues to write.

Exile continues to emerge as a major theme in recent books. The hero of *MF* (1971) is a type of sixties' protester who is thrown out of college for public fornication and heads for the Caribbean island of Castita where he almost marries his own sister. *Napoleon Symphony* (1974) culminates with the emperor's exile on the island of St. Helena, where he languishes and finally dies of liver complications. In *The Clockwork Testament or Enderby's End* (1975), Burgess brings his poet Enderby (who had appeared in two novels in 1963) from England to New York City, where, while working as a visiting professor of creative writing at the University of Manhattan, he is killed. The transplantation across the ocean is not unlike Burgess's own American transplantation and academic career in the early seventies. *Abba Abba* (1977) chronicles John Keats's death in a foreign land. *Earthly Powers* (1980) concerns the self-imposed exile of a homosexual who leaves England to avoid a scandal. The hero wanders to Paris, Malaya, Chicago, Berlin, and New York before returning to England to live a quiet life with his sister. The novel mirrors in a sense Burgess's belief that no Englishman can live in England until it is time to die. Burgess has also dabbled in historical fiction. A life of Christ, *Man of Nazareth* (1979), was used as the basis of the television production "Jesus of Nazareth." *Moses* (1976) retells the story of the biblical figure in loose blank verse.

In the past decade, Burgess has continued to publish at least one book per year. *Enderby's Dark Lady* (1984) was written "to placate kind readers of *The Clockwork Testament or Enderby's End*, who objected to my casually killing my hero," as Burgess notes on the title page of the novel. It brings to four the number of Enderby novels. The first part of Burgess's autobiography, *Little Wilson and Big God*, appeared in 1986. It covers his life to the age of forty-two. A second volume is called *You've Had Your Times, Being the Second Part of the Confessions of Anthony Burgess* (London, 1990). Other nonfiction includes *Flame into Being: The Life and Work of D. H. Lawrence* (1985) and *But Do Blondes Prefer Gentlemen?* (1986). The latter volume reprints one-third of Burgess's journalistic output for the years 1978–85 from the *Times Literary Supplement*, the *New York Times*, and the *Observer*. The essays concern women, travel, language, film and literature. More recent works include *The Kingdom of the World* (1985); *The Pianoplayers* (1986); and *Any Old Iron* (1988). Burgess published a new collection of stories, *The Devil's Mode*, in 1989 and co-wrote a dramatization of his *A Clockwork Orange*, which was produced in London in 1990.

Consult: Samuel Coale, *Anthony Burgess* (1981); Paul W. Boytinck, *Anthony Burgess: An Annotated Bibliography* (1985).

GEORGE KLAWITTER

BURROUGHS, William S. Born February 15, 1914, in St. Louis, Missouri; he has returned to the United States. Burroughs, a scion of the wealthy Burroughs adding machine family, traveled widely in Europe after his graduation from Harvard. The accident in 1951 in Mexico in which he shot and killed his wife, Joan Vollmer Adams, led to his expatriation to Tangier, where he is said to have taken up residence in a male brothel. (Burroughs is bisexual, and during this troubled period had many male lovers and unhappy affairs.) From Tangier he went to South America in search of a final fix, the right amount of drugs that would either kill or raise him to euphoric heights. He completed his famous novel *Naked Lunch* in Paris in 1959; later he lived in London, where he was cured of his drug habit. He moved back to Tangier in the 1960s and was part of the coterie that included Jane Bowles,* Paul Bowles,* and Alfred Chester.*

Burroughs is another kind of expatriate from the American writers who went to Paris in the 1920s. His is the odyssey of a man in demonic pursuit of a vision of wholeness through the illusionary eye of the needle of drugs; his Promethean bout with the demigods of his raging guilt and incessant moral necessities provoked him into writing some of the finest descriptions of the hell in which moral outcasts and self-appointed lepers live, and to become an enormous influence on the Beat literary movement in the United States. Burroughs is more rightly to be placed beside Charles Baudelaire and Arthur Rimbaud in their search for sensation as a means to depth of feeling than he is to be associated with European culture-seekers like Ernest Hemingway, Scott Fitzgerald, or Henry Miller.*

Burroughs's *Naked Lunch,* written in exile, is one of the significant works of his generation. Along with Allen Ginsberg's *Howl*, it signified a depth of alienation and anxiety of the aware artist and his desperate clutching at drugs or fantasy as a restorative of vision. Using both fantastic allusion and a cutup method of writing, which if he did not invent he perpetuated, Burroughs created a world in which the primal scream demanded to be heard. The naked lunch in Burroughs's imagery becomes the bare truth of want, loss, and sexual frenzy and drug-induced euphoria as disguise of such truths. The disguise is rendered in a series of cutups, placements of seemingly random but in some way fated coming together, which at some point produce a startling illumination of insight.

Burroughs's work has become conventional with time, just as his revolutionary techniques have been more widely practiced by other writers. His work emanates from a philosophic decision to explore drugs to the point of no return but to survive the experience before the last Faustian gasp. Burroughs seems to have passed through this rationale of drug experience and to have entered a new phase in which he writes more conventionally ordered stories in terms of both technique and content.

Selected Titles: *The Soft Machine* (1966); *The Ticket That Exploded* (1967); *Nova Express* (1981); trilogy: *Cities of the Red Night* (1981); *Place of Dead Roads* (1985); *The Western Lands* (1988).

Consult: Ted Morgan, *Literary Outlaw: The Life and Times of William S. Burroughs* (1989); Jennie Skerl, *William Burroughs* (1985).

C ———————————

CABRERA INFANTE, Guillermo. Born April 22, 1929, in Gibara, Cuba, Cabrera Infante now lives in London and describes himself as ''the only English writer who writes in Spanish.'' Though a prolific author, he has won an international reputation mainly through his two long novels, *Three Trapped Tigers* (1964; English, 1971) and *Infante's Inferno* (1979; English, 1984).

Cabrera Infante attended the University of Havana's School of Journalism and in the 1950s wrote film reviews and essays and translated Mark Twain, William Faulkner, Ernest Hemingway, James Joyce, and others into Spanish. He published a collection of short stories about Fulgencio Batista's Cuba in 1960 and supported the new government of Fidel Castro. He was named editor of *Lunes*, the literary magazine of the Revolution, but was fired when he and others protested the government's banning of a documentary film about Havana nightlife. He was posted to the Cuban embassy in Brussels as a cultural attaché, a job he describes as little more than that of a porter but one that allowed him time to write.

In 1964 his novel *Three Trapped Tigers* (English, 1971) won the prestigious Biblioteca Breve prize, but was not well received in Cuba, even occasioning a controversy which revolved around Cabrera Infante's praise for poet Heberto Padilla. The next year, Cabrera Infante returned to Havana for his mother's funeral; he found Cuba further changed under Castro's repressive measures and his own book banned. He left, never to return, and settled in London. His physical exile predates his definitive self-exile in 1965 and could justify regarding *Three Trapped Tigers* as a novel written in exile.

Three Trapped Tigers is not, however, openly political: it merely re-creates the adventures of three young men in Havana in 1959 on the eve of Castro's coup. It never comments directly on the politics of its moment, but instead depicts the high energies of its characters as they enjoy Havana, women, music, literature, and talk—mostly talk. "It is a political novel, because it is a-political," Cabrera Infante has explained. Not merely banned, but "considered anathema" in Cuba, it celebrates its characters' individuality. "There isn't a more apolitical novel in the whole history of Latin American literature. Perhaps that is the reason and unreason of this prohibition: all freedom is subversive. Totalitarian regimes are more afraid of individual liberty than vampires are of crosses" (*Seven Voices*).

Cabrera Infante's style is often identified with a profusion of puns and literary allusions and with parody; in fact, in a mock-chronology of his life, he adopts a parody of Stephen Dedalus's credo: "insolence, exi(s)le(s), and punning" (*Review*, 30). Even the style may be considered an exile's political strategy; Carlos Fuentes* has described the style of *Three Trapped Tigers* as a search for a new language that will capture the complexity of contemporary realities and form an authentically revolutionary literature. With the openness and plurality of meanings and the verbal slapstick of punning, art is desacralized; Cabrera Infante exposes all the "academic pachyderms" of a senescent world whose "canonical, medieval, and heirarchical" explanations are incapable of expressing the multivocal disorder of real life and genuine fiction (*La Nueva Novela Hispanoamericana*).

Infante's Inferno (1984) begins in 1941 with the relocation of the then twelve-year-old and his communist parents from Oriente to a tenement in central Havana and follows his sexual "ventures, adventures, and misadventures" into the 1950s. The novel recaptures the texture and detail of Batista's Cuba: an erotic, violent, decadent world of poverty, prostitutes, pederasts, and pimps; but above all, for the young narrator, Havana is a city of movie theaters. Its life teems with the color, energy, eccentricity, and vitality of a large metropolis which, though it may have no real culture of its own, offers the freedom of youth's attempt to imagine one or escape into the erotic and exotic fantasies of Hollywood films. Again, Cabrera Infante recreates but does not glorify Old Havana and never directly or specifically engages the political, but the narrator clearly enjoys the liberty of inventing himself and pursuing his pleasures. Again, parody, puns, and allusions form a bawdy and dense fabric of ironies and associations, but here they are more controlled because the adolescent narrator has replaced the more experimental use of many voices in *Three Trapped Tigers*.

Memory is itself a political instrument, a resistance to the forces of oblivion; in fiction the reconstruction of the past becomes the exile's imperative. In contrast, Cabrera Infante has openly and vigorously denounced the Castro regime in essays and interviews and sees himself as more of a true exile than other Latin American writers (such as Julio Cortázar, Carlos Fuentes, Gabriel García Márquez*) who continue to sympathize with the Cuban Revolution.

Cabrera Infante's recent work, *Holy Smoke* (1986), is his first book written in English. An irreverent look at the growth and industry of tobacco (Cabrera Infante says he is a lover of lost causes), it contains the author's usual display of puns; the change in language has not affected Cabrera Infante's sense of humor. Cabrera Infante has become a naturalized British citizen.

Selected Titles: *Vista del amancer en el tropico* (1974; *A View of Dawn in the Tropics*, 1978); *O.* (Barcelona, 1975); *Exorcismos de Estilo* (Barcelona, 1976; 2nd ed., 1982); *Asi en la paz como en la guerra* (Bogotá, 1987).

Interviews and Essays: Rita Guibert, *Seven Voices* (1973); "Bites from the Bearded Crocodile," *London Review of Books*, June 1981; "El exilio invisibile," *El Herald* (Miami, Florida), April 7, 1982.

Consult: Carlos Fuentes, *La nueva novela hispanoamericana* (Mexico City, 1969); David Gallagher, *Modern Latin American Literature* (1973); Seymour Martin, *Prose Fiction of the Cuban Revolution* (1975); Raymond D. Souza, *Major Cuban Novelists* (1976).

DONALD GWYNN WATSON

CAI Qi-jiao. Born 1918 in Fujian, China. In 1926, Cai emigrated with his parents to Indonesia, returning to China by himself at age eleven to attend school in Fujian. After high school, he went home to Indonesia, returned to China again in 1938, and later walked with friends from Wuhan to Yenan. He worked among soldiers in the New Fourth Army, then entered Lu Hsun Arts Academy, where he studied literature. He began to teach in 1940 and to write poetry in 1941. When the novelist Ting Ling founded the Central Literature Training Institute in 1952, he headed its teaching research office of foreign literature.

His seven collections of poetry include three published during the Hundred Flowers and Anti-Rightist era of 1957–58: *Echo, The Sound of Waves*, and *A Further Collection to Echo*. At that time he was criticized for writing mainly about scenery, people, and love, with too little regard for Party political ideology. His prolific publication since the Cultural Revolution includes the poetry collections *Prayer, Songs of Life, Facing the Wind*, and *The Drunken Stone*. Recently he has been working at the Fujian Federation of Literary and Arts Circles.

EDWARD A. MORIN

CALLAGHAN, Morley. Born February 22, 1903, in Toronto, Canada; died August 25, 1990, in Toronto. Callaghan spent only one year (1928–29) in Paris but is identified as an expatriate his associations there and his notorious acquaintanceship with Ernest Hemingway, an association that thrived on boxing and either Hemingway's knockout punch or Callaghan's lighter-weight victory over machismo, depending on which writer's ring a reader chooses to enter. Although the story is frequently repeated, Callaghan never knocked out Hemingway in the boxing ring. The two did box together in Paris, during the heady year before the stock market crash of 1929, but had become friends long before, while both were reporters for the Toronto *Star*. Callaghan joined the expatriate crowd in Paris on the strength of his early stories and first novel, *Strange Fugitive* (1928); he recounted his experiences abroad in *That Summer in Paris* (1963), one of his few works set outside North America (only one of his novels, *A Passion in Rome*, published in 1961, is set outside Canada).

That Summer in Paris is clearly a corrective vision. Callaghan describes the Paris expatriates long after the fact, as a survivor of the social turmoil, self-destruction, and moral giddiness that engulfed them. He elicits Paris in the terms it conveyed for expatriates in general: "what it offered to us was what it had offered to men from other countries for hundreds of years; it was a lighted place where the imagination was free." Yet his memoir is curiously mannered. If Callaghan's later fiction generated energy from the disjunctions between the forces of determinism and the consolations of transcendent morality, the roots of that vision are evident in *That Summer in Paris* as an inability to be touched, and as sharp contrasts between the commentator and his subjects. *That Summer in Paris* is essentially an allegory, presenting personalities in the forms of various temptations, from the body of Kiki to the spirit of Marcel Proust, towards which the narrator remains solid, controlled, and nearly disengaged. To remain in Paris, Callaghan says, would have required immersion in its life; his rejection of that initiation and his return to Canada in 1929 reinforce the detachment evident in his work from the outset of his career.

Selected Titles: *It's Never Over* (1930); *Morley Callaghan's Stories* (1959); *A Fine and Private Place* (1975); *Close to the Sun Again* (1977); *The Lost and Found Stories of Morley Callaghan* (Toronto, Exile Editions, 1985); *O Wild Man on the Road* (Toronto, 1988).

Consult: Victor Hoar, *Morley Callaghan* (1969); P. Morley, *Morley Callaghan* (1978); Edmund Wilson, *O Canada* (1964); George Woodcock, *A Choice of Critics* (1966).

JOHN SCHECKTER and MARTIN TUCKER

CALVINO, Italo. Born 1923, Santiago de las Vegas, Cuba; he died 1988, in Rome, Italy. Calvino was a partisan in exile, fighting in Piedmont, far from his native habitat of Rome. All his works were published after his experience of the devastation of war. He lived in France for more than 15 years as a publishing executive and may be viewed as an expatriate by virtue of career.

Consult: Lucia Re, *Calvino and the Age of Neorealism: Fables of Estrangement* (1990).

CAMARA LAYE. *See* LAYE, Camara

CAMPBELL, Roy. Born October 2, 1901, in Durban, South Africa; he died April 23, 1957, in an automobile accident near Setubal, Portugal. He was on his way home from a vacation with his family in Spain. Campbell left South Africa for England after graduation from Durban High School and after serving in the South African army during World War I. He attended Oxford University in 1919 but did not complete his degree. He married Mary Garman in 1922. In 1924, with the publication of *The Flaming Terrapin*, he became an instant celebrity as the first South African poet of international fame. He returned to

South Africa in 1924; the following year he founded the literary journal *Voorslag*, with William Plomer* and Laurens van der Post* (the journal made its premier appearance in 1926). He returned to England in 1927 after both Plomer and van der Post had left South Africa and *Voorslag* ended its brief but important life. He produced his first satire of literary life, *The Wayzgoose* (1928), this time directed against the South African establishment; after the brouhaha over this volume Campbell moved to Provence and southern France. In 1930 he published his extraordinary volume of lyrics and satires, *Adamastor*; in 1931 he published his second satire, *The Georgiad*, this time scoring the literary establishment in England as effete, weary, and overintellectualized. In 1932 Campbell moved to Spain, where in the words of Alan Paton, another South African writer, Campbell gave "his heart to the Spanish people, the Roman Catholic church, and finally to General Franco." He became a convert to Catholicism in 1935, but in 1936 returned briefly to England before moving again in 1937 to Spain, and later that year settling in Portugal. He volunteered to fight with the British Armed Forces during World War II (he was stationed mainly in Kenya), and after the war worked as a BBC producer and moderator for three years. In 1952 he moved back to Portugal in a display of flagrant farewell; in his last years he idealized Portugal as a source of primitive, traditional loyalties and strengths. Ever the isolate, daring fighter, he remained committed to his ideal of the flaming terrapin, the crusading knight, the irredeemable literary outcast fighting his lonely battle against a horde of compromisers.

Campbell may be viewed as a double exile, first in leaving South Africa, where he was, at the time, opposed to the prevailing Afrikaner doctrine of white supremacy; significantly, he later championed such a racist program when he was in exile from the land about which he was writing. Campbell's various departures from England become another example of his instinctive drive to play the glittering toreador taunting the vulgar crowd and/or a devitalized establishment. He insisted, for whatever personal reason and/or philosophic necessity, on alienating those who had helped him and on defending fascism, militarism, and violence. In 1936 he issued his attack on left-wingers in his book of poems, *Mithriac Emblems*. In 1939 he antagonized the entire literary world and practically every humanist in England with his volume of verse in defense of Franco, *Flowering Rifle*. After the war, when he had accepted life in Britain for three years and been accepted as the extraordinary poet he was, he again drew notoriety to himself with the publication of his autobiography *Light on a Dark Horse* (1951, a reworking of an earlier autobiography, *Broken Record*). Alan Paton in his collection of short writings, *Knocking On Any Door*, says that Campbell saw himself in his autobiographies as "the flail, the scorpion, the lash" who had to chastize mediocrity in life and in poetry. Paton writes:

Campbell totally misunderstood the real meaning of Fascism and Hitlerism, and saw true modernity working in them. This he was later to regret, but I could not go so far as to say he repented . . . . He called Calvin and Luther crooks, and thought his praise of

Afrikanerdom would be appreciated by the Afrikaners, who were Calvinist almost to a man. He despised Jews and Quakers. He thought that the killing of bulls should be reserved for the aristocrats of mankind, the people whom he called equestrian. He despised democracy, egalitarianism and any kind of socialism. He defended the virtues of illiteracy—he whose own literacy had opened to him so many doors. His hatred of communism and the Communists amounted to a mania. He boasted of his own exploits, the kind that befitted a man.

Paton sums up the enigma of Campbell in these concluding words: "We must leave the mystery there, of how so sensitive a poet could write so foolishly, so aggressively, about the affairs of mankind." Campbell remained forever his own man, and inevitably drew further into his self-exile from his English and South African contemporaries. His last years were spent mainly in translating, from the Spanish, works of deep religious instinct and feeling.

Selected Titles: *Talking Bronco* (1946); *Portugal* (1957); *Selected Poems* (1982); *Collected Works*, 4 vols. (Craighall, South Africa, 1985–86).

Consult: Alan Paton, "Roy Campbell," in *Knocking on the Door: Shorter Writings* [of Alan Paton], ed. Colin Gardner (1975); John Povey, *Roy Campbell* (1977); Rowland Smith, *Lyric and Polemic: The Literary Personality of Roy Campbell* (1972); David Wright, *Roy Campbell* (1961).

CANETTI, Elias. Born July 25, 1905, in Rustschuk, Bulgaria; he lives in Zurich, Switzerland. A wanderer rather than a refugee, though uprooted from his homeland; a scholar and commentator on the human condition rather than a chronicler or entertainer; a British citizen by choice who writes in German, remaining spiritually a European (above all, Viennese), Canetti does not fit readily into accepted literary categories. The award of the Nobel Prize in 1981 acknowledged his eccentric but incontestable distinction. In boyhood he had spoken the antiquated Spanish of the Sephardic Jews while also learning German from his mother. Bulgaria left little trace on his work, though a short story, "Der Mordanschlag" (The Murder Attempt), conveys the Danubian background and, significantly, introduces an Armenian refugee from Istanbul. Canetti first visited England when only six but was educated mainly in Zurich and Vienna, where he studied chemistry. Abandoning Austria in 1938, he lived first in France, then England. London and Zurich have since become his chosen cities.

Canetti had little success with his early play *Hochzeit* (1932, Wedding), though the later *Die Befristeten*, which examines the fear of death, was performed in London as *The Numbered* in 1956. His reputation as a writer of fiction rests on his singular and solitary novel, *Die Blendung* (1935), published in English as *Auto da Fé* in 1946; the translation by the historian C. V. Wedgwood was made "under the personal supervision of the author." This formidable extravaganza is stamped with the dynamism of youth. The claustrophobic atmosphere owes much to Franz Kafka.* Scenes of low life in Vienna, with their grotesque characters, are painted with a remorseless eye for repellent detail. The hero, Dr. Peter Kien, a renowned sinologist, is portrayed as a second Leibnitz and "the

Jacob Burckhardt of eastern cultures," a pointer to Canetti's own interest in Chinese philosophy. Obsessively preoccupied with his library, Kien becomes increasingly paranoid, regarding his books as the last stockade against womankind; misogynism is indeed shown as a bond between men who otherwise have little in common. Kien's willed petrifaction and self-diminution are typically Kafkaesque; but his ultimate self-immolation amid his blazing library is also a comment on the book-burning rites of the Nazis. *Auto da Fé* beguiles the reader with its blend of the realistic and the fantastical, achieving in its climaxes a Gothic bleakness of vision spiced with black humor. The work is also a philosophical novel that probes the social dilemmas of our time and includes authorial reflections on that "huge, wild, full-blooded warm animal in all of us." Contending that we ignore this animal, a symbol of man's lower gregarious instincts, at our peril, Canetti set himself the task of exploring the phenomenon in depth in his unique treatise *Masse und Macht* (1960; *Crowds and Power*, 1962). His approach combines data gleaned from wide research in the fields of sociology, psychology, philosophy, and anthropology and is notable for many unusual insights. The tone is markedly didactic. Much of what Canetti here reports may seem axiomatic, but the thrust of his argument is always toward important and often original conclusions. In the present context his analysis of "the flight crowd" is particularly suggestive. Though *Crowds and Power* covers a much broader spectrum, it clarifies many of the forces that have shaped literature of exile. The book ends with a paradox: the survivor, usually presented as a hero, may, it is argued, become a threat to mankind, since the urge to survive might trigger a nuclear war. Both Canetti's major works convey disturbing messages for an age characterized by fear and indifference. In temper and inspiration they belong to the disintegrating world not only of Kafka but of Robert Musil* and Karl Kraus.

Selected Titles: *Die Stimmen von Marrakesch* (1968; *Voices of Marrakesh*, London, 1978); *Der andere Prozess* (1969; *Kafka's Other Trial: The Letters to Felice*, London, 1974); *Die Provinz des Menschen* (1973; *The Human Province*, London, 1985); *Die gerettete Zunge* (1977, The Tongue Set Free); *Die Fackel im Ohr* (1980; *The Torch in the Ear*, 1982); *The Conscience of Words* (London, 1986); *Das Augenspiel: Lebensgedichte 1931–1937* (Munich, 1985); *The Secret Heart of the Clock* (1989); *The Play of the Eyes* (London, 1990).

Consult: Dagmar Barnouw, *Elias Canetti* (Stuttgart, West Germany, 1979); Yaier Cohen, "Elias Canetti: Exile and the German Language" in *German Life and Letters*, vol.17 (Oxford, 1988–89); Idris Parry, "Elias Canetti's Novel *Die Blendung*," in *Essays in German Literature*, vol. 1 (London Institute of Germanic Studies, 1965).

CEDRIC HENTSCHEL

CAREW, Jan. Born September 24, 1925, in Agricola, Guyana (then British Guiana); he lives in Evanston, Illinois, and teaches at Northwestern University and Princeton University. Kwame Dawes, in *Fifty Caribbean Writers*, writes:

His travels, starting at age nineteen, began what was to become a life of "endless journeyings" and searching for Jan Carew. He has visited five continents: North and

South America, Europe, Asia and Africa. While in Africa he lived for a few years in Ghana, where he did some writing. . . . In 1962 he moved to Jamaica with his wife, novelist Sylvia Wynter, and lived there until 1969. He then returned to the West Indies. . . . Carew's journeys have enhanced his work significantly.

Selected Titles: *Black Midas* (London, 1958); *The Last Barbarian* (London, 1960); *Moscow Is Not My Mecca* (London, 1964; *A Green Winter*, 1965); *Save the Last Dance for Me* (1976; stories); *The Twins of Llora* (1977).

Consult: Wilfred Cartey, "The Rhythm of Society and Landscape: Mittelhlzer, Carew, Williams, Dathorne," *New World* (Guyana Independence Issue) (1966); Hena Maes-Jelinek, "The Myth of El Dorado in the Caribbean Novel," *Journal of Commonwealth Literature* 6 (June 1971).

CARPENTIER, Alejo. Born December 26, 1904, in Havana, Cuba; died April 24, 1980 in Paris, France. Carpentier was born of a Russian mother and French father two years after his parents settled on the island. He spent his life writing novels set in Latin America and the Caribbean and in which he explored the theme of Latin American identity. He may be said to be an ironic case of dislocation—a child who wished himself a Caribbean native but who, because of his ethnic heritage, felt outside the pale of Cuban nativeness. Perhaps in reaction, Carpentier began his literary career as a passionate Afro-Cuban poet-participant in cultural nationalism movements.

Carpentier left Cuba in the early 1930s on a forged passport (unknowingly supplied by a visiting friend) and traveled to Europe, where he joined various groups of Latin American expatriate writers in France and Spain. For some critics he provides a rare corner of the prism of ethnic exoticism; for others he is an opportunist who exploited his rarefied circumstances.

Selected Titles: ¡*Ecue-Yamba-O*! (1933); *El reino de este mundo* (1949; *The Kingdom of This World*, 1957); *El siglo de las luces* (1962; *The Century of Enlightenment*, 1963).

Consult: Roberto Gonzalez-Echevarria, *Alejo Carpentier: Bibliographical Guide* (1983, bilingual edition).

CARRINGTON, Leonora. Born 1917, Crookhey Hall, Lancaster, England; she lives in Mexico and travels to the United States frequently. Known both as writer and painter, Carrington has in recent years also been active as spokesperson on feminist issues. She left England in 1937 when she eloped with the painter Max Ernst (who left his wife for the event); she was nineteen, he was forty-one. Carrington and Ernst lived in Provence until the French government arrested Ernst as an enemy alien during the German invasion (Ernst had been living in France for seventeen years). Carrington was able to secure Ernst's release from a concentration camp, but he was rearrested. Carrington crossed the border with friends into Spain in 1940; she suffered a nervous breakdown and was locked up in a Lisbon (Portugal) asylum. She managed to survive the horrors of her incarceration and to arrive at a safe haven in the United States in 1942; she left for Mexico in 1943. Since the time of her refuge she has won international recognition for her surrealist, and postsurrealist, writings and paintings and frescoes. Two volumes of her stories and novellas were issued in 1989 in London, on which occasion David Gascoyne wrote in *Times Literary Supplement* (August 4–10, 1989, p. 856) that Carrington "has led a life of singular creativity, active as an artist, writer and feminist in New York and Chicago as well as Mexico." Gascoyne quoted Octavio Paz's "fitting" tribute to her: "Romantic heroines, beautiful and terrible . . . come back to life in women like Leonora Carrington."

Carrington's publications record is confusing. She often wrote her works in either English or French (and at least on one occasion in both languages); publication of the original version was often delayed, and a translation was instead published first. As outlined by Marina Warner, in her introduction to *The House of Fear* (1988), the history of *Down Under* is a case in point of the confusing chronology. The original English version of *Down Under* was rejected by Janet Flanner* for a New York publishing company. Carrington was encouraged by a French exile doctor, and member of the Surrealist circle in France, Pierre Mabille, to tell the story again in 1943, this time verbally in French while Mabille's wife wrote it down. This French version became the official text, and it was translated into English for publication in the February 1944 issue of *VVV*, the surrealist journal edited by David Hare in New York, two years before the French manuscript was published. Another example is Carrington's first novel, *Little Francis*, written in English in the south of France in 1937–38, but first published in a French translation, *Histoire du Petit Francis*, in 1986, and only in an English version in 1989.

Selected Titles: *The Hearing Trumpet* (1985); *The House of Fear: Notes from Down Below* (1989); *The Seventh Horse and Other Tales* (London, 1989).

Consult: Marina Warner, Introduction in *The House of Fear* (London, 1989; New York, 1990).

CASONA, Alejandro (pseudonym of Alejandro Rodriguez Alvarez). Born March 23, 1905, in Bessullo, Spain; died September 17, 1965, in Madrid, Spain. Casona left Spain in 1937. He toured Latin America, where his plays enjoyed a huge success. In 1939 he emigrated to Buenos Aires, Argentina. Casona returned to Spain in 1962, with the restoration of civil freedom there. A blend of fantasy and social observation, his plays (and his earlier poetry) contain pointed moral lessons. The son of a teacher, and an occasional teacher himself, Casona saw drama as a tool for moral education.

Selected Titles: *La dama del alba* (1944, The Lady of the Dawn); *La barca sin pescador* (1945, The Boat with No Fishermen); *Los arboles mueren de pie* (1949, Trees Die Upright).

Consult: Harold K. Moon, *Alejandro Casona, Playwright and Poet* (1970). See Arturo Sanchez-Rojas, "Bibliographia de Alejandro Casona," in *Boletin del Instituto de Estudios Asturianos* 27 (1972).

CASSIAN, Nina. Born November 27, 1924, in Galatz, on the Danube, Romania; she lives in New York City. One of Romania's leading poets, with over fifty books published during her lifetime, Cassian made her debut in 1947 with a volume of poems, *La scara 1/1* (Scale 1/1), which provoked three angry reviews in *The Spark*, the official Communist party newspaper. Critics accused Cassian of "bourgeois decadence and contempt for the people" because she had written of private emotions in an oblique and/or experimental way. Since 1947 Cassian has published a large number of books in differing styles, confusing her critics who look for labels; she has been called, variously, lyrical, cerebral, discursive, hermetic, and ludic. Parallel with her poetry writing, she has composed music and had a prolific career as a critic and reviewer of literature, music, visual arts, film, choreography, and the theater. Cassian witnessed the evolution of her country to increasing dogmatism and cultural repression, and she was often a target in critical attacks that served as public trials. She stopped writing poetry between 1954 and 1956, finally refusing to adjust to the language of socialist realism, and devoted herself instead to musical composition. When the Romanian "thaw" took place in 1956, she resumed her writing of poems with recuperative fervor, abandoning music for approximately seventeen years. Since 1973 her double career as writer and composer of music has continued without interruption. Her output includes sixteen individual collections of poems, six volumes of selected poems published with her own illustrations; many children's books, puppet plays, some musical compositions, and short stories. Of her works published in Romania, *De indurare* (Have Mercy) won the Bucharest Writers Union Award in 1982, and *Numaratoarea inversa* (Count Down) won the Bucharest Writers Union Award in 1983. Cassian has also published numerous translations into Romanian of Bertolt Brecht,* Vladimir Mayakovksy, Guillaume Apollinaire, Paul Celan,* Yannis Ritsos,* Jean Cocteau, Max Jacob, and Shakespeare.

Cassian, a Jew, married Vladimir Colin, a science fiction writer and fabulist in 1943; they were divorced in 1948, the year in which she married Al. I. Stefanescu, publisher, dramatist, and fiction writer. Stefanescu died in 1984, leaving her a widow after thirty-six years of marriage. In 1985 she came to the United States as an exchange professor in New York University's Graduate Writing Division. In 1986 she won a Fulbright grant, enabling her to stay in the country teaching at New York University. During her absence from Romania, one of her friends was arrested and tortured to death in prison; the government confiscated the friend's diary, which implicated Cassian in political protest by quoting Cassian's attitudes toward and sarcastic poems about the Romanian dictatorship. Out of fear of consequences Cassian elected to remain in the United States in exile.

Cassian is currently working on a journal (*Jurnalul unui jurnal*, Diary of a Diary) that covers the years 1948 to 1985 and integrates fragments from an original diary with commentary created approximately twenty-five years later. Not only is the diary valuable testimony to her own literary and musical creativity and relationships, but it serves as a survey of events relating to the cultural policies of her homeland over a span of forty years; her chronicle is recounted from the angles of both naive youth and mature lucidity. Living in exile allowed

Cassian to work on her memoirs without fear of reprisal from the Romanian government.

Cassian's musical compositions have been performed in Romania's major concert halls as well as in New York and Boston. Of her many books Cassian herself favors *Ambitus* (1969), poems of polemics and magical incantations, and *Confidente fictive* (1974, Fictive Collections), a collection of her stories told from a first-person viewpoint and dealing with individual dramas of failure and betrayed ideals.

Selected Titles: *Blue Apple* (1981); *Lady of Miracles* (1983). Cassian is featured in an anthology of Romanian poets in translation, *Silent Voices* (London, 1986); *Call Yourself Alive? The Love Poems of Nina Cassian* (1988); *Life Sentence: Selected Poems* (1990).

DANIELA GIOSEFFI

CASSIRER, Ernst. Born 1874 in Breslau, Silesia, Poland; died 1945 in Princeton, New Jersey. The eminent scholar and academic theorist arrived in England in 1933 as a political refugee. He moved to Sweden in 1935, and in 1940 reached the United States, where he taught for many years at Princeton University.

Selected Title: *The Myth of the State* (1946).

CAVAFY, Constantine P. Born April 17, 1863, in Alexandria, Egypt; died April 29, 1933, in Alexandria. Constantine Cavafy was the youngest of many children of Peter John and Chariclea Photiady, both of well-to-do families in Constantinople. Peter John migrated to Alexandria in 1850 to establish a commercial house dealing in grain and cotton. According to the poet's genealogy, Cavafy and Sons was one of the largest commercial houses of its kind in Egypt. Peter John set up branches of Cavafy and Sons in Liverpool, Manchester, and London, to handle the export of Egyptian cotton. Peter John was prominent in the religious and commercial life of the Greek Orthodox community in Alexandria.

Peter John died in 1870 when Constantine was seven, leaving "very little." Chariclea took her family to England, where they spent the next seven years in Liverpool and London. In 1879, the firm of Cavafy and Sons was dissolved, and Chariclea returned to Alexandria with six of her sons. George, the oldest, chose to remain in London. Chariclea now enrolled the sixteen-year-old Constantine in the Hermes Lyceum, a business school. In his genealogy Cavafy states that he was tutored at home in French and English.

In June 1882, an antiforeign, anti-Christian outbreak in Alexandria forced Chariclea and her sons to leave for Constantinople. There she stayed at the home of her father, a dealer in diamonds. Five sons returned to Alexandria, but Constantine and Chariclea spent the next three years in Constantinople. At the home of his grandfather, George Photiady, Cavafy came to know his maternal Phanariot forebears. Here he also continued his studies in Byzantine and Hellenic history and became interested in demotic Greek. In the manuscript notes of Rita Singopoulos, wife of the heir to Cavafy's poetry, we learn that Cavafy's "homo-sexuality began to manifest itself in Constantinople with his cousin George Psilliary in 1883" (Robert Liddell, *Cavafy* [1976], p. 45).

Chariclea and Constantine returned to Alexandria in 1885, and moved to a house on Rue Tewfik. Constantine found Alexandria oppressive. The prejudices of the Greek Orthodox community required him to hide his homosexual predi-lections. The testimony of Basil Athanassopoulos asserts that Cavafy "bribed the servant to ruffle up his bed on Rue Tewfik," to conceal his tracks from his mother, while he spent whole nights away from home. Some of his erotic poems, inspired by these nocturnal escapades, were among those Cavafy distributed in broadsheets to friends and a select group of writers, a procedure he continued throughout his life. Two of these are "I Went" (1913) and "He Swears" (1915). In the morning, realizing how low he had fallen at night, he repented; yet when night came again he went back to his "fatal joy," disregarding his oath.

Cavafy found it prudent not to show his friends all his erotic poems. Those that he regarded as too daring he kept in archives marked "not for publication, but may remain here." George Savidis discovered these erotic poems in Cavafy's archives in 1967, and had them published in Greek under the title *Anekdota Poiimata* (Unpublished Poems) in 1968.

Cavafy felt he was a sociocultural exile in the city where he was born. As late as 1907, when he was forty-four years old, he was ambivalent about spending the rest of his life in Alexandria. In a note discovered by George Savidis in Cavafy's archives, dated April 28, 1907, the poet wrote, "By now, I've gotten used to Alexandria and it's very likely that even if I were rich, I'd stay here. But in spite of this, how the place disturbs me. What trouble, what a burden small cities are—what lack of freedom. I'd stay here (then again I'm not entirely certain I'd stay) because it is like a native country for me, because it is related to my life's memories."

Cavafy decided to give voice to his own past homosexual passion by focusing on Hellenic motifs through historic characters. It was a "hedonistic doctrine through a historical perspective," in the words of critic Francis Golffing ("The Alexandrian Mind," *Partisan Review* [Winter 1955]: 76). "Theater of Sidon A.D. 400" (1923) and "Days of 1896" (1925) are two examples. Cavafy ca-tegorized his poems as "erotic, philosophical and historic." But he regarded himself as a historical poet. "I am a poet-historian. I could never write a novel or a play, but I feel inside me 125 voices telling me that I could write history." Cavafy finally found the way out of his isolation and sense of stagnation by drawing upon the whole Hellenic world with Alexandria as the focal point, and the Greek language as "the collective consciousness (and conscience) of civilized mankind" (Golffing, p. 78). But he cherished only those passages in history that aroused his sympathy and his compassion for those who had failed or were defeated. In "Alexandrian Kings" (1912), he focuses on the child Caesarian, son of Julius Caesar and Cleopatra who was assassinated in 30 B.C. by the Romans; in "The God Forsakes Antony" (1911), one of his finest poems, Cavafy feels compassion for Antony's loss of Alexandria; in "The Trojans" (1905), he relates the dirge of the Trojans to "the sad memories of our own days"; in "Expecting the Barbarians," his most mature poem, the poet muses on the inhabitants of an imaginary city who think they can find happiness by returning to the life of a primitive civilization; in "Che Fece . . . il gran rifuto" (written before 1911), Cavafy upholds the moral values of the great refusal. "In Cavafy," writes George Seferis, "there is a feeling of temporal identification. Past and present are united with them, perhaps the future as well" (*On the Greek Style* [1966], p. 140).

Examples of Cavafy's historical poems that blend "with an indissoluble mixture of feeling, learning and thinking" (Seferis, p. 40) are "Those Who Fought for the Achaean League," printed on February 2, 1922, on the eve of the catastrophe of Asia Minor; and "The Battle of Magnesia 190 B.C." (1916) in which Antiochus the Great, King of Syria from 223 to 187 B.C. was defeated by the Romans.

The last historical poem Cavafy wrote in the year of his death was "The Suburbs of Antioch" (1933).

Selected Titles: *Poimata* (Athens, 1952); *Anekdota Poimata* (1882–1923); *Complete Poems*, trans. and ed. Rae Dalven (1961).

Consult: Francis Golffing, "The Alexandrian Mind: Notes toward Definition," *Partisan Review* (Winter 1955): 73–83; Edmund Keeley, *Cavafy's Alexandria* (1976); Robert Liddell, *Cavafy, a Critical Biography* (1976); George Seferis, *On the Greek Style: Selected Essays in Poetry and Hellenism* (1966); Gregory Jusdanis, *The Poetics of Cavafy* (1987).

RAE DALVEN

CELAN, Paul (pseudonym of Paul Ancel, Antschel, or Anczel). Born November 23, 1920, in Chernovtsky, USSR (then Cernăuti, recently ceded to Romania and formerly, as Czernowitz, a part of the Austro-Hungarian Empire). Died May 1, 1970, of drowning in the Seine in Paris, presumably a suicide. Celan was born to a German and Yiddish-speaking Jewish family in the old imperial city in the Bukovina, shortly after it became part of Romania following World War I. Although his father was Orthodox, Celan attended Romanian schools, then went to France in 1938 to begin medical studies at Tours. He returned home the next summer to study Romance languages shortly before the Bukovina, and Czernowitz, became a part of Russia. He studied one more year, but in 1942 Czernowitz was occupied by Nazis and his family was ghettoized, deported, and then killed. Celan managed to escape, spent some time confined in a labor camp, then returned to Czernowitz (now Chernovtsky), which had again been occupied by the Russians in December 1943. He continued his university education there—in Russian—until 1945, when the war ended, and he left the Soviet Union for Bucharest, where he began his literary career in publishing and translating. It was here that his first poems were published, under the pseudonym of Paul Celan (an anagrammatic reconstruction).

In 1947 Celan made his way to Vienna, where he settled and in 1948 published a first collection of poems, *Der Sand aus den Urnen* (The Sand from the Urns), under the name of Paul Anczel. But he withdrew the collection and moved to Paris, where he undertook the study of German literature and, after he gained his license, taught German at the École Normale Supérieure and worked as a translator, notably of French and Russian poetry.

Celan lived in Paris for the remainder of his life. It was there that with *Mohn Und Gedächnis* (Poppy and memory, 1952) and his most famous poem, "Tödesfuge" (Fugue of Death), he gained recognition. With *Von Schwelle zu Schwelle* (From Threshold to Threshold, 1955), *Sprachgitter* (Language Grill, 1959), and *Die Niemandrsrose* (No Man's Rose, 1963), he built upon it to establish a reputation without peer as a lyricist in the German language. Celan wrote in German, the language of those for whom he sustained the most intense of his hatreds. In 1952 he began a sustained dispute with the widow of his benefactor, Yvan Goll,* the German-French poet. Mental illness, the product of his internment and various exiles, plagued him until his suicide in 1970.

As a writer Celan was almost defined by his experience of exile. His year in a forced labor camp of which he always avoided speaking lay somehow at the center of that experience. "Tödesfuge" is centrally concerned with the imposition of musical order upon that experience, and yet it was the very language of that poem, the "black milk" metaphor, which became the subject of the charges and countercharges of plagiarism in his dispute with Claire Goll.

Celan lived and wrote on the borders of language. His knowledge of Russian and French, the language in which he lived and studied, were inevitably conditioned by his knowledge of Romanian, the language of his schooling. His knowledge of German was similarly conditioned by Yiddish, which he spoke as a child and which imposed an awareness of an earlier German, that of the Middle Ages. Thus, Celan was constantly reminded of the tendency of language to enclose as much as to disclose meaning. He was a poet of neologisms, by which he escaped the restraints imposed by conventional German. Yet these word formations contain within them evidence of Celan's unceasing study of the etymologies of words. Michael Hamburger, one of Celan's translators, speaks of the problems encountered in translating a poem from *Atemwende* (1967) entitled "Einmal" (Once), and its verb formation, *ichten*, which, as Celan explained to him, is related to the personal pronoun "ich" (I) but was also formed with the Middle High German "iht" (aught) in mind.

In the 1950s and 1960s, as one might expect, Celan, an émigré living in Paris among such "pure" poets as Paul Éluard and René Char and deeply affected by the poetry of Rainer Maria Rilke* and as well by French surrealism, resisted "engagement" in political or ethical commitments and developed in the direction of the hermetic and the increasingly obscure. This movement, manifest in *Atemwende* (Breath Turn, 1967) and *Fadensonnen* (Sun Thread, 1968), and in the posthumous collections *Lichtzwang* (Light-farce, 1970) and *Schneepart* (Snow Share, 1971), was to alienate him from his poetic audience, who were increasingly engagé in the 1960s and 1970s. The hermeticism also fed in Celan an ironic distrust even in the very possibility for truth implicit in language itself. Certainly, in the beginning was no *logos* for Celan; he distrusted Christianity and its assumptions almost as much as he despised Germans and, as a Jew, was enthralled by the Holocaust. It was this distrust that led Celan, for all his linguistic awareness, to find order not in words, but only occasionally in music; it was his ironic awareness that seemed, especially in his late poems, to exile him from language, the very matter of poetry.

Celan had articulated this awareness as early as 1948, at the very beginning of his career as a poet, in *Edgar Jene: Der Traum von Traume* (Edgar Jene: The Dream of a Dream), in which he spoke of man, languishing in the chains of reality, gagged and unable to speak. It is this awareness, manifest throughout his work, that is at the center of Paul Celan's terrible and beautiful postwar— and profoundly postmodern—poetry, a poetry in exile from language itself.

Selected Titles: *Gedichte in 2 BD* (1975, Poems in two volumes); *Zeitgehoft* (1977, Time Farm).

Translations: *Speech-Grille and Selected Poems* (1971); *Prose Writings and Selected Poems* (1977); *Poems: A Bilingual Edition* (1980); *Last Poems: A Bilingual Edition* (1990, repr. of 1970 ed.).

Consult: Jerry Glenn, *Paul Celan* (1973).

MILNE HOLTON

CÉLINE, Louis-Ferdinand (pseudonym of Louis-Ferdinand Destouches). Born May 27, 1894, in Courbevoie, France; died July 4, 1961, in Meudon, France. Céline has been damned as a collaborator with the Germans during the French occupation period of 1940–44. A prominent doctor who rose from a humble background, he had served in the French army during World War I, worked in the French passport office in London after being demobilized for war wounds, and worked for a year in 1916 as a commercial agent in the Cameroons, West Africa. He received his medical degree in Rouen in 1924; he worked for the League of Nations, traveling to Switzerland, England, the Cameroons, Cuba, Canada, and the United States; he studied working conditions in the Ford factory in Detroit, Michigan. Céline began his writing at about the same time he established a private practice in the working-class Parisian suburb of Clichy in 1928.

With the exodus of German forces in 1944, Céline fled to Germany to escape execution by French Resistance partisans; in 1945 he moved to Denmark, where he had smuggled his savings. Denmark imprisoned him for a year on charges of collaboration with the Nazis; he was forced to remain in that country when France refused permission for him to reenter its borders. Exiled for six years, Céline returned to France in 1951 and spent the last ten years of his life in a Paris suburb, Meudon, where he practiced medicine and wrote fiction that many critics consider modern masterpieces. Embittered and impoverished, Céline poured all his gall onto pages describing the decadence of modern France, which in turn became a microcosm of the modern world for Céline.

Consult: Patrick McCarthy, *Céline* (1976).

CERNUDA, Luis. Born September 21, 1902, in Seville, Spain; died November 5, 1963, in Mexico City, Mexico, of a heart attack. Cernuda published in 1934 the first of four editions called *La Realidad y el deseo* (Reality and Desire). In each succeeding edition (1936; 1958; 1964) he revised earlier work and added new poems. Thus "Reality and Desire" in its evolution may be seen as Cernuda's autobiography, for in his poetry he revealed himself through veiled codes and recurrent images. Some critics—Derek Harris in particular—see in Cernuda's work a persistent flight from admission, and desire to admit, his homosexuality. The tension between his desire, whether expressed in yearning for physical consummation and emotional fulfillment, and his reality—his awareness of a world hostile, or at best condescending, to a sexual outsider—runs through his body of work and gives it a current of urgency. In his first book of poems, *Perfil del aire* (published as a supplement to the magazine *Litoral*, 1927), Cernuda revealed his adolescent vision of sentimental homoeroticism. When critics scoffed at his gifts—though they admitted his talent—Cernuda retreated into a poetic silence that lasted several years. He attempted to balance his wounded pride with, among other activities, political and social duties to the Spanish Republic. He was on a fund-raising mission in England for Republican forces when the Republican government surrendered to General Franco. Cernuda never returned to Spain. He became, first, a teacher in a school in Surrey, then in 1939 a university lecturer in Spanish at Glasgow University, Scotland, and in 1947 he moved to the United States to become a professor of Spanish at Mount Holyoke College. In 1952, after a vacation in Mexico, he settled there permanently, although he continued to teach at various times in California. Cernuda died, prophetically, of a heart attack at the age of sixty-one; he feared death at that age because of a family history in which most members had died at age sixty. He wrote his volume of poems *Desolacion de la Quimera* (Mexico City; The Disconsolate Chimera, poems written 1956–62) as a testament by which to be remembered.

In 1928, after the death of his widowed mother, Cernuda left Seville for a six-month stay in France, where he taught in Toulouse. He then worked in a bookstore in Madrid until the eruption of the Spanish Civil War. His first collection published in exile, *Les Nubes* (Buenos Aires; The Clouds, poems written 1937–40), contains little lament for the political situation, just as Cernuda wrote no direct political poetry during the Civil War. Instead, the familiar loneliness of the exile is felt in Cernuda's views of the Scottish landscape, the cold north of his refuge, and the contrasting pictures drawn from his memory of the Andalusian sun. Loneliness drove Cernuda further into a search for his own strengths, particularly as he became less reliant on Christian faith as a means of easing his pain. While not rejecting Christianity, he turned to poetry and its objectifying rituals as his new faith. One of his important volumes of poems arises out of this consciousness of self, *Como Quien Espera el Alba* (Buenos Aires, 1947; Like Someone Waiting for the Dawn, poems written 1941–44). Other volumes that draw on this chastened reserve are *Vinar sin Estar Viviendo*

(Buenos Aires, 1949; Living Without Being Alive, poems written 1944–49), begun in England and completed in Mount Holyoke, where Cernuda taught in 1947); and *Con Los Horas Contados* (Mexico City, 1956; With Time Running Out, poems written 1950–56).

Some biographers believe Cernuda had an intense love affair in Mexico in the summer of 1951, a physically satisfying affair in which Cernuda threw his furtiveness to the winds. The experience resulted in a spur of creative energy and romantic lyricism, reflected in a number of short poems and odes he wrote and collected in *Poemas Para Un Cuerpo* (Malaga, 1957; Poems for a Body).

Anthony Edkins and Derek Harris, the editors of the collected poems of Cernuda in the English version, *The Poetry of Luis Cernuda* (1971), write in their Preface that Cernuda was

obsessed by a dream of a perfect existence where reality and desire were one, where the division between self and world was obliterated, and he sought in a variety of ways to make this dream come true. This often gives to his poetry a strongly evasive character, since when faced with a reality hostile to his dreams he frequently attempted to retreat into his personal realm of desire rather than compromise the dream. But this is not a sign of an effete personality, that fragile ''man of glass'' several critics have tried to make of him. As the successive attempts to realize the dream failed one by one, he used the experience of failure to teach himself to come to terms with the gulf between that dream of a perfect existence and the imperfect reality in which he had to exist. He came finally to understand that the dream itself was merely a pretext, a vehicle for self-affirmation. (p. v)

Selected Titles: *Donde Habite El Olvido* (Madrid, 1934; Where Oblivion Dwells); *Invocaciones* (Madrid, 1934; Invocations); *La Realidad y el deseo*, 3rd rev. ed. (Mexico City, 1958), 4th ed. (Barcelona, 1964); *Perfil del aire, Con otras obras olvidadas inéditas, documentos y epistolario*, ed. Derek Harris (London, 1971); *Epistolario inédito*, ed. Fernando Ortiz, 1981.

Translation: *The Poetry of Luis Cernuda*, ed. Anthony Edkins and Derek Harris (1971).

Consult: Salvador Jiminez-Fajardo, ed., *The Word and the Mirror: Critical Essays on the Poetry of Luis Cernuda* (1989); Derek Harris, Introduction to *The Poetry of Luis Cernuda*, ed. Anthony Edkins and Derek Harris (1971).

CÉSAIRE, Aimé. Born 1913, in Martinique; he lives in Fort-de-France, Martinique. With Léopold Sédar Senghor* and Léon-Gontran Damas,* Césaire initiated the concept that bears the name *négritude*; he created the word in his novel *Cahier d'un retour au pays natal* (first published in *Volontés*, no. 20, 1939; definitive version in *Présence Africaine*, 1956; *Return to My Native Land*, 1971). *Négritude* —the name given to the consciousness of African identity: the totality and profundity of African essence—was born out of the meeting of three lonely students in Paris; they explored the consequences of the colonial experience that had shaken their national, cultural, and personal histories. Each became a master poet. Césaire also has written several distinguished plays, while

Senghor became the president of his country (Senegal) as well as the foremost Francophone poet of Africa.

Césaire went to France on a government scholarship when he was eighteen years old. He received a teaching degree in 1931. He became acquainted with the literary movements that were swirling in Paris at the time: surrealism, modernism, the American Negro Renaissance; he studied with the anthropologist Leo Frobenius, whose vision highlighted the achievement of African culture in precolonial history. Césaire wrote his first work, a poem-novel in free verse, in 1938; it appeared in journal form a year later, and created an underswell of literary current in Paris that reached a wave of public attention in 1947 when it was reprinted with an introduction by André Breton.* Césaire's writings, and his distinguished career as a politician-statesman, follow his expatriate period (he returned to Martinique soon after receiving his teaching degree), but the expatriate experience informs all of his work. His early announced goal of using his writing to "reunite Black people to their history" may be seen as the consequence of consciousness aroused by a foreign land's misappropriation of black achievement.

Césaire retired from teaching in 1944; after his retirement he was elected deputy for Martinique to the French National Assembly in Paris. He also was elected several times to the mayoralty of Fort-de-France, Martinique. Although he has repeatedly called for a distinctive appreciation of African and West Indian culture, he led the group that elected Martinique to statehood in the French assembly and rejected political independence. Earlier in his career Césaire had been a member of the Communist party, but he resigned from that affiliation in 1956 after the invasion of Hungary by Soviet troops. (Césaire discusses his disillusionment with the gulf between goal and practice in communist ideology in *Lettre à Maurice Thorez* (Paris, 1956; *Letter to Maurice Thorez*, 1957.)

Césaire stopped writing poetry in the 1950s and became actively involved in dramatic writing. Several of his dramas have received wide attention and numerous productions, among them *Toussaint Louverture* (1962); *Une Saison au Congo* (Paris, 1965; *Season in the Congo*, 1969), a treatment of Patrice Lumumba, Dag Hammarskjöld, and Moishe Tshombe in thinly veiled disguise; and *Une Tempête* (Paris, 1969; *The Tempest*, 1970), a play on Shakespeare's theme in which the Prospero character is delineated as an ineffectual colonizer, while Caliban becomes the true and black hero.

Selected Titles: *Les Armes Miraculeuses* (Paris, 1946; repr. 1961, 1970); *Soleil cou coupe* (Paris, 1948); *Corps perdu Fragrance* (Paris, 1949); *Discours sur le colonialisme* (Paris, 1950); *Et les chiens se taisaient* (Paris, 1956; an earlier version appeared in *Les Armes Miraculeuses*); *Ferrements* (Paris, 1960); *Cadastre* (Paris, 1961; this volume includes *Soleil cou coupe* and *Corps perdu*); *La tragedie de roi Christophe* (Paris, 1963); *Moi, laminaire* (Paris, 1982). See *Oeuvres completes*, 3 vols. (Fort-de-France and Paris, 1976; *Complete Works*, 3 vols., 1976).

Consult: A. James Arnold, *Modernism and Négritude: The Poetry and Poetics of Aimé Césaire* (1981); André Breton, *"Un Grand Poète noir,"* Preface to *Cahier d'un retour au pays natal* (Paris, 3rd ed., 1971); Thomas Hale, *Les écrits d'Aimé Césaire: Biblio-graphie Commenté*, special issue *Études Françaises* (Montreal, 1978); Lilyan Kesteloot and Barthélemy Kotchy, *Aimé Césaire, l'homme et l'oeuvre* (Paris, 1973); Clement Mbou, *Le Théâtre d'Aimé Césaire* (Paris, 1979); M. and M. Ngal and Martin Steins, eds., *Césaire 70* (Paris, 1984; this volume is published in homage to Césaire and contains critical essays on his work as well as an annotated bibliography by A. James Arnold); Ronnie Leah Scharfman, *"Engagement" and the Language of the Subject in the Poetry of Aimé Césaire* (1980).

CHANG, Eileen. Born September 20, 1920, in Shanghai, China. She now lives in Hollywood, California. Chang was a member of an affluent bourgeois family at a time when China was undergoing tremendous social and political changes. Her early education, in addition to routine schooling, consisted of self-study of Chinese literary classics, especially the eighteenth-century work *Dream of The Red Chamber*, which exerted considerable influence on her writing. Her college education in Hong Kong in the mid–1930s acquainted her with Western literary works. During the latter part of World War II in Shanghai, Chang began to contribute stories and essays to literary magazines and newspapers; her work won immediate popular and critical acclaim. Her first two collections, *Romances* (stories) and *Gossip* (essays), which were published in Shanghai in 1947, were pirated in various versions. The authorized edition of *Collected Stories of Eileen Chang*, which appeared in Hong Kong in 1954, depicts bourgeois life in cos-mopolitan Shanghai and Hong Kong. In these stories and essays, Chang's sar-donic wit, unusual visual imagery, and tragic awareness of historical events are clearly seen. In the early 1950s Chang left China for Hong Kong, where she published two novels, *Rice-Sprout Song* and *Live in Redland* (both in 1954). In these novels she draws realistic portraits of peasants and the petty bourgeois under communist rule. Chang came to the United States in the mid–1950s and has written sparsely since then. The few original pieces she has published show little of her earlier creative sensibility. In recent years, Chang has been living the life of a recluse in self-imposed silence. She will be remembered best as a storyteller of exquisite prose; her most memorable story is " The Gold Cangue," a chronicle of the bitter, anguished life of a woman from youth to old age.

Consult: C. T. Hsia, *A History of Modern Chinese Fiction,* 2nd ed. (1971).

DOROTHY TSUNGSU WEISSMAN

CHAO Chi-kang. Born April 2, 1931, in Chechiang, China. She lives in Queens, New York. Chao grew up in Chungking, Szechuan, during China's war against Japan's invasion, 1937–45. Descended from a family of petty bour-geois intellectuals, Chao was persecuted during the 1957 anti-Rightist movement and sent to a remote rural region for reeducation and reform. Intellectuals with bourgeois backgrounds and/or overseas connections were doubly suspect; Chao, whose older brother was a professor at Stanford, suffered guilt by association. During the Cultural Revolution Chao spent several years in various parts of

China's rural regions, especially the southwest, where she collected the folklore of minority tribes. In her work she sometimes assumed the pen names of Chi Kang or Ta Chi; she published movie scripts in addition to stories and essays before her exile. One of her scripts, *Five Golden Flowers*, won the Chinese Golden Festival Award in Beijing in 1961. Her novel, *The River of Sorrow*, a story of the struggles of the minority Tai tribe in southwestern China, was published in Beijing in 1982.

Since Chao left China early in 1985 she has contributed stories and essays to magazines and the literary supplements of Chinese newspapers in Taiwan and the United States. Like most newly exiled writers, Chao's recent works are reminiscences of bygone times and places. Her eloquent prose style makes those remembrances memorable.

DOROTHY TSUNGSU WEISSMAN

CHAPLIN, Charlie. Born April 16, 1889, in East Lane, Walworth, London; died December 27, 1977, in Corsair sur Vevey, Switzerland. His earthly remains were stolen from his grave on March 1, 1978, but were recovered by Swiss police on March 17, 1978. Screenwriter, memoirist, autobiographer, composer, and film comedian, Chaplin was born to an acting couple, who separated shortly after his birth. His half-brother and he spent time in a workhouse when their father refused to support them. Chaplin became a theater actor early in life, playing comic roles in touring vaudeville companies. He came to the United States first in 1910 as a member of a theatrical company; he returned with the troupe in 1912. In 1913 he joined the Keystone Film Company as an actor; he made his debut in 1914 with release of *Making a Living*. His film career spanned thirty years, and he became the best-known film comic of his era. Chaplin never applied for U.S. citizenship, preferring to remain a permanent, resident alien.

An autodidact, he read voluminously, partly to improve his writing techniques and partly to come to more informed literary, social, and cultural judgments. An outspoken critic of indifference to poverty, he suffered no adverse consequences for his progressive, and sometimes radical, views until the 1950s when a climate of accusations of un-Americanism was induced by investigations led by Senator Joseph McCarthy and the House Un-American Activities Committee. Part of Chaplin's troubles may have stemmed from publicity about his extramarital affairs: he was accused of fathering a child with a teenager. Indicted under the Mann Act on federal charges of criminal immoral behavior with a minor, he was found innocent. Later he was ordered by a California court to support the child.

Chaplin left Hollywood with his fourth wife, Oona O'Neill Chaplin, daughter of Eugene O'Neill and more than forty years younger than her husband, on September 17, 1952, on a trip ostensibly to attend the premiere of his newest film, *Limelight*. While en route on the luxury liner *Queen Elizabeth*, Chaplin heard the news that the U.S. attorney general had revoked his entry permit and decreed that Chaplin would have to appear for new hearings before the Immigration and Naturalization Service "to determine" if he were eligible for re-admission to the United States. The attorney general cited the U.S. Code of Laws on aliens and citizens, Section 137, Paragraph C, which allowed for exclusion of aliens on the grounds of "morals, health, or insanity, or for advocating Communism or associating with Communist or pro-Communist organizations."

The Justice Department action clearly was a means whereby to rid the United States of its cultural dissidents. Most observers assign the events to a political pattern of Red-baiting in the United States during the cold war years. Chaplin had in 1947 been subpoenaed by the House Un-American Activities Committee; the U.S. Justice and State departments and the Catholic War Veterans Association had demanded his deportation. In waiting till he was out of the country, the Immigration Service was able to "deport" him by threatening public humiliation if he attempted to return.

Chaplin and his family lived in London briefly before emigration to Switzerland in 1952, where Chaplin wrote and produced films for his remaining twenty-five years. In 1954 Oona O'Neill Chaplin renounced her American citizenship (she later regained it and now lives in the United States). Many honors were heaped on Chaplin in the latter part of his life. He received a belated Special Academy Award from the motion picture industry in Hollywood in 1972; he was knighted by the British government, and Oxford University conferred an honorary degree on him in 1962.

Chaplin's *My Autobiography* appeared in 1964.

Consult: Jerry Epstein, *Remembering Charlie: A Pictorial Biography* (1989); Charles J. Maland, *Chaplin and American Culture: The Evolution of a Star Image* (1989).

CHASE-RIBOUD, Barbara. Born in the United States; she lives in Paris, France. Chase-Riboud graduated from Yale and has received an honorary degree from Temple University. She has lived in Paris since the 1970s after her marriage to a Frenchman. Her first published work was a collection of poems, *From Memphis & Peking* (1974), in which she drew on her many journeys as thematic, emblematic devices. In her poems she showed her first strains of expatriatism and her black consciousness of separation from the Western mainstream. At the same time, her poems, in their varied and intricate forms, urge a reconciliation of the wounding gulfs imposed by history on her people and their oppressors. In 1979 she published her biographical novel, *Sally Hemings*, an account of the gifted black slave woman who became Thomas Jefferson's mistress. She has continued to write on Hemings and that extraordinary woman's period of black history, forming a "chronicle" of novels on the historical era. The second novel in the series, *Valide*, concerns white slavery. The third novel, *Echoes of Lions* (1989), treats an early nineteenth-century rebellion aboard the slave ship *Amistad*, led by one of the intended slaves Joseph Cinque. The mutinous cargo kill the captain and the crew of the slave ship, but find themselves marooned in Sag Harbor, Long Island (New York), in a craft they do not have the ability to move and operate. After negotiations with American forces, the ship is allowed to proceed/return to Africa with her "slaves".

Chase-Riboud has continued to write poetry as well in the intervening years since her first published book. Her second collection, *Portrait of a Nude Woman as Cleopatra*, was awarded the Carl Sandburg Prize in 1988.

CHAUDHURI, Nirad C. Born 1897 in India; he lives in England. Chaudhuri's first book, *The Autobiography of an Unknown Indian* (1951), catapulted him into fame. The autobiography, which is as much social commentary as personal history, describes his growing up in a changing India and his engagement in the "new politics" of the 1920s that allowed for questioning of hierarchy and caste and for a development of Mohandas Gandhi's philosophic revolutionary pacifism and civil disobedience. Chaudhuri's acerbic and witty prose made him a favorite of English critics, and he moved to England in the early 1950s. He has remained in England since that time, though he travels to the European continent frequently and has made extensive revisits to India. He has written two further book-length essays on manners as a means of defining the history of national character, *A Passage to England* (1959) and *The Continent of Circe* (1967). *A Passage to England* describes the reality after his anticipations of experience in England. *The Continent of Circe* is a more generalized and personalized observation of both English and Indian behavior in political frenzy and mutual confusion.

In a 1988 interview in a Sunday illustrated newspaper, Chaudhuri described himself as an English gentleman living in an English country village. Clearly he has adapted to the British style of living and extracted its virtues for amalgamation into his personal life. In his first book he wrote: "No great political concept has ever governed political life in India which has not been created by foreigners, and none but foreigners have ever been able to establish and maintain stable political regimes in this country." Given Chaudhuri's view, which he apparently still holds, he finds in England that version of India he prefers.

Selected Titles: *The Indian Intellectual* (1968); *To Live or Not to Live* (1970).

Consult: K. R. Srinivasa Iyengar, *Indian Writing in English,* 2nd ed. (1973).

CHEN, Jo-hsi. Born November 15, 1938, in Taipei, Taiwan. She lives in Berkeley, California. Chen started her writing career while attending National Taiwan University in Taipei by contributing stories to magazines and literary supplements of local newspapers. In 1960 Chen and a few classmates started the magazine *Modern Literature* as a showcase for major Western literary trends, and thus launched the so-called literary modernist movement in Taiwan. Chen came to the United States for graduate studies in the early 1960s. A native-born Taiwanese who had never been to mainland China, she was emotionally and spiritually drawn to her mother country. When, in 1966, Chen and her husband went to China on a sentimental journey in search of ancestral roots and a sense of identity, they expected an experience of great meaning. The timing, however, proved unfortunate because the Cultural Revolution was being launched, and

China was in turmoil. After seven years Chen and her family left China, disenchanted. From her experiences came the book *Magistrate Yin*, a collection of tales of the Cultural Revolution, published in Taipei in 1976. It has been translated into many languages. Since she left China more than a decade ago, Chen has been writing at the rate of one book a year, among them collections of stories, essays, and novels; two of these novels are *Breakthrough* (1983, Taipei) and *Far Sight* (1984, Taipei and Hong Kong). Chen's more recent work has focused on Chinese life in the United States, and a remarkable shift of emphasis may be seen from novel as technique to novel as vehicle of presenting social issues. *Magistrate Yin* remains her best-known work; as the first eyewitness account of the torments of the Cultural Revolution, it retains impact.

DOROTHY TSUNGSU WEISSMAN

CHEN Kaige. In exile in New York City. Chen is an internationally acclaimed filmmaker and screenwriter who now makes his home in New York City. He is the producer of the award-winning film *Yellow Earth* and two other major cinematic works, *Big Military Parade* and *Kingdom of Children*. In exile he has been writing his first book.

CHESTER, Alfred. Born September 7, 1928, in Brooklyn, New York; died July 28, 1971, in Jerusalem. Chester spent most of his adult years as an underground writer living abroad. His publications include two novels, a dozen short stories, and many book reviews. He attended New York University. At age twenty-three he left the United States and settled for nine years (1951–60) in Paris. He socialized with a group of writers at the Café Tournon and published his first stories in the *New Yorker, Evergreen Review*, and the *Paris Review*.

In 1955 four of his stories were printed in Paris as *Here Be Dragons*, and ten were collected and published in New York under the title *Behold Goliath*. The central theme is the celebration of the flesh, sensual instincts, and sexual passions. Chester's stories are peopled by social misfits and deviants: child murderers, paranoid hallucinators, jilted homosexuals, transvestites, pederasts, sodomists, voyeurs, fortune-tellers, and gypsies. Yet the bizarre sensualists in this carnal underground live in a natural state that Chester prefers to the sterile existence of conventional middle-class society. He satirically depicts straight people as slaves, marionettes, empty raindrops, and unreal ghosts.

In 1957 Chester's first novel, *Jamie Is My Heart's Desire*, was published in New York. The narrator is Harry Sutton, an unloving undertaker's assistant who values nothing but his desires of the flesh. He indulges his animal instincts and sexual passions but refuses to love because "love is not a natural thing: it's something made up—like the idea of God." Normal, considerate people are portrayed as silly hypocrites and charlatans tending a dying young boy, Jamie, who exists as a fantasy that everyone but Harry can see.

Most reviewers were put off by the sordid characters and morbid cynicism of Chester's fiction, but several stories won awards and resulted in a Guggenheim fellowship (1957–58). In 1960 Chester returned to New York for three years and penned his reputation as the enfant terrible of the book review columns. He wrote reviews for *Book Week*, the *New York Times*, and *Herald Tribune* and published stories in *Esquire* and the *New Yorker*.

Chester quickly tired of the New York literary scene and in 1963 left for Morocco. This period of his life is chronicled by Norman Glass in "The Decline and Fall of Alfred Chester," *Paris Review* (Fall 1977): 88–125, and in a collection of his letters published in *Confrontation* (Spring 1988): 305–17. Glass sketches a portrait of Chester as an explosive, paranoid individual given to sudden outbursts of rage. Ostracized by the large community of expatriate writers living in Morocco at the time, he supported himself by writing book reviews, including perceptive pieces on contemporary authors for *Commentary*.

In Morocco Chester drank heavily, smoked *kief*, and took hallucinogenic drugs. His mental disorientation is reflected in the novel he completed in spurts at this time, *The Exquisite Corpse* (1967). An avant-garde work in the French tradition, the novel takes its name from a famous surrealist parlor game, Cadavre Exquis, in which different players contribute parts of a drawing or sentence. Chester's fragmented novel is a disconnected series of scatological scenes and fantasies in which four homosexual characters reappear under any one of many names, sexes, and identities.

Following the unfavorable reviews of his last work, Chester began a nightmarish descent into drug and alcohol dependency. Friendless and tormented by "the little green people" of his imagination, he was treated briefly at Ronald Laing's psychiatric clinic in London. He divided the last few years of his solitary life among living quarters in Tangier, Paris, New York, and Jerusalem. On July 28, 1971, his body was discovered in his Jerusalem apartment; he had died of a heroin overdose. Jewish-born, he had come home to the land of his ancestors to die. His exile was one of self-imposed solitary confinement, rooted in a deviant lifestyle, paranoid delusions, and contempt for all facades of normalcy in society.

Consult: Theodore Solotaroff, *The Red Hot Vacuum and Other Pieces on the Writing of the Sixties* (1970). See also *Alfred Chester Newsletter*, ed. Edward Field.

R. DARBY WILLIAMS

CHIARAMONTE, Nicola. Born 1905, in Rapolla, Potenza, Italy; died 1972, in Rome, Italy. Chiaramonte earned a law degree at the University of Rome; he wrote for Italian journals in the 1920s but found himself isolated by his antifascist views. He emigrated to Paris in 1934; in 1936 he enlisted in André Malraux's air squadron to fight on the side of the Loyalists in the Spanish Civil War. In 1940 he came to New York, where he wrote cultural commentary for leading American intellectual journals; he also coedited *Italia libera* with Enzo Tagliacozzo and Gaetano Salvemini. Returning to Europe in 1949, he worked for UNESCO in Paris for three years, and then moved to Rome, where he wrote drama criticism and coedited with Ignazio Silone the review *Il Tempo Presente*.

Chiaramonte's intellectual explorations in both the novel and the drama grow from moral and ethical persuasions. In *La situazione drammatica* (1960, The Dramatic Situation) he examined the correspondence between authorial belief and historical reality in the work of thirty dramatists from the seventeenth to the twentieth century. In *Credere e non credere* (London, 1970; translated into English as *The Paradox of History*, repr. 1985), he posits the view that bondage to empirical knowledge without recourse to a superrational belief unique for each era leads to petty morality and to what Chiaramonte described as an age of ''bad faith''; he applied this term to twentieth-century history.

The six essays comprising *The Paradox of History* were first delivered as lectures at Princeton University. In them Chiaramonte states his view that the events of history lead to progress and to the greater freedom and individuality of human beings only with the awareness that moral constraints, or patterns of ideals, must of necessity shape human vision and its understanding of an event. The paradox of history lies in the knowledge that history must rely on a faith which involves doubt and return to the ''primal disorder'' of new awakenings; this, Chiaramonte posits, the novelist understands better than the philosopher, who misconceives history as a science. In Chiaramonte's view the novelist gives a truer picture of the experience of history than the philosopher or social scientist or historian because his primary interest is in the way an individual perceives an event rather than in the event itself.

Chiaramonte's views reflect a perspective gained by exilic experience and a yearning for a wholeness not shattered by the blunt boots of history.

Selected Titles: (posthumous) *The Worm of Consciousness and Other Essays* (1976); *Silenzio e parole* (1978).

CHIPASULA, Frank Mkalawile. Born October 16, 1949, in Malawi; he teaches at Brown University in Providence, Rhode Island. Chipasula studied at the Universities of Malawi and Zambia, and came to the United States in 1980 to enroll in the creative writing program at Brown University. He received his Ph.D. from Brown University but has not returned to Malawi because of the political situation there; he refers to himself as an ''exiled poet.'' Chipasula is the editor of two major anthologies of Central and Southern African poetry, *A Decade in Poetry* (Zambian poetry) and *When My Brothers Come Home: Poems from Central and Southern Africa* (1985). He writes in English and has published two volumes of his own work, *O Earth, Wait For Me* (Johannesburg, South Africa, 1984) and *Nightwatcher, Night Song* (London, 1989).

CIORAN, E. M. (Emile M.). Born in 1911 in the Carpathian (Romanian) village of Rasinari, where his father was a Greek Orthodox priest; he lives in Paris. Cioran graduated from Bucharest University, where he continued to study philosophy until 1936. In 1933 he published *On the Summits of Despair*, which earned him the Prize for Young Rumanian Writers. He has lived in Paris since 1937, when he went there assisted by a scholarship from Bucharest's French

Institute. He has written in *The Temptation to Exist*, "I have no nationality—the best possible status for an intellectual."

Cioran began writing in French in 1947. His style has been likened to that of some of the great masters of brief personal statement—La Rochefoucauld, Oscar Wilde, and Friedrich Nietzsche—as well as to such contemporary spiritual allies as Samuel Beckett,* Antonin Artaud,* and Eugène Ionesco,* the latter, like Cioran, a Rumanian who has chosen to spend his life in Paris.

Cioran's fervent partisans have included Susan Sontag, W. H. Auden,* Saint-John Perse,* and Claude Mauriac. The qualities they have found to admire in his work include an uncompromising skepticism and intellectual rigor, the astonishing erudition of a man at home in virtually all civilizations (though comfortable in none), and his paradoxical ability to describe in fresh prose the futility of all thought and the nullity of argument. In aphoristic formulations notable for their wit and what may be termed playfulness, Cioran expresses an almost ecstatic revulsion for every aspect of the human situation.

Cioran's literary strategies have guaranteed him a limited appeal. In addition to his unrelenting pessimism and his mistrust of sequential argument, Cioran consistently violates readers' expectations that an author be cordial and reliable and that an essay lead to a conclusion. His learning, for example, is used to demonstrate the futility of learning, and his essays pile doubt on doubt. In the words of John Updike, he makes the reader "uncertain as to what he has read, or, indeed, whether he has read anything" (*The New Yorker*, May 12, 1975).

Living a semireclusive life on Paris's Left Bank, eking out a modest sufficiency as a translator and publisher's reader, Cioran personifies the *via contemplativa*. His disgust with the human animal has made him virtually a voluntary exile from common humanity, linking him with the ascetic traditions of hermits and Desert Fathers.

Selected Titles: *Précis de décomposition* (Paris, 1949; *A Short History of Decay*, 1976); *La Tentation d'exister* (Paris, 1956; *The Temptation to Exist*, 1968); *La Chute dans le temps* (Paris, 1964; *The Fall into Time*, 1970); *Écartelement* (Paris, 1971; *Drawn and Quartered*, 1984); *Le Mauvais Demiurge* (*The New Gods*, 1975); *Aveux et anathèmes* (1988).

MARTIN BELLER

CLARKE, Arthur C. Born December 16, 1917, in Minehead, England; Clarke, the distinguished science fiction writer, novelist, and social analyst, moved to Sri Lanka in 1979. He is Chancellor of the University of Moratuwa in Colombo.

Selected Titles: *Childhood's End* (1954); *Profiles of the Future* (1962), nonfiction.

CLARKE, Austin C. (Chesterfield). Born July 26, 1934, in Barbados; he lives in Toronto, Canada. According to an interview Clarke gave Daryl Cumber Dance in Toronto on December 6, 1979, Clarke's mother did not marry Clarke's father because she felt that he, as a classless artist, was "two or three social levels below her." Clarke studied economics in Toronto after graduation from private high school in Barbados. He was cultural attaché to the Barbadian embassy in Washington in 1974 and was advisor to the prime minister of Barbados from 1975 to 1976. This latter experience provided the core of his novel *The Prime Minister* (London, 1977). Clarke taught at American universities, among them Yale, Duke, Brandeis, and Indiana universities, from 1968 to 1973.

Clarke has written five novels, a collection of stories, and an autobiography, *Growing Up Stupid Under the Union Jack* (Havana, 1980; Toronto, 1980).

Daryl Cumber Dance, in *Fifty Caribbean Writers*, writes that Clarke's

major theme is exile. Indeed, even those works which are set in Barbados, before exile begins, lay the foundations for this exploration. His first novel, *Survivors of the Crossing* (1964), relates the attempts of Rufus, a Black peasant worker on a sugarcane plantation, to revolt against the White-controlled establishment, a revolt at least partially inspired by rumors about the outside world—Canada and the United States. Clarke's second novel, *Among Thistles and Thorns* (1965), focuses on a young Barbadian boy who runs away. His efforts at flight are obviously a desire for exile. . . . Most of Clarke's male exiles in their quest for goals motivated by Canadian (or Western) society's materialistic symbols of success (a big bank account, a big car, a house in Rosedale) continue that process of repudiation and denial of self begun in their childhood education in Barbados.'' (p. 117). ''Destroyed by their denial of self, their loss of humanity, their futile efforts at assimilation, and their obsessions, most of Clarke's males either lose their lives or their sanity. . . . Clearly there is not much promise of continued life for Clarke's Barbadian exile community in cold Canada'' (pp. 116–17).

Selected Titles: *The Meeting Point* (London, 1967); *When He Was Free and Young and He Used to Wear Silks* (Toronto, 1971); *Storm of Fortune* (1973); *The Bigger Light* (1975); *Nine Men Who Laughed* (1985); *Proud Empires* (1986).

Consult: Gareth Griffiths, *A Double Exile: African and West Indian Writing between Two Cultures* (London, 1978); Donald E. Herdeck, ed., *Caribbean Writers: A Bio-Bibliographical-Critical Encyclopedia* (1979); Kenneth Ramchand, *An Introduction to the Study of West Indian Literature* (London, 1968).

CLEAVER, (Leroy) Eldridge. Born August 31, 1935, in Wabbesheka, Arkansas. He lives in Berkeley, California, where he was a candidate for city council. Cleaver received an education courtesy of Southern primary schools and the California penal system. His prison essays, *Soul on Ice* (1968), call for a liberation of black Americans through the overthrow of social, military, and economic institutions of the government. Cleaver eventually espoused Marxism in *Post Prison Writings and Speeches* (1969), as schisms developed in Black Muslim teachings, which he had studied in prison, and as the leaders of the Black Panther Party were imprisoned. Rather than face jail himself for parole violations, he fled to Cuba and then to Algeria. At the invitations of the governments of North Vietnam, North Korea, and the People's Republic of China, Cleaver traveled to these countries and observed how Marxism had been betrayed by what he viewed as tyrannical practices. He became disillusioned with communism, and he and his wife Kathleen Neal, the daughter of a U.S. Foreign Service officer, settled in France. There he experienced acceptance of his intellectual ideas, and such reception led him to reinterpret his political stance. This reinterpretation forms the basis of his apologetic *Soul on Fire* (1978), a predominantly Christian gloss of the events that led to his return to the United States.

Cleaver voluntarily returned to America, faced trial, and was sentenced to serve more than 2,000 hours of community service in California, where he now lives. Since completing that sentence, he has lectured widely throughout the United States and spoken on many local and national political issues. He is currently at work on a fourth book.

Consult: Lee Lockwood, *Conversations with Eldridge Cleaver* (1970).

DAVID G. SARLES

CODRESCU, Andrei. Born 1946 in Sibiu, Transylvania, on the Hungarian-Romania border; he lives in Baton Rouge, Louisiana. Codrescu claims that on the border where he was born he ''could see the barbed wire all through my infancy.'' Given to hyperbole and the pose of an *enfant terrible* in his public declarations/interviews, Codrescu defends his outlandish behavior as the means by which he expresses the spirit of his vision. In an interview he gave Jacques Servin in July 1989 for this study, Codrescu replied in this fashion to questions put by the interviewer:

Servin: You write in English, yes?

Codrescu: You could say that. You can assume that.

Servin: Are you confident in writing in other languages?

Codrescu: Well, I'm sure I would be confident if I had to. I mean if there was a gun to my head and it said, ''Write in Hungarian,'' I would. What's confidence? Confidence is simply the knowledge that limits are there and can be transgressed. It's simply knowing that the enemy is a smaller person than you are. It's knowing that whoever you're going to beat up can't stand up for more than two rounds. I have infinite confidence. I've got an eternal metaphysical muscle stretching way past those borders. Especially linguistic ones. The prison house of language is nothing to me. I hop in and out all the time. Being a confidence man is a whole different story though. Natives are there to be conned. Natives don't exist for any other reason. Natives exist to defend their property and nomads exist to take it from them.

Servin: So you're at ease in English?

Codrescu: I'm at ease in English because English has provided me with all the nouns I need to be specific in the world.

Servin: When did you get that feeling?

Codrescu: About thirty seconds after I got to the United States of America. As soon as I knew three words, I put them together and I made a poem. ''It, thou, and them.''

Codrescu left Romania in 1965, during the brief period of liberalization in Eastern and Central Europe that ended with the Prague Spring of 1968. Considered a Hungarian Jew, he had been expelled from the University of Bucharest.

He went to Italy "for a year," then to France "for another year." He moved to the United States in 1966, according to his calculation,

because a European year is shorter, because Einstein was a European and when he figured out that time gets dense he was speaking from a uniquely European perspective: it does get turned inward. So when I said a year in France and a year in Italy, I meant six months in Italy, six months in France, but I speak with the wisdom of hindsight, which is American. We've got real time here."

When he came to the United States, Codrescu

tried to put to use the only English sentence I knew, which I had put together in Italy, with my friend Julian, which was, "Why don't you kill yourself?" I went to New York and tried that sentence out for a while, it didn't work very well. . . . I did a number of odd jobs, bookstores, and I went to Detroit, Michigan, to be in Céline's territory, and I thought I'd go to such a hell and I did and then I went to New York and took over the New York School of Poetry. New York-Detroit-New York-California, San Francisco and Northern California, Northern California-Europe, Paris for another year, Baltimore, Maryland, for about five years, Baton Rouge, Louisiana, New Orleans. If you look at it it's a perfect symmetrical cross. Same thing described by Indian migrations to the continent. I was deliberately though unconsciously following a path that is time-hallowed.

Codrescu believes that the experience of exile has enriched his life. He said in his interview that exile is

the ideal condition of consciousness. Consciousness does not exist unless it is in exile. To be out of place is to think on place. All meditation, place and being is made by someone who's been taken out of it. So in a way the way I think about exile is the way I think about food: it's something necessary to my spiritual being. I propagate it. I'm an advocate of it. I recommend it. If they make a pill called "exile" I'll take it.

Codrescu is currently working on "understanding my mother. She's a complicated and older person from an older world, a woman I call the Vortex, and I'm working on a book called *Mother Baby*. It's not a book about psychology or self. It's about my mother, which is neither psychology nor self, actually the mascot of a universe apart."

Codrescu has published sixteen volumes of poetry, three works of fiction, and two volumes of autobiography. He has hosted a program of his volatile commentary for National Public Radio's "All Things Considered," and was editor of the now-defunct literary journal, *Exquisite Corpse*. He claims in his Transylvanian moments to be "1,040 years old." In his American moments he is a professor at Louisiana State University.

Codrescu visited Romania briefly in 1990 for National Public Radio to report on the fall of the Nicolae Ceauşescu regime.

Selected Titles: *License to Carry a Gun* (1970); *A Craving for Swan* (Columbus, Ohio, 1986); *Comrade Past and Mister Present: New Poems and a Journal* (1986); *American Poetry Since 1970* (1987); *Monsieur Teste in America and Other Instances of Realism* (1987, stories); *Raised by Puppets: Only to be Killed by Research* (1989).

COFFEY, Brian. *See* Irish Modernists.

CONRAD, Joseph (Josef Teodor Konrad Korzeniowski). Born December 3, 1857, in Berdyczow (also spelled Berdichev), Poland, then part of the Russian Empire; he died August 3, 1924, in Bishopsbourne, near Canterbury, England. Conrad is regarded as an exile par excellence in that he chose a third language, English, as his medium of expression and wrote about psychic exile in a manner that has profoundly influenced writers who came after him. Among the many writers who have acknowledged their debt to Conrad in the invidious area of isolation are William Faulkner,* Ernest Hemingway,* Graham Greene,* André Gide, Anthony Powell, Ngugi wa Thiong'o,* and Albert Camus.

Conrad's father was an impoverished Polish nobleman who translated Shakespeare, Victor Hugo, and others into Polish. He and his wife, who came from a wealthy bourgeois family, were patriotic signers of manifestos against the czarist domination of their country. When Conrad was four years old, his father and mother were arrested for subversive activities and deported to northern Russia, where Conrad watched his mother die of tuberculosis. He was brought back to Poland to be raised by his maternal uncle, Tadeusz Bobrowski. Bobrowski exerted a strong influence on his nephew, instilling in him a sense of necessity for prudence and discipline. Conrad was also strongly influenced by the image of his father—the quiet rebel dedicated to the patriotic cause of a free, united Poland. Throughout his work and his life, this pull between conservative and impulsive conditions of reaction to circumstance may be seen: irresolution is what defines one part of the Conradian rendering of reality. Conrad's ambivalence, complexly layered in fine lines of distinction, also defines the kind of exilic experience he presented to his world audience, for Conrad turned exilic unease into the means by which to explore modern man's frustrating search for harmony.

Conrad's father was released from penal exile shortly before he died in 1869; he and Conrad lived together in the Austrian-ruled part of Poland for a short period, and Conrad was again impressed with his father's triumph over adversity through dedication to cultural and national ideals. Conrad was admonished by his uncle, whose concern for Conrad is indisputable, to reject the impractical, albeit noble, example his father represented, and to become a man of responsibility. Conrad's teenage life and young manhood is not fully recorded, but it appears he had moments of abandon during a pattern of generally conformist behavior. As an adolescent Conrad dreamed of going to sea, a dream that was likely one of escape and withdrawal from the steady demands of the ordered life held out to him by his uncle; the dream also represents a world Conrad had never experienced: he did not see the sea in his landlocked Poland until he went on vacation in 1873 to Western Europe. When he was seventeen years old, Conrad left Poland for Marseilles against the advice of his uncle (but ultimately with his uncle's financial support) and joined the French maritime service. For the next four years he served as an ordinary sailor in journeys to many parts of the world, among them the West Indies, which was to serve as the locale for one of his masterpieces, *Nostromo* (1904). It was during this period that Conrad may have engaged in gun-running activity for the Spanish/Carlist monarchist cause; he also suffered a chest wound in Marseilles, which most biographers now believe was self-inflicted and the culmination of a half-hearted despair and suicide attempt over his gambling debts. Conrad attempted to clothe this experience in romantic mystification in *The Arrow of Gold* (1919) and to mislead future biographers into perceiving the wound as a result of a duel in an amorous affair over a mysterious lady. Conrad used the motif of a duel in several other works as well; his imagery exploits the features of romanticism, but reveals, when the stylistic layers are penetrated, a need for some protest within the long wail of silent acquiescence to intolerable psychic conditions.

Conrad's uncle traveled to France in 1878 to ensure his nephew's recuperation and to implore him to mend his ways. Conrad secured a berth on a British freighter in 1878, and arrived in Lowestoft for his first sight of England. Significantly for someone of Conrad's ironic temperament, he witnessed as his welcoming sight the capsizing of a dinghy taking sailors ashore. Conrad obtained his master seaman's license in 1886 and became a naturalized British citizen that same year. He sailed on British ships for sixteen years and journeyed to the Far East and South Pacific; he also made a trip to the Belgian Congo in 1890 that was to serve as the embryonic veil of meaning for *Heart of Darkness* (1902).

Conrad married Jessie George in 1896 shortly after his return from the Congo trip, from which he became afflicted with a long illness. Two sons, Boris and John, were born of their union. In 1893 Conrad showed John Galsworthy, a passenger on the ship of which Conrad was serving as an officer, the manuscript of what he had so far written of *Almayer's Folly*. Encouraged by Galsworthy, Conrad began writing seriously. He published his first novel in 1895 when he was thirty-eight years old. Conrad followed this novel with *An Outcast of the Islands* in 1897, *Nigger of the Narcissus* in 1897/1898, and *Lord Jim* in 1903. Although Conrad has often been described as a slow writer, he managed to produce some thirty-five volumes over a course of 30 years of literary activity; these include novels, novellas, dramatizations of his fiction, short stories, essays, memoirs, and prefaces and notes. Conrad himself complained of his instability as a producing writer: the terror of the blank page was one of his nagging nightmares. Perhaps as a means of coping with his anxieties and neuroses, Conrad began writing several works at one time. Whenever he was stymied with one project, he worked on another. Critics have explained his approach, or more accurately, approaches, to writing as his way of coping with financial worries and his anxious refusal to depend on the fortune of any one project, but Conrad's working methods also represent, in essence, the exile who cannot depend on any one land or source, and consequently must plan on several possible routes and resources. The alternative is always necessary in Conrad, for a world without alternatives is an unbearable hell. Some critics have given the name of Janiformity to Conrad's plural need of circumstance.

Conrad received wide critical acclaim early in his career. His first two novels proved popular, but from *Lord Jim* until *Chance* he was a writer more admired than widely read. He lived with his family in Kent in the south of England, and enjoyed association with a group of English and American émigré writers who lived nearby—Galsworthy, Arnold Bennett, Rudyard Kipling, Ford Madox (Hueffer) Ford,* Henry James,* and Stephen Crane. Conrad had a great need for the correspondence of ideas that association with one's peers and colleagues brings; perhaps Conrad's uncertainty with the English language in which he was creating his profound art may be responsible for his oft-expressed cries for companionship in personal and/or epistolary shape. During the latter part of his life, Conrad traveled little, content to live in his garden of English soil. He visited his native land in 1914; stranded there by the outbreak of World War I, he was aided in his return to England by the offices of the American ambassador to Vienna, Frederick C. Penfield. In gratitude Conrad dedicated his novel *The Rescue* (1920) to him. Conrad visited the United States in 1923 for the first and only time on a triumphal reading tour. In 1924 he was offered a knighthood by the British government, which he declined. His refusal to accept the commitment of a lord of the manor of English literature may be viewed as a refusal for final identity with any one land. In keeping himself free of titles, he kept his options open. The closed door, no matter how much beauty lies behind it, was a fearsome confinement for Conrad.

Conrad's place in exilic history is demonstrated on several levels—as a Polish child deported to the outer borders of the ruling imperial entity; as a young Pole émigré to France; as a Pole forsaking his citizenship to become a naturalized Briton. From a literary view, Conrad first exiled himself from his native language for French, and then, in a willful gesture of commitment, to English. Conrad wrote about exile in many guises. His early isolate heroes are stranded in the Far East or South Pacific, estranged from native lands and customs. Conrad shows their disintegration as stemming from an exilic base: a sense of psychic separateness without any new source of corresponding strength. Almayer (in *Almayer's Folly*, 1895) loses his beloved daughter by trying to hold onto his world of prejudice and prejudgment; with her loss he also loses his props of steadiness, since they were based on temporal illusion and he has no resources to replace them. In *An Outcast of the Islands* (1896) Willems is reduced to treachery and betrayal by his own greed and envy but also by his lack of central vision beyond the optics of daily responsibilities and personal ambitions. With *Lord Jim*, Conrad began the series of novels that would distinguish him as the delineator of modern man's existential plight. Jim becomes a refugee from himself after indulging in one instance of impulse; the expression of impulse is by definition an act of freedom but its consequences are those of constraint. Jim's impulsive act is uncharacteristic—that is, as a Conway public school boy, he behaved unlike a gentleman and officer in jumping from the *Patna* when he thought the ship was going to sink. For the rest of his life Jim will atone for his act, and only in his death will he come anywhere near a healing point. Characteristically ironic, the Conradian hero causes destruction most when he tries to avoid it. In Jim's case he gets a second chance to be a leader: he succeeds as magistrate on the island of Patusan, but in hesitating to kill a band of invading gangsters (his hesitation is in part an avoidance of the impulsiveness of his *Patna* youth), he becomes involved in the death of the island's young prince. In turn Jim is killed by the dead man's father, the tribal chief of the island. The father's bullet pierces the center of Jim's being to bring Jim finally to a certain peace.

Conrad treats alienation, isolateness, and psychic exile in *Heart of Darkness* (written 1889) as well. In this work he employs the good-natured social character of Marlow as an alternative to the egomaniacal zealot Kurtz, who jumps into his activities with complete fervor. It is instructive to remember that Conrad constantly deals with the *jump* into an act. He employs the image to suggest flight and exile *from* community as well as desire to fly *into* the abandon of high ideals. In his *jump* Kurtz becomes a barbarian unable to return home to Europe. Marlow's search for Kurtz—a search that is more than a job, though Marlow has been employed to find and return Kurtz—represents a more moderate and perhaps preferable dance with life. If Kurtz becomes an exile from society in his descent into barbarity, Marlow becomes the bridge that may allow passage over the grounds of exile.

Conrad's pervasive sense of the terror of exile and the fear of the jump that will proclaim its ineradicable condition of consequent statelessness is apparent in *Nostromo* (1904), *The Secret Agent* (1907), *Under Western Eyes* (1911), and *Victory* (1915), and in his often-anthologized stories, particularly "Amy Foster" (written 1900) and "The Secret Sharer" (written 1909). In these works the protagonists are estranged from their selves and their circumstances until they accept the darker and impulsive characters of their being alongside the orderly demands of membership in a community. In *Nostromo* the hero is "whole" so long as he resists the temptation of silver glistening over the republic of the novel's site; he is a man of the people, "our man" as in the title. Once he allows any corruption, even the slightest invasion, the act will prove as toxic as self-deception; only death will be able to reclaim his integrity. In *The Secret Agent* the characters are literal exiles, but more significantly, they exhibit the wounds of characterological exile. The angles from which they delude themselves will not cohere, except paradoxically in the simple circles drawn by the idiot Stevie, whose inadvertent death will unfold them all into a conclusive void.

Under Western Eyes also treats literal exile. In this work Conrad came closest to rendering his complex of attitude to his native land and to his departure from it. The protagonist, Razumov (his name signifies a man of reason), wishes merely to go his way into the world as a quietly successful member of society; he wishes not to be immersed in the distractions of history. Ironically, as characteristic of his creator, Razumov must enter the society he is trying to evade. In keeping silent in his university classroom, Razumov is mistakenly assumed to be a revolutionary whose secret sympathies are with those trying to overthrow the czarist autocracy. After the revolutionary Haldin assassinates a high government official, he takes refuge in Razumov's apartment. Razumov must now choose between informing on Haldin, an act detestable to his morality, or suffering the consequences of silent accomplice to a fact he never wished to possess. In working out Razumov's conflict between inner peace, morality, political suasion, and personal love, Conrad treats the conflict that attends exile life as a fact of political and personal condition. Significantly, the resolution in this case takes place not in the contentment of peace through death but in deafness and its accompanying volumes of silence.

Conrad's last great work is one in which a victory over exile and its displacement is achieved. Heyst, the protagonist of *Victory*, has withdrawn from any profound human contact; he credits his self-imposed exile to his father, a philosopher who saw the snares of human involvement and counseled isolation to his son. Heyst's return to community—that is, to a tie with another human being—is realized in an ironic series of events. He befriends a young woman whose job as part of a string quartet in a seedy south Asian restaurant may be a brief moment away from concubinage via the quartet's orchestrator. Heyst offers Lena the opportunity of flight to his island home—only he and a few servants live on the deserted island that plays home to an inoperative, abandoned mine. The island is Heyst's bulwark against entrapment from daily humanity on the shores of the mainland. Heyst's act, an impulsive and generous outburst of compassion, becomes the start of a revolution in feeling that will turn his world upside down.

What Heyst learns is that no act, even the most kingly and kindly one given in the aura of charity, is a single event separate unto itself. All acts have their reverberation; once exile is breached with one slice of compassion, it cannot be made isolate again. In the course of *Victory* Heyst will discover his greatest allegiance is to the woman he has come to love, and for whom he is ready to die in a battle with armed gangsters hired to avenge her desertion from her former employer. Ironically, as in all Conradian fiction, Heyst's willingness to sacrifice himself for the first time in his life to a declaration of pure commitment without any limits of emotional withholding is foiled. The woman Lena sacrifices herself for him and suffers the bullet wound intended for Heyst. As Heyst holds the dying Lena in his arms, he admits and thus realizes his love for her.

The theme of exile in Conrad's many shorter works is most clearly seen in ''Amy Foster,'' in which the protagonist suffers complete ostracism because he cannot communicate in a new language, and in ''The Secret Sharer,'' in which the hero must accept the ambivalence of his dual nature, both his striving toward benevolence and his impulse to outlawry.

Conrad's great love of Shakespeare is illustrated in his portraits of Hamlet-like figures in their ambivalent affections for words as dividing points between the self and the self's language. (One of Conrad's characters in *Under Western Eyes* says that words ''are the great foes of reality.'') Conrad's legacy in the kingdom of exilic perception may best be seen as a vision of alternatives in the drama of recuperative catharsis.

Consult: Joseph Conrad, *Collected Letters*, ed. Frederick Karl and Laurence Davies, 3 vols.(1983–88; further works in progress); Zdzislaw Najder, *Joseph Conrad: A Chronicle* (1983) [completed 1977]. See also *Joseph Conrad: Selected Essays*, ed. Ludwik Krzyzanowski (1960, Polish Institute of Arts and Sciences in America).

COPE, Jack (Robert Knox Jack Cope). Born 1913, South Africa; he lives in England. Novelist, poet and editor, Cope is highly honored for his short stories. He founded and edited the bilingual journal *Contrast*, still operating in South Africa. Cope remained in South Africa for many years as a dissident critic of South African racial policy; he went into self-imposed exile in the early 1980s as a protest against such policies. One of his recent works, *The Adversary Within* (1982), is a tribute in the form of literary analysis to Afrikaans-language writers who have expressed dissatisfaction with their government's edicts and laws.

Selected Titles: Stories: *The Tame Ox* (1960); *The Man Who Doubted* (1967); *Alley Cat* (1973); Novels: *The Fair House* (1955); *The Golden Oriole* (1958); *The Road to Ysterberg* (1959); *Albino* (1964); *The Rainmaker* (1971); *The Student of Zend* (1972); Poetry: *Marie: A South African Satire* (1948); *Recorded in the Sun* (1979); Anthology: with Uys Krige, *The Penguin Book of South African Verse* (1968).

CORVO, Baron. *See* ROLFE, Frederick

CORTÁZAR, Julio. Born August 26, 1914, in Brussels, Belgium; died February, 1984, in Paris, France, of cancer. Cortázar's parents were Argentinians in Europe on business when he was born; they returned to Argentina four years later. Cortázar studied in Argentina, and was an active protester against the dictatorship of Juan Perón (he was briefly jailed for taking part in a demonstration). Cortázar moved to Paris in 1952, where he worked as a free-lance interpreter for UNESCO.

Jorge Luis Borges's influence on Cortázar was both literary and practical: Borges, as editor of *Los anales de Buenos Aires*, published Cortázar's first story, "Casa tomada" (House Taken Over), in 1946. Cortázar took from Borges, and from his own natural tendency, the world of the fantastic as his realm of rendition, but his fantastic milieu is mixed with commonplace events and allusions to real, daily and historic events. The mixture becomes an inextricable web of real and unreal, nightmare and day autobiography, a world in which there are not two distinct worlds of reality and fantasy, but one of phantasmagoria and unsettling and/or illuminating sunlight.

As Cortázar's craft matured, he turned to a felicitous blend of humor and verbal playfulness along with an acceptance of the supernatural element in human life that melded logic into a humanistic faith. In his later years Cortázar grew increasingly concerned with the fate of political prisoners in Latin America, and, in empathy, shared their exile from their homeland. He donated proceeds from sales of his novel *Libro de Manuel* for use by families of political prisoners in Latin America.

His most famous work, *Rayela* (1963; *Hopscotch*, 1966) is an amalgam of realism and superrealism. His hero attempts to live his life through self-willed experiences rather than through externally imposed circumstances. Harming no one (or in Cortázar's view, taking the world on his shoulders for his own good ride), the hero attains to a suspension of reality, in itself an achievement, since he has made—or remade—the world to his heart's desire at least for a brief respite from the trampling footsteps of history.

Although Cortázar lived as an expatriate for thirty years in France, he retained his vital concern with his country, making himself a blend of the real and the distant-phantasmal, an expatriate of contemporary Argentina and a native Argentinian at heart. He took an active interest in politics, supporting Salvador Allende in Chile and Fidel Castro in Cuba, but he never treated *realpolitik* in his work, preferring instead an allusionary approach to socialism.

Translations: *62: A Model Kit* (1972; orig. published 1968, *62: Modelo para armar*); *End of the Game and Other Stories* (1967; republished as *Blow-Up and Other Stories*, 1968); *A Change of Light* (1980).

Consult: J. Alazraki and Ivar Ivask, eds., *The Final Island* (1978); Evelyn Picon Garfield, *Julio Cortázar* (1975); Rita Guibert, *Seven Voices* (1972).

COWARD, Noel. Born December 16, 1899, in Teddington, Middlesex, England; died March 26, 1973, in Jamaica, West Indies. Coward left England in 1956 to reside in Jamaica; his decision was based largely on financial (income tax) reasons and also on a preference for the climate of the Caribbean over that of London. He travelled frequently throughout his life, and set the action of his plays, fiction, and sketches in world capitals, principally London, Paris, and New York. Coward was knighted in 1970.

Selected Titles: *The Noel Coward Diaries*, ed. Graham Payn and Sheridan Morley (1982); *Autobiography*, ed. Sheridan Morley (1980), consists of *Present Indicative*, London, 1937; *Future Indefinite*, London, 1954; and uncompleted *Past Conditional*.

Consult: Frances Gray, *Noel Coward* (1987); Robert Greacen, *The Art of Coward* (1953); Robert F. Kiernan, *Noel Coward* (1986); Cole Lesley, *The Life of Coward* (1976); William Marchand, *The Privilege of His Company: Noel Coward Reconsidered* (1975); Sheridan Morley, *A Talent to Amuse: A Biography of Coward* (1969). For bibliography, see *Theatrical Companion to Coward: A Pictorial Record of the First Performances of the Theatrical Works of Coward*, compiled by Raymond Mander and Joe Mitchenson (1957).

COWLEY, Malcolm. Born August 24, 1898, Belsana, Pennsylvania; died March 27, 1989, Westport, Connecticut. Educated at Harvard, Cowley volunteered, like many of his literary colleagues, for ambulance service on the European front during World War I. He remained in France to edit a little magazine, *Cessation*, as well as to serve as editor of the expatriate literary journal *Broom* in 1923. Later, when he returned to the U.S., he became literary editor of *The New Republic*. Although his stay in Europe was briefer than many of his expatriate friends and associates, he, more than most, understood the forces that drew American writers to expatriate life in France after the Great War. He drew these ideas into his seminal study, *Exile's Return: A Narrative of Ideas*, which he published in 1935; the work was reissued as *Exile's Return: A Literary Odyssey of the 1920s* in 1951. Cowley later reviewed in retrospect the same group of writers and their period of awareness in *A Second Flowering: Works and Days of the Lost Generation*, which he published in 1973. Cowley was a poet as well, issuing three collections: *Blue Juniata* (1929); *The Dry Season* (1941); and *Blue Juniata: Collected Poems* (1968).

Selected Title: *The Literary Situation* (1954); *Selected Correspondence of Kenneth Burke and Malcolm Cowley, 1915–1981*, ed. Paul Jay (1989); *The Portable Malcolm Cowley*, ed. Donald W. Faulkner (1990).

CROSBY, Caresse. Born 1892, New York; died 1970, Rome, Italy.
CROSBY, Harry. Born 1898, New York; died 1929, New York. Caresse and Harry Crosby were patrons of the literary arts in Paris in the 1920s. Caresse continued her patronage through the mid–1930s after her husband's death by suicide in a New York hotel room in 1929. Both were intelligent, sophisticated and supportive patrons and helped the careers of D. H. Lawrence, Henry Miller, Ezra Pound, T. S. Eliot, and others. Harry was himself a writer, who published nine books of his poetry (largely through his own Sun Press). He published his autobiography in serial form in *transition* through 1920–30; after his death Caresse edited the pieces for book publication into three volumes. Caresse wrote her memoir, *The Passionate Years* (1951, 1979), recording the couple's sense of liberation and exhilaration at the creative freedom in Paris in the 1920s (the couple had jumped *onto* ship from Boston to escape that city's confining customs). Caresse also recorded the adventures of her years after her return home in the mid–1930s. Although Caresse and Harry wrote and reflected the expatriate experience, they remain best known as friends of the arts through their Sun Press, and through Caresse's continuing, if sporadic, generosity to writers during the Depression and after.

CSOKOR, Franz Theodor. Born September 6, 1885, Vienna, Austria; died January 5, 1969, Vienna, Austria. Csokor left Austria after the Anschluss in 1938 to begin a roving life until the end of World War II. He had become a target of the National Socialist bureaucracy, who were resentful of his protests against censorship and book-burning celebrations in 1933. He lived in Poland, Romania, and Yugoslavia until he returned to Vienna in 1946. He served as president of the Austrian PEN Club from 1947–1969.

Csokor is remembered for his *Europaische Trilogie* (published in one edition in 1954, European Trilogy). Part I was published after Part II had appeared, and Part II was written during Csokor's exile: Part I, *3. November 1918* (1936); Part II, *Besetztes Gebeit* (1930, Occupied Zone); Part III, *Der verlorene Sohn* (1947, The Prodigal Son). He also wrote of his escapes from Nazi discovery and arrest in *Als Zivilist im polinischen Krieg* (1940; *A Civilian in the Polish War*, 1941) and *Als Zivilist im Balkankrieg* (1947, A Civilian in the Balkan War); the two volumes were published in a single edition *Auf fremden Strassen* in 1958. Csokor wrote all his work in German.

Selected Titles: *Satans Arche* (1940, Satan's Ark); *Zeuge einer Zeit: Briefe aus dem Exil 1933–1950* (1964, Witness of an Epoch: Letters from Exile, 1933–50.

Consult: Jethro Bithell, in *German Life and Letters 1954–55*.

CUADRA LANDROVE, Angel. Born August 29, 1931, in Havana, Cuba; he lives in Miami, Florida. Lawyer, poet, and early supporter of Fidel Castro, Cuadra served as legal advisor to the Cuban Institute of Artists and Writers in Havana for several years before his arrest in 1967. Charged with conspiracy against the state, he was given a death sentence, later commuted to fifteen years at hard labor. Cuadra was released from detention in 1976 but arrested again in 1977 on a charge he had smuggled his poems out of the country and published them abroad; the poems were deemed subversive.

In 1982 he shared with Armando Valladares* and Jorge Valls* the International Prize of the Hispanic–Puerto Rican Pro-Culture Association, given for high achievement in the arts under physical and social duress. Cuadra was granted permission to go into exile in the United States in the 1980s. One collection of Cuadra's poems, *Impromptus*, was published in the United States in 1977.

CULLEN, Countee (pseudonym of Countee Leroy Porter). Born May 30, 1903, in Kentucky? Baltimore, Maryland?; he died January 9, 1946, in New York City. A pivotal figure in the Harlem Renaissance, Cullen was a respected writer and teacher during the later part of his life, but little is known about his parents, his birth, or very early childhood. An orphan in New York City, he was adopted by the Reverend and Mrs. Frederick A. Cullen. He graduated from New York University in 1925 (B.A.) and from Harvard in 1927 (M.A.). He used the proceeds of a Guggenheim fellowship, awarded in 1928, to live and work in France from 1928 to 1930, while also studying at the Sorbonne in Paris. Cullen's experiences in France were profound—French culture provided him with a role model at the same time it helped him shape his identity. Cullen believed that black writers should draw on West European traditions as well as on their distinct third world of consciousness. He became part of the vocal excitement of ideas exchanged round café tables in Paris by black artists and writers; central to their talk was the issue of assimilation and the resolution of attitude to the black disapora.

Cullen may be said to be a part of that exilic dilemma characteristic of the black experience and all diaspora descendants. African writers like Léopold Sédar Senghor* and Léon Damas-Gontran* and the West Indian poet Aimé Césaire* were in Paris at the time arguing over how to resist the benign sweep of cultural assimilation. The empirical attitude that turns black and white colonials into clones of one bias, and thus eliminates plural prejudice, provides an umbrella view that erases the reign of diversity; in this process of graduated tolerance, the black (or any minority class in a polymorphous grouping) loses his history, however bitter that history may be. Cullen's attitudes in the continuing debate were somewhat ambiguous, but he was clearly vocal against separatism of black cultural achievements; he believed the black writer should be part of larger European traditions, informed by awareness of history, colonial and otherwise.

Cullen's annual summer visits to France (he taught French and English in a New York City junior high school during the regular academic year) were interrupted by World War II. Somewhat neglected toward the end of his life, but now valued as a significant American writer, Cullen represents the plight of the invisible outsider. A gifted artist, he had to draw for his materials on those aspects of his racial past he wished to put behind him in the quest for an artist's world in which color is a flowering image and no longer a sore prejudice.

cummings, e. e. (Edward Estlin Cummings). Born October 14, 1894, in Cambridge, Massachusetts; died September 3, 1962, at Joy Farm, New Hampshire). Cummings served with a volunteer ambulance unit in France during World War I. He was interned without trial for three months by the French government on suspicion of pro-German sympathies and treason. Cummings recorded his experiences of this horrendous error in his first novel, *The Enormous Room* (1922). After the war Cummings journeyed often to Paris. He felt a sense of creative freedom in France that his Puritan upbringing denied him in his native locale.

In addition to creating some of the finest lyrics in the twentieth century and to shaping new concepts of rhythm and typography in American poetry, Cummings was also a painter of merit. In his early years he studied painting in Paris; in his later years he had several one-man shows in New York and Paris.

Selected Titles: Prose: *EIMI* (1933, report of trip to USSR); Poetry: *Tulips and Chimneys* (1923); *Collected Poems* (1938); *Selected Letters* (1969); *Complete Poems 1913–1962* (1972).

Consult: George J. Firmage, *E. E. Cummings: A Bibliography* (1974 [repr. of 1960 edition]); Norman Friedman, *The Magic Maker* (rev. ed. 1964).

CURREY, R. N. (Ralph Nixon Currey). Born 1907, Mafeking (now Maxikeng), South Africa; he lives in England. Currey has lived in England since he came to Oxford as a student. He served with the British Royal Artillery in World War II; after demobilization he taught in Colchester. Many of his works deal with a sense of cultural exile and isolation; one of these is his radio play, *Early Morning in Vaaldorp* (1961). He is by turns ironic and lyrical in his writing. Currey won the Viceroy's Poetry Prize in 1945 and the South African Poetry Prize in 1959. He was initiated into the Royal Society of Literature in 1970.

Selected Titles: Poetry: *Tiresias* (1940); *The Other Planet* (1945); *Indian Landscape: A Book of Descriptive Poems* (1947); *Formal Spring: Translations of French Resistance* (1950); *The Africa We Knew* (1973); Verse Drama for Radio: *Between Two Worlds* (1947).

CZAYKOWSKI, Bogdan. Born 1937, in Poland; he lives in Canada. Czaykowski achieved renown as the editor of the London-based exile journal *Kontynenty*. He now teaches political literature in Canada.

D ———————————————————————

DAMAS, Léon-Gontran. Born 1912, in Cayenne, French Guiana; died 1978, in Washington, D.C. Humor, quick wit, and fiery compassion mark the poetry and life of Damas; so, too, do anger and bitterness over the history of French colonialism in the West Indies and in Africa. A gifted student who early had become a cultural Francophile, Damas left for university studies in Paris after graduating from high school in Martinique. In France, for the first time, he felt a foreigner, the consciousness of which initiated his awareness and celebration of native West Indian and African cultural achievement. His first influence of cultural separatism came from his fellow Guyanan and Paris-based student, Etienne Léro. Damas voiced support for Léro's manifesto, *Légitime Défense*, which called for an end to French colonial dominance (and the elimination of all past West Indian literature, since it was tainted with invidious colonialist bias). Damas also came under the sway of surrealism and the enthusiasm in Paris for the American Negro Renaissance. Like a number of students in Paris at the time, he became an enthusiast of the Russian Revolution, seeing in the event a promise of vibrant change. When Damas became more closely associated with Léopold Sédar Senghor* and Aimé Césaire,* his political activism waned in the ensuing focus on African consciousness. With the two other poets, he founded *L'Etudiant Noir* (The Black Student), a journal devoted to black awareness. Although it was Césaire who coined the catchword *négritude* that came to stand for the new language, style, and vision of adherence to a pride in an older African identity, the concept was clearly fermenting in the minds of all three writers. Damas's first volume, *Pigments* (Paris, 1937), appeared one year before Césaire's prose poem, *Cahier d'un retour au pays natal*, and is the first volume of Négritude verse. In this work Damas proved characteristically iconoclastic in social and political matters as well as in style and form: he called on Africans to reject the barbed niceties of European dominance, even going so far as to suggest a liberating invasion of Senegal and a passive resistance by black men to French military conscription. The French government responded by banning the book in French West Africa.

Damas continued to live in France, working at various jobs. From 1945 to 1951 he served as deputy from Guiana to the French Assembly. He also worked for UNESCO in Paris, served on the editorial board of *Présence Africaine* (based in Paris), and lectured in the United States, Africa, Haiti, and Brazil. In 1970 he moved to Washington, D.C., with his wife, where he lived till his death.

Damas is the least recognized of the trio—Césaire and Senghor are the other members—who brought awareness to African achievement through a first stage of cultural separatism. The lack of recognition may stem from his distinctive, but demanding, characteristics: blunt language, layered puns, passionate and coruscating critiques of human behavior and social life. Damas also antagonized factions in literary politics by his criticism of Africanism and Africanist exploitation. His bitterness in later years may have grown as a result of his literary quarrels, but in personal company he showed consistent brilliance of wit and a certain good humor about human fallibility.

Damas, Césaire, and Senghor represent that twentieth-century phenomenon of having to leave home to find it. Damas remained true to his rootlessness, as Senghor and Césaire did to their roots, for the latter two stayed home once they had come home. Césaire became a deputy to the French Assembly, and the mayor of Fort-de-France, Martinique; Senghor became president of the Senegal republic. Damas, in contrast, remained in France most of his life and then moved to the United States; he did not return, after his one-term as a deputy, to the French Assembly. All three writers are responsible for the awareness of Africanness that is now an accepted being of cultural pluralism. Through their concerns, the depth of African and West Indian identity and achievement has pervaded both indigenous and foreign shores.

Selected Titles: *Retour de Guyane* (Paris, 1938, Return from Guiana); ed., *Poèmes nègres sur des airs Africains* (1948, Songs of Love, War, Grief and Abuse); *Graffiti* (1952); *Black Label* (1956); *Nevralgie* (1966, Neuralgia).

Consult: Ellen Conroy Kennedy, ed., *The Negritude Poets: An Anthology of Translations from the French* (1975); Daniel Racine, *Léon-Gontran Damas: l'homme et l'oeuvre* (Paris, 1983); Keith Q. Warner, ed., *Critical Perspectives on Léon-Gontran Damas* (1988).

DARWISH, Mahmud. Born 1942 in the village of al-Birwah, Palestine, which became part of Israel in 1948. He opted for "external" exile in 1970 and lived for the most part in Beirut, Lebanon, until the Israeli invasion of 1982. Presently he resides in Paris, France, where he edits a Palestinian literary journal, *al-Karmil*. Darwish is a poet of two exiles, internal and external. Like the rest of the relatively small Palestinian community that was not displaced in 1948 and came under Israeli rule, he lived for the next two decades in a political and cultural quarantine: "I am the exile behind the fence and the gate," he wrote in his collection, '*Ashiq min Filastin* (A Lover from Palestine) in 1966. His verse in this early period represents what he calls his poetical childhood and adolescence. One can discern in this early work the genetic material of Darwish's later, mature writings. His poem "A Lover from Palestine," with its call for the rebirth of cultural nationalism, propelled him into the role of a national Palestinian poet. The startling concise imagery, incantatory repetition, and modulation between rhyme and nonrhyme found in this celebrated early poem prefigure the techniques of his later work; the poem also encapsulates Darwish's themes of estrangement, defiance, affirmation of Palestinian identity, and rootedness in his magical land. Darwish left Palestine after a period of imprisonment and harassment; his departure is also concerned with a craving for linkage with the main currents of Arab and international literature.

As an external exile, Darwish commemorates in his work the traumas and triumphs of a nation in exile and projects its dreams of tranquillity and return, or as he puts it, "going forward." Whether he is writing about Beirut, Paris, an assassinated friend, poetry, or an erotic encounter, his eye remains fixed on the mythic presence of Ithaca and Penelope. Although his poetry has become more elegiac, he can also be playful or sardonic, and remain at base lyrical. A masterful technician who draws on a multitude of prosodic resources, from both Arabic and Western tradition, he employs language close to common speech. But in contrast to his earlier equating of poetry's value with its clarity of line, his later work often succumbs to the modernist allure of ambiguity and difficulty.

In 1986 Darwish was awarded the French government's Ordre des Arts et des Lettres with the rank of Chevalier. He has produced more than ten volumes of poetry, a book of essays, and numerous articles and commentaries. Among his Arabic collections are '*Ashiq min Filastin* (1966, A Lover from Palestine); *Al-'Asafir Tamutu fi al-Jalil* (1966, Birds Perish in the Galilee); *A'aras* (1977, Weddings); and *Wardun Aqal* (1986, Fewer Flowers).

Translations: *The Music of the Human Flesh* (Washington, D.C., 1986); *Sand and Other Poems* (1986); and in the anthologies, *Victims of a Map* (London, 1984) and *Modern Arabic Poetry* (1987).

SHARIF S. ELMUSA

DATHORNE, O. R. Born November 19, 1934, in Georgetown, Guyana; he lives in the United States. The oldest of seven children, Dathorne was born to a lower-middle-class family who supported his efforts at writing and at formal education. In 1946, in search of employment, Dathorne's father emigrated with his family to England. Dathorne worked there for two years before enrolling at the University of Sheffield, where he received his B.A. in 1957. In 1959 he received a teacher's certificate from the University of London, married, and took on an assignment as a lecturer in English at the University of Ahmadu Bello in northern Nigeria.

Dathorne's work as a critic of African literature (*The Black Mind: A History of African Literature*, Minneapolis, 1974; *African Literature in the Twentieth Century*, Minneapolis, 1975) and of Caribbean literature (*Dark Ancestor: The Literature of the Black Man in the Caribbean*, Baton Rouge, 1981) is highly regarded. He is also a novelist who aims at a comic pose in his presentation and view of human material and incident. Dathorne has taught at many American universities as well as at the United Nations. He founded in 1979 and still edits the *Journal of Caribbean Studies*.

Selected Titles: *Dumplings in the Soup* (London, 1963); *Dele's Child* (1986).

Consult: Ngugi wa Thiong'o, *Homecomings: Essays on African and Caribbean Literature, Culture and Politics* (1972); Michael Hughes, *A Companion to West Indian Literature* (London, 1979); Robert E. McDowell, *Bibliography of Literature from Guyana* (Arlington, Texas, 1975).

DELIUS, Anthony. Born Simonstown, South Africa; he lives in England. Delius is a graduate of Rhodes University in Grahamstown, South Africa; he served with the South African Intelligence corps in World War II. He worked as a journalist in his homeland as well as served as the English editor of the journal *Standpunte* until 1956. He moved to England that year and has lived there since. He is both a novelist and poet, and often employs South African milieus and expatriate themes. One of his prose satires, *The Day Natal Took Off* (1963) is a fictional treatment of the rivalry between "liberal English" residents and fiercely conservative Afrikaners; Delius ridicules the cant in both their stands and stances.

Selected Titles: Poetry: *The Last Division* (1959); *A Corner of the World* (1962); *Black South Easter* (1965); Novel: *Border* (1976); Play: *The Fall: A Play about Rhodes* (1960).

DEMETZ, Hana. Born 1928 in Czechoslovakia; she lives in Connecticut. Demetz survived the Holocaust to become in 1949 an editor for Radio Free Europe broadcasting in German. She lectured in Czech at Yale University. Her best-known work is *The House on Prague Street* (1970), the semiautobiographical novel of a half-Jewish girl in prewar Czechoslovakia who becomes a victim of the Nazi terror. An adolescent at the time of Hitler's annexation of her country, she survives the Holocaust and war years, but her entire family disappears in the camps. After the war the heroine returns to what had been a beautiful home and childhood in Prague to exorcise the spirit of her past. Demetz's novels are written and published in German; only a few have been translated into English.

DEVLIN, Denis. *See* Irish Modernists.

DINESEN, Isak (pseudonym of Baroness Karen Blixen; other pseudonyms: Tania Blixen, Osceola, Pierre Andrezel). Born April 17, 1885, in Rungsted, Denmark; died September 7, 1962. Famous for her tales of Africa and her legends of a long-ago Denmark, Dinesen is a curious example of a woman who chose to leave her ancestral home for Kenya (in 1914) and for marriage to a brother of the man she loved. In Kenya she grew to admire the Kikuyu people and to feel a fulfillment in that continent's landscape. Her marriage proved difficult (her husband was a philanderer, though he has his supporters, among them the expatriate aviatrix, Beryl Markham). Dinesen contracted syphilis from her husband, was cured of the disease but rendered sterile in the process, and in later years took a younger lover, Denys Finch-Haddon, who died in an airplane crash in central Africa. The fortunes of weather fell against her when alternate sequences of drought and flood ruined her coffee plantation, and she was forced to relinquish the property. She returned to Denmark in 1931. Through her writing, both those of African memoir and Danish legendary material, she found a catharsis and form for expression that turned her into a significant phenomenon and possibly a major writer.

Dinesen is among those expatriates who may be viewed as exiles in their own land, yet who triumphed over memory of loss by force of will. Perhaps her true home was in the castle of aristocracy, that tower of reserve holding off the blasts of cold life and sweeping misfortune.

Selected Titles: *Seven Gothic Tales* (1934); *Den afrikannske farm* (1937; *Out of Africa*, 1937); *Vinter-eventyr* (1942; *Winter's Tales*, 1942); *Sidstefortoellinger* (1957; *Last Tales*, 1957); *Sygger pa groesset* (1960; *Shadows on the Grass*, 1960); *Efterladte fortoelllinger*, 2 vols. (1975; *Letters from Africa*, 1981).

Consult: Robert Langbaum, *The Gaiety of Vision: A Study of Isak Dinesen's Art* (1961); William Maxwell, *The Outermost Dream* (1989); C. Svendsen and F. Larson, *The Life and Destiny of Karen Blixen* (1970).

DIPOKO, Mbella Sonne. Born February 28, 1936, in Mudngo, near Douala, Cameroon; he lives in France. Son of the paramount chief Paul Sonne Dipoko, Dipoko was raised by his uncle, a man of stern Protestant faith, on a farm in Missaka on the Mungo River. He went to school in Nigeria from 1952 to 1956. He returned to Cameroon to work for his country's Development Corporation in Tiko, then moved to Nigeria to work for the Nigerian Broadcasting Corporation. In September 1960 he moved to Paris, still on the staff of the Nigerian Broadcasting Corporation, but he quit his job to take a staff position on the journal *Présence Africaine* and to devote himself to his writing. Dipoko also made plans to study law at the Sorbonne, but did not follow through with them. In 1969 he traveled through England, Spain, Morocco, and France.

Dipoko's first book was a volume of poems printed locally. His first novel, *A Few Nights and Days* (Paris, 1966), set in France, was characterized by Paul Theroux as "a French novel about France by a man who writes like a European woman." In his second novel, Dipoko turned to an African locale; in *Because of Women* (1969) a young Cameroonian fisherman must make a choice among several women in his flight to and from maturity. Both these novels and Dipoko's poetry (see *Black & White in Love*, London, 1972) are written in English.

Selected Title: *Overseas* (1968) (play).

DÖBLIN, Alfred. Born August 10, 1878, in Stettin, Germany (today Szczecin, Poland); died June 26, 1957, in Emmendingen, West Germany. Döblin studied medicine both in Berlin and Freiburg. He worked as a physician in Regensburg, Berlin, and during World War I in two military hospitals in the Alsace. His early publications were novels and short stories, reflecting traits of both German impressionist and expressionist style between the turn of the century and the end of World War I. During the Weimar Republic he became one of Germany's most productive and highly respected literary figures. Besides short stories, novels, and dramas, he published many literary and political essays. Under the pseudonym of Linke Poot (Left Paw) he expressed his satirical views on the political shortcomings and bureaucratic ways of contemporary life in Germany. He achieved his greatest fame, which he was not able to match again during his lifetime, with his novel *Berlin Alexanderplatz* (1930). The bustling capital of Germany during the 1920s forms the backdrop and also the subject of this work, important no more for its social implications (the protagonist, Franz Biberkopf, is a former prisoner who finds himself incapable of entering into a normal bourgeois existence) than for its stylistic experimentation in surrealist description, stream of consciousness, and montage technique of narration. Following Hitler's rise to power in 1933, Döblin tried at first to register his protest against censorship and tyranny—for example, the expulsion of Heinrich Mann* and Käthe Kollwitz from the Prussian Academy of Arts. Finding himself powerless in this regard and also endangered himself, he crossed the border on March 1, 1933, into Switzerland, soon to be followed by his wife and children. They initially lived in Zurich, but moved on to Paris later the same year and fled before the advancing German troops in 1940 to southern France. During the years of his European exile, Döblin took up the cause of the persecuted Jews and, despite the outspoken atheistic tendencies of his earlier period, expressed pride in his identification with his Jewish heritage. During a temporary separation from his family, Döblin had a mystical experience in the cathedral of Mende which one and half years later led to his conversion to Catholicism.

From September 1940 until October 1945, Döblin lived in the United States, mainly in Hollywood, where he was supported in turn by a stipend from the European Film Fund and voluntary aid by fellow exiles. After the war, Döblin returned to Germany as a cultural officer of the French military authorities. While living in Baden-Baden and later in Mainz, he published his own journal, *Das Goldene Tor*, between 1946 and 1951, and then returned to Paris. During the last four years of his life, Döblin lived again in Germany, but with rapidly failing health and in disappointment over the slow growth of his recognition in his native country.

Of several works which Döblin wrote during his exile, the novel *Babylonische Wandrung oder Hochmut kommt vor dem Fall* most vividly reflects the experiences of the homeless writer, albeit in the guise of a Babylonian god who was cast from heaven and whose final abode becomes France, the country where Döblin finished this work in 1934. Less directly, though still present, is the experience of exile in the *Südamerika-Roman*, a novel in three parts depicting the prehistoric wanderings of Indian tribes in the Amazon region and the historic development of the Jesuit republic in Paraguay in the first two parts (published in Amsterdam, 1937); the plot of the third part, entitled "Der neue Urwald" (The Modern Primeval Forest), is set in the twentieth century and gives a very critical view of the consequences of modern civilization on man's moral thinking and behavior.

The largest exile work written by Döblin is a novel in four parts entitled *November 1918*. However, instead of speaking of exile, Döblin gives the reader a fictionalized historic account of the events leading up to the revolution in Germany at the end of World War I. The revolution's thwarted success was for Döblin the cause of many events to come and eventually necessitated the flight of him and many of his fellow German citizens from their homeland. Only the first part of this novel, *Bürger und Soldaten* (Townspeople and Soldiers), was published before the defeat of Germany (Amsterdam, 1939), while the remaining three parts had to wait for publication in Munich in 1948, 1949, and 1950 respectively.

Interest in Döblin's works has been steadily growing during the last two decades. A new edition of selected works, the publication of which began in 1960, has now reached twenty-two volumes.

Selected Titles: *Jüdische Erneuerung* (Amsterdam, 1933); *Pardon wird nicht gegeben* (Amsterdam, 1935; *Men without Mercy*, London, 1937); *Die deutsche Literatur (im Ausland 1933)* (Paris, 1938); *Schicksalsreise: Bericht und Bekenntnis* (Frankfurt, 1949); *Hamlet oder Die lange Nacht nimmt ein Ende* (Berlin, 1956).

Consult: Patrick James O'Neill, *Alfred Döblin's Babylonische Wandrung: A Study* (Bern, Frankfurt, F.R.G., Las Vegas, 1974); Matthias Prangel, *Alfred Döblin* (Stuttgart, 1987).

HELMUT F. PFANNER

DOMENCHINA, Juan José. Born 1898 in Spain; died 1959 in Mexico. Domenchina went into exile with the advent of the Civil War. His earlier poetry, highly crafted and intellectualized, was followed by a more intense and passionate expression of exile. Much of his poetry is nostalgic, harking back to a land to which he can no longer return. In essence, Domenchina refused to begin a new life in a foreign land because the surrender of the dream of return to Spain would have been a betrayal to his existential definition. Thus he became a man both tortured and sustained by a yearning for a past moment, a refugee determined to believe in another revolution that would return him to his native Castille. He spent his exile in Mexico, but in spite of the common language of his resting place and his birth land, he remained fixated on his alienation.

Selected Titles: *Tres Elegias Jubilares* (Mexico, 1946); *Perpetuo Arraigo* (Mexico, 1949); *La Sombra Desterrado* (Mexico, 1950); *Neuve Sonetos y Tres Romances* (Mexico, 1952); *El Extranado* (Mexico, 1958); *Poemas y Fragmentos Ineditos* (Mexico, 1964); *Poesia 1942–1958* (Madrid, 1975).

Consult: Gerardo Diego, ed., Introduction to *El Extranado y Otros Poemas* (Madrid,

1969) by Domenchina; Robert Warner, "The Non-Life Style of an Exile: The Poetics of Juan José Domenchina," *Hispanofila* 76 (September 1982).

DOMIN, Hilde. Born July 27, 1912, in Cologne, Germany; she lives in Heidelberg, Federal Republic of Germany. Domin left Germany with her family in 1931 to escape political and religious persecution. She did not begin her writing career until she wrote her first poem after twenty years in exile. The time and place of exile was 1951 in Santo Domingo; the language in which Domin wrote, and has continued to write all her work, is German. She believes passionately that she must "write as a German poet speaking to fellow Germans" because, as in a letter she wrote to Nelly Sachs,* another exiled German Jewish poet, one's native language keeps alive "humanity's memory."

Domin returned to (West) Germany in the late 1950s after two earlier plans to return were aborted by her ambivalence over what her country had done to its people during the Nazi era. Yet, in moving back to Germany and in accepting the role of the poet as the conscience of her country, Domin has found a restorative of creative energy. The term she uses is *Doppelkopfigkert jeder Erfahrung*, or the ineradicable double-sidedness of every experience. Domin thus accepts the paradox of being a citizen of humanity that has often been barbarously inhumane. Her poetry becomes in the process a witness to history; its major theme remains the pain and transcendence of exile.

In the introduction to her anthology *Four German Poets* (1979), Agnes Stein writes of Domin: "Domin generalizes the pain of exile to the human condition, the loneliness of the human spirit in a bureaucratic and technological world, while keeping a keen eye on the walls that threaten to separate the individual from a common humanity" (p. 2).

Selected Titles: *Ich will dich; Gedichte* (Munich, 1970); *Von der Natur nicht vorgegehen: Autobiographisches* (Munich, 1974); *Aber die Hoffnung: Autobiographisches aus und uber Deutschland* (Munich, 1982); *Gesammelte Gedichte* (Frankfurt, 1987, Poems).

Consult: Agnes Stein, ed., *Four German Poets: Gunter Eich, Hilde Domin, Erich Fried, Gunter Kunert* (1979).

DONLEAVY, J. P. (James Patrick). Born April 23, 1926, in Brooklyn, New York; he lives in County Westmeath, Republic of Ireland. Donleavy did his early schooling in New York, then became a college student at Trinity in Dublin. He later utilized his experiences in his first and hilarious novel, *The Ginger Man* (Paris, 1955; 1958), which remains his most popular work. It has gone through many censored editions; it appeared in a "complete" edition in London in 1963 and in New York in 1965. Donleavy also turned the work into a play (produced in 1961 and published 1962), which had a more limited success. He has followed this pattern of dramatizing his novels after their publication as well with *A Singular Man* (1964, drama 1965); *The Beastly Beatitudes of Balthazar B.* (1969, drama 1981); *Summer of Samuel S.* (1967, drama 1972); and *Fairy Tales of New York* (1961; drama, *A Fairy Tale of New York*, 1973). All his work continues to portray the rebellious anti-hero given to pranks on conventional society. In *The Ginger Man* and *A Singular Man*, Donleavy's great energy and appetite overwhelmed the reader into acceptance of the appeal of his resilient young and stylized heroes and of Donleavy's brand of cloacal, impolitic nonsense. Yet Donleavy's critics have consistently maintained that, unlike other comedic writers, his works have little meaning beyond their shock value, and that Donleavy's protagonists are less anti-heroes of an angry age than immature college pranksters of any era. His middle work shows a resonance of the limitations of waning energy, but in the last decade Donleavy has succumbed to a willful mockery of all he surveys, including his readers. The result is a contest between a shrill performer whose tricks have become somewhat tedious and a resistant audience.

Donleavy served in the U.S. Navy during World War II, then moved to the land of his ancestors; he was also taking advantage of liberal Irish tax laws for writers. In 1967 Donleavy became an Irish citizen. Donleavy may be said, then, to be neither an exile nor an expatriate, but a citizen, unlike James Joyce,* returning to his native land. Yet physical union with his roots has not quietened the anxiety and alienation of Donleavy's voice. Ironically it has been accompanied with the loss of comic tone and the substitution in its place of a hectoring posture.

Selected Titles: *Meet My Maker the Sad Molecule* (1964) (stories); *The Onion Eaters* (1971); *The Unexpurgated Cody: A Complete Manual of Survival and Manners*, illustrated by Donleavy (1975); *The Destinies of Darcy Dancer, Gentleman* (1978); *Schultz* (1979); *A Singular Country* (1990 [travel book, memoir of Ireland]).

DONOSO, José. Born October 5, 1924, in Santiago, Chile. He now lives and works in Chile. Donoso, the most widely known Chilean prose writer both at home and abroad, has been translated into English and many other languages. Before settling in Europe, Donoso lived for short periods of time in different parts of Latin America and the United States. These stays confirmed his dislike of the oppressive atmosphere of upper middle-class Chilean society. He finished his B.A. in English at Princeton University (1949–51), where he published his first short stories. He left Chile again (1958–60) to spend two years in Buenos Aires, where he found the literary atmosphere vital and stimulating. There he met the most important writers of the period. By then he had already published his first novel, *Coronación* (1957; *Coronation*, 1965), which continued the concerns established earlier in his short stories: alienated individuals as products of their environment, in this case, upper middle-class Chile.

During the next few years, Donoso attended various writers' conferences where he came to know the most important Latin American writers and their works. His contact with authors like Carlos Fuentes* (Mexico), Mario Vargas Llosa* (Peru), Julio Cortázar* (Argentina), and Gabriel García Márquez* (Colombia) was crucial in helping Donoso to establish his style.

His attempt to finish a particular work while teaching at the Writers Workshop at the University of Iowa (1965–67) led Donoso to the conclusion he could engage in only one activity at a time. In 1967 Donoso moved to Spain with his wife, adopted a daughter and settled in Mallorca, although he made several moves within Spain during his thirteen-year stay.

His main goal now was to finish the novel started several years ago in Chile. The process was delayed by Donoso's recurring problems with stomach ulcers. But by 1970 *El obsceno pájaro de la noche (The Obscene Bird of Night*, 1973) was published and established him as a major figure in Latin American literature. His first novel published in Spain, the work marks a move away from traditional plot, character, and thematic development to a deeper concern with the internal workings of the human psyche. The world of the surreal, absurd, and irrational become more prominent, as does Donoso's dour outlook on the human condition. The novel is regarded by many as a highly complex, enigmatic, and hermetic work where man seems to fall helplessly downward into a vortex of nothingness. Donoso's purpose in the novel may be the presentation of a life completely void of reason, where nothing is resolved and where instinctual sensations dominate. The move to Spain proved the catalyst that allowed Donoso free rein in his major obsessions and concerns.

In *Historia personal del "boom"* (1972; *The Boom in Spanish American Literature, A Personal History*, 1977), Donoso speaks about the boom period of Latin American literature, a period from approximately 1960 to 1970, during which time the novel replaced poetry as the major genre in the continent's literature. In this book Donoso discusses his personal reasons for having left Chile, reasons that had nothing to do with politics. His explanation centered on the following: (1) the difficulty of getting works published in Chile; (2) the deep sense of isolation from the mainstream of Latin American literature; (3) the tradition of living abroad, in voluntary exile, established over the years by major Latin American writers; and (4) the importance of being part of that cohesive community of Latin American writers living in exile. Donoso felt that he must establish contact with writers outside Chile in order to grow as a writer. Thus his voluntary exile may be said to stem from a personal need to flee an oppressive environment that inhibited him.

Tres novelitas burguesas (1973; *Sacred Families*, 1977) reflects Donoso's residency in Barcelona from 1969 to 1971 in its use of the city in all three novellas. The novellas are clearly not as dramatic as *The Obscene Bird of Night*; they indicate a secondary concern with the superficial world of upper middle-class Spanish couples. The primary concerns are those found in his previous work: the search for identity within a world in which order and chaos are in conflict and the human personality is subject to disintegration. In the same year as the book's publication Donoso canceled his visit to Chile as a protest against the military takeover of the government. In 1975 he returned for a short visit but vowed he would never again visit his country until its repressive state was mitigated.

In 1978, Donoso's *Casa de campo (A House in the Country*, 1983) was hailed as another major work. Critics differed over its primary significances, particularly its allegorical reflection of the Chilean political situation, but all were in agreement that the novel was a showcase for an impressive array of style, technique, and imagination. Donoso is concerned with the nature of personal relationships, the struggle for survival in a world intent on annihilation, the search for individual identity, and life as a series of fraudulent experiences. The novel has been compared to William Golding's *Lord of the Flies* in its parallel of children protagonists whose deficient upbringings result in their destruction.

El jardín de al lado (1980) marks a turning point in Donoso's career as its publication takes place just after his return home to Chile. It is his first work of fiction to deal openly with the question of exile in its attempt to explain the reasons for his departure and return. Donoso's biographical novel suggests there has been a need on the part of Latin American writers to create a sense of uprooting in leaving their homelands. That sentiment serves as motivation to write in a place, usually Spain, where publishing houses abound. Thus the framework for return is inherent in the move away. Once published, the author can return freely to his country as a successful writer. On a more personal level is the experience of the author-protagonist who discovers he cannot run away from himself. His most profound desire is to find and accept his destiny and in so doing to discover happiness and salvation. That destiny is tied not to an exterior place but to his inner self. The protagonist's journey to find his heart's desire leads him back to the beginning, to his roots.

Donoso's last work written in exile indicates his stay has been a necessary and successful one. The demons that pursued him in the writing of *The Obscene Bird of Night* have abated, and he has ended his journey with a more explicit statement on his experiences.

Since returning to Chile, Donoso has published *Cuatro para Delfina* (1982), which contains four novellas, one of which, *Suenos de mala muerte*, has been presented successfully as a play. The new work proves a return to the type of fiction Donoso wrote before going into exile: the settings are obviously Chilean. Allegory, savage humor, and grotesque exaggeration abound in his portraits of daily life within contemporary Chile.

Although Donoso has insisted on his indifference to politics and his emphasis on the abstract and irrational world of the subconscious, critics continue to debate the social and political elements inherent in his work. Whatever that debate, most critics agree on the impressive level of his literary achievement.

Selected Titles: Novels: *Este domingo* (Santiago, 1966); *El lugar sin limites* (Mexico, 1966); *La misteriosa desaparicion de la marquesita de Loria* (Barcelona, 1980); Short Story Collections: *Veraneo y otros cuentos* (Santiago, 1955); *El Charleston* (Santiago, 1960); *Los mejores cuentos de José Donoso* (Santiago, 1965).

Translations: *This Sunday* (1967); *Hell Has No Limits* (1972); *Charleston and Other Stories* (1977); *Curfew* (1988).

Consult: George R. McMurray, *José Donoso* (1979); Ricardo Gutierrez Mouat, *José Donoso: Impostura e impostacion* (Gaithersburg, 1983).

ERICA FROUMAN-SMITH

DOOLITTLE, Hilda (H. D.). Born September 10, 1886, in Bethlehem, Pennsylvania; died September 29, 1961, in Zurich, Switzerland. H. D. was the child of orthodox Moravian parents. She was twenty-six years old when she left New

York, where she had been working after her college studies in Bryn Mawr and the University of Pennsylvania, for travel in Europe and, later, residence in London. She would make only brief and infrequent visits to her home country although she was proud of the American recognition and honors bestowed on her at the end of her life. H. D.'s first love may have been Ezra Pound,* whom she met in 1905 and to whom she was briefly engaged; although she claimed a vacation as the reason for her first trip to Europe, the real motivation may have been to visit Pound. H. D.'s friendship with Pound continued through the years and during Pound's trials with the American government.

H. D.'s first husband, with whom she lived in Europe, was the British writer Richard Aldington; she was also a great friend of Winifred Bryher, the wealthy British novelist, who assisted H. D. when she was in financial need and who left much of her fortune to H. D. and her daughter. H. D. spent her last years in a nursing home in Switzerland.

H. D. was part of the expatriate movement that saw in Europe the ideas of high literary endeavor. Pound was her mentor, counseling knowledge of world literature, ancient and modern; her associates were the wide world of brilliant writers that included James Joyce,* Gertrude Stein,* Ernest Hemingway, and Djuna Barnes. Novelist, short story writer, translator, and cinematographer as well as poet and memoirist, she is likely to be remembered first for her poetry. All her work explores the profound mystery in the simplest instant of reality, and the mythic communication between an artist's perception and his later rendering of human experience.

Selected Title: *H. D.: Collected Poems, 1912–1944*, ed. Louis L. Martz (1988).

DORFMAN, Ariel. Born 1942 in Argentina. A Chilean citizen, he divides his residence between the United States and Chile. Dorfman was brought by his family to the United States in 1945. From 1954 until the military takeover in 1973, Dorfman lived in Chile, where he became a citizen and obtained the equivalent of a master's degree from the University of Chile. Before finishing his studies, he was a research scholar at the University of California at Berkeley from 1968 to 1969. From 1970 to 1973 Dorfman taught Spanish-American literature at the University of Chile. Since then he has wandered through the United States and Europe. During the 1970s he taught Latin American literature at the Sorbonne in Paris and at the University of Amsterdam. In the 1980s he was a fellow at the Wilson Center (Smithsonian Institute) and a visiting scholar at the Institute for Policy Studies, both in Washington, D. C. He officially returned to Chile in 1983 at the time when many exiles were allowed (and encouraged) to return. He justified his move by claiming that his place was among his people where he could be nourished spiritually and linguistically. His plans changed when he was arrested and deported from Chile in 1987. Subsequently, he was allowed to return; he now divides his time between the United States and Chile, but considers himself an American resident.

Dorfman teaches at Duke University in North Carolina. Like many Latin

American writers, he finds an insufficient market for his works in his native land, and he is better able to survive economically on the writings he publishes abroad, particularly in the United States. He is a regular contributor to the *New York Times*, the *Village Voice* (newspaper of New York City), the *Los Angeles Times*, and the *Washington Post*. His most widely read work remains the series of trenchant essays on the human penchant for deception of self as well as others that he collected under the title *Para leer al Pato Donald* (with Armand Mattelart) (1970; *How to read Donald Duck*, 1975). Recently the English-language version of *La ultima canción de Manuel Sendero* (1982) was published to wide critical acclaim (*The Last Song of Manuel Sendero*, 1986). Dorfman's theatrical version of his novel *Viudas* (1981; *Widows*, 1983) appeared in production in August 1988 in Williamstown, Massachusetts, and in September 1989 in Los Angeles. Its narrative concerns a group of women in a war-ravaged nation whose husbands have disappeared from their village. When the bodies of the men wash onto shore, one by one, day after day, the women seize them for proper burial in defiance of the local military law that has branded them traitors. In Dorfman's words, the play is about military repression under the government of General Augusto Pinochet and about the civil war then tearing Chile apart, but it is also more than a reference to Chile's past and present; it is a work that treats the fates of millions who disappear without attention, people who have become obscure casualties of historical catastrophes.

Dorfman's latest novel, *Mascaras* (1988; *Mascara*, 1988), which he wrote simultaneously in Spanish and English, is an allegory of exile and evil. He remains a politically and socially committed writer who has incorporated his views on the experience of exile into many different genres—short stories, novels, poetry, essays, and plays.

Selected Titles: Prose fiction: *Cría ojos* (Mexico, 1979); *Dorando la píldora* (Chile, 1985); Essays: *La última aventura del Llanero Solitario* (San Jose, Costa Rica, 1978); *Hacia la liberacion del lector americano* (1984); *Sueños nucleares* (Buenos Aires, 1985); *Matando la inocencia* (Santiago, 1985); Poetry: *Desaparecer* (Federal Republic of Germany, 1979); *Pruebas al canto* (Mexico, 1980).

Translations: Poems: *Missing* (London, 1982); *Last Waltz in Santiago* (1988); Essays: *The Empire's Old Clothes* (1983); *Missing Continents* (1990); Stories: *My House Is on Fire* (1990).

Consult: Juan Claro-Mayo, "Dorfman, cuentista comprometido," *Revista Iberoamericana* 47, nos. 114–15 (January-June, 1981): 339–45; Naín Nómez, "Hacia la liberación del lector latinoamericano," *Revista Canadiense de Estudios Hispanicos* 12, no. 3 (Spring 1988): 498–503.

ERICA FROUMAN-SMITH

DOS PASSOS, John (Roderigo). Born January 14, 1896, in Chicago, Illinois; died September 28, 1970, in Baltimore, Maryland. Dos Passos journeyed to Spain in 1916 on his graduation from Harvard. He remained in Europe to serve as an ambulance driver in the Norton-Harjes Ambulance Unit in Spain and Italy. He was dishonorably discharged from the American Red Cross in 1918 because of alleged pacifist, anti-war comments he made in letters sent home to friends in the United States. He enlisted in the regular American army, served in France and was discharged in 1919. He stayed in Paris to attend lectures at the Sorbonne. Dos Passos drew on these experiences in his first novel, *One Man's Initiation* (1920).

Dos Passos returned to the United States in 1922. He began his lifelong interest in social causes, first as a member of the radical Left and later as a supporter of conservative Right movements. He was a passionate defender of the immigrant anarchists, Sacco and Vanzetti, who had been convicted of treason against the United States in 1927, and who he and many other American intellectuals felt had been wrongly judged. With Edna St. Vincent Millay and others, he marched in Boston to protest the conviction and the death sentence meted out to Sacco and Vanzetti, but the protests were unavailing. He visited the Soviet Union in 1928 and Spain during the Civil War there. He lost his wife, and the sight of one eye, in an automobile accident in 1947.

Dos Passos continued writing throughout his life. His literary achievement is secure, though critics argue over the quality of his later fictional work.

Selected Titles: *Rosinante to the Road Again* (1922, travels in Spain); *U.S.A.* (1938) [trilogy including *The 42nd Parallel*, 1930; *1919*, 1932; *The Big Money*, 1936]; *The Ground We Stand On* (1941); *District of Columbia* (1952) [trilogy including *Adventures of a Young Man*, 1939; *Number One: A Novel*, 1943; *Grand Design*, 1949]; *The Head and Heart of Thomas Jefferson* (1963).

Consult: John H. Wren, *John Dos Passos* (1962).

DOUGLAS, Norman. Born December 8, 1862, in a village of the Vorarlberg, a province in Austria; died February 9, 1946, in Capri, an island off the coast of Italy. A multiple expatriate, Douglas was born in a distant province of Austria of a half-Scottish, half-German mother; his father was a Scottish cotton miller who preferred residence in Austria to Scotland. Douglas did not see Scotland until he was taken there at the age of six by his mother after his father had died in a mountain-climbing accident. He studied in private schools in England and later in Karlsruhe, Germany, where he exhibited a superior talent for languages. By the age of twenty he had working knowledge of English, German, Greek, Latin, French, Italian, and Russian. He was also a gifted pianist and a serious botanist-naturalist.

Douglas made his first trip to Italy and Capri in 1888; he visited Greece and the Lipari Islands and developed the affection for Magna Graecia that was to persevere for the rest of his life. Douglas joined the British Foreign Office; from 1894 to 1896 he served in St. Petersburg, where he got into his first sexual imbroglio, this one with a Russian woman, and fled the scene for Naples. Douglas traveled several times to Tunisia and Ceylon; he wrote scientific essays, usually on biology. He married in 1898, divorced in 1904, the year he moved to Capri, where his homosexual adventures began playing a dominant role in his life. Douglas made no attempts to hide his pederasty, and Capri served as a home base for him for the rest of his life, allowing him a return whenever he got into difficulties because of his sexual escapades as well as providing a nurturing enclosure from distraction for his writing. Douglas was so liked by the local populace that he was made one of the few honorary citizens of the island.

Douglas was forty when he began writing his first book, *Siren Land* (1911). His fiction, travel writing, and memoirs evoke the world of a happy expatriate; clearly he was satisfied to live the life of a man of means pursuing the discipline of a writing career. His great interest in Roman culture was evidenced in several of his books; it also revealed another characteristic of the expatriate-exile: the choice of distant and foreign civilizations over his birthplace as sources of identity. His work is distinguished for its classical scholarship and cool style; the early books—*Siren Land; Fountains in the Sand* (1912); and *Old Calabria* (1915), his most popular travel work—disclose an artistic control of material and a brio that proved endearing even when daunting. His most famous work, the novel *South Wind* (1917), is a witty satire of expatriates on an island inescapably Capri though going under another name; in this work Douglas presents a world of double exiles, people who choose foreign shores to escape from inhospitable societies that reject them because of their sexual proclivities and/ or personal eccentricities. The misfits adapt so well to their foreign clime that they become acceptable eccentrics, but again they are excluded from responsibility for determining the laws of their habitat. The characters of *South Wind* do not mind their exclusions; their creator shared their view. Douglas did not think of himself as an outcast yearning for home, but in the words of one of his critics, George Woodcock, as a "glad exile."

Selected Titles: *They Went* (1920); *Alone* (1921); *Experiments* (1925); *Looking Back* (1934).

Consult: Mark Holloway, *Norman Douglas* (1976); George Woodcock, "Norman Douglas: The Willing Exile," *Ariel: A Review of International English Literature* 13, no. 4 (October 1982).

DOVLATOV, Sergei. Born September 3, 1941, in Ufa, Bashkiria, USSR; he lived in the Forest Hills section of Queens, New York City until his death on August 24, 1990. Dovlatov described his growing up in an eccentric family (certainly by Soviet norms) in his memoir, *Ours: A Russian Family Album* (1989). His father was a theater director and gag writer; his mother, an aspiring actress. Dovlatov's Aunt Mara was a powerful editor at a literary house who, Dovlatov says, hid her self-censorship by various rationales. His grandfather Isaak was shot as a spy because he played host to his émigré son's friend from Belgium; the friend was a Stalinist who had come to the Soviet Union to celebrate communism in its habitat. The absurdities of incongruity in the Soviet way of life impressed Dovlatov increasingly as the bright young man grew more aware of his surroundings. He described his cousin Boris, who ended up in prison, probably by self-destructive willfulness, and suggests the appeal of Boris's existential "solution" of crime as a way out of the kind of state in which the contemporary

Soviet citizen lives. Seeking experience by which to resist his foregone conclusions of invidious political, social, and personal amorality in his country, Dovlatov worked as a newspaperman-satirist during the Brezhnev era and became a master at summing up an adversary in a few punch lines. (Dovlatov used his experiences as background material in his novel, *The Compromise*). Dovlatov also worked as a guard in a labor camp, where he observed criminals whom he saw as representative not merely of Soviet society but of universal types. (He turned these experiences into material for his novel *Zona* (1982, Russian version; *The Zone: A Prison Guard's Story*, 1985). One of his stories, ''Predstavlenie'' (The Performance), included in the original Russian version, *Predstavlenie i drugie rasskazy* (published by Russica House, New York, 1988), concerns a play put on by the convicts to celebrate the jubilee of the October Revolution. In assigning the roles of Soviet heroes from Lenin downward to the inmates, Dovlatov was able to invest startling irony in his tale and to turn it into an archetypal fiction as well as a reflection of the grand Russian tradition spanning Fyodor Dostoyevsky, Leo Tolstoy, and Aleksandr Solzhenitsyn.* At the same time, Dovlatov's absolute refusal to conform to imposed social codes without first mocking them gives his story a pathos uniquely his and representative of his generation, both within the Soviet Union and in the third wave of émigrés.

Dovlatov's work suggests what seems at first an antisocial streak (and indeed was interpreted as such by Soviet authorities, who tolerated it as long as they felt it did not get out of hand). A protester of official Soviet policy, Dovlatov was not so much against any one policy as against the system *qua* system. He believed—given the history of his family and the aftermath of the Revolution—that a life of goallessness was as meaningful as the goal-striving that previous generations had wholeheartedly accepted. (Dovlatov defined the condition by the Russian term, *tseloustremlennost.*) In 1978 he apparently went too far in his joking criticism and his samizdat fiction, and he was asked to leave the country or go to prison. In exile, a state that Dovlatov found at first bewildering but exciting enough as experience, he continued his writing and was able to publish his fiction openly for the first time. A student, Ann Frydman, asked to translate one of his stories, sent it off to the *New Yorker* magazine, and it was promptly accepted (Dovlatov was paid $3,000 for his first published work). Dovlatov accepted the pleasant happening as one of the ''well-organized accidents'' that determine his, and all, human behavior. He celebrated this accidental fatalism as a limitation to be enjoyed; he saw his life as remaining forever capable of surprise and profound paradox.

Dovlatov continued to write in Russian while he worked as an announcer for Radio Free Europe in New York. His humor made him one of the most popularly appreciated of the Soviet-émigré writers. His attitude of mockery and self-mockery—or the groundwork of irony by which he roils all pretensions of language and system—is singular in his mastery of it but representative as well of a Soviet generation that chooses withdrawal, in the form either of apathy or of exile/

emigration, as a way out of the dogmatic fences, and defenses, of Socialist demands on the individual.

Dovlatov's recent fiction, *Inostranka* (in Russian, New York, 1980), treats in his comic manner the disarray in the lives of several Soviet émigrés, all of them Russian Jews, in the Forest Hills section of Queens, New York City. (Dovlatov, a Russian Jew, lived in Forest Hills, a community that now houses some 7,000 Soviet émigrés.) In reviewing the novella, Sally Laird, in the *Times Literary Supplement*, wrote: "Singularly lacking in purpose or principle, attaining to something like consciousness only in occasional fits of irritation, Marusya [the heroine] is the kind of constitutional foreigner for whom emigration is a permanent temptation—a substitution for thought, a bid for life after death—and who is unlikely to find herself at home anywhere except in Dovlatov's fiction" (p. 135).

Selected Title: *The Invisible Book* (1979).

Consult: Sally Laird, *Times Literary Supplement*, February 12–18, 1988; Seth Mydans, "Writing Without Roots," *New York Times Book Review*, September 23, 1984; Suzanne Ruta, "Russia Without Tears," *New York Times Book Review*, April 30, 1989.

DRABEK, Jan. Born May 5, 1935, in Prague, Czechoslovakia; he lives in Vancouver, British Columbia, Canada. Drabek emigrated with his parents in 1968 to the United States after the communist seizure of power. He studied at several American universities and traveled to India for philosophic explorations. On his return, he left the United States for permanent residence in Canada.

Drabek's best-known work is the novel *Whatever Happened to Wenceslav?* (1975), a bittersweet treatment of a wealthy Prague family's emigration to New York. Drabek's exile may be completed, as he now writes only in English except for Canadian broadcasts beamed to Czech audiences.

Selected Titles: *Report of the Death of Rosenkavalier* (1977); *The Statement* (1982).

DRUZHNIKOV, Juri. Born 1933, in Moscow, USSR; he lives in California. Druzhnikov graduated from the Moscow Pedagogical Institute in 1955, taught Russian and Soviet literature and history, was a journalist and editor, and was elected to the Union of Soviet Writers in 1971.

Prior to his emigration, eight of his books were published in the USSR. Among them are *In Quest of Archimedes* (1969) a collection of short stories; *Nothing Ever Goes My Way* (1971); the novel *Wait till Sweet Sixteen* (1976), and several children's books. Two of his plays, *Teacher in Love* (1976) and *Bear's Service* (1977), were staged in public productions. Not one of these works was published or appeared as written by the author. Half of Druzhnikov's novel was excised and the ending changed; one of his plays was banned during its premier run. In an article in *Izvestia* (August 16, 1974), Druzhnikov was accused of a "harmful philosophy" and of distorting the character of the Soviet people. He announced his intention to emigrate in 1977 but was subjected to harassment and was unable to secure a permit to leave until 1987. At that time an open letter by several Soviet writers demanding that his civil rights be restored was published, and Druzhnikov's case was included in the giant exhibition ''A Decade of Exclusion of Writers from Soviet Literature'' in Moscow.

Druzhnikov's recent book, *The Myth of Pavlik Morozov* (London, 1988), is the result of a historical and literary investigation into the murder of an adolescent boy who had denounced his father to the Soviet police. The boy had become a celebrated child-hero in the Soviet Union; in Druzhnikov's treatment the informer becomes a means by which the author comments on the ethics and morality of Soviet culture. Druzhnikov also has published a novel, *Angels on the Head of a Pin* (1989), about the Prague Spring and the ''Prague Autumn'' in Moscow, 1968 and 1969, in which he exposes ideological state machinery of Soviet administrators during the occupation of Czechoslovakia and purge of its independent thinkers. Druzhnikov's most recent publication is a collection of stories, *A Crack in the Pink Lampshade* (1989). He teaches at the University of California at Davis.

MARK A. POPOVSKY, translated by Zoric Ward

DUBNOV, Eugene. Born 1949 in Tallinn, then Estonia. He has been living in England since 1975. Dubnov was educated at the University of Moscow and published widely in his country before he emigrated to Israel in 1971. He studied at Bar-Ilan University in Israel and received his Ph.D from the University of London, with a dissertation on T. S. Eliot* and Osip Mandelshtam.* His poems and stories have been translated into Hebrew, English, and many other languages. His books of poetry in Russian are *Ryzhiye monety* (1978, Russet Coins) and *Hebom i zemleyu* (1984, By Sky and Earth). He is compiling an anthology of Russian poetry translated in collaboration with John Heath-Stubbs.

DU BOIS, W. E. B. (William Edward Burghardt). Born February 23, 1868, in Great Barrington, Massachusetts; he died August 27, 1963, in Accra, the capital of Ghana. Du Bois graduated from Harvard in 1890 and pursued graduate studies at the University of Berlin on a Slater Fund fellowship from 1892 to 1894. On his return he taught at Wilberforce University in Ohio. Later he earned his doctorate from Harvard and taught at the University of Pennsylvania and Atlanta University. Du Bois's interest in the black diaspora, and his passionate search into its history, became evidenced early in his teaching and writing career and during his leadership role in the Pan-African movement. With the rank of special envoy, he attended the inauguration of Charles B. King as president of Liberia in 1924. Du Bois was also one of the prime movers in the founding of the National Association for the Advancement of Colored People.

Du Bois's belief that the black man could find his place in society only through consciousness of roots was part of his fabric of historical determinism. In accepting the history of his origin as a slave in the Western world, and in transcending that circumstance into personal achievement, the black man finds his peace of identity, Du Bois argued. Conversely, the black man draws upon the regality of his African origins to shore himself against the anguish of present exile. Du Bois's views on Pan-Africanism, which led in part to the Back-to-Africa movements of the 1920s (and again in the 1960s), are also related to his Marxist analytic tools and to an earlier quarrel with the distinguished black inventor, George Washington Carver, over the proper course for a black man in finding his way in America. Carver declared that a black man should accept second-class citizenship and menial labor as temporary goals in a gradual process to equality and freedom. Du Bois called for protest and defiance even if such acts led to setbacks of personal or political injury.

Du Bois believed the black man would find his surest strength in group solidarity emphasizing the joys of sharing in physical and intellectual ferment. His grasp of the powers of fraternity and his approach to economics led him to join the Communist party in 1961. Membership, however, may have been more nominal and flaunting than committal, for Du Bois loved the country in which he was born, but had become a victim of its political persecution in the 1950s. Charged as an agent of a foreign power in 1951, he was acquitted, but he continued to suffer harassment and government surveillance; he also was treated as a pariah and cast out from his country's social and political activities.

In 1961 Nwame K. Nkrumah, president of Ghana, invited Du Bois to Accra to organize and administer an encyclopedia of African history and achievement. Du Bois worked on this project until his death two years later. He became a Ghanaian citizen and was given a state funeral there.

Consult: John Edgar Wideman, *Du Bois* (1990).

DUČIC, Jovan. Born February 17, 1871, in Trebinje, Yugoslavia; he died April 7, 1943, in Gary, Indiana. Dučic wrote poetry (in Serbian) while in the diplomatic corps, where he was variously stationed from 1907 to 1918 in Istanbul, Sofia, and Athens. He worked for the Yugoslav government after World War I as a delegate to the League of Nations; he also was Yugoslavia's ambassador to Egypt, Italy, Romania, and Portugal. In 1941, with the collapse of the Yugoslavian monarchy and the German conquest of his country, he emigrated to the United States.

Dučic was also an accomplished essayist and memoirist (*Gradovi i himere* [1932, Cities and Chimeras]).

Selected Titles: *Stihovic proza* (1952); *Izabrana dela* (1964).
Consult: A. Kadíc, *Contemporary Serbian Literature* (1964).

DUO Duo (originally Li Shizheng). Born 1951, he has lived most of his thirty-eight years in Beijing, China; he now lives in London, England. Duo was among the student protesters in Tiananmen Square on June 4, 1989, who brought world attention to their prodemocracy movement. He left one day after the army began shooting at the protesters, in order to fulfill a teaching-reading engagement in Rotterdam, The Netherlands. Thus he was spared the arrest, humiliation, and possible torture and death, which many of his colleagues experienced. Duo now considers himself a writer in exile and foresees a period of repression in China for many years. Although as a leading modernist poet he has written little direct people's poetry or "engaged literature," he feels it his mission to speak out about the state of oppression in his country. The memory of Tiananmen Square remains vivid to him, and one of his celebrated lines, reflecting the horror of the army's brutality in quelling the student protest, sums up his nightmare: "the troops keep coming through the clouds." Duo has said in public appearances in London that as soon as the shooting started in Tiananmen Square, "what was killed was the Communist Party."

Duo now lives in London, where he teaches Chinese literature at the University of London. He is a professional painter, and has trained as an opera singer. He began his writing career as a journalist for the government-owned *Peasant's Daily*.

In a recent panel discussion at the PEN International Congress in Toronto, Canada, in September 1989, 100 days after he became an exile from China, Duo spoke of the need for writers to remain the conscience of their country. The paradox, Duo said, is that they must remain silent in order to speak, or go into exile where their voices will no longer be heard in their country. Duo also said that in exile in the West he had learned a new attitude to the concept of freedom from that which he had held in his thirty-eight years in China. Freedom in China, he explained, is an idea that has not been realized; it thus possesses a burning vitality as an image and currency of emotional force. In the West, where freedom, though it is limited, is a real thing, a property of the human condition, it is less valued and less impelling. For Duo the prodemocracy movement in the past seventy years in China was aimed at the idea, not the reality, of it; in June 1989 the reality of freedom suddenly seemed possible before it was wiped away.

At present, Duo is pessimistic about the writer's role in China, believing no writer will be encouraged in his pursuit unless he puts state security and people's interests above private conscience and aesthetic values. Such a primacy of view, Duo believes, dissembles the writer's search for individual truth and individual vision into a propaganda of well-intentioned ideals of social progress, a propaganda of values that thrive on uniformity and intolerance of dissent.

Only one volume in English translation of Duo's poetry is currently available: *Looking Out from Death: From the Cultural Revolution to Tiananmen Square*, published in 1989 by Bloomsbury Press in London.

DURRELL, Lawrence. Born February 27, 1912, in Darjeeling, India, to Anglo-Irish parents who had never seen England; died November 7, 1990, in Sommières, France, of emphysema. Durrell's father was an engineer who worked on the construction of the Darjeeling railway line skirting the Himalayas; the family had been in residence in India for three generations. When Durrell was twelve, he left India, where he had attended the College of St. Joseph, for further education in St. Edmund's School in Canterbury, England. After secondary school, according to Durrell's own account, he purposely failed the entrance examination to Oxford four times, a conscious rebellion against his father and England. He became a jazz pianist in a London nightclub while aspiring to be a writer. He found life intolerable in England, which he has described as "that mean, shabby little island . . . [that] tried to destroy anything singular and unique in me." He married the artist Nancy Myers in 1935.

Durrell's literary guides have been largely expatriate writers. He admired D. H. Lawrence,* who, like Durrell, left England and wandered round the world. Durrell's discovery of the works of his senior expatriate Henry Miller* produced a tremendous effect on his writing. Durrell also felt a kinship with T. S. Eliot,* with whom he kept up a correspondence in the 1930s. In 1938, after censorship problems had complicated its British Isles publication, Durrell's *The Black Book* appeared in an edition by Obelisk Press in Paris. Durrell has been grateful to the French ever since, claiming that this book made him what he calls a "serious writer."

In 1936 Durrell persuaded his family to move to Corfu. He disliked the English climate and the prewar class system. However, worried about supporting his family, he managed to join the British Council even though he had not attained a university degree. In 1939 he accepted a teaching appointment at the British Institute in Athens, but the onset of the war and the constant shifting of battle lines forced him to move to Crete and eventually to Egypt. From 1941 to 1944, Durrell was the British foreign press officer in Cairo; later he became press attaché in Alexandria, the setting of his most famous work, *The Alexandria Quartet*. In Alexandria he published, with Robert Felding, the magazine *Personal Landscape, a Magazine of Exile*. (It is interesting to note that in *Clea* Durrell calls Alexandria "the city of exiles.") After his stay in Alexandria, Durrell went to Greece and Rhodes as a public information officer. He lectured in Argentina and Yugoslavia for the British Council (1947–49), and settled in Cyprus in 1953. When that island suffered the throes of revolution in 1956, he returned to Dorset, England, but forsook his native land again for Provence and the south of France, where he has been living since. Durrell, who said when he turned fifty that he had not lived in England for more than eight continuous years, has visited his home country on occasion but remains a committed expatriate.

Durrell proclaims his displacement and sense of exile openly. His major work, *The Alexandria Quartet*, concerns itself with a group of exotic characters from different social levels and countries, among them an Irish schoolmaster, a Greek cabaret dancer, a Coptic millionaire banker, a retired English sailor, a brilliant English writer, and a born-again Jewish heroine. These people exhibit many varieties of extreme intellectual, religious, and sexual passion in the brilliant depraved society of Alexandria. They are characterized by profound suffering and a dissatisfaction resulting, mainly, from their sense of displacement. At the end of Durrell's narrative, some of the characters—disoriented, desperate, and displaced at the beginning—find what they are seeking through love. Durrell has said, "There is such a thing as modern love, but I hope to suggest that it is in itself only a way of growing" (Harry T. Moore, *The World of Lawrence Durrell* [1962], p. 157). It is significant that those characters who find a release into an exuberance of spirit do so by leaving or in the act of departing from Alexandria.

Durrell has written many volumes of fiction, both short stories and novels; he has also written highly praised works of poetry and travel books as well as biography and literary criticism. The Mediterranean inspires almost all of his important work.

Selected Titles: See Robert Potter and Brooke Whiting, comps., *Lawrence Durrell: A Checklist* (Los Angeles, 1961); *The Durrell-Miller Letters 1935–1980*, ed. Ian S. MacNiven (1988).

Consult: G. S. Fraser, *Lawrence Durrell: A Critical Study* (1968); Alan Warren Friedman, eds., *Lawrence Durrell and the Alexandria Quartet* (Norman, Oklahoma, 1970); Harry T. Moore, *The World of Lawrence Durrell* (1962); John Unterecker, *Lawrence Durrell* (1964); John A. Weigel, *Lawrence Durrell* (1965).

FRANCESCO CESARI and MARTIN TUCKER

E

EDWARDS, Jorge. Born 1931 in Santiago, Chile. Edwards renounced Chile in 1973 after a military coup destroyed the democratic government of President Salvador Allende. At the time of the coup he was a diplomat serving the Allende regime in Paris. He spent most of his exile years in Spain, returning to his native land in 1979.

Selected Title: *Persona Non Grata* (Barcelona, 1973; *Persona Non Grata*, 1977).

EHRENBURG, Ilya. Born January 27, 1891, in Kiev, Russia; died September 1, 1967, in Moscow, USSR. Ehrenburg was a biological phenomenon searching for some form of spiritual commitment but permitting his dubious intelligence to play underhandedly with any faith he might acquire along the way. His path is strewn with recantations, intermittent bursts of revised zealotry, and rationalizations of extraordinary persuasion. That he survived, and survived well, is a testament to his ingenuity. The larger questions of his sincerity, his right to eccentricity within the conformism demanded by his new society, remain intriguingly unanswered. Ehrenburg may well be the archetypal exile, at home nowhere and possessing the faculty to be accepted as a guest anywhere. The son of a prominent Jewish beer brewer, he was educated at the Moscow Gymnasium (the family had moved from Kiev when Ilya was five years old). In his teens he joined a revolutionary cadre, was arrested by the Czarist government, and spent six months in jail. On release he went to Paris where he lived the life of a young bohemian; he chose, significantly, François Villon as his bohemian better-self to translate into Russian. His first book of poems, *Poems*, appeared in 1910 in Paris. In 1914 he became a newspaper correspondent, covering the hostilities on the World War I battlefronts. He returned to Russia in 1917, with the overthrow of the Czar, but wrote of his fears of revolutionary violence and emasculation of Russian traditions in "Prayer for Russia" (1917). This publication was the first of many whose consequences Ehrenburg would have to juggle, since the work put him outside the pale of Red enthusiasm. He recanted the work but left the country again in 1920 for exile in France. It was during this period that he published his first novel, *The Extraordinary Adventures of Julio Jurenilo and His Disciples* (1922), a work that has remained one of his important fictions. The eponymous rogue Mexican hero travels through Paris, Rome, Mexico City, Moscow, and a provincial Russian city during the Civil Wars in 1919–22 in a picaresque journey representing Ehrenburg's ironic observations of what was happening to his country. As "teacher" to his disciples, Jurenilo advises that a new slavery is necessary for a new world freedom, and, like Thomas Carlyle, he urges his disciples to put on the "yoke" demanded by the Revolution. Whether the novel is satire, or serious exhortation, has been debated by critics since its appearance, and its perverse ability to withstand resolute analysis may prove its value rather than diminish it. Particularly in its closure, when Jurenilo is robbed and then murdered by thugs, the mystery of Ehrenburg's attitude to the revolution and its triumphs becomes a source of perplexing stimulation. Ehrenburg's outspoken protest against the military horrors of the Revolution may also be seen in his novel *The Stormy Life of Lazik Roitschwantz* (1928), in which he describes the tyranny of a new Soviet power and the continuing deprivation of the Russian people. In another novel, *Protochny Lane* (1927), he reiterates the failure of the Soviet dream in its desertion of the humanitarian values that spawned the Russian Revolution and made possible its appeal to peasants, the middle-class and aristocratic theorists alike.

As a result of Ehrenburg's published attitudes, he was accused of bad faith in the Soviet dream, and of backsliding into the hated "revisionist" camp. He also was charged with the dangerous tendency to sentimentalize the young days of the Revolution and to malign the more difficult times that follow the first fruits of victory. As a consequence—Ehrenburg was always a realist, and/or opportunist, who knew he had to appease those in power when he most disagreed with them—Ehrenburg turned to historical fiction. In writing about the past, he presented his commentary on the present. Several of Ehrenburg's following books praised the Russian/Soviet Revolution. These were published during the most brutal period of Stalinist discipline. Among these works are *The West Is Dying* (1929), *Moscow Does Not Believe in Tears* (1936), and *White Coals, or the Tears of Werther* (1928). By the mid–1930s Ehrenburg was questioning the direction of the Revolution, and began to employ the imagery of slavery without the literal expression of it. He published his observations of the Spanish Civil War in two separate books and his view of *The Fall of Paris* (1940), in which, predictably, the Communist forces become the heroic manifestation of progress. But with the fall of France, Ehrenburg's attitude again showed a nostalgia for the end of an era—that period of capitalist democracy and culture which had produced nineteenth-century realistic triumphs. In lamenting the fall of France, Ehrenburg was expressing an ambivalence about the decline of a century.

Ehrenburg returned to the Soviet Union in 1940, where he served on the battlefront as a correspondent for several Soviet newspapers. After the war he wrote several novels set in contemporary times, and in which he treated the direct effect of politics on ordinary, daily living. Throughout this later work—*The Thaw*, in particular—Ehrenburg returned to that humanitarian ambivalence regarding manipulation of power for an ameliorative end. In *The Thaw* (first published serially in *Znamya* in May 1954; the second volume appeared in the same journal in April 1956) he confronts two artists—one is successful, the other lives in anonymous poverty. One has accommodated himself to revisions demanded by politic society; the other has kept faith with his first timeless sight of principles. The tale is an allegory of the Russian/Soviet revolution, and its placement of human values. Significantly, the work appeared after Stalin's death, when such questions, long suppressed by that dictator's regime, began to manifest themselves. In the end, Ehrenburg remained true to one guiding doubt characteristic of him from the start of his career: the inescapable sense of loss with the passing of any tradition that had sustained itself for a period of history, no matter into what state of decadence that tradition has fallen.

Consult: Vera Alexandrova, *A History of Soviet Literature, 1917–1962: From Gorky to Yevtushenko* (1963); A. Goldberg, *Ilya Ehrenburg: Revolutionary, Novelist, Poet, War Correspondent, Propagandist: The Extraordinary Epic of a Russian Survivor* (1984).

EKELUND, Vilhelm. Born 1880, in Stehag, Sweden; died 1949, in Saltsjobaden, Sweden. Ekelund left Sweden in 1908 after becoming involved in a brawl in a public establishment; he preferred flight to notoreity and possible incarceration. He spent four years in Berlin, often poor and lonely; he later lived in Denmark for nine years, where he fell seriously ill. On his recuperation Ekelund returned to Sweden to play the role of a spiritual advisor to the young, but he found himself with no larger following than a small band of devoted adherents.

Ekelund's exile was concurrent with the end of his poetry career. Whether exile prompted his decision to stop writing poetry, or whether he went into exile because his poetic vein had dried up, remains indeterminate. What is clear is that in Ekelund's case exile turned him into a philosophic writer who wished desperately to enter through some door into his country's halls of popular culture. He did not find the entranceway.

ELAGIN, Ivan (pseudonym of Ivan Venedictovich Matveev). Born December 1, 1918, in Vladivostok, USSR; he died February 8, 1987, in New York City. Elagin's father was a futuristic poet, his grandfather a journalist and author of essays about the history of the city of Vladivostok; his niece N. Matveeva is a well-known Soviet poet. After completing high school, Elagin entered the Kiev Medical Institute, but World War II interrupted his medical studies. He was captured, while working as student medic, by the advancing German army near Kiev in 1942, and for several years was a prisoner of war, then an inmate in a displaced persons camp. Hunger, cold, homelessness, and the depression-despair experienced in those years were to be mirrored in the small books of poems, which Elagin miraculously managed to have printed in the late 1940s—*Journey from There* and *Thou* and *My Century*. The young poet had no desire to return to the Soviet Union, since he was aware that Stalin had issued orders that all soldiers and officers who had fallen captive to the German military be confined in detention-labor camps. Elagin also had not forgotten that in 1937 the Soviet secret police had arrested his poet father, who died in prison. One of Elagin's best-known poems, "Stars," is dedicated to the memory of his beloved father.

In 1950 Elagin received permission to enter the United States, where he enrolled in university studies. He received his doctorate in Slavic languages and literatures from New York University in 1969. Later he taught at Middlebury College, New York University, and the University of Pittsburgh. In 1953 he succeeded in having a small volume of his poems published, largely a reprint of the work published in Munich, under the title of *Journey from There*. His next collection, *Nocturnal Reflections*, appeared ten years later in 1963. *Slanting Flight* (1967) and *Dragon on the Roof* (1973), two further collections, followed.

Of his work Elagin has written: "I have lived a great part of my life in America. The American city, as in a theatrical stage-set, has become my poetical backdrop. Lyrical experience placed not within a landscape but in the midst of a stage set, among the wondrous constructions of a world no longer hostile but still alien to me, has become a familiar compositional technique in my poetry" (*Under the Constellation of the Axe*, 1976). Elagin's later work, the poems of the 1960s and 1970s, present these spiritual yearnings set amid the metaphoric stone forests of giant metropolitan centers. His special mood is an ambivalent one. In the midst of a cityscape, for example, "The Skyscrapers Were Hiding in the Haze" or "Greenwich Village," scenes of his abandoned motherland surge up: the seashore in the Crimea, the family house in Kiev. The poet is clearly struggling with a nostalgia that he is both resisting and fondling.

Elagin's poems issue out of a long-honored Russian tradition in which the poet seeks not only beauty but truth. Thus, in his work, a certain moral fervor prevails, and Elagin appears to have no problems in presenting political and moral credos and pedagogy in his creative work. In 1959 in Munich he published a book of political feuilletons (broadsides) in verse in which he criticized what he called the totalitarian structure of his homeland. In defense of his aesthetic views Elagin has written: "In art, as in a large house, there are many different rooms from the attic to the cellar. I am drawn to those rooms whose windows look out on the street, on people. From here comes my general acceptance of life and at times my pamphleteering and proselytizing. Art for me is not only self-expression, but in a larger form, personal contact. Perhaps it's because of this that I translate. I think that translation is the true cultural exchange. My most important work is the translation of the epic poem of the American poet, Stephen Vincent Benét—'John Brown's Body.' I worked on my translation for five years.''

Elagin's later work—his collection of poems *Under the Constellation of the Axe* (Frankfurt, 1976) and *In the Amphitheater of the Universe* (Hermitage, 1982)—shows a further growth in his craft. At the same time, a bitterness and frustration, a sense of corrosive loss, are also felt in this later work. Elagin has written that the theme of modern man and his disruption/separation/exile is what ''palpitates'' his creativity, and that his poetry represents an attempt to heal the damage of emigrant and exile existence.

Elagin's poems are simple in vocabulary and sentence structure, and are traditional in form. He aims for accessibility with his readers and rejects any attempt to bring intellectual abstraction into his poems. His approach has proved popular with readers of Russian-language newspapers and journals both in the USSR and in the West. Shortly before his death, this poet, who has been called the major phenomenon of the ''second emigration,'' prepared for publication the most complete collection of his verse, *Heavy Stars* (Tenafly, New Jersey, 1987). All of Elagin's work was written in Russian.

MARK A. POPOVSKY, translated by Zoric Ward

ELIADE, Mircea. Born March 9, 1907, in Bucharest, Romania; died April 22, 1986, in Chicago, Illinois. Eliade, whose lifelong work was the expression of literature and religious instinct through the focus of religious symbolism as evidenced in religions and literatures throughout history, studied philosophy in Bucharest. He received his master of arts degree from the University of Bucharest with concentrated study on the (European) Renaissance and its philosophical tenets. In 1928 he journeyed to Calcutta to explore Eastern religion in one of its places of origin, studying with Surendranath Dasgupta. He returned to Romania to earn his Ph.D. in 1933, with a dissertation on Yoga. He taught for six years at the University of Bucharest and served in the diplomatic corps from 1940 to 1945, first as cultural attaché in London, and later, during World War II, in Portugal. In disagreement with the state socialism of his new government, Eliade emigrated to Paris, where he lived from 1945 to 1956; many of his books are written in French as well as in his native language. He taught at the Sorbonne and other European universities and participated in the yearly Ancona meetings of the Eranos group. In 1956 he accepted an invitation to a professorship of history of religion at the University of Chicago, where he taught the history of religion for many years. Eliade received various honors and academic distinctions during his lifetime.

The centrality of Eliade's thought lies in the kingdom of nostalgia for a state in which religious symbols play so vital a part they heal the wounds of exile and division into which self-awareness has led its followers. Eliade, who completed the third volume of his mammoth *History of Religious Ideas, From Muhammad to the Age of Reforms* shortly before his death, saw himself as a scientist of religion presenting man's ever-recurrent wish for and attempts at annihilation of the dualism in his nature. All religions, and the myths that precede them, are seen by Eliade as guises and disguises throughout the ages against an ineradicable core of religious instinct. This religious instinct is represented in the religious symbol, but the symbol may come before the religious experience and may determine the shape and history of the experience.

One critic, A. M. Piatigorsky, sees Eliade as a historian who objectifies his findings through the prism of his assumptions and prior knowledge. Whether Eliade is to be viewed as an objective scientist or a partisan seeker after a working but nonverifiable truth, it is clear that his aesthetic—his totality of cultural vision—is based on the presence and expression of a religious core in the essence of humanity. Though Eliade's yearning for the paradise that predates man's duality is not a consequence of historical exile, it reflects an even more primal experience of exile—the exit from God's garden.

One of Eliade's last works, *Briser le toit de la maison: La creativities et ses symboles* (Paris, 1987), reveals another instance of his intimate relationship to exile and his yearning to bridge it. In this collection of essays and reviews written between 1949 and 1985, Eliade posits the concept that man has lost his ability to scale new heights of being, to "break through the roof of his house," because he has taken scientific methodology as his guide into the mysteries of the universe. In reducing wonder to technical adaptability in the universal scheme of things, man has, Eliade is saying, lost both the quick of religious awe and the slowness of time that permits mystery to reveal itself in chronic wonder.

In Eliade's early years as a writer, his main output was narrative fiction characterized by a quest for (and questionings of) knowledge. Some of his fictional works are clearly outgrowths of musings from the journals he kept of his experiences and intellectual probings. Among these are *Isabel şi apele diavolului* (1930; Isabel and the Devil's Waters), a reflection of Eliade's psychosexual obsessions, and *Maitreyi* (1933, Maitreyi) and *Şantier* (1935, Work in Progress), both drawing on his years in India. The novels have a typical protagonist: a young intellectual torn between the pursuit of the progressive rationalism of the West and a yearning for the timeless a-historicism of the East. One of Eliade's most important critics, Matei Calinescu, says that the most "forward-looking" of Eliade's early works is his least praised one, *Lumina ce se stinge* (1934, The Light That Fails), a work with "fantastic" or "epiphanic" dimensions. In this novel and the ones that followed, among them *Întoarcerea din rai* (1934, Return from Paradise), *Domnişoara Christina* (1936; Miss Christina); *Şarpele* (1937, The Snake), *Secretul Doctorului Honigberger* (1940; *Two Tales of the Occult*, 1972), Eliade explores consciousness on two planes, the rational and the superrational, the fields of perceived knowledge and illuminated belief. The terms "fantastic" and "fictional realism" as two polarities of literary technique and profound authorial response to the material of human life have also been used to characterize the two essential, dualistic aspects of Eliade's writing and thinking.

Eliade did not forsake fiction after World War II—he produced twenty shorter works of fiction during that period from 1945 to his death—but he placed greater emphasis on his scholarly and philosophical pursuit of religious planes of existence and being in humankind. Among the many celebrated works of this period are *Le mythe de l'éternel retour* (1949; *The Myth of the Eternal Return*, 1954); *Traitré d'histoire des religions* (1949; *Patterns in Comparative Religion*, 1958); *Le chamanisme* (1951; *Shamanism*, 1964); *Yoga, Immortalité et liberté* (1952; *Yoga: Immortality and Freedom*, 1964); and *A History of Religious Ideas* (1976–83), written in English, in three volumes.

Eliade's fiction during this later part of his life and fame contrast sharply with his earlier creative works. The later works rely more on symbols of quest and initiation while at the same time they are spare in style and confident in the suspended realities of fantastic universes conjured for Eliade's narrative journeys. There is much less autobiographical reference and texture, and a seeming naturalness, a stance in which the storyteller becomes a part of his story without intrusion of an authorial voice. Part of this sense of grace may stem from Eliade's acceptance of the keys to the lost worlds of meaning through communion with comparative mythology. It is clear that in the later fiction, all dealing with the fantastic world of another reality than the modernist, ironic view and the observable surface of timely events and accepted fact, Eliade exhibits no sense of existential anguish, a feature of his earlier quests.

Eliade also published several volumes of autobiography during his later years, among them *Fragments d'un journal, 1945–1969* (1973; printed in English in a variant edition as *No Souvenirs, Journal 1957–1969*, 1977); *Fragments d'un journal II, 1970–1978* (1981); *Autobiography, Volume I* (1981), and *Autobiography, Volume II: 1937–1960, Exile's Odyssey* (1988) in which he writes of his new homeland in the United States.

Eliade's work, in sum, is the exploration of a universe, and its many constituent worlds, in which the dualities of human consciousness are resolved through philosophy or religious instinct and abiding undercurrents of insight. His work posits two worlds—one in which surface reality demands its due, and the "other," the world of miracle and myth. Eliade's reliance on myth—and the double process of demythification and then remythification (invention, or reinvention of a new viable form of the old decadent myth)—is crucial to any understanding of his work. Eliade himself believed that man was in a state of exile and loss until he regained creative power through the embrace of and surrender to mythic sustenance. In his words:

Every exile is a Ulysses traveling toward Ithaca. Every real existence reproduces the *Odyssey*. The path toward Ithaca, toward the center. I had known all that for a long time. What I have just discovered is that the chance to become a new Ulysses is given to *any* exile *whatsoever* (precisely because he has been condemned by the gods, that is, by the "powers" which decide historical, earthly destinies). . . . But to realize this, the exile must be capable of penetrating the hidden meaning of his wanderings, and of understanding them as a long series of initiation trials (willed by the gods) and as so many obstacles on the path which brings them back to the hearth (the center). That means: seeing signs, hidden meanings, symbols, in the sufferings, the depressions, the dry periods in everyday life. Seeing them and reading them even *if they aren't there*; if one sees them, one can build a structure and read a message in the formless flow of things and the monotonous flux of historical facts. (*No Souvenirs, Journal 1957–1969* [1977], entry for January 1, 1960, p. 84)

A thorough study of Eliade's characteristic approach to his later fiction may be found in the introduction by Matei Calinescu to *Youth Without Youth and other Novellas* (1988), Eliade's most recent translation published in the United States; much of the information on Eliade's later fiction given in this entry was provided by Calinescu's fine study. The volume, edited as well by Calinescu, contains the eponymous novella and two other celebrated works, "The Cape" and "Nineteen Roses." Eliade wrote all his fiction in Romanian, and said in one of his journal entries that his chief goal was to be a "Romanian writer."

Translations: *The Old Man and the Bureaucrats* (1979; first published in 1968 in Romanian); *Tales of the Sacred and Supernatural* (1981; parts of this work appeared in French in 1963 and 1976); *Two Strange Tales* (1986; reprint of *Two Tales of the Occult*, 1972, a translation of *Secretul Doctorului Honigberger*, 1940).

Consult: Douglas Allen and Dennis Doeing, *Mircea Eliade: An Annotated Bibliography* (1980); N. J. Girardot and M. L. Ricketts, eds., *Imagination and Meaning: The Scholarly and Literary Worlds of Mircea Eliade* (1982); J. Kitagawa and C. Long, eds., *Myths and Symbols: Studies in Honor of Mircea Eliade* (1969; contains essays by E. M. Cioran, V. Horia, G. Spaltmann, and others).

ELIOT, T. S. (Thomas Stearns). Born September 26, 1888, in St. Louis, Missouri; died January 4, 1965, in London, England. Eliot's distinguished family included the Elizabethan prose writer Sir Thomas Elyot and a grandfather who founded Washington University in St. Louis. He moved to England, after receiving B.A. and M.A. degrees from Harvard in English literature and philosophy, in order to work on his Ph.D. dissertation on the philosopher F. H. Bradley. He completed the dissertation in 1916 while in residence at Oxford, but did not pursue a formal degree. Instead he taught in an English prep school, then worked in Lloyds Bank for several years until he suffered a breakdown and journeyed to the Continent for recuperation. It was during this period that he worked on his masterpiece, *The Waste Land*, and received inestimable help and advice on the manuscript from his friend, Ezra Pound.* After his return to England, Eliot began working for Faber and Gwyer (later Faber and Faber, now Faber), and in the course of more than a generation became one of the most powerful literary statesmen in publishing and cultural history. He worked as editor of the *Criterion* from 1922 to 1939, selecting for attention many young and unknown writers; he wrote reviews for a number of select journals that often decided the literary fate of an aesthetic movement or author. His pronouncements set the thermometer for readings on John Milton, John Donne, George Herbert, Lord Byron, Rudyard Kipling, and other figures. While Eliot was oracular as a literary arbiter, he was often both personally attentive to beginning writers and quietly generous in his defense of them with the literary establishment.

Eliot was very much at home in England; possibly he was at home in England because it represented the cultural traditions he valued, while also keeping him at a distance from the demands of his Unitarian forebears in St. Louis. In any case Eliot became an Anglo-Catholic in 1927 and a British citizen in 1928. The conversion to orthodoxy gave Eliot relief from the terrors of emptiness that had dogged him since young manhood and that were not assuaged by his marriage to Vivienne Haigh-Wood, a highly neurotic and demanding person; Eliot's reserved personality and Vivienne's need of attention produced misery for both of them.

Although Eliot kept very much in contact with American colleagues and thus could be said to have found a perfect residence—that is, the habitation of high English and American worlds of honor, respect, and intelligence—he may be viewed as an expatriate, as an emigrant, and as a self-exile till he found himself through conversion to Anglo-Catholicism and to British nationality. His later work is a celebration of his newfound state of identity, which issues from his realization of wholeness. Critics disagree on which Eliot—the early one of despair and dry, rasping pain, the one never at ease, or the later Eliot, the man of religious faith and statesman-like surety—is the greater Eliot. The earlier Eliot is the one who took counsel in exile and exploited his self-banishment in the fog of taunting yellow reckonings; the later Eliot is the one who questioned less and justified more his own satisfaction with life. He received the Nobel Prize for Literature in 1948.

Selected Titles: Poetry: *Poems* (London, 1920); *The Waste Land* (1922); *Poems 1909–1925* (1925); *Collected Poems 1909–1935* (1936); *Four Quartets* (1943); *Old Possum's Book of Practical Cats* (1979); *The Complete Poems and Plays* (1952, enlarged ed. 1962); *Collected Poems 1909–1962* (1963); *Poems Written in Early Youth* (1967). Criticism: *The Sacred Wood* (London, 1920); *Selected Essays 1917–1932* (1932); *After Strange Gods* (London, 1934); *Elizabethan Essays* (London, 1934); *The Idea of a Christian Society* (1939); *Notes Towards the Definition of Culture* (1948); *Selected Essays* (1950); *On Poetry and Poets* (1957); *To Criticize the Critic, and Other Writings* (1965). Plays: *The Rock* (London, 1934 [choruses only]); *Murder in the Cathedral* (London, 1935); *Family Reunion* (London, 1939); *The Cocktail Party* (1950); *The Confidential Clerk* (1954); *The Elder Statesman* (1959); *Collected Plays* (1962). Letters: *Letters*, vol. 1, 1898–1922, ed. Valerie Eliot (1989).

Consult: Peter Ackroyd, *T. S. Eliot: A Life* (1988); Bernard Bergonzi, *T. S. Eliot* (1972); Helen Gardner, *The Art of T. S. Eliot* (1950); Lyndall Gordon, *Eliot's Early Years* (1977 [vol. 1]), *Eliot's New Life* (1988 [vol.2]); A. Walton Litz, ed., *Eliot in His Time* (1973); F. O. Matthiessen, *The Achievement of T. S. Eliot* (1935); D. E. S. Maxwell, *The Poetry of T. S. Eliot* (1952); Christopher Ricks, *T. S. Eliot and Prejudice* (1989); Allen Tate, ed., *T. S. Eliot: The Man and His Work* (1967); Derek Traversi, *T. S. Eliot: The Longer Poems* (1976).

ELYTIS, Odysseus (pseudonym of Odysseus Alepoudhélis). Born 1912, in Hērákleion, Crete; he lives in Athens, Greece. The son of a well-known industrial family from the Greek island of Lesbos, Elytis studied law and political science

at the University of Athens. He was second lieutenant in the Greek army during
the Albanian campaign against Mussolini's fascist troops, 1940–41. He represented Greece in 1938 at the Eleventh International Writers Congress in Geneva
and in 1950 at the First International Congress of Art Critics in Paris. Elytis
lived in France (mainly Paris) 1948–52 and 1969–71; he toured the United States
in 1961 and the Soviet Union in 1962. His *Axion Esti* won the National Prize
for Poetry in 1960. Some of its lyric poems, set to music by Mikis Theodorakis,
became popular songs accepted throughout Greece as pleas for liberty and justice
and indictments of the dictatorship in power from 1967 to 1974. Elytis witnessed
government-ordered destruction of his books and took up residence in France in
1969. He has written over fourteen books of poems and five books of biography,
art and literary criticism, and translation of European poetry into Greek. He has
also made paintings and collages, some of which have appeared as illustrations
in his books. He received the Nobel Prize for literature in 1979.

Elytis's "exile" periods total only about seven years. Yet his wartime military
service on a foreign front shook his worldview, and his two sojourns in France
rejuvenated the creative impulses of this cosmopolitan writer. After reading a
book of poems by French surrealist Paul Éluard at age seventeen, Elytis adopted
a belief in surrealism, which he calls "the last available oxygen in a dying
world" because surrealism liberates the senses, which rationalism has stifled in
the West since the Renaissance. Together with Byzantine Greek Christianity,
surrealism inspires the poet to recast two coexisting worlds—physical and spiritual—into a "third state" or "borderland" of dreams accessible through poetry.

His first two books, *Orientations* (1938) and *The Primal Sun* (1943), established his reputation as "Poet of the Aegean," envisioning an idyllic natural
world unsullied by human institutions or industrialism. In these strikingly beautiful and romantic works, Elytis's devotion to his country's natural beauty and
rich traditions amounts to what some admirers have called Helenolatry. Withdrawn from human concourse, the poet finds personal revelation in a surrealistic
metamorphosis of nature.

World War II ended the poet's youthful erotic innocence. Pain, loneliness,
and estrangement during the Albanian campaign introduced tragic vision to his
work and heightened his moral awareness. Snatched away from his former
solitary life, Elytis confronts the demands of wider social responsibility in his
fourteen-poem sequence, "Heroic and Elegiac Song for the Lost Second Lieutenant of the Albanian Campaign" (1945). In this poem, the landscape itself
forebodes the lieutenant's death, which causes desperation in his family and
shocks the poet more than any previous event in his life. One man's death
diminishes the whole world, and after lamenting the soldier's unfinished life,
the poet imagines his transfiguration and resurrection.

In 1948, Elytis settled in Paris, studied literature at the Sorbonne, and associated with surrealist poets André Breton,* Éluard, Tristan Tzara,* René Char,
Henri Michaux, and Giuseppi Ungaretti, and with modernist artists Henri Ma-

tisse, Pablo Picasso, Alberto Giacometti, and Giorgia De Chirico. During these four years in France, Elytis remade his writing style and did not break poetic silence until the publication of his magnum opus, *The Axion Esti*, in 1959.

This epic-like collection of lyric and prose poems shows extensive growth over earlier work in Elytis's command of plotting and coherent discourse. It combines classical, Byzantine, and demotic Greek dictions in a tripartite book structured along lines of the Orthodox mass: "The Genesis" presents the pristine beauty of the natural world, "The Passion" agonizes over Greece's national predicament of being "devastated . . . by the tribes of the Continents," and "The Gloria" rediscovers what is worthy of praise in "this small world the great." With uniquely cosmopolitan nationalism, Elytis expresses personal feelings and general group consciousness. He has probably been more successful as a "representative poet" winning the hearts of the educated and the masses in Greece than Walt Whitman was in America.

Elytis's second extended stay in France (1969 to 1971) occurred during the zenith of the Greek military government's power and ended with the publication of two poetic sequences that may have been composed or at least begun much earlier. "The Light Tree and the Fourteenth Beauty" uses materials and themes of his earlier work, developing a "Solar Metaphysic" that restates the central place of light in Elytis's Aegean aesthetic. Another sequence of seven love poems entitled "The Monogram" reveals passions of youth and maturity via intricate mathematical structures of line and stanza. Both these works show Elytis's characteristic portrayal of natural settings without reference to the artifacts of industrial consumer society.

His next major work, conceived if not begun during the final exile period, confronts the promise and vulgarity of mass-production society. *Maria Nepheli* (1978) is a book-length antiphonal dialogue in verse between a young woman, Maria (whose last name is the Greek word for "cloud"), and the poet. Believing in the consumer gratifications of the "me" generation, Maria seems alienated from the natural world of fresh air and sea; the poet halfheartedly defends tradition but concedes that "everything is preferable to my slow murder by the past." This tragicomic confrontation across the generation gap is the first work in which Elytis extensively uses profane, abusive, and unpoetic diction. While Maria drops brand names, the poet quotes the wisdom of ancient and modern worthies. The speakers' multilingualism reveals a culture become more functional but less articulate and coherent. The two understand each other better by the end of the book and anticipate the promise and aggressive vulgarity of the coming decade. This book was immediately popular with the younger generation of Greek readers, who felt that it expressed their values and frustrations, but Elytis's established public of older readers sees it as a work unworthy of their "Poet of the Aegean."

Translations: *The Axion Esti* (1973); *The Sovereign Sun* (1974); *Maria Nephele: A Poem in Two Voices* (1981); *Selected Poems*, ed. Edmund Keeley and Philip Sherrard (1981).

Consult: *Odysseus Elytis: Analogies of Light*, ed. Ivar Ivask (1981, repr. of Autumn 1975 issue of *Books Abroad*); *Elytis: Life and Works* (1982/1983; double issue of *The Charioteer: An Annual Review of Modern Greek Culture*, nos. 24–25).

EDWARD MORIN

EMECHETA, Buchi. Born in 1944 near Lagos, Nigeria; she returned to Nigeria in 1981 to teach at the University of Nsuku. She lives in England six months of the year and teaches in Nigeria the other six months. Daughter of a railroad station porter, Emecheta was orphaned early. Perhaps because of this traumatic childhood experience Emecheta chose to marry early; she bore her first child before she was seventeen years old. She went to London in 1962 after her husband had gone there for study. The marriage floundered in England, and Emecheta, on her own initiative and without help from her husband, raised her five children and attended night school. Her first book, *In the Ditch* (London, 1972), was a collection of columns she wrote for the *New Statesman* about her marriage, its breakup, and her life on the dole (welfare). She graduated from London University with a master's degree in sociology; her novel, *Second Class Citizen* (London, 1974; 1975), served as her master's thesis requirement.

In her autobiographical first novel, *Second Class Citizen*, Emecheta relates how she came to England as a young wife, following her Nigerian student husband's move there in search of professional advancement. She was a second-class citizen in both her husband's demands of subservience to him and in the English attitude to African immigrants. When her marriage faltered, she had a choice of striking out on her own in a foreign country or returning to her native community, where her needs would be little recognized. She chose the more immediately difficult role, managing to secure a job in London and to put herself through night school. Eventually, she became a published writer and today, on campuses in the United States and England, she is a leading African spokesperson for women's rights and African matters. She has published more than ten books since her first novel appeared in 1974.

Critics have noted the gritty vibrancy of her early work in which her heroines, still young and naïvely tough, battle their way through overwhelming odds in a style that remains obdurately unpolished. In her more recent work, Emecheta shows artful contrivance and a certain professionalism that moderates her tone. She has always been a compassionate feminist with sympathy for men's problems as well as women's issues. Her sympathetic quality is particularly evident in one of her stronger works, *Double Yoke* (1983), where she treats the difficulties men undergo when their chauvinistic world is threatened by liberated women and when they too experience the double yoke of tradition and modernity's modes. The novel is set on the University of Calabar campus where Emecheta spent a year. In its narrative unfolding of a young Nigerian woman with intellectual goals who finds herself caught between two lovers—a manipulative older professor and a tradition-bound young fiancé—the work treats the anxiety of assimilation and the ever-present politics of sex and culture in modern Nigerian society. The heroine, Nko, must face the awesome conflicts between fulfilling the primary role of a wife and mother and subjugating her own desires for intellectual and personal growth or giving priority to her own needs. Only in the aftermath of her affair with the venal professor-lover do she and her fiancé face the demands of their real selves. In Emecheta's work and vision, such conflicts of personal-social wishes and demands cohere into a meaningful break for freedom when they are expressed in the commitment of love. Thus, both women and men in Emecheta's novels are subjugated to social politics until they transcend them through an act of love and into the awakening of their freedom from the yokes of imposed custom.

In a review in *Confrontation*, the literary journal of Long Island University (nos. 27–28, 1984), Marlene San Miguel Groner wrote:

Emecheta explores the central dilemma of modern African women—how to reconcile the past with the present and how to carve a place for themselves in a society that tolerates a woman's intellectual and economic advancement only as long as she remains subservient to the desires of husband, family and tribe. Emecheta, a Nigerian who makes her home in London and periodically returns to her homeland to serve as guest lecturer at one of its universities, is well aware of the difficulties facing such women. (p. 133)

In 1982 Emecheta published what many critics consider her major novel, *Destination Biafra*. Using the Nigerian Civil War as backdrop for her examination of divided human motives and yearnings, and writing on a broad canvas of different types and varieties of characters, Emecheta centered her novel on a young, rich heroine, someone who had until the crisis that enveloped her country led a sheltered, unquestioning life. In meeting the trials of civil war, and the personal sacrifices demanded of each person caught in the conflict, the heroine comes to a richer and tragic understanding of the world about her. In 1981 she returned to Nigeria to teach at the University of Calabar in Nigeria; she describes her twenty-year stay in England in her autobiography, *Head Above Water* (1987).

Consult: Charlotte and David Bruner, "Buchi Emecheta and Maryse Conde—Contemporary Writing from Africa and the Caribbean," *World Literature Today* 59, no. 1 (Winter 1985); Roberta Rubenstein, "Buchi Emecheta, Second Class Citizen," *World Literature Written in English* 16, no. 2 (1977); Marie Umweh, "African Women in Transition in the Novels of Buchi Emecheta," *Présence Africaine* 116 (1980).

EMPSON, William. Born September 27, 1906, in Howden, England; he died April 15, 1984, in London, England. Empson was an expatriate by reason of academic service. He taught English literature in Tokyo from 1931 to 1934, and at Peking National University from 1937 to 1939. During World War II he worked as editor in the Chinese section of the British Broadcasting System in London. He moved again to Peking in 1947, where he taught Western languages for six years. In 1953 he was appointed to the Chair of English Literature at the University of Sheffield.

Empson's most known critical work is *Seven Types of Ambiguity* (1930), a collection of essays that has had a profound impact on modern criticism. His poetry draws from his knowledge of foreign shores as well as his native English roots.

Selected Titles: *Collected Poems* (1949); *Using Biography* (1985).

ENRIGHT, D. J. (Dennis Joseph). Born March 11, 1920, in Leamington, England; he lives in England. Enright is an expatriate by reason of academic service and preference. He has taught in West Berlin, Alexandria (Egypt), Bangkok (Thailand), and Singapore. In 1948, during the Suez crisis, he was arrested as a Jewish spy; this was the period when many British nationals resident in Egypt were rounded up by Egyptian forces in a wave of hysteria following the joint British-French-Israeli military seizure of the Suez Canal. Enright was freed soon after his arrest. Before he came home to residence and work in London, he also lived and worked as a lecturer and unaffiliated scholar in Japan, Hong Kong, Bangkok, and Singapore. Best known for his poetry and criticism (he reviews widely for English literary periodicals), he also is a novelist.

Selected Titles: *Literature for Man's Sake: Critical Essays* (Tokyo, 1955); *The Apothecary's Ship* (1959); *Memories of a Mendicant Professor* (1969); *Daughters of Earth* (1972); *The Joke Shop* (1976).

Consult: Jacqueline Sims, ed. *Life by Other Means: Essays on D. J. Enright* (1990).

ENZENBERGER, Hans Magnus. Born November 11, 1929, in Kaufbeuren, Germany; he lives in Munich, West Germany. Enzenberger has been a sojourner in many lands in his exploration of human behavior. His upbringing in Nazi Germany—he was drafted into the Volksturm in 1944—and his witnessing of the defeat of Germany at the end of World War II—he sold on the black market, earning his living on the streets—shook up whatever tenuous codes of behavior he had struck by that time. After studying literature and philosophy in three German universities and at the Sorbonne, and after two years of working as a radio writer and editor, he began his travels. He lived in the United States, Mexico, and in Rome on a government stipend, from 1957 to 1960. In 1961 he moved to Norway, and in 1965 emigrated to Berlin, with time away for many trips, mainly to the United States. He gave up a fellowship at Wesleyan University, Connecticut, in protest against American policies in Vietnam; he visited Cuba in 1968 and 1969, after which he returned to Germany to live in Munich.

Enzenberger has been called one of the angry young moralist poets of his generation. He objects to the term *angry*, preferring to think of himself at that time as a critic of Nazism. He felt a responsibility to assess responsibility, but he did not wish to become a professional Germanist specializing in German guilt. As a consequence, he left Germany in 1961 for travels abroad.

Enzenberger dislikes confinement in any form, and he sees in specialization a danger to intellectual inquiry. His own practice of involvement in many literatures and travels—he speaks and reads seven languages—mandates a constant journeying into new territories. He has been involved in many protests against military policies of the West and East, and particularly of the use of military force in Vietnam and Latin America. Although he has been associated with political causes and revolutionary social movements, his stand lies in the ground of independent critical observation. He believes in an awareness that strips away hypocrisy and opens up a dialogue for unfettered truth. His vision, while sometimes expressed in strident language, is often resigned. Enzenberger is an abrasive critic searching out error and danger rather than a goodwilled tyrant with a magic resolving wand. Yet his poetry, criticism, and essays show an unrelenting concern with morality and, by such concern, express a plea for resolution.

In the view of one of his critics, Rosmarie Waldrop, Enzenberger is a careful craftsman, using considered parallels and syntactical allusions and imagery even when he spurns traditional verse forms. His highest poetic achievement in verse is probably *Mausoleum* (1975; *Mausoleum*, 1976). Other volumes are *Verteidigung der wölfe* (1957, Defense of the Wolves, Enzenberger's first collection), and his most politically oriented collection, *Blindenschrift* (1964, Braille). His criticism includes *Einzelheiten* (1962; *The Consciousness Industry*, 1974); *Politik und Verbrechen* (1964; *Politics and Crime*, 1974); and a more popular undertaking, *Der Untergang der Titanic* (1978, The Sinking of the Titanic).

Enzenberger's newest work, *Europe, Europe* (1989), is a collection of essays on different European cultures, emphasizing the pluralism of modern times. Enzenberger believes the old American Empire, which he once fervently attacked as an establishment monolith, is gone, and in its place is a variety of lesser but potent forces. Yet Enzenberger just as acerbically dismisses the European Community, which he says is an imposition from politics on high, not a natural unity growing out of shared roots. The concluding essay, a fictional narrative, is set in the year 2,000 in which Europe is alive and kicking, but with many different suitors showering her with gifts; she is no longer married to either the United States or the USSR. In writing the piece, Enzenberger has said, he wished to open a door to speculation, not to close his book with a prophecy. His newest work, like his earlier work, remains provocative and unsettling, the features he believes are requirements of writers and intellectuals. In his journeys to provocation, he is perhaps seeking an antidote to the exile that he first felt when he saw Germany dismantled and new states put in its place.

Enzenberger is also the editor of *Kursbach* (Railroad Timetable), a journal of ideas.

Translations: *Poems* (1966); *Poems for People Who Don't Read Poems* (1968).

Consult: R. Grimm, "The Commitment and Contradiction of Hans Magnus Enzenberger," *Books Abroad* 47 (1972); B. Keith-Smith, ed., *Essays on Contemporary German Literature* (1968).

ESFANDIARY, F. M. *See* Iranian Writers in Exile

ESPIRU, Salvador. Born 1913, in Spain. He died February 22, 1985, in Barcelona, Spain. Espiru is an exile in that he chose a banned language, Catalan, in 1939 as the means by which he would be heard, and reheard, in his native country. Generalissimo Franco and his forces had triumphed in the Spanish Civil War. Punishing Catalonia for its support of the Loyalist/Second Republic forces, Franco's government forbade use of the Catalan language in public schools, the press, and public offices; the history of Catalonia was similarly erased from official recognition. Espiru had witnessed the outpouring of creative talent in Catalan when his land was granted autonomy for the first time since its absorption two centuries earlier by Spain. Making his vow of silent opposition, though silent only in sound and not in signified language, Espiru chose poetry as his form of expression, forsaking a prominent career as a popular narrative fiction writer. Undoubtedly the Spanish Civil War was the climactic event that determined Espiru's turn to poetry, but his interest had for some time been turning to what he felt was the essence of Catalan identity, an essence he believed could only be captured in the spare evocative lyric genre. His poetry is, not surprisingly, hermetic and jeweled in its concentration of meaning through precise and resonating imagery. His linking symbol is the cemetery in Sinera (an anagram of Arenys, where Espiru lived out his childhood); the mourning for his land's fate (Catalonia) is summed up in the deaths that pass through Sinera in all of Espiru's volumes of poetry (see particularly *El libre de Sinera* [1963, The Book of Sinera]). His most widely read volume is *La pell de brau* (1960, The Bull's Skin), a more accessible work that has been read by critics as political and social commentary (though Espiru denied any labels attached to his work). Espiru's last volume was *Holy Week*, in which his recurrent fatalism is communicated in a characteristically transcendent and severe pose.

Espiru's work in Catalan was allowed publication in 1954, when Catalan was once more acknowledged by Spain as a distinct culture.

Selected Title: *Les horas* (1952, The Hours).

Translation: *Selected Poems*, ed. Magda Bogin (1985; original-language volume c. 1985).

Consult: Francesc Vallverdu, Introduction in Espiru, *Selected Poems* (1985).

ESSLIN, Martin (Julian). Born June 8, 1918, in Hungary; he lives in London, England. Esslin emigrated to England during World War II; he became a British citizen in 1947. He is best known for his dramatic criticism and in particular for his studies of theater of the absurd and "epic theater." He writes often for periodicals and has been head of drama at the BBC in London.

Selected Titles: *The Theatre of the Absurd* (1961); *Bertold Brecht* (1969).

Consult: *Contemporary Literary Criticism*, ed. Carolyn Rilar and Phyllis C. Mendelson (1977).

F

FALUDY, George. Born September 28, 1910, in Budapest, Hungary; he resides in Toronto, Canada. The noted Hungarian poet is also a novelist, journalist, translator, philosopher, human rights activist, poet laureate of Canada, and a frequent nominee for the Nobel Prize for Literature. Faludy began contributing to Hungary's leading Social Democratic and other liberal papers in his early twenties, and by 1938 had published five books. His first volume of poems, *A Pompei Strázsán* (1938; *Guarding the Gates of Pompei*, 1980), which warned of the coming of World War II and the ethical collapse of modern society, was publicly burned by the Nazis; the second edition in 1950 was pulped by the Hungarian communist government. Faludy's volume of translation, *An Anthology of European Poets* (1938), presenting 150 poems of pacifist and liberal attitudes, and *Dicsértessék* (1939, Laudetur), a collection of Medieval Latin poetry, was well received, but his major public and critical success was his translation of *Villon's Ballads* into Hungarian (1937). In this work he wrote his own verse about freedom and justice and cried out against oppression in the style and tenor of the fifteenth-century vagabond French poet. The first edition sold out in two days; the eleventh edition, two years later, was again burned by the fascist bureaucracy; the fifteenth edition was confiscated by the communists, and the thirty-first edition was being typed and xeroxed for Hungarian samizdat distribution. Finally, in 1988, it was again released by an official publishing house in over 100,000 copies.

In 1938, Faludy fled his country after being sentenced to eight years imprisonment for anti-Nazi activities. His first exile began in Paris; he lived erratically in various places in North Africa to avoid internment; in 1941 President Franklin Delano Roosevelt invited him to the United States. In New York Faludy worked for the Free Hungary Movement and also served in the American army. In 1950, four years after his return to Hungary, he was arrested on unsubstantiated charges and sentenced to twenty-five years of hard labor. In the death camp Recsk, he taught, consoled, and encouraged his prisonmates; poetry became the sustenance of their spirit. Since paper and pencil were forbidden, Faludy composed his poems orally, recited them to his fellow prisoners, who then memorized them. After Stalin's death Faludy was released, but following the Revolution of 1956, he entered his second period of exile. He stayed briefly in Vienna and Paris, then settled in London, where he edited a literary journal and completed his monumental autobiography, *My Happy Days in Hell* (1962), in English; his story of an adventurous, rich life is presented in a vibrant tone. The poems in his subsequent collection, *Memoir of Red Byzantium* (1961), reveal a hitherto unexpressed existential current coupled with a Kafkaesque vision of hopelessness in the shadow of the hydrogen bomb.

Following his settlement in Canada in 1967, Faludy taught at several American and Canadian campuses, including Columbia, Princeton, and the University of California at Los Angeles, and completed a critical biography, *Erasmus of Rotterdam* (1970). He released a giant collection of poetry (600 pages) in Hungarian, *Összegyüjtött Versek* (1980); concurrently he began publishing his poems in English with the help of English, Canadian, and American poet-translators. A collection of Faludy's translations of 1,400 poems from world literature was published in Budapest in 1988. During his second exile he has published, so far, eighteen books; received many honorary doctorates; and become accepted as the leader of exiled Hungarian writers, a legendary bard and symbol for the young in Hungary. His is the vision of the exile, reviled in his native land but welcomed outside it. In his works Faludy emerges as a man who must write on behalf of those who are not permitted to do so; thus he has enhanced not only the literature of Hungary but widened the awareness of foreigners to his native literature. In 1989 he returned to Hungary and was awarded the Republic's Medal of Honor on his eightieth birthday, September 28, 1990.

Selected Titles: *Tragedies of a People* (1959; a documentary of the 1956 Hungarian Revolution); *Karoton* (1966, *City of Splintered Gods*, 1966, historical novel); *East and West* (1978, poems); *Learn This Poem by Heart* (1983; poems); *Twelve Sonnets* (1983); *Collected Poems* (1985); *Notes from the Rainforest* (1988, diary fragments).

Consult: Barbara Amiel, "You Should Know Something about George Faludy," *East and West* (Toronto, 1987); John R. Colombo, *George Faludy* (Toronto, 1987); Lajos Szakolczay, "The Poems of Gyorgy Faludy," *Mozgó Vilag* 9 (1982).

CLARA GYORGYEY

FANON, Frantz. Born in 1925, in Martinique, West Indies; died in 1961, in Washington, D.C. Fanon studied medicine in France; his discipline was psychiatry. At 27, he published his first book based on his observations as a black psychiatrist in the Antilles, *Peau noire, masques blancs*, in France (1952, *Black Skin, White Mask*, 1967). During the French-Algerian wars, he was assigned to a hospital in Algeria; the experience led to the awakening of consciousness of his African/black heritage and his subsequent exposures of colonial tyranny and pseudo-myths of European cultural dominance. He published *L'an V de la Révolution Algérienne* (A Dying Colonialism) in 1961; that same year he was sent to Washington, D.C., for treatment of cancer, but medical help was unable to reverse his terminal illness. His most influential work, *Les damnés de la terre*, was published posthumously in 1961 in Paris; it was translated into English as *The Wretched of the Earth* in 1963, and has had a profound impact on black consciousness movements throughout the world. Although Fanon did not live in exile, he experienced it in his awareness of cultural displacement. His perceptions of this experience of exile and diaspora for black and West Indian people created a revolution of language and imagery that continues to reverberate in analyses of post-colonial cultural traditions and separatist ideologies.

FAQIR, Fadia A.M.A. Born August 21, 1956, in Amman, Jordan; she lives in England. Faqir received her B.A. in English literature from the University of Jordan in 1983. She came to England in 1984 for her M.A. in creative writing; she received her degree from the University of Lancaster in 1985. In 1986 she began work on her Ph.D. in critical and creative writing at the University of East Anglia. She considers herself an expatriate. In a March 8, 1989, letter to the editor of this volume, Faqir wrote: "I needed the uncomfortable distance of expatriatism to be able to judge my familiar surroundings and gain a detached perspective."

Faqir's first novel, *Nisanit*, was published in England in 1988. After its publication she wrote:

After interviewing three Palestinian ex-prisoners for the "Jerusalem Star" in Amman, Jordan, I started writing my first novel *Nisanit*. Anger, love, and sheer helplessness were and still are the demonic trinity behind my writing. Human beings are tortured all over the world: anger. The Arab world, oblivious to its profound culture and civilization, is fumbling around in the dark: love. I could not do anything: helplessness. I held the pen and started writing away my fears and nightmares. (Personal note to the editor)

Faqir's second novel, *The Yarn-Spinner*, is being considered for publication. Although she has experienced some despair from public reaction to her work, she continues to believe in the power of writing. In a personal note she entitled "Second Thoughts," she wrote: "The publication of *Nisanit* led to only one metamorphosis: mine. I was put in a cage with a swinging sign saying, 'An Arab woman writing in English!' ... Despite the frustration, the heartache and 'You write in English. How sweeet!' I still blindly believe that my scribbling will improve the status of Arab women, will set them free, will even change the shape of the old, corrupt sand dunes."

FARAH, Nuruddin. Born in 1945 in Baidoa, Somalia; he now lives in Uganda. Farah worked in the Ministry of Education before leaving for India to study philosophy and literature at the University of Chandigarh. He returned to Somalia in 1970 to teach at the University of Mogadishu, then moved to England in 1974, where he taught at the University of London and at Essex until 1976. His play, *The Offering*, was produced at the Royal Court Theatre in London during this time, and several of his radio plays were broadcast over BBC. Fearing imprisonment should he return to Somalia, Farah moved to Rome in 1976. He lived in Italy working as a teacher and translator until his recent move to Uganda. Farah writes in English, knows his native Somali (which has existed as a written language for only a quarter of a century), and is fluent in Italian, Arabic, and Gujurati.

Farah's novels have earned him respect from both literary and human rights circles. He has protested oppression of women in Muslim Somali society; one critic, Kirsten Holst Petersen, calls him "the first feminist writer to come out of Africa in the sense that he describes and analyzes women as victims of male subjugation." His first novel, *From a Crooked Rib* (London, 1970), treated the story of a young Somali girl sold several times for her protection. Since Somali women, before the Revolution of 1969, had no legal rights, they were without protection if they were unmarried or not living with a male family member. In *From a Crooked Rib*, the heroine runs off defiantly to the city (Mogadishu) and finds a husband, but he, a student, goes off to Italy, leaving her behind to fend for herself. The outlook for the heroine is grim, but she shows stoic courage in her fight for independence. Farah further angered official and traditional critics with his portrait of the Revolution of 1969, which resulted in laws guaranteeing equal rights of inheritance for women. The bloodless coup, occurring nine years after Somali achieved its independence from Italy, was engineered by military forces trained in the USSR and with announced Marxist goals of equalization of wealth and land distribution. Farah, however, saw not a socialist dream coming into shape but another betrayal of ideals—he portrays the military repression of civilian dissent and the personal corruption in the armed forces.

In both *A Naked Needle* (London, 1976) and *Sweet and Sour Milk* (London, 1980), he treats the revolution as a frightening whip over the people, with the educated elite serving as willing pawns in the game of power. *A Naked Needle*, set in a single day in Mogadishu, concerns the fate of the young hero, Koschin, as he walks through the city to meet various people; the novel's structure and motifs have been compared to James Joyce's *Ulysses* in their unities of time, place, and concentrated theme and in the similarities between Farah's hero and Joyce's Stephen Dedalus (each brooding, intellectual, poor, and given to personal dirtiness; both at odds with their schoolmasters and dissatisfied with their teaching jobs). Koschin, living in Mogadishu in the early days of the revolution, experiences great conflict in the demands of communal duty made on him by the revolutionary government. His conflict is brought to a climactic point by an unexpected visit of an English girl, whose presence causes him to face the choices he has been avoiding. In *Sweet and Sour Milk*, possibly his strongest novel, Farah employs twin brothers as his agents of examination of the 1969 Revolution. One is idealistic and supports the revolutionary government in complete dedication; he is killed. His brother, the more pragmatic of the two, a political activist because it is in his self-interest, investigates the killing and in the process turns against the revolutionary government, members of which are responsible for his brother's death.

Farah's views made him persona non grata in his country, and he fled to England, and later to Italy, as a consequence. His is a rare African voice in that he praises Western rationalism and liberality of attitude and chastises traditional Somali, Muslim patriarchal views on social programming and personal rights. His particular fervency is seen in his animus to the patriarchal figure, whom he regards as the obdurate force holding women and dissidents in subjection through fear of banishment and/or imprisonment. (In *Sweet and Sour Milk* the informer is the patriarch; he is strong only in his social web, and weak once removed from the imposed social-religious structure propping him up.) In Farah's next novel, *Sardines* (London, 1982), he used a woman reporter-editor, Medina, as his mouthpiece for the wrongs of the revolution: she is the editor of the country's leading newspaper, but when she expresses her individual views, which run counter to government policy, she is fired. At the end of the novel she stands alone with her child, bereft of husband, status, and home. The outlook Farah again presents is bleak, for equality in a slave state brings no particular freedom.

Given Farah's views on his country's policies and its military administration, it is not surprising he remains in exile. Even in the changing political climate (a civilian administration headed by President Mohammed Sian Barre is ruling the country), guarantees of personal liberties and the right to dissent do not seem an option. Kirsten Holst Petersen writes of Farah in *Ariel* (1981): "modern nomad from Somalia, moving from there to India, Italy, England, Germany, and now Nigeria, nevertheless can see exile as a condition of the mind as much as a physical displacement: a tyrannical regime may in a sense place a nation in exile."

Selected Title: *Maps* (1986).

Consult: Ian Adam, "Nuruddin Farah and James Joyce: Some Issues of Intertextuality," *Books Abroad*, 24, no. 1 (Summer 1984); Charles Larson, *World Literature Today* 54, no. 3 (May 1980); Kirsten Holst Petersen, "The Novels of Nuruddin Farah," *Ariel* 12, no. 3 (July 1981).

FARHI, Morris. Born July 5, 1935, in Ankara, Turkey; he lives in London, England. Farhi moved with his family to Istanbul when he was eleven years old, and received his secondary and university education there. Farhi's mother was a Greek Jew who followed the customs and traditions of her Mediterranean heritage. Farhi began his career as a college journalist writing in Turkish, which he considers a second language since he first spoke and wrote Ladino, taught to him by his mother. He moved to England in 1954 when he was nineteen, both in protest against Turkish military policy (he was liable for conscription and feared possible mistreatment on account of his religious minority status) and against Turkish punitive taxation on ethnic minorities. In London he studied at the Royal Academy of Dramatic Arts, and became in his words an "unsuccessful actor.'' After ''osmosing'' into English culture in the 1960s, he began writing in English; he became a British citizen in 1964. He feels, however, that he is ''outside'' the British tradition and is thus in a form of exile from the land of his rooted feelings. Characteristic of his pervasive attitude is his attempt to form a PEN Club of Romany gypsies and to provide a home base for their wandering culture. In sum, Farhi feels as committed to the wandering gypsy tradition as to the land of his birth and naturalization, or to his religion, which he admires in principle. The sense of his own need for separation or distance from a national or religious loyalty prompted his decision to move to England rather than to Israel when he left Turkey.

Farhi's best-known novel is the recent *Journey through the Wilderness* (London, 1989), set in a mythic South America. Farhi claims he was able to ''understand'' South America though he has never visited the continent because of the ''mythic'' field of his personality and of the Southern Hemisphere. Farhi is also the author of two previous novels, *The Last of Days* (London, 1983), set in the milieu of the Arab-Israeli conflict, and *The Pleasure of Your Death* (London, 1972), a ''romp'' he created out of an earlier playscript. (All quotes are from an interview given to the editor in September, 1989, in Toronto, Canada.)

FENG Zhi. Born in 1905 in the province of Hopei, China. Feng Zhi graduated from Beijing University. After publication of two collections of poems, *Songs of Yesterday* (1927) and *Northern Wanderings* (1930), he studied German literature at the University of Heidelberg. After years of silence he began writing again; his work from this period shows the influence of Rainer Maria Rilke.* An exile by virtue of separation from his native land because of professional and possibly personal reasons, he later became a professor of German at Lienta.

EDWARD MORIN

FEUCHTWANGER, Lion. Born July 7, 1884, in Munich, Germany; died December 21, 1958, in Pacific Palisades, California. Son of a wealthy Jewish industrialist, Feuchtwanger studied German philology and history of literature at the Universities of Munich and Berlin; he also studied ancient and modern languages, and in 1918 completed his Ph.D. dissertation on Heinrich Heine's work ''Rabbi von Bachrach.'' At this time he founded a literary journal, *The Mirror*, which concentrated on contemporary literature emphasizing social-progressive idealism and revolutionary artistic technique. Traveling extensively in Italy, he wrote his novel *God of Thunder*. In 1912 he married Marta Loeffer, and together they left Germany. In 1914 he was taken prisoner in the war in Tunisia, but managed to escape and return to Germany, where he served briefly in the army. During World War I he wrote two plays, *Vasantasena* and *Warren Hastings*, both of which were banned but later had great success on the stage. Several later plays, among them *Prisoners of War* and *Peace*, were also suppressed before they saw successful stage productions. His drama *Thomas Wendt* (later retitled *1918*), which he wrote in 1918, describing the betrayal of the German Revolution and the end of the Great War, created a disturbance at its first performance and was subsequently banned.

In 1921 Feuchtwanger finished what was to become his most known work, the novel *Jud Sus* (1925; *Power*, 1927). He could not find a publisher for it until four years later. It proved an immediate and lasting success. In 1925 Feuchtwanger and his wife moved to Berlin. Two more novels, *Die hässliche Herzogin Margarette Maultasch* (1923; *The Ugly Duchess*, 1928) and *Erfolg* (1930; *Success*, 1930), appeared in Germany to favorable notice. In 1931 Feuchtwanger began his *Josephus* trilogy. In 1933 his entire fortune, including his house, was confiscated by the National Socialist (Nazi) government. Feuchtwanger moved to France, where he wrote another of his well-known works, *Die Geschwister Oppenhiem* (1933; *The Oppermans*, 1934). This novel traces the tragic fate of an integrated German-Jewish family caught in the Nazi web of prejudice and oppression; its pages contain a thinly veiled satire of Adolf Hitler's Munich "Beer Hall Putsch" in 1923, an account that especially angered the Nazi propaganda bureaucracy. In 1937 Feuchtwanger moved to Moscow and began writing a new novel, *Exile*, but returned to France shortly thereafter. When France capitulated to the German army, Feuchtwanger was interned in a French concentration camp. Through the efforts of Franklin D. Roosevelt, president of the United States, and Eleanor Roosevelt, Feuchtwanger managed to escape from confinement. Disguised as a woman, he was smuggled out of the camp; he and his wife walked through the French Pyrenees to the border and eventual freedom/ exile in the United States. *The Devil in France*, published first in translation (1941; *Unholdes Frankreich*, 1942), gives Feuchtwanger's description of his concentration camp experiences.

After Feuchtwanger's death his widow Marta wrote her autobiography *Nur eine Frau: Jahre, Tage, Stunder* (Munich, 1983; Only a Woman: Years, Days, Hours), a work widely acclaimed in Germany. A headnote to an excerpt from her book translated into English for the collection *Women of Exile: German-Jewish Autobiographies since 1933*, edited by Andreas Lixl-Purcell (1988), states that "her memoirs read like an object lesson on the art of exile politics, something every refugee had to master if she wanted to survive in a world full of hostility, distrust, and human exploitation. Marta Feuchtwanger's personal courage, political reason, and social skills secured them [the Feuchtwangers] free passage from France into Spain and Portugal in 1946."

On the occasion of the hundredth anniversary of Feuchtwanger's birth, many celebrations were held in Germany.

Translations: *The Oil Islands* (1928); *Warren Hastings* (1928); *Josephus* (1932); *Three Plays* (1934); *The Jew of Rome* (1935); *Marianne in India* (1936); *The Pretenders* (1937); *Josephus and the Emperor* (1942); *Double, Double, Toil and Trouble* (1943, on Nazi Germany); *Simone* (1944, on occupied France); *Proud Destiny* (1947); *This Is the Hour* (1951); *'Tis Folly to Be Wise* (1953).

Consult: L. Kahn, *Insight and Action: The Life and Work of Lion Feuchtwanger* (1975); John Spalek, ed., *Lion Feuchtwanger: The Man, His Ideas, His Works* (1964).

                                                                                    STELLA HERSHAN

FIGES, Eva. Born Eva Unger in 1932 in Berlin, Germany; she lives in London, England. Figes came to England with her Jewish family in March, 1939. Her father was an assimilated German Jew who ran a successful business. After Kristallnacht (November 1938), his business was confiscated and he was imprisoned in Dachau. He managed to buy a visa for his family and himself to England. Figes describes her awkwardness and difficulties of adjustment to English life in *Little Eden: A Child at War* (London, 1978); her memoir of one year of growing up evokes the evacuation of a group of London children to Cirencester in the bucolic Cotswolds and their education there during the Blitz of Britain in 1940–41. Figes writes of her feeling of statelessness, a condition felt more profoundly by her (then) inability to speak more than a few words in English.

Figes did not become a writer until after the breakup of her first marriage; in her first published novel, *Equinox* (London, 1966), she describes a year of crisis in the heroine's life. Figes also gained an advanced university degree during this period and began teaching at university level in London. She has taught at several British and American universities and is presently a co-editor of a Women's Writing series for an American publisher. Although she has written several novels, the work that has brought her most prominence is *Patriarchal Attitudes: Women in Society* (London, 1986), a feminist study of contemporary social attitudes. That book, and Figes's continuing feminist work, have made her a recognized figure on the British intellectual scene. Figes views the woman's position in modern, as well as in earlier times, as one of exile from the mainstream of power, though she sees gains for women as a result of the feminist movement. While her nonfiction is witty and rational, her novels tend to be elliptical in presentation and bare in style, concentrating on a spare line and a nexus of symbols rather than realistic detail or fleshed-out characterization. Her work reflects a sense of inner division caused by social and historic circumstance characteristic of modern exile.

Selected Titles: *Sex and Subterfuge: Women Writers to 1850* (1982); *Light* (1983); *Nelly's Version* (1985); *The Seven Ages* (1986); *Ghosts* (1988).

FITZGERALD, F. Scott (Francis Scott Key Fitzgerald). Born September 24, 1896, in St. Paul, Minnesota; died 1940, in Hollywood, Los Angeles, California. Fitzgerald and his wife Zelda moved to France in 1921, believing the rate of exchange would enable them to live beyond their means without going into further debt; in spite of Fitzgerald's popularity and command of high fees, they already were in serious financial binds. They lived in France and Italy through 1925. During their residence Fitzgerald gathered material for his novel *Tender Is the Night* (1934) of a self-defeating psychiatrist and his wealthy, neurotic wife. Fitzgerald also met with Ernest Hemingway and others in cafés and bistros favored by the bohemian expatriate set; he made the *de rigeur* visit to Gertrude Stein and Alice B. Toklas in their Parisian flat. He left Paris in the summer of 1927 to work in Hollywood; he spent the following year with Zelda in Paris. When Zelda's mental illness worsened, he moved her to a sanitorium in Switzerland, where she remained till she was transferred to a home in Georgia. (She died in a fire which swept through the Georgia site March 10, 1948.)

Fitzgerald's increasing despair and sense of guilty waste manifested in his alcoholism, but chastened with a new resolve, he began to work on what many critics consider would have been an even greater triumph than his early masterpiece *The Great Gatsby*. At his death by heart attack in 1940 he left the uncompleted manuscript of *The Last Tycoon*, which was posthumously published through the editorial aid of Fitzgerald's friend, the critic Edmund Wilson.

Fitzgerald's stay of expatriatism is a curious instance of irony. A midwesterner, and a Catholic in a predominantly and socially prejudiced Protestant community, he found in Europe the glamor to fly above his self-perceived humble origins. Yet he did not appreciate Europe for its culture but for its ambience of wealth and station. His reputation, however, as an expatriate has largely invested him with an aura of cultural hierarchy. At base, he remained an American who knew his European sojourn was a frock of manners he was collecting for exhibit for the folks back home.

Selected Titles: *The Great Gatsby* (1925); *Afternoon of an Author*, ed. Arthur Mizener (1957, uncollected stories and essays). See *Three Novels: The Great Gatsby*, ed. Malcolm Cowley; *Tender Is the Night*, ed. Malcolm Cowley; *The Last Tycoon*, ed. Edmund Wilson (1951). See also *Letters of F. Scott Fitzgerald*, ed. Andrew Turnbull (1963). A special facsimile edition is *F. Scott Fitzgerald Manuscripts*, 18 vols. (1990).

Consult: Frances Donaldson, *Scott As I Knew Him* (1987); Sheila Graham, *Beloved Infidel* (1958); Alfred Kazin, ed., *F. Scott Fitzgerald: The Man and His Work* (1951); Arthur Mizener, *The Far Side of Paradise* (1951); Andrew Turnbull, *F. Scott Fitzgerald* (1962). See also special issues devoted to Fitzgerald of *Princeton University Library Chronicle* 12 (Summer 1951) and *Modern Fiction Studies* 7 (Spring 1961).

FLANNER, Janet (pseudonym Gênet). Born March 13, 1892, in Indianapolis, Indiana; died January 7, 1978, in New York City. Flanner went to Europe in 1921 with her lover, Solita Solano, after deserting her husband in New York, where the couple had moved from Indianapolis. In Paris she became part of the artistic bohemian circle that included Djuna Barnes and Natalie Barney; she was friends with Gertrude Stein and Alice B. Toklas. She began writing her celebrated letters from Paris for *The New Yorker* magazine, under the pseudonym of Gênet, in 1925. She later published several collections of memoiristic essays which surveyed and commented on local customs as seen by a foreigner and on foreign customs as seen in the local land she was inhabiting at the time. She also wrote *Pétain: The Old Man of France* (1944), a study of the World War I military hero who became the collaborationist political leader of Vichy France after his country's defeat by Germany in 1940; and a reflection in *Men and Monuments* (1957) on the achievements of André Malraux. Flanner was knighted by France's Legion of Honor.

Selected Titles: *Paris Was Yesterday, 1925–1939* (1972, adapted for the stage by Paul Shyre, 1978); *Paris Journal*, ed. William Shawn (1977, reissued 1988); *Janet Flanner's World: Uncollected Writings 1932–1975*, ed. Irving Drutman (c. 1979); *Darlinghissima: Letters to a Friend*, ed. Natalia D. Murray (1985).

Consult: Brenda Wineapple, *Gênet: A Biography of Janet Flanner* (1989).

FORD, Ford Madox (until 1919 Ford Madox Hueffer). Born December 17, 1873, in Merton, Surrey, England; died June 26, 1939, in Deauville, France. A major figure of the Edwardian and modern age, Ford spent the last years of his life as an expatriate because of financial hardship and a weary retreat into resignation. At the end of World War I, he was depleted emotionally by his military experiences (he had sought and received a commission in the infantry in 1915 at the age of forty-two) and financially by various marital troubles. He tried his hand at cottage farming in Sussex, England, and when these enterprises failed, he moved to southern France, and then to Paris. In the last decade of his life he was a visiting lecturer at Olivet College in Michigan. The literary lion of his age in his youth—he was a poet, editor, novelist, critic, and raconteur par excellence who knew everybody and wrote about his knowledge of everybody—Ford was a lonely and impoverished figure, though he apparently never lost his sense of humor or exaggeration. Whenever he could, he visited the south of France, where he died.

Selected Title: *A History of Our Own Times*, ed. S. Beinfeld and S. J. Stang (1988).

Consult: Frank MacShane, *The Life and Work of Ford Madox Ford* (1965); Arthur M. Mizener, *The Saddest Story: A Biography of Ford Madox Ford* (1971); Thomas Moser, *The Life in the Fiction of Ford Madox Ford* (1981); S. J. Stang, ed., *The Presence of Ford Madox Ford: A Memorial Volume of Essays, Poems, and Memoirs* (1981).

FORNES, Maria Irene. Born May 14, 1930, in Havana, Cuba; she lives in Greenwich Village, New York City. In 1945 Fornes left Cuba with her mother and sister; she has lived in the United States since, except for a three-year period from 1954–57 when she studied painting in Europe. On her return she worked as a textile designer. In 1960 she began writing plays; her first play was produced in 1961. She claims no sense of exile from her birthplace; she considers herself a Spanish-American writer who is an American citizen. She writes in both English and Spanish, and her work is often performed by Spanish-language theatrical companies in the United States and in Latin America. Her work reflects a Latin-American consciousness but not a sense of invidious exile from the mainstream; her work concentrates on wry touches of individual frustration in modern and mid-life America, and she flings the saving humor of self-mockery into her scenes of potential savagery. In terms of form she characterizes her work as "instinctive." In terms of content, her distinctive voice draws much of its uniqueness from the immigrant/emigrant experience: she is aware of what exodus has meant to her extended Cuban and Latin-American family. Like Walter Abish*, Eva Hoffman*, Bharati Mukerjee*, and Lore Segal*, she may be viewed as part of the phenomenon of the American immigrant in the twentieth century. Accepting her Spanish Americanness in a declared identity, she eschews provocative separatism. In 1990 she was awarded the New York State Governor's Award for Cultural Achievement.

Selected Titles: *La Viuda* (Havana, 1961, The Widow); *Promenade and Other Plays* (includes *Tango, The Successful Life of 3, Promenade, A Vietnamese Wedding, Dr. Kheal, The Red Burning Light,* and *Molly's Dream*) (1971); *Fefu and Her Friends* (in *Performing Arts Journal* 2, Winter 1978).

Consult: Bonnie Marranca, "Interview," *Performing Arts Journal* 2 (Winter 1978); Richard Gilman, Introduction to *Promenade and Other Plays* (1971); *Orchards: Stories* (1986).

FRANK, Bruno. Born June 13, 1887, in Stuttgart, Germany; died June 20, 1945, in Beverly Hills, California. Frank received a Ph.D. in German literature in 1912; he travelled throughout Europe for several years. In 1924 he moved to Munich where he lived until he fled Germany in 1933 immediately after the burning of the Reichstag. Frank emigrated to the United States in 1937, after living in Austria, England, France and Switzerland.

Frank wrote in many genres. His poetry career was concentrated in his early years, and his novel writing heavily in evidence in his middle period. He came to playwriting late, but the form proved a popular one for him. In exile he wrote several novels and essays of literary criticism. Frank's prose is simply put, but it harbors a complex and cosmopolitan layering of humanistic faith. He wrote little literature *engagé* but in his most powerful novel, *Politische Novelle* (1928; *The Persians Are Coming*, 1937) he treated contemporary social and political issues directly. In the process he portrayed the perverse appeal of fascist brutality, the erosion of humanism in greed-pits of capitalism, and the adulteration of history by robotic texts.

Frank remained an eclectic all his life, attempting a synthesis of historical struggles through means of ethical values in their dissemination through literature. In his study of Miguel de Cervantes, *Cervantes* (1934; *A Man Called Cervantes*, 1934), he brought his own such view of literature to the fore, that of a crossing into a liberating frontier no matter what the constraints and chains along the way.

Selected Titles: *Sturm in Wasserglas* (1930; *Tempest in a Teapot*, 1936); *Der Reiseplass* (1937; *The Lost Heritage*, 1937); *Die junge Frau Conti* (1938; *Young Madame Conti*, 1938); *Die Tochter* (1943; *One Fair Daughter*, 1943); *Ehre Vater und Mütter* (1944; *Honor Thy Father and Mother*, 1944); *Gesammelte Werke* (1957, Collected Works).

Consult: H. von Hofe, "German Literature in Exile: Bruno Frank," *German Quarterly* 18 (1945); T. A. Kamla, "Bruno Frank's *Der Reiseplass*: The Exile as an Aristocrat of Humanity," *Monatshefte* 67 (1975).

FRANKLIN, Miles (Stella Maria Miles Franklin). Born October 14, 1879, in "Talbingo," near Tamut, New South Wales, Australia; died September 19, 1954, in Sydney. Franklin's family were pioneering landholders in the mountains of New South Wales. This was fertile ground for a writer whose continuing interests would be social interaction and the influence of environment; wealthy "squatters" replicated, or magnified, many of the class assumptions of the English gentry, while their employees were busy refining the egalitarian and nationalistic notions that form a large part of the bush tradition of Australian literature. Franklin wrote in appreciation of the high-mindedness and grand enterprise of the pioneer squatters, while democratically insisting that similar traits would be found at all social levels. Her first novel, *My Brilliant Career* (1901), established the complex characterization and ironic style that mark most of her writing; these subjects and treatments were carried forward into *All That Swagger* (1936), *My Career Goes Bung* (1946), and *Childhood at Brindabella* (1963).

In 1905, Franklin left Australia to live for several years in Chicago, where she coedited the feminist-socialist journal *Life and Labor*. In World War I, she served as a nurse on the Macedonian front. She lived in England from the end of the war until her return to Australia in 1933.

In the preface to *Up the Country* (1926), Franklin depicts the ghosts of her Australian past crowding around her reader's desk at the British Museum, begging her to write their story. She accedes, but with a twist: she writes *Up the Country* and five subsequent novels under the name "Brent of Bin Bin," a pseudonym that gives her both an identification with her subject and a distance from it (indeed, Franklin never admitted she was Brent, although her identity is now undisputed). Importantly, those ghosts demand that the writer treat them as fully rounded characters, noting the past in its complexity. Thus, Franklin's novels are hardly dominated by the simple nostalgia often cited by her critics; rather, she allows nostalgia its place in a very wide range of responses to Australian experience. The pioneering past has its lost grandeur, but Franklin qualifies her admiration by showing the fright, punctiliousness, and lack of imagination that have historically undermined the Australian version of idealism. The ironic depiction of complex responses in part explains a continuity of national temperament and behavior despite changes of environment or social configuration.

Consult: Marjorie Bernard, *Miles Franklin* (1967).

JOHN SCHECKTER

FRANQUI, Carlos. Born 1921, in Clavellinas (Las Villas), Cuba; he lives in Puerto Rico. Franqui was born to a peasant family on a sugar plantation; he joined the Socialist Youth organization when he was a teenager. He began his professional career as a proofreader on the communist newspaper *Hoy* and rose in the ranks to a position on the editorial board there; he also wrote for *Carteles*. Because of an embarrassing printer's error, he was fired from *Hoy* and expelled from the Communist party. The novelist Guillermo Cabrera Infante,* in an introduction to Franqui's *Family Portrait with Fidel* (1984, from the Spanish original *Retrato de familia con Fidel*, Barcelona, 1981), describes the event as one in which Franqui took the blame though he was not present at the time of the error. The failure to catch the error resulted in the publication of the word *never* in place of (the correct written copy) *ever* in a declaration about the success of Communist party goals in Cuba.

In 1947 Franqui joined the Cayo Confites military expedition to the Dominican Republic in an attempt to topple the Trujillo regime; another member of the expeditionary force was Fidel Castro. Both men met again as soldiers in the July 26 (1953) uprising in Santiago (Cuba), an unsuccessful coup against the Batista dictatorship. Although Franqui escaped capture (Castro was imprisoned for two years), he later was arrested and tortured by the Batista forces for his role as founder and editor of the newspaper *Revolución*. Released in 1955, Franqui went into exile in Mexico and in New York City. He returned secretly to Cuba to join Castro forces in the Sierra Madre. When Batista fled from the capital on January 1, 1959, Franqui entered Havana and reopened the *Revolución* office. For eleven years he served in Castro's government, holding high official positions, but he increasingly voiced his objections to newly instituted repressive laws. Fearful of his probable imprisonment, he went into self-imposed exile in 1968 through a subterfuge that allowed him passage to Europe; he wandered over the Continent before settling in Italy. Recently he moved to Puerto Rico.

Franqui's accounts of his relationship with Castro, and of his own disillusionment with the direction of the revolution, have a particular immediacy and depth of detail. He has written little beyond the most important experience in his life, the revolution that betrayed his Cuban dream.

Selected Titles: *Cuba, el libro de los doce* (Mexico, 1966; the work was published first in a French translation, *Cuba, le livre des douze*, Paris, 1965; it appeared in English, *The Twelve*, 1968); *Diario de la revolución cubana* (Barcelona, 1976; *Diary of the Cuban Revolution*, 1980).

Consult: Guillermo Cabrera Infante, Introduction, *Family Portrait with Fidel* (1984); Daniel C. Materos and Marnesba D. Hill, *Cuban Exile Writers: A Biobibliographic Handbook* (1986).

FRIED, Erich. Born May 6, 1921, in Vienna, Austria; he lives in England. A Jew, Fried began his exile in 1938, with flight to England after the annexation of Austria by the Germans and the murder of his father by the Gestapo. He worked for the German desk of the BBC from 1952 to 1966; he resigned from his position in 1966 as a gesture of political protest against Western involvement in Vietnam.

Fried's work is provocative and controversial. His poetry is often harshly satirical, while his fiction draws on political substance in a spirit that refuses to tread softly. His novel, *Ein Soldat und ein Madchen* (written 1946, published 1960, A Soldier and a Girl) posits the possibility of a love affair between a

Jewish-American soldier and a German woman condemned to die for her crimes as a concentration camp guard. The novel offended Fried's colleagues on the Left and on the Right. Fried also was an activist against American incursion into Vietnam; in his moral zealotry he proved intractably rude to his opposition and to those Germans whose complacency he compared to an earlier generation that had permitted the spawning of the Holocaust.

Fried's work is characterized by social, political and religious commitment. At the same time he shows an appreciation of the fantastic and of apolitical imaginative wonder as surcease from the rigors of artistic responsibility. In addition, Fried loves to engage in jousts of wordplay, in a style that is combative and reeling. He has said that by leaving Austria he was able to remain truer to his expressionist credo than if he had remained in his native land. Although his command of English is thorough, he writes his poetry in his native language; he has, in addition, translated Shakespeare, Dylan Thomas, and other English poets into German and has written criticism in his original language. Fried's poetry, influenced by both Bertold Brecht* and W. H. Auden,* is savagely satiric in its expressionistic evocation of the hypocrisies of Austro/German society before and after the Holocaust. He is after the essential truth rather than the representation of realistic detail, although all his cries of poetic expression flow from observations of real human behavior.

Selected Titles: *Deutschland* (1944, Germany); *Osterreich* (1945, Austria); *Genugung* (1947, Moderateness); *Gedichte* (1958, Poems, first of Frank's books published in Germany); *Reich der Steine* (1963); *Kinder und Narren* (1965, Children and Fools); *und Vietnam und* (1966, and Vietnam and); *Befreitung von der Flucht* (1968, Freedom from Flight); *Unter Nebdenfeinden* (1970, Among Close Enemies); *Liebesgedichte* (1979).

Translations: *Last Honors* (1968); *On Pain of Seeing* (1969).

Consult: Helen Adolf, on *und Vietnam und* in *Books Abroad* (now *World Literature Today*) (1967): pp. 320–21; Michael Hamburger, *After the Second Flood: Essays on Post-War German Literature* (1986); Wieland Schmid in *Handbook of Austrian Literature*, ed. Frederick Ungar (1973); Agnes Stein, ed., *Four German Poets: Gunter Eich, Hilde Domin, Erich Fried, Gunter Kunert* (1979).

FREUD, Sigmund. Born May 6, 1856, in Freiburg (now Pribor), Moravia, Austria; died September 23, 1939, in London, England, of cancer. Freud came to England in 1938 in flight from the Nazis and their announced program of liquidation of Jews. As the principal figure in the field of psychoanalysis, Freud had an extraordinary impact on twentieth-century literature. He believed in the power of literature to shape minds, and he drew many of his brilliant insights into human behavior from myth and literature.

Selected Title: *The Standard Edition of the Complete Psychological Works of Sigmund Freud*, ed. James Strachey, 24 vols. (London, 1964).

FUENTES, Carlos. Born November 11, 1928, in Mexico City, Fuentes has published almost thirty volumes, among them novellas, plays, screenplays, collections of short stories and essays, books of literary criticism (on the Latin

American novel and on Miguel de Cervantes) and cultural and political commentary, but is best known for his thirteen novels. He has also written extensively about film, art, and international politics for the periodical press and is often mentioned as a possible Nobel laureate. Though Fuentes is not always thought of as an exile writer, he has lived almost, if not more than, half of his life outside of Mexico, and now divides his time between Cambridge, Massachusetts, where he lectures on comparative literature at Harvard University, and his home in the San Angel district of Mexico City. Although outspokenly critical of Mexican politics throughout most of his life, Fuentes has also served at various times as a government bureaucrat and diplomat; his various periods of exile have been voluntary and intentional.

Fuentes spent his early life in a kind of involuntary exile. His father, Rafael Fuentes Boettiger, was a career diplomat for the Mexican government, posted to Montevideo and Rio de Janeiro from 1929 to 1934 and to Washington from 1934 to 1940. In interviews Fuentes has frequently related anecdotes about his discovery of his Mexican identity: as an outcast in Washington when Mexico expropriated foreign-owned oilfields; as a ten-year-old representative of Mexico when President Franklin Delano Roosevelt staged an international pageant of children from all nations against the European invasions of Germany; as a young patriot when he saw the actor Richard Dix as Sam Houston at the Alamo in a 1939 film and shouted, "Death to the gringos! Viva Mexico!" Each incident and its affective, residual memory helped to forge his identity as a Mexican. Later with his father in Santiago and Buenos Aires (1941–43), he began to rediscover the Spanish language and to connect literature and politics after the examples of Pablo Neruda* and Gabriela Mistral. He returned to Mexico in 1944. About the effect of this long absence, Fuentes said in a *Paris Review* interview: "You must understand that I am a peculiar case in Mexican literature because I grew up far from Mexico, because Mexico is an imaginary space for me, and has never ceased to be so. . . . My Mexico and my Mexican history take place in my mind" (p. 147).

His first novel, *Where the Air Is Clear*, was not published until 1958. In the meantime, through the urging of his father who (rightly) could not believe that a Mexican could earn a living as a writer, Fuentes finished high school, college, and law school in Mexico City and entered the diplomatic service, rising through the Ministry of Foreign Affairs to head its Department of Cultural Relations. On the side, he contributed frequently to newspapers and journals in Mexico and abroad, founded and edited several literary reviews, and wrote short stories. In 1959 he published his second novel, *The Good Conscience*, and resigned from the Ministry. His third, *The Death of Artemio Cruz* (1962), became his greatest success and still remains his best-known work, a portrait through the deathbed meditations of one man of the failure of Mexico to live up to the promises and ideals of Revolution of the 1910s.

In 1965 Fuentes chose to live in Paris to avoid the cultural isolation of Mexico. Citing Henry James,* Ernest Hemingway,* F. Scott Fitzgerald,* and others as well as joining his colleagues Octavio Paz* and Julio Cortázar,* Fuentes said during these years that voluntary exile was necessary for the regeneration of the writer and that national literatures had always been moved forward by émigré writers (Monegal, 120–22). In the late sixties Paris was home for many Latin American exiles or expatriates—Paz, Cortázar, Alejo Carpentier,* Mario Vargas Llosa,* José Donoso,* Gabriel García Márquez*—many of whom wrote for *Mundo Nuevo*, a journal founded and edited in Paris by the Uruguayan Emir Rodriguez Monegal. Fuentes's novels during the period 1965–68, especially *Change of Skin* (1968), show the influence of the French *nouveau roman* and its multiplication of identities and deliberate frustration of the reader's certainty about what happens in the story. The other émigrés, particularly Cortázar and García Márquez, also influenced Fuentes, as most certainly he did them. As the narrator of *Distant Relations*, Carlos Fuentes, says: "France is the final homeland of every Latin American" (24). The varieties of modernism and the desire for technical innovation had been hallmarks of Fuentes's novels from the beginning, and these international cross-currents apparently encouraged his narrative experimentation.

Fuentes moved back to Mexico City in 1969, back to Paris in 1972, and spent 1974 in Washington as a fellow in the Woodrow Wilson International Center for Scholars, a year in which he finished his longest and most difficult novel, *Terra Nostra* (1975). From 1975 to 1977 he served the Mexican government of Luis Echeverría as ambassador to France, resigning upon the appointment of former president Díaz Ordaz as ambassador to Spain, the man whom Fuentes held personally accountable for the Tlatelolco massacre of students in Mexico City in 1968.

After remaining briefly in Paris, Fuentes moved to Princeton, New Jersey, in 1977 and since then has taught and lectured at Princeton, Columbia, University of Pennsylvania, Harvard, Cornell, and other universities in the northeastern United States, an area in which he finds a concentration of great minds. Within this corridor of intellectual power, Fuentes continues to be an outspoken critic of United States foreign policy toward Mexico and Central America.

Fuentes has said that he finds the linguistic element of exile challenging: "I grew up with American English and yet I was able to maintain my Spanish. Spanish became something I had to maintain and recreate. When I am outside of Mexico, the same sensation of being alone with the language and wrestling with it becomes extremely powerful, whereas when I am in Mexico, it is immediately debased into asking for coffee, answering the phone, and whatnot" (*Paris Review*, p. 148).

Fuentes has seldom directly addressed the problems of exile in his novels, although *Distant Relations* (1981), in taking up many of the problems of writing and of narrative, engages the narrator more straightforwardly than is usual in relationships between the cultures of the Old World and the New, France and Mexico. The earlier novels attempt to recover the Mexican past as it survives (or fails to survive) in its present: the colonial and Mediterranean heritage, the

Aztec mythology, the revolution. The later novels, *Terra Nostra* and *Distant Relations*, for example, also concentrate upon the European origins of the Americas and stress the interdependence of European and Latin American cultures. *The Hydra Head* (1978), a Third World spy thriller about international oil, curses both the superpowers and counsels Mexico to seize its chance to regain control of its national destiny through its natural resources of petroleum. In *The Old Gringo* (1985), Fuentes pits the hypocrisy and villainy of the United States against the vigorous revolution of and for the people of Pancho Villa's rebels, a tale of 1914 partly meant as a commentary on the policies of the Reagan administration. Fuentes has recently expressed his hope for a polycultural and pluralistic world.

Fuentes's interest in Mexico's history, identity, culture, and future has remained constant. What his periods of voluntary exile have added are a wider range of formal innovations in narrative technique and experimentation with storytelling, of modernist, postmodernist, and antinovelistic methods, and a more sophisticated approach to the Mexican and Latin American place within international politics. This combination of political and social criticism with a formal eclecticism, which may include Marcel Proust and Alain Robbe-Grillet as well as Jorge Luis Borges and Julio Cortázar, makes Fuentes's novels consistently surprising. Fuentes's continues to write in Spanish. He published his most recent novel, *Christopher Unborn*, in 1989.

Interviews: In Emir Rodriguez Monegal, *El arte de narrar: Dialogos* (Caracas, 1968); with Bill Moyers, WNET/PBS, June 19, 1980; *Paris Review* 82 (Winter 1981); *Kenyon Review* 5 (Fall 1983).

Essays and Criticism: *La nueva novela hispanoamericana* (Mexico City, 1969); *Tiempo mexicano* (Mexico City, 1970); *Don Quixote or the Critique of Reading* (1976); *Myself with Others* (1986).

Consult: Robert Brody and Charles Rossman, eds., *Carlos Fuentes: A Critical View* (1982); Wendy Faris, *Carlos Fuentes* (1983); Daniel de Guzman, *Carlos Fuentes* (1972). See also special Fuentes issue, *World Literature Today* 57, no. 4 (Autumn 1983).

DONALD GWYNN WATSON

FÜLÖP-MILLER, René (also René Fülöp-Müller). Born March 17, 1891, in Caransbee, (then) Hungary; died 1963, in Westport, Connecticut. Novelist, essayist, historian, and literary and psychological theoretician, Fülöp-Miller was a seminal force in European intellectual circles in the 1920s and 1930s before his departure for exile in the United States. His writings on Dostoyevsky and parricide influenced Sigmund Freud's theories of guilt; his studies of Bolshevism, the role of the Catholic church in modern politics, and the brutalization of the humanities by fascist forces had a significant following. Fülöp-Miller was also trained as a chemist/pharmacologist (his father was a pharmacist), and wrote studies in the field of medicine. He was a medic in the Austrian army during World War I. Previous to his conscription, he had run away from home when he was fourteen years old and traveled over the Balkans before settling in Vienna in poverty. He moved on to Paris, where he became a university student. Later he took courses in medicine, psychiatry, pharmacy, and chemistry at various universities throughout Europe. After World War I he worked as a foreign correspondent; his assignments took him to Asia, Africa, and North America. In 1938 he went into exile in the face of the growing danger of Nazi territorial advances in Europe; in 1939 he was among the group of brilliant European refugees toiling away at scriptwriting for the Hollywood studios. He moved to the East Coast after World War II, where he wrote both fiction and biographies. His last novel published before his death was *The Silver Bacchanal* (1960), a story of faith regained through struggle against doubt.

Fülöp-Miller wrote all his work in German.

Selected Titles in Translation: *Lenin and Gandhi* (1927); *The Mind and Face of Bolshevism: An Examination of Cultural Life in Soviet Russia* (1928); *Ghandi, The Holy Man* (1931); *Leaders, Dreamers, Rebels: An Account of the Great Mass Movements of History and of the Wish-Dreams That Inspired Them* (1935); *The Power and Secret of the Papacy* (1937; in England, 1937, *Leo XIII and Our Times: Might of the Church-Power in the World*); *Fyodor Dostoevski: Insight, Faith and Prophecy* (1950); *The Web* (1950, stories); *The Night of Time* (1955, novel).

FUNDOIANU, Barbu. Born 1898, Moldavia, Romania. Fundoianu felt estranged in his native country, both as a Jew and as a poet who believed he had more in common with French literary tradition than with Romanian culture. In his youth he proclaimed that Romanian culture, except in its folklore, did not exist as a cohesive force, and, in consequence, the Romanian writer had to turn to the cultural esthetics of France, a country with whom Romania had historic ties. As part of his creed, Fundoianu wrote in both French and Romanian; his poems in each language are distinct in mood and tone as well as in literary expression. In general, Fundoianu's Romanian poems, written early in life, draw on culturally fixed forms and traditional perspectives. His French poems, products of his later age, are experimental in technique and language. He also wrote provocative essays, and, as in his poems, tended to keep distinct his Romanian subjects and his French concerns. He may be viewed as a cosmopolitan writer in search of a familial-rooted base, or as an exile from what he perceived as the limits of Romanian parochialism. As his analytic criticism evolved, he became an assimilationist, one who wished to hold onto Romanian traditions that produced a richness of unadulterated custom while partaking also of the liberating experiments of modernism. Another example of the Romanian *enfant terrible*, no more and no less a *provocateur* than Eugène Ionesco,* E. M. Cioran,* or Tristan Tzara,* Fundoianu is little known today. His first work, a collection of "books and images from France," appeared in 1922; his first book of poems, *Privelisti* (Landscapes) appeared in 1930 in Paris. A collection of his poems, edited by Paul Daniel, his brother-in-law, was published in 1974, and a collection of nonfiction, largely dealing with Romanian concerns and "images," was issued in 1980.

Consult: Mircea Martin, *Inroducdere in opera Lui B. Fundoianu* (Bucharest, 1986).

FURST, Henry. Born in the United States; died 1967, in Italy. Furst joined the circle of Gabriele D'Annunzio after receiving his degree from the University of Padua. He was with D'Annunzio's forces when they invaded Fiume (now Rijeka, Yugoslavia); later he served as D'Annunzio's secretary. Furst remained in Italy until the 1930s, when he returned to teach at Vassar and at the Library of Congress in Washington, D. C. He returned to Italy at the end of World War II and made his home in Rome, where he became a close friend of Eugenio Montale, the poet who was to be awarded the Nobel Prize. Furst is better known as a figure in a literary *cause célèbre* than as a writer: he ghostwrote feature articles and reviews for Montale in the late 1950s under Montale's name. The pieces were published regularly in *Corriere della sera*. The scandal over a Nobel Prize writer having a ghostwriter for, admittedly, peripheral work erupted in 1989 on the publication of Mario Soldati's memoir, *Rami Secchi* (Barren Branches), in which Soldati quoted from Montale's letters asking for Furst's help. Soldati suggests that Montale felt too harried to write the demanded monthly number of features yet wished both the financial and public rewards of his contractual agreement with the newspaper. Throughout the escapade, Furst seems to have played a willing part; he was no exile to the art of literary juggling.

G

GABIERA, Fernando. Born 1941 in Juiz de Fora, State of Minas Gerais, Brazil; he returned to Brazil in 1979. Gabiera was arrested in February 1970 for participating with a revolutionary Marxist group in the kidnapping of the American ambassador to Brazil, Charles Burke Elbrich, in 1969. He was sent into exile in 1970 when he was flown with thirty-nine other Argentinian political prisoners to Algeria as part of an agreement with leftist groups for the release of the kidnapped West German ambassador to Brazil. Gabiera left Algeria for Cuba, where he lived for eighteen months and grew increasingly critical of that island's revolutionary dictatorship and its repressive attitudes in regard to blacks, religion, homosexuality, and women's rights. He lived in West Berlin under an assumed name for a year, and in 1973 left for Chile. When the Salvador Allende government was overthrown by a military junta a few months after his arrival, Gabiera fled to Buenos Aires, but the Argentine government refused him permission to remain in the country. He moved to Sweden in 1973, where he was granted asylum, and remained in Western Europe until the 1979 Brazilian amnesty.

The author of several nonfiction books and essays on social theory, Gabiera is now committed to the process of democratic change, arguing that revolutionary violence and armed struggle is not a viable alternative in the contemporary arena of civil rights. Attacking both leftist and rightist ideologues, whom he accuses of inability to change their rigid formalism, Gabiera has taken up many social issues as part of his new political regimen. He has defended the legalization of abortion and the use of marijuana. He has condemned both the Soviet invasion of Afghanistan and the United States' bombing of Libya; he has also expressed doubt about the revolutionary struggle in Nicaragua and Cuba, claiming that revolutionary violence is self-perpetuating. Gabiera remains a staunch socialist, but he demands democratic procedure. In 1986 he ran as a candidate of the Rio de Janiero coalition P.T.-Green Party for Governor of Rio de Janiero state, but lost the race.

Selected Titles: *"O Que E Isso, Companheiro?"* (1979, "What's This, Partner?"); *Crepusculo do Macho* (1980, Sunset of Machismo); *Diario de Salvaco do Mundo* (1982, Diary of the Salvation of the World).

Consult: Alan Riding, "Exile, Back in Rio, Agitates for Change on the Left," *New York Times*, August 5, 1986, p. A2.

GALEANO, Eduardo (Hughes). Born 1904, in Montevideo, Uruguay; he returned to Uruguay in 1984. Galeano began his writing career as a political cartoonist for the socialist weekly *El Sol* under the name "Gius." He also served as editor of the weekly *Marcha*, the daily *Epoca*, and several other periodicals. Before moving into exile in Argentina in 1973, he wrote and published *Open Veins of Latin America* (1971); in Argentina he founded and edited the journal *Crisis*. He moved to Spain in 1976, and lived there until his return to Uruguay in 1984. Galeano's early novels *The Song of Ourselves* (1975) and *Days and Nights of Love and War* (1978) both won the Cuban Casa de las Americas prize. His trilogy of novels, under the collective title of *Memory of Fire*, issued in complete form in three volumes in English translation (London, 1989), is a unique rendering of the history of Latin America through brief fictional units in which historical characters and events mingle with anachronistic colleagues and thematically paralleled but disparate events to provide an illumination of truth in the narrative telling. Galeano's view of the evolution of his continent is one filled with rape, torture, violence, and the great falsehood of silence on the genocide of the Latin American peoples. Volume 1 of the trilogy, *Genesis* (1982), treats events from 1492 to 1700 but refers to myths and vatic texts composed prior to Columbus's setting sail for the New World; much of this first volume is given over to the exposure of barbarity and its glorification in those centuries by both European and Central/South American Indian cultures. Volume 2, *Faces and Masks* (1984), treats events in the eighteenth and nineteenth centuries that determined the face of the continent and gave rationale to the various masks that the victorious and the defeated put on in the wake of those events; it surveys the dissolution of one kind of empire, the triumph of another more virulent one, that of foreign capitalist-industrialist lordships and new native oligarchies; the peasant revolutions, and the military dictatorships. Volume 3, *Century of the Wind* (1989), begins its historical narrative with the twentieth century and continues through events of 1984. In providing documentation and yearly headnotes for each unit portrait, Galeano is signifying his work is not merely satirical exaggeration but fact grounded in "narrative, essay, epic poem, chronicle, testimony," as Galeano describes his methodology in the preface to the third volume. As a reflection of the conditions that led to tyranny and exile as well as progress and achievement, the trilogy is a kaleidoscope of experimental techniques and polished prose; it has the breadth of the continent's magic realism and Galeano's outrageous humor and intelligent outrage at the dominant conditions of the Americas in the past five centuries.

Galeano's unique mode emphasizes moral incongruities of historic fact, as in the following excerpt from one unit, "1939: Washington in the Year Nine of the Trujillo Era," in *Century of the Wind*: "General George Marshall offers Trujillo a banquet on board the *Mayflower* and President Roosevelt receives him in the White House. Legislators, governors, and journalists shower this exemplary statesman with praise. Trujillo, who pays cash for murder, acquires his eulogies likewise, and lists the disbursements under the heading 'Birdseed' in the executive budget of the Dominican Republic" (p. 119).

Ronald Wright, reviewing the trilogy in the *Times Literary Supplement* (London, October 20–26, 1989, p. 1165), described the work as a "subversive history" employing the techniques of both the traditional historian and the poet. Wright called Galeano "one of South America's most daring and accomplished authors."

All of Galeano's titles listed above have been translated into English, with the exception of *The Song of Ourselves*. Dates given are those of the original Spanish-language publication.

GALICH, Alexander (pseudonym of Alexander Ginzburg). Born October 19, 1919, in Ekaterinoslav (now Dniepropetrovask); died December 15, 1977, in Paris, France. Galich spent his childhood in Sevastopol, Rostov-on-Don, Baku, and other towns in the south of Russia before his family moved to Moscow in the mid–1920s. Early influenced by Alexandr Pushkin, Galich published his first poems in Soviet children's magazines (one of them was the *Pioneer*); like Pushkin, he was also attracted to the theatre and to musical drama. He won a scholarship to study with Konstantin Stanislavsky and the Moscow Arts Theatre in 1935. When Stanislavsky died in 1938, Galich moved to the Moscow Theatrical Studio. His first play, *City of the Dawn*, a drama drawing on the collective ideal of literary collaboration in the service of the community, was produced in 1941. He was found unfit for military service and spent World War II as an entertainer playing for the troops on the front and for civilians in war-torn cities. During this period Galich began reciting his poetry to his own accompaniment of guitar music. His performances proved popular, and his plays, which were put on after the war, established him as a celebrity. Two of his most popular plays of this period are *Podschastlivoi zvezdouio* (1954, Under a Lucky Star) and *Pokhodnyi marsh* (1957, Campaign Marsh); both focus on Soviet youth and their successful striving for the idealistic goals of socialist vision. In the 1960s Galich began writing songs for Russian musicals and became one of the star entertainers in the country for his solo performances. He also began writing "street" (or "mass") songs, lyrical pieces dealing with *byt* or everyday life, and with the effects of Soviet politics on ordinary living. At the same time Galich was becoming aware of anti-semitism in the Soviet Union and its effects on the average Jewish household. A consequent feeling of obligation as a Jewish artist to speak

out about the spectre of racial/group prejudice took root in him, and he began
publishing some of his anguished satires in samisdat form (underground press).
Galich's mood of invidious bitterness was deepened by the banning of his play,
Malrosskaiatishina (Sailor's Rest) during its run in Moscow; the first version
had been written in 1945, but the first production of a revised script took place
a decade later. (When the play was revived in London, England, in 1988, it
bore the title, *My Big Land*.) The drama concerns three generations of a Jewish
family and the ''crimes'' against them by the Soviet state. The play is set in
four acts—each one delineating a decade (1920, 1937, 1944, 1955) and its anti-
semitic offenses.

In the late 1950s and 1960s Galich began sending his manuscripts into Western
Europe for publication; *Sphinxes* was published in *Grani*, the exile journal based
in Frankfurt. In 1968 he performed his ''Pasternak in Memoriam'' song before
2,500 people in Akademgorodok, Siberia. Official Soviet response was a stern
warning to cease and desist from such public display of dissidence, but Galich
continued on his provocative way. He published his *Songs*, a collection of lyrics
about the daily enervations and frustrations of Soviet life and the oppressive red
tape of Soviet bureaucracy, in Frankfurt, West Germany. On December 29,
1971, he was expelled from the Writers Union (on express orders of a member
of the Politburo) and denied access to theatrical employment. He wrote his
memoir, *The Dress Rehearsal*, during this time (in 1973; it was published in
the West in 1974). He signed an open letter in defense of Alexander Solzhenitsyn
in 1974; the result was further harassment from official Soviet bureaucracy. He
applied for an emigration visa but was denied one. Finally, in June 1974, after
protest from PEN International, the PEN Club of France, and other human rights
organizations, he was permitted to leave the country. He and his wife moved,
first, to Norway, then to Munich; he made a successful singing tour of Italy in
1977. Returning home to his flat in Paris on December 15, 1977, he accidentally
electrocuted himself while trying to repair a tape recorder. Galich's last book,
When I Return, was published a week after his death.

As suggested by Gerald Stanton Smith in his detailed introduction to Galich's
first English-language collection, *Songs and Poems* (1983), Galich's life was a
tragic one, but perhaps, like tragedy, proved uplifting in its cathartic ending.
From a lionized entertainer to a scorned dissident, from a performer who could
anticipate enthusiastic audiences of 2,000 or more to a playwright whose works
could not be performed in the USSR, Galich nevertheless achieved a triumph
in his final self-awareness. Once he identified himself and the role he wished to
play—that of a bard of the people and not a puppet of the state media—he
achieved a power his work previously lacked. Probably his self-awareness began
or in some measure arose from a sense of guilt at having enjoyed luxury and
special privilege while others of his religion were suffering discrimination. Whatever Galich's motives and psychoanalyses, he found a contentment in his work
and life after his trials with Communist bureaucracy intensified. That he should
have died in a freak accident after discovering his deep sense of commitment

provides a concluding irony in a career built on Galich's own ironic and witty observations of human nature.

Selected Title: *General' naya repetitsiya* (Frankfurt, 1974).

Consult: Deming Brown, *Soviet Russian Literature Since Stalin* (1978); Rosette C. Lamont, "Homer's Heirs: Beyond Censorship in the Soviet Songs of the *Magnitzdat*," *World Literature Today* 53 (1979); Gerald Stanton Smith, Introduction in *Songs and Poems* by Galich (1983, Ann Arbor: Ardis); Victor Terras, *Handbook of Russian Literature* (1985).

GALLANT, Mavis. Born August 11, 1922, in Montreal, Canada; she lives in Paris, France. One of Canada's most impressive expatriate writers, Gallant has lived in Europe for the past forty years, thirty of them in Paris. She left Montreal, where she had begun working in the editorial department of the *Montreal Standard*, in 1950. Her characters tend to be emotionally disinherited, adrift in a limbo between soothing recall and ambivalent recollection of their withdrawal into self-exile. Employing the ironies of attenuated impressions is another of the characters' devices for coping. Best known as a short story writer, Gallant is also a novelist and essayist (see particularly her *Paris Notebooks: Essays and Reviews*, 1986). Like Henry James,* she uses Europe and Canada/America as foils for expression of states of mind: her Canadian and American protagonists sink into a further land of withdrawal and apathy, conditions from which they had hoped Europe would rescue them.

In 1981 Gallant received the Order of Canada and Governor Generals Award for *Home Truths: Selected Canadian Stories*. She is at present working on her third novel and also a study of the nineteenth-century French Jewish army officer Alfred Dreyfuss, who was wrongly accused and convicted of treason in a military court and sent to Devil's Island for confinement; he was later pardoned by the government and exonerated of any crime.

Selected Titles: *The Other Paris: Stories* (Toronto, 1970); *The Pegnitz Junction* (1973); *The End of the World and Other Stories* (Toronto, 1974); *From the Fifteenth District* (1979); *Green Water, Green Sky* (1983); *Overheard in a Balloon* (Toronto, 1985; 1987); *In Transit* (1988).

Consult: Robert Weaver, Introduction to *The End of the World* (1974).

GARCÍA MÁRQUEZ, Gabriel. Born March 6, 1928, in the remote village of Aracataca, Magdalena Province, near the northern Caribbean coast of Colombia. He resides currently in Mexico City. Amid the intense diversity of Latin American literature, García Márquez is recognized as an author of extraordinary talent and international acclaim based primarily on the reputation of his narrative epic *One Hundred Years of Solitude*. Novelist, short story writer, and journalist, García Márquez, perhaps more than any of his contemporaries, has created a corpus of work that constitutes a unique blend of vibrant creativity and social consciousness. A political activist, he has long been an outspoken critic of domestic oppression and foreign exploitation of countries within the Third World, and opposition to his own government in Colombia has made him a self-exile for most of his adult life.

Emerging at the height of a literary renaissance in Latin America, he has attempted in his fiction to create the reality of a continent in transition through a dreamlike, surrealistic world of the imagination. Inheriting an artistic tradition from his maternal grandparents, he published his first stories as a student at the University of Bogota. His formal education was interrupted by the outbreak in 1948 of *la violencia*, a state of undeclared civil war that would ravage Colombia for more than a decade. As a result he went first to Cartagena to continue his studies and to Barranquilla to pursue a career in journalism. Deeply affected by the social and political upheaval of *la violencia*, he later would incorporate the conflict within the context of a wide selection of his fiction. Returning to Bogota in 1954, he went to work as a journalist. Publication in 1955 of his first novel, *La hojarasca* (*Leaf Storm and Other Stories*, 1972), was of seminal importance to his fiction, but he received more attention for a series of articles appearing in *El Espectador*; these articles embarrassed the government of Gustavo Rojas Pinilla, the dictator of Colombia. In fear of reprisal, García Márquez went abroad as a foreign correspondent and was on assignment in Paris when *El Espectador* was closed down by the Rojas dictatorship. Stranded in Europe, he was reduced to virtual poverty while completing a new novel, which eventually became *La mala hora* (*The Evil Hour*, 1979), as well as the novella *El Colonel no tiene quien le escriba* (*No One Writes to the Colonel*, 1968).

He returned to Latin America in 1957 to live in Caracas, Venezuela, where he worked in journalism and continued to write short stories. Renewing his political commitment to write short stories, he returned to Colombia in 1959 to align himself with Prensa Latina, the official press agency of Fidel Castro's Cuba, first in Bogota, then in Havana, and later in New York City. Beginning in 1961, he took up residence in Mexico City and entered a period of transition lasting until 1965, during which time he wrote no fiction. Then in a sudden burst of creative energy, he produced in eighteen months *Cien años de soledad* (*One Hundred Years of Solitude*, 1970). Greeted with critical acclaim, the novel is structured as a family saga set in the fictionalized Aracataca of García Márquez's birthplace. Hailed as a modern masterpiece, although criticized in part for evading social and political issues, the novel is considered an allegorical microcosm of Colombia if not all of Latin America, attempting to chronicle the paradoxical nature of human experience from innocence to apocalypse. Since the publication of the novel, García Márquez has been identified as Latin America's premier author, overshadowing other prominent writers.

Having mastered a style of "magical realism" in his fiction, he has continued to enhance his literary reputation, most notably with his novel *El otoño del patriarca* (1975; *The Autumn of the Patriarch*, 1975) and the recent novella *Crónica de una muerte anunciada* (1981; *Chronicle of a Death Foretold*, 1982). As a public figure García Márquez openly acknowledges enlisting his literary fame to advance his political sentiments but denies repeated accusations of being either a Communist or an instrument of the Left. Fiercely critical of American intervention in Latin America, he has been refused unrestricted entry into the United States. In contrast, although optimistic about the changing political climate in his native Colombia, he is understandably cautious about the future, having fled the country during a 1981 visit, fearing arrest by the government. Steadfast in his efforts to improve the social and economic conditions in Colombia, he remains an expatriate and currently resides in the Pedregal section of Mexico City after living for a time in Barcelona, Spain. With the award in 1982 of the Nobel Prize for Literature, he and his work have been assured lasting literary attention. Through the richness and strength of his artistic vision his work has permitted to the wider world an access into the essence and mystery of his heritage. In this achievement García Márquez has fulfilled his political and intellectual commitment to the transformation of Latin America.

Selected Titles: *Innocent Erendira and Other Stories* (1978); *Collected Stories* (1984); *Clandestine in Chile: The Adventures of Miguel Littin* (1987); *The Story of a Shipwrecked Sailor* (1986, repr. of 1970 story ghostwritten by García Márquez); *Love in the Time of Cholera* (1988); *The General in His Labyrinth* (1990; orig. Spanish, 1989); *Collected Novellas* (*Leaf Storm, No One Writes the Colonels, Chronicle of a Death Foretold*) (1990).

Consult: Regina Janes, *Gabriel García Márquez* (1981); George R. McMurray, *Gabriel García Márquez* (1984); Stephen Minta, *García Márquez: Writer of Colombia* (1987); Raymond Williams, *Gabriel García Márquez* (1985).

STEVEN SERAFIN

In his recent novel, *Love in the Time of Cholera* (1988), García Márquez employs the conceit of love as a disease much like cholera, or at least showing the same symptoms—shaking, flailing, fever, pain, distraction, obsessional concern, perpetuity of infection, profundity of illness. In a series of chapters that serve as periodic biographies of the love lives of the three protagonists, García Márquez returns again and again to the meaning of love and sexuality and the understanding that passes forgiveness. The comedy of a man who waits more than four decades to propose again to the woman he loves (he has been waiting for her husband to die); the comedy of a woman who married her husband neither for love nor money but gained both; the comedy of the doctor-husband who loved his wife, understood her resistance to him, and found pleasure elsewhere—all three comedies of human passion, and their unity of one, are gathered into a circle that permits no exit. García Márquez's concerns with family, tradition, progress, change, and the abiding values that move all changes into their proper places remain constant: his is a novelist's thread in the seams and seemings of life's garments. His newest fiction shows a more chastened weaver of tall tales—some of the hyperbole reads like self-parody, and some of the novelistic twists issue from strained and mannered lines. Yet García Márquez's unique blend of realistic detail and winking exaggeration continues to exert its appeal. What keeps the world going, he seems to be saying, is its circumference—laughter and sorrow move into more laughter and sorrow; love and cholera hold fast to their places on the circumference yet move with all the turnings of the circle. This view reveals a more mellow, possibly sentimental García Márquez; it may be read as the report of a traveler who sometimes thinks he would like to come home.

García Márquez's interest in films manifested itself publicly in the summer of 1989 as well. Six features films based on his stories or story ideas were released in an omnibus unit, *Amores Difíciles* (Dangerous Loves) at the Latino Festival in New York in August 1989. García Márquez reputedly worked on the stories or story ideas at the same time and in between breaks from his novel writing earlier in the day and other work in the evening. Some of the stories were revisions of early work, others were new work, and others were simply ideas he gave to the movie scriptwriters; García Márquez also collaborated on the filmscripts. The films were scheduled for individual showings at theaters and for broadcasting on Public Service Television.

GAZDANOV, Gaito (Georgy Ivanovich). Born December 6, 1903, in St. Petersburg, Russia; died December 5, 1971, in Munich, Germany. Gazdanov, who came from an upper middle-class family of Osetian origin, spent his childhood in different parts of Russia: Siberia, White Russia, Ukraine, Caucasus, and Crimea. In 1911, Gazdanov entered the Poltava Cadet Corpus, and from 1912 to 1919 he attended the Kharkov Gymnazium. At the age of fifteen, Gazdanov joined the Volunteer Army and left for the front. In November of 1920 along with remnants of the Army of Baron Wrangel, Gazdanov left Russia heading toward Constantinople. He spent his first year in exile in Gallipoli in the military camp. In 1923 he graduated from the Russian gymnazium in a small Bulgarian town, Shuman. By the end of 1923, at the age of twenty, Gazdanov arrived in Paris. At first he worked at a factory; for a while he attended the Sorbonne. From 1928 to 1952 he worked as a night taxi driver. In 1932 he joined the Parisian Russian Freemasonary Lodge the Northern Star, and from 1932 to 1939 he was a member of the unofficial Masonic group the Northern Brothers. In October 1936 Gazdanov married Faiona Gavrishev. During World War II Gazdanov lived in Paris and helped to save the lives of his friends through underground work; he also wrote for an underground Russian newspaper. From 1953 to 1971, he worked at the Russian desk of Radio Liberty. Gazdanov is buried in the Russian cemetery of Sainte-Geneviève-des Bois near Paris.

Gazdanov began writing at the age of eight. He matured as a writer in Paris during the 1930s. He belonged to the "unnoticed generation" (in V. Varshavsky's phrase) of Russian Parisian literature of the time that has been described by another Russian writer of that generation as an "extraordinary decade" (V. Yanovsky). Gazdanov wrote nine novels, thirty-seven short stories and critical articles on Vladimir Nabokov,* Alexei Remizov,* among others, *The Diary of a Writer*, and about fifty of his articles are in the Radio of Liberty catalogue. Gazdanov's best-known novel is *An Evening with Claire* (1929); it was published in English in 1983, with a reprint in 1988. His second novel, *The History of a*

Journey, was written in 1934–35 and published serially in the Russian Parisian journal *Sovremenie Zapisky* (1936, vols. 58–59). His novel *The Night Roads* was written in the 1930s and also published serially in *Sovremenie Zapisky* (1939, vol. 69) under the title *Nochnaya Doroga* and as a book by the Chekhov Publishing House, New York (1952). His other novels have appeared in Russian or in translation subsequently: *The Specter of Alexander Wolf (Prizrak Aleksandra Wolfa)* in the *New Review*, vols. 16–18, New York, 1951 (English translation, 1951); *Buddha's Return* (*Vozrashtshe-nie Buddy*) (1946; English translation, 1951); *Pilgrimy*, in the *New Review*, vol. 33, 1953, under the title *Piligrim* (English Pilgrims). The last two novels, *The Awakening* and *Eveline and Her Friends*, were written between 1950 and 1964. Gazdanov has never been published in the Soviet Union.

Shaped by two cultures, Russian and French, and influenced by the Neo-Romantic school of his country, Gazdanov was able to penetrate through his sense of the dark curtains of life into a realm of colorful emotion-laden imagery.

ARKADY ROVNER

GEOK-LIN LIM, Shirley. Born c. 1955 in Malaysia; she lives in New York State. "I am a Malaysian woman writer now living in the United States, a marginal 'object' in ego-political terms, to whom and in whom poetry is the supreme subject," Geok-lin Lim wrote in a biographic statement for *Contact II* magazine (Summer/Fall 1989, p. 47). She won the Commonwealth Poetry Prize for her first collection, *Crossing the Peninsula* (London, 1980). Her second volume, *No Man's Grove*, was published by the National University of Singapore in 1985; her third volume of poems, *Modern Secrets: New and Selected Poems*, was issued in London in 1989. She has also published a collection of stories, *Another Country* (1982). In her statement she further wrote: "I grew up in a colonized literature; I am not convinced that a third-world writer must abandon the English language to achieve post-colonial autonomy. Mothered by a foster-language, I will take whatever I need in order to live. Language suicide is not my game, despite whatever regressive ideologies suggest I do."

GHOSE, Zulfikar. Born 1935, in Sialkot, Pakistan; he lives in Austin, Texas. Ghose graduated from Keele University in England in 1956 and worked as a sports writer for the London *Observer*, before returning to Pakistan. He came back to London in 1962, married in 1963, and emigrated to the United States in 1969, largely for career and personal reasons. Now a professor of English at the University of Texas in Austin, he is the author of four volumes of poems, two of criticism, ten novels, and an autobiography. He has always written in English. Of his first novel, *The Murder of Aziz Khan* (1969), Martin Tucker wrote:

It is partly Ghose's combination of oldfashioned stately rhythms and modern thematic counterparts that accounts for Ghose's success in provoking sympathy. He has taken traditional themes and invested them in modern stock situations. The constant flow—it is never a shift or break—between the contemporary and the traditional gives his book a fable-like quality. And Ghose has contributed to this air by his use of the narrator's voice. . . . It is Ghose's achievement that Aziz Khan seems as much a real man as he does a symbol, particularly in the final chapters when he has been deprived of his land and his family, and he walks wraith-like alongside the barbed wire that keeps him from entering his house. . . . If the novel is at one level a revelation of the corruption of Pakistani progress, it is on another and deeper level a restatement of the human condition and its quiet defiance of tragedy (*Commonweal*, pp. 117–118)

Moving his fictional locales to other areas of the world, Ghose has continued to explore both human weakness and strength. In his novel *A New History of Torment* (1983), he employed the lure of El Dorado in his tale of a fabulously wealthy South American rancher who wishes for a vision beyond the glitter of his vast material wealth. The rancher and his children are manipulated through appeals to their sentimentality into providing a sixteenth-century map of El Dorado, funds from the sale of which will supposedly aid in a socially progressive revolution to sweep across the continent. Ghose loads his novel with allusions to the poetry of Pablo Neruda* and César Vallejo* as well as to the El Dorado myth in order to provide a reverberating legendary tone, but the effort sometimes proves more strain than ore. In *Figures of Enchantment* (1986), also set in South America, Ghose put in motion a fusion of dreamscape and reality as two men, one the father of a woman and the other her lover, go on separate journeys but keep crossing each other's path.

Ghose is also a widely published critic of world literature in English. In one of his full-length studies, *Hamlet, Prufrock and Language* (1979), he explores the shaping of reality as determined by language. Ghose's thesis that language precedes idea and thus is responsible for the perspective or attitude of the writer, who in turn shapes the reality of his reader, is buttressed with reference to works by Bertolt Brecht,* Patrick White, Wallace Stevens, Wittgenstein, and G. E. Moore.

Consult: Alamgir Hashmi, *World Literature Today* 62 (Winter 1988); Martin Tucker, *Commonweal*, April 11, 1969.

GIBRAN, Kahlil. Born December 6, 1883, of Christian Maronite parents in Bisharri, Lebanon; died April 10, 1931 in New York City. In 1895 Gibran (at the age of twelve), his brother, and two sisters were brought over to relatives in Boston's immigrant South End by their mother. They left their homeland partly to escape the poverty and restrictions of Ottoman rule, partly to escape from a drunken husband and father. Gibran had had little education in Lebanon, and living among his fellow Arabic-speaking immigrants, he was able to absorb as much of American culture as he did over a short three-year period from a series of fortuitous acquaintances. Jessie Fremont Beale, a social worker at the Denison Settlement House, noticed his skill in drawing and introduced him to Fred Holland Day of the publishing firm of Copeland and Day, who encouraged Gibran and introduced him to the works of William Blake, John Keats and Percy Bysshe Shelley, Ralph Waldo Emerson and Walt Whitman. Gibran met also

Josephine Preston Peabody, a young poet, whose conversation and example inspired him to a life in the arts. He was encouraged by Day to return to Lebanon to understand his heritage better, and he spent three years (1898–1901) at the Al-Hikmat School in Beirut. He returned to America to suffer, at the age of nineteen, the deaths in quick succession of his sister, brother, and mother. For the next ten years, Gibran drew and painted, and wrote poems and essays in Arabic for Near Eastern and Arab-American newspapers and journals. A friend and patron, Mary Haskell, headmistress of a girl's school in Boston, paid for a year of advanced schooling in art in Paris in 1909, and helped him thereafter to learn English well enough to contemplate the future writing of his prose poems, parables, and aphorisms in the language of his adopted country. In 1912 Gibran moved to a studio apartment on West 10th Street in Manhattan, where he lived for the rest of his life, painting with a good deal of commercial and critical success, and writing, beginning in 1919, seven small books of prose poetry in English, illustrated by himself and all published by Alfred Knopf.

The continuity of tone that runs throughout the Arabic and English works of Gibran is that of lonely alienation, of a yearning for connections. Beneath all his prophetic masks, Gibran's lyric cry for connection reveals his most authentic voice. Gibran fundamentally finds solace only in the poetic consciousness or imagination. *The Prophet* (1923), however, is an extended flight on the wings of an idea that he derived from Blake, Whitman, and Friedrich Nietzsche, that the evolving godliness in man is god enough for exultant worship. More often his poems before and after *The Prophet* show a melancholic poet who wants to deliver wisdom to "his" people (sometimes the Lebanese, sometimes the world), but fears that he is bringing them poison or gall, that he is a "false alarm." Rather than "Forerunner," he sees himself as a bitter, weary "Wanderer." Gibran's visual arts are illustrative of this same tonality, pervaded as they are with sadness, alienation, and longing. With respect to Gibran's stature with "his people"—the Arabic world in general, and more specifically the Christian-Lebanese and Lebanese-American worlds—there is a great deal of pride in the native son and an appreciation of his pioneering work in introducing forms and themes of Western romanticism into Arabic literature. The price for his American and world success came high, however, as Gibran often wrote of the pain of his "exile"; his total work encompasses the drama of the talented émigré who was at home neither in the Old Country or the New World.

Consult: Suheil Bushrui, *Kahlil Gibran of Lebanon* (1988); Jean Gibran and Kahlil Gibran [the author's cousin], *Kahlil Gibran* (1974) (contains bibliography); Kahlil Hawi, *Kahlil Gibran: His Background, Character and Works* (Beirut, 1963); Eugene Paul Nassar, "Cultural Discontinuity in the Works of Kahlil Gibran," *Melus* 7:2, reprinted in *Essays: Critical and Metacritical* (1983).

EUGENE PAUL NASSAR

GIPPIUS, Zinaida. *See* HIPPIUS, Zinaida

GLATSTEIN, Jacob (pseudonym of Yankev Glatshteyn). Born August 20, 1896, in Lublin, Poland; died November 19, 1971, in New York City. Glatstein emigrated to the United States in 1914 because of anti-Semitic pogroms. He stayed in New York, where he wrote poetry, criticism, and essays in Yiddish. He returned briefly to Lublin when his mother was dying.

GLOWACKI, Janusz. Born 1938, in Poland; he lives in New York City. Glowacki received his master's degree in literature from the University of Warsaw; shortly after, his one-act plays were produced on Polish radio, and he began writing filmscripts for Polish studios. He became an active voice in the Polish Union of Writers and was a leading supporter of Lech Walesa's Solidarity movement. His first published volume was the novel *Moe trichleje* (1981; *Give Us This Day*, London, 1983; 1985), a narrative of the Solidarity movement in terms of several of its adherents' lives and the hostility of the Polish military and political bureaucracy to the movement. Banned by the censors in his country, it was published there in underground fashion in 1981 and smuggled out of the country for several language editions in Western Europe; it was published in New York in 1985 to acclaim. The novel is different in tone from his later dramatic work, which has taken on an abrasively satiric tone. His plays, produced throughout Poland, proved popular during this time, though their bitter tone was critical of bureaucrats who refused to consider inequities in the Polish socialist system.

In *Kopiuch* (1981; *Cinders*, produced 1981, London; published New York, 1985), still possibly his most strikingly original and powerful play, Glowacki dramatized the visit of a fashionable Polish film director to a girls' reformatory school, where the girls were being obliged to mount a stage production of *Cinderella*. The director, seizing the opportunity to make his fame through a documentary of the girls' lives as played against the *Cinderella* fairy tale enlists the school's administration in making each girl submit to an interview and tell her sad, terrible story on film. The worse the story, the better the documentary, the director consoles the girls. All the inmates comply, realizing they will be rewarded for their rendition of woe (some of them throw in, gratis, new, irrelevant, and often fanciful details), but one girl, Cinders, stubbornly holds out, and on to, in her view, her faith in herself. Glowacki's play forces the audience to ponder the claims of integrity and perversity in exhibiting a director who exploits misfortune for the sake of his artistic fortune and a rebellious outcast who refuses to conform to a society she has rejected. In the drama that unfolds, the girl slits her hands on camera as the film director is interviewing her; he does not yell "cut" until he has his shot of the bloodletting climax. With *Cinders* scheduled for production at the Royal Court Theatre in London in 1981, Glowacki left for England on December 13 to attend rehearsals. While he was there, martial law was declared in Poland. Glowacki's wife, who was scheduled to join him in England, was not permitted to leave. In 1984 his wife and daughter joined him in New York.

Glowacki came to the United States in 1982 after receiving invitations to teach at Bennington College in Vermont and at the University of Iowa. After his teaching stints, he moved to New York City's Lower East Side, a site he utilized in his recent play, *Hunting Cockroaches* (produced 1987; published in *American Theatre*, May 1987). In this dark comedy an exiled Polish couple—an actress and her writer-husband—live out one sleepless night of their new tenement city life. Both have found the going rough in exile; the actress cannot find a role proper to her talents, and the writer has a "block" as well as an awareness of the general lack of his recognition. In *Hunting Cockroaches* and the play preceding it *Fortinbras Gets Drunk* (1985)—the first play he wrote in the United States—Glowacki seems to be traveling a path familiar to observers of exilic progression: mockery, self-mockery, and desperation are constant companions, each intruding on the other to make of a person's world such a maze that the puzzling in life becomes commonplace, and the commonplace becomes another opportunity for confusion and puzzle. The result of such reckless admixtures of moods is often hilarity drowning out tender cries of anguish; survival becomes, if not all of a person's concern, then the dominant sustaining myth of humanity.

Glowacki has written several works in which he draws on his literary and theatrical experiences, and in which he universalizes the conflicts in an artist's life to those of any man who must face the question of his integrity. *Cinders* is about the dangers to integrity posed by a thoughtless socialist dictatorship and by human greed; *Hunting Cockroaches* plays with the frustrations every artist starting a new life in exile faces, where a new language and new milieu demand an overwhelming fresh start. Glowacki treated the issue of integrity in two of his shorter plays as well. In "Journey to Gdansk" his journalist protagonist vacillates on whether to travel to Gdansk to cover the strike of shipyard workers there: if he goes, he may end up in prison and/or without a job; if he does not go, his colleagues and he will know him as a coward. In "Flashback" Glowacki draws on the same situation, but in this script his protagonist is an older, respected writer who remembers the time when he did not speak out against tyranny; he saved his professional status and his surface freedom, but the knowledge of his cowardice has taken root beneath every surface he inhabits. Glowacki, then, may be said to have always written about the artist and his responsibility to society, but in exile the voice of protest seems to be opting for moderation.

Glowacki continues to write in Polish. He has written more than six plays, ten books, twenty radio plays, and four produced screenplays, as well as journalistic articles and essays. His plays have as yet been produced only off-Broadway.

In an interview granted to Jasna Peručic in December 1989, Glowacki commented on his exile status and on his attitude to the current situation for Polish artistic freedom. The report of that interview is given in Professor Peručic's words:

Glowacki considers himself a voluntary exile. He has thought of returning to Poland but has decided to remain in the United States. He believes that he has come "a long way" and that there is too much at stake for him in the United States at the present time for him to leave it. However, he said that "When Poland becomes a normal country, going back will not be a big decision, just a matter of ordinary choice." He does not feel he can write better or any differently in Poland than in the United States, though, of course, he points out that he travels with his native culture all the time in his mind.

Glowacki returned to Poland for a visit in June, 1989, the first time he had seen his native land in seven years. He said that he was happy to see that his audience still missed him, and he admitted that things have changed considerably in his country. His plays are scheduled for production again, first in Moscow, and then in Poland. His novel, *Give Us This Day*, which had to be published in underground *samisdat* form, is going to be published in an official Polish edition. Glowacki was also getting ready to leave for a two-week visit to Moscow as a member of the official Polish delegation, headed by the Polish vice minister of culture, to the Theatre Festival there; on his way back, he was planning to visit Poland for a week.

Glowacki admitted he was "jealous" that he was not in Poland during what he called "the most important moments in the history of my country—the beginnings of democracy." A playwright works with language, and Glowacki felt he had missed the moment when the language changed. Going back to Poland, he discovered that people were using words and phrases that had their gestation and birth during the martial law period.

Glowacki said that coming to the United States was a second birth for him. At home he was well-known, respected, rich, and oppressed. In the United States he was a nobody, no one knew his work. It was a difficult adjustment, but one he found challenging. Paradoxically, the hardships and struggle gave him bitter inspiration and produced a new language in him, a new script of irony. He finds irony the perfect means of communicating with the world and the most effective mode of expressing tragic depth. He believes his play *Hunting Cockroaches* embodies his new "language" and is, in this sense, "an American play, an American dream turned upside down. It is about Polish intellectual aristocracy coming to the United States, confronted with a new culture, new system of values, and hitting the bottom." Glowacki believes part of the problem with adjustment to America is the creation of the myths about America. " 'For years they lied about the West, so people didn't believe it was a paradise! But, once you're a part of the new wave of emigration, you gain a new perspective that eludes you at home, especially if you happen to be famous.' "

Glowacki said he was very frightened of the United States at the time of his arrival here. He remembered the opening night of his first play in the United States—he felt he was fighting for his life. He believes audiences like his plays because they are "honest and without self-pity." Glowacki no longer lives in a *Hunting Cockroaches* tenement flat. However, he has remained faithful to the lower East Side, because, he says, he works well in a "depressing landscape." He has written a new play about New York, and a collection of stories about the lower East Side. He says: "Where else can you find such a fascinating panorama of characters: a mixture of struggling artists, madmen, prostitutes, and drug dealers of all nationalities?"

Glowacki does not believe he will ever write in English. He feels he can best express himself in Polish, and that what used to be the final step in an emigré writer's life—the completion of a manuscript—has now become only the beginning of a slow and painful process of translation. Glowacki also said that he does not believe "one can make a living in the United States as a playwright." He has adopted the alternative route of teaching—he is an instructor at Columbia University in dramatic writing.

In an article Glowacki wrote for the *New York Times* (March 4, 1990) on the exile-emigré writer amidst the changing circumstances of a new decade, he mentioned that his banned novel *Give Us This Day* was scheduled for a print run of 100,000 copies in an "official" edition. His play, *Cinders*, has been performed by sixteen Soviet theater companies, and Glowacki himself has been a guest of the Soviet Union as a distinguished visiting artist. Nevertheless, Glowacki reiterated his decision to remain in residence in the United States where he has established a new homeland; paradoxically, Glowacki referred to Poland as "my country" in the same article.

Consult: Janusz Glowacki, "Polish Odyssey: Warsaw to Off-Broadway," *New York Times*, February 15, 1987; James Leverett, "From Killing Flies to Hunting Cockroaches," *Village Voice*, March 3, 1987; *London Theatre Record*, December 3–31, 1981.

JASNA PERUČIC and MARTIN TUCKER

GOETEL, Ferdynand. Born May 15, 1890, in Sucha, Austro-Hungarian Empire; died in London in 1960. Goetel's life is a series of forced, involuntary residences. As a child he went to school in Cracow and Lvov; later he studied architecture in Vienna, after which, in 1912, he moved to Warsaw and began his literary career while earning a living as a tutor. An ethnic Pole, an Austrian citizen in Russian-ruled Warsaw at the outbreak of World War I, he was deported to Tashkent, where he was a construction worker for five years. He was drafted into the Red Army when the Russian Revolution erupted, and served in the Caucasus during the Civil War in 1920. Returning to Poland by way of Persia and India in 1921, he lived and wrote about his travels and his observations in human psychology. He served as president of the Polish PEN Club from 1926 to 1934. Accused of collaboration with the Nazis, he fled to London in 1946, where he lived for the rest of his life. Although his vision grew progressively impaired, he managed to eke out a living as a free-lancer for émigré papers.

GOGARTY, Oliver St. John. Born August 17, 1878, in Dublin; died September 22, 1957, in New York City. Gogarty did not become an exile in any convincing sense until the age of sixty-one, when he left Ireland for the United States. Even then, he thought of staying only temporarily, and not until much later did he decide to become an American citizen. Certainly by the time he arrived in New York, his best work had already been done, though he now nourished hopes of living exclusively by his pen. A man of unflagging exuberance and diverse skills, Gogarty had given up a successful medical practice in Dublin with the idea of finding new adventures in a new world, hoping especially that his reputation as an Irish wit and as one who had hobnobbed with the literary and political giants of the Celtic revival during the first three decades of the century would prove financially lucrative both on the American lecture circuit and in a variety of published reminiscences. He found that old memories paid better in America than in Ireland, but without the steady income from his medical practice and without his family, who remained in Ireland, Gogarty spent his last years in comparative poverty and loneliness. Indeed, the height of Gogarty's fame (as writer, wit, and politician) had been reached in Dublin, and in many ways his eighteen-year stay in New York made him something of an exile manqué.

Gogarty, the eldest son of Dr. Henry Gogarty and Margaret Oliver Gogarty, entered Royal University in 1896, but soon transferred to Trinity College, where he came under the spell of several dons renowned for their erudition and wit, notably J. P. Mahaffy and R. Y. Tyrrell. Despite his interest in the arts, particularly poetry, Gogarty pursued a career in medicine, the same career followed by his father, grandfather, and great-grandfather. In 1904 he spent two terms at Worcester College, Oxford, making an unsuccessful attempt to win the Newdigate prize for verse. He soon returned to Dublin, married Martha Duane in August 1906, took his medical degree in June 1907, and set off for a year of postgraduate work in Vienna. He returned to Dublin in 1908 and began a thirty-one-year practice as a specialist in ear, nose, and throat surgery.

Gogarty's student days witnessed two events that had a lasting influence on his life and literary career. First, he met, probably in 1901, William Butler Yeats, who many years later included a selection of Gogarty's poems in his *Oxford Book of Modern Verse* (1936) and described him in the preface as "one of the great lyric poets of the age," a remark often quoted, sometimes in very skeptical commentaries on Gogarty's poetry. Second, in the summer of 1904, Gogarty moved into Martello Tower at Sandycove, just outside Dublin, and took in James Joyce* as one of his roommates. Joyce did not stay long, but he remembered his tenancy and immortalized Gogarty as the "Stately, plump Buck Mulligan" in the opening chapter of *Ulysses*.

Gogarty had, however, made a reputation for himself long before Joyce's novel was published in 1922. Indeed, Gogarty had found himself brought to life by others' pens as early as 1912 in *Salve*, the second volume of *Hail and Farewell*, George Moore's comic account of the Irish literary renaissance. In addition, Gogarty wrote three minor pieces for the Abbey Theatre in the late teens (*Blight* [1917], *A Serious Thing* [1919], and *The Enchanted Trousers* [1919]); he became a member of Sinn Féin; and in 1922 he was appointed senator of the newly formed Irish Free State. In January 1923 he was kidnapped at gunpoint from his home; though he made a heroic, and much-publicized, escape, he was advised to move his medical practice to London until the political situation had stabilized. He resumed his practice in Dublin the following year, allotting his time to his medical career, his senatorial duties, and his poetry. Some of his best poetry was produced during these years, most notably *An Offering of Swans* (1923) and *Wild Apples* (1928).

During the early 1930s, Gogarty began to reduce his medical practice and write for various Irish and English periodicals. In 1937, at the age of fifty-nine, he published his first major prose work and the one by which he is still most remembered, *As I Was Going Down Sackville Street*, a loosely structured and half-fictional account of the Dublin milieu. He quickly followed this work with *I Follow Saint Patrick* (1938) and *Tumbling in the Hay* (1939), both autobiographical works dressed up in the language of fiction.

In the fall of 1939, not long after having his application to join the Royal Air Force rejected, Gogarty left for New York. According to his biographer, J. B. Lyons, in *Oliver St. John Gogarty* (1976), Gogarty's main motive for going to the United States was not, as is sometimes speculated, the expensive libel case he lost when an angered friend sued him for offensive passages in *Sackville Street*, but rather his "long-submerged conflict between the frustrated artist and the reluctant clinician." When he first arrived in the United States, Gogarty found that his reminiscences, or more often rewritings of reminiscences, paid comparatively well, and he sold a number of pieces to such journals as *Atlantic Monthly* and *Harper's Bazaar*. Some of his writings in America were essays on the returned exile, most notably "Dublin Revisited," first published in *Tomorrow Magazine*, reprinted in *Mourning Became Mrs. Spendlove* (1948), Gogarty's first collection of essays, and later expanded for inclusion in the autobiographical *Rolling Down the Lea* (1949).

Like Joyce and other exiles, Gogarty wrote very little about the country in which he took up residence. Instead, he looked to the past, producing undistinguished historical romances (*Mad Grandeur* [1943], *Mr. Petunia* [1945]) and essays on things Irish, both in his accounts of his occasional visits to Ireland and in his very readable account of his younger, more celebrated years in *It Isn't This Time of Year at All! (An Unpremeditated Autobiography)* (1954).

Gogarty deals most explicitly with the theme of exile in *Going Native*, his 1940 novel narrated by Gideon Ouseley (who also narrates *Tumbling in the Hay* and who is a thinly disguised portrait of the author). Oddly enough, the novel is not about "going native" in America but in England (as Gogarty had done in 1923–24). The narrator is exhorted by Yeats, the "chief vessel" of the Irish imagination, to "fly with the wild geese," for the war of independence has "brought havoc and destruction to the comely life of Ireland." Ouseley concurs that in order to rid himself of the "vacuous and the dreamy" he must "go amongst the strivers and the builders." Much of the novel is a gentle satire on the English, the satire depending largely on the dreamy Irishman encountering the practical English. It is important to keep in mind that the novel was published after Gogarty had been in the United States for less than a year; many of his comments about the English he no doubt found equally applicable to the Americans he was meeting in Manhattan.

Gogarty made the best of his life in New York, but there is general agreement that he produced little of value during his exile and that he did not enjoy the celebrated status he had hoped for. Especially revealing of his last years in America is W. R. Rodgers's *Irish Literary Portraits* (1973), which provides a transcript of a 1961 BBC broadcast in which a variety of Gogarty's friends (including Austin Clarke* and Denis Johnston*) and two of his children discussed his life and career. There is little doubt that Gogarty planned to return permanently to Ireland, but the last of Ireland's wild geese, as he has been called, died unexpectedly in New York. His remains were taken back to Ireland.

Selected Titles: *Intimations* (1950); *Collected Poems* (London, 1951; 1954); *Start from*

Somewhere Else: An Exposition of Wit and Humor Polite and Perilous (1955); *A Weekend in the Middle of the Week and Other Essays on the Bias* (1958).

Consult: Gerald Griffin, *The Wild Geese: Pen Portraits of Famous Irish Exiles* (London, 1938; repr. 1978); A. Norman Jeffares, *Anglo-Irish Literature* (1982); J. B. Lyons, *Oliver St. John Gogarty* (1976); Ulick O'Connor, *The Times I've Seen—Oliver St. John Gogarty* (1963).

DAVID B. EAKIN

GOLDMAN, Emma. Born June 27, 1869, in Kaunas, Lithuania; died May 14, 1940, in Toronto, Canada. Although Goldman achieved her greatest fame as speaker, organizer, and publisher in the United States, she made her most lasting contribution in exile as author of an epic autobiography, *Living My Life*, published in 1931. Her cult of personal politics laid the foundation for this anarchist classic. Born to a middle-class Jewish family in Lithuania, educated in the Realschule in Konigsberg, exposed in St. Petersburg to the ideals of the Russian Populists, she came to America late in 1885 at the age of sixteen, full of elevated immigrant expectations. She was radicalized by her contacts with the harsh realities of American industrial capitalism, and by the Haymarket affair of 1886–87, when four anarchists were executed for allegedly inspiring a dynamite explosion in a downtown Chicago square. Joining the anarchist circle around Johann Most in New York, she quickly became famous as a charismatic speaker on such subjects as birth control, motherhood, and the modern European drama. An accomplice of Alexander Berkman in his attempt to assassinate Henry Clay Frick during the Homestead steel strike of 1892, Goldman escaped conviction but later served prison terms for leading hunger demonstrations, lecturing on birth control methods, and opposing the draft during World War I. Vehemently opposed to all forms of state authority, she never advocated violence against the state, but her romantic defense of political terrorists made her position an equivocal one, and she was often wrongly accused of fomenting violence. Her defense of free love, her celebration of sexuality, and her attacks on the institutions of marriage and monogamy aroused the anxious fears of conservatives and the enthusiasm of many liberals and radicals, especially young women eager to throw off the bonds of Victorian womanhood. From 1912 until 1918, she circulated her ideas in a monthly anarchist little magazine, *Mother Earth*, which attempted to attract native-born Americans to the primarily immigrant anarchist movement, and helped to bring together labor and political activists with artists and intellectuals.

Deported with Alexander Berkman and other immigrant radicals to Russia in December of 1919, at the height of the post–World War I Red Scare, Goldman quickly turned against the Bolshevik regime she had championed so warmly since October of 1917. Although she refrained from active opposition and continued to work throughout 1920 gathering material for a museum of the revolution, she was sharply critical of increasing Bolshevik centralization, the growing repression of other parties on the Left. With the crushing of the Kronstadt sailors' revolt in March of 1921, both Goldman and Berkman became outspoken critics of the regime, and in December 1921, they left for Germany.

During the next decade, living in England, France, and Canada, Goldman devoted most of her energies to a campaign against the Bolsheviks and to efforts on behalf of Russian political prisoners. She first elaborated her critique in the anarchist press. To the dismay of her comrades, she then published a series of articles in March-April 1922 issues of the *New York World*. She later turned the articles into a book, *My Disillusionment in Russia* (1925), which she incorporated, in more dramatic form, in her autobiography. Goldman argued that the Bolsheviks had betrayed the libertarian promise of the October Revolution, and that a state dictatorship, held in place by terrorism, followed inevitably from Marxism. Attacking what she and Berkman called "the Bolshevik myth" of a workers' utopia that had mesmerized Western leftists, Goldman helped promote another myth of the monolithic, unchanging Bolshevik tyranny, ignoring the many oppositional movements for greater democracy that existed within the Bolshevik party during the 1920s. Focusing exclusively on Bolshevik failures, she denied their significant achievements during the early years of the revolution, particularly in the arts, in health, and education and on behalf of women. As anticommunist polemic, *My Disillusionment in Russia* reflects the abyss that the October Revolution opened between anarchists and Marxists, which contributed to the tragic events in Spain twenty years later.

More successful was Goldman's autobiography, written for an American audience, partly in hopes of returning to that country. Goldman drew on her agitator's gift for caustic repartee and dramatic confrontations with the police to write an emotional narrative, casting herself as Antigone battling Creon in cities and towns across America. If the detailed, thousand-page memoir lacks intimacy and introspection, and passes too quickly over her formative childhood years, it gives, through its account of Emma's free speech fights, a powerful Tocquevillean portrait of American conformity and sexual anxiety in the late Gilded Age and the Progressive era. It offers as well an idiosyncratic view of the tiny but influential anarchist movement in America during the decades when American radicalism achieved its greatest strength. *Living My Life* is filled with nostalgia for America, personified in the memoir by the energetic, flamboyant, unpredictable Dr. Ben L. Reitman, a Chicago physician who became her lover and manager. It also traces her deepening experience of exile, from her unhappy childhood feeling that she had been banished from the world of love, to the spiritual exile she felt she shared with all "pioneers of human progress," to the successive political exiles she suffered in the wake of the Red Scare and the triumph of Bolshevism. This sense of exile lay at the heart of Goldman's compassion for outsiders, dissidents, and despised people everywhere. "The Tragedy of the Political Exiles" (*The Nation*, October 12, 1934) was her final poignant lament for all homeless wanderers, like herself, "cast out and a stranger everywhere."

Living My Life helped Goldman get a three-month visa to visit the United States in 1934, but it did not enable her to remain. The last great campaign of her life was the Spanish Civil War. She traveled to Barcelona in the fall of 1936,

1937, and 1938, returning each winter to London, where she served as agent of the anarcho-syndicalist Confederación Nacional del Trabajo, Spain's most powerful labor confederation, affiliated at that time with the Federación Anarquista Iberica (CNT-FAI). On behalf of the beleaguered anarchists, she raised money, organized publicity, and wrote endless letters, articles, and speeches (many of which are published in David Porter's anthology, *Vision On Fire: Emma Goldman on the Spanish Revolution* [1983]). Though she never learned to speak or read Spanish, and communicated in French or through an interpreter, she instantly fell in love with the Spanish anarchists and experienced exaltation she had not felt before.

With the defeat of the Republic in 1939 (the anarchists had been defeated by the communists in Barcelona in 1937), Goldman returned bitterly to Canada, aiding Spanish and Italian refugees from fascism, still hoping for a visa to the United States yet refusing to cooperate with the Dies Committee, which tried to enlist her in their anticommunist schemes. After she died in Toronto in May of 1940, U.S. immigration authorities allowed her body to be transported to Chicago, for burial in the only country she felt was her home.

Selected Titles: *Red Emma Speaks: Speeches and Writings of Emma Goldman*, ed. Alix Kates Shulman (1973); *Nowhere at Home: Letters from Exile of Emma Goldman and Alexander Berkman*, ed. Richard and Anna Maria Drinnon (1975); *Emma Goldman Papers* (1990).

Consult: Richard Drinnon, *Rebel in Paradise* (1961); Alice R. Wexler, *Emma Goldman in Exile: From the Russian Revolution to the Spanish Civil War* (1989). See also *The Emma Goldman Papers* (1990; available from The Emma Goldman Papers Project, Institute for the Study of Social Change, University of California at Berkeley); Candade Falk, *Guide to the Emma Goldman Papers* (Cambridge: Chadwyck-Healy, 1988).

ALICE R. WEXLER

GOLL, Yvan (also spelled Iwan) (orig. Isaac Lang; pseudonyms: Iwan Lassang, Iwan Lazang, Tristan Torsi, Johannes Thor, Tristan Thor). Born March 29, 1891, in St. Dié, Alsace; died February 27, 1950, in Paris, France. Born of Jewish parents who spoke only French at home, Goll was educated in a German school in Metz, Alsace. He studied law in Strassburg, Freiburg, Munich, and Lausanne, where his literary career began. Like so many other young Europeans, Goll was influenced by the French pacifist writer Romain Rolland. In Switzerland Goll met the poet Claire Studer, who later became his wife. From 1919 until 1939, the Golls lived in Paris, where Goll started writing in French. Goll, who began as a German expressionist poet, soon became acquainted with many major European writers who influenced his career. Among them were James Joyce* and Guillaume Apollinaire, whose literary cubism Goll tried to revive in the periodical *Surréalisme*. Goll's relationship with the Austrian poet Paula Ludwig resulted in the *Chanson Malaise* (1935, Malayan Songs), a collection of erotic poetry.

Goll wrote surrealist novels (*Lucifer Vieillisant*, 1934, Aging Lucifer) and plays (*Methusalem oder Der ewige Bürger*, 1924, Methusalem or The Eternal Bourgeois) which are precursors to both the *nouveau roman* of Alain Robbe-Grillet and Eugène Ionesco's absurd theater. Goll's main work consists of French and German poetry, focusing on his continuing theme, the role of the artist as a spiritual leader of society. His poetry consists mainly of rewritten ancient myths concerning Ahasver, Orpheus, or Hiob.

Since Goll considered himself a German as well as a French poet, his exile began after he went to New York in 1939. His main work, *Jean sans Terre* (1936–44, John Lackland), a five-volume collection of poems, describes his experience as a European intellectual in the United States. The cycle of poems demonstrates how his attention shifts from the problems of the old continent to a more optimistic America where he initially saw a future for himself. With *Jean sans Terre*, Goll re-created the medieval Everyman as an twentieth-century exile. Goll's Everyman Jean goes beyond his own sufferings as well as beyond the experiences of the exiled Europeans in the 1930s as a representative manifestation of modern times.

In New York Goll founded and directed the French-American literary magazine *Hémisphère* from 1943 to 1946, which featured poems and articles by Saint-John Perse,* André Breton,* Henry Miller,* and others. In 1947, Goll returned to Paris, where he published his last volume of surrealist poetry in German, *Traumkraut* (1950, Dream Weeds), a work that reflects his struggle with leukemia.

Selected Titles: *Der Panama-Kanal* (1914, The Panama Canal); *Der Neue Orpheus* (1918, The New Orpheus); *Le Microbe de l'Or* (1927, The Microbe of Gold); *Métro de la Mort* (1936, Subway of Death); *Le Mythe de la Roche Percée* (1947, The Myth of the Pierced Rock); *Abendgesang Neila* (1954, Evening Song).

Consult: Francis J. Carmody, in Yvan Goll, *Jean sans terre* (University of California Publications in Modern Philology, vol. 65, 1962); Vivien Perkins, *Yvan Goll: An Iconographical Study of his Poetry* (Bonn, 1970); Vera B. Profit, *Interpretations of Iwan Goll's Late Poetry* [with annotated bibliography] (Berne, 1977).

REINHARD ZACHAU

GOMBROWICZ, Witold. Born August 4, 1904, in Maloszyce, near Opatow, 200 kilometers south of Warsaw; died July 25, 1969, in Vence, southern France, of complications from asthma. Son of a landowner and industrialist, Gombrowicz was born into an old Catholic gentry family, who moved, after the 1863 anti-Russian uprising, from their native Zmudz to the Kielce region in central Poland. In 1911 Gombrowicz and his parents moved to Warsaw, where he graduated, first, from St. Stanislav Kostka Gymnasium and later, in 1927, from Warsaw University with a degree in law. During the period 1927–29 he studied philosophy and economics at the Institut des Hautes Études Internationales in Paris, but, because of what his family considered Gombrowicz's frivolous and provocative behavior, his allowance was canceled and his studies discontinued. Gombrowicz spent six months in the Pyrenees and then returned to Warsaw, where he worked briefly in a Warsaw court. He then turned to writing as a full-time profession. Several of his stories ("Krajkowski's Dancer," "The Memoirs of Stefan Czarniecki," "Premeditated Murder," "Virginity," "The Feast at Countess Fritter's," "Adventures," "The Kitchen Stairs," and "Events on H.M.S. *Banbury*") were collected and published in 1933 in Polish under the title *Pamietnik z okresu dojrzewania* (A Memoir Written in Puberty; revised edition, *Bakakaj*, 1957), but this first book did not attract any substantial attention. Gombrowicz's first novel, *Ferdydurke*, published in 1937 (Eng., 1961), however, became a literary sensation in Warsaw. An absurd, surreal social satire about a thirty-two-year-old man who is turned back into an adolescent, the novel expresses the author's view that man, although a social creature by necessity, longs to be a spontaneous, free spirit divorced from entanglements with other adults. In this novel of the grotesque, Gombrowicz outlined the major themes of his future work while unveiling his attitude to various sociocultural patterns and conventions. Following the success of *Ferdydurke*, Gombrowicz earlier-written play, *Iowa, ksiezniczka Burgunda*, first published in the review *Skamander* in 1935 (Eng., *Yvona, Princess of Burgundia*, 1969), received critical acclaim. (The play, often produced in Paris, Berlin, and London during the 1960s as part of the theater of the absurd phenomenon and most recently in New York's Off-Broadway in 1987, again stressed Gombrowicz's belief that social institutions affect, in an unnatural way, the behavior of individuals entrapped within them.)

During the 1930s Gombrowicz also contributed to newspapers and journals, especially *Kurier Poranny*, and was a literary personality often to be found at the fabled Café Ziemianska in Warsaw. After a trip to Italy in 1938 and a stay in the Tatra Mountains, he was invited by a Polish shipping company to be its guest on the maiden voyage of the *Chobry*, which left for Buenos Aires on August 1, 1939. With the outbreak of World War II, Gombrowicz was cut off from Poland; his "free ride" was to become a period of exile until 1963, when he left Argentina to return to Europe. He learned Spanish (he was also fluent in French, German, and Russian), but remained aloof from the community of Polish émigrés, living by his wits and on borrowed money. For many years he remained a solitary figure, largely unnoticed in Polish conservative circles and largely neglected as a writer. To support himself he took a position as a secretary at a Polish bank in Buenos Aires. He did little writing until 1947, when he published his play *Slub* (Marriage), two short stories ("The Banquet" and "The Rat") and began work on a novel, *Trans-Atlantyk* (Paris, 1953; Warsaw edition with his commentary, 1957), all written in Polish. Gombrowicz's play is a parody of Shakespearean tragedy in a dream-vision form; his second novel explores the appeal of cult heroes and the lure of romanticism, and represents in essence Gombrowicz's ambivalence to his Polish cultural heritage.

In 1955 Gombrowicz left his position with the Polish bank to devote himself to writing his third novel, *Pornografia*, and his musical satire, *Operetta*, which dealt with, in his words, "the monumental pathos of history." *Pornografia*, completed in 1957 and published in a Polish-language edition in Paris in 1960 and in English in 1966, was a counterpart to *Ferdydurke* and was based again on the tension between the experience and wisdom of age and the spontaneity and innocence of youth. In its treatment of the fascination with youth that can lead to amorality, sadism, and murder, Gombrowicz's work has been compared to Vladimir Nabokov's *Lolita* and to the visions found in the work of Jean Genet. Gombrowicz set his novel in a phantasmagoric Poland dominated by Nazi tyranny. *Pornografia* missed the International Literary Prize by one vote.

The Polish postwar regime expressed its displeasure with Gombrowicz's stress on the "individual" as opposed to the "communal" spirit by banning his novels and plays. Only a few of his works were known in Poland, and this knowledge was gained through private circulation of banned copies and manuscript or typescript versions. However, following a brief political thaw in 1956–57, *Ferdydurke* was republished in Warsaw, and Gombrowicz's plays were again performed. Gombrowicz was compared by many Polish critics to Samuel Beckett* and Eugène Ionesco.* With the coming of the Wladyslaw Gomulka regime, Gombrowicz's work was again banned and disappeared from public view until the late 1970s. During this period Gombrowicz's reputation spread in Western Europe and the United States, and his works were translated into many Western languages.

In 1963 Gombrowicz was invited by the Ford Foundation to spend a year in Berlin, and on April 8, he left Argentina after twenty-three-and-a-half years of residence there. In his following novel, *Kosmos* (Paris, 1965; *Cosmos*, 1967), which did win the International Literary Prize, he utilized his knowledge of erotic psychology to comment on the interplay between the accidental and the fated, the lasting moment and the transient one. Gombrowicz's last play, *Operetka* (Paris, 1966; *Operetta*, 1971) proved a grotesque parody on the meaning of history. In the same year he published his third volume of *Dziennik* (vols. 1–3, Paris 1957–66; *Diary*, vol. 1, 1988), probably the most original literary self-portrait in Polish literature, a work that mixes philosophical exploration, polemical stances on literature, and personal and trivial diary jottings.

Gombrowicz's works concentrate on form as a signifier of meaning and on immaturity as an agency that takes on new meanings throughout a person's life. In his view, as shown in *Ferdydurke*, man is never his own self; he is subject to his neighbors' perceptions of him, he yields to the forms (conventions, schemes, patterns) of habit and intellect that are dominant in the society in which he lives. An individual can only guess at the inner logic of the development of these forms, never knowing if he is facing illusions of his own making (as implied in *Kosmos*). Freedom of the individual thus becomes for Gombrowicz man's ability to destroy those forms that constrain and constrict him. One of these methods of destruction is laughter, and the ability to use laughter as a subversive force leads Gombrowicz to the discovery that the source of the forms is not to be found in transcendence (God, Nature, Historical Necessity) but in the makings of a concrete person, sometimes despite an individual's fear of his own power (see *Slub*). Life vacillates between the dying form and its alternative, amorphousness or chaos. The agents of this progression to breakthrough are, paradoxically, immaturity and an individual sense of inferiority, which again, paradoxically, is loaded with creative energy. The obsession with immaturity—for Gombrowicz the source of beauty—leads him to concentrate on the complements of beauty: ugliness (*Iwona ksiezniczka Burgunda*), boyishness (*Ferdydurke*), and primitivism of Polish gentry as a manifestation of patriotism. Eroticism becomes an increasingly fixed feature of this obsession with beauty and its various parts in Gombrowicz's late works (*Pornografia, Operetka*).

Art originates in the fascination with the unformed, unshaped, but it crystallizes in the completed form. Following this assumption, Gombrowicz advocates a youthful and skeptical distance toward form as a means to cope with its inherent contradictions. In the *Diary*, in an attempt to combine the petty and the great, laughter and seriousness, whim and order, he postulates a psychological model of dynamic and ambivalent personality. Authenticity of an individual (a writer) is measured not by the fixity of psychological constitution or by intellectual views, which Gombrowicz considers a sign of stagnation, but by the individual's ability to change according to any challenge thrown his way.

Gombrowicz's writing is characterized both by his critical assessment of contemporary culture and by a highly conscientious spiritual attitude that he attempts to impose on his readers. His oeuvre shows some affinities with existentialism, but differs in its stress on anarchism and skepticism as methods of insight. His literary manner is also of a different character from the existential mode in its adherence to parody and the exquisite taste of grotesque humor.

Since 1960 Gombrowicz's output has attracted worldwide attention. After the long controversy concerning the publication of his works in Poland, his collected writings were printed in an (almost) unabbreviated edition in 1986.

In his *Diary*, Gombrowicz wrote:

It is very painful not to have readers and very unpleasant not to be able to publish one's work. It certainly is not sweet being unknown, highly unpleasant to see oneself deprived of the aid of that mechanism that pushes one to the top, that creates publicity and organizes fame, but art is loaded with elements of loneliness and self-sufficiency, it finds its satisfaction and sense of purpose in itself. The homeland? Why, every eminent person because of that very eminence was a foreigner even at home. Readers? Why, they never wrote "for" readers, always against them. Honors, success, renown, fame: why, they became famous exactly because they valued themselves more than their success. (vol. 1, p. 39)

Selected Titles: Vol. 1 of *Diary* was published in English in 1988; vol. 2 published in 1989.

Consult: F. Bondy and C. Jelenski, *Witold Gombrowicz* (1978); G. de Roux, *Gombrowicz* (1971); E. Thompson, *Witold Gombrowicz* (1979).

JAN BLONSKI, translated by Marek Kedzierski
with additional notes by Henry Sikorski

GONZÁLEZ-ECHEVARRÍA, Roberto. Born November 18, 1943, in Sagua la Grande (La Villas), Cuba; he lives in Connecticut. González-Echevarría left Cuba in 1959 for the United States, where he has taught at several universities since. He is now a professor at Yale University. He is both a critic and translator (of Julio Cortázar* and Severo Sarduy,* among others). He is best known for his study of Alejo Carpentier,* *The Pilgrim at Home* (1977); he has also compiled *Alejo Carpentier: Bibliographical Guide/guia bibliografica* (1983, bilingual edition).

GORKY, Maxim (pseudonym of Aleksi Maximovich Peshkov). Born March 28, 1868, in Nizhny, Novgorod (now Gorky), Russia; died June 18, 1936, in Gorky, near Moscow. Gorky was arrested by czarist police for antigovernment activities before he was twenty-one years old. In 1901 he was charged with subversion after his poem "The Stormy Petrel" had appeared in the periodical *Zhizn* (Life); the charge resulted in suspension of the magazine. Gorky was also accused of setting up an underground press. Leo Tolstoy's intervention led to Gorky's release, but he was deported from his native town. The forced removal of Gorky led to near riots, and the train carrying him had to be rerouted around Moscow. In 1905 Gorky was again arrested, this time for promoting the overthrow of the czarist government. When the 1905 Revolution failed, Gorky emigrated to Western Europe in 1906 and then to the United States, where he proselytized and raised funds for the Russian Socialist Democratic Labor party (RSDLP). Gorky's efforts were not highly successful; in the United States, Russian embassy pressure resulted in a cancellation of a meeting with President Theodore Roosevelt, and, on a more mundane level, cancellation of Gorky's hotel room. Gorky never forgot his American treatment; his satiric treatment in return is recorded in his collection of stories about American life. After his failure as a fund-raiser he moved to Capri for what became a seven-year exile, returning to Russia in 1913 after a promise of amnesty by the czar.

Gorky's first exile period had a significant impact on his literary work. Among major work written during this period are his plays *Nadne* (1902; *The Lower Depths*, 1912); *Meshchane* (1902; *The Smug Citizen*, 1906); *Dachniki* (1905; *Summer Folk*, 1905); *Deti solntsa* (1905; *Children of the Sun*, 1912); *Varvary* (1906; *Barbarians*, 1945); *Vragi* (1906; *Enemies*, 1945); his novels *Mat* (1906; *Mother*, 1907); *Ispoved* (1908; *A Confession*, 1909); *Zhizn Matveya Kozhemyakina* (1910; *The Life of Matvei Kozhemyakin*, 1959); the first volume of his autobiography, *Detstvo* (1913; *My Childhood*, 1914). (The other two volumes were published later: *Vlyudakh* [1914; *In the World*, 1917]; *Moi universitety* [1922; *My University Days*, 923].)

Gorky also engaged at this time in an intense schedule of political programmatic activity: he attended the Fifth Party Congress in London; wrote pamphlets, manifestos, and committee reports for the Party Congress; and began his correspondence with Lenin, which was interrupted in 1913 when he and Lenin quarreled over the place of religion in a communist state.

Gorky left his native land again in 1921, this time at Lenin's request. (Gorky denounced Lenin in several of his writings as an autocrat who arrested anyone opposed to him.) He lived for a time near Sorrento, Italy. He visited the USSR several times and returned there for permanent stay in 1933.

Gorky's strong sense of realism and local color—his ability to pile detail on detail of the poverty and forced ignorance of the working and peasant Russian class in contemporary czarist times and the corresponding willful ignorance and indifference to such conditions by the aristocracy and complacent bourgeois class—brought him fame both in the West and in the Soviet Union. His pen name, which means "bitter" in Russian, represents a self-critical stance to the material he was treating. Though Gorky was a pioneer of literary naturalism, his work has consistently been praised or derided as either relevant pathos or propagandistic socialism. Some critics see in it a harbinger of later Soviet Realism heavy with suffering and broad strokes of victimization and villainization. Others see it as distinct from obsessively socially conscious dicta and find a compassion in Gorky that allows for subtlety of human error and goodwill in all kinds of people. Gorky's latest biographer, Henri Troyat (*Gorki*, 1989), portrays him as a naive and flawed man who traded his role as artist for that of honored bureaucrat and who became a "literary functionary" of government brutalities. (Gorky apparently approved of a hard line on writers whose freethinking jeopardized social programming.) Troyat lists enough brutalities in Gorky's early life to account for Gorky's "bitter" attitude: his father died of cholera when Gorky was four; his mother of tuberculosis when Gorky was eleven; Gorky stabbed his stepfather, hated his grandfather who beat him, and lived a life of extreme poverty. He worked as ragpicker and earned extra money as a pickpocket. Later he worked as a watchman on a construction project. He also had a job as a songbird-catcher, trapping the birds for sale to wealthy czarist clients, and in his twenties began writing for newspapers. Gorky's death remains shrouded in mystery. He died officially of pneumonia, but whether his natural death was induced by government doctors under orders from Joseph Stalin or whether he was murdered by opposition Trotskyites continues an irksome question. A third speculation is that Gorky's natural death was exploited by Stalin as a "mystery" to throw suspicion on opposition forces within with the government.

Selected Titles: (from 1921 to 1933) *Vospominania o Lve Nikolaeviche Tolstom* (1919; *Reminiscences of Leo Nikolaevich Tolstoy*, 1920); *V. I. Lenin* (1924; *Days With Lenin*, 1932); *Sobranie sochineny*, 21 vols., 1923–28.

Translations: *Stories of the Steppe* (1918); *Tales* (1923); *The Last Plays of Maxim Gorki* (1937); *Articles and Pamphlets* (1951); *Untimely Thoughts: Essays on Revolution, Culture, and the Bolsheviks, 1917–1918* (1968).

Consult: Dan Levin, *Stormy Petrel: The Life and Work of Maxim Gorki* (1965); I. Weil, *Gorki: His Literary Development and Influence on Soviet Intellectual Life* (1966); Bertram D. Wolfe, *The Bridge and the Abyss: The Troubled Friendship of Maxim Gorki and V. I. Lenin* (1967). See also special issue *Yale Theatre* 2 (1976).

GOYTISOLO, Juan. Born January 5, 1931, in Barcelona, Spain; he lives in New York and Marrakesh, Morocco. Goytisolo is considered one of the most innovative and articulate of contemporary Spanish novelists. His novels exemplify the anger and frustration brought on by the Spanish Civil War and its repressive aftermath. Although Goytisolo was only five years old when the Civil War began, the fighting left indelible scars on his life. His mother was killed in 1938 in an air raid by Franco's forces while she was crossing a Barcelona street, and his father, imprisoned for a time during the fighting, fell sick immediately after being released; he did not recover until well after the war ended. Several of Goytisolo's novels, particularly the early ones, are haunted by memories of the Civil War, and of the political and religious censorship that followed.

Goytisolo spent the war years in Barcelona and in the Catalan village of Viladrau, where his father owned a small farmhouse. The house was used as a shelter for refugee children, and served as the setting for his early novel *Duelo en el Paraiso* (1955; Children of Chaos). Goytisolo's first book to bring him international recognition was the partly autobiographical *Juegos de manos* (1954; The Assassins), which explored problems of delinquency among children of upper-class families with vast material but little spiritual resources. His other early novels—*El circo* (1958; The Circus), *Fiesta* (1958), and *La resaca* (1958; Undertow)—are also highly autobiographical commentary on the troubled existence of Spanish society in the postwar era.

Goytisolo is a writer of alienation, having lived in self-imposed exile from the age of twenty-six (first making his home in Paris, and then in more recent years dividing his time between New York and Marrakesh). His protagonists reflect his own attempts as a young intellectual to come to grips with exile and estrangement.

Goytisolo's novels written in the 1960s—*La isla* (1961; The Island), *Fin de fiesta* (1962; Holiday's End)—and his collection of short stories *Para vivir aqui* (1963; To Live Here) further develop his earlier themes to the point at which even normal human passions and sympathies are so frustrated or exaggerated that they cease reflecting humanistic values. Goytisolo's most celebrated novel from this period, *Senas de identidad* (1966; *Marks of Identity*, 1988), focuses on the problems of exile and the process of alienation. *Reivindicacion del conde don Julian* (1970; The Vindication of Count Julian) and *Juan sin tierra* (1973; Landless Juan) complete a trilogy linked by literary style rather than narrative, and seek to break down the barriers of genre in which "the creative imagination of the writer manifests itself not through an outside referent in reality, but through the use of language."

Contiguous with his fictional efforts, he has been working on a series of literary and political essays that have been collected into several books, including *Presentacion critica de la "Obra Inglesa" de Blanco White* (1974), *Disidencias Sahara* (1977), *Libertad, libertad, libertad* (1978), and *El problema del Sahara* (1979). His later novels—*Makbara* (1980) and *Paisajes despues de la batalla* (1982; Landscapes after the Battle)—signify his increasing occupation with form and language, and are a testament to his efforts to construct a literature beyond the conventional, where creative work is linked to the exercise of a critical faculty encompassing and reflecting upon the political, artistic, and philosophical framework of the society in which it is created.

Goytisolo published his memoir *Coto vedado* in 1985. It appeared in an English translation, *Forbidden Territory: The Memoirs of Juan Goytisolo 1931–1956*, in 1989.

Selected Title: *Paisajes después de la batalla* (1982, Landscapes After the Battle).

Consult: Abigail Lee Six, *Juan Goytisolo: The Case for Chaos* (1990); Julio Ortega, "An Interview with Juan Goytisolo," *Review of Contemporary Fiction*, Summer 1984; Kessel Schwartz, *Juan Goytisolo* (1970); Michael Ugarte, *Trilogy of Treason: An Intertextual Study of Juan Goytisolo* (1981).

SUSAN SCHREIBMAN

GRADE, Chaim. Born April 15, 1910, in Vilna (then Vilnius), Lithuania; died June 26, 1982, in New York City. Grade fled from the USSR in 1941, where he lived, to Vilna, where he had been born, and then to Soviet Central Asia in his attempt to escape the Nazi menace threatening Soviet soil in World War II. At the end of the war he left the Soviet Union for a brief stay in Paris and emigrated to the United States in 1948. A poet, novelist, and autobiographer, he wrote only in Yiddish. Several of his works have been translated into English, among them a group of three novellas issued in one volume, *Rabbis and Wives* (1985), and a memoir, *My Mother's Sabbath Days* (1986). In his memoir Grade tells of returning after the Holocaust to Vilna, once a great center of Yiddish culture, and visiting the house in which he was born. His mother had been killed by the Nazis during their occupation of the city, and Grade's visit was an attempt to revisit his memory before putting it away from his present. Grade describes the various inhabitants of the Jewish ghetto in Vilna he knew: those who stayed were killed by the Nazis, while those who fled to the USSR were separated from their culture by place and lack of ritual. He describes his own wanderings in Central Soviet Asia, and the dangers he encountered there.

Grade is best known as a poet, clear and direct in his imagery and expressing an unquenchable aspiration for the breath of freedom he believed was due humankind. In reaction to his strong religious upbringing (his father was a rabbi), Grade became a believer in the power of literature to carry ethics and values and to triumph over barbarism in the world. His works became a testament to the ethical service of the creative artist.

Selected Titles: Poetry: *Yo* (1937, Yes); *Doyres* (1945, Generations); *Pleytim* (1947, Refugees); *Elegiye ozf di Sovetish-yidishe shraybers* (1962; Elegy for the Soviet-Yiddish Writers, 1969).

Consult: S. Liptzin, *The Maturing of Yiddish Literature* (1970).

GRAF, Oskar Maria. Born July 22, 1894, in Berg on Lake Starnberg, Bavaria, Germany; died June 28, 1967, in New York City. Following his apprenticeship in the family bakery and mistreatment by his tyrannical older brother, Graf ran away from home and joined the Munich bohemia at age sixteen. He was drafted into the German army in 1915 to serve on the eastern front. He protested a nonsensical command by a military officer by feigning insanity and was committed to a mental institution. After his discharge, he returned to Munich, where he participated in the revolution of 1918–19. His success as a writer grew rapidly during the Weimar Republic, when he published, at first, poems and, later, short stories, novels, and autobiographical prose works. Of the latter, *Wir sind Gefangene: Ein Bekenntnis aus diesem Jahrzehnt* (Munich, 1927; *Prisoners All*, 1928) gained him international recognition. In the aftermath of Hitler's rise to power in 1933, Graf protested the recommendation of his books (with the exception of *Prisoners All*) to German readers by Nazi authorities; he publicly declared a preference for his books to be burned along with those of other banned writer colleagues. His open letter "Verbrennt mich!" ("Burn Me Too"), published by the Viennese *Arbeiterzeitung* on May 12, 1933, was reprinted and quoted in many countries.

From 1933 till 1934 Graf lived in Austria, from which country he fled to Czechoslovakia after the suppression of the uprising of Austrian workers by the Engelbert Dollfuss regime. His stay in Brno from 1934 till 1938 was interrupted in the fall of 1934 when he participated in the First Congress of Socialist Writers in Moscow and in a guided tour to the southern parts of the USSR. While living in Vienna and Brno, Graf served as one of the editors of the German exile periodical *Neue deutsche Blätter*, published in Prague. He also wrote his novel *Anton Sittinger*, which was published by the German exile publishing company Malik (London, 1937). It is a satirical portrait of a typical minor German government employee who tries to stay out of politics, but who always manages to change his party affiliation and arrive on the side of those in power. In 1938 Graf and his second wife, Mirjam Sachs (a cousin of Nelly Sachs,* whom he had known since his days of the Munich Revolution when his brief first marriage broke up), fled to New York. There, living for some time in the artists colony of Yaddo near Saratoga Springs, he completed his biographical novel *Das Leben meiner Mutter* (*The Life of My Mother*, 1940; first Germ. ed., Munich, 1946), in which he painted a broad panorama of life in Germany from the rule of Bismarck to that of Hitler. After the war, Graf was long prevented from returning to Germany by his lack of an American passport (his German citizenship had been taken away by the Nazis); because of his unwillingness to sign the clause requiring a commitment to fight for the United States, if needed, as required by the Oath of Allegiance, a passport had been denied him. When in 1958 the said clause was removed from his papers, he became an American citizen and was able to visit his homeland four times during the following years. After the death of his wife, Mirjam, in 1959, he was married once more in 1963, this time to Gisela Blauner, another German exile.

Among several new books published by Graf after the war, are the novels *Unruhe um einen Friedfertigen* (1947), the story of a Jewish cobbler who lives fully integrated in a Bavarian village until he is killed by the Nazis; *Die Eroberung der Welt: Roman einer Zukunft* (Munich, 1949, repub. as *Die Erben des Untergangs*, Frankfurt, 1959), a futuristic account of life on the earth after an atomic war; and *Die Flucht ins Mittelmässige* (Frankfurt, 1959), a depiction of a group of German exiles in New York after the war, and of their state of permanent diaspora as a consequence of their unwillingness to return to Europe or to become a part of American life. Graf served as president of the German-American Writers Association during its one year of official existence in 1938–39.

Graf wrote in German. He did not learn to speak English though he lived in the United States for nearly thirty years.

Selected Titles: (written in exile) *Der Abgrund: Ein Zeitroman* (London, 1936); *Der Quasterl und andere Erzählungen* (1945); *Der ewige Kalender: ein Jahresspiegel* (1954); *An manchen Tagen: Reden, Gedanken und Zeitbetrachtungen* (Frankfurt, 1961); *Der grosse Bauernspiegel* (Vienna, 1962); *Altmodische Gedichte eines Dutzendmenschen* (Frankfurt, 1962); *Gelächter von aussen: Aus meinem Leben* (Munich, 1966); *Oskar Maria Graf in seinen Briefen*, eds. Gerhard Bauer and Helmut F. Pfanner (Munich, 1984); *Reden und Essays aus dem Exil*, ed. Helmut F. Pfanner (Munich, 1989).

Consult: Gerhard Bauer, *Oskar Maria Graf: Gefangenschaft und Lebenslust*. Eine Werk-Biographie (Munich, 1987); Sheila Johnson, *Oskar Maria Graf: The Critical Reception of His Prose Fiction* (Bonn, 1979); Helmut F. Pfanner, *Oskar Maria Graf: Eine kritische Bibliographie* (Berne, 1976).

HELMUT F. PFANNER

GRAHAM-YOOLL, Andrew. Born January 5, 1944, of Scottish descent in Buenos Aires, Argentina; lives in London, England, and visits Argentina periodically, where he owns a house in Buenos Aires. Graham-Yooll edits *Index on Censorship* and has written for the *San Francisco Chronicle, Miami Herald, Newsweek,* and the *New York Times*. As poet, literary critic, and memoirist, he writes both in Spanish and English and often translates his work from one language to the other. He is best-known for his *Portrait of an Exile* (London, 1981; *Retrato de un exilio*, Buenos Aires, 1985), an account of the period in Argentina when a military coup toppled the Isabel Péron government and a reign of terror ensued. He left Argentina in 1976 to escape possible torture as a "subversive." His employer in England, the *Daily Telegraph*, assigned him to cover Argentina in the mid-1980s. He was beaten by a gang of political hoodlums in Buenos Aires and left Argentina soon after. Today Graham-Yooll travels freely to the country of his birth and lives in his adopted one.

Selected Titles: In English: *Day to Day* (Buenos Aires, 1973, poetry); *The Forgotten Colony* (London, 1981); *Small Wars You May Have Missed* (London, 1983); *A State of Fear* (London, 1986). In Spanish: *Tiempo de Tragedia, Argentina 1966–1971* (Buenos Aires, 1972); *Se habla spangles* (Buenos Aires, 1972, poetry); *Tiempo de Violencia, Argentina 1972–1973* (Buenos Aires, 1974); *Arthur Koestler, del Infinito al Cero* (Madrid, 1978); *De Péron a Videla, 1955–1989* (Buenos Aires, 1989).

GRASS, Günter. Born October 16, 1927, Danzig (now Gdansk), Poland; he lives in West Berlin. Of Kashubian forebears, an ethnic group tied both to Germany and Poland but distinct in its Swabian ancestry from each, Grass grew up in a city that was Polish only since the end of World War I and had been Prussian before that time. During the period of Grass's adolescence the city was invaded and conquered by German forces, a takeover that Grass welcomed, believing in the propaganda of strength through youth and spiritual cleanliness as a shibboleth of Nazi vision. He was drafted into the German air force in 1944 and wounded on duty in 1945. While recovering from his wounds he was taken captive by American forces. Confined to a hospital bed in Marienbad that overlooked the Dachau concentration camp, he was forced to consider the horrors that had taken place within that camp. When he revisited his native city some time later, he found it destroyed. Grass decided at that point to build a new life out of the ashes of his history and to dedicate himself to the processes of creativity, both in writing and in drawing, which might heal his and Germany's sufferings and aid in transcending the past. He worked at odd jobs in West Germany for several years before enrolling at the Dusseldorf Academy of Arts in 1949; in 1952 he moved to West Berlin to study at the Berlin Academy of Art. (Grass's drawings as well as his fiction and poetry have brought him world renown.) In 1952, penniless but refusing to submit to despair, he moved to Paris with his close friend Anna. While she trained in ballet, he began writing *The Tin Drum*. Grass visited Gdansk for detail for his novel, but the visit wrenched him emotionally. He returned to Paris to discover he had tuberculomas, or bonelike nodules, in his lungs. He survived the illness, although he jokingly refers to its consequence as getting "fat." He began working on a play, *The Wicked Cooks* (Grass's food imagery is a marked feature of his work; the protagonist of one of his novels is a fish, and he has likened himself to a snail in several of his essays; the first title of his celebrated novel *Dog Years* was "Potato Peelings").

In 1960 Grass returned to West Berlin and since then has actively supported the Social Democratic party in the Federal Republic of Germany, serving as a speech writer and campaign publicist.

Grass is thus an exile from his past since in his own words it no longer exists for him or for any Kashubian from Danzig. He cannot trust to his memory, since memory in Grass's view is subject to both purposeful and whimsical revision.

Grass has become one of Germany's most significant postwar writers. Some critics rank him higher than Heinrich Böll, to whose more pacific style Grass is profoundly opposed. Loud, satirical, hard-hitting, and irredemiably compassionate, Grass's work continues its agonizing (and sometimes agonizingly funny) spotlight on the contrarieties of man's soul—his wickedness and his good nature, his loyalty and his greed, his will to power and his easy accommodation with subjugation. He is essentially, in the words of Salman Rushdie,* a "migrant," one in search of new roots to replace the displaced tendrils of his beginnings. In an introduction to Grass's book *On Writing and Politics 1967–1983* (1985), Rushdie summed Grass up as "migrant from his past," and not merely because Grass's native city had disappeared into a new name and new national appropriation, but because Grass's entire world had been shattered. In Rushdie's words, Grass

grew up . . . in a house and milieu in which the Nazi view of the world was treated quite simply as objective reality. Only when the Americans came at the war's end and the young Grass began to hear how things had really been in Germany did he understand that the lies and distortions of the Nazis were not the plain truth. What an experience: to discover that one's entire picture of the world is false, and not only false, but based upon a monstrosity. What a task for any individual: the reconstruction of reality from rubble. (page xii)

Rushdie suggests that Grass, as a migrant from an old self into a new one at the end of World War II, underwent a "triple dislocation." The first was the loss of home, nation, place. The second dislocation was linguistic. Rushdie writes:

We know—and Grass has written often and eloquently—of the effect of the Nazi period on the German language, of the need for the language to be rebuilt, pebble by pebble, from the wreckage; because a language in which evil finds so expressive a voice is a dangerous tongue. The practitioners of 'rubble iterature'—Grass himself being one of the most prominent of these—took upon themselves the Herculean task of re-inventing the German language, of tearing it apart, ripping out the poisoned parts, and putting it back together. (p. xiii)

Grass's last dislocation was both social and personal, a realization that the society in which he had grown up and in which he had once believed had betrayed him. He thus was bereft of support from physical place, from family, from language, and from his former associations and group. Rushdie concludes his portrait of Grass with these words:

I see Grass, then, as a double migrant: a traveler across borders in the self, and in Time. And the vision underlying his writing, both fiction and nonfiction, is, I believe, in many ways a migrant's vision. This is what the triple disruption of reality teaches migrants: that reality is an artifact, that it does not exist until it is made, and that, like any other artifact, it can be made well or badly, and that it can also, of course, be unmade. What Grass learned on his journey across the frontiers of history was Doubt. Now he distrusts all those who claim to possess absolute forms of knowledge; he suspects all total explanations, all systems of thought which purport to be complete. (p. xiii)

Today Grass is a national literary hero, and thus he has a great deal of supportive praise. But the question may well be asked as to which group he belongs. He is a West German, but his roots remain in East Germany. He is fearful of a Germany that still may be reunited into the old Germany of power and violence. He is a committed democratic socialist, in love with the workers of Europe and yet increasingly less active in his support of political programs. He remains a controversial figure in East-West German affairs, often accusing West Europe and the United States for what he calls their hypocrisy and capitalist deviousness; at the same time he is fearful of communist totalitarian tendencies. Clearly he remains a man of vital, surging uncertainties, forever in search of truth and finding that loneliness and isolation are inevitable companions of truth-seeking journeys.

Translations: *The Tin Drum* (1962); *Cat and Mouse* (1963); *Dog Years* (1965); *Selected Poems* (1966); *The Plebeians Rehearse the Uprising: a German Tragedy* (1966); *Four Plays* (1967); *New Poems* (1968); *Local Anaesthetic* (1970); *From the Diary of a Snail*

(1973); *The Flounder* (1978); *The Meeting at Telgte* (1981); *Headbirths*, or *The Germans Are Dying Out* (1982); *Collection of Graphics and Writings/Poetry: Drawings and Words 1954–1977* (1983); *On Writings and Politics 1967–1983* (1985); *The Rat* (1987); *Show Your Tongue* (1989); *Two States—One Nation?: Against The Unenlightened Clamoring for German Reunification* (1990).

Consult: Philip Bradley, Timothy McFarland, John J. White, *Gunter Grass's Der Butt: Sexual Politics and the Male Myth of History* (Oxford, 1990).

GRAVES, Robert. Born July 24, 1895, in London, England; died December 7, 1985, in Deya, Majorca. Graves was educated at Charterhouse and Oxford University. He became an officer in the Royal Welsh Fusiliers during World War I and wrote several memorable works drawing on his experiences. Financial exigency drove him into teaching at the Royal Egyptian University in Cairo in 1926; he had come to Egypt (as he would go to other places in the Near East) for reinvigoration of his love of antiquity and Greek and Roman history. He lectured at Oxford and many universities in Europe and the United States through the 1930s. In 1929 he moved to Majorca with Laura Riding (later Jackson), who was to become his second wife some years after they began their liaison. During the Spanish Civil War he left the island but returned to it at the end of World War II; there he spent the remainder of his life with brief interruptions for lecturing and visits to receive honors and awards throughout the world. He spent the year 1961–1962 as professor of poetry at Oxford.

Graves was an extraordinary craftsman who achieved distinction in many genres: poetry, novel, criticism and mythography, translation, and biography. He found in travel and in life outside England the stimulus and the calm that afforded him the right mix for his creative talents. In the Balearic Islands, where he spent the last forty-five years of his long life, he found an enriching blend of classical purity, Mediterranean warmth, and Christian-Judaic tradition.

Consult: D.N.G. Carter, *The Lasting Poetic Achievement* (1988); Richard Perceval Graves, *Robert Graves: The Assault Heroic 1895–1926* (1989); *The Years with Laura, 1926–40* (1990) (two volumes in a planned trilogy).

GREEN, Julian. Born September 6, 1900, in Paris, France. Green is an example of an expatriate born of American parents on foreign soil; his father was the European agent for the Southern Cotton Seed Oil Company. Green went to French lycées and at age eighteen moved to the United States to become a student at the University of Virginia for three years. He returned to Paris in 1922, and wrote his novels, plays, and journals there, both in English and in French, his native and adopted languages.

With the advent of World War II, he returned to the United States, serving the war effort through his staff position with the Office of War Information. He also lectured and taught at several colleges. When the war ended, Green, feeling more at home abroad, returned to Paris.

Green's writing has a select but passionate following and reflects the world from unconventional angles.

Selected Titles: Novels: *Moira* (1950; *Moira*, 1951); *Chaque homme dans sa nuit* (1960; *Each in His Darkness*, 1961). Autobiography: *Journal*, 9 vols. (1938–72); *Memories of Evil Days* (1976); *Ce qu'il faut d'amour a l'homme* (1978).

Consult: J. M. Dunaway, *The Metamorphosis of the Self in the Works of Julian Green* (1978); Marilyn Gaddis Rose, *Julian Green: Gallic-American Novelist* (1971).

GREENBURG, Uri Zvi. Born September 22, 1896, in Bilikamin, Austro-Hungarian Empire; died May 8, 1981, in Tel Aviv, Israel. Greenburg began his career as a bilingual poet, aware that both Hebrew and Yiddish, which were to become his sources of expression, had a limited audience. He spent a year in Berlin before he emigrated to Palestine in 1924.

GREENE, Graham. Born October 2, 1904, in Berkhamsted, England; he lives mainly in Antibes, France. Greene became a tax exile in 1966 after half of his savings were embezzled by his accountant. He emigrated to Paris, then to Antibes, France. Michael Meyer, in his memoir, *Words through a Windowpane: A Life in London's Literary and Theatrical Scenes* (1989), describes Greene's new role in this manner:

Although his French never became really good, Graham settled into his new surroundings with an ease which surprised me. I knew how content he could be in hotel rooms with a few books, but I did not think he would so readily acclimatize himself to lifelong exile. (As a tax-exile he was allowed to spend, I think, only ninety days a year in England.) (p. 219)

Greene has continued to travel extensively, and his writing production schedule shows no strains of abatement as a result of his chosen exile.

Selected Titles: Novels: *Travels with My Aunt* (1967); *The Honorary Consul* (1973); *Lord Rochester's Monkey* (1974); *The Human Factor* (1978); *Doctor Fischer of Geneva: or, The Bomb Party* (1980); *Monsieur Quixote* (1982); *The Captain and the Enemy* (1988). Stories: *Collected Stories* (1973); *The Last Word and Other Stories* (1990); *Reflections*, ed. Judith Adamson (London, 1990). Essays and Studies: *Collected Essays* (1969); *The Pleasure Dome* (1972; in U.S., *The Collected Film Criticism of Graham Greene*); *Getting to Know the General* [Omar Torrijos Herrera] (1981); *Another Mexico* (1982); *Collected Essays* (1983). Autobiography and Interview: *A Sort of Life* (1971); *Ways of Escape* (1980); *The Other Man: Conversations with Graham Greene* (1983); *Yours, etc.: Letters to the Press 1945–89*, ed. Christopher Hawtree (London, 1989).

Consult: Biography: Norman Sherry, *Graham Greene*: vol. 1, *1904–1939* (1989); Bibliography: J. D. Vann, *Graham Greene: A Checklist of Criticism* (1970). See also Grahame Smith, *The Achievement of Graham Greene* (1985).

GREGOR, Arthur. Born November 18, 1923, in Vienna, Austria; he lives in New York City and Châtillon-sur-Loire in central France. Gregor left his native Vienna when he was fifteen. His father, a well-to-do businessman, was reluctant to leave his homeland till he had amassed a sizable sum of money abroad to carry his family through the hazards of exile; he postponed the passage out of

Austria as he gambled on business deals. The family escaped from Vienna before the borders were closed; they were in Paris the day France declared war on Germany. A hair-raising taxi drive brought them to Rotterdam, where they set sail on the last passenger ship from Europe. When they arrived in New York, Gregor had one possession from his old elegant life—his dog, Fifi. A few months later the dog was killed by a passing car. Gregor worked in New York in various jobs, a change of life for him from his gilded boyhood, and grew to appreciate the freedom that America offered him. He continued his abiding love affair with his adopted country but criticized what he saw as the American penchant for fast spiritual food and easy satisfaction. His talent for writing was recognized by the time he was in his early twenties, and he achieved success with a number of lauded volumes of poetry, among them *Declensions of a Refrain* (1957), *Basic Movements* (1966), *Figure in the Door* (1968), *A Bed by the Sea* (1970), *Selected Poems* (1971), *The Past Now* (1975), *Embodiment and Other Poems* (1982), *Secret Citizen* (1989).

In his search for a more meaningful sense of substance in his life, one beyond a national and even democratic consciousness, Gregor journeyed to India to study with a Vedantic guru. He also traveled widely in France. After several years as an editor in trade publishing in New York, he switched careers and became a professor of English at Hofstra University, from which he recently took early retirement in order to live half the year in his home in France. Gregor has written plays (*Fire!*, 1951, *Continued Departure*, 1952, *The Door Is Open*, 1970); books for children (*The Little Elephant*, 1956; *Animal Babies*, 1959); and a memoir, *A Longing in the Land: Memoir of a Quest* (1983). In his memoir he re-creates his past in its linear moments but glides the sequences into a ladder flowing to a point of question, or as he calls it, a quest. He is pursuing the understanding of wholeness, the moment before exile from the garden of youth. In Gregor's case it was not only adulthood or compromise that he had to accept; it was also expulsion from a society that had shaped his profoundest longings. When the first anti-Jewish laws were promulgated in Vienna, Gregor felt both a sense of outrage and stupefied wonder. His memoir, as his life, shows a quest for ''return'' that has not abated. Even his visits to India seem attempts to regain a spirit that exile from central European civilization sundered.

Consult: *Contemporary Authors*, vol. 10 (1990).

GREGOR-DELLIN, Martin. Born June 3, 1926, in Naumburg/Salle, Germany; he died of cancer after a protracted illness on June 23, 1988, in Munich. Gregor-Dellin wrote poetry, novels, a play (Eng., Luther's Marriage, 1987), and literary criticism but is best remembered for his biography of Richard Wagner (1980) and his edition of Cosima Wagner's diaries (1976–77). Gregor-Dellin himself was irked that his nonfiction studies ranked higher in public estimation than his other work. He was early influenced by Klaus Mann* and edited several volumes of Mann's posthumously published fiction and essays as well as wrote introductions to these editions. He also wrote on his experiences as a young student growing up in the Third Reich. After the defeat of Germany, he remained in his native area, which became part of the German Democratic Republic, and taught there, but in 1958 he defected to the Federal Republic of Germany, seeking asylum in Beyreuth. In 1962 he moved to Munich, where he lived till his death.

Gregor-Dellin earned his living as a free-lance writer from 1966, with occasional stints in radio writing, for which he received national awards. He became a member of the Bavarian Academy of Fine Arts in 1980, and was president of the PEN Center of the Federal Republic of Germany when it hosted its International Congress in Hamburg in 1986. A highly regarded personality, widely respected for his firm gentleness and passionate moderation, Gregor-Dellin nevertheless engaged in most of the national and cultural dramas attendant on both Germanies in the aftermath of World War II. Many of his critics believe his novel *Fohn* (1974, Warm Wind) represents his greatest achievement; the novel uses a bank robbery as the premise for a moral examination of German mores.

Selected Titles: Novels: *Judisches Largo* (Germany, 1956; repr. as *Jakob Haferglanz*, 1963); *Der Nullpunkt* (1959); *Der Kandelaber* (1962); *Einer* (1965). Other works: *Wagner-Chronik* (1972); co-editor with D. Mack, *Cosima Wagner: Die Tagebucher*, 2 vols. (1976–77); *Deutsche Schulzeit* (1979); *Richard Wagner: seine Legen, sein Werk, sein Jahrhundert* (1980); *Was ist Grosse? seiben Deutsche und ein deutsches Problem* (1985); *Italienisches Traumbuch* (1986).

Consult: Wilhelm Kosch, *Deutsches Literature Lexicon; Who's Who in Germany* (1968-ongoing; 11 vols, published through "P").

GRUNTHAL, Ivar. Born 1924, in Estonia; he lives in Sweden. A medical doctor, Grunthal was editor of *Mana*, the Estonian literary exile journal, in Sweden. An urban poet and careful craftsman, Grunthal often employs erotic content as symbolic meaning in his work.

Selected Titles: *Must puhapäev* (1954, Black Sunday); *Peetri kiriku killad* (1962, The Bells of St. Peter; a novel in verse).

Consult: Ivar Ivask, *World Literature since 1945* (1973).

GRUSA, Jiri. Born 1928, in Czechoslovakia; he lives in the Federal Republic of Germany. Grusa left Czechoslovakia in the 1970s after serving time in prison for the crime of publishing his novel *Dotaznik* in Czechoslovakia in 1970 (1982, *The Questionnaire, or Prayer For a Town and Friend*). He is associated with those first-generation-independence writers who witnessed both the Nazi annexation of their country and the Stalinist dominance of post-World War II politics; the collective identity of "Generace 35–45" has been given to their work. Most of these writers published in the underground journal *Tvar* (The Face); many showed an admiration for achievements of pre-World War II Czechoslovakia and a sense of tragedy at what had happened to their country with the advents of Nazism and Communism. As a member of the privileged minority of the new intelligentsia in the Soviet-dominated Czech hierarchy, his apolitical, esthetic stance both angered and grieved the ruling Czech bureaucracy. Many of these writers had experienced a wave of popularity under Alexander Dubček in the Prague Spring of 1968, but were jailed and/or harassed with the crushing of Dubček's government by Soviet troops later that year. Most of these writers left their country to go into exile in Western Europe, Canada, or the U.S., but a few remained behind to work within the system as invidious humanists. With the liberalization of the Czech government at the end of 1989, some of these writers returned to Czechoslovakia. Grusa is also the author of *Franz Kafka aus Prag* (Frankfurt, 1983; *Franz Kafka of Prague*, London, 1983).

Consult: Karel Hvizdala, ed., *Generace 35–45* (Munich, 1988). See also review in *Times Literary Supplement* (October 1, 1982) of *The Questionnaire*; review of *Generace 35–45* in *Times Literary Supplement* (1988) by Vaclav Pisecky.

GU Cheng. Born 1957, in Beijing, China; he lives in Auckland, New Zealand. The son of the poet Gu Gong, who was a cultural worker with the army before the liberation of 1949, Gu Cheng was moved with his entire family in 1969 to Shandong Province, where he was assigned by the government to work as a swineherd. In 1974, he was reassigned to carpentry in a Beijing street repair station. His first poems were published in 1979, a year before his work unit was disbanded. By 1983 he had published 300 pieces, but the Beijing Writers Association refused to assign him a job. In the space marked "Occupation" on his membership card, he wrote the standard phrase for unemployment: "Waiting for Work." One of the best known Obscurist poets, he published *Selected Lyrics of Shu Ting and Gu Cheng* in Fujian in 1982; *Selected Poems by Bei Dao and Gu Cheng* was published by Good Book Press in Sweden in 1983. Other collections are *Dark Eyes* (Beijing: People's Literary Press, 1986), and *Collected Poems of Gu Cheng* (New Horizon Press, 1987). He is a member of the Chinese Writers Association.

By 1988 Gu was again unemployable in China; he made his way to Hong Kong and emigrated with his wife and child to Auckland, New Zealand. He visited the United States briefly in late 1988 as part of a poetry-reading tour. Currently, he teaches Chinese language and literature at the University of Auckland.

Translations of his poems have appeared in several issues of *Renditions: Chinese Literature in English Translation* (Hong Kong); in no. 11 of *Frank: An International Journal on Contemporary Writing and Art* (Paris, 1989); and in *The Red Azalea: Chinese Poetry since the Cultural Revolution*, ed. Edward Morin (Honolulu, 1990). A French translation of his poems, entitled *Les Yeux Noirs*, was published in Paris by Les Cahiers Confluent in 1987, and a Danish translation (1989) is entitled *Gu Cheng Sorte Ojne*. An English translation is *Selected Poems of Gu Cheng* (Hong Kong: Renditions Press, 1990).

EDWARD MORIN

GUILLÉN, Jorge. Born January 18, 1893, in Valladolid in Old Castle, Spain; died February 6, 1984, in Malaga, Spain. Guillén began his travels as a student. He attended secondary school in Mexico; college in Fribourg, Switzerland; grad-

uate school in Madrid and Granada. He received his doctor of letters degree
from the University of Madrid in 1924. An academic expatriate, he taught at
the Sorbonne (1917–23) and Oxford University (1929–31), with positions in the
interim at the Universities of Murcia and Seville. In 1936 he was arrested and
imprisoned in Pamplona; after his release he continued to teach, but in 1938 he
left the country in voluntary, and ultimately permanent, exile. He taught in the
United States at Middlebury College in Vermont, then at McGill University in
Montreal (1939–40). From 1940 until his retirement from active teaching, he
held positions at many universities in North and South America, among them
Yale, University of California at Berkeley, Harvard, University of the Andes in
Bogota, Colombia, and University of Puerto Rico in San Juan. He married
Germaine Cahen in 1961; fourteen years after her death he married Irene Mochi
Sismondi in Bogota. In his later years he maintained residences in France and
Italy and visited the United States frequently. Among his many recognitions are
the Award of Merit from the American Academy of Arts and Letters in 1955
and the Poetry Prize given by the City of Florence in 1957.

Exile did not daunt Guillén's work or attitude to life. He believed in what he
called "integral poetry," a coherence of all knowledge into a totality of experience without division of disciplines of learning, or in his words, "the whole
man with the stirrings of his imagination and feeling." His partisans have called
him both a "universal Castilian" and a poet of "planetary consciousness."
Guillén himself wrote that "exile has not been for me a totally alienating experience, because I find anywhere on earth the essential things: air, water, sun,
man, human companionship. I have never been able to consider myself completely exiled. I am always in this home country called the planet earth" (Introduction, Ivask and Marichal, 1969). Whatever labels are attached to Guillén,
it is clear that he saw his goal as a fusion of particularities into an ontology of
worldliness; his journeys in many countries and cultures were meant as pathways
to an understanding of universal poetic being.

Selected Titles: Poetry: *Cantico* (Madrid, 1928; 2nd enlarged ed., Madrid, 1936; 3rd
enlarged ed., Mexico City, 1945; 4th enlarged ed., Buenos Aires, 1950; first complete
edition, Buenos Aires, 1962; 2nd complete ed., Buenos Aires, 1964); *Clamor: I: Mar-
emagmun* (Buenos Aires, 1957); *Clamor: II: . . . Que van a dar en la mar* (Buenos Aires,
1960); *Clamor: III: A la altura de las circunstancias* (Buenos Aires, 1963); *Suite italienne*
(Milan, 1964; 2nd enlarged ed., Verona, 1968); *Seleccion de poemas* (Madrid, 1965);
Homenaje (Milan, 1967); *Aire Nuestro: Cantico, Clamor, Homenaje* (Milan, 1968).
Prose: *Federico en persona. Essay (semblanza) e correspondence* (Buenos Aires, 1959);
Lengage y poesia: Algunos casos espanoles (Eng., *Language and Poetry: Some Poets
of Spain*, Cambridge, Mass., 1961).

Translations: *Cantico: A Selection*, ed. Norman Thomas Di Giovanni (Boston and
London, 1965); *Affirmation: A Bilingual Anthology, 1919–1966*, ed. Julian Palley (Norman, Okla., 1968).

Consult: Ivar Ivask and Juan Marichal, eds., *Luminous Reality* (Norman, Okla., 1969—
this is an expanded version of "An International Symposium in Honor of Jorge Guillén
at 75," first published in *Books Abroad* 42, no. 1).

GUILLÉN, Nicolás. Born July 10, 1902, in Camaguey, Cuba; died July 17, 1989, in Mexico City, Mexico. Guillén, a mulatto, lived in exile in Latin America for five years from 1953 to 1958. He had gone to Chile for a visit, but was forbidden re-entry on orders of the Cuban dictator, Fulgencio Batista. When Fidel Castro came to power, Guillén returned to Cuba, where, for more than twenty-five years, he served as director of the Union of Writers. He has been called Cuba's national poet: his work celebrates the Communist Revolution in Cuba and the participation of all groups in it. Guillén saw the new Cuban society as a many-colored coat of ethnic mix woven into an integrated socialist fabric.

Selected Titles: *Motivos de son* (1930, Cuban Dance Motifs); *Songoro Cosongo* (1931; Songoro Cosongo); *West Indies Ltd.* (1934); *Summa Poetica* (Madrid, 1976).

Consult: Richard L. Jackson, *The Black Image in Latin American Literature* (1976); George McMurry, *Spanish American Writing Since 1941: A Survey* (1987).

GURNAH, Abdulrazak. Born 1948 in Zanzibar, Tanzania; he lives in England. His first novel, *Memory of Departure* (1987), is a lyric rendering of an African boy's coming of age, and his decision to fly to new horizons. Joycean in feel as well as African in setting, the familiar pain of growing up and growing apart from what-has-been is etched in compassionate detail and style. The novel is autobiographical in spirit and tone if not in literal fact; Gurnah left his homeland for personal reasons, or as his hero, Hassan, says: "Perhaps because I saw nothing but the misery and defeat of my people. I saw nothing but a clinging to old habits" (p. 157). In a letter to a friend in Kenya, the hero writes:

I think a good deal about home and about my people, and about the way things were with them. I feel such pain about leaving that place. Who would have thought it? I never thought I would miss that land. Now I'm afraid that I might forget it all. Drama, more drama! I'm homesick. I even miss seeing the old man brothel-keeper who lives next door to us. Sometimes names escape me, even after such a short time. I try to recall the streets and the colours of the houses. I'm in exile, I tell myself. It makes it easier to bear this feeling because I can give it a name that does not shame me. (pp. 158–59).

Gurnah lives in Canterbury, England, where he teaches literature at the University of Kent. His new novel, *Dottie*, was published in 1990.

GYORGYEY, Clara. Born 1938 in Budapest, Hungary; she lives in Orange, Connecticut, and works as a master teacher of English and drama at Yale University. Gyorgyey is a translator, playwright, and critic. She has written in English a definitive study of one of her fellow Hungarian writers in exile, *Ferenc Molnár* (1980); several of her plays have seen production in the United States. Her translation of *Cats Play* by the Hungarian playwright Istvan Orkeny has been performed in various U.S. theaters including a run on off-Broadway. Gyorgyey's latest volume, *With Arrogant Humility*, a collection of criticism, was published in 1987. She has been president of the Writers in Exile chapter in America of PEN International for many years, and has brought attention to exile writers and their conditions in the United States.

H

HABE, Hans (pseudonym of Jean Bekessy). Born February 12, 1911, in Budapest, Hungary; died September 30, 1977, in Ancona, Switzerland. When Habe began his literary career in Vienna during the early 1930s, he changed his name from Jean Bekessy in order to overcome the stigma of his father's involvement in an embezzlement scandal. Although Habe was raised in the Christian religion to which his parents had converted soon after their marriage in Hungary, his Jewish ancestry was known in Austria, where he tried to make a career as a journalist and newspaper editor. He therefore did not return to Austria from Switzerland, where he was working as a foreign correspondent for a Czech newspaper when the Anschluss occurred in 1938. Instead, when the war broke out between Germany and the Western powers of Europe, he went to France and joined the French military forces. As a member of the Regiment of Foreign Volunteers, Habe witnessed the poorly organized attempts of the French army to stem the Nazi invasion of France and the debacle of defeat; he was himself detained for several months in the transitional German camp for French prisoners of war at Dieuze of the Lorraine. Habe was successful in concealing his Austrian-Jewish background by using the false name of Maurice Pionnier (Napier in the English-language version of his autobiographical account that was published during the war) and his excellent command of both French and German, which enabled him to act as an interpreter for the French prisoners of war in Dieuze and the German camp guards. As a prisoner, he enjoyed certain privileges with the German army, among which were frequent trips to the commercial center of Nancy for the sake of procuring rare goods on the black market.

On one of these trips, Habe escaped under adventurous circumstances, at first spending a night in a brothel for German soldiers and then fleeing through the occupied zone of France into the free southern part, from where he made his way across the Pyrenees into Spain and Portugal, and finally, still in 1940, to the United States. Habe's account of his involvement with the ''drôle de guerre'' and ensuing circumstances both as a prisoner of war and illegal refugee were first published in English translation as *A Thousand Shall Fall* (New York, 1941); the publication of the German original entitled *Ob Tausend fallen* came two years later (London, 1943), and a revised new German edition (which lists the real names of the people whose identities had previously been protected by the use of false names) appearing after the war (Stuttgart, Hamburg, 1947). This book takes a critical view not only of the Nazi war of aggression, but also of the defeatist attitude of the French, some of whom openly proclaimed they preferred Hitler to their own Socialist president Léon Blum. The book also reflects Habe's role as a perpetual outsider on different planes despite his constant efforts to establish some sort of national and ideological identity.

Already in a previous work that Habe had written and published in Switzerland, *Drei über die Grenze: Ein Abenteuer unter deutschen Emigranten* (Geneva, 1937; *Three over the Frontier*, 1939), he had made an important contribution to exile literature—for this novel presented one of the earliest typologies of the exiles of this period by showing how the larger percentage consisted of people who had left their homelands for ethnic, religious, economical, or psychological reasons, and only a smaller percentage consisted of politically active persons. Two of the three protagonists of the book belong to the former group; a wealthy capitalist and an easygoing, young Jewish woman; and the third, an engineer and Communist party member, represents the political activists. The plot takes the reader through some of the major German exiles' locations in Europe—Czechoslovakia, Austria, France, Switzerland, and England—and it ends with the marriage between the young woman and the engineer and their escape into a mystical rural idyll, which led some critics to relate it to Nazi blood-and-soil literature.

During the years of American exile until 1954 (with various interruptions in the service of the U.S. Armed Forces in Europe), Habe wrote several more books and gave frequent speeches as warnings against totalitarianism (in turn, national socialism and communism). In the first few years after the war, he directed the German program for Radio Luxembourg and then became chief editor of the Allied-controlled German newspaper concern *Die neue Zeitung* in West Germany. Soon after his final return from America, Habe published his autobiography, *Ich stelle mich* (Munich, 1954; *All My Sins*, London, 1957). He remained a prolific novelist during the final period of his life when his political beliefs became increasingly conservative and he used his writings as attacks against the ideological Left.

Selected Titles: *Eine Zeit bricht zusammen* (Geneva, 1938); *Katherine: A Novel* (1943); *Aftermath: A Novel* (1947).

Consult: Robert C. Jefferson, ''Hans Habe,'' in *Deutsche Exilliteratur seit 1933*, vol. 1, *Kalifornien*, ed. John M. Spalek and Joseph Strelka (Berne and Munich, 1976).

HELMUT F. PFANNER

HACKS, Peter. Born March 21, 1928, in Breslau, Silesia, then Germany, now Wroclaw, Poland; he lives in East Germany. Hacks grew up in Silesia, a territory ceded to Poland at the end of World War II. He lived in Munich after 1946, where he studied philosophy, sociology, literature, and theater, and attained his doctoral degree in 1951 on nineteenth-century German drama. In 1955 he moved to East Germany as a testament of his political allegiance, and there worked with the Berliner Ensemble Theatre and later as playwright in residence with the Deutsches Theatre in Berlin. His work employs a concentration on Marxist determinism but also acknowledges the abiding strength of earlier, bourgeois myth and thus insists on the inevitability of conflict in East Germany. In 1963 Hacks was forced to leave his post with the Deutsches Theatre after his plays were criticized for their negativism of spirit and their author's tendentiousness of observation about conditions in his socialist land.

Hacks, along with Walter Kaufmann, has been an enthusiastic member of the German Democratic Republic PEN Club of PEN International. His wide-ranging concepts and visions dictate ongoing international dialogue.

Selected Titles: *Moritz Tascow* (1961, Moritz Tassow); *Adam und Eva* (1973, Adam and Eve); *Ein Gesprach im Hause Stein uber den abwesenden Herrn von Goethe* (1976, A Conversation in the Stein House about the Absent Mr. Goethe).

Consult: Lowell A. Bangerter, *Encyclopedia of World Literature*, vol. 2 (1982); Hermann Laube, *Peter Hacks* (1972); W. Schleyer, *Die Stucke von Peter Hacks* (1976).

HALPERN, Moyshe Leyb. Born 1886 in Zloczow, Austro-Hungarian Empire; died 1932 in New York City. Halpern was born in eastern Galicia and went to Vienna to study applied art when he was twelve years old. While visiting Vienna he began writing verse in German. When he returned to Zloczow in 1907, he was persuaded to write in Yiddish. He emigrated to New York in 1908, where he began publishing in Yiddish journals.

HANDKE, Peter. Born December 6, 1942, in Griffen, province of Carinthia (Kärntnen), Austria; he lives in Austria. Handke first received recognition at a 1966 Princeton meeting of Group 47, a who's who of postwar German writers, when he intemperately attacked established writers for their excessive reliance on realistic form and their persistent moral concern. One year later Handke's first full-length play, *Kaspar*, appeared, thrusting him into the forefront of younger German-language writers. Though he had written stories in his university days and now prefers writing novels, his reputation for a number of years was primarily based on his plays. When Handke left Austria in 1966, he moved from city to city in Germany for seven years, then moved to Clamart, a suburb of Paris, returning to Austria in 1979. Much of his career, then, has been spent outside his native land, though he often refers to Graz, where he studied law and where his mother committed suicide.

Handke's obsession with language resulted in six short plays (the *Sprechstücke*, or "speech plays") and three full-length plays, *Kaspar* (1967; *Kaspar*, 1969),

Der Ritt über den Bodensee (1970; *The Ride across Lake Constance*, 1972), and *Die Unvernünftigen sterben aus* (1973; *They Are Dying Out*, 1976), each of which explores *how*, not what, verbal and nonverbal signifiers mean. Handke's drama differed so radically from established drama that most critics failed to understand what he was attempting. From the start he has tried to expose the conventions of the theater in order to establish a new theater that would be free of institutionalization. *Publikumsbeschimpfung* (1966; *Offending the Audience*, 1969), for example, attacks the audience through abusive epithets in order to challenge its complacency.

In *Kaspar*, based on the story of Kaspar Hauser, Handke creates a dramatic character equipped with just one sentence. As disembodied voices teach him to speak, he becomes increasingly adept at expressing himself verbally, but he eventually finds that language, while making the world accessible, divides him from it as well. In *Der Ritt über den Bodensee* Handke continues his inquiry into language, exploring how daily speech and behavior solidify into conventions; our system of coordinating perception and meaning, the play suggests, is only a provisional form of order. In *Die Unvernüftigen sterben aus*, a capitalist-poet laments the loss of a time when humankind and nature were in harmony and poetry expressed that union. The nostalgia for a lost time, literature, and language that Quitt experiences in this play characterizes Handke's major novels of the 1970s as well.

Spare in style and lacking psychological judgments, Handke's novels appeal primarily to an intellectual elite. His coldly analytic prose has led older German writers to condemn his writing as ''dry'' and ''lifeless''; yet he is acknowledged as a major avant-garde influence and is widely credited with extending the form of the German novel beyond social and political concerns.

Following two early novels, *Die Hornissen* (1966, *The Hornets*) and *Der Hausierer* (1967, *The Peddler*), Handke published the Kafkaesque *Die Angst des Tormanns beim Elfmeter* (1970; *The Goalie's Anxiety at the Penalty Kick*, 1972), in which he analyzed the semiotics of experience by carefully recording the actions and observations of Josef Bloch following his seemingly gratuitous murder of a cinema clerk. In *Der kurze Brief zum langen Abschied* (1972; *Short Letter, Long Farewell*, 1974), an unnamed traveler across the United States associates America's history and geography with his own narrative, seeking his identity through a self-imposed analogy. The novel achieves a subtle leveling of fiction, imagination, reality, and dream.

In *Wunschloses Unglück* (1972; *A Sorrow Beyond Dreams*, 1974), Handke examines the life of his mother, who lived in a small Austrian town till, at age fifty-one (in 1971), she killed herself. In searching for a language to describe his mother's life and reflect his own response to her suicide, Handke dismantles narrative clichés. In *Die linkshändige Frau* (1976; *The Left-Handed Woman*, 1978; Handke directed the 1978 film version of this novel), he examines the life of Marianne, who first tells her husband of her vision of his leaving her, then lives her life without him. At novel's end, Marianne has withdrawn from the understanding of others and found security in the solitary space she has carved out for herself.

Handke's more recent works are increasingly autobiographical, yet suggestive of the same concerns found in his earlier work. *Das Gewicht der Welt* (1977; *The Weight of the World*, 1984), Handke's journal of his life in and around Paris from November 1975 to March 1977, is an inventory of hundreds of observations about daily life and about mortality. *Langsame Heimkehr* (1979; *Slow Home-coming*, 1985, also including *The Lesson of Saint-Victoire* [*Die Lehre der Sainte-Victoire*, 1980]) and *Children's Story* [*Kindergeschichte*, 1981]) is a narrative or epic poem that attempts to connect the forms of consciousness, language, and the world. And *Nachmittag der Schriftstellers* (1987; *Afternoon of a Writer*, 1989) is about a nameless writer who walks through his city, hating humankind yet hoping for human contact. In the course of his journey, he asks myriad questions about existence, concluding that the writer must remain an alienated observer, unable to participate in life.

Handke has remained faithful throughout his career to his statement that the only thing that concerns him as a writer is language. Over the years, though, his vision of language has matured, with his early anger tempered and his analysis of the limitations of language yielding to an examination of its possibilities. His fiction today touches a range of linguistic and aesthetic concerns barely suggested in the early plays. And while his drama will remain important, the narrative form of the novel, in which he has said he has always felt freer, seems to offer richer potential for him.

Selected Titles: *Publikumsbeschimpfung und andere Sprechstücke* (Frankfurt, West Germany, 1966 [includes *Publikumsbeschimpfung* (Offending the Audience), *Selbstbez-ichtigung* (Self-Accusation), and *Weissagung* (Prophecy)]; *Hilferufe*, in *Deutsches Theater der Gegenwart. 2*, ed. Karlheinz Braun (Frankfurt, 1967); *Begrüssung des Aufsichtrats: Prosatexte* (Salzburg, 1967); *Prosa Gedichte Theaterstücke Hörspiel Aufsätze* (Frankfurt, West Germany, 1967); *Deutsche Gedichte* (Frankfurt, 1969; *The Innerworld of the Out-erworld of the Innerworld*, 1974); *Das Mündel will Vormund sein* (Frankfurt, 1969; *My Foot My Tutor*, included in *The Ride across Lake Constance and Other Plays*, 1977); *Offending the Audience* (London, 1969); *Quodlibet* (Frankfurt, 1970); *Ich bin ein Be-wohner des Elfenbeinturms* (Frankfurt, 1972); *Als das Wünschen noch geholfen hat* (Frank-furt, 1974; *Nonsense and Happiness*, 1976); *Calling for Help*, in *Postwar German Culture: An Anthology*, ed. Charles E. McClelland and Steven P. Scher (1974); *Über die Dörfer* (Frankfurt, 1981); *Der Chinese des Schmerzes* (Frankfurt, 1983; *Across*, 1986); *Die Wiederholung* (Frankfurt, 1986; *Repetition*, 1988); *Das Spiel vom Fragen, oder, Die Reise zum sonoren Land* (Frankfurt, 1989); *Nachmittag emes Schriftstellers* (Frankfurt, 1989; *The Afternoon of a Writer*, 1989); *Versuch über die Mudigkeit* (Frankfurt, 1990); *Langsam in Schatten* (Frankfurt, 1990); *Versuch über die Jukebox* (Frankfurt, 1990).

Consult: Richard Gilman, "Peter Handke," *American Review* 17 (May 1973), repr. in *The Making of Modern Drama: A Study of Büchner, Ibsen, Strindberg, Chekhov, Pirandello, Brecht, Beckett, Handke* (1974); Ronald Hayman, *Theatre and Anti-Theatre: New Movements since Beckett* (1979); Nicholas Hern, *Peter Handke: Theatre and Anti-Theatre* (London, 1971; *Peter Handke*, 1972); Linda Hill, *Language as Aggression:*

Studies in the Postwar Drama (Bonn, 1976); Jerome Klinkowitz and James Knowlton, *Peter Handke and the Postmodern Transformation: The Goalie's Journey Home* (1983); Hugh Rorrison, "The 'Grazer Gruppe': Peter Handke and Wolfgang Bauer," in *Modern Austrian Writing: Literature and Society after 1945*, ed. Alan Best and Hans Wolfschütz (London, 1980); June Schlueter, *The Plays and Novels of Peter Handke* (1981).

JUNE SCHLUETER

HARRIS, Wilson. Born March 24, 1921, in New Amsterdam, British Guiana (now Guyana); he uses London as his home base and travels frequently to the United States, Canada, Europe, and Asia. Harris's ancestry is multiracial, a paradigm of his country's history of Asian, African, European, and Amerindian citizenry. His family was part of the prosperous middle class, with a colonial attitude of respect for things British. Harris was sent to the prestigious Queen's College in Georgetown, from 1934 to 1939, where he developed his interest in English and classical literature. He became a land surveyor in 1944 and before giving up his civil service position reached the rank of senior surveyor in 1955. He also began to publish his literary work—in his early career his focus was on poetry—in *Kyk-over-al*, the Guyana journal (1945–61) edited by Arthur Seymour. In 1951 his first volume of poems, *Fetish*, appeared under the pseudonym Kona Waruk; his second volume, *Eternity to Season*, published privately, appeared in 1954.

Harris married in 1954, but the marriage lasted only five years. He moved to England in 1959, where he met and married Margaret Burns, a Scottish writer. Thus in one climactic season Harris divorced himself from his old personal life, his job as land surveyor, and his country, for a new physical and spiritual landscape. He turned as well from one literary craft to another: from this point he concentrated on novel writing. His first fiction, *Palace of the Peacock*, appeared in 1960; it was followed by three other novels with a Guyanese setting and a land surveyor as the central image in work exploring identity and loss and the exile of spirit. These novels—*Palace of the Peacock, Far Journey of Oudin* (London, 1961), *The Whole Armour* (London, 1962), *The Secret Laddder* (London, 1963)—are often referred to as Harris's "Guiana quartet" and were issued in a single edition.

Harris's prolific output has included some additional twelve novels, five volumes of literary and cultural criticism, and a revised and enlarged edition of his volume of poems, *Eternity to Season* (London, 1978). Harris is an avid traveler and a frequent lecturer and writer-in-residence on American, European, and East Indian campuses. It is fitting that Harris, in his emphasis on integration of culture into what he conceives as the benefits of "cross-cultural imagination" should be a part of the world scene: in one sense he is, and promulgates, the spirit of internationalism; in just as profoundly invidious another sense, he retains and sparks off his peculiar West Indian being of identity. Harris has written extensively, particularly in *The Womb of Space: The Cross-Cultural Imagination*

(1983), on fertilization of ideas that allows for unity of diversity (and diversity of unity) in literary and cultural "space."

Harris's fiction and criticism are the work of a writer who began publishing in these genres after his thirty-ninth year. His experiences and his intellectual questionings of things past are reflected in a maturity of outlook that has changed little in perspective since he adopted his new career. The image of land surveyor—that of an intellectual journeyer charting out unplumbed territory—pervades his work; the processes of cognates of intercultural invigoration infuse at the deepest levels his use of comparative mythology. Harris's interest in myth is a part of his natural search for unifying elements in man's cultural history and in the cultural parallels of human sustenance. His interest in natural beauty and the landscapes of density and clearing are also part of his complex of vision; from the jungles comes the path to the inner waterfall of cleaning and restoration. From difficulty comes the way to transcendence; from mythology and history comes the possibility of understanding of self.

Harris's novels have been called obscurantist by some critics, and merely difficult by others. Given the scope of his search through Christian and pre-Christian mythos and into the profuse identities of his various characters, it is not surprising that Harris takes unconventional liberties with chronology and employs unconventional unifying leaps of creative will. Yet, as Anthony Boxill says in his essay in *Fifty Caribbean Writers* (see below), Harris's ideas "do not change so much as they grow in depth and sophistication. They become fuller and more complex, and they embrace more of the paradoxes of life with each new work." Harris himself says in *The Womb of Space*, his apologia for a new kind of literature, the kind he wishes to write and to have fostered as a beacon for Guyanese writers: "The paradox of cultural heterogeneity, or cross-cultural capacity, lies in the evolutionary thrust it restores to orders of the imagination, the ceaseless dialogue it inserts between hardened conventions and eclipsed or half-eclipsed otherness, within an intuitive self that moves endlessly into flexible patterns, areas or bridges of community" (p. xviii). Such a view illuminates Harris's obsession with the powers of literature, and the difficulties his direction away from naturalism into less chartered literary paths brings to his readers.

In Harris's case, his decision to relocate, his literal displacement and replacement of base and stimulus, did not result in conventional melancholy but in an outburst of creative energy and in a flowing production of his many cultural journeys.

Selected Titles: Novels: *Heartland* (London, 1964); *The Eye of the Scarecrow* (London, 1965); *Tumatumari* (London, 1968); *Ascent to Omai* (London, 1970); *The Sleepers of Roraima* (London, 1970); *The Age of the Rainmakers* (London, 1971); *Black Marsden* (London, 1972); *The Secret Ladder* (1973); *Companions of the Day and Night* (London, 1975); *Da Silva da Silva's Cultivated Wilderness and Genesis of the Clowns* (London, 1977); *The Tree of the Sun* (London, 1978); *Explorations* (1981); *The Angel at the Gate* (London, 1982); *The Infinite Rehearsal* (1987); *The Four Banks of the River of Space* (1990). Criticism: *Tradition, the Writer and Society* (London, 1967); *History, Fable and*

Myth in the Caribbean and Guyana (Georgetown, Guyana, 1970); *Fossil and Psyche* (Austin, Texas, 1974); *Explorations, ed. Hena Maes-Jelinek* (Aarhus, Denmark, 1981); *The Womb of Space* (Westport, Conn., 1983).

Consult: Rolstan Adams, "Wilson Harris: The Pre-Novel Poet," *Journal of Commonwealth Literature* 13 (April 1979); Joyce (Sparer) Adler, "Wilson Harris and Twentieth-Century Man," *New Letters* 40 (October 1973); Anthony Boxill, "Wilson Harris," in *Fifty Caribbean Writers*, ed. Daryl Cumber Dance (1986); Sandra Drake, *Wilson Harris and The Modern Tradition* (Westport, Conn., 1986); Michael Gilkes, *Wilson Harris and the Caribbean Novel* (London, 1975); C.L.R. James, *Wilson Harris—A Philosophical Approach* (Trinidad, 1965); Bruce King, *The New English Literatures: Cultural Nationalism in a Changing World* (London, 1980); Hena Maes-Jelinek, *Wilson Harris* (Boston, 1982).

HARTOG, Jan de (pseudonym of F. R. Eckmar). Born 1914, Haarlem, The Netherlands; he lives on the Isle of Wight and in Paris. Hartog is a sailor-journeyman traveler. He left home at an early age to work as a cabin boy and ordinary seaman on Dutch freighters. In 1946 he moved to the Isle of Wight and to Paris as his main residences. A best-selling author whose novels are translated into many languages, he writes sea stories in which heroes must face the challenge of a storm and prove their mettle, but beneath the popular surface of adventure in his tales is a moral exploration of knowledge beyond the wanderer's ordinary ken. His plays have been produced throughout the world; *The Fourposter*, produced on Broadway in 1951, which stands or falls in its lines on one kind of bed and the people who lie in it, remains his most durable success.

HARWOOD, Ronald. Born 1934 Johannesburg, South Africa; he lives in London. Harwood left South Africa in his youth; he has lived in London since, and is now president of the English PEN Centre. Significantly, his first published book, *George Washington September Sir!* (London, 1961) and his most recent work, the play *Another Time* (which opened in London in September 1989), draw on his South African experiences. His first novel is a seriocomic treatment, in the vogue of Joyce Cary's *Mr. Johnson* (London, 1939), of a charming black native destroyed by prejudice in spite of his willingness to accede to all demands made on him. His most recent play treats a South African musical artist living in London who must confront the dilemma of returning to South Africa when he is offered a musical engagement there. In making his decision, the protagonist must face his own social and ethical values and expose his principles, or lack of them.

Harwood has published fiction, criticism, and biography (of Sir Donald Wolfitt and Sir John Gielgud). He is widely known for his drama, *The Dresser*, which appeared in London in 1981, and which deals with the victim-oppressor relationship of a theater "star" and his dresser/assistant.

Selected Titles: *Articles of Faith* (London, 1973); *The Genoa Ferry* (London, 1976); *A Family: A Play* (London, 1978); *All the World's A Stage* (London, 1984); *Tranway*

Road (Oxford, 1984); *The Deliberate Death of a Polish Priest* (London, 1985); *Interpreters: A Fantasia on English and Russian Themes* (London, 1986).

HASENCLEVER, Walter. Born 1890, in Aachen, Germany; died June, 1940, in Les Milles, Aix-en-Provence, France. Novelist, dramatist, and poet, Hasenclever was deprived of his German citizenship in 1933 and emigrated to southern France. He continued his wandering, with residence in Dubrovnik in 1935, London in 1936, Nice in 1937, and Florence and London from 1937 to 1939. He spent his last year in Cagnes-sur-Mer in southern France and was interned twice by French authorities. He committed suicide in June 1940 at the refugee camp in Les Milles as the Germans were overrunning the region.

Consult: Alfred Hoetzel, *Walter Hasenclever's Humanitarianism: Themes of Protest in his Works* (London, 1988); Stephen S. Stanton, "Hasenclever's Humanism: An Expressionist Morality Play," *Modern Drama* 13, no. 4 (February 1971); Peter Bruce Waldeck, *The Split Self from Goethe to Broch* (1979).

HASSAN, Marwan. Born in Lebanon; he lives in Canada. Hassan is a Lebanese exile in Canada, brought there by the horrors of the civil war in his country. In 1989 he published his first book, *The Confusion of Stones*, a collection of two stories about the exile condition and spirit. In a review of the book, in *Books in Canada* (August-September 1989), the reviewer (B.S.) wrote:

The first [story] is about a young Lebanese peasant named Falah Azlam who is forced to emigrate to Canada, and the second is about a Canadian doctor of Lebanese extraction who is nearing the end of a nearly year-long stay in Lebanon, where he has been teaching at a university. The style of the two stories is fastidious, intensely concentrated; and in each the themes are cultural confusion and the despair of exile, the despair of being an Arab in Canada, an Arab in Lebanon. These are great themes, and Hassan explores them with contained passion. (p. 5.)

HÁY, Julius (Gyula). Born 1900, in Budapest, Hungary; died 1975, in Ascona, Switzerland. The only internationally known Hungarian playwright of communist persuasion, Háy was Hungary's most experienced refugee. He spent more time in exile in various parts of the world for various reasons than in any one homeland. Son of a rural teacher, he joined the working-class movement at an early age. In 1919, during the short-lived Communist Revolution, he served as a junior liaison officer in the Educational Soviet (Council). After the revolution was defeated, Háy escaped into Germany where he studied drama and worked in theaters in sundry capacities; thus his first exile trained him for dramatic writing. Fearing the Nazis on the rise in Germany, he fled to Austria; he fled Austria into the Soviet Union because of his participation in the 1934 labor revolt. In 1940, in the USSR, his first play was performed: *Isten, császár, paraszt* (God, Emperor, Peasant), an allegoric historical play set in the late fourteenth century and treating such issues as the conflict of state and religion, absolutism and the effect of power upon the poor. The play launched Háy's career in the theater.

His subsequent plays emulated the rational irony of G. B. Shaw and the theatrical techniques of German expressionists, particularly those of Gerhart Hauptmann. Among his noteworthy plays of this second period of exile are *Gát a Tiszán* (1933, Dam at the Tisza), *Tiszazúg* (1936), and *Az itélet éjszakája* (1943, The Night of the Verdict).

With the Communist party in power after World War II, Háy returned home in 1945 and plunged into the cultural programs of the new socialist country. His plays were widely performed; he became a full professor at the Budapest Drama School, and an important party functionary. By 1956 Háy had turned against the Communist regime; he joined the revolutionary youth during the Revolution on October 23. When Soviet tanks reestablished the status quo, Háy was sentenced to a six-year term of imprisonment. International pressure led to his pardon in 1960. In the ensuing five years Háy wrote several historical plays, among them *Mohács* (1960), *Attila éjszakái* (1963, Attila's Nights), and a complete volume of *Királyrámák* (1964, King Dramas), focusing on the conflicting historical forces in different centuries in his Central European nexus. Each of these plays carried a thinly disguised social message: protest against oppression, protest against the exploitation of the masses. In 1965 Háy entered his last exile: he settled in Switzerland's picturesque Ascona, where at last he felt free of political/ social pressures and obligations. Here he wrote his two-volume autobiography in German, *Geboren 1900* (1971, Born in 1900), and republished many of his plays in various languages. During the last ten years of his life he enjoyed a serenity and rest hitherto rare to him. All the major Hungarian periodicals in exile featured his work and promoted his lesser-known writings. Together with Tamas Aczel* and Tibor Méray, Háy belongs to that group of Hungarian writers who abandoned their earlier communist beliefs and continued to write. Háy's death was officially mourned in Hungary, a rare occurrence for a writer in exile.

Selected Titles: *Az élet hídja* (1951, The Bridge of Life), *Varró Gáspár igazsága* (1955, Justice for Gaspar Varro).

Individual plays and two major collections: *Öt szindarab* (1954, Five Plays); *Sorsok és harcok* (1955, Fates and Fights).

CLARA GYORGYEY

H.D. *See* DOOLITTLE, Hilda

HEAD, Bessie. Born 1937, in Pietermaritzburg, South Africa; died of hepatitis April 17, 1986, in Serowe, Botswana. As startling evidence of the inhumane apartheid system of South Africa, Head's birth occurred in the insane asylum where her white mother had been confined by her family because she was pregnant by a black man. Raised in foster homes, Head was orphaned at six by her mother's suicide. Her mother had provided for her education, however, and she was trained in missionary schools, eventually graduating from teachers college and pursuing a teaching career in Natal. She moved to Johannesburg, worked as a reporter for the black newspaper *Golden City Post*, then was transferred to the Cape Town office, where she married a fellow reporter, Harold Head. After unsuccessful attempts to obtain a passport, she was finally granted an exit permit from South Africa and left for Botswana in 1964, where she lived, except for brief visits abroad, until her death. There, she gave birth to a son, but divorced Head. Having applied unsuccessfully for Botswana citizenship in 1977, she finally had it granted in 1979. As might be expected from a writer with such a background of alienation and uprootedness, the topic of exile is central to her work.

Head's treatment of exile may be viewed from four related perspectives through which she examines the corollary issues of tribalism, individualism versus communalism, Pan-Africanism, Christianity, witchcraft, rural development and, most particularly, male-female relationships. These four foci are national, racial, sexual, and artistic isolation and powerlessness. In addition to brief pieces, Head published three novels, *When Rain Clouds Gather* (1968), *Maru* (1971), and *A Question of Power* (1974); a series of short stories, *The Collector of Treasures* (1977); and *Serowe, Village of the Rain Wind* (1981), a compilation of historical sketches and oral narratives documenting the past and present history of her adopted Botswana village.

When Rain Clouds Gather recounts the psychological and geographic journey of Makhaya, a former journalist, imprisoned for terrorism in South Africa, who escapes to Botswana after his release. In Golema Mmidi, he links forces with Gilbert, the visionary but practical Britisher, who successfully introduces methods of cooperative farming to villagers impoverished by the ancient heritage of subsistence farming and the exploitation of chiefs. Through his work and his love for Pauline, Makhaya is led to a sense of personal and social wholeness.

Revealing the Botswana prejudice against the traditionally enslaved Masarwa, *Maru* focuses upon an outsider, Margaret Cadmore, who, despite her sense of self-worth, is subjected to cruel isolation and humiliation. Her marriage in the end to Maru, the village chief, signals not only Margaret's personal transcendence over alienation but also Head's optimistic prediction of the eventual rejection of prejudice in African society.

A Question of Power, described by the author as "my only truly autobiographical work," traces the mental breakdown and recovery of Elizabeth, a colored refugee to Botswana from South Africa, whose background replicates Head's own. Elizabeth's tortured struggle to ensure her sanity is expressed through grotesque, hallucinatory sexual and religious conflicts that reflect not only her personal quest for peace but the political power struggles of contemporary African society. Elizabeth's racial and gender powerlessness is overcome by her ultimate realization that "there is only one God and his name is Man." Her deep awareness of fraternity, brought about by genuine friendships and successful work on a collective farm, effects a psychological healing. As she falls asleep at the book's end, it is not to cringe before nightmares; instead, "she placed one soft hand over her land. It was a gesture of belonging."

The Collector of Treasures opens with a legend of exile and wandering. It goes on to present portraits of African women in conflict with men and with tribal and colonial laws dispossessing them of power, but developing life-sustaining friendships with other women and with "another kind of man in the society," like Makhaya, "with the power to create himself anew."

In a 1964 sketch, Head writes of "the green tree," a hedge cultivated by the villagers that "came here as a stranger and quickly adapted itself to the hardness of our life. It needs no water in the earth but draws into itself the moisture of the air for its life." The symbol of this plant, dedicated to its own survival, is so potent that she returns to it, in greater detail, in 1981 in her last book, *Serowe, Village of the Rain Wind*, a paean to the village that provided her with meaningful work and the accompanying air of peace that allowed her to develop as an artist. Before moving there, she lived her life in "scattered little bits"; in the village she experienced a "sense of wovenness, a wholeness in life." This sense of place and acceptance grew from her participation in the educational, social, and agricultural reform taking place in Serowe and, especially, from her opportunity to carry on the African tradition of storyteller, poet, and historian. At the end of her life, Head, like the green tree, though transplanted into semi-arid soil, put down her roots as a productive member of her adopted land.

Consult: Susan Gardner and Patricia E. Scott, comps., *Bessie Head: A Bibliography*. National English Literary Museum Bibliographic Series, no. 1 (Grahamstown, South Africa: National English Literary Museum, 1986); Craig MacKenzie, *Bessie Head: An Introduction*. National English Literary Museum Series, no. 1 (Grahamstown, South Africa, National English Literary Museum, 1989); *The Tragic Life*, ed. Cecil Abrahams (1990).

ARLENE A. ELDER

HEDAYAT, Sadeyh. *See* Iranian Writers in Exile

HEIFETZ, Michael Ruvimovitch. Born January 18, 1934, in Leningrad, USSR; he lives in Israel. Heifetz graduated from the Faculty of Russian Languages and Literatures of the Herzen Pedagogic Institute in Leningrad in 1955. He was a teacher at village schools in the Altai area for two years and later taught in the Leningrad area. His attempts to attain a scientific degree were foiled when he was excluded from postgraduate enrollment at the Pedagogic Institute because of political statements he had made during a literary symposium. Professionally, he became a journalist in 1966, when the magazine *Knowledge-Power* (translation of Russian title) printed his documentary-historical novella, *The Shot of Hell*, an account of the revolutionary People's Freedom Movement of the nineteenth century.

The historical-documentary essay became for Heifetz the form in which he found his greatest creativity. In this genre he wrote his only book to be published in his homeland—*The Secretary of the Secret Police* (Moscow, 1968), a study of the nineteenth-century revolutionary hero, Kletochnikov. Heifetz also published in the USSR a long essay, *The President of the Far East*, and a biocritical sketch of the nineteenth-century writer-social democrat, V. Bervi-Flerowski, "Greetings and Brothers" (this essay is included in Heifetz's collection, *Roads into the Unknown*, 1970). In 1972 and 1973 Heifetz wrote several film and television scenarios based on historical themes and figures. In 1970 he was admitted into the Leningrad Union of USSR writers.

Heifetz was arrested by the KGB on April 22, 1974, in Leningrad, and the following September was sentenced to four years in a labor camp to be followed by two years of internal exile. The charge presented against him was that he had engaged in anti-Soviet propaganda by writing the foreword to a five-volume collection of poetry by the banned-poet Joseph Brodsky. Brodsky's friends wished to distribute the work in samizdat form (underground circulation of the typescript). Heifetz was accused of writing in his foreword (he was taken prisoner while the essay was still in "rough" form) that Brodsky's "Roman" poems might be compared to the feelings Czech citizens experienced about occupation of their country in 1968. Heifetz's arrest was viewed by many observers as a scare tactic against dissident opinion.

While imprisoned in the political Mordavski camps, Heifetz wrote, and smuggled out, the manuscript of *Place and Time*, in which he described his camp experiences. Published in Paris in 1978 (in Russian), the book received wide attention in the exile community. In a preface to the book, V. Marazin wrote:

Let the reader imagine what it is like to write a book in a labor camp: Always hungry, worn out by senseless physical labor, one has to write with a small hand on little sheets of paper, hiding the manuscript and then hiding it again, not having the possibility of re-reading it, risking every moment that someone, on discovering it, will inform about it, or that it will be destroyed out of hatred for revealed truths.

Heifetz subtitled his work, "Jewish Notes," out of his conviction that he was being punished both as a Jew and as a dissident. Critics have noted that Heifetz writes with attention and understanding to the plight of Russian, Armenian, and other ethnic groups undergoing punishment for their convictions, but that he identifies himself primarily as a Jewish writer and with the problems of Jewish culturalism in the USSR. The reviewer of *Place and Time* in *Kontinent* magazine, N. Yuzheva, wrote in the November 18, 1978, issue: "From the first pages one is penetrated by a feeling of trust in the author because this author—resembling no one, becoming like no one—is yet friendly. . . . In him and in his book, one feels the purity of thought, an inborn worth of a real intellectual."

Upon release from confinement in 1980, Heifetz left with his family for Israel. He worked for the Center for the Study of Eastern Judaism in 1982, and since 1983 has been a member of the editorial board of the magazine *22* based in Tel Aviv. In 1985 he was appointed literary editor of the magazine *The People and the Land*, based in Jerusalem. Heifetz also completed several book-length manuscripts, among them *Ukrainian Silhouettes* (1983) and *The Prisoner of War Secretary* (London, 1985), and edited *The Image of a Fortunate Man, or Letters from the Camp of a Special Regime* (London, 1985), the work of the imprisoned

Soviet writer A. Murzhenko. Heifetz's commitment to advancing the publication of politically confined fellow-Soviet writers, among them the Ukrainian poet Vasili Stus (recently deceased in a labor camp) and those whom Heifetz calls "Russian freedom fighters," has been praised by several publications (see *World Literature Today*, no. 2, 1985). Heifetz's book *The Russian Field*, published serially in *Kontinent* (nos. 27–28) and other journals, describes his continuing activities in this role. Heifetz has also published widely on social and national issues in Israeli magazines, among them *22*, *Aleph*, *The Circled*, and *The Jerusalem Courier*, and in European periodicals.

The first part of Heifetz's novella *Travel from Dubrovlag to Ermak* was published in 1987 in the Russian literary magazine *Grani* no. 141. A reviewer in the Paris-based Russian newspaper *Russian Thought* wrote of it:

Michael Heifetz does not stop at describing his hardships in prisons and camps, but shares with the reader his thoughts about a whole range of subjects. These thoughts merge with factual information and are striking in their clarity, consistency, balanced judgment and combination of humanism with inevitable ruthlessness. It would seem that the literature about the camps has been exhausted and that there is nothing to add to the thousands of pages written by victims, historians, and novelists. Yet Heifetz has managed to add a great deal of new and invaluable substance to the theme.

Aleksandr Solzhenitsyn* responded to Heifetz's text with a personal letter to Heifetz, in which he said, "I am glad you continue to describe the Gulag so vividly in modern times (including the current publication in *Grani*). Let this memory remain with us." In 1989 Heifetz published, in Russian, a book about his impressions of Israel, *Looking at Israel* (Jerusalem, 1989). He continues to write in Russian.

                                        MARK A. POPOVSKY, translated by Zoric Ward

HEMINGWAY, Ernest Miller. Born July 21, 1899, in Oak Park, Illinois; died July 2, 1961, in Ketchum, Idaho. Hemingway ran away from home twice before he became a reporter for *The Kansas City Star* in 1917. He volunteered the following year for ambulance duty in the Red Cross on the Italian front; he was badly wounded in the knee at Fassalta di Piave. After the war he found living in Europe both cheaper and more liberating than in the United States. He became friends with Ezra Pound,* Gertrude Stein,* F. Scott Fitzgerald,* Sylvia Beach, and James Joyce,* among other notable figures in the expatriate group in Paris in the 1920s. Although he often satirized them, his writing immortalizes those individuals he characterized as the "lost generation." Many critics believe he could not have achieved his success as a writer if he had not been an expatriate, free from the constraints that would have enervated him in his homeland.

Hemingway grew rich and famous in the 1930s and lived abroad much of the time, though he also established a home base in Key West, Florida. During World War II he served as a war correspondent with the U.S. Third Army. After the war he and his fourth wife Mary purchased a home near Havana, Cuba, a residence he left reluctantly in the face of Cuban political instability. Hemingway was awarded the Pulitzer Prize in 1953 for *The Old Man and the Sea* and the Nobel Prize for Literature in 1954. He committed suicide by shooting himself in the mouth on a cold morning in his home in Idaho; he had been suffering from depression for a long time and had stopped writing altogether.

Hemingway's biography is a record of flight outward. He left the United States for work on a Canadian newspaper. He became the most celebrated American literary expatriate of the 1920s. He covered the Spanish Civil War in the late 1930s. During both world wars he fought heroically. In the early 1950s he spent long periods at his hacienda in Cuba; only in the late 1950s did he spend any significant time in the United States, and these residences were necessitated in the main by conditions of illness, either at the Mayo Clinic in Minneapolis, Minnesota, or recuperation at his home in Idaho. His love of foreign soil has many roots, but his need for freedom from his childhood origins—the confining grounds of Oak Park, Illinois, and the bourgeois stratifications of his mother's dominating personality—is certainly one of them. Expatriatism became for Hemingway a way of life, and quite possibly a rejection of national and personal responsibilities unless he was able to shoulder such burdens in a public display of personal heroism. War and battle thus served not only as a matter of survival for him but as a field on which his code of honor and courage could flower.

Selected Titles: *The Sun Also Rises*; *A Farewell to Arms* (1929); *For Whom the Bell Tolls*.

Consult: Carlos Baker, *Ernest Hemingway: A Life Story* (1969); Kenneth Lynn, *Hemingway* (1987); Jeffrey Meyers, ed., *Hemingway: The Critical Heritage* (London, 1982); Gerald B. Nelson, *Hemingway: Life and Works* (1984); Michael Reynolds, *Hemingway: The Paris Years* (1989).

HERBERT, Zbigniew. Born October 29, 1924, Lvov, Poland [now USSR]; he lives in Paris, France. Herbert moved to Paris in the 1970s. His work was highly regarded in his country, but his association with liberal reform and Polish dissident writing and writers, among them Czeslaw Miłosz,* put him in difficulty with Poland's bureaucracy, particularly during the martial law period. Herbert has visited the United States on occasion for readings and has visited other European countries as well as his homeland. With Miłosz (the two of them read for the first time in the United States together on the same evening at the Y.M.H.A. in New York in the 1960s), he is considered one of Poland's major contemporary poetic voices.

Selected Title: *Selected Poems*, ed. Bogdana Carpenter and John Carpenter (1977).

Consult: Stanislaw Baranczak, *A Fugitive from Utopia: The Poetry of Zbigniew Herbert* (1988).

HERMLIN, Stephan (pseudonym of Rudolf Leder). Born April 13, 1915, in Chemnitz, Germany; he lives in East Berlin. Educated in Berlin, he has traveled widely in Europe and North Africa. He fought on the Loyalist side in the Spanish

Civil War. During World War II he was in exile in France and Switzerland. He returned to Germany in 1947, where he lived for two years in the Western sector. Hermlin's socialist ideals led him to defect to East Germany, where he joined the Socialist Unity Party. He has been a prominent literary figure in East Germany—vice-president of the Writers Union, president of the East German PEN Center, and vice-president of International PEN.

Hermlin is a courageous writer willing to take a humanistic stand in literary/ political matters even at the cost of offending ideological bureaucrats. His poems and novels bear this impress of profound humanism that knows no affiliation other than the common grounds of the search for meaning in life.

Hermlin may be considered an exile in that any postwar German writer felt himself in exile from the other half of his expropriated land. Hermlin's case is particularly apt in touching on the essential issue of the two Germanies: born in the East, he came to the West to return again to the East. Today he travels round the world on literary missions and has achieved the continuity of a resident world traveler, but the simple fact of the division of his native land adds continuing depth to his vision.

Selected Titles: *Zwölf Balladen von den grossen Stadten* (1944, Twelve Ballads of the Great Cities); *Zweiundzwanzig Balladen* (1947, Twenty-two Ballads); *Der Leutnant Yorck von Wartenburg* (1946, Lieutenant Yorck of Wartenburg); *Mansfelder Oratorium* (1950, Mansfield Oratorio).

Consult: W. Ertl, *Stephan Hermlin, und die Tradition* (Germany, 1977); J. Flores, "Stephan Hermlin: 'Volkstumlichkeit' and the Banality of Language," *Poetry in East Germany* (1971); T. Huebener, *The Literature of East Germany* (1970); Silvia Schlenstedt, *Stephan Hermlin* (West Berlin, 1985).

HERSHAN, Stella K. Born in Vienna, Austria; she lives in New York City. Hershan fled her native country in January 1939 after its annexation by Nazi Germany (Anschluss) in March 1938. Nearly twenty years later she enrolled in creative writing programs at New York University and the New School for Social Research; she received a certificate in general education from New York University in 1962 for an original novel. She published her first work, *Eleanor Roosevelt—A Woman of Quality*, in 1970. In 1972 her first novel, a historical fiction, *The Naked Angel*, was published. This work, translated into eight languages, uses the Congress of Vienna during Metternich's sway of influence as a backdrop for the love story of an innocent girl who grows into maturity through her various love affairs. Hershan's latest manuscript, a novel, "Daughter of the Revolution," is being translated into German for publication by a Munich firm. Hershan was the editor for ten years of *Talent*, a newsletter published by the American Council for Émigrés in the Professions.

HESSE, Hermann. Born July 2, 1877, in Calw, Swabia, Germany; died August 9, 1962, in Montagnola, Switzerland. Hesse's father was a naturalized German citizen of Russian birth; his mother (Marie Gundert) was a German born in

Talatscheri, India. His paternal grandmother was Slavic; his maternal grand-mother came of Swiss-French stock. Hesse's international caste of character may thus be seen in these players of his origin. He spent much of his young adult life in Switzerland, near Lake Constance. His early journey to the Orient—to India and the Malay archipelago in 1911—had a profound effect upon his world-view and his writing, although the effect did not become fully apparent till a decade later when he was writing *Siddhartha* (1922; English, 1951) and other tales exploring the wisdom of the Orient as it related to Western history and Western historical potential. Hesse's commitment to the meditative spirit of the East is total, but he rejects the Buddhist denial of earthly pleasures. Instead Hesse called for an infusion of the spirituality of the East with the sensualism and pleasure-pain principles of the West. In all of Hesse's work may be seen this exploration of the conflict between spirituality and sensualism, between physicality and the ineffable. Young readers have taken to Hesse's tales of temptation and redemption with a swelling and a passion that have made his work among the most discussed in modern literature, particularly his novels *Demian* (1919; English, 1923) and *Steppenwolf* (1927; English, 1929).

When Hesse's unhappy marriage ended in 1919, he moved to Montagnola, Switzerland, and became a Swiss citizen six years later. Though Hesse was not an exile and possibly not even an expatriate, his books explore the necessity for the wandering spirit to complete a journey through far distant lands of mystery in order to arrive at self-knowledge. The journey to the wide-ranging area must at some point take a corresponding tollway into depth. Hesse, after his worldwide travels, stayed pretty much at home in the narrow confines of Switzerland—he was vilified by both the Nazis and the Jewish humanitarian groups for his retreat to an apolitical stance and for his refusal to involve himself in the temporal world situation of the 1930s to the 1950s. Hesse declared himself a poet whose task demanded aloofness from sociopolitical causes and extraliterary scenes.

Although Hesse received his greatest recognition in the late 1940s and 1950s (he was awarded the Nobel Prize in 1946), his popularity waned in Europe after the 1950s, possibly as a result of his refusal to commit himself on public issues. His popularity remains steadfast in the United States.

Consult: Joseph Mileck, *Hermann Hesse: Life and Art* (1978; full bibliographies).

HEYM, Stefan (pseudonym of Hellmuth Fliegel). Born April 10, 1913, in Chemnitz, Germany (now Karl-Marx-Stadt, German Democratic Republic). He lives in East Germany, though his writings were banned there until the collapse of the regime in 1989. Heym's defiance of society was noticed early: he was expelled from high school for writing a pacifist poem. Later he wrote for *Die Weltbühne* (The Worldstage), whose editor, Karl von Ossietzky, won the 1936 Nobel Prize for Peace while interned in a Nazi concentration camp. Heym, who had made public his opposition to Hitlerian policies, fled to Prague in 1933; he stayed there for two years, barely earning a living from his writing. He con-tributed poems to such exile publications as *International Literature, Neue*

Deutsche Blätter (New German Papers), *Die Sammlung* (The Collection), and *Das Wort*. Heym also wrote a play, *Die Hinrichtung: Sayers Grosses Abenteuer* (Tom Sawyer's Great Adventure), which was performed in Vienna in 1937. The University of Chicago offered Heym a scholarship intended for "brilliant students whose education had been interrupted by the coming of National Socialism to Germany." When he could not pay for the journey, Czech and exile writers collected the necessary funds for transportation. Heym completed his M.A. at Chicago in 1936, worked at various jobs, and served as editor of a small New York antifascist weekly, *Deutsches Volksecho* (Echo of the German People). During this time he wrote *Nazis in the U.S.A.: An Expose of Hitler's Aims and Agents in the U.S.A.* (1938).

Heym learned English in exile, and within seven years he had mastered the language so well that he wrote his first novel in English. *Hostages* (1942), which deals with the Nazi occupation of Prague, became an instant success both as book and film (1943). In 1943 Heym began serving in the psychological warfare division of the U.S. Army. As part of his task, he edited *Frontpost*, an American publication for German soldiers. Heym's second novel, *Of Smiling Peace* (1944), added to his growing reputation as a popular writer; it was written in English, as were most of his later novels. At the end of World War II, Heym was sent to Germany where, as a part of the reeducation program in the U.S. Occupied Zone, he cofounded the *Neue Zeitung* (New Newspaper) in Munich. He also became editor of the *Neue Ruhr-Zeitung* in Essen. During the postwar period Heym wrote a number of popular novels that reflected his assimilation to life in America, as well as his unbroken faith in socialism: *The Crusaders* (1948); *The Eyes of Reason* (1951); *Goldsborough* (Leipzig, East Germany, 1953; 1954).

In spite of his successful publications and his position as chief of the American delegation at the World Peace Conference in Warsaw (1950), Heym was transferred back to the United States in 1952 to face an investigation into his alleged procommunist leanings. Unwilling to expose himself to further accusations by Senator Joseph McCarthy and his committee, Heym moved to East Berlin. As a gesture of defiance, the former refugee returned to the American government his war decorations along with his American passport.

Although hailed in the German Democratic Republic for his stories and novels, which were seen as examples of "socialist literature," Heym stopped writing novels for ten years. Instead, he produced editorials, articles, and reports, mainly in praise of East Germany and the German-Soviet friendship. In one of his articles he defended Soviet experiments in atomic weaponry. Rewarded for his politically "correct" writing, Heym was allowed to publish children's fairy tales and short stories, like his English-language collection *The Cannibals and Other Stories* (Leipzig, 1953; 1957) and *Shadows and Lights* (Leipzig, 1960; London, 1963). Although never a member of the Communist party, Heym became one of the most important writers in emerging East German literature, together with Bertolt Brecht * and Anna Seghers.* He was awarded several prizes by East German authorities, among them the Heinrich Mann Prize (1953), the 1956

Literature Prize of the FDGB (Federation of Free German Unions), and the National Prize (1959).

In 1963 Heym wrote *The Lenz Papers* (Leipzig and London, 1964), his last novel to be published in East Germany. On February 5, 1965, West Germany's influential weekly *Die Zeit* (The Times) printed Heym's article on Stalin's declining importance and impact on communism. The piece signaled the beginning of another exile for Heym—the exile of his work. East German authorities, now outraged by Heym's stance, no longer supported his writings. Although he had used historical characters and settings for many of his works, Heym's dissenting voice could be clearly heard. No longer allowed to communicate publicly in his own country, he arranged for his stories, essays, and novels to be published in the Federal Republic of Germany, England, and the United States. Most of his writing became illegal in East Germany until the end of 1989.

Heym's list of best-selling novels, all printed in Western Europe, England, and/or the United States, include *The King David Report* (Munich, 1972; 1973); *Uncertain Friend* (London, 1969; *Lassalle*, Munich, 1969), in which intellect and integrity confront power and the personality cult; and *Five Days in June* (London, 1977; Munich, 1979), which deals with the historic but futile uprisings of East Germans against the regime in 1953. In *Collin* (Munich, 1979; 1980), Heym presents his hero as an author who overcomes the past by writing about it, irrespective of the consequences. Collin can say that the world has changed for him as a result of his total honesty. Heym's latest novel, *The Wandering Jew* (1984; original German title: *Ahasver*, Munich, 1981), may be considered his most mature work, perhaps his testament. In it he presents not only a panorama of human fallibility and suffering, but also shows that individuals, despite the circumstances, are free to change, and, in the process, are capable of changing their society. This guiding attitude, especially with its unusual combination of brutal irony and farce, its implicit and explicit attacks on dogmatism, and its surreal mysticism, all controlled by powerful language, have helped to make Heym one of the most challenging figures among German exile writers of this century.

In June 1979 Heym was expelled from the German Democratic Republic Writers Guild. Once influential and respected, he was taken to court in 1979 and punished for a "breach of exchange control regulations." Those writers who subsequently came to his defense were also ousted from the Writers Guild and deprived of professional privileges.

The defiant "work in exile" situation for writers like Heym is awkward and dangerous, yet he has endured. This German exile who still writes most of his novels in English before he translates them into German once wrote: "There is no reason to write German." (Heym: "*Es hatte keinen zweck Deutsch zu schreiben*," *Wie Ich Anfing*, ed. Hans Daiber [Düsseldorf, West Germany, 1979], pp. 145–54, originally published with a different title in *Eröffnungen*, ed. Gerhard Schneider [East Berlin, 1974], pp. 81–90).

In 1988 Heym published in the Federal Republic of Germany his autobiography of nearly 850 pages, *Nachruf* (Obituary); it has not yet appeared in English. The volume reveals again a man intensely committed from an early age to the power of reason and the ideal of synthesis of varying ideologies into a liberating compromise.

HENRIK EGER

On October 7, 1989, the fortieth anniversary of the creation of the German Democratic Republic, Heym reflected on the growing crisis in the political division of the two Germanies. In an interview printed in *The Globe and Mail* (a national Canadian newspaper based in Toronto), he said that the government of East Germany had still not created the state that its peoples wanted, although the uprising in 1953, the exodus in 1961 that resulted in the construction of the Berlin Wall as an attempt to stem the tide, and the current exodus through travel to other Communist countries in Eastern Europe and then flight to West Germany, provided continued evidence of pleas for an altered state. Heym has indicated no desire to move from his chosen habitat, but has admitted his sorrow at the failure of the East German socialist dream to inspire its young people and to provide a moral spirit with which they can engage.

Selected Title: *Einmischung*: Gespräche, Reden, Essays, ed. Inge Heym and Heinfried Henniger (Munich, 1990).

HIKMET, Nazim. Born 1902, in Selanik (then an Ottoman city, now Thessaloniki, Greece); died June 3, 1963, in Moscow, after a massive heart attack. Turkey's greatest modern poet became, after the early 1950s, synonymous with "exile unto death" and "death in exile." In the 1920s his name was associated with radical revolutionary Marxism-Leninism. In the late 1930s and throughout the 1940s, his work epitomized the best of *de profundis* literature. He was released from prison after having served thirteen years of a twenty-five-year sentence, and fled Turkey in 1951 to avoid being drafted into the armed forces at age forty-nine with a severe heart condition. He was in exile in the USSR, Poland, Bulgaria, and other socialist countries for twelve years until his death. Having been stripped of his Turkish citizenship, he took up Polish citizenship. His poetry and plays were extensively translated into all major languages and dozens of minor languages. There have been protracted periods when his work was totally banned in Turkey. Since the 1960s his complete works have been appearing in Bulgaria (in the Turkish originals) in a multivolume series, but the project remains to be completed. Since 1954, ten volumes of Hikmet's selected poems have been published in English translation.

Hikmet is known internationally more than any other contemporary Turkish writer, and possibly is the single most known Turkish poet outside his country from the past ten centuries. Among world figures who have paid homage to his work and spirit are Jean-Paul Sartre, Miguel Asturias, * Ilya Ehrenburg,* Louis Aragon, Tristan Tzara* (who has also translated him into French), Hans Magnus Enzenberger,* Philippe Soupault, and Pablo Neruda* (with whom he shared the Soviet Union's International Peace Prize in 1950). Hikmet remains, in addition to his poetic stature, his country's most famous Communist. His plays, many of which introduced avant-garde and experimental theater to Turkey in the 1930s, have been popular as well in the Soviet Union and in France. Hikmet's newspaper articles and brief essays are notable only for their rhetorical flourish, and his few novels, hastily written for newspaper serialization, are singularly inept.

From age twenty to twenty-four, Hikmet studied sociology and economics at the University of the Workers of the East in Moscow. While there he developed an abiding interest in Soviet communism and came under the literary influence of Sergey Yesenin, Vladimir Mayakovsky, and the constructivists. This orientation inspired him to compose revolutionary poems in free verse. No other figure has exerted a greater influence on Turkey's poetic modernization since Hikmet's emergence in the 1920s.

Hikmet's best work appeared before 1951 when he went into exile. This corpus includes a very large number of short poems and several verse epics. Many of the poems in the collections he published during a fecund period from 1929 to 1936, and those he wrote in prison until 1950 (some were published after his death), are among his best achievements. *The Epic of Sheik Bedreddin*, about an early fifteenth-century Anatolian Islamic sect and its revolutionary goal to establish a quasi-communistic state, is considered by many as the apogee of Hikmet's success and the most important long Turkish poem of the twentieth century. *Human Landscapes*, an epic consisting of more than 17,000 lines, is a "poem-novel" which Denise Levertov has likened, in some respects, to Homer.

The campaign to free Hikmet from prison in 1950 was supported by such world figures as Bertolt Brecht, *Pablo Picasso, Paul Éluard, Sartre, Halldor Laxness, Neruda, and Jorge Amado.* Hikmet's escape to the Soviet Union a year later marked the beginning of the dissipation of his creative powers. There is very little documentary evidence to show whether he was favorably impressed by or disillusioned with Soviet communism and East European socialism in action. He produced a considerable number of propaganda poems that lack not only literary value but also ideological conviction. Most of his effective poems written outside Turkey are testaments of exile and longing. They tend to lend credence to the assumption that his nationalist sentiments outweighed his vision of world communism.

Hikmet studied French at Istanbul's French-language lycée and presumably knew Russian, but he never wrote in these two languages nor adapted any of his poems into them. He was totally committed to the Turkish language as his personal vehicle and his creative tool. Unlike some other writers who are able to employ two or more languages and even flourish in exile, Hikmet suffered in his separation from his national milieu and language. Except for a number of poignant poems of nostalgia and depictions of his private life, his twelve years in exile yielded very little that possesses the impressive merit of his earlier career.

Selected Title: *Selected Poetry, 1902–1963* (1988).

Consult: Terence Des Pres, "Poetry and Politics: The Example of Nazim Hikmet," *Parnassus* 6, no. 2 (1978); Talat Sait Halman, "Nazim Hikmet: Lyricist as Iconoclast," *Books Abroad* [now *World Literature Today*] 43 (1969). See also special issue of *Europe*, nos. 547–48 (1974) devoted to Hikmet.

TALAT SAIT HALMAN

HIMES, Chester. Born July 29, 1909, in Jefferson City, Missouri; died November 12, 1984, in Benissa, Spain. Himes studied at Ohio State University in 1926. In 1928, at the age of nineteen, he was arrested, found guilty of armed robbery, and sent to federal prison. Released in 1936, he wrote for the Federal Writers Project and sold stories to *Esquire* and *Coronet* magazines. In 1953 he moved to Paris, and later to the south of Spain. In France Himes had a reputation as a serious writer; in addition, he was considered a popular writer there, particularly with his series of detective novels, which the French public and literary critics consider an American art form. Himes published his two-volume autobiography, *The Quality of Hurt* (1973) and *My Life of Absurdity* (1976), and received serious attention for the first time in the United States. He chose to continue to live abroad, but his status was more an exilic one than a version of expatriatism, since, as a convicted felon and a black man, he was rejected by the society in whose mainstream he at least wished to sail, if not to find harbor.

Consult: Wilfried Feuser, "Prophet of Violence," *African Literature Today* 13; James Lundquist, *Chester Himes* (1976); Stephen F. Milliken, *Chester Himes: A Critical Appraisal* (1976).

HIPPIUS, Zinaida (also spelled Gippius). Born November 20, 1869, in Belev, Russia; died September 9, 1945, in Paris, France. Hippius was the wife of Dmitry Merezhkovsky,* prominent Russian novelist, poet, and theorist of symbolism. They emigrated from Russia to Poland in 1919, and later settled in Paris, where they were leaders in Russian émigré circles.

Hippius wrote literary criticism in French, but continued to write in her first language when creating novels, stories, and plays.

Selected Titles: *Collected Poetical Works*, vol. 1, *1899–1918*, vol. 2, *1918–1945*, ed. Temura Pachmuss (Munich, 1972); *Collected Dramatic Works*, ed. Temura Pachmuss (Munich, 1976).

Translation: *Selected Work of Zinaida Hippius*, ed. Temura Pachmuss (1972).

Consult: Temura Pachmuss, *Zinaida Hippius: An Intellectual Prophet* (1971); Renato Poggioli, *The Poets of Russia: 1890–1930* (1960). For bibliography, see *Bibliographie des oeuvres de Zenaide Hippius*, compiled by A. Banda (Paris, 1975).

HIRSON, Denis. Born August 25, 1951, Cambridge, England; he lives in Paris, France. Hirson was born in Cambridge, England, where his father was a student of physics. The family returned to South Africa in 1953. Hirson, who read anthropology at the University of the Witwatersrand, holds an Honours degree in this discipline. He left South Africa in 1973 with his family after his father's release from prison for political crimes against the state. Since 1975, he has lived in Paris (he teaches English there); he has had a long association with the Chaudron Theatre, an activity he recently relinquished in order to devote more time to his writing. His poetry has been published in many journals, and his translation of the Afrikaans poetry of Breyten Breytenbach* was issued in London in 1978 as *Even the Flies Are Happy*. His first novel, *The House Next Door to Africa* (Manchester, England, 1986; also published in South Africa), draws on his family's experience in South Africa. An evocation of the growing up of a South African consciousness, one which will issue into a voice of exile, the novel reads like a prose poem in which intensity of image plays a stronger role than narrative or realistic portraiture. Hirson paints the memory of a family, exotic in its designations—Russian Jewish immigrants washed ashore on the wilds of South Africa and making their way to middle-classdom in the Afrikaner world. The narrator is a young man awakening to the prejudices round him and to the awareness of his limitations; his world is not at the center of South Africa, and yet by location of its periphery, the moral and psychological consequences of racial exclusion become painfully sketched.

HLASKO, Marek. Born January 4, 1934, in Warsaw, Poland; died June 14, 1969, in Wiesbaden, West Germany. Hlasko's work chronicles the lives of disillusioned, rootless young men who refuse to give up their emotional pain or surrender their sense of loss by forging a new future. Instead, his heroes engage in forgeries of various kinds in a present tense that becomes an eternity of human hell for the rest of their lives. Some critics have called Hlasko's protagonists "losers": young men who are lonely, painful, self-defeating, but stoic in their self-defense. Other critics have noticed Hlasko's love of Ernest Hemingway and of the world of celluloid illusion, with its spare dialogue, that was presented in film noir, grade B American movies of the 1940s.

Whether it be called film noir, black comedy, or pale tragedy, Hlasko's world is a dark one reflecting the enclosure in which the young male victim turns corrupt and deceitful in his apathy of survival and moves into a world of habit, of evasion and running. Hlasko's heroes cannot be said to struggle for a better world, since they have no belief that such a world is open to them, given their circumstances of history; they retain, however, their dreams of a garden of meaning, a vision that comes upon them fitfully even as they are invoking the schemes and routines by which they extend the days of their lives. This pathetic vision of a world beyond their will to grasp at it is encapsulated in Hlasko's constant references to love as the saving force of life—love as a form of belief that has no institutional body but whose power is spread through an all-pervading spirit. Unfortunately, in Hlasko's life and in his work, the force of love was defeated by the deadly quiet blows of a loveless, careless universe. In all his work, from his first story published when he was only twenty, to his last novel, published posthumously after he committed suicide at the age of thirty-five, Hlasko's sad heroes engage in a vain search for capture of a sustaining love force; their failure results in suicide or in a living death, a continuance of rootless behavior without hope of future bloom. A maddening, courageous blend of self-pity, vanity, suffering nobility, stoic passivity, and the routine of the damned and godless exile from the joys of ordinary comfort shape the trademark of the Hlasko protagonist. As he wrote in his most recent book translated into English, *Killing the Second Dog* (New York, Cane Hill Press, 1965), "Why haven't I ever said or written that there is no greater misery than living without awareness of God, contrary to His commandments? I don't know. And why haven't I ever said that the worst sin is to betray the love of another human being? I don't know" (pp. 116–17).

Hlasko's life parallels his fiction but suggests that the narratives of his art may have preceded the story of his life. What comes first, however, is indisputable: that is, the cruel sadism of circumstances that presented Hlasko with national acclaim before he was twenty-one but stripped him of those Polish honors in which he deeply believed despite his show of casual indifference to praise. As a child Hlasko witnessed the coming of the Nazis into power over Poland (he was seven years old at the time of the German invasion); as a young teenager he witnessed the Communist sweep of his country. He worked at various jobs in his later teens—as a bellboy in a Warsaw hotel, as a lumberjack, bargeman, truck driver, and taxicab driver for six years. He became editor of the student newspaper *Po Prostu*, which he turned into a national organ of student criticism, before it was silenced by government decree. Before he turned twenty, he published his first major story (in 1954) and became the writer of and for young Poles, someone who understood their frustrations and sense of separation from an uncaring system. In the two years that followed, he published his first novel, *The Eighth Day of the Week* (1956) and a collection of stories, *A First Step in the Clouds* (1956). Both volumes, which treat the world of the young and their struggles of closet rebellion and open survival, were greeted with wild enthusiasm, and Hlasko became a national celebrity. The State Publishers Literary Prize was awarded to *A First Step in the Clouds*, and *The Eighth Day of the Week* was translated into fifteen languages and made into a prize-winning (Cannes Festival, 1958) film. In a survey taken in Poland at the time, Hlasko was voted the most important writer of his generation and second only to the premier, Wladyslaw Gomulka, in popularity. A tall, handsome blond man, dressed in jeans and continually smoking, he looked like, and became for his young Polish fans, the James Dean of their group portrait.

Hlasko was given a two-month visa to the West in 1958, where he attended the Cannes film festival (and reportedly went on a wild spending spree). Yet, in spite of his acclaim, Polish censors refused permission for publication of Hlasko's two short novels, *The Graveyard* and *Next Stop—Paradise*, even though *Next Stop—Paradise* had already been made into a movie in Poland. Hlasko published the two novellas in the Polish émigré journal *Kultura*, based in Paris, and was attacked at home for this "crime," particularly in view of *The Graveyard's* direct criticism of Stalinism in Poland. When Hlasko asked for an extension of his visa and was refused one, he decided on self-exile. He traveled through France, Italy, Switzerland, and West Germany the following year, much like a Beat generation figure. He moved to Israel in 1959 in search of a new home, a new state in which he could find, again, a passion of commitment. In Israel, having spent all his publisher's advances and royalties, he worked illegally as a truck driver, a manual laborer, and possibly, if he is not exaggerating in his autobiography, *Piekni duridziestoletni*, as a pimp. He also met again the woman who had played the leading female role in the movie version of *The Eighth Day of the Week*; they married in 1962 and moved to West Germany. The years from 1962–66 proved productive ones for Hlasko: he wrote several stories, two short novels, an autobiography and a novel set in Poland during the hard-line Stalinist period of the 1950s. In 1966, Hlasko and his wife separated, and he moved to the United States, where he again worked illegally; his jobs were, necessarily, itinerant and manual. During this three-year period he wrote only one work, an autobiographical novel about life in the United States. In 1969 he seemed to have found a new resolve, a determination to revive his life; he made plans to return to Israel, but on June 14, 1969, in Wiesbaden, Germany, he killed himself with an overdose of sleeping pills.

Hlasko's death, like that of the mythic American screen rebel, James Dean, was romanticized into legend. The fire of the young star burned out at age thirty-five, the indifference of the bourgeois and/or Communist bureaucracy to an alien artistic spirit became a matter of reference to Hlasko, but in both the West and in Poland, attention soon stopped being paid to him. What little was given referred to Hlasko as a talented romantic unable to grow into maturity, as a sad case of a self-defeating, self-pitying macho sentimentalist. While there is substantiation of Hlasko's sentimentalism behind the clipped sentences of his spare Hemingway-like prose, there is also depth to his work, and the same courage that Hemingway showed in his relentless camera-eye style. Hlasko, like the early Hemingway, is a writer of a lost generation; in his case it is a lost generation under Stalinist Polish rule, a generation denied spiritual and emotional release by a rigidly programmed regime. Like Hemingway, Hlasko committed suicide when he could no longer believe in and propagate his visions. Unlike Hemingway, he could not long sustain his faith, or suspend it while waiting for belief, in a world of stoic nature. His self-exile, while it was one of surface choice, became the cause of his ruin because Hlasko knew he could never return to the country of his expansive youth. He faced imprisonment at the worst for his "crimes" of mis-representation; at the least, he would be forbidden publication as an unregener-ative deviationist or else have to become a docile convert to the socialist cause. Constitutionally, Hlasko was incapable of such a faithless commitment; he clung to the dream of the pervasion of love from some source on high or below that would reinvigorate him and re-focus his genius.

Killing the Second Dog, written during Hlasko's two-year inspired period in exile in West Germany, reflects clearly the author's views on love and on the pain of exile from the community of the common. The two protagonists are con-men exiles in Israel, playing out their swindles of American women looking for new husbands, a second chance at love and life. The narrator, Jakob, referred to by name only once in a reference by another character, bares Hlasko's tired, sad, pitying-romantic voice. He plays the swindle game out of the necessity of gaining some money for his living, but he has lost faith in living. Since the con-game consists of the deception of women victims that the man they are about to "rescue" has lost faith in himself, the irony of the narrator's view becomes resonant of Hlasko's romanticism of loss. The scene in which the narrator is reduced to killing the only creature he can any longer love—his dog—becomes Hlasko's final statement of the itinerant exile's non-passage to home; the swindle game the two con-men have mapped out mandates that one of them shoot a "beloved" dog to gain the sympathy of the conned onlooker as the climax of each affair. Each game thus becomes another death of love.

Consult: Thomas Bradley, Introduction in *Killing the Second Dog* by Hlasko (1990).

HOBAN, Russell. Born in 1925 in Lansdale, Pennsylvania; he lives in London with his family. Hoban was an illustrator before he turned to writing in 1958. He moved to London in 1969 for personal reasons. He is the author of two acclaimed novels, *Riddley Walker* (1980) and *Pilgermann* (1983). *Riddley Walker* is set in a future world that has parallels to the caveman beginnings of the universe and uses the narrative convention of a young boy growing up amid the rubble to find the meaning of his existence. *Pilgermann* is set in a "space called time" that is more medieval fantasy than Middle Ages reality and involves the mystery of illumination that accompanies one crusader's pilgrimage to Jerusalem in the eleventh century. Hoban deals with themes of alienation, loneliness, and physical exile in terms of man's willful destructiveness and his disregard of spiritual awe. One of his favorite ploys is his adaptation of the science fiction technique of a bomb, in whatever form of conflagration, that ends civilization as Western man has known it, and the posing of the question: Where does man go from this end to what new beginning? Hoban also employs "time" as a warp or hurtling passage that can manifest itself at will or happenstance in one's journey through life. His work may then be said to utilize the trappings of science fiction while exploring wider confines of religious questioning.

Hoban's recent novel, *The Medusa Frequency* (1987), is a satiric takeoff on writers and publishers in present-day London. Hoban is also a children's story writer (with more than forty titles to his credit). In this genre he employs a lighter tone and forgoes the invention of a mock-language of barbarities symbolizing man's fallen grace. His best-known children's book is probably *The Mouse and His Child*.

Selected Title: *The Lion of Boaz-Jachin and Jachin-Boaz* (London, 1973).

Consult: Christine Wilkie, *Through the Narrow Gate: The Mythological Consciousness of Russell Hoban* (1989).

HOCHWALDER, Fritz. Born May 28, 1911, in in Vienna, Austria. A "non-Aryan" dramatist, Hochwalder fled from Austria into exile when Hitler annexed his country. He succeeded in reaching Switzerland, where he settled in Zurich.

Consult: Martin Esslin, "Introduction: Hochwalder, Mastercraftsman of Ideas," in *The Public Prosecutor, and Other Plays* (1980), by Fritz Hochwalder.

HÖEL, Sigurd. Born December 14, 1890, in Odal, Norway; died October 14, 1960, in Oslo, Norway. Höel was forced to take refuge in Sweden during the Nazi occupation of Norway in the 1940s. After the war he returned to his country. He wrote novels, essays and criticism, and dramas.

Consult: H. Beyer, *History of Norwegian Literature* (1956); Amanda Langemo, *Encyclopedia of World Literature*, vol. 2 (1982).

HOFFMAN, Eva. Born July 1, 1945, in Cracow, Poland; she lives and works in New York City. Hoffman left her birthplace in April 1959 for Canada, when she was thirteen years old, with her parents and her nine-year-old sister. They arrived first in Halifax and disembarked in Montreal; after a stay there during which Hoffman began her English language study, they moved to Vancouver. Hoffman grew up in the British Columbia city, in her own words, first as "exile," then as "immigrant." Loss through the awareness of memory is a part of the first condition; consciousness of difference and holding onto memory is a part of the second. Thus, Hoffman felt, from age thirteen until her college education at Rice University in Houston, Texas, a Polish-Jewish stranger; she also knew she had been a Jewish "stranger" in Poland. She said of one encounter in her childhood in Cracow, "I gradually came to understand that it is a matter of honor to affirm my Jewishness and to do so with my head held high. That's what it means to be a Jew—a defiance of those dark and barbaric feelings. Through that defiance, one upholds human dignity" (p. 33).

Even after graduate school at Harvard University, where she received her doctorate in English literature, Hoffman has written that she felt "different" from her first lover, a blond, blue-eyed Texan. It was not until she came to New York City, where she wrote reviews and feature articles for magazines, that she began to think of English as her first language, though she has never written for publication in any other tongue. In her memoir of growing up Canadian and American—or rather, growing into the English language, since language for Hoffman is the profound text of identity—she has written that when English words began appearing in her dreams, she knew she was experiencing a transformation into a different consciousness/person.

Hoffman considers dislocation and spirit of place as essential constituents in consciousness of being. In reconciling her Polish heritage and her Canadian and American experiences, she became aware that all consciousness imposes loss; holding onto the memory of loss keeps one a stranger or "immigrant" in a new land. Transmuting memory into a nourishing undercurrent of the river of self while flowing ahead into a new language or way of being is what signals (or signifies) the arrival of citizenship in an assimilated culture. (Hoffman wrote, significantly, in her memoir, *Lost in Translation: A Life in a New Language* [1989], that the English word *river* first sounded cold and foreign to her, without resonance, not at all like the Polish word she had known and used as a child in Cracow. Today she can immerse herself in this English image in waves of associations.)

Hoffman's memoir thus becomes not only a narrative of one person growing into awareness, but a discursive journey into the meaning and complexity of the stages of exile, immigration, and arrival at a sense of belonging again. Hoffman ends her memoir with the cautionary advice: "All immigrants and exiles know the peculiar restlessness of an imagination that can never again have faith in its own absoluteness. 'Only exiles are truly irreligious,' a contemporary philosopher has said" (p. 275).

Today Hoffman works as an editor at the *New York Times Book Review*. She has published only one volume as yet, her widely praised memoir, but has appeared in a number of periodicals.

Consult: Peter Conrad, "Lost in Translation," *New York Times Book Review*, April 1, 1989; Carole Rumens, "Tongues of Men and Angels," *Times Literary Supplement* (London), November 17–23, 1989.

HONWANA, Luis Bernardo. Born 1942, in Mozambique; he lives in Malagasy Republic. Honwana was imprisoned from 1964–67 by the Portuguese government for his revolutionary/independence activities. He lived in Portugal, Switzerland, Algeria, and Tanzania before returning to his country after it achieved independence from Portugal.

Selected Title: *Nos Matamos o cao Tinhosa* (1969, We Killed Mangy-Dog, and Other Mozambique Stories).

Consult: Donald Burness, ed., *Fire: Six Writers from Angola, Mozambique, and Cape Verde* (1977).

HOPE, Christopher (Christopher David Tully Hope). Born 1944, Johannesburg, South Africa; he lives in England. Hope worked as a journalist in Durban after graduating from Witwatersrand University in 1963, where he studied genetics. In anguish at the racial policies of his country, he left South Africa in 1974, one year after winning his country's distinguished literary prize, the Thomas Pringle Award. In England he has worked as a teacher and free-lance reviewer. His novel, *A Separate Development* (London, 1980), was briefly banned by South African authorities. He has also written the novel *The Hottentot Room* (London, 1986), and several collections of short stories, essays and journalistic pieces, among them *Private Parts and Other Tales* (Johannesburg, 1981/ London, 1982) and *Kruger's Alp* (London, 1984). He is well known for his poetry, for which he received the Cholmondeley Prize in 1979; his volumes of verse include *Cape Drives* (London, 1974) and *In the Country of the Black Pig* (London, 1981). In his long satirical poem, *Englishmen* (London, 1985), he draws on his experience as an colonial "immigrant" who has to get used to English ways in a spoofing tradition exemplified in *In Pursuit of the English*, the recollections of another South African writer, Doris Lessing.* In his recent memoir, *White Boy Running: A Book About South Africa* (1988), Hope recounts his visit to South Africa in 1987 and raises the inevitable questions of whether it was a return home or a journey to a now-alien context. In essence, Hope is exploring the issue of his expatriatism (he is free to return to South Africa whenever he chooses) or self-exile (he knows he has broken with his roots, whatever new journeys he may take and thus is "banned" from what he once owned as his heritage). Hope's telling takes into account his minority English status in a Boer-dominated South Africa, making him neither a member of the white South African minority nor the black South African majority but a third-world citizen like the Cape Coloureds, Indians, and Hottentots/Bushmen. He writes in this context that he "went into exile long before we left home." His sense of dislocation not eased by his South African journey, Hope is continuing his pattern and his generation's pattern of "white boy running."

Consult: Stephen Watson, "The Great Bereavement," *Times Literary Supplement*, March 11–17, 1988, p. 270.

HORVATH, Odon von. Born 1901, in Fiume (now Rijeka), Yugoslavia; died June 1, 1938, in Paris, France. Horvath was the son of a Hungarian diplomat father and a Czech-German mother. He moved to Berlin in 1924 and became a highly successful and popular playwright and novelist: in his lifetime he wrote eighteen plays and four novels as well as filmscripts, poems, and essays. In 1933 the Nazis banned production of any of his theater works in Germany (his "last" play in Germany, *Volksstück, Glaube, Leibe, Hoffnung,* a portrait of a repressive bureaucracy, was halted as the play was being mounted in Berlin; the play was produced for the first time three years later in Vienna). He joined the Reichsverband Deutsche Schriftsteller (the writers union officially approved by the Nazis) in order to continue working in the German film industry, but he himself fled to Vienna in 1933 for his personal safety. He returned briefly to Berlin in 1934 in an attempt to comprehend the Nazi phenomenon and possibly make some accommodation to it.

In Vienna and Zurich Horvath's plays were performed in small theaters and cabarets. When the Germans annexed Austria in 1938, Horvath fled to Paris, where he died shortly after his arrival, the victim of a falling tree on the Champs Elysées.

Horvath's most serious work reveals a commitment to the theme of responsibility and guilt for things not done. His work was anathema to the Nazis because of its democratic-radical views. Horvath particularly despaired over what he called *Bildungsjargon*, the language of slogans, posters, and shibboleths that obscured, purposefully, or paid little meaning to truth. *Bildungsjargon* was used by the undereducated as an easy way of communicating prejudice and anger; it was exploited by the political arms of fascist bodies of government and political suasion to discredit unwanted ideas. As Horvath saw it, the perversion of such language was an act of irresponsibility, for which all intellectuals bore guilt unless they demonstrated against its infernal use. Because of his continuous attack on demagoguery in the form of *Bildungsjargon*, Horvath became a prime target of the Nazis, who scorned even the prestigious German literary award, the Kleistpreis, when it was awarded to Horvath in 1932.

In his self-exile in Austria, Horvath experienced a growing attack of guilt and self-accusation. He expressed this anguish for things not done, for struggles not fought against oppression, in a number of works in which his heroes bare their troubled conscience to the audience. In his play translated as *Judgment Day*, written in 1936–37 (and given a London production in 1988), he draws a scene in which the protagonist, a trainman, may be responsible for the death of eighteen people and injury to many others. The trainman has in the past always done his duty, but this time he may have been careless; his carelessness, in turn, may have been caused by the frustration of a repressed life in which he never yielded to passion. Before the tragedy, the protagonist, fourteen years younger than his wife and with whom he has led a chastened, if not chaste, life, meets up with a young seductress, determined to carry him off as her trophy. In the ensuing contest, the train tragedy occurs. Some critics have seen in this work, and in other of Horvath's plays, an apology for his willingness to accommodate himself to Nazi barbarism, an awareness of his failure to oppose the Nazi threat to civilization.

In the last two years of his life Horvath turned to novel writing, both as a personal release to express his concerns and as a means of earning a livelihood (the banning in Germany and the limited resources of theater production in Vienna and Switzerland had strained his resources). He wrote two short first-person narratives about the evils of Fascism, one of which, *Jugend ohne Gott* (1939, Youth Without God), achieved wide popularity and critical attention.

Horvath's work has recently received renewed attention in England, where several of his plays have been produced in London's off-West End theaters during the past few years. One of these productions was Christopher Hampton's translation, under the title *Faith, Hope, Charity,* of Horvath's 1933 play *Volkstück Glaube, Liebe, Hoffnung.* Based on a story told to Horvath by a court reporter, the play follows a young woman whose life has disintegrated into a series of petty crimes and betrayals, but the playwright's profound concern is with the world of ''*die kleinen Paragraphen*'' (the ''little laws''). This world is one of petty compromise and demeaning conformism, of people afraid to protest their little sentences or rationalized corruption and the perverse manipulations of laws handed down by higher authorities. In portraying this world, Horvath used his trademark language of evasive commentary and deceptive verbal ballistics, *bildungsjargon.* The rationalizations of the ordinary German willing to pervert his/her integrity out of a lack of moral courage becomes the familiar double-talk of contradiction and gibberish uttered with authority; the techniques of *bildungsjargon* thus prefigure the corruption of language George Orwell presented in his ''double-think'' and ''newspeak.'' Perhaps, because of Horvath's mastery of portraiture of corruption on a grand scale, his work continues to appeal to new generations of theater-goers.

Selected Titles: *Gesammelte Werke*, ed. Trangott Krischke, 4 vols. (vol. 1, *Plays 1920–30*; vol. 2, *Plays 1931–33*; vol. 3, *Plays 1934–37*; vol. 4, *Prose and Verse, 1918–1938*) (Frankfurt, F.R.G., 1988).

Translation: *Four Plays*, ed. Martin Esslin (1989).

Consult: Ian Huish, *Horvath: A Study* (1980); Joseph Strelka, *Brecht—Horvath—Durrenmatt: Wege und Abwege des modernen Drames* (1962); K. Winston, *Horvath Studies: Close Readings of Six Plays* (1977).

HUCHEL, Peter. Born April 3, 1903, in Berlin, Germany; died April 30, 1981, in Staufen/Baden, West Germany. Huchel grew up in rural Mark Brandenburg. He studied literature and philosophy in Berlin, Freiburg, and Vienna, then worked as a translator and farmhand in France, the Balkans, and Turkey. After service in the army during World War II, he became artistic director of East Berlin Radio. Between 1949 and 1962 he was editor-in-chief of the influential East German literary journal *Sinn und Form*. His refusal to conform editorial policies to Communist party policies led to his dismissal and to eight years of imposed isolation in Wilhelmshorst near Potsdam. He was allowed to emigrate to West Germany in 1971, where he settled in Staufen near Freiburg.

As editor of the leading East German organ of literary and cultural opinion, Huchel was in charge of its three most significant issues—the opening 1949 number, which was devoted to Bertolt Brecht* and contained the first publication of Brecht's *The Caucasian Chalk Circle*; the 1951 issue devoted to Johannes R. Becher,* who had suggested the title of the journal; and the 1952 issue devoted to Arnold Zweig,* who had returned from Israel to East Germany. All three issues were thus devoted to exile writers who, in returning to East Germany, were reconfirming their allegiance to a national spirit and to the spirit of Marxist socialism. Huchel's policy was never one of communist evangelism, but his journal served as a vehicle for "reconnecting" German literature and culture with its past and as a forum for moving forward from its most recent history.

Selected Titles: *Gedichte* (1948, Poems); *Gezahlte Tage* (1972, Numbered Days); *The Garden of Theophrastus and Other Poems* (1983); *Sinn und Form: Beitrage Zur Literatur* (West Berlin, 1989).

HUGHES, Langston. Born February 1, 1902, in Joplin, Missouri; died May 22, 1967, in New York City of a stomach ailment. Hughes's father left Hughes's mother before Hughes was born; he grew up in Lawrence, Kansas, under the watchful care of his grandmother, Mary Langston (she is the model for Aunt Hagar Williams in Hughes's autobiographical novel, *Not Without Laughter* [1930]). From his grandmother he heard stories about the family lineage: one grandfather was an admired politician and abolitionist, and Hughes's Aunt Mary's first husband had fought with John Brown in the raid on Harpers Ferry, West Virginia. Hughes's mother took him to Cleveland, Ohio, where he attended high school, but when he was fourteen years old, his mother again abandoned him. He supported himself through menial jobs and spent summers with his father in Mexico. In 1920 he went to live for a year in Mexico with his father, but they quarreled, sometimes bitterly. Hughes returned to the United States to attend Columbia University but quit after a year and shipped out as a deckhand on freighters to Africa and Spain. In 1924 he spent six months in Paris, working as a waiter and doorman and imbibing the heady bohemian expatriate life of the City of Light. When he returned to the United States, he enrolled at Lincoln University in Pennsylvania, receiving his B.A. there in 1929. Hughes traveled through the United States, the Soviet Union, and the Orient during the 1930s, and covered the Spanish Civil War for American newspapers. He lived the remainder of his life in New York City; he never married.

Hughes is one of the significant black writers in the first half of the twentieth century. He published eighteen collections of poems; his first collection, *The Weary Blues* (1926), attracted immediate attention with its African, Afro-American, and jazz rhythms, and showed itself very much a part of the Harlem Renaissance. Hughes also published two novels, several children's books, and an autobiography, *The Big Sea* (1945), and saw his plays produced in the United States and abroad. For twenty-three years he wrote for the *Chicago Defender* what was probably the most popular column in black journalism—"Simple" (Jesse B. Semple), a black Everyman who, with a little reflection, can be seen as a universal common man devoid of exclusionary color. Hughes's humility, his face of simple emotion, and his partisanship in the fights for civil rights from the 1920s on are typified in the figure of Simple—a black man who can never be exiled from America's cityscape though bigots continually try to turn him into an invisible inner émigré. Hughes also translated modern French and Spanish writers.

Hughes is another instance of the black American expatriate writer who found French culture not only sympathetic but stimulating in its respect for black achievements. Yet it is instructive that Hughes returned to the United States and lived in Harlem, where he struggled with his art as he fought his literary and social battles as well as fighting for amelioration of the black man's condition in America. Like Richard Wright,* Hughes became a model whom the younger black writer either emulated or challenged in a contest for new literary supremacy. Lorraine Hansberry, for instance, took the title of her play, *A Raisin in the Sun* (1959) from Hughes's celebrated poem, "Dream Deferred," while James Baldwin openly admitted it was Hughes he had to "disprove" for a new generation of black writers to emerge.

Selected Titles: Poems: *Fine Clothes to the Jew* (1927); *The Dream Keeper* (1932); *Fields of Wonder* (1947); *Montage of a Dream Deferred* (1951); *Ask Your Mama: 19 Moods for Jazz* (1961); *The Panther and the Lash* (1968). Fiction: *Laughing to Keep From Crying* (1952, stories); *Tambourine to Glory* (1958, novel); "Simple" series: *Simple Speaks His Mind* (1950); *Simple Takes a Wife* (1953); *Simple Stakes a Claim* (1957); *Simple's Uncle Sam* (1965). Plays: *Don't You Want to Be Free?* (1938); *The Gospel Glory: A Passion Play* (1962); *Emperor of Haiti* (1963). Opera: *Troubled Island*, libretto by Hughes (1951, c. 1949). Autobiography: *The Big Sea* (1945); *I Wonder As I Wander*

(1956). Nonfiction: *The Ways of White Folks* (1934); *Fight for Freedom: The Story of the NAACP* (1962); editor: *An African Treasury* (1960); with Christiane Reygnault, *Anthologie Africaine et Malgache* (Vichy, 1962).

Consult: Arnold Rampersad, *The Life of Langston Hughes*, 2 vols., vol. 1: *1902–1941, I, Too, Sing America*, vol. 2, *1941–67, I Dream a World* (1988); Webster Smalley, ed., Introduction, in Langston Hughes, *Five Plays* (1963).

HUTCHINSON, Alfred. Born 1924 in Hectorspruit, Eastern Transvaal, South Africa; he lives in England. Hutchinson's maternal grandfather was a Swazi chief; his paternal grandfather was an Englishman. Under South African law, he was of "mixed" heritage, and thus could attend only segregated schools. After obtaining a B.A. degree in education at Fort Hare University College, Hutchinson taught at a high school in Johannesburg. He has written radio plays, short stories, and nonfiction studies; he is best known for his full-length play *The Rain Killers* (London, 1964) and his autobiographical *Road to Ghana* (London, 1960). Hutchinson left South Africa in 1956 after being arrested in a sweep-up of blacks in Johannesburg by the South African government; he had been teaching at the Central High School at the time of his arrest. He jumped bail, fled to East Africa, and then moved to Ghana, where he met his wife, an Englishwoman, Hazel Slade. In 1960 he moved to Brighton, England, where he reentered the teaching profession and worked as a free-lance writer. Hutchinson's work was banned in South Africa during the 1960s under terms of the Suppression of Communism Act.

I ───

IONESCO, Eugène. Born November 26, 1912, in Slatina (near Bucharest); he lives in a retirement house in France. The son of a Romanian lawyer and French mother, Ionesco was taken to Paris by his family in 1914 when he was eighteen months old. His father left Paris in 1916 with plans to enlist in the Romanian army in Bucharest. His mother, hearing no news of him, assumed he had died in the war; she supported the family through factory work. In 1921 Ionesco, at age 10, developed amnesia and was sent to a country village for treatment and recuperation. He returned to Paris in 1922 and began writing plays, poems, a film scenario, and a memoir that might establish for him his identity. His father, who had returned to Paris, divorced Ionesco's mother and was granted custody of the children, whereupon the father took the children with him to Romania. In his new surroundings Ionesco proclaimed himself a Romanian patriot and dedicated one of his plays to his fatherland. His sense of "home," however, was severely disturbed by his father's remarriage. In 1929 Ionesco ran away from home (he was seventeen) and enrolled at Bucharest University, where he pursued a degree in French literature. He was influenced at this time by surrealism and particularly by the works of the Belgian playwright Maurice Maeterlinck. His desire for knowledge of French literature, and thus a French identity, may be seen in psychological terms as an attempt to regain his mother's *place* in his affections. Perhaps this split in Ionesco's life between two opposing and sometimes hostile approval-masters may illuminate the profound sense of absurdity in his comedies. At base in Ionesco's plays is a void, yet people carry on the pretense of substance; piercing the emptiness may result in unbearable, inescapable anonymity. In his early work Ionesco continued to tilt at these assumptions of identity; only with his later maturity has he faced the emptiness of assumed personae. His characters achieve a triumph over emptiness if survival may be construed as victory. At the same time, Ionesco shows that such triumph is a fancy of the mind.

From 1930 to 1937 Ionesco published poems and essays in Romanian journals; his book of literary criticism, *Na* (1934, No), characterized his wit through his technique of utilizing a crescendo of shifting definitions before the words have had time to be heard, much less pondered. In *Na*, for example, he damned three Romanian writers in the first part of the book; in the second part, without explanation for the contradiction, he praised the same three writers for the same reason he had detracted them. Thus, in Ionesco's work, a reader/viewer must accept Ionesco's sense of contradiction as a center. Only then can its nonsense and its sense be appreciated.

Ionesco married Rodica Burileano, a student, in 1936, shortly before his mother died. He returned to France after he obtained a French government grant to write a thesis, "The Themes of Sin and Death in French Poetry since Baudelaire." He found writing in French a difficult task, but he claimed to have disciplined himself to his goal through lecturing and writing in French on Franz Kafka,* Gustave Flaubert, and Marcel Proust in Marseilles, where he lived from 1940 to 1943. He also acknowledges a debt to the French writer Emmanuel Mounier.

Ionesco moved to Paris in 1944 after the birth of his daughter, Marie-France. He worked in a publishing house as a proofreader from 1944 to 1947. His first play, *The Bald Soprano*, was written in 1948; *The Chairs* was completed in 1951. Although *The Chairs* did not at first prove popular in France, it became a *cause célèbre* when, first, Samuel Beckett* and Raymond Queneau praised it, and later Jean Anouilh called it a masterpiece. Ionesco's name became world-known, and his next play, *The Killers*, his first full-length drama, received serious attention. It was Ionesco's following play, *Rhinoceros*, written in 1958, that proved his masterpiece, in its depiction of rhinoceritis—that is, the unstoppable flood of words foaming in the mouths of cult leaders and followers who have become afflicted with the disease of malleable, meaningless words.

Ionesco was elected to the French Academy in 1970. He has acted in films of his own work and written memoirs and short stories. His latest work, *La Quête Intermittente* (1988, The Intermittent Quest), is a bitter memoir of a lonely man who feels forgotten by the audience that once cheered him on. Although painful, the real-life situation (Ionesco lives in a retirement house and complains bitterly at the world's treatment of him) is an inevitable consequence and ironic paradigm of his dramatic legacy. This irony may be seen most pointedly in *The Lesson* (1951), where the lesson to be learned is that there is nothing of significance to be learned from formal education except an abundance of absurdity in the rhetoric of formality. Significant knowledge—for Ionesco, the kind that provides meaning—has become so formalized in the modern era that its content has receded into arcane confines of ritual whose codes are now vaguely lost to a new generation. Ionesco's world is thus subject to the despair that arrives with the awareness of absurdity of man's position vis-à-vis knowledge. Yet Ionesco continues to believe in the possibility of knowledge; a gleam of light pervades his world of doubting constants. The light is seen clearly in his humor, which dictates that his work be viewed as active comedy in which man goes on his routinely amusing ways rather than as passive participation in assumptions of permanently insubstantial disbeliefs.

Selected Title: *Fragments of a Journal* (1990).

Consult: Richard N. Coe, *Ionesco: A Study of His Plays* (new ed., 1971); Ronald Hayman, *Eugene Ionesco* (1976); Rosette C. Lamont and Melvin J. Friedman, eds., *The Two Faces of Ionesco* (1978).

ISHERWOOD, Christopher (William Bradshaw). Born August 26, 1904, in High Lane, Cheshire, England; died January 4, 1986, in Santa Monica, California, U.S.A. After an uneventful British public school and Cambridge University education, Isherwood became a tutor in London. His first novel, *All the Conspirators* (1928), describes the psychological disorientation caused by the conflicts an artist must resolve with his family and with his personal goals. His own alienation from self and family led Isherwood to Berlin, where he taught English from 1930 to 1933. He experienced this expatriation as a form of psychological exile but transformed it into two popular novels, *Mr. Norris Changes Trains* (1935) and *Goodbye to Berlin* (1935). The extremely episodic structure of these novels is a consequence of the naturalistic, first-person point of view that Isherwood adopted to break down the barriers between fiction and the reality of decadent Berlin as he had experienced it.

After Berlin Isherwood seems never to have felt completely at ease with conventional English culture, and after 1938 he did not regularly reside in his native country. A sojourn in China with comrade-in-literary-arms W. H. Auden* produced the travel book *Journey to a War* (1939, with Auden). Isherwood also wrote about his travels in Greece, South America, and India. Finally he settled in California, becoming an American citizen in 1946. The novel *Prater Violet* (1949) describes the sense of dislocation that filmmaking produces in a sensitive individual aware of both daily realities and the illusions fostered by the cinema world.

The psychological explanation for Isherwood's need to live abroad is revealed in *Christopher and His Kind* (1976). In this book and in the brilliant mosaic of materials for an autobiography, *Kathleen and Frank* (1971), Isherwood discusses his homosexuality frankly and describes the effect it has had on his life and work. *Christopher and His Kind* opens with a statement that *Lions and Shadows* (1938), ostensibly the story of his life to the time when he decided to leave England for good, is not, in fact, "truly autobiographical." *Christopher and His Kind* is intended as a "frank and factual" record of his feelings of psychological exile from his native society because of its inability to accept his sexual nature. As Isherwood explained in a *New York Times* interview, "Any sort of concealment that an artist puts up about his life injures him as an artist, just as it injures him as a man."

After his film days, Isherwood supported himself by writing and teaching at several California colleges. Although such fictional works of his American period as *The World in the Evening* (1952), *Down There on a Visit* (1959), *A Single Man* (1964), and *Memorial* (1978) do not live up to his early promise, he achieved a consistent readability by continuing use of autobiographical materials. Also unsuccessful is *A Meeting by the River* (1967), a fictionalization of Isherwood's experience in a Hindu monastery in India. He did apparently find an acceptance of his homosexuality in Hindu culture that he found nowhere in Western society. Thus he was able to resolve his expatriate experience and psychological exile through the artistic expression of his awareness.

Consult: John Lehmann, *Christopher Isherwood: A Personal Memoir* (1989); Claude J. Summers, *Christopher Isherwood* (1980).

CHARLES KOVICH

ISHIGURO, Kazuo. Born 1954, in Nagasaki, Japan; he lives in London, England. Ishiguro came to England with his parents in 1960 when he was five years old (his father was a scientist who came to Britain for what he considered a job's temporary residence); Ishiguro has lived in London since that time. He writes in English and has published three novels—*A Pale View of Hills* (1982), his first novel set in Nagasaki during the 1950s and an exploration of the dislocation caused by the atomic bomb without any mention of the bombing itself; *An Artist of the Floating World* (1986), in which the complex of tradition and change in modern Japan is viewed through a painter's dilemma caused by his past support of Japanese imperialism; and his third, highly praised novel, *The Remains of the Day* (1989). In this recent work Ishiguro utilizes an English butler's viewpoint to create a portrait of a social class sinking into moral decline by its obdurate clinging to a remote aristocratic system in the period just before and after World War II. The butler becomes a figure of self-repression who, in denying his emotional growth, contributes to the pathos of the dying class system he fervently wishes to preserve. Ishiguro's novel becomes another tale in his body of work of alienation and isolation of minority figures from the larger communities around them. In his most recent novel the minority figure is a subordinate whose true love lies in his pecking order, and who, in a gasp at epiphany, sees only peril in a less socially classified world.

IVANOV, Vyacheslav Ivanovich. Born February 28, 1866, Moscow, Russia; died July 1949, Rome, Italy. Ivanov's first exile ended with his return to Russia in 1903 after fifteen years abroad; he had been a liberal opponent of Czarist policies. During the period from 1903 through the Russian Revolution of 1917, he was accepted not only as one of Russia's leading poets but as a great salon talker and influence on Russian poets, particularly Alexandr Blok, and on the course of Russian futurism. He was also acknowledged as one of his country's outstanding literary theoreticians, classical scholars, and philosophers. He was an early enthusiast of the October 1917 Revolution, but fell out of favor with the Soviets because of his refusal to domesticate his work to state concerns. He left the Soviet Union in 1921 for Italy, where he converted to Roman Catholicism. He became both a translator and profound scholar of Dante Alighieri, whose life became a role model for Ivanov's literary and philosophic development. Dante took the place for Ivanov of earlier role models of the Hellenic age, who had inspired in Ivanov an aesthetic single-mindedness and a devotion to classical harmony and formal craft. Ivanov's poetry is dense with metaphor and hermetic in its aesthetic shelter; both the early and later work reflect the author's commitment to art as an entity without recourse to specific social construction. Because of his inimical attitude to social realism, Ivanov's work was not published in the USSR during the Stalin period; he is little known in the Soviet Union today.

Ivanov left a vast novel unfinished at his death. The work, under the title *Povest o Svetomire Tsareviche* (Account of Tsarevich Svetomir), was published with the collaboration of Ivanov's companion, Olga Chor (herself a writer under the pseudonym of O. Deschartes), in Ivanov's *Collected Works* (1971) in Russian.

Consult: Pamela Davidson, *The Poetic Imagination of Vyacheslav Ivanov: A Russian Symbolist's Perception of Dante* (1989); Simon Karlinsky and Alfred Appel, Jr., eds., *The Bitter Air of Exile: Russian Writers in the West 1922–1972* (1977); Harold B. Segel, *Twentieth-Century Russian Drama: From Gorky to the Present* (1979); J. West, *Russian Symbolism: A Study of Gregory Ivanov and the Russian Symbolist Aesthetic* (1960).

IVASK, Ivar. Born December 17, 1927, in Riga, Latvia, of an Estonian father and Latvian mother; he has been teaching at the University of Oklahoma (Norman) since 1967. Ivask graduated from the Estonian Gymnasium in Wiesbaden, Germany, then studied art history and comparative literature at the University of Marburg in the Federal Republic of Germany from 1946 to 1949. He married the Latvian poet and critic Astrid Hartmanis in 1949, and immigrated with her to the United States the same year; he became an American citizen in 1955 and served in the U.S. Army Medical Corps from 1954 to 1956. He has taught at several American universities and has been professor of modern languages and literatures at the University of Oklahoma and editor of the international literary quarterly *World Literature Today* (formerly *Books Abroad*) since 1967. Among the special issues on exiled writers for the journal he has edited are those on Jorge Guillén,* Gabriel García Márquez,* Odysseus Elytis,* Julio Cortázar,* and Czeslaw Miłosz*; the journal has also published special issues on exile writing, Baltic letters, and modern poetry from Eastern Europe. Ivask has also been the head of the committee that awards the biennial Neustadt International Prize for Literature since its inception in 1969; the value of the prize is put at $25,000 today. Among exile writers who have been honored with the prize are Gabriel García Márquez, Czeslaw Miłosz, and Josef Skvorecky,* and such expatriate writers as Elizabeth Bishop and Raja Rao.*

Ivask has published eight collections of his own verse in Estonian, among them *Tähtede tähendus* (Lund, 1964, The Meaning of Stars); *Päev astub ku-kesammul* (Lund, 1966, The Day Arrives with a Rooster's Steps); *Ajaloo aiad* (Lund, 1970, The Gardens of History); *Oktoober Oklahomas* (Lund, 1973, October in Oklahoma), which won the Henrik Visnapuu Prize that year; *Verikivi* (Lund, 1976, Bloodstone), with the author's illustrations; *Verandaraamat* (Lund, 1978, The Veranda Book); and *Tänusõnu* (Lund, 1987, Words of Gratitude). He has published two chapbooks in English, *Snow Lessons* (Norman, Oklahoma, 1986) and *Baltic Elegies* (Norman, 1987), the latter of which has been widely translated. He has published many volumes of literary criticism, and more than 150 book reviews in *Books Abroad* and *World Literature Today*. He is also a visual artist and photographer whose works have been exhibited in several European countries and the United States. He was awarded a Citation of Commendation by the Oklahoma House of Representatives in 1978 and the Oklahoma Governor's Art Award in 1985.

Selected Titles: *Gottfried Benn als Lyriker* (1950, 1972); *Hugo von Hofmannsthal also Kritiker der deutschen Literatur* (1953); with J. Marichal, *Luminous Reality: The Poetry of Jorge Guillén* (1969); with J. von Wilpert, *World Literature since 1945* (1973); *The Perpetual Present: The Poetry and Prose of Octavio Paz* (1973); *Odysseus Elytis: Analogies of Light* (1981).

J ————————————————————————

JABÈS, Edmond. Born April 16, 1912, in Cairo, Egypt; he lives in Paris. Jabès lived in Egypt until the expulsion of the Jews at the time of the Suez crisis (1957). Since then, he has been living in Paris, where he is regarded as an important contemporary writer. In 1970 he received the coveted Prix des Critiques, in 1982 the Prize for Arts, Letters and Science of the Foundation of French Judaism, in 1983 the Pasolini Prize, and in 1987 the Cittadella Prize and the Grand Prix National de Poésie.

Jabès began writing poems in the wake of the surrealists and Max Jacob, which he collected under the title *Je bâtis ma demeure* (1957, I Build My Dwelling). The poems and their collective title indicate that his sense of exile preceded its history. The actual experience of exile triggered his major work, the great cycles of ''The Book'': *Le livre des questions* (Paris, 7 vols., 1963–73; *The Book of Questions*, 1976–84) and *Le livre des ressemblances* (Paris, 3 vols., 1976–80, The Book of Resemblances).

In Jabès's concept, exile is a consequence of being ''other,'' the Jewish condition par excellence, experience of a people without a country. Such an experience is moreover exemplary of the condition of individuation, of man who finds himself a stranger to other beings and knows that he is headed toward the ultimate exile: death. Jabès sees exile more in its existential and metaphysical dimensions than in its historical and political instances.

Jabès's work is sui generis: an untold story forms the pretext for rabbinical commentaries, poems, aphorisms, wordplay with philosophical implications, and reflective, densely metaphorical prose. Shifting voices and constant breaks of mode let silence have its share of the language and allow for a fuller meditative field than possible in linear narrative or analysis.

In the first three volumes (*Le livre des questions*, 1963; *Le livre de Yukel*, 1964; *Retour au livre*, 1965—*The Book of Questions*, 1976; *The Book of Yukel/Return to the Book*, 1977), the untold story that emerges from the commentaries is a Holocaust story in which two young lovers are deported to Nazi camps. The images of the desert with its inevitable dispersion and, complementarily, the image of the concentration camp—grotesque historical parody of an impossible ontological center—dominate these volumes and are perhaps always the focal points of Jabès's elliptical thought. The succeeding three volumes (*Yaël*, 1967; *Elya*, 1969; *Aely*, 1972—*Yaël/Elya/Aely*, 1983) show, on a more allegorical level, man rejected by and exiled from the word. The word takes the shape of a woman, Yaël. This woman cannot be faithful because the word implies the possibility of ambiguity and falsehood. The narrator thinks he has killed Yaël in his rage against the other, in his rage for truth. But one cannot kill the word. The only one reduced to silence is the stillborn child, Elya. The narrator finds that he is not only rejected but also changed by the word, and that he is himself turning into the other. *El ou le dernier livre* (1973); *El or the Last Book*, 1984) is a meditation on the point as God's first manifestation, which expanded to encompass all of creation, and to which all creation returns. If this seems to hold out hope of an ultimate unification, Jabès suggests that it is at the price of existence.

The cycle of *The Book of Resemblances* consists of three volumes: *Le livre des ressemblances* (1976; *The Book of Resemblances*, 1990); *Le soupçon/le désert (1978; Intimations/The Desert*, 1991); and L'ineffaçable/l'inaperçu (1980; *The Ineffaceable/The Unperceived*, 1992). It marks a further turn of involution in its use of the *Book of Questions* as the basis for its meditations. This "book which resembles a book" probes the nature of analogy that is at the root of thought and language, yet proves to be a tenuous support for man created in the image of a god who does not exist. In these books, man is exiled even from his own myths and metaphysical origin.

Clearly the experience of exile has led to the extraordinary fusion of traditions in Jabès's work. He draws on the Mishnah as well as on French poetry and current linguistic theory for an innovative work that defies classification. Jabès's work not only treats basic human questions with great intellectual and emotional power, but challenges the unifying tendency of our thinking, which is at the base of intolerance and leads to the recurrence of exilic history. It does this through the theme of man's singularity (given in the exemplary otherness of the Jew), but also through opening the discourse to fragmentation and discontinuity, opening language to a silence that calls the word into question.

Selected Titles: *Le petit livre de la subversion hors de soupçon* (1982, The Little Book of Subversion beyond Suspicion); *Le livre du dialogue* (1984; *The Book of Dialogue*,, 1987); *Le Parcours* (1985, The Journey); *Le livre du partage* (1987; *The Book of Shares*, 1989); *Un Etranger avec, sous le bras, un livre de petit format* (Paris, 1989).

Consult: E. Gould, ed., *The Sin of the Book: Edmond Jabès* (1985); J. Guglielmi, *La ressemblance impossible* (Paris, 1978); Mary Ann Caws, *Edmond Jabès* (Amsterdam,

1988); Warren F. Motte, Jr., *Questioning Edmond Jabès* (1990); Richard Stamelman and Mary Ann Caws, eds., *Écrire le livre: Autour d'Edmond Jabès* (Seyssel, France, 1990).

ROSMARIE WALDROP

JACOBSON, Dan. Born March 7, 1929, in Johannesburg, South Africa; he lives in London. Jacobson, born into a middle-class Jewish family in which the traditions of liberalism, mercantilism, and democratic optimism play a large role, grew up in Kimberley. He attended the University of Witwatersrand, and worked as a teacher, journalist and businessman. He taught at a private school in England in 1950 and at Stanford University, California, in 1957. He emigrated to England in 1954, though he visited the United States on teaching engagements through the 1950s and 1960s. In 1975 he decided to teach permanently at the University College of London. His work reflects his concern with South Africa's color bias and its apartheid policies. Although never a political animal, Jacobson spoke out forthrightly against his government's policies in such early works as *The Trap* (London, 1955) and *The Price of Diamonds* (London, 1957). His short story "The Zulu and the Zeide" (reprinted in the collection under the same name, London, 1959) captures the anguish of prejudice in its ironic depiction of the closeness between an old Jewish man and his black servant; in Jacobson's rendering both are the victims of racist historicism, both are caught in the punitive vise of impersonal governmental decrees even if one person is on the surface "free" and the other a second-class citizen. Jacobson's novel *Evidence of Love* (1960) presents the story of an interracial affair, its depth of human commitment, and its consequence of imprisonment for violating the law against cohabitation. Significantly, as in a number of tales by South African writers, the personae return to South Africa to face punishment after they have reached another country in which they are free to live out their lives together without opprobrium. Early twentieth-century South African literature—that is, literature published through the 1960s—reflects this patient optimism that Christian forebearance and humility—whether practiced by Christian or non-Christian—will unshackle the bars of nationally decreed racial bias. The characteristic is most apparent in South African Jewish writing (see Nadine Gordimer's eponymous heroine Rosa Burger [*Rosa Burger*, 1979], who returns to her country to face imprisonment for her activities on behalf of color equality and socialism).

Jacobson's concern with freedom and equality has never lessened, but his novels from 1970 to 1988 showed less concern with the immediate present and with direct representation of contemporary South African policy. Perhaps his creative spirit needed another route of expression, perhaps he felt he had said all he could say in fiction about apartheid, and perhaps he wished to explore human nature in other historical eras of oppression during the period of the 1960s after he left South Africa to settle in England. His last novel (before 1989) with a South African setting is probably his masterpiece, *The Beginners* (1966), in which he traces the rise and fall from political and social grace of a prominent Jewish family. Jacobson said in an interview with Martin Tucker that he felt "exhausted" in terms of South African portraiture and naturalistic representation of events after the completion of this novel. In his following fiction he turned to a biblical theme and more metaphoric language, *The Rape of Tamar* (London, 1970), a novel which Jacobson said, in his interview in 1982 in London, was his "favorite" work. In this work Jacobson turned to his Jewish roots through a probing into the incestuous passion of an otherwise exemplary Jewish prince for his sister and his subsequent rape of her. Jacobson also published in 1982 a history of the Jewish people, *The Story of the Stories: The Chosen People and Its God*.

When the Republic of South Africa left the Commonwealth, Jacobson, as a British resident, chose to remain in England; he has since become a British national. He feels that if he has "a home anywhere, it is here," in England (personal interview in 1982). He thinks of himself, however, not as an exile but as an expatriate. He also considers himself an English don: he has worked as a department tutor in charge of student problems at the University of London as well as taught, while continuing to write both fiction and informative prose. Two of his works that received wide attention in the 1970s are *The Wonder-Worker* (London, 1973), an exposure of contemporary London life, and *The Confessions of Josef Baisz* (1977), a portrait of the power of authority as it mutes an outspoken, compassionate man. Jacobson says the country in *Josef Baisz* is not South Africa (though readers have seen parallels with it in Jacobson's novel) but a tyrannized East European land. Jacobson's most recent fiction marks a return to an African setting.

As a South African Jew living in England, Jacobson feels "detached" both from his country and from identification as a "Jewish writer." He claims to be a writer who happens to be Jewish, and that while Jewish themes enter his work both consciously and subconsciously, the creed he serves is that of humanism rather than religious affiliation or nationalism. In a series of autobiographical essays published together in the collection *Time and Time Again: Autobiographies* (London, 1985), and particularly in the essay "Time of Arrival," which was first printed in *Time of Arrival and Other Essays* (London, 1962; 1965), Jacobson demonstrates how "unaided recollection" continues relentlessly to infiltrate his being and to shape his present view. Jacobson can be said to represent a modern example of the Romantic Wordsworthian spirit, an expatriate who drinks from the fountain of troubled recollection in a more tranquil land.

Selected Titles: Stories: *A Long Way from London* (London, 1958); *Beggar My Neighbours* (London, 1964); *Inklings* (London, 1973); *Her Story* (1987). Travel: *No Further West: California Revisited* (London, 1959; 1961); *Adult Pleasures* (1988).

Consult: Myra Yudelman, *Dan Jacobson: A Bibliography* (Johannesburg, 1967); Martin Tucker, *Africa in Modern Literature* (1967).

JAHNN, Hans Henny. Born December 17, 1894, in Stellingen, near Hamburg, Germany; died November 29, 1959, in Hamburg, West Germany. Jahnn changed his family name of Jahn after his family and he came to blows over his homoerotic relationship with his schoolmate and (later) life friend, Gottlieb Harms. Jahnn's sense of alienation from society, combined with his homophilia, became key factors in his life and in his work. He saw art and love—"the little eternities"— as a defence in the battle against decay to which he believed all human life was doomed.

Lifelong pacifists unwilling to be drafted, Jahnn and his friend Harms went into their first exile in Norway in 1915 where they stayed until the end of World War I. Jahnn's dramatic works, mainly written in Scandinavia at the beginning of his literary career, have been characterized as "poetic visions of a creation that has been recognized as tragic, full of heathen, anti-Christian culture-critique" (Uwe Schweikert, quoted in *Metzler Autoren Lexikon: Deutsche-sprachige Dichtler und Schriftsteller vom mittelalter bis zur Gegenwart* [German-Speaking Poets and Writers from the Middle Ages to the Present], Stuttgart: J. P. Metzler, p. 312). The writing of his first play, *Pastor Ephraim Magnus* (1916–17), was guided, in Schweikert's words, by his intention to write "no literature like the one they all write, not that which they drill into you as literature at school, not that kind of language" (p. 313). Response to *Pastor Ephraim Magnus* ranged from condemnation as originating from the "underworld" and unnecessary in its terrifying explosion of dementia—one critic wrote that its state of "being nothing but a grandiose, ghastly document of an extreme con-dition" had nothing to do with theater and that the script should be kept under lock and key in the "poison chest of humanity" (Julius Bab, quoted in Schwei-kert)—to the coveted Kleist Prize and a production under the direction of Bertolt Brecht in 1920.

Written in exile, *Pastor Ephraim Magnus* led to heated controversies in Jahnn's native country. The controversy grew out of Jahnn's attacks on Christian mo-rality, his protest against the "violence" of "bourgeois order," his willingness to portray aspects of pubescent erotica, and his expressionistic depiction of physical desperation. The eponymous hero of Jahnn's drama undergoes castration and crucifixion before he can pass through his soul's journey. The work, as well as Jahnn's experience of exile, spurred on his lifelong wrestling with language and the beginning of his stream-of-consciousness writing. In exile, Jahnn also developed his utopian vision of Ugrino—a community of fellow believers in the rebirth of an archaic culture which he and his friend Harms founded in Eckel in northern Germany in 1920. Ugrino did not survive, however, except for the Ugrino Music Publishing Company, which, among others, produced Buxtehude's complete works. Jahnn became well-known as an inventive and productive organ builder and worked for the city of Hamburg as its organ expert. In 1933 he was dismissed for "political unreliability."

Jahnn's second exile period began in Switzerland in 1934 and continued into Denmark where he lived as a writer, farmer, horse breeder, bio-scientist, phi-losopher, and visionary. Apparently he did not see himself as an emigrant and, consequently, did not seek out the company of other literary exiles. Jahnn in fact kept his passport, traveled to Germany, and had some of his work published there during the Third Reich. During the German occupation of Denmark in the 1940s, Jahnn was left unharmed by the Nazis.

In 1950 Jahnn returned to Hamburg and became active in the literary and political world there, including association with the German PEN Club and the anti-nuclear and anti-rearmament movements. His visionary despair is perhaps best represented by Gustav Anias, the main character in his homoerotic novel *Die Niederschrift des Gustav Anias Horn* (1949/50, The Apologia of G. A. Horn), in which a sailor murders the fiancé of Horn (who is a composer), and through his intimate relationship with the survivor (the composer) finds forgiveness for his crime. Horn, in turn, is convinced that his relationship with the murderer is modelled on the love of Gilgamesh and Engidu of the ancient Sumeric Gilgamesh epos. It is in this exile-inspired novel that Jahnn, through the character of Horn, expresses one of his visions of the terrible: "on the weak spot of the single human, a renegade who tries to think . . . in whose ears the words reverberate which one speaks, [which one] teaches, [words] in whose name one judges, with which one dies—and [the renegade] no longer believes them. . . . In vain I bless a single creature the horse. In vain I vote for the party of the weak and conquered—I can save nobody—it is as it is" (*Lexikon der deutschesprachigen Gegenwartsletints*, Munich: Nymphenburger, p. 245).

Indeed, it may be said that in his epic trilogy, *Fluss ohne Ufer* (1949–61) of which *Die Niederschrift des Gustav Anias Horn* is a part and whose *Epilog* (1961) was published posthumously, Jahnn was attempting to bring together those compartmentalizations of reality which have splintered modern men into beasts of power and monsters of indifference. He saw the decline of German society as an inevitability of the pursuit of the divisiveness of the Western world into fields of science and humanity. Trained as a biological scientist, and self-trained as a musician-organist, Jahnn utilized his interdisciplinary experience as a continuing method of awareness. Throughout his early fiction, from the experimental *Perrudja* (1929) through the trilogy *Fluss ohne Ufer*, Jahnn pursued a notion of totality that included reason, super-reason, and an illumination of reason that was positioned so far beyond it that it might be called Ur-reason or meta-reason. In this forest world of the soul, this tossing sea of knighthood and darkness through which a ghostly ship must pass, the baptism of the hero is invariably accompanied by symphonic-like passages of exaltation, which draw on Jahnn's vast knowledge and love of music. His heroes must undergo initiation into violence, passionate sexuality, and even murder as a passage through the dark center of the journey into being. Jahnn thus posited that reason, once it is shorn of its companionship with the mythic, undergoes a decadence in its sanity. At the same time he recognized that madness is inevitable without the profound healing presence of reason. His view was a tragic one: he saw evil as triumphant in its corruption of society, a corruption the artist could not prevent, yet against which the artist was obliged to struggle.

Critics continue to remain in separate camps about the value of Jahnn's work and his literary heritage. Some champion him as a writer of mythic power; others see his vision as morbid and grotesque. Many readers cannot fathom his multitudinal talents and forms, his sexual orientation, and his experimental language. He is often labelled an outsider in the German literary canon. Yet a steadily growing number of critics compare his work to Alfred Döblin* and James Joyce,* and see in Jahnn's prose "one of the greatest writers of the German language in our century" (*Autorenlexikon*, Hamburg: Rowohlt, 1988). As in the past, Jahnn remains an enigma; at the same time, one of his critics, Uwe Schweikert, believes that his future as a great modern author is in the process of gestating.

Selected Titles: Trilogy, *Fluss ohne Ufer*: consists of *Das Holzschiff* (Hamburg, 1949, *The Ship*, 1961); *Die Niederschrift des Gustav Anias Horn* (2 vols., Hamburg, 1949–50, Gustav Anias Horn's Written Narrative); *Die Nacht aus Blei* (Hamburg, 1955, The Night Made of Lead); *Epilog* (Hamburg, 1961).

Consult: Raymond Furness, *The Twentieth Century 1890–1945* (1978); Hans Henny Jahnn, *Buch der Freunde*, ed. R. Italiaander (Hamburg, 1960, Book of Friends); Hans Henny Jahnn, *Schriftsteller, Orgelbauer, 1894–1959* (Wiesbaden, 1973, Writer, Organ Builder [includes posthumously published documents]); Hans Henny Jahnn, *Werke und Tagebucher*, 7 vols. (Hamburg, 1974, Works and diaries); Jochen Meyer, *Verzeichnis der Schriften von und über Hans Henny Jahnn* (Neuwied, Berlin, 1967, List of publications by and about Jahnn); Hans Wolffheim, *Hans Henny Jahnn: Der Tragiker der Schoepfung* (Frankfurt, 1966, Hans Henny Jahnn, The Tragic Writer of Creation). Also see *Das Hans Henny Jahnn Lesebuch* (Hamburg, 1984, The Hans Henny Jahnn Reader).

HENRIK EGER and MARTIN TUCKER

JAMES, C.L.R. (Cyril Lionel Robert). Born January 4, 1901, in Port of Spain, Trinidad; he died in June, 1989, in Trinidad. This eminent political theorist, biographer, union spokesman, philosopher, and fiction writer has also written unique works on cricket, and has been the cricket correspondent for several newspapers, among them the *Manchester Guardian* and the *Glasgow Herald*. James's interest in literature began also at an early age; as a student in high school he wrote an essay, "The Novel as an Instrument of Reform," using an angle of view he was to advance all his life and to which he was to bring what he saw as Black Marxist justification. His fiction was immediately popular; his first novel, *Minty Alley* (written 1929; published London, 1936; 1971) remains a staple in West Indian literature.

James and his friend, Alfred Mendes,* formed a little magazine, *Trinidad*, in 1929 that published work by emerging Trinidadian writers. The following year they published another journal, the *Beacon*, which also promoted the work of young Trinidadian writers. In 1932 James and Mendes both left Trinidad, and their magazines folded. James went to England, Mendes to the United States.

James's wanderings began at this point, but they were largely confined to the United States, England, and return to Trinidad. His profound commitment to political literature and the social progress of the black man revealed itself in his work, ranging from biography, autobiography, political tracts, fiction, and literary criticism. He talked with Leon Trotsky in England, a discussion he never forgot and which became the spur for his various works on black workers in a capitalist world.

James lived in the United States for fifteen years, but was expelled from this country in 1953 because of his socialist views. He moved back to England, where he lived for five years and became active in the Pan-Africanist movement. He returned to Trinidad in 1950, but was placed under house arrest there when he disagreed with Trinidad's head of government, Dr. Eric Williams. He returned to England in 1962, wrote an autobiographical book on cricket, *Beyond the Boundary* (1962). In 1965 he came back to Trinidad as a cricket correspondent; again he was placed under house arrest, but public protest forced the government to release him. The experience of political in-fighting drove him back to England; from there he moved to the United States.

James's influence on West Indian culture and the vast public support his adherents bring to the cause of literature that he has celebrated all his life make him a seminal West Indian figure. His fiction is a prototype of later West Indian fiction in its portrayal of the alienation of West Indian intellectuals from their island people. James's fiction also provided a model for later writers in its portrayal of the colonial past and the need to find a path forward to a unity of concern between the intellectual and the common man.

Selected Titles: *The Life of Captain Ciprian: An Account of British Government in the West Indies* (London, 1932); *The Case for West Indian Self-Government* (London, 1933; 1967); *World Revolution 1917–1936: The Rise and Fall of the Communist International* (London, 1937); *The Black Jacobins: Toussaint L'Ouverture and the San Domingo Revolution* (1938, repr. 1963); *Mariners, Renegades and Castaways: The Study of Melville and the World We Live In* (1953); *Nkrumah and the Ghana Revolution* (Westport, Conn., 1977); *The Future in the Present: Selected Writings* (London, 1977); *Spheres of Influence: Selected Writings* (Westport, Conn., 1980).

Consult: Paul Buhle, ed., *C. L. R. James: His Life and Work* (London, 1987); Eugenia Collier, "C. L. R. James," in *Fifty Caribbean Writers*, ed. Daryl Cumber Dance (1986); Michael Gilkes, *The West Indian Novel* (1981); C. L. R James Interview in *Interviews with Three Caribbean Writers in Texas, Kas-Kas* (Austin, Texas); Kenneth Ramchand, *The West Indian Novel and Its Background* (1970); Reinhard W. Sander, *The Trinidad Awakening: West Indian Literature of the Nineteen-Thirties* (1988).

JAMES, Henry. Born April 15, 1843, in New York City; he died February 28, 1916, in London, England. James was educated privately. His father, a well-read man who knew his Swedenborg profoundly and who counted Ralph Waldo Emerson as one of his close friends, arranged for James to board in Europe while receiving tutorial instruction. James visited Europe several times, from 1855 to 1860, and in 1869 and 1872, before embarking on his decisive voyage to emigration in 1875. He spent one year in Paris and then moved to England, where he lived for the rest of his life. He became a British citizen in 1915, both to show his allegiance to a country fighting to maintain a world of tradition under siege and to protest American's lack of involvement in the Great War. He was awarded the Order of Merit by the British government in 1916 shortly before he died.

All of James's work was written after his emigration/self-exile from American shores, with the exception of a juvenile novel, *Watch and Ward* (1871). He remained committed to his profound belief that manners distinguished character in a lifelong balance sheet between American innocence and European sophistication, American vitality and European measured expression. In the end, James's reserve of values celebrated both America and Europe, innocence and knowledge, and most of all, generosity of impulse and the tutoring of emotional response.

Selected Titles: *The American* (1877); *The Europeans* (1878); *Washington Square* (1880); *The Portrait of a Lady* (1881); *The Bostonians* (1885); *The Lesson of the Master* (1892, stories); *The Real Thing and Other Stories* (1893); *The Spoils of Poynton* (1896); *What Maisie Knew* (1897); *The Sacred Fount* (1901); *The Wings of the Dove* (1902); *The Ambassadors* (1903); *The Golden Bowl* (1904); *The Novels and Stories of Henry James*, 35 vols. (1921–23); *The Art of the Novel: Critical Prefaces* (1934); *The Notebooks of Henry James* (1947); *Complete Plays of Henry James* (1949); *Complete Tales*, 12 vols. (1962–64).

Letters: *Letters of Henry James*, 2 vols. (1920); *Letters of Henry James*, ed. Leon Edel, 3 vols., (1974–80); *Henry James and Edith Wharton Letters: 1900–1915*, ed. Lyall H. Powers, 1990.

Consult: Van Wyck Brooks, *The Pilgrimage of Henry James* (1925); Leon Edel, *The Life of Henry James*, 5 vols. (1953–72); Leon Edel and Dan Laurence, eds., *A Bibliography of Henry James*, 2nd ed. (1961); Percy Lubbock, *The Craft of Fiction* (1921); F. O. Matthiessen: *Henry James: The Major Phase* (1944); F. O. Matthiessen, ed. *The James Family* (1947); Richard Poirier, *The Comic Sense of Henry James* (1961).

JARNES, Benjamin. Born October 7, 1888, in Codo, Saragossa, Spain; died August 11, 1949, in Madrid, Spain. Jarnes left Spain in 1939 with the collapse of the Republicans in the Civil War. From France he sailed to Mexico, where he taught and wrote for Spanish emigré magazines. Aware of his imminent death, he returned to his homeland in 1948.

The pain that Jarnes as novelist, essayist, and translator suffered in exile— his loss of familiar personal surroundings and the understanding of colleagues in profound games of intellectual discourse—strengthened his conception of art as an analytical tool for perceiving reality. Jarnes came to believe more firmly in the insubstantiality of mass doctrine as a means of reflection of truth and, conversely, in the concreteness of abstract truth and mathematical objectivism. One critic, Paul Ilie, describes Jarnes's style as a form of intellectual cubism, a manner of laying out observations on mathematical planes of view before arriving at moral weighing-stations. While paying homage to Jarnes's artistic and moral integrity, Ilie questioned whether Jarnes's "objective" scientific and mathematical approach brought art into an area of dehumanization.

Selected Titles: *Poeta de su siglo* (1942); *Stefan Zweig: cumbre apagoda, retrato* (1942); *Venus dinamica* (1943, Dynamic Venus); *Cervantes: Bosquejo biografico* (1944).

Consult: J. S. Bernstein, *Benjamin Jarnes* (1972); Paul Ilie, "Benjamin Jarnes: Aspects of the Dehumanized Novel," *PMLA* 76 (1961); Emilio de Zuleta, *Arte y vida en la obra de Benjamin Jarnes* (Madrid, 1977).

JHABVALA, Ruth Prawer. Born May 7, 1927, in Cologne, Germany, of Polish parents; she lives mainly in New York. Jhabvala came to England in 1939 with her parents in flight from the Nazis; she was twelve years old. She received an M.A. degree from London University. In 1951 she married an Indian architect and moved to New Delhi. Since 1975 she has divided her time between New York and London. Jhabvala is no stranger to displacement, having suffered it involuntarily as an alien in Germany and voluntarily as an adopted Anglo-Indian in New York and Europe. She began writing and publishing her fiction after her move to India, and her themes have remained consistent, though her tone has changed from sardonic amusement to bittersweet irony. Her subject is local customs and manners as observed through a distanced eye, and often in terms of the marriage or alliance of an Indian and a Westerner. In her early work the city of New Delhi and its variety of inhabitants were treated with humor and sympathy. In her later work both Indians and the European/American visitor come under her scalpel for a rarely benign diagnosis. In the course of her development, Jhabvala tended at first to see the Indian as innocent and hapless, while the European/colonial was portrayed as repressed and controlling. In her later work the European and the American characters exhibit their own brand of naïveté, one that causes disorder and is just as willful as the Indian tendency to mysticism and acceptance of unknowingness as a position of action. In her recent novel, *Three Continents* (1986), she encapsulated her portraiture (some have called it caricature) of three kinds of people: (1) Indians ruthless in their greed for power and money and exploiting their hold on exotic religious teachings (Jhabvala is severe on gurus who deceive disciples with promises of cultish nirvana); (2) Americans, wealthy and spoiled, who indulge their dilettantish pleasures with a "try" at Indian philosophies; (3) the psychically dispossessed and sexually stranded in both these groups. (Jhabvala is sympathetic to her sexually ambivalent characters, who appear a number of times in her fiction, though she delineates their inevitable victimization with a clear, unswerving hand.) Jhabvala's tone in her most recent work is thus at a remove from that in her earlier work in which marriage, courtship, and social status were predominant concerns in a comedic universe. (See particularly *Esmond in India* [1956].) Jhabvala, however, always had an eye out for fraudulent mystics in the Indian subcontinent, and a review of her work shows her ambivalence to the spiritual Indian leader who proslytizes a faith beyond the rational world. In *The House-holder* (London, 1960) Jhabvala poked fun at gullible Westerners in India. In *Get Ready for Battle* (London, 1962) she showed goodwill to the guru of integrity in the subcontinent and elsewhere. In *A Backward Place* (London, 1965) the hostility to swamis is again in evidence. In *A New Dominion* (London, 1973;

U.S., *Travelers*, 1973) Jhabvala's tone becomes bitter in her portrait of a corrupt swami who demands total obeisance from those under his control. In one of her best-known works, *Heat and Dust* (London 1975), the examination of the depth and force of Indian religious appeal is layered into the story of a love affair between an Englishwoman and an Indian bandit, who segregates her high on a mountain while he descends to practical living below. The Englishwoman's willingness to sacrifice her Western liberty for her new condition of servility draws, years later, her granddaughter from England to India. This descendant will try to resolve the mystery and allure of a foreign faith and a dead woman's choice of experience of what for some is profound humility and for others a form of victimized passion. The issue of passion and consummation in its conflict with asceticism and sacrifice continues to permeate Jhabvala's explorations of character and individual will.

It is apparent that since *Heat and Dust* Jhabvala's struggle with the demands of India have exhausted her to the point of retreat from the subcontinent. She wrote in 1986, in a preface to her volume of stories *Out of India*, "I have lived in India for most of my adult life. My husband is Indian, and so are my children. I am not, and less so every year." Perhaps Jhabvala's sense of inability (or her confession of it, whether it be true or not) to grasp the nonrationality of Indian philosophy and way of life after all her years in the country is at base the reason for her current residence in New York and on several locations with the Merchant-Ivory production company. (Jhabvala has collaborated with the producers and directors on several distinguished scripts/films, among them *Shakespeare Wallah, Autobiography of a Princess, Heat and Dust*, and E. M. Forster's *Room with a View*.) Significantly, she did not return to England, her first refuge; she has lived in the United States now for almost fifteen years. Jhabvala is, then, that rare example of a gifted, sophisticated outsider in most of her adult experiences, a person aware of her foreignness and yet intimately sympathetic with her surroundings. Although she has been compared to Jane Austen, Anton Chekhov, and Henry James* in her attention to manners, and to the single telling understatement of pathos in human life, and to the ironies of two cultures rubbing against each other in an embrace meant to obscure identification of motives, she is also an example of the elegant displaced rationalist standing apart to observe familiar relations.

Selected Titles: Novels: *To Whom She Will* (London, 1955; in U.S., *Amrita*, 1956); *The Nature of Passion* (London, 1956); *Esmond in India* (London, 1956). Stories: *Like Birds, Like Fishes* (1963); *How I Became a Holy Mother* (1976); *A Stronger Climate* (1968); *An Experience of India* (1972).

Consult: Yasmine Gooneratne, *Silence, Exile and Cunning: The Fiction of Ruth Prawer Jhabvala* (London, 1983); K. R. Srinivasa Iyengar, *Indian Writing in English*, 2nd ed. (1973); V. A. Shahane, *Ruth Prawer Jhabvala* (1976); R. S. Singh, *The Indian Novel in English: A Critical Study* (1977); E. de Souza, "The Expatriate Experience," in *Awakened Conscience: Studies in Commonwealth Literature*, ed. C. D. Narasimhaiah (1978).

JIMÉNEZ, Juan Ramón. Born December 23, 1881, in Moguer, Spain; died May 29, 1958, in San Juan, Puerto Rico. Jiménez spent most of his life in Spain, with visits to southwestern France. The theme of exile in his work lies in the assumed premise of melancholy as a condition natural and constant to humankind. Jiménez was stimulated rather than debilitated by such a view, and he enjoyed his role as mentor to a younger generation of Spanish poets. His last years were marked by disappointment; the generation he had nurtured seemed to be turning to new modes and views, and he in turn felt rejected by them.

While his literary manner was rarefied, his inner warmth responded to the needs of the Spanish populace for democratic and diverse expression. Although he withdrew from public activity, he considered it a poet's duty to be informed of public issues and to serve common goals through the enriching expressions of literary art. When the Spanish Civil War erupted, he moved into exile in Puerto Rico, aware that he needed distance to live out the tragedy of his country. Jiménez's work, as one critic, Marshall S. Schneider, has put it in the *Encyclopedia of World Literature*, Leonard Klein, general editor, volume 2 (1982), was an attempt to come to full consciousness of the many realities about him. Thus he attempted to combine the apprehensions of love passionate and etheralized and experience physical and mystical in his poetic work. In his middle years, after his marriage in New York, he freed himself from the restraints of rhyme and meter to deal unreservedly with the metaphysical universe that claimed him.

Jiménez also wrote several prose works, among them the popular *Platero y yo* (1914; *Platero and I*, 1956), about the travels he and his donkey took together, and *Espanoles de tres mundos* (1942, Spaniards of Three Worlds), a series of expressionistic literary portraits written over many years.

Selected Titles: *Diario de un poeta reciencasado* (1918, Diary of a Newlywed Poet); *La estacion total con canciones de nueva luz* (1936, The Total Season with Songs of New Light); *Animal de fondo* (1949, Animals of Depth); *Romances de Coral Gables (1939–42)* (1948); *Tercera antologia poetica* (1957); *El Modernismo: Notas de un curso* (1962); *Cartas 1898–1958* (1962); *Primeras prosas 1890–1954* (1962); *La colina de los chopos 1913–1928* (1965).

Translations: *Fifty Spanish Poems* (1950); *Selected Writings* (1957); *Three Hundred Poems 1903–1953* (1962); *Forty Poems* (1967).

Consult: L. R. Cole, *The Religious Instinct in the Poetry of Juan Ramón Jiménez* (1967); D. F. Fogelquist, *Juan Ramón Jiménez* (1976); John C. Wilcox, *Self and Image in Juan Ramón Jiménez* (1989).

JOHNSON, Uwe. Born July 20, 1934, in Kammin, Pomerania, Germany (now part of Poland); died February 23, 1984, in Skeerness, England. Johnson fled with his family in 1945 from the German section of Pomerania to a rural area near Mecklenburg in what is now East Germany. He studied at the University of Leipzig from 1952 to 1954, and established a reputation as a bright young East German writer. In 1959 he chose to emigrate to West Germany and live in West Berlin, where he felt his freedom of expression would be less subject to censorship and harassment. His first novel, *Mutmassungern uber Jakob* (1959;

Speculations about Jakob, 1963), was published in West Germany and received the Fontane Prize of West Berlin. The novel uses a protagonist speculating on his own death by a railway train as a means of exploring current social and political issues in the two Germanies and their relationships with the rest of the world; in exploring the social issues Johnson is also exploring the personal and psychic responses of his countrymen. In 1971 Johnson was awarded the Georg Buchner Prize; he also received the International Publishers Prize for *Das dritte Buch uber Achim* (1961; *The Third Book about Achim*, 1967).

Johnson spent several years in the United States before he returned to West Germany. He taught at Wayne State University in Detroit and at Harvard University in 1961. From 1966 to 1968 he lived in New York City and worked as a textbook editor at Harcourt Brace Jovanovich. Johnson had long wished to live in the United States not as a visiting writer but as a job-holding citizen, "a working New Yorker." His last work, the multivolume *Jahrestage* (vol. 1, 1970; vol. 2, 1971; vol. 3, 1973), grew out of this wished-for experience; Johnson began writing it on Third Avenue in New York City. The novel's central character is its heroine, Gesine Cresspahl, a refugee from East Germany who has lived and worked in New York for seven years. Gesine finds safety in the anonymity of New York after a childhood under a Nazi banner and her youth under a Red flag. Remembering the horrors of persecution, false charges, imprisonment, and torture to which she was a witness, the heroine finds a peace in her present time raising her young daughter and working in a secure, bland job at a bank. Johnson was praised for the irony and humor in this fiction and for turning the "most familiar sight into a revelation" as well as for rendering the imprint of specific events on human consciousness.

Johnson's last work is in contrast to his earlier work, but only in tone; the tonal difference, however, is vast between the earlier and later fiction. The early work is satiric and direct in its charges. The later work is more slowly paced, more subtle in its wanderings, and more compassionate in its clipped wires of interrogatory composites. Ultimately Johnson's final novel seems a more resigned acceptance of circumstance in the twentieth century. Interestingly, Gesine Cresspahl is the protagonist's lover in Johnson's first novel and the heroine in his last; indeed, all of Johnson's fictional characters in his earlier work reappear in this last mammoth undertaking. Thus the orbit in which Johnson was examining his German state of identity—and the conflicting ethos of East and West responsibilities and demands—come full circle in his last work. It is important to note that Johnson did not complete his last novel, even though it already ran into three published volumes. (The English edition was published in this order: *Anniversaries I* [1975]; *Anniversaries II* [1987].)

Consult: R. Baumgart, ed., *Uber Uwe Johnson* (1970); R. Post-Adams, *Uwe Johnson* (1977); N. Riedel, *Uwe Johnson, Bibliographie*, 2 vols. (1976, 1978).

JOHNSTON, Denis. Born June 18, 1901, in Ireland; he lives in the United States. Johnston moved to the United States in 1960. A major Irish playwright who employs folklore, myth, and his own sense of literary expressionism, Johnston is best known for his often-produced play, *The Old Lady Who Says No*, produced in 1929, and first published in *The Moon* and *The Yellow River* (Dublin 1931; 1932).

Selected Titles: *Collected Plays* (1960); *Dramatic Works 1977–79*.

JOHNSTON, George. Born July 20, 1912, in Australia; died July 22, 1970, in Sydney, Australia, of tuberculosis. Johnston began his career as a journalist in Melbourne. He served as a war correspondent from 1942 to 1945, first for Australian newspapers and later for *Life* and other American magazines. After the war, Johnston attempted to find various jobs in journalism in Europe and Australia. In 1955 he settled on the Greek island of Hydra for ten years, producing several novels in collaboration with his wife, Charmian Clift, and several on his own (*The Darkness Outside*, 1959; *Closer to the Sun*, 1960). Following the success of his memoiristic novel *My Brother Jack* (1964), Johnston returned to Australia, where he worked on two weaker sequels, *Clean Straw for Nothing* (1969) and *A Cartload of Clay* (posthumous, 1971).

My Brother Jack was immediately recognized in Australia as a masterpiece; the work is now included in standard reading lists of Australian fiction. Its reception puzzled Johnston, for much of the widely praised evocation of Melbourne life between 1920 and 1945 runs counter to commonplace images of Australia as "the lucky country." David Meredith, the narrator, describes his brother as representing those positive images: Jack is strong, free-spirited, earthy, and self-sacrificing. But Jack is also shortsighted, uncultured, arrogant, and intolerant. David, in contrast, desires all of the sophistication and self-awareness that seem to him so rare in Jack's Australia, but he also accuses himself of being a malicious moralist, elitist, and opportunist. Meredith notes at painful length, for instance, that his personal success as a war reporter depends directly upon mass violence. In subsequent volumes of the autobiographical Meredith trilogy, Johnston continued to probe David's mixture of pride and self-accusation, which the reader may come to understand as a deeper, more genuine representation of Australian character.

Consult: Greer Johnson and Chris Tiffin, "The Evolution of George Johnston's David Meredith," *Australian Literary Studies* 11, no. 2 (1983); Garry Kinnane, *George Johnston: A Biography* (Melbourne, 1986); Geoffrey Thurley, "*My Brother Jack*: An Australian Masterpiece?", *Ariel* 5, no. 3 (1980).

JOHN SCHECKTER

JONES, James. Born November 6, 1921, in Robinson, Illinois; died May 9, 1977, Southampton, Long Island, New York. Jones lived with his wife Gloria and two children in Paris, France, from 1958 to 1974; he returned to the United States to teach at Florida International University in Miami. The following year he bought a home in the chic Hamptons community of Sagonponack. His "geography" spans a birth and childhood of deprived circumstance (he spent time in an orphanage) to the glamour and wealth of literary celebrity. His first novel,

From Here to Eternity (1952), written in Indiana (with the financial support of an older, ambitious Midwestern would-be patron of the arts, Lowney Handy) and New York (through the advice of Jones's writing teacher at New York University, Dr. Frank McCloskey), achieved world recognition for its recreation of a young soldier's initiation into barracks discipline and the perils of romance with a beautiful, intelligent and ambitious prostitute. (It was made into a hugely successful film in 1953.) The novel remains Jones's one undisputed achievement; his later work reveals an earnest but less transmuted autobiographical narrative art. His strength remained in his memorable renditions of his early army life, and the ardor of male camaraderie, a consciousness to which he returned in two later novels—*The Thin Red Line* (1962) and *Whistle* (1978, published posthumously).

During his expatriate period—a self-conscious attempt to parody his idol Ernest Hemingway's choice of experiential venue and, in addition, to provide a tax benefit—Jones wrote several failed novels of upper bohemian life in Paris and Europe, and one artful novella of military life, *The Pistol* (1960). In his later years, Jones tried his hand at poetry and published two nonfiction works, *Viet Journal* (1974) and *WWII* (1975), as well as toiled at Hollywood screen treatments.

Selected Titles: *The Merry Month of May* (1971); *To Reach Eternity: The Letters of James Jones*, ed. George Hendrick (1989).

Consult: Frank MacShane, *Into Eternity: The Life of James Jones: American Writer* (1985).

JOYCE, James. Born February 2, 1882, in Dublin, Ireland; died January 13, 1941, in Zurich, Switzerland. In the closing chapter of *A Portrait of the Artist as a Young Man*, Stephen Dedalus asks Davin, an ardent Irish nationalist, "Do you know what Ireland is? . . . Ireland is the old sow that eats her farrow." The anger and ambivalence of Stephen's remark has been accepted as profound autobiography. Choosing permanent self-exile from his native country in 1912, at the age of thirty, Joyce cherished Ireland as his spiritual mother, yet despised her as the murderer of artistic creativity. He could come to grips with her only in imagination, from a safe distance, in exile.

The eldest of the ten children of John Stanislaus Joyce and May Murray Joyce, Joyce witnessed in his youth the steady decline of the family's fortunes, from genteel respectability to out-and-out poverty. His father lost his political job after the Irish leader Charles Parnell fell from power; the father subsequently mortgaged his inherited family properties, pawned family belongings, and took to heavy drinking. Joyce was schooled by Jesuits, first at Clongowes Wood College and then, thanks to a waiver of tuition, at Belvedere College. He flirted very briefly with joining the priesthood, but rejected Catholicism, instead dedicating himself to the "priestly" vocation of art. He matriculated at University College, Dublin, in 1898 and graduated in 1902. He moved to Paris shortly afterward, ostensibly to study medicine; in fact, he spent most of his time reading at the Bibliothèque Ste. Geneviève, writing poetry and epiphanies, and steeling himself in his resolve to be a writer.

Joyce returned home in April 1903, having received the news that his mother was dying. He stayed on in Dublin for more than a year after her death, working on various writing projects, teaching at the Clifton School in Dalkey (Ch. 2, *Ulysses*), living in Martello Tower at Sandycove (Ch. 1, *Ulysses*). On June 16, 1904, the day subsequently immortalized as "Bloomsday," Joyce first courted Nora Barnacle, a Galway girl working at Finn's Hotel. On October 8, he and Nora left Ireland together for the Continent, where they lived the rest of their lives. They were married twenty-three years later.

Joyce and Nora settled first in Trieste, where Joyce supported them by giving English lessons at the local Berlitz school. Their son, Giorgio, was born in July of 1905; their daughter, Lucia, in July of 1907, a crucial year for Joyce's writing. He published *Chamber Music*, his first book and his major collection of poetry; he wrote "The Dead," thus putting *The Dubliners* into its final form; he scrapped *Stephen Hero* and began to reconstitute his autobiographical material into *A Portrait of the Artist as a Young Man*. In 1909, Joyce made two short return trips to Dublin, largely to sign contracts with Maunsel and Company for the publication of *Dubliners*. This agreement was the second of two ill-fated attempts to get *Dubliners* into print. Nearly nine years elapsed between Joyce's first offer for the book from a publisher in 1906 and its eventual appearance in 1914; these years of frustrated anticipation, quarreling and humiliation culminated on September 11, 1912, when the Irish printer, enraged at the "unpatriotic" sentiments in *Dubliners*, burned the proofs. Joyce left Dublin that night, never to set foot on Irish soil again. He blamed Ireland and her values very directly for censorship, calling her "This lovely land that always sent / Her writers and artists to banishment." *Dubliners* was eventually published in 1914, oddly enough by Grant Richards, who had first contracted for it. During the same year that *A Portrait of the Artist as a Young Man* was serialized in London (it was published as a book in New York in 1916), *Ulysses* began to take shape, and Joyce began to write his only drama, *Exiles*. After the outbreak of World War I, Joyce and his family moved to Zurich, where he wrote the bulk of *Ulysses*. The Joyces moved permanently to Paris in 1920, where Joyce completed *Ulysses* and arranged for its publication by Sylvia Beach in 1922.

With the move to Paris and the publication of *Ulysses*, both accomplished with the help of Ezra Pound,* Joyce suddenly found himself a famous and sought-after author, rather than a hounded language teacher who happened to write on the side. He held court in Paris for the next twenty years, fighting to have *Ulysses* published in the United States (1933), writing the numerous installments for *transition* magazine that added up to *Finnegans Wake* (1939), and living largely on the largesse of the American heiress Harriet Weaver. He and Nora were married in 1931; their first grandchild was born in 1932. When France fell to the Nazis in 1940, Nora and Joyce left their home in exile, moving back to neutral Zurich. He died there a few months later, after surgery on a perforated ulcer.

Joyce's self-imposed exile from Ireland was a matter of both personal compulsion and creative integrity. On one level, Joyce believed that Ireland was no place for a man with his literary goals. He vowed to write the truth, especially when "the truth" meant unmasking hypocrisy and portraying human beings in all their natural habits. Joyce also vowed to maintain absolute artistic independence, renouncing allegiance to all religious and political institutions. This latter determination brought Joyce into collision with the Roman Catholic church and the forces of Irish nationalist politics. It placed him at odds with the Dublin literary establishment—William Butler Yeats, AE, John Millington Synge, Oliver St. John Gogarty,* and others—who were largely immersed in Celtic myth and symbolist poetry. As Joyce wrote of them in "The Holy Office" (1904), a poetic statement of termination of contract with his intellectual roots: "That they may dream their dreamy dreams / I carry off their filthy streams."

Joyce's emotional makeup also demanded that he exile himself from his native land. An arrogant and quirky man, he was quick to feel slighted and apt to see himself as victimized by lapsed friends and by those in authority. He could take stock of himself and his persecutors only from a safe distance, in exile. Further, Joyce quite simply throve upon his self-righteous absence from home. As Richard Ellmann puts it: "Joyce needed exile as a reproach to others and a justification of himself. His feeling of ostracism from Dublin lacked, as he was well aware, the moral decisiveness of his hero Dante's exile from Florence, in that he kept the keys to the gate . . . he was in fact to go back five times. . . . But, like other revolutionaries, he fattened on opposition and grew thin and pale when treated with indulgence. . . . Joyce, as he dimly recognized already, throve on the incursions he could make upon conventions, and upon the resistance he could stimulate. Departure from his country was a strategy of combat."

Joyce's commitment to exile pervades his work as a preoccupation with the themes of betrayal, usurpation, and necessary separation. The first of these concerns is already apparent in *Dubliners*, whose stories were written sporadically from 1904 to 1907, and thus bridge Joyce's last period of residence in Dublin and first migration to the Continent. *Dubliners* maps the people and values of the city that drove Joyce away; Joyce advertised it to potential publishers as a "moral chapter in the history" of Ireland. Its opening story, "The Sisters," invokes three words that haunt the young narrator: "paralysis," "simony," and "gnomon." As the collection unfolds, these talismanic words reverberate through the stories in various guises, with "simony" and "paralysis" especially becoming a diagnosis of Dublin's moral disease.

"Simony" comes to represent every aspect of the buying and selling of sacred things, every manifestation of the betrayal, for personal gain, of human beings and human values. The stories in *Dubliners*, like the city of Dublin as Joyce saw it, are pervaded by betrayals. The most obvious simony appears in "Two

Gallants,'' in which Corley betrays a poor servant girl by bartering her affection for him for money. She risks her situation by stealing for him; he acknowledges having bought her, body and soul, when he triumphantly displays a stolen gold coin to his friend at the story's close. Varieties of simoniacal betrayal also dominate "The Boarding House" and "A Painful Case." In the former, a young man is seduced by his landlady's daughter and then forced to marry her. The girl's body becomes the barter in a deadly exchange of easy virtue for a doomed marriage. In "A Painful Case," James Duffy betrays both Mrs. Sinico and himself by leaving her, thus trading off their chance at emotional fulfillment for his own obsession with order and solitude. Betrayal hovers over "Ivy Day in the Committee Room" in a more ghostly way, in the unspoken presence of the dead Parnell, whom Joyce saw as a Christ figure, sold to a mob of priests.

If Joyce saw Dublin as fraught with betrayal, he saw it equally stricken with "paralysis." The priest in "The Sisters" suffers a stroke, which paralyzes him before he finally dies; his physical condition becomes a metaphor for his spiritual sterility, and the stifling effect of the Catholic church in Ireland. In "Eveline," the heroine simply can't move: confronted with the opportunity to escape her wretched life by sailing to South America with her lover, she freezes at the dock, immobile, "passive, like a helpless animal." Most of the stories in *Dubliners* depict people who are trapped in some way—by poverty, by family circumstances, by hypocritical values. Even Gabriel Conroy in "The Dead," the most affluent and self-conscious protagonist in the collection, finds himself trapped by his past and the absence of passion in his temperament.

The Ireland that emerges from *Dubliners* is a country Joyce wanted to put behind him. By the time he wrote *A Portrait of the Artist as a Young Man*, in Trieste from 1907 to 1914, distance had considerably softened his feelings for his old home; his changed attitude can be seen in his ironic treatment of Stephen Dedalus's hatred for Ireland and in the humor he directs at Stephen's developing sense of superiority to Dublin's priests. Yet exile is still necessary to both Joyce and his protagonist. Joyce was beginning to see exile and separation as the general condition of the modern writer; he makes Stephen Dedalus sacrifice his entire life to his art, swearing priestly allegiance to "silence, cunning and exile."

Portrait is a largely autobiographical work that retells the tale of Joyce's early life and reasons for leaving Ireland, emphasizing literary and personal themes crucial to the author. Stephen Dedalus is, like Joyce, in love with words, and arrogant and fearful of being caught in the Irish "nets" of nationalist politics and Roman Catholicism. Equally important, Stephen sees himself as being "betrayed"—by the girl he courts, by Irish culture, by his closest friend, Cranly. (Cranly is modeled upon J. F. Byrne, a Dublin friend Joyce accused, somewhat questionably, of betrayal.) The forces of personal compulsion, cultural alienation, and circumstance combine to propel Stephen away from his native land, to Paris, a place where he can make himself into "a priest of eternal imagination." As Stephen tells a friend: "I will not serve what I no longer believe, whether it call itself my home, fatherland or my Church." But *Portrait* is about more than physical exile from Dublin. As Joyce lived in the alien culture of Trieste, isolated from the familiar and set apart by language and habits, the experience of exile became more and more a metaphor for the necessary distance a writer must put between himself and his artistic material. To create successfully, the artist must separate himself from the raw material of his art; he must also leave no trace of personality in the finished artistic product. Richard Ellmann addresses one side of the question when he notes that "Writing was itself a form of exile for [Joyce], a source of detachment." Stephen Dedalus approaches the matter from another angle in *Portrait* when he formulates his theory of the lyrical, epical, and dramatic forms of art, and concludes the dramatic is most preferable because, in it, the artist most nearly "exiles" himself from his artwork: "The artist, like the God of the creation, remains within or behind or beyond or above his handiwork, invisible, refined out of existence, indifferent, paring his fingernails."

It would be a mistake to identify Stephen Dedalus's artistic theories in *Portrait* totally with Joyce's views, especially since *Ulysses* opens with Stephen at home in Dublin from Paris, having failed miserably at living the life of the artist-in-exile. *Ulysses*, written largely in Zurich from 1914 while World War I raged, and completed in Paris in 1921, teaches Stephen to soften his rejection of Ireland and to lessen the distance between himself and the raw material of his art. On the other hand, *Ulysses* vastly expands the centrality of the themes of betrayal, alienation, and necessary separation in Joyce's work, since exile becomes the fundamental experience not only of the artistic vocation, but of the human condition.

Exile is crucial to the structure of *Ulysses*. The novel's plot is patterned on the struggles of the exile Odysseus to get home after the Trojan War; the novel's characters have confrontations that parallel Odysseus's adventures with the Sirens, Nausicaa, Circe, and others. Joyce anchors his epic of modern life by locating the entire action in Dublin on a single day: June 16, 1904. Many critics argue that Joyce uses his epic parallels ironically, to point up the radical deflation of modern life, in which epic heroism in the Greek style is no longer possible. Other critics insist, perhaps more persuasively, that Joyce's epic parallels are comic but serious, and meant to highlight the magnificent small heroisms possible and necessary in daily life in the twentieth century.

The protagonist of *Ulysses*, Leopold Bloom, is an exile in his own country. A Jew in Catholic Dublin, Bloom is set apart from his fellow Dubliners by barriers of history, culture, and temperament. He is a victim of numerous betrayals, the most notable of which is at the hands of his wife, Molly, who consummates an affair during the novel's course. Yet, for all his alienation, Bloom is a resilient personality. He is intelligent and pragmatic; he is sensitive and kindly; he is a very ordinary good man, an Everyman figure who wanders Dublin in search of peace of mind.

Stephen Dedalus is also an exile in his native land. Having returned from Paris, where he failed to become an artist, he finds himself at odds with everything in Dublin. He holds an enervating teaching job; he cannot live in his father's house. Stephen feels betrayed by his closest friend, Buck Mulligan, whom he calls a "usurper," and senses himself cast out of the Martello Tower on which he has paid the rent. Stephen is even alienated from his vocation as an artist: though he struggles with aesthetic theories, he produces only a few paltry poetic images, scribbled on scraps of paper.

Stephen is fatherless; Bloom is sonless; both are, symbolically, keyless. Their meeting constitutes the novel's climax, a sort of temporary homecoming for both. Through it, Bloom seems to gain some equanimity about his situation and Stephen seems to reinvolve himself with the dailiness of Dublin life, the experience that should constitute the material of his art. Molly Bloom is the presence hovering behind their meeting, a character who, though not seen directly until the novel's last chapter, represents the human desire for passionate immersion in the flux of experience.

But though Bloom and Stephen both symbolically "come home" in *Ulysses*, the weight of their experience as exiles informs the book, and stands as Joyce's most definitive statement about the situation of man in the modern world. As *Ulysses* closes, Bloom has been transformed into "Sinbad the Sailor and Tinbad the Tailor and Jinbad the Jailer"—an archetype of all wanderers through the cosmos. And Stephen, though having found the ground of his art at home where he left it, remains fatherless, friendless, keyless, homeless, and soon to be jobless. Spurred in part by his own life as an exile, and even more by his grasp of the politics and culture of the twentieth century, Joyce came to see modern man as the perpetual wanderer, privy only to the very temporary haven of human contact.

Joyce wrote one surviving dramatic work: *Exiles* (Trieste, 1914–15). *Exiles* uses the idea of exile almost allegorically, since every major character in the play is an exile in some sense—from country, from family, from self. What differentiates *Exiles* from Joyce's other works is that it features a successful writer, self-exiled, who returns to Dublin in triumph rather than defeat. Joyce always nursed a special affection for his only play: though *Exiles* was never a dramatic or commercial success, he campaigned for performances and formed a theatrical company in hopes of producing it. Begun in 1914, when Joyce's first major works were just beginning to be published, *Exiles* sums up the extremes of hope and disappointment that were to remain with Joyce for the rest of his life. On one hand, *Exiles* expresses his longed-for relation to his native land: affectionate acceptance, triumphal return. On the other hand, *Exiles* depicts what Joyce saw, and continued to see, as the reality of his situation: the prospect of rejection, the possibility of betrayal, the necessity of renewed exile. In Joyce's daily world, as in his fictive world, from his early work through his mature career, triumphal return from exile would always remain a luxury of the imagination.

Consult: Bernard Benstock, *James Joyce: The Undiscover'd Country* (1977); Richard Ellmann, *James Joyce* (1959; rev. ed., 1982). See also: Jacques Aubert and Maria Jolas, eds., *Papers from the 5th International James Joyce Symposium, Paris, 16–20 June 1975*,

2 vols. (Paris, 1979); Helene Cixous, *The Exile of James Joyce* (1968); David Daiches, "James Joyce: The Artist as Exile," *College English* 2, no. 3 (1940); Doris L. Eder, *Three Writers in Exile: Pound, Eliot and Joyce* (1985); *James Joyce Quarterly* 9 (1972): 207–49, Joyce and Trieste issue; Willard Potts, ed. *Portraits of the Artist in Exile: Recollections of James Joyce by Europeans* (Seattle, 1979).

KATHERINE C. HILL-MILLER

Joyce's last work was known as *Work in Progress* until its issue in book form in 1939 as *Finnegans Wake*; a corrected edition of *Finnegans Wake* appeared in 1945. (See below for genesis of fragments of *Work in Progress* to *Finnegans Wake*.) Its first serial appearance was in 1925 in the French journal *La Navire d'Argent*; other portions of the work appeared in the Paris-based, English-language little magazine *transition*. An epic rendered in a style of circular flux, it is probably the only extant work of fiction in which all the characters appear in a state of sleep. Joyce structured this work around the drunkenness that follows in the wake of the death of Finnegan (Finn-again), a modern Irishman whose identity may be paralleled in ironic contrast to that of the Irish hero, Finn MacCool. Among the work's archetypal figures are H.C.E. (variously standing for Haveth Childers Everywhere, Humphrey Chimpden Earwicker, Here Comes Everybody, or a specimen of the human plant similar to the comic Bloom of Dublin); Shem and Shaun, two brothers under the skin of their opposing personalities—one wild and irresponsible (the artist), the other conscientious and considerate (the societal man); and Anna Livia Plurabelle, who stands for motherhood in her river-run flow of acceptance of all things. Anna Livia is distinct from her creative but no longer procreative kin Molly Bloom, in that she is all-embracing without any links to self-centered sexuality, which the vibrant, lusty Molly encapsulates. Anna Livia is the bodiless body of the River Liffey, which runs through Dublin and is its source of revitalization.

Profoundly influenced by the eighteenth-century historian Giambattista Vico and his concept of the cycles of history and *ricorso* (return), *Finnegans Wake* erupts and interrupts in epic sweeps of wild humor. Like the subconscious entity that it portrays, the work becomes a transformation of dramatic fantasy and linguistic play into overwhelming shapes of psychic concerns and profoundly private signs. It represents Joyce's closest capture of harmony through the regenerative function of mythic memory. In this subconscious state between life and death, slumber and awakening, in this limbo of becoming where all things rush by in a slow march to their appointed destinies, the author achieves a different kind of epiphany from his earlier ones: an awareness of belonging in a fluid succession of timeless presence, a sense of contemplation of his own identity without intrusion of another's judgment. After Joyce's long dwelling in the house of exile—from his first volume of poems with their lyric laments through the bleakness of *Dubliners*, the growth of strata of consciousness in *A Portrait of the Artist as a Young Man*, and the profoundly wonderful aspects of ordinary comic behavior in *Ulysses* —this last work is a journey outward through the inner being to unmapped areas of language and narrative structure; it reveals the author's sensibility of a self-accepting pace of private symbolism.

Critics differ on whether Joyce is more at home in his almost solitary humors and peculiar humanities of language in *Finnegans Wake*, or whether he is less querulous and more in touch with his humanity in accepting the foibles of his fellows. There is general agreement that in his final work Joyce is more inclusionary and less critical of human folly than in his earlier, more questing personae.

Consult: Joseph Campbell and Henry Morton Robinson, *A Skeleton Key to "Finnegans Wake"* (1944, repr. 1961); Thomas F. Connolly, ed. *Scribbledehobble: The Ur-Workbook for "Finnegans Wake"* (1961); David Hayman, ed., *A First Draft Version of "Finnegans Wake"* (1963); Ellsworth Mason and Richard Ellmann, eds., *The Critical Writings of James Joyce* (1959); John J. Slocum and Herbert Cahoon, *A Bibliography of Joyce* (1953). See also: *Letters of James Joyce*, vol. 1, ed. Stuart Gilbert (1957); vols. 2 and 3, ed. Richard Ellmann (1966).

K

KAČUROVS'KYJ, Ihor. Born September 1, 1918, in Nižyn, Černihiv region, Ukraine. He is a poet, novelist, translator, and literary scholar who currently resides in Munich. Unable to conform to the norms of socialist realism while living in the Soviet Union, Kačurovs'kyj began his literary career in exile in 1946. His first collection of lyric poetry, *Nad svitlym džerelom* (Above the Lucid Spring), published in Salzburg in 1948, revealed the then-young poet's wondrous vision of the West and his profound yearning for his native Ukraine. Toward the end of 1948, Kačurovs'kyj left Austria for Argentina, where he stayed until 1969. Here he published his second collection of poetry, *V dalekij havani* (1956, In a Distant Port), in which motifs of yearning and nostalgia alternate with praise of Argentina's landscape and its exotic beauty. In due course, influences of Spanish and Italian poetry became more palpable in his work, while the yearning for his native land subsided in intensity. Following his return to Europe in 1969, Kačurovs'kyj's poetry assumed a more optimistic note. His verse resounded with an exuberant affirmation of life in the West with its freedom, its natural splendors, and its cultural resources; the exiled poet became a citizen of the world. While Kačurovs'kyj's poems show this remarkable evolution, his prose continues to be steeped in the tradition of literature in exile. His novel *Šlyax nevidomoho* (1956; *Because Deserters Are Immortal*, Doncaster, Australia, 1979) is a moving account of a young Ukrainian trapped between Russians and Germans, who ultimately overcomes his existential despair and finds the meaning of life in an absurd world through acceptance of suffering. Kačurovs'kyj continues to write poetry characterized by a classical form and a manifold rhythmic and strophic variety. He is a member of Argentine (SADE) and German (FDA) Writers Associations.

Selected Titles: Fiction: *Dim nad kručeju* (1966, House over the Cliff). Poetry: *Pisnja pro bilyj parus* (1971, White Sail Song). Translation: *Francesco Petrarcha: Vybrane* (1981, Selected Poems).

Consult: C. H. Andrusyshen and Watson Kirkconnell, *The Ukrainian Poets* (Toronto; University of Toronto Press, 1963), pp. 484–86, provides a biographical note with an English translation of the poem "The Rainy Night"; Bohdan Bojčuk and Bohdan T. Rubčak, *Koordynaty* (Munich, 1969), II; 192–202, 462, is a comprehensive and annotated anthology of contemporary Ukrainian written in the West; Dmytro Chub, *In the Mirror of Life and Literature* (Melbourne, 1982), pp. 110–18, offers basic data on the poet's life and works.

LEONID RUDNYTZKY

KAFKA, Franz. Born July 3, 1883, in Prague, then Austro-Hungarian Empire; died June 3, 1924, in Kierling, Austria-Hungary. Kafka never lived in literal or physical exile, but he may be considered an archetypal figure of psychic exile in that his most intimate thoughts are those of yearning for a harmony to end his affliction of separateness from humankind. Except for short trips to Germany and Switzerland, he lived out his short life in his native land, and largely in his native city of Prague. He died a victim of tuberculosis, but managed to leave a body of work profoundly affecting the aesthetic vision of the twentieth century. Fortunately, his last instructions to his friend and executor Max Brod to destroy his unpublished manuscripts were not carried out. Singularly, Kafka wrote only in German, thus making him acutely aware of exile from language.

Kafka's major works are "In der Strafkolonie" (1919; "In the Penal Colony," 1941); *Ein Hungerkunstler* (1924; *The Hunger Artist*, 1928); *Amerika* (1927; *Amerika*, 1938 [written between 1912 and 1914]); *Der Prozess* ([begun in 1914] 1925; *The Trial*, 1937); *Das Schloss* ([begun 1921] 1926; *The Castle*, 1930). Each treats the exilic sense of isolation and condemnation of "foreignness" within a community where everyone else has a seemingly common understanding with the other. In *The Trial* the crime that the hero commits is never made known; the crime is the dangerous depth of his outsidedness; the hostility he incurs, without effort on his part, is that of his strangeness, or what he and others perceive as his unnatural nature. This sense of difference, raised to profoundly grotesque heights, is encapsulated in Kafka's masterpiece, *Der Verwandlung* (1915; *The Metamorphosis*, 1936), the tale of a man who turns into a beetle/roach. The physical transformation is Kafka's metaphor for the hero's secret knowledge that bursts forth to claim him and expunge him from the bosom of family or friend.

Kafka's influence on modern literature has been enormous both in the use of his symbolic technique and imagery and in his unfree choice of the irrepressible theme of the self's repression out of fear of communal rectitude and scapegoat justice.

In April 1989 it was announced that Kafka's work was again allowed to be published in Czechoslovakia. Odeon, a large publishing house, will issue an ongoing multivolume collection translated from the original German into Czechoslovak. The first of the volumes was scheduled to appear in late 1989, with a supplement of thirty-two previously unpublished letters written by Kafka.

Consult: *Reading Kafka*, ed. Mark Anderson; Max Brod, *Franz Kafka: A Biography* (1947); Stanley Corngold, *Franz Kafka: The Necessity of Form* (1989); Martin Greenberg, *The Terror of Art: Kafka and Modern Literature* (1968); Ernst Pawel, *The Nightmare of Reason* (1984); Heinz Politzer, *Franz Kafka: Parable and Paradox* (1966); Shimon Sandbank, *After Kafka* (1989); J. P. Stern, *The World of Franz Kafka* (1980).

KAISER, Georg. Born November 25, 1878, in Magdenburg, Germany; died June 4, 1945, in Ascona, Switzerland. One of Germany's outstanding expressionist playwrights and novelists, Kaiser fled into exile in 1938. He had remained in his native land until that time although the opprobrious labels "cultural Bolshevism" and "Jewish tendencies" had been attached to his work by Nazi critics, and his books and plays were banned in Germany. Kaiser moved first to Amsterdam, and then to Switzerland. He had hoped to obtain a visa for the United States, but even with vouchers of recommendation from Albert Einstein and Thomas Mann,* he was excluded from American soil. The reason has never been made official, but Kaiser's politically radical beliefs are said to have frightened some influential American bureaucrats.

KALLAS, Aino. Born August 2, 1878, in Viipuri, Finland; died November 9, 1956, in Helsinki, Finland. Kallas married an Estonian scholar, Oskar Kallas, in 1900; they lived in Tartu, Estonia, till 1918. During these years of exile by reason of marriage, Kallas observed peasant life in Estonia and absorbed the history and traditions of her new country; hers was not an exile into fields of alien corn, but an opportunity to grow into a new old culture.

Kallas became an expatriate by reason of her husband's diplomatic service, when he was appointed ambassador to England with the advent of Estonia's independence after World War I; they lived in London from 1922 to 1934. She and her husband fled to Stockholm from Estonia in 1944, and stayed there through 1953, during the last year of the German occupation of Estonia and its subsequent annexation by the USSR. In Stockholm during her only period of literal exile she published six volumes of diaries and memoirs. Her books were written in the Estonian language, and have been translated into Dutch, Italian, Swedish, German, and Hungarian. Fittingly, after a long life in other lands, she returned to the country of her birth to die.

KANE, Cheik Hamidou. Born 1928, in Senegal; he lives in Senegal. Kane studied in Paris from 1952 to 1959. *See* Francophone African Writers in Exile.
Selected Title: *L'aventure ambiguë* (Paris, 1961; *Ambiguous Adventure*, 1961).
Consult: Wilfred Cartey, *Whispers from a Continent* (1969).

KANGRO, Bernard. Born September 18, 1910, in Vana-Antsla, Estonia; he lives in Sweden. Kangro is a novelist, poet, playwright, and editor of the leading émigré publishing house, Estonian Writers Cooperative, in Lund, Sweden. Ivar

Ivask writes that Kangro's poetry is characterized by "symbolism of native soil, alienation, and patriotism." Kangro has written more than thirteen volumes of verse; from 1949 to 1971 he wrote twelve novels. His plays were collected in *Merre vajunud saar* (Island Lost in the Sea) in 1968.

Consult: Ivar Ivask and J. von Wilpert, eds., *World Literature since 1945* (1973).

KATILIŠKIS, Marius (pseudonym of Albinas Vaitkus). Born September 15, 1915, in Gruzdžiai, northern Lithuania; he died December 17, 1980, in Chicago, Illinois. A self-taught writer, Katiliškis worked on road gangs and as a lumberjack in Lithuania. After military service he became a librarian in a small town and read extensively. In 1944 he left Lithuania and later settled in the United States, where he made a living from blue-collar work. His first collection of stories, *Prasilenkimo valanda* (1948, The Hour of Passing By), in part nostalgic and lyrical, in part sardonic, described life in refugee camps after World War II. His next book, *Užuovėja* (1952, The Shelter), was dedicated to his native village and its people, and depicted, in the vein of Knut Hamsun, their bond with country life. Its rich and innovative style attracted the attention of émigré critics. His full-length novel *Miškais ateina ruduo* (1957, Autumn Comes through the Forests) is probably his magnum opus. Showing the influence of Scandinavian writers, the novel also is reminiscent of William Faulkner in its concerns with universal passions and the confrontation of nature and civilization. In his next novel, *Išėjusiems negrįžti* (1958, Point of No Return), Katiliškis describes the experience of Lithuanians forced to serve in the German army in 1944–45; in his choice of uncommon material and his ironic style, this work has been judged a major achievement. His stories in the collection *Šventadienis už miesto* (1963, Holiday in the Countryside) draw upon the experiences of Lithuanian émigrés in the United States. At the end of his life Katiliškis had developed into an accomplished writer who influenced Lithuanian literature not only in exile but in his homeland. His novel *Miškais ateina ruduo*, reprinted in Lithuania in 1969, was a great success there.

Consult: R. Šilbajoris, *Perfection of Exile* (1970).

TOMAS VENCLOVA

KAZANTZAKIS, Nikos. Born February 18, 1883, in Herakleion, Crete; died October 26, 1957, in Freiburg, Germany. The only son of Michael Kazantzakis, a simple peasant, and Maria Christodoulaki, a kindly, saintlike woman, Kazantzakis attended school in Herakleion until 1897, when the Cretan Revolution forced the family to take refuge in Naxos. There he spent the next two years (1897–99) at the French School of the Holy Cross directed by Franciscan monks. In 1899 he continued his studies at the gymnasium at Herakleion and graduated in 1902; he studied law in the University of Athens from 1902 to 1906. In 1906 he published his first book, *The Serpent and the Lily*, a novella written under the name Karma Nirvami, and dedicated to Toto, the pet name he had for Galatea Alexiou whom he married in 1911.

From 1907 to 1909 he studied philosophy at the Sorbonne in Paris, and with Henri Bergson at the Collège de France. In 1908 he wrote his dissertation, *Frederick Nietzsche and the Philosophy of the Right*, published in Herakleion in 1909. In 1908 he wrote a tragic play entitled *Sacrifice*, which received the Lassaneiou Award. It was published in 1910 as *The Master Builder*, dedicated to the Greek diplomat Ion Dragoumis; the play later became the libretto of the first opera by Manolis Kalomiris.

In 1911 he translated Bergson's *Laughter*. In the Balkan War of 1912–13, Kazantzakis enlisted as a volunteer serving in the office of Eleuthérios Venizélos, who enacted a policy in defense of the demotic language. It was decided to introduce the demotic language in the first three classes of elementary school. A competition was announced. Kazantzakis and his wife Galatea entered the competition, wrote a primer and five books, all of which won awards.

With the money he had received from these awards Kazantzakis began his extensive travels. In 1914–15 he made a pilgrimage to the Holy places of Greece with the poet Anghelos Sikelianos. From 1916 to 1917 he was in Mani with Alexis Zorbas exploring the lignite mine at Prestova, a trip that resulted in the novel *Alexis Zorba*. In 1919 he was appointed director general of the Ministry of Public Welfare, a post he held to November 1920. In 1920–21 he traveled to Crete, France, and Germany; in 1922, to Vienna and Germany.

From September 22 until December 31, 1923, he was in Berlin, "immersed in communist ideas and possessed by the revolutionary fervor enveloping Germany of that time" (Georgopoulos, 179). However, influenced as he was by Bergson's philosophy, he could not fully accept Marx's basic thesis that economics constitutes the absolute foundation of the socio-political structure and is the reason and cause of any change. In Berlin, Kazantzakis embarked on a mystical work entitled *Spiritual Exercises* (translated by Kimon Friar as *Saviors of God*), which he wrote between the end of December 1922 and the end of 1923. He called his *Spiritual Exercises* his "Meta-communist Credo," higher in the spiritual scale than either capitalism or communism. *Saviors of God* is concerned with the ascension of the soul to God. As soon as the book was published, he was accused of "atheism."

On January 18, 1924, Kazantzakis left Germany and traveled to Italy. In 1924 he and Galatea were divorced. In Herakleion in the autumn of 1924, he took part in an unsuccessful, illegal political action with the local communists and was arrested. All that remains of that experience is his "Apology" to the examining magistrate, which Prevelakis calls a "synopsis of Kazantzakis's political views."

In October 1925 he left for the Soviet Union. This trip lasted three and a half months. On his second visit to the Soviet Union, October-December 1927, he went as an officially invited guest (the only person from Greece) for the tenth anniversary of the Russian Revolution, and participated in the Communist World Congress by expressing his convictions about the threat of a new world war. Kazantzakis argued that the proletariat should prepare for it; this was in disagreement with the view held by the other delegates, who believed that such a war should be avoided.

In the spring of 1928 he made a third trip to the Soviet Union, where he met Panait Istrati in Kiev. He left the Soviet Union on April 19, 1929, stayed for about three weeks in Berlin, and on May 10 settled in Gottesgab, Czechoslovakia. Here he began to write *Toda Raba* in French. *Traveling: Russia*, a one-volume edition of his impressions, was published in Athens soon after his return from his last trip to the Soviet Union.

With Panait Istrati and D. Glynos, a leading intellectual of the left, Kazantzakis organized a meeting at the Alhambra where both he and Istrati spoke on "the Russian fate." It aroused a passionate response in the audience. Three days later, the public prosecutor ordered an investigation. Istrati was asked to leave the country; a trial date was set for Glynos and Kazantzakis, but it was repeatedly postponed. Nonetheless, Kazantzakis was accused of being a Russian agent, even though his books were banned in the Soviet Union. The Greek Communist Party refused to include him in its ranks, labeling him bourgeois, decadent, and even fascist.

Kazantzakis had been working on his heroic epic *The Odyssey* (translated by Kimon Friar as *The Odyssey: A Modern Sequel*), from the completion of the first draft on September 22, 1927, through four versions until its first publication in 1938. Written in twenty-four books, one for each letter of the Greek alphabet, it starts from Odysseus's return to Ithaca and goes to his death. Its central theme is modern man in search of a soul and God.

During the years of the German occupation (1941–44) Kazantzakis lived in Aegina. In the spring of 1941 he wrote *Buddha*, "a hymn to the pride and dignity of man." At the end of May 1941 Crete fell to the Germans. In the autumn of 1941 Kazantzakis attempted to join the partisans in the mountains but was rejected. In Aegina he wrote *Alexis Zorba, Kapodistrias, Prometheus Trilogy*, and *Constantine Palaeologus*.

The Civil War followed almost immediately after the liberation of Greece. In May 1945 he was elected the first president of the Socialistiki Ergatiki Enosi (Socialist Labor Union). The same year he became minister without portfolio in the Sophoulis government, a position he resigned from a few months later. On November 11, 1945, he married Eleni Samios, with whom he had been living for eighteen years. In the summer of 1946, while Kazantzakis was in England, a plebiscite brought back the king. Disheartened by the victory of the royalists (to whom he was always anathema), and embittered by the situation in Greece, he moved to France, never to see Greece again. In May 1947 he was appointed to the post of director of translations of the classics in Paris. He resigned this post on March 25, 1948, and moved to the south of France, where he turned to his literary activity.

"Now I am crossing the stage—will it be the last?—that I call freedom. No shadow whatever, only my own *long, dark, black ascending* pole" (Prevelakis, *400 Letters*, 465). His wife calls this period (1942–57) the period of the great novels and the two monumental translations of Homer's *Iliad* and *Odyssey*, the former completed in close collaboration with Professor Kakridis. With the exception of *Alexis Zorba*, all his novels date from this time; all of them express the force of his heritage that he called "The Cretan Glance": *Sodom and Gomorrah* (1948), *The Greek Passion* (1948), *Freedom or Death* (1950), *The Last Temptation* (1951), *The Poor Man of God* (1953), *Fratricides* (1954), and *Report to Greco* (1956–57).

In 1956 he received the National Drama Award for his two volumes of dramatic works. The International Peace Prize was bestowed on him in Vienna on June 29, 1956. He was invited to the People's Republic of China. In his homeland, however, the vilification of Kazantzakis continued with much talk about his antireligious heroes. *The Last Temptation* was put on the Papal Index. The Holy Synod banned the circulation of the book in Greece. Herakleion alone defended its offspring by placing a commemorative plaque on the wall of the house where he was born and naming the street after him. It was *The Last Temptation* that led the Greek Orthodox Church in Athens to refuse burial to Kazantzakis within its province. The poet was given a "legendary burial" in Herakleion on the Martinengo rampart overlooking the city.

At the time of his death in 1957 his works had been translated into some thirty languages.

Consult: Peter Bien, *Kazantzakis: Politics of the Spirit* (1989); Kimon Friar, Introduction, *The Odyssey: A Modern Sequel* by Kazantzakis (1958); N. Georgopoulos, "Marxism and Kazantzakis," in *Byzantine and Modern Greek Studies*, vol. 3 (1977); Pantelis Prevalakis, *Nikos Kazantzakis and His Odyssey: A Study of the Poet and the Poem* (Athens, 1958, 1961); Pantelis Prevalakis, *Tetrakosia Grammata tou Kazantzakis ston Prevelaki* (Athens, 1965, 400 Letters). For biography, consult Helen Kazantzakis, *Nikos Kazantzakis* (1968); see also Elly Alexiou, *Gia Na Ginei Megalos* (Athens, 1966, Bent on Greatness); Peter Bien, *Kazantzakis and the Linguistic Revolution* (1972); Peter Bien, *Kazantzakis: Politics of the Spirit* (1989); Peter Bien, *Nikos Kazantzakis: Novelist* (1989); Kazantzakis, *Suffering God: Selected Letters to Galatea and Papastephanou*, eds. Philip Ramp and Katerina Anghelake Rooke (1979); Nikephorus Vrettakos, *H Agonia tou kai ta Erga Tou* (Athens, 1960).

RAE DALVEN

KEDZIERSKI, Marek. Born September 9, 1951, in Lodz, Poland. He maintains residences in New England and in Baden-Baden, Federal Republic of Germany. Kedzierski is a scholar-writer who took his training at the University of Warsaw (Ph.D., 1979, modern tragedy). His main field has been contemporary drama, with particular emphasis on Samuel Beckett,* and theory of literature. In 1986 he resigned his post at the University of Warsaw and moved to West Germany. He has held guest lectures at German universities, written contributions for Polish and West German radio (a version of Beckett's *Company*, among others), and many articles on Beckett. Kedzierski is the author of two books on Beckett's oeuvre, one with Jan Błoński, and is at work on a third. In 1981 he retranslated Beckett's *Endgame* into Polish for a production at the Stary Theater in Cracow, which he codirected with Walter D. Asmus. While in Germany, he prepared the 1990 Thomas Bernhard issue of the Warsaw magazine *Literatura na Swiecie* (World Literature).

An excerpt of his novel *lucid intervals, blind summits*, written directly in English, appeared in a limited edition in New York in 1986. The novel is rendered in what may be considered an exilic genre—that is, a tale by a composer in exile about an artist who has chosen to remain behind, thus becoming an "obscure" personage in a conformist land. Kedzierski's view of displacement and identity is rendered through distance of observer in spheres both of time and place, with memory in its willful selectivity serving as a guiding half-light in the discourse of discovery.

KENEALLY, Thomas. Born October 7, 1935, in Sydney, Australia; he lives in Sydney. Keneally taught English in high school before succeeding as a writer with *Bring Larks and Heroes* (1967). *The Chant of Jimmie Blacksmith* (1972) secured his place in Australian literature of alienation. He then spent a decade in England and the United States, during which time his interest in moral outsiders and historical watersheds moved into new geographical areas.

As a historical novelist, Keneally is preoccupied with the displaced individual, especially when that displacement comes on behalf of a lost cause. Thus, his early works focus upon the mistakes and misunderstandings that lead to extreme action in a repressive society: *Bring Larks* deals with the penal colonization of Australia, *Jimmie Blacksmith* with a rampaging murderer of mixed white and Aboriginal ancestry, and *Blood Red, Sister Rose* (1974), with Joan of Arc. The authenticity of physical detail in these works is striking—Keneally is a thorough researcher—but the characters' attributed concerns and patterns of expression often seem modern overlays.

Keneally's residence abroad extended the range of his historical interests, while adding coherence to his characterizations and sometimes enlivening the rather wooden prose that marked the early works. His issues have remained consistent: *Gossip from the Forest* (1967) examines the end of World War I from the German point of view; *Season in Purgatory* (1977) is concerned with Yugoslavian partisans in World War II; *Confederates* (1979) depicts the American Civil War; and *Schindler's List* (1982; *Schindler's Ark* outside the United States) deals with the rescue of European Jews from the Nazis. Despite continuing problems with style, Keneally has a remarkable eye for events. His work is most accomplished when he provides genuine characters who respond to outrageous circumstances of history.

Keneally discusses his motivations and techniques of historical fiction in "Doing Research for Historical Novels," *Australian Author* 7, no.1 (1975).

JOHN SCHECKTER

KERRIGAN, Anthony. Born March 14, 1918, in Winchester, Massachusetts; he lives in South Bend, Indiana. Kerrigan was brought up in Havana, Cuba, with schooling in the United States. He served in the U.S. Army Intelligence

Corps during World War II. Since 1951 he has lived in France, Spain, and Ireland, and now resides in Indiana, where he is a senior research fellow at the Helen Kellogg Institute for International Studies at Notre Dame. Kerrigan wrote in a letter to the editor: "Six children trace an exilic trajectory: Michael (born Hollywood), Antonia (born Paris), Camilo (born Palma de Mallorca), Patrick (born Palma), Elie (born Dublin, Ireland), Malachy (born Palma)." Kerrigan has held American university posts and considers the United States "the definitive refuge remaining for permanent exiles from whatever country." He describes himself as having come "out of Cuba a Communist in his teens" and claims that his "Red record, released from the F.B.I. through the Freedom of Information Act, cost him dearly, just as his vigorously evolving anti-Communist stance subsequently cost him dearly."

Kerrigan is an outspoken writer often embroiled in controversy. He is a poet, an art critic, and a translator (with some fifty titles to his credit). He is best known for his translation of the seven-volume edition of *The Selected Works of Miguel de Unamuno*, for which he has received several prestigious awards and prizes.

More expatriate than exile, Kerrigan claims a kinship with the outsider and reflects, proudly, this sense of lonely polemicism in his work.

KESTEN, Hermann. Born January 28, 1900, in Podwoloczyska, near Tarnapol in Austrian Galizia; he lives in Basel, Switzerland. Kesten wrote his dissertation on Heinrich Mann at Erlangen University but never finished it. From 1927 to 1933 he was reader, then chief literary editor at the Kiepenheuer publishing company where he nurtured such writers as Bertolt Brecht, Gottfried Benn, and Anna Seghers. His own work, mainly novels, had been translated into several languages before the Third Reich came into existence.

Kesten, who was not a religious man, was attacked in the Nazi press for his Jewish background. He moved to Paris in 1933 and from there to Amsterdam, where he founded the German literature division at Allert de Lange's publishing company (he stayed there, as editor-in-chief of that division, until the invasion of Holland by the German army). In 1935 his books were banned in Germany; in response to growing censorship, Kesten co-founded the Union of Free Press and Literature, the association of independent German writers and literature in exile. In 1940, while visiting Paris, he was caught in the German invasion and was interned by the occupiers. However, after five weeks, Kesten was able to escape. He fled to New York, where he became active in assisting endangered writers. He collaborated with Thomas Mann and other writers in operating the Emergency Rescue Committee to aid refugees in their emigration to the United States. He wrote for exile publications, including the *Aufbau* (Rebuilding), *Deutsche Blätter* (German Papers), *Mass und Wert* (Measure and Worth), *Neue Deutsche Blätter* (New German Papers), *Das Neue Tagebuch* (The New Diary), *Die Neue Weltbühne* (New World Stage), *Die Sammlung* (Collection), and *Die*

Zukunft (Future). Kesten became an American citizen and remained in the United States through 1949.

From 1949 to 1951 Kesten lived in various European cities; in 1952 he moved to Rome, and in 1977 he returned to the United States, only to return again to Italy in the 1980s—"a poet in exile who has never returned home." In 1975 he turned down an offer by the city of Munich to return there; however, he did accept an honorary doctorate from the University of Erlangen and the presidency of the German PEN Center (1972–76).

Kesten devoted much of his artistic vision to the flaying of bourgeois hypocrisy, and particularly to those middle-class values which exalted safety and comfort over honesty and resistance to tyranny of whatever devious kind. His postwar fiction is often the emotional reflection of a witness to acquiescence to barbarism. At times savagely sketched, his work makes up in passion what it may lack in subtlety. Many of his critics went through gyrations of reaction over his postwar writing; some of them could not relate to Kesten's unusual combination of the erotic and the political, the satiric and the non-theatrical, the entertaining and the poetic. In sum, Kesten's writings defy many conventions, and as a result of his political engagement and refusal to honor taboos and self-censorship, he has been criticized by some critics as frivolous. Given German literary traditions, such antagonism comes as little surprise.

At his best, Kesten was a deeply philosophical and poetic voice. "Slowly the tree bends under snow and the weight of life," he wrote in his volume of poems, *Ich bin der ich bin: Verse eines Zeitgenossen* (Munich, 1974, I am who I am).

Selected Titles: *Josef sucht die Freiheit* (Potsdam, 1927; London, 1950, *Joseph Breaks Free*); *Einer sagt die Wahrheit* (Berlin, 1930, One Says the Truth, drama); with Ernst Toller, *Wunder in Amerika: Mary Baker Eddy* (Berlin, 1931; *Mary Baker Eddy*); *Der Gerechte: Roman* (Munich, 1934, The Just); *Die Kinder von Guernika: Roman* (Munich, 1939: The Children of Guernica: A Novel, 1939); *The Twins of Nuremberg* (1946; Amsterdam, 1947, *Die Zwillinge von Nürnberg: Roman*); *Meine Freunde, die Poeten* (Vienna, 1959, My Friends, the Poets); *Die Abenteuer eines Moralisten: Roman* (1961, Adventures of a Moralist); *Lauter Literaten: Portraits, Kritik an Zeitgenossen, Erinnerungen* (Vienna, 1963, All Literary Types: Portraits, Critique of Contemporaries, Memoirs); *Die Zeit der Narr En: Roman* (1966, The Time of the Fools); *Die Lust am Leben: Bocaccio, Aretino, Casanova* (Munich, 1968, The Joy of Living); *Ein Mann von sechzig Jahren* (Munich, 1972, A Man of Sixty Years); *Heine im Exil* (Cologne, 1972, Heine in Exile). See *Ausgewählte Werke in 20 Einzebanden*, 20 vol (Frankfurt, 1980–84, Collected Works).

Consult: Walter Seifert, "Exil als politischer Akt: Der Romancier Hermann Kesten," in *Die deutsche Exilliteratur 1933–1945*, ed. Manfred Durzak (Stuttgart, 1973); John M. Spalek, *Guide to the Archival Materials of the German-Speaking Emigration to the United States after 1933* (Charlottesville: University of Virginia, 1978); Hans-Albert Walter, *Deutsche Exilliteratur 1933–1950* (Darmstadt, 1972).

HENRIK EGER and MARTIN TUCKER

KGOSITSILE, Keorapetse (William Kgositsile). Born 1938 in Johannesburg, South Africa; after living in the United States he has returned to Africa to teach at the university level in Dar es Salaam, Tanzania. Kgositsile worked on the journal *New Age* in Cape Town before leaving South Africa for Dar es Salaam, Tanzania, where he worked on *Spearhead* magazine. He studied at several universities in the United States; he was at the New School for Social Research in 1962 and at Columbia University later; he also attended Lincoln University in Pennsylvania, where a number of other African writers and scholars were students. During the past two decades he has taught and lived in several areas of the United States. Kgositsile's collections of poems include *Spirits Unchained: Paeans* (1969); *For Melba* (1969); and *My Name Is Afrika* (1971). His is a voice full of energy and anger; his early work sparked real enthusiasm, but his recent work has seemed less inventive.

KHAZAHNOV, Boris (pseudonym of Gennadi M. Faibusovich). Born in 1928 in Leningrad, USSR; he lives with his family in Munich, Germany. Khazahnov studied classical philology at Moscow University from 1945 to 1949. In his fifth year at the university he was arrested and sentenced to eight years in a labor camp on a charge of anti-Soviet propaganda. He remained in the correctional labor camp, Unzhlag, in Unza until 1955. In 1961 he graduated from the Medical Institute in the town of Kalinin, and for the next sixteen years he worked as a physician, first in the rural areas and later in Moscow. In 1967 he received a master's degree in medical science. From 1967 to 1981 he was a feature editor for the popular science magazine *Chemistry and Life*, sponsored by the Academy of Science of the USSR.

Khazahnov was the editor-author-consultant of the underground magazine *Jews in the USSR* until its liquidation in 1980. Because of his samizdat operations and his outspoken writings published abroad, he was subject to harassment and persecution. The threat of new imprisonment impelled him to emigrate with his family in August 1982.

Khazahnov published *The Extraordinary Consultation* (1976) and *The Boy at the Ocean's Shore* (1981), a biography of Isaac Newton, in the USSR, but his work "An Inquiry into the Matter of Cause," a study of the problems of medical philosophy, was banned, and existing copies destroyed, when the author emigrated.

Khazahnov has published in Russian *The Scent of the Stars* (Tel Aviv, 1976) a collection of stories and essays, and *Walking on Water* (Munich, 1985). Also in 1985, *I Am the Resurrection and the Life*, a collection of two novellas, was issued in Russian by a New York publishing house. The novella *I Am the Resurrection and the Life* treats the period of mass arrests ordered by Stalin in 1937 and centers on a child who bears witness to the atrocities. The companion novella *Anti-Time*, which was confiscated by the KGB and later rewritten by the author, is a story of love that unites three young people and is told many years later by the only remaining participant. Khazahnov has also written short fiction utilizing as its grim setting the Soviet concentration and labor camps of the Stalinist era. To this group of related settings belong "The Scent of the Stars," "Look into My Stern Eyes," "On the Deaf Mute Taiga," and "The Road to the Station.'' One critic has characterized Khazahnov's work in the following manner: ''With the same laborious persistence that Robinson Crusoe exhibited in recreating around himself the symbols of his lost civilization, Khazahnov creates his narratives, stories, essays out of the condition of the 'uninhabited Russia,' the splinters of European humanism.'' The same critic asserts that a willed loneliness permeates Khazahnov's work, a sense of alienation in Khazahnov's self-imposed identity as a Jew and intellectual outsider.

Khazahnov utilizes contemporary techniques in his fiction and nonfiction. He does not shun symbolism and/or fantasy, yet writes in a clear and laconic language, creating with varied materials a one-and-the-same life situation, the loneliness of a man forsaking his dignity before the menacing forces of an inexorable history, a despotic government, and/or the depths of his own emotional state. Khazahnov's work is ultimately more analytical than ideological in its concerns. Khazahnov has likened his attitude to that of the Russian poet Alexandr Blok: ''The soul is harassed by Russia in the twentieth century.''

Commentary on Khazahnov's work may be found in *Syntax*, no. 17; *Studies in Soviet Thought*, vol. 33, and in *Kontinent* (1977). Y. Mal'tsev devoted a section in his study *Free Russian Literature* (1980, German edition) to Khazahnov's work.

Khazahnov is an editor of the Russian-language magazine, *The Country and the World*, founded in 1984.

MARK A. POPOVSKY, translated by Zoric Ward

KHODASEVICH, Vladislav Relitsianovich. Born May 16, 1886, in Moscow, Russia; died June 14, 1939, in Paris, France. Khodasevich believed Russian culture had slipped into an era of decadence with its emphasis on experimentation and new and mixed forms of expression. He regarded it as his goal to restore the traditions of classical Russian harmony and versification to his country's aesthetic. An apolitical person to the core, he left the USSR in 1922 to carry his program into the camp of young exiles in Paris. His personal circumstances of poverty and loneliness took their toll, and he became an anachronistic figure preaching a prophecy of the Old Order. Khodasevich supported himself in meager fashion by writing articles and criticism for refugee and émigré journals.

Khodasevich left behind him a body of work that included poetry, criticism, essays, memoirs, and translations. Although he died feeling himself irrelevant to a world blinded by barbarism and vulgarity, he has been heralded in recent years as a craftsman of an extraordinary order. In *Sovremennye zapiski*, volume 59 (Paris, 1939), Vladimir Nabokov called him ''the greatest Russian poet of our time. . . . The pride of Russian poetry as long as its last memory lives.'' In 1973 Nabokov translated his commentary into English for inclusion in his volume of literary essays, *Strong Opinions*.

Selected Title: *O Pushkine* (1937).

Consult: Robert Hughes, ''Khodasevich: Irony and Dislocation: A Poet in Exile,'' *Triquarterly* 28 (1973), reprinted in *The Bitter Air of Exile: Russian Writers in the West*

1922–1972, ed. Simon Karlinsky and Alfred Appel, Jr. (1977); Vladimir Nabokov, "On Khodasevich"[1939], in *Strong Opinions* (1973).

KIM, Kyung Jae. Born November 3, 1942, in Soonchun (or Sunchon), South Korea; he lives in New York City. While a political science major at the National University of Seoul, Kim took part in the April Revolution of 1960, which overthrew the government of President Syngman Rhee. In 1971 Kim joined the political campaign of opposition leader Kim Dae Jung as press secretary in the latter's presidential bid against Park Chung Hee. Park's military government narrowly won the election. Soon afterward Kim was arrested by military police and tortured while in detention. After the Park government reversed its policy of detaining dissidents, Kim was released and ordered to immediate exile. He came to the U.S. in 1972 and studied political science at the University of Pennsylvania. In 1974 he persuaded Kim Hyung Wook, former chief of the Korean CIA, to collaborate with him on a book that would expose the clandestine activities of the Korean CIA in the United States. The "Korea-gate" book, which was to take two years to write and be based on numerous secret documents and taped interviews, was subject to approval by Kim Hyung Wook. When the former Korean CIA official disappeared in Paris in 1979, Kim felt he was released from his vow of silence and published his three-volume study, *Revolution and Idol.* Although the work was banned in South Korea, Kim persuaded a publisher friend in his country to issue 150,000 copies of the book. The Chun Doo Hwan government suspended the license of the publishing house, and the publisher went into hiding.

Kim's literary endeavors include short stories and essays he wrote before exile, and his one longer work of fiction, *The Midnighters* (Seoul, 1977), a realistic treatment of farmers, laborers, and intellectuals under dictatorial rule. In many of his creative works, Kim assumes the name of Saul Park in admiration of the Nobel Laureate Saul Bellow. At present Kim writes educational columns and social commentaries for the *Korean Independent Monitor*, a weekly paper in New York, of which he is publisher and editor.

DOROTHY TSUNGSU WEISSMAN

KIM, Richard E. Born March 13, 1932, in Hamhung City, Korea; he teaches in Shutesburg, Massachusetts. Kim was educated in South Korea and, at age eighteen, became an officer in the South Korean army during the Korean War in the 1950s. He emigrated to the United States in 1954; he published his first novel, *The Martyred,* written in English, in 1964. It is the story of a young captain in the South Korean army who is ordered to investigate the mystery of fourteen Christian ministers who had been held captive by the Communists, of whom only two survived. In the course of his investigation, the young officer uncovers evidence that causes him to question his own categories of right and wrong, belief and hypocrisy, patriotism and treason. Kim uses the Korean War as background for his descent into the paradoxes of morality; he writes his tale in a spare style akin to that of Albert Camus (to whose inspiration he pays tribute in the dedicatory page). Kim has his protagonist end his report with the death of Mr. Shin, one of the two surviving ministers, whose last words are: "Love man, Captain. Help him!" But the novel ends with a coda in which the young captain must face the further mystery of Shin's resurrection in North Korea as a vision seen of a Christian ministering angel, and of the death of a young Korean marine officer who had doubted the good works of Christianity. Ultimately Kim's novel is about conscience and admission of belief. In raising the curtain on the mystery of belief, the novel attempts no answer other than a nourishing speculation.

The Martyred, although rejected many times by American publishers, was published in 1964 to critical acclaim and became a best-seller. Kim teaches creative writing at the University of Massachusetts in Amherst. He became an American citizen in 1964.

Selected Titles: *The Innocent* (1968); *Lost Names: Scenes from a Boyhood in Japanese-Occupied Korea* (1988, stories).

KINCAID, Jamaica. Born May 25, 1949, in St. John's, Antigua; she lives in New York City. Kincaid says that as early as her ninth birthday she prayed to be sent to America. She came to the United States in 1966 and achieved early success with her pieces for the *New Yorker* magazine. She joined the staff of that magazine in 1976 . She has published four books, all dealing with the theme of exile and displacement: *At the Bottom of the River* (1983), a collection of stories; *Annie John* (1985), a novel; *A Small Place* (1989), an essay on the West Indian diaspora; *Lucy* (1990), an autobiographical novel in which the heroine attempts to cross the divides of her various exiles, those from childhood to adulthood, those from a Caribbean island to an American metropolis, those from the comforts of parochialism to the frustrations of a larger quest for meaning.

Consult: Anne Tyler, "Mothers and Mysteries," *New Republic* 189 (December 31, 1983); Leslie Garris, "Through West Indian Eyes," *New York Sunday Times Magazine*, October 7, 1990.

KIPPHARDT, Heinar. Born 1922, Germany; died 1982, Federal Republic of Germany. Kipphardt was an enthusiastic supporter of the German Democratic Republic after the close of World War II; his play *Shakespeare dringend gesucht* (1953, Shakespeare Urgently Needed) was particularly popular in the GDR. He moved to West Germany in 1963 in disillusionment. His documentary drama, *In der Sache J. Robert Oppenheimer* (1964, *In the Matter of J. Robert Oppenheimer*, 1967), has been produced frequently in the United States in translation. His other dramatic work includes *Der Hund des Generals* (1963, The General's Dog); and two other documentary dramas, *Joel Brand* (1965, Joel Brand) and *Bruder Eichmann* (1982, Brother Eichmann).

KIRSCH, Sarah. Born April 16, 1935, in Limlingerode/Harz, Germany; she lives in West Berlin. Kirsch was one of several writers and intellectuals who emigrated from the German Democratic Republic to the Federal Republic of Germany in 1977 to protest against the expulsion of the dissident writer Wolf Biermann. In Kirsch's case she moved from one part of Berlin to another part separated by a great wall. She had published several volumes of poetry in East Germany; in West Germany she continued her personal and intense explorations of existential issues, using as a literary device the balm of nature as a restorative to worldly pain. She also published several novels and volumes of nonfiction.

Kirsch's book, *The Panther Woman: Five Tales from the Cassette Recorder*, appeared in the United States in 1989. The compilation, based on talks, recorded on cassette, with five women in East Germany who tell about their lives, emphasizes Kirsch's role in the European women's movement. Among the "speakers" who tell their "tales" are a tamer of circus panthers, a political activist imprisoned in World War II who later became a leader in building a socialist society, and a commercial manager who interjects comments on her frustrated love life as she describes her goals, her education, and her "professional choices."

Selected Titles: *La Pagerie* (1980, The Pagery); *Erdreich* (1982, Earth Domain); *Katzenleben* (1984, Cats' Lives).

Consult: Silvia Volckmann, *Zeit der Kirschen? Das Naturbildinder deutscher Gegenwartslyrik: Jürgen Becker, Sarah Kirsch, Wolf Biermann, Hans Magnus Enzenberger* (Konigstein, 1982).

KIŠ, Danilo. Born February 22, 1935, in Subotica, Yugoslavia; died October 15, 1989, in Paris, France. Kiš died of cancer of the lungs after a long illness to which he refused to surrender his spirit. Two months before his death he was still planning to attend the PEN International Congress in Toronto/Montreal, Canada, in September 1989; he had, to outward appearance, beaten the cancer in one lung caused at least in part by his earlier heavy smoking. The cancer returned to ember out the life in mid-career of what many critics consider a major world writer.

Kiš's father was a Hungarian Jew; his mother came from Montenegro. He was baptized into the Orthodox faith in 1939 in Novi Sad, Yugoslavia, a conversion that saved his life in Nazi-occupied Hungary, where the family lived until after World War II. At thirteen, he moved with his mother to Yugoslavia. He graduated from the Philosophic Faculty in Belgrade with a degree in comparative literature; his first published texts were in literary journals in 1953. Kiš taught Serbo-Croatian language and literatures in France (Strasbourg, Bordeaux, Lille) in the 1960s and 1970s. Afterwards he alternatively lived in Paris (France) and in Belgrade, convinced that a double identity was necessary for a poet's spirit to survive. Throughout his work he glorified the myth of the exile in literature. He wrote in 1983, with a characteristic touch of understatement, a definition of his self-imposed exile: "During the last few years I've been living in Paris, in the ninth arrondissement and I am not homesick. When I wake up in the morning I usually don't know where I am. I can hear my countrymen yelling in the street. From their cars, parked under my window, the accordion is shrieking loudly from their record-players.''

Kiš's father was the author of a standard European railway guide, a work that became a personal cult-book for Kiš and one often quoted in his own work. In Kiš's fictional/factual genealogical tables his father's name was transposed into Eduard Sam, who went to school in Dublin, the birthplace of one of Kiš's literary idols, James Joyce,* and of Joyce's character Mr. Virag, the ancestor of the wandering Irish Jew Leopold Bloom. From his mother, Kiš inherited, proudly, a dislike of romantic fiction—novels particularly—because of the "falsehood" and "lies" implicit to her in the genre. This dislike led in Kiš's poetics to his special form of "faction," or documented fiction.

Kiš's entire family, with the exception of his mother and himself, were exterminated in Auschwitz. Through his unusual sense of humor and balance, Kiš was able to transmute this experience into high literature, employing both factual and imagined detail. In discussing his own philosophic/aesthetic work, *Homo poeticus* (Belgrade, 1983), he wrote that banality lasts longer than a synthetic bottle; the remark was both an artistic warning to himself and an awareness of the power of common facts.

Kiš translated literary texts from Russian, contemporary and classical French, and from the Hungarian; Arthur Koestler* was another of his literary idols. In 1962 he published his first novel. It consisted of two units: "Mansarda, Satirička poema" (The Attic: A Satiric Poem), a work full of optimism and joy at the coming world, and "Witz," a portrait of the author as a young man. His following novel, *Psalam 44* (Psalm 44), published in the same year (1962), is characterized by what became his dominant preoccupation: the Holocaust and the suffering of the Jewish people. *Psalam 44* is structured as a series of seemingly real (factic) documents. His next novel, *Bašta, pepeo* (1969; *Garden, Ashes*, 1975), begins a genealogical cycle to which Kiš will return in later works; it represents his aesthetic homage to his family, and metaphorically to all suffering people throughout history. The novel draws on the myth of the Wandering Jew as well as the history of the Holocaust and its awesome horrors. The boy narrator must face the phantoms of his subconscious history and the realities of his biography—in particular, a father who collects railway and airplane timetables of many lines and at a certain point begins to disappear into his own mysterious journeys, resurfacing into his family's life when they have begun to lose track of him. The father is, for example, lost in the miasma of the tales that the family hears of the Holocaust victims, yet like a legendary figure of patriarchal vitality, he continues to return to the clearing of his natal village. In Kiš's rendering the father becomes a dominant figure of history that the boy must learn to face and to pass by in order to create his own, new history. The symbolism in Kiš's first novel is sometimes apparent and intrusive, but the passionate sincerity of his tone captures the reader in a sweep of lyric narrative. The work catapulted Kiš into the first rank of Yugoslavian literary figures, and his succeeding works were greeted with praise from official quarters as well as independent literary organs.

Garden, Ashes was followed by *Rani jadi: Za decu i osetljive* (Belgrade, 1970; *Early Sadness and Other Stories*, 1984), a collection of fictionalized memoirs of childhood. In *Peščanik* (1972; *The Hourglass*, 1990—the title may also be translated as The Sandglass), named the best Yugoslav novel of the year, Kiš reconstructed, on the basis of one seemingly real letter, the life of a Central European family. It is important to note again that in spite of Kiš's passion for documentation, his literary expression surpasses mere historical recitation and brings to his fiction a universality and an aesthetic authority.

Kiš's problems with Yugoslav officialdom and certain members of the Yugoslav press began with the publication of his documentary novel, *Grobnica za Borisa Davidovicá* (1976; *A Tomb for Boris Davidovich*, 1978). A confederation of stories cohering around the destiny of a victim of one of Stalin's pogroms, the stories brought Kiš international acclaim but at the same time severe polemics in his country about the legitimacy of his poetics and techniques. Questions were raised as to whether he was "creatively" writing or merely establishing the verity of his fiction by documentary evidence. He was charged with failure to provide clear indication of when and where he was reprinting others' work and when and where he was presenting his own words. In the public discussions that followed, critics argued the responsibilities of a writer in this new genre of documentary fiction to disclose sources even if they were obscure pamphlets and/or uncopyrighted government memoranda, and to give attribution. The controversy grew to such heat when the Yugoslav Writers Union condemned the book that Kiš felt a personal ostracism, and moved with his family to Paris. He visited Yugoslavia regularly in the following decade, sometimes staying there for months at a time. (In Paris he practiced what he regarded as another dictum of his poetics: the experience of exile as a spur to and revelation of vision.) Two years later Kiš's virtuous answers to the invectives hurled at him in the controversy were presented in *Čas anatomije* (1978, Lecture on Anatomy).

Kiš's next work of fiction, *Enciklopedija mrtvih* (1983; *The Encyclopedia of the Dead*, 1989), is, more than ever, faithful to his mother's legacy: "Give no credence to the fiction, only to the facts!" Because of Kiš's glorious talent in inventing facts of anachronism that retained their truth from the day before, he was able to reconstruct the lives and deaths of representative Yugoslav citizens under the pretense of having found such biographic accounts in an encyclopedia of the dead in Salt Lake City, Utah. He took the narrative position that he was merely and humbly transcribing a sacred text. Kiš's entire poetics may be said to be focused in these stories on his predominant topic: "the death"; that is, the tragedy of Central European Jewishness, the absurdity of the human being, his general skeptical attitude and, paradoxically, his immense optimism and sense of humor. In *The Encyclopedia of the Dead* Kiš continued both his exploration of the roots of Semitic identity and his essence of realistic fantasy: flights from mountaintops that start in symbols but ring with the weight of physical death;

processions of disorderly marches fueled into mindful energies. Kiš's eerie and lofty style, and his combinations of realistic detail with mythic allusiveness, have made him a figure to be reckoned with such other Jewish moralist-fabulists as Isaac Bashevis Singer* and Cynthia Ozick. At the same time, he is regarded as one of the prime exemplars of the fact-fiction phenomenon. His work has been called "non-novel" by those critics who see a paradox of genre in Kiš's craft. Most critics agree with Kiš's own assessment of his work (in an autobiographical note for publication of his last book) that he was expressing what he could not suppress in his aesthetic vision of experience: a spiritual anxiety that became his consuming shadow, one to which Sigmund Freud* gave the name *Heimlichkeit*.

Kiš wrote all his major work in Serbo-Croatian, though as a translator he was particularly literate in French, a language in which, during his last years, he wrote occasional short pieces for publication. At a memorial service held in New York on December 14, 1989, at the Yugoslav Press and Cultural Center, Kiš was lauded for his achievements both as a Yugoslav writer and as a world writer and translator. Among those who spoke at the service were the Nobel Prize laureate Joseph Brodsky,* Susan Sontag,* and the Yugoslavian writer Brana Crnčevic, who said that Kiš held a never-ending dialogue with the past in his "scrutiny of evil." Crnčevic said that Kiš never "arrested" any one in his investigation of evil; he only "arrested evil ideas." Darmir Grubiša, director of the Yugoslav Press and Cultural Center, proclaimed Kiš's work as a shaper of Yugoslavian consciousness, but he, and all the other speaker-writers present, added that Kiš's stature raised him from a local writer to a figure of world renown. The dual sides of Kiš—as Yugoslav and as a world figure in exile—were emphasized by Maja Herman-Sekulić, an essayist, poet, and translator, who pointed out Kiš's love of James Joyce* and his similarity of exilic temperament with Joyce. She also spoke of Kiš's identity with exile even in the name given to him at birth: Danilo/Daniel, the exiled biblical singer writing his "book." Such a solid symbolic presence, she added, was a beacon for Yugoslav culture, a light out of the "darkness of local and national strife" afflicting Yugoslavia at the present time. Susan Sontag spoke of her memories of Kiš, when the two met in a favorite Parisian café of Kiš's, and held marathon dialogues about craft over coffee and cigarettes, and conversations of sly, warm parries of varied concerns. Sontag particularly lamented the early death of Kiš, who, unlike John Keats, "secreted things slowly": Sontag felt that Kiš was still evolving from the center of his field of profound and profoundly growing vision. Sontag also announced for the first time in public that Kiš had won the prestigious Bruno Schulz prize, given in the United States for work by a foreign writer not yet well known on American shores.

Kiš left behind his widow and family in Yugoslavia, and a faithful companion-translator, Pasqual, in Paris.

Selected Title: *Po-etika* (Belgrade, 1971).

MIRJANA STANČIĆ and MARTIN TUCKER

KISHON, Ephraim (originally Franz Hoffman). Born August 23, 1924, in Budapest, Hungary; he resides in Tel Aviv, Israel. Son of a Budapest banker, Kishon early in his life experienced anti-Semitic prejudices endemic in Central Europe in the 1930s. Yet, in spite of his family's and his own tragic experience during World War II, he became a prolific writer of humorous sketches for radio, cabaret, and theater. He wrote first under the pseudonym of Ferenc Kishont. In 1949 he escaped to Israel via Austria. When an inflexible Israeli immigration officer changed his name into Hebrew, he became Ephraim Kishon, and according to his own statement was "newborn." He did not speak a word of Hebrew prior to his arrival, but learned it so well that he soon began writing editorials for the influential Israeli daily newpaper *Maariv*.

In his early work as an exile Kishon depicted themes from his diaspora experience, criticizing religious and moral taboos of his new home country. (See *Look Back Mrs. Loot*, 1962; *Noah's Ark, Tourist Class*, 1963; *The Seasick Whale*, 1965; the book of the Six-Day War and its aftermath, *So Sorry We Won!*, 1968 and *The Fox in the Chicken Coop*, 1969.) A rare example of a writer referring to his exile as "a land of laughter," he has proven that freshness of primary perception can be articulated in the universal manner of humor. Consequently, he has devised a special form, what he calls the "ironic short story." In this ironic mode he reveals various aspects of his content of Jewishness, particularly what makes it so special, and so available for laughter (see *Blow Softly from Jericho*, 1970; *Wise Guys, Solomon*, 1972; and *No Oil, Moses*, 1974). Avoiding mystification, he gives an epiphany of exile in a country that by its history stands for exile itself.

Like most European-born ironists, Kishon is sentimental about his European roots; however, it is precisely his cultural heritage that has made him a critic of contemporary politics and global issues as viewed through the prism of tolerant humor. Kishon is a writer who, in the final analysis, would sacrifice almost anything in his arsenal of craft for a good joke. He is also a very popular dramatist and screenwriter. His full-length play *Ha-ketubbah* (The Marriage Contract) had one of the longest runs in the history of Israeli theater. Two collections of his plays have been published in Hebrew: *Shemo Holekh Lefanov* (1953) and *Ma'arkhonim* (1959).

Selected Titles: Stories: *Unfair to Goliath* (1967); *One Eden for Rent* (1979). Feature Filmscript: *Salah*.

MIRJANA STANČIĆ

KLEN, Jurij (pseudonym of Oswald Burghardt). Born September 22, 1891, in the village of Serbynivci, Podillja region, Ukraine, then part of the Czarist Russian Empire; died October 30, 1947, in Augsburg, Germany. Born to German parents living in the Ukraine, Klen mastered German, Ukrainian, and Russian while still in his youth and wrote in all three languages. The bulk of his work is in Ukrainian. His oeuvre includes poetry, short prose, essays, and translations from the French and English. Following his philology studies at the University of Kiev, Klen, as a German citizen, was exiled to the Arkhangelsk region in 1914. He returned to Kiev after four years, joined the group of Ukrainian neo-classicists comprised of such prominent poets and men of letters as Maksym Ryl's'kyj (1895–1964), Mykola Zerov (1890–1941?), Pavlo Fylypovyč (1891–1937), and Myxajlo Draj-Xmara (1889–1939), and wrote poetry in a serene neoclassical style. To escape persecution, Klen migrated in 1931 to Germany, where he taught Slavic languages and literatures at various universities.

His poetry may be divided into two categories: exotic poetry, imbued with a timeless beauty, and philosophic poetry, in which the poet comes to terms with cataclysmic upheavals and tragedies of the age. The latter category includes his long narrative poem *Prokljati roky* (1937, The Damned Years), a moving attempt to overcome the burning memories of the suffering of his people during Stalin's reign of terror; a collection of poems, *Karavely* (1943, The Caravels), in which he seeks a philosophical perception of the world while trying to postulate an intrinsic relationship between permanent values and transience; and the epic poem *Popil imperij* (The Ashes of the Empires), written in the 1940s but published posthumously in 1957. Modeled on Dante's *Inferno*, *Popil imperij* reveals the horrors and suffering of multitudes under twentieth-century totalitarian regimes while seeking to fathom the apparently absurd mystery of human existence. Unadorned and pitiless in its realism, Klen's work also conveys a classical sense of simplicity and quiet grace and affirms an absolute belief in God and immortality. A sui generis Christian *amor fati* informs Klen's work; while damning those who cause suffering and those who strike a compromise with the enemy, the poems evidence a charitable forgiveness for all. The notions of a benevolent God and ultimate forgiveness of sin mitigate the rancor of his exile experiences.

Selected Title: *Dijabolični paraboly* (1947, Diabolical Parabolas, written under the pseudonym of Porfyrij Horotak in collaboration with other writers).

Consult: Josefine Burghardt, *Oswald Burghardt Leben und Werke* (Munich, 1962); Igor Kaczurowskyj, "Goethes '*Faust*'—Motive bei Jurij Klen (Oswald Burghardt)," in *Mitteilungen* 18 (Munich, 1981, a study of Goethe's influence on the poet, with bibliographical notes; Karl Siehs, "Oswald Burghardt—Jurij Klen," in *Mitteilungen* 18 (Munich, 1981, an analysis of the author's poetic works.

LEONID RUDNYTZKY

KLITGAARD, Mogen. Born 1906, Valby, Copenhagen, Denmark; died 1945, Aarhus, Denmark. Klitgaard fled the Nazi invasion of his country in 1940, and received asylum in Sweden. He returned to Denmark after World War II, but died soon thereafter. A social realist, he was a spokesman for liberal causes in the 1930s and personally aided in the resettlement of German refugees in that decade preceding the second World War.

KNIGHT, Eric. Born April 10, 1897, in Menston, West Riding, England; died January 15, 1943, in Dutch Guiana (now Suriname). Though best known for one book that in various incarnations has become one of the best-loved children's books of all time, *Lassie Come-Home* (1940; London, 1941), Knight was a versatile writer in various genres, and in book after book he explored the Yorkshire of his English childhood, though ironically he changed citizenship from British to American and back a total of six times, becoming an American again just three months before he died. All his books were written while he was resident in the United States, and all are set partially or wholly in England.

Herrie Champion, the hard-luck hero of *Song on Your Bugles* (1936), is a sketch of a young Knight using the visual arts to survive grueling work in a bottling factory and a textile mill. *Lassie Come-Home* contains his memories of the lonely, ruggedly beautiful moors ringing Menston and Halifax, and his adaptations of an uncle's yarns about conniving breeders who trained dogs they sold to return to them; hence the hyphenated word in the title suggestive of specially trained animals with a finely developed homing instinct.

The same uncle is the physical model for Knight's most whimsical, and recurring, character. Sam Small is Knight's version of a mythic figure whose elastic exploits he absorbed in Yorkshire. Sam, in several stories and one novel, is a squat, walrus-mustachioed curmudgeon whose fondness for ale and boasting leads to outrageous adventures. Besotted, he clangs into a lamppost and divides into two: yearning for an escape from nutty California, he begins to fly; convinced that he knows more about Americans than the author of a guide to the United States, he is outwitted by a Yankee soldier. In many cases, Sam was a pick-me-up for a creator victimized by homesickness and work blockages.

In each of his novels Knight demands socioeconomic equality and the creation of a caste system run on dignity and merit. This view was colored by a slum upbringing in Leeds and a 1938 research trip to depressed coal-mining areas in Great Britain. On his first return to his native country since 1912, Knight discovered squalor often accentuated by laissez-faire policies. In *The Happy Land* (1940; in England, *Now Pray We for Our Country*), Thora Clough, another of Knight's feisty young protagonists, lobbies to improve the diet of the miners' families. A rigid nurse informs her that top-grade milk can be distributed only if a child is near death.

Even *Lassie Come-Home* features a minitreatise on the dangers of capitalism. On the dole because of an inefficient, often closed coal mine, Sam Carraclough must sell his prized collie to pay for food, clothing, and fuel. Family stability is eventually restored, in large part due to his animal-training talents and the family's stoicism.

Knight proposed solutions to world problems in his last literary projects. In *This Above All* (1941), his most notorious fiction, a moonlighting British soldier continually explains why war transforms England from a kitten into a tiger, whitewashing a number of ills in the process. In scripts for the "Why We Fight" orientation films (produced by Frank Capra for the film-production unit of the

U.S. Army's Special Services branch), he explains why and how American soldiers should beware Axis forces, especially their propaganda. "A Short Guide to Great Britain" is another of Knight's attempts to cement the bond between traditional allies. A humane, sane food-distribution plan, described briefly in *The Happy Land* and *This Above All*, is the bedrock of "World of Plenty," a 1943 documentary written by Knight and Paul Rotha. Knight, though, never saw "World of Plenty." On a military mission to North Africa for the U.S. Army, where he served as a major, he was killed in an airplane crash near Paramaribo.

Selected Titles: *Invitation to Life* (1934); *Song on Your Bugles* (London, 1936: rev. ed., U.S., 1937); *You Play the Black and the Red Comes Up* (London, 1938; under pseudonym of Richard Hallas; 1938); *The Flying Yorkshireman*, title work in collection of five novellas by five authors (London, 1938; 1940); *The Happy Land* (1940; revised as *Now We Pray for Our Country*, London, 1940); *Sam Small Flies Again* (1942; London, 1943; later editions titled *The Flying Yorkshireman* and *Other Sam Small Stories*); *Portrait of a Flying Yorkshireman; Letters from Eric Knight in the United States to Paul Rotha in England*, ed. Paul Rotha (London, 1952).

Consult: A. S. Burack, *Writer's Handbook* (1946); *Current Biography 1942*; Goeff Gehman, "50th Anniversary of 'Lassie Come-Home': Belief in Dog and Humanity No Far Fetched Philosophy," Allentown (Pennsylvania) *Morning Call*, December 17, 1988; Granville Hicks and others, "There is No Formula to Life; Eric Knight and *This Above All*," *Wilson Library Bulletin* 17, no. 8 (April 1943); Paul Rotha, Foreword to *Portrait of a Flying Yorkshireman: Letters from Eric Knight in the United States to Paul Rotha in England*, ed. Paul Rotha (London, 1952); Edmund Wilson, "The Boys in the Back Room," in *Classics and Commercials: A Literary Chronicle of the Forties* (1950).

GEOFF GEHMAN

KOESTLER, Arthur. Born September 5, 1905, in Budapest; died March 3, 1983, in a double suicide with his third wife, Cynthia, in their London, England, apartment. Koestler was an only child whose mother was a descendant of a chief rabbi of Prague. His parents moved to Vienna in 1914–15 when his father's business suffered severe financial losses. Koestler's primary interest during his early school years was science, although he evinced an interest in linguistics. During the years when he was a polytechnic student in Vienna, he became a follower of Vladimir Jabotinsky, a Zionist ideologue who championed militancy and activism. In 1926 Koestler renounced his matriculation and left Vienna for Palestine where he performed menial jobs as proof of his commitment to Jabotinsky's Revisionist party. In 1927 he began his career as a correspondent for a German newspaper. For the next three years he served as correspondent and science editor for newspapers in Paris and Berlin; he was the only journalist invited on the *Graf Zeppelin* Arctic expedition. However, because of his membership in and work for the German Communist party (he joined on December 31, 1931), he was dismissed from his job. Koestler then moved on to the USSR, where he wrote a play, since destroyed. He returned to Budapest for a visit in 1933, but spent the years from 1933 to 1935 mostly in Paris working for international communism. During 1936 and 1937 he made three trips to Spain to report on the Civil War; he clearly was a spokesman for the Left in his reports. After his capture by Franco forces in Malaga he was sentenced to death, but freed as a result of strong British protest. Koestler published *Spanish Testament* a short while later, in 1937.

Koestler's belief in communism wavered after the ordeal of his imprisonment and the lack of a strong communist party protest against his death sentence. He resigned from the Communist party in 1938 and began concentrating on his fiction. He published his first novel, *The Gladiators*, in 1939 and was working on *Darkness at Noon*, which would become his best-known fiction work, in 1940 when French police arrested him and sent him to a camp for aliens. Again, British protest led to his release. Before the Germans marched into Paris he joined the French Foreign Legion and fled to England, where he worked in the British Pioneering Corps, an organization that employed loyal Allied residents of prior enemy nationality. In 1941 *Darkness at Noon* was published in its English translation to wide critical acclaim as well as to charges of Koestler's political ambition and historical revisionism. Koestler's account of his infatuation with, his commitment to, and his denunciation of communist ideology and ideals would continue for a long time; it can be said to be one of the grand passions of his life. During this time Koestler revised his earlier *Spanish Testament* into a new edition under the title *Dialogue with Death* (1942). He also wrote and published in 1941 a depreciation of his internment period in France in *Scum of the Earth*. This work earned him further fame and controversial notice.

Koestler's exile may be divided into several stages: the first was his conscious decision to be a roving reporter, a stateless person more interested in the world than in local or national habitation. The second was his commitment to international communism, a commitment that deprived him ideologically of a native home but attempted to replace the loss with a belief in a universal cosmos of brotherhood. A further stage began in the early years of World War II when Koestler was interned by the French even though he had chosen the Allied cause as his cause. Throughout this period, it was the British who spoke out for him, and it is not surprising that Koestler, when he found the opportunity to start a new life, chose England as his venue.

In 1943 Koestler published his first novel written in English, *Arrival and Departure*. From this time on he wrote only in English. (One of his friends and editors, Melvin J. Lasky, wrote in *Encounter* magazine, September-October 1983, that Koestler wished to become an Englishman but realized such a goal was futile for a ''foreigner'' in England; Koestler resigned himself to remaining a ''rootless cosmopolitan.'') Koestler took a position as correspondent for the *London Times* in order to monitor the situation in Palestine. By this time he had again become an ardent Zionist. He published *Thieves in the Night*, a pro-Zionist novel (and, according to some critics, an anti-Jewish one), in 1946. *Promise and Fulfillment: Palestine 1917–1949* (1949) is his overview of the Zionist state of Israel. During Israel's first years of independence Koestler commented on its state of affairs in various English, American, and French periodicals.

Koestler's increasing fame—particularly after the French edition of *Darkness at Noon (Le Zéro et l'Infini*, 1946)—led him to participate in many panels and seminars on world matters with a number of other intellectuals. These included an attempt to form a League for the Rights of Man with George Orwell and a debate with Jean-Paul Sartre and Simone de Beauvoir on political action. Koestler's provocative comments became the subject of further debates and media attention. His memoir in the collection of essays *The God That Failed* (1950, a composite reflection on various disillusionments with the Marxist dream) caused an intense fervor of response.

Koestler began publication of his autobiography in 1952 with the initial volume, *Arrow in the Blue, 1905–1931*. He and his second wife, Mamaine Paget, were divorced in 1953; her death by suicide in 1954 and his appreciation of her are recorded in a moving tribute in the preface to his collection, *The Trail of the Dinosaurs and Other Essays* (1955); their relationship is also detailed in her volume of published letters, *Living with Koestler: Mamaine Koestler's Letters 1945–51*, edited by Celia Goodman (1985).

The Trail of the Dinosaurs may be said to mark still another phase in Koestler's career. It is the last of his work that emphasizes political content in his intellectual explorations—from this point, Koestler's work will be absorbed in other causes. *Reflections on Hanging* (1956) is a testament against capital punishment. Eastern mysticism and its roots of healing unity are the subject of *The Lotos and the Robot* (1961). Psychology, parapsychology, and the processes of creativity take their place among Koestler's final speculations.

Koestler was an inveterate traveler, perhaps by nature, certainly by design. His consistent subversive speculations into ordered thinking and activity led him to the brink of intellectual loneliness and the putative role of the outcast. In his later years he seemed more easy in tone and less inimical in stance. He received many honors in England, where he lived from the mid–1950s. He married his third wife, Cynthia Jefferies, in 1965. Like T. S. Eliot* he left no children but reaped a contentment late in life with a younger wife who had been his assistant for many years.

Koestler committed suicide with his wife in 1983. He left a note that indicated he did not wish to bear the ravages of Parkinson's disease and leukemia, from which he was suffering.

Koestler summed up his career in *Janus: A Summing Up* (1978) and in his collection of papers, *Bricks to Babel* (1980). He published *The Thirteenth Tribe: The Khazar Empire and Its Heritage* (1976), a more kindly appraisal of Jewish identity than that found in his earlier commentaries. After his death the incomplete third volume of his autobiography, *The Stranger in the Square*, was published in 1984, edited and with an introduction by Harold Harris. This work touchingly exemplifies the end of Koestler's exile. In its coauthorship with his third wife, the book reveals a harmony achieved in the dissolution of separateness.

Selected Titles: Koestler's works are being issued in a uniform Danube edition by Hutchinson of London. Included in the series are his novel *The Call-Girls* (1972) and an early autobiographical work, *The Invisible Writing* (1954).

Consult: Iain Hamilton, *Koestler* (1982); Harold Harris, ed., *Astride the Two Cultures: Arthur Koestler at 70* (London, 1975); Mark Levene, *Arthur Koestler* (1984); Murray A. Sperber, ed., *Arthur Koestler: A Collection of Critical Essays* (1977).

KOHOUT, Pavel. Born July 20, 1928, in Prague, Czechoslovakia; he lives in Vienna, Austria. Kohout graduated from the Philosophy Faculty of Charles University in Prague in 1952. While earning his degree he worked in Czech radio as playwright, publicist, and director from 1947 to 1949; he was a cultural attaché to Moscow from 1949 to 1950; he served as editor-in-chief of the satirical magazine *Dicobraz* from 1950 to 1952. During this time he also wrote in the many genres for which he later achieved world fame—drama, fiction, poetry, children's books, screenplays, song lyrics, and translation. In the late 1950s he worked as director and program advisor for several Prague theater groups, among them Theater in Vinohrady, Realistic Theater, and Theater of St. K. Neumann. He traveled abroad frequently for the staging of his plays in the USSR, East Germany, Switzerland, Greece, Austria, the United States, England, and France. He became a member of the Union of Czechoslovak Writers, the Union of Czechoslovak Newspapermen, and the Union of Czechoslovak Theater Artists.

Kohout's first published literary works were poems in 1945; several of these appeared in the magazine *Halo Soboto*. His poetry was influenced by his political ideology, and in turn induced other young Czech poets to further politicizing of their work. His early success as a playwright led to worldwide fame, and his works had great popular success in the United States and Western Europe as well as in Eastern Europe. He experienced a loss of faith in both his political and artistic creeds during the Prague Spring in the 1960s; with the advent of reform and freedom in cultural vision characteristic of that era, he began to have doubts about his commitment to dogmatic socialism. In 1977 he signed the Charter 77, along with Vaclav Havel, Jan Patocka, Jaroslav Seifert, and others; that historic document called for freedom of expression in political and cultural ideas. Those courageous enough to sign the proclamation were soon persecuted either by outright harassment or by more subtle pressures. Kohout was allowed to leave Czechoslovakia in 1978 to work in Austria for one year as director of Vienna's Burgtheater, where he was awarded an Austrian national prize. When he tried to return to Czechoslovakia in October 1979, he was divested of his citizenship.

Since his exile Kohout has written several plays full of dark humor and a tone of comic absurdity. The absurdity of his situation and the feeling of helplessness to change it has produced works both Hamlet-like and comic in their pathetic attempts at resolution. Like a number of other Czech writers, Kohout has used words to confound words in order to live with words tilted in their misuse by political hacks and spokesmen. His satire has grown increasingly bitter at the same time it has grown abstract and removed from pithy detail, yet the genius of his wordplay continues to exert the shock of recognition of personal suffering.

Kohout has returned to Czechoslovakia since the peaceful overthrow of the Communist Party government in 1990, but has not, as yet, made a decision whether to remain in exile or to return permanently to his homeland.

Selected Titles: *Verse a pisne* (1953, Verses and Songs); *Treti sestra* (1961, Third Sister); *Z deniku kontrarevolucionare* (1969, From the Notebook of a Counterrevolutionary); *Valka ve tretim poschodi* (1971, The War on the Third Floor); *Ta muz a ten zena* (1973, Poor Murderer); *Ruleta* (1976, Roulette); *Katyne* (1978); *Napady sv. Klary* (1982, Ideas of St. Claire).

MARTIN TUCKER and ANDRE VLCEK

KOKOSCHKA, Oskar. Born March 1, 1886, in Pöchlarn, Austria; died February 22, 1980, in Villeneuve, Switzerland. Because he achieved renown as a painter, Kokoschka's early contributions to expressionist drama are sometimes overlooked. A rugged individualist (he rejected the term *expressionism* in favor of *expression*), Kokoschka illustrates the close links that existed between the radical literary school and the visual arts, not least in the series of portrait sketches printed in the avant-garde journal *Der Sturm* between 1910 and 1916. After being seriously wounded on the Russian front in World War I, he returned to Dresden and later settled in Vienna. Disliking the Schuschnigg regime, he left for Prague. Proscribed under Adolf Hitler as an exponent of degenerate art, Kokoschka became a refugee and spent the rest of his life chiefly in England and Switzerland. He became a British citizen in 1947 but retained a link with Austria through the foundation of his School for Seeing in Salzburg.

Apart from plays and an autobiography, Kokoschka wrote articles and stories marked by resolutely unorthodox vision and the nonconformity of a rebel in exile. In *Lettre de Voyage* he imagines the three Kings from the East visiting Stockholm in 1917 to attend a peace conference: Hjalmar Branting, later awarded the Nobel Peace Prize, gives them a frosty reception.

Selected Titles: *Das schriftliche Werk*, ed. H. Spielmann, 4 vols. (Hamburg 1973–76); *Mörder, Hoffnung der Frauen* (1907, Murderers, the Hope of Women); *Der brennende Dornbusch* (1911; The Burning Thornbush)—both plays repr. Leipzig, 1917.

Translations: English trans. of *Lettre de Voyage* in *"X," a Quarterly Review* (London), March 1960; *A Sea Ringed with Visions* (London, 1962).

Consult: *Künstler und Poeten*, ed. Hans-Maria Wingler (Feldafing, 1954); R. Brandt, *Figurationen und Kompositionen in den Dramen Oskar Kokoschkas* (1968); Frank Whitford, *Oskar Kokoschka: A Life* (London, 1986).

CEDRIC HENTSCHEL

KOLB, Annette. Born February 13, 1870, in Munich, Germany; died December 3, 1967, in Munich. Kolb underwent two periods of exile when she protested her country's policies. In the first, as a young writer espousing pacifism during World War I, she fled to Switzerland out of fear of imprisonment in her native Bavaria. Kolb's troubles were exacerbated by her unrelenting attacks on both

Germany and France as participants in the struggle against a pacifist aesthetic society. She remained in Switzerland till the end of the war and then returned to Bavaria. Kolb worked to repair the division between Germany and France, two countries whose culture represented for her the possibility of aesthetic repletion. Her background led naturally to her Franco-German sympathies: her mother was a French concert pianist who inspired in the daughter a sense of the richness of French culture; her Bavarian father was a distinguished landscape architect whose circle included artists, intellectuals, and aristocratic philosophers. In her youth Kolb met many composers and writers in her mother's salon, and their company stimulated her studies in music and literature.

Kolb again became a disputant with her government's policies in the early 1930s when she protested Nazi tyranny. In 1933 she left Germany and lived in the United States for a few, unhappy years. She returned to Germany at the end of the war to live out her life as a celebrated woman of letters.

Kolb's literary writings include three novels, *Die Last* (1918), *Daphne Herbst* (1928), and *Die Schaukel* (1934), as well as essays, pamphlets, and critical commentaries.

Selected Titles: *Dreizen Briefe einer Deutsch-Französin* (1916, Thirteen Letters of a Franco-German Woman); *Die Schaukel* (1934, The Swing); *Mozart: Sein Leben* (1937, Mozart: His Life); *Franz Schubert: Sein Leben* (1941, Schubert, His Life); *Memento* (1960); *1907–1964—Zeitbilder* (1964).

Consult: R. Lemp, *Annette Kolb: Leben und Werk einer Europäerin* (1970).

KONING, Hans (originally Hans Koningsberger). Born July 12, 1921; he lives in Connecticut. Koning was in high school when the Germans invaded Holland. He was smuggled out of the country through occupied France into England, where he joined a unit of the British commandos, serving in the British Army from 1943–45. He returned to school in Amsterdam in 1946 but felt "too old"; he moved to Indonesia and from there by freighter to Los Angeles. He wrote his first novel, *The Affair* (1958), in English in California while earning a living as a journalist.

When Koning's mother died in 1964, he felt his last link with Holland, the place of his youth and school years, had been cut. New York was the place of his adult life, his marriage, children, and profession. At this same time Koning became involved with the worldwide antinuclear movement, but he did not feel any sense of isolation from the larger American community. In 1986 he wrote in a letter to the editor of this study that "it was different with the anti-Vietnam war movement. Increasingly, and especially after we founded 'Resist' in 1967, I found myself at odds with my surroundings, with former friends, with the very reasons for writing novels. Novel-writing seemed an indulgence to me then, and America, while I did not stop seeing it as 'my country' became a place drenched in blood. When the war began to wind down, I began to disengage myself from my activities, and on May 1, 1975, when the Vietnamese armies entered Saigon, I left for England on what I called to myself a self-imposed exile." From 1975 to 1988 he lived most of the time in England. He made tentative moves to return to the United States, but claimed "the barriers are enormous, both emotional and technical—it is now virtually impossible for a writer with small children and my income to live in New York City." Koning further wrote: "I have in a sense cut myself off and continue in what remains an exile, as I live in London with my eyes on the U.S., writing for a U.S. public, with very few local contacts or links, the way the British used to live in India." Koning saw himself at the time as an "anomalous animal, a Dutch-born American writer living in exile in London."

In 1988 Koning and his family returned to the United States; they live in Connecticut.

Selected Titles: *An American Romance* (1960); *A Walk With Love and Death* (1961); *Love and Hate in China* (1966).

KOPELEV, Lev. Born 1907 in Borodyanka, Ukraine; he lives in Cologne, Federal Republic of Germany. Kopelev's stature as an intellectual, his fierce commitment to Marxist ideology, and his strength of character have been acknowledged in various commentaries and memorialized in Aleksandr Solzhenitsyn's portrait of him (as Lev Rubin) in *The First Circle*. Kopelev was refused reentry to the USSR after a visit to West Germany in 1980.

Kopelev was born to Jewish middle-class professional parents in the Ukraine near Kiev; his father was trained as an agronomist. Kopelev's love of things German—in cultural and historical achievements—began in his own words when he was ten years old. In the wake of the Bolshevik Revolution, he witnessed in his native village of Borodyanka successive occupations by the White Army, the Red Army, German invading forces, and a Polish squadron that took, as compensation for years of Russian occupation, a vengeful pillaging of the area. Kopelev found the German soldiers the kindest of all the conquerors. He held onto this memory for the rest of his life. His greatest passion, however, was for Bolshevism, and its promise of a new society. Breaking with his family and entering into the sphere of political engagement, Kopelev ran afoul of communist bureaucracy during Joseph Stalin's reign in the 1930s. He was placed in a *sharashka*, a special prison camp for intellectuals and scientists and politicians, who were to put their skills to work for the state while serving their sentences. It was in one such *sharashka* that Kopelev met Aleksandr Solzhenitsyn.* Kopelev and Solzhenitsyn were separated when Solzhenitsyn was transferred. They met again when Solzhenitsyn came to him years later with the manuscript of his first novel, *One Day in the Life of Ivan Denisovich*, and asked his help in getting it published. Kopelev spoke with Alexandr Tvardovsky, the editor of *Novy Mir*, and the book appeared in that journal, the most important literary organ in the USSR.

Kopelev supported the Soviet system throughout the decade in which Solzhenitsyn had his gravest problems with the state (just as he had continued to support the Stalinist regime during his own wrongful imprisonment). He justified his defense of a system that contained error as long as attention could be called to such error, and he did not lose faith in the capacity of the system to progress into a more popular democracy. He refused to leave his country even when such a move was suggested to him by censorious overseers who were upset at the publication of his first volume of memoirs published in Germany in 1976. (The English-language edition is *To Be Preserved Forever*, 1977.) In this work Kopelev brought to public attention the shameful record of Soviet mistreatment of German prisoners of war during World War II. In addition to the offense his book caused in official circles, Kopelev was actively involved in protesting the treatment of harassment against Andrei Sakharov in the late 1970s. After Kopelev accepted an invitation to lecture in the Federal Republic of Germany in 1980 and left the USSR, he was informed he could not return. Although his wife, the literary critic Raisa Orlova, had accompanied him on the trip, he was effectively cut off from his children, his family, and friends in the USSR.

Kopelev's stature has enabled him to serve as a liaison between East and West German writers and social groups. He is often seen at literary and intellectual conferences in Germany, where he remains a symbol of personal integrity, refusing to condemn his country because it has wrongfully found him guilty of enmity. Kopelev, however, is a lonely figure, appreciative of a foreign citizenry that honors him and does everything to make him feel at home, but that can never make him feel he *is* home.

Sovietologist and critic Mark Priceman wrote, in an analysis of *Ease My Sorrows: A Memoir* (1983) for *Confrontation* magazine (nos. 27–28, 1983):

In Kopelev's *To Be Preserved Forever* (English, 1977), he told how his principled defense of human decency in dealing with defeated Germans resulted in direct experience of the Soviet judicial and penal systems. In *The Education of a True Believer* (English, 1980), we learn, among other things, what it was like to grow up: the author was born in 1912—in the Russia of the NEP, of Stalin's rise to absolute power, and of the "liquidation of the Kulaks as a class." This to me was the most revealing part of the memoirs. It may not explain "Rubin" as a long-time ideological hold-out to everybody's satisfaction, but it certainly furnishes key elements to a better understanding.

Readers of *Ease My Sorrows* will be rewarded, also, by a view of the young Solzhenitsyn—not yet a confirmed anti-Marxist but a passionate anti-Stalinist and a questioner of Lenin's historic stature. Solzhenitsyn had "human relations" problems rooted in his character which also led to his early transfer out of the *sharashka*. After both he and Kopelev were freed in the mid–1950s, they resumed their friendship and Kopelev was instrumental in getting his friend's *One Day in the Life of Ivan Denisovich* published. "In the seventies, however, [their] paths diverged. But that's another story. And the time to tell it has not yet come." Perhaps it will have with the volume Lev is now preparing with wife Raisa Orlova.

For the present, Kopelev tells movingly where he now stands and sketches briefly the path which led him there. By the early sixties he "began to realize" that "Stalin's policy was flawed . . . in its entirety. . . . " He still upheld Marxism-Leninism, and found Khrushchev's exposé of the "cult of personality" superficial, not Marxist. It took numerous further shocks, his experiences as a militant dissident and much reading for him to conclude that "the forecasts of Marx and Engels were utopian." In 1968 he was expelled from the party. In 1980 he and his wife left Russia for West Germany, where he was welcomed as a proven friend.

For the lost ideal of socialism, Kopelev appears to have substituted that of tolerance. Laudable as that ideal is, one wonders how it can fill the void his earlier faith must have left. (pp. 139–40)

In August 1990, Kopelev's Soviet citizenship was restored to him by a direct order of Mikhael Gorbachev.

Translations: *To Be Preserved Forever* (1977); *No Jail for Thought*, Foreword by Heinrich Böll (1977); *The Education of a True Believer* (1980; first published in Russian, *I Sotvoril Sebde Kumira*, Ann Arbor, Michigan, 1978); *Ease My Sorrows: A Memoir* (1983; first published in Russian, *Utoli Moia Pechali*, Ann Arbor, Michigan, 1981).

Consult: Robert G. Kaiser, "A Note on Lev Kopelev," in *Ease My Sorrows* (1981).

KOROVIN, Konstantin. Born 1860 in Russia; died 1939 in USSR. Korovin moved into exile in Paris when the Czarist regime fell in 1917. He applied his primary creative energies to the medium of painting until 1930. From 1930 to 1939 he wrote his memoirs, which he published in émigré journals and periodicals in Paris. The memoirs centered on his life as a painter and his friendships with visual artists, opera stars, composers, and writers. His work has never been collected in book form in the West. In 1971 his memoirs, under the title *Konstantin Korovin vspominaet* were published in Moscow. Korovin is not a major literary figure, but he is representative of the first wave of twentieth-century Russian émigré writers.

KORZHAVIN, Naum. Born 1939, USSR; he lives in Boston, Massachusetts. Korzhavin emigrated to the United States in 1974. While popular as a writer in his own country, he has published little since his emigration.

KOSINSKI, Jerzy. Born June 14, 1933, in Lodz, Poland; he lives in New York City. Kosinski's literary achievements are unquestionable. In his first novel, *The Painted Bird* (1965; 2nd ed., 1976), he presented a graphic delineation of the horror of the Holocaust. A young boy—possibly Jewish, possibly gypsy—is given by his parents to peasants in Nazi-dominated Poland in an attempt to save him from life in (and death at) a concentration camp. The boy's adventures, from one hiding place to another, culminate in his rescue by Communist soldiers and therapeutic attention in an American military hospital. Kosinski's powers of description are uncanny: portraiture of the demon world of the grotesque in realistic, graphic language. Significantly, the boy passes through both Communist and Western hands; he is reunited with his parents, and his voice is restored after the horrors of his experience have turned him mute. Kosinski indulges in the exilic wish for restoration of the family of origin, but the indulgence in no way mars the power of his narrative; conversely, it reflects the triumph of will over transient history.

Kosinski's second novel, *Steps* (1968), showed a direction in which he would travel for many years, and one that would lead to both his literary fame and his notoriety as a public persona. In *Steps*, which won the National Book Award in 1969 and was highly praised by American and European critics, the method of presentation is that of fragmentary entries by a narrator who directs events by the force of his will. The Kosinski hero may be said to have been conceived at the end of the *Painted Bird* in the boy's wish for a world he could make; it was born in *Steps*, a novel in which the hero achieves dominion over his world by manipulating other human beings and by casting events into the service of his own scenario. The Kosinski hero is not, however, a premeditated thinker; he operates on the factor of whim and chance and arranges his schedule of resolutions according to situations into which he has been pushed or shoved, or into which he has fallen. Kosinski's heroes triumph over challenges because they shape their environmental battles with scalpels of will and knives of immense ambition that enable them to cut down adversaries, whether real, self-ordained, chosen at random, or imagined for sport.

All of Kosinski's work since his second novel features this kind of hero—a subterranean *Ubermensch*, an agent of vengeance on the crimes and hypocrisies of modern society. His targets are the excesses of malfeasance in both the Communist and the Western worlds. In one of his novels, a Communist prize skier is driven to distraction by the thought that a spot of semen has stained his beautifully immaculate ski pants; the thought so unnerves him that he loses his grip on a jump and falls to his death at the end of the slope; the Kosinski hero, waiting behind him on the top of the ski run and the one who had planted the false semen rumor, goes on to win the competition. In another narrative a protagonist implants the seed of cancer in the body of a nagging mistress by positioning her in the full blast of an airplane's poisonous engine exhaust.

Kosinski's extraordinary imagination and tactics of morality have resulted in constant debate about his values. His stance is provocative, and while his narratives are presented as expressionistic fancy, his repeated use of sexual fantasy and manipulation of human desire has offended some readers. Ultimately Kosinski is an exploiter of the grotesque. Whether this exploitation is done in the service of a higher cause of philosophic fiction remains an unresolved issue; he has his detractors, but many critics believe him to be a serious moralist in his sly way.

Kosinski's personal image has occasioned almost as much debate as his work. A figure often seen at literary gatherings (he was president of PEN American Center from 1973 to 1975 and remains active in this writers organization as well as in other groups), he is also known to have adopted many disguises for the purpose of provoking response. These often ingenious and usually amusing ploys are found in his novels sooner or later, and it is unclear which comes first—the fiction of them or the experience that led to their rendering into fiction. Kosinski seems to wish to throw his readers into ambiguities where they are not sure what has been imagined and what has happened in fact. Kosinski appears to believe firmly in the indistinct line wavering between verifiable fact and creative invention. His persona (the Kosinski hero) and his many recognizable guises of deception for later unmasking may stem from the demands of his early real life. He was sent into hiding with a Polish farming family by his parents as a means of survival; he may have suffered muteness for a period of several years after his rescue by Communist soldiers at the end of World War II in Europe.

With the war's end in 1945, Kosinski returned to school and earned honors in university training. He felt he was an inner émigré because he was unable to speak his mind. To ensure artistic survival and to avoid the harassments of censorship, Kosinski turned to photography and became a skilled craftsman who exhibited throughout Poland. The interest of this craft soon palled, and Kosinski emigrated to the United States in 1957 in hope of wider freedom, whether or not through the ruse he tells of having "invented" officials who "signed" his travel documents (he claims he was able to emigrate because of these "invented" dossiers, which contained letters recommending he be allowed to leave the country). In 1958 he was awarded a Ford Foundation fellowship. During these early years in the United States he wrote two books of nonfiction under the pseudonym Joseph Novak: *The Future Is Ours, Comrade* (1960) and *No Third Path* (1962). In these works he proclaimed the possibility of triumphing over the accidents of fate through the development of programs of social alternatives.

Kosinski has taught at various universities—among them Yale, Wesleyan, and Princeton, and he has a popular following among students. He married the widow of the founder of one of the largest steel companies in the United States, Mary Hayward Weir, in 1968; she died tragically of incurable brain disease a few years later. In 1986 Kosinski married Kiki von Frauenhofer, a public relations executive who had been his assistant for the previous twenty years. He has returned to Poland only once since his departure—in 1988 he was invited by the Communist government as a guest of the state.

Kosinski's latest novel, *The Hermit of 69th Street*, appeared in 1988 after an interval of six years of publishing silence. It is both a stunning departure from Kosinski's spate of recent fiction and a return to the pyrotechnic brilliance of his first two novels. Kosinski employs again the carrot of fact/fiction: his protagonist is a writer, Norbert Kosky, who has left behind his "working papers." The editor of the collected papers is Jay Kay. The papers are footnoted endlessly: in them are references to Kosinski's own fiction (as Kosinski); to Kosky's work; to work said to be written by Kosky and immediately recognizable as published work by Kosinski; and to discussions of exile, the Holocaust, Jewish identity, Polish identity; the many facets of Joseph Conrad* and of Conrad's critics; philosophic and metaphoric reality; and levels of vision and meaning. Clearly Kosinski is working out philosophic ideas by his fictional means. His postmodernist technique permits him to establish a fascinating medley of historic documentation, outrageous claims of humor, fantastic leg-pulling, and profound rationales of human behavior. Kosky is a "hermit" much like the hero of Kosinski's third novel *Being There*: by withdrawing he sees more, and sees more objectively. Kosky is also Kosinski in Kosinski's Hollywood days (and nights) as a screenwriter for the movie version of *Being There* (for which Kosinski won an Academy Award) and as an actor in director-producer Warren Beatty's much-lauded film *Reds*. As Kosinski, Kosky is wickedly funny about Hollywood, about Beatty (under another name), and about the movie scene. Yet some of Kosinski's brilliant fiction reads like a self-parody—at times he outdoes himself in a performance meant to show how much he can do.

Kosinski writes only in English. He is now an American citizen. His second marriage took place in the apartment of Marion Javits, the widow of the revered late U.S. senator from New York. Kosinski is chairman of the board of the American Foundation for Polish-Jewish Studies, and has twice been elected president of PEN American Center. Clearly Kosinski is no longer an exile in material terms. In spiritual matters he retains the essence of exile.

Selected Titles: Novels: *The Devil Tree* (1973); *Cockpit* (1975); *Blind Date* (1977); *Passion Play* (1978); *Pinball* (1982). Essays: *Notes of the Author* (1965); *The Art of the Self* (1968).

Consult: Paul R. Lilly, Jr., *Words in Search of Victims* (1988).

KOSSAK-SZEZUCKA, Zofia. Born August 8, 1890, in Kosmin, Poland; died April 9, 1968, Gorki Wielkie, Poland. Born into a Polish Catholic family (her maiden name was Szatkowska), Kossak-Szezucka worked with a Catholic underground organization to provide aid and hiding for Jews in Poland during the Holocaust. In 1943 she was arrested and interned in Auschwitz under an assumed name; she was freed in July 1944 by Allied forces. She wrote about this experience in her autobiographical work *Zotchani* (From the Abyss). She lived in England until 1956, and then for a few months in France. Nostalgia for her homeland drove her back to Poland.

Kossak-Szezucka's chief works are historical novels which show an intense interest in religion and history, particularly in *Krzyżowy* (The Crusaders); *Złota Wolność* (Golden Freedom). Her popularity derived from the richness of her detail and easy narrative style.

Selected Titles: *Przymierze* (1946; *The Covenant*, 1951); *Puszkarz Orbano* (1947); *Suknia Dejaniry* (1948).

Consult: W. Bartoszewski and Z. Lewin, eds., *Righteous Among the Nations: How the Poles Helped the Jews* (London, 1969); Adam Gillon and L. Krzyzankowski, *Modern Polish Literature* (1964); Teresa Prekerowa, "The Just and the Passive," *Yad Vashem Studies* 19 (1988).

KOSTETZKY, Eaghor. Born May 14, 1913, in Kiev, Ukraine; died June 14, 1983, in West Germany. Kostetzky studied acting in Leningrad and Moscow and worked as an actor in the Urals. After World War II as an émigré in Western Europe he began to publish stories, reviews, essays, and plays in Ukrainian. He also made translations primarily from German and English, among them the first complete Ukrainian translation of Shakespeare's sonnets, his *Romeo and Juliet*, and selections from T. S. Eliot. He published these translations largely through his own publishing house, Na hori. With his wife, the German poet Elizabeth Kottmaier, he translated literary works from Ukrainian into German. His own plays and essays were translated into Bengali, Byelorussian, Dutch, English, German, and Polish. He also edited and published a periodical in Ukrainian, *Ukrayina i svit*.

Initially Kostetzky translated his own works into German, and then began writing in German in the 1970s, especially his radio plays. All his work displays a certain playfulness in the use of unusual words, phrases, syntax, and dialogue. One of his consistent themes is the lack of communication between people. Present also is a parody of the political systems and political movements that Europe had recently experienced. This element of parody is particularly notice-able in his play *The Twins Shall Meet Again* (1947). Because of his special kind of humor and his demanding vocabulary and form, Kostetzky's work has not found a wide audience.

A Play about a Great Man (1948) represents Kostetzky at his most charac-teristic. A "mysterium" with three acts and two *intermediae* in the Ukrainian dramatic fashion of the Baroque era, it follows the form of a "crown of sonnets," with the last line repeated in the scene that follows and the final remark repre-senting the initial line of the work. In the play a group of adventurers decides to convince a simple, middle-aged man that he is a *great* man. The man believes what he has been told, and soon becomes a great architect, editor, political activist, and speaker, and finally president of the country. The experiences bring him no satisfaction; indeed he begins to see that greatness, or individuality, may be found only within one's inner self. He returns to his modest home. The play also contains two superimposing planes of time: one that is progressive (with speed relative to events), the other that is both progressive and regressive, thus allowing for the last scene to return to the first scene. The two levels of awareness of time finally unite, with the present becoming the past and the past becoming the present. Thus Kostetzky suggests that one can begin life anew if one is willing to free himself from the constraints of historical chronology. His work represents some basic elements of the philosophy of existentialism, though with a different and mocking tone from the works of Jean-Paul Sartre and Albert Camus.

Selected Titles: *Opovidannya pro peremozhtsiv* (1946, stories); *Tam de pochatok chuda* (1948, stories); *Teatr pered tvoyim porohom* (1963, plays); *Die Nonnen* (1966); *Das Spiel vom grossen Man. Ein Mysterium in drei Tagen* (1967).

Translations: *A Play about a Great Man*, in *An Anthology of Modern Ukrainian Drama*, ed. L. Onyshkevych (forthcoming, Canadian Institute of Ukrainian Studies, University of Alberta, Canada); Igor Kostecki, *Surowe sonety*, trans. Jerzy Niemojowski (1976).

Consult: Vasyl' Barka, "Ekspressionistychna proza Ihorya Kostetskoho," *I. Kostets'-kyi. Zbirnyk de 50-richchya* (1964); Cord Henrich, "In Hamburg gehort," *Die Welt* 125 (June 1967); Ivan Koshelivets', "Styl' surmoderne," *Litavry* 2 (1947); Larissa M. Z.

Onyshkevych, "Diystvo pro velyku lyudynu," *Suchasnist'* 10 (1969); Hryhoriy Shevchuk, "Pravo na eksperyment i yoho mezhi," *Ukrayins'ka trubyna*, February 16, 1947; Yar Slavutych, "Shekspirovi sonety," *Shakespeare Quarterly* X (1959).

LARISSA M. L. ONYSHKEVYCH

KOTT, Jan. Born October 27, 1914, in Warsaw, Poland; he now lives on Eastern Long Island. Kott received a classical European education and, after taking a law degree, studied in Paris, where he was associated with leading figures of both the surrealist and the progressive Catholic movements, such as Tristan Tzara* and Jacques Maritain. He returned to Poland a month before the outbreak of World War II, taking part in his country's defense first as a soldier and later as a member of the resistance to the German occupation. (By his own account, in information provided by *World Authors 1950–1970*, published in 1975, he earned his living "by illegal currency transactions," and he also edited an underground newspaper.) He was one of a group of people who established Poland's first postwar printing press.

Kott joined the Communist party during the war, but during the 1950s became increasingly active among those who opposed the cultural theory generally known as socialist realism. He formally resigned from the party in 1957, in the aftermath of the "Polish October" of 1956 and the suppression of free expression that followed it. During the next ten years, Kott traveled and lectured widely, especially after his international reputation was secured with the French translation of his Shakespeare studies (1962). He settled permanently in the United States in 1966, and from 1969 on has been professor of comparative drama at the State University of New York at Stony Brook.

The works for which Kott is known in the West represent a small part of his productive efforts. His bibliography occupies thirty-four typed pages, and his wide cultivation is evident in the range of subjects he has treated. (Kott speaks eight languages). He published two volumes of poetry while an undergraduate, and during his doctoral studies, produced *Mitologia i realizm* (1946), a sort of intellectual autobiography. During the next fifteen years, Kott wrote books on the classics and Victor Hugo in addition to numerous critical editions and anthologies of Polish literature and translations of European and classical authors into Polish. These labors earned for him the State Prize in Literature and Literary Studies for 1951 and 1955.

Kott's emergence as a figure of international significance dates from the publication of *Szkice o Szekspirze* (Sketches on Shakespeare, translated into English under the title *Shakespeare Our Contemporary*). In this and subsequent works— *Theater Notebook 1947–67* (1968), *The Eating of the Gods: An Interpretation of Greek Tragedy* (1973), *The Theater of Essence and Other Essays* (1984), and *The Bottom Translation: Marlowe, Shakespeare, and the Carnival Tradition* (1987)—Kott combined a deep erudition with an equally profound immersion in contemporary life.

The essence of Kott's approach to Shakespeare is embodied in three linked notions: first, that what is mimed in the theater is life itself, so that the proper context for discussing plays is the human condition as a whole; second, that every age finds in Shakespeare a reflection of its own preoccupations, anxieties, and self-perceptions; and third, that the critic's work must bear the stamp of his or her own personal history.

Kott left his homeland (and forfeited an assured place among its most honored literary figures) after the age of fifty. His identity as an exile is inseparable from his achievement as a critic.

MARTIN BELLER

KOVALENKO, Ludmyla. Born on September 29, 1898, near Mykolayiv, in the Ukrainian steppe area near the Oziv Sea; died June 13, 1969, in Trenton, New Jersey. A popular émigré writer, as well as an activist in the Ukrainian women's movement and in the Ukrainian Orthodox church, Kovalenko began her participation in humanitarian and civic causes early in life. She interrupted her college studies to serve in the Red Cross during World War I. Her impressions of events in Kiev during the war and during Ukraine's struggle for independence are described in her trilogy of novels, *Nasha, ne svoya zemlya* (1964–68, Ours, But Not Our Own Land).

Kovalenko's first works were written when she was in her early twenties. After the arrest of her husband, the writer Mykhaylo Ivchenko, by the Soviet government, her works were labeled unacceptable for publication, and she turned her hand to translations from the French. During World War II Kovalenko was in charge of aiding Ukrainian prisoners of war. Escaping to the West with her daughter Lesya, she saw the end of the war in Western Europe. There, in the displaced persons camps she became active in the Ukrainian women's movement (she served as vice-president of the Association of Ukrainian Women) and edited their periodical, *Hromadyanka*. She continued to write stories and plays. (Some of Kovalenko's satirical stories were written under the name of L. de Marini.)

After emigrating to the United States, Kovalenko worked as an editor at the Voice of America. She also compiled and edited *Ukrayina: Entsyklopediya dlya Molodi* (1971, Ukraine: An Encyclopedia for Youth). Of her six plays, two have been staged: *Domakha* (in West Germany in 1947–48 by V. Blavatsky's theater and the Ukrainian Theater in Australia); *Ksantippe* (by "Zahrava" in Toronto, in 1969 and 1973). While Kovalenko depicted in her work, after World War II, some of the difficulties émigrés faced in displaced persons camps, she expressed hope for a new and better life. This hope may be seen especially in her science fiction novel, *Rik 2245* (1958, The Year 2245) and *Heroyinya pomyraye v pershomu akti* (1948, The Heroine Dies in the First Act). With missionary zeal she pursued a goal to record and transmit through literature various historical elements and figures dealing with twentieth-century Ukraine, for she felt it a responsibility of writers in exile to leave for posterity that information which could not be published in their homeland. Thus the trilogy of novels about the period of Ukrainian independence and works based in Ukraine in earlier centuries.

Consult: Larissa M. L. Onyshkevych, "Literaturna tvorchist' Ludmyly Kovalenko," *Suchasnist* 1 (1970); Yuriy Sherekh, "Z krytychnoho shchodennyka," *Novi Dni* (July-August 1956).

LARISSA M. L. ONYSHKEVYCH

KRISTOF, Agota. Born in Hungary; she lives in Switzerland. Kristof has published one novel, *The Notebook* (1989), a work akin to Holocaust fiction. It employs the premise of a mother abandoning her twin children to the care of their grandmother, because she believes the children will be more likely to endure the horrors of World War II in Central Europe in a remote village than in a metropolitan center. The children are abused by their neighbors, and they, in turn, become abusive in their progression of survival. Mirrored in their amorality, and in the amorality of their tyrants and/or victims, the novel shapes itself into a record of the brutalizing of modern European civilization. Kristof's fiction has its affiliation with such earlier works as Jerzy Kosinski's *The Painted Bird*; Jakov Lind's* *Landscape in Concrete* and *Soul of Wood*; Günter Grass's* *The Tin Drum*; and Primo Levi's* studies of concentration camp morality. Kristof emigrated to Switzerland in 1956 after the invasion of Hungary by Soviet troops. She is now a Swiss citizen.

Consult: Ariel Dorfman, *The New York Times Book Review*, January 15, 1989.

KUHNER, Herbert. Born March 29, 1935 in Vienna, Austria; he lives in Vienna, and makes frequent trips to the United States. Kuhner is a poet, novelist, and essayist who writes only in English though he has now returned to Austria, where he was born. Kuhner left his native country with his Jewish parents in 1939, when he was four years old. He published his first novel, *Nixe*, in the United States in 1968. In October 1963 he decided to return to Vienna, where his mother had reemigrated. He has been active in promoting the work of Jewish Austrian writers and has edited several anthologies of postwar Austrian writing. Kuhner is a writer in exile as a Jew who fled from Nazism and now as an Austro-American living in permanent residence in a country of which he is no longer a citizen but was once a native. In an unpublished work, "Memoirs of a 39er," which Kuhner calls a "novel of sorts," he writes: "In 1939, when I was four, my parents left Austria before the juggernaught could crush us. In 1963, I came back to Austria to live. Surely I can't be blamed for being born in Austria, but I must take the blame for returning. Going from New York to Vienna was like going from the frying pan into the fire. When I lived in New York, I thought I'd been uprooted. After I moved to Vienna I knew I'd been uprooted."

Selected Titles: editor, with Feliks J. Bister, *Carinthian Slovenian Poetry* (Columbus, Ohio: Slavica Publishers, 1984); with Milne Holton, *Austrian Poetry Today* (1985).

KUNDERA, Milan. Born April 1, 1929, in Brno, Czechloslovakia; he lives in Paris. Son of Ludvik Kundera (1891–1971), a classical pianist-professor of music, Kundera attended high school in Brno, then studied philosophy at Charles University in Prague for several semesters; he did not complete his degree. In his teens, soon after World War II, he joined the Czech Communist party but was expelled from it in 1948 when the Russian sphere of influence swallowed Czechoslovakia into its hegemony. In 1958 he completed requirements in the film division of Prague's AMU (Prague Institute of Advanced Cinematographic Studies). After graduation he became a staff member of the faculty; he taught world literature and later was promoted to senior lecturer. He lost his position after the Russian invasion of Czechoslovakia in 1968 because of his activities during the "Prague Spring," a period of artistic experimentation under the liberal Alexander Dubček regime with few political restraints. His work was banned from publication in 1971, and copies of his books—his first novel, *The Joke*, and a collection of stories, *Laughable Loves*, had been published earlier in Czech—were removed from Czechoslovak libraries. In 1975 he accepted an offer to teach at the University of Rennes in France. In 1979 the Czechoslovak government stripped him of his citizenship. He now teaches at the University of Paris.

Kundera is without question one of the widely read and acclaimed Czech authors of the twentieth century. His work first appeared in Czech magazines in 1946, and his book of poems, *Monologs* (1957), became a text of expression for young poets throughout his country. Kundera has also worked as editor and translator from the Ukrainian and French, in particular the work of the French surrealist poet Guillaume Apollinaire. He has adapted some of his work for the screen as well as written original screenplays; his dramatic work, *Sister of My Sisters*, was produced in Prague in 1963. He has also published many short stories.

Best known in Western Europe and the United States for his novels, particularly those written during his exile period, Kundera explores in depth and at length the absurdities of psychological rationale and rationalization, which his characters put forth for their behavior. His work is deeply moral, but it is covered with a surface of playful wit. Kundera often employs the comic grotesque to make his point that contemporary man is willing to sink to the most ingenious hypocrisies in order to avoid blunt consequences of truth. His black humor and seeming cynicism are counterbalanced by his humanism and compassion for victims who create their own tyrannies. His irony is subtle, perhaps because in his high humor Kundera means what his words say, but the context in which they are placed makes the reading painful; recourse is made to laughter as an exit from intolerable revelation. In his early novel *The Joke* (1968) Kundera uses as his premise the notion that a man who writes a silly comment on a postcard is foolish enough to believe that his satire will not be taken seriously by literal-minded over-the-shoulder bureaucrats. The protagonist's persecution becomes a deadly joke; the consequences of a light-hearted lark develop into a clipping not only of innocent wings but eventually of a man's free voice.

Kundera's later work shows the influence of modern French absurdism although the settings of the novels continue in Czechoslovakia. While Kundera's emphasis has never centered on the political as distinct from the run of common daily activity, his work clearly shows that no man is isolated from politics, particularly the man who withdraws into absurd isolation (absurd in Kundera's view because isolation is impossible in a communist state) or absurd community (absurd in Kundera's view because the individual man, as an individual, is too eccentric to fit into group routines of behavior). Rather than politics proper, Kundera uses the impact of politics on the cultural milieu as the sounding board by which his characters' eccentricities are defined. Thus in *The Joke* and *Laughable Loves* (1963–68; English, 1978, c.1974) the characters are drawn in their reactions to the atmosphere of the 1950 monolith of ideology and its cult of personality in the Czechoslovak Socialist Republic. In his later work, most apparent in *The Unbearable Lightness of Being* (1982), the Soviet invasion of Czechoslovakia becomes the background that paints everything around it in traumatizing colors.

Some critics see in *The Unbearable Lightness of Being* a decline in Kundera's power, or rather a thinning-out of his extraordinary talent to capture the strokes of comic absurdity in a frame of compassionate pathos. The novel concerns four characters who move in and out of their native land, reduced to varying levels of economic and professional mediocrity, and always holding onto a sustaining memory, whether it is that of love or of family or of country. In his previous novel, *The Book of Laughter and Forgetting* (1978), Kundera treats the same theme in tighter, more poetic guise, and makes telling the power of bureaucratic weight to erase history. Merely by allowing the passage of time to erode awareness, a country becomes accomplice to the loss of its history and uniqueness. Thus the identity of Czechoslovakia is more likely to be dismembered by the slow censorious process of the deletion of historical references to real events in school texts and newspapers and journals than by Russian tanks or soldiers. In a score of years, Kundera suggests, no one will remember a history that has been sequestered, condensed, and powdered into the finest of invisible print.

Kundera's elegant wit is probably most evident in *The Farewell Party* (1976) his satiric tour de force in which a high communist official is found murdered; the humor is abetted by unexpected juxtapositions of elegant style with heavy-language commitment to state socialism.

By continuing to write only in his native tongue, Kundera is demonstrating his commitment to the need of keeping his national language alive and flourishing, and thus making it inaccessible to entropy and oblivion, the two great dangers posed in his view by the condition of exile.

Of Kundera, the critic Janet Malcolm (*New York Review of Books*, May 10, 1984) has written: "His need to experiment with form is surely connected to his personal vendetta against the puerilities of 'socialist realism' and its 'free world counterparts'. . . . His novels have all the unpredictability and changeability of mountain weather, and are marked by an almost compulsive disregard for the laws of genre" (p. 3.) Terry Eagleton, in an essay in *Salmagundi* (No. 73, Winter 1987), writes :"The dissonance in Kundera between a conventionally romantic subject-matter and a decidedly non-romantic handling of it has itself a political root. For if on the one hand his astonishingly subtle explorations of personal relationships redeems that which Stalinism expels, the ironic pathos with which such relationships are invested is just the reverse of that triumphalistic sentimentality which is Stalinism's ideological stock-in-trade" (p. 31).

Selected Titles in Translation: *Last May* (Prague, 1955, poems); *Owners of the Keys* (Prague, 1962–63, criticism and translations); *Ptakovina* (Prague, 1969), translation); *Jacques and His Master: Honor to Denis Diderot* (Paris, 1970; English, 1985, criticism); *Life Is Elsewhere* (1972, novel); *The Art of the Novel* (1988, essays). See also *L'Immortalité* (Paris, 1990).

Consult: Special Issue, *Salamugundi*, no. 73 (Winter 1987).

MARTIN TUCKER and ANDREJ VLCEK

KUNENE, Daniel. Born 1929 in Johannesburg, South Africa; he teaches at the University of Wisconsin in Madison. Kunene is a well-known scholar of African literature and linguistics. He left South Africa in the 1960s for the United States, where he now teaches. His translation of Thomas Mofolo's *Chaka* (1981) is now accepted as the authoritative text. Kunene has also published poetry and a short-story collection, *From the Pit of Hell to the Spring of Life* (Johannesburg, 1986).

Selected Titles: *Heroic Poetry of the Basotho* (Oxford, 1971); *Pirates Have Become Our Kings* (1978, poems); *The Ideophone in Southern Sotho* (Berlin, 1978); *A Seed Must Seem to Die* (Johannesburg, 1981, poems).

KUNENE, Mazisi. Born 1930 in Durban, South Africa; he teaches at the University of California at Los Angeles (UCLA). Kunene received his master's degree from Natal University in Durban, and later became head of the Department of African Studies at University College in Roma, Lesotho. He went to England in 1959 to complete his thesis on Zulu poetry. Kunene was a founder member of the antiapartheid movement in the United Kingdom. His participation in African rights movements has remained active over the years, particularly in his role as representative of the African National Congress both in the United Kingdom and in the United States. In an interview conducted by Deborah J. Wilkes and printed in the spring 1986 issue of the African Studies Center/UCLA journal, Kunene responded to the question about the role his poetry played in the African struggle in this way:

Only history, not my personal judgment, will decide what role my works played in the struggle. I hope that my poetry and my other writings will continue to play a role for many centuries. I do believe that the struggle is not only a physical one, but also an intellectual one. In the period of reconstruction we shall also need a literature that will create the correct perspective. My commitment to writing is not an act of self-glorification, but of self-sacrifice for the generations to come.

Kunene has translated Zulu epic poetry into English as well as published his own verse, *Zulu Poems* (London, 1970); significantly, the title of Kunene's own work connotes the importance of tradition in his creations. He believes that the role of the modern poet remains that of the traditional African bard—a glorification of Africa's epic history as an instance of individual African pride. His translations from Zulu epic poetry are *Emperor Shaka the Great* (London, 1979), and *Anthem of the Decades* (London, 1981); a third work, of lyrics, *The Ancestors and The Sacred Mountain* (London, 1982), is both a translation and Kunene's imaginative adaptation of the Zulu originals. In his introduction to *The Ancestors* Kunene writes:

This collection of poems translated from Zulu to English is . . . an attempt to focus on one of the greatest resources for an African writer or artist: few societies have projected the past with such philosophic and creative intensity as the African. Where other societies describe social and material progress in identical terms of growth from lower levels to higher levels, African society separates the two, depicting the ethical element and the technological aspects as often capable of moving in opposing directions. . . . In short, the instruments or tools for modelling man's material environment do not necessarily improve the ethical quality of the society. (p. xi)

As a poet of African consciousness, Kunene warns in his introduction that

the highlighting of literary works not representative of African classical literature and traditions has undermined the emergence of authentic contemporary African literature. The literary principles and techniques that have enriched African literature are as a result obscured. The erosion of the African literary classic and philosophy may yet deprive the world of one of the greatest contributions to human civilization (p. xix).

Although Kunene is an activist exile engaged in the struggle against South African racism, some of his work was published in South Africa before the liberalization of 1989 and 1990.

Consult: O. R. Dathorne, *African Literature in the Twentieth Century* (London, 1976); Christopher Heywood, *Aspects of South African Literature* (London, 1976).

KUNERT, Gunter. Born March 6, 1929, in Berlin, Germany; he lives in Itzehoe, Federal Republic of Germany. Under the Nuremburg laws of Nazi Germany, Kunert was allowed to attend only one segregated school in Berlin. He did not complete his senior year of high school because of war conditions. His house was bombed in 1943; in 1944 he was found unfit to serve in the army reserve. He survived the end of the war by hiding in a cellar of a deserted house. With the Soviet occupation of (East) Germany, Kunert began his studies in graphic arts at the Academy for Applied Arts in Berlin-Weissensee (1946–49). His poems began appearing in 1947; his first volume, *Wegschilder und Mauerinschriften*, appeared in 1950. His early work was highly praised by East German authorities, and he became one of the state's cultural stars. He was sent on several European tours, lectured at the University of Texas in Austin in 1972, and was writer in residence at the University of Warwick, England, in 1975.

During this period Kunert's prolific output was evidenced in the genres of the short story, novel, poetry, essay, graphic arts, and film and television writing. Kunert's independent and forceful views, however, ran counter to official policy in the 1970s, and he was expelled from the Sozialistische Einheitspartei Deutschlands in 1976. In 1979 he moved to Itzehoe, West Germany, with a travel visa valid for 1,050 days; his stay has lasted more than ten years. In 1982 he became a member of the Academy for Language and Poetry in Darmstadt; in 1985 he received the Heinrich Heine Prize of the City of Darmstadt, and in 1988 he was awarded an honorary degree from Allegheny College, Pennsylvania.

While Kunert's work has since been castigated in East Germany, it is becoming more widely read in West Germany, where he is recognized as a poet of major stature. Some critics see in his work two distinct stages. The first, exhibited in such volumes as *Unter diesem Himmel* (1955, Beneath This Sky) and *Tagwerke* (1960, Daily Work), declares an unwavering pledge to universal progress signaled in a style of calm assurance. These writings reverberate with dialectical and epical trappings; they also draw on other traditional German expressionist techniques. His later work, evidenced in such books as *Unterwegs nach Utopia* (1977, On the Way to Utopia), *Abtgotungsverfahren* (1980, Mortification Procedures), and *Stilleben* (1983, Still Life), exclaims an ineradicable skepticism about human progress in a style correspondingly private and melancholy. The later works also draw on silence as a meaningful point of communication. The critic Lowell Bangerter claims that Kunert's lyric productions are among the most important of the past forty years.

In a memoir printed in *Suddeutsched Zeitung* (January 21/22, 1984), Kunert's friend and colleague Erich Loest wrote:

Are you homesick, Gunter? I don't dare to ask him. From his first day here he has stressed that he just moved from one German district to another, within the same language area, and country and people treat him with friendship. In East Berlin, where the authorities keep stepping on his poetry, his typewriter could not function properly, but in Itzehoe it resumed its usual clatter right away. He speaks softly, carefully, as he always did. Only Heiner Muller can be so polite among us. Sarah Kirsch* and he live in former village school houses, complete with classrooms and teacher's apartment and an outdoor privy, now used for bicycles and watering cans. Gardens and fences all around, fields and meadows on all sides. Within a short hour, says Kunert, he is in Hamburg at the airport; in about three hours he manages the distance between Marianne waving goodbye from their door to the Academy in West Berlin. And in the evening he is back again. Loneliness? What does that mean nowadays? But whoever wants to visit him should call him beforehand. It is not that close after all. (English translation by Christine Friedlander)

Loest's comment encapsulates the exilic dilemma that afflicted Kunert and other German writers from both east and west sides of the political/geographic dividing line before the reunification of Germany on October 3, 1990.

Selected Titles: *Mein Lesebuch* (Frankfurt, West Germany, 1983); *Leben und Schreiben* (Frankfurt, 1983); *Zuruck ins Paradies* (Munich, 1984); *Berlin Beizeiten* (Munich, 1987); *Fremd Daheim* (Munich, 1990; A Stranger at Home).

Translation: *Windy Times: Poems and Prose* (1983).
Consult: Lowell A. Bangerter, *German Writing since 1945* (1988).

KUNZE, Reiner. Born August 16, 1933, in Celsnitz, Germany; he lives in West Germany. Kunze studied philosophy and journalism in Leipzig from 1951 to 1955; he taught for four years while writing and publishing several widely noticed works, among them *Vogel uber dem Tau* (1959; Birds among the Dew). Kunze's criticism of the bureaucracy and of government policy brought him official chastisement and harassment; he gave up his teaching duties in 1959 and lived as a professional writer in East Germany until 1977, when he emigrated to West Germany. During this period, a productive one for his writing, he published *Widmungen* (1963, Dedications), *Sensible wege* (1969, Sensitive Ways), *Zimmerlautstarke* (1972; *With the Volume Turned Down, and Other Poems*, 1973), and *Brief mit blauem Siegel* (1972, Letter with Blue Seal); *Die Wunderbaren Jahre: Prosen* (1976; *The Wonderful Years,* 1977); *Auf eigene Hoffnung: Gedichte* (1981); *Gesprach mit der Amse* (1984); *Eines Jeden einziges Leben: Gedichte* (1986).

In 1977 Kunze won the Buchner Prize awarded for high literary distinction. His later work shows an increasing lyricism and personalism, a willingness to treat the conflicts of his complex allegiances. In particular, *Auf eigener Hoffnung* (1981, In Personal Hope) demonstrates Kunze's refusal to be beaten by the circumstances of exile.

Although his two Germanys are now re-united into one, Kunze sees no easy reconciliation among former "East" and "West" German intellectuals and writers. Kunze believes the German writer-intellectual is innately a soldier of ideology rather than a freedom fighter of sniper thought. While he sees the wounds of twentieth-century German separatism as transient and factional, he is concerned about what he considers the permanent condition of German intellectual rigidity. He expresses his views in an interview in Bonn in July, 1990, as reported in *The New York Times*, August 24, 1990 (p. A7); he characterized the German intellectual as a "tin soldier" in an army of "closed systems of thought" for whom ideology becomes one's "fatherland."
Consult: Lowell A. Bangerter, *German Writing since 1945* (1988).

KUZNETSOV, Anatoli. Born August 18, 1929, in Kiev, USSR; he lives in West Germany. Kuznetsov escaped from the USSR in 1969 after suffering harassment for his writings: he had been subject to several police searches and interrogations. He is best known for his work, *Babi Yar* (1970, English edition), a documentary fiction detailing the climate of anti-semitism in the Soviet Union that reached its horrendous climax in the mass slaughters of Jews and gypsies at Babi Yar outside Kiev in September 1941. Commemorating in ignominy the site where the butchery took place, the work was published in a censored version in the USSR in 1966; many of the episodes which revealed the guilty participation of Russian and Ukrainian citizens in the events leading to the slaughter were ordered cut from the manuscript by the Central Committee of the Soviet Communist Party. Out of fear that the uncut manuscript would be confiscated and that he would be charged as a political criminal for writing and holding onto his work, Kuznetsov photographed the original copy before burying it in a secret hiding place. He was able to smuggle out the photographic film with him when he fled from the Soviet Union. The work has been translated into many languages, and several English language editions have appeared since 1970. In the foreword to the 1971 paperback edition, Kuznetsov wrote that everything in the work he was presenting to the reader "happened," and that he had invented "nothing but the truth." Kuznetsov's statement may be taken at both a metaphorical and a literal level. Although Kuznetsov denies that he is "bothering about any literary rules," the fact remains that his work is an instance of literary achievement as well as indisputable factual evidence of political and racial horror. While it is, as Kuznetsov claims, a "document," it is also a transcendence into a literary and imaginative masterpiece.

In 1957, twelve years before his fall from grace with the Soviet authorities and his flight into exile, Kuznetsov published his novel *Continuation of a Legend*, a work reflecting the author's faith in the Soviet system. Katerina Clarke, in her study, *The Soviet Novel*, writes that the work is a "classic example of the youth novel and its official progenitor until the author defected" (p. 228). In this early work, Kuznetsov places his young hero on his first day of work at the Irkutsk power station; the novel traces the hero's journey from an untried innocent to an experienced worker who has passed through doubt and hard work to achieve a lasting faith in the Soviet system. In this and other youth novels of the period (also called Stalinist novels by Western critics), the hero has a mentor whose idealism guides the system forward; characteristically, the mentor must die in order that the young hero may in turn become a spiritual guide to a following generation.

Consult: Katerina Clarke, *The Soviet Novel: History as Ritual* (1981); Ivar Ivask and J. von Wilpert, eds., *World Literature Since 1945* (1973).

L

LA GUMA, Alex. Born February 20, 1925, in Cape Town, South Africa; died 1985, in Havana, Cuba. Deeply influenced by his father, the known communist activist Jimmy La Guma, Alex La Guma showed an early passion for political action. He was a member of the Communist Party Cape Town District Committee until 1950 when the government banned it. (La Guma's membership in the Party was discovered in 1955.) He was a leader of the Coloured People's Congress, and helped to draw up the Freedom Charter of the African National Congress in 1955. In 1956 he was among 156 people accused in a treason trial. Although he was not found guilty (the charges were dropped five years later), he was harassed and detained. In 1962 he was put under house arrest, subject to surveillance twenty-four hours a day for five years; he lost his job at the Cape Town newspaper *New Age*, and his work was banned from publication. He spent four months in prison in 1966 for organizing a strike against the government. After his release he left for exile in London. La Guma moved to Cuba when he was invited there by Fidel Castro to join the Cultural Affairs Division. He served in the capacity of representative of the African National Congress for Latin America and the Caribbean from 1978 to his death.

La Guma's first story appeared in the South African periodical *Fighting Talk* in 1956, and his novella *A Walk in the Night* was published by Mbari Press in Nigeria in 1962. *And a Threefold Cord* was issued in English by an East Berlin publishing house in 1964. La Guma's proletarian views are clearly seen in his early work, largely set in urban slums amid the violence that afflicts victims of racial, cultural, and economic bias. La Guma's teenage street heroes possess a vitality that enables them to survive the despair of an oppressive situation; their bravado and macho *shebeen* talk, while illusionary, serves as a source of fraternity in their struggles.

Because the South African government had listed him as a known communist, La Guma's writings were banned, and while he was known in West African and English literary circles, it was not until the reissue of *A Walk in the Night* (with other stories) by the English publisher Heinemann in 1968 that he achieved a world following. All his stories and subsequent novels are pervaded by a political awareness and a striving for the awakening of revolutionary consciousness in his native land. His later novels *In the Fog of the Season's End* (1972) and *Time of the Butcherbird* (1979) reveal an increasing call for militancy and subversion.

La Guma's exile provoked him into an activist attitude that encouraged his tendency to dogmatism. As his exile lengthened, his work became didactic; the vibrant sociopolitical commentary of his youthful passions was succeeded by a propagandistic moralism.

One of his most astute critics, Abdul R. JanMohamed sees in La Guma's work an example of reactionary cultural paradox. He writes:

Yet the irony of his fiction-as-social-praxis is that the South African people, who would find his novels most useful and pertinent, cannot read them because all his works and utterances are banned by the government.

This political excommunication renders La Guma's novels completely marginal. In the first place this is true because, as we have seen, his fiction is preoccupied with depicting the political, social, personal, and emotional marginality of the disfranchised South Africans. Second, his fiction is marginal in its style and substance: his style is simple and succinct, and his novels are short and terse—they lack the digressions and embellishments born of luxury and plenitude. Third, his novels are marginal in the sense that they limit themselves to a naturalistic and realistic depiction of the political facts of life in South Africa and contain a minimal amount of "fictional" elaboration: they are lean and sparse novels that constantly speak of lack and fortitude. Finally, his fiction is marginal because . . . in West Europe and the United States there is little demand for political fiction. Those who are inclined to read political novels tend not to be interested in La Guma or Nadine Gordimer, preferring instead the fiction of Alexander Solzhenitsyn, which revives the legacy of the Cold War by once more valorizing the freedom of Western institutions against the restrictive practices of the Russian "other," or the fiction of V. S. Naipaul, which revives the legacy of colonialism by further valorizing the goodness and civilization of the West against the unredeemable evil and barbarity of the Third World "other" (p. 262, reprinted from *Manichean Aesthetics: The Politics of Literature in Colonial Africa*, by Abdul R. JanMohamed [Amherst: University of Massachusetts Press, 1983] © 1983 by The University of Massachusetts Press).

Selected Title: *The Stone Country* (East Berlin, 1967).

Consult: Robert July, "The African Personality in the African Novel," in Ulli Beier, *Introduction to African Literature* (1967); Bernth Lindfors, "Form and Technique in the Novels of Richard Rive and Alex La Guma," *Journal of the New African Literature and the Arts* 2 (Autumn 1966).

LAMMING, George. Born 1927 in Barbados; he has returned to Barbados, and travels regularly to England and elsewhere. Lamming moved to Trinidad in 1946 to teach there and also in search of wider intellectual horizons. In Trinidad he deepened his knowledge of literature and social ideas through association with other writers and intellectuals. In 1950 he moved to England, still pursuing intellectual stimulation and an informed view of his situation as writer, as West Indian, and as teacher and propagator of ideas. In seeking wider spheres of opportunity he did not forsake his allegiance to Barbadian peasant consciousness; indeed, his writing shows an increasing awareness of the need to find a West Indian identity integrative in its experiences but distinct from recent colonial dominance. In England he worked at factory jobs and wrote scripts for the BBC's "Caribbean Voices" program. He published his first, and autobiographical, novel, *In the Castle of My Skin* in 1953, in which he idealized the peasant community of Barbados and saw in such community the means by which to transcend colonial history. In an introduction to the book, Richard Wright* signaled Lamming's novel as a "symbolic repetition of the story of a million simple folk who, sprawled over half of the world's surface and involving more than half of the human race, are today being catapulted out of their peaceful, indigenously earthy lives and into the turbulence and anxiety of the twentieth century."

Lamming's corpus shows a growing vision of the need for synthesis in West Indian culture, not only in a multiracial society but in a milieu in which traditional views as exemplified in peasant consciousness or roots mingle with progressive political, social, intellectual, and cultural achievements. Thus much of his fiction involves satire of West Indians who attempt to rise up the ladder of social and economic success and who ape their former English masters in their prestige-climbing. Lamming also renders compassionately those artists and peasants who refuse to surrender to expediency or cultural exploitation.

Lamming particularly expresses his sense of the gulf between his dream of an integrated society without color and class prejudice and the reality of West Indian political turbulence, individual corruption, and/or foolish pandering. The need for the artist/intellectual to associate with the West Indian peasant and with his profound commonality of values becomes in Lamming's novels his guiding exhortation, though Lamming has only recently involved the writer/artist as an active participant in the struggle; in the earlier work the artist provided the vision while the politician engaged in gritty methodology. Yet, in his later fiction, Lamming pushes the artist into the political/social struggle and clearly delineates the artist's responsibility as a social activist, whether through writing or through engaged social action. By Lamming's association of all classes into a web of Caribbean society, the possibilities of a new Caribbean history are defined, one in which the colonial past is put to rest. In the shaping of such a new world the artist loses his sense of exile in communion of experience with his people.

Lamming's arsenal of ideas and ideals sometimes, and for some critics, creates a schematology heavy with the freight of symbols. One of these critics is V. S. Naipaul, who in the *New Statesman* (December 6, 1958, p. 827) praised Lamming as one of the finest prose writers of his generation but also claimed that Lamming had suppressed his emotions in his search for identity and had thereby turned his struggle into a diminished intellectual matter. Naipaul also claimed that Lamming's vision masked a willful ignorance of West Indian political realities. Other critics, however, see in Lamming one of the most significant West Indian writers of this century and one whose novels show a constant growth of portraiture and intellectual exploration.

Lamming's first novel remains his most popular and most wittily engaging. His style in his early work is filled with personal, romantic allusion; his later fiction shows a more severe allegoric mood and frame of reference. His second novel, *The Emigrants* (1954), is generally considered the weakest in execution and most apparent in ideological framing. In this work a number of West Indians embark for England in hope of wider opportunities; their travels will end in disillusionment and ostracism, another world of exile from the promised land of beauty and self-sufficiency they had been seeking on their native island and from the arms of their supposed English motherland. It is probable that this novel served as Lamming's clearinghouse of lingering colonial loyalties, and that the novel was meant to disabuse Lamming of the notion of a mother England who accepted her colonial children with welcoming arms; at best she gave them condescension; at her most usual gesture she allowed them to drift into poverty and the shacks and shackles of urban ghettos. In both this novel and in *Natives of My Person* (1972), Lamming used the setting of a ship as his conveyance for a conglomerate cast of characters of different types and ranges of awareness, but in the later work the mood is triumphant, as diversity provides richness through shared experience.

Lamming is also profoundly conscious of the African diaspora and the African legacy of the West Indian; it is this sense of heritage that Lamming shapes into his "peasant consciousness" and that underlies his work.

In 1960 Lamming published his informal autobiography, *The Pleasures of Exile*, in which he put to good use the putative wounds of separation from one's land and people. Through exile, he was able to realize, comes the opportunity to begin constantly anew. Nothing is lost if the individual and collective consciousness subsumes the past, without rejecting or obscuring it, into a new fabric. Lamming has followed the import of his own flag of words, having returned to Barbados, where he is working on new fiction. He also makes regular visits to the United States, England, Africa, and Europe, giving lectures and observing humankind in its many varieties.

Selected Titles: *Of Age and Innocence* (London, 1958, repr. 1981); *Season of Adventure* (London, 1970, repr. 1979); *Water with Berries* (1972); *The Pleasures of Exile* (1984).

Consult: Cecil Abrahams, "George Lamming and Chinua Achebe: Tradition and the Literary Chroniclers," in *Awakened Conscience: Studies in Commonwealth Literature*, ed. C. D. Narasamiah (New Delhi, n.d.); Wilson Harris, *Tradition, the Writer and Society* (1963, 1967); Bruce King, ed., *West Indian Literature* (1979); Ian Munro, in *Fifty Caribbean Writers*, ed. Daryl Cumber Dance (1986); Ngugi wa Thiong'o, *Homecoming* (1972); Sandra Pouchet Paquet, *The Novels of George Lamming* (London, 1982); Ivan Van Sertima, *Caribbean Writers: Critical Essays* (London, 1968).

LANDSBERGIS, Algirdas. Born June 23, 1924, in Kybartai, Lithuania; he lives in Freeport, Long Island, New York. Landsbergis studied Lithuanian literature at the University of Kaunas and English literature at the University of Mainz. He emigrated to the United States in 1949. In 1957 he received a master's degree in comparative literature from Columbia University. Since 1965 Landsbergis has been teaching English and comparative literature at Fairleigh Dickinson University.

Landsbergis started his literary career as a poet, but is known primarily as a novelist, short story writer, and a playwright. He belonged to the avant-garde group of Lithuanian intellectuals, including Jonas Mekas and others, who wrote experimental literature and criticized Lithuanian émigré society for its conservative outlook. In his novel *Kelionė* (1954, The Journey), Landsbergis describes the experiences of a young slave laborer in Germany during the last months of the Nazi regime. He uses modern psychological and narrative techniques: the events are seen through the prism of a traumatized consciousness. The novel is also noted for its innovative style. *Ilgoji naktis* (1956, The Long Night), a book of short stories, is an investigation, in an existentialist vein, into extreme human situations during the years of guerrilla war and totalitarian terror in Lithuania. The same motifs form the core of Landsbergis's best-known play, *Penki stulpai turgaus aikštėj* (1966, Five Posts in the Marketplace); the English-language version was presented off-Broadway and also in Chicago and Toronto in 1961. His other plays, for example, *Meilės mokykla* (1965, School of Love), *Paskutinis piknikas* (1970, The Last Picnic), as well as his collection of stories *Muzika įžengiant i neregėtus miestus* (1979, Music While We Enter the Unseen Cities), use surrealist and avant-garde techniques to touch upon the paradoxes of existence in exile. Landsbergis is one of the main proponents of absurdist drama in Lithuanian literature. He has also coedited several anthologies of Lithuanian and Baltic literature in English, for example, *The Green Oak* (1962); *The Green Linden* (1964).

Consult: R. Šilbajoris, *Perfection of Exile* (1970).

TOMAS VENCLOVA

LASKER-SCHÜLER, Else. Born February 11, 1869, in Elberfeld [now a part of the integrated city of Wuppertal] Germany; died January 22, 1945, in Jerusalem. Daughter of a banker, granddaughter of a chief rabbi of the Rhineland, Lasker-Schüler, in revolt against her bourgeois origins, joined the bohemian literati prominent in Berlin during the 1890s. Consorting with Theodor Däubler, Franz Marc, Georg Trakl, and Peter Hille (the German Verlaine), she became "the Scheherezade of the Café des Westens." Her second marriage, to Herwarth Walden, linked her with the expressionists, and she began to publish poetry and prose in *Die Fackel* (The Torch), *Der Brenner* (The Burner), and *Der Sturm* (The Storm). *Die Wupper* (1909, People of the Wupper) was an isolated exercise in proletarian drama, but her later play *Arthur Aronymus und seine Väter* (1932, Arthur Aronymus and His Fathers), based on her own family history, expressed more durable associations with Hebraic themes. When the play was banned in 1933, Lasker-Schüler emigrated to Zurich. A first visit to Palestine inspired a travel book, *Das Hebräerland* (1937, Land of the Hebrews). The outbreak of hostilities in 1939 found her once more in Palestine, where she spent the remainder of her life.

Though condemned to poverty, Lasker-Schüler does not fit into the stereotype of the refugee. Her powerful, erotically charged verse owes more to cosmic alienation than to a sense of banishment. At home in a self-created psychic environment, rather than in her physical surroundings, she claimed spiritual descent from the Thebes of ancient Egypt. Oriental imagery, often based on the Old Testament, is evident in much of her work, especially in her *Hebräische Balladen* (1913, Hebrew Ballads), which she considered her finest achievement. Yet her attitude to life in Palestine was often ambivalent. She scolded her fellow immigrants for not being sufficiently "Hebrew," and in the poem "Mein Volk" (My People) complained that the rock on which Jewish faith was founded had grown brittle ("morsch"). Her creativity was too firmly rooted in the German language to permit full identification with an embryonic Israel. Significantly, her poem "Die Verscheuchte" (The Woman Driven Away), written after her escape to Switzerland, is a sentimental evocation of the past rather than an accusation against her evictors. Lasker-Schüler's status as a poetess is still controversial, and it is unfortunate that her declamatory, hyperbolic style lends itself to parody. Franz Kafka* charged her with contrived verbosity; for Gottfried Benn she was preeminent, greater even than Annette Elisabeth von Droste-Hülshoff. Peter Hille's early vision of her as "the black swan of Israel, whose world has been shattered" is a valid summing-up of her anguished career.

Selected Titles: *Styx* (Berlin, 1902); *Das Peter-Hille-Buch* (Stuttgart, 1906); *Der Prinz von Theben: Ein Geschichtenbuch* (Leipzig, 1914, The Prince of Thebes: Tales); *Mein blaues Klavier: Neue Gedichte* (Jerusalem, 1943, My Blue Piano: New Poems); *Gesamtausgabe*, 10 vols. (Berlin, 1919–20, Collected Works); *Gesammelte Werke*, 3 vols. (Munich, 1959–62); *Sämthliche Gedichte* (Munich, 1966, Complete Poems); *Hebrew Ballads and Other Poems* (1981).

Consult: S. Bauschinger, *Else Lasker-Schüler, Ihr Werk und Ihre Zeit* (Heidelberg, 1980); M. Schmid, *Lasker-Schüler: Ein Buch zum 100 Geburtstag der Dichterin* (Wuppertal, Germany, 1969), a centenary commemoration.

CEDRIC HENTSCHEL

Before her exile from 1933 to 1945, Lasker-Schüler wrote hundreds of poems and prose pieces, many of which appeared in leading journals. Thirty volumes of her poetry, prose, and plays were published by 1933. For some of these works Lasker-Schüler chose imaginary male names for herself as symbol of the artist as a royal being; she sometimes signed these names in her correspondence with lovers, friends, financial supporters, and critics. Throughout her life she put feeling above intellect and invariably triggered strong reaction in her readers and listeners through her innovative language and her dramatic and eccentric manner of performance. Karl Kraus preferred some of her poems to those of Heinrich

Heine. Georg Trakl, Franz Werfel,* and Gottfried Benn dedicated works to her. Franz Marc and Oscar Kokoschka* painted her. Theodore Herzl, the founder of Zionism called her one of the "36 just beings, holy people walking on earth naively, angels!" but Franz Kafka was discomforted by her bohemian lifestyle. A newspaper critic called her "the most radical representative of modern radical poetry." In spite of these mixed reactions, Lasker-Schüler was awarded Germany's prestigious Kleist Prize in 1932.

Soon after Adolf Hitler came to power, her works were banned and burned. When the sixty-four-year-old poet was physically attacked in the spring of 1933, she fled to Zurich, Switzerland, the same day. Unable to visit the graves of her parents in her beloved hometown of Wuppertal, or the grave in Berlin of her only child, Paul, Lasker-Schüler never again returned to her homeland.

Swiss police found Lasker-Schüler sleeping on a bench in a park without any money and papers, arrested her, and published their report in the daily newspaper. Such was the embarrassment of her exile, which was to continue until her death.

The three visits Lasker-Schüler made to Jerusalem may be seen as an exile's desperate attempts to make her vision of the Land of the Hebrews come true, and to make her writing a contribution in "the building of Palestine; I have not been idle in God's work" (cited in J. Hessing, "Else Lasker-Schüler and Her People," *Ariel* 41 [1976], p. 67). Yet she also concluded: "I have imagined my being in Jerusalem differently . . . and I will die here of sadness. . . . There is no warmth here." As a work of love and reconciliation between Jews and Arabs, she wrote her last prose collection, *Das Hebräerland* (1937, The Land of the Hebrews), in her Swiss exile.

Whether in Switzerland or Palestine, Lasker-Schüler was aware that "foreign hedges surround [the exile's] heart" (Lasker-Schüler's diary, cited in Sigrid Bauschinger, *Else Lasker-Schüler: Ihr Werk Und Ihre Zeit*, Heidelberg, 1980). After decades of *Fernwehdichtung* (poetry of painful longing for that which is far away), her exile writing became a form of *Heimwehdichtung* (poetry of homesickness). After her second visit to Palestine in 1937, the Jewish Kulturbund in Switzerland no longer offered her financial support. Deprived of her German citizenship in 1938, she felt newly betrayed, and left Zurich to visit Jerusalem for a third time in 1939. Unhappy with life in Palestine, Lasker-Schüler applied for a return visa to Switzerland, but her application was denied.

Twice exiled and unable to leave Jerusalem, Lasker-Schüler—now over seventy years old, impoverished but still dressing herself as Prince Yussuf—became an object of derision among Jewish settlers and intellectuals. In return, she referred to her once beloved "Erez-Israel" (Land of Israel) as "Erez-Miesrael" (Land of Erez Misery-el). Filled with her visions, Lasker-Schüler continued writing, drawing, giving readings, and forming a literary salon called "Kraal," which Martin Buber,* the philosopher, opened on January 10, 1942, at the French Cultural Center. Although she attracted some of the leading writers and promising poets to her literary programs, Lasker-Schüler soon faced a ban of her readings and lectures because they were held in German. In a letter to the head of the German synagogue in Jerusalem, she begged him to let her use his *Gotteshaus* (house of God) one more time: "Wherever I was, German is not allowed to be spoken. I want to arrange the last Kraal evening for a poet who is *already* broken, to recite from his translations [into German] of a great Hebrew" (Letter to Rabbi Kurt Wilhelm, Else Lasker-Schüler Archive, Jerusalem, cited in Bauschinger, p. 270).

In her final years Lasker-Schüler worked on her drama *IchundIch* (IandI), which was to remain a controversial fragment. However, she finished her volume of poems, *Mein Blaues Klavier* (1943, My Blue Piano). This collection of privately printed poems appeared, under difficult circumstances, in a limited edition of 330 copies; her literary farewell became her last attempt to overcome the loneliness of exile. Significantly, she dedicated the work to "my unforgettable friends in the cities of Germany and to those, like me, exiled and dispersed throughout the world, in good faith." In one of her final acts, she asked that her hometown of Wuppertal and its surrounding area be spared from Allied bombing.

Few of her poems and prose works have been translated into English. However, her work has been shown increasing attention by American scholars.

Translation: See section on Lasker-Schüler in A. Durchslag and J. Litman-Semeestere, eds., *Hebrew Ballads and Other Poems* (1980).

Consult: Sigrid Bauschinger, *Else Lasker-Schüler: Ihr Werk und Ihre Zeit* (Heidelberg, 1980); Jakob Hessing, "Else Lasker-Schüler and Her People," *Ariel* 41 (1976); Heinz Politzer, "The Blue Piano of Else Lasker-Schüler," *Commentary* 9 (1950); Michael Schmid, ed., *Lasker-Schüler: Ein Geburtstagsbuch* (Wuppertal, 1969); Wolfgang Springmann, ed., *Else Lasker-Schüler und Wuppertal* (Wuppertal: Stadtbibliothek, 1965).

HENRIK EGER

LAWRENCE, D. H. (David Herbert). Born September 11, 1885, in Eastwood, near Nottingham, England; died March 30, 1930, in Vence, France. Lawrence's humble origins are well known through his rendering of them in *Sons and Lovers* (London, 1913). He was born of a coal-miner father (who rose to become a subcontractor, a position of some note in his field, and whose managerial abilities are nowhere paid tribute in Lawrence's work), and an intellectual, strong-willed mother who had been a schoolteacher. Lawrence studied at schools in the English midlands and earned a teachers certificate from Nottingham University. His first novel, *The White Peacock* (London, 1911), received favorable critical attention. The novel is, as is usual in Lawrence's work, a transmutation of personal experience whose surface similarity to real events of biography is apparent. The novel concerns the dissolution of a marriage between a weak-willed, physically strong and charming man and a demanding woman who knows merely what she is missing and not yet what she is seeking. The outlines of what would later prove graphic strokes in Lawrence's portrait of the quest for identity and the need for a merging, or flow (Lawrence's term), into a mystic, ineffable communion can be seen from this earliest novel. His second novel, *The Trespassers*

(London, 1912), proved less effective; it is the story of a doomed love affair told to him by Helen Corke, one of the several women with whom he enjoyed an emotionally intimate relationship. In this work the male lover in an extramarital affair—he is a married father who has fallen in love with a younger woman—shoots himself as an end to the affair. Perhaps because it was someone else's story, and not one in which Lawrence really shared, the novel lacks the characteristic passion of his other prose.

Lawrence's mother died of cancer in 1910. The marriage of his parents that Lawrence had witnessed exhibited a blast of quarrels and a sulky compromise that was less forgiveness than a convenient repression of hostility and a lingering, irrepressible affection. Lawrence's affection for his mother, and his partisan view of her marital trials, show clearly in his work and in his enormous sense of loss after her death. The loss may well have influenced his quandary over whether to continue teaching or to go into full-time writing, as he wished. In seeking an answer Lawrence went to visit his teacher friend, Professor Ernest Weakly, at Nottingham University for counsel. While there he met Weakly's wife, born Frieda von Richthofen, a German baroness and the cousin of the German aviator ace who was to shoot down enough Allied planes during the course of World War I to justify lasting public attention. Frieda and Lawrence spent an afternoon together while waiting for Weakly to finish his lectures, and thus began their famous lifelong love affair and their unique marriage of polarized beings.

Lawrence and Frieda ran off to Germany in 1912, leaving her three children behind with Weakly. Their plans for a secret tryst were shattered into public knowledge when they had to appeal for letters of confirmation and identity in their difficulties with German police agents on the eve of World War I.

Lawrence's choice was made for him at this moment, and he took up the challenge—he began the end of one life and the exile into another grandly. He and Frieda returned to England, where he completed *Sons and Lovers* (some critics, particularly Frank O'Connor,* posit that the novel is bifurcated in mood and vision as a result of its author's awareness of new experience). He began the composition of a new novel, "The Sisters," which several years and several versions later appeared in the form of *The Rainbow* (London, 1915) and *Women in Love* (London, 1920). The two novels explore the growth and experience of several generations of an English midlands family, and mark the kind of new fiction characteristic of this major writer in modern British literature.

Lawrence's physical wanderings began in 1919, with the end of World War I. During the war he and Frieda had been hounded in London; Frieda's cousin, the German ace Baron von Richthofen, and his war record, made Frieda a suspicious alien to the British government. Because of their economic condition and because Lawrence desired to find a quiet place where he could work, they chose to move to a cottage in Cornwall, where accommodations were quite cheap. Lawrence, in addition, was saying a repeated farewell to the bohemianism of London (later it would be other worldly cities), which he detested but was drawn to like a fascinated mimic. Frieda's German affiliations again proved a provocation for surveillance by English security agents, and she and Lawrence were harassed on several occasions during this period of continual rumors of German submarine invasion. At this time Lawrence conceived the idea of a utopian society in which his concepts of polarization would create a perfect modus vivendi for human beings to realize their potential for spiritual fulfillment. In effect Lawrence's notion of polarization is the erasure of the exilic feeling in human beings; it is a union of psychic awareness for the purpose of the creation of a sense of wholeness and fulfillment. Lawrence's notion allows for the retention of the self and its unique qualities in the merger with the universe and its holistic harmony. The concept is thus Lawrence's drawing of the kind of marriage his parents failed to achieve in their self-centered quarrels without a unifying resolution; it also represents the kind of society that for Lawrence would make a world in which wars and ostracism would become anathema. Together with Bertrand Russell and John Middleton Murry, Lawrence wrote prospectuses of the utopian colony they were going to found in Florida; Lawrence called it Ranamin, and the philosophy guiding it, Pantisocracy. Predictably, the utopian society ran into administrative problems before it took root, and Russell and Lawrence quarreled violently about it and inevitably about their variant views of philosophy. For Lawrence the concept of Ranamin may be seen as a lasting vision that issued into the rainbow that Ursula in *The Rainbow* had to walk through; in *Women in Love* it is reflected in the successful union of Ursula and Birkin.

Walking, journeying, traveling, motion—the features of a quest—are part of the Lawrentian canon from this point on. Lawrence traveled to Australia, Ceylon, San Francisco, New Mexico, Mexico, Italy, Capri, and southern France in his journey outward to a journey inward that both enclosed him and Frieda and freed them to their individual identities and a universal referent. Lawrence's views on the sense of the outcast and wanderer may be seen in *Aaron's Rod* (London, 1922), a short novel (written shortly after the appearance of *Women in Love*) in which a lower middle-class English father leaves his family to wander through Europe and play his flute, thus obeying the music of siren calls in his personal odyssey. Although not a major work, the novel explores Lawrence's sense of quest openly. The biblical name of the hero is significant as well as the rod in the title, since the rod is both a staff on which to lean and an implement of higher, and corporal, education. As a journeyman must wander in fields of exile before he can come home to a sense of himself, Lawrence ends the novel without any clear sense of Aaron's destination, perhaps because the point of the journey was not a terminus but a motion.

Lawrence and Frieda both said that Taos, New Mexico, was the geographical spot in which they experienced their greatest and most sustained contentment. They lived there from 1923 to 1924 at the invitation of Mabel Dodge Sterne Luhan, the American heiress, in her home; later, from 1924 to 1925, she provided them a cottage 2,000 feet above the village. In spite of their monumental quarrels in New Mexico and old Mexico (Mexico City, Lake Chapala, and Oaxaca, 1923–24, and 1925), Lawrence and Frieda responded to their new lands with great amatory passion. The record of their stay here is filled with the transiency of constant search for the perfect place, for Lawrence's Ranamin in spirit if not in establishment. Frieda had Lawrence's ashes brought from France to Taos; the ashes were placed in an urn in the cabin they had shared, along with his typewriter and other memorabilia. Frieda lived in Taos in a house nearer to the village for some twenty-six years after Lawrence's death; she died in 1956 and is buried in Taos.

The fields of wandering that cover the hegira of Lawrence's vision prove curiously ironic. Lawrence's life began in the English midlands; he wandered over half the world in his short lifetime. His life was filled with controversy, and he rarely earned enough money from his writing for subsistence. He married a German baroness of learning and quick wit. His fiction often presents the story of a humble or working man in a relationship with an upper-class and/or wealthy and titled woman. Although Lawrence always put feeling above intellect, and the rank of natural pose above class and station, he also paid tribute to learning and education. In his early work he clearly champions the victimized woman of little learning and great potential hemmed in by the demands of poverty and an ill-educated mate and their narrow surroundings. In his later life he exalted the qualities potent in his father's figure—the natural man, the gamekeeper Mellors whose common sense could raise a lady's spirit to heights unavailable in the richly material world of wit and sophistication provided by her sterile husband, Lord Chatterley. It is significant that in Lawrence's fiction the rich and titled heroine must be humbled into a naturalness that has no memory of material wealth; only thus is she freed to achieve her full potential as a human being. The means of her deliverance is a primitive rite issuing out of a pristine civilization. Thus the coal-miner father figure, in the trajectory of Lawrence's childhood memory, is given his due finally, perhaps in compensation for the earlier rejection of the vulgar man when pitted against the bourgeois claims of his protective mother.

Lawrence's works over the years have amassed a publishing fortune. On a metaphoric level the distribution of the proceeds has its ironies as well. The working-class Englishman's legacy, or royalties, went to a German baroness, who married an Italian army major after Lawrence's death; the major and Frieda's English-born children received the proceeds of her legacy. Lawrence might well have enjoyed the polarity of his sales script.

Among Lawrence's other works written during his period of wandering are *The Lost Girl* (London, 1920), his most conventional novel in which a bourgeois English girl joins a circus in Italy and marries a poor Italian man and finds fulfillment enough in her connubial love in a cold hut; *The Boy in the Bush* (London, 1924; a rewriting of a novel by an Australian admirer, M. L. Skinner, who sent Lawrence her manuscript and asked for his help in revising it); and *Kangaroo* (London, 1923), which explores the tempting appeals of fascism through the allure of the militant instinct in men and the equally appealing note of trade unionism and brotherhood. This last novel grew out of Lawrence's trip to Australia and reflects his apprehension of the contemporary Australian social scene. Ultimately Lawrence rejects both the militant fascist underground army group and the activist socialist organization he observed in his travels in Australia. He finds each wanting in the essential quality of immaterial spiritual kinship. Lawrence's late novel *The Plumed Serpent* (London, 1926) also treats the appeal of darkness, mystery, and primitiveness as one way for man to shed his nagging sense of loss of human potential and to clothe himself in the pristine state of feelingful hope and euphoria. His last novel, *Lady Chatterley's Lover* (Florence, 1928), is probably his best-known work largely because of its controversial publishing history. It was written and published in three versions during the final years of his illness in Italy and France. Each version is distinct, but all offer a resolution to psychic exile through the harmony of physical and social love. The class structure is broken by the affair of a titled lady and her gamekeeper and healed by their union on the high planes of natural love. The authorized third manuscript version, which Lawrence had privately printed in Italy, was republished in 1959 by Grove Press of New York and led to a famous court case in which the right to publish the book was sustained over the charges of pornography leveled against it.

In his short stories—a genre in which he is acknowledged as a master— Lawrence presents the theme of alienation and exile particularly in "The Princess," "The Woman Who Rode Away," and "Sun." Lawrence is also a major poet, and his lyrics, odes, and pensées on death and rebirth reveal the theme of the wanderer and his necessary experiential exploration essential to the coming and becoming of peace. His *Collected Poems* was first issued in 1928.

His travel books, among them *Mornings in Mexico* (London, 1927), *Etruscan Places* (London, 1932), and *The Spirit of Place*, edited by Richard Aldington (London, 1935), are extraordinary in their molding of the history of a place with the spirit of that place; these works present a place that is at once past and present. Lawrence also wrote plays still performed in England, the United States, and elsewhere, but he is not considered a major dramatist. He was a painter as well, and several reproductions of his paintings have been collected in variously issued volumes. His paintings, particularly those of the final period of his life when he was writing/rewriting *Lady Chatterley's Lover*, have been described as passionate, throbbing, erotic, and primitive. Like his fiction, they portray men and women in the act of joyous sexuality. Like his novels, they suffered harassment through acts of banning and censorship: the entire showing of his work at the Warren gallery in London in 1929 was confiscated by police on charges of obscenity.

Selected Titles: *Fantasia of the Unconscious* (1922); *England, My England* (1922), stories; *Studies in Classic American Literature* (1923); *Birds, Beasts and Flowers* (1923), poems; *Little Novels of Sicily by Giovanni Verga* (1925), translation; *Sun* (London, 1926); *Selected Poems* (1928); *Cavalleria Rusticana*, by Giovanni Verga (1928), translation;

The Paintings of D. H. Lawrence (London, 1929); *Pansies* (London, 1929); *Pornography and Obscenity* (London, 1929); *The Escaped Cock* (Paris, 1929), later *The Man Who Died* (London, 1935); *Last Poems* (Florence, 1932); *Phoenix: Posthumous Papers* (1936); *Complete Short Stories*, 3 vols. (London, 1955); *The Complete Poems of D. H. Lawrence*, ed. Vivian de Sola Pinto and F. Warren Roberts, 2 vols. (1964); *The Complete Plays* (1965). Letters: James T. Boulton, general editor, 5 vols. published by 1989: vol. 1, *1901–1913*; vol. 2, *1913–16*; vol. 3, *1916–19*; vol. 4, *June 1921–March 1924*; vol.5, *March 1924–March 1927*; further volumes in progress. See the authoritative editions of D. H. Lawrence's writings being published by Cambridge University Press, each volume edited individually; General editors James T. Boulton and F. Warren Roberts. Several titles have been issued. See also E. W. Tedlock, Jr., comp., *The Frieda Lawrence Collection of D. H. Lawrence's Manuscripts: A Descriptive Bibliography* (Albuquerque, 1948); E. W. Tedlock, Jr., ed., *Frieda Lawrence: The Memoirs and Correspondence* (1964).

Consult: Harry T. Moore, *The Intelligent Heart: The Life of D. H. Lawrence* (1954, rev. 1962); Edward Nehls, ed., *D. H. Lawrence: A Composite Biography*, 3 vols. (1959).

Bibliography: James C. Cowan, ed., *D. H. Lawrence: An Annotated Bibliography of Writings about Him*, 2 vols. (1982); Warren Roberts, comp., *A Bibliography of D. H. Lawrence*, The Soho Bibliographies (London, 1963).

LAWRENCE, T. E. (Thomas Edward). Born August 15, 1888, in Tremadoc, North Wales; died May 19, 1935, near Clouds Hill, England, after a motorcycle accident. Lawrence developed an early fascination for archaeology and for military strategy while studying at Oxford. These interests, combined with a desire for independence, led him to study French medieval fortresses in Syria for his thesis topic. With little money, he made his first trip to the Middle East in the summer of 1909, traveling from castle to castle on foot and mingling with Arab villagers. Later work on the Carchemish archaeological excavation provided further knowledge of Arab manners and customs. Lawrence's experiences on these journeys proved a profound influence; he became committed to freeing the Arabs from Turkish and European dominance, and to helping in establishing an independent state.

When World War I broke out, Lawrence got himself assigned to the British military intelligence unit in Egypt, and in October 1916, he joined the Arab leader Feisal and his revolt against Turkish rule. For the next two years Lawrence led a guerrilla campaign against the Turks. His military exploits brought him fame in both the Arab and European worlds. Yet he was not able to accomplish what he had set out to do, that is, establish an independent Arab state. Despite his eloquent pleas, the British and French governments in the Treaty of Versailles parceled out for themselves the lands for which Lawrence and the Arabs had fought. It was not until two years after World War I that Lawrence managed to persuade Winston Churchill to establish Feisal as king of Iraq.

During this postwar period, Lawrence began his second massive undertaking, the writing of a literary epic. One of his biographers, Vyvyan Richards, claims Lawrence wanted, first, to create a work of art that presented the Arab campaign in graphic detail and, second, to reveal his own inner heart and mind. *Seven Pillars*, a prodigious feat of individual endurance, is nearly a half million words long. The first draft was almost complete when Lawrence lost the manuscript in Paris. He rewrote the text from memory and notes, then revised the entire rewrite, producing as many as 30,000 words in twenty-four hours. This feat was succeeded by a private edition, which Lawrence arranged, of about 100 copies of the text containing specially commissioned illustrations and detailed bindings. Costs for the elaborate printing enterprise were funded in part by proceeds from the sale of *Revolt in the Desert*, a popularized condensation of *Seven Pillars*. Despite the efforts that went into *Seven Pillars*, the book never achieved the literary renown Lawrence had sought.

Lawrence was an exile in two notable ways: politically and personally. He was a political exile in his single-minded determination to establish an independent Arab state in spite of lack of support in European capitals in the early twentieth century. He was a personal exile in his difficulty in coping with the widespread fame he had earned as a military leader, and in refusing to make any personal profit from his wartime exploits, whether in the form of medals or money. He went so far as to enlist twice in the British military (once in the army, once in the air force) as a private in order to preserve the anonymity he desired.

Consult: John E. Mack, *A Prince of Our Disorder* (1976); Vyvyan Richards, *T. E. Lawrence* (1939); Stanley Weintraub and Rodelle Weintraub, eds., *Evolution of a Revolt* (1968).

TIMOTHY E. DYKSTRA

LAWSON, John Howard. Born September 25, 1894, in New York City; died August 14, 1977, in San Francisco. Playwright, screenwriter, dramatic theorist, film theorist, social critic. Lawson was best known through the end of the World War II as a playwright, theorist, and screenwriter. Though he was successful and reasonably well known, it was his identification with the Hollywood Ten— a group of screenwriters including Dalton Trumbo,* Ring Lardner, Jr., Alvah Bessie, and Albert Maltz accused by the House Un-American Activities Committee (HUAC) of communist affiliations and sympathies—that led to his subsequent notoriety, imprisonment, exile in Mexico and brief stay in the Soviet Union and East Germany.

In addition to several early plays written before and after college, Lawson wrote numerous dramatic works following his service in World War I that reflect experimental efforts and borrowings from German expressionism. He was active in Hollywood for some twenty years from the late 1920s onward; he wrote the screenplay for Cecil B. DeMille's first talkie, *Dynamite* (1929), and over twenty other screenplays (dialogue for some, collaboration on others). He was also founding president of the Screenwriters Guild. He continued writing for the theater throughout the 1930s, and had four of his plays successfully produced.

Roger Bloomer (1923), his first important play (and, since it preceded Elmer

Rice's *The Adding Machine* by a few weeks, the first American expressionistic play), is a conventional, somewhat satiric story of a young man who goes to New York City to seek his fortune. While there he becomes involved with a hometown girl who kills herself but who reappears, along with others from his hometown, in a dream vision that frees him from his guilt and helps him understand the necessity of accepting his situation. *Processional: A Jazz Symphony of American Life* (1925) is experimental in its attempts to combine jazz and vaudeville with the satiric thrust found in *Roger Bloomer*. Lawson's social activism is evident in the play's focus on a brave worker in a mining town who is blinded for his efforts to organize labor.

From the late 1920s onward, Lawson's plays began to reflect explicitly his political activism and social beliefs. *Nirvana* (1927) is an expressionistic search for a new world religion; *Loudspeaker* (1927) is a farcical examination of politics. *The International* (1928) is an uneasy mixture of exotic setting (Tibet), elements from musicals, and a radicalized protagonist who becomes a martyr because of his love for a Russian woman. *Success Story* (1932) focuses on a radical, in this case a New Yorker who compromises his beliefs by pursuing a career in advertising. Innocence is ruined in *The Pure in Heart* (1934) as a young woman, drawn into unethical circles as she embarks on a theatrical career, finds that love does not in fact conquer all. *Gentlewoman* (1934) more explicitly attacks the decadence of American society, though the proletarian protagonist escapes destruction. *Marching Song* (1937) is the most explicitly preachy of Lawson's plays, clearly intended to convert uncommitted viewers: capitalism in its excesses and lack of feeling is exposed in a company town, with polarized characters (vicious exploiters on the one hand, brave, heroic workers on the other).

As Lawson's work turned more doctrinaire, it also became correspondingly didactic and undramatic, with stereotyped characterization, stilted dialogue (even from the mouths of proletarian workers), and with ideology supplanting technique. Yet his screenwriting was often free of such ideology, with some of his films—*Blockade* (1938), *Algiers* (1938), *They Shall Have Music* (1939), *Babes in Arms* (1939), *Action in the North Atlantic* (1943), *Sahara* (1943), *The Jolson Story* (uncredited, 1946), and *Smash-Up: The Story of a Woman* (1947)—achieving genuine feeling and depth of characterization.

Lawson's 1947 encounter with the McCarthyist tactics of the HUAC, in which, as an "unfriendly" witness, he defended the Bill of Rights as it applied to the film industry and to his own beliefs, ultimately made him better known than had any of his writings. Found in contempt of court, Lawson was one of only two of the Hollywood Ten (the other was Dalton Trumbo) to be tried immediately, and he served a year in federal prison in 1947–48, after which he wrote the unproduced *Thunder Morning*, a play about black ghetto life, and *The Hidden Heritage: A Rediscovery of the Ideas and Forces That Link the Thought of Our Time with the Culture of the Past* (1950), an underappreciated cultural synthesis.

Immediately blacklisted after his release in 1948, Lawson, along with others of the Hollywood Ten, found it impossible to work under his own name in

Hollywood. He went into exile in Mexico, as did Trumbo, and wrote for the cinema under assumed names. He wrote the screenplay for *Cry, the Beloved Country* (1952), for example, and wrote a few additional, forgettable films, such as *Terror in a Texas Town* (1958), all at a fraction of his previous earnings of $75,000 per script, but had little such work otherwise. He subsequently taught at various colleges and universities (Reed, San Fernando State, Stanford, Loyola) and over a two-year period (1961–63) spent time in the Soviet Union and East Germany, where he saw a revision of his 1939 play, *Parlor Magic*, produced.

Selected Titles: *Theory and Technique of Playwriting* (1936, rev. ed., *Theory and Technique of Playwriting and Screen Writing*, 1949); *Film in the Battle of Ideas* (1953); *Film: The Creative Process: The Search for an Audio-Visual Language and Structure* (1964, rev. ed., 1967).

Consult: Garry Carr, *The Left Side of Paradise: The Screenwriting of John Howard Lawson* (1984); Lester Cole, *Hollywood Red* (1982); Bernard F. Dick, *Radical Innocence: A Critical Study of the Hollywood Ten* (1989); Gordon Kahn, *Hollywood on Trial* (1948); Victor Navasky, *Naming Names* (1980); Robert Vaughan, *Only Victims: A Study of Show Business Blacklisting* (1972).

PAUL SCHLUETER

LAYE, Camara (also Camara Laye). Born 1928 in Kouroussa, Guinea; died February 4, 1980 in Dakar, Senegal. Camara Laye, a descendant of the black Sudanese who founded the Mali Empire, was raised in the Muslim faith and in the animist faith of his parents. His mother and father were highly respected members of their tribal community, and each was thought to possess supernatural powers. In the ancient city of Kouroussa, where Laye grew up, he learned his father's trade of goldsmithing and described its wondrous forms and shapes in his novel/memoir, *L'enfant noir* (Paris, 1953; *The Dark Child*, 1954; *The African Child*, London, 1955). He attended technical high school in Conakry and was awarded a French government scholarship for further study in France. Against the wishes of his mother, who feared not only the physical separation of her son from her but his loss of native traditions, Laye went to Argenteuil, France, where he earned a degree in automotive technology. He moved to Paris to study automotive engineering and worked in a Renault automobile factory to earn money to live on; he was often poor and hungry, and felt the oppression of homesickness. He thus began his first period of exile as a young man, which ended in 1956 on his return to Guinea. Laye describes the magic and wonder of his childhood in his first book, a work that has received worldwide recognition as one of the outstanding memoirs of an African in transition from a traditional, nonmechanized village to a different modern world. Filled with a consciousness of African identity, the work extols the beauty and stability of childhood faith in the rituals of growing up African, in being in touch with nature and its roots, and in feeling the enrichment of animal, particularly snake, worship. Laye's first book is often regarded as the perfect example of negritude—a work that illuminates the essence of African identity—but he did not believe in the separatism that the negritude movement spawned. His ideal was a unity of culture, just as the hero of his last work, *The Guardian of the World: Kouma Lafolo Kouma*, united the many kingdoms of the upper Niger into the flower of the Mali Empire.

Laye wrote his second and most complex work in France as well, *Le regard du roi* (Paris, 1954; *The Radiance of the King*, 1956), an allegorical novel in which a white wanderer seeks salvation from a black king who finally smiles on him the radiance of forgiveness for the white man's past sins. The novel is a brilliant literary paradigm of colonial experience, a surreal allegory in which are mixed Christian redemption, Islamic allusiveness, Kafkaesque imagery, and African spiritualism. The roles of victim and tyrant are reversed, and the hope of a brighter, newer political and social climate for the victims and tyrants of European-African history is conveyed. The narrative follows a white beggar who wanders in search of a black king who will liberate him by the radiant smile that smites all sickness in a troubled soul. Laye's second work is allegorical, Kafkaesque, and African in a way unique to him, a powerful and disturbing exploration of exile, quest, and reconciliation with a power greater than logic and reason.

On his return to Guinea, Laye worked in a technical capacity for the French colonial regime, and after Guinean independence, he became a close associate of the country's first president, Sékou Touré. He was sent on several diplomatic missions and later became director of the study and research center in the Ministry of Information in Conakry. A quarrel ensured between Touré and Laye, and Laye fled in 1965 to Senegal. The second exile of Laye began at this point. He was tried in absentia in Guinea for treason and received a death sentence. His wife was arrested when she returned to Guinea to attend her father's funeral and spent time in prison there. During this second period of exile Laye wrote a bitter fictionalized memoir—it has also been called an autobiographical memoir—*Dramouss* (Paris, 1966; *A Dream of Africa*, London, 1968), in which he lamented the deterioration of postindependent Guinea. The novel continues the narrative at the point where *The Dark Child* left off: Laye's years in Paris, his dream of an independent, proud country, his return home to a dream that ends in betrayal by corruption and venality and political compromise. *A Dream of Africa* is a hastily written work and proved disappointing to Laye's critics after the high achievement of his earlier two novels. It was his first full-length fiction since 1954; during the years of his government service he had published only one story, "Les yeux de la statue" (1957; "The Eyes of the Statue," 1959).

In 1978 Laye published *Le maître de la parole* (Paris) after a long silence partly due to a serious illness over the years. This work, translated into English as *The Guardian of the Word: Kouma Lafolo Kouma*, and published in London in 1980 and New York in 1984, is a legendary tale of the first emperor Sundiata, who ruled Guinea in the fourteenth century. Laye called this work an adaptation of the oral rendering by the famous griot Babu Conde. More influence than adaptation of literal borrowing, the work represents Laye's renewed commitment to the oral tradition in Africa (griots began as court minstrels, but the tradition is identified today with village and street storytellers). In drawing on Africa's mythic and historic past, Laye was returning to a source that could not be sundered from him even in exile. Praise poems, apostrophes to divinities, choral chants, and proverbs of instructional import fill his griot's lively tale. Laye also acquaints his readers with the characters' *tana* (the forbidden object that destroys one) and totem (their representative images of strength). He suggests that the totem is but one way of describing the psychological double, or subconscious; both in this last work and in his earlier works the double/totem becomes a device cognate with European expressionistic tools.

Laye also wrote "L'exil," a memoir, in which he attacked Sékou Touré and the Guinean government and which could not be published for political reasons while his wife Marie remained in a Guinean jail. (After her release she and Laye separated and divorced.)

Laye's last years were lonely ones; he died of ill health exacerbated by homesickness.

LEE Sang (pseudonym of Kim Hae-Kyung). Born 1910, in Korea; died 1937, in Tokyo, Japan. Lee Sang studied architecture at Tokyo University but felt segregated and abused as a second-class Korean colonist (Korea was an occupied colony of Japan at the time). He abandoned his architectural studies to return to Korea in 1933; in Seoul he worked as an assistant engineer for the Japanese government, but he soon quit this job to devote himself fully to a writing career. He moved to Hyo-Ja-Dong, where he met Keum Hong, a singing and dancing girl who also sold sexual favors, and became obsessed with her. He opened a tea house as a way of holding onto her and providing her with the money she demanded. In 1934 he became a member of the Society of Nine People and began writing his poems and novels. He was forced to close the tea house because of financial losses, and his economic and personal life deteriorated rapidly. In 1935 he wrote his famous and bitter poem, "The Epitaph of Paper"; in 1936 he wrote several novels, among them *The Wing*, *The East Sea*, *The Unhappy Heritage*, *The Dark Room of a Map*, and *Ji Ju Hoi Si*. His personal life was brightened that year by a new love, Byun Dong Lim, whom he married. In the short time after his marriage and his imprisonment by the Japanese government as a political offender and his subsequent release for reasons of poor health, he wrote the remainder of his total output of twelve novels and three major poetic sequences. His poetry may be characterized by three distinct stages, each one summed up by his relationship to the three women with whom he was contemporaneously involved—Keum Hong, Kwon Soon Oak, Byun Dong Lim.

Lee Sang used a pseudonym both to protect himself from political persecution by the imperial Japanese government and because he felt a false name symbolized exile from roots he felt as a subject native. By creating his work and withdrawing his authorship from it, he was proclaiming ambivalence in publishing any work in Japanese-occupied Korea.

Lee Sang's fiction employs modern Western techniques—paradox and self-mockery, psychological subject matter as a locus of identity or lack of it, and autobiographic reference transmuted into ironic commentary of the isolate self trapped in a community dominated by aliens. His poetry contains this spirit of isolateness and weariness as well, but it is characterized less by accretion of realistic detail and more by a surreal tenderness. His work ridiculed the Japanese occupation as a transient show of power, but his epiphanal expression brought him no personal transcendence. Broken in health, he died in the hospital of Tokyo University, driven by his hunger to feed an impregnable military empire on native traditions they indifferently refused to consume.

The remains of Lee Sang, who was not yet twenty-seven years old when he died, were returned to Korea.

LENGYEL, Menyhért Melchior. Born January 3, 1880, in Balmazujváros, Hungary; died October 25, 1974, in Budapest, Hungary. Lengyel was an imaginative, prominent, and versatile Hungarian dramatist whose plays and movie scripts had a wide range of subjects and were well known throughout the world. His thriller-play *Tájfun* (1909; *Typhoon*, 1913) exposed a Japanese scientist who lacked moral courage. In 1917 he wrote *Czarina*, a satirical comedy depicting the life of the Russian empress Catherine the Great. Ernst Lubitsch filmed it in 1924 as *Forbidden Paradise* with Pola Negri. A later version of the film appeared under the title *A Royal Scandal*. His plays boldly exposed social problems and examined the fate and the passions of individuals. Many of his plays were translated into leading languages and performed on stages from Broadway to Paris, some of them directed by Max Reinhardt. Perhaps his most famous play was the libretto *A csodálatos mandarin* (The Miraculous Mandarin), written in 1919, upon which Béla Bartók based his pantomime. Lengyel also wrote in 1919 *Sancho Panza királysága* (The Kingdom of Sancho Panza); the comedy's English adaptation was staged in 1921. A later play published in 1957 was *Csendes ház* (Quiet House). He was also a contributor to *Nyugat*, an important periodical in support of progressive literary movements.

Lengyel left Hungary during World War I and lived during the turbulent war years in Switzerland. He returned later to Hungary as theater director in Budapest. In 1931 he moved to London, and in 1937—prior to the outbreak of World War II—he settled in the U.S. After World War II he went back to Europe, first to Rome, where he received the Grand Prix in 1963, and later to his native Hungary where he died.

Lengyel wrote numerous filmscripts for Hollywood, among them *To Be or Not to Be* (with Jack Benny), *Angel* (with Marlene Dietrich), and *Ninochka* (with Greta Garbo).

ELIZABETH MOLNÁR RAJEC

LERNER, Laurence (David). Born 1925, Capetown, South Africa; he lives in England. Lerner was educated in the universities at Capetown, South Africa, and Cambridge, England. Before settling into a professorship at the University of Sussex in 1970, he taught in Belfast and in Ghana. He is a South African expatriate writer who often concerns himself with South African themes and with the accompanying expatriate rhythms of nostalgia and ambivalent anger. He has published both fiction and poetry; one of his novels, *The Englishman* (1959), is an ironically titled treatment of his experiences growing up in Cape-town.

Selected Titles: Poetry: *Domestic Interiors* (1959); *The Directions of Memory: Poems 1958–1962* (1963); *Selves* (1969); *The Man I Killed* (1980); Novel: *A Free Man* (1968).

LERNOUX, Penny. Born 1940, in New York; died October 8, 1989, in Mt. Kisco, New York. Lernoux was well known for her research and writing on the Roman Catholic Church in Latin America, and the role it played in the worker priests and democratic movements in that hemisphere. She had lived in Bogota, Colombia, from 1962 to 1989, returning to the United States for treatment of the lung cancer that proved fatal. She was the author of several volumes of nonfiction; her work appeared regularly in such periodicals as the *Nation* and *Newsweek*.

Selected Titles: *Cry of the People* (1980); *People of God: The Struggle for World Catholicism* (1989).

LESSING, Doris. Born October 22, 1919, in Kermanshah, Persia (Iran); she lives in London, England. Lessing was born to British parents in Persia (now Iran) who moved to Southern Rhodesia (now Zimbabwe) when she was a child. She published her first book after she emigrated to England in 1949. Her early novels and stories were set primarily in colonial Africa, and Africa remained a frequent topic or setting in several later works. Her one return visit to Rhodesia and South Africa in 1956 resulted in *Going Home* (1957); she was thereafter banned as an undesirable alien because, as someone born in Iran, she was classified as an Asian. She has lived in London since she came to England.

Lessing's first novel, *The Grass is Singing* (1950), is conventionally realistic in its description of a colonial farmer and his wife who cannot adjust to the rigors and racial customs of Rhodesia; the woman's cruelty and insecurity lead to her murder by a black houseboy. Four of the five parts of the ''Children of Violence'' *Bildungsroman* are also set in colonial Africa: *Martha Quest* (1952), *A Proper Marriage* (1954), *A Ripple from the Storm* (1958), and *Landlocked* (1965). The series follows the life from adolescence to old age and death of Martha Quest, a woman contemporaneous with Lessing herself, focusing on changing racial, political, sexual, and social circumstances, with Quest emi-grating to England in 1949 and, in an apocalyptic final volume (*The Four-Gated City*, 1969), with the end of the world.

The Golden Notebook (1962) is commonly considered Lessing's masterpiece. A multileveled novel concerned with the fragmented psyche of Anna Wulf, it shows how Wulf divides her narrative into ''notebooks'' reflecting various parts of her life and with a therapeutic ''golden'' one enabling her to reconcile her various "selves." A short, conventional novel, "Free Women," separates and serves as counterpoint to the parts of the various "notebooks," lending perspective to Wulf's search for wholeness through various commitments, through therapy, and through the act of writing.

Lessing's ventures into "inner space," or further explorations into the necessity of psychic wholeness, include *Briefing for a Descent into Hell* (1971), a claustrophobic work somewhat indebted to psychiatrist R. D. Laing in its focus on mental imbalance and psychic phenomena; in this novel Lessing probes into the life of a male professor who experiences a number of previous "existences." Following *The Summer Before the Dark* (1973), a realistic account of a woman leaving her family for a series of experiences before she returns home, Lessing wrote *Memoirs of a Survivor* (1974). *Memoirs* is an important work about a woman's solitary survival following a cataclysmic war; she must care for an adolescent girl who quickly, circumstantially matures and who, with her lover, becomes a pioneer in enabling others to survive the end of civilization. The woman's "walking" through her apartment wall to "see" various tableaux about her own presumed earlier life enables her to alter her thinking and behavior.

Lessing has published a series of "space fiction" narratives, collectively called "Canopus in Argos: Archives," five volumes of which have appeared thus far, in which she depicts Earth's history as a war zone for opposing forces of ageless aliens. *Shikasta* (1979), a sequence of reports and records telling of Earth's history from a cosmic perspective, is allegorically impressive though unconvincing in fictional terms. *The Marriages between Zones Three, Four and Five* (1980), by contrast, is a fascinating, moving allegorical account of the rise and fall of civilizations told through a love story. *The Sirian Experiments* (1981) includes many of the same kinds of documents found in *Shikasta* but also offers a lesser deity, a female, who changes as she gradually understands the forces running the universe and the consequences this has for Earth. *The Making of the Representative for Planet 8* (1982), in telling of the world's eventual death through freezing, also suggests that even celestial "Overlords" are subject to cosmic forces. *Documents Relating to the Sentimental Agents in the Volyen Empire* (1983) includes various "records" as part of a partially successful satire about the debasing of language in the rise and fall of societies.

Lessing published two novels under the pseudonym Jane Somers as part of an experiment to see whether books could be published on their merits instead of on an author's reputation. *The Diary of a Good Neighbour* (1983) and *If the Old Could . . .* (1984) are realistic books, the first focusing on a fashion editor's relations with a dying older woman and the second on an abortive love affair, but because of trite characterization, sentimental plots, and lack of any larger purpose or vision, neither is exceptional.

The Good Terrorist (1985), a reversion to the kind of realism found in Lessing's early works, concerns an idealistic though insecure young woman who works with a gang of terrorists who prefer to fight the system through talk, parasitism, and demonstrations; though the woman misguidedly takes the revolution into her own hands, the book lacks emotional conviction and compelling characters. *The Fifth Child* (1988), Lessing's tribute to horror fiction, is predictable and only partially successful as it presents a family's struggle to understand their abnormal, malevolent fifth child; as the boy matures, their simple, happy world is radically altered.

Lessing's work has changed radically over some thirty years, and she has moved far from her initial emphases and interests, though in retrospect one can see that she has always been concerned with the integrated, whole personality. Always a serious writer, she early on had a reputation as a Cassandra, a prophet of doom, and now increasingly seems a prophet whose increased interest in and dedication to Sufism colors her work. At her best, as when she focuses on a solitary, compulsive character (usually female) who exists in a moment of crisis, she is able to dramatize a personal revaluation of identity and search for wholeness. Her fiction is sometimes repetitive, prolix, and didactic, but her depth of character analysis and commitment have secured her a place among the most compelling, enduring writers of her time.

Selected Titles: *The Habit of Loving* (1957); *Each His Own Wilderness*, in *New English Dramatists: Three Plays*, ed. E. Martin Browne (1959); *Fourteen Poems* (1959); *In Pursuit of the English: A Documentary* (1960); *Play with a Tiger* (1962); *A Man and Two Women* (1963); *African Stories* (1964); *Particularly Cats* (1967); *A Small Personal Voice: Essays, Reviews, Interviews*, ed. Paul Schlueter (1974); *Collected Stories* (London, 1978; *Stories*, 1978); *Prisons We Choose to Live Inside* (1986); *The Wind Blows Away Our Words* (1987); *The Doris Lessing Reader* (1989).

Consult: Katherine Fishburn, *The Unexpected Universe of Doris Lessing: A Study in Narrative Technique* (1985); Carey Kaplan and Ellen Cronan Rose, eds., *Doris Lessing: The Alchemy of Survival* (1988); Mona Knapp, *Doris Lessing* (1984); Roberta Rubenstein, *The Novelistic Vision of Doris Lessing* (1979); Paul Schlueter, *The Novels of Doris Lessing* (1973); Claire Sprague, *Rereading Doris Lessing: Narrative Patterns of Doubling and Repetition* (1987); Ruth Whittaker, *Doris Lessing* (1988).

PAUL SCHLUETER

LEUNG Tung. Born August 22, 1946, in Shanghai, China. He lives in Oakland, California. Leung's education was interrupted by the Cultural Revolution of 1966. Toward the end of the movement in the early 1970s, Leung was sent to remote rural regions to be "re-educated." In 1975, bitter and disillusioned, he swam across the waters to Hong Kong. In Hong Kong he and a group of former Red Guards published the magazine *Pei Dou* (Northern Star). His stories, realistic and issuing from personal experiences with the Cultural Revolution, also appeared in the anthology *Anti-Revisionist Building* (Hong Kong, 1979); the title comes from one of Leung's stories contained therein. Since 1980 Leung has resided in Oakland, California, and contributes frequently to newspapers and magazines in Hong Kong and Taiwan. He writes in a lucid and moving style, with occasional indulgences in emotional outpourings. As a voice of the generation of China's youth who took part in and suffered from the Cultural Revolution, Leung's writings bear valuable witness to that period in Chinese history.

Off Broadway, a collection of stories about Chinese life in alien lands, was published in Taipei in 1986. His newest book is *Posted Telegram* (Taipei, Taiwan, 1988).

DOROTHY TSUNGSU WEISSMAN

LEVI, Carlo. Born 1902, in Turin, Italy; he died 1975 in Rome, Italy. A practicing physician who received his medical degree from the University of Turin, Levi was arrested for subversive activities against the fascist state of Italy in 1935 and sentenced to internal exile in Gagliano in the southern province of Lucania. During his sentence he became aware of the Italian peasants of the region; in his personal and philosophic memoir, *Christ Stopped at Eboli* (1945; 1947), the work that brought him world fame, Levi paid attention to and exposed their sore conditions. Levi lived in voluntary exile in France after his release from penal exile in Gagliano; he returned to his native land in 1944, choosing Florence as his residence. Like only a few other victims of fascism, he triumphed over his adversities to become an influential voice in his native land in his later years.

Selected Titles: *Paura della liberta* (1947, Of Fear and Freedom); *L'orologio* (1950, The Watch); *Il futuro her un cuore antico* (1956, The Heart of the Future Lies in the Past: journal of Levi's visit to U.S.S.R.); *La doppia notte dei Tigli* (1959, The Two-Fold Night: A Narrative of Travel in Germany).

LEVI, Primo. Born July 31, 1919, Turin, Italy; he died April 11, 1987, in Turin, Italy by suicide. Levi was separated from his native region when he joined the partisans in 1943. In 1945 he was captured and sent to Auschwitz. He wrote all his published work after World War II. Now recognized as one of the great humanistic voices in Italy in the twentieth century, he published his first book, *Se questo e un uomo* in 1959 (If This Is a Man), a work to be regarded as philosophical speculation rather than autobiography. Other works include *Se non ora, quando?* (1982; *If Not Now, When?* 1985), *Lilit e altri racconti* (1984, Moments of Reprieve); *Survival in Auschwitz and The Reawakening: Two Memoirs* (1985); *The Periodic Table* (1984); *Opere* (Turin, 1987, Works); *Collected Poems* (1989); *I sommersi e i salvati* (1987; *The Drowned and the Saved*, 1988); *Other People's Trades* (1989).

Consult: H. S. Hughes, *Prisoners of Hope: The Silver Age of the Italian Jews* (1983); Alvin H. Rosenfeld, *A Double Dying* (1980).

LEVITIN-KRASNOV, Anotoly Emmanuilovich (pseudonym of Anotoly Emmanuilovich Levitin). Born September 21, 1915, in Baku, Russia; he lives in Lucerne, Switzerland. Levitin-Krasnov's father was a district judge who converted from Judaism to Christianity; his mother was a descendant of Russian nobility. In 1920 the family moved to Petrograd (now Leningrad), where Levitin-Krasnov graduated from the Pedagogical Technical Institute named after A. Herzen. He began teaching Russian language and literature when he was nineteen years old. He was a socialist by belief but opposed to Soviet policies; he joined an opposition group in 1934, and was arrested three times. He spent ten years in prisons and labor-camps on charges of political crimes. Under pressure from the KGB, he emigrated from the USSR in 1974.

After World War II, during a period of thaw in the relationship of the government and the Orthodox Church, he was able to publish his writing in the magazine *Herald of the Moscow Patriarchy*, but most of his workbooks, pamphlets, speeches, and various essays have been distributed through samizdat, that is, circulated through typescript form. Among these samizdat publications is his historical account, in coauthorship with V. Shavriv, "The History of Church Discord" (from 1920 to 1940). Levitin-Krasnov later organized this material into more than 1,000 pages of printed text in three volumes printed in the West; he has published fifteen other books during his exile.

Levitin-Krasnov's writings provoked sharp irritation in the Soviet bureaucracy during the time they were circulating in samizdat form. The official Soviet organ, *Science and Religion*, labeled him "the most active of the graphomaniacs." In the West, even before his emigration, his works were greeted enthusiastically. *The Defense of the Faith in the U.S.S.R.* was published in Paris in 1966; *Dialogue with Churchly Russia* was issued in Paris in 1967; and a collection of essays was issued under the title *Stomas* by the Posev publishing house in 1972.

After his emigration to the West, Levitin-Krasnov wrote on other than religious subjects. He published *Native Space* in 1981; he wrote a critique of Aleksandr Solzhenitsyn* and V. Mazimov under the title *Two Writers* (Paris, 1983). In *The Star Major*, a series of novellas, he described the life of young people in Leningrad during the 1930s. His other works include *Hard Times* and *In Search of the New City* (Tel Aviv, 1980). All these works were published in Russian-language versions.

Levitin-Krasnov's outspoken views have shocked a number of Russian/Soviet émigrés. In "Revolutionary and Mystic," an article in *Posev* magazine (no. 9, 1983), a critic complained of the difficulty of "placing" him in any measurable category while admitting that he was the most original of the Russian émigré writers. Other critics appear alienated by his mysticism and his continuing predictions of bloody revolution in the USSR in the twenty-first century. Another group of critics assert that his commitment to socialism is dubious.

Perhaps Levitin-Krasnov may be best perceived through three categories he imposes on himself in the epilogue to his work *The Star Major*: "My religion, my socialism, and my Russia." He writes:

My religion—I have always perceived God in the form of Christ. I love Christ endlessly and am accustomed to see him as a friend, a brother, an older comrade. . . . *My socialism* —I have always disliked any authority, teachers and school directors, government officials and bishops, and Tsars and generals, millionaires, Stalin, and all and sundry powerholders. Any pompous, puffed-up earthly majesty has always seemed to me funny. What I like best about socialism is the withering away of the state and the realization of equality and fraternity. . . . *My Russia*—it was in my childhood that my love for Russia was born, for the simple Russian people (I just don't like intellectuals). Russia, my native land, is filled with kind, warm, simple people; this Russia has stayed in my soul. This Russia has nothing to do with lying, indifferent, shallow government officials.

In his seventies, Levitin-Krasnov continues to work on a number of projects, one of them an evaluation of his ten-year stay in the West. He has published the first and second volumes of his work *From Another Counter* (Paris, 1985), in which he reflects on his meetings with the "strange" and "new" Russians living abroad, all of them suffering, as he does, the inevitable loss occasioned by exile.

In the last few years Levitin-Krasnov's views have undergone an evolution. In a letter sent from Lucerne to the head of the Soviet Union, Mikhail S. Gorbachev, in April 1989, Levitin-Krasnov requested permission, as a citizen of the USSR, to return to the Soviet Union. He wrote: "I was compelled to leave my native land by provocative attacks on my religious, political, and democratic convictions." He also declared: "The Soviet government and you, Michael Sergheevich, can rest assured that in all your efforts toward a democratic reconstruction [*perestroyka*] of Soviet society you will find in me a zealous, convinced and, in spite of my age, an energetic supporter."

MARK A. POPOVSKY, translated by Zoric Ward

LEWICK, Halpern. Born 1888, in Minsk, Poland; died 1962, in Los Angeles, California. Lewick's early enthusiasm for social causes was shown in his participation in the *Bund*, a Jewish socialist organization, activities for which he was arrested and sentenced to life imprisonment in Siberia. Although Lewick was subject to privation, he wrote many poems while in Siberia, some of which were published later. He managed to reach New York in 1913 after escaping from confinement; here he worked as a paperhanger and wrote plays, poems, and articles for Jewish newspapers. His health broke down, and he suffered attacks of tuberculosis in 1920 and in 1932; in 1958 he was devastated by a paralytic stroke, from which he died four years later. Ultimately, Lewick thought of himself as neither Russian nor American but as a wandering Jew.

LI Tuo. Born 1939 in Hohot, Inner Mongolia; he lives in exile in the United States. A member of the Daur national minority, Li moved to Beijing in 1947. He worked as a fitter in a metalworking factory in Beijing for more than twenty years; he first began publishing his fiction in the mid–1960s. Li resumed writing in 1976, and since 1986 has been the executive editor of the literary journal *Beijing Literature*. He has published many essays of literary and film criticism and edited several anthologies of new Chinese fiction.

Selected Title: Li's work appears in *Spring Bamboo*, an anthology edited by Jeanne Tai (1989).

LIDDELL, (John) Robert. Born October 13, 1908, in Tunbridge Wells, Kent, England. He lives in Athens, Greece. After completing three degrees at Oxford University, Liddell worked as a manuscript librarian in the Bodleian Library, Oxford, and taught in Finland and Egypt. Since 1953 he has taught in Athens as British Council lecturer, and for five years he was head of the English Department of the University of Athens. He has written a number of novels in addition to studies of Jane Austen, Ivy Compton-Burnett, Elizabeth Taylor, Barbara Pym, and Constantine Cavafy,* and critical analyses of the craft of fiction. His travel books include observations on Greece and Turkey, and he has translated works on Greek literature and a work from French into English.

Liddell's novels are quiet domestic dramas peopled with middle- or upper-middle-class characters whose inherited wealth enables them to live comfortably in small British towns; occasionally he ventures abroad, as in *Unreal City*, set in Caesarea, Israel (London, 1952). He resists contemporary settings, preferring the simpler world before World War II and the coming of the "welfare state"; his bias against modernity may be seen, in minuscule, in his description of his politics for *Contemporary Authors*: "anti-left."

Some of the criticism Liddell's fiction has received is similar to that which Kingsley Amis accorded Liddell's book on Compton-Burnett: brilliant dialogue, limited inventiveness, gentle comic sense. His examinations of family manipulations and attempts at domination, his exposure of pretentiousness and pomposity, are always presented sardonically.

Liddell's first novel, *The Almond Tree* (London, 1938), is prototypical in its use of domestic allusions found in his later works, among them *Kind Relations* (London, 1939; in the United States, *Take This Child*); *Watering Place* (London, 1945); *An Object for a Walk* (London, 1966); *Stepsons* (London, 1969); and *The Aunts* (London, 1987). *The Gantillons* (London, 1940) may be his best-known work, centering on a family dominated by a spinster who orders others in the family about as if they are servants.

Selected Titles: *A Treatise on the Novel* (London, 1947; Bloomington, 1948); *Some Principles of Fiction* (London, 1953; Bloomington, 1954); *Aegean Greece* (London, 1954); *The Novels of Ivy Compton-Burnett* (London, 1955); *Byzantium and Istanbul* (1956); *The Rivers of Babylon* (London, 1959); *The Novels of Jane Austen* (1963); *Mainland Greece* (1965); *Cavafy: A Critical Biography* (London, 1974); *A Mind at Ease: Barbara Pym and Her Novels* (1989); *Twin Spirits: The Novels of Emily and Anne Brontë* (1990).

PAUL SCHLUETER

LIND, Jakov. Born 1927 in Vienna; he lives in New York City, Deya, Majorca, and London. The jacket copy of the first American edition of Lind's first-published book, a collection of short stories, *Soul of Wood* (1964; *Eine Seele Aus Holz*, West Berlin, 1962) reads:

the son of Jewish parents who were deported and killed after Hitler annexed Austria. Lind, then only eleven, escaped to Holland. After the Germans invaded that country, he hid for a time and then escaped deportation by posing as a Dutch national volunteering for work on a Rhine barge. Later, he became "assistant" to a spy, employee of a food rationing office, fisherman in the Mediterranean, construction worker in Jerusalem, beach photographer in Tel Aviv, orange picker in Nathanya, aircraft inspector with the Israeli air force, publisher of a small Vienna newspaper, private detective, film agent in London, traveling salesman in Scandinavia, France and Italy.

Although some of these jobs were of short duration and are perhaps hyperbolic publicity copy, they indicate the peripatetic nature of Lind's youth and the impact of the Holocaust on him.

After the publication of his book in Germany, England, and the United States, his reputation was assured. Maxwell Geismar, in the *New York Times Book Review*, called him "the most notable short story writer to appear in the last two decades," and William Hogan in the *San Francisco Chronicle* wrote that the book was "without doubt the most shattering work of fiction I have read in years." *Soul of Wood* was called more grotesque and fierce in its vision than Günter Grass's equally expressionistic impressions in print. Like Grass, and like other German, Austrian, and Jewish writers of the period attempting to transcend the Holocaust experience, Lind employed a catalog of grotesque elements in his fiction: men and women who perform the most horrendous of acts without any sense of shame or without awareness of breaking codes of civilized behavior. His list of sinful acts included incest, mass murder, cannibalism, animal abuse, and mutilation, among others, in a style that mockingly glorifies the actors as performers on a world stage of amorality.

Lind's intense whipping of sins into public exposure continued in his next work, his first-published novel, *Landscape in Concrete* (1966; *Landschaft in Beton*, West Berlin, 1963). In a style like his earlier stories—that of a fairy tale or allegory to lessen the physical horror of the realism of the tale—Lind rendered the story of an enlisted man in the German army at the close of World War II, trying desperately to make amends for having failed his country by losing his regiment in a battle with the Allied enemies. Lind creates a picaresque mood and structure as the sergeant, who has been discharged from the *Wehrmacht*, travels across his demoralized country in search of a regiment that will allow him to assert his part in the fatherland's fight. In his fable-like story Lind is reviewing the history of appeal of German militarism and nationalism on German youth during the 1930s and early 1940s. While all of Lind's work is an indictment of the nationalized madness in which he grew up, and to whose temptations of psychological, mass hysteria he fell prey, this novel and his later work show an extraordinary, and agonizing, understanding of the appeal of Nazism on German youth, an appeal that traded on legitimized violence and the trappings of Wagnerian music and boots as well as the identification of military clothing with camaraderie and patriotism. *Landscape in Concrete* and *Soul of Wood* utilized imagery grotesque in their placement of conventional opposites and in narratives always on the border of howling laughter and the pain of howling indignity.

These satires refused to let go the issue of responsibility for Germany's acts under Hitler; Lind indicted German society, or at least put it on trial in his work.

Ergo, Lind's second novel (1967; *Eine bessere Welt*, West Berlin, 1966), is a narrative of two men seeking to destroy each other by destroying that part of themselves they cannot face. The novel has its share of execrement in its description of the shack in which one of the heroes, Wachholder, lives. There are hundreds of thousands of unused sheets of government paper. Wachholder crawls over them, sleeps among them, and carries on his assignation with a buxom government minister in the midst of them. Wachholder has to destroy Wurz, his alter ego, because Wurz, by hiding in his hermetically sealed house, is constantly (as Wachholder construes it) holding Wachholder up to ridicule. Wachholder writes nasty letters to Wurz and arranges a mock-trial of him, but he cannot force Wurz out of his *assumed* identity. What defeats Wachholder is not entirely clear: partly it is his two adopted sons who have their own problems of identity and in the moment of crisis refuse to strip any man of the artifice of his choice.

If, however, Wachholder's "children" betray him, he is not alone in his dilemma. Wurz's two step-children also betray him by adopting their own devices: they pimp on public buses. Wurz's "children" destroy the social and ultimately moral retreat that Wurz has constructed by forcing themselves on public attention, and thus bring Wurz to public accountability. From the hard concrete and wooden souls of his earlier work, in which the setting is a Germany on the brink of military defeat but still dominant in its psychic state, Lind comes in *Ergo* to a postwar divided Germany reeling from the split to its national and psychic soul. The title is ironic—the disaster of Germany was inevitable if Germany's past is viewed from a humanist viewpoint that believes in the ultimate triumph of humanism over barbarity—and yet there is no "ergo" to events in Lind's work: all is drift and attempt at survival; what comes later comes later and reflection does not precede action. Thus German response to its crime is indeed a pleading of lack of premeditation. The awesome issue is that of guilt in refusal to meditate on circumstances.

Lind married an English book editor in the 1960s; they lived in London, where they raised their two children. His wife died of brain cancer in the 1970s. He has written many books in the two decades since his early acclaim, including two volumes of autobiography, and several plays. His first work in English, *Travels to the Enu* (1982), is a tribute to England and the United States, where he has lived for the past twenty-five years (he also spends time in Majorca). This novel is a parody of *Gulliver's Travels* in which Lind's hero is shipwrecked on an island and observes modern customs from his peculiar eye. In an introduction to an excerpt from the playscript that Lind adapted from his novel, published in *Confrontation* magazine (nos. 25–26, 1983), Jeanne K. Welcher wrote:

Travels to the Enu is a chilling, funny, acidly rational *jeu d'esprit*. It tells of Mr. Orlando, as ordinary an Englishman as a writer can be, who goes on a pleasure cruise to the South

Seas early in 1980, arrives unexpectedly in the land of the Enus, and then late in 1981 is rescued and restored to England. The first-person narrative is circumstantially precise with names and backgrounds of fellow travelers, geographic references specified to the latitudinal minute, and times to the day and hour. As a setting, Enu Island is an ad-man's dream of Polynesia. But subject to the whimsical sadism of the natives, life there is one long, though varied, ordeal. The utopian and dystopian become wildly entangled in Lind's special blend of surrealism and satire. His major preoccupations are language, literature, and literary personalities. He gives nearly equal time to political ideals versus realities. He examines secret and investigative agencies and "the big porno plot." He ridicules pedantry and pseudosciences, human engineering, female liberation, electronic inventions and modern architecture. Along the way few twentieth-century attitudes escape without at least an ironic overtone.

Lind himself has said that "this present tale is my first voluntary plunge into a new world: English fiction—and it will not escape some astute critics that *Travels to the Enu, Story of a Shipwreck* is 'pure' literature in the sense that it is about words, about language and to be more precise about the English language." Given Lind's stated aims, it is not surprising that this novel shows less the deftly crushing hand of social satire than an elegance of language in its concentration of view.

Lind's adaptation of *Travels to the Enu* was announced for production in 1983, but it has not been mounted in full production as yet. His other plays have had concert readings but no American productions.

Lind now writes mainly in English. His new and second novel to be written in English, *The Inspector* (London, 1987), is, like its immediate predecessor, a fabulistic tale. The direction in which the author wishes his reader to follow his symbolic narrative, if indeed the novel has a central focus, is unclear. Lind seems intent in this fiction on its parts as tales cabalistically satisfying in themselves, at one point teasingly telling the reader he is not sure, as the creator of the tales, of their significance or of his conscious intent in writing them. From a symbolic landscape and an expressionistic style, Lind has moved into the postmodern camp with ironies that flirt their subtextual meanings in a dense world.

Lind, who admits to the influence of Elias Canetti* in his satiric and pluralistic philosophy of life and that of Stefan Heym* in his willingness to experiment with variant approaches to truth, said in an interview with Martin Tucker in Lind's Chelsea Hotel (New York) apartment in late 1982 that roots come not from the country of birth but from the soil of cultural and ethnic spirit. Perhaps because of the painterly milieu of Majorca, where he has sojourned regularly part of the year for many years, Lind has tried his hand at watercolor painting; some of his work has been exhibited in galleries in California.

Selected Titles: *Counting My Steps: An Autobiography* (1969); *The Silver Foxes Are Dead, and Other Plays* (1969); *The Inventor* (London, 1987; 1988).

LIU Da-ren. Born February 5, 1939, in the Chaing-hsi Province of China. He lives in Westchester County, New York, and works at the United Nations as a translator. With the fall of mainland China to communist rule in 1949, Liu's family took refuge in Taiwan. Liu published his first stories and essays while attending National Taiwan University and saw his first collection of stories, *Impressions of Red Earth*, published in 1970. In the mid–1960s he came to the United States for advanced studies; in the early 1970s he took active part in the Tiao Yu Tai protest movement of Chinese overseas students against U.S. ac-quiescence to Japan's claims of sovereignity over the Tiao Yu Tai Islands (Sen-kaku in the U.S. press) as part of the Ryukyu chain. The movement, originally begun as a nationalistic voice asserting Chinese patriotism, turned into a com-petition vying for popular support between China and Taiwan. One of the leading organizer-activists of the movement, Liu became persona non grata to the Taiwan government until the 1980s, when the government relaxed its policies regarding dissidents. His second book of stories, *The Cuckoo's Song of Sorrow* (Taiwan, 1984), suggests a wished-for end to his decade-long estrangement from Taiwan, during which time his books were banned on the island. In his latest book, Liu presents a wide range of characters from different walks of life, set against the various backdrops of Taipei, the metropolitan United States, and urban China. In his novel *The Plankton Community* (Hong Kong, 1983), the first of a trilogy, Liu's focus is on the life of Chinese intellectuals in Taiwan in the 1960s. Many of these intellectuals are offspring of mainlander Chinese who took refuge in Taiwan during the 1949 Deluge; an acute sense of nostalgia, vulnerability, and rootless impermanence permeate the novel's world. This nostalgia may also be seen in Liu's third book of collected stories, *Autumnal Sunshine Mellow as Wine* (Taiwan, 1986). Like most Chinese writers in exile, Liu writes in Chinese and almost exclusively about Chinese people.

DOROTHY TSUNGSU WEISSMAN

LIU Zaifu. Lives in exile in the United States. Liu is considered the dean of Chinese literary critics. He is a member of the faculty of the University of Chicago.

LIYONG, Taban lo. Born 1939, Uganda; he lives in Kenya. Kenya. Iconoclastic and exuberant, Liyong broke literary ground in several ways. He was the first African in the writing program at the University of Iowa; he also studied at Howard University and at Knoxville College (Tennessee). He wrote the first book of literary criticism published in East Africa, *The Last Word* (Nairobi, 1969). His works generated controversy, and his satiric bite lent additional flavor to his writings and appearances. He taught in Kenya in self-exile during the Idi Amin dictatorship of Uganda; he taught for several years, beginning in 1978, at the University of Papua New Guinea, and later at Juba University in the Sudan. Fearful of arrest and/or harassment should he return to his native land, he grew less enthusiastic about the power of the writer's word to change social conditions than he had been in his youthful and bravado days. His profound concern with African literature, and its progenitors, gives his critical writing an authenticity; his illuminating passion continues to inform his writing even after the declamatory flauntings are lifted from his judgmental ore. He is a gifted poet and fiction writer whose works in these genres have received less attention than his critical pronouncements.

Selected Titles: *Fixxions, and Other Stories* (London, 1969); *The Last Word: Cultural Synthesis* (Nairobi, 1969); *Eating Chiefs: Lwo Culture from Lolwe to Malkal*, selected, interpreted and transmuted by Liyong (London, 1970); *The Uniformed Man* (Nairobi, 1971); *Frantz Fanon's Uneven Ribs, with poems, more and more* (London, 1971); *Another Nigger Dead: Poems* (London, 1972); compiler, *Popular Culture of East Africa: Oral Literature* (London, 1972); *Offenses Against Our Enemies* (Nairobi, 1973); *Ballads of Underdevelopment: Poems and Thoughts* (Kampala, 1976); *Meditations of Taban lo Liyong* (London, 1978).

LOWRY, (Clarence) Malcolm. Born July 28, 1909, in Merseyside, Cheshire, England; died July 27, 1957, in Ripe, Sussex, England. Lowry's father was a cotton broker of some means. As a child Lowry had a vision problem that tormented him until it was corrected by an operation. Having attained full use of his eyes, he decided to become a sailor to further his aspiration to a career in writing. He shipped out as a deckhand at the age of seventeen. This act was the first of a long series of separations from his native land. He returned to England to complete his education, taking a degree from Cambridge University in 1933. His first novel, *Ultramarine*, based on his sea voyage, was written while he was at Cambridge and was published the year he graduated.

Lowry felt himself a man isolated from his society and moved to Paris, where he married an American woman. In 1935 he went to the United States without his wife and became enamored of the movie community in Hollywood. His wife joined him in Cuernavaca, Mexico, where he began to work on his masterpiece, *Under the Volcano*, the atmosphere of which owes much to the city in which it was written.

After Mexico, Lowry returned to Hollywood and there met Margerie Bonner, who became his second wife. The need to wander again possessed him, and he moved with Margerie to a beach cabin near Vancouver, British Columbia, Canada, in 1940. Although he suffered from alcoholism, he was able to make extensive revisions on the manuscript of *Under the Volcano*, revealing a profound influence of cinematic techniques; the book was published in 1947 to critical acclaim but poor sales. The need to move on came upon him again, and Lowry left Canada with his wife in 1954. They lived for a time in Italy and then returned to England, where he died in 1957.

Much of Lowry's work appeared in print only after his death: *Hear Us O Lord from Heaven Thy Dwelling Place* (stories) in 1961; *Selected Poems*, 1962; *Selected Letters*, 1965, edited by his widow and Harvey Breit; *Dark as the Grave Wherein My Friend Is Laid* (novel), 1969; and *October Ferry to Gabriola* (novel), 1971. These works were well received, possibly because *Under the Volcano* had achieved the status of an underground classic.

Under the Volcano more than justifies its reputation, and Lowry's depth of feeling has made him a name to be reckoned in English literature. In this work the dreadful tyranny of the human self caught in unrelenting alienation overwhelms the protagonist, who comes to realize that destructive tendencies are native to the human spirit; obsessed by his sense of apartness, he succumbs to bouts of alcoholism. Many critics have seen in the protagonist a reflection of Lowry.

Consult: Douglas Day, *Malcolm Lowry* (1973); Richard K. Cross, *Malcolm Lowry: A Preface to His Fiction* (1980).

CHARLES KOVICH

LUDWIG, Emil. Born January 25, 1881, in Breslau, Germany; died 1948. Ludwig's father, Hermann Cohn, was a professor at Breslau University and an eminent ophthalmologist. Ludwig was raised as a cultured German and thought of himself as a nondenominational Deist. Though he never denied his Jewish origins, he was more a secular ethicist than a religious spirit. He received his law degree from Heidelberg University in his early twenties, but by the age of twenty-five was a full-time writer. During World War I he was a correspondent on the front lines for a German newspaper. After the war he wrote several plays that proved popular on the German stage. In the later 1920s he began writing many of his popular biographies, starting with one of his cultural heroes, Goethe, and going on to political leaders like Kaiser Wilhelm I, Napoleon, and Tomáš Garrigue Masaryk (the first president of Czechoslovakia); he continued his personalized biographical volumes during World War II with a study of Franklin Delano Roosevelt, one of his new heroes. Ludwig wrote in a creative biographical style during the time when, influenced by Lytton Strachey, biography used the techniques of fiction and psychoanalysis. It was a time distinct from the postmodern age in which biography utilizes the techniques of journalism to mock historical chronology while appearing to imitate it. Ludwig also was a popular novelist, who provoked attention with his exploration of morality in contemporary times. Among his novels are *Diana* (1929) and *The Case against Mr. Crump* (1926), a tale of a timid man who revolts against the dominance of his tyrannical wife by murdering her. In portraying Crump's side of the story Ludwig suggested to some readers a justification of his protagonist's actions. The novel has remained controversial since its appearance and has been, at various times, banned.

A humane man who claimed the defense of rationalism in his approach to the workings of the individual in society, Ludwig consistently was involved in controversy during his lifetime. He supported the cultural revolutions spurred in the Weimar regime in Germany during the 1920s, though he found some of the artistic movements excessive for his moderate taste. His own style, traditional in form, was quietly subversive in content in allowing for the breaking of conventional morality by individuals of higher talents, and capable in rare instances, like Mr. Crump, of reaching higher plateaus of experience. His works were the subject of protracted legal fights before Hitler's coming to power, but with the new Nazi government in control of Germany in 1933, Ludwig knew he had to flee from the country, both as a Jew and as an "immoral" artist in the pronouncements of the National Socialist party. He emigrated to Ascona, Switzerland, where he had lived during the summers since 1922; from Switzerland he moved to the United States in 1938, and lived on both the East and West coasts. Ludwig continued to write in German during World War II, devoting himself to liberal, psychological studies of men who changed the course of history. In his later years he was largely silent; personal difficulties with one of his sons caused him some sorrow.

Exile in Ludwig's case drew from him a new reserve of strength to fight one more enemy of humanism. Exile did not profoundly change Ludwig's view of life or lead to a new way of perception: he remained a rational and compassionate man who, on occasion, touched, as in *Mr. Crump*, profound depths of ambiguity and tragedy.

Selected Titles in Translation: *Genius and Character* (1927); *Napoleon* (1927); *Bismarck* (1927); *Goethe* (1928); *Defender of Democracy: Masaryck of Czechoslovakia* (1936); *The Nile* (1936); *Cleopatra: The Story of a Queen* (1937); *Roosevelt: A Study in Fortune and Power* (1935); *Three Portraits: Hilter, Mussolini, Stalin* (1940); *Bolivar* (1942).

LUKÁCS, György. Born April 13, 1885, in Budapest, Hungary; died June 4, 1971, in Budapest, Hungary. Lukács is one of the significant humanist Marxist critics of the twentieth century, a philosopher–literary analyst who wrote theory that demanded of his readers a participation in classical humanism and Hegelianism as well as Marxist dialectics. Aware of the dangers that might entrap a critic who refused Marxist conformism, he suggested through his critical studies a different path for Marxism from that of socialist realism. His major work, *Der historische Roman*, was written in exile in the Soviet Union in the winter of 1936–37 and published in Russian translation shortly after. In an introductory note for the 1960 edition he wrote,

What I had in mind was a theoretical examination of the interaction between the historical spirit and the great genres of literature which portray the totality of history—and then only as this applied to bourgeois literature; the change wrought by socialist realism lay outside the scope of my study. In such an enquiry it is obvious that even the inner, most theoretical, most abstract dialectic of the problem will have an historical character. My study is confined to working out the main lines of this historical dialectic: that is, it analyzes and examines only the typical trends, offshoots and nodal points of this historical development, those indispensable to a theoretical examination. Hence it does not aim at historical completeness. The reader must not expect a textbook on the development of the historical drama or the historical novel. (p. 13)

Lukács was attempting in this dialectical examination of the specifics of historicism and the universalisms of genre (to use his terms) to find insight into the workings of both artistic form and social history. In sum, he was attempting (he emphasizes his use of the word *essay* as a trial run in a hoped-for progression of later examinations by other critics) to discover how art and history follow each other in intimately linked embraces of action. For Lukács, genre is a universalism of form, while history is filled with the specificities of event. He wished to know why the historical novel became so important in the era of bourgeois capitalism, rather than, for example, historical drama; in exploring this question, he hoped to see how society causes direction in artistic form, and art correspondingly causes direction in the society in which it gestates. As Lukács perceived it, history infuses an emphasis on one literary form to the distinction of another, and conversely, the altered form alters the consciousness of an age. In Lukács's dialectic, history affects the artist and the artist affects history, but not in a chronology of direct primacy but in an intimate, subtle series of reactions to the feel of both history and art. The role of the humanist critic is to illuminate the history and drama of those reactions, to bring back to a later age the awareness of those revolving forces that at some point in their circles of change provided an impetus for a greater revolution in history and of artistic form/genre. Lukács claims only modesty for his role—that is, he provides representativeness rather than formulaic analysis—and in so doing, he and all critics who follow in the same path declaim not only past events but suggest a "great realism," that understanding of variant possibilities and meanings of experience.

Lukács's representative novelists were Sir Walter Scott, Honoré de Balzac, and Leo Tolstoy, the great writers of nineteenth-century bourgeois culture. His choice of twentieth-century "historical novelists" were Thomas Mann* (whom he apotheosized), Stefan Zweig,* Lion Feuchtwanger,* and Romain Rolland. He specifically avoided treating the works of Soviet authors, claiming that as a critic who did not read Russian as a first language, he could not judge a writer's work in that language. Such a universal noble gesture rings true as an abstract truth, but it has its limitations in Marxist historicist dialectics: very likely Lukács chose to avoid trouble with the authorities during Joseph Stalin's brutal reign in the 1930s and 1940s by evading comment on Soviet literature and socialist realism. Thus Lukács survived his period in exile in the Soviet Union through abstention. He is not to be blamed for this lack of act, or for his lack of entrance into Stalin's prison camps as a result of a prior commitment, but his abstract statement of rationale—that judgment must be based on a reading ability in the original language of the writer—cannot be understood only as a statement of artistic code. It has its deeper truth in biography, history, and personal morality as well.

Lukács was born into a wealthy Jewish family in Budapest. He studied with Max Weber at the University of Budapest, and from 1912 to 1916 lived in Heidelberg, associating himself with adherents of Weber. In 1911 he published his first work, *Die Seele und die Formen* (The Soul and the Forms), a work strongly grounded in neo-Kantianism. In 1917 he returned to Budapest and became two years later the people's commissar for public education in the short-lived Hungarian Communist Republic. When that government fell within a year, he fled to Austria; twelve years later he moved to Berlin. With the rise to power of Adolf Hitler, he fled to the Soviet Union. He remained in exile there until the close of World War II. He was in exile, then, from 1919 to 1945 before returning to his native land; on his return he worked at the Institute of the Academy of Science and as a professor of aesthetics and cultural history. In the 1956 uprising, during which Imre Nagy succeeded to the head of the government for a few weeks, Lukács was appointed minister of culture. After the uprising was crushed, Lukács was deported to Romania, where he remained for one year before being allowed to reenter Hungary. In his final years Lukács eschewed any public statements and/or political activity.

Lukács's writing during his career in exile was marked by several official Communist party objections. In 1923, after publication of *Geschichte und Klassenbedwusstsein* (1971, *History and Class Consciousness*), he was charged with "revisionist" tendencies. Again in 1929 the same charge was leveled against him. At this point he withdrew from public activity and two years later moved to Berlin, where he lived from 1931 to 1933.

Lukács's other significant work, *Die Theorie des Romans* (1971, *The Theory of the Novel*), was completed in 1916, and published in German in 1920. In this work as in his other "essays," he states his theory of "great realism"—that is, the belief that art does not mirror reality but provides a way to reflect on it and thus to achieve an understanding of it. In this work Lukács used the terms *naturalistic* and *formalistic* in a unique way that has taken on wide acceptance. *Naturalism* is the limited manner in which novelists reproduce reality without providing any of their own vision; *formalism* is the limited manner in which novelists re-create a world that is more their style than it is representation of reality. Lukács was again calling for a balance between the two poles, for he believed that art was more than socialist realism—it had a dynamic that included the currents of history, politics, social consciousness, and form as well as the artist's unique shaping imagination. Thus art for Lukács became a continuum of all the currents in an artist's being, and by the artist's imagination such currents were cohered into a gift for the public. Such a gift is a form of communality, an entranceway into a house of belonging, and a party card into a communist fraternity. The personal thus becomes fused with the social dynamic, and a new form is born. In Lukács's examination of the historical novel, he wrote as his concluding lines: "The historical novel of our time must above all negate, radically and sharply, its immediate predecessor and eradicate the latter's traditions from its own work." Lukács was suggesting that no "great realism" or art stands still but is born in every age, or as he put it, the "renewal in the form" will come, in a "phrase from Hegel's terminology," in "the form of a negation of a negation."

Selected Titles: *Geschichte und Klassenbewusstsein* (1923; *History and Class Consciousness*, 1971); *Die Theorie des Romans* (completed 1916, published 1920; *The Theory of the Novel*, 1971); *Der historische Roman* (published in Russian, 1937; German, 1955; *The Historical Novel*, 1962, repr., with introduction by Frederic Jameson); *Goethe und seine Zeit* (1947; *Goethe and His Age*, 1969); *Der junge Hegel* (1948; *The Young Hegel*,

1976). See *Werke: Gesamtausgabe*, 17 vols. (1962–81); *Ausgewahlte Schriften*, 4 vols. (1967–70); *Politische Aufsatze*, 3 vols. (1975–77).

Selected Translations: *Political Writings 1919–1929* (1972); *Essays on Realism* (1980).

Consult: Ehrhard Bahr and R. G. Kunzer, *György Lukács* (1972); Peter Demetz, *Marx, Engels and the Poets: Origins of Marxist Literary Criticism*, rev. ed. (1967); Mary Gluck, *George Lukács and His Generation* (1985); Frederic Jameson, *Marxism and Form: Twentieth Century Dialectical Theories of Literature* (1971); I. Mészáros, *Lukács' Concept of Dialectic, with Biography, Bibliography, and Documents* (1972); G.H.R. Parkinson, ed., *György Lukacs: The Man, His Work and His Ideas* (1970).

LUSTIG, Arnost. Born December 21, 1926, in Prague, Czechoslovakia; he lives in Washington, D.C. After the German occupation of Czechoslovakia, Lustig, as a Jewish child, was not permitted to continue his schooling. He became a tailor's apprentice in 1941, and in 1942 he was rounded up and sent to Terezin, a Jewish ghetto town set up by the Nazis in north Bohemia, and from there to the concentration camps of Auschwitz, where his father died in the gas chambers, and to Buchenwald. In March 1945 he escaped from a prisoners' transport for liquidation in Dachau, and managed to stay in hiding in Prague until the Czech uprising two months later. He studied politics and social sciences at Prague University; after graduation he became a journalist and broadcaster. He was sent to Israel as a correspondent to cover the Arab-Jewish war in 1948. After his return he became a director for the Czechoslovak radio in Prague. He worked as editor of the magazine *Mlady Svet* from 1958 to 1960 and then as a screenwriter for the Czechoslovak state film industry. He fled to Yugoslavia after the Soviet invasion of Czechoslovakia in 1968, and then moved to Israel; he accepted an invitation to the International Writing Program at the University of Iowa in 1970. He and his wife now live in Washington, D.C., where he is a professor of literature at American University.

Lustig has written a number of prose works on the theme of the Nazi persecution of the Jews: *Diamonds of the Night* (1958, in Czech, English, and Polish editions); *The Street of Lost Brothers* (1959, in Czech and Polish editions); *Dita Saxova* (1962, in Czech, English, and Polish); *The Prayer for Katarina Horovitzova* (1964, in Czech, English, and many language editions—the third Czech edition of 1970 was ordered to be shredded by the Czechoslovak authorities). In the United States his work has appeared under the series title *Children of the Holocaust* (1977–78)—*Night and Hope; Darkness Casts No Shadow;* and *Diamonds of the Night*. His latest work, published in English, is *The Unloved* (1986). Four feature films based on his work were made in Czechoslovakia in the 1960s; two of these films were awarded major prizes at West European film festivals. Among his many novels in translation and written in exile are *Darling* (1969); *Oleander Trees* (1978); and *A Man the Size of a Postage Stamp* (1978).

Lustig is part of the extraordinary phenomenon of contemporary Czech literature, which over the past twenty years has had a "threefold existence": (1) as officially permitted literature published in Czechoslovakia; (2) as banned literature circulating in Czechoslovakia in typed (samizdat) copies; and (3) as émigré Czech literature printed by small publishing houses in the West or published in the West in translation in West European languages.

Selected Titles: *Z deniku sedmnactilete Perly Sch.* (1979, From the Diary of 17-year-old Perla Sch.).

Consult: V. D. Mihailovich, ed., *Modern Slavic Literatures*, vol. 2 (1976).

LVOV, Arkady. Born 1931, USSR; he lives in Washington, D.C. Lvov emigrated to the United States in 1976. He wrote and published 16 novels before leaving the Soviet Union. At the time of his departure, he had written an 800-page novel set in the Stalinist era 1936–1953, which explored the lives of several families in an Odessa tenement building; the novel, meant as a microcosm of Soviet society, contained overtly critical passages regarding Stalin's repressive policies and government-sanctioned anti-Semitism. Lvov hid a microfilm copy of the manuscript in a shoeshine kit and was able to take the microfilm copy with him out of the country. Thirteen years later it was published in the U.S. (1989) under the title *The Courtyard*.

M

MAALOUF, Amin. Born Lebanon; he lives in Paris with his wife and three children. Formerly the director of the Beirut daily newspaper *an-Hahar*, Maalouf moved to Paris to work as editor of the periodical *Jeune Afrique*; he has since retired from his editorial position to write full-time. His first novel, published in Paris in 1986 to great acclaim, *Leo Africanus* (1989), is a historical chronicle that ranges in time from Moorish Granada, Arab Fez, Cairo, and the Turkey and Italy of the Renaissance era.

MacGREEVY, Thomas. Born October 26, 1893, in Tarbert, County Kerry, Ireland; died March 16, 1967, in Dublin, Ireland. *See* Irish Modernists

McKAY, Claude. Born September 15, 1889, in Sunny Ville, Jamaica; died 1948, in Chicago, Illinois. McKay left his island home of Jamaica in 1912; he never returned. He had established himself that same year with the publication of his first two volumes of poetry, *Songs of Jamaica* (Kingston, Jamaica, 1912) and *Constab Ballads* (London, 1912). Both of these volumes drew on McKay's Jamaican experiences and his African heritage. *Songs of Jamaica* concentrated on the joys and sorrows of the island's mountain and farming people; *Constab Ballads* focused on urban realities of the island's largest city and capital. Both works found their base in the "folk" of the island. McKay's kinship with "folk" and their legends proved his rooted experience of life and made him a radical poet in several senses. He was impelled into sympathy with Marxist goals and liberationist policies, but more profoundly, he identified himself with the striving poor and the undaunted hopeful sufferers of misfortune. Radical in technique as well, McKay initiated dialect and slangy, jazz rhythms into his odes and paeans. While he never lost admiration for English literary tradition and conventional verse forms, he believed in an admixture of the informal and formal. McKay may then be said to be more a synthesist, or syncretist, than a revolutionary, but at the time of his entrance into the literary world, his innovations appeared startling and iconoclastic. He became celebrated as one of the pioneers of the Harlem Renaissance.

McKay lived in New York City through World War I, working at various menial jobs and suffering both racism and poverty. He had encountered neither in Jamaica as a child growing up on his father's farm; he had seen some poverty when he lived with his elder brother in Kingston, but McKay's early life was a tranquil one. He wrote poetry by the time he was ten, and he was encouraged in his work by several people, among them the English scholar Edward Jekyll. In 1920 McKay moved to London, where he worked as a reporter for the Marxist journal the *Workers Dreadnought*. He published his third volume of poems, *Spring in New Hampshire*, in London in 1920. In 1921 he returned to the United States to work as the editor of the American Marxist periodical the *Liberator*. He published his first book in the United States, the volume of poems *Harlem Shadows*, in 1922. His brief marriage was suffering difficulties, and when his wife moved to New York that year, McKay left the city for Europe, where he lived and worked for the next eleven years. To earn money he posed as a model for art students in Paris; he also traveled to Germany, Spain, Morocco, and the USSR (in the Soviet Union he was accorded great honor). During this expatriate period he turned from poetry, as his main genre of expression, to fiction writing. His three celebrated novels—*Home to Harlem* (1928); *Banjo: A Story without a Plot* (1932); and *Banana Bottom* (1933)—belong to this period. In these novels McKay explored the anguish of race relations, particularly as it affects blacks and whites attempting to avoid surface slashes of prejudice. In *Home to Harlem* a black army (World War I) deserter comes home to try for a new life; in *Banjo* black workers in Marseilles find their lives constrained by self-conscious do-gooder whites; and in *Banana Bottom*, a white couple adopts two black children in an attempt to raise them from their marginal worlds of poverty, disease, and prejudice; the experiment fails because the white couple is willing to accept only their own standards as the measure by which compassion and civilization are weighed. All three novels, and McKay's poetry, show his profound tie to these issues of racial and color-group ostracism. His plea of understanding—and its seemingly inevitable failure/tragedy in America—defines the compassion in his corpus.

McKay returned to the United States in 1933 at the depth of the depression; he became an American citizen in 1940. In later life he found increasing solace in Catholicism; he moved from Harlem to Chicago to teach in a Catholic school there. Although he continued to write until his death—he left a number of unfinished manuscripts—his lasting work stems from his earlier expatriate period.

Selected Titles: *The Negroes of America* (Moscow, USSR, 1923); *Gingertown* (1932), stories; *A Long Way from Home* (1937), autobiography; *Harlem: Negro Metropolis* (1940); *Selected Poems* (1953); *The Passion of Claude McKay: Selected Poetry of Claude McKay, 1912–1948*, ed. Wayne F. Cooper (1973).

Consult: Addison Gayle, *Claude McKay: The Black Poet at War* (1972); James R. Giles, *Claude McKay* (1976).

MACKUS, Algimantas. Born February 11, 1932, in Pagégiai, Western Lithuania; died December 28, 1964, in an automobile accident in Chicago, Illinois. Mackus left Lithuania as a child toward the end of World War II. After a few years in Germany he came to the United States, where he attended Roosevelt College, 1957–59, and worked for the Lithuanian press and radio. His first book of poems, *Elegijos* (1950, Elegies), printed under the pen name Algimantas Pagégis, was conventional. The second book, *Jo yra žemé* (1959, His Is the Earth) was a radical departure toward modern writing. It expressed the tragic experience of solitude in exile through an innovative and elaborate system of symbols, in vers libre instead of the traditional Lithuanian syllabo-tonic meter. The next book, *Neornamentuotos kalbos generacija ir Augintiniai* (1962, The Generation of Unornamented Speech and the Wards) contributed further to his reputation as the most original Lithuanian émigré poet. Mackus wrote about the loss of native roots, the crisis of language and national identity, and the incommunicability and alienation of the exile condition. In his poems, the problems of exile became a model for contemporary man's destiny. He dedicated major poetry cycles to the fate of blacks, the descendants of the slaves, and to a Jewish boy murdered by the Nazis, drawing parallels between their experience and the Lithuanian experience. Often nihilistic and blasphemous, Mackus's poetry reminds one of T. S. Eliot* and the American beatniks, though it also makes highly original use of Lithuanian folklore. His last book, *Chapel B*, was dedicated to the memory of Antanas Škéma,* a Lithuanian émigré writer who perished in a highway accident, the same fate that befell Mackus; his book, which became a veritable funeral dirge not only to Škéma but also to himself, was published posthumously in 1965. That book consists in part of paraphrases of Federico García Lorca, Dylan Thomas, and others. Mackus's collected poems were published in Lithuania in 1972 and in Chicago in 1984.
    Consult: R. Šilbajoris, *Perfection of Exile* (1970).

                                                                      TOMAS VENCLOVA

MACLEISH, Archibald. Born May 7, 1892, in Glencoe, Illinois; died April 20, 1982, in Boston, Massachusetts. Following the Pulitzer Prize award in 1923 for his narrative poem, in free terza rima, *Conquistador*, MacLeish broke with family tradition and convention and left a Boston law practice. His background included a prestigious preparatory school in Connecticut, undergraduate work at Yale, and a Harvard Law degree. MacLeish took his family with him to Europe, and for six years he worked in seclusion, without the distraction of any other employment. During this period he completed four volumes of poetry. In 1928, he returned to the United States, where he began work as a reporter for *Fortune* magazine. He served as Librarian of Congress during the administration of Franklin Delano Roosevelt (from 1939–44) and held several government posts in the following decade; he was an assistant Secretary of State when he retired in 1945. MacLeish also taught at Harvard University, holding the Boylston Chair of Rhetoric and Oratory from 1949–62.

MacLeish's strong and intellectual poetry has earned him a wide following. He also wrote dramatic verse, and received the Pulitzer Prize for his drama, *J. B.*, a modern rendition of the Biblical Job story.

Selected Titles: *Collected Poems, 1917–1952* (1952); *Collected Plays* (1962); *New and Collected Poems, 1917–76* (1976); *Six Plays* (1980).

Consult: G. Smith, *Archbald MacLeish.*

MADARIAGA (y Rojo), Salvador de. Born July 23, 1886, Corunna, Spain; died December 14, 1978, in Locarno, Switzerland. Madariaga early became a traveler. He studied in Paris from 1900 to 1910, was a mining engineer in Spain from 1911 to 1916, and worked as a journalist in London from 1916 to 1920. He held several distinguished posts at the League of Nations from 1921 to 1927 (among them the secretariat, the press secretary, and official Spanish delegate) and headed the Chair of Spanish Studies at Oxford University from 1928 to 1931. He served as Ambassador of the Spanish Republic to the United States in 1931 and to France from 1932 to 1934. When Franco came to power at the end of the Spanish Civil War, Madariaga went into self-imposed exile, living mostly in England. He returned to Spain in 1976 after Franco's death.

Madariaga served in an official capacity as an ambassador of Spanish culture during his term of exile. Novelist and poet as well as intellectual analyst, he is known primarily for his criticism, philosophic commentary, and biographical essays. He was adept at and wrote in three languages, Spanish, English, and French.

Selected Titles in Translation: *Shelley and Calderon and Other Essays on Spanish and English Poetry* (1920); *Don Quixote* (1934); *Christopher Columbus* (1939).

MALAN, Rian. Born December 1, 1954, in Vereeniging, South Africa; he lives in Los Angeles, California. Malan's family came to South Africa in 1689; its pedigree includes the founder of apartheid (Malan's great-uncle was D. F. Malan, Prime Minister of South Africa in 1948 when new racist restrictions were voted) and the country's present Defense Minister as well as other members of high government and social station. He grew up in Johannesburg, which he calls in a press release for his book, *My Traitor's Heart: A South African Exile Returns to Face His Country, His Tribe and His Conscience* (1990), "the generically western whites-only moonbase in Africa." After graduation from college he worked as a copper prospector, a rock and roll band musician, and a crime reporter for the *Johannesburg Star*. His experiences on the *Star* proved traumatic—he felt he was on the front lines of an undeclared civil war every working day. In 1977 he fled to the United States, and thereby avoided being drafted into the South African army, a move interpreted by family and friends as a rejection of his heritage and country. Eight years later he returned to South Africa to resume his job in an attempt to learn how to cope with life in South Africa. When he felt he had concluded his self-journey, he left South Africa again, and traveled widely in England, France, Israel and Canada. He is now a resident of the state of California.

Malan's autobiography is not, in his words in an official press release, "about an Afrikaner coming to terms with his tribe. It is about one white man's internal and subjective struggle to come to terms with Africa. I thought that the key to living in South Africa might lie in the way black and white South Africans killed each other. And it did." His book is a moral journey by extension in its study of three murders in contemporary South Africa, and of resort to violence as a relief from pressures of apartheid. Malan ends his book on a note of hope in that a Zulu ceremony is given to honor two murdered whites: thus, though tragedy is a concomitant in South African life, hope of reconciliation between races is also a continuing presence. Yet Malan also sees the repressive political administrations of his country as rooted bulwarks against history: unless new policies are put into effect, South Africa becomes, in essence, an exile from modern civilization, and its white inhabitants become practitioners of perverted Calvinist ethics. Clearly Malan does not see an easy road to progress, and he has chosen exile from his country's state of transition.

MALANJUK, Jevhen. Born January 20, 1897, in Elysavet, Kherson region, Ukraine, then part of the Czarist Russian Empire; died February 16, 1968, in New York City, after suffering a massive stroke. A prominent poet and essayist, Malanjuk served as an officer in the army of the Ukrainian National Republic from 1917 to 1920. Following the collapse of the Ukrainian state, he obtained a degree in engineering at the Ukrainian Technical Institute of Poděbrady in 1923. Toward the end of World War II, he emigrated to Germany, and after the war he came to the United States. During his Polish exile, Malanjuk, together with another Ukrainian poet Jurij Darahan (1894–1926), founded the journal *Veselka* (1922–23), where he published his own works. His first collection of poetry, *Stylet i stylos* (Stylet and Stylus), in which he expressed his poetic and ideological credo, was published in 1925 in Poděbrady, Czechoslovakia. Throughout his émigré life, Malanjuk kept in close contact with his native Ukraine, both spiritually and intellectually. Influenced by Dmytro Doncov (1883– 1973), the ideologue of Ukrainian nationalism, Malanjuk's poetry enunciates a deep-seated yearning for a free and independent Ukrainian people to achieve statehood. Malanjuk excoriates his fellow Ukrainians for their various "sins" and chastizes them for their lack of discipline and their excessive emotionality. Conscious of his nation's numerous defeats through the centuries, he bewails the history that cursed his people, but never loses faith in a brighter future. His poetry is a call to moral regeneration; he seeks to imbue his countrymen with a spirit that will lead them to freedom and statehood. While bemoaning his personal fate, stuck "in the sands of the émigré desert," Malanjuk's poetry holds onto its martial ethos and reiterates a messianic calling. His vision of Ukraine, based partially on Johann Gottfried von Herder's idea of Ukraine as a "new Greece," is a product of his exile imagination. Like Herder, Malanjuk sees Ukraine as the Hellas of the Steppes, but unlike Herder, who saw it through the prism of an Apollonian vision, Malanjuk sees it as a land in which the harmonious Apollonian elements vie for supremacy with frenzied Dionysian forces lurking beneath the surface. Malanjuk's poetic-mythic symbol for Ukraine is the ancient Greek figure of Nike, characterized by ineffable beauty and boundless dynamism but lacking a head. The task of the Ukrainian people, according to Malanjuk, lies in reconciling these disparate elements, and this task can be accomplished through the establishment of Ukrainian statehood. Banned until recently in his native land, Malanjuk's poetry has played an important role in Ukrainian émigré life.

Selected Titles: *Poeziji* (1954, Poetry); *Ostannja vesna* (1959, Last Spring); *Knyha sposterežen'* (1962, A Book of Observations, essays).

Consult: Oksana Kerch, ed., *Jehven Malanjuk* (Philadelphia; Ulana Steciuk Foundation, 1983); Bohdan Rubchak, "Homes as Shells: Ukrainian Émigré Poetry," in *Old Roots— New Soil*, ed. J. Rozumnyj (Winnipeg; Ukrainian Free Academy of Sciences in Canada, 1983); Leo D. Rudnytzky, "Yevhen Malanjuk," in *Modern Slavic Literatures*, vol. 2 (1976).

                                                                                    LEONID RUDNYTZKY

MANDELSHTAM, Osip Emilievich (also spelled Mandelstam). Born January 15, 1891, in Warsaw, Poland; died December 27, 1938, in near Vladivostok, USSR. Mandelshtam was arrested and sentenced in 1934 to a three-year term of prison exile in Voronezh for criticizing, in one of his poems, Joseph Stalin. He was rearrested in May 1938 and sentenced to five years of penal servitude in a labor camp. Mandelshtam's poems composed during the horrors of his prison experience were preserved by his wife, Nadezhda Yakovlevna Mandelshtam, who often memorized them in fear of their confiscation by Soviet guards. Mandelshtam's later work, vast in output, expresses an unquenchable hope for survival of the spirit against the overwhelming forces of political and cultural tyranny.

Selected Title: *Sobranie sochineny*, 3 vols. (1964–71).

Translations: *The Complete Poetry of Osip E. Mandelshtam* (1973); *The Complete Critical Prose and Letters* (1979).

Consult: Clarence Brown, *Mandelstam* (1973); Nadja Mandelstam, *Hope Against Hope* (1970); Nadja Mandelstam, *Hope Abandoned* (1974).

MANEA, Norman. Born 1936 Bukovina (now Rumania); he lives and teaches in New York State. Manea left Rumania in 1989 on a grant from the Ford Foundation to teach at Bard College. He has chosen to remain in the United States. His first book in English is a collection of stories centering on a concentration camp inmate as he grows from youth to maturity during the Holocaust and the succeeding years in a Stalinist-dominated Rumania. The book is scheduled for publication in 1991. A Jew, Manea was imprisoned in a concentration camp in the Ukraine when he was five years old; he was freed in 1945. In the years of the Nikolae Ceauşescu regime he was subjected to attacks on his orthodoxy. In 1987 he was the target of an anti-Semitic press campaign after he had criticized the complacency of Romanian intellectuals to civil rights and humanitarian issues. The Prize of the Writers Union of Romania, which had been awarded to him for a collection of essays in 1986, was withdrawn by the government. When he was offered an opportunity to teach abroad for one year, the government gave him and his wife permission to leave. Manea's decision to remain in the United States in spite of the overthrow of the brutal Nikolae Ceauşescu regime, indicates that, for him, Romania remains in a state of transition. Manea has published ten books, most of them novels, which have been translated into German, Dutch, Hebrew, Spanish and Swedish.

MANN, Erika. Born November 9, 1905, in Munich, Germany; died August 27, 1969 in Kilchburg, Switzerland. Erika Mann, the daughter of Thomas and Katja Mann, studied acting with Max Reinhardt in Berlin, and appeared as one of the two female leads in her brother Klaus Mann's first play, *Anja and Esther*, in 1925 (the other female lead was played by the daughter of playwright Franz Wedekind). She married Gustaf Grundgens, an actor known for his participation in left-wing social and political causes who later became a prominent Nazi sympathizer and spokesman; the couple's political disagreements led in large part to their divorce a few years later. Erika began a strenuous regime of acting, writing, and traveling in the early 1930s; her revue, ''Peppermill,'' in which she played the lead and which she directed, opened in Munich in 1933. When Adolf Hitler and the National Socialists took control of the government, the revue was moved on to other countries, including the United States; it proved popular for several years. She left Germany in 1933, warning her father (who was out of the country) not to return; she smuggled out, in her escape, the manuscript of her father's *Joseph* novel. She lived in Czechoslovakia from 1933 to 1936; in 1935 she married W. H. Auden,* a marriage largely of convenience. In 1936 she came with her mother and father and her brother Klaus, for whom she held a deep affection, to the United States; here, she and her brother lectured at various universities (they had performed this kind of work earlier in 1928 when they were touring in a stage production; Klaus Mann wrote about their experiences in his book *Rundherum*, 1928, Roundabout). Her writing after exile in the United States was largely in analytic, sober non-fiction; the bright spark of satirical wit that characterized her earlier literary output withdrew from public evidence in her exile period.

Selected Title: *Briefe und Antworten*, ed. and with Introduction by Zanco Prestel (Munich, 1984, Correspondence and Selections).

Translations: *School for Barbarians* (1938); with Klaus Mann, *Escape to Life* (1940); *The Lights Go Down* (1940).

Consult: Zanco Prestel, Introduction, *Briefe und Antworten* by Erika Mann (Munich,

1984); *Current Biography* 1940; Stanley J. Kunitz and Howard Haycraft, eds., *Twentieth-Century Authors* (1942).

MANN, Heinrich. Born March 27, 1871, in Lübeck, Germany; died March 12, 1950, in Santa Monica, California. Considered by some critics to be the only German writer of his generation to fully develop his democratic thinking, he was a prolific author of novels, novellas, plays, satires, and political essays highly critical of bourgeois values. He was also an antifascist moralist who sharply attacked authoritarian arrogance and the subservience of subject classes. He frequently clashed with his younger brother, Thomas Mann,* over values and *Weltanschauungen.*

Mann published numerous essays, among them "Diktatur de Vernunft" (1923, Dictatorship of Reason), and many satirical novels, including *Professor Unrat* (1903, Small Town Tyrant)—filmed as *Der blaue Engel* (*The Blue Angel*). He was elected president of the Writing Section of the Prussian Academy of Arts in 1930. During a time of heightened nationalism that swept over Europe, Mann published his essay "Bekenntnis zum Uebernationalen" (1932, Confession for the Supernational), and a book-length study, *Der Hass: Deutsche Zeitgeschichte* (1933, The Hate: German Contemporary History).

After he, Albert Einstein, and the artist Käthe Kollwitz publicly urged the unification of the Social Democratic and Communist parties as a means of slowing the Nazi tide, Mann was forced to resign from the Academy. He fled to France (Paris and Nice) in 1933 and worked against fascism there, with Ernst Bloch, André Gide, and others.

His exile publications in France include novels and essays. Sensitive to censorship throughout his life, Mann used historical figures and epochs to exemplify modern democratic, rational principles based on "humanistic socialism," especially in his masterpiece, the two-volume novel *Henri Quatre, the King of France* (*Young Henry of Navarre*, 1935, and *Henry, King of France*, 1938). King Henry, for Mann, becomes a Renaissance Bolshevik, the forefather of modern revolutionary socialism. At pivotal moments in the German novel, Mann inserted "moralités," or conclusions in classical French, attempting to unite intellectually his native Germany with France, the land of his exile.

Heinrich Mann published several essays while he was in France: *Der Sinn dieser Emigration* (1934, The Sense of This Emigration), which contains "Schule der Emigration" (School of Emigration); *Es kommt der Tag: Deutsches Lesebuch* (1936, The Day Will Come: A German Reader); "Hilfe fuer die Opfer des Faschismus" (1937, Help for the Victims of Fascism), a speech; *Was will die deutsche Volksfront?* (1937, What Does The German Volksfront Want?); and *Mut* (1939, Courage). Reflected in many of Mann's satirical essays is his belief that literature and politics are inseparable and that writers must concern themselves in their texts with intellectual freedom and political conscience.

Threatened by the invading German army, Mann fled France in 1940 and settled in the United States, where he initially worked as a filmscript writer in

Hollywood (1940–41). His penchant for abrupt changes from neutral descriptions to grotesque exaggerations created an epic alienation effect enhanced by his new experiences of the American movie world.

Mann's novels written in American exile include *Lidice* (1943), the story of the Czech resistance to Heinrich Heydrich's oppressive regime; *Der Atem* (1949, The Breath), an autobiographical work which condenses events into a few days at the outbreak of World War II; *Empfang bei der Welt* (posthumous, 1956, Reception of the World), a satire in fairy tale form; and the incomplete *Die traurige Geschichte von Friedrich dem Grossen* (posthumous, 1960, The Sad Story of Frederick the Great), a critique of Prussian-German history in the form of filmic dialogue.

Although Mann openly presented socialistic interpretations of the events he described, he did not argue an extreme communist or Marxist point of view. During the latter part of his life, he shifted from aggressive political engagement to a more skeptical stance in which human conflicts were displayed in an elegant style his brother Thomas termed a "product" of Heinrich's "sage avant-garde"["*Produkt eines Greisen-Avantgardismus*"].

Mann's autobiography *Ein Zeitalter wird besichtigt* (My View of an Epoch) appeared in 1946. Four years after the end of World War II, he wrote, "I anticipated what was to become of Germany. Afterwards I was accused of it as if I had been responsible" (Letter to K. Lemke, May 27, 1949). Eleven years after his burial in Santa Monica, California, his remains were flown to East Berlin. His manuscripts and papers are at the Literary Archive of the German Academy of Arts in Berlin and in the Schiller-Nationalmuseum in Marbach, Germany.

Consult: U. Weisstein, *Heinrich Mann* (Tuebingen, 1962); E. Zenker, ed., *Heinrich Mann Bibliographie* (East Berlin, 1967).

HENRIK EGER

MANN, Klaus (Klaus Heinrich Thomas Mann). Born November 18, 1906, in Munich, Germany; died May 21, 1949, in Pacific Palisades, California. Thomas Mann's second child, Klaus Mann distinguished himself early in his literary endeavors. He published several stories and dramatic criticism and reviews in Berlin newspapers in 1924 and 1925. He published his first book, a collection of stories, *Vor dem Leben* (Before Life) in 1925; a novel, *Der Fromme Tanz* (The Pious Dance) was also issued in 1925 as was his play *Anja and Esther*. He worked as an actor as well, travelling with his sister Erika on theatre and lecture tours. He published his recollection of their tour together under the title *Rundherum* (1928, Roundabout). His output continued at a steady pace, with two novels and two plays issuing in the period from 1929 to 1933. In 1933, before he left Germany in March, he published his memoir of childhood life, *Kind Dieser Zeit* (Child of Our Time). Mann became a citizen of Czechoslovakia after he was deprived of his German citizenship by Nazi fiat. He lived principally in Amsterdam, from 1933 to 1936, editing a literary journal, *Die Sammlung*

(The Collection), there. He emigrated to the United States in 1936 and volunteered for service with the United States Army during World War II. After the war he edited an influential cultural journal, *Decision*, in New York. He grew despondent in his last years, possibly over psychosexual conflicts, and committed suicide at the age of forty-three.

Mann's most famous fiction is *Mephisto*, the tale of a minor left-wing actor who sells his talent to the Nazi cause and in the process is rewarded with high administrative posts. A loosely allusive tale of corruption through unprincipled ambition, of Satan as an actor in the drama of Nazi corruption, the work achieves a special intensity through its bold expressionistic strokes. Mann based the novel on the life of his one-time friend and former brother-in-law (Erika's husband); all three—Erika, Klaus and "Mephisto" had shared success and intimacy in the mid–1920s. In dramatizing the fall of an actor, he was also painting the autumn of German civilization. The novel was published in German, first in Amsterdam in 1936, then in Prague in 1937; it was issued in English in 1977. Its first German publication was in 1956 in Berlin; it has been reprinted in Germany many times.

Translations: *The Fifth Child* (1927); *Alexander* (1930); *Pathetic Symphony* (1938); (with Erika Mann) *Escape to Life* (1939); (with Erika Mann) *The Other Germany* (1940); *The Turning Point* (1942, autobiography).

Consult: Michel Grunewald, comp. *Klaus Mann 1906–1949: eine Bibliographie* (Bern/Frankfurt, 1984).

MANN, (Paul) Thomas. Born June 6, 1875, in the Hanseatic town of Lübeck, Germany; died August 12, 1955, in Zurich, Switzerland. Mann believed that the contrast between his sensitive, southern, artistic, Germanic-Creole mother and respectable merchant father had created in him a personality in which artistic, sickly, decadent, self-conscious aloofness was complicated by an undertone of bourgeois guilt and a longing for unreflective stability and social acceptance. He projected this dualistic mode of thought universally. In his first novel, *Buddenbrooks* (1901; English, 1924), he contrasts a family's strong, elder, bourgeois, merchant generations with the decadent, artistic strain of its heirs.

Throughout his life, Mann perceived a duality between artist and society. He saw himself as different, an outcast from bourgeois normalcy in every area; for example, in his abysmal academic career, and in his personal relations—his notebooks describe a lifelong conflict between a passionate (though apparently unconsummated) homoerotic love for various young adult boys, and the dutiful, though finally nonsexual, warm devotion to his wife.

This sense of being an outcast probably diminished his "rootedness" in German soil. In his fictionalized account of leaving Lübeck at seventeen for Munich (with his bereaved mother), Mann writes that the protagonist "with nothing but derision in his heart, had left his native town. . . . he felt no pain to go." Mann further distanced himself from Germany when he followed his older brother Heinrich to Italy (in 1895, 1896–98), where he devoured Scandinavian and Russian literature, wrote some important short stories, and began writing *Bud-*

denbrooks, a book whose fidelity to real events and persons, and ironic style, were perhaps encouraged by geographical distance.

Yet this distance from German soil and literary influence contrasts sharply with his deep, almost fanatical absorption of the German Tradition in the form of Richard Wagner, Arthur Schopenhauer, and especially Friedrich Nietzsche. From Wagner and Schopenhauer, Mann acquired the Romantic pessimism and sympathy for decadence and death that pervades his early work. Through Nietzsche he applied his own sexual and spiritual disorientation, his acedia, his "serious plans for suicide," to German and European society at large.

Mann's brilliant novella *Der Tod In Venedig* (1912; *Death in Venice*, 1925) exemplifies his paradoxical conservation of a radical national tradition in a foreign setting. Gustave Aschenbach, a dignified, established, aging, and sickly writer vacations at a Venice resort where he is attracted—Platonically, aesthetically, he tells himself—to a frail, beautiful fourteen-year-old boy. Venice, once the cradle of culture, now has declined to a decadent tourist trap, whose denizens (abetted by the artist) conspire to cover up a spreading epidemic. The artist realizes that his Platonic, mythological musings (and perhaps his art itself) are merely a delusive rationalization of the truth—of his raging, perverted lust for this boy. Soon, sitting in a beach chair staring at the distant object of his absurd love, he dies. This deeply confessional, fact-based story met with great public acclaim in part because it precisely conveyed the then-current feeling of Nietzschean sexual and spiritual decadence, as well as the sense of alienated "foreignness" and the licentiousness such anonymity engenders. Simultaneously, Mann created a sultry, sickly sweet atmosphere that captures the voluptuousness of surrender, the secret fascination with death and decay.

In *Death in Venice* Aschenbach's career fulfilled his craving for recognition (as had Mann's through the huge success of *Buddenbrooks*); now he could "administrate his fame"—maintaining his public bourgeois dignity while surreptitiously revealing his darkened soul. Aschenbach's "exile" to Venice was a dreamed-for escape from this deceit. Yet exile's license for Aschenbach ends by revealing a still deeper level of deception: the artist's self-deception that his tradition and craft are meaningful—his wrapping of base, primitive desires in mythological rationalizations. Aschenbach's journey from home leads to the bestial core of his soul—this self-knowledge destroys him.

Mann's unique and historically important chronicling of Germany's Nietzschean decadence gained further significance with the outbreak of World War I, which he and most Germans welcomed eagerly. He temporarily abandoned his art to become a public figure with the antidemocratic treatise *Betrachtungen eines Unpolitischen* (1918; *Reflections of a Non-Political Man*, 1983). Yet his dualistic mode of thought, so valuable in deepening or complicating his art, rendered his political statements ambiguous, contradictory, and ineffective, a problem exacerbated by the invariably reactive, personal, and aesthetic motivations behind his politics.

Following World War I, Mann rather suddenly evolved from imperialist into the "socialist" intellectual spokesman (beginning ca. 1923) for defeated Germany's democratic Weimar Republic. Critics debate whether this apparent political reversal is an opportunistic siding with the war's socialist "winners," or a cosmetic, equivocal covering of his guilt over his own protofascist leanings, or a genuine, wholehearted renunciation of youthful mistakes in favor of enlightened liberalism or leftism. (Mann himself usually claimed there was no change in his views.) His hopelessly subjective and aesthetically oriented concept of "socialism," even of "freedom," renders somewhat inconclusive the purely political aspect of this debate. The question of whether the fifty-year-old Mann completely shook off all of the Nietzschean demons of his "youth", however, bears upon the relative importance of the work of the 1930s (which seems to repudiate Nietzsche's influence in favor of Goethe's) and the post–1942 work (which seems to revert to Nietzschean themes).

The early stages of Mann's self-announced transition to Goethe's influence may be seen in his extremely popular novel *Der Zauberberg* (1924; *The Magic Mountain*, 1927), started in 1913, interrupted by the *Betrachtungen*, then resumed in 1919. As in *Der Tod In Venedig*, Mann begins in a foreign setting, with the personal, autobiographically inspired realism of the Nietzschean obsession with sickness and death: he fictionalizes his 1912 visit to a Swiss mountain sanitorium, where a "higher" realm of idle intellectuality and sensibility intertwines with sexuality, sickness, and death. From the bourgeois flatlands below arrives a Goethean naif, Hans Castorp, who will be "educated" by Settembrini and Naptha, who respectively represent the progressive European Enlightenment and the German Romantic positions that Mann juxtaposed in the *Betrachtungen*. Here, however, Mann attempts to balance the aesthetically true and heartfelt Romantic position with the socially necessary arguments of a democratic, humanistic optimist of Enlightenment. Though the Romantic man wins the many dry and encyclopedic debates, his inwardness leads to totalitarianism and self-destruction. Thus Dionysian death and sickness, the dark power of will and desire, are acknowledged by Mann but are balanced with Apollonian civilization. Castorp's dream teaches this balance in the "Schnee" (Snow) episode in which two hags in a temple devour baby flesh while those outside accept but ignore the alluring horror. This achievement of precarious unity through grudging acknowledgment of every possible opposing view seems ironically undercut as Castorp stumbles blindly, finally observing enlightened social duty, toward ambiguous death as a *German* soldier in World War I.

Mann had thought that his earlier system of dichotomies, in which he emphasized the artist and culture (tradition) over society and politics (modernity), would protect the elite aesthetic tradition from the vulgar liberal-democratic masses. However, his elite constituency of decadent artists and outcasts was so representative of the times that it grew into exactly the kind of mindless mass movement he had feared, and began to vulgarize his treasured tradition. Thus Mann's sudden political involvement does *not* represent a change in his thinking, and *is* opportunistic, cosmetic, and dutiful rather than heartfelt, in the sense that it remains a means to his fundamentally aesthetic ends. Yet his deep feelings for the primary importance of artistic tradition (and thus of himself) to humanity justify or complicate whatever egoism and opportunism may appear to underlie his politics.

The twelve-year writing of *Der Zauberberg* documents a transition, heartfelt or not, from Nietzschean dichotomous (and therefore relativist or nihilistic) decadence to Goethean striving for unification, initially through a long-winded, all-encompassing thoroughness. Publicly, this transition meant an apparent movement from conservative, nationalistic, individualistic aestheticism, to progressive, Pan-European, politically involved humanism—a loosening of his ties with Germany symbolized by his controversial Paris visit (1926), where he was treated like a foreign dignitary. Artistically, Mann moved toward new goals, subjects, and stylistic vices: from chronicling (and indulging in) Nietzschean dualism to constructive attempts at unification and synthesis, from inverted sexuality to chaste morality, from cold pessimism to increased ironic humor and parody, from realism to symbolism and mythology, from personal confession to psychological abstraction, from subtle observation to ostentatious erudition, and from egocentric selectivity to epic-scale inclusivity.

When the nihilistic "disease" that Mann believed enhanced his genius was first mirrored in the back alleys of civilization, he reveled in the secret adventure of its forbidden license, and mocked the hypocritical efforts to cover it up. But in the 1920s he saw the epidemic spread in earnest—saw it grow from a sultry, aristocratic heightening of sensibility, a dilettante exploration of darker desires, to the massive, uncontrolled barbarism of Hitler's biologicalization and vulgarization of Nietzsche, Wagner, and pre-Christian Germanic myth into "blood" and "soil" and "national destiny." (He later called Hitler his "brother . . . artistic genius.")

Mann recognized and "fled" this usurpation of his German tradition as early as 1926 when he first followed Goethe's suggestion to expand the biblical Joseph tale by beginning the tetralogy *Joseph und seine Brüder* (1933–43; *Joseph and His Brothers*, 1934–44). Mann's writing of the series' first two novels was often interrupted by various political activities, more frequent lectures and travels, his winning of the 1929 Nobel Prize, and his concern over the increasing power of the National Socialist party in Germany's parliament. Hitler's enormous gains in the 1930 elections prompted Mann's disrupted speech, *Ein Appell an die Vernunft* (1930; *An Appeal to Reason*, 1942), in which he announced his support for (without joining) the Social Democratic party, an unusually clear position that led to the first major disillusionment with him by the fascist press.

On February 10, 1933, eleven days after Hitler became chancellor, Mann gave a surprisingly resented Munich lecture, *Leiden und Grösse Richard Wagners* (1933; *Sufferings and Greatness of Richard Wagner*, 1933) and repeated the lecture in Amsterdam, Brussels, and Paris, resting afterwards with his wife in the Swiss town of Arosa. Here he learned to his surprise of the Reichstag's burning, Hitler's 288-seat landslide of March 5, the Nazi book burnings (in which his books were spared), and, through his daughter, of rumored accusations of his "pacific excesses" and "intellectual high treason," the seriousness of which convinced him to remain in Switzerland (eventually settling in Küsnacht). Mann's unrivaled stature created enormous pressure from his politically divided fellow émigrés (whom he in general publicly disowned and deeply angered) to denounce the Nazi murders and torture (of which he was quite aware). However, since the Nazis sought propaganda advantage through permitting the continued sale and publishing of his books, he remained silent for three years, apparently in hopes that his yet-to-be-published *Joseph* novels might contribute to some sort of oppositional uprising. (Again, his ever-dominant aesthetic priorities make this political naïveté credible, though some suggest that the considerable, tainted profits contributed to his silence.)

On February 3, 1936, in an open letter to Eduard Korrodi, Mann made his first clear statement of opposition to the Nazi regime, for which he and his family were later deprived of German citizenship (Mann became a Czech citizen in 1936 and an American citizen in 1944). A similarly outspoken reply (December 31, 1936) to the Bonn University dean who withdrew his honorary doctorate was published around the world. During Mann's fourth trip to the United States, Hitler annexed Austria, which helped convince Mann to accept a chair as part-time lecturer at Princeton University (from 1938 to 1941). In addition to sporadic lectures at Princeton, Mann aided other emigrants, produced an unusually large number of incidental pieces, continued to work on the *Joseph* novels, and toured the country speaking in favor of America's entering the war. In July 1941, he began building a house in Pacific Palisades, California, where a significant colony of German émigrés had settled. Here, after sixteen years in the writing, *Joseph* was finished.

Joseph began as a presciential fantasy of exile as a providential rebirth, an escape from one's treacherous brothers to husband their essence in foreign isolation, and later redeem and rescue them from destruction, thereby exchanging their envious rejection for worship. (Joseph is sold into exile/slavery by his brothers and rises to power in Egypt, where he stores the food that will be needed by his brothers during the famine he has foreseen.) *Joseph* encapsulates and completes the transition Mann began with *Der Zauberberg*. His personal confessions and fictionalized reality have become communal Jungian archetypes, whose actions are interspersed with parodically vast compilations of scholarship and commentary. The artist-figure's isolation now derives not from decadence but from self-confidence of election of "God". Thus, to integrate with society he need only mature, naturally sparking his social concern, which society now reciprocates with grateful obedience. As Mann claimed, "The contrast of the artist and the bourgeois . . . is reconciled in this fairy tale." As a "counter-myth" to Hitler's dark pre-Christian Germanic myth of lust, violence, and destiny, Mann offers a light, rational, psychological modernization of Judeao-Christian myth—but Mann's vague, man-made, relativist God, who changes to meet man's evolving needs, seems much like Nietzsche's dead God. (And while Mann called himself a "nonbeliever," Hitler's followers believed fervently in their brutal mythology.) As in *Der Tod In Venedig*, mythology and religion become rationalizations for bestial primitive passions and "the stranger [pagan] god"; but now, aided by Freud's scientific light on our darker regions, these rationalizations form the foundation of a humanist, agnostic "faith." Mann's theology may then be said to obscure responsibility. If Joseph's brothers' evil is part of God's plan, so could be Hitler's evil. The sudden, contrived resolution of Mann's lifelong artist/society duality through "maturity" seems limited, since maturity leads to decay, death, and, in societies, to the "cultural lateness" evidenced by the novel's descent into ever-increasing self-conscious parody.

Joseph's huge sales continued Mann's virtually uninterrupted worldwide success, stature, and financial security, rendering him uniquely unaffected by exile in material terms. He was singularly unaffected emotionally by exile because of his characteristic personal aloofness. (The fourth novel contains the most direct American influence of Mann's works in its portrayal of the Roosevelt-like Joseph the Provider's use of New Deal economic policies.)

Between the third and fourth *Joseph* novels, Mann crystallized his ultimately unconvincing attempts to connect himself with Goethe (as writers, they were opposites), through writing *Lotte in Weimar* (1939; *The Beloved Returns*, 1940). Again, the duality of artist and society is "resolved" through the "election" (here, genius) of the artist, through his ability to contain all things, including evil, within his vast intellect and spirit. Here, however, there are reminders of an earlier Mann—he returns to Aschenbach's problems of hypocrisy and stature. As in *Joseph*, there are incidental allusions to the war, but now also allusions to Mann's earlier dualism: "For [the Germans'] best always lived in exile among them, and in exile only . . . will they develop all the good there is in them." Also, Mann has Goethe decry the intrusion of any temporal political "tinder" into art. While the sixteen-year prolongation of *Joseph* was in part an exotic "refuge" from the European émigrés' demands for purely political involvement (of the kind that embittered and corroded so much of their own art, and that in part prompted Mann's further "escape" from those demands to America), Mann's reception in America as more of a cultural ambassador, the vessel of the Good German Tradition, no doubt encouraged this experiment in the historical novel.

Mann's Goethe period was, as he said of *Joseph*, "a refuge . . . a homeland." By 1942, with the true suicidal barbarism of Hitler's now-declining efforts revealed, Mann permanently turned from his always resented political "duties" and Goethean attempts to dissociate himself from his actual nature and tradition, to courageously tell the truth—that Mann more than anyone since Nietzsche understood, foretold, and aesthetically prepared the way for his "brother . . . artistic genius," Hitler, and was thus implicated in the resulting barbarism far more deeply than could be self-absolved through superficial political vacillations. In the artist-protagonist of his deeply autobiographical novel *Doktor Faustus* (1947; *Doctor Faustus*, 1948), Mann interweaves himself, Nietzsche's life and thought, the German Tradition, and the German people: all made a pact with "the Devil" (or with themselves—the question of responsibility is again clouded), or renounced humanity and love in favor of intellectual, aesthetic obsessiveness, which leads inward to nihilistic despair and self-destruction. Mann's multilayered novelistic overreaching results in ethical inconsistency which could be the point —the damned Faustus, and so, Germany, seems Christ-like at times and worthy of resurrection—but more seriously, the dissociative layers of prolixity, montage, evasion, and narrative distance built up over the Goethe period ultimately detract from the novel's conceptual brilliance. Here Mann more convincingly "solves" the outcast-artist/society dichotomy through the integration of society into the artist—into an outcast nation presided over by its insane brother-artist. Mann's theology gains in relevance if not credibility through his theory that once one reaches the utter nadir of sin, grace may become the only possible next step. The novel ends with a heartfelt prayer for the man who made prayer impossible—Nietzsche—whose damnation (repudiating Goethe's Faust's salvation), with that of his race, fulfills both his own terrible prophecy and Mann's fundamental aesthetic-historical destiny: Mann becomes the modern chronicler of the decadence and demise of the German nation and tradition.

One effect of exile for Mann was the enormous personal and "critical" adulation for him as the Good German by many Americans, perhaps easing their justification of killing bad Germans. With the war over, this adulation seemed abruptly revoked: the critics almost universally damned Faustus, to Mann's bitter disappointment, which combined with his fear and anger over the anticommunist hysteria of the 1950s (though he was never a communist, his ever-present political ambiguity provoked some criticism) to prompt what he called his "second exile," to Switzerland (near Zurich) in 1952.

Here exile provided the geographical and emotional distance to write the bitter novella Die Betrogene (1953; The Black Swan, 1954), which, among other things, exposes America as an attractive but inwardly sick provider of cosmetic, false rejuvenation, rather than of a cure (as Mann had suggested in Joseph) for Europe's mortal disease. (In the novella an older woman believes her love for a young American has restarted her monthly cycle—she dies from cancer of the womb.) Exile's distance allowed Mann to fictionally "burn his bridges" to America as he did those to Lübeck (with Buddenbrooks in Italy) and to Germany with Faustus: only in exile could he unsentimentally chronicle the demise not only of his nation, but also of his treasured German Tradition, which is to say, of his own life. For in 1901 Mann had planned Faustus as his final summation of his life's work—now he called it "a bookend . . . all that follows is postscript."

Mann accurately said he was the chronicler of a decadence he sought (but failed) to overcome. During his anomalous Goethe period, he pretended or deluded himself (so as to distance himself from Hitler's usurpation of decadence) that he had happily overcome the Nietzschean dichotomies (e.g., artist/bourgeois, mind/spirit, culture/politics, etc.) that had formed him as an artist and man and that integrated him with the German Tradition. Mann believed this tradition was great *because* it was divided (dichotomous) and decadent, just as he and Nietzsche believed their genius was enhanced by their physical sickliness and their exile, both perceived and real. Some critics suggest that the Goethean political period represents the "true" Mann, an assessment that makes him a more attractive and heroic character, but dismisses much of his work and detracts from his deeper cultural-historical significance within the development of the essentially Germanic, Nietzschean relativism that continues to dominate the twentieth century.

Selected Titles: The tetralogy *Joseph und seine Brüder* (Joseph and His Brothers), was published in this order: *Die Geschichten Jaakobs* (Berlin, 1933; *The Tales of Jacob*, 1934), vol. 1, written between ca. December 1926 and October 1930; *Der junge Joseph* (Berlin, 1934; *Young Joseph*, 1935), vol. 2, written between ca. December 1930 and June 1932; *Joseph in Ägypten* (Vienna, 1936; *Joseph in Egypt*, 1938), vol. 3, written between ca. July 1932 and August 1936); *Joseph, der Ernährer* (Stockholm, 1943; *Joseph the Provider*, 1944), vol. 4, written between ca. August 1940 and January 1943.

Other Selected Titles: *Order of the Day: Political Essays and Speeches of Two Decades* (1943); *Der Erwählte* (Frankfurt, 1951; *The Holy Sinner*, 1951); *Bekenntnisse des Hochstaplers Felix Krull. Der Memoiren erster Teil* (Frankfurt am Main, 1954; *Confessions of Felix Krull, Confidence Man: The Early Years*, 1955); *Die Entstehung des Doktor Faustus* (Berlin, 1955; *The Story of a Novel: The Genesis of Doctor Faustus*, 1961 [written between July and October 1948]); *Tagebücher 1946–1948*, ed. Inge Jens (Frankfurt, 1990).

Consult: Bruce M. Broerman, *The German Historical Novel in Exile after 1933* (1986); Henry Hatfield, *From the Magic Mountain: Mann's Later Masterpieces* (1979); Erich Heller, *Thomas Mann: The Ironic German* (1979); Klaus W. Jonas, *Fifty Years of Thomas Mann Studies: A Bibliography of Criticism* (1955); Klaus W. Jonas and Ilsedore B. Jonas, *Thomas Mann Studies*, vol. 2: *A Bibliography of Criticism* (1967); Helmut Koopman, "German Culture Is Where I Am: Thomas Mann in Exile," *Studies in Twentieth-Century Literature* 7 (Fall 1982); Egbert Krispen, *Anti-Nazi Writers in Exile* (1978); Herbert Lehnert, "Thomas Mann in Exile: 1933–1938," *Germanic Review* 38 (1963); J. M. Ritchie, *German Literature under National Socialism* (1983). See also *The Letters of Thomas Mann, 1895–1955*, ed. Richard and Clara Winston (1990).

STUART HAMILTON SMITH

MANSFIELD, Katherine (Katherine Mansfield Beauchamp). Born October 14, 1888, in Wellington, New Zealand; died January 9, 1923, near Fontainebleau, France. Mansfield rebelled explosively against the upper-middle-class assumptions of her family, and at fifteen was sent to England for schooling. Back in Wellington, three years later, she was so unhappy that her family remitted her again to England. She entered the bohemian life of Europe in 1908 with the energy of rebellion; she married in 1909 but left her husband the next day, had a variety of affairs and at least one abortion, lived with and eventually married the editor John Middleton Murry, acted as film extra and chorus girl, and contracted the tuberculosis that killed her at the age of thirty-four. She also began writing. Most of her work before 1915—"smart set" sketches and satires of the bourgeoisie—were published in little magazines edited by Murry or their friends: the satires were collected as *In a German Pension* in 1911. Both the tinges of hollowness or alienation among the bohemians, and the violence of her attack upon the middle class are attributable to the same cause: having grown up without ready access to long-established cultures, she was pained to see culture abused by those who had such easy access.

Mansfield's career turned sharply in 1915, when her brother was killed in France. She had fled New Zealand in disgust, but now reimagined the country of her youth in order to find the security she felt ought to have existed there and to examine the roots of her current, pervasive alienation. In such stories as "Her First Ball" (1921) and "The Garden Party" (1922), she depicts a social landscape that is deep and lush but that can insulate its inhabitants from unhappiness only if they limit their expectations to superficiality and material well-being. These later works typically involve an adolescent or young adult who acquires a sudden recognition of underlying forces, a vision similar to the epiphanies in the stories of James Joyce* from the same period. Mansfield appears to have arrived at the technique independently, for she consciously sat outside the critical discussions that Murry was fond of conducting with D. H. Lawrence,* Leonard and Virginia Woolf, and other modernist writers. She tapped instead the many layers of loneliness—her upbringing, her expatriation, her poverty, her failing health—and wrote of a world which yet includes small, quiet opportunities for tenderness.

The adoring Murry published Mansfield's journals, letters, and miscellany throughout his lifetime; most Mansfield criticism before his death in 1957 tended toward hagiography. Recent critical and biographical studies have placed her in a clearer perspective.

Selected Title: *Poems*, ed. Vincent O. Sullivan (1990).

Consult: Anthony Alpers, *The Life of Katherine Mansfield* (1982); Kate Fullbrook, *Katherine Mansfield* (1986); Jeffrey Meyers, *Katherine Mansfield* (1978); Claire Tomalin, *Katherine Mansfield: A Secret Life* (1988).

JOHN SCHECKTER

MÁRAI, Sàndor. Born April 11, 1900, in Kassa, Hungary (now Kosice, Czechoslovakia); he committed suicide February 21, 1989, in San Diego, California. In its notice of his death *Irodalmi Ujság* (Literary Magazine) of Hungary called Márai "the greatest Hungarian writer of our time" (no. 2, 1989), while another obituary called him "the spirit of the twentieth century in Hungary." During earlier decades of strict communist rule Márai was, however, consistently derided as a mere stylist—for example, the entry in *Magyar Irodalmi Lexikon* (Hungarian Literary Lexicon) stated in its 1965 edition: "Márai clings desperately, at the dawn of the new era, to declining middle-class values and literary world-views. He could not develop in the direction of progress" (p. 125). In spite of its denigration, the same encyclopedia devoted three pages to Márai's prodigious output.

Márai was the scion of a professional upper-middle-class family of German origin. He studied at the Universities of Frankfurt and Berlin and simultaneously became the foreign correspondent of a Vienna paper, working first from Germany and later from Paris. His first novel, *A mészáros* (The Butcher), was published in Vienna in 1924. He returned to Budapest and there achieved immediate success with *Bébi vagy az elsö szerelem* (Baby or First Love) in 1928. It was the earliest appearance in Hungarian literature of Freudian concepts and Proustian style, and the twenty-eight-year-old author had a galvanizing effect on young intellectuals of his time. By the time he reached his thirties, Márai personified the ethos of the literate bourgeoisie of Hungary, the essence of Central Europe. His auto-biographical novel, *Egy polgár vallomásai* (Budapest, vol. 1, 1934, vol. 2, 1935, Confessions of a Bourgeois), and its sequels, *Féltékenyek* (1937, The Jealous) and *Sértődöttek* (3 vols., 1947–48, The Injured), are not merely chronicles but seek to vindicate values Márai felt were in danger of disintegration. In the war years, as he watched barbarism eclipsing Europe, his drama *Kassai polgárok* (The Burghers of Kassa) played for a full year at the National Theater of Budapest in 1942.

When the Nazis overran Hungary Márai left Budapest for the countryside; the excesses of the subsequent communist regime drove him abroad. In 1945 he began to write a diary that he continued till 1982; this work was later published in exile. The diary begins with his last year in Hungary and follows his fate in Italy and from there to New York. The first part, published under the title *Geist im Exil* (Spirit in Exile) in its German translation (Hamburg, 1959), offers a diagnosis of the spiritually uprooted writer living in exile.

Márai did not stop writing in exile, but his work began to mirror his new predicament: he declared that his homeland was his language, that is, Hungarian. Unlike Joseph Conrad* or Arthur Koestler,* he never wrote in another language. In Naples he defiantly published two new novels himself. *San Gennaro vére* (published in German translation: *Das Wunder des San Gennaro*, Baden-Baden, 1957, The Blood of San Gennaro) and *Judit* both deal with the hopelessness and later the resignation that overtook him. The hero commits suicide because the familiar world embodying his values has disappeared. This rejection may have strengthened a suicide impulse awakened in Márai since his departure from Hungary. His beloved wife had died, and his only son had committed suicide in the United States. Yet, even before this time, the hero of his novel, *The Blood of San Gennaro*, who is an émigré writer, throws himself off the rocks in Posilipo (where Márai had once lived), because the Europe he believed in had ceased to exist.

Márai's shattering poem *Halotti Beszéd* (Sermon over the Dead) reached Hungary in 1951 from Italy (where Márai was then living). The medieval *Halotti Beszéd* is the first literary document found in the Hungarian language, and Márai's poem, using an umbrella title, describes the slow death of an exile who cannot adapt to a new environment even as his old roots are withering away. Márai's poem is the first specimen of samizdat literature in Hungary; typewritten copies of the poem may have contributed to the Hungarian will to revolution in 1956.

When Márai moved from Italy to the United States, a Hungarian publisher in

Toronto, Vörösváry, took over his work and republished his great novel-cycle based on the professed values of the cultured upper class. In this sense Márai remained an unashamed elitist. He valued culture above money, power, and technological superiority.

Márai also wrote several profound psychological novels analyzing the relations between the sexes. In all of them—*Válás Budán* (1935, A Divorce in Buda), *Vendégjáték Bolzanóban* (1941, Guest Performance in Bolzano), and *Az Igazi* (1941, The Real One)—he maintained the position that human beings rarely understand each other and remain creatures of obscure instincts.

The publishing house Griff, in Munich, led by the Hungarian Sándor Ujváry, republished all of Márai's work, except his last manuscript, a crime story, written when Márai was eighty-five years old. This was Márai's first experience in rejection. Interestingly, his earliest book, published in Vienna, had also been a murder story, a refashioning of a famous German crime.

Márai's books have been translated into English, German, Czech, Danish, Finnish, Flemish, French, Dutch, Polish, Italian, Portuguese, Spanish, Swedish, Serbo-Croatian, Slovenian, and Turkish. He himself has no monument: his ashes were scattered in the Pacific.

On his eightieth birthday a Festschrift was compiled in his honor for *New Europe* (Munich); it began with a laudation written by Otto Habsburg. The heir to the Habsburg dynasty, having learned to speak Hungarian as a child, chose Márai as the ideal model for anyone seeking to employ the Hungarian language with distinction.

ÉVA BOLGÁR

MARCUSE, Herbert. Born July 7, 1889, in Berlin; died July 29, 1979, in Starnberg, West Germany. Marcuse, son of prosperous Jewish parents, is perhaps the foremost and most widely read contemporary philosopher to emerge from the ranks of German academics who were in exile in the United States during the Third Reich. After attending the gymnasium, he studied philosophy, literature, and economics at Berlin and Freiburg from 1922 to 1929. In Freiburg, Marcuse was a student of the two great thinkers of early twentieth-century German philosophy, Edmund Husserl and Martin Heidegger. With the publication in 1932 of *Hegel's Ontology and the Foundation of a Theory of Historicity*, Marcuse attracted the interest of a group of left-wing noncommunist German intellectuals, who would come to be known as the Frankfurt School, or the exponents of "Critical Theory." Marcuse was soon invited to be one of their collaborators at the Institute of Social Research, first in Geneva, then in Paris, and finally in New York. His decision to join the institute in Geneva in 1933 marked the beginning of his emigration and exile from Germany. In 1934 he joined the institute in New York, where together with Theodor Adorno,* Max Horkheimer, Leo Lowenthal, Friedrich Pollack, and others, Marcuse helped to formulate the central ideas of the "Critical Theory of Society" that helped to revitalize Marxism in particular and social theory in general. In 1941 Marcuse published *Reason and Revolution: Hegel and the Rise of Social Theory*. The

1941 study on Hegel, which constituted some of the fruits of Marcuse's years of exile and his work at the institute in New York, was an attempt to rescue Hegel from his image as a philosophical and political conservative. In his interpretation of Hegel, Marcuse discovered beneath the surface of Hegel's more authoritarian statements a radical core, namely "the dialectical theory of negativity." This philosophical approach, first gleaned from Hegel, has played a central role in Marcuse's analysis and critique of existing ideologies and institutions.

Although many of Marcuse's writings were completed in exile between 1934 and 1941, he first gained wide acclaim in the late sixties and early seventies. In 1964 he published his now famous *One Dimensional Man*, which, among other things, branded advanced industrial civilization as unfree and oppressive. Toward the end of *One Dimensional Man*, Marcuse spoke of what he termed the "Great Refusal," a protest and struggle against an advanced industrial civilization, which Marcuse denigrated as obscene. Not only a perceptive and convincing critic of advanced industrial civilization, particularly in its capitalist form,. Marcuse was also an adamant opponent of the Vietnam War. This Marxist Jewish philosopher, who some thirty-seven years earlier had fled Germany, became known internationally as the Father of the New Left. *One Dimensional Man* was followed by *An Essay on Liberation* (1969), *Counter-Revolution and Revolt* (1972), and *Aesthetic Dimension* (1978). Students of Marcuse, fascinated and influenced by his writings on revolt, liberation, and aesthetics, discovered the earlier and important study on Sigmund Freud,* *Eros and Civilization* (1955), and the seminal essay from Marcuse's period of exile, "The Affirmative Character of Culture." Marcuse's early work through 1940, such as "Über den affirmative Charakter der Gesellschaft," was written in German; the essay was first published in *Zeitschrift für Sozialforschung*, vol. 6 (1937). It later appeared in English in a volume of Marcuse's essays, *Negations: Essays in Critical Theory* (1968). During the period of World War II and after the war until German publishers and journals resumed operations, Marcuse's writing was restricted, for the most part, to an English-reading audience. His major works, *Reason and Revolution* (1941), *Eros and Civilization* (1955) and *One Dimensional Man* (1964), were all written first in English and then translated into German. However, in the mid–1950s Marcuse again began to write in German; at the height of his fame he was writing in both languages.

Consult: John Fry, *Marcuse—Dilemma and Liberation* (1974); Douglas Kellner, *Herbert Marcuse and the Crisis of Marxism* (1984); Robert Pippin, Andrew Feenberg, and Charles P. Webel, eds., Marcuse: *Critical Theory and the Promise of Utopia* (1987); Kurt H. Wolff and Barrington Moore, Jr., eds., *The Critical Spirit: Essays in Honor of Herbert Marcuse* (1987).

RICHARD CRITCHFIELD

MARKANDAYA, Kamala (pseudonym of Kamala Purnaiya Taylor). Born 1924, Chimakurti, India; she lives in England. Markandaya moved to England in the 1950s when she married an Englishman, and has lived there since. A major novelist whose themes revolve around the opposition of Eastern and Western values, she characterizes her heroes and heroines in the light of both stoicism and humor: they refuse to surrender their struggles for accommodation of differing and distinct values within their one and changing world. Her first book, the novel *Nectar in a Sieve* (1954, repr. 1982) emphasized the intransigeance of those oppressed and imperialist peoples who refuse to rise beyond inculcated group response. In her continuing discovery of conflict and catharsis in the historical universe of twentieth-century India, she has refined her vision into a narrative of lyric prose and inexorable ballad-like rhythm.

At a Commonwealth Writers Conference in 1976, Markandaya discussed her sense of a writer's identity and feeling of isolation and exile. In her integrated and "ambivalent" (a term she uses) acceptance of both the sense of belonging (the universal) and the sense of alienation (the colonized separation), Markandaya feels no paralyzing loss of connection with society or expression of her communal roots. Her attitude, stated fourteen years ago, remains paramount in her writing today. These were her concluding remarks at the conference: "There is one belief to which I have remained fairly constant. It is tied in, paradoxically, with the shifting balance of power in the world. At one time there were the accepted metropolitan areas, in the West, and there were colonies and later the Commonwealth. On the whole the Commonwealth looked to the metropolis for its standards, and the metropolis, confident of its values, was content that it should. But now there are fewer certainties. A good deal of soul-searching is going on. The Commonwealth has its own theses to put forward, and the metropolis is willing to listen. In this climate I cannot share the gloomy views for Commonwealth literature expressed elsewhere'' ("One Pair of Eyes: Some Random Reflections," in *The Commonwealth Writer Overseas: Themes of Exile and Expatriatism*, p. 32).

Selected Titles: *Some Inner Fury* (1955); *A Silence of Desire* (1960); *Possessions* (1963); *A Handful of Rice* (1966); *The Nowhere Man* (1972); *Two Virgins: A Novel* (1974); *The Golden Honeycomb* (1977); *Pleasure City* (1982); *Shalimar* (1982).

Consult: K. R. Srinivasa Iyengar, *Indian Writing in English*, 2nd edition (1973); Alastair Niven, ed. *The Commonwealth Writer Overseas: Themes of Exile and Expatriatism* (Brussels, 1976).

MARKOV, Georgi I. Born 1920, Bulgaria; died summer 1978, London, England. Exile did not prove a haven for Markov. After his defection from Bulgaria in 1969, he worked for the British Broadcasting Company's World Service in England. While waiting for a bus on a London street in the summer of 1978, he was stabbed by a poisoned umbrella stick; he died four days later from the wound. The murderer was never apprehended; Markov's widow, and others, believe the assailant was a hired agent of the Todor I. Zhivkov regime in Bulgaria, whose repressive policies Markov had outspokenly described in a series of broadcasts over Radio Free Europe earlier in 1978. The texts of the broadcasts were published in the United States and Great Britain under the title, *The Truth That Killed* (1984, c. 1983).

In 1990 Markov's widow, the British writer Annabel Markov, petitioned the reorganized Communist Party government in Sofia to investigate the matter officially and to assess the culpability of the former Zhivkov government for the crime.

Selected Titles: *Dimcho Debelianov (lichnost; tvorchestvo)* (Sofia, 1974); *Studii za bwlgarskata kritika* (Sofia, 1983); *Tvorbi i kritika* (Sofia, 1987); *Bitka za literaturni printsipi* (Sofia, 1987).

MARON, Monika. Born June 3, 1941, in Berlin, Germany; she lives in Hamburg, West Germany. Maron made her first trip to West Germany in 1983. In 1988, accompanied by her husband and 21-year-old son, she left East Berlin with a three-year visa for residence in West Germany. Her two novels, *Die Überläuferin* (Frankfurt, 1986; *The Defector*, 1988) and *Flugasche* (Frankfurt, 1987), were banned in East Germany until the events of December 1989 toppled the Communist monopoly of power. *The Defector* delineates the life of a citizen whose personal freedom has been usurped by the state.

Maron, a descendant of a Polish-Jewish family, said in an interview in the *New York Times* (March 8, 1990), that she was not frightened that reunification of Germany might produce a new wave of anti-semitism. She was quoted as saying that although her grandfather was killed by the Nazis, her son "is German. But he didn't kill my grandfather. And I don't need to be afraid of him" (page A12). In Hamburg, Maron has been writing a series of features for West German newspapers and magazines discussing the phenomenon of German guilt.

MARTINEZ, Tomas Eloy. Born 1935 in Argentina; he has returned from exile to Argentina. A former magazine editor who spent time in exile, Eloy is wary of the invidious effects of tyranny in his country. Although he now resides in his native land, he claims that many writers and intellectuals, particularly those who remained behind in their land during the infamous military dictatorship of the 1970s and early 1980s, speak only in the voices of careful fear. Freedom of speech remains submerged in Argentina, he believes, though on the surface it appears vocally unorchestrated.

Consult: Mitchell Levitas, "Writers and Dictators," *The New York Times Book Review*, August 14, 1989.

MATSHIKIZA, Todd. Born 1921 in Queenstown, Cape Province, South Africa; died 1968 in Zambia. Matshikiza's father was a church organist and civil servant. Matshikiza was educated at the prestigious black private academy, St. Peter's in Rosettenville, and after graduation worked as a wine steward, a clerical assistant, a barbershop's sweeper, a music teacher, a razor blade salesman, and bookseller and journalist; he had a feature column in *Drum* magazine. In following years Matshikiza achieved renown both as writer and as composer. He wrote a choral work with orchestra for the Johannesburg Festival and the score for the musical *King Kong*, which ran in Johannesburg in 1959 before it went on to London, New York, and other world capitals. He also collaborated with Alan Paton on another musical, *Mkhumbhane*, in 1959. He left South Africa in 1960 and lived in England before moving to Zambia. He wrote one novel, *Chocolates for My Wife* (London, 1961, repr. 1982), in which he alluded to his reasons for his departure and his resultant ambivalence. Matshikiza's work was banned in South Africa during the 1960s under terms of the Suppression of Communism Act. Exile proved a trying experience for him, and in his last years he was unable to feel and/or to communicate the spark that had characterized his early work. He worked as a broadcaster in Zambia in his last years.

MATSUBARA, Hisako. Born Japan; she lives in Cologne, Germany. The daughter of a Shinto priest, Matsubara grew up in Kyoto and studied comparative religion and literature at International Christian University in Tokyo. She came to the United States for graduate work in theater arts and earned her doctoral degree in Germany in the history of thought. She moved to Germany when she married Friedemann Freund, a physicist. Within five years Matsubara taught herself to write so well in German that she became a weekly columnist for *Die Zeit*. She has written three novels and five nonfiction books, all in German. Among her titles are *Samurai* (1979), which has been translated into eight languages, and *Cranes at Dusk* (1985).

MAUGHAM, Robin (Robert Cecil Romer, Second Viscount of Hartfield). Born May 17, 1916, in London; died March 31, 1981, in Brighton, England. Son of a lord chancellor and nephew of Somerset Maugham, Robin Maugham received a traditional upper-class education at Eton and Trinity College, Cambridge, becoming a barrister at Lincoln's Inn, London. Wounded in North Africa in World War II, he began his literary career during a lengthy recuperation. For much of the remainder of his life, he lived in the Mediterranean, on Ibiza, part of the Balearic Islands. Social and sexual exile play a prominent role in his fiction, in which "abroad" suggests greater social, emotional, and sexual freedom as well as lowered class, gender, and age barriers. The exile theme is adumbrated in *Line on Ginger* (1949) by an anticipated escape from class-ridden England (the barrister protagonist hopes to settle somewhere abroad with a working-class war mate). Homosexual exile is explored more explicitly in *Behind the Mirror* (1955), where a Foreign Office official abandons career and friends to enjoy in Kenya a relationship with a young man that would have been socially unacceptable in London. Morocco provides settings for later novels exploring both homosexual (*The Wrong People*, 1971) and heterosexual (*The Dividing Line*, 1979) passions. An accomplished and varied treatment of exile can be found in a collection of four novellas, *Lovers in Exile* (1977), where Maugham tells the reader directly that his subject is people exiled from England for the sake of love: romantic love, obsessive love, procreative love, and godly love.

Although his autobiographical *Conversations with Willie* (1979) firmly establishes his homosexuality, his themes are not exclusively homosexual. In later works one sees increased diversity in types of passions and settings (Los Angeles, Italy, Sri Lanka, Australia, the Holy Land). Interestingly, while all Maugham's fiction encourages autobiographical speculation, Spain, his chosen place of exile, plays no role in his fictional world. Exile, however, pervades even those novels like *The Servant* (1948), *The Rough and the Smooth* (1951), and *The Corridor* (1980) where characters do not escape from conventional barriers as internal exile. Whether foreign or domestic, exile for Maugham's characters is libidinally therapeutic but rarely results in settled happiness.

BRUCE R. S. LITTE

MAUGHAM, W. [William] Somerset. Born January 25, 1874, in the British Embassy in Paris; died December 16, 1965, in Cap Ferrat, France. One of the most widely read English writers during his lifetime, and a prolific author of novels, short stories, plays, essays, and travel books, Maugham spent much of his life traveling over the world; although he always defined himself as an Englishman, he never settled permanently in England. His most lasting home, Villa Mauresque, where he spent his last years, was in France. Maugham's recent reputation has depended primarily on his fiction, much of which centers on characters who live in voluntary exile from their native countries. *The Moon and Sixpence* (1919) is characteristic of Maugham's fiction of exile. The hero, Charles Strickland, is closely modeled on the painter Paul Gauguin. Strickland, like Gauguin, abandons a conventional career in midlife to devote himself to art, and begins to lead a meaningful life only after he has left London for permanent exile on Tahiti. A similar breakthrough by means of voluntary exile occurs in *The Razor's Edge* (1944), in which the main character, an American named Larry Darell, travels to India to attain spiritual enlightenment. Although Larry returns home, his travels in India make up the most significant period of his life. Self-fulfillment of this kind is, however, rare in Maugham's work. For the most part his exiled characters are isolated in foreign cultures and are powerless either to control their circumstances or to understand the cultures in which they find themselves.

Many of Maugham's short stories turn on the inability of missionaries, colonial officers, and other displaced Europeans to adjust to the conditions of the Far East. His most subtle treatment of this kind of exile is in the figure of Willie Ashenden, the central character in a series of short stories published in book form as *Ashenden* (1928). As a British secret agent, Ashenden lives in voluntary exile as part of his job, but in spite of his competence as a spy, he rarely has much knowledge of events around him or control over them, and can only carry out his job more or less mechanically. Because he deals in deception and violence and is isolated from the normal moral standards of society, Ashenden is tainted by his profession and becomes a repellent person; however, his coldness and protective cynicism are not unique to this book but are characteristic of the emotional tone that pervades most of Maugham's fiction. The characters in his novels and stories are isolated from any lasting or secure human community; their success or failure as persons depends on their actions outside the societies into which they are born; thus exile for them is not only a matter of physical separation from their homelands, but a spiritual precondition of life. Maugham's frequent use of exotic settings for his fiction was, in part, indicative of his sense that everyone spends his life in exile and must work out his life in a world that is essentially alien. As Frederic Raphael wisely said in the *Times Literary Supplement* (March 31–April 6, 1989, p. 330), Maugham "was never entirely at home anywhere; his conformity was the measure of his alienation."

Consult: Robert Calder, *Willie: The Life of W. Somerset Maugham* (1990); Robin Maugham, *Somerset and All the Maughams* (1975, c. 1966); Ted Morgan, *Maugham: A Biography* (1980); M. K. Naik, *W. Somerset Maugham* (1966); Frederic Raphael, *Somerset Maugham and His World* (London, 1977, repr. London, 1990, as *Somerset Maugham*).

EDWARD LENSE

MAURINA, Zenta. Born October 15, 1897, in Lejasciems, Latvia, then part of Russia; she died April 25, 1978, in Basle, Switzerland. A doctor's daughter, Maurina was stricken with polio at the age of five and remained bound to a wheelchair throughout her life. In adolescence she experienced the German and Russian invasions that preceded the establishment of an independent Latvia after World War I. Despite her physical disability, Maurina completed a doctorate in philology at Riga University and embarked on a career as teacher, critic, and translator. Bilingual in Lett and German, she wrote in both languages. When Latvia was annexed by Soviet Russia in World War II, she went into permanent exile, spending her remaining years in Sweden (chiefly Uppsala) and later in Germany, though also lecturing widely in Europe.

Maurina's critical writings, which include studies of Dante and Fyodor Dostoyevsky, as well as Scandinavian and Latvian authors, reveal her exceptional acquaintance with European literature and philosophy. The three volumes of her autobiography, *Die weite Fahrt* (1951, The Long Journey), *Denn das Wagnis ist schön* (1953, Brave Venture), and *Die eisernen Riegel zerbrechen* (1957, The Iron Bars Are Shattered), constitute her most substantial and original achievement. The subtitle, *A Passion*, of the first volume, points to her unrelenting efforts to come to terms with her unusual fate; she shows herself to be a shrewd observer of external incident as well as of her own predicament. In addition to numerous translations from French, English (e.g., Thomas Hardy's *Tess of the D'Urbervilles*), Russian, and Norwegian into Lett, Maurina also translated into German a novel trilogy composed by her companion in exile, the Latvian writer Konstantin Raudive.

Maurina exorcized the demons of her peculiar solitude as a lame refugee by recourse to belief in the sovereignty of the Will; in this she was a disciple of Nietzsche. Her spirituality, at once refined and tough, was founded on a deep though undogmatic religious faith. It was a cruel irony that the debt she acknowledged to German culture proved an unpopular message in postwar Sweden. The vicissitudes of her Swedish sojourn are explored in the two volumes of her diaries, covering the period 1946–58. Ever eager to take the positive view, she sees the Swedes as the kinsmen of Linnaeus and Dag Hammarskjöld, just as in her eyes the Germans are above all the children of Goethe, Friedrich Hölderlin, and Beethoven.

Little of Maurina's work is available in English translation, apart from *A Prophet of the Soul: Fyodor Dostoievsky* (London, 1939).

Consult: *Buch der Freundschaft: Zenta Maurina zum 70 Geburtstag*, (Memmingen, 1967), festschrift.

CEDRIC HENTSCHEL

MAXIMOV, Vladimir. Born 1932, in the USSR; he lives in Paris, France. Maximov published *Sem dnei Tvoreniy* (*Seven Days of Creation*) in 1973 in the West. The work is an ironic treatment of what has been called by literary critics a Stalinist novel. It portrays an idealistic and committed young Soviet worker who becomes disillusioned with the Communist regime and its practices and stated goals. Instead of a journey to commitment, the hero works out his passage to disillusionment within the communist system. The subtitle of Maximov's work, ''A Journey to Find the Self,'' reflects the focus of his work. He left the USSR one year after publication of the book, on his own journey to discover a faith in which he could immerse himself. Maximov became editor of the exile journal *Kontinent* in Paris, and continued with his fiction writing. His second novel, *Quarantine* (published in 1973 in the West), exploits the Boccaccian premise of a group of people confined to quarters because of an epidemic; in Maximov's novel it is a cholera epidemic that forces passengers on a train to Moscow to live with each other for a protracted period of time and to interact through story-telling. In his third novel, *Farewell from Nowhere*, also published in 1973 in the West, Maximov returns to the theme of lost faith: the hero is in search of some kind or form of commitment, some substitute for God or an alternative faith now that his belief in socialism has waned.

Consult: Edward J. Brown, *Russian Literature since the Revolution* (1982).

MEDINA, Pablo. Born August 9, 1948, in Havana, Cuba; he currently teaches in Washington, D.C. Medina came with his parents to the United States in 1961, attended schools in the Bronx, New York, and took a bachelor's degree in Spanish (1970) and a master's degree in English from Georgetown University (1972). Twice married, he has a son, Pablo IV.

In 1975 Medina published the first collection of poems in English by a Cuban exile in the United States, *Pork Rind and Cuban Songs*. One critic called his ''a complex, exultant, melancholic, utterly challenging new poetic voice.'' The book explores the meaning of family and self, and includes a five-page narrative, ''Miguel Medina,'' in which 100 years of exilic history spanning Spain and the

Americas is presented. "The Taino Male's Elegy to Himself"—one of the most powerful dramatic monologues since Randall Jarrell's "The Woman at the Washington Zoo"—is a thinly veiled treatment of those who suffered regimentation, by staying on in Cuba, from Fidel Castro's regime. On the other hand, in "To the Cuban Exiles to Make Much of Time," Medina directly addresses those who fled their homeland to take with them their middle-class amenities to a place where "the weeding of cuticles [is] far more technically advanced." Medina waited fifteen years to publish a second book of poems, *Arching into the Afterlife* (1990). In it the Brooklyn Bridge itself is doing the arching—the book is a serious, surrealistic elegy to the failed hope of America where he finds "Freedom / more alive than you." Medina also has written fiction, including one of the few extant novels in English by a Cuban American, *The Marks of Birth*. Part of it was excerpted in the 1989 anthology *Cuban American Writers (Los Atrevidos)*, edited by Carolina Hospital, who said Medina's "talent and integrity as a writer have served as a strong role model." Medina has been an assistant professor of Spanish and English at Mercer County Community College, Trenton, New Jersey, since 1974. He was writer-in-residence at George Washington University in 1990–1991.

Selected Titles: "A Manifesto of the Post-Absurd," *Courier*, May 1971; "Arrival," *Confrontation*, nos. 27–28 (1984); "Grandfather Pablo," *Antioch Review*, Spring 1985; *Pork Rind and Cuban Songs* (1989); *Arching into the Afterlife* (1990); *Exiled Memories: A Cuban Childhood* (1990); *Everyone Will Have to Listen* (poems of Tania Diaz Castro), co-edited and translated with Carolina Hospital (1990).

Consult: Carolina Hospital, "Los Atrevidos," *Linden Lane Magazine*, October-December 1987; Gregory Orfalea, "Waiting Out the Faraway Sun: The Poetry of Pablo Medina," *Margins* 1/2/3 (1976).

                                                              GREGORY ORFALEA

MEHTA, Ved Parkash. Born 1934, India; he lives in the United States. Mehta went blind early in childhood. His father, determined to give his son opportunities equal to those enjoyed by people with normal vision, sent him to a school for the blind in Arkansas, where he benefitted from therapeutic treatment. Mehta later studied at British and American universities.

Mehta used the metaphor "continents of exile" as the subtitle of his recent autobiography, *The Stolen Light* (1989); he sees himself as a citizen of exile on several shores—as a blind man different from the normal visionary, as a writer separated from the herd of conventional animals and yet roped to that herd by a common thread of humanity, and as a gifted individual who missed the ordinary pleasures of growing up, even to the point of having to find his way blindly to sexual fulfillment. Mehta has spent his entire life trying to bridge the gulfs between these various worlds. He remains a compassionate seeker after unity, but history and autobiography keep him aware of the commanding presence of psychic exile in the universe both about and within him.

Selected Titles: *Face to Face* (1957); *Fly and the Fly-Bottle: Encounters with British*

Intellectuals (c. 1962, 1983); *The New Theologians* (1966); *Portrait of India* (1970); *John Is Easy to Please: Encounters with the Written and Spoken Word* (1971); *Daddji* (1972); *Mahatma Ghandi and His Apostles* (1977); *The New India* (1978); *Mamaji* (1979); *A Family Affair: India Under Three Prime Ministers* (1982); *Vedi* (1982); *The Ledge Between the Streams* (1984); *Sound-shadows of the New World* (1985).

LEE MHATRE

MEMMI, Albert. Born December 15, 1920, Tunis, Tunisia; he lives in Paris, France. Memmi writes in the preface to his *Portrait of a Jew* (1962) that his father was a harness maker and that the family lived in the large ghetto outside the city. As a youth, he engaged with the politics of Zionism and its promise of a Jewish homeland; at the same time he acknowledged the appeal of traditional apolitical and ghettoized Jewry. He was interned in a forced labor camp in Tunisia during World War II, but escaped and hid from the Germans. At the end of the war he studied at the University of Algiers and at the Sorbonne in Paris, where he received a degree in Philosophy. He has taught both in Paris and in Tunis. His first novel, *The Pillar of Salt*, appeared in translation in the United States in 1955; his second novel, *Strangers*, appeared in the United States in 1959. Memmi's fiction is oblique as well as direct in its intensity. In both *Strangers* and *The Pillar of Salt* the intensity of relationships is made the stronger by the ambivalence in them; in *Strangers* the portrait of a marriage achieves its clarity through descent into a maze of conflicting emotions.

Memmi has written that as a Zionist who believed in a Jewish homeland he felt obliged to support Tunisian independence from France. Yet, when the Moslem religion was proclaimed the official religion of the state, he felt a conflict of identity. In attempting to come to terms with his identity as a Jew, as a Tunisian, as a human being—who once had been a universalist and later admitted to nationalism—he wrote his famous self-scrutiny, *Portrait of a Jew*, his third published work. In his own words, Memmi wrote the book because "I wanted to understand who I am—as a Jew—and what the fact of being a Jew has meant in my life." Yet, characteristically, Memmi admits the book "caused me the greatest pain. I detest it."

Memmi's contrarieties of emotion have established him as a paragon of alienation and dislocation. A Tunisian novelist who writes in French; a Jew who lives in a psychic ghetto in a predominantly Christian society; a North African who feels alien in France because of his colonialist background, Memmi also feels that he is ostracized as a colonialist Frenchman in North Africa. Léopold Sédar Senghor* has hailed Memmi's work, *Portrait d'un colonisé précedé du Portrait d'un colonisateur* (1957, *The Colonizer and the Colonized*), as a necessary tool in the understanding of the psychic legacy of colonialism; Jean-Paul Sartre has also called for attention to Memmi's analysis of the North African complex of conflicting loyalties. Memmi's ideas often parallel those of Frantz Fanon in their rock bottom lines of cultural division caused by the advent of colonialism.

Selected Titles: *Portrait d'un Juif* (1962; Portrait of a Jew); *La Liberation du juif* (1966; The Liberation of the Jew); *La terre intérieure: Entretiens avec Victor Malka* (1976, The Inner Ground: Interviews with Victor Malka).

MENDES, Alfred H. Born November 18, 1897, in Trinidad; he lives in Barbados. Mendes's wealthy businessman father was of Portuguese heritage. He sent his son at eight years old to England for his education. During World War I, Mendes volunteered for action, but grew disillusioned with the militarism he felt was part of the capitalist system. He saw hope in the Russian Revolution of 1917 for a new kind of society.

Mendes wrote two novels and edited *Trinidad* and the *Beacon*, two journals he founded with C.L.R. James* in 1929 and 1930. He lived in the United States from 1932, where he worked for the Federal Writers Project, to 1940, when he returned to Trinidad. When Mendes retired from his position as general manager of the Ports Service Division in Trinidad, he moved to Mallorca with his wife, but they grew homesick for the West Indies and returned to Barbados to live.

Selected Titles: *Pitch Lake* (London, 1934); *Black Fauns* (London, 1935).

Consult: Kenneth Ramchand, *The West Indian Novel and Its Background* (1970).

MEREZHKOVSKY, Dmitry Sergeyevich. Born August 14, 1865, in St. Petersburg, Russia; died December 7, 1941, in Paris, France. One of the founders of Russian symbolism, Merezhkovsky was poet, novelist, philosopher, literary critic, and public figure. His father was an important court official. His first poems appeared in 1881. In his first collection, *Poems* (1888), and in his second book, *Symbols* (1892), he evidenced the influence of such decadent modes as ennui, discord, satiation, and ironic wit. In 1892 he published his article "On the Causes of Decline and the New Currents in Contemporary Russian Literature," in which he discussed the primary elements of the new art of symbolism. In 1900 Merezhkovsky married Zinaida Gippius (*see* Hippius, Zinaida), a distinguished poet who became his collaborator until his death. From his travels to Athens and Constantinople he gained a sense of the clash between the two "most contrary ideas, Man-god and God-man, Apollo and Christ." He traced the struggle of Christ and Antichrist in his trilogy *Christ and Antichrist*.

Merezhkovsky employed his new critical method of antithesis in his collection of essays *The Eternal Companion* (1897), in which he presented portraits of his "eternal contemporaries," Marcus Aurelius, Montaigne, Gustave Flaubert, Henrik Ibsen, and Alexandr Pushkin. In his critical work *Lev Tolstoy and Dostoyevsky* (2 vols., 1901–2), Merezhkovsky brought to a direct confrontation "the religious consciousness of flesh" of Tolstoy and "the religious contemplation of spirit" of Dostoyevsky, and declared a necessity for a "religious synthesis." Renouncing "historical Christianity," he proclaimed the apocalyptic Christianity of the Third Testament, in which a new synthesis will be achieved when rational history has come to an end. Merezhkovsky took part in 1903–4 in the founding of the Religious-Philosophical Meetings society aimed at bringing together Orthodox clergy and atheistic intelligentsia. At the same time he, together with Dmitry Filosofov, published the monthly magazine the *New Way*, a tribune for the ideas of Russian symbolism.

After the Revolution of 1905 Merezhkovsky and Zinaida Gippius were exiled from Russia; they settled in Paris. At that time they believed a social revolution would lead to a religious social order and to the Kingdom of God on earth. Among Merezhkovsky's essays of this period are "La tsar et la revolution" (1907) and *The Coming Ham* (1906), the work in which he predicted an approaching era of mediocrity.

Merezhkovsky and Zinaida returned to Russia before World War I; he published his historical novels, *Alexander I* (1913) and *December the Fourteenth* (1918) there. His *Diaries* (1910–14) were published in 1915 and (1914–16) in 1917. In 1919 he and Zinaida left the Soviet Union and returned to Paris, the place of their first exile. Together with Zinaida and with D. Filosofov and N. Zlolin, Merezhkovsky published a study of the Russian Revolution entitled *The Kingdom of Antichrist* (1921). In Paris Merezhkovsky completed his cycle of historical novels, *Tutankhamen in Crete* (Prague, 1925; *The Birth of Gods*, 1926), in which he proclaimed the reconciliation of opposites and the synthesis of "the religious consciousness of flesh" along with "the religious contemplation of spirit"; and *Messiah* (Paris, 1927; *Akhnaton, King of Egypt*, 1927; and several historical dramas. In his works *The Mystery of the Three: Egypt and Babylon* (1925), *The Secret of the West: Atlantis-Europe* (1930, trans. 1933), *Jesus the Unknown* (2 vols., 1931; 1934), and *Jesus Manifested* (1935; 1936), Merezhkovsky worked out and developed his main prophetic themes of the Third Testament and of the imminence of the new Revelation. He also wrote, in the 1920s and 1930s, a series of biographies, primarily those of Christian saints, religious thinkers, poets, prophets and heroes: *Napoleon* (1929), *Paul, Augustine* (1936), *Francis of Assisi* (1938), *Jeanne d'Arc* (1938), *Dante* (1939), *Luther* (1940). His famous "Green Lamp Meetings" in Paris attracted writers, artists, and public figures, among them Georgy Adamovich,* Boris Poplavsky,* Juri Felzen, Ivan Bunin,* and Vasily Yanovsky.* Merezhkovsky, who called himself "an early prophet of a slow spring," was a second candidate (after Ivan Bunin) for the Nobel Prize for Literature. His work published in Russia before the Revolution has never been reprinted in the Soviet Union; books of his Paris period are forbidden and unknown in his homeland.

Selected Titles: Merezhkovsky's two trilogies are (1) *Christ and Antichrist*, Parts 1–3, 1896–1905, consisting of *Smert Bogov: Yulian Atstupnik* (1896; *The Death of Gods: Julian the Apostate*, London, 1901); *Voskrsshie Bogi* (1902; *The Romance of Leonardo da Vinci: The Forerunner*, London, 1902); and *Antkrist: Piotr i Alexey* (1905; *Peter and Alexis*, London, 1905); and (2) *Pavel I* (1908); *Alexander I* (1913); and *Chetyrnadtsatoye decabrya* (1918; *December the Fourteenth*, London, 1923, repr. 1929).

Translations: *Tolstoi, as Man and Artist*, with an essay on Dostoyevsky (Westminster,

England, 1902); *The Life of Henrik Ibsen* (London, 1915); *Joseph Pilsudsky* (London, 1921); *The Life of Napoleon* (1929); *The Secret of the West* (1931).

Consult: C. H. Bedford, *The Seeker: Dmitry Sergeevich Merezhkovsky* (1975); B. G. Rosenthal, *Merezhkovsky and the Silver Age* (1975).

ARKADY ROVNER

MIHAJLOV, Mihajlo. Born September 26, 1934, in Pancevo, near Belgrade, Yugoslavia; he lives in Washington, D.C. A literary scholar and dissident writer, Mihajlov became a refugee in the United States after thirteen years of government harassment and detention on charges of incitement by ideas through the publication of his writings. He was born of Russian parents, each of whom had emigrated to Yugoslavia from the Soviet Union during the years of famine that occurred immediately after the Russian Revolution. His father fought as a partisan in World War II and was a director of the Yugoslav Scientific Institute after the war; his mother was a schoolteacher. Mihajlov studied at Zagreb University, served in the Yugoslav army, worked as a translator, and taught Russian literature at Zagreb University while his dissertation was in progress. He developed a reputation as one of the important specialists on Fyodor Dostoyevsky and in post-Stalin literature.

Mihajlov's troubles with the government began with the publication of his essay "Moscow Summer 1964" in the Belgrade literary journal *Delo*. Mihajlov had toured Moscow and Leningrad for five weeks in a cultural exchange program between Yugoslavia and the Soviet Union. In his recounting of his talks with post-Stalin Soviet writers, Mihajlov referred to Soviet concentration camp literature and suggested that the Soviets ran extermination camps before the Nazis instituted their annihilation programs; he also posited that Stalin practiced genocide against minority tribes in the southeastern areas of the Soviet Union. Unfortunately for Mihajlov, a rapprochement between the Soviet Union and Yugoslavia was in the making, and the Yugoslav government acceded to pressure by the Soviet Union to ban the magazine and to bring charges against Mihajlov. At his trial for "damaging the reputation of a foreign state" and, further, for sending a copy of his banned work abroad for publication (Mihajlov's essay was published in Italy and the United States), Mihajlov argued that he was guilty of no lies, and that all evils, whether fascist or communist, were states of evil to be exposed. Mihajlov's conviction and sentence of nine months in jail were later reversed by the Yugoslav Supreme Court.

Mihajlov's troubles, however, were far from ended. He was fired from his teaching job and shunned by the country's literary establishment. Mihajlov's work sent abroad, however, received wide intellectual attention in the United States through publication in *The New Leader* and other journals, and through its appearance in book form. Mihajlov argued for a restoration of the awareness of the Christian rock of values on which socialism stood. He also declared that while Yugoslavia was closer to political democracy than any other Eastern bloc country, it was controlled by a one-party government and therefore subject to dangers of totalitarianism on the Left.

Mihajlov was rearrested in 1965 after proposing the establishment of a magazine that would print ideas in opposition to prevailing communist doctrines. He argued that such an exposure would improve the country's political and philosophic health. Although his proposed journal was not named in the indictment against him—only his foreign publication of the banned essay "Moscow Summer" was listed in the formal charge—many observers feel Mihajlov's proposal of free exchange of ideas terrified Yugoslavian bureaucrats and sent them into a paranoid rampage against the provocateur they saw in Mihajlov.

Mihajlov was sentenced to one year in prison at his first trial on the newly brought charges in 1966. In 1967 he was tried on new charges of spreading false propaganda in foreign countries and sentenced to four and a half years in prison, with a subsequent four-year ban on his work and public appearance. His sentence was reduced on appeal—he was given leniency because his actions were judged those of a "psychopathic" personality. He was again sentenced to prison in 1975—this time for seven years at hard labor—but freed in a public amnesty of political prisoners in 1977.

Mihajlov secured a visa for the United States in 1978 by a direct appeal to Marshall Josef Tito, president of Yugoslavia. While he was abroad, a warrant for his arrest was issued. Fearing further imprisonment, he has remained in the United States, where he has taught at several universities (Yale, Virginia, and Ohio State among others). His mother and sister emigrated to the United States years before his difficulties with the Yugoslav government began.

Mihajlov is committed to a recognition of spiritual values as the base of communal values. In the preface to his collection of essays *Underground Notes* (1976), he writes that the essence of his lifelong studies lies in "the theme of religious renaissance, the first rays of which one can presently observe in Russia and Eastern Europe."

Some critics have found in Mihajlov's work an erratic quality, not unlike the nervous dynamism of his idol Dostoyevsky, which can jar an otherwise potent argument of reason. Most critics see in Mihajlov a literary critic-philosopher who exemplifies his tenets of courage in the face of ideological opposition and a willingness to allow for diversity of view in order to continue the exploration into multiple human values. Mihajlov is more of an impressionistic thinker than a logical theoretician, but he has earned the right to be a historian of all he has witnessed.

Mihajlov writes in his native Croatian; all his work is published in translation. His productivity in recent years has been slight, and it may be possible that exile from the intellectual ferment of his native land has achieved what intolerable prison conditions and official bureaucratic displeasure could not: the wearing down of a passionate seeker of morality through literature and religion into the sporadic silence of weariness.

Translations: *Moscow Summer* (1965); *Russian Themes* (1968); *Underground Notes* (1976); *Tyranny and Freedom* (1979).

MIKES, György (George). Born February 15, 1912, in Siklós, Hungary; died 1987 in London, England. Mikes was that rare phenomenon, a happy exile, whose popularity as a writer was based on his ability to poke fun at foreigners and alien environments. He began his career as a reporter in Budapest and became a well-known and highly respected journalist. A Jew, in 1938 he found it opportune to emigrate to London to report on the rape of Prague (Czechoslovakia) from a new vantage point. He stayed in England, together with another refugee, his schoolfriend Andre Deutsch, who started his own publishing house in England. Their first joint venture was Mikes's *How to Be an Alien* (1946), a benevolent satire of Mikes's new compatriots whom he had observed while working in England for the Hungarian section of the British Broadcasting Company. The slim volume became an instant success. He next wrote *How to Scrape Skies*, in which he subjected the United States to an equally witty analysis; both books elicited a congratulatory letter from Albert Einstein. In all, he repeated his entertaining formula thirty-three times, selecting among other targets Germany (*Über Alles* [1953]), France (*Little Cabbages* [1955]), Japan (*The Land of the Rising Yen* [1969]), and Israel (*The Prophet Motive* (1969).

For the Hungarians Mikes became an Anglicized emigrant, while for the English he came to represent the arch-Hungarian, the ur-Central European. In his last book, *How to Be Seventy* (1982), Mikes summed up his recipe for a successful life: "Don't take it seriously."

ÉVA BOLGÁR

MILLER, Henry. Born December 26, 1891, in New York City, of German ancestry; died June 7, 1980, in Pacific Palisades, California. Miller lived in France from 1930 to 1939, returning home before the start of World War II. Earlier, he had worked in the business world (Western Union) and detested it; he tried in 1924 to become a full-time writer, but was unable to earn a living. His first trip to Europe was made with his second wife, June Smith Miller, the money for which came from one of her "benefactors." He and June returned to the United States several months later; in the depths of the depression, nearly broke, they lived in a dark basement flat in Brooklyn Heights, New York City. Miller scraped up enough money to return to Europe a second time in 1932. It was during this nine-month period that he wrote *Tropic of Cancer* (1934) and *Tropic of Capricorn* (1939) and met Anaïs Nin,* who helped pay for the cost of publication of his books. Miller's financial state was dire in the summer of 1930 when he arrived in Paris, and Nin helped him find a job through her husband's influence.

Miller had at first resisted a European sojourn, considering it "dilettantish," but it was his expatriate spell that freed his creative energies. While he went on to write many novels and travel books and essay collections after his return to the United States, his major work remains the two Tropics, which have weathered the reign of censorship imposed on them, and *Quiet Days in Clichy* (1956), a fictionalized autobiography with emphasis on his expatriate days told in a characteristically Millerian style of rambling narrative, explicit detail, and essayistic discursiveness. Both Tropics are autobiographical without much attempt at disguise, as is all of Miller's work, and immensely barbaric in their yawping demands for freedom from the ropes of sexual restraint and for a sense of picaresque adventure along the urban roads of experience. Miller represents that aspect of the Lost Generation that saw in experience a constant movement to growth without the necessity of ordering it into disciplines of response. From his example, his disciples grew, and some of them became influential in the later Beat movement in the United States and in its expatriate counterparts in the 1950s, among such American writers as Robert Creeley and Paul Blackburn.

Selected Titles: *Aller Retour New York* (1938); *The Cosmological Eye* (1939); *My Life and Times* (1971).

Consult: A. K. Baxter, *Henry Miller, Expatriate* (1961); Lawrence Durrell and Alfred Perlès, *Art and Outrage: A Correspondence about Henry Miller* (1959); Ihab Hassan, *The Literature of Silence: Henry Miller and Samuel Beckett* (1968); E. B. Mitchell, ed., *Henry Miller: Three Decades of Criticism* (1971); Gunther Stuhlmann, *A Literate Passion: Letters of Anaïs Nin and Henry Miller, 1932–1953* (1987).

MIŁOSZ, Czeslaw. Born June 30, 1911, in Seteiniai, Lithuania, then part of the Russian Empire (until the end of the eighteenth century the Grand Duchy of Lithuania and the Polish Kingdom constituted one commonwealth). He is professor emeritus at the University of California at Berkeley, where he lives. Polish poet, essayist, novelist, literary critic, and translator, Miłosz grew up in Wilno (Vilnius), which belonged to the restored Polish state during the period between World War I and World War II. He studied law at the King Stefan Batory University in Wilno. He made his publishing debut in 1930 in the journal *Alma Mater Vilnensis*; in 1931 he became a cofounder of the avant-garde literary group Żagary. That year he also traveled for the first time to Paris, where he met his relative, the French metaphysical poet Oscar V. de L. Milosz, whose influence on Milosz has proved long-lasting. Miłosz's first volume of poems, *Poemat o czasie zastygłym* (1933, A Poem on Time Frozen), received an award from the Polish Writers Union. In 1934 he went to Paris on a fellowship. In 1936 he was employed at Polish Radio in Wilno. His second volume of poems, *Trzy zimy* (1936, Three Winters), is considered one of the most representative works of "catastrophism" in Polish literature; it is saturated with symbolic visions of calamities eschatological in nature. *Trzy zimy* marked a shift from Miłosz's early avant-garde inclinations toward classical clarity and conciseness; it contains features of his later lyrics, "a preference for dialogue or at least for polyphonic utterance . . . a pressing search for an ever-retreating truth" (in the words of one of his critics, Jan Błoński). In 1937, after visiting Italy, Miłosz worked with Polish Radio in Warsaw. In 1940 he returned to Wilno and in the same year, when Lithuania was incorporated into the USSR, Miłosz left his native land, the landscape of which, in his own words "has always been the core of his imagination," as it was for his predecessor, the great Polish Romantic poet

Adam Mickiewicz, to whom, as Miłosz admitted, "every line of his verse was indebted." During World War II, Miłosz lived in occupied Warsaw and clandestinely published a volume of poems (1940); edited an anthology of anti-Nazi poetry *Pieśń niepodległa* (Invincible Song); translated Jacques Maritain's anti-collaboration essay *À travers le désastre*; and translated T. S. Eliot's *The Waste Land*. He wrote in 1943 a cycle of "naive poems," *Świat* (The World), which he described, as an "effort to resist the temptation of utter despair" and an attempt to oppose the forces of destruction and terror by recourse to the harmony of the happy world of childhood. One of the first volumes of poetry published in postwar Poland was Miłosz's collected poems, meaningfully entitled *Ocalenie* (1945, Rescue). This volume contained the cycle "Głosy biednych ludzi" (Voices of Poor People), "dedicated to the victims of oppression," and included poems on the destruction of Warsaw and the Warsaw ghetto.

Because of the recognition that Miłosz gained as a poet and the tendency in his early work to social criticism, he was offered in 1945 a diplomatic position in the Polish consulate in New York; in 1947 he served as cultural attaché in Washington, and in 1950 as secretary in Paris. Foremost in Miłosz's poems written during these years is a new tone of biting irony and moral indignation against the postwar intellectual and political situation in Poland and in the world. "Dziecię Europy" (The Child of Europe), written "in fury and anger"; "Traktat moralny" (Treatise on Morals), "deriding the rule by terror"; the short poem "Który skrzywdziłeś człowieka prostego" (You Who Have Wronged a Simple Man), chosen to serve as an inscription on the monument erected in Gdańsk during the days of Solidarity's great strength and promise; and others were collected in 1953 in the volume *Światło dzienne* (Daylight); this was the first volume of Miłosz's poems published in exile.

In 1951 when the dogmatism of socialist realism was imposed on Poland, Miłosz asked for political asylum in France; he remained there until 1960 as a free-lance writer and contributor to the émigré monthly *Kultura*. In 1953 Miłosz published the book that brought him international fame, *Zniewolony umysł* (1953; *The Captive Mind*, 1953), which he described as "an analysis of the mental acrobatics Eastern European intellectuals had to perform in order to give assent to Stalinist dogmas." In the same year his political novel *La prise du pouvoir*, a treatment of the communist seizure of Poland, won the Prix Littéraire Européen. In 1955 this novel was published in Polish as *Zdobycie władzy*, and in English as *The Seizure of Power*.

Miłosz's great achievement as a novelist is *Dolina Issy* (1955; *The Issa Valley*, 1981), which in his own evaluation is "a novel close to the very core of his poetry. It has been called 'pagan' because of its childish amazement with the world; but this story of childhood in Lithuania with its simple images of nature is somewhat deceptive, as underneath lurks a Manichean vision." In 1958 Miłosz published his intellectual autobiography *Rodzinna Europa (Native Realm: A Search for Self-Definition*, 1968) as an attempt to explain to the Western European world "the corner of Europe from which he came." *Traktat poetycki* (1957,

Treatise on Poetry) is Miłosz's penetrating overview in verse form of the development of Polish literature and history since the end of the nineteenth century from the vantage point of contemporary time.

Miłosz moved to Berkeley in 1960, where he became professor of Slavic literatures. Before his move, he published a volume of essays and translations of poetry, *Kontynenty* (1958, Continents), and a translation of selected writings of Simone Weil,* to whose works, he admits, he is "profoundly indebted." Miłosz's years in California have proved fruitful and productive: a succession of his poems appeared first in journals, later to be gathered into volumes such as *Król Popiel i inne wiersze* (1962, King Popiel and Other Poems), *Gucio zaczarowany* (1965, Bobo's Metamorphosis), *Miasto bez imienia* (1969, City Without a Name), *Gdzie wschodzi słońce i kędy zapada* (1974, From the Rising of the Sun Unto the Going Down of the Same), *Hymn o perle* (1983, The Hymn on the Pearl), *The Separate Notebook. Osobny zeszyt* (1984), *Nieobjęta ziemia* (1984; *Unattainable Earth*, 1986), *Kroniki* (1987, The Chronicles). The works present a variety of forms and are in accordance with Miłosz's declaration: "I do not want new poetry but new diction." In these later volumes formal poetics are minimized and accepted divisions between the genres of poetry and prose abandoned. Miłosz's themes in these works embrace the mystery of the world, eternity and transience, the succession of historical epochs, and the future of mankind. He explores man, his destiny, his faults and suffering; expresses compassion for the fragility of everything human; and deals with the frightening forces of evil and tyranny, with the fascination with the beauty of the world, and with human greatness and goodness. Miłosz scrutinizes poetry, its inability in naming the world, in describing the uniqueness of being, and its integrity, its craft, its power in the service of virtue. He has described "the sources of his poetry as his childhood memories, Christmas carols, the liturgy of the Month of Mary devotion and of Vespers, and the Bible." Clearly apparent in his later poems is a growing return to these early and lasting sources of influence, the result of which may be seen in his rendering into Polish of the Gospel According to St. Mark, the Psalms, the Book of Job, Song of Songs, Ruth, Lamentations, Ecclesiastes, and Esther from the original Greek and Hebrew.

One recurrent theme in Miłosz's poetry is exile, exile in general, and exile from his native Lithuania and his native city of Wilno. Many allusions, lines, entire poems, and two cycles entitled "City Without a Name" and "From the Rising of the Sun" show his unextinguished memory of that city "defenseless and poor," which "kept offering itself" to him, which became to him a myth, and a memory to which he must bear witness and defend from loss. Miłosz's memory thus becomes a point of view, a location from which, independently of where he physically stands, his world and his destiny are to be viewed. Drawing from the tradition of antiquity, from the Bible, from Polish romantic poetry, and above all from his own and his generation's afflictions, Miłosz looks at exile in universal terms as a predicament of modern man.

Miłosz's view of exile is also present in his many collections of essays, all of which contain autobiographical molding. *Człowiek wśród skorpionów: studium o Stanisławie Brzozowskim* (1962, A Man among Scorpions: A Study of Stanisław Brzozowski) is a book about a philosopher whose influence Miłosz acknowledged. *Widzenia nad Zatoka San Francisco* (1969; *Visions from San Francisco Bay*, 1982) presents Miłosz's impressions of a wide range of American contemporary life and culture and its significance for the future of civilization; he also speaks here of his experience as an émigré in the United States. In *Prywatne obowiązki* (1972, Private Obligations) Miłosz comments on Polish literature, Jean-Paul Sartre, T. S. Eliot,* O. V. Milosz, and includes translations of poems by W. B. Yeats and C. Cavafy.* In *Ziemia Ulro* (1977; *The Land of Ulro*, 1984) Miłosz reflects in restrospect on his life and his epoch. In this philosophical meditation on the roots of the crisis in contemporary civilization, on the disinherited mind of the man of our age, he invokes William Blake's symbolic land of disinherited spirits, of "crippled man" whose thinking was shaped in the Age of Reason, when a world of religious disinheritance, of materialistic culture, and of a permissive society was created, reaching catastrophic proportions in the twentieth century and leading to a progression of nothingness, to Samuel Beckett's *Endgame*. Most of the pages of *The Land of Ulro*, which contains also Miłosz's thoughts on Fyodor Dostoyevsky, Simone Weil, and others, as rebels against the laws of Ulro, are devoted, according to Miłosz, "to those who at the cost of madness have sought exit from it to Swedenborg, Blake, Mickiewicz and O. V. Milosz," in order to restore the sacred correspondence between God and the human spirit, to create "a civilization in which man will be freed from the servitude of Ulro."

Miłosz published *The Emperor of the Earth: Modes of Eccentric Vision* also in 1977, a collection of essays mostly concerning Polish and Russian writers and philosophers and a continuation of the themes found in *The Land of Ulro*. Different in character is his next volume of essays, *Ogród nauk* (1979, The Garden of Knowledge), in which along with meditations on devotion, transience, the Seven Deadly Sins, and Hell, along with essays on Polish language and literature, he presents examples of his craft as a translator through the works of Charles Baudelaire, O. V. Milosz, Yeats, Walt Whitman, Robinson Jeffers, Nuchim Bomse, and Tomas Venclova. *Zaczynając od moich ulic* (1985, Starting from My Streets), a collection of essays, memoirs, obituary tributes, and speeches written during the past forty years, included also his recurring thoughts on exile in the essays "The Dictionary of Wilno Streets," "To Tomas Venclova," and "Notes on Exile."

As a consequence of Miłosz's belief that good translations are equal and sometimes more important than original works, he has been active in translating his own poems as well as those of his Polish contemporaries into English, and American and other-language poets, and several books from the Bible, into Polish. He is also the author of the comprehensive *History of Polish Literature* (1969) and editor of an anthology, *Postwar Polish Poetry* (1965). He has been awarded many honors in Poland, France, and the United States, among them the Neustadt International Prize for Literature in 1987. In 1980 he received the Nobel Prize for Literature.

Selected Titles: Miłosz's collected work, *Utwory poetyckie*, was published in 1976 in Polish in Ann Arbor, Michigan; *Dzieła zbiorowe*, vols. 1–12, appeared in Paris in 1980–85.

Translations: *Selected Poems* (1973); *Bells in Winter* (1978); *Nobel Lecture* (1980); *The Witness of Poetry* (1983); *Collected Poems, 1931–1987* (1988); *Unattainable Earth* (1986).

Consult: Special Miłosz issues; *World Literature Today* 3 (1978); *Ironwood* 2 (1981); *Teksty* 3–4 (1981). R. Volynska and W. Zalewski, eds., *Czesław Miłosz: An International Bibliography 1930–1980* (1983); *Poznawanie Miłosza* (Cracow, 1985, Studying Miłosz); Donald Davie, *Czesław Miłosz and the Insufficiency of Lyric* (1986); E. Czarnecka and A. Fiut *Conversations with Czesław Miłosz* (1987); A. Fiut, *Moment wieczny: Poezja Czesława Miłosza* (Paris, 1987; *An Eternal Moment: The Poetry of Czesław Miłosz*, Berkeley, 1989); E. Możejko, ed., *Between Anxiety and Hope: The Poetry and Writing of Czesław Miłosz* (1988).

SAMUEL FISZMAN

MISTRY, Rohinton. Born 1952, Bombay, India; he lives in Toronto, Canada. Mistry emigrated to Canada in 1975. He worked for ten years in a bank while studying English literature and philosophy at the University of Toronto. His first volume of fiction, a novelistic collection, *Swimming Lessons and Other Stories from Firozsha Baag*, appeared in 1989. The stories radiate from a sustaining site of an apartment complex and reflect the different lives within the building over a period of ten years; in effect, Firozsha Baag becomes a microcenter of Bombay and city life in western India. The hero—a cricket player who appears in several of the stories—has left India for Toronto in an attempt to escape poverty and provincialism. In Canada he writes nostalgically of his childhood and sends his stories home to his parents to read. His mother thinks her son must be unhappy because all he writes about is Bombay and his childhood; his father comments that out of such material comes a writer's truth. They await the visit of their son, but his ambivlance resists the opportunities of his journey home to primal memories, and he goes back to Canada as confused as when he left it. Mistry's admitted autobiographical tale of growing up and facing the forms of exile that constitute separation from family as well as exile from geographical territory gains in relevance by its puissant comic tone.

MITTELHOLZER, Edgar. Born December 16, 1909, in New Amsterdam, British Guiana; died by suicide in 1965 in Farnham, Surrey, England. Mittelholzer spent most of his life in Guiana. He indicates in his autobiography, *A Swarthy Boy* (1963), that his parents felt ashamed of his dark coloring, since it suggested Negro blood somewhere in the family's ancestry. Whatever the truth, Mittelholzer apparently felt great conflict about his identity and a corresponding need to prove himself. He moved to England in 1947 and lived there until 1952. He spent the following year in Montreal, Canada, and returned to Barbados in

1953. He returned to England in 1956, where he lived until he poured kerosene over his body and set himself aflame.

Mittelholzer's work, and his place in West Indian literature, is controversial. Some critics see him as a sensationalist, a provocateur exploiting sexual stereotypes, and an opportunist. Others see in his troubled characters and violent melodrama a reflection of his own sense of loss and his angry reaction to his deprivations of psychic comfort. Most critics are willing to concede his enormous narrative sweep and sense of characterization. Some see in his work the clash of desire for order—instilled in him as a Germanic virtue by his Swiss-German parentage and upbringing—and a need for expression of self, a need that Mittelholzer repressed until it burst forth into rage.

Selected Titles: *Corentyne Thunder* (London, 1941, repr. 1970); *A Morning at the Office* (London, 1950; *A Morning in Trinidad*, 1950); *Shadows Move among Them* (London, 1951); *Kaywana Blood* (London, 1958; *The Old Blood*, 1958); *The Wounded and the Worried* (1962); *The Aloneness of Mrs. Chatham* (London, 1965).

Consult: "An Artist in Exile—From the West Indies," *New World Forum* 1 (November 12, 1965); Michael Gilkes, *The West Indian Novel* (1981); Colin Ricards, "A Tribute to Edgar Mittelholzer," *Bim* 11 (January—June 1966); Arthur J. Seymour, "An Introduction to the Novels of Edgar Mittelholzer," *Kyk-over-al* 8 (December 1958).

MODISANE, Bloke (William Modisane). Born in 1923 in Johannesburg, South Africa; he grew up in the slums of Sophiatown. He died in 1986 in London, England. Modisane worked in bookstores in Johannesburg after publishing his first short story, "The Dignity of Begging," in 1951. He changed his pen name to Bloke Modisane when he left South Africa in the early 1960s. He worked in London as an actor and broadcaster as well as wrote stories and articles for many English periodicals; he was in the London production of Jean Genet's *The Blacks*. He was at work on a study of the Maji Maji Rebellion in German-colonized Africa when he died.

Modisane defended his decision to leave South Africa by his statement that "because I love humanity more than I hate oppression, I could not stay to face the possibility of slitting throats." Modisane's work was banned in South Africa during the 1960s under terms of the Suppression of Communism Act. His decision to leave his country, which was still then part of the British Commonwealth, and live in England, produced in him a terrible conflict that he was never able to resolve and that drained him of emotional and creative energies, leading to an early death. In his only completed book, *Blame Me on History* (London, 1963, repr. 1990), he described the conflict between self-interest, self-awareness, and fear of violence whatever the cause, on one hand, and his identification with his people's struggles for their rights, either through clandestine means or as a participant in their suffering. He expressed his guilt in a severe sentence on himself: "I hate all violence, mental and physical, and no rationalization can cease its stark horror; I am a moral coward who cannot take a gun and go to war." Like Arthur Nortje,* another South African exile (who committed suicide in exile at a young age), Modisane died, if not of a broken heart, then at the least of a depleted one.

Consult: Es'kia Mphahlele, "Bloke William Modisane—A Tribute to a Great Artist," *Staffrider* 6, no. 4 (1987).

MOLNÁR, Ferenc. Born January 12, 1878, in Budapest, Hungary; died April 1, 1952, in New York City, of cancer. The celebrated Hungarian playwright was also a distinguished journalist and prolific prose writer. As a newspaperman he valued keen observation, precise description, and wit. His vibrant urban stories, mainly about the battle of the sexes, reveal an astute narrative talent and a rare skill with dialogue. From among his twelve novels, widely popular when first published, only one, *A Pál-utcai fiúk* (1907; *The Paul Street Boys*, 1927), a moving juvenile tale about gangfights in Budapest, is likely to last as literature of distinction. Molnár's most significant contribution to world literature is in the field of drama. Called "The Prince of the Theater" at home and abroad, Molnár was the first Hungarian dramatist to become internationally famous. Most of his forty-two plays have been performed around the world; twenty-six motion pictures and five musical comedies have been based on his works. By fusing Hungarian stage tradition and Western influences into a cosmopolitan amalgam, Molnár emerged as a playwright whose *Zeitgeist*, unerring dramatic instinct, and style proved uniquely his own.

The first play to bring him world fame was *Az ördög* (1907; *The Devil*, 1908), which was translated into all major languages. In this comedy Molnár launched his theories about women, marriages, and jealousy, topics he would expand in endless variations in later plays. From powdered dandies and scheming ladies, Molnár turned to thugs and servants for his next and best-known play, *Liliom* (1910; English, 1921). *Liliom*, a symbolical drama, examines the question of redemption while portraying human suffering and sacrifice in Budapest's contemporary underworld. This allegory has been staged and filmed several times throughout the Western world; both the play and its musical version, *Carousel* (1946), with music by Richard Rodgers and lyrics by Oscar Hammerstein II, have become classics. Molnár's ability to contrast relative and absolute truth, and his skill in creating a theater-within-a-theater situation, abound in his comedy *A testőr* (1910; *The Guardsman*, 1924), written for and about his actress-lover. An apotheosis of jealousy, it presents the predicaments of a famous actor who feels he is not loved for what he is and needs to masquerade as what he believes his wife covets. *Játék a kastélyban* (1926; *The Play's the Thing*, 1927) shows further evidence that in Molnár's consciousness the line between theater and life was beginning to disappear: truth is only an illusion, illusion may prove a truth. Molnár's cynical farce marked the zenith of his career; he was besieged by admirers and contracts from around the world. Similarly dazzling were his facile farces presenting romance among the aristocracy: *A hattyú* (1921; *The Swan*, 1929), a beguiling satire of a princess compelled to forsake a genuine love for family interests, and *Olympia* (1928, English, 1928), which elaborated a similar theme.

As a celebrity Molnár traveled extensively, surrounded by the trappings of fame and success almost all his life. Living away from home was part of his lifestyle, yet during these periods of separation from his homeland he was perpetually depressed. In the 1930s, fearing the approaching debacle of the West against fascism and communism, Molnár made his absences from his beloved Budapest longer; he moved from country to country with his companion, Mrs. Wanda Bartha. As a Jew he sought refuge, finally, in the United States. He arrived in New York in January 1940 and moved into the Plaza Hotel, where he stayed till his death. In his new home Molnár wrote constantly—though a heart attack in 1943 slowed him down momentarily. When he learned of the tragic fate of his Jewish friends and of his country, he became misanthropic, and the suicide of Mrs. Bartha further depressed his mental condition. The sophisticated raconteur felt rootless, finding solace only in hard work. He wrote assiduously until his final collapse: the celebrated Hungarian hedonist died in exile as a forlorn American. In the final analysis it was old age, illness, nostalgia, and personal tragedy rather than exile that proved responsible for Molnár's decline in America. His weltanschauung during his final years was expressed in his opening statement at parties: ''We are all dead people, we refugees: we walk around, shadows among shadows, ghosts of what we were, in a world that does not know us and we only faintly comprehend.''

The numerous works written during Molnár's twelve years of exile rarely show his innate talent and wit. The late work unfortunately comprises the sad residue of a rich life and/or the therapeutic activities of a disillusioned man. *Farewell My Heart* (1945; *Isten veled szivem*, 1947) was the first Molnár novel to appear in English first and later to be translated into Hungarian. The story, narrated by a nostalgic Hungarian journalist on his deathbed in a New York hospital, is a transparent autobiographical fragment. The plot is a variation on the familiar theme of an ageing man's anguished infatuation with a much younger woman. Incontestably, *Companion in Exile* (1950; *Utitárs a számüzetésben*, 1958) is Molnár's most dolorous work. This loosely constructed autobiographical elegy is a pathetic tale of an old man's tragic love. Meant as Molnár's final tribute to Mrs. Bartha, it regrettably presents the heroine sometimes in an unattractive light. One chapter expostulates against the condition of exile, another chapter describes fellow émigrés in less than generous-spirited tones. The wordy passages of description unveil Molnár's paranoid fears and his vanity. Despite its flaws, this memoir is the most important writing he produced in his exile. It serves as evidence of the changes for the worse that Molnár and his art underwent during his final years. His last theatrical pieces also reflect a man at the end of his tether, yet the veteran stage magician managed to produce some noteworthy drama—he left behind five unfinished plays and seven filmscripts.

Selected Titles: *The King's Maid* (1941), symbolic tragedy; *Waxwork or Panoptikum* (1941), drawingroom comedy/fantasy farce; *The Emperor or the Last Role* (1942; A császár, 1945), tragedy; *Game of Hearts* (1943), comedy; *The Captain of St. Margaret's: Twenty-Five Chapters of Memoirs* (1945), story collection; *Romantic Comedies: Eight Plays* (1952), dramatic collection, posthumous.

CLARA GYORGYEY

MOORE, Brian. Born August 25, 1921, in Belfast, Northern Ireland; he lives in California. Moore was raised a Roman Catholic in Northern Ireland, emigrated to Canada in 1948 (and became a citizen of that country in 1953), and has lived in the United States since 1959 (first in New York City, subsequently in southern California, where he is professor of English at the University of California at Los Angeles and lives in Malibu). Moore's widely praised and diverse novels are noted for their emphasis on the dispossessed and displaced among ordinary folk in the three countries he has called home, and regardless of specific setting he minutely explores various forms of cultural and religious isolation. He probes into the conflicts that defy easy resolution, such as hope and despair, individual freedom and the need for security, religious faith and profound despair and doubt, consistently avoiding easy solutions to complex emotional and cultural dilemmas.

Like Graham Greene, Moore decided early to distinguish his serious fiction from his more popular work. After producing two pulp mysteries under his own name, he wrote three more under the pseudonym Bernard Mara and two under the pseudonym Michael Bryan; none of these is more than competent, workmanlike formula fiction, comparable to his later writing of screenplays in Hollywood.

His first serious (and possibly most important) work, *Judith Hearne* (published in the United States and Canada as *The Lonely Passion of Judith Hearne*), is one of several novels set in Belfast, focusing on isolation, repression, closed-mindedness, and bigotry in that troubled city. Moore has said that his "loneliness when living as an exile in Canada all focussed in this novel to produce what he felt the climate of Ulster to be" (quoted in Hallvard Dahlie, *Brian Moore*, New York: Twayne, 1981, p. 43). Judith Hearne, like others in Moore's early novels, is sexually repressed, incapable of engaging life in any meaningful fashion, and doomed to a grim, joyless existence as a single middle-aged woman in a male-dominated world, in a narrowly circumscribed, parochial world of boarding-house, Roman Catholic church, and provincial city. Hearne's brief, hopeless relationship with James Madden, who has returned from the United States (one of several characters in Moore's fiction who no longer fit well in any society), leads her again to her one secret solace, alcohol, as respite from what she perceives as rejection by those around her.

The equally distinguished *The Feast of Lupercal* (1957; republished as *A Moment of Love*, 1960) centers on Diarmuid Devine, also an *isolato*, though unlike Hearne he is socially more experienced with Belfast society as a teacher and theater coach. More conscious than Hearne regarding his repression, limitations, and difficulties, he still cannot summon the courage to confront openly and directly the "scandal" caused in his Jesuit school by his chaste liaison with an easygoing Protestant woman, an irreconcilable breach between two totally alien ways of thinking and living. Another Belfast novel, written after Moore had moved to the United States, is *The Emperor of Ice-Cream* (1965). This and his subsequent work have been uniformly free of the bleakness and bitterness in the other two novels, with admittedly autobiographical details in the twenty-five-year-old protagonist, Gavin Burke. Burke searches for release from the same repressive Belfast forces, though, as he attempts to understand his confusing "duty" to family, church, the military (he serves in the Home Guard), and conventional morality. A comic novel offering a serious examination of the wretched life of another anti-hero, this book is warmer though ultimately no more hopeful than its predecessors.

Moore's best-known novel, *The Luck of Ginger Coffey* (1960), is the first of his books set in North America and centers on an Irish immigrant in Montreal. A comic picaresque work, it explores ways in which Coffey dreams of achieving business success, and although he only partially succeeds in matching his optimism with accomplishment, along the way and through various wild, impressionistic adventures (including being arrested for drunkenness and indecent exposure), he eventually recognizes who he is, the importance of his family, and the sharp contrast between the values of the Old World and the New. The more complex *An Answer from Limbo* (1962) is also about the search for self-knowledge experienced by an exile to North America, in this case New York City: Brendan Tierney is more successful than Coffey, though he too, a writer, attempts to ascertain matters of illusion and identity. Much of the book is concerned with family relationships, especially as the various members reflect a spectrum of religious and personal values.

Fergus (1970) is set in Los Angeles and again contrasts the influence of the past on the present. A thirty-nine-year-old novelist hired to adapt one of his books for the film, Fergus lives with a twenty-two-year-old woman who leaves him, prompting a series of reflections on irresolvable uncertainties from his Belfast origins such as family and religious tensions. Fergus's "ghosts" in time enable him merely to continue living as he is doing, ultimately resolving nothing but offering a kind of muted hope.

With *Catholics* (1972), Moore moves from the past to the future. Set in a remote island abbey near Ireland, this novel suggests that the Roman Catholic church he grew up with will metamorphose dramatically by the century's end. The contrast between a young priest's progressive thinking and an old abbot's conservatism offers what is ultimately a dire prophecy. Another case of the past impinging on the future is found in *The Great Victorian Collection* (1975), which, even more than *Fergus*, offers a complex allegorical, hallucinatory vision about a "miracle" in which a young history professor's dream of a prize collection of Victoriana materializes in a motel parking lot.

Moore's subsequent books have been considerably more concerned with probing into his characters' introspection. *I Am Mary Dunne* (1968), for example, tells of a lonely hairdresser's complex day, from her first customer of the morning to midnight flirting with thoughts of suicide; as she attempts to recall every detail of her day, she reflects on her life, her three marriages, her mother, and a myriad of memories. *The Doctor's Wife* (1976) is a complex love story about a conventional older woman's seeking some idea of her identity by deserting her happy marriage for an affair with a young man. *The Mangan Inheritance* (1979) also presents a wife's leaving her husband but with the focus on the husband, whose reflections on his past, real and imagined (he identifies with his ancestor, the nineteenth-century poet of the same surname), constitute the book's plot.

In 1981 Moore published *The Temptation of Eileen Hughes*, again set in Northern Ireland. Hughes, generously taken to London for a holiday by the wealthy owners of the store where she works, concludes guiltily after the husband takes an excessively personal interest in her that she has to return home; however, she remains involved in saving the man's life with the help of a young American man, and, in an epilogue set in the future, learning of the husband's suicide. *Cold Heaven* (1983) returns to Roman Catholicism and ambiguous miracles as a means of a woman's discovery of her identity. Again focusing on a physician's wife who intends to leave her husband, she discovers instead, after he "dies" in an accident in which his body disappears along with passport and airline ticket, that he has escaped, changed, to California. The book is a striking combination of realistic detail with metaphysical speculation about miracles and rebirth.

The historical novel *Black Robe* (1985) dramatizes the disastrous attempts by Jesuits in the seventeenth century to convert and civilize several tribes of North American Indians. In 1987 Moore published *The Colour of Blood*, a Hitchcockian suspense novel set in Eastern Europe (though suggestive of Ireland); since Moore had written the screenplay for Alfred Hitchcock's *The Torn Curtain* (1966), he had experience with the thriller genre. In this novel Moore tells of a Roman Catholic cardinal's three-day ordeal with attempted assassination, kidnapping, and pursuit.

Moore's books rarely repeat themselves except occasionally in setting, and he is noted for consistent readability that sometimes disguises his seriousness of intent, his metaphysical exploration of psychic and physical isolation, and his profound concern with his characters' moral and ethical dilemmas, especially as these are connected to family and religious and national bonds. One could conclude that his mature career blossomed after he became an exile and was able to purge himself of his origins, and the fact that he has returned to Northern Ireland in some recent writing suggests that the purgation is complete after some forty years away from Ulster.

Selected Titles: *Wreath for a Redhead* (1951); *The Executioners* (1951); [as Bernard Mara] *French for Murder* (1954); [as Bernard Mara] *A Bullet for My Lady* (1955); [as Bernard Mara] *This Gun for Gloria* (1956); [as Michael Bryan] *Murder in Majorca* (1957); *Canada* (1963); *Lies of Silence* (1990).

Consult: Terence Brown, "Show Me a Sign: The Religious Imagination of Brian Moore," *Irish University Review* 18, no. 1 (Spring 1988); Hallvard Dahlie, *Brian Moore*

(1981); Jeanne Flood, *Brian Moore* (1974); John Wilson Foster, *Forces and Themes in Ulster Fiction* (Dublin, 1974); Michael P. Gallagher, "The Novels of Brian Moore," *Studies* 60 (Summer 1971); Paul Goetsch, "Brian Moore's Canadian Fiction," in *Studies in Anglo-Irish Literature*, ed. Heinz Kosok (Bonn, West Germany, 1982); John A. Scanlon, "The Artist-in-Exile: Brian Moore's North American Novels," *Eire/Ireland* 12 (Summer 1977). See also Brian McElroy, "A Brian Moore Bibliography," *Irish University Review* 18 (Spring 1988).

PAUL SCHLUETER

MORAES, Dom. Born 1938, Bombay, India; he lives in Bombay. The son of Frank Moraes, a sophisticated writer and world traveller, Dom Moraes early imbibed the life of a foreign traveller-resident. With his father he saw various parts of Sri Lanka, Australia, New Zealand, and Southeast Asia; he studied at Oxford University after graduation from a secondary (Catholic Missionary) school in India. At age 15 his poems were heralded by Stephen Spender (who published some in *Encounter*), by Karl Shapiro (who published some in *Poetry*), and by W. H. Auden; at nineteen Moraes published his first book of poems, *A Beginning* (1957). This work won the Hawthornden Prize; Moraes became the youngest and the only non-English poet to win the prize. Moraes has always written in English; he declared in his autobiography, *My Son's Father*, that he went to England to "polish and harden my tools, and extend my powers"; the resulting experiences of association with the British Commonwealth characterize his work but do not exclude his confessional voice of earlier intimacies, those epiphanies of youthful awakenings in India. Moraes attempts a synthesis in his work of the personal note with universal traditions of growth and awareness; he does not emphasize regional, group or national consciousness. At the same time, since his return to India in recent years, he has acknowledged the power of the native tradition, the unconscious memory of identity that at some point surfaces to claim its occupancy in a writer's domain.

Moraes has undergone several transitions and periods of awakening: from 1967 to 1985, a period of seventeen years, he published no poetry (with the exception of a privately printed volume, *Absences*, Bombay, 1983). He occupied himself during this period editing journals in London, Hong Kong, and New York, and writing nonfiction works (he has published more than twenty-three such print works and twenty television documentaries); he also served in an official capacity as a writer with the United Nations (he wrote the text for the UN publication, *A Matter of People*). Such activity has given him an opportunity for replenishing his inner substance while allowing him to explore surface realities of temporary, and contemporary, life.

Moraes writes in a tradition that has, until recently, been called Anglo-Indian; among others in this "category" are Kamala Markandaya,* Nizzim Ezekiel, R. K. Narayan, Anita Desai, and Santha Rama Rau.* The tradition does not mandate residence outside India and inside England, but implies a cross-fertilization of two cultures; those who practice it are Indian by birth and culture who write in English and who reflect a leavening of English values in their Indian consciousness. Recently, some critics have insisted on calling this tradition Indo-Anglian, finding the earlier term redolent of British Empire days and a stale political odor; the newer term emphasizes the dominance of the Indian consciousness over any shapings of British import.

Selected Titles: *Poems* (1960); *John Nobody* (1965); *Poems 1955–1965* (1966); *Beldam and Others* (1967); *From East and West: A Collection of Essays* (1971); *The Tempest Within: An Account of East Pakistan* (1971); *The Open Eyes: A Journey through Karnataka* (1976); *Mrs. Ghandi* (London, 1980); *Answering Flutes: Reflections from Madhya Prades* (Bombay, 1983); *Trishna* (Bombay, 1987); *Collected Poems 1957–87* (1987).

Consult: K. R. Srinivasa Iyengar, *Indian Writing in English*, 2nd ed. (1973); Dom Moraes, Introduction in *Collected Poems* by Moraes (1987).

MORAVIA, Alberto (pseudonym of Alberto Pincherle). Born 1907, Rome, Italy; he died September 26, 1990, in Rome. Moravia spent many years from the 1930s to the end of World War II in travel and in flight from Fascist harassment. From 1930 to 1935 he lived in England and France; he visited the United States and Mexico in 1936, and lived in China and Greece from 1936 to 1937. As a Jew and anti-Fascist he fled to Fondi in 1943.

The English translations of the works he wrote during his exilic period are: *Bad Ambitions* (1935); *The Good Life* (1935); *The Swindle* (1937); *The Unhappy Love* (1943); and *Hope, or That is to say, Christianity and Communism* (1944).

MORGAN, Ted (new legal name of Sanche de Gramont). Born 1932, Paris, France; he lives in New York City. Sanche de Gramont was eight years old when he watched German troops march into Paris. His father was killed while flying a mission for the Free French in 1943. With his mother, he emigrated to the United States after the war. He worked as a reporter for *The New York Herald-Tribune* and *The New York Times* under his first name. He changed names when he became an American citizen in 1977; he describes the event in *On Becoming American* (1978).

A popular biographer of, among others, Churchill and W. S. Maugham, Morgan published *An Uncertain Hour: The French, the Germans, the Jews, the Klaus Barbie Trial, and the City of Lyon 1940–45* in 1989. This study of the Frenchman who was responsible for sending hundreds of Jewish children to concentration camps and probable death and who aided in the capture of the French resistance leader, Jean Moulin, served, in Morgan's words, as his *crise d'identité*. By reliving his own dilemma as a French national through the reports of the trial and through interviews with surviving witnesses, Morgan came to an awareness of the past he had tried to exile. Barbie became for him not only a monster of the Holocaust, but, like Sanche de Gramont, a French Christian whose depths he had to pursue.

MORTON, Frederic. Born in 1925; he lives in New York City. Born Fritz Mandelbaum, Morton left Austria after Germany's annexation of the country. He lived in England till 1943, when his family moved to the United States. He worked as a baker's apprentice near New York City's theatrical West Side and has described his experience as a fifteen-year-old youth roaming the bright lights of Broadway dreaming his dream of fame and worldly acceptance. Significantly, his first great popular success was *The Rothschilds: A Family Portrait* (1962; c. 1961), the story of an immigrant Jewish family that went on to become financial leaders of the Western world. Morton has called *The Rothschilds* saga "an antidote to exile" (in a talk given to a conference on German Writers in Exile, held in Lincoln, Nebraska, April 1989) in that his eponymous heroes created a new home out of their wanderings. Perhaps even more significantly for him, the musical adaptation of his book (produced on Broadway in 1970 and revived off Broadway in 1990) brought him transient fame and celebrity status, and then rejection and post-theatrical depression, a condition that opened him again to the anguish of exilic loss.

Morton wrote several highly regarded novels before he turned to biography and autobiography; he has continued to write fiction while writing in these nonfiction genres. Among his novels are *The Hound* (1947); *The Darkness Below* (1949); *Asphalt and Desire* (1952); and *The Witching Ship* (1960). His most autobiographical novel is probably *Asphalt and Desire*, the story of a young apprentice who must choose between integrity and material wealth; the choice involves a compromising of his ideals or the loss of the dream of material comfort. The hero is influenced in his decision both by the woman he loves, a bright young savvy girl from the Bronx, and by her idealistic, artistic brother. Whichever way he chooses, he must forsake some of his luxuries; he must experience loss as he grows to maturity. Morton's recent work, *Crosstown Sabbath: A Street Journey through History* (1987), is a memoir-novella in which he discusses the sense of exile felt by his protagonist; it is basically a dialogue with the persona and his selves as he rides a crosstown bus in Manhattan on a Saturday afternoon to pick up his daughter to take her to a "select" party on Fifth Avenue. During the course of his peripeteia the protagonist ponders the questions of his identity as a Jew and his resolutions, both those already forged and those newly made. Morton says of his protagonist's pervasive longing: "Nostalgia literally means a pain caused by one's absence from home. As a rule this is a home we never had. If we had ever had it, it would, even after we'd left it, abide in our soul; then its parting wouldn't be so total and so painful. . . . In the crosstown wilderness of Manhattan I long for a home I never had" (pp. 10–11). Morton calls his fiction a return to the "therapeutic story" shattered by Laurence Sterne and those who followed him in the blurring of the clarity between good and evil, hero and villain, value and insignificance.

Morton writes only in English. He became an American citizen and has taught at New York University, the New School for Social Research, Johns Hopkins, and the University of Utah. Since 1959 he has been, in his words, a "free-lance writer."

Morton has written two impressionistic histories/travelogues of his ancestral city: *A Nervous Splendor: Vienna, 1881–1889* (1979) and *Thunder at Twilight: Vienna 1913–1914* (1989).

Selected Titles: *The Schatten Affair* (1965); *Snow Gods* (1968); *An Unknown Woman* (1976); *The Forever Street* (1984); with Marcia Morton, *Chocolate, an Illustrated History* (1986).

MOSS, Rose. Born January 2, 1937, Johannesburg, South Africa; she lives in Newtonville, Massachusetts. Moss left South Africa in 1964 "to get away from the political environment." She became an American citizen in 1972. For years, in her words, she has been trying to "shake off the shadow of South Africa." She now accepts the legacy of her past. All quotes are from an interview given to Martin Tucker in 1988.

Moss's first novel, *Family Reunion* (1974), set in Nice, uses as its premise a gathering of family members from all parts of the world for a birthday party on a declining summer day before the end of the world. An apocalyptic fiction, it sums up the end of the era of American empire; in Moss's view, all empires must come to their time-appointed end as a natural consequence of history. Her second novel, *The Terrorist* (London, 1979), ironically is her only work published in South Africa (1981), where it was issued as *The Schoolmaster*. The work is loosely based on a real incident: a white man, who set off a self-made bomb in a railroad station, has been arrested and interrogated; the novel becomes the dialogue of his rationale. Moss wrote it out "of a feeling at the time that nothing would change the situation except the attention paid to violence," though she was aware, then and now, that violence would not resolve the racist problems of South Africa. Her novel thus became "an argument with myself." Moss believes the novel was allowed by the censors to appear in South Africa because of its innocuous title.

Moss's novella *Exile* (1971), repeatedly anthologized, has been optioned for the movies.

She is currently at work on a nonfiction study (the working title is "Through the Fire") based on the transcript of two people found guilty of treason in South Africa; one of them is the leader of the largest organization opposed to apartheid. Again, as in her fiction, Moss is examining the pressures of conscience in the unnerving conflict between peaceful and violent means of ending oppression.

MPHAHLELE, Es'kia (formerly Ezekiel). Born December 17, 1919, in Pretoria, South Africa; he now lives in Johannesburg, South Africa. Mphahlele has been one of the most versatile and influential of African authors. As literary critic, autobiographer, journalist, short story writer, novelist, dramatist, and poet, he has probably contributed more than any other individual to the growth and development of an African literature in English. After leaving South Africa he traveled widely, stopping to teach for a year or more in five different countries: Nigeria, Kenya, Zambia, France, and the United States.

In South Africa Mphahlele wrote mainly short stories about life in the urban black ghettos where he had grown up and spent most of his adult years. The events in these stories were based on his personal experiences and reflected a wide variety of responses to the people and places he knew best. There were humorous sketches and satirical vignettes as well as more serious stories about human or social problems. Later, as stringent apartheid legislation made life more difficult for urban blacks, Mphahlele began to write angry protest fiction. By the mid–1950s he felt stifled in his home country and applied for an "exit permit," a document allowing him to leave South Africa on the condition that he never return. The South African government granted his request in 1957, and he roamed in exile for the next twenty years. He returned to South Africa in 1978.

His first major piece of writing abroad was an autobiography, *Down Second Avenue* (1959), in which he tried to work off the emotional creative energy that had been building inside him during his last years in South Africa. A moving story, it is told with candor and compassion for his people. In 1962 he published a pioneering work of literary criticism *The African Image*, part of which had been written in South Africa as an M.A. thesis. He also brought out two collections of short stories and produced a manual for aspiring fiction writers. His first novel, *The Wanderers* (1971), examined the plight of the black South African intellectual in exile, a depressing tale constructed out of the debris of his personal life. A second novel, *Chirundu* (1979), which appears to have been inspired by his years in Zambia, dealt with postcolonial power politics in an independent African state. In 1972 he published another volume of perceptive literary criticism, *Voices in the Whirlwind and Other Essays*.

During his years in exile Mphahlele was able to arrive at the kind of emotional balance and aesthetic distance from his subject matter that he found impossible to achieve as a young man living in South Africa. But after a time he began to feel increasingly restless, angry, and politically impotent abroad, so he elected to return to his homeland in 1977, despite the hazards and frustrations that he knew would confront him there. In recent years he has been extremely prolific, producing a sequel to his autobiography, a children's book, another manual for writers, and a new collected edition of his short stories and poems. These books have contained forthright protest, yet he has managed to get them all published in South Africa. Also, some of his earlier works have been unbanned there. In addition, a volume of his letters has appeared, and he has been the subject of a locally written biography. Repatriation, like exile, has obviously served as an intense creative stimulus for him, releasing pent-up energies of passionate self-expression. Instead of aiming for aesthetic distance, he now seeks close emotional engagement with the people and places that serve as primary sources of his inspiration. After decades of wandering, he has rediscovered his roots as a South African writer.

Selected Titles: *The Living and the Dead and Other Stories* (Ibadan, 1961); *A Guide to Creative Writing* (Nairobi, 1966); *Afrika My Music* (1984); *Bury Me at the Marketplace: Selected Letters 1943–1980,* ed. N. Chabani Manganyi (1984); *Renewal Time* (London, 1989, contains a discursive essay on his return to South Africa, and earlier stories written in South Africa and Nigeria, with an afterword).

Consult: Ursula A. Barnett, *Ezekiel Mphahlele* (1976); N. Chabani Manganyi, *Exiles and Homecomings: A Biography of Es'kia Mphahlele* (1983). D. Catherine Woeber and John Read, *Es'kia Mphahlele: A Bibliography.* National English Literary Museum Bibliographic Series No. 2 (Grahamstown, South Africa, National English Literary Museum, 1989).

BERNTH LINDFORS

MROŻEK, Sławomir. Born March 26, 1930, in Borzecin near Cracow; he has made Paris his home since 1968. Mrożek's father was a postman in the small town where Mrożek was born. After graduating from gymnasium in Cracow he studied architecture there, and in 1950 began writing journalistic contributions for the Cracow press. Gradually he turned to creative genres and published humorous short stories and poems. He was also a cartoonist. His short stories brought him popularity, and his literary reputation grew further when he took to writing for the stage in the late 1950s. With the publication and staging of several plays between 1958 and 1963, he became a recognized dramatist in the West. After 1957 he frequently traveled abroad, and in 1963 he left Poland, a voluntary exile. He lived first in Italy, and in 1968 moved to Paris.

Mrożek's early stories—*Słoń* (1957; *The Elephant,* 1962), *Wesele w Atomicach* (1959, Wesele in Atomtown), and *Deszcz* (1962, Rain)—seem products of some logical machine capable of turning every concept into the absurd. The distortions in social life brought about by simplistic notions of rationality and modernity are presented in bravura narratives in which the author indulges in parodying styles and paradoxes. While many of the paradoxes pertain to human nature in general, the author's frame of reference is clearly the Polish People's Republic (where such paradoxes can be found in abundance and concentration). In his later prose (e.g., *Dwa listy,* 1970, Two Letters), Mrożek, not discarding his penchant for paradox, turned from social satire to psychological introspection.

In drama Mrożek has written more than twenty important works. His earlier plays include *Męczeństwo Piotra Oheya* (1959; *The Martyrdom of Piotr Ohey,* 1967); *Indyk* (1960, The Turkey); *Na pełnym morzu, Karol, Striptease* (1961; *Out at Sea,* 1967, *Charlie,* 1968, *Striptease,* 1972); *Zabawa Czarowna noc* (1963; *Enchanted Night,* 1972); *Tango* (1964; 1968); *Policja* (1968; first published in English, *The Police,* 1967). All these works appeared first in *Dialog,* a Warsaw drama journal founded by Adam Tarn* in 1956 in a period of political "relaxation"; the journal published works of the Parisian avant-garde and theater of the absurd. Often labeled a Polish absurdist, Mrożek also owes much to the tradition of the Polish avant-garde, especially S. I. Witkiewicz and Witold Gombrowicz.* Mrożek derides belief in language, mocks traditional logic, distrusts (or shows distrust of) ideology, unveils political manipulation, and rebels against fixed values as a tenet of belief. By these works, Mrożek challenged the naturalistic conventions of drama and in their place celebrated the grotesque and the elements of parody, irony, and parodox. His plays center on an individual portrayed in romantic loneliness without accompanying romantic pathos. Mrożek sets his individual against the conforming institutions in which he finds himself, and in adherence to Polish literary tradition, uses the image of the aristocratic spirit in battle with an insensitive, vulgar brute. A superb stylist, Mrożek parodies both Polish Romantic drama and Shakespeare while achieving and maintaining his individual voice.

Mrożek's later plays—among others *Drugie danie* (1968; *Repeat Performance*, 1972), *Vatzlav* (first published in English translation, 1970; first Polish edition, Paris, 1982), *Szczęśliwe wydarazenie* (1973), *Garbus* (1975, The Hunchback), *Pieszo* (1980), *Ambasador* (Paris, 1982; *The Ambassador*, n.d.), *Alfa* (Paris, 1984), and *Portret* (1987, The Portrait)—assume a somewhat less facetious and more somber tone. There is less experimentation, less parody, more sarcasm and open bitterness to be found in these works; they also show a direct rapport with political issues. *Alfa* is a play about the Solidarity movement, with Lech Walesa disguised as the titular hero, while *Portret* touches directly on the moral issues of conformism and betrayal in the face of political repression (Stalin and Poland are explicit references in the work).

Among Mrożek's best plays are *Tango* and *Emigranci* (1974; *The Emigrants*, 1984). *Tango* presents an idealist who, in his search for the meaning of life and his efforts to aid in mankind's happiness, falls victim to an uncivilized brute. A family drama on the conflict of generations and attitudes, *Tango* is also a bitter parable of European intellectual history from modernism to totalitarianism. *Emigranci*, theatrically Mrożek's most accomplished play, presents the conflict of a political exile and a greedy "*gastarbeiter*"—both are products of Poland's complex present history, each is unable to communicate with the other, yet they are condemned to stay together. This psychological study of the phenomenon of alienation and exile also shows the diversity of issues related to Poland, which Mrożek sees both through a Polish and a Western perspective.

Mrożek continues to write in Polish, and although his works have been translated and staged throughout the world, his principal audience remains in Poland. Despite his long stay out of his native country, he remains a force in Poland's cultural life, and he is his country's most-often-staged contemporary dramatist. He avoids loud political gestures but does not hesitate to express criticism of the communist government; for example, he publicly condemned martial law in 1981. Mrożek claims not to have been politically persecuted or to have been forced to leave Poland, and has often given "private" grounds as the basis for his living abroad. His adolescent years passed in the shadow of World War II, during a time of brutal rule, and his youth was the experience of slow but relentless destruction of personality by the political force of a totalitarian regime. These memories, he confesses, obsess him as a writer. He is always influenced by contemporary events as part of his personal experience, but rather than describe such events directly, he projects them onto what he conceives as more universal situations. His plays are built around a central character who, like the romantic hero, refuses to be subordinated by politics, which Mrozék sees as "the law of the stronger."

Mrozék is also the author of many feuilletons (those written for *Dialog* were published in book form, *Małelisty*, in 1981), one radio drama (*Rzeźnia*, 1973, The Slaughterhouse), and two film scenarios.

Selected Titles: Selected stories from *Deszcz* (1962, Rain) and *Dwa listy* (Paris, 1970, Two Letters) appeared in English translation as *The Uqupu Bird* (1968).

Consult: Daniel Gerould, *Introduction to Twentieth-Century Polish Avant-Garde Drama* (1977); Jan Blonski, *Romans z tekstem* (Cracow, 1981).

MAREK KEDZIERSKI

MTSHALI, Mbuyiseni Oswald Joseph. Born 1940, Vryheid, Natal; he has returned to South Africa. Mtshali worked as a messenger boy for several years while submitting his poems to small literary journals in South Africa. His first volume of poems, *Sounds of a Cowhide Drum* (Johannesburg, 1971), brought him instant attention and became a best-seller in his country; it has also been issued in the United States and the United Kingdom. He left South Africa in 1975 to study at Columbia University. He returned to South Africa in 1979 and worked on the Johannesburg newspaper, *The Star*, as a roving critic. While his first volume is filled with humor and a wry hopefulness, his later work shows signs of a loss of optimism and sustaining faith. The poems in his second volume, *Fireflames* (1980), banned for a short period in South Africa, often speak in apocalyptic allusions.

Mtshali was awarded the Olive Schreiner prize in 1975.

Consult: Es'kia Mphahlele, "Mtshali's Strident Voice of Self-Assertion," in *Soweto Poetry*, ed. Michael Chapman (Johannesburg, 1982).

MUKHERJEE, Bharati. Born 1932, in Calcutta, India; she lives in New York. Mukherjee arrived in England when she was eight; she returned to India three and a half years later to attend a fashionable school and "to live a colonial life in a post-colonial world." In a P.E.N. American Center panel discussion on exile and immigrant writing, held in New York in 1988, she declared she no longer writes about a "lost homeland" but is in search of a new land, the United States, to which country she has given her loyalty as an immigrant. Mukherjee said she could have gone to France with a grant for university study when she was eighteen years old but instead decided to come to the United States on her own resources. She has lived in Canada and the United States since she was twenty years old, and her fiction explores the theme of identity and self-illumination. Her writing is a part of her own quest, since she "no longer knows which part of me is English or Indian or Canadian.'' (All quoted remarks were made by Mukherjee at the PEN panel discussion.)

Mukherjee's third novel, *Jasmine* (1989), deals explicitly with the difficulties an Indian exile experiences in the United States. A widow at sixteen, she leaves her homeland for Florida and later Iowa. When the heroine marries a midwestern American banker, the author changes her name to Jane, but the all-American name does not prevent new troubles in the promised land, including the wheelchair confinement of the heroine's husband as a result of a bank shooting, and the tribulations resulting from Jane's and her husband's angry, adopted Vietnamese daughter. As in her earlier work, particularly the widely praised collection, *The Middleman and Other Stories* (1987), Mukherjee's work centers on the outsider, a person willing to fight the battle of adventures that may lead to a new and better life. Mukherjee's characters often do not find success, as measured in conventional terms, but they remain "reckless with hope," and they insist on looking ahead, rather than back into their past. Mukherjee herself believes all experience is useful in shaping a present form, and she considers herself an expectant immigrant. She is not, however, a reckless optimist. Often her characters remain cool and controlling, no matter what the circumstances in their lives, and thus they may be considered survivors rather than transcenders of cataclysmic adventures. Her insights into the collision of cultures—a pervasive content in Anglo-Indian writing—provide sharp, glittering perceptions and a stubborn determination to resist despair, but her characters are often more concerned with their survival than with compassion for the misery of those with whom they are thrown into contact.

Selected Titles: *The Tiger's Daughter* (1971); *Darkness* (1985); *Wife* (1987). Nonfiction: *Kautilya's Concept of Democracy: A New Interpretation* (Calcutta, 1976); with Clark Blaise, *Days and Nights in Calcutta*, 1977; with Clark Blaise, *The Sorrow and the Terror* (1985, report on the Air India Flight 182 Incident in 1985).

MURAVIN, Victor. Born 1929 in Vladivostok, USSR; he emigrated to the United States in the 1970s. Muravin was an agricultural laborer and horse wrangler, a member of the communist youth organizations, the Pioneers and the Komosol, and an ardent young Stalinist. In 1937 his father was imprisoned as a German spy; although the father was later released, the family was kept under surveillance, and when Muravin joined the merchant marine he was not allowed to sail abroad. He spent nine years in the Soviet Pacific and Arctic circle as a deck boy, sailor, and radio officer, after which he worked as a stevedore and learned English at night school. He later became head of the English Department at the college where he taught, and wrote two English-language textbooks that were adopted in about 300 colleges in the Soviet Union. In the late 1960s he requested a visa for his mother for medical treatment in the United States. His mother was granted the visa, but Muravin was declared "an enemy of Soviet power"; fortunately the KGB declaration was lifted and Muravin was not arrested. He petitioned the government for an exit visa, and a year later was granted permission to leave. He spent a year in Europe and then moved to the United States.

Muravin has said he did not want to emigrate. He wanted to go back to sea and regain his personal freedom; such a course was available to him only outside the USSR. During the year he waited for his visa he wrote a 900-page typescript on the "ordinary Soviet citizen" and the first two volumes of a trilogy on the life of Captain Angarov; in exile in the West he wrote the third volume. The trilogy covers the years from 1914 to 1970, when Angarov dies, and serves as an informal history of Russian life from the time just before the revolution to contemporary events. Muravin published *The Diary of Vikenty Angarov*, the second volume in the trilogy, in the United States in a private edition in English translation in 1975; in 1978 it was issued in a regular edition. He dedicated the book "To Russia."

Muravin has not published any further fiction in English translation. His health, which had broken down over the many strains in his life, improved during his exile years in New York City, and he returned to university life in pursuit of a doctorate in political science. He has said he is now apolitical.

Like Joseph Conrad,* who was stricken with illness after his trip down the Congo River at the beginning of the century, Muravin still dreams of returning to sea as soon as his health improves. He is working in the meanwhile as a translator and teacher, and was last reported living in Queens, New York City.

Consult: Abraham Ascher, Preface, to V. Muravin, *The Diary of Vikenty Angarov* (1978).

MUSIL, Robert Edler. Born November 6, 1880, in Klagenfurt, Austria; died April 15, 1942, in Geneva, Switzerland. An Austrian of partly Czech descent, Musil fled to Switzerland in 1938 to avoid Nazi persecution; his wife was a Jewish painter. In addition, Nazi ideology and Austrian anti-Semitism were anathema to his creed of philosophical speculation and the consciousness of noncommitment as a step to higher and deeper knowledge of man's place in the universe. His early work reflected the problems of his childhood: Musil could not bring himself either to accept his engineer father's dedication to practical concerns or to make a break with his family and pursue his more immaterial ambitions. Musil attended military school and attained the rank of second lieutenant but resigned his post to become an engineering student. Soon after graduation as an engineer in 1901, he became a student of philosophy and experimental psychology at the University of Berlin. During all this time he remained financially dependent on his parents. He rejected a university appointment but accepted a position as a librarian when his free-lance writing situation proved precarious. It was at this time, 1911, that he married. After four years of librarianship at the Technical University in Vienna, he moved on to an editorship at *Die neue Rundschau* in 1914 but was conscripted into the army soon after. His military service was brief: illness was a reason for his discharge. With the end of the war he found work as a government employee in the foreign and defense bureaus. In 1924, buoyed by his comparative critical and pecuniary success as a published writer, he resigned his government job. Much of Musil's great novel *Der Mann ohne Eigenschaften* (1930–43; partial translation *The Man without Qualities*, 1953) was written during this period when he and his wife subsisted on the subsidies of friends and appreciators.

Musil's first novel, *Die Verwirrungen des Zöglings Törless* (1906; *Young Torless*, 1955), was a popular success. Set in a military school, it deals with a cadet's experiences of military life, its brutalities, and its spartan ideals. Musil explored the polarities of his teenage hero's desires—for reason and order and for the knowledge that the mystery and inchoateness of intellectual freedom bring. In this early work his style was richly symbolic but accessible. In his second work *Vereinigungen* (1911; Unions), a collection of two stories, "Die Vollendung der Liebe" (The Perfecting of Love, 1966) and "Die Versuchung der stillen Veronika" (The Temptation of Quiet Veronica, 1966), he attempted to provide narration largely through the use of metaphoric devices and to forsake linear plots. The work, a remarkable tour de force, achieved a limited following.

In midcareer Musil turned to writing plays. Both *Die Schwärmer* (1921; The Enthusiasts) and *Vinzenz und die Freundin bedeutender Männer* (1923, Vincent and the Girlfriend of Important Men) are satirical studies of bourgeois customs; what distinguishes them is Musil's introduction of a new kind of hero, the noncommitted man who, because of his radical assumption of freedom from conventional social responsibilities, is able to transcend the conflicts that attend bourgeois morality. Musil portrayed a hero who could show love for others without a hidden agenda in his file of motives, even if his act was whimsical and sometimes short-lived.

Musil's greatest work, *The Man without Qualities*, was published in three stages. The first part appeared in 1930; a second volume containing thirty-eight chapters of Part 2 was issued in 1933. A remaining twenty chapters were set in proof in 1938 but never reached publication because Musil's publishing house, a Jewish firm, was confiscated by the Nazis. These chapters and parts of Part 3, on which Musil worked in exile in Switzerland, were published posthumously by his widow in 1943. The novel, huge as it is, was not completed at the time of Musil's death.

In the first half of the novel Musil explores the intellectual and moral life of Ulrich, ironically a man with many qualities but one who cannot integrate them into a socially distinguished career. Like Musil, Ulrich has been a soldier, engineer, and mathematician; he is a skeptic who relies on scientific training. Ulrich is constantly seeking a rationale for life. The novel sets up Ulrich against a number of broad historical backdrops that suggest Musil's views, or specu-lations, on twentieth-century history. The chief setting is Kakanien, Musil's name for the Austro-Hungarian monarchy; a meeting of the Parallelaktion Society in 1918 to celebrate the sixtieth anniversary of Franz Josef's rule provides the novelistic means for an ironic discussion of the failure of the grand empirical ideal. Yet behind the social-political failure is a success as well—that is, the ideas that the grand experiment of a multinational empire generated into an awakening of human possibility.

Musil's complex of ideas may be seen in this failure that is not necessarily a failure. Indeed, in Musil's presentation of realities, little may be deemed failure if experience provides intellectual reward or a possibility for intellectual journey. The controversy over Musil's attitude to the legacy of the Austro-Hungarian Empire as well as his conflicting nostalgia for and satire of the empire's historic and spiritual triumphs remains current. Musil's views on openness of intellectual attitude and his belief in an irresolution that is not a failure of character or of communication are the reasons both for such continuing controversy and for the justification of Musil's refusal to be bound by ordinary logic or rhetoric.

In an attempt to illuminate his perceptions, Musil introduced a sister for Ulrich in the third part of his novel; he gave her the reverberative name of Agathe. Agathe is Ulrich's "other" side and at the same time inseparable from him; only by accepting their differences, which are not really differences but complements of a grand ideal, can the reader progress to that "other" state of unity, a state that exists for those allowing themselves to discover it.

Because Musil did not complete the novel, it is difficult to assign the shapes of finished commentary to the relationship of Agathe and Ulrich. Yet the pattern of unity by complementary opposition seems apparent to many critics. Musil saw a complex of differences in meaning and insight in what lay before him. He was less obsessed by the need to discover a revelation of truth that would mandate a priority of reasonable acceptances than he was absorbed in the re-generative process of duality, irony, and balance of polarities. For Musil, the inability of Ulrich to come to terms with any particular issue is less consequential than the loss of mysterious soul-satisfaction that would obtain in the closure of stimulating thought. Both in style and in philosphic content Musil posits the need for a flow of consciousness, a rich river of intuition and observable fact, a continuum of balancing opposites. Joseph P. Strelka, one of his critics, has said of him: "The importance that such a consequent thinker and great intellect as Musil puts upon precision and truth excludes from the beginning any kind of oversimplification and any kind of black and white representation that would tend to incline towards untruth." Frank Kermode has written that "Musil's is notoriously a world in political collapse, the end of a great empire; but more central to his poetic writing (at times he makes one think of a prose Rilke) is the sense of a world in metaphysical collapse, a universe of hideously heaped contingency, in which there are nonetheless transcendent human powers. These he represents always by the same complex and various images of eroticism, which reaches its fullest expression in the big novel."

Exile for Musil was painful, but in a curious way it did not affect him pro-foundly, for in his nature he was ironically at home wherever he found himself—ironically, because he never was at home in any one physical state. Though his last years were marked by poverty and the neglect of the literary-cultural world, Musil continued with his old habits. He was well aware of the fabled worth of trying on an emperor's new clothes.

In 1988 *Posthumous Papers of a Living Author* was published in English for the first time (London). Originally published in 1936 (*Nachlass zu Lebzeiten*), the work is a collection of sketches, fables, and meditations on cultural issues which Musil wrote mainly during the 1920s and which he published in various German-language periodicals. In the preface to the collection, he speaks of a "loitering sensibility," that pervasive condition within him that held onto memory as the means of ordering his life. Musil's spirit of identity has also been characterized as *andere Zustand*, that "other condition," a sense of exile from the mainstream, of difference from the bourgeois norm. Both phrases sum up Musil's invidious commitment to the exploration of modern consciousness and its reliance on memory in preference to observation.

Selected Titles: *Gesammelte Werke* (1978); *Briefe 1901–1942* (1981).

Translations: *Five Women* (contains stories from *Drie Frauen*, 1925—"Grigia," "The Lady from Portugal," and "Tonka"—and from *Vereinigungen*).

Consult: D. S. Luft, *Robert Musil and the Crisis of European Culture 1880–1942* (1980); F. G. Peters, *Robert Musil: Master of the Hovering Life* (1978); B. Pike, *Robert Musil: An Introduction to His Work* (1961).

MZAMANE, Mbuelelo Vizikhungo. Born 1948, Brakpan, South Africa; he lives abroad, mainly in England. Mzamane was educated at the Universities of Botswana, Lesotho and Swaziland (at Roma). He left South Africa after the Soweto protest in 1976 for black human rights, and has lived abroad since. He has been a lecturer at the new University of Botswana, and in Nigeria; he has pursued research and taught at Sheffield University in England. Some Africanist critics consider his trilogy, *The Children of Soweto* (Johannesburg, S.A., and Harlow, Essex, U.K., 1982), the finest fictional rendition of that era in South African apartheid policy, both in its portrait of the brutal repression of the Soweto protest and of the "children" who witnessed the atrocities. Mzamane has also published a collection of stories, *Mzala* (Johannesburg, 1980), which focused on black township life; the volume was reissued in 1981 under a new title, *My Cousin Comes to Jo'burg*. He has edited *Hungry Flames and Other Black African Short Stories* (Harlow, Essex, U.K., 1986); he wrote an introduction for, as well as edited, the *Selected Poems* of Wally Mongane Serote.* (Johannesburg, 1982). Mzamane won the prestigious Thomas Mofolo-William Plomer literary Prize in 1979.

N ————————————————————

NABOKOV, Vladimir Vladimirovich. Born April 23, 1899, in St. Petersburg, Russia; died July 2, 1977, in Montreux, Switzerland. Nabokov's parents were members of the aristocratic gentry of Old Russia. They are reputed to have lost a fortune when their estates were confiscated during the Revolution of 1917. Nabokov emigrated with his father (who had been an important liberal politician) and brother to Germany; Nabokov went on to Cambridge University, from which he graduated in 1922. Nabokov's father was killed by an assassin at a political rally in 1923 in Berlin when the bullet intended for another political leader hit him.

Nabokov lived in Berlin from 1923 to 1937, earning his living as a private tutor. Here he started to publish his novels, short stories, plays, and poems in Russian; he wrote, until 1940, under the pseudonym of V. Sirin. Later he would publish under his own name and write in English; his knowledge of many languages and his ability to participate in their nuances were extraordinary.

Nabokov's first novel, *Mashen'ka* (1926; *Mary*, 1970), is set in Berlin in a colony of Russian emigrants. His consciousness of past and present chronology, of memory, reality, and history as units of shifting time, are features that characterize his work throughout his life and may be seen in his first novel. The protagonist, a young Russian emigrant, Ganin, chooses his gift of memory over the shock of real experience when he refuses to meet, again, his now-married former lover, Mashen'ka, whom he believes can only be a shadow of his memory of her. In his second novel, *Karol, dama, valet* (1928; *King, Queen, Knave*, 1968), Nabokov contemplates the idea of life as a toss-up of cards and of self-inflicted wounds turning against their initiator. Composed as a contemporary detective story, it reflects a Russian émigré's sharp impression of European manners. In *Zashohita Luzhina*, (1930; *Defence*, 1964), Nabokov moves from card symbolism to the chessboard; he examines the means of artistic defense against the hostility of the social community. The protagonist, a chess master, attempts to transcend the barrenness of life, and its stream of repetitive mechanical events, through an intellectualized system of chess moves. He converts his life into an endless chess game; his suicide may be interpreted as an ultimate transcendence of reality or as a defeat of character, an ambiguity characteristic of his style and posing of issues.

Nabokov's sense of ambiguity may be detected in later works as well when he deals with the fact of emigration and exile—should the flight be viewed as defeat by circumstances or victory over them? Nabokov's answer turns on the strength of the protagonist's values: it is victory and release if philosophical, metaphysical, and/or aesthetic values survive and retain their sustaining power; it is both defeat and victory by reason of recurrent loss of the event turned into insubstantial memory. In his novel *Kamera obskura* (1932; *Laughter in the Dark*, 1938), Nabokov deals with blind forces of passion and with his concept of slavery as a complex resulting from rigidity of view and irony of circumstance. In the novel *Podvig* (1932; *The Feat*, 1971), he examines the phenomena of exploitation, heroism, and moral behavior and recognizes in their public and private executions the mechanisms of social and historical determinism. The plot concerns a young Russian idealist who gives up the solitude of aristocratic withdrawal from the public arena and chooses direct political action; he decides to cross the borders of Soviet Russia to fight a battle in which he must engage. The novel's dramatic ending imparts a tone of stoicism and martyrology not common in Nabokov's other work. *Otchayanie* (1936; *The Despair*, 1937), written in first-person point of view, treats the contemporary leveling of values, the lack of profound joy and its converse, real disaster; all are reduced in Nabokov's eyes to a perfect ''anthill.'' This novel reflects his growing concern with man as a double being who never is one person till he accepts his duality; the dualism is that of the person who breaks the shell of conformity to find his individual voice.

Nabokov's next novel, *Invitation to a Beheading* (1938; 1959), was first published serially in the leading Russian émigré journal in Paris, *Sovremenye zapisky*; it is a dystopia in which human life is overwhelmed by the listless process of death and the stultification of political tyranny. Cincinnatus, the protagonist, lives in a prison where his consciousness of day and night blend, and the invitation to his own beheading becomes the possibility for catharsis, activity, and, ultimately, for freedom. Nabokov's longest novel in Russian, *Dar* (written 1937–38, published 1952; *The Gift*, 1963), was also first published in *Sovremenye zapisky*. In this work the object of artistic contemplation becomes the most valuable and at the same time the most vulnerable instrument for transformation of life; it becomes a gift for the artist and the artist's gift to his fellow beings. Filled with autobiographical reminiscences (the young poet's life in poverty and exile, his first love, and the death of his father), the novel is centered on the conflict between the gift of an artist and the inertia of mediocrity, the latter manifested in the voice of public opinion as embodied in the Russian radical critic Chernishevsky. *The Gift* is probably the most overt manifestation of Nabokov's dazzling gifts of literary imagination—allusions, puns, word puzzles, anagrams, teasing associations, and words of different levels climb and play their way throughout the text.

The first book written by Nabokov in English is *The Real Life of Sebastian Knight* (1941). It is apt that in changing languages with this work, he chose as his theme the question of identity and the roles that memory enacts in human lives. Nabokov had come to the United States in 1940 and supported himself by teaching jobs in American colleges. In *The Real Life of Sebastian Knight*, the protagonist, V. (compare his name to Nabokov's pseudonym, V. Sirin, a pseudonym Nabokov forsook on the publication of this book), tracks down his brother's life as if plotting out a detective story. The roles are reversed for imaginative play: the brother becomes the well-known novelist, and V. takes on an unknown quality. Nabokov shows in the course of V.'s adventures that V. must follow in his brother's footsteps in order to gain an awareness of self. At the end of the novel the reader is not sure if the brother really existed, or whether the brother's physical existence matters at all, since the brother is a vehicle for the protagonist's necessity to attain a sense of brotherhood. In *Sebastian Knight* Nabokov is clearly, if obliquely in technique, dealing with the questions of exile and identity attendant upon repatriation, and with memory as gain and potential for a new vision. By allowing imagination to gain the perspective of memory, re-vision becomes new vision.

During this period in his adopted country, Nabokov also wrote *Pnin* (1957), a comic, episodic novel based loosely on his teaching experiences at Cornell University. He published *Bend Sinister* in 1947, a novel with political concerns similiar to those in *Invitation to a Beheading*. The story is set in a Slavic country where absolutism provides for a surface of mediocrity running deep into everyone's bones. Danger is not dramatic in this novel; the real danger, Nabokov may be saying, lies in the loss of the contemplation and experience of danger. *Lolita* (1958), Nabokov's third book written in English, brought him world fame and fortune. The story of a middle-aged college professor who becomes infatuated with an American "nymphet," it aroused storms of controversy concerning its scenes of sexual behavior (and its premise of sexual liaison between a teenager and a much older man). Its hilarious presentation of scandalous material and its generous offerings of high style and ingenious wit rewarded Nabokov with great popularity and fortune (a film was made of it), and allowed Nabokov to retire from teaching duties. Characteristically, Nabokov moved to a hotel suite in Montreux, Switzerland in 1961, and lived and wrote there until his death. He retained his American citizenship.

Nabokov's following books include *Pale Fire* (1962), a satirical fantasy consisting of a long poem and a commentary written by a mad New England scholar who believes himself the exiled king of a mythical Balkan country. Nabokov's complex of Russia and America is manifested (and joined) in the fantasy world of his most complex work, *Ada or, Ardor: A Family Chronicle* (1969), where geography, chronology, history, and artistic recollections of family life are mixed in a capricious manner. Nabokov's literary translations and his volumes of criticism also form a significant part of his contribution to English-language culture. He developed a theory of literary translation in his translation of *The Song of Igor's Campaign: An Epic of the Twelfth Century* (1960). Carl R. Proffer, a leading Slavic critic, wrote that Nabokov's translation of Aleksandr Pushkin's *Eugene Onegin* (in four volumes with commentaries, 1964) "is a unique gift from one culture to another."

After 1930 Nabokov published 300 poems in Russian throughout his lifetime. A collection of them, *Stikhi*, was issued in 1979 (Ann Arbor, Michigan). Nabokov's son, Dmitri, reported in the summer of 1989 that a new collection of Nabokov's poems written in Russian and never issued in translation was in preparation. Also announced for publication in late 1989 was a collection of Nabokov's letters edited by his son and Matthew J. Bruccoli, one of Nabokov's students at Cornell University (and a writer and editor in his own right). The book, *Vladimir Nabokov: Selected Letters 1940–1977*, contains some 400 previously unpublished letters, many of them written in English, and covering a wide variety of interests.

Nabokov wrote two major plays, *Sobytiye* (1938, The Event) and *Isobreteniye Valsa* (1938; *Waltz Invention*, 1966). Among his critical works are *Notes on Prosody* (1964); *Nikolay Gogol* (1944); and *Mikhail Lermontov, A Hero of Our Time* (1958). In Switzerland he wrote two novels in English, *Transparent Things* (1972) and *Look at the Harlequins* (1974).

Nabokov's wonderfully evocative book of autobiography, *Speak Memory* (1966), was originally written and published as *Conclusive Evidence* (1951; *Drugie berega*, 1954) and later revised. It is required reading for an understanding of how he perceives memory as an agent for a perspective on history and as a reinvigoration of present time. Nabokov also has written short stories in which his language reaches a wondrous level of fluidity. He published three collections of stories, *Vozvrashtshenie Chorba* (1930; *The Return of Chorb*, 1976); *Soglyadatsy* (1938, Russian Recession); and *Vesna v Fialte* (1956; *Spring in Fialta*, 1956). An English-language edition of stories, *Tyrants Destroyed*, was issued in 1975.

Selected Titles: *Poems* (1959); *Poems and Problems* (1970); *Lolita: A Screenplay* (1974); *The Nabokov-Wilson Letters 1940–1971* (1979); *Lectures on Russian Literature* (1980; new collection with same title, 1981). Stories: *A Russian Beauty* (1975); *Details of a Sunset* (1976); *The Enchanter* (1986 [written 1939]). See also *Selected Letters 1940– 1977*, ed. Dmitri Nabokov and Matthew J. Bruccoli (1989).

Consult: Alfred A. Appel, Jr., *Nabokov's Dark Cinema* (1974); Alfred A. Appel, Jr., and Charles Newman, eds., *Nabokov: Criticism, Reminiscences, Translations, and Tributes* (1970); Brian Boyd, *Vladimir Nabokov: The Russian Years* (vol. 1 of planned 3-volume biography) (1990); L. S. Dembo, ed., *Nabokov: The Man and His Work* (1967);

Andrew Field, *Vladimir Nabokov: The Life and Art of Vladimir Nabokov* (1967; rev. ed.,
London, 1987). See also Andrew Field, comp., *Nabokov: A Bibliography* (1973).

ARKADY ROVNER and MARTIN TUCKER

NADERPUR, Nader. *See* Iranian Writers in Exile

NAIPAUL, Shiva. Born February 25, 1945, in Port of Spain, Trinidad; died
August 13, 1985, in London, England. Naipaul's grandfather was a former
indentured laborer on a Trinidadian sugar plantation who made good. Naipaul
saw the Trinidad where he spent the first nineteen years of his life as a disintegrating society where sham spiritualism could on occasion be used to justify
the virulently materialistic superstructure of the colonial outpost. From 1964 to
1966, Naipaul attended University College, Oxford, where he got a degree in
Chinese, and a young English wife as well. His first two works were novels:
Fireflies (London, 1970) and *The Chip-Chip Gatherers* (New York, 1973). Both
received wide critical acclaim for their uncommitted, ironic, traditionally narrative depiction of Trinidadian society. In 1970, he won both the Jock Campbell
New Statesman award and the Winifred Holtby Memorial Prize. In 1971, he
received the John Llewellyn Rhys Memorial Prize and in 1973 the Whitbread
Award for Fiction. Naipaul's next works were documentary, rather than fictional,
and were less enthusiastically received by the critics. The first of them, *North
of South: An African Journey* (New York, 1978), documents Naipaul's travels
in Kenya and Tanzania, where he recorded the effects of postcolonialism and
its politics. Written as a string of encounters with African natives, *North of
South* was unfavorably compared to the travel works of Paul Theroux. In his
anger at the Africans for the way they perpetuate white privilege at the expense
of Asian dignity, Naipaul alienated many readers. His *Journey to Nowhere* (New
York, 1981) is probably the best extended piece of investigation of the Jim Jones/
Guyana massacre, although charges of insensitivity to the black victims have
been raised. Naipaul also wrote a fictional account of Guyana in *Love and Death
in a Hot Country* (London, 1984) that was praised for its descriptive powers and
realistic portraits. Though Shiva Naipaul is almost never considered in his own
right without obligatory mention of his famous older brother, V. S. Naipaul,*
Shiva Naipaul's views on the personal effects of racist society merit distinct
attention.

Selected Titles: *The Chip-Chip Gatherers* (London, 1982); *Fireflies* (Middlesex, England, 1983, c. 1970); *Beyond the Dragon's Mouth* (1984), stories and sketches; *An
Unfinished Journey* (London, 1986).

Consult: *Contemporary Literary Criticism*, vol. 32 (1973); David D'Arcy, "Lost in a
Landscape of Neglect," *New Leader* 67, no. 9 (May 28, 1984); John Darnton, "Black
and White and Middleman," *New York Times Book Review* (May 6, 1979).

JUDITH M. BRUGGER

NAIPAUL, V. S. (Vidiadhar Surajprasad). Born August 17, 1932, in Chag-
uanas, Trinidad; he lives in London and travels frequently round the world as a
journalist. Naipaul may be viewed as a triple exile—born of Brahmin parents

on a West Indian island, he was a member of neither the black majority nor the white power structure. Within the milieu of his family, he felt as great a sense of isolation. His kin's Hindu practices, customs, and beliefs had become, in Naipaul's eyes, absurd shadows of their original potency. From an early age (in a hyperbolic moment he placed it before his first decade), Naipaul said he wanted to be a writer—the act of writing gave form to a life composed of illusions. By age eleven he wanted to leave his birthplace for London, the great center of the Western empire—here he would find, he believed, the focus that would enable him to return one day to the insular spoke of the wide wheel of literary fulfill-ment.

Naipaul left his island home in 1950 at age eighteen to study at Oxford University on a scholarship. During this period his father, Seepersad Naipaul, with whom Naipaul had established, in his words, the "big relationship," died. Naipaul was profoundly grieved; he wrote that "My father was extremely im-portant in my childhood; nearly everything that I am, I am because of this great link I felt with him, and a lot of my work—especially my early work—I meant to be dedicated to him." After graduation, Naipaul worked as a journalist in London; he met his future wife, Patricia Ann Hale, in a canteen at the British Broadcasting Company offices, where both were employed.

Naipaul is not a wanderer in search of roots. He knows that each place has unique displacements that must be accepted as part of the nature of the universe. He has seized the task of putting things into place through observation and writing, of establishing order in a chaos of pluralistic decadence, as a necessity for his own psychological salvation. His first four books reveal a gently comic ironist. In these works he re-creates the Trinidad of his youthful mind, full of tricks and self-deceptions but also warmth and sheltering modes. Naipaul's first-written book (it was published after two later-written works), the collection of stories *Miguel Street* (London, 1959), is patterned after his father's only published fiction, *Gurudeva and Other Indian Tales* (Port of Spain, Trinidad, 1943). In this collection, as in *The Mystic Masseur* (London, 1957) and *The Suffrage of Elvira* (London, 1958), the two novels that preceded its publication, linked characters and ideas suggest a pattern of quest as an alternative to the confusion aswirl in the Trinidadian milieu. In these three early works that fantasy is an easy antidote to a life of poverty and debased culture. The trickster—both the street rogue and the rogue minister/swami/guru of Hindu culture and "Scientific Thought"—becomes the people's royalty until these villainous clowns are un-masked in turn. Naipaul is not sentimental in these novels, but he is kind to his devious characters because they fill a need in a decadent society. If their rituals are shoddy vestiges they provide, at least, some contact with a spirit beyond the presence of their physical and material worlds. Ultimately both deceiver and deceived will be exposed in Naipaul's novels, but their end is comedic and their world continues the next day with another foible: the fables of their lives are not transformed.

In his third novel, *A House for Mr. Biswas* (London, 1961), Naipaul completed the first stage of his exilic journey. Writing of Trinidad in London, writing of his childhood (the novel is autobiographical), Naipaul put his "house" of memories into order. The work is dedicated to his father and is a tribute to that gentle, bumbling man who created a world of intrinsic value while everyone else thought him a foolish failure. The climax of the novel comes with the acquisition of a house—through its possession one comes home to die in the dignity of one's appointed place in the universal scheme of things. Mr. Biswas's search for a house, or rather the means to buy one, and the many houses other people occupy, tear down, or rent out in their lack of respect for radiating forms of tradition, represent Naipaul's tribute to the values by which his father lived. Foolish though Mr. Biswas may have been in the world's eyes, saddled with debts he could not shake off, he achieved his dream and left it behind for his family.

After *A House for Mr. Biswas* Naipaul felt a certain depletion, inevitable in that he had consumed his creative energy in the shaping of a vision to serve as the foremost link with his father. The novel triumphs over exile by the creation of a house/home, but curiously—or perhaps not so curiously in the canon of exile—its completion began another odyssey of wandering for Naipaul. He traveled to India and Trinidad, wrote nonfiction accounts of his visits there in his characteristic employment of travel as a field of puzzling facts to be put into journalistic reports. (See *The Middle Passage: The Caribbean Revisited* [London, 1962] and *An Area of Darkness: An Experience of India* [London, 1964]). He published two books of fiction, the novel *Mr. Stone and the Knights Companion* (London, 1963) and the short story collection *A Flag on the Island* (London, 1967), parts of which had been written earlier. These two books reveal Naipaul in feeble style and spirit.

Naipaul's second breakthrough, or stage of battle with exile, surfaced in 1967. With the publication of *The Mimic Men*, Naipaul showed he had turned from a subtle and personal treatment of displacement, and the cunning by which artists of eccentric shapes and rogue kinds live, to a more direct encounter with social and political forces by which strong protagonists are tested. *The Mimic Men* treats of a West Indian political leader in exile in London writing his memoirs. Unlike the pattern in *Mr. Biswas*, the hero realizes he cannot hold onto what has irretrievably become a thing of the past.

Like other colonialist and postcolonialist writers, Naipaul uses the history of place as a setting-point for his fictional explorations. After *The Mimic Men* he needed new fields to stimulate his quest, and Africa became his locus as well as Trinidad. In the two novels and one collection of stories that appeared between 1971 and 1979, he used Africa as an illustration of exploitation. This exploitation is no longer to be seen so much in Africa's rape by imperialist forces but in the manipulation of African natives by homegrown dictators with the support of alien mercenary fantasists who prefer the illusion of an African refuge to the alternative of bleaker realities at home. In the title story in *In a Free State* (London, 1971), three "displaced" persons find no change in their sense of freedom in a newly independent country since their inner states remain unplowed.

In *Guerrillas* (London, 1975), possibly Naipaul's most bitter work, a revolutionary activist (modeled on Adam Malik/Michael X) murders an English girl in sympathy with the commune's stated aims, but Naipaul's portrayal, at least in part, ridicules the truths of her beliefs by presenting them as a cover for sexual and political titillation; correspondingly, Jimmy, the activist, is presented as a man filled with his own doubts about the motivations of his political actions. In *A Bend in the River* (London, 1979), Naipaul's black strokes of anger are grayed by a wash of compassion for the displaced and confused protagonist, Salim, a young Indian businessman. Salim has bought a shop in an independent Central African state from another Indian merchant shrewd enough to sell out before the political winds topple his investment. Both the protagonist and his foil are parallel characters to the two distinct types of personality in *A House for Mr. Biswas*—the foolish but compassionate Indian open to experience and yearning for meaning to shape his malleable forms of understanding, and the mercantile mind that sees all experience in the primacy of economic success and/or failure. Salim loses his shop, but he will move on to another bend in the river, like Mr. Biswas; social and economic failure will not diminish his self-value, and his own values in an at best indifferent society. A far worse fate awaits a European couple, the wife of whom is having an affair with Salim. Both she and her husband, dependent for their sense of worth on their political status, are cast aside by the new dictator of the country. Having only a materialist scale of values, they have no recourse. They become the new displaced people—the white European colonialists who think they can make a deal with the progress of history and find they are beyond redemption as far as a role in African society is concerned.

Naipaul's view of the world as seen in his later work is bleak. All the world is a void and all the world is in exile, for displacement is the natural condition of historic determinism. Naipaul sees all alternatives as wanting, since no moment can be more than a dated fact in a currency of report. Rituals are necessary as a satisfaction of human need, but the rituals are vital only so long as the faith they conjure up in the image reflects a corresponding belief. In Naipaul's experience ritual and belief have not been constant companions, and alternatives—which are the desperate crutch of an exile losing his place of identity—have no certitude of continuity. What Naipaul presents is a world that cannot be trusted, a world in which alternatives inevitably prove devious.

Yet the fact that Naipaul keeps writing is proof he has not given up on postcolonial mankind. What follows surrender to indifferent determinism can be only an apathy of silence: Naipaul's rage at the world's stupidities, limited to no one group but enveloping Indian and African history as well as the data on political independencies that have followed the collapse of modern imperialism, represents a plea for an end to evasions employed to deny the presence of emptiness. Naipaul has not found a resolution to his perceived awareness of all alternatives leading to the same void through different swamps, but his anger and his bitterness of expression show he is not ready to give up on his struggles for the achievement of a sustaining vision through literary art.

Naipaul has also written essayistic commentary that is more personalized observation than social and historical analysis. Among his studies are *The Loss of El Dorado: A History* (London, 1969), *The Overcrowded Barracoon, and Other Articles* (London, 1972), and *India: A Wounded Civilization* (London, 1977). In his recent novel, *The Enigma of Arrival* (1987), he sums up his exilic stance in the image of a Giorgio De Chirico painting: a lone traveler on a high sea before a strange door. Danger lurks beyond the door, but the other world, the one promising strange new knowledge, beckons. In Naipaul's recounting of his dream vision, he is rescued from the danger before he steps into it, but when he looks again at the De Chirico painting he realizes he cannot find the door in it; that door has been shut to him. In Naipaul's parallel to the exilic experience— he further describes an Englishwoman whose letter he will not answer because to do so will bring up the past of their association, a moment between them that cannot be recaptured thirty years later—Naipaul is drawing again on the protectionist device of closing doors on memory's pain. The territory of the exile, in Naipaul's case, is displacement, and given its nature, it cannot be removed since memory always brings it back. That is its paradox, and the strength of Naipaul's painful, grating art.

Naipaul may be compared to James Joyce* as a cultural exile. Both writers fled their native lands for a larger European metropolis; both used exile and cunning as tools in their journey outward to inner revelation and psychological awareness of the void that lies in wait for them. Yet they differ in that Joyce provided a home for his bumbling hero, Leopold Bloom, in *Ulysses* and a rest, whether through sleep or awakening, for HCE in *Finnegans Wake*. Naipaul is more despairing and angry in his later work than in his earlier fiction; Joyce became more comedic as his works in progress shaped their ends. Joyce provided through Bloom and his wife Molly an alternative to the void in the midst of human intercourse. In Naipaul's universe the void is presently triumphant over any attempts to fill it.

Selected Titles: *The Return of Eva Peron with the Killings in Trinidad* (1980); *Among the Believers* (1981); *Finding the Center* (1984); *A Turn in the South* (1988); *India: A Million Mutinies Now* (London, 1990).

Consult: Robert Boyers, ed., *Salmagundi* 54 (Fall 1981), Special Naipaul issue; Andrew Gurr, *Writers in Exile: The Creative Use of Home in Modern Literature* (Brighton, England, 1981); Richard Kelly, *V. S. Naipaul* (1989); Maureen Warner, "Cultural Confrontation, Disintegration, and Syncretism in *A House for Mr. Biswas*," *Caribbean Quarterly* 16 (1970).

NAJDER, Zdzislaw. Born October 31, 1930, in Warsaw, Poland; he lives in Munich, West Germany. Najder was educated at the University of Warsaw, where he earned his master of philosophy degree in 1954, and at Oxford University (B.Litt., 1963); he holds a doctorate from the University of Warsaw (1970) and the D.Hab. from the Polish Academy of Sciences (1977). He was senior assistant at the Institute of Literary Research (Polish Academy of Sciences,

Warsaw) from 1952 to 1957, and senior assistant in the Philosophy Department at the University of Warsaw from 1958 to 1959. Najder spent a great part of his professional career lecturing abroad following his dismissal from the University of Warsaw during the purges of the 1960s. Because of his distrust of the Polish communist regime, and as a result of his affiliation with the underground intellectual coterie in Warsaw (he was a cofounder of the Polish League for National Independence), he was banned from work within Poland's borders. His scholarly reputation led to the intervention of the U.S. State Department in gaining an exit visa for him to teach in the United States. He has lectured at Columbia University (1966), Yale University (1966), University of California at Berkeley (1967) and at Davis (1968, 1970), and Stanford (1974–75), among others. He was coeditor of the critical journal *Tworczosc*, published in Warsaw, from 1957 to 1981. Najder is a member of the Polish PEN Club and was a member of the Polish Writers Union from 1957 to 1983.

In 1981, just prior to the institution of martial law and fearing arrest because of his activities with the Solidarity Union movement, Najder fled from Poland for permanent exile. He was tried in absentia in 1983 by the government on charges of spying for U.S. intelligence services; found guilty, he was sentenced to death.

Najder was director of the Polish service of Radio Free Europe from 1982 to 1990 and together with his wife, the translator Halina Teresa Carroll, lived in Munich. His writings include *Conrad's Polish Background* (London, 1964); (editor) *Joseph Conrad, Dziela* (Works), 27 vols. (Warsaw, 1972–74); *Values and Evaluations* (Clarendon, 1975); *Joseph Conrad, Congo Diary and Other Uncollected Pieces* (1975); *Joseph Conrad, A Chronicle* (1983), considered the standard Conrad biography.

HENRY SIKORSKI

On January 16, 1990, Polish television announced all charges against Najder had been "disproved" and his death sentence dissolved. Najder returned to Poland in February and is now president of Citizens' Committee for Lech Walesa.

NAZARETH, Peter. Born April 27, 1940, in Kampala, Uganda, of Goan (East Indian) parents; he lives and teaches in Iowa City, Iowa. Nazareth's father came from Goa, then ruled by the Portuguese, to Uganda; his mother was Goan but born in Malaysia, where her father had settled as a professional Western classical musician. As "Asians" Nazareth and his wife and children were expelled by the Idi Amin government in 1972. Nazareth's citizenship was taken away shortly after the expulsion order. Nazareth, who was senior finance officer in the Ministry of Finance at the time, wrote in a letter to the editor of this study that he believed Uganda was "my country and I believed (and there was evidence every day to prove I was right) that the majority of Ugandan Africans did not hate me or Asians in general. Eventually, my Ministry obtained for me an Exemption, which meant that I could stay on in the country and work, although I was stateless.

The head of my department in the Ministry of Finance told me to stay cool and to present a case for my citizenship a few weeks after the expulsion deadline. However, I received the Seymour Lustman Fellowship to Yale University and had to leave in January 1973 with my wife and two daughters: it was too soon to present a case to get back my citizenship, but the British came through and gave me a British passport (I was British before independence)."

Nazareth's first novel, *In a Brown Mantle*, was ironically published at the same time as his loss of Ugandan citizenship. As he describes it,

Actually, the announcement of the expulsion of Asians was made by Idi Amin nine days after my novel *In a Brown Mantle* was launched with full publicity by the East African Literature Bureau [EALB] in the Regional Headquarters of the East African Community in Kampala, with a write-up and photo on the front page of the *Uganda Argus* and with publicity on radio and T.V. My novel was handed to the publishers before Amin's coup but was published in mid–1972. It turned out to be prophetic of both the coup and the Asian expulsion. I was trying to maintain a very low profile, which was not easy to do as I was Senior Finance Officer in the Ministry of Finance: but the EALB said this was its first important novel and it wanted maximum publicity....

Finally, with the assistance of the American Ambassador, Thomas Melady, a writer on Africa himself, I left, with the intention of returning, but I have not returned physically to date. Instead, I came to Iowa and am currently Professor of English and African-American World Studies and Advisor to the International Writing Program. But I have returned through my writing. I wrote one of my most important essays, "Waiting for Amin: Two Decades of Ugandan Literature," for G. D. Killam, *The Writing of East and Central Africa* (London, 1985) at Iowa. I could not have written it in Uganda because the materials would not have been available. At the same time I returned to my ancestral home through writing: I edited the first major anthology of Goan literature. I have discovered myself that history can be real: that even if you do not want to go into exile, your history can send you into it. But exile has its rewards, to echo George Lamming*: I can do more in my writing and have more of a global vision than I could have had if I were at home. And from my experience with the writers of the world I have met in the International Writing Program at the University of Iowa, I have discovered that it is possible to be in exile at home. The ending of exile is an African and a Goan historical imperative.

Nazareth tells his expulsion story in fictional terms in his second novel, *The General Is Up*, which was accepted for publication by the Tanzanian successor to the East African Literature Bureau. The work was due out in 1980, with three sets of proofs being produced, but it has not yet appeared. An informal edition was issued by the Writers Workshop of Calcutta, India, in 1984.

In addition to his two novels, Nazareth has written radio plays, literary and critical commentary—*Literature and Society in Modern Africa* (East African Literature Bureau, Nairobi, Kenya, 1972; 2nd ed., 1980; published in the United States as *An African View of Literature*, 1974) and *The Third World Writer (His Social Responsibility)* (Kenya Literature Bureau, 1978)—and essays and short stories. He has edited two anthologies: *African Writing Today* (published by *Pacific Mona Quarterly*, 1981); and *Goan Literature: A Modern Reader* (published by *Journal of South Asian Literature*, Michigan State University, 1985, the only such anthology in print).

NEKRASOV, Viktor. Born July 17, 1911, in France of Russian émigré parents who had fled from czarist oppression; he returned to the USSR in 1921 with his parents; he lives in Paris, France. Nekrasov went into exile in the aftermath of a famous denunciation by Nikita Khrushchev, in which the Soviet leader decried the gulf of generations in contemporary Soviet society and laid part of the blame on writers like Nekrasov. The oration, dubbed the "fathers and sons speech" by Soviet analysts, linked Nekrasov to Ivan Turgenev's heroes in *Fathers and Sons* as a gifted intellectual unaware of the damaging chasms he was creating in his passive disavowals of Communist party goals. Khrushchev called on Nekrasov, as a prodigal son, to return to the fold of that society which had nurtured him and to which he owed his gifts.

For his part, Nekrasov had emphasized from his earliest works the human successes and the profound failures of the Soviet program, particularly in his re-creations of daily circumstance and human response to it; he refused to propagate the ethics of vision of official policy. In remaining truer to his artist's creed than to his role as a social realist, Nekrasov was seen by rigid theorists and party hacks as an enemy of the people; at best he was regarded as a debunker of Soviet myth. His first novel was *Vokopokh Stalingrada* (1946; it has been translated under various titles: *In the Trenches of Stalingrad*; *Front-Line Stalingrad*, and *Stalingrad*). The documentary fiction first appeared serially in the September and October 1947 issues of *Znamya* magazine and drew on Nekrasov's battlefield experiences (he was wounded in Lublin, Poland, fighting the invading Nazi armies). Although the work won the Stalin Prize, it was scored for its depiction of error and incompetence by Soviet army officers. In Nekrasov's version the courage of the Soviet people won the battle while the army barely missed losing it. Nekrasov's second novel, *Vrodnom gorode* (1945; it has been translated variously as *In the Native City* and *Back Home*), was published first in the October and November 1954 issues of *Novy Mir*. It occasioned a similar, ambivalent response among Soviet officialdom: a lukewarm praise for Nekrasov's portrait of Soviet soldiers coming home to a postwar weary and famished world, and a covert disapproval of Nekrasov's denigration of Soviet bureaucracy. *Kira Georgievna*, published in *Novy Mir* in July 1961, brought Nekrasov further difficulty. The tale described the love of a young woman sculptor for a twenty-year-old art student; they are separated when he is arrested and sent to a labor camp for twenty years. On his release the man and woman meet again, and the tragedy of their wasted lives—the man had been an innocent victim of Stalinist paranoia—becomes overwhelmingly apparent.

In 1962 Nekrasov published *Po obje storony okeana* (On Both Sides of the Ocean), a collection of essays in which he called on Soviet writers to express their views honestly and on Soviet censors to allow open criticism of social issues. The essays drew a heated response and controversy, which continued in the various reactions to a new Soviet phenomenon: a generation of youth no longer holding the same zealousness for the goals of their fathers and no longer willing to conform to a discipline that demanded political commitment to the point of exclusion of aesthetic satisfaction. In 1956 Khrushchev had denounced Stalin and Stalinist methodology and terrorism in what he termed the "cult of personality"; at the same time he pleaded with Soviet youth, Nekrasov among them as a leading voice, to stop profaning the imagery of socialist realism and to continue drawing portraits of the Revolution's glorious common men. In effect, Khrushchev was asking of a whole new generation that it shift its enthusiasm of response to poetry and art back to the first-generation barricades of communist solidarity. Nekrasov refused to renounce his artistic credo, and although he was not imprisoned, he found himself outside the pale of publishability.

Nekrasov left the Soviet Union for France when it became apparent to him that he could not do as his "fathers" and bureaucracy asked; his desire for freedom of expression was too strong to allow curtailment of it for whatever reasons. In France Nekrasov has continued writing but has not found much of a public for his work. He is reported to have said that going into exile was not only a tragedy for him, but a professional mistake.

Selected Title: *Pervoe Znakomstvo* (1958, First Acquaintance).

Consult: Vera Alexandrova, *A History of Soviet Literature, 1917–1962: From Gorky to Yevtushenko* (1963); Edward J. Brown, *Russian Literature since the Revolution* (1982); E. L. Crowley and Max Hayward, *Soviet Literature in the Sixties* (1965).

NERUDA, Pablo (pseudonym, adopted 1920, of Neftalí Reyes). Born July 12, 1904, in Parral, Chile; died September 23, 1973, in Santiago, Chile, of cancer. Neruda was born in a remote town surrounded by forests and valleys in the southern part of the country. His family was of limited means—his mother, a schoolteacher, died when he was a month old; his father was a railroad worker. A precocious child and an avid reader, he learned more from direct observation and contact with peers than from formal schooling, although he studied briefly with the exceptional teacher, writer, and Nobel Prize winner Gabriela Mistral. After finishing high school in Temuco, a nearby city, he went to the capital, Santiago, to continue his studies; he was planning to become a teacher of French language and literature. Neruda's personal philosophy at this time was close to anarchism. In 1927 he was appointed honorary consul of Chile in Rangoon, Burma. From 1927 to 1932 he lived in the Orient: Rangoon, Colombo, Calcutta, and Batavia. Basically without salary, lonely and depressed, he lived more like an expatriate than a diplomat. This period of self-exile was motivated mainly by a desire to escape his distressing economic situation in Chile; it gave birth to most of the best poems of one of Neruda's most famous books, *Residencia en la tierra*, published in Buenos Aires in a first limited edition in 1933 (translated into English as *Residence on Earth*, 1946). The poems are nightmarish cries haunted by disintegration and death, and employing many avant-garde techniques, especially those of surrealism. Neruda never acknowledged his debt to the surrealist movement; indeed he criticized surrealism bitterly. He was drawn instead to the communist movement during his years in the Orient, but he did not join the party at that time; he believed the surrealists, under André Breton,* were evolving into a Trotsky-like, inimical group.

Neruda's *Residence* poems, although difficult in technique and often in need of extended examination, make a powerful impact upon the reader. They express the loneliness and terror of man in an infinite world totally alien and hostile; they can be compared to an Inferno without promise of redemption and Paradise. Less structured and anchored in tradition than T. S. Eliot's *The Waste Land*, the poems nevertheless are equally important to the twentieth-century canon: if loneliness and anxiety are typical of the modern age and of this century's political and cultural "times of trouble," these poems are perhaps unsurpassed in expression of such existential attitudes. They generalize the emotions of alienation and despair that are very much part of the life of exile.

After his return to Chile in 1932, Neruda was appointed to a consular position in Buenos Aires in 1933. There he met Federico García Lorca, who was visiting Argentina, and started a friendship that would end only with Lorca's death in 1936 at the hands of a Francoist death squad.

It was probably the deep loneliness that Neruda experienced in the Orient that propelled him slowly but insistently to search for the solidarity of a common social cause. Unofficially since the years in the Orient, officially only in 1945, he felt himself bound by the ideals and goals of the Communist party. In 1934 he traveled to Spain as consul in Barcelona and later in Madrid. The politically charged atmosphere was to explode into the Spanish Civil War (1936–39), during which Neruda espoused with enthusiasm the cause of the Spanish Republic, raising money for it in France, in Chile, and elsewhere, helping resettle Spanish Republican refugees after the war was lost, contributing books and articles to the cause. *España en el corazón* (1937, Spain in My Heart), which was distributed to front-line Republican soldiers, expressed his solidarity with the Spanish Left and his condemnation of fascism. Back in Chile in 1945, after a period of diplomatic activity in Mexico, Neruda saw the need for a vast poem that would depict the whole American continent. This poem, begun as a hymn to Chile, would expand to embrace almost every country in Latin America and become the great *Canto General* (General Canto).

In 1946, after joining the Communist party and being elected senator, he gave his support to candidate González Videla for the presidency of Chile, assuming he was backing a man of the Left. Once elected, Videla switched to a conservative stance; Neruda became an embarrassment to the newly Rightist president. When Neruda complained about Videla's behavior, he was indicted as a seditious rebel and his parliamentary immunity was lifted: he went into hiding and soon afterward, in disguise, having grown a beard, he crossed the Andes and became an exile. He attended a peace congress in Paris, made his first visit to the Soviet Union, where he took part in the celebration of the 150th anniversary of Aleksandr Pushkin's birth, visited Poland and Hungary, traveled to Mexico with the French surrealist poet Paul Éluard, and took part in the Latin-American Congress of the Partisans for Peace. In Mexico he met for the second time Matilde Urrutia, a beautiful, intelligent, and sensitive compatriot he had first met in 1946, and their love affair, which was to last all their life, inspired some of his most passionate love poems. In 1950 *Canto General* was published in Mexico City, with illustrations by the artists Diego Rivera and David Alfaro Siqueiros. Although this book had been started in Chile, it was exile that allowed Neruda to see his continent in its grandeur and that gave the book its final shape. As a centerpiece of this book stands the poem "Heights of Machu Picchu," a fusion of nature and history, one of the essential poems in the Spanish language.

Neruda returned to Chile in 1952; he witnessed the beginning of a new era in Chilean politics, with his friend Salvador Allende serving as president of the country. Neruda died a few days after Allende was shot in the Presidential Palace while fighting an armed rebellion led by General Augusto Pinochet. Allende's administration was succeeded by the military takeover that has finally after many bitter years evolved into a democracy under President Aylwin.

Neruda wrote forty-two books of poems and his *Memoirs*. Many critics consider the two volumes he wrote in exile, *Residence on Earth* and *General Canto*, his finest work. His *Obras Completas* was published in Buenos Aires in 1962.

Consult: René de Costa, *The Poetry of Pablo Neruda* (1979); Manuel Duran and Margery Safir, *Earth Tones: The Poetry of Pablo Neruda* (1981).

MANUEL DURAN

NEUMANN, Robert. Born May 22, 1897, in Germany; he died 1975, in England. Neumann's wit early distinguished his writing. He remained a humorist and parodist throughout his literary career. His satires developed a darker humor during his exile, but his trademark qualities—a parody of his own voice and style, as well as accurate and satiric parodies of other writers—never exited from his literary domain. Neumann was an expert in writing an entire novel in the voice of any one of his characters. Like James Joyce,* he shifted point of view and tonal, linguistic ambience to achieve a juncture of seemingly disjointed effects. Like Joyce, he was a comic virtuoso not able to resist a pun or a chance to play with words. If, unlike Joyce, he did not reach profound heights, he produced a number of solid comedic social and political satires.

Neumann was one of many German-language writers whose works were burned by the National Socialists in their public conflagration in 1933 of "decadent" culture. After his flight to England in 1934, he wrote in both German and English, and became a British citizen. Some of his work appeared first in English.

As a youth Neumann had studied chemistry and German literature in Vienna; in his young manhood, he managed a chocolate factory and later became an officer in a large corporation. He lost all his savings when the corporation failed; he took to the high seas, working round the world as an able-bodied seaman.

After he published his good-humored satire, *Mit fremden Federn*, he grew rich again, and famous for the first time. The ability to laugh at personal circumstances remained a guiding principle in Neumann's life. He refused to allow exile to daunt him or to produce melancholy within him. Yet while he thrived on adaptation, and wit as a means of adaptation, he spurned any compromise with the acknowledgement of the moral perversity of National Socialism. Consequently he remained in England after World War II, refusing to return to the country which had first nurtured his talents.

Selected Titles: *Sir Basil Zaharoff: Der Konig der Waffen* (1934, The Munitions King); *Struensee* (1935, republished 1953 as *Der Favorit der Konigin*, The Favorite of the Queen); *By the Waters of Babylon* (London, 1939); *Scene in Passing* (1942); *Children of Vienna* (1946; German version *Kinder von Wien*, 1948); *Die Puppen von Poshansk* (1952, The Dolls of Poshansk); *Madame Sephardi* (1960); *Olympia* (1961); *Festival* (London, 1962); *Damon Weib* (1969, Demon Women).

Parody: *Unter falscher Flagge* (1932).

Memoirs: *Mein altes Haus in Kent* (1957, My Old House in Kent); *The Plague House Papers* (London, 1959).

Commentary: *Twenty-three Women: The Story of an International Traffic* (London, 1940); *Deutschland diene Osterreicher. Osterreich, deine Deutschen* (1970, Germany, Your Austrians. Austria, Your Germans). See also *Gesammelte Werke in Einzelausgaben* (1959–   , Collected Works in Single Editions).

Consult: Kurt Desch, ed., *Robert Neumann: Stimmen der Freunde. Der Romancier und sein Werk* (1957).

NGUGI wa Thiong'o (formerly James Ngugi). Born January 5, 1938, in Limuru, Kenya; he lives in London. Kenya's foremost novelist and dramatist earned a B.A. in English at Makerere University in Uganda in 1964 and then worked as a journalist for Nairobi's *Daily Nation* for half a year before leaving Kenya again to continue his studies in literature at the University of Leeds in England. He returned home in 1967 and taught in the English Department at Nairobi University College until January 1969, when he resigned in protest during a students strike. He lectured in African literature at Northwestern University in Illinois in 1970–71, then resumed teaching at Nairobi University College, where he soon was appointed acting head of the English Department. In December 1977 he was arrested by the Kenyan government and detained for a year; no formal charges were ever filed against him, but it is assumed that his involvement in an adult literacy campaign aimed at raising the political consciousness of peasants and workers in his hometown of Limuru led to his imprisonment. When he was released, he was unable to regain his position at the university. In 1982 he went to England at the invitation of his publisher (Heinemann Educational Books) to launch a novel he had written while in detention. During his absence there was an attempted coup in Kenya, after which a number of his friends and associates fled the country. Since that time Ngugi has lived in exile in London.

Ngugi's literary works have been concerned with major social, cultural, and political problems in Kenya, past and present. His first two novels, *Weep Not,*

Child (1964) and *The River Between* (1965), set in the colonial period of his childhood, focus on the traumatic effects of the Mau Mau uprising on Gikuyu family life and on the impact of the independent schools movement on rural Gikuyu society. His third novel, *A Grain of Wheat* (1967), written while he was a student at Leeds, combines memories of the Mau Mau era with a depiction of Kenya on the eve of independence. It was a time of great bitterness, Ngugi claims, "for the peasants who fought the British yet who now see all that they fought for being put on one side." In *Petals of Blood* (1977), his longest and most complex novel, he describes in even greater detail the exploitation of Kenya's masses by its own established elite. Ngugi has always sympathized with the oppressed and underprivileged people in his nation. Before independence this included most Kenyans, for the country was being ruled by foreigners, but after independence he showed that it was the poor, rural, working-class people who suffered most, this time at the hands of their more fortunately placed compatriots who controlled all the levers of political and economic power. Ngugi's primary target of criticism has thus shifted from colonialism to neo-colonialism.

This stance is most evident in the works he wrote after *Petals of Blood*. For the adult literacy campaign in Limuru he coauthored in Gikuyu a musical, *Ngaahika Ndeenda* (1980; *I Will Marry When I Want*, 1982), which exposed the hardships of the landless poor and the greed and arrogance of wealthy landowners. In a subsequent Gikuyu novel, *Caitaani Mutharaba-ini* (1980; *Devil on the Cross*, 1982), he turned to allegory and transparent symbolism to indict the evils of capitalism in contemporary Kenya. Another of his Gikuyu musical dramas that stirred controversy in Kenya in 1981, *Maitu Njugira* (Mother, Sing for Me), has not yet been published. Ngugi has said that it was his imprisonment that persuaded him to persist in writing novels and plays in Gikuyu so that he could convey his message directly to the exploited masses among his people.

However, he continues to write his political and cultural essays in English in order to reach a broad international audience. His miscellaneous pieces have been collected in four volumes: *Homecoming: Essays on African and Caribbean Literature, Culture and Politics* (1971), *Writers in Politics* (1981), *Barrel of a Pen: Resistance to Repression in Neo-Colonial Kenya* (1983), and *Decolonising the Mind: The Politics of Language in African Literature* (1986). He has also produced an autobiographical work based on his year behind bars (*Detained: A Writer's Prison Diary*, 1981) and an essay on educational policy (*Education for a National Culture*, 1981). In all of his writings Ngugi has attacked injustice and oppression and championed the cause of the poor and dispossessed in Kenya. This has earned him a reputation as an opponent of the current Kenyan regime. He is East Africa's most prolific and most politically engaged author.

Selected Title: *Matigari* (1989).

Consult: David Cook and Michael Okenimpke, *Ngugi wa Thiong'o: An Exploration of His Writings* (1982); G. D. Killam, *An Introduction to the Writings of Ngugi* (1981);

David Maugham-Brown, *Land, Freedom and Fiction: History and Ideology in Kenya* (London, 1986); C. B. Robson, *Ngugi wa Thiong'o* (1979). See also Carol Sicherman, *Ngugi wa Thiong'o: A Bibliography of Primary and Secondary Sources, 1957–1987* (1989).

BERNTH LINDFORS

Practicing what he preaches, Ngugi's newest novel, *Matigari* (London, 1989), was written first in Gikuyu (during Ngugi's exile in London in 1983), then translated into English. The creative procedure represents Ngugi's pervasive concern for identification by native roots and obliteration of his colonial past. Agitprop in its use of stern political moralisms, the novel treats the story of a Mau Mau leader, released from prison, who returns to a postindependent Kenya and finds he is not welcome there. Matigari also finds that the new Kenyan government is as corrupt as the old colonialist one, preferring ease and comfort to the austerity of a communist-inspired social program for the people. However, Matigari finds his reward in the support of the peasants, who revere both the memory of his past struggles and his continuing ideals; his fame and support continue to grow among them. The field between easy corruption and puritan vision becomes ripe for open trenches of warfare, and Matigari must face, once again, the choice between a struggle for a pure Marxist-Leninist dream and a compromising, adulterated political future. In making his choice, Matigari becomes aware once more of how rapacious and prosecutorial a postindependent bureaucracy, and its army support, can be to people who oppose its policies.

NIN, Anaïs. Born February 21, 1903, in Neuilly, France; died January 14, 1977, in Los Angeles, California. Nin's father was the Cuban composer, Joaquin Nin; her mother was of Danish birth. When her father deserted the family in 1914 in Paris, Nin's mother took the family to the United States. Nin began keeping a diary from this time on, first writing in French and then some six years later in English. She was educated in Europe, returned to New York where she married a Scotsman, Hugh Guiler, in 1923. In 1925 the couple left for Paris, where Guiler worked in finance in the French capital. After the stock market crash of October 1929, the couple was obliged to change residences from their expensive Paris flat to a house in Louveciennes, a suburb west of Paris. Despite their reduced circumstances, Nin continued as a patron of the arts who kept a diary of her meetings with writers and her personal reflections on art and aesthetics. (The *Diary*, later published in seven volumes, was to prove her lasting monument.) She studied psychology with Otto Rank in 1934–35 and underwent extensive analysis; the analysis influenced her literary work, most apparent in her fiction, and the training led to professional occupation in New York in the 1940s, when Nin was in need of money.

Nin was a believer in open expression of sexuality as a way to personal well-being. Like Ernest Hemingway,* she believed that morality was what you felt good after doing. She denied any prohibition in human relationships that was based on social, rather than independent, judgment and charity. Nin practiced her beliefs not in a promiscuous manner but in a long literary, intellectual, and briefly sexual relationship with her friend, Henry Miller,* whom she helped to publication (with borrowed funds, she paid the printing costs in Paris of *The Tropic of Cancer*). Nin's relationship with her husband continued both before and after her meeting with Miller; the Nin-Guiler marriage came to an end only with Nin's death. Nin also had an affair with Miller's second wife, June Edith Smith, who had come to Paris to visit Miller in 1932. After her one night with June, Nin consummated her relationship with Henry Miller in a dingy Paris hotel. She describes the climactic event in her diary.

Nin returned to the United States with the advent of World War II. Her fiction, dominated by the consciousness of psychological determinism, found little audience in war-stricken America, and publishers were reluctant to print her work. She founded her own press, the Gemov Press, to publish her works in the early 1940s. By the mid–1950s she had achieved a limited reputation, and in the 1960s her work began to prove popular, both through its own merit and through her association with Henry Miller and the circle of psychoanalysts she had known and frequented in Paris and the United States. *The Diary* (7 vols., 1931–1974) brought her a celebrity status and many public speaking engagements. Nin's work, situated in a density of psychological tissue, is permeated with an awareness of the role of psychology in creativity.

At the end of her life Nin could be said to have come home. The aristocratic insider was welcomed as a celebrated and brave eccentric who had rubbed her elegant shoulders with the rough and vital Henry Millers of the world and not only survived, but gained a dynamism all her own. With her psychoanalytic scalpel she presented a direction for the new young generation.

Selected Titles: Novels: *House of Incest* (1936); *Cities of the Interior* (1959, enlarged version, 1974 [consists of five novels: *Ladders to the Fire*, 1946; *Children of the Albatross*, 1947; *The Four-Chambered Heart*, 1950; *A Spy in the House of Love*, 1954; *Solar Barque*, 1958, reissued in enlarged edition as *Seductions of the Minotaur*, 1961]). See also *D. H. Lawrence: An Unprofessional Study* (1932); *A Woman Speaks: The Lectures, Seminars, and Interviews of Anaïs Nin* (1975); *Henry and June* (1986).

Consult: Evelyn Hinz, *The Mirror and the Garden: Realism and Reality in the Writings of Anaïs Nin* (rev. ed. 1973); Bettina Knapp, *Anaïs Nin* (1978); Henry Miller, *Letters to Anaïs Nin* (1965); Gunther Stuhlmann, Introduction in *A Literate Passion: Letters of Anaïs Nin and Henry Miller 1932–53*, ed. G. Stuhlmann (1987).

NKOSI, Lewis. Born 1936 in Durban, South Africa; he lives in Lusaka, Zambia, and teaches at the University of Zambia. Nkosi attended Zululand public schools and enrolled at a technical college in Durban for a year before turning to professional journalism. He worked on a Zulu-English weekly, *Ilanga lase Natal* (Natal Sun); in 1956 he began writing for *Drum* magazine and served as an editor of the *Golden City Post* in Johannesburg. Nkosi came to the United States in 1961 on a Nieman fellowship for independent journalism study at Harvard University; after his departure the government refused him permission to reenter South Africa.

Nkosi's work was banned in South Africa under terms of the Suppression of Communism Act. Nkosi lived and worked in England for several years as a journalist and television moderator for African literary programs and transcription services. He also taught at the University of California at Irvine and elsewhere before moving to Zambia. He has written two books of literary criticism, *Home and Exile and Other Selections* (1965) and *Tasks and Masks* (1981), as well as collected editions of his plays.

In 1986 Nkosi published his first novel, *Mating Birds*; it tells the story of a condemned twenty-five-year-old black man's recollections of his obsession with a white woman as he awaits execution for his alleged rape of her. Ndi Sibiya reflects in his jail cell how he met Veronica Slater on a Durban beach, he on the "colored only" side, she on the border of the "white beach." They did not speak but made contact in pantomime every day through the hazy air that communicated their erotic passion and established its psychological and worldly consequences. At the end of a week of simulated sexuality on the hot beach, separated from each other by the color "bar," Sibiya followed Veronica to her home, entered her bedroom, and consummated their affair. On leaving the house he was observed by a neighbor and beaten and taken into detention. Nkosi filters his tale through the words of Sibiya and through the observations of a Swiss pathologist, a supposed outsider, who has become obsessed with understanding the riddles and contrarieties of apartheid. In showing how apartheid, like Shakespeare's villain Iago in his progress of lies, weaves a web that entraps all—victims and supposed victors alike—Nkosi shows a compassionate anguish and ambivalence more pronounced than the anger found in his early dramatic work. As seen through his protagonist Sibiya's suspended view of an ever-present sun hanging above the unyieldingly dry South African landscape, the novel is reminiscent of Albert Camus's *The Stranger*, in which colonial, racist prejudice and fear dam the yearning of individuals of two cultures, one temporarily dominant and the other temporarily subject, to unite in an embrace. Nkosi's story may also be read as a portrait of miscegenation and liberalism's refusal to accept responsibility for the continuation of apartheid. In dealing with the complex of miscegenation and the master-slave relationship, Nkosi has written, in the words of Henry Louis Gates, Jr., "a political indictment of racist South Africa" (*New York Times Book Review*, May 18, 1986, p. 5).

NORTJE, Arthur. Born in 1942 in Oudtshoorn, Cape Province, South Africa; he committed suicide through an overdose of prescribed drugs in Oxford in 1970. Nortje was classified as a "Cape Coloured" by the South African government— that is, as any mixture of indigenous South African heritage (Hottentot or Bush people) and/or European/Asian background. As a "Coloured" he was allowed to attend only segregated schools (he graduated from University College of the Western Cape in 1964) and taught English briefly before leaving for Jesus College of Oxford University in 1965. In 1967 Nortje went to Canada to teach in British Columbia and in Toronto. He returned to Oxford to work for a doctorate, but despondent over his status as a "marginal" person, one forever sentenced to inner exile, he killed himself in 1970. His work has received renewed attention recently. In *English in Africa* (May 1984), Jacques Berthoud, a fellow South African writer-scholar in exile, wrote: "Nortje is pre-eminently a poet of the sixties; his work seems to me to be a classic expression of the character of that decade—of that interval of immobility and silence between the collapse of liberalism and the rise of black consciousness, when the might of the state seemed everywhere unchangeable and unchanging..." (p. 6). Berthoud claims that Nortje's poetry is not protest poetry,

but the poetry of nightmare: the poet is altogether too implicated in what he describes. We know, of course, that the despair of political impotence tends to turn society into nature. This is an effect of projection: it is to be doubted whether the political refugees whom Nortje thinks of as burnt offerings were as "broken" as he represents them.... Nortje's poetry, then, is a symptom as well as a diagnosis; to this double office it owes a good deal of its status as an expression of the consciousness of his epoch. Its ambivalence cannot be understood outside its author's history as a so-called coloured; by virtue of its location in his personal biography, his neurosis has public resonances. Unlike the black, or for that matter the white, who have access to their own myths and who can distance themselves without loss of definition from an equally distinct opponent, Nortje sees himself as the inheritor of both traditions. (p. 7).

Berthoud believes that Nortje's exile poetry is of important critical concern because

it raises in an acute form the question of the use of literature. Professor R. N. Egudu provides a direct illustration of this. In an essay on responses to apartheid published five years ago [*Modern African Poetry and the African Predicament*, London, 1978] he says of Nortje's verse that it is "mainly concerned with self-pity resulting from loneliness in exile and general racial discrimination," and that its final effect is to "sap the energy for action." That this objection is not only political but also critical Egudu makes clear by placing Nortje with those poets who have, as he says, "merely sung their sorrows," and whose singing sounds "like a weak-limbed dirge." If Nortje's poetry slackens the springs of action, it is the genre to which it belongs that is partly to blame. Nortje's case would seem to require us to call into question a whole conception of poetry dominant in post-Romantic Europe, of which the confessional lyric is the type. (p. 2).

In the words of M. F. J. Chapman, Nortje realized after his departure from South Africa that "alienation is ultimately not a matter of geography, but of temperament: an inability to form enduring personal relationships." Nortje's exile is then both self-imposed and the result of color persecution.

Selected Titles: *Dead Roots* (London, 1973); see also *Lonely Against the Light*, ed. Guy Butler and Ruth Hartnett, in *New Coin Poetry* (Grahamstown, S.A.) 9, nos. 3–4 (1973).

Consult: M.F.J. Chapman, "Arthur Nortje: Poet of Exile," *English in Africa* (Grahamstown) 6, no. 1 (1979): 60–71; Charles Dameron, "Arthur Nortje, Craftsman for his Muse," in *Aspects of South African Literature*, ed. Christopher Heywood (London, 1976), pp. 155–62; R. G. Leitch, "Nortje: Poet at Work," *African Literature Today*, no. 10 (London, 1979): 224–30.

NOVAK, Jan. Born 1953 in Kolin, Czechoslovakia; he lives in Chicago, Illinois. Novak left Czechoslovakia at age sixteen when his family emigrated in 1969. They lived for a year in Traiskirchen, a transit camp 25 kilometers south of Vienna, and in June 1970 received permission to enter the United States, whereupon they came to Chicago. Novak tried to hold onto his Czech heritage, in part through writing all his poems in Czech. In the mid–1970s he began translating his poems into English, ostensibly to enter them in American poetry contests. He now realizes that his conversion of language was the beginning of a new phase, a self-mandate to write for American readers in English about his American experiences, and the parallel forsaking of writing about Czechs in Czech for Czech exile readers. Novak also moved from poetry to fiction writing as his principal genre. In 1983, as he decided to stop writing a novel in Czech and to begin writing it in American English directly without the distancing of translation, the material "poured out of me." He realized consciously that he was "trading languages," particularly when he began dreaming in English and even his Czech friends (in his dreams) began speaking in English. Out of these experiences he fashioned his first published novel *The Willys Dream Kit* (1985). His second novel, *The Grand Life* (1987), provided the final step of baptism into American English. In this novel about the American corporate world, no Czechoslovakians played significant parts in the theme, and Novak chose to replicate only, and peculiarly, American English.

Novak now considers himself a "Chicago writer," though he still teaches his children Czech (so they will not forget their heritage), and he still breaks into Czech on occasion and without premeditation, largely when he is excited or disturbed. He refers to the present stage of his life as an apron of linguistic schizophrenia, a condition exacerbated when he reads the Czech translations done by others of his work written originally in English. At such moments, he says, he feels the confusion of not knowing what he has lost, and that he must find what he has lost, since he misses it even if he doesn't know what it is.

Consult: Jan Novak, "The Typewriter Made Me Do It," *The New York Times Book Review*, April 2, 1989.

NYKA-NILIŬNAS, Alfonsas (pseudonym of Alfonsas Čipkus). Born July 15, 1919, in Utena, Eastern Lithuania; he lives in Baltimore, Maryland. Nyka-Niliŭnas studied Romance languages and literatures as well as philosophy at the Universities of Kaunas and Vilnius, graduating from the latter in 1942. After leaving Lithuania in 1944, he did postgraduate work at the Universities of Tübingen and Freiburg. In 1949, he arrived in the United States, where he joined the editorial board of the Lithuanian cultural monthly *Aidai* (Echoes), and was one of the founders of the avant-garde literary magazine *Literatŭros lankai* (The Literary Folios, 1952–59). For many years, he was employed at the Library of

Congress. Nyka-Niliūnas has published five volumes of poetry: *Praradimo simfonijos* (1946, The Symphonies of Loss), *Orféjaus medis* (1954, The Tree of Orpheus), *Balandžio vigilija* (1957, The Vigil of April), *Vyno stebuklas* (1974, Miracle of Wine), and *Žiemos teologija* (1985, Winter's Theology). Four of these books have won literary awards. His poetry has been influenced by Friedrich Hölderlin, Charles Baudelaire, Oscar L. Milosz, and Czesław Miłosz,* among others, but he has developed a highly original poetic diction, classical and surrealist at the same time, expressing existential conflicts and the anguish of exile. His work has been instrumental in shifting Lithuanian poetry from traditional to modern patterns. He was also one of the first writers to introduce contemporary philosophical themes into Lithuanian literature. Nyka-Niliūnas is an outstanding critic and translator; his Lithuanian versions of Shakespeare's *Hamlet* (1964) and of Virgil's *Georgica* (1984) are of high value.

Consult: R. Šilbajoris, *Perfection of Exile* (1970).

TOMAS VENCLOVA

O

O'BRIEN, Edna. Born December 15, 1932, in County Clare, West Ireland; she lives in London and teaches creative writing in New York City part of the year. O'Brien has written more than fifteen volumes of fiction, screenplays, stage plays and reportage since her first novel, *The Country Girls,* appeared in 1960. The central character of most of her fiction is an Irish expatriate asserting her independence in either an indifferent or hostile world. Such a heroine is in exile from what O'Brien has posited as the stultifying parochialism of Ireland; in her portrayals such a heroine becomes a dislocated transient in her pilgrimage to newer worlds. Nevertheless, her heroines experience what they cannot avoid— the pain of the breaking of national, local and personal ties, no matter how plucky their strings of rhetoric. As one of her interviewers, Richard B. Woodward, recently wrote: "The pain of exile, even self-imposed, can't be under-estimated. In her stories, the lives of thwarted women are dramatized with bitter compassion. Her characters share an urge to flee, and a fear of being mired in one place."

O'Brien moved to London from County Wicklow in 1960 with her husband, the novelist Ernest Gebler (they have since divorced). She has lived abroad since that time, mostly in London but also traveling widely and visiting New York City regularly. Like her fellow exile, James Joyce,* she feels, in the words of Woodward, "permanently scarred by her homeland." Yet she has, like Joyce, written little about anything other than Ireland, Catholicism, and the requirements of loneliness for the role of literary observer Her most recent title is *Lantern Slides* (1990).

Consult: Richard B. Woodward, *The New York Times Magazine*, March 12, 1989.

O'CASEY, Sean. Born March 30, 1880, at 85 Upper Dorset Street, Dublin, Ireland; died September 18, 1964, in Torquay, England. The last of thirteen children (only five of whom survived infancy) O'Casey was born to a Protestant minority working-class family in the Dublin slums and christened John Casey. Caught up in the Gaelic revival movement, he gaelicized his name to Sean O'Cathasaigh in his twenties, anglicizing his surname to O'Casey when the Abbey Theatre produced his first play, *Shadow of a Gunman*, in 1923. In 1926, following the turbulent reception of *The Plough and the Stars* in Ireland, he exiled himself to England, where he spent the remaining thirty-eight years of his life, writing often about Ireland in the vivid recollection of his six-volume autobiography and in his nine remaining full-length plays. Those plays, experimental in technique, suffered somewhat from O'Casey's loss of a theater in which to test his work, but he was able to confront the world's problems from Devon in a way that Dublin would never have permitted.

Prior to his self-exile, O'Casey was an alien in his own country: a celebrator of life among a puritanical people, a believer in the future amid a revivalist culture, a Protestant in a Catholic country, a working-class playwright in a theater dominated by aristocratic leanings, individualist concepts, and aesthetic concerns. What finally drove him, in 1926, from the country of his impoverished birth was the riot in the Abbey Theatre when nationalists interrupted the performance of his *The Plough and the Stars* with catcalls and stench bombs for his ironic treatment of the Easter Rising. W. B. Yeats called the demonstration one that resembled the riot attendant on the Abbey Theatre presentation of J. M. Synge's *Playboy of the Western World* nineteen years earlier, and said it was O'Casey's "apotheosis." Yeats himself helped to confirm O'Casey's exile when he turned down O'Casey's next play, *The Silver Tassie*, telling him that in a play "the whole history of the world must be reduced to wallpaper in front of which the characters must pose and speak."

By the time of his self-exile, O'Casey had produced a trilogy of pacifist plays, the action of each succeeding play built around an ever-expanding radius of involvement, from the lone would-be poet Donal Davoren, caught up in *The Shadow of a Gunman* in the guerrilla war between the IRA and Black and Tan auxiliaries; to the family of *Juno and the Paycock*, ravaged in the Civil War of 1922; to *The Plough and the Stars*, where the Easter Rising of 1916 sweeps the working-class tenement dwellers of Dublin into the savage maw of death and destruction. Surmounting the pathos of war in each of these tragedies is the comic vitality of characters who triumph over despair by their wit and wits.

Exile gave O'Casey less opportunity for working in the theater than he had at the Abbey but more freedom for experiment; the result was often imperfect innovation. Perhaps the most striking and successful of these innovations was written before he left: *The Silver Tassie*, with its combination of realistic and nonrealistic techniques for the transformation of the symbolic hero Harry Heegan from athlete-soldier to bitter impotent cripple under the terrific impact of the expressionist second-act avatar of modern war.

Four prophetic plays—modern moralities about the relationship between man and society, beginning with the subject of the Great Depression and ending with

World War II—followed: *Within the Gates* (1933), *The Star Turns Red* (1940), *Red Roses for Me* (1942), and *Oak Leaves and Lavender* (1946). In these works individual eccentrics like Fluther and the Covey and Joxer Daley tended to be replaced by Man with a capital M, and society became not a web of action but a set of preconceptions. The second and the last of these plays are full of heavy-handed didactic speeches, and an excess of sentimental morality maims the drama into oversimplified combat between Right and Left. However, *Within the Gates*'s violent attack on the fabric of civilization, symbolized by and within Hyde Park, has moments of touching beauty in the frenzied dance of the dying whore Jannice, a dance that leaves its mark on the park's convincingly representative world; *Red Roses for Me* transforms a well-remembered "dear dirty" Dublin into an "epiphany of joy" when Ayamonn and the poor of the city break into a spontaneous dance on the banks of the Liffey.

As David Krause says, "the joyous dance of life, the liberation of mind and body," freed O'Casey from the trammels of a restrictive environment by exile. This joyous dance persists as the theme of his last four comic fantasies. *Purple Dust* (1940) is a pastoral parody in which the lively spirit of pagan Ireland, incorporated in a group of jesting, prankish workingmen, triumphs over wealthy antediluvianizers who are finally overwhelmed in a deluge. *Cock-a-Doodle Dandy* (1950) is an exile's revenge on a joyless, priest-ridden Irish village, Nyadnanave (Nest of Saints), in the persona of a demon cock, a symbolic embodiment of the life force, a dancer got up in feathers. *The Bishop's Bonfire* (1955) celebrates the return of Bishop Mullarky to Ballyoonagh in a workman's antic revel that runs counter to the intended formal, official rite, a ceremony to be touched off by a great bonfire of "evil" books. *The Drums of Father Ned* (1958), which was to have opened the Dublin International Theatre Festival in 1958 and was canceled by censorship (along with a play based on James Joyce's work and Samuel Beckett's *All That Fall*), is the least intense of the group, a drama of good-natured merriment, "just fun from beginning to end" as O'Casey described it.

In exile, deprived of a regular theater audience, O'Casey poured himself into thousands of letters, unconsciously creating a self-portrait that may in fact be, as his editor David Krause says, "one of the greatest characters he created."

In the autobiography, published in six volumes between 1939 and 1954 and brought together as *Mirror in My House* in 1956, it is not so much his own character, presented impersonally from a third-person point of view as Johnny Casside—in the later volumes, Sean—that stands out as it is the teeming sense of Dublin working-class life, poignantly recalled. Pain, hardship, death, and song rise like a flood from the pages of *I Knock at the Door* (1939) and *Pictures in the Hallway* (1942). These first two volumes, covering his childhood and adolescence, show the suffering of the near-blind child confronting a hostile world where inadequate medical care is grudgingly administered, routinized education is indifferently provided, harsh religious imperatives are always insisted upon, and hunger lurks everywhere. The sense of life that prevails is the one nourished by Sean's mother, widowed when he was six, a ray of maternal strength and hope for the future.

Drums under the Window (1946) takes O'Casey as a young man, into the labor movement under its "promethean" leader Jim Larkin, who led the general strike of 1913 and inspired O'Casey's socialism and anticlericalism. It also takes him into the Gaelic revival, turning him from Johnny to Sean, under the influence of Michael O'Hickey, the "lost leader" in the struggle for the revival of the Gaelic language.

Inishfallen Fare Thee Well (1948), beginning with the touching elegy on his mother's death, "Mrs. Casside Takes a Holiday," surveys the turbulent years of guerrilla warfare against the Black and Tans and the Irish Civil War—subjects of his early plays—and ends with his journey into exile: "He would be no more in exile in another land than he was in his own," Sean reflects. "He was a voluntary exile from every creed, from every party, and from every clique."

The last two volumes of the autobiography, *Rose and Crown* (1952) and *Sunset and Evening Star* (1954), are less dramatic than the others, less various in their modes of presentation, less poetic, but no less lively. O'Casey celebrates, sometimes naïvely, always at the top of his voice, the new world (according to Karl Marx), comrades in the struggle against oppression, the young (in spirit and in flesh), and all who bring joy into the world instead of despair.

Selected Titles: *Letters of Sean O'Casey*, ed. David Krause, vol. I (1975), vol. II (1980), vol. III (1989).

Consult: David Krause, *Sean O'Casey, the Man and His Work* (1960, enlarged ed. 1975); David Krause and Robert Lowery, eds., *Sean O'Casey: Centenary Studies* (1980); Garry O'Connor, *Sean O'Casey, A Life* (1988). See also *Modern Drama* 4, no. 3 (December 1961), special issue devoted to O'Casey.

WILLIAM A. FAHEY

O'CONNOR, Frank (pseudonym of Michael Francis O'Donovan). Born September 17, in a Cork, Ireland, slum; 1903, died March 10, 1966, in Dublin. O'Connor's decision to write under a pseudonym signified his need to distance himself from the unaesthetic parochialism, religious and political, of his origins. James Matthews, his literary biographer, writes that O'Connor's alienation was similar to that of his contemporaries, George Bernard Shaw, Sean O'Casey,* and Samuel Beckett* in that "he was close to home and far away, always loving it, always hating it" (3). O'Connor was prolific—a poet, a translator from the Gaelic, a dramatist and novelist, a biographer, a literary critic, and a member of the board of directors of the Abbey Theatre briefly in the 1930s, but he is best known for his masterful short stories, which he referred to as his "voices." O'Connor's activities in the IRA, for which he was interned, engendered his first and well-received volume of stories. The title story in *Guests of the Nation* (1931) is among his best, and the exile theme is evident, not only in the ironic title, but in the concluding observation of the narrator, an IRA novice and accomplice to the execution of two English hostages, "the little patch of black bog with the two Englishmen stiffening into it . . . was [as though] a thousand miles away from me, . . . and I was somehow very small and very lonely. . . . I never felt the same about [anything] again'' (*Collected Stories* 12).

Because of O'Connor's attention to detail and his realistic portrayal of Irish provincialism, Richard Ellmann, in his introduction to the *Collected Stories*, typifies O'Connor as a "Flaubert among the bogs" (vii); Ellmann detects the implied theme "that flexible people can suddenly become fixed, that the other side may be less the enemy than one's own incrustation" (vii) in many of the stories. As O'Connor found, attempts to chip away at such incrustation are met with stiff resistance from the Irish authorities; his books were banned, and he was harassed by the "paudeens." During World War II, O'Connor's income from his writing was cut off, and he was forced to assume yet another pseudonym, "Ben Mayo," in order to get articles published because, writes Maurice Sheehy, "the Irish government couldn't make up its mind whether Frank O'Connor was a Nazi, a Communist or a spy for the imperialist Allies" (179). O'Connor finally fled such harassment, first to England, and then, in June of 1954, he sailed for America, where he held a succession of teaching positions at Harvard, Northwestern, and Stanford.

Although he continued to write stories, such as "A Bachelor's Story" and "Fish for Friday," filled with nostalgic re-creations of Irish life, and he published with Knopf, his American publisher, yet another collection of stories, *Domestic Relations* (1957), which, according to Matthews, "blurred the line between fiction and autobiography" (315), much of his exile writing is atypical, suggesting that separation from Ireland encouraged him to try new forms. *A Mirror in the Roadway* (1956) is a critical examination of the style, narrative technique, and characterization of some major nineteenth-century novelists such as Charles Dickens, Stendhal, William Makepeace Thackeray, and Jane Austen; and *The Lonely Voice* (1962) is his study of the modern short story.

O'Connor also began to write in exile his autobiography, sections of which first appeared in the *New Yorker*, one of the many American magazines and journals for which O'Connor wrote. Much like the *Autobiographies* of W. B. Yeats, his friend and associate, O'Connor's autobiography is not marked by slavish adherence to facts, but rather serves as a vehicle for the imaginative re-creation of his life and his quest for himself as an artist. For example, a passage of childhood reminiscence from *An Only Child* (1961) exemplifies his dual identity as Michael/Frank: "It was a strange double life, and small wonder if it comes back to me only as a hallucination. . . . I said good-bye to my real self, . . . he rejoined me, a boy exactly like myself except that no experience had dinged or dented him . . . —the perfection of the poet's dream of escape" (177). Troubled by his exile, O'Connor returned to Eire in the fall of 1961, where melancholia possessed him. In November of 1965, a few months before his death, he wrote to his son Myles, "How I got into this melancholy vein you can guess. I feel like Emily Dickinson, too long confined to Amherst. Not comparing Amherst to this place, where flogging etc. have been fully restored to the curriculum officially . . . '' (Matthews 370). After his fatal heart attack, O'Connor's second volume of autobiography, *My Father's Son* (1968), was published. It concludes, ''At once I resigned from every organization I belonged to and sat down, at last, to write'' (235).

Consult: James Matthews, *Voices* (1983); Maurice Sheehy, ed., *Michael/Frank* (1969), a collection of essays by friends and acquaintances of O'Connor, contains an extensive bibliography of O'Connor's canon. Richard Ellmann's Introduction to O'Connor's *Collected Stories* (1981) is a concise assessment of O'Connor's literary accomplishments.

DAVID JAMES MORIARTY

O'FLAHERTY, Liam. Born August 28, 1896, in the village of Gort na gCapall, Inishmore Island of the Aran Islands, Republic of Ireland; he died September 7, 1984, in Dublin, Ireland. O'Flaherty was educated at Jesuit schools and the National University in Dublin. He joined the Irish Guards (of the British army) in World War I and was shell-shocked in battle in Belgium. Discharged in 1917, he spent the next few years traveling round the world, earning his passage by working on freighters and tramp steamers to South America, the Mediterranean, Canada, and the United States. He returned to Ireland in 1922 to fight with the Republicans in the Irish Civil War; on one occasion he led a four-day insurrection in Cork during which he raised the Red flag over the city. At the close of the Civil War, he felt Ireland had succumbed to debased bourgeois domination, and with Francis Stuart and others he called for a radical transformation of the country: an end to the tyrannies of capitalism, Catholicism, and sexual prudery. When his calls went unheeded, O'Flaherty left Ireland and wandered around North America and Europe; he spent a large part of his years from 1935 in the United States, and only in his later years returned to Ireland, where he lived in Dublin, largely unnoticed and mostly silent as a writer.

Although O'Flaherty was never in literal exile, he suffered a sense of separation from his fellow beings, except when he was fighting in a dramatic cause with them. His most prominent achievement is the novel *The Informer* (1925), a tale of an Irish coward who informs on the IRA to the British. On the surface the novel is about a man tempted by greed to betray his community in a strife-torn land, but more profoundly it is the perception of the psychological injury inflicted by war on its participants. Erosion of ideals in the face of carnage proves lethal to the human spirit; what began as a dream vision of patriotic glory ends an ordinary nightmare of civil violence.

O'Flaherty's first two works, *Thy Neighbour's Wife* (London, 1923) and *The Black Soul* (London, 1924), utilized his native Aran Islands as background. His later work centers on mainland Ireland, its tormented history of violence and strife, and the terrible destruction wrought by civil war. *Famine* (London, 1937; repr. 1965), one of his lasting achievements, treats the history of Ireland through its cataclysmic event, the potato famine in the nineteenth century, a decimation and trauma from which, O'Flaherty believed, the Irish people never recovered.

Selected Titles: Novels: *Mr. Gilhooley* (1927); *Skeritt* (1932); *The Martyr* (1933); *The Land* (1946). Memoir: *Shame the Devil* (1934).

Consult: Thomas Flanagan, Afterword in *Famine* (1982 ed.); Patrick F. Sheeran, *The Novels of Liam O'Flaherty: A Study in Romantic Realism* (Dublin, 1976); John Zneimer, *The Literary Vision of Liam O'Flaherty* (1970).

OKRI, Ben. Born 1960 in Nigeria; he lives in London. Okri came to England to study at the University of Essex and has remained in England since. At nineteen he completed his first novel, *Flowers and Shadows* (London, 1980). He published his second novel, *The Landscapes Within*, in 1981 (London). Both works concentrate on the theme of corruption in modern Nigeria, particularly as its seeds are passed from one generation to the next. In Okri's first novel, an idealistic and only son, Jeffia Okwe, must face the truth of his businessman father's corruption and mendacity in order to begin his own life; his triumph comes in his ability to move beyond suffering and disappointment. His most recent work has been in the short story genre: *Incidents at the Shrine* (London, 1986) and *Stars of the New Curfew* (1989), a work that has received wide praise in the United States for its stark portrait of modern urban Nigerian life.

Okri worked for the BBC's Africa Department and was poetry editor of the cultural journal *West Africa*, headquartered in London, before becoming a full-time writer. He treats both cultural exile and native alienation in his narratives of the gifted educated young African, a protagonist who is always apart from his community by virtue of his superior qualities and who disappoints the expectations of the community, whether through venal corruption or through his own agenda of personal needs. The tradition of such theme-weaving, particularly in relation to the expectations of the community and their sense of betrayal, may be discerned in the fiction of such earlier Nigerian writers as Chinua Achebe, Wole Soyinka,* and Cyprian Ekwensi.

Okri won the prestigious Commonwealth Prize for Africa award in 1987.

Consult: Adewale Maja-Pearce, Introduction, in Okri, *Flowers and Shadows* (London, 1981); Hans Zell et al., *A Reader's Guide to African Literature* (1983).

OLES', Oleksander (pseudonym of Oleksander Kandyba). Born December 5, 1878, on the Kandyba estate near Kryha, Sumy area, Ukraine; died July 22, 1944, in Prague, Czechoslovakia. One of the most popular Ukrainian lyrical poets of the twentieth century, Oles' was a practicing veterinary doctor, served on the editorial boards of several literary periodicals, and wrote children's stories. His first collection of poems *Z zhurboyu radist' obnialas'* (Joy Embracing Sorrow) appeared in 1907, followed by six others, as well as several editions of his collected works; many of his poems have been set to music by Ukrainian composers. Oles' also wrote plays in verse, among which the symbolist *Podorozi v kazku* (1910, Along the Road to a Fairytale Land) is best known; his last published work was a play in verse, *Nich na polonyni* (A Night in the Mountain

Plains). Oles' published his satires under a second pseudonym, V. Valentyn. He also translated from Byelorussian and English into Soviet Ukrainian.

Oles' left Ukraine in 1919 and emigrated to Budapest, then to Vienna, and finally settled in Prague. While some of his works were published in Soviet Ukraine, they were heavily criticized and, on occasion, censored.

LARISSA M. L. ONYSHKEVYCH

ONDAATJE, (Philip) Michael. Born September 12, 1943, in Columbo, Ceylon (now Sri Lanka); he lives in Toronto, Ontario, Canada. Ondaatje's parents divorced when he was three years old. He was sent to England when he was eleven to attend Dulwich College (the same school P. G. Wodehouse* attended and epitomized as the private school of every proper English boy's dreams/ nightmares). He began writing when he was 19 and published his first book, *The Dainty Monsters*, in 1967. He received a B.A. from the University of Toronto and an M.A. from Queens University in Canada (his thesis was on the Scottish poet Edwin Muir). He taught at the University of Western Ontario in Toronto from 1967–71, when he was let go because he had not completed a doctoral degree. At the time he had published three volumes of poetry and a critical study of the Canadian poet-songwriter Leonard Cohen. Two days after his dismissal, he was given the Governor-General's Award for his unique work of poetry-prose, *The Collected Works of Billy the Kid: Left-Handed Poems* (1970). Ondaatje also dramatized *Billy the Kid* in 1970, and has appeared on Canadian stages to perform from it in solo readings. He has written film scripts, memoirs, short prose fiction, and novels.

Ondaatje made his first return trip to Sri Lanka in 1978; he visited again in 1980. Both these visits exercised a spirit of return to memories of childhood, and led, in part, to his later memoir, *Running in the Family* (1982). Ondaatje received the Governor-General's Award for a second time in 1979 for *There's a Trick I'm Learning to Do: Poems 1963–1978*.

Selected Titles: Poetry: *Rat Jelly* (1973); *Coming Through the Slaughter* (1976); *Secular Lore* (1984). Novel: *In the Skin of a Lion* (1987).

Consult: Leslie Mundwiler, *Michael Ondaatje: Word, Image, Imagination* (Vancouver, B.C., 1984).

ONETTI, Juan Carlos. Born July 1, 1909, in Montevideo, Uruguay; he has returned to Montevideo. Political reasons led Onetti to leave Uruguay in 1975 for Spain; earlier he had worked in Buenos Aires as an advertising executive from 1955–1957; he also was editor of the journal *Vea y Lea*, based in Buenos Aires, from 1946–1955. Onetti was honored in 1962 with the National Prize for Literature in Uruguay. Onetti left Uruguay in 1975 after he was refused permission by the government to attend a presentation ceremony in Italy of an award for *El Astillero* as the best foreign work translated in 1975 (Onetti's novel was originally published in Spanish in 1963). Resigning his position as director of municipal libraries, he went into self-exile in Spain. In Spain, in 1979, he won the Critics Prize for his novel *Dejemos hablar al viento* (Let's Speak with the Wind); in 1980 he was awarded the Miguel de Cervantes Prize for his body of work.

Much of Onetti's work centers on people inhabiting marginal worlds and living out their presence in fantasies of the past. Often his characters choose suicide as a resolution to their existential agonies. Stylistically, he exemplifies in striking fashion one direction of modernism, or postmodernism. In a world in which doubt has become one of the few certainties available to all, Onetti's characters take away their stories from their creator and begin writing, or rewriting, the narratives of themselves. Often, in Onetti's work, characters are created by characters, and the novel which a reader is perusing is revised at will by a fictional character, or even a committee of fictional characters. Such disguises, or guises, of reality make Onetti's work difficult and esoteric, but he has gained a fervent public for his tales of disintegration, psychic exile, separatism and survival in a grim world. His works show an indebtedness to John Dos Passos* (particularly *Manhattan Transfer* and *The USA* trilogy) and to William Faulkner in the conceptualization of mythic regions and town documents of pseudo-life histories. Onetti, however, is more extreme than either of the American writers in his cubes of fragmentation. His physical locales, for example, are not created as mythic background complementing character development; they become creations created by characters as means of escape from authorial confinement. Onetti returned to Uruguay in the 1980s after a civilian government replaced the military dictatorship.

Selected Titles: *La vida breve* (Buenos Aires, 1950; *A Brief Life*, 1976); *El astillero* (Buenos Aires, 1961; *The Shipyard*, 1968); *Juntacadaveres* (Buenos Aires, 1964; *Body Snatcher*, 1990); *Cuentos completos* (Buenos Aires, 1967, revised 1973); *Novelas* [and Cuentos] *cortas completas*, 2 vols. (Caracas, 1968); *Obras completas* (Montevideo, 1970); *Réquiem por Faulkner* (Montevideo, 1975); *Tan triste como ella y otros cuentos* (Barcelona, 1976); *Tiempo de Abrazar y los cuentos de 1933 a 1950* (Barcelona, 1983, Time to Embrace and Stories from 1933 to 1950).

Consult: M. Ian Adams, *Three Authors of Alienation: Bombal, Onetti, Carpentier* (1975); Yvonne P. Jones, *The Formal Expression of Meaning in Juan Carlos Onetti's Narrative Art* (Cuernavaca, 1971); Djelal Kadir, *Juan Carlos Onetti* (1977); Mark Millington, *Reading Onetti* (Liverpool, 1985); Jorge Ruffinelli, Introduction, in *Tiempo de Abrazar* by Onetti (Barcelona, 1983); Kessel Schwartz, entry in *Encyclopedia of World Literature*, ed. Leonard Klein, vol. 2 (1983); See also Special Section, *Review* 16 (1975), on *A Brief Life*.

ORTEGA, Julio. Born 1942, in Peru; he lives in the United States. Ortega left Peru to teach at several American universities, but his decision was a political as well as personal one. He continues to write fiction in Spanish, but lately has written criticism directly in English. In discussing one of his short-short fiction pieces, ''Las Papas,'' collected in *Diario imaginario* (published by the Universidad de Antioquia, Colombia, and reprinted in the anthology, *Sudden Fiction International* [1989], edited by Robert Shapard and James Thomas) he wrote:

"Potatoes originated in Peru, my country, but also adapted themselves quite well in many other parts of the world. This metaphor from cultural preservation in exile interested me—cooking is not a melting pot if you care for flavor— *Saber y sabor* (knowledge and flavor)—are together in Latin America from the very beginning. In fact, the first poem written in the New World was a Cuban recipe a Spanish cook sent back to Spain" (p. 331).

Selected Titles: *Poetics of Change; García Márquez and the Powers of Fiction.*

Consult: "Afternotes," *Sudden Fiction International*, ed. Robert Shapard and James Thomas (1989).

ORTEGA y Gasset, José. Born May 8, 1883, in Madrid, Spain; died October 8, 1955, in Madrid. Ortega received his doctorate from the University of Madrid in 1904. He traveled to Germany for postgraduate study in Leipzig and Berlin in 1906 and pursued research with Hermann Cohen in Kantian philosophy in 1908. He joined the faculty of metaphysics at the University of Madrid in 1910, remaining there until his self-exile in 1936. During his exile period he lived in France, Holland, Portugal, Argentina, and the United States. He returned to Spain after the close of World War II.

Ortega was a lecturer and guest professor at many universities during his exile years, among them the Aspen Institute for the Humanities. From his first lecture tour to Buenos Aires in 1916, he became an influence on the intellectual history of South America. The influence of Ortega's ideas on intellectuals in Spain as well as in Latin America was also, and largely, spread through his editorship of *Revista de Occidente*, which he founded in 1923.

Two recent studies of Ortega and his work by Andrew Dobson and Rockwell Gray, as reviewed by Raymond Carr in the *Times Literary Supplement* (October 13–19, 1989), indicate that while Ortega felt abandoned by the nature of events in his country, he found exile from it more painful. He felt it was the artist-intellectual's duty to lead the "mass" even if, and usually when, such leadership was not recognized. Ortega's concept of leadership involved an assumption of a "select minority" (one of Ortega's terms) and a hierarchy of values reflected in a hierarchy of leadership roles and a "docile" mass. The "docile" mass, according to Ortega, were not interested in much else than material self-satis-faction. In effect, Ortega rejected the mass appeal of both fascism and socialism because of their slighting of the liberal aristocratic ideal of disinterested judgment. He chose to continue to propagate a new kind of elitist liberalism to replace what he called the tired bourgeois liberalism of his time. Reacting to the dec-adence of insularity spawned by the defeat of Spain in the Spanish-American War and by the intellectuals of the Generation of 1898, who called for a return to "Spanishness," Ortega instead called for an opening up of Spain, and par-ticularly German, culture. In writing of the need to "level the Pyrenees," and thus rescue Spain from its debilitating inwardness, Ortega turned to those special people, "authentic" and "exemplary" men who could lead the masses to a new vision and their "radical reality."

Ortega's distinction between the mass and "exemplary men" and/or "creative minority" is a moral one rather than an economic or social-class determination. In his view some men are given the rare ability to lead, while the vast majority of others must follow or remain mired in a mass of cultural and spiritual dimness. Ortega thus continues the nineteenth-century concept of the Great Man as History, but he also believed that art, by its revelations whether immediately intelligible or not, helped to shape the national climate; such shaping remained afloat in the air of ideas, eventually "trickling" down to the people. Because of this sense of the tension between leader and mass and between artist and mass, Ortega grudgingly accepted socialism as a national movement that might unite divisive factions within Spain in the twentieth century. He later saw the military takeover of the government by Primo de Rivera in 1923 as the way to national unity; Rivera's military dictatorship became a Caesarian maneuver that would rescue the country from its petty politicians who promoted "particularism" and special interest goals rather than "national" goals and rewards. Trusting to a strong leader who would do away with the tolerance and frustrations of factionalism, Ortega lent vocal support to both Rivera and the Falange party that he led. Because of this support, Ortega was accused of writing philosophy that "fed fascist minds." Stung by the criticism, he signed a statement of support in 1936 for the Republican cause. Seeing himself as a beleaguered aristocrat cast out from his country by its two popular "mass" movements, socialism and fascism, he left Spain for exile later that same year. On his return to his native land years later, Ortega began to accept the idea of federalism; he at least conceded the need for political satisfaction of regional and cultural-ethnic demands within a larger, national Spain (see his work *La Redencion de las provincias*).

In reviewing these two new studies on Ortega, Raymond Carr wrote: "Ortega was no fascist. He was a patrician conservative, a liberal for whom the tension between liberalism and the egalitarian implications of democracy were central to his whole thought" (p. 1114).

Selected Titles: *Espana invertebrada* (1922; *Invertebrate Spain*, 1937); *La deshumanizacion del arte* (1925; *The Dehumanization of Art*, 1948); *Estudios sobre el Amor* (1939; *On Love: Aspects of a Single Theme*, 1957); *Historia como sistema* (1941; *Toward a Philosophy of History*, 1941, repub. as *History as a System*, 1961); *Del imperio romano* (1946; *Concord and Liberty*, 1963); *El hombre y la gente* (1957; *Man and People*, 1957); see also *Obras completas*, 11 vols., 1946–69.

Consult: Andrew Dobson, *An Introduction to the Politics and Philosophy of José Ortega y Gasset* (1989); Rockwell Gray, *The Imperative of Modernity: An Intellectual Biography of José Ortega y Gasset* (1989); R. McClintock, *Man and His Circumstances: Ortega as Educator* (1971); F. Niedermayer, *José Ortega y Gasset* (1973).

OUSMANE, Sembene. Born 1923 in Ziguinchor, Southern Senegal; he lives near Dakar, Senegal. Son of a fisherman and a mother from rural country in Casamanche Province, Ousmane worked in many blue-collar and laboring jobs. He served in the French colonialist army but was discharged (possibly for striking an officer) and then worked as a docker in Marseilles for several years. During this time he became active in union organizing of black dockers; he also developed an interest in Marxism. After the publication of his first novel, *Le Docker Noir* (Paris, 1956), he returned to Senegal. Ousmane is also a noted filmmaker; most of his films are written as well as directed by him. His work, from his first novel to his current film, shows a strong tendency to ideological communalism, a desire to convert his fellow Africans from a personal pronoun emphasis to an awareness of the joys of solidarity in the struggle against economic tyranny of white or black bosses and impersonal capitalists.

Consult: Per Wastberg, ed., *The Writer in Modern Africa* (1969).

OYONO, Ferdinand. Born 1929, Cameroon; he lives in Cameroon. Oyono was a student in France in the late 1950s. He wrote his two early novels concurrently in France in 1956—*La vieux nègre et la médaille*, which he claims to have completed in three days, and *Une vie de boy*, which he found difficult to finish. Both books were published in Paris in 1956. They appeared in English translation as *Houseboy* (1966) and *The Old Man and the Medal* (1969, c. 1967).

P ───────────────────────────────

PADILLA, Heberto. Born January 20, 1932, in Puerta del Golpe in the province of Pinar del Rio, Cuba; he lives in Cambridge, Massachusetts. When he was seventeen he emigrated to the United States and often traveled as a foreign correspondent until 1959, when he became one of the editors of the literary magazine *Lunes de Revolución*. In 1961 *Lunes* was repressed, and its three editors were censured and given foreign assignments—Padilla as a journalist in Prague and Moscow. The experiences of the preceding decade left their mark on Padilla's first major collection; *El Justo Tiempo Humano* (1962). Here the poet, often isolated in foreign countries, reflects on modern war, the Holocaust, political persecution, and exile; he admits his doubts about human history, although he does not give up hope in a just future. This hope was put to a severe test in the next decade. Defections and increasing repression, including the expulsion of Allen Ginsberg, who had been invited to serve as a judge in a poetry competition, led to the "Padilla case." In 1967 Padilla sharply criticized Lisandro de Otero's novel *Pasión de Urbino*, a work favored by the government, and defended *Tres Tristes Tigres*, the novel by Guillermo Cabrera Infante,* which had not been published in Cuba even though it had defeated *Pasión de Urbino* in the 1964 Siex Barral Competition in Barcelona. Shortly thereafter, Padilla lost his job and was not allowed to make a trip to Italy.

In 1968 Padilla's second major book, *Fuera del Juego*, won a major poetry prize, forcing the Cuban Union of Writers and Artists to compromise—they decided *Fuera del Juego* could be published with a prologue that proclaimed it counterrevolutionary. Padilla's second book presents, with clarity and irony, a cyclical view of history. The poet is a "suspicious person" and an exile, either in his own land or abroad; disillusioned with the old promises, he can no longer hide his skepticism, nor can he find an escape from imminent political violence and the threat of nuclear war. What he affirms is the common humanity of all, whether friend or enemy of the revolution. Although *Fuera del Juego* was defended as a constructive critique of Cuba, the government never accepted it. On March 20, 1971, Padilla was arrested and held until April 27, when on the very evening of his release, he was forced to make a public confession of his "error," in which he accused himself, his wife, and friends of antirevolutionary attitudes. Around the world writers and intellectuals came to his defense, but all appeals failed, and Padilla was forced to live as an "interior exile" in Cuba, working as an obscure translator of technical material, until 1980, when he became an official exile in the United States.

Padilla's later poems, *Provocaciones* (1973) and *El Hombre Junto al Mar* (1980), continue to examine dehumanization and exile; they also find the promise of healing in ordinary experience and human relationships. His novel, *En mi Jardín Pasten los Héroes* (1981), combines extensive dialogue with surreal dream sequences to show how its main characters, trapped by their past and their language, live in an atmosphere of paranoia and suffer aesthetic, erotic, and political estrangement, ultimately becoming the victims of historical forces they cannot control. The autobiographical foreword provides a stark account of how the Cuban authorities interrogated and coerced Padilla and also how he smuggled the only surviving manuscript of his novel out of the country.

A summary of the "Padilla case" may be found in Seymour Menton's *Prose Fiction of the Cuban Revolution* (Austin/London, 1975).

Translations: *Legacies: Selected Poems* (1982); *Heroes Are Grazing in My Garden* (1984); *Self-Portrait of the Other* (1990).

Consult: Luis Quesada, "*Fuera del Juego*: A Poet's Appraisal of the Cuban Revolution," *Latin American Literary Review* 3, no.6 (1975): 89–98.

MICHAEL MANLEY

PAGIS, Dom. Born 1930 in Bukovina (formerly part of Austria, then Romania, now in USSR); died 1986 in Jerusalem, Israel. Pagis was an inmate of a Nazi concentration camp for three years; he was among the first group of survivors to be sent directly from the camps to Israel. He became a professor at Hebrew University and also taught at Harvard University of California at San Diego and Berkeley, and at the Jewish Theological Seminary in New York. Pagis transcended his experience of exile into a new citizenship and an old identity as a Jew. He is considered by many critics as one of the outstanding poets of the modern Israeli state. In 1990 his first collection of poems in the United States, *Selected Poetry*, was published posthumously.

PAI Hsin-yung. Born July 11, 1937, in Kwang-hsi, China; since 1963 he has been living in Santa Barbara, California. Like a number of other transplanted mainlander-Chinese writers, Pai fled to Taiwan with his politically prominent family in 1949. In the early 1960s, when he was in his junior year in college, he and a few colleagues started the literary magazine *Modern Literature*, which was to have a considerable impact on developments in Taiwan's literary scene. As the publisher and main contributor to *Modern Literature*, Pai has been considered the most representative of the Modernist school, a loosely connected group of young writers whose work exhibit clear influence of Western literary trends. Pai's collection of stories [The Taipei-ners] was published in Taipei in 1971 and received wide critical acclaim; its English version, published under the title *Wandering in the Garden, Waking from a Dream: Tales of Taipei Characters*, was published in the United States in 1982. The stories deal with the wasted lives and vanquished psyches of displaced mainlanders who fled to Taiwan from China in the wake of the change in government on the mainland. Pai's first full-length fiction, *The Prodigal Son*, treats the subculture of homosexuals and teenage prostitutes in Taipei; it was published in Taiwan in 1983.

DOROTHY TSUNGSU WEISSMAN

PARIZEAN, Alia. Born 1930 in Luniniec, Poland; she lives in Canada. Parizean was freed from the Bergen-Belsen concentration camp in 1945 with the arrival of the Allied armies. She moved to Paris to study political science and law. A professional lawyer, she is as well a prize-winning novelist and a critic whose range of commentary extends to literary and social-political issues. The first *Prix européen de l'Association des écrivains de langue français* was awarded in 1982 to her novel *Les Lilas fleurissent a Varsovie*. She moved to Canada in 1980.

PARKS, Tim. Born 1954 in Manchester, England; he lives in Verona, Italy. Unique as his work may be, Parks represents a well-worn British and American expatriate tradition—leaving home in one's mid- or late twenties for Europe, writing one's fiction or poetry after hours of teaching, usually English-language skills, at a low salary that allows a high degree of freedom of movement. Parks's themes are also consistent with the expatriate tradition: the early work relying on his native origins, the later novels utilizing his experiences in Europe to provide a texture for portraits of foreign life. His first novel, *Tongues of Flame* (1985), treated the hysteria that afflicts a seemingly complacent suburban town when a religious zealot sets its fears aflame with sexual guilt and consciousness of sin. His second novel, *Loving Roger* (1987), draws on the relationship of a brilliant young ambitious writer who exploits an ordinary young woman's infatuation with him to the point beyond a return to his self-centered life. In a chilling climax the writer realizes he cannot manipulate human beings as he does characters in his fiction. Parks's third novel, *Home Thoughts* (1988), profiles that combination of traits and *distraits* he sees as the exile complex. He calls his characters "ex pats," expatriates who long ago took flight into psychological exile; physical flight is the final flag in their race for distance from shadows of identity. Parks's cast of characters, a variant on a new lost generation, are self-willed, self-destructive, lonely, and searching for companionship in unlikely places; fascinating in their bright, shiny postgraduate wit and their indestructible innocence in the onslaught of moral issues, they are well-heeled, spoiled, and yet endearingly charming young people (almost no one is beyond the age of thirty), fleeing from a Thatcherite England that rankles their liberalized consciences.

Parks, the son of an Anglican clergyman, graduated from Cambridge University with a degree in English literature. He received his M.A. degree from Harvard and worked for National Public Radio in the United States for a brief period. Since 1980 he has lived in Italy, where he teaches at the University of Verona. He is also a translator from the Italian.

Selected Title: *Family Planning* (London, 1989).

PARRA, Nicanor. Born September 5, 1914, in Chillán, Chile. Parra was trained as a physicist in Chile, the United States, and England, and has, since 1952, taught physics in both Chile and the United States. He has also become famous as an advocate of antipoetry. Parra has made erotic, political, and spiritual estrangement a major concern of his antipersonae.

Severed from his provincial origins by his education, Parra developed an ironic voice through a dialogue with foreign cultures and writers. Like others of his generation, he wanted a poetry of daily life in a common language. When he was at Brown University (1943–45), he tried to create a Whitmanian hero, but the hero disintegrated, and "an antihero struggled to get into the poem." Parra turned to Franz Kafka* and Charlie Chaplin,* and at Oxford (1949–51), he read English poetry and was profoundly influenced by John Donne. While recovering from a mysterious illness, he completed *Poemas y Antipoemas* (1954). Mocking the poet, the reader, and himself, the anti-hero repeatedly talks about women's deceit and imprisonment of him, his own obsessions, and art; after a series of grotesque and absurd experiments, he emerges from his prison as the voice of contradiction, aware of his own irremediable spiritual exile.

Parra continued to emphasize the absurd in *La Cueca Larga* (1958), written in a traditional Chilean form, and *Versos de Salón* (1962). While the earlier antihero is a victim, the dominant antipersona of *Versos de Salón* is an "energumen" defying the world but affirming that, if we all share spiritual exile, we also share a common language. To those who rejected the book, Parra responded characteristically: "No one is a poet in his own land." In 1963, he visited the USSR and China, and the resulting *Canciones Rusas* (1907) is elegiac and nostalgic, but not without sharp political satire. Parra resumed a savage tone in the later 1960s, making his poetry as concise as a theorem, and earning the title he himself gave to the antipoet—persona non grata.

Because of his essentially anarchist position, Parra by the 1970s found himself estranged even from the Marxists who formerly had supported him. While he has advocated social radicalism (*Discursos*, 1962), he has always refused to subordinate poetry to politics, just as he has refused to subordinate his antipoems to his own antipoetic theory. This refusal is clearly demonstrated by *Los Artefactos* (published as a boxed collection of postcards in 1972). If the antipoems result from the explosion of the traditional poem, "the artifacts result from the explosion of the antipoem" and they constitute Parra's most severe critique of metaphor, the unified voice, and the poet as creator. The poet, or "prefabricator," as Parra has preferred to call him, now becomes a collector, and the artifacts are found objects, parodying all forms of speech and writing.

Parra insisted on his artistic independence during the Chilean political crises of the 1970s, and *Hojas de Parra*, a 1977 "happening" based on his work, was censured by the authorities and closed after a bombing. Meanwhile he was completing a major satire of the human condition and of the repressive Pinochet government—*Sermones y Prédices del Cristo de Elqui* (1977 and 1979). Based on a historical figure, Domingo Zarata Vega, a construction worker who became a preacher, the persona of those poems is at once charlatan and prophet, jongleur and stand-up comic. An exile in his own land, like Parra himself, he finds his way to speech beyond exile, continuing the antipoetic project of aesthetic and political subversion while addressing a community that endures political injustice. Recently Parra has shown great concern for ecology and disarmament and has given these issues priority in his latest artifacts, "sermons," and poems.

For Parra, the antipoetic conversation has no beginning; it can already be heard in the work of Archilochus and Aristophanes, and it suggests that men and women have always been exiles and that authentic speech is also an exile lost in language itself.

Translations: *Emergency Poems* (1972); *Sermons and Homilies of the Christ of Elqui* (1984); *Antipoems: New and Selected*, ed. David Unger (1985).

Consult: Elizabeth Grossman, *The Antipoetry of Nicanor Parra* (1975); Leonidas T. Morales, *La Poesia de Nicanor Parra* (Chile, 1972).

MICHAEL MANLEY

PAU-LLOSA, Ricardo. Born May 17, 1954, in Havana, Cuba; he lives in Miami. Pau-Llosa left Cuba as a child when his family emigrated to the United States. He is a poet, literary critic, and art historian. He teaches at Florida International University in Miami and is the senior editor of *Art International*.

Selected Titles: *Veinticinco poemas* (Miami, 1973, *Twenty-Five Poems*, bilingual ed.); *Sorting Metaphors* (1983, poems, published originally in English).

PAVESE, Cesare. Born 1908 in Santo Stefano Belbo, Province of Piedmont, Italy; died 1950, by suicide, in Turin, Italy. In 1935 Pavese was arrested and confined at Brancaleone in the extreme southern province of Calabria for his Communist activities. He was freed from prison in 1936. While in confinement he wrote *Zavorare Starca*, which was published in 1936. Because of his strong allegiance to the north of Italy, a region he considered distinct from the southern half of the country, he regarded his incarceration as one of exile as well.

PAZ, Octavio. Born March 31, 1914, in Mexico City; he lives in Mexico, though he travels widely and often. Because of his diplomatic service, and his inclination to journey into foreign cultures, Paz has spent a great part of his life abroad. He has served as his country's ambassador to India, studied on a Guggenheim fellowship in the United States, and has been a guest lecturer and reader of his poetry at many universities in North and South America and Europe over the past three decades. He resigned as ambassador to India to protest his government's brutal crackdown of the student uprising at the University of Mexico in 1968. In disengaging himself from official Mexican policy, he became even more of an "outsider" in his own country than he had been earlier as an iconoclastic critic. Paz has said of himself (in a recent interview in *Boulevard* magazine, vol. 3, no. 2–3, 1988) that *there*, inside Mexico, he feels most an "outsider."

Paz's interests, as he describes them, are three-fold. He believes the poet must act in concert with a social conscience, and thus must participate in both protest and celebration of politico/social events. He also has been influenced by the works of Sor Juana Ines, a Baroque theologian, poet, and nun who took the vows of silence and renunciation in her last years (Paz has edited and commented on her works). Paz also has been both a part of and a critic of Surrealism, differing with André Breton* on many issues but employing Surrealistic techniques in his own poetry and in championing Surrealist aesthetics. Marcel Duchamp is one of his idols, particularly the Duchamp who renounced painting to find its entity in silence and bare canvas. Paz has also edited several literary journals, dedicating himself to the promotion of young and ignored writers.

With his colleague Carlos Fuentes,* Paz may be said to be an expatriate by virtue of intellectual journeying. Both writers reflect their profoundest Mexicanness through their expression of it in a rebellious stance. Paz was awarded the Nobel Prize for Literature in 1990; he is the first Mexican author to win the prize.

Selected Title: *The Collected Poems, 1957–1987*, ed. Eliot Weinberger (1987).

Consult: Rita Guibert, *Seven Voices* (1973); Ivar Ivask, ed., *The Perpetual Present: The Poetry and Prose of Octavio Paz* (1973); Wilson Jason, *Octavio Paz: A Study of His Poetics* (1979); John M. Fein, *Toward Octavio Paz: A Reading of His Major Poems, 1957–1976* (1986).

p'BITEK, Okot (Okot p'Bitek). Born 1931 in Gulu, Northern Uganda; he died July 19, 1982, in Kampala, Uganda. Okot's father, Opii Jebedyo, was a teacher from the pa-Cua clan of the Patiko chiefdom and his mother, Lacwaa Cerina, was from the Palaro chiefdom of the Acholi people; they had become Protestant worshippers. Although he studied with missionaries and went to Gulu High School and the prestigious English-styled King's College in Budo, and between 1952 and 1954 to the Government Training College in Mbarara, Okot remained indebted to his Acholi oral and folk traditions. His mother, who was a composer and singer, was a dominant influence in his childhood, and she taught him many tribal songs, some of which he used in spirited ways in his various "Songs." In addition to being a superb student, Okot was a gifted athlete. He first went abroad to play on the national soccer team in England and stayed there to attend

Bristol University (he majored in Education). Okot later read Law at Aberystwyth, Wales, and took a degree in Sociology and Anthropology at Oxford University. He returned to Uganda to teach at Makerere University; he would later teach in the United States and in Kenya. He founded the Gulu Festival, instituting a policy of native drama production in which a mix of music, song, poetry, and dance along with the playscript, or in place of it, was followed. During his tenure as director of the National Theater and Cultural Center in Kampala, he revamped the policy of presenting traditional modern British comedy (e.g., Noel Coward,* Terence Rattigan) and putting in its place indigenous drama in Lwo, Acholi, other East African, and English-language productions. In 1971 Okot was appointed to the post of senior research fellow at the Institute of African Studies in Nairobi and remained for the rest of his life part of the administrative scene involved in the sociocultural life of East Africa.

Okot was a man of many distinctions, but his chief mode was a tone of what has been called "lightness" and "mischief." In his creative work, from his first novel, *Lak Tar*, written in Lwo in 1953 and set in Acholiland, to the completion of his Song Cycle, this mood of mischievousness is apparent. The lightness becomes heavier as Okot's awareness of suffering and ineradicable conflicts of public and private interest grows in his later years. *Song of a Prisoner* and *Song of Malaya* are, for example, tragic and dirge-like in comparison to the winking asperities of the voice in *Song of Lawino* and the comic ironies unveiling the pomposity of the persona in *Song of Ocol*. Part of Okot's increasing bitterness— the quality became marked because Okot had been the kind of teasing bard who joined disputants rather than polarized them—was the result of internecine attacks on his approach to literature and to social and cultural policies. Okot remained a man who could sum up a friend or opponent in simple but nakedly comic analysis; on one such occasion on a trip to Zambia, he made pointedly mocking remarks about his government. Okot was told his life was in danger (another source claims that the planned punitive action against Okot was the result of politicians' anger over criticism of them in *Song of Lawino*). Okot fled to Kenya. During the last years of his life, the toll of the experience of exile proved beyond his means. He wrote little, and his joyous-mischievous tone was whittled into despairing bitterness or silence.

Okot may be seen both as as intellectual-cultural administrator, who was highly educated in Western technology (and jargon, which he satirized), and as a poet who refused to surrender his folk source of vitality. He published three scholarly works—*African Religions and Western Scholarship* (1970); *Religions of the Central Lwo* (1971); and *Africa's Cultural Revolution* (1973)—as well as wrote many administrative reports and studies. As a poet (and as distinct from his creative life in the theater of mixed media as director-producer and cultural consultant) he is remembered for his "Songs." The first, *Song of Lawino*, was written in 1954 in Acholi (*Wer pa Lawino*); it was translated by Okot and published in English in 1966. Lawino, bemoaning the way her native Africa is changing, is bewildered by all these "new" things that have come into her hometown, and she cannot (or does not wish to) adjust to an adulterated Africa. She is a fundamentalist of sorts who cannot follow her husband's obeisant and aping modern European ways. Lawino is no Yahoo, however; she is an intelligent commentator expressing a profound discontent at the imposition of alien standards on a subject and all-too-willing people. Okot uses the device of Lawino's and her husband Ocol's quarrels to highlight their differences of personal, political, cultural, and social views; Ocol wants to leave Lawino to live with his more "progressive," European-bandwagon mistress, Tina. The desertion is expressed in the poem's subtitle: "A Lament." But the poem itself is not a lament—it is a celebration of things East African in general and Acholi in particular, and an uproarious exposure of European ways (missionaries, religion, teachers, education, politics and politicians, and African toadies of Western culture come in for a call-down by Lawino in her comic hyperboles about the states of New Africa). The poem proved such a success with both its African and English readers that it was followed in 1970, with Ocol's side of the matter, *Song of Ocol*, but the sequel is not as humorous as its predecessor, largely because Okot was intent on allowing Ocol to do his own exposing. The resultant tone is an irony more layered and questionable as Ocol speaks in his pompous and bewildered manner of his wrongs and Lawino's betrayal of him.

In 1971 Okot published *Song of a Prisoner* (with an introduction by Edward Blishen), his most agonizing poem, in which a man's arrest becomes the basis for a confession of crimes against the state by one of its innocent, guilt-induced victims, crimes that on examination turn out to be the work of tyrants of social policy and programmed response and the desire of outcasts to be reaccepted into the group through penitence. Much like Franz Kafka's *The Trial* in its beginning questions (and much unlike it in its African unfolding of the issues), the poem exposes the heart-rending irony of freedom's cost. The protagonist is a victim of his new, independent government and its new ways, which have swept aside older notions of justice and due process of law in a program of Africanization; in effect Okot's prisoner is a prisoner of *Uhuru* (freedom). In a review in *Parnassus* (Spring-Summer 1973), Michael G. Cooke said of it that "the singer operates as much in his own mind as in relation to his audience (judge, jailer, etc.). The cycle takes the form of a set of pleas—plangent, pungent, indignant, humble, conceited, incredulous, tender. . . . Associated with drink and dancing, poetry and rain, this catholicity carries an affirmation of human life in terms of fertility, the creative powers of language and music, beauty and vitality, community and hospitality" (p. 117).

Song of a Prisoner may have had its genesis in the experience of arrest and brief imprisonment that Okot suffered one night on a return trip home to Kisumu from Nairobi. Although he spent only one night in jail, he learned something he could not forget: guilt is induced as well as deduced in the name of various kinds of justice. This consciousness evident in *Song of a Prisoner* led to Okot's fourth song, *Song of Malaya*, in which he takes on the voice of a prostitute and bewails the decline of his country. Thus, from the personal and joyous, albeit by transference to the African communal ideal, Okot went to the symbolic, and from there to the socially conscious poem.

Okot wrote his poetry in both Acholi/Lwo and in English, and did his own translations into English. He also edited and translated two collections of Acholi writing, *Horn of My Love* (1974, poetry) and *Hare and Hornbill* (1978, stories and poetry). The interplay between his native language and folk/oral traditions and his worldly English language and education kept him aware of sources of creativity and led to informal study of theories of literature. Okot never polarized or chose one theory over another; he was a syncretist, an amalgam maker (Ogo A. Ofuani calls him a "traditional modern poet"). He did, however, understand the difficulties of transposing an oral art into a written one, and the losses, as well as the gains, involved; the same processes and difficulties occur in transposing nonverbal Acholi/Lwo/African culture into verbal/Western/written form. Okot discussed these problems, and his resolution of them, in his essay "What Is Literature?" (*Busara* 4, no. 1 (1972): 21–27). For him literature is a "festival," as demonstrated by and in the celebrations of his Acholi brothers and sisters; it is open, communal participation, and is not sealed in private enterprise. As Okot put it, "A song is a song whether it is sung or written down. . . . The aim of any literary activity must be to ensure that there is communication between the singer and the audience, between the story-teller and his hearers. There must be full participation by all present" (quoted in *African Studies Review* 28, no. 4 (December 1985): 89).

It seems of little wonder (though of much sorrow) that Okot lost his buoyant spirit in exile—he needed his local countrymen as a spur for his constructive detonations because he was a part of their local customs and was identifying with them as well as laughing at human absurdities. His mischievous satires were in effect praise poems in their affirmation of viable native customs in the modern world. The Uganda government in denying him safe passage in his own country took away his vitality and life force. Okot could go on criticizing, but the sounds would be meaningless to him. For he would now be an outsider chattering about others, and he was not interested in others—he was interested in the Acholi/Lwo/Uganda/East African self. But, and the "but" remains an important butt of Okot's satire, he recognized that no identity in modern times can ignore Western omnipresence. To ignore the modern, in Okot's eyes, was as much cause for satire as to glorify the tribal past without an awareness of the need for change in a changing world.

In 1982 Okot returned to Uganda to teach at Makerere University in Kampala, but he died within five months of his return home.

Selected Title: *Acholi Proverbs* (Nairobi, 1985).

Consult: D. Duerden and Cosmo Pieterse, eds., *African Writers Talking* (1972); G. A. Heron, *The Poetry of p'Bitek* (London, 1976); Albert Lord, *The Singer of Tales* (1976); Ogo A. Ofuani, "The Traditional and Modern Influences in Okot p'Bitek's Poetry," *African Studies Review* 28, no. 4 (December 1985): 87–99. See also Introduction by G. A. Heron in *Song of Lawino and Song of Ocol* (London, 1984).

PELTSMAN, Michael (pseudonym of Mikhail Armalinsky). Born April 23, 1947, in Leningrad, USSR; he lives in St. Louis, Missouri. Peltsman emigrated from Leningrad in 1976, where he had earned a master's degree in electrical engineering, which, in his words in a letter to the editor of this study, he "hated," and had written "a lot of poetry," of which little was published in the Soviet Union. In 1982 he began writing exclusively in prose. He has published six books since 1974, all in Russian.

PERETZ, Isaac Leib. Born 1851 in Lublin, Poland; died 1915 in New York. Peretz wrote first in Hebrew, then turned to Yiddish as his language of literary expression. *Monish* is the first verse novel in modern Yiddish. His *Complete Works* was published in 1929.

PIETERSE, Cosmo. Born c. 1925 in South West Africa (now Namibia). Pieterse was educated at Capetown University. He was active in both literary and social protest as an expatriate in the United States and in England. He was ordered to leave the United States in the 1980s, where he had been teaching at the university level in Ohio, because his visa had expired; in England he also experienced resident alien difficulties with the authorities. Pieterse is best known as an editor, though he has published a number of his poems in periodicals over the years.

Selected Titles: (with Donald Munro) ed., *Protest and Conflict in African Literature* (1969); ed., *Seven South African Poets and Poems of Exile* (1971); ed., *Five African Plays* (1972).

PINSKI, David. Born 1872 in Mohilev, Ukraine; died 1959 in Haifa, Israel. Pinski and his family moved to Moscow in 1885. In 1891, on his way to Vienna, Pinski stopped in Warsaw to show his Yiddish stories to the famous Yiddish writer Isaac L. Peretz,* whose encouragement so moved Pinski that he returned to Warsaw in 1892 to become the assistant editor of Peretz's anthology, *Yomtov Bletter.* Pinski left for further studies in Berlin in 1896 and emigrated to New York in 1899, where he edited several Yiddish Labor periodicals as well as participated in the Labor-Zionist movement.

Pinski was the first president of the Yiddish PEN Club. In 1949 he moved to Haifa, where he continued writing his stories, plays, articles, and commentary until he died ten years later.

PLANTE, David. Born March 4, 1940, in Providence, Rhode Island; he lives in London. The sixth of seven sons of French-Canadian and American Indian stock, Plante had a Catholic grammar and high school education. He earned a B.A. in French from Boston University. From 1961 to 1962 he taught English as a foreign language in Rome, and then returned to the United States, where he was a researcher and guidebook writer for *Hart's Guide to New York*. From

1965 to 1966, he taught French in a Massachusetts preparatory school. Since then, he has lived in London.

Plante's first publication, in 1967, was a short story, "The Buried City." He has published eight novels, a biographical memoir, and numerous short pieces. The consensus is that he is a talented experimental novelist who retains a concern for details of realism, but that he tends toward a dense humorlessness.

Plante's first five novels are inspired by earlier American writers whose voices he transports into a modern *nouveau roman* idiom. The inspirational voice of *The Ghost of Henry James* (1970) is obvious; *Slides* (1971) uses Nathaniel Hawthorne; and *Relations* (1973), *The Darkness of the Body* (1974), and *Figures in Bright Air* (1976) are visited by Gertrude Stein.* In his trilogy of the Francoeur family, clearly based upon his own family, the voice becomes Plante's own, and the style becomes more traditionally narrative. The novels, *The Family* (1978), *The Country* (1981), and *The Woods* (1982), examine the dynamics of a loving but difficult family and explore themes of faith and loyalty through the sensitive eyes of the autobiographical figure, Daniel. Plante has also written a biographical memoir of three *Difficult Women* (1982), Jean Rhys,* Sonia Orwell, and Germaine Greer.

The Family reveals in Daniel's perceptions why he has chosen expatriation: "foreigners, he thought, live in worlds that don't have particulars, live in vast, sharp, clear, general worlds" (133). Both Daniel and his creator seem to believe that as an alien one gains the ideal novelist's perspective.

There have been no critical articles or books published on Plante other than entries in reference works, such as the thorough one by John R. Kaiser in *The Dictionary of Literary Biography Yearbook 1983*, and a bibliography, "David Plante: A Bibliographical Checklist," by George Bixby, in *American Book Collector*, November–December 1984.

Selected Titles: *The Catholic* (1986); *The Native* (1988).

JOAN GORDON

PLIVIER, Theodor (in exile: Plievier). Born February 17, 1892, in Berlin-Wedding, Germany; died March 12, 1955, in Avegno, Switzerland. After early voyages to Australia and South America, Plivier served throughout World War I as a sailor in the German navy and participated in the Wilhelmshaven mutiny of November 1918. His best-seller *Des Kaisers Kulis* (1929; *The Kaiser's Coolies*, London, 1932), which was translated into eighteen languages, reflects his disillusionment with naval service and reveals the radical political commitment that prompted him to join an anarchist publishing venture. After Adolf Hitler's accession to power, Plivier fled to Moscow, where he became a member of the National Committee for a Free Germany. He returned to Berlin in 1945 in the wake of the victorious Soviet army, but after working for the Walter Ulbricht regime for only two years, he reemigrated to West Germany.

Plivier's reputation rests on a grandiosely conceived trilogy: *Stalingrad* (Moscow, 1945; Mexico City, 1946), *Moskau* (Munich, 1952), and *Berlin* (Munich,

1954). These interrelated novels, in which the same characters intermittently appear, describe in horrific, Goya-like detail the disintegration of the Third Reich from the collapse of the German army at Stalingrad to the ultimate Russian triumph in the capital of a now-demoralized enemy state. In his realistic narrative, Plivier strives to strike a balance between the opposed parties and occasionally achieves panoramic effects worthy of Émile Zola. Amid the chaos of total warfare individuals seem mere "puppets on a stage as the curtain falls." The verisimilitude of his account is based on interviews conducted with prisoners of war. In this sense, Plivier may claim to be a pioneer of the documentary school of fiction. His political struggle as an exile, defector to the Russians, and re-defector to the West raises intricate questions as to the nexus between loyalty and betrayal, between treason and true patriotism, and between exile as a sanctuary and exile as an ideological prison.

   Translations: Plivier's trilogy is available in English: *Stalingrad* (London, 1948); *Moscow* (London, 1953); *Berlin* (London, 1956).

   Consult: H. Wilde, *Theodor Plivier: Nullpunkt der Freiheit* (Munich, 1965).

CEDRIC HENTSCHEL

PLOMER, William (Charles Franklyn). Born December 10, 1903, in Pietersburg, Northern Transvaal; died September 22, 1973, in London, England. Plomer was taken to England in 1904 when his mother became ill. He returned to South Africa in 1905. In 1908 he was taken again to England by his mother and put in care of his Aunt Hilda, who arranged his schooling until 1911, when his mother brought him back to Johannesburg, where he attended St. John's College. In 1917 he left for England again to attend Rugby; in 1919 he returned to Johannesburg as a "day boy" at St. John's College. Thus, within his childhood and youth, he experienced a succession of journeys that promoted a sense of rootlessness. In 1921 he lived on a farm (Marsh Moor) near Molteno, where he worked as a sheep-shearer, enjoying the discipline and the silent landscape. When Plomer's father retired in 1922, Plomer was asked to help him establish a native trading post at Entumeni (The Place of Thorns) in an isolated area in Zululand. Plomer's experiences here were expropriated for much of his African fiction, particularly his first novel, *Turbott Wolfe* (London, 1926). That publication brought him to the attention of Roy Campbell,* who issued an invitation for Plomer to visit him and his wife at their home, Umdoni Park. It was here that Plomer wrote "Ula Masondo," one of the key stories in his second book, *I Speak of Africa* (London, 1927). In 1926 Plomer met Laurens van der Post,* and the three of them—Campbell, van der Post, and Plomer—joined forces to publish a literary magazine, *Voorslag*, that had a brief life but lasting influence in its provocation on young South African writers. Plomer and Post sailed for Japan on September 2, 1926, Post to cover a story for a Durban newspaper and Plomer to see the country. Post returned in a few weeks, but Plomer stayed in Japan for almost three years and kept in contact with Japanese friends for most of his life. In 1929 Plomer returned to England via Korea, Siberia (he crossed the territory in ten days of train travel), and Europe. By this time he had published five books and was a well-known literary figure. Although he traveled intermittently the rest of his life, England—and London literary life—became his profound home.

Plomer is a mixture of South African and English heritage, and the mixture is apparent in the liberal attitudes expressed in his African fiction, where he speaks with English tolerance of the dignity and rights of black oppressed victims. In his later years he drew pleasure from editing and writing introductions for several South African works, among them Pauline Smith's *The Little Karoo*; Hans Reich's *South Africa*; H. C. Bosman's *Unto Dust*; Guy Butler's edition of *South of the Zambesi: Poems from South Africa*; Zelda Friedlander's *Until the Heart Changes: A Garland for Olive Schreiner*. He also edited the first edition in English of *The Dark Child* (London, 1955) by Camara Laye.* He revisited South Africa, however, only once, in 1956 at the invitation of the University of Witwatersrand.

Plomer may be said to be a wanderer, or a constitutional exile, one who feels slightly outside the community in which he lives. He expresses such exilic feelings, and such ambiguities of allegiance, in his two autobiographical works, *Double Lives* (London, 1943) and *At Home* (London, 1958), as well as in his fiction and poetry. Plomer also retained his fond interest in Japanese literature and customs and edited several volumes in English by Japanese writers. He wrote and edited biographies (*Cecil Rhodes* [London, 1933]; *Kilvert's Diary*, 2 vols. [London, 1938–39], one-vol. ed., 1944) and wrote four libretti for music by Benjamin Britten—*Gloriana* (London, 1953), for the coronation of Queen Elizabeth II; *Curlew River* (London, 1965), based on a Japanese Noh play; *The Burning Fiery Furnace* (London, 1966); and *The Prodigal Son* (London, 1968). He was given the Order of the British Empire in 1968.

Although Plomer is likely to be remembered for his many roles and faces, and as an example of the constitutional exile, his first novel, *Turbott Wolfe*, serves as his lasting achievement. His view in this work is radical but pessimistic. The hero, Wolfe, dies a few days after telling his story to the "I" narrator, who by a realistic, symbolistic touch is given the name "William Plomer." The tag "Chastity Wolfe" with which the natives label Turbott (because he seems to shun sexual activity) is an apt symbol as well: his life has been a rejection of experience, and that rejection has led to the void that encloses him. In *Africa in Modern Literature* (1967), Martin Tucker writes:

Today, it is easy enough to understand why *Turbott Wolfe* stimulated so much controversy on its first publication. And, because the novel calls for the abolition of the color bar in a violently sexual manner, the book has remained controversial. Plomer's next book, *I Speak of Africa*, was less controversial but no less influential. A collection of three short novels, it introduced a new kind of hero in Ula Masondo. "Ula Masondo" is the story of a native who tries to adapt to Christian and Western standards and who fails because his eagerness to please cannot adapt itself to white immorality and sloth. The story is the record of another instance of failure in the relationship between black and white: the

African who has loved and respected, and who has tried to imitate, his white masters is brutally mistreated by them. . . . Plomer is a novelist of violence because he views the South African scene as an environment of tension and repressed hostility which cannot be altered by quiet good will. It is action, and not sentiment, which affects South Africa in his fiction. (pp. 210–11)

Consult: John Robert Doyle, Jr., *William Plomer* (1969).

POPLAVSKY, Boris Yulianovich. Born 1903 in Moscow, Russia; died 1935 in Paris, France. Poplavsky's active literary career spans only six years in exile in Paris in the 1920s, but his remarkable output during a very short life has earned him a world reputation. He left Russia in 1919 when he was sixteen; he spent the second half of his life in Constantinople and Paris. In Constantinople, to which he fled with his father, he became a fervent adherent of Russian Orthodoxy. In 1921 he and his father emigrated to France, where Poplavsky became a frequenter of the émigré artistic circle in Paris; he was part of the network of gifted artists that included Marina Tsvetaeva* and Alexei Remizov.* His literary influences, with the exception of Aleksander Blok, however, are non-Russian: Charles Baudelaire, Guillaume Apollinaire*, and James Joyce*. His best-known work is *Homeward from Heaven*, a hybrid form of fiction and autobiography written in Russian that treats Poplavsky's life in Paris.

Translation: Selections in *Modern Russian Poetry*, ed. Vladimir Markov and Merrill Sparks (1967); in *Russian Poetry: The Modern Period*; eds. John Glad and Daniel Weissbort (1978).

Consult: Gregory Adamovich, "Literaturrnye besedy," *Zveno* 4 (Paris, 1928); Temura Pachmuss, *A Russian Cultural Revival* (1984); Victor Terras, *Handbook of Russian Literature* (1985).

POPOVSKY, Mark Alexandrovich. Born July 8, 1922, in Odessa, Ukraine; he lives in Washington Heights, New York City. Popovsky was an army medical officer in World War II. After the war he earned a degree in philology from Moscow University in 1952. A free-lance journalist not affiliated with the state press, he wrote articles for *Pravda*, *Izvestia*, *Literary Gazette*, and many Soviet magazines; he was a member of the Union of USSR Writers from 1957 to 1977. A collection of his sketches on outstanding Russian scientists, physicians, agronomists, and pharmacologists was issued in book form under the title *The Master of the Sunflower*; two other similar collections, *When the Physician Dreams* and *The Way to the Heart*, were published in the USSR. For several years he gathered material on the life of the bacteriologist Vladimir Harkin (1860–1930), the man who developed the first vaccine against cholera and the bubonic plague. Popovsky's documentary account of Harkin's career, *The Fate of Doctor Harkin* (1963), and his novel *Five Days of One Life* (1965) helped to establish Harkin's reputation in his native land.

Popovsky has published fourteen books of biography and scientific history in the USSR, among them *In the Footsteps of the Dissenters* (1961; the title may also be translated as *In the Footsteps of Those Off the Beaten Path*); *Over a*

Chart of Human Sufferings (1971), and *"Hurry!"* (1968), a biography of the biologist Nicholas Vavilov. The last book Popovsky published in the USSR was *Panacea, the Daughter of Aesculapias* (1973).

Popovsky has said that in 1964, while continuing to publish in the Soviet Union, he began writing books not destined for Soviet publication. For several years he collected information on the career of biologist Vavilov, who perished in a Soviet prison from hunger. Popovsky claims to have succeeded in gaining access to confidential KGB material on Vavilov, but has been unable to publish more than a fraction of what he has seen. The excerpt published in the magazine *Space*, nos. 6–7 (1966), entitled "A Thousand Days in the Life of Academician Nicholas Vavilov," resulted in Popovsky's official state censure, and he was unable to publish any of his work in the Soviet press for two years. His entire manuscript on Vavilov was later published in German, *N. Vavilov und die Biologische Diskussion in der Ud SSR* (Berlin, 1977); in a Russian-language edition in the United States in 1983; and in English as *The Vasilov Affair* (1984), with a foreword by Andrei Sakharov.

In 1979 Popovsky published in Paris his study *The Life and Writings of Voino-Yasenetsky, Archbishop and Surgeon* in his original Russian version. He had written the manuscript in the Soviet Union and had traveled to the Arctic Circle for his research as well as interviewed more than 150 people. The book is a testament to the courage of a famous scientist (he won the Stalin Prize for Medicine) who refused to surrender his religious faith under extensive pressure and harassment by government officials. The archbishop spent twelve years in prison and labor camps, and is reported to have replied to Soviet officials when they asked him to remove his cross and cassock: "You will remove this cassock only with my skin."

Because of Popovsky's association with dissidents and his disfavor among censorious bureaucrats, he was subjected to harassment. He was not allowed to publish in magazines or newspapers; his manuscripts, which previously had been accepted for publication, were returned to him. Shortly before he left the Soviet Union in 1977, he discovered the archives of the peasant-followers of Leo Tolstoy and smuggled out to the West some 3,000 pages of manuscript material. He incorporated this material into his book, *Russkie Muzhiki Passkazyvaiut. Posledovateli L. N. Tolstovo v Sovetskom Soiuze v 1918–1977* (1984; Russian Peasants Speak).

Popovsky has lived in New York since his defection from the Soviet Union. There he published *Manipulated Science* (1979, in English), which he wrote in the Soviet Union; the work is an indictment of the current situation in the Soviet Union in which Party policy manipulates objective science, and it is a grim warning of the possibility of the destruction of Soviet science. Popovsky has also written scripts for Radio Liberty and is an editor of *Grani* (Facets), the Russian-language exile journal published in Frankfurt, West Germany.

Popovsky's newest work is a reportorial account, *Tristiy Lishny. On, Ona i*

Sovetary Rezhim (1985, The Superfluous Third: He, She, and the Soviet Regime), in which he prints interviews with 250 recent emigrants from the USSR. One of the book's major themes is the distortion of intimacy and personal relations in the Soviet Union because of bureaucratic invasion into the daily lives of Soviet citizens.

Consult: *Free Voices in Russian Literature—1950–1980, a Biographical Guide* (1987); *Writers Directory 1984–1986*.

ZORIC WARD

PORTNOY, Alicia. Born 1955 in Argentina; she lives in Washington, D.C. Portnoy was among the intellectuals and writers arrested by the military government during what is known as Argentina's "dirty war." The testimony about prison camp conditions she gave to the United Nations, Amnesty International, and other human rights organizations led, in part, to the conviction of several junta generals. Portnoy's own stories and poems, which were smuggled out of prison, were published anonymously to protect her against further torture by the authorities. In 1986 she published under her name a memoir of her incarceration, *The Little School*, a work that received wide attention for its portrayal of the undaunted human spirit under duress. Portnoy is also the editor of *You Can't Drown the Fire* (1988), an anthology of poetry, short fiction, essays, and testimonials by Latin American women living in exile.

POUND, Ezra Loomis. Born October 30, 1885, in Hailey, Idaho; died November 1, 1972, in Venice. At the age of four, Pound was moved from the frontier town of his birth to the genteel environs of Philadelphia, which his mother felt to be more consonant with her social needs. Pound's father soon followed the example of wife and son, and through his wife's family's connections, landed a job at the U.S. Mint, where he worked until retirement. Pound was an odd child, ostracized by his peers, who called him "The Professor." His parents raised him in the Presbyterian faith; they themselves did missionary work among the poor Italians of Philadelphia. In 1901, at the age of fifteen, Pound entered the University of Pennsylvania, where he was mentored by William Brooke Smith, a tubercular artist to whom Pound later dedicated his first published volume of verse, *A Lume Spento* (Venice: privately printed for the author, 1908). Included in this volume is "The Tree," which anticipates Canto XC in his Rock-Drill Sequence.

Pound transferred to Hamilton College (Pennsylvania) in 1903, receiving a Ph.B. degree there in 1905. He then reenrolled at the University of Pennsylvania, where he met H. D.,* Marianne Moore, and William Carlos Williams. In general, though, Pound had few friends. Williams said of him, "Not one person in a thousand likes him, and a great many people detest him, and why? Because he is so darned full of conceits and affectation. . . . It is too bad, for he loves to be liked, but there is some quality in him which makes him too proud to try to please people" (*Autobiography* [New York, 1948], p. 58).

Pound briefly worked at Wabash College (Indiana), his only U.S. teaching position, but left there in January 1908 because of the scandal created by his having harbored an abandoned chorus girl in his apartment. On February 8, 1908, "hungry for his own kind," Pound sailed by cattle ship via Gibraltar (see Canto XXII) and Venice to London, where he was to remain for the next thirteen years. There, in December, at the age of twenty-three, he published his second volume of verse, *A Quinzaine for This Yule* (London: Pollock, 1908). In 1909, he began giving lectures on medieval and Renaissance themes at the Regent Street Polytechnic, where his work attracted the interest of Olivia Shakespear, novelist, and her daughter, Dorothy, whom Pound married on April 20, 1914. She bore him a son, Omar, on September 10, 1926.

Pound was a tireless literary impresario in London, where he was midwife to the careers of T. S. Eliot,* Robert Frost, James Joyce,* Ford Madox Ford,* Wyndham Lewis, and others, often sending them clothes and money when he himself had little. He invented the term *"les Imagistes"* in 1912, at the age of twenty-seven, in a discussion of T. H. Hulme in his *Ripostes* (London: Swift, 1912). By the time he left for Paris in 1921, "il miglio fabbro," as Eliot dubbed him, had written for the *Dial*, the *Little Review, Egoist*, the *Atheneum, New Age, Poetry*, and *BLAST!*, and had published seventeen books, the most celebrated of which are *The Spirit of Romance* (London, 1910) and *Hugh Selwyn Mauberly* (London: Ovid Press, 1920). He had already established a reputation for quarrelsomeness, flamboyance, and philandering in England, a reputation which followed him and grew on the European continent. The more he offended the staid British establishment, the fewer were his opportunities to publish, and the greater his embitterment in the face of bourgeois capitalism.

His reputation as a poet began to suffer a downturn in Paris, where he only lasted four years, 1921–25. There he read, approved, translated, and postscribed Rémy de Gourmont's *Natural Philosophy of Love* (1922). The *Philosophy* fit in well with Pound's criticism of Christianity's ("Xtianity's") condemnation of the sensual, and his belief in the primitive, vatic graces of ritually sanctioned sex. For Pound the Muses were living, sexually available women. While in Paris, he also strengthened his ties to music, both collaborating with and writing about composer Georges Antheil. He also championed the American expatriate violinist Olga Rudge. Rudge later bore him a daughter, Mary (b. July 9, 1925), and was living with him at the time of his death. Pound was not as centrally situated in Paris as he had been in London, and he wasn't publishing much. At parties where the Baroness Elsa von Freytay-Loringhoven could appear in a gown made of pots and pans, Pound's earring and malacca cane were decidedly understated. And he was getting bad reviews. Gertrude Stein* said of him, "He's like the village explainer, which is fine if you're a village, and if not not."

In 1925, Pound settled in Rapallo, Italy, where he lived for the next twenty years. He, Dorothy, and, eventually, his parents lived in one house, and Olga lived in another up the hill. Pound shuttled back and forth between houses, and even, when the Germans requisitioned his own home, moved Dorothy and his parents into Olga's for a while. The isolation of Rapallo did two things for Pound. First, it let him concentrate on the imperishably beautiful and revolutionary verse of the *Cantos* (New York, 1970), nearly half of which he wrote there. Published incrementally in 1919, 1928, 1937, 1940, 1948, 1955, 1959, and 1965, the *Cantos* embodies Pound's self-contradictory rejection of what he once called "an old bitch gone in the teeth / a botched civilization." His substitute for the "botch" was a glorious transmutation of his dead heroes into ever-present historical symbols. His readings of François Villon, Guido Cavalcanti, Sigismundo di Malatesta, Confucius, and Thomas Jefferson bear the narcissistically personalized patina of a Poundian mask, a persona. Malatesta, for example, who was little more than a "velvet-coated bully and thug," Pound transformed into an arts patron and managerial genius (c.f. Pound's Mussolini). The second thing Rapallo did for Pound was to deprive him of an intellectual milieu sufficient to dissuade him from his ever-more virulent anti-Semitism and crank economics.

Arrested in 1945 for his rabidly incoherent radio broadcasts over Rome Radio—difficult amalgams of Confucius, Provence and empty pockets, which Pound actually believed would spur President Franklin D. Roosevelt to call him into America's ruling circle—Pound was declared insane. He then spent the next thirteen years holding a kind of literary court in St. Elizabeth's Hospital for the Criminally Insane (Washington, D.C.), styling himself an "internal exile." During this time, largely due to the efforts of T. S. Eliot, Pound received the Bollingen Prize for his Pisan Cantos. That this prize, awarded by the Library of Congress, should go to an officially insane individual under indictment for treason, a capital offense, astounded some of his contemporaries. The periodicals hummed with debate. In 1958, largely due to the efforts of Robert Frost, Pound was released into the custody of his wife, whom he quitted shortly thereafter to live with his former mistress, Olga Rudge.

About 1960, Pound began to be oppressed by his sense of contrition. He began referring to his entire work as a "botch," and he wrote the famous last cantos (CX-CXVII) with their poignant refrains on failed achievement. From 1962 on, he gradually left off writing, and even talking. He died quietly in his sleep and is buried on the cemetery island of San Michele.

Pound saw himself as quintessentially American, despite the large portions of his life spent abroad. In his twin desperations to keep himself at the center of the world's attention at the same time as he castigated its philistinism, he sabotaged the brilliance of his poetic gifts. He left a permanent mark on twentieth-century poetry, nudging it toward a concern with voice, hermeneutics, and original patterning. The Old Testament tone of his economic harangues and the fervency of his aesthetic beliefs are still important in contemporary ideological debates.

Consult: Donald Gallup, *A Bibliography of Ezra Pound* (London, rev. ed. 1969); Donald Davie, *Ezra Pound* (1976); Hugh Kenner, *The Poetry of Ezra Pound* (1951);

Noel Stock, *The Life of Ezra Pound* (1970); E. Fuller Torrey, *Roots of Treason* (1984); J. J. Wilhelm, *Ezra Pound in London and Paris (1908–1925)* (1990).

JUDITH M. BRUGGER

POWYS, J. C. (John Cowper). Born October 8, 1872, in Shirley, Derbyshire, England; he died June 17, 1963, in Merionethshire, Wales. Powys lived in the United States for thirty years, traveling to various parts of the country on lecture/reading tours and imbibing the exhilaration of cultural observation. He elected to live away from his homeland, and in 1929 he moved for five years to a house in rural upstate New York. During World War II, after his return to Wales, he became known as a solitary wanderer among the hills who often spoke with American soldiers stationed nearby.

Powys is part of the prolific Powys writing family that includes his brothers Llewelyn Powys (who also lived abroad, and who wrote travel books, reportage, and fiction) and T. F. Powys, a recluse who found enough material for his fiction in his small natal village.

Selected Title: *The Diary of John Cowper Powys, 1930* (London, 1988).

Consult: G. Wilson Knight, *Visions and Vices: Essays on John Cowper Powys* (London, 1990).

PREZIHOV, Voranc (pseudonym of Lovro Kuhar). Born 1893 in Kotte, Yugoslavia; died 1950, in Maribor, Yugoslavia. Prezihov, a Slovene, was drafted into the Austrian army during World War I but escaped to Italy in 1916 in a vain attempt to join the enemy forces against the Austro-Hungarian Empire. He joined the Communist party in 1920 and took as his dual mission in life the writing of politically oriented fiction and the activism of a political revolutionary. In 1930 he fled from Yugoslavia to avoid arrest; he lived in Vienna, Prague, Paris, Norway, and Rumania. He returned secretly to Slovenia when World War II broke out in 1939 to help in partisan and underground activities, but was arrested and sent to the Sachsenhausen and Mautheusen concentration camps. After the war he was honored for his cultural and political activities by the new Yugoslavian state.

PRINCE, F. T. (Frank Templeton). Born 1912 in Kimberley, South Africa; he lives in England. Prince received his secondary schooling in South Africa; he left the country when he was nineteen years old to study at Oxford University, and never returned. He served in the British Intelligence Corps during World War II. Now retired, he was Professor of English at Southampton University; he has been accorded high recognition for his scholarly studies of John Milton (*The Italian Element in Milton's Verse*, 1984) and Shakespeare. As poet, he is best known for his first volume, *Soldiers Bathing* (1954). He has published ten volumes of poetry, "all distinguished," in the words of one critic, "by classical restraint, subtle craftsmanship and religious profundity."

In the National English Literary Museum Newsletter (*Nelm News*), published in South Africa, the issue of F. T. Prince as a South African poet is discussed in the terms of "the relationship between national identity and the creation and reception of imaginative literature" (November 13, 1988). The report summarizes an interview conducted by Stephen Devereux in Prince's home in Southampton in 1988, and repeats Prince's answer to Devereux's question, whether there is "still some corner of [his] life that is, forever, South African." Prince's response was that his first 19 years belonged to South Africa, "and nothing can ever replace, or be the equivalent of, your childhood"; Prince also said that "you can never have that relationship to another country, however much you devote yourself to it, and however much you take it for granted." Prince however admitted that he could not resolve the issue of national identity or dislocation, an issue which is the "prerogative" of the reading public and not of the author. Interestingly, Prince is omitted from two recent general anthologies of South African literature. Yet, as Michael Chapman writes in his Introduction to one of them, *The Paperbook of South African Poetry* (1986), the omission is not one based on Prince's decline as a poet but on the fact that his "interests, revealed by [his] poetry, have remained marginal to the life" of South Africa. The *Nelms* editor sums up the discussion in these words: "It is probably otiose to continue to ask whether 'South Africanness' is intrinsic to a poem, a matter of theme, setting, and idiom, or whether it is extrinsic, concerning the author's place of birth or residence, or the poem's place of composition or publication."

Selected Title: *Collected Poems* (1979).

PUIG, Manuel. Born December 28, 1932, in the small town of General Villegas in Buenos Aires Province, Argentina; died July 22, 1990, in Cuernavaca, Mexico. Puig recalled that as a child he went to the movies five nights a week and sat in the same seat on each visit to the theater. Hollywood films provided him with an escape from the repressive atmosphere of small-town life, an escape that he believes was redemptive. Drawn to the spiritual exile of escapism, Puig longed for physical exile as well. His family sent him to high school in Buenos Aires, and in 1951 he entered the University of Buenos Aires. In 1957 he traveled to Rome to study on scholarship at the Cine Citta (Experimental Film Center). Both environments were disappointing to him to the extent that he encountered what he considered similar repressive situations.

Puig's subsequent attempts at film directing and scriptwriting in the late 1950s and 1960s proved unsatisfactory. Because of the continued relation in his mind between film and fantasy, he acknowledged that his scripts were romantic copies of the films of his childhood. Puig then turned to realism in writing about his childhood. An exercise in re-creating the voice of an aunt grew into *La traición de Rita Hayworth* (1968; *Betrayed by Rita Hayworth*, 1971), the first of seven novels, all of which are autobiographical, according to Puig, in that they focus on an unresolved personal problem. In his first novel the spiritual exile of the child Puig is portrayed in the character of Toto Casals; the mundane, tedious reality of middle-class small-town life in Argentina is filtered through the consciousness of the sensitive boy. Though not in strictly chronological order, the novel traces his story from infancy in 1933 to 1948. Puig uses a variety of narrative techniques to develop the theme of repression as experienced by Toto. He feels an emptiness that is only partly relieved by the escapism of moviegoing.

Puig's second novel, *Boquitas pintadas* (1969; *Heartbreak Tango*, 1973), offers a cast of characters who base their lives on the model of those in soap opera and popular romance. At the heart of the book is Juan Carlos Etchepare, a charming but shallow Casanova, who (as the story opens in 1947) has died of tuberculosis. Nélida, a married woman who had known him ten years before, convinces herself that Juan Carlos is the only man she ever loved. She writes a number of tactless letters to his mother, reconstructing her romance with the son in terms of cliché and fantasy. Other characters' lives touch that of Juan Carlos: a friend seeking to emulate him impregnates a servant girl, who then murders her lover; a teacher, whose family employs the servant girl, becomes sexually involved with both Juan Carlos and the friend. Against these shallow characters two genuine figures are contrasted: the well-meaning though dull husband of Nélida and a widow who nurses Juan Carlos before his death.

The Buenos Aires Affair (1973, English title; Eng. edition, 1976) again portrays two spiritual exiles. Gladys D'Onofrio seeks a perfect love that includes a deep spiritual commitment, but her model is based on contemporary advertisements and Hollywood films. Unsuccessful in personal relationships, she suffers a nervous breakdown. In contrast, Leo Druschovich thrives on purely sexual conquest; when a woman accepts a relationship with him, he becomes impotent. Leo is driven by a deep guilt stemming from a homosexual experience that ended with his attacking, possibly killing, his partner. Whether his guilt derives from latent homosexuality or genuine fear over the violence of his aggression is not clear.

An Argentine prison cell is the place of exile in *El beso de la mujer araña* (1976; *Kiss of the Spider Woman*, 1980). The principal characters, the homosexual Molina and the political prisoner Valentín, are exiled from their normal milieus and, as the experience of sharing a cell begins, are spiritually exiled from each other by the distinctly different motivating forces of their lives. The chief way employed to survive the tedium of prison life is Molina's recounting of the plots of movies. Puig includes the plots of three actual Hollywood films and three invented plots. Valentín learns the power of fantasy and realizes the inadequacy of his political self-image. In turn, Molina becomes more political and agrees to engage in a mission for Valentín after the former's release from prison. In his manipulation of prison officials in a ruse to obtain goods in exchange for providing information about Valentín, Molina reveals himself a character of greater complexity and substance than the reader at first perceives. Thus, the central movement of the novel is the development of a friendship, which makes possible a transformation of both men.

The only Puig novel with a non-Latin setting, *Maldicion eterna a quienes lean estas paginas* (1981; *Eternal Curse on the Reader of These Pages*, 1982), offers the author's only traditional exile in the character of Juan José Ramirez, a seventy-four-year-old Argentine political prisoner recovering from amnesia in a New York nursing home. Ramirez is also spiritually exiled in that not only has he forgotten certain facts of his past, but he has lost the ability to experience certain feelings. In order to effect a recovery, he asks an attendant, a failed college history instructor, to re-create for him certain, mainly sexual experiences. In turn, the attendant feels gratification in communicating these experiences. In a note on the novel's jacket, Puig says that the work grew out of a series of interviews with a young, handsome man he met at a gymnasium, interviews that revealed the man as "morally bankrupt."

In his novel *Sangré de amor correspondido* (1982; *Blood of Requited Love*, 1984), set in Brazil, the character Josemar, like other Puig characters, feels repression and failure as a result of the masculine, materialistic society in which he moves. He creates fantasies of himself to boost his ego, including one in which he ruins the life of a young girlfriend by roughly forcing her into sexual submission and then abruptly breaking off the relationship. Josemar's need for such fantasies is evidence of a spiritual exile, but his exile is also partly physical: to spend time in his hometown is for Josemar painful because he must face his own failures there.

Pubis angélical, written in 1979, was published in English in 1987. In the last decade of his life, Puig wrote only one original play, *Under a Blanket of Stars*, but he authored several adaptations of his own fiction and that of other authors. The latter group includes a film version of *Heartbreak Tango* and a stage adaptation of *Kiss of the Spider Woman*. After living in various European capitals and in New York City, Puig settled in Rio de Janeiro, but moved to Mexico in his last years. Several of his books were banned at one time in Argentina. Now Puig saw no problem in returning to his native country, though he had chosen not to live there after the return of Juan Perón to power. Puig can be considered a chronicler of the ways, for good or ill, that people use to deal with frustration, failure, and guilt in middle-class life. His treatment of this theme, combined with his sophisticated, inventive narrative techniques, establishes him as a contemporary Latin American writer of importance.

Consult: Lucille Kerr, *Suspended Fictions: Reading Novels by Manuel Puig* (1987).

LADD KELLEY

Q ————————————————————

QABBANI, Nizar. Born 1923 in Syria; he lives in France. Qabbani, a Syrian diplomat at the time, began experiencing troubles with his government when he published a book of poems and commentaries on the Six-Day War between Israel and Arabs in 1967, *Footnotes to the book of the Setback*. The volume was issued in *samisdat* form by an underground press because of its critical/controversial nature. As a result of its publication, Qabbani's work was banned in his country, and he suffered disgrace and ostracism as did many Arab intellectuals in several countries; previous to this time, Qabbani had been one of the most popular Arabic writers. He fell out of favor with the Arab intellectual establishment again in 1970 when he published poems celebrating the policies and image of the Egyptian leader Gamal Abdel Nasser; although these pro-Nasser poems generated popular acceptance and enthusiasm, Qabbani found himself isolated in his intellectual milieu. He moved to Lebanon in 1971, where he formed a publishing house. He left Lebanon for France in 1987.

Consult: *Index on Censorship*, December 1981; September 1986; June 1990.

R ──────────────────────────────

RADAUSKAS, Henrikas. Born April 23, 1910, in Cracow, Poland; died August 27, 1970, in Washington, D.C. Radauskas studied Lithuanian, German, and Russian literature at the University of Kaunas, then worked as a radio announcer and an editor. He left Lithuania in 1944, lived in Germany, and emigrated to the United States in 1949. After a decade of work as a blue-collar laborer, he joined the staff of the Library of Congress, where he was employed until his death. Never a prolific writer, Radauskas published four books of poems: *Fontanas* (1935, The Fountain), *Strelé danguje* (1950, Arrow in the Sky), *Žiemos daina* (1955, The Winter Song), and *Žaibai ir véjai* (1965, Lightnings and Winds). A posthumous volume of his later poetry appeared in 1978. His poems have been translated into several languages, including English (by Randall Jarrell). Radauskas is considered by some critics the best Lithuanian poet of the twentieth century. His poetry has been compared to Paul Valéry's, Wallace Stevens's, and that of Osip Mandelshtam.*

Since he never subordinated his art to patriotic or philosophical concerns, as was the common practice of the Lithuanian letters in his time, he was often labeled an "aesthete." His poems, in their own way, express the basic themes of the modern era, the fragility of human beings and of culture, as well as the indomitable strength of humanity in the face of totalitarian challenge. Radauskas uses classical meters to attain a precise balance of imagery, rhythm, and sound. His major themes are love, human loneliness, and art itself, especially painting. Everyday life, mostly urban reality, in Radauskas's poetry undergoes a metamorphosis that achieves magical properties: more often than not he employed mythical and fairy-tale motifs. His work also displays an inclination toward subtle irony and the grotesque. Radauskas undoubtedly was the Lithuanian poet who more than any other overcame the borders of his language and tradition, joining the ranks of poets of universal significance. In this journey, he was assisted, rather than constrained, by his bitter experience of exile. A volume of his collected poems, published in Lithuania in 1980, has achieved extraordinary success.

Consult: Ivar Ivask, "The Contemporary Lithuanian Poet Henrikas Radauskas," *Lituanus* 5, no. 3 (1969); R. Šilbajoris, *Perfection of Exile* (1970).

TOMAS VENCLOVA

RADITSA, Bogdan. Born August 26, 1904, in Split, Yugoslavia; he lives in New York City. Raditsa came to the United States in 1946. He had served as a partisan with Marshal Tito during World War II, but preferred not to live under Tito's socialist rule. He has worked with the exile press in the United States, Canada, Australia, and Argentina, and has published several works of social commentary and autobiography. Among his works are *Diary 1944–1975* (1948) and *The Mediterranean Return*, both published in Croatian. In 1940 he published *The Agony of Europe* in Belgrade in the Cyrillic script; this work is a collection of linked interviews with literary figures, philosophers and intellectuals about the great crisis facing Europe, among them Thomas Mann,* Benedetto Croce, Andre Gide,* Georges Duhamel, Julian Bender, Paul Valéry, and François Mauriac. The work was banned by the Germans during their occupation of Yugoslavia and by the succeeding Tito administration. His two-volume autobiography appeared in 1984; vol. I covers his life in Europe, vol. II, his life in America.

RAFFAT, Donné. *See* Iranian Writers in Exile

RAMA, Angel. Born c. 1920 in Uruguay died November 27, 1983, in an airplane crash outside Madrid, Spain. Rama was literary editor of *Marcha* from 1958 to 1968, and also served in an editorial capacity on *Revista Iberoamericana de Literatura*. He went into self-exile in 1972 in Venezuela after the military coup in his country. He founded and was codirector of *Escritura*.

In 1981 Rama, who had been offered a tenured position at the University of Maryland, applied for permanent resident status in the United States. He had been living in the United States since 1979 and had been named Distinguished Scholar of Latin-American Literature at the University of Maryland. The U.S. Immigration and Naturalization Service (INS) denied the request on the grounds that Rama was a subversive as defined in the provisions of the McCarran-Walter Act. Rama appealed the charges, but the INS refused to disclose its sources of allegation; the INS asked Rama to show proof of "having evidenced an active opposition to communism for the previous five years." Rama refused to do so, declaring that such actions on his part would be tantamount to "recognizing the guilt that I am denying." Rama offered to request residency in the United States as a defector, but during the time of his appeal he died in an airplane crash outside Madrid, Spain.

RAMA RAU, Santha. Born 1923 in India; she lives in the United States. Rama Rau's autobiographical and journalistic flair created early attention to her writings; she also dramatized E. M. Forster's *A Passage to India*, which became a Broadway success. In recent years she has published little.

Selected Titles: *Remember the House* (1956); *My Russian Journey* (1959); *Gifts of Passage* (1961, autobiography).

RANDALL, Margaret. Born 1936 in Scarsdale, New York; she lives and teaches in Albuquerque, New Mexico, after having won her fight against the U.S. Immigration and Naturalization Service to deport her. Randall's family moved to New Mexico shortly after her birth. She attended the University of New Mexico, lived three years in New York City, and moved with her ten-month-old son to Mexico, where she met and married Sergio Mondragon, a Mexican national and poet. She gave up her American citizenship—a decision she regretted later—in order to secure work to support her son and her two daughters from her marriage to Mondragon. Together she and Mondragon edited the bilingual literary journal, *El Corno Emplumado* (The Plumed Horn), an influential publication both in Latin America and on the small-press scene in the United States, from 1962 to 1968; she coedited it with the American poet Robert Cohn for one further year. The journal served as a vehicle for introducing Spanish-language writers of Latin America (among them Octavio Paz* and Ernesto Cardenal) to English readers and for bringing the work of Allen Ginsberg, Denise Levertov, Paul Blackburn, and Diane diPrima, among other North American poets, to the attention of Latin American readers. When her marriage with Mondragon ended in 1968, Randall continued to live in Latin America, reporting on the political and social struggles she witnessed in Mexico, Cuba, and Nicaragua. She returned to Albuquerque on a visitor's visa in 1984 and married an American writer, Floyce Alexander, and began teaching at the University of New Mexico. Her book, *Albuquerque: Coming Home to the U.S.A.*, is a diary-journal of her impressions of her homeland after a twenty-three-year absence.

In 1984 Randall applied for permanent residency status in the United States. At her hearing before the U.S. Immigration and Naturalization Service (INS) on October 11, 1984, she testified: " . . . as I grow older, I believe more and more in people and their capacity to understand the truth when they're presented with different sides and I think it's healthy to be presented with different sides and I would prefer a country in which all those sides could be presented." Her application was denied one year later, and she was requested to leave the country; she appealed the decision. Her case was taken up by a wide variety of human rights advocates, civic groups, and literary associations, among them PEN American Center; twenty-nine writers, among them Donald Barthelme, E. L. Doctorow, and Denise Levertov, sent the following cable to INS Commissioner Alan C. Nelson:

On behalf of our writer colleagues in this country and abroad we ask you to grant permanent residency status to writer and former U.S. citizen Margaret Randall. Delay in her application is apparently connected to INS question October 11 last year which was targeted almost entirely at her published ideas and intellectual associations. We object to American officials still impugning writers and intellectuals under the ideological exclusion provisions of the McCarran-Walter Act, and we urge you to respect her as we do: as an asset to our best American traditions of ideas freely formed and transmitted in spite of political upheavals between nations.

On August 28, 1986, an Immigration Service ruling ordered that Randall be deported because her "writings advocate the economic, international, and governmental doctrines of world communism"; she was given until December 1, 1986, to leave. In protesting the decision to Attorney General Edwin Meese, PEN American Center sent a letter of protest, signed by Norman Mailer, Susan Sontag, Rose Styron, William Styron, Kurt Vonnegut, Hortense Calisher, Wesley Brown, Frances Fitzgerald, John Irving, and Hilary Masters, which asserted that Randall's ideas were being punished, and that her deportation would be an abridgment of the American right to free expression. The letter noted that the Immigration judge (Martin Spiegel) made his decision, by his own admission, on ideas expressed in Randall's books. Randall won a first round in her case in 1988 and was assured of continued residency in the United States, but the Immigration Department requested an appeal of the decision.

In his introduction to Randall's book, *Part of the Solution: Portrait of a Revolutionary* (1977), Robert Cohn summarized Randall's career and life from a rich Scarsdale, New York, girl to a rebel in Europe to a revolutionary in Latin America and eventually to a return home to Albuquerque. Cohn lived with Randall in hiding in Mexico in 1969, when both feared assassination by Mexican police and/or rightists. Randall and Cohn, who became coeditor of *El Corno Emplumado* after Randall's husband Mondragon left the journal, had angered Mexican authorities by the magazine's open support of the Mexican student uprising in 1968. Cohn tells in his introduction that Randall's parents were worldly, well-traveled, liberal sophisticates; in reaction, Randall adopted as many loyalties of awkward small-town-mindedness and controversial, provocative causes as she could discern. She married a wealthy ice hockey player, whom she met at the University of New Mexico, and spent a year with him in Spain (he ended up in a mental institution after the breakup of their marriage). From 1958 to 1961 she lived on the Lower East Side of New York City, working as a secretary in a feather factory, as an art model, as a court interpreter, and at the Spanish Refugee Aid headquarters run by Nancy McDonald. She also worked as a waitress in Amagansett, Long Island, one summer. When not working, she collected unemployment insurance benefits, which enabled her to write articles in favor of Fidel Castro and the Cuban revolution and to associate with both abstract expressionist painters and Beat poets of the decade, among them Robert Creeley, Paul Blackburn, and Charles Olson. Her first child was born in 1961 in New York before she left for Mexico, where she met Sergio Mondragon. The marriage became strained after the birth of their two daughters; the profound cause of separatism probably lay in Sergio's generally apolitical views and

Randall's contrasting social activism. He edited the Spanish-language section of *El Corno Emplumado*, Randall edited the English-language section; a review of their separate editorial accomplishments shows a wide difference between Randall's publication of "committed" work and Mondragon's encouragement of private, abstract expression. The breakup of their marriage was spurred by Randall's visits to Cuba in 1967 and 1968 to attend cultural congresses there, after which her decision to emphasize social poetry took on the spirit of a cause. Cohn became both her lover and coeditor on her return to Mexico. In 1969 Randall's passport was stolen, rendering her unable to visit Cuba. She and Cohn went into hiding and managed to reach Cuba in September 1969. In Cuba Randall became intimately involved in socialist experimentation, women's issues (and their triumphs in revolutionary activities), and with Third World politics. She moved to Nicaragua in July 1979 to write about women who helped the Sandinistas win their war. In December 1980 she moved to Managua to live with her youngest daughter, then eleven years old. All during this time she wrote diaries, poems, social tracts, and reflective essays.

In 1984, when she decided to return home, she had been away from the United States for twenty-three years. She said on her return: "I had not planned this nearly-quarter-century as one of expatriatism or exile. . . . I often thought of myself as a kind of hybrid, with as much of Latin America as of North America within me, and with values which reflected both cultures. . . . But I always thought of Albuquerque, New Mexico, as my home. . . . This city where my mother and father live, and my brother runs a bookstore."

Randall's case was returned, on her appeal, to the Immigration Board of Appeal, after the U.S. Supreme Court denied her appeal for a hearing. In August, 1989, the INS voted 3–2 that she has always been an American citizen. Thus Randall is free to live in the United States and travel abroad, if she chooses.

Randall is author of more than forty books; she is a poet, photographer, editor, publisher, translator, critic, and teacher.

Selected Titles: *Water I Slip Into at Night: Poems* (Mexico City, 1967); *Getting Rid of Blue Plastic: Poems Old and New* (Calcutta, India, 1968); *Spirit of the People* (Vancouver, Canada, 1975); *Carlotta: Prose and Poems from Havana* (Vancouver, Canada, 1978); *El Pueblo no solo es testigo: la historia de Dominga* (Puerto Rica, 1979); ed. and trans., *Breaking the Silences: An Anthology of 20th Century Poetry by Cuban Women* (Vancouver, Canada, 1980); *Women in Cuba, Twenty Years Later* (1981); *Sandino's Daughters: Testimonies of Nicaraguan Women in Struggle* (1981); *Risking a Somersault in the Air: Conversations with Nicaraguan Writers*, ed. Floyce Alexander (1984); *Women Brave in the Face of Danger: Photographs and Writings by Latin and North American Women* (1985); *Albuquerque: Coming Back to the U.S.A.* (Vancouver, Canada, 1986).

RANNIT, Aleksis. Born October 15, 1914, in Kallaste, Estonia, then a Russian province; died January 5, 1985, in New Haven, Connecticut, of a heart attack. An Estonian poet, scholar, and art critic, Rannit published much of his scholarly and critical work in English and also wrote some poems in English. Rannit studied art history and literature at the universities of Tartu (Estonia) and Vilnius (Lithuania), classical archaeology and aesthetics later at Freiburg (Germany), and after his immigration to the United States in 1953, library science and comparative literature at Columbia University. He was curator of Russian and East European studies at Yale University from 1960 until his retirement shortly before his death. Rannit held honorary doctorates from the universities of Stockholm and Seoul (Korea), and was elected a member of the International Academy of Arts and Letters in Paris in 1962.

Rannit's oeuvre is defined by two basic traits, a lifelong devotion to art in its variety of forms and a highly conscious and vigorously positive assertion of his status as an exile. As a literary critic and scholar, Rannit used his broad erudition and intimate familiarity with every modern art form to develop a unique synesthetic approach to the works of several twentieth-century poets, specifically the Estonians Marie Under (1883–1980), an exile like himself, and Heiti Talvik (1904–47); the Lithuanian Henrikas Radauskas* (1910–70), another exile; the Russians Anna Akhmatova and Nikolai Zabolotskii, "inner émigrés" both, and the Austrian Rainer Maria Rilke, on whom Rannit may have patterned his life and his poetry. Rannit's art criticism features the same synesthetic traits. His vision of the Lithuanian painter Čiurlionis and the Estonian graphic artist Wiiralt was determined by verbal and musical associations.

Rannit's poetry is pointedly synesthetic. It captures land and seascapes as a painter would see them, or it deals with works of art—paintings, sculptures, musical compositions—in an effort to translate their peculiar effect into the language of poetry. At the same time, many of Rannit's poems are attempts at a definition of poetry, or of the creative process. An eminently conscious craftsman, Rannit cultivated the euphonic aspect of his verse and introduced many innovations in the technique of Estonian verse, including the metric principle of tonic-quantitative verse and a type of rhyme that is often identified by his name. Rannit added to Estonian poetry, which had started with Romanticism, a distinctly Parnassian and classicist strain. He also succeeded in turning exile into an asset by conquering ever-new regions of world culture and world art for the Estonian word. At the same time he was able to introduce Estonian poetry to many international audiences. His poetry has appeared in book form in translations into English, German, Russian, Hungarian, and Lithuanian.

Selected Titles: *Akna raamistuses* (1937, In the frame of a window); *Käesurve* (1945, A handshake); *Suletud avarust* (1956, Closed expanses); *Kuiv hiilgus* (1963, Dry radiance); *Kaljud* (1969, Cliffs); *Sõrmus* (1972, A ring); *Helikeeli* (1982, Sound language); *The Violin of Monsieur Ingres: Some Hieratic and Erratic Estonian Lines in English* (1983); *Mikalojus Konstantynas Čiurlionis, Lithuanian Visionary Painter* (1984); *Valimik* (1985, A selection). Further volumes in English: *Line* (1970); *Dry Radiance: Selected Poems* in *New Directions 25: An International Anthology in Prose and Poetry* (1972); *Donum Estonicum: Poems in Translation* (1976); *Cantus Firmus* (1978, bilingual).

Consult: A. Willmann, "The Perceptional World of Aleksis Rannit's Poetry," *Estonian Learned Society in America Yearbook IV, 1964–1967* (1968); V. Terras, "The Poetics of Aleksis Rannit: Observations on the Condition of the Émigré Poet,'' *Journal of Baltic Studies* 5 (1974); V. B. Leitch, ''Modernist Poetry: A Phenomenological Reading of Aleksis Rannit's English Works,'' *Journal of Baltic Studies* 10 (1979).

VICTOR TERRAS

RAO, Raja. Born November 8, 1908, in Hassana, state of Mysore, India; he lives in Texas. Son of an old Brahmin family, Rao was sent to a Muslim school for his primary education; here he learned English. Retaining his interest and skill in his native Kannada/Sanskrit language, he studied English and history at Madras University and at Hyderabad. In 1929, at the age of nineteen, he won a Hyderabad state scholarship to study abroad; he moved to the University of Montpellier in France that year and later studied at the Sorbonne. In 1931 he met and married a Frenchwoman (the source of inspiration for the heroine Madeleine of *The Serpent and the Rope* [London, 1960; 1963]). During this period Rao gave up formal schooling and turned his attention to research and writing. He published four scholarly articles written in Kannada and several stories written in either English or French. (All of Rao's later work, from 1950, is written in English.) Rao's separation from his first wife and his return to India occurred at the same time; both were intimately involved with his quest for understanding of self and pursuit of knowledge higher than scientific objective reality. In his quest Rao lived in an ashram in India in 1933.

Though Rao constantly pays attention to the physical sciences and mathematics as part of his reality, his interest is in that totality of understanding that places knowledge in a distinction-less universe of being as well as on measurable scales of definition and category. In effect, he has been in search of a guru and a philosophy that will show him the way to subsume knowledge without obtrusion of divisive disciplines.

Rao lived in India during World War II, spending time in ashrams there and journeying through the subcontinent from the Himalayas to Cape Comorin in the south. (*The Serpent and the Rope* traces this journey-quest in the pilgrimage of its hero Ramaswamy, who has married a Frenchwoman, lost their two-year-old child to a fatal illness, and left his wife to return to India. The novel, autobiographical in narrative outline, is Rao's spiritual odyssey to a faith he has not yet allowed himself to surrender to.) Rao also was active in underground activities against the British during these years; his life, spent in search of a unity of meaning and desire, is filled with dualisms of a brilliant nature that cannot shut out the dark arrows of opposing loyalties. Thus, the philosopher-mystic, seeking to put the middle world of politics and power not so much behind him as underneath him in his lofty/humble concerns, was capable of engaging in several temporal acts that contradicted his soulful quest for the pure spirit of active passivity, the goal of powerful passive acceptance of all things, worldly and otherwise. (Some critics see in Rao's quandaries a battle between the active and passive forces recognized in Indian philosophy as the dynamic Feminine and the transcendental Masculine Absolute.)

After independence and the partition of India in 1947, Rao moved back to France but visited and lived in India for long intervals as well. He moved to the United States in 1963 to teach at the University of Texas (he first visited the United States briefly in 1950). In the late 1960s he married one of his American students, Katherine Ann Jones, now a successful playwright and short story writer and formerly an actress. They have one son. Recently they separated. Rao continues to live in Texas, though he retired from his university post in 1980. He has received several prestigious awards, among them one from the Indian Academy of Literature and the Neudstadt Prize in 1988, administered by *World Literature Today* and the University of Oklahoma at Norman.

Rao's award from the Indian Academy of Literature marked only the second time the honor was given to a writer working in the English language. It is important to emphasize that Rao is primarily an Indian writer writing in English. The distinction must be made between such a writer and the more familiar (to the Western reader) Anglo-Indian writer. Rao is not of mixed literary blood, nor an Indian writing primarily for an English-speaking audience. He is a writer who, as early as his twenty-first birthday when he was writing his first novel, *Kanthapura*, knew that Indian English was a separate language from either of its parents and a full, if not yet adult, one. In the foreword (written in 1937) to the original 1938 edition of *Kanthapura*, Rao wrote:

We are all instinctively bilingual, many of us writing in our own language and in English. We cannot write like the English. We should not. We cannot write only as Indians. We have grown to look at the large world as part of us. Our method of expression therefore has to be a dialect which will some day prove to be as distinctive and colorful as the Irish or the American. Time alone will justify it. (p. vii in the 1963 reprint edition)

In *Kanthapura*, Rao's vast erudition is compressed into the simple words of an old village woman whom he employs as his narrator—she tells the story of her village, Kanthapura, in the south of India, its comings and goings, its rhythms and dissonances when violence erupts in the wake of nonviolent protests during the years of Gandhi's Independence movement before World War II. The hero is a young city idealist who learns in the ensuing tragedy that accompanies his pacifist teachings—police and landlords turn a peaceful protest into a bloody riot—that transcendence of temporal defeat must be a constant in one's life. In Rao's third novel, *The Cat and Shakespeare* (1965), he says clearly that *real* victory comes proven in time, but the time lies in the soul of the beholder.

Rao continues his use of the humble narrator and his simple language in *The Cat and Shakespeare* (first published in *Chelsea* magazine in New York in 1959), a tale told by a lowly clerk (he cannot manage to earn more money at the end of his career than at the beginning of his employable state, though he does achieve his desired bride). The hero finds enlightenment through a guru who counsels him into the way of the kitten: by forgetting dominion and status, as the kitten does with the dominant mother cat, all things fall into a unity of action without strife or opposition. The union of kitten and cat and, by extension, man and master, requires more than rational (and demeaning) labels; the relationship between dominance and subjection must be illuminated by more than the victories recorded on surface battlefields, Rao seems to be saying. Some inner play—and delight in that play—occurs in Rao's rendering of Advaita Vedanta, the philosophical belief and guide of action that may be defined as the absence of all dualisms, the embrace of a timeless day. When the novel was first issued, Rao wrote of it: "It is a metaphysical comedy, and all I would want the reader to do is to weep at every page, not for what he sees, but for what he sees he sees. For me it is like a book of prayer."

Rao is not an exile, though he may be viewed as an expatriate. He lived for many years in France; he has lived in the United States for more than twenty-five years. Although he returns to India, and in the past has sought refuge in ashrams in his native land, he also has journeyed perilously close to Western shores of subversive rationality. He is a seeker after truth, and his journeys have crossed terrains of philosophy, history, and many academic and intellectual disciplines in many countries through time and geography. Lawrence Durrell* has said Rao has "honored" English literature in "writing in our language"; E. M. Forster has called *Kanthapura* "perhaps the best novel in English to come from India." *The Serpent and the Rope*, Rao's second novel (after an absence from long fiction for more than twenty years) has been judged a masterpiece by various critics. In treating the journey of a young Indian who goes to France to pursue his research in French medieval history, marries a Frenchwoman, and leaves her to return to India, aware of the great gulf that separates the consciousness of East and West, no matter how willing each may be in rational and physical desire, Rao re-created the philosophical dilemma of his generation in his own terms. Indeed Rao is after that most mystical and mythical of events: the meeting of East and West on the planes of communication and the flights of language; in his packbag are years of study of Western and Eastern philosophy, knowledge of European and Indian history. His quest in the novel takes him to Mysore, the Midi, Paris, Cambridge, and London as he continues his search for the serpent and the rope. As his hero says at one point, either one believes in the serpent or one believes in the rope. Either the world is real and every object in it is real (and thus we are at the mercy of the world's reality), or each man creates the reality of his world, each man climbs his rope to a growing understanding of what he sees before and behind him. At the end of *The Serpent and the Rope* it is unclear if the hero Ramaswamy will find *his* answer, but the quest has been made amid the real objects in the world, the quest has not been an escape from temporal daily responsibilities. Ramaswamy says as he is ending his tale: "And we went back to the plush chairs. The chocolate was very good."

Rao also has written brilliant short stories, issued in two collections, *The Cow of the Barricades and Other Stories* (London, 1947) and *The Policeman and the Rose* (New Delhi, 1978), which contains seven of the stories printed in the earlier collection. Rao's novella, *Comrade Kirillov*, written in French and published in Paris in 1965 (New Delhi, 1976), is presently receiving renewed attention. It provides a confrontation of two views of the world, that of Advaita Vedanta and that of modern communism, as the two philosophies grapple for the belief of the hero. Rao sees the Vedanta as a way of believing that opens up the individual; communism, in contrast, is a closed system. The protagonist, a South Indian Brahmin former teacher who has learned Russian in order to read Lenin in the original, has seemed to some readers a self-portrait by Rao.

Rao also has written plays, though most of the work in this genre was done in his youth. In reviewing Rao's only published volume of dramatic work, *Apavada*, in the *Indian PEN*, P. Ramanand wrote:

[*Apavada*] is a play in one scene in blank verse, dealing with the naive conceit that Sita may have been Ravana's own daughter. The skill of the author has made this conceit very plausible, but it is a pity that the theme has been given a dramatic form instead of a narrative one. The play is mainly a dialogue between Ravana and Mandodari concerning the birth of Sita, and in the course of their conversation it comes out that Sita is after all their own daughter. The situation is sufficiently dramatic, but the effect is weakened by the narrative character of the dialogue and the inanity—from the dramatic point of view— of most of the observations made by those characters when not narrating. . . . (September, 1938, p. 101)

Rao has been reported at work on several new projects, but he has published little in the past twenty years. One of his projects, a nonfiction work titled "Ganges and Her Sisters," was announced two decades ago but has not appeared. A newer manuscript, completed but not yet published, is reportedly a novelistic conversation between a Brahmin and a rabbi on the meaning of the Holocaust and the ways to transcend the memory/experience of it.

Selected Titles: ed., with Iqbal Singh, *Changing India: An Anthology* (London, 1939); with Iqbal Singh, *Whither India?* (1944); *Soviet Russia: Some Random Sketches and Impressions* (Bombay, 1949); *The Chessmaster and His Moves* (New Delhi, 1988). See also Selected Bibliography (1931–1988) compiled by R. Parthasarathy in special issue of *World Literature Today* 62, no. 4 (Autumn 1988) devoted to Rao.

Consult: P. C. Bhattacharya, *Indo-Anglian Literature and the Works of Raja Rao* (New Delhi, 1983); Janet Powers Gemmill, "Rhythm in *The Cat and Shakespeare*," *Literature East and West* 13 (1969); M. K. Naik, *Raja Rao* (1972; rev. ed., Bombay, 1982); C. D. Narasimhaiah, *Raja Rao* (New Delhi, 1973); R. Parthasarathy, "Tradition and Creativity: Stylistic Innovations in Raja Rao," in *Discourse across Cultures: Strategies in World Englishes*, ed. Larry E. Smith (London, 1987); K. K. Sharma, ed., *Perspectives on Raja Rao: An Anthology of Critical Essays* (Ghaziabad, India, 1980); Paul Sharrad, *Raja Rao and Critical Tradition* (New Delhi, 1988).

RATUSHINSKAIA, Irina (also spelled Ratushinskaya). Born March 4, 1954, in Odessa, Ukraine, USSR; she lives in Illinois. Ratushinskaia, who was born of Polish noble forebears, was discouraged by her parents from identifying herself with her Polish or her Catholic ancestry; her grandparents were forbidden to talk with her in Polish or of Catholic matters. She was given extensive education in secondary school, where she was a celebrated honor student. In 1971 she was admitted to Odessa University; her university experience marked the first real physical separation from her protective parents. She studied physics and mathematics and graduated with honors. (One unconfirmed report is that she was asked by the KGB, and refused, to serve as an informer on her student and faculty colleagues.) She taught mathematics and physics on the high school level and in 1977 was promoted to the faculty of Odessa Pedagogical Institute. The first of her many difficulties stemming from her idealistic conceptions of honor without regard to expediency began at this point. After objecting to the clear anti-Semitism of the admissions policies of the institute, she was demoted from her prestigious instructorship to a laboratory assistantship. During the same year she was accused of anti-Soviet tendencies because of a play she had cowritten, which was banned after its premiere in Odessa.

Ratushinskaia married Igor Gerashchenko in 1979 and moved to Kiev. When the pair protested the inner exile of the eminent scientist Andrei Sakharov to Gorky in 1980, they were warned to cease their activities. More practical difficulties ensued when Gerashchenko was fired from his post. Ratushinskaia and her husband survived by free-lance tutoring and by doing menial labor. (One of her stories, ''Senia the Dream Maker,'' draws from experiences of this period.) Her first arrest occurred on December 10, 1981, after she and Gerashchenko had gone to Moscow to participate on Soviet Constitution Day in a protest for human rights. She spent ten days in a Moscow jail for disturbing the peace.

Ratushinskaia was again arrested with her husband on September 17, 1982, when, after they had signed on as apple pickers during harvest time, they were accused of ''preparing and distributing anti-Soviet materials.'' The exact charge, according to Aleksandr Aloits (''Ugolovnoe delo Iriny Rushinskoi [Violations of Soviet Law in the case of Irina Ratushinkaia],'' *Novoe russkoe slovo*, June 24, 1986), was ''the authorship of poetry, documents in defense of human rights, and articles concerning the Polish labor movement published in the bulletin of SMOT [Free Inter-Professional Union of Workers]; the possession of anti-Soviet literature (which included the works of the poet Maks Voloshin, d. 1932), and oral agitation and propaganda'' (as quoted in *A Tale of Three Heads*). Ratushinskaia was sentenced six months later at the conclusion of a three-day trial to seven years of prison and five years of internal exile. She was twenty-nine years old.

Ratushinskaia's prison experiences were particularly harsh. She was sent first to Barashevo Corrective Labor Colony in the Morovian Region, a restricted isolation center for political prisoners. She engaged in a hunger strike and was beaten and force-fed. On one occasion she suffered a concussion from a beating by prison guards and was handcuffed while she lay unconscious and as warders threw liquid down her throat. As a result of her maltreatment she became afflicted with kidney disease, dropsy, an inflamed ovary, and periodic loss of consciousness.

Worldwide protest from writers throughout the world, and particularly from PEN American Center, PEN International, Amnesty International, and other human rights groups, followed news of her successive ordeals. At one point

Soviet administrators responded, to pleas from PEN, that Ratushinskaia was not a bona fide writer and that her writings had nothing to do with her incarceration and treatment. Shortly before her release by the Soviet government in 1986, she was awarded the highest honor of the Poetry International Festival in Holland for her achievements in poetry.

Ratushinskaia's work has been translated into English, French, German, and other languages, but it is not voluminous, as is to be expected. She wrote most of her work while in prison, and this work was distributed in samizdat fashion and smuggled abroad. Her translators point out that she cannot be judged as a "finished" writer since she had no chance to polish or revise her work. Her stories have a passionate intensity and are drawn from the dreams and daily activities of people in town life. Many of her tales are immersed in fantasy and fable, two territories where she felt freer to wander in her exploration of ideas. Ratushinskaia renders nightmare as well, as a constant of life in a world where pseudotruth and pseudoknowledge trample spirit and understanding.

On October 9, 1986, Ratushinskaia was released from prison and allowed to emigrate. She flew first to England and then came to the United States a short time later. She lived briefly in the New York–New Jersey area and moved in 1988 to Northwestern University as poet-in-residence.

Beyond the Limit (*bhe jinmhta*), a volume of poems translated by Frances Padorr Brent and Carol J. Avins, was published in 1987. This volume constitutes material from a Russian typescript of poems written by Ratushinskaia when she was in camp Zhkh 385/34 in Barashevo in 1985, material distributed in the USSR in samizdat fashion. In a foreword to the volume, Brent writes: "The poems are a gesture against oppression and the subordination of the individual; they register outrage and record what survives" (p. xi). The poems, according to Brent, were "written with a sharpened matchstick on a bar of soap. When they were memorized, the poet washed her hands and the palimpsest was erased. The poems were composed sporadically over a period of 14 months."

Ratushinskaia's stories have been collected in the bilingual edition *A Tale of Three Heads* (English and Russian, Tenafly, N.J., 1986). The title story is typical fable/dream/nightmare material, the tale of a metaphysical three-headed dragon who filches drinks from urban drifters. The volume contains a succinct history of Ratushinskaia's life and her work by the editor, Diane Nemec Ignashev.

In 1988 Ratushinskaia published her prison autobiography, *Grey Is The Color of Hope*, translated from her unpublished Russian-language manuscript. She describes in detail the brutal treatment she and other women prisoners suffered in the prison camps.

Ratushinskaia's poems have also been collected in an early edition, *Stikhi* (Ann Arbor, Michigan, 1984). A British edition of her work, *No, I'm Not Afraid* (Newcastle upon Tyne, 1986), contains biographic information and an Amnesty International report on conditions in the Barashevo women's labor camp.

RAYGORODETSKY, Roman. Born April 26, 1929, in Kiev, USSR; he lives in Brooklyn, New York. Raygorodetsky emigrated to the United States in September 1988. Before his departure with his wife and son, he had headed the

Young Writers Division of the Kamchatka Writers Organization (USSR Writers Union) and had worked as both scriptwriter and film producer for studios in Moscow. His literary works, all published in the USSR in Russian, include *Fishing Season* (1964); *Getting Up before Nine* (1966); *The Bay of Doubt* (1974, repr. 1988); *Manhunters* (1974, repr. 1988); and *Express Russia* (1980). He has also worked as an anchorman on Soviet television and radio. He left the Soviet Union, in the words of his colleague Mark Popovsky,* as a "refugee."

REED, John Silas. Born October 20, 1887, in Portland, Oregon; died October 17, 1920, in Moscow, of typhus. After graduation from Harvard, where he belonged to several socialist groups, Reed began writing for struggling socialist magazines in New York, building a reputation with reports on the labor movement and as a war correspondent, and becoming popular with the radicals and artists in Greenwich Village. Reed's stories supported rebel movements, causing him to be fired from several magazines, jailed, deported from several countries, and indicted for sedition in the United States. Reed's importance as a propagandist for the Bolshevik Revolution led to his involvement in Soviet politics and in the formation of the American communist movement, but he was becoming increasingly disillusioned with the directions of both before he died in 1920. He is the only American buried in the Kremlin.

Most of Reed's poems (*The Complete Poetry of John Reed*, 1983 and *Collected Poems*, 1985) are amateurish. His short stories (*Adventures of a Young Man*, 1963) typically use encounters between street people and the middle class to question who is the real outsider. Reed's best play, *Freedom* (1916), is a heavy-handed comedy in which three prisoners reject freedom to preserve the middle-class beliefs that have exiled them from society.

As a reporter, Reed condemns capitalism and praises the workers and peasants who revolt against oppression. He first won acclaim with stories and a Madison Square Garden pageant celebrating the 1913 IWW (Industrial Workers of the World) strike in Paterson, New Jersey. His two major books, *Insurgent Mexico* (1914) and *Ten Days That Shook the World* (1919), celebrate proletarian revolutions led by former exiles, Pancho Villa and Lenin. Though both works are marred by his imperfect knowledge of the language and ideologies of Mexico and Russia and by a naive, romantic view of the people, they are powerful descriptions of the events and the leaders, soldiers, and civilians caught up in them. Although *The War in Eastern Europe* (1916, with illustrator Boardman Robinson) is less dramatic and effective, it harshly condemns a war that Reed believed exemplified the inhumanity of capitalism.

Consult: David C. Duke, *John Reed* (1987), contains annotated bibliography.

JAMES C. McDONALD

REGLER, Gustav. Born May 25, 1898, in Merzig/Saar, Germany; died January 14, 1963, in New Delhi, India. Regler fought and was wounded in World War I. Though a son of the Rhineland and deeply influenced by Catholicism, he joined the German Communist party in 1928. Accordingly, his writings tend to probe the frontiers between traditional and radical values. Deprived of his German citizenship in 1934, Regler led a roving life as a political activist in France, Russia, and Spain before reaching Mexico in 1940. An early novel, *Wasser, Brot und blaue Bohnen* (1932, Water, Bread and Bullets), explores the iniquities of the prison system, while *Der verlorene Sohn* (1933, The Prodigal Son) suggests a biblical dimension in the theme of exile. A further novel, *Im Kreuzfeuer* (1934, Crossfire), concerns Regler's native Saarland, the territory disputed between France and Germany. Incensed by Stalin's show-trials, Regler grew disillusioned with Soviet communism, but his antifascist stance prompted him to join the International Brigade during the civil war in Spain. When the brigade was disbanded, he was interned in France. Powerful friends, including Ernest Hemingway* and Eleanor Roosevelt, helped him to escape to Mexico. Some of his experiences in Spain were later incorporated in Hemingway's *For Whom the Bell Tolls*.

Though his fiction now commands little attention, Regler retains importance as a privileged eyewitness of the prelude to World War II. In his lively autobiography he covers the Moscow writers congress of 1934 as well as the 1935 Paris congress, recording the conflicting opinions of Maxim Gorky,* André Gide, André Malraux, and Louis Aragon; the views of some notable fellow exiles, including Anna Seghers,* are also reported. Subtly and sentimentally interwoven with this contemporary reportage is the story of his marriage with the artist Marie Louise Vogeler.

Regler's account of his lengthy sojourn in Mexico examines possible socioeconomic and religious reforms, though often in an ambivalent mood. Despite the obsessive death cult shared by the Mexican Indians and their Spanish conquerors, Regler was initially more inclined than Bruno Traven* to take a benign view of his new country, seeking escape as a farmer from the collectivist follies of Europe, but he soon noted the friction between church and state in a land where liberation from Rome had been won four centuries after Martin Luther. His novella "Love, Destructive Goddess," the story of a mestizo's struggle against clerical and political obscurantism, forms a striking episode in his book on Mexico.

Regler belongs to that constellation of politically motivated writers, led by Arthur Koestler,* who as apostates from communism agonized over "the God that failed" and looked elsewhere—including the Third World—for alternative utopias.

Translations: *A Land Bewitched* (London, 1955 [*Verwunschene Land*, Mexico]); *The Owl of Minerva* (London, 1959, New York 1960 [*Das Ohr des Malchus*, 1958]).

Selected Titles: *Verwunschene Land, Mexico* (Munich, 1954; *A Land Bewitched*, 1955); *Das Ohr des Malchus* (1958; *The Owl of Minera*, London, 1958).

CEDRIC HENTSCHEL

REMARQUE, Erich Maria (pseudonym of Erich Paul Remark). Born June 22, 1898, in Osnabruck, Germany; died September 25, 1970, in Locarno, Switzerland. Remarque, who wished to become a teacher and lead a contemplative life, was drafted into the German army during World War I and was subsequently wounded while on duty. He taught school briefly after his demobilization and then became editor of *Sport im Bild* in Berlin, a position he held for almost ten years. In 1929 he published his most famous work, *Im Westen nichts Neues* (*All Quiet on the Western Front*). In its portrait of the horrors of the Great War and its compensating comradeship of soldiers in the trenches, the novel achieved lasting renown; it is still read and taught today in secondary schools and universities and has been translated into forty languages. Many regard it as a statement of pacifism, though Remarque refused such a label; all critics agree it is a criticism of the presumed need for war. Remarque published a sequel, *Der Weg Zuriche* (1931; *The Road Back*, 1931), which was set in the milieu of a defeated Germany and the problems that the returning soldier faced—economic decline, demoralization, and loss of national pride. He continued with this focus of milieu in his next novel, *Drei Kameraden* (1937; *Three Comrades*, 1937), in which the sustaining force in a deeply troubled land becomes male friendship and the camaraderie gained in the demands made by the experience of war and military life.

Aware of the dangers National Socialism presented in his times and to a populace disenchanted with the artistic success of the anarchic-minded Weimar Republic and its liberal social policies, Remarque left for Switzerland in 1931. In 1933 his citizenship was revoked by the newly installed Nazi government, and his books were burned and banned. He emigrated to the United States in 1937; he became an American citizen in 1947. He married the actress Paulette Goddard at about this time. He returned to Switzerland in the late 1950s, in part in reaction to the cold war policies of the decade. In 1967 he was awarded the Federal Republic of Germany's high honor, the Great Service Cross, for his service to humanity through his writings.

Remarque's focus on exile and the pitiless conditions that refugees were forced to endure is the undercurrent in most of his work after the rise of the Nazis to power in 1933. In particular, in three novels he centered on refugees and exiles and the way they cope with their displacement—*Flotsam*, published first in English in *Collier's* magazine in 1939 and in book form in 1941 (German, *Leibe deinen Nachsten*, 1941); *Der Funke Leben* (1952; *Spark of Life*, 1952); *Arch of Triumph* (1945; German, *Arc de Triomphe*, 1946). In these works he drew portraits of people who refused to surrender to the demons of history pursuing them, and who drew strength from inner resources untapped until adversity revealed them. Remarque's awareness of history's impact on the daily lives of its victims, his broad canvas of historical events, and his psychological realism made him a popular writer during his lifetime. Although his later work is undistinguished in its popular typecasting (the villainous Nazi, the psychologically scarred refugee hero, the supporting cast of collaborators and resistance fighters), and although he is not an innovator in his craft, he is likely to be remembered for his realistic, compassionate renderings of life in Germany during and after the World War I period.

REMIZOV, Alexei Mikhaylovich. Born June 24, 1877, in Moscow, Russia; he died November 26, 1957, in Paris, France. Remizov's involvement in protest demonstrations for freedom causes began in his student days. In 1897 he was expelled from his university and exiled to Penza for two years. Subsequent arrests, imprisonment, and exile brought Remizov to such places of internal exile as Vologda, Ust-Sysolsk, Kharlov, Kiev, and Odessa. His internal exile resulted in the artistic benefit of his association with and exploration of indigenous peasant life in central Russia; his series of folktales on the mythologies of the region was printed in Russian in 1908 under the title *The Midnight Sun.*

Remizov left Russia in 1921 because of what he called unbearably painful headaches; thus his exile may be classified as medical, but the headaches were obviously psychosomatic, the result of tension and conflict over his country's politics and his desire to remain out of the political arena, a decision he had made some years earlier during his internal punitive exile.

Remizov lived briefly in Estonia, then an independent country, and moved to Germany for two years. From there he emigrated to Paris, where he lived until his death in 1957. He published more than forty volumes while in exile; many of them had already appeared in his native country or been written while he was resident there. Remizov may be said to have shaped a hybrid genre: the memoir-chronicle, a combination of personal, subjective reminiscence and objective or objectified historical and biographic commentary along with the fantastic images of the dreamworld of his mind.

RHYS, Jean (pseudonym of Ella Gwendolyn Rees Williams). Born August 24, 1890, on the British West Indian island of Dominica; died May 14, 1979, in Exeter, England. When she was sixteen, Rhys left for an English schooling, not to return to her birthplace except for a brief visit twenty-five years later. Her father died soon after her arrival in England, and she became a chorus girl, changing her name to Jean Rhys; at this time she began the diaries that later would be transformed into fiction. During the 1920s Rhys eked out a subsistence in Paris where she became a protégée of Ford Madox Ford,* and in London. Rhys had three husbands, two children, one of whom died soon after birth, and a life marked mostly by poverty, obscurity, and heavy drinking, but in the last fifteen years, by modest comfort and fame. Between 1939 and 1966 Rhys wrote nothing, living a completely nonliterary life in England, worrying about her declining finances and health. She died in 1979, having published four collections of short stories, five novels, and an unfinished autobiography.

The novels, on which her reputation most solidly rests, are luminous portrayals of autobiographical anti-heroines whose lives are miserable and anxious. Rhys's novels are *Quartet* (1928), *After Leaving Mr. MacKenzie* (1930), *Voyage in the Dark* (1934), *Good Morning, Midnight* (1939), and *Wide Sargasso Sea* (1966).

In all of Rhys's novels, the sensations of the exile are examined in a tense, controlled, deceptively simple prose—feelings of insecurity, isolation, and remoteness; the sense of impermanence of relationships; and that void of feeling often a concomitant of the experience of misery. In every novel the protagonist, always a woman, is a figurative exile, an outsider to respectability, love, and happiness. Rhys's passive women are easily and willingly manipulated by men and their money; feminists therefore find her novels philosophically and politically compelling. In *Voyage in the Dark* and *Wide Sargasso Sea* the protagonists are literal exiles, each a woman transported against her will from the West Indies to England. *Wide Sargasso Sea* is both a radical departure from her more closely autobiographical style, since it is a retelling of *Jane Eyre* from the perspective of the first Mrs. Rochester, and a transfiguration of Rhys's autobiography. As a transfiguration it offers a universally applicable vision of the damage that transplantations—from a land, from a way of life, from understanding—can wreak.

A valuable omnibus, *Jean Rhys: The Complete Novels*, with an introduction by Diana Athill, presents its material in an arrangement that clarifies the relationship of Rhys's novels to her life. *Smile Please: An Unfinished Autobiography*, written with the help of David Plante,* offers less than would be gained by an autobiographical reading of Rhys's fiction.

Selected Titles: *Letters of Jean Rhys*, ed. Francis Wyndham and Diana Melly (1984).

Consult: Grace Schneck Babakhanian, "Expatriatism and Exile as Themes in the Fiction of Jean Rhys," Ph.D. dissertation, University of Illinois at Urbana, 1976; Nancy R. Harrison, *Jean Rhys and the Novel as Women's Text* (1988); Elgin W. Mellown, *Jean Rhys: A Descriptive and Annotative Bibliography of Works and Criticism* (1984); Thomas Staley, *Jean Rhys: A Critical Study* (1979).

JOAN GORDON

RIBEIRO, Aquilino. Born 1885 in Portugal; died 1963 in Portugal. Ribeiro spent his early years in exile in France, where he studied at the Sorbonne. An outspoken critic of dictatorship and political tyranny, he was imprisoned several times for his writings and public statements. He returned to Portugal in midlife to carry on his struggles for a free society in his country. His only book translated into English is *When the Wolves Howl* (1985); the original title is *Quando os Lobos Vivum*.

RICHARDSON, Henry Handel (pseudonyn of Ethel Florence Lindesay Richardson Robertson). Born January 3, 1870, in Melbourne, Victoria, Australia; died March 20, 1946, in Sussex, England. Richardson grew up in comfortable surroundings; her father had established a successful medical practice after failing to find quick wealth in the gold rushes of the 1850s. On the strength of her early promise in music, though with few hopes of a concert career, Richardson was sent to study piano in Leipzig. During the remainder of her life she returned only once to Australia, as a visitor. Her early novel, *Maurice Guest* (London, 1908), ends with the suicide of a failed musician, and her last novel, *The Young Cosima* (London, 1939), deals with the frustrations of a life overshadowed by the romantic, if heartless, geniuses of Franz Liszt and Richard Wagner. Her marriage to the philologist, J. G. Robertson, seems to have been stable and mutually enriching.

Maurice Guest broadened the scope of Australian letters by demonstrating that a native-born writer could deal knowledgeably with Europe; Richardson's masterwork trilogy, based upon her father's career, deepened Australian tradition immeasurably, by demonstrating that native materials could support probing psychological examination. *The Fortunes of Richard Mahony* (omnibus ed., 1930), comprising *Australia Felix* (1917), *The Way Home* (1925), and *Ultima Thule* (1929), is the tragedy of an Irish immigrant physician who casts his mind adrift in a world that demands secure anchorage in social identity. Mahony, thoughtful and intellectually daring, simply cannot provide the bedside friendliness and social openness expected in Richardson's Australia. He realized on his abortive return to England that Australia has in fact led him beyond the invidious narrowness of his upbringing. He had hated Australia for lacking the lushness of European culture and landscape; now, he finds, the remembered lushness was nostalgic fabrication, a green covering over impoverished rot and ruin. With nowhere to fit in, distrustful even of his own impressions, Mahony collapses emotionally, and is reduced to manic, rocking repetition of his medical credentials, as if wondering how such promise could be crushed so easily. Richardson's portrait of splendid, tragic isolation comes, at last, to stand for all who have left behind the homelands of childhood, idealism, and unquestioned self-confidence.

Richardson's incomplete autobiography, *Myself When Young*, was published posthumously in 1948.

Consult: W. D. Elliott, *Henry Handel Richardson* (1975); Dorothy Green, *Ulysses Bound: Henry Handel Richardson and Her Fiction* (1973); see also *Henry Handel Richardson 1870–1946: Papers Presented at a Centenary Seminar*, Australian National University, 1972.

JOHN SCHECKTER

RICHLER, Mordecai. Born January 27, 1931, in Montreal, Canada; he lives in Montreal. Richler lived in Paris 1951–52 and in England 1954–72; he returned to Canada in 1972. A satirist who draws on both his Jewish background and his expatriate experience, he is best known for his novel *The Adventures of Duddy Kravitz* (1959). His most recent novel is *Solomon Gursky Was Here* (1990).

Consult: A. E. Davidson, *Mordecai Richler* (1983); George Woodcock, *Mordecai Richler* (1983).

RILKE, Rainer Maria. Born December 4, 1875, in Prague (then part of the Austro-Hungarian Empire); died December 29, 1926, in Valmont, Switzerland. Rilke published his first book of poems while still in school (he attended a military academy and a business school). He began his wanderings in 1896. He traveled with Lou Andreas-Salome and her husband to Russia (where they met Leo Tolstoy and other distinguished writers and public figures). He moved to

Paris in 1902, where he existed for years in poverty and ill health. He was invited to Duino Castle by Princess Marie von Thurn und Taxis in 1911 and stayed in the castle both in 1911 and 1912. He lived in Switzerland from 1918 till his death. Exile, or rather a sense of invidious displacement, was a profound current in his view of life. His work was an attempt to span the divisions in his soul.

RIPOLL, Carlos. Born March 31, 1922, in Havana, Cuba; he lives in New York. Opposed to Fidel Castro, Ripoll went into exile in the United States, and studied at the University of Miami; he received his Ph.D. degree from New York University in 1964. He is a professor of literature at Queens College in New York City and has written several works of criticism on Spanish, Cuban, and Latin American literature. He is also a translator into English of Cuban writers, perhaps the most famous among them his friend Armando Valladares.*

RISTIKIVI, Karl. Born October 16, 1912, in Paadiema, Estonia; died July, 1977, in Stockholm, Sweden. Ristikivi escaped from Nazi-occupied Estonia in 1943 into Finland and reached Sweden in 1944. He worked as an insurance clerk in Stockholm, and was an avid traveler to the Mediterranean and southern Europe.

Aleksis Rannit* said that Ristikivi was filled with a profound "religious" sense and that the act of writing was in essence a form of devotional prayer. Severe in its pure line and shorn of all decorative imagery, Ristikivi's poetry and prose exhibit a serenity akin to religious experience.

Selected Titles: *Viimme linn* (1962, The Last City); *Kaspar von Schmerzburgi Rooma päevik* (1977, Roman Diary of Kaspar von Schmerzburg).

Consult: A. Magi, *Estonian Literature* (1968); E. Nirk, *Estonian Literature* (1970).

RITSOS, Yannis. Born May 1, 1909, in Monemvasia (Laconia), Greece; he lives in Athens. The youngest of a family of four, two boys and two girls, Ritsos completed elementary school in Monemvasia; in 1921 he entered Gytheio High School in a neighboring town. That same year his brother and his mother died of tuberculosis. His father, a well-to-do landowner, was ruined by the Greek defeat in Asia Minor in 1922 and went insane.

Upon graduation from Gytheio High School in 1925, Ritsos left for Athens, where he found work as a typist, then as a copyist for a lawyer. In the winter of 1926 he became seriously ill with tuberculosis and returned to Monemvasia. Upon recovery he returned to Athens and found work as a library assistant in a lawyer's office. In January 1927, he suffered another relapse of tuberculosis and was hospitalized at the Sanitorium Sotiria in Athens, where he remained till September 1930; the rest of the year and the next he spent in a sanitorium in Crete.

Ritsos returned to Athens in October 1931 and joined the left-wing *Ergatiki Leschi* (Workers' Club), dedicating himself to the people's struggle. *Tractor* (1934) and *Pyramids* (1935), his first two collections of poems, are influenced by political events in Europe as well as in Greece. The Marxist publisher Konstantinos Gavostis employed Ritsos as a reader and proofreader, services Ritsos continued to perform for Gavostis for the next twenty years. *Epitaphios* (1936), written in the elegiac mode of the Greek folk song, is a moving threnody of a mother over her son killed in a demonstration of tobacco workers on strike in Salonika. (*Epitaphios* was confiscated by Ioannis Metaxas at a public book burning; Mikis Theodorakis set it to music in 1958.)

In 1937, Ritsos suffered another relapse of tuberculosis, and was hospitalized in the sanitorium of Mt. Parnitha, where he remained until 1938. Gavostis published his next three books: *Song of My Sister* (1937), dedicated to his then-ailing sister; *Spring Symphony* (1938); and *March of the Ocean* (1939–40).

During the years of the Nazi occupation (1941–44) Ritsos wrote several works stemming from his political beliefs. *The Last Century B.H.* [Before Humankind] (1942), celebrates the heroes of the Albanian campaign; *Trial* (1945), a collection of short poems, treats the years 1935–43, which witnessed the battle against fascism.

The First Civil War followed almost immediately after the liberation from the Germans at the end of World War II. In 1945, Ritsos joined the EAM (National Liberation Front) and went with a group of actors and writers to Kozani, where he set up a People's Theater. The Civil War ended in victory for the government forces, and Ritsos returned to Athens and began work on his militant poem *Romiosini* (1945–47, Greekness), written in the spirit of the demotic folk song, a tribute to the valor of the liberation fighters in the EAM-ELAS. *Romiosini* did not appear until 1954. Mikis Theodorakis set *Romiosini* to music in 1958.

For the next four years, from 1948 to 1952, Ritsos was in exile, first at the prison camp in Lemnos, where he wrote *The Blackened Pot* between December 1948 and February 1949. In Lemnos he made objects of stones, bones, and bits of wood. In an article entitled "Stones, Bones, Roots," he explained his fascination for objects. "Men in exile," he wrote, "especially men confined and isolated, forced to silence, found that stones made good company, secrets were exchanged and real friendships formed between them" (*Shenandoah* 27, 1–4, Fall 1975-Summer 1976).

In 1949 he was transferred to the 'Institute for National Reeducation' on the island of Makronisos, where he endured physical and psychological torture for refusing to sign the "declaration of repentance." In Makronisos he buried his poems in bottles to save them from confiscation by the camp authorities. The most celebrated piece written at this time is the "Letter to Joliot Curie," dated November 1950, and smuggled out of Greece without the poet's knowledge. In 1951 the poet was transferred to the less rigorous Aghios Efstratis (Ai Strati), where he was detained until 1952.

From 1952 to 1967, a most productive period that Ritsos calls the Fourth Dimension, no less than twenty-eight separate collections of new works were published. In 1954 he married Falitsa Georgiadi, a doctor practicing in Samos. Their daughter, Eri, was born in 1955. Ritsos celebrated her birth with *Morning*

Star, a collection he subtitled "a small encyclopedia of diminutives." In 1956 he wrote *Moonlight Sonata*, a dramatic monologue on the theme of loneliness that won the National Poetry Prize. That year Ritsos visited the Soviet Union with a delegation of writers. In 1958 he visited Hungary, Bulgaria, Czechoslovakia, Germany, and Romania, where he wrote *The Architecture of Trees*. He spent three months in Prague because of a relapse of tuberculosis, and there began his translation of an anthology of Czech poetry, which was completed in 1961 but not published until 1966. His work up to 1960 was collected in three massive volumes of *Poiimata* (1930–1960), which run to 1,500 pages.

In the early 1960s Ritsos turned to classical myths "to add meaning to hollowness and to do so in a largely undefinable metarational way consistent with his vision of life's complexity" (Bien, *Myths*, 17). Dramatic monologues presenting mythic personalities are *The Dead House* (1962, Electra), *Beneath the Shadow of the Mountain* (1962), *Philoctetes* (1965), *Orestes* (1966), *Ismene* (1972), *Chrysothemis* (1972), and *The Return of Iphigeneia* (1972).

During these years he also wrote several collections of short poems: *Testimonies A* (1963), *Testimonies B* (1966), *Testimonies C* (1966–67), all of which evoke the everyday life of contemporary Greece. On February 10, 1963, Ritsos participated in the Bertrand Russell Peace rally, which presented *Epitaphios*.

Immediately after the colonels' military coup of April 21, 1967, Ritsos was arrested and sent to the prison camp at Yiaros. All his books were banned. In September of that year Yiaros was shut down, and Ritsos was sent to Leros. In 1968 the military doctors at Leros diagnosed cancer; he was sent to an anticancer center in Athens; further tests showed he did not have cancer, and he was returned to Leros, where he underwent surgery. In 1969 he was transferred to Samos because he had become seriously ill and because of the petitions of writers and artists (including Pablo Picasso, Günter Grass,* Arthur Miller, Pablo Neruda,* and Jean-Paul Sartre) against his maltreatment. In Samos he wrote *Corridor and Stairs* (1969), a series of short poems describing that bleak period in Greek history. *The Wall in the Mirror* (1972), which consists of a series of short poems about the camp at Leros, is political in spirit. Finally he was permitted to return to Athens, but he was prevented from accepting invitations extended by the Festival of Two Worlds at Spoleto and the Arts Council of Great Britain. Eventually the government granted him a passport with restrictions, which Ritsos would not accept.

Ritsos has been widely recognized in Europe. In November 1970, he was elected to the Meinz Academy of Letters and Science. In the French bilingual edition of *Stones, Repetitions, Railings* (1972) Louis Aragon stated in his prologue that Ritsos was "the greatest living poet." In 1972 Ritsos was awarded the Grand International Poetry Prize of the Biennale of Knokke-le-Zoute, Belgium. In May 1974 the National Council of Bulgaria bestowed on him the Georgi Dimitrov award for his dedication in the struggle for peace, democracy, and progress, the first time this award has been given to a writer. In June 1975, Ritsos was honored in Paris with the Alfred de Vigny award for poetry. On June

10, 1975, the University of Salonika granted Ritsos an honorary doctorate in philosophy. In 1976 he was awarded the International Poetry Prize of Etna-Taormina, Sicily. In 1977 he was awarded the Lenin Prize and elected member of the Mallarmé Academy. He has been nominated for the Nobel Prize at least ten times. His poetry has been translated into twenty-four languages.

Ritsos is a lyrical poet, a master of metaphor, who writes without bitterness in the demotic tradition, for the freedom and equality of all peoples. He lives on Koraka (Crow) Street observing the life of the people around him in Athens.

Selected Titles: *Exile and Return: Selected Poems*, trans. Edmund Keeley (1985, repr. 1989); *Fourth Dimension: Selected Poems of Yannis Ritsos*, ed. Rae Dalwen (1977).

Consult: Peter Bien, Introduction in *Yannis Ritsos: Selected Poems*, trans. Nikos Stangos (London, 1974); Edmund Keeley, *Ritsos in Parentheses* (1979).

RAE DALVEN

RIVE, Richard. Born 1931 in District Six, Cape Town, South Africa; died June 1989 in Cape Town, South Africa. Rive grew up in poverty in a black ghetto, but, through scholarship and grants, graduated from the University of Cape Town. His literary talent was noticed early, and he published his first collection of stories, *African Songs*, in 1963. His best-known work, the novel *Emergency*, was published in 1964; a tale of the Sharpeville riots, and how a decent black man turned to violence as his only weapon against apartheid; it was banned by the white South African government. He moved to the United States in the late 1960s to attend Columbia University for a master's degree. He moved to England to study for his Ph.D. degree from Oxford University. His doctoral dissertation on Olive Schreiner led to the publication of an edition in 1988 of Schreiner's letters (only one volume appeared before his death). After receiving his degree, and after twenty years of exile, he returned to South Africa, where he taught and wrote before he was murdered in his house. He published a memoir, *Writing Black*, in 1981 and several other works, but some critics feel he did not fulfill his potential because of his innate humanism: unable to lay blame on any one side as a villain purely of impurities, Rive suffered the agony of a Hamlet-like qualifying observer. The pain of indecision, or measured judgment, ate at him and quite possibly inhibited his writing talent. Other critics have hailed his cautious humanism; on the appearance of his collection of selected stories, *Advance, Retreat* (London, 1983), in the United States in 1989, Rive was called a major South African voice.

Selected Titles: *Make Like Slaves* (1972, play); *Selected Writings* (London, 1977).

Consult: David Adey et al., *Companion to South African English Literature* (1986).

ROA BASTOS, Augusto. Born June 13, 1917, in Iturbe, Paraguay; he lived in exile from 1947 to 1989, when he returned to Paraguay. Roa learned both Spanish and Guaranti, the language of the Guaira peasants, in his childhood. He graduated from a military school in Asunción but decided to pursue a career as a journalist, going to London on a scholarship in 1944 to study there. He returned to Paraguay at the end of World War II, but fled his country in the wake of the civil war as he was a prominent target of the rightist, militarist forces. He lived in Argentina for several years, and then taught at the University of Toulouse in France until his retirement in 1985. After the coup that unseated General Stroesser's administration, he returned to his native land and was acclaimed a national hero. Roa has written short stories, filmscripts, and journalism in addition to the two novels that have made him his country's most illustrious writer.

Roa's early stories, in which he idealizes the common man and peasant and denigrates the capitalist and landowner in Paraguay, are often sentimental, no matter how sincere the author's vision may be. It is not until his first novel, which channels the same tributary of idealism into deeper currents, that his work flows into moving art. *Hijo de hombre* (1960; *Son of Man*, 1965, repr. 1989), is a novelistic portrait of the history of Paraguay from the nineteenth century to contemporary times. Roa saw in the solidarity of a Christian vision of brotherhood and self-sacrifice an antidote to the mercenary evils of his country. His novel glows with a sense of ultimate triumph over human betrayal and prostitution of morality (the image of the redeemed prostitute is seen throughout the work).

The protagonist of Roa's best-known novel, *I the Supreme* (1987; written in Spanish and published originally in 1974 under the title *Yo el Supremo*), is a dictator for life in a mountain-clad country whose geographical isolation effectively separates it from the pressures of international civilization. A supreme being in a godless land, he is at the zenith of his power, having eliminated his opposition by imprisonment, torture, and/or execution. Vulgar and crafty, he boasts of his conquests over the compunctious aristocracy of his country. (Roa may have a particular bias against aristocrats and capitalists, whom he presents as blinded by their greed for status and/or wealth.) The character is based on a specific person, Dr. Jose Gaspar Rodriguez de Francia (1761?–1840), and set in the Paraguay of the nineteenth century after independence was wrested from the Spanish Empire, but the tone of the novel clearly draws parallels with modern tyranny. The Supreme in Roa's novel is so entranced with his own achievements and convinced of his own goodwill to the people that he believes he has brought democracy to his country and rid the land of the oppressors of the church, the aristocracy, and the mob. In telling the Supreme's story through his own voice, and thus allowing the author to get inside the general's megalomania, Roa is able to give the perfect inverse myopia of a man who cannot be dissuaded of his achievements: the Supreme is a titan who believes he has brought a New Land to his country. The force of Roa's telling lies not in the exaggeration of the dictator's deeds nor even in realistic description (graphic as the scenes of torture and bloodshed are), but in the citizenry's rationalized acceptance of the Supreme's brutality and warped vision.

Selected Titles: *El naranjal ardiente: nocturno paraguayo* (Asunción, 1960); *El baldio* (Buenos Aires, 1966); *Lucha hasta el Alba* (Asunción, 1979); *Antologia personal* (Mexico City, 1980), collection of stories and essays; *Madera quemada* (Asunción, 1983); *Hijo de hombre* (Asunción, 1983).

Translation: *On Modern Latin-American Fiction*, ed. John King (1989).

Consult: A. Roa Bastos, *Yo El Supremo* (1986), with introduction, chronology, and bibliography by Carlos Pacheco. See also "Seminario sobre *Yo, el Supremo* de Augusto Roa Bastos," Université de Poitiers, 1976 (Centre de recherche latino-américaines de l'université de Poitiers, 1976); David William Foster, *The Myth of Paraguay in the Fiction of Augusto Roa Bastos* (Chapel Hill, 1976).

ROBAKIDSE, Grigol. Born October 28, 1884, in Sviri, Georgia, Russia; died November 19, 1962, in Geneva, Switzerland. Accused of supporting Adolf Hitler and National Socialist policies during World War II, Robakidse, a playwright and essayist, emigrated in 1945 to Switzerland. Some of his work was written in German while he was still living in the USSR, for example, *Hitler* (1939) and *Mussolini* (1941). Robakidse was also charged in the press with avoiding punishment for writing anti-Bolshevik novels, among them *Die gemordete Seele* (1933) in which an unflattering portrait of Joseph Stalin is drawn, by writing such work in German. His work was banned in the Soviet Union.

ROBERTS, Sheila. Born May 25, 1942, in Johannesburg, South Africa; she lives in Milwaukee, Wisconsin. Roberts left South Africa in 1977 following the Soweto uprising, "when things looked so hopeless," and went directly to a teaching job at Michigan State University in East Lansing. A widow with two young children, she decided to emigrate to a land where a future was brighter for them. The impact of exile has had a deepening effect on her in that, in her words, "the crisis is happening now—I feel I may be losing touch with South Africa." Although she continues to set many of her stories in South Africa, she has also gone on to other climes in her work, and the possibility of loss of passion for her subject—her native South Africa—"does bother" her. At the same time she calls herself a South African expatriate, "one who cannot rinse the South African experience out of her imagination." Her remarks were made in a written interview and by phone with the editor of this study.

The author of three novels, two collections of stories, a volume of verse, and a study on fellow–South African expatriate Dan Jacobson,* Roberts teaches English literature at the University of Milwaukee, Wisconsin. She received her doctorate from the University of Pretoria, South Africa, in 1977, with a dissertation on the Australian writer Patrick White.

One of Roberts's novels, *He's My Brother* (Johannesburg, 1977), was banned by South African censors after its publication, and then "unbanned" in 1982; it was issued in New York under the title *Johannesburg Requiem* in 1980.

Selected Titles: *Outside Life's Feast* (Johannesburg, 1975), stories; *The Weekenders* (Johannesburg, 1981); *Dan Jacobson* (1982); *This Time of Year* (Johannesburg, 1983), stories; *Dialogues and Divertimenti* (Johannesburg, 1985), poetry; ed., *Still the Frame Holds* (1986), essays on women writers; *Jacks in Corners* (Johannesburg, 1987).

Consult: *Between the Lines: Interviews with Bessie Head, Sheila Roberts, Ellen Kuzwayo, Miriam Tlali*. National English Literary Museum Interviews Series, no. 4 (Grahamstown, South Africa: National English Literary Museum, 1989).

ROLFE, Frederick (William Serafino Austin Lewis Mary). Also known as Baron Corvo. Born July 22, 1860, in London; died October 23, 1913, in Venice, Italy. Rolfe dropped out of school at age fifteen and converted to Roman Catholicism. He supported himself after a fashion as artist, photographer, schoolteacher, tutor, and finally writer. His life was a succession of spiritual exiles in which he alienated himself from one friend after another and destroyed all his opportunities for success by hopeless litigation, malicious letter writing, and paranoid suspicions of various patrons and collaborators.

Rolfe's first books, *Stories Toto Told Me* (1898) and *In His Own Image* (1901), are collections of dialect saints' lives supposedly narrated by a precocious Italian servant boy to his expatriate English master. These books earned Rolfe a certain early reputation. His next works were experiments in more arcane baroque prose, including a perverse but gripping historical work, *Chronicles of the House of Borgia* (1901). This work offers an apologia for the Borgias and presents a sympathetic portrait of the exile of Cesare (whose Borgia paternity is, however, called into question by Rolfe). A related work is *Don Tarquinio* (1905), a minutely reconstructed day in the life of a Renaissance soldier of fortune in the period of the Borgias. The hero has been suffering under a papal ban. He returns in secret from his exile to redeem himself in the eyes of Pope Alexander VI. The twin terrors posed for a man of such an age by excommunication and loss of his native city are poignantly realized in this book, and the mannered Renaissance prose is a tour de force. A similar work written in even more mannered prose is *Don Renato* (printed 1909, released for sale 1963).

Hubert's Arthur (1935, with C.H.C. Pirie-Gordon) is another work with a theme of traditional exile. It is a medieval reconstruction of an imagined life of Arthur, Duke of Brittany, had he escaped death at the hands of King John. Arthur goes into a long exile, finally winning distinction as a crusader in the Holy Land and marrying the heiress of the Kingdom of Jerusalem. But in the true spirit of romance, he eventually returns to England and wins the crown of that kingdom in a trial by combat with John's son, Prince Henry. Another collaboration with Pirie-Gordon is *The Weird of the Wanderer* (1912). This unsatisfactory work recounts the psychological exile and disorientation of repeated reincarnations.

For many years Rolfe tried unsuccessfully to be accepted as a candidate for the priesthood. The particular frustration he felt in this futile pursuit of ordination is captured beautifully in his autobiographical masterpiece *Hadrian the Seventh* (1904). In baroque satirical prose, this novel tells the story of George Rose, like Rolfe an expelled seminarian. The long story of Rose's tribulations is an indictment of the church for failure to recognize his vocation. The quality of life led by Rose—and by Rolfe during the equivalent period of his life—has all the worst features of exile, including poverty and wandering. It has all the features of exile except, that is, loss of country. The paranoia Rolfe developed in his own period of ecclesiastical exile is given a strange twist in the novel, for Rose is elected pope as a compromise candidate in a deadlocked election. By this stroke, he becomes an exile in the more traditional sense since he then can never return to England as an ordinary citizen. Pope Hadrian VII inaugurates an era of international peace, ending his predecessors' diplomatic stalemate with Italy over the occupation of the Papal States. He dies finally at the hand of an anarchist, a martyr to the grandeur of his theopolitical vision.

Rolfe experienced no such improbable translation. He did apparently keep a vow of celibacy for fully twenty years in an obsessive and perhaps ostentatious attempt to validate his vocation, but on the expiration of the period he gave himself over to the sensuous attractions of pederasty in Venice. The friends he distrusted tried to do what they could to pay his hotel bills and his passage home, but he turned on everyone who came to his aid. He completed several novels in Venice, but he filled *The Desire and Pursuit of the Whole* (published 1934) and *Nicholas Crabbe; or, The One and the Many* (published 1958) with venomous portraits of everyone he had ever known—including the unsuspecting expatriates who had given him shelter after he had been turned out into the canals. Thus he added an element of aesthetic exile to the ecclesiastical, geographic, and erotic estrangements already separating him from his origins. These late works, although less explicit than the *Venice Letters* (published 1974) composed at the same time, celebrate the decadent androgyny of turn-of-the-century Venice. The sensuous texture of these last two novels and Rolfe's absolute control of even his most perverse stylistic flourishes give these works an interest for modern readers now that time has dissipated the specific point of the satire.

Rolfe has acquired a considerable cult following, beginning with A.J.A. Symons's *Quest for Corvo* (1934). A major stylist of decadence, Rolfe fueled his career by a paranoia that not only drove him into every form of exile but also provided the subject matter for his works and perhaps influenced the distinctive excesses that are the hallmarks of Corvine prose.

Consult: *English Literature in Transition* 23 (1980); this contains an annotated bibliography.

                                                          EDMUND MILLER

ROTH, Joseph. Born September 2, 1894, in Brody, Galicia, then part of the Austro-Hungarian Empire, now Poland; died May 27, 1939, in Paris, France. The glory and demise of the international Hapsburg monarchy was both the surface and the profound content of Roth's historical fiction. He called the Austro-Hungarian Empire the only homeland he ever had and described as the most traumatic experience of his life the fall of the empire at the end of World War I. His childhood in the little town of Brody became the focal point from which all events derived in his novels. Located in the province of Galicia, which was one of the poorest of the Austrian states, Brody was 10 kilometers from the Russian border and 800 kilometers from the empire's capital, Vienna.

Roth studied for a short time at the University of Lember (Lwow) in 1913, and later at the University of Vienna, from 1914 to 1916, where he specialized in German literature. He served in the Austrian army from 1916 to 1918; after the war he became a journalist, first in Vienna and then in Berlin, from 1920 to 1923. His first novel, *Das Spinnennetz* appeared in the Social-Democratic newspaper *Arbeiter-Zeitung*, after his return to Vienna in 1923. (*The Spider Web*, with *Zipper and His Father*, was issued in one volume in London in 1989.) The protagonist of *Spinnennetz* is a veteran of World War I whose life both during and after the war is examined against the backdrop of a hungry land and a newly imposed national identity. Roth utilized the pattern of a World War I veteran as protagonist in his next five novels—*Hotel Savoy* (London, 1988), *Die Rebellion, Die Flucht ohne Ende, Zipper und sein Vater* (London, 1989), and *Rechts und Links*. Many of the major characters in these novels are exiles journeying from Eastern Europe to the West because their birthplaces have been expropriated into new national territories. Roth's sympathies at this time were with the political Left, and in 1925 he joined the "Gruppe 25," a group of Leftist writers to which, among others, Alfred Döblin,* Ernst Toller,* Bertolt Brecht,* and Kurt Tucholsky,* belonged. However, as early as 1926, Roth lost his enthusiasm for the group. After his journey to the USSR in 1926 as a reporter for *Frankfurter Zeitung*, he gave expression to his disillusionment in his novel *Der stumme Prophet* (written 1929) (1966; *The Silent Prophet*, 1980), which represents in Roth's narrative exploration his most direct confrontation with communism. His protagonist, Friedrich Kargan, helps to bring the Russian Revolution to a victorious conclusion, but Kargan becomes the victim of a despotic tyranny into which, in Roth's view, the 1917 Revolution turned.

Roth was a traveling reporter–foreign correspondent for the *Frankfurter Zeitung* from 1925 to 1929, moving from hotel to hotel in country after country. In 1929 the Kiepenheuer Verlag began paying him a monthly allowance as an advance against royalties for future novels. Though his economic situation changed for the better, he became melancholic over the incurable, chronic illness of his wife and the worsening social, economic, and political conditions in Europe. In 1927 his volume of essays, *Juden auf Wanderschaft* (Wandering Jew), which foreshadowed the excesses of the German Third Reich, was published; in this collection he openly allied himself with his once-scorned Eastern European Jewish roots and tradition. In 1928 his essay on Franz Josef I appeared in the *Frankfurter Zeitung* and warned against the rising power of fascist and communist forces in Europe. In his early novels Roth had described the collapse of rational order and the onslaught of barbarism attendant on the advent of World War I; now he turned away from realistic detail of socio-political-economic spheres of behavior to the consoling faith of his religion and the old traditions of the Austro-Hungarian Empire. His following two novels—probably his two greatest single literary achievements—*Hiob* (1930; *Job*, 1931), his most Jewish book, and *Radetzkymarsch* (1932; *Radetsky March*, 1933), his most Austrian book, may appear aimed in different directions, but they represent two aspects of one prismatic vision. They also signal the fateful change for Roth from the simple realistic style of "Neue Sachlichkeit" (the new functionalism) to the more visionary characteristics of the neo-Romantic style he would not forsake for the rest of his life. Roth now began to draw strength from his memories of childhood in Brody and identified with that which he had suppressed for years, his roots as a Jewish Austro-Hungarian. The forgotten emperor of Austro-Hungary was reborn for him as a glorious father figure, which not by accident in Roth's imagination took two images—one that of a Hasidic mystic, Nachum Roth (Roth's father), and the other that of an officer of the Austrian army. What stands behind both images—drawn from the religious and political past alike—was the childhood world of the little town of Brody, which for Roth became a free world in which Jews and Poles, Ruthenians and Germans, Hasids and agnostics lived together in a multicultural empire of goodwill.

The protagonist of *Hiob* is an Eastern Jew, Mendel Singer, who is obligated to suffer more than the rest of his tribe—as Roth felt he himself had to do—because he is a chosen person. Singer, who had eaten pork to "offend" his God, is able to transcend his sufferings and achieve religious exaltation. The story of *Radetzkymarsch* concerns a "grandson," the lieutenant Carl Joseph Trotta in the pre–1918 Austrian army, who is physically weaker than his ancestors and frailer in his hold on life. The Radetzky march becomes the background music of his death, of his time coming to an end with the consignment of his era to history.

In 1933 Roth moved from Austria to Paris. He once said of himself: "I could not write if I had a permanent residence." During his time of exile he changed residences many times only to return to Paris. Between 1933 and 1979 he lived in Salzburg, Rapperswil, Zurich, Marseilles, Nizza, Sanary-sur-mer, Amsterdam, Brussels, Ostende, Steenockenzeel, Wilna, Lwow, Warsaw, and Vienna. It was for a good reason that he called himself a "hotel-citizen."

Roth's later novels continue in the vein of *Hiob* and *Radetzkymarsch* by taking up either the Brody/Galician/Austrian theme in *Tarabas* (1934; *Tarabas: A Guest on Earth*, 1987); *Die Büste des Kaisers* (1934); *Das falsche Gewicht* (1937, The False Weight); and *Der Leviathan* (1940); or the Vienna/Austrian theme in *Die Kapuzinergruft* (1938, The Crypt of the Capuchin Monks) and *Die Geschichte von der 1002 Nacht* (1939, The Story of the Thousand-and-Second Night). East European memories and the presence of his French exile are characteristics of his *Beichte eines Mörders* (1936; *Confessions of a Murderer Told in One Night*, 1937).

Roth traveled to Vienna in 1938 in a final attempt to persuade the Austrian chancellor to recall Otto von Hapsburg to Austria and declare a monarchy as a last resort in unifying the Austrian people against Hitler and subsequently enlisting foreign aid and support against Hitler's annexation of Austria. He returned to Paris without success. The fate of his beloved Austria was sealed when Hitler's troops marched into the country one month later.

Roth was elected vice-president of the *Liga fur das geistige Osterreich* (League for the Spiritual Tradition of Austria), a society that was trying to keep viable the Austrian heritage. Grief-stricken by the turn of events in Austria, Roth indulged more and more in heavy drinking and certainly in the last year of his life was an alcoholic. When the news of his friend Ernst Toller's suicide reached him, Roth suffered a nervous breakdown. He was taken to the pauper's ward of the Necker hospital in Paris when he succumbed to delirium tremens; he died after pneumonia raged through his body. His funeral became a demonstration for the unity of all anti-Hitler groups in Paris, a unity that he had always championed. At his funeral, tensions between Jews and Catholics, communists and monarchists flared. An Austrian communist and close friend of Roth, Stefan Fingal—who edited a journal, *Nouvelles d'Austriche* (Austrian News), which advocated and promoted Popular Front policies—claimed Roth's corpse. According to Fingal, Roth had been planning to forsake his writing for the Monarchist journal *Osterreichische Post* (Austrian Post) and to begin writing for *Nouvelles d'Austriche*. Fingal claimed that only he knew about Roth's conversion (or reconversion) to the Left, but Roth's death had prevented the move. Fingal's version of the event has been questioned by Roth's associates.

One of Roth's last narrative works was *Die Legende vom heiligen Trinker* (1939; *The Legend of the Holy Drinker*, 1943), in which a "holy drinker" kills a man who has attempted to murder the woman the drinker loves. After his release from prison he becomes a homeless *clochard*, a vagabond in permanent exile. He cannot forget his love even in drink; he drinks both to remember her more vividly and to forget her through the oblivion of drink. His sorrow becomes so overwhelming that not even the possibility of miraculous faith can save him. Roth's obsession with his memory of the lost world of Brody/Austria may be seen as parallel to this fictional rendering of a man who drank himself to death, as some have said Roth did. Roth is buried in the Cimetière Thiais in Paris. His funeral and gravesite expenses were paid by Stefan Fingal. Since 1947 the new Republic of Austria has cared for his grave.

Consult: David Bronsen, *Joseph Roth* (Cologne, West Germany, 1974); Rudolf Koester, *Joseph Roth*, (Berlin, 1982).

JOSEPH P. STRELKA, with Martin Tucker

ROZIMIR, Felix Yakovliewich (also spelled Feliks Yakovlevich Roziner). Born September 17, 1936, in Moscow, USSR; he lives in Boston, Massachusetts. Rozimir's mother and father were taken from Russia to Palestine when they were children; they met and married in the 1920s after their return to the Soviet Union. Soon after Rozimir's birth, his mother was arrested; she spent two years in prison on a charge of "political crimes." During his childhood Rozimir studied the violin, and later he attended a conservatory. His love of music remained with him into his adult life. Nevertheless, he embarked on an engineering career: he graduated from the Polygraphic (Printing) Institute in Moscow and received the degree of engineer-designer (master of science) for printing presses. He worked as an engineer-designer from 1958 to 1967; during these years he also wrote poetry and played with amateur symphony orchestras. His first poem appeared in print in 1962. In 1967 he became a free-lance writer, with music as his specialty. His accounts of conversations with George Faier, the famous conductor of the Bolshoi Theater (*George Faier about Himself, on Music and Ballet* [Moscow, 1970]), received high praise in musical and theatrical circles.

During the next ten years Rozimir followed his first book with six more books mainly about musicians. He considers his principal books published in the USSR the fictionalized biographies of the composers Edvard Grieg and Sergey Prokofiev, *A Saga about Edvard Grieg* (Moscow, 1972) and *A Toccata of Life: S. Prokofiev* (Moscow, 1978), as well as a biography of the Lithuanian painter Čiurlionis, *Hymn to the Sun* (Moscow, 1974).

From 1971 to 1975 Rozimir worked on a long novel under the manuscript title of "Dust in the Wind." The novel is concerned with events among Moscow intelligentsia in the early 1960s. Rozimir was aware his novel could not be published in the USSR, and he consequently issued it in samizdat form. After he left the USSR with his family in 1978 and settled in Israel, the novel, under the new title *A Certain Finkelmeyer*, was published by Overseas Publications of London in 1981 in the Russian version. In an interview in the magazine *Israel* Rozimir said: "Of course in my novel there is the upper stratum, if one may so express oneself—it's Soviet reality. But if one sees only this stratum, perhaps we will perceive only one more accusation against the regime. However, my novel is, first of all, a novel about creation, about the creative personality, about the painter, the conflict of the painter and reality, an eternally tragic conflict." A saga about the life of a poet born in the USSR who dies under dramatic circumstances in the prime of his talents, the novel's concern with the artist's gifts and his society's clearly apparent rejection of them. The work has been translated into French and Hebrew and was scheduled for American publication in 1989. Even before publication, the manuscript was awarded the Vladimir Dal literary prize of 1980.

Rozimir's family odyssey, *The Silver Cord*, was issued in the original Russian version in 1983 by the Israeli publishing house Bibiloteka Aliya. Devoted to seven generations of the author's family, the work was written for a contest with the theme of "My Paternal House in Russia," announced by the Center for Research of Eastern European Judaism at the University of Jerusalem; it received first prize in the competition. Rozimir writes in his final chapter:

Concerning history, the physicist Einstein said, "It is drama, the drama of ideas." Following him I can say the same about the history of several generations in my family: "It is drama, the drama of ideas." My great-great-grandfather—a rabbi-sage in Bobrujsk, living completely by the idea of the Torah; my great-grandfather made the first step to social world perception; my grandfather, captured by ideas of Zionism for communistic internationalism; and finally the children and grandchildren, witnesses to so many idealistic catastrophes that they prefer to live today not believing in the pure idea nor in experimentalism.

Rozimir has published in Russian a collection of twelve poems under the title *One Hundred and One Words*. He calls this chapbook a work of "experimentationalism and word-coining" (Jerusalem, 1983, Facsimile Edition). A collection of his stories, *Triptych* (London, 1986), contains three works that belong to the genre of "documentary prose." One, "The Poppies of Kargopol," narrates the author's trip in 1976 to northern Russia and his encounters there with Russian peasants. Rozimir's conclusion from his observation of moral and social consciousness in the USSR is grim: he does not hold out hope for change in the abuses he perceives in the social system of his native land.

MARK A. POPOVSKY, translated by Zoric Ward

RUSHDIE, Salman. Born 1947 in Bombay, India; he lives in hiding. As of this moment, Rushdie remains in hiding, a marked man under a death threat issued by the Ayatollah Ruhollah Khomeini on February 14, 1989. Rushdie's exilic troubles began with the publication of *The Satanic Verses* (London, 1988; 1989). Declaring the work blasphemous, Khomeini called on all faithful Muslims to assassinate Rushdie, thus sending him to hell. The sentence of death has not been lifted by the successors of Khomeini, who died in June, 1989.

Immediately after the call for Rushdie's death was issued, Rushdie went into hiding with his American expatriate wife, Marianne Wiggins. Both lived under police protection in a secret location in the United Kingdom until she announced her separation from him; Rushdie now changes his residence regularly to avoid detection. By this turn of events Rushdie became an exile as well as an expatriate. He was born into a Sunni Muslim family in Bombay; his wealthy father had gone to King's College, Cambridge University. Rushdie's father sent him, after a brief stay at Cathedral High School in Bombay, to England for study at Rugby and, later, Cambridge. Rushdie liked Cambridge University in the 1960s decade of change and "rethinking things." After graduation in 1968 he returned home to his family, who had emigrated to Pakistan and were living in Karachi. He stayed, however, only a few months, finding Pakistan parochial and antagonistic to his intellectual explorations. Back in England, he worked with multimedia groups and as a free-lance journalist; he held down a job as a copywriter in advertising agencies for over ten years while he wrote fiction at night. He visited Pakistan and India frequently during these years but he no longer considered returning there permanently: he had become an expatriate. Rushdie's first marriage to an Englishwoman ended in divorce after several years. He and his second wife, the novelist and short story writer Marianne Wiggins, had been married less than a year when the storm over *The Satanic Verses* broke into their lives.

It is clear that Rushdie, like many gifted students and intellectuals of his generation, suffered emotional trauma from the partition of India. All his work, long before the sensationalism attendant on *The Satanic Verses*, reveals this unrelenting grasping for closure on the fissures of political, spiritual, and geographic division. Rushdie apparently has been willing to go to any lengths in his writing to satiate his appetite for reparation of his wounded psyche.

Although most American readers assumed *Midnight's Children* (London, 1980; 1981) was Rushdie's first novel, and heralded his appearance on the scene as a major new talent, that book was his second novel. His first, *Grimus* (London,

1975; 1979; out of print), was an adolescent but prescient piece of work that shows Rushdie's spectacular talent for hyperbole and satire. The work is more Swiftian and intellectual than are his later unique stylistic integrations of Indian fable and German/European expressionism. *Grimus* is a fantastic story in which physical death is a transient thing while the death of an idea is irrevocable, but rare; the converse is more likely, that an idea is less likely to die and more likely to reappear at fated moments. Rushdie calls these ideas or emblematic manifestations of the personal spirit the "I" within the person. Essentially his first novel is a struggle between the "I" of two opposed forces: Grimus represents tyranny in its most constructive form—that is, as a construct of a perfectly working island—while Flapping Eagle, a stranger washed onto the shores of Grimus's Calf Island, represents the spirit of humanism, the priority of sequence by natural surprise over the constraints of willed and predictable order. The narrator of the tale is a constantly amorphous being, Joe-Sue, a hermaphrodite alien in color to the Ancoma Indians into whose society he has been born; he is an orphan as well. All these traits deny Joe-Sue a common bond with his group, but they enable him to gain a perspective on those alien to him. In Rushdie's vision in *Grimus*, the free spirit wins out by sheer purpose of waywardness; the consequence, however, is a loss of the conceptualizations that art and history provide. In the process of working out his thematics, Rushdie plays with such characters as Mr. Virgil Beauvoir Chanakya Jones, an Indian-cum-European, in love with the married and the beautiful Dolores O'Toole. Ideas and thematics in Rushdie's first novel are capable of abstraction because Rushdie's craft has not yet rendered them in their potent complexity and subtlety; perversely, it is the abstract quality of Rushdie's prose and craft that robs this novel of the vitality conveyed in his later work.

While Rushdie's craft has advanced magnificently, his fixity of theme and obsessional pursuit of identity through a dialectical mode remains in evidence through his latest work. He is angry at the fate history has dealt him, particularly the partition of India, which in its divisiveness has sealed his fate of orphanage. He declares his anger in *Midnight's Children*, appropriating Independence Day of India (August 14–15, 1947, midnight) as the birthday of his protagonist and comparing his protagonist's face to the map of India. His novel bears the influence of postmodern literary displacement as well—Rushdie interrupts his narrative constantly and teasingly to tell the reader the story is a joke, or that he, Salman Rushdie, is the real hero/character, or to give parallels with contemporary Indian history to the incidents in his narrative. He sets the action of his novel in Bombay in the time between 1947 and 1977, the years of Indian partition/independence and the emergency period that resulted in the imprisonment of 30,000 people under Indira Gandhi's orders. He thus gives his hero the symbolic age of Jesus when he awoke to his destiny (Rushdie is shameless in his allusions, taking from whatever source his fertile imagination brings him); the age may also be that of Rushdie when he was writing the novel (he took nearly four and a half years to complete the manuscript). In using these explicit and implicit parallels he gives his work a larger than narrative quality. Indeed, *Midnight's Children* is an example, as Rushdie says, of autobiography through history, and of history dislodged from chronology to get at its truths; the same displacement occurs in the physical attributes of Rushdie's characters: they are at times disembodied and/or put to death so that they can reappear later in other and the same guises. In using this technique and attitudinal guile Rushdie is appropriating from the Arabian Nights tradition of his youthful reading, a point he makes explicit in stating that 1,000 other people (1,001 mid- *night* babies) were born at midnight on August 15, 1947.

Midnight's Children issues then from a magnificent collection of stories, incidents from contemporary history (Rushdie is without pity in his attacks on Indira and Sanjay Gandhi), and fabulous impossibilities of hyperbolic escapes and escapades. Essentially it is the story of Saleem, the child of an Indian, European-oriented doctor and his darker, Indian-core wife. But Saleem is not Saleem in that he was given Saleem's identity by his future ayah, Mary Pereira, a Catholic woman obsessed with good works, and her communist lover, who repeatedly told her to do her part for the equalization of wealth. Mary Pereira switches babies in the hospital when no one is looking: the baby of poor parents becomes the rich baby, and the rich baby becomes the poor baby in an instant. Echoes of Oscar Wilde and Mark Twain, Eastern fable, and Rushdie's sardonic wit all play under the surface of this and other incidents of the matter of identity. Is Saleem not Saleem because he was not born in Saleem? Can he not be made Saleem by becoming what everyone believes Saleem to be? Later in the novel, Saleem and the real Saleem (that is, the baby in the hospital who was the Saleem born of his parents) will pursue each other in deadly rivalry. One of the Saleems (which, the reader may ask, is the real Saleem?) dies; the narrator-protagonist, who was given Saleem's identity in the switch at birth, lives on—in constant doubt about his *real* identity.

At an earlier point in the narrative, the other Saleem, who has risen to become a general in the Indian army and taken to assaulting troublesome relics of Indian life, like its beggars, gypsies, magicians, prostitutes, and street vendors, impregnates a poor and beautiful whore, Parvati. General Shiva shudders when the pregnant whore tries to marry him; he fears a descent into the world of poverty from which he has extricated himself through his own talents and ambition. (It is likely that it was not by accident that Rushdie chose the name of General Shiva's wife-to-be as Parvati; in Hindu mythology Parvati is the wife of the god Shiva.) Saleem, the switched baby, loves the whore and marries her; he is impotent, and thus he gains a wife he loves and a child he cannot have. But he has a child—Shiva's son; he has a wife—Shiva's wife, who was consecrated and consummated in Shiva's love. Shiva's son is his son, just as Shiva is Saleem and Saleem is Shiva. Saleem ponders the question: when the son marries, the grandchild will be the true grandchild of the two grandparents, but the son will be the true son of only one of the two parents. Such are the games Rushdie plays brilliantly, fast and loose in *Midnight's Children*, and the novel is an extraordinary display of courage in craft and dissident opinion. The use of hyperbolic imagery, which Günter Grass* used before him, is much in evidence, and it is clear there is a lot of Grass in Rushdie's book on Bombay, an influence Rushdie admits readily, since he has written essays elsewhere on Grass's stature as a major twentieth-century writer.

What is fascinating in Rushdie's work is his vast imagination splaying out from a few spokes of his wheel of technique. *Midnight's Children, Shame* (1983), and *The Satanic Verses* all use the following device: two characters, brothers in their similarities and even more in their opposition to each other, fight each other to the death. One of the brothers lives, the other dies. The survival may be seen either as Rushdie's acceptance of a world that demands maturity through the experience of loss or as Rushdie's inability to resolve the dilemma of his dialectic mode. For each brother makes claim on the other and on the world; each brother has a right and has been wronged. One, however, proves more antisocial, and he is the one eliminated, though he may be the more honest, the more oppressed, and/or the more brilliant.

The use of this divided self/dialectic technique is another example of how the partition of India has affected Rushdie with the virus of exilism, a germ of viewpoint never riddled out of his work. In *Shame* the two brothers are Raza Hyder and Iskander Harappa, two titans of modern India and Pakistan, who must end their rivalry in the death of one and the flight of the other. In *Shame* Rushdie moved from India to Pakistan, again a significant move in the dialectic of his identity-seeking—first he attacked India, then he probed Pakistan. In each novel he flagelated corruption and the betrayal of the dream of independence. In damning both India and Pakistan, Rushdie moves to that center stage which Shakespeare called the exile of the spirit; he portrayed it in Lear, in Timon, and in Coriolanus, among others. Rushdie's humor in *Shame* is less bitter than in Shakespeare's foul-mouthed tragic heroes, but it is uproariously shameless in its exposure of the secrets of hypocrisies in low and high castes of characters. Thinly veiled portraits of Benazir Bhutto and Ali Bhutto, of General Mohammad Zia ul-Haq and of Pakistani society pervade the book and provide the historic parallels for the "shame" of the Pakistan Rushdie is exposing.

Less fabulous than *Midnight's Children* but more damningly satiric in its swipes, the novel uses the character Omar Khyam Shakil as the narrator and possible protagonist; significantly, Omar lives on the margin of things, so a marginal character is quite possibly the protagonist of modern Pakistan in Rushdie's postmodern thematics. Omar, as narrator, says the story he is telling is a modern fairy tale, one "told at a slight angle to reality." Omar lives in two worlds, the fifteenth century and the twentieth (Rushdie uses even a dialectic of time periods); he is a poet in one and a doctor in the other. He is conceived at the house in which the wake of his grandfather (to-be) is taking place, the first and only time the three daughters of the dead father have opened the house to entrants from the streets of Bombay. The three daughters all suffer morning pain, for no *one* will admit to the shame of seduction; three pregnant women make possible no pregnant woman, since there is no one body that gives birth, as all three make moans and gasps and go through the agonies of childbirth, and when the baby is born no one knows from which of the three reclining women it has come. Thus, in destroying shame through a triplicate of identity, Rushdie makes comment on a world that allows quantity to serve as its measure of worth. At the end of the novel, in a true circle of modern fiction as accepted by modern circles of critics and as a circle of unity accepted in the Pakistan-Persian-Urdu fabulistic tradition of court song, Omar is murdered in the same house in which he was conceived. Such is Rushdie's narrative craft that the novel also becomes the story of his writing the novel.

The Satanic Verses, which has occasioned such grief for Rushdie, is not a new literary or thematic departure for him. The novel is no more blasphemous, if it is at all blasphemous, than his two earlier works of fiction. It is more concentrated in its attacks on hypocrisy within the Islamic faith and community, and it has specific reference to Khomeini and other mullahs and Ayatollahs. It is, like Rushdie's earlier work, the story of two men, or "brothers" under the skin—one is a famous leading actor, the other an established character actor. The plane on which they are passengers is bombed in mid-air by a terrorist and Gibreel Farishta and Saladin Chamcha fall to earth, 30,000 feet below (the same number of people rounded up by Indira Gandhi during the emergency period). In Rushdie's novel, they glide to earth and are either reborn or find new awarenesses in themselves. The gaiety of satire and the exuberance of attack are mounted strongly in Rushdie's latest fiction, but by this time Rushdie is after an India that has grown fat with the decay of romance and commerce to feed on, and with the adoption of tawdry traditional and Western values. Rushdie's world is a world, it must be emphasized, in which no one side is blamed, for there are always two sides to every blame. In this novel Rushdie scores movie moguls, psychoanalysis, hypnotism, and color prejudice. His main subject in the novel is religion and spiritualism. It is a real irony (real in the sense that Rushdie would find most real) that Rushdie, in digging deeper into himself and exposing his doubts and desires for communion, should have suffered the greatest indignity—a curse on his life. For in having Gibreel Farishta and Saladin Chamcha fight out their battles with the world and with each other, Rushdie was trying to find the angel that would redeem him with his country. Only, it may be asked, which is Rushdie's country—India, Pakistan, England, the country of the mind, the country of a writer's imagination, or the country of blinding vision? While *The Satanic Verses* is more difficult in style—it is Joycean, in contrast to the Rabelaisian air of *Shame* and *Midnight's Children*—it is a magnificent attempt at a journey to the destination of its own beginning, a shutting out of exile from within the circle of forgiveness, and a closing to the tempest of Rushdie's and India's partition. Rushdie's journey in this novel, an airplane flight, may be compared to Bloom's and Dedalus's walk through Dublin (and earlier in the flight of Dedalus from the net of artistic constraint); Rushdie takes his flights in midair, in crazed and visionary illuminations, and in the anguished comedy of two actors who never get their parts right after their fall from the sky (and from ignorant grace). One shoots himself in despair, and the other "stands at the window of his childhood" and looks out to the Arabian Sea. Childhood is over for him, and he is now leaving his past to move on to a different age. *The Satanic Verses* is Rushdie's most mature work in that his dialectic has been resolved on the last page of the novel in one of the brothers moving on, purposefully, to a new beginning, while the other, the one that cannot survive in the present, dies. What an irony, one that surely Rushdie must appreciate even in his terrible exile, that the novel in which he is saying goodbye to the deconstruction of his past and attempting to progress to a more positivist view, is the one that has imprisoned him outside the world he was at last trying to enter.

Rushdie's attacks on religion and politics are comic, exaggerated, and ingenious. Sometimes they are filled with savage yawps of expression, as if Rushdie were a scourge, an Indian Savonarola out to burn all bridges of excuses before him. Like Jonathan Swift, he works most effectively in spinning fables as if they were travel reports or observations of social reality; like Swift he is obsessed with hypocrisy, finding no apology acceptable for it. Unlike Swift, however, he has little concern for orderly narrative and less concern for the appearance of logical reason in his telling trial of injustices. He is a postmodernist in technique and spirit, believing that passionate, speculative teasing and trickery are ways to outwit the treason of rationality.

Rushdie's attacks and his poses are sometimes tasteless, and some of his fabrications are without any thread but that of his prosecutorial imagination. In his scathing portraits of Indira Gandhi, General Zia, Ali Bhutto, and the Ayatollahs of Iran, he whips without mercy (though not without wit). The subject of any one of his attacks is likely to be offended; Rushdie's prose, both the language and the passionate, denunciatory core of argument, are bound to be offensive to individuals who, after all, are being ridiculed without benefit of counsel or reply time. Yet there is nothing immoral, pornographic, licentious, or of such hateful, incendiary matter as to make his writing unsafe to read. His novels are not protocols of blasphemy nor designs for insurrection (though of course as literature they are subversive agents of thinking). Much less are they agents of heresy—they issue from an acolyte so shaken by what he sees that he cannot remain quiet. Rushdie is abrasive and has his own brand of fanaticism— as an author he keeps swinging the tail (tell/tale) of his subjected subjects. But it is apparent his view is that of the bitter commentator trying desperately to keep from sinking into the swamp of misanthropy; it is apparent that Rushdie is a child of the 1960s, an idealist still angry at the betrayal of the flowering ideals of his generation and who finds in his novels the means to express his apocalyptic warning.

It is also apparent that, as Rushdie expresses it in *Midnight's Children* —"Is this an Indian disease, this urge to encapsulate the whole of reality?" (p. 75)— that he is writing the same kind of novel each time he writes a novel: for always his novel is a loose narrative in which time moves many ways rather than in one chronological line, and he allows himself the space to comment on history, his characters, and social issues. His central subject is the redemption of the coupon of promised, aborted dreams. His motifs repeat themselves: blushes, color codings, perforated sheets (in *Midnight's Children* it is the means through which Dr. Aziz first views his bride-to-be; in *Shame* it is the means by which Rani Harappa sees the corpse of her husband); in pickles and jars and genies and magic and magic troupes; and in soothsayers, mystics, future-tellers, and seers. Compare Captain Talvar Ulhaq, who can see into the future in *Shame*; Saleem, who can smell the coming event in *Midnight's Children*; and Gibreel (the angel Gabriel?), who hears the future through his trumpet in *The Satanic Verses*. The fatalism Rushdie implies in his use of clairvoyants suggests that he must have been aware that the abuses he scored in his work and his defiant manner would lead to difficulties for him. In *The Satanic Verses* he employs Baal-the-poet, who is excommunicated and sentenced to death for his songs; before he is caught, he hides in a whorehouse and dresses as a woman. There is other evidence as well that Rushdie expected troubles, but when the pronouncement on his death came, he must have been shocked at the actual call to murder by a religious leader, the first such appeal for assassination by a religious leader in the twentieth century. Some critics may argue that religious riots, wars, and crusades have been a part of history since religion and history entered the universe with man and woman, and that assassination for religious or political reasons has been a known policy since the coining of the word *assassin* from its root *hashish*. Yet such arguments deny the fact that assassinations in the past were carried out by secret order from government or quasi-government actors, and that out of shame (as Rushdie might use the word) such orders were not made public. It is a dismaying notion to compare the relative (or absolute?) virtues of hypocrisy versus open admission of assassination policies based on religious instruction. Some critics may also argue that Rushdie willed his fate— he must have had warnings about his flamboyance in the face of religious orthodoxy; his satires had been smarting many people for years, and the cumulative anger was audible. Certainly Rushdie had a good thing going in the Western reception to his work (or perhaps the sentence should read too much of a bad press in the Eastern world). In any case Rushdie goaded his opposition to the breaking point, at which he knew the pieces would have to be those of his own life. There is also speculation that the Ayatollah Khomeini may have had a more political agenda in mind when he called for Rushdie's death, since the first and main riots concerning Rushdie occurred in Pakistan on publication of *The Satanic Verses*. While Rushdie criticized Khomeini and Iran, that criticism was but a speck on the canvas of his Indo-Pakistan paintings. It is significant to remember that with Khomeini's decree he became again the authority to whom appeals throughout the world would have to be made for a man's life. Khomeini in effect had a new hostage through whom he could make his putative power felt again in the world outside the confines of his Iranian theocracy.

In an article in the *Guardian* (Manchester, England, February 3, 1989), the

Jordanian novelist Fadia Faqir* wrote that Rushdie's version of a Mohammad of flesh and blood with the name "Mahound" becomes a businessman in a city of businessmen (Jahilia), and that he employed three henchmen—Salman the Persian, Bilal the black muezzin, and Khalid—to spread his word. This earthly holy trinity are characterized as "scum" and "riff-raff." Rushdie further questions the authenticity of the Word of God (according to Faqir) in the Prophet's failure to save the victims of a pilgrimage to Mecca (they attempted to walk on the ocean floor from Titlipur) and in the Prophet's inability (or willing ignorance) to notice that Baal-the-poet is mistranscribing the Prophet's words in the Divine Text. Faquir concludes:

Rushdie's rewriting of the canonised version of Muhammad's biography urges Muslims to rethink their theological position. His use of obscene language is designed to shock and to make the reader re-examine her/his attitudes towards unquestionable mythologies of history. Some of its writing is as offensive to Orthodox Muslims as the film "The Last Temptation of Christ" is to devout Catholics. The film was not stopped from being shown and *The Satanic Verses* should also be published and read. If some Muslims in Britain and elsewhere find the book abusive, it is time for them to be intellectually militant in their positions, to launch a scholastic offensive to refute Rushdie's argument, and present their point of view in an equally powerful way. (p. 29)

Rushdie has also written one nonfiction work, the journalistic account of his visit to Nicaragua in 1986, *The Jaguar Smile: A Nicaraguan Journey* (1987). By consensus this is a work better forgotten, lacking in any real distinction except for the fact that a distinguished writer wrote it. It is a biased defense of the Sandinista government that while open in its biases shows no depth of analysis; mostly what appears is a tired litany of anti-American diatribe, particularly against the CIA and its covert/overt operations in Nicaragua. Rushdie is sincere in his causes, but this work is unfortunately an oration rather than an examination.

Before his religious troubles, Rushdie was a familiar figure on the barricades of protest marches on behalf of harassed writers and intellectuals; he served for many years on committees of English PEN and other rights groups. Now he has become his own subject of protest. It remains to be seen what effect the banishment of ordinary life by decree of religious zealotry will have on his writing. *Haroun and the Sea of Stories*, his first book since the Khomeini decree calling for his assassination, was published in September 1990 in London. The work is a children's fable, drawing on the magic and wonder implicit in its genre and steering clear of adult allegorical possibilities.

Consult: Lisa Appiganesi and Sara Maitland, eds. *The Rushdie File* (1990); Timothy Brennan, *Salman Rushdie and The Third World: Myths of the Nation* (London, 1990); Salman Rushdie, "In Good Faith," in (London) *Independent on Sunday*, February 4, 1990; Salman Rushdie, *Is Nothing Sacred?* special *Granta* (New York and London) magazine pamphlet, March 1990; Daniel Pipes, *The Rushdie Affair* (1990); Malise Ruthven, *A Satanic Affair* (London, 1990); W.J. Weatherby, *Salmon Rushdie: Sentenced to Death* (1990).

S

SACHS, Nelly. Born December 10, 1891, in Berlin, Germany; died May 12, 1970, in Stockholm, Sweden. In contrast to the many exiled writers whose strong political motivation involved them in turbulent careers, Sachs followed a path of quietist resignation. Daughter of a Jewish industrialist, she was to achieve belated recognition as a poet, translator, and dramatist. A few of her early experimental verses in the romantic tradition were accepted by the *Vossische Zeitung*. Remaining in Germany long after most Jewish writers had left, she escaped in 1940, with the assistance of Prince Eugen Bernadotte and Selma Lagerlöf, to neutral Sweden. Adopting Swedish citizenship, Sachs made Stockholm her second home, and she began her studies in Swedish literature. Some of her poems appeared in Swedish and Finnish periodicals, but the bulk of her original work found publishers only after the conclusion of World War II, initially outside West Germany. Thus the two volumes of poetry *In den Wohnungen des Todes* (1946, In the Habitations of Death) and *Sternverdunkelung* (1949, Eclipse of the Stars) were respectively printed in East Berlin and Amsterdam. *Eli*, a mystery play dealing with the sorrows of Israel, followed in 1951. In 1957 she received a Swedish literary award in acknowledgment of her substantial role as a translator of modern Swedish poetry. Further honors marked her growing reputation: the Droste Prize in 1960; the institution of a Nelly Sachs prize by the city of Dortmund in 1961; and finally, in 1966, the award of the Nobel Prize.

Sachs's poetry, obsessively focused on the trials of the Jewish people in the twentieth century, forms an austere monument fashioned from intractable material: expulsions, homesickness, torture, the obscenities of the concentration camps, and the Holocaust. Though she viewed the horrors of genocide from her privileged refuge in Sweden, their impact was climactic, inspiring poems of surreal vividness, vibrant with pain and anguish, but also with dignity and compassion. In accord with her quietist philosophy she shuns thoughts of retribution. The special flavor of her verse stems in part from close acquaintance with the Cabbala, but more significantly from imaginative powers able to pierce the veil of contemporary circumstance and reach out to eternity. The opening lines of "In der Flucht" (Fleeing)—"I hold instead of a homeland / the metamorphoses of the world"—illustrate this gift for exploring wider horizons and widening implications. Often, as in "Landschaft aus Schreien" (Landscape of Screams), she is driven to apostrophizing the ultimate enigmas: "O hieroglyphs of screams / engraved at the entrance gate to death." Her rhetoric, combined with an insistent elegiac note, derives strength from her reliance on ancient models. She sees the disasters that have afflicted the Jewish people as linked by predestination with the ancient Jewish heritage; in the final analysis she conceives the martyrdom of Israel as the price to be paid for God's election of his Chosen People.

Sachs's awareness of Sweden was necessarily colored by the enormity of events in Germany. In the poem "Und wir, die ziehen" (And we who move away), the bleakness of the Scandinavian winter is attuned to the pervasive themes of exile and death:

> Myself here,
> where earth is losing its lineaments
> the Pole, death's white dead nettle
> falls in the stillness of white leaves

She greatly admired modern Swedish poetry, a debt she repaid through her translations into German of works by J. Edfelt, G. Ekelöf, E. Lindegren, and K. Vennberg. This achievement, augmented by several anthologies, reinforced her claim to the Nobel Prize, which she shared with the Polish-Israeli novelist S. Y. Agnon.* The pairing of these two writers in the 1966 award was appropriate in that Agnon, no less than Sachs, was profoundly influenced by Hebrew traditions enshrined in the Bible.

Selected Titles: *Legenden und Erzählungen* (Berlin, 1921, Legends and Tales); *Aber auch diese Sonne ist heimatlos* (Darmstadt, 1957, This Sun too Is Homeless [contemporary Swedish poetry]); *Flucht und Verwandlung* (Stuttgart, 1959, Flight and Transformation); *Späte Gedichte* (Frankfurt, 1965, Late Poems); *Verzauberung* (Frankfurt, 1970, Enchantment [late dramatic works]); *Briefe der Nelly Sachs* (Frankfurt, 1984, Letters of Nelly Sachs).

Translations: *Selected Poems, including the verse-play Eli*, with Introduction by H. M. Enzensberger (1967, Bilingual edition).

Consult: *Nelly Sachs zu Ehren: Zum 75. Geburtstag* (Frankfurt, 1966, In Honor of Nelly Sachs on her 75th Birthday); H. Falkenstein, *Nelly Sachs* (Berlin, 1984).

                                                                           CEDRIC HENTSCHEL

SAID, Edward W. Born November 1, 1935, in Jerusalem, Palestine, then under rule of the British Mandate; he lives with his wife, Mariam, and two children, Wadie and Najla, in New York City. Unique in the annals of American literary criticism, and perhaps in American letters in general, Said has achieved stature as one of the most important and original critics of his time, and as a key figure in exile of a political revolution. Since 1963, Said has been Parr Professor of English and Comparative Literature at Columbia University; as an American member of the Palestinian legislature-in-exile, the 400-member Palestine National Council (PNC), he helped draft the Declaration of Independence announced by Yasser Arafat at the PNC meeting in Algiers on November 15, 1988. The declaration was monumental—forty years after U.N. Resolution 181 partitioned Palestine into both Arab and Jewish states, the Palestinian resistance leadership accepted that decision officially, as well as U.N. Resolution 242. A month later on December 13, addressing the United Nations in Geneva on behalf of the PLO, Arafat explicitly accepted Israel's right to exist as a state. Said was a major voice of moderation in this difficult evolution for Palestinians, many of whom (750,000) left or were expelled from their homeland in the war that created Israel in 1948. The Algiers vote (253–46–10) indicates that coexistence of two states triumphed in the opinion of a vast majority of the five million Palestinians worldwide, three million of whom live in diaspora. Said's multicultural upbringing in Jerusalem, his long sojourn in New York City and exposure to progressive traditions in Jewish diasporic culture and letters, as well as to freedom as an American, all contributed to his leavening influence in the Palestinian leadership. In *Before the Flames: A Quest for the History of Arab Americans* (1988) by Gregory Orfalea Said notes he is of two minds concerning return to Palestine when and if Israeli troops withdraw from the West Bank and Gaza, enabling the new state to be established. "Force of habit" has imbued him with "a sense of exile and rootlessness" and "New York . . . enhances that."

Said's father, Wadie (or William), actually left Palestine in 1911 to avoid the Ottoman Turkish draft, which would have put him in battle in Bulgaria. Preferring to fight for democracy rather than autocracy, the elder Said became an American doughboy in World War I. He returned to Jerusalem, however, coming back to America only in 1951 to escort son Edward to school. Edward Said has spoken fondly of growing up in Palestine amid a large extended family with relatives in Ramallah, Jaffa, and Haifa, as well as Jerusalem. He particularly enjoyed summer trips to Safed and swimming in the Sea of Galilee as a boy. Said has not, however, been back to any part of historic Palestine since 1966, when he attended a wedding in Ramallah. The Said family left Palestine in 1947 at the onset of the war that created Israel, going to Cairo, where the family business in office machines and publishing had a branch office. A brilliant student, Said had a rebellious streak—he was expelled from a Cairo prep school run by the colonial British, and was thrown out of a posh country club there run by the British for being an "Arab," though his family actually were club members, an early lesson he later said of "the importance of race over class" (Orfalea, p. 156).

After being taken to Massachusetts to finish prep school, Said graduated from Princeton University in 1957; he received his doctorate from Harvard University in 1964. His first book, *Joseph Conrad and the Fiction of Autobiography* (1966), dealt with an author whose experience of multiple dislocation resembled his own; Conrad was "born in one society and wrote in another . . . about a third one." Said was struck by Conrad's attempt to write about "a reality slipping away" (Orfalea, p. 154). Said's broadside volley against the detached solipsism of the New Critics is contained in essays he collected in *The World, the Text, and the Critic* (1983). Here Said argues passionately for an approach to literature that is engaged and informed by a strong sense of history, politics, and changing mores, what he terms "secular criticism." He rebukes the clean-room jargon of obsessive textuality that avoids consideration of the human life and culture from which both author and work spring. His experience as an exile is crucial to his perspective; he quotes favorably, with great admiration, from Eric Auerbach,* the German Jewish refugee who produced *Mimesis* in exile in Istanbul: "Our philological home is earth; it can no longer be a nation." Said puts it himself: "Criticism must think of itself as life-enhancing and constitutively opposed to every form of tyranny, domination, and abuse." In a word, Said's criticism is oppositional to the self-congratulatory, static, and chauvinistic— manifestly the viewpoint of someone who has lived in exile, at a distance from the excesses of nationalism.

At the same time as these writings, another "track" of Said's critical life was coming to fruition, one that would paradoxically transform him into one of the shapers of a new nation. Beginning with his *Orientalism* (1978)—a watershed examination of Western attitudes toward the Near East since the Napoleonic Wars—Said published a quartet of books converging ever more intensely on the Palestinian-Israeli conflict. In *The Question of Palestine* (1980)—dedicated to two Palestinian exiles, one of whom died in a fire in a New York rooming house—Said presents the most widely disseminated history of the Palestine dilemma from a Palestinian perspective published to date in the United States. The book is an eloquent plea for the two-state solution to the problem. The last of the quartet, and perhaps the most moving volume, *After the Last Sky: Palestinian Lives* (1986) is both a penetrating commentary on Jean Mohr photographs of Palestinians around the world, and an elegiac meditation on the lives Palestinians lead today in the wake of a fifty-year history of massacre, exclusion, explusion, and exile. Said exchanges his formidable powers of exegesis and argument for a work of the heart. Here an exile faces the hardest truths of loss and time; it may well be, literarily, his most stirring book (though *Orientalism* is generally acknowledged to be his masterpiece). Said muses on Palestinian authors and poets such as the celebrated Mahmoud Darwish* from whose poetry Said's book title derives; Emile Habiby; Ghassan Kanafani; Sahar Khalife; Hanan Ashrawi; Raja Shehaheh; and others. He considers life in exile for his family members—father, mother, an aunt who was called "the Mother of Palestine." He connects to the Palestinian experience two poems of William Butler Yeats— "Leda and the Swan" and "Among School Children"—and culls from the latter a sense of limits, age, and destiny. He sees Palestinians not as "disembodied presences of Sorrow or Homelessness" but finds their "truest reality . . . in the way we cross over from one place to another. We are migrants and perhaps hybrids in, but not of, any situation in which we find ourselves." Being Palestinian often entails "mastery without domination, pleasure without injury to others." Palestinians, he concludes, "live in a protracted not-yet." A mature idealism and empathy—qualities Said embodied in his own intellectual and spiritual odyssey—were brought to bear in the great compromise enshrined in the 1988 Declaration of Independence. Few American authors have been on the cutting edge of historic change as has Said. At fifty-five, he has amassed an original body of work increasingly influential in both literary and foreign policy circles.

Selected Titles: "Reflections on Palestinian Self-Determination," *Nation* 223 (December 5, 1981); "Palestinians in the Aftermath of Beirut," *Journal of Palestine Studies* (Winter 1983); "Reflections on Exile," *Granta* 13 (Autumn 1984); "The Mind of Winter: Reflections on a Life in Exile," *Harpers* (September 1984); "Michel Foucault, 1927–1984," *Raritan* 4 (Fall 1984).

Consult: James Clifford, *Predicament of Culture: Twentieth Century Ethnography, Literature and Art* (1988); John Kucich, "Edward S. Said," *Dictionary of Literary Biography*, 67; John Kucich, in *Modern American Critics since 1955*, ed. Gregory Jay (1988); Gregory Orfalea, *Before the Flames: A Quest for the History of Arab Americans* (1988).

GREGORY ORFALEA

SAINT-EXUPÉRY, Antoine de. Born June 29, 1900, in Lyon, France; died July 21, 1944, near Corsica (missing in action). Saint-Exupéry spent much of his younger life as a mail pilot in Africa, and later in Argentina as an executive of an air service firm. He engaged in several air competitions around the world. Despite many injuries sustained on his commercial flights and in his aviation competitions, he enlisted for military service at the start of World War II when he was thirty-nine years old. After the defeat of France, he managed to reach New York, where he lived for a few years in exile. When American forces invaded North Africa, he requested permission to rejoin his squadron. He was killed on his eighth mission as he was flying back to his base in Corsica.

In exile the ever-active Saint-Exupéry had opportunity to write and/or rewrite much of his best-known work, for example, the charming *Le petit prince* (1943; *The Little Prince*, 1943); the compassionate *Lettre à un otage* (1944; *Letter to a Hostage*, 1950); as well as the philosophic *Pilote de guerre* (1942; *Flight to Arras*, 1942).

Selected Titles: *Citadelle* (1948; *The Wisdom of the Sands*, 1950), a posthumous collection of notes left by Saint-Exupéry.

Consult: C. Cate, *Saint-Exupéry, His Life and Times* (1970); G. Pelissier, *Les cinq visages de Saint-Exupéry* (1951); *Wartime Writings, 1939–1944* (1986).

SAINT-JOHN PERSE (pseudonym of Alexis Saint-Leger Leger). Born May 31, 1887, in Saint-Leger-les-Feuilles, Guadeloupe; died September 20, 1975, in Giens, France. Saint-John Perse fled Paris after its capitulation to the invading

Germans in 1940. He lived in Washington, D.C., where he wrote many of his major poems, until 1967, when he returned to France. He received the Nobel Prize in 1960.

His first poem written in exile in the United States, "Exil," appeared in *Poetry* magazine in 1942. Saint-John Perse's exile poems explore the demands made on the poet both by his personal nature and by his sense of social responsibility. In *Exil* (1942, Exile and Other Poems), he finds solace in exile through a transcendence of its condition into a consciousness of gain of experience. His later work continues his mythic vision of history as a voyage of discovery into renewal of spirit. Saint-John Perse worked in the Library of Congress.

Selected Titles: *Eloges* (1944); *Exile* (1949); *Winds* (1953).

SALIH, Tayeb. Born 1927 in Northern Province of Sudan; he lives in Qatar. Salih, who comes from a background of small farmers and religious teachers, has spent most of his life outside the Sudan. He studied at the University of Khartoum and later at the University of London. After graduation he worked briefly as a teacher, then joined the BBC, where he became head of drama of the Arabic Service. He lived in Paris while on the staff of UNESCO, and moved to Qatar on appointment as head of Information Services in the Qatar government.

Salih writes in Arabic and is recognized as one of the leading voices in contemporary Arabic literature. His collection of three interrelated stories, *The Wedding of Zein* (1985, first published in Arabic in Beirut, Lebanon, in 1966, *Urs-az-Zain wa sab' qisas'*), treats village life in a rapidly changing world; the Arabic movie version of the title story won a Cannes Film Award in 1976. Salih's novel *Season of Migration to the North* (1989) employs a classic premise of exile and return: the narrator of the novel has returned to a remote area of Sudan after seven years of European education. He meets Mustafa, a creature like him, who also had left and returned to the Sudan; in the period since his return, Mustafa has succumbed to a kind of madness in his failure to accommodate his Western knowledge to his Sudanese claims. The novel's atmosphere and narrative hangs on the tension between the narrator's struggle to avoid a fate similar to that of Mustafa and to the temptation of the unknowable vortex that Mustafa represents.

SALINAS, Pedro. Born November 27, 1891, in Madrid, Spain; died December 4, 1951, in Boston, Massachusetts. Salinas accepted a visiting professorship at Wellesley College in Massachusetts in 1936. With the outbreak of the Spanish Civil War, and with the defeat of the Republican forces, he decided to remain in the United States. He became a professor of Hispanic literature at Johns Hopkins University in 1940. He never returned to Spain. Salinas wrote in Spanish all his life.

Consult: Gustav Pérez Firmat, "Pedro Salinas, Mundo Cérrado, and Hispanic Vanguard Fiction," in *La Chispa* 1981: Selected Proceedings (New Orleans: Tulane University, 1981).

SALKEY, Andrew. Born January 30, 1928, of Jamaican parents in Colon, Panama; he lives in Massachusetts. Salkey was taken to Jamaica when he was two years old and raised by his grandmother, and later by his mother. He rarely saw his father, who became a successful businessman spending a great deal of time outside Jamaica. Salkey says he met his father for the first time in 1960 when he, Salkey, returned to Jamaica on a Guggenheim fellowship.

Salkey went to school in Jamaica, became aware of the oral and folk traditions of the island, particularly the Anancy tales. He went to England in 1952, where he earned his B.A. at the University of London. Like many West Indian writers his sense of exile began with his formal education and his ensuing sense of separation from his people and their folk traditions. Salkey has worked for the BBC, served as editor for a number of little magazines in the United States (he founded *Savacou*), and teaches at Hampshire College in Amherst, Massachusetts. He has written five novels, eight children's books, four volumes of poems, a collection of stories, and two travel books. He has, in addition, edited nine anthologies of West Indian literature.

Daryl Cumber Dance, in her essay on Salkey in *Fifty Caribbean Writers*, writes:

Though the quest for identity and the need for revolution are probably the major themes that permeate most of his work, the style and tone of the treatment and development of these themes and the nature of the world in which they are developed vary greatly as the novelist moves from one genre to the other. After *A Quality of Violence* (1959), his later adult novels generally focus on a weak, aimless, lost, ineffective middle-class young man, for all intents and purposes fatherless, unable to determine who he is and what he wants, struggling in a world that is basically corrupt, racist, evil and absurd. They end in despair. . . . His poetry is very romantic and also political. It focuses on the beauty of the West Indies as place, on the love and attraction this homeland retains for its children in exile (this latter is an especially dominant theme in *Away*, 1979).

Selected Title: *The Late Emancipation of Jerry* (1982).

Consult: Bill Carr, "A Complex Fate: The Novels of Andrew Salkey," in *The Islands in Between*, ed. Bruce King (1979); Daryl Cumber Dance, in *Fifty Caribbean Writers* (1986); C. R. Gray, "Mr. Salkey's Truth and Illusion," *Jamaica Journal* 2 (June 1968).

SANCHEZ, Florencio. Born January 17, 1875, in Montevideo, Uruguay; died November 7, 1910, in Milan, Italy. A playwright who focused on the country poor (with some work centered on the urban working class), Sanchez left his native country permanently in 1898. He was a moralist protesting the debasement of traditional values at the same time that he called for social change and progressive economic revisionism. With an output of over twenty plays and his own theater group in Buenos Aires, Sanchez created a vogue for social realism in his adopted country of Argentina.

SÁNCHEZ ALBORNOS, Claudio. Born 1904 in Spain; died 1985. The eminent scholar and intellectual apologist for the Spanish Republic left Spain in 1936 when the Civil War began, for a chair at the University of Bordeaux,

France. In 1940 he fled France before the invading German army occupied the country. In 1942 he was given a special institute at the University of Buenos Aires for his studies on Christianity in Spain during the medieval period. He also served as president of the Republic of Spain in Exile from 1962 to 1971. After Franco's death he returned to Spain in 1976. Many honors were accorded Sánchez Albornos in his last years, among them the Feltrinelli Prize in 1971.

Sánchez Albornos was a prolific, painstaking scholar. In his exile years, isolated from his sources on medieval Spain, he relied on the voluminous notes (and little else) he had taken with him in his flight to the New World. He produced in the pages of *Cuadernos de Historia de Espana*, the journal he edited in Buenos Aires, one of the great repositories of honed scholarship on the Christian-feudal past of his country from the eighth to the twelfth centuries. Sánchez Albornos proved not only indefatigable in his literary-scholarly efforts, but also in his many pronouncements and activities in academic matters.

Selected Titles: *Cuadernos de Historia de Espana* (Buenos Aires, Argentina, 1950–1960); *Espana: un enigma historico* (Buenos Aires, 1956); *Origenes de la nacion espanola*, 3 vols. (Buenos Aires, 1972–75).

Consult: *Estudios en Homenaje a Don Claudio Sánchez Albornos en sus 90 anos*, 2 vols. (Madrid, 1984); Peter Linehan, "A History of Isolation," *Times Literary Supplement*, October 11, 1985.

SANCHEZ-BOUDY, José. Born October 17, 1927, in Havana, Cuba; he teaches in Greensboro, North Carolina. Sanchez-Boudy is a novelist, poet, lawyer, former diplomat, and university teacher. He practiced law in Cuba until his exile in 1961.

Selected Titles: *Cuentos grise* (Barcelona, 1966); *Poemas de otoño e invierno* (Barcelona, 1967); *Cuentos blanco y negros* (Miami, 1983); *Poema del parque* (Miami, 1984).

Consult:Woodrow W. Moore, *Cuba and Her Poets* (Miami, 1974); Manuel Laurentino Suarez, *La narrativa de José Sanchez-Boudy (Tragedia y folklore)* (Miami, 1983).

SANG Ye (pseudonym of Shen Dajun). He lives in New York City. Sang was forced to work as an apprentice in a small factory as a result of the Cultural Revolution's assignment program. He became an electrician and later a salesman. He lived in Hong Kong, where he continued his technical training; later he wrote for the Hong Kong press. He now works as a feature writer for *China Daily News*, a newspaper published in New York City.

Selected Title: with Zhang Xinxin, *Chinese Lives: An Oral History of Contemporary China* (1989).

Consult: Introduction by W. J. F. Jenner and Delia Davin, eds., in *Chinese Lives: An Oral History of Contemporary China* (1989).

SANTAYANA, George. Born December 16, 1863, in Madrid, Spain; died September 26, 1952, in Rome, Italy. Santayana's mother brought him to the United States when he was nine years old. Santayana, however, never became an American citizen. In nationality and in all other categories of his extraordinarily varied career, he refused to be pinned onto a label. In his last years, after much wandering through Europe and after many controversies and academic skirmishes, Santayana placed himself in the English Catholic order of the Blue Sisters in Rome and gained a sense of inner calm.

SARDUY, Severo. Born February 25, 1937, in Camaguey, Cuba; he lives in France. Sarduy had completed one year of medical study when the University of Havana was ordered to close its doors by the Fulgencio Batista regime. After the Cuban revolution he wrote art criticism for various journals, among them *Lunes de Revolución* and *Diario Libre*; in 1959 he was given a scholarship by the Castro government to study art history in Europe. He stayed briefly in Madrid and then moved to Paris, where he has been an émigré since. In France he fell under the influence of Roland Barthes, under whom Sarduy took courses at l'École des Hautes Études, and with Philippe Sollers, with whom Sarduy worked on the journal *Tel Quel* and with whom he continues to collaborate on French translations of his text.

Sarduy's work, since his stay in France, is profoundly mired in semiotics, linguistic philosophy, and the concept of intertextuality. He believes in a polyphonic literature which suggests pluralities of texture and meaning, and is least concerned with linear, chronological narrative. For Sarduy the intertext, or that which is conveyed but not transcribed, is the core of meaning, and its language must be explored for hidden codes, signifiers, and felt ideas. In Sarduy's view, language is an entity unto itself and the core of literature's reality, not its mechanistic and technical servant. At the center of literary and visual art lies a language, but since language is an assumption based on other assumptions, the center of art becomes a shifting and unverifiable base. Sarduy's theories provide, by the nature of their core, little certainty of fact. To proceed, one must constantly move into new areas of perception, much like acts of sexual discovery and erotic satisfaction, references that Sarduy makes throughout his fiction and in his two books of speculative essays: *Escrito sobre un cuerpo: ensayos de crítica* (Buenos Aires, 1969, Written on a Body) and *Barroco* (Buenos Aires, 1974, Baroque).

Sarduy's major works are *Gestos* (1963, Gestures); *De donde son los cantantes* (1967; *From Cuba with a Song*, 1972); *Cobra* (1972; *Cobra*, 1975); and *Maitreya* (1978; *Maitreya*, 1987). All have been influenced by the nouveau roman tradition of Alain Robbe-Grillet, Roland Barthes, and the *Tel Quel* group. All three novels revolve on an axis of viewpoint: as the world turns, the point of view is shifted, or conversely, the author-narrator's view turns the world into its inescapable wheel of event and circumstance. All use the technique of a camera eye spanning, panning, moving in and out of range of vision of its subject matter, so that a reader cannot place anything on a grounded map of information. All is circle and play in Sarduy's wheel of fiction, but the circles ultimately make a point through semiotic and referential codings. In *Gestos* a black woman terrorist is on her way to plant a bomb in a crowded Paris site; the novel follows her scene by scene; the import is not her success or failure, but a revelation of reaction among the members of each scene. The truth of Sarduy's tale lies not in what happens, but in a kind of "what if it happens?" In *De donde son los cantantes* the world of post-Castro Cuba is seen as a junction, disjunction, and conjunction of three beings—the African, the Spanish, the Chinese—as three characters, two women and one man, play out roles given them by the narrator. In acting out the narrator's biographies of the Cuban being, the characters indulge their appetite for machismo, eroticism, religious zealotry, political dominance and power, all part of the characterological fabric of Cuba as Sarduy views it. In *Cobra* the technique of serial/circular identity is played out against a world of projection and fantasy as the main character changes/is transformed, like a salamander shedding skin to reveal a new layer of skin-deep identity. Among the identities assumed in the hallucinatory light of core meaning are a human female, a manufactured doll, a human male, and a transsexual: throughout *Cobra* the notion of the double or Janus-psyche prevails. Sarduy's brilliance resides in the power of control of the games he is playing, games that the reader, in terror of self-annihilation, cannot dismiss as a void of inconsequential fantasy. Sarduy continues to write in Spanish.

Selected Titles: *Big bang; Para situar en órbita cinco máquinas; pour situer en orbite cinq machines de Ramón Alejandro* (Montpellier, 1974); *Colibrí* (Buenos Aires, 1984).

Consult: Suzanne Jill Levine, Foreword to Sarduy's *Cobra* (1975); Oscar Julian Montero, "The French Intertext of *De donde son los cantantes*" (Ph.D. diss., University of North Carolina at Chapel Hill, 1978); Julian Rios, ed., *Severo Sarduy* (Madrid, 1976); José Sanchez-Boudy, *La tematica narrativa de Severo Sarduy* (Miami, 1985); Enrico M. Santi, "Textual Politics: Severo Sarduy," *Latin American Literary Review* 8, no. 16 (1980). See also the special section on Sarduy in *Review* 13 (1974).

SARRAUTE, Nathalie. Born Nathalie Tcherniak on July 18, 1900, in Ivanovo Voznesinsh (now Ivanovo), USSR; she lives in France. Sarraute was shunted back and forth between her mother in Geneva and her father in Russia after the breakup of her parents' marriage. In 1908 she went to live with her father in Paris, where he had emigrated. She studied at the Sorbonne and received a degree in law from the University of Paris. She practiced law until 1940, when the Germans took over Paris. She survived the occupation by posing as a governess for her own three children; she convinced the Germans that the Jewish mistress had disappeared.

SAVARIUS, Vincent. *See* SZASZ, Bela

SCHAEFER, Albrecht. Born 1885 in West Prussia; he died 1950. Schaefer left Germany because of fear of Nazi persecution. He achieved critical success as a writer of short fiction, and also published poetry, criticism, dramas, and essays.

Selected Title: *Elli oder Sieben Treppen* (1920, Elli, or the Seven Steps).

SCHLAUCH, Margaret. Born September 25, 1898, in Philadelphia, Pennsylvania; died July 1986 in Warsaw, Poland. A distinguished linguistic scholar and critic of early English and medieval literature, Schlauch left the United States in 1951 during the Cold War period of the 1950s for exile in Poland. Fearful of persecution for her communist beliefs and unwilling to give information to the House Un-American Activities Committee, which had subpoened her for questioning, she disappeared from her office at New York University (she had been a professor there for decades). She resurfaced in Warsaw and was granted asylum by the Polish government. She received many awards from the Polish government for her Scholarly and linguistic achievements.

Selected Titles: *The Gift of Tongues* (1942); *Who Are the Aryans?* (New York: Anti-Fascist Literature Committee, 1940); *English World Literature and Its Social Foundations* (Warsaw, 1956); *Modern English and American Poetry: Techniques and Ideologies* (London, 1956); *The English Language in Modern Times, since 1400* (Warsaw, 1959); *Antecedents of the English Novel* (Warsaw, 1963).

Consult: *Studies in Language and Literature in Honour of Margaret Schlauch*, ed. Mieczysaw Brahme, Stanislaw Helsztynski and Julien Krzyzanowski (Warsaw, 1971).

SCHREINER, Olive. Born March 24, 1855, in Wittebergen, Basutoland, South Africa; died December 11, 1920, in Wynberg, near Cape Town, South Africa. Schreiner left South Africa at age twenty-six to earn her living in England. She had been a governess in South Africa and written *The Story of an African Farm*, the novel that was to give her a lasting reputation as her country's chief literary painter, before she was twenty-one years old. She also wrote an earlier, unfinished novel, *Undine* (published posthumously in 1929), in between her teaching and household duties on two large farms in the Rand. She published *The Story of an African Farm* (London, 1883) under the pseudonym Ralph Iron, and became famous overnight. In England, Schreiner missed her kopjes and hills of the veldt landscape and returned home in 1889. In South Africa she stood apart from any side in the growing divisions of Anglo and Boer and black camps. (Schreiner's father was a German missionary who met and married his English wife in England; they came to South Africa shortly after their marriage.) She became an apologist for the Boer cause in South Africa, believing that they had some right to the land that they had trekked and settled, but she allied herself with the more liberal Anglo tradition in civil and political rights. Schreiner was also an early feminist (her work *Woman and Labor* [London, 1911], remains a testament to her part in the women's movement). Ultimately Schreiner may be seen as a characterological exile who always felt and delineated the wounds of psychic apartness and remained dubious of any healing future, though she continued to believe and exclaim it. Schreiner died as and remains an honored spokeswoman of South Africa.

Selected Titles: *Dreams* (London, 1891); *Dream Life and Real Life* (London, 1893); *Trooper Peter Halket of Mashonaland* (1897); *An English-South African's View of the Situation: Words in Season* (London, 1899); *Stories, Dreams and Allegories*, ed. S. C.

Cronwright-Schreiner (London, 1923); *Thoughts on South Africa* (London, 1923); *Letters, 1876–1920*, ed. S. C. Cronwright-Schreiner (London, 1924); *From Man to Man* (1926); *Undine: A Queer Little Child* (London, 1929).

Consult: Ruth First and Ann Scott, *Olive Schreiner* (1980); Doris Lessing, Afterword to *The Story of an African Farm* (1968); Martin Tucker, *Africa in Modern Literature* (1967).

SCOTT, Paul. Born March 25, 1920, in a suburb of London, England; died March 1, 1978, in London, England, of cancer. Scott worked as an accountant for five years before joining the intelligence unit of the British army, in which he served from 1940 to 1942; from 1943 to 1946 he was stationed in India and Malaya. On his demobilization he again worked as an accountant. In 1950 he became a literary agent, while writing his radio plays and novels concurrently. In 1964 he revisited India; he made a third return in 1969, and a final visit in 1972. His revisits inspired him to write his most famous work, *The Raj Quartet*, consisting of *The Jewel in the Crown* (1966), *The Day of the Scorpion* (1968), *The Towers of Silence* (1971), and *A Division of the Spoils* (1975). Scott wrote a fifth novel concerning the British raj in India, *Staying On* (1977), the story of an English couple adrift in an exilic sea of feeling after India regains its independence from the British Crown in 1947. They belong neither in a new England nor in the new India; having no home to go to, they "stay on" in a place no longer there.

Scott was a world journeyer who enjoyed his travels. He wrote several other novels in addition to his *Quartet* (which became a celebrated television series in Great Britain and the United States), and some literary and autobiographical volumes.

Selected Titles: *My Appointment with the Muse: Essays 1961–1975*, ed. Shelley C. Reese (1986); *On Writing and the Novel* (1987).

Consult: K. Bhaskara Rao, *Paul Scott* (1980); Shelley C. Reese, Introduction to *My Appointment with the Muse: Essays 1961–1975* (1986).

SEGAL, Lore (born Lore Groszmann). Born March 8, 1928, in Vienna, Austria; she lives in New York City. Segal fled Austria in 1938 because she was Jewish; she was ten years old when she arrived in England with her parents and family. At age twenty she moved to the Dominican Republic, where she stayed at the home of a Jewish lawyer and his wife who were friends of the family. In 1951 she came to the United States and has lived mainly in New York, though she commutes to the Chicago campus of the University of Illinois as a professor of English there. Segal married the prominent editor David Segal, who died tragically early of a heart attack. A widow, a mother of two children, she is a naturalized American citizen and proud of her status, though she reserves the right to criticize her new country's foreign and domestic policies. She is known for her sophisticated wit, as evidenced particularly in her two novels, *Lucinella* (1976), an exaggerated but real satire of a fashionable writers colony in the northeast United States, and *Her First American* (1987), a warmly sad comedy of a love affair in New York City between a European-Jewish refugee and a black American novelist suffering from bouts with alcoholism. She also has achieved a high reputation for her children's stories, among them *Tell Me a Mitzi* (1970), *All The Way Home* (1973); *The Juniper Tree and Other Tales* (1973, adapted by Segal from the Brothers Grimm and with illustrations by Maurice Sendak); *Tell Me a Trudy* (1977); *The Story of Mrs. Lovewright and Purrless Her Cat* (1985); *The Book of Adam to Moses* (1987).

SEGHERS, Anna (pseudonym of Netty Reiling Radványi). Born November 19, 1900, in Mainz, Germany; died June 1, 1983, in East Berlin, GDR. By virtue of her longevity, sustained achievement, and ideological "correctness," Seghers became the unrivaled high priestess of letters in the German Democratic Republic. Daughter of a Jewish art dealer, Seghers adopted communism as an escape from narrow nationalism and the reactionary forces that paved the way for National Socialism. In 1925 she obtained a doctorate at Heidelberg, writing a thesis on Jewish elements in the work of Rembrandt (hence "Seghers," the name of a Dutch artist). She achieved early success with *Aufstand der Fischer von St. Barbara* (1928; *The Revolt of the Fishermen*, London, 1929), for which she was awarded the Kleist Prize. This novella, airing the grievances of exploited seafolk, was adapted as a Russian film in 1934. *Auf dem Wege zur Amerikanischen Botschaft* (1930, On the Way to the American Embassy) voiced a protest against the death sentences passed on Nicola Sacco and Bartolomeo Vanzetti. *Die Gefährten* (1932, The Companions) follows the mixed fortunes of communist sympathizers living in exile, after World War I, in Hungary, Poland, Italy, Bulgaria, and China. The book heralded her own future, for after her arrest in 1933 she sought asylum in France, Austria, Madrid (1937), and Mexico (1940). She returned to Germany in 1947.

Mexico proved a refuge rather than a source of exotic inspiration, serving as a spur to sharpen her vision of contemporary Germany. She wrote there her most popular book, *Das siebte Kreuz* (1942; *The Seventh Cross*, London, 1943), a minutely recorded picaresque tale of a multiple escape from the Nazi concentration camp Westhofen. At one level a suspense story about a manhunt, it was also politically the right book at the right time and became an instant best-seller in America and Britain. In Mexico Seghers also completed *Transit*, 1943 (*Transit Visa*, London 1945), a novel detailing the adventures of emigrés waiting for a ship in Marseilles. By now Seghers had grown skilful in deploying a large cast of characters against a broad canvas, a pattern well suited to her epic intent, which at times betrays echoes of John Dos Passos. The epic approach was to be elaborated after her return to Germany in *Die Toten bleiben jung* (1949; *The Dead Stay Young*, London, 1950); (1968, Trust) *Die Entscheidung* (1959, The Decision); and *Das Vertrauen*, (1968, Trust). This trilogy attempts a comprehensive portrayal of the development of German society, after 1945, from a supposedly moribund capitalism to a buoyant socialism. Seghers shows herself politically committed to furthering this process of social change; but what some might view as ideological gain was bought at the expense of a blinkered view and consequent artistic loss. By espousing the cause of the GDR, on her return from foreign exile, Seghers was to exile herself spiritually from her cultural roots in West Germany. A late work, the three tales published in 1972 as *Sonderbare Begegnungen* (Strange Encounters) might be interpreted as an escape from this dilemma into realms of fantasy. Her purposeful flouting of chronology permits E. T. A. Hoffmann, Nikolai Gogol and Franz Kafka to meet in a Prague café. The plurality of truth revealed in their discussions suggests that, towards the end of her combative life, she may have doubted the infallibility of the strict party line.

Selected Titles: *Gesammelte Werke*, 12 vols. (East Berlin, 1975; FRG, 10 vols., 1977, Collected Works); *Der Bienenstock*, 3 vols. (GDR, 1963; FRG, 2 vols., 1963–64), The Beehive [collected stories] twelve stories omitted from the FRG edition.

Consult: K. Franke, *Literatur der DDR* (Munich, 1971); H. Neugebauer, *Anna Seghers* (Berlin, 1959, rev. 1970).

CEDRIC HENTSCHEL

SELVON, Sam (Samuel Dickson). Born May 20, 1923, in South Trinidad; he lives in Canada. Selvon's parents were a mix of ancestries: his father's family was East Indian, his mother was half-Indian and half-Scottish. The family did not have the means to send Selvon to college, and after high school he served in the British navy during World War II. After the war, from 1946 to 1950, he worked as a journalist in Trinidad. In 1950 he moved to London. (He records his immigrant experiences in his novel *The Lonely Londoners*, 1956.) He worked in the Indian embassy when he was unable to gain admittance to the National Union of Journalists; during this period he worked as a free-lancer. In 1952 he was stricken with tuberculosis and spent fifteen months in recuperation. His first novel, *A Brighter Sun*, had appeared in 1952, and buoyed by its reception, he decided to write full-time.

Selvon also has taught and lectured in various locations. In 1978 he and his family moved to Calgary, Alberta, Canada.

Selvon has published ten novels; one collection of short stories; radio, television, and film plays; and many magazine articles. Sandra Pouchet Paquet has written of him that

After more than thirty years in Great Britain and Canada, Selvon is essentially a writer-in-exile, but paradoxically what distinguishes Selvon as a writer is his continuing Caribbean focus. . . . Like other major writers of the English-speaking Caribbean, among them Wilson Harris* and Derek Walcott,* Selvon is committed to the idea that Caribbean man, whatever his ancestry, possesses a distinct sensibility and potential. Living in the Caribbean, Selvon explains, "you become Creolized, you not Indian, you not Black, you not even White, you assimilate all these cultures and you turn out to be a different man who is the Caribbean man." For Selvon, as for Walcott and Harris, the loss of Old World traditions is no cause for despair, but an opportunity for rebirth and renewal.

Selected Titles: *The Housing Lark* (1965); *Those Who Eat the Cascadura* (1972); *Moses Ascending* (1975); *Moses Migrating* (1983).

Consult: Edward Braithwaite, "Sir Galahad and the Islands," *Bim* 7 (July-December 1957); Michel Fabre, "The Queen's Calypso: Linguistic and Narrative Strategies in the Fiction of Samuel Selvon," *Caribbean Essays and Studies* 3 (1977–78); Sandra Pouchet Paquet, in *Fifty Caribbean Writers*, ed. Daryl Cumber Dance (1986); Kenneth Ramchand, "Sam Selvon Talking: A Conversation with Kenneth Ramchand," *Canadian Literature* 95 (Winter 1982).

SEMPRUN, Jorge. Born ca. 1920 in Spain; he has returned to his native country. Semprun is a radical left-wing novelist given to Goyaesque descriptions of the horrors of war. He fought on the Republican side in the Spanish Civil War and emigrated to France when Generalissimo Francisco Franco and his forces triumphed in the war. He fought with French resistance forces after the fall of France in 1940. Captured by the Gestapo, he was sent to Auschwitz. After surviving the concentration camps, he was reluctantly readmitted to France at the close of World War II; the French government viewed his politics with unwelcome eyes and with surveillance. Semprun's slashes of imagery, blunt, horrific, and painful, and the ugly realities of death camps, firing squads, air raids, and bleeding and unlimbed soldiers and civilians, place him in a postwar school of realism exemplified by Cursio Malaparte and Louis-Ferdinand Celine in the novel and Roberto Rosselini and Pier Passolini in the cinema.

Semprun returned to Spain after the constitutional monarchy was established in his country. In 1989 he became the minister of culture in the socialist cabinet. Semprun writes in French, and only recently has begun to write in Spanish as well. He published his first book when he was 40 years old. After his denunciating portrait of the Spanish Communist Party Appeared in his *Autobiography of Frederico Sanchez* (Semprun's pseudonym), he was expelled from the party. He remains an active socialist.

Selected Titles: *La deuxième mort de Ramon Mercader* (Paris, 1960; *The Second Death of Ramon Mercader*, 1973); *L'Evanouissement* (Paris, 1967); *The Long Voyage* (1974); *Stavisky* (1975, text for film by Alain Resnais); *Autobiografia de Federico Sanchez: novela* (Barcelona, 1977; *The Autobiography of Federico Sanchez and the Communist Underground in Spain*, 1979); *Quel beau dimanche* (Paris, 1980); *Aquel domingo: novela* (Barcelona, 1981; *What a Beautiful Sunday!* 1982); *L'Algarabie: roman* (Paris, 1981).

SENDER, Ramón. Born February 3, 1901, in Chalamera de Cinca, Aragon, Spain; died January 16, 1982, in Los Angeles. Sender was a prolific writer. His bibliographer, Charles King, lists 102 book titles, including 64 novels, 23 compilations of essays, 5 books of plays, 2 volumes of poetry, and a host of short pieces and journalistic articles. Sender's background, reflected in numerous semi-autobiographical novels, was that of a small village in Aragon. After desultory studies in Zaragoza, Teruel, and later at law school in Madrid, he was drafted in 1923 for service with the army in the ill-fated "War of Reconquest" in Morocco. *Imán* (1930), his first published novel, was a bitter indictment of the war and by extension of the dictatorship of Primo de Rivera (1923–30). Several of the themes to be repeated in his later works stem from this period: his hatred of authoritarian rule (including that of the church), his dislike of his unfeeling father, the symbol of the social ills in so much of Spain, and his rejection of the status quo.

Imán was a considerable success and was soon translated into more than ten languages. His second novel, *Orden público*, based on his imprisonment without trial for a period of three months, was published in 1931. There followed a steady stream of impassioned essays and newspaper articles supporting the Republican position, though not uncritically. The outbreak of the Civil War in 1936 marked a personal as well as a national tragedy; Sender's wife, Amparo, the mother of his two young children, was executed by the Nationalists, as was his brother Manuel. Sender fought bravely during the savage conflict, rising to the rank of major, despite growing differences with the communist faction. In the spring of 1938 the hard-pressed Spanish government sent Sender on a visit to the United States to enlist support; by the end of the year, Sender found himself in French exile, and early in 1939, en route to New York with his two children. There followed two years in Mexico City before he settled in Santa Fe, New Mexico, in large measure due to the award of a Guggenheim fellowship. Sender later taught Spanish literature at several American universities, most notably at the University of New Mexico (1947–63) and at the University of Southern California (1965–71). His earlier novels on the Spanish Civil War, such as the powerful *Contraataque* (1937), evolved into more poetic evocations of the conflict; in this latter style are the sensitive *Mosén Millán* (1953) and the popular trilogy *Crónica del alba* (1963–66), a nostalgic reminiscence of his Aragonese childhood. Many of his later works are imbued with a fantastic, almost ethereal quality in contrast to the severe style of his earlier writing. Unlike a large number of his fellow Spaniards in exile, Sender remained a productive writer to the end of his life. The high plateau country of New Mexico, the archaic forms of the Spanish spoken in the pueblos, the sharp contrasts in climate, all reminded him of his native Aragon. In a real sense, Sender took a part of Spain with him; his personal library was stocked with rare editions of Spanish works and an extensive collection of Spanish folk music.

Many of Sender's novels are readily available in translation, making him perhaps the best known of all the Spanish exile writers.

Consult: Charles L. King, *Ramón J. Sender* (1974); Charles L. King, *Ramón J. Sender: An Annotated Bibliography, 1928–1974* (1976); Michael Ugarte, *Shifting Ground: Spanish Civil War Exile Literature* (1989); Mary S. Vásquez, ed., *Homenaje a Ramón J. Sender* (1987).

DOUGLAS HILT

SENGHOR, Léopold Sédar. Born October 9, 1906, in Joal, Senegal. Senghor was a major participant in the political events preceding the independence of France's African colonies; he became president of Senegal from its independence in 1960 until his resignation in 1981. After four decades, he continues to be an important figure in the development of contemporary African literature. His writing includes several volumes of published poems and numerous essays dedicated primarily to literary, social, and political topics. With Aimé Césaire* and Léon-Gontran Damas,* he was one of the founders of Negritude, a movement that affirmed the existence and value of black cultural heritage. Far more than the other Negritude writers, Senghor has succeeded in defining the specific nature of that heritage. He has also emphasized the merits of cultural *metissage*, or crossbreeding, and has consistently sought recognition for what Africa might contribute to the future of civilization.

The son of a prosperous cultivator, Senghor spent his early childhood immersed in the African setting with its characteristic customs and beliefs, but by the age of seven, he had become a pupil in the missionary school at Joal and had left behind the carefree years he refers to in his poetry as "the kingdom of childhood," that period prior to his acquisition of a European education when he yet remained wholly African. In the case of Senghor, the term *exile* relates only in part to the actual physical separation from home and family that came about as a result of studies that took him from Joal to N'Gazobil to Dakar and, finally, to Paris in 1928 to pursue a university education and to become in 1935 the first African *agrégé*. More significant in terms of Senghor's work as a poet is the sense of cultural exile that was the necessary result of having been born an African during the period of French colonial dominance. His first collection of poetry, *Chants d'ombre* (Shadow Songs), published in 1945, deals with the poet's attempts to come to terms with the question of his identity as an African and as a black, more specifically as a black African living in France and educated under the French policy of assimilation that explicitly affirmed Western cultural supremacy and denied that the African had a significant civilization of his own. Senghor had thus been taught that he was culturally tabula rasa, waiting to be imprinted with Western values, but in *Chants d'ombre*, he recognizes that this attitude threatens his very identity. He confronts the issue in poems that articulate his feelings as an exile and reaffirm the values of his African heritage. These early poems represent the resolution of the poet's own identity crisis and ultimately become a commitment to rehabilitate Africa and to represent her people, a resolution that figures prominently in later works.

The theme of exile, although it occasionally appears elsewhere with interesting variations, never again resounds so strongly, but the positive images of Africa evolved during this period and the related dichotomy he establishes between Africa and the West remain an essential part of his poetic vocabulary in future poems. His second important collection, *Hosties noires* (Black hosts) appeared in 1948 and deals primarily with the experiences of World War II from an African perspective. The theme of exile is less important here but returns in some of the poems recounting the poet's own suffering as a prisoner of war and in the descriptions of the African soldiers serving the cause of a country and civilization that is not their own. The end of the war coincided with the beginning of Senghor's political career, and from 1946 to 1960, he represented Senegal in the French National Assembly. The year 1946 also marked the year of his marriage to Ginette Eboué. The couple would have two sons before their divorce in 1955. *Chants pour Naëtt* (Songs for Naëtt), published first in 1949 and reissued in 1961 as "Chants pour Signare" in the collection *Nocturnes*, consists of a cycle of love poems that depict the poet in quest of a woman. Her evident association with Africa and the recurring themes of separation and absence sometimes suggest a parallel between these works and the nostalgic poems of *Chants d'ombre*.

In 1960, Senghor was elected as the first president of the newly independent Republic of Senegal. *Ethiopiques* (1956) contains poems written during a period of vigorous and successful political activity in which the poet increasingly identifies himself with Africa and its people; in addition to reprinting most of the previously published love poems, *Nocturnes* (1961) groups together several elegies dealing primarily with the subjects of nationhood and leadership. In 1956, Senghor married Colette Hubert, a Frenchwoman. His *Elégie des Alizés* (Elegy of the tradewinds), published in 1969, is dedicated to her, and in *Lettres d'hivernage* (1973), he celebrates their relationship in a series of epistolary poems. The elegies in *Elégies majeures* (1979) constitute a record of the events of the poet's later years in the presidency; also included is the richly symbolic "Elégie pour la Reine de Saba" and, in the 1984 edition, an extremely moving poem on the death of his son by Colette Hubert. Senghor retired from office in 1981. In 1984, he became the first black member of the French Academy.

Senghor's collected poems are available under the title *Poèmes* (Paris: Editions du Seuil, 1984). Many of his early theoretical essays are collected in *Liberté I: Négritude et humanisme* (Paris: Editions du Seuil, 1964).

Consult: Sylvia Washington Ba, *The Concept of Negritude in the Poetry of Léopold Sédar Senghor* (1973); Janice Spleth, *Léopold Sédar Senghor* (1985); Janet G. Vaillant, *Black, French, and African: A Life of Léopold Sédar Senghor* (1990).

JANICE SPLETH

SERGE, Victor (pseudonym of Victor Lvovich Kibalchich). Born December 30, 1890, in Brussels, Belgium; died November 17, 1947, in Mexico City, Mexico. Serge's life was filled with tribulations and flights of exile from his birth to his death. His parents fled Russia to France after the assassination of Czar Alexander II in 1881; Serge's father had been in sympathy with the Narodnik movement, members of whom had plotted the czar's assassination. In France as a child Serge read a vast collection of revolutionary literature in his father's library; the reading proved a substitute for public schooling, a system Serge's father condemned as self-perpetuating bourgeois control. Not surprisingly, Serge joined a socialist youth organization and lived for a while in an anarchist utopian commune (in the Ardennes). In 1908 he moved to Paris, where three years later he became the editor of an anarchist magazine, *Anarchie*. In 1912 he was arrested for complicity in the terrorist Bonnot gang series of bank robberies and abductions throughout the Paris region. Although he had not been a participant in any of the violent crimes of the "Tragic Bandits" Bonnot group, he was sentenced to five years in prison. In 1917, on his release, he was expelled from France; he found asylum in Spain. In Barcelona he wrote the first piece he signed as Victor Serge. Later that year he returned to France to join an army unit of Russian exiles that had been formed to fight on the side of the revolutionaries, but he was arrested by the French police and put in a concentration camp as a Bolshevik agent. In 1918 he was exchanged in a hostage sweep for French officers who had been detained by the Soviets.

Arriving in Petrograd in 1917, he worked with the Red Army and was one of the prime organizers of the Communist International (Comintern), for which he worked as a secret agent from 1923 to 1926 in Berlin and Vienna. Serge also edited the journal *Imprekor* during this time. He returned to the USSR in 1926 and began a series on the Chinese Revolution. In 1927 he protested Stalin's lack of support of Mao Zedung and Stalin's complacence vis-à-vis the threat of Kuomintang power in China. By 1928 he had become suspect in Stalin's eyes; later in the year he was expelled from the Communist party and prohibited from work in the USSR. During the period of this prohibition he wrote several of his major novels—*Men in Prison* (1930); *Birth of Our Power* (1931); *Conquered City* (1932)—and the history *Year One of the Russian Revolution* (1930). All these works were published in Paris in French-language editions, since Serge was forbidden publication in the USSR. For the "crime" of sending his works abroad, Serge was arrested and deported to Orenburg in Central Asia, where he remained till world protest succeeded in gaining his release. In 1936 he was expelled from the USSR, and all his manuscripts were confiscated. He lived briefly in Brussels, then returned to Paris; in the following year he published *From Lenin to Stalin* and *Destiny of a Revolution*, both in French and issued in Paris. Elected a counselor to POUM (the Independent Marxist party in Spain), he was one of the few socialist-minded intellectuals to protest the Moscow Purge trials.

With the Nazis outside Paris in 1940, Serge fled to Marseilles, where he tried to obtain a visa. He was among those aided by Varian Fry, the American scholar who went to France at the behest of the U.S. government to rescue scholars from Nazi and fascist persecution. Because of Serge's Communist Party record he was not able to to get into the United States, but he found refuge in Mexico, where from 1940 to 1947 he lived in poverty. During this time he wrote *The Case of Comrade Tulayev* and *Memoirs of a Revolutionary*, works he knew he could not publish immediately because of the political situation around him. He collaborated with the widow of Leon Trotsky, Natalia Sedova Trotsky, in a biography of the exiled Russian leader, *The Life and Death of Leon Trotsky* (Paris, 1951; London, 1975). Serge died shortly after completing this project; he is buried in the French section of the Mexico City cemetery.

Serge's work, both his nonfiction and fiction, is a record of personal experience and a social history. His first novel, *Men in Prison*, is a partly autobiographical account of his five years in French jails from 1911 to 1917. His second novel, *Birth of Our Power*, describes the Barcelona populist uprising in 1917 and Serge's attempt to return to his country to fight on the side of the revolutionaries. His next novel, *Conquered City*, draws on the situation in Petrograd in 1919 (the time he arrived there), while his popular novel *Midnight in the Century* documents, in a manner both Arthur Koestler* and, later, Aleksandr Solzhenitsyn* employed in their work, the sufferings of imprisoned or deported socialist idealists discarded by the Stalinist autocracy.

Serge wrote at least twenty books and witnessed, as active participant as well as intellectual observer, two world wars, the Russian Revolution and its ensuing civil wars, and the Spanish Civil War. He remained a firm believer in the possibilities of humankind. He said in 1943, when he was a stateless citizen and without financial means, "I have more confidence in mankind and in the future than ever before." Although his style is often clumsy (he is reported by his biographer Richard Greeman to have said that he had no time for literary polish or the niceties of literary craft), his novels show sensitivity to and compassion for human error and human striving. This compassionate expression may be seen in Serge's statement quoted in *Carnets* (Paris, 1952): "Writing becomes a search for poly-personality, a means of living several destinies, of penetration into others, of communicating with them."

Because of his secret agentry and his political agenda, Serge often engaged in subterfuge for what he considered higher aims; his critical and political opposition sees him, however, as manipulative and untrustworthy. Basically a believer in individualism (his first adherence was to anarchism and early individualist-oriented movements in the Russian Revolution), he submerged those beliefs for group solidarity with the Bolsheviks. He has remained a controversial figure but one consistently forgotten and much maligned: while many of his articles appeared in journals during the period from 1937 to 1950 (among them *Partisan Review*, *Politics*, and *New International*), he is rarely listed today in literary histories, and most of his books are out of print. At his death Serge left manuscripts of several novels, historical and political writings, poetry, and letters, as well as the materials confiscated by the Soviet censors at the time of his expulsion from the USSR.

Serge was fluent in French and Russian and wrote in both languages. He translated Lenin, Trotsky, and Alexander Zinoviev* into French.

Selected Titles: *What Everyone Should Know about Repression* (*The Okhrana*) (Paris, 1925; repr. 1979); *The Case of Comrade Tulayev* (Paris, 1948; London, 1968); *The Long Dusk* (New York and Montreal, 1946); *Duel of the Opposition: The Serge-Trotsky Correspondence*, ed. Peter Sedgwick (London, 1982).

Consult: Richard Greeman, Introduction to *Midnight in the Century* (London, 1982; this edition contains a chronology of Serge's life and a bibliography of his work).

SEROTE, Mongane Wally. Born 1944 in Sophiatown, South Africa; he lives in London, England, where he works in the Department of Art and Culture of the African National Congress. Serote was imprisoned in South Africa in 1969 for nine months without trial. He went into exile in 1974 and studied at Columbia University in New York in 1976. He lived in self-imposed exile in Gaborone, Botswana, where he co-founded the Media Arts Ensemble. The news of the Soweto uprising and the brutality by South African police in 1976 affected him deeply, and although he was in demand in the United States as a reader of his poetry, Serote decided to turn to fiction to express his outrage. He began *To Every Birth Its Blood* in New York in 1975 and finished the manuscript in Botswana, where he was then living as a Fulbright scholar. It was published in South Africa in 1981 and promptly banned there (it was later unbanned); it appeared in the United States only in 1989. The novel is an arrangement of attitudes of three generations of South African blacks to white oppression as told by a black African journalist. The protagonist, Molope, works for a newspaper in Alexandra township (the same township in which Serote grew up); he reflects on his grandfather, who never dreamed of achieving, in his time, freedom from the white Boer minority (or at least kept any such dream within his own head) to his father who believed prematurely that independence in South Africa must follow independence elsewhere in Africa to the most brutal era of all—Soweto and its aftermath.

While Serote has not recently written poetry on the scale of his early achievement, he continues to work in the genre. His early poems were lyrical, jazzy, and rallying cries for an enthusiasm of protest. His later work is both more somber and reserved. Among his poetry titles are *Yakhsl' inkomo* (Johannesburg, Renoster Books, 1972); *Tsetlo* (1974); *No Baby Must Weep* (1975); *Behold Mama, Flowers* (1978); *Selected Poems*, ed. Mbuelelo Vizikhungo Mzamane (1982).

Consult: Lionel Abrahams, "Black Experience into English Verse," *New Nation* 3, no. 7; Nadine Gordimer, *The Black Interpreters* (Johannesburg, 1973); Es'kia Mphahlele, "Mongane Serote's Odyssey: The Path That Breaks the Heels," in *English Academy Review* 3 (Johannesburg, 1985).

SHEED, Wilfrid. Born December 27, 1930, in England; he lives in Sag Harbor, Long Island, New York. Sheed came to the United States at the beginning of World War II with his parents, the distinguished publishers Frank Sheed and Maisie Ward. He became a permanent resident in 1947, after a year's return to England in 1946 because of self-imposed difficulties as "a surly fifteen-year-old war refugee" (as Sheed describes himself in his most recent collection, *Essays in Disguise*, 1990). Sheed interrupted his stay in the United States for university study at Oxford. He is best known as a trenchant critic and essayist, though he has also published many witty novels, among them *Max Jamison* (1970); *People Will Always Be Kind* (1973); and *Transatlantic Blues* (1978). His collections of essays and biography/commentary include *The Morning After* (1971); *Three Mobs: Labor, Church and Mafia* (1974); *Muhammad Ali: A Portrait in Words and Photographs* (1975); *The Good Word and Other Words* (1978); *Clare Boothe Luce* (1982); and *The Boys of Winter* (1987).

SHEPARD, Sam (pseudonym of Samuel Shepard Rogers VII). Born November 5, 1943, in Fort Sheridan, Illinois; he lives in California and Minnesota. Shepard spent four years of self-imposed exile, from 1971 to 1974, in England in an attempt to rediscover his artistic spirit and to refine his place in American culture. Shepard's early success—his first produced plays, *Cowboys* and *The Rock Garden*,were performed off-off-Broadway shortly before his twenty-second birthday—was followed by a series of popular failures and his own sense of a void in his life. He was suffering domestic problems at the time, living with rock singer Patti Smith while visiting his wife and son Jesse nearby. He returned to his family and took them to England, where he continued writing and began playing in rock and roll bands there. Music became an integral part of his plays, and poetry, which had always issued into his vision (or in part created it), increasingly replaced the prose lines of his dialogue. Shepard's four years of finding himself through distance is exemplified in the plays he wrote during this time—*The Tooth of Crime* (produced in 1972); *The Geography of a Horse Dreamer* (produced in 1974); *Little Ocean* (produced in 1974); *Action* (produced 1975), and in his collection of poems, stories, and monologues, *Hawk Moon* (1972). After his return to the United States, he moved to the San Francisco area, and later became the intimate friend of the movie actress, Jessica Lange; they have lived together since 1983. It was during this period that Shepard also became a movie star, receiving high praise for his dramatic talent and his rugged good looks.

Shepard's work after his self-exile period has shown a more definable realism and a more conventionally ordered narrative; confusion and yearning in his plays are rendered from a controlled and distilled authorial viewpoint. The mythic, however, has not disappeared from his work, for, in essence, Shepard is writing about the myth of exile through the cowboy, isolate hero, a protagonist who must stand apart in order to survive. That Shepard sees the integrity of the cowboy hero as an irrelevance in the modern world testifies to a vision of a country bereft of the values of individual responsibility and individual strength. The "natural" or the spontaneous also remains in evidence in Shepard's plays, a characterological quality necessary to Shepard's belief in intuitive logic or a will of the spirit to survive all apocalypses of self-knowledge into regenerative bodies of artistic meaning.

Selected Titles: *Seven Plays* (1981); *Chicago and Other Plays* (1981); *Motel Chronicles* (1982); *Fool for Love and Other Plays* (1984); *A Lie of the Mind* (1986; also contains *The War in Heaven*, written by Shepard and Joseph Chaikin, 1984).

Consult: Bonnie Marranca, ed., *American Dreams: The Imagination of Sam Shepard* (1981); Richard Gilman, Introduction to *Seven Plays* by Shepard (1981); Ron Mottram, *Inner Landscapes: The Theater of Sam Shepard* (1984); Ellen Oumano, *Sam Shepard: The Life and Work of an American Dreamer* (1986).

SIGAL, Clancy. Born 1927 in Chicago, Illinois; he lives in London, England, an expatriate since 1956. Sigal grew up in Chicago and was intimate with working-class attitudes from childhood when he observed his mother and father in their trade union organizing activities. In his teens he boasted he was a "zoot suiter," a "gang boy," and a radical socialist. Whatever the proportions of his masculine imagery, it is apparent Sigal identified with American labor in its 1950s dominant pose of virility. He also flirted with communism and was investigated for un-American activities during the Joseph McCarthy era of Red-baiting. He worked at various jobs, one of them as a well-paid writer at a Hollywood studio, but he took time out to travel "on the road" across America; he also stayed faithful to his inner pledge to organize American labor into a viable economic and social force. An idealist, more militant socialist than beatnik, he left for Europe after the Russian invasion of Hungary in 1956.

Disillusioned with Soviet Marxism, he decided to do the traditional writerly thing—that is, to take a boat to Paris and live there. His experience in France proved comic rather than bohemian, but his London excursion, planned as a brief stay, lengthened into more than thirty years and is still transpiring. Sigal left America not in flight but clearly unhappy with the cold war mood and with Soviet tyranny over its East European neighbors. In a sense he was reenacting the childhood memory of his parents' divorce—in love with the best of each of them, in anger with the betrayal of his trust by both of them. In England, not quite apolitical but an independent thinker without any organized base or system of support except his individual morality, Sigal completed his still best-known work, *Going Away: A Report, a Memoir* in 1961 (it was published in 1962). In a recent reflection he wrote: "Sometimes I think I stay simply because it's there. It may be a question of literary distance, the same reason why so many writers have to leave home to see it more clearly" (*San Francisco Review of Books*, Winter 1987–88, p. 15).

Selected Titles: *Weekend in Dinlock* (1960); *Zone of the Interior* (1976).

SILONE, Ignazio (pseudonym of Tranquilli Secondo). Born 1900 in Pescina di Marsi, Aquilla; he died 1978 in Gereval, Italy. Silone participated in the founding of the Italian Communist party, but left it by 1930. His anti-Fascist activities forced him to remain in Switzerland from 1930 to 1945, where he wrote *Fontamara* (1930; *Fontamara*, 1930); *Pane e Vino* (1936, *Bread and Wine*); and *Il seme sotto la meuve* (1942; *The Seed Under the Snow*). *Emergency Exit* was published in London in 1969.

SIMON, John. Born May 12, 1925, in Subotica, Yugoslavia; he lives in New York City. Simon came to the United States when he was fifteen. He was educated at Harvard (B.A., 1946; M.A., 1948; Ph.D., 1959), served in the U.S. Air Force during World War II, and has taught at several universities. He has written extensively for the *New Leader, Hudson Review, Commonweal,* and *New York* magazine. Although he has lived in the United States for almost half a century, he thinks of himself as part-exile. He said in a recent interview that he would rather "be an exile here" than a "citizen over there."

Selected Titles: *Acid Test* (1963); *Private Screenings: Views of the Cinema of the*

Sixties (1963); *Movies into Film* (1971); *Singularities: Essays on the Theatre 1964–74* (1976).

SINGER, Isaac Bashevis. Born July 14, 1904, in Leoncin, Poland; he lives in Miami Beach, Florida. The son and grandson of rabbis, Singer is the third child of Bathsheva and Pinchas Mendel Singer. When Singer was four years old, his parents moved from Leoncin to Warsaw, where Rabbi Singer set up court on Krochmalna Street in the densely populated Jewish ghetto. From early childhood the would-be writer was exposed to his father's "mystical intensity" and his mother's "rationalistic strain," a philosophical difference, which, along with other contradictions generated by the particular lot of Jews in an alien land, came to be prominently reflected in Singer's literary work. Rabbi Singer's efforts to limit his son's education to the Torah and the Talmud, and his condemnation of secular subjects, especially Yiddish literature that was "leading the Jews to heresy," could not prevent the exposure of his children to the modernity of the outside world. The first to abandon the orthodox household was Israel Joshua Singer,* Singer's elder brother, who became a convert to Jewish Enlightenment and an ardent follower of socialist doctrine. He was also the first to introduce Singer to "heretical" literature by presenting him with a copy of Fyodor Dostoyevsky's *Crime and Punishment.*

In 1917 Singer and his mother moved to the small town of Bilgoray. Depressed by its unworldliness, Singer found solace in teaching Hebrew and in writing poetry in Hebrew. While rebelling against his isolation from city life, he nevertheless absorbed the spirit of Bilgoray that was to nourish his artistic imagination. In his memoir *In My Father's Court* Singer admits that "In this world of Jewishness I found a spiritual treasure trove. I had a chance to see our past as it really was. . . . I lived Jewish history."

In 1921, to avoid moving with his parents to yet another shtetl, Singer enrolled in the Tachkemony Rabbinical Seminary. His education ended a year later, when he concluded he could not comply with the strict tenets of organized religion. After a brief sojourn to Bilgoray, Singer returned to Warsaw in 1923 and began working as a proofreader for *Literarishe Bletter.*

As Singer's memoir *A Young Man in Search of Love* (1978) and his autobiographical novel *Shosha* (1978) show, the road on which an aspiring Jewish writer composing in Yiddish traveled was a difficult one. Poland was between two world wars, and the 800-year-old Polish Jewish community was caught between Polish anti-Semitism and nationalism on one hand and the threat of Nazi barbarism on the other. Torn between Hasidism and Haskala, the Polish Jews looked for a way either to come to terms with their sense of exile or to find a means of transcending their "unnatural state of existence." The Jewish intellectual, especially the writer, was expected to lead the way in political and social causes, and the responsibility provided a spawning ground for conflict. Singer could not compromise his own sense of artistic integrity, for he believed true relevance comes from artistic integrity and the products of that integrity. Although his first novel, *Satan in Goray*, was set in seventeenth-century Poland and treated the theme and concept of perverted messianism, a subject at first glance seemingly removed from prewar realistic conditions in Poland and of the modern Jew, a discerning reader can see in Singer's rendering how much the young writer was preoccupied with the fate and strivings of his Jewish people to return to the Holy Land and to transcend their "exile."

Singer did not witness the publication of his first novel in Poland. In 1935 his brother, now a prominent Yiddish writer in New York, invited him to work for the Yiddish daily newspaper *Der Forverts* (The Forward). It is clear from Singer's autobiographical writings that his decision to leave Poland did not rest solely on a promise of a successful literary career. "I saw that the Jews were in great danger in Europe," Singer stated in an interview (1975). "Warsaw was a doomed city. I was thirty-one. I left with two valises of clothing and manuscripts. It was Passover." His personal exodus was further underscored by his understanding of the role a Jewish writer plays in the fate of his people. In *Shosha*, Singer's double and mouthpiece, Aaron, comes to a conclusion he shares with many friends: "We are running away and Mount Sinai runs after us. This chase has made us sick and mad." Most of Aaron's coreligionists refuse to run anymore. They don't "want to rest in a strange cemetery." Yet these homeless people beg Aaron to escape—they desire a rememberer who through his writings will make future generations aware of the Polish-Jewish milieu and of the fate they know is coming with the Nazi invasion.

Upon his arrival in the United States, Singer was stricken by a disease familiar to exiled intellectuals—artistic paralysis, whose symptoms are an inability to compose, a failure to make contact with new audiences, and a weakened confidence in one's native language. Singer's state of psychic illness was exacerbated by his acute awareness of the impending destruction of the world he had left behind, as well as by the pain he felt for the decline of Yiddish. It took Singer eight years to regain his creative potency. In 1943 he published *Satan in Goray*, along with five new stories, in Yiddish. That same year he started his fruitful association with the Yiddish paper *Der Forverts*. He assumed the pen name Isaac Warshofsky for his nonliterary contributions to the paper while publishing his fiction under the name of Isaac Bashevis. He signs his translated work as Isaac Bashevis Singer.

Singer's worries about the fate of the Yiddish language have never abated. He is aware that the Holocaust has claimed millions of potential readers. Although his knowledge of English is superb, he continues to use Yiddish as a means of artistic expression, because Yiddish is "a language of Jewishness." Writing in Yiddish for Singer is a point of morality and ethics: had he abandoned Yiddish, he believes he would have betrayed the memory of those who never lived to experience the richness of their culture.

Singer is among the few exiled writers fortunate enough to see his works translated and also to gain vast literary success. After being serially published in *Der Forverts*, *The Family Moskat* was issued in both Yiddish and English in

1950. The two other parts of this family saga that resurrect Jewish life in prewar Poland—*The Manor* and *The Estate* —became available in English translation in 1967 and 1969. Three years after publishing *The Family Moskat*, Singer reached a point in his career in which his contact with American audiences grew even greater: in 1953, *Partisan Review* published Saul Bellow's translation of "Gimpel the Fool."

Many of Singer's novels and stories are inhabited by demons and dybbuks, spirits and ghosts. When invoking such fantasy-like creatures, the writer asserts that not everything in life can be explained through rational means. The truth, Singer implies, is embedded in the surreal, rather than in sociology, history, psychology, or philosophy. The truth his characters are searching for can be found when the answer to the question of how one remains a Jew, a human being, in an age of which the Holocaust is a part, is found. This inquiry into the event that defies imagination is intimately connected to the issue of exile that runs through his fiction; the two are merged in Singer's major achievement, *The Slave*, a novel set in seventeenth-century Poland.

In *The Slave* Singer departs from ambiguity and offers his protagonist, a survivor of the Chmielnicki atrocities, a concrete way to transcend his exiled state and to shake off the bondage of slavery. Jacob, in his search to understand fully the prayer "Thou has not made me a slave" is given an opportunity to combine his powerful artistic imagination with his faith in Judaism, a merger that leads to his repatriation to the Holy Land, where he and his son prosper. When he returns twenty years later to Poland, his strength abates, and he dies without fulfilling his mission to retrieve the bones of his wife and bury them in Jerusalem. Exile, Singer suggests, inevitably leads to death, be it in spiritual or physical form. This resolution is also drawn in *Enemies, A Love Story*, a novel set in the United States and populated by characters not only exiles but Holocaust survivors as well. Most of them are doomed, for they cannot strike an equilibrium between their past and present, a prerequisite for survival. Only an elderly couple is allowed to survive through emigration to Jerusalem.

In his fiction Singer seems to be asserting that there is a way for a whole transplanted nation—the Jewish people—to survive their exile: they must retrieve their own land, with its language, laws, and art, the basic elements of a new and liberated identity. In his nonfiction, however, Singer admits there are no easy answers to Jewish concerns. He recognizes a "contradiction between the Jewish exile and Jewish statehood that can never be ignored or glossed over." Israel, he maintains, may not always be the state "the Jew has prayed for in the long night of exile." What he apparently hopes for is that the "spirituality" and "saintliness" the Jews have acquired in the Diaspora will be complemented, rather than negated or diffused, in the establishment of a Jewish homeland.

In recent years Singer has published *The Penitent* (1983) and a number of collections of stories, *Love and Exile* (1983) among them, books that once more underscore his preoccupation with Jewish fate. Exile as a subject remains close to Singer, and he continues to treat it not only as a Jewish phenomenon but as a prevalent condition of modern existence.

Selected Titles: *Gimpel the Fool and other Stories* (1957); *The Spinoza of Market Street* (1961); *A Little Boy in Search of God: Mysticism in a Personal Light* (1981), written in English; *Collected Stories* (1982); *The King of the Fields* (1988); *The Death of Methusaleh and Other Stories* (1988).

Consult: Edward Alexander, *Isaac Bashevis Singer* (1980); Irving Buchen, *Isaac Bashevis Singer and the Eternal Past* (1968); Irving Malin, *Isaac Bashevis Singer* (1972); Asher Z. Milbauer, *Transcending Exile: Conrad, Nabokov, I. B. Singer* (1985).

ASHER Z. MILBAUER

SINGER, Israel Joshua. Born November 30, 1893, in Leoncin, Poland; died February 10, 1944, in New York City. Israel Joshua Singer was the older brother of Isaac Bashevis Singer,* and until the 1960s was far better known than his younger brother. Bashevis called Joshua his "master" as a writer, and if Joshua lacked his brother's imaginative reach, he was a more artful stylist and achieved his own reputation as an essayist, playwright, and novelist. He brought his family from Poland to the United States in 1934; his physical exile from Eastern Europe to New York stimulated some of his best work at the same time that it provided comfort to his family and himself. Abraham Cahan, editor of the Yiddish daily *Der Forverts* (The Forward), serialized Joshua's first successful novel, *Yoshe Kolb*, in 1931. A successful theatrical version followed, as did a series of remarkable novels that are still his claim to fame. Though his early years in the United States were marked by his continuing sadness over the death of his eldest son, Jacob, he loved the freedom that he found in his adopted country—it liberated his vision of what he considered the world of exiles, the world of Jews in Poland during the twentieth century.

Israel Joshua Singer came from two learned rabbinic families—his father was a pious, unworldly Hasid while his mother's family was "Russian." (Singer uses quotes mark around this word in his autobiography, *Of A World That Is No More*, published in Yiddish in 1946 and in English translation in 1970. The Singer family came from Wolyna, and the maternal grandfather served as a rabbi in Maciejow. Given the shifting borders of these places, "Russian" is a general designation provided by the Jews of Galicia, which was itself in an area of shifting borders.) Singer also described his mother's family as a "family of rationalists" (see I. B. Singer, *In My Father's Court*, New York, New American Library, 1967, page 18). Singer was given a rabbinic training, but in *Of A World That Is No More*, he described his longing for the freedom of nature and his dislike of religious schooling. When in 1908 his father left the small towns, where he had served as a rabbi, for the bustle of Krochmalna Street in Warsaw, Singer quickly dropped his traditional garb and tried to establish himself as a painter and writer.

What followed was a quest for new ideals and causes. In his autobiography, Isaac Bashevis Singer gives fragments of the new ideas that his brother was bringing home: there was no God; only a universe existed that worked like a mechanism in which humans, like animals, followed the laws of nature. Having abandoned Hebrew, the holy language, Israel Joshua Singer was uncertain about what language to use as a writer. For a time, before establishing himself in the Yiddish literary life of Warsaw, he advocated abandoning Yiddish for German. But his return to Yiddish brought with it a return to the Jewish materials of his youth. His early stories reveal what he called his ''passion for realism.'' With the German occupation of Poland in 1915, he was conscripted for forced labor, an experience that he was to describe vividly in his proletarian novel *Steel and Iron* (1927; English, 1935).

That experience prepared him to welcome the Russian Revolution in 1917 with the enthusiasm felt by socialists throughout the world. Abandoning Poland, he emigrated to Kiev, where he worked as a proofreader and writer. He married Genia Kupferstock there in 1918, but after three years, disillusioned with the revolution, he returned to Warsaw. In 1922 his first volume of short stories, *Pearls*, brought him to the attention of Abraham Cahan, who hired him as a correspondent for his paper, *Der Forverts*. Though his column, written under the pseudonym Kupfer, was a notable success, he was bitterly disappointed by the failure of his call for unity among Yiddish writers. The success of *Yoshe Kalb* in America made him leave Poland with few regrets, especially since the threats against the Jews from both Hitler and the Polish fascists suggested that East European Jewry was on the edge of a cataclysm.

Thousands of miles away from Poland and Russia, he found his natural novelistic voice. In *The Brothers Ashkenazi* (1936), he depicted the history of a family of Polish Jews approaching a destruction that would ultimately engulf an entire people. In *East of Eden* (1939), he drew upon his experiences in Russia to show how the czar's oppression had been replaced by a Soviet tyranny that victimized the very workers who created the revolution. In his last novel, *The Family Carnovsky* (1943; English, 1969), he presented his best work on the theme of exile and return. Three generations of the Carnovsky family move from Hasidism to an enlightened form of Judaism, then to only token religious gestures, and finally to a self-hating anti-Semitism. That the novel ends in America with the rescue of the young Carnovsky from his insane flirtation with the Nazis suggests an optimism about his adopted country. Written just a year before Singer's death, this novel suggests that he had come to terms with his exile. But perhaps this conclusion is merely the utopian hope of fiction. Only a year before, Singer had written a bitter essay in *Die Tsukunft* about the prevalence of anti-Semitism, even in America, arguing that the Jew must return from exile (*galut*) to his own land.

Consult: Irving Howe, Introduction to *The Brothers Ashkenazi* (1980); Charles Madison, *Yiddish Literature* (1971); Clive Sinclair, *The Brothers Singer* (1983); Isaac Bashevis Singer, *Love and Exile* (1984).

ESTELLE GERSHGOREN NOVAK and MAXIMILLIAN E. NOVAK

SINYAVSKY, Andrei Donatovich (pseudonym Abram Tertz; also spelled Abrama Tertz). Born October 8, 1925, in Moscow, USSR; he lives in France. Sinyavsky was a relatively unknown but working critic in the USSR before he was unmasked as Abram Tertz. He graduated from Moscow University in 1952, after which he pursued research at the Gorky Institute of World Literature in Moscow. He wrote reviews for *Novy Mir*, co-wrote a book on Pablo Picasso, and wrote an introduction to a collection of poems by Boris Pasternak in 1965. (Sinyavsky's courage in attending Pasternak's funeral, when Pasternak was vilified by Soviet official circles, is of note.)

Sinyavsky went into exile after serving almost all of a seven-year prison term meted out to him for publishing his work abroad without permission from Soviet authorities. His colleague, Yuly Daniel (1925–89) (pseudonym of Nikolai Arzhak), received a lesser term (five years) and remained in the USSR after his release from prison. The three-day trial of Sinyavsky and Daniel in 1965 provoked worldwide attention, consternation, and protest at the severe sentences handed out to the two writers. Found guilty in effect were their works that criticized present conditions in the Soviet Union. Sinyavsky and Daniel were sent to separate labor camps in the Dubrovlag Gulag, about 300 miles east of Moscow, a special gulag for political prisoners. Sinyavsky wrote several manuscripts while in captivity, which have since been published, both in the original Russian and in translation. The best-known volume is *Golos'z khora* (1973; *A Voice from the Chorus*, 1976), a loosely connected series of reflections based on letters Sinyavsky sent out to his wife, and, out of necessity, they contain no specific criticism of camp life or of Soviet policy—Sinyavsky could be punished for writing anything deemed contrary to the Soviet state's goals and policies. What has impressed many critics is Sinyavsky's call for an understanding of one's enemies without rancor. A spiritual calm, in which the jailed accepts the jailer, a kind of Dostoyevskian air of forgiveness of the shackler as well as of the errant prince and prodigal son, pervades Sinyavsky's pages. Prior to this work, and before his unmasking by Soviet agents, Sinyavsky had published *Unguarded Thoughts* in the West (*Mysli vrasplokh*, 1966; *Unguarded Thoughts*, 1972). This volume, also a loosely structured collection of philosophic musings and observations of daily Soviet life, expressed the need for some guiding faith beyond the social realism of the Soviet Union and the collective goals of the Communist party. Sinyavsky's illumination of his need for individual identity within the larger social mass through service to one's inner god (a god that was not merely the state or technology or social/economic amelioration) aroused wide interest. It was shortly after publication of this book that Sinyavsky and Daniel were unmasked.

Sinyavsky's works, however, that caused an adverse reaction against him by Soviet bureaucrats were the book-length essay *On Socialist Realism*, first printed in the French journal *Esprit* in 1959, and *The Trial Begins*, a short novel, published in Russian [*Sud idyot*] in the Polish émigré journal *Kultura* (based in Paris) in 1960 and shortly afterwards in English in *Encounter* (London). *On Socialist Realism* decries the loss of vision that the Soviet cultural policy mandates, because "socrealism" (as Sinyavsky calls it) takes from the artist and from his individual reader all choice and will. In "socrealism," goals for the good of all are decreed, and personal vision becomes a subversive state crime. In *The Trial Begins* Sinyavsky writes a novel in which the protagonist is never quite sure of what crime he has committed; the crime is his wavering thought, not any specific act of wrongdoing.

Sinyavsky also published abroad before his arrest and conviction a collection of five stories, *Fantastichesky mir Abrama Tersta* (1967, The Fantastic World of Abram Tertz, or Fantastic Stories), and a short novel, *Lyubimov* (1964; *The Makepeace Experiment*, 1965). Both these works show a phantasmagoric universe in which reality and fantasy are mixed, and in which truth is shaped according to varying needs of state policy. Sinyavsky is not propagandizing in his work; the phantasmagoria of his world is his way of showing national and individual misshaping; his presentation represents a cry not for reshaping what has been lost or gained by "socrealism" but for a newer world in which individual concerns are given attention. For example, in *The Makepeace Experiment*, a small town is brought to the brink of apocalypse by the hypnotic powers of a bicycle mechanic. As told in the first person by two people with the same surname, one of whom is alive and the other dead, the novel issues a warning against the hysteria made possible by the perversion of reality through official state policy.

When Sinyavsky was released from prison in 1971, he applied for an emigration visa, which was granted. He lives in France and continues to write in Russian; most of his work in his exile period has been in nonfiction. He has also worked as an editor and commentator for several émigré journals. In resigning from one journal, *Kontinent*, to help form another, *Syntaxis*, in Paris, Sinyavsky wrote "Pluralism and tolerance are of especial importance for the development of independent thought in present-day Russia" (*Encounter* 51 [September 1978], p. 80). His words are a fitting summation of the philosophy by which he has lived and through which he has expressed his spiritual and literary voice.

Goodnight!, the English-language version of Sinyavsky's manuscript written in Russian in the early 1980s and published in Paris several years ago, was issued in 1989. In his recollections, told in fictional guise and through (in his case) the objectifying tranquility of memory, Sinyavsky proves himself a scrupulously honest man who still refuses to allow himself to be exploited as a martyr in the West and who remains in exile to keep alive the ideals which his native country nurtured in him. As Sinyavsky describes his condition, he lives in a house near Paris but in a spiritual home, through memory, in his native Russia. Thus he is not in exile even when he is in exile. Sinyavsky also concedes that he broke Soviet law and committed a crime by sending his manuscripts abroad for publication without permission in the 1960s, yet at the same time he protests he would break such a law again, given another chance. In thus examining his rights as a creative artist, as a humble Soviet citizen, and as a watchdog of human rights, Sinyavsky reveals all the more his personal courage and willingness to suffer for a credo that exasperated not only Soviet bureaucratic opposition, but his own less dispassionate supporters. Significantly, Sinyavsky defines his view of himself in the pseudonym he chose for his foreign-publishing escapade—Abram Tertz, a name he adopted after reading the work of Osip Mandelstham* and reflecting on the persecution of that Jewish writer by Joseph Stalin and his subordinates. Although Sinyavsky is not Jewish, he chose a Jewish hero in an Odessa street song as his literary identity. The device is meant to draw attention to the power of the word for Jews in their struggles of survival and an equal attention to himself as an associate of a persecuted minority who refuse to accept their shackles.

Sinyavsky now writes publicly under both his names, Sinyavsky and Tertz. Sinyavsky is for what he calls his "academic" pursuits and Tertz is for his fictional renderings. He has said that Soviet officialdom encouraged him to leave the USSR when he was released from prison on the grounds that his Jewishness was embarrassing, but they could not deport him because he was not legally Jewish (only the phantom "Tertz" was). He left the USSR in 1973, by mutual agreement with the authorities, to teach at the Sorbonne in Paris. He has visited the United States, Israel, and several European countries, and made one visit to the USSR, in January 1989, for the funeral of Yuly Daniel, his friend and co-defendant in the 1965 trial. When Sinyavsky was asked if he would consider returning to live in the USSR, he replied that each person's *exile* is an individual act consisting of many decisions. He believes his place now, after twenty-five years in France, remains in France, though he writes in Russian, teaches Russian literature in Russian at the Sorbonne (he speaks only a few words of French), reads only Russian books, and has a circle of Russian friends (his wife edits, as well, a Russian-language literary journal). Sinyavsky said that in spite of his 25-year-old son's assimilation into French culture, he, Sinyavsky/Tertz, would speak only in Russian to his grandchildren.

Selected Titles: *Progulki s Pushkinym* (1935; Strolling with Pushkin [written in prison]); *V teni Gogolya* (1975; *In the Shade of Gogol Rozanova*, 1982 [written in prison]); *Kroshka Tsores* (1980; Little Tsores, fiction).

Consult: L. Labedz and Max Hayward, *On Trial: The Case of Sinyavsky (Tertz)* (1967); Richard Lourie, *Letters to the Future: An Approach to Sinyavsky-Tertz* (1975); Mihajlo Mihajlov, *Russian Themes* (1968).

SKÁRMETA, Antonio. Born November 1940, in Autofagasta, Chile; since 1975 he has been living in West Berlin, FRG, for six months every year and teaching literature at Washington University in St. Louis for the other six months.

He left Chile after the military coup against the Salvador Allende government in September 1973, but has returned for at least two visits. He said in an interview with Mitchell Levitas, of the *New York Times*, in 1988 that "you can write whatever you want [in Chile]. At the same time you can get killed." Skármeta gains his perspective through a mix of fantasy and insight into the real paradoxes of daily behavior and ritual. Of a recent work, *Burning Patience*, the reviewer Michael Skakun wrote in *Publishers Weekly* (March 13, 1987, p. 79): "Puncturing local and national pomposities with unfailing wit, Skármeta draws parallels between [the hero's] private life and the public turbulence and violence that gradually overtake Chile, bringing this sunny, erotic fantasy to a tragic close with the 1973 murder of President Salvador Allende and the death of [Pablo] Neruda."

Selected Titles: *El entusiasmo* 1967, Enthusiasm); *Soné que la nieve ardia* (1975; *I Dreamt the Snow was Burning*, 1985)

Consult: Mitchell Levitas, "Writers and Dictators," *New York Times Book Review*, August 14, 1988.

ŠKÉMA, Antanas. Born November 21, 1911, in Lodz, Poland; died September 11, 1961, in a highway accident in Pennsylvania. In 1921 Škéma's parents opted for Lithuanian citizenship and moved with their son to Lithuania. Škéma studied at the University of Kaunas. In 1936 he started an acting career that led to work in the Lithuanian theater until 1944, when he moved to Germany; in 1949 he came to the United States. Working in New York as an elevator operator he dedicated his spare time to writing, acting in, and directing Lithuanian plays. He gained a somewhat controversial fame in the Lithuanian émigré community as one of the most modern and "nihilist" writers in exile. Škéma published several collections of stories, for example, *Šventoji Inga* (1952, Saint Inga); plays, for example, *Pabudimas* (1956, presented in an English version off-Broadway as *Awakening*); and a novel, *Balta drobulé* (1958, The White Shroud). His *Raštai* (Collected Works, 3 vols.) appeared in 1967–85. Škéma had much in common with existentialist and absurdist writers, as well as with the American Beat generation. He was deeply interested in the problem of evil and the totalitarian experience. Škéma's work, especially his novel, ranks with the best of East European writing concerning Stalinism and exile. An innovator in Lithuanian fiction with his employment of Joycean stream of consciousness, he applied the technique for a depiction of the gradual disintegration of an immigrant unable to free himself from the pressures of the past or to adapt to an alien society. Škéma also was noted for his sardonic style, inclination to parody, intensity of language, and explicit treatment of sexual behavior. He was and remains a major influence on less conformist Soviet Lithuanian writers.

Consult: R. Šilbajoris, *Perfection of Exile* (1970).

                                                                    TOMAS VENCLOVA

SKVORECKY, Josef. Born September 27, 1924, in Náchod, Bohemia, Czechoslovakia; he lives in Toronto, Canada. Skvorecky's father, a bank clerk, was imprisoned by both the Nazis and communists for his nationalistic-patriotic activities. After his graduation from high school in 1943, Skvorecky worked in factories producing spare parts for airplanes; he also served briefly as a trench digger and cotton miller before the end of World War II. Skvorecky studied medicine at Charles University in Prague in 1945 but switched to the Philosophical Faculty after one year; he received a Ph.D. in American philosophy, with a dissertation on Thomas Paine, from Charles University in 1949. He taught at a girls high school from 1950 to 1951, was drafted into the Czech army and served for two years in a tank division stationed near Prague. On his return to civilian life he worked for the publishing house Odeon.

Skvorecky early showed a preference for surrealism and avant-garde writing and painting; in the 1950s he associated with Prague underground artistic circles that included Mikuláš Medek, Jiří Kolář, and Bohumil Hrabal. His first novel, *Konec nylonového věku* (The End of the Nylon Age), was banned by Czech censors in 1956 before its ultimate publication in 1958; his second novel, *Zbabělci* (1958, 1964, 1966, The Cowards, 1980), which he had written in 1948–49, produced a controversy resulting in Skvorecky's loss of his job on the magazine *World Literature*; the loss of jobs of the editorial directors of the house that published Skvorecky's novel; and a purge that spread deep into the Czech intellectual community. The novel outraged Czech authorities by its use of slang, its irreverence, and its satirical portraits of both the German surrender to the Allies in 1945 and the subsequent Soviet occupation of Czechoslovakia.

Five years later Skvorecky was allowed to publish the novella *Legenda Emöke* (1963, The Legend of Emöke); the book became a major seller in the midsixties, though it was chastized by the Communist party. His following novel, *Lvíče* (Miss Silver's Past), scheduled for 1966, was banned before publication, and only allowed to be printed during the liberal Dubček regime in early 1969. When the Dubček regime fell, Skvorecky's novel fell with it: a second printing of some 80,000 copies was destroyed in 1970.

Considered a difficult problem, Skvorecky was watched by the authorities throughout his career but was finally allowed into the Czech Writers Union in 1967. He was also allowed to travel to the United States in 1965 with fellow writer Josef Nesvadba to attend an International Writers Conference at Long Island University.

Skvorecky's experience with censorship in his native country extended to other literary activities. A filmscript he wrote with Milos Forman in 1959–60 was banned by the president of Czechoslovakia and never produced; the script was based on Skvorecky's story "Eine kleine Jazzmusik," which had been banned in 1957, and was probably the cause of police censorship of *Jazz Almanach* magazine, in which the story first appeared. Skvorecky did, however, write scripts that were not only produced but proved successful; he worked with the directors Jiří Menzel and Evald Schorm, among others.

Skvorecky and his wife, Zdena, a singer, actress, and novelist (*Summer in Prague*) left for exile in 1968 after the Soviet invasion. They stayed briefly in the United States before emigrating to Canada, where Skvorecky was invited to teach at the University of Toronto. In 1971 Skvorecky and his wife founded the Czech-language publishing house Sixty-Eight Publishers Corporation, which to date has published more than 100 books by Czech dissident writers, among them Milan Kundera,* Vaclav Havel, Ludvik Vaculík, Jan Skácel, Pavel Kohout,* Jan Beneš, Václav Černý, Ivan Klima, and Alexander Kliment. The printing record of Sixty-Eight Publishers makes it the major publishing house of Czech writers in the world. In a recent interview, Skvorecky said that his emigré publishing firm is likely to fade away in a year or two, because the new climate of freedom in Czechoslovakia makes it obsolete. Skvorecky said, however, that he does not plan to return to Czeschosvakia because he is ''now a Canadian.''

Since his exile Skvorecky has written and published more work—he writes in the genres of novel, short story, play, filmscript, poetry, essay, memoir, review/critique, and translation—than he completed during the previous twenty years of his adult life in his native land. His style is distinguished by a gentle, playful wit, an ease of seeming naturalness, and the rhythms of modern jazz (Skvorecky is an accomplished saxophonist and has played in bands). Exile has not corroded his sense of humor; his quiet satire, which sustains him, continued to exacerbate authorities in Czechoslovakia until the fall of the Soviet-dominated government in 1989. Skvorecky was stripped of his Czech citizenship in 1978.

Skvorecky's recent work includes the well-received *Pribeh inzenyra lidskych dusi* (Toronto, 1977; *The Engineer of Human Souls*, 1984) a collection of stories, and *Dvorak in Love* (1987), his first attempt at a documentary novel, in which he re-creates the famous composer's trip to America and the composition of the ''New World'' Symphony.

Skvorecky is also an accomplished translator, teacher, and critic. He has translated into Czech and written prefaces for the work of such American writers as Henry James,* Ernest Hemingway,* William Faulkner, Saul Bellow, Ray Bradbury, Sinclair Lewis, and Dashiell Hammett. He lists his membership in the Mark Twain Society of America proudly.

Skvorecky is the recipient of the Neustadt International Prize for Literature (1980), a Guggenheim fellowship (1980), and the 1985 City of Toronto Book Award for *The Engineer of Human Souls*. He was elected a Fellow of the Royal Society of Canada in 1984.

Selected Titles: *Bassaxofon* (1967; *The Bass Saxophone*, 1979), a collection of stories; *Tankový prapor* (Prague, 1969, The Tank Corps; this edition was banned and confiscated; reprinted 1971, 1980, Toronto); *All the Bright Young Men and Women* (Toronto, 1972), a personal history of the Czech cinema; *Prima sezóna* (1975; *The Swell Season*, Toronto, 1982; London, 1983); *The End of Lieutenant Boruvka* (1990); *Talkin' Moscow Blues*, ed. Sam Soleki (London, 1990), essays written in English sincę 1969 on jazz, modern literature, film, politics.

MARTIN TUCKER AND ANDRE VLCEK

SLAVOV, Atanas Vasilev. Born ca. 1925 in Sliven, Bulgaria; immigrated to New York in 1976; he lives in Bethesda, Maryland, as a permanent resident of the United States. Slavov received a candidate of sciences degree in 1965 in theory of literature with his dissertation, "Function of Rhythm in Metrical Speech," from the Institute of Literature of the Bulgarian Academy of Sciences. He also earned two master's degrees from the University of Sofia, Bulgaria, during 1949–53, one in Russian philology and one in English philology. He is the recipient of several academic honors from Moscow State University, the Polish Academy of Sciences, the Wilson Center in Washington, D.C., the Ford Foundation, and the International Research and Exchange Board in New York (for postdoctoral work in the future of culture). His films and literary work have earned him honors; he has published more than twelve books of nonfiction and five novels, some of them science fiction, a genre in which he is particularly interested. Slavov was part of Bulgaria's intellectual and literary elite, and when publication of his poetry and fiction was discouraged in the early 1960s, he turned to academic work; he has served as teacher, editor, and writer. He stayed in the United States after his international fellowship ended because he felt that, in spite of Bulgaria's literary "thaw," a stultifying bureaucracy was enveloping creative activity in his country. Slavov has served as a member of the executive board of the International PEN Club for Writers in Exile, American branch.

Selected Title: *With the Precision of Bats* (1986, autobiography).

SLONIM, Mark (pseudonym of Mark Lvovich). Born 1894 in Russia; died 1976 in Switzerland. Best known as a literary historian and critic of European literature, Slonim also served as an editor of an emigré newspaper, *Novaya Gazeta*, for several years. He left the Soviet Union in the early 1920s and lived in Prague, Czechoslovakia, before emigrating to the United States. He has been a distinguished professor at several universities.

Selected Titles in Translation: *Russian Theatre: From the Empire to the Soviet* (1962); *Soviet Russian Literature: Writers and Problems, 1917–1977*, 2nd rev. ed. (1977).

SMITH, Rita. Born November 14, 1932, in Madras, India; she lives in Wichita, Kansas. Smith graduated from Doveton-Corrie Girls High School in Madras. She left India in 1953 when she met and married an American psychologist, Dr. Steve Pratt. They settled in Larned, Kansas, and later moved to Wichita, Smith's present home. After her first husband's early death, she married Ray Smith. In 1975 she returned to school, but a broken leg curtailed her activities; it was in her literature courses that she began to take her writing seriously. Her first story appeared in *Redbook*, her second in *Intro #11*, and her third in *Confrontation*. Her first novel, *In the Forest at Midnight*, published in 1989, is, in her words, "a coming-of-age story of an English girl growing up, with a parallel narrative of India's coming into independence." The action of the novel is set in the urban center of Madras in the south and Srinagar in the north as well as in a small village in the southern part of the subcontinent.

Smith considers herself an expatriate writer: although she writes only in English, her stories are all located in India, and her most vivid memories are those steeped in the colorful and dramatic events of her childhood. She feels close ties to India and has returned there several times, but she considers the United States her home; she became an American citizen in 1961. She is at work on a novel about a middle-aged housewife in America. The change of place in this fiction may also signify her movement toward "immigrant" literature as distinct from the "expatriate" writing of her past.

LEE MHATRE

SOKOLOV, Sacha. Born 1950 in USSR; he lives in New York. Sokolov's *School for Fools*, published in the West in 1976, proved a triumphant introduction into the literary world for the author. With its mixture of moods and tones and its seemingly random but vibrant associations of imagery, the satiric novel displayed an innovative style and a humorous talent in sketching Soviet bureaucracy and its tentacles reaching into Russian life. Sokolov emigrated to the United States in 1978 after suffering harassment for his views about Communist rules, regulations and goals. His second novel published in the West, *Between the Dog and the Wolf* (1980), showed a continuing effective satirical wackiness, but his most recent novel, *Astrolabia* (1989), rendered as a putative memoir of a hermaphrodite Soviet bureaucrat, Palisander Dahlberg, in which fictional and historical characters interweave, and in which the historical characters are given new and questionable motives, produced a chorus of disapproval. The criticism of Sokolov's latest work, particularly the objections to Sokolov's use of pranks when dealing with serious history, suggested that exile had perhaps isolated the author from the taste of contemporary events and that he remained mired in the once-fresh attitudes of his youth.

Consult: Edward J. Brown, *Soviet Literature since the Revolution* (1982).

SOLDATI, Mario. Born 1906 in Turin, Italy; he lives in Italy. Soldati was a resident in New York from 1929 to 1931, where he was a professor at Columbia University. He wrote about his American experiences in *America, My First Love* (1935). Ironically, he later was barred from entering the United States because of his purported Communist beliefs; he thus became, under the provisions of the McCarran-Walter Act, a banned foreigner.

Selected Title: *Rami Secchi* (Milan, 1989, Barren Branches).

SOLZHENITSYN, Aleksandr Isaevich. Born December 11, 1918, in Kislovodsk in the Caucasus, USSR, and christened there in the Church of St. Pantaleimon while the Civil War raged. His Orthodox father, Isaaki, a peasant's son who had worked his way up through Moscow University and had served faithfully as an army officer in World War I, had been killed in a hunting accident the previous June. An orphan in a religious family living in what soon became an outspokenly atheistic state, young Solzhenitsyn felt himself a kind of exile from birth. His father, many relatives and family friends, and much of his early life—especially the dozen harsh years in Rostov when he and his mother lived in a tiny, half-rotten shack without plumbing—are depicted in his novel *August 1914*.

Solzhenitsyn exploded onto the literary scene with his first published literary work, a short novel titled *Odin den' Ivana Denisovicha* (One Day in the Life of Ivan Denisovich), published in the November 1962 issue of the leading Moscow literary journal, *Novy Mir* (New World), at that time edited by the poet Aleksandr Tvardovsky. The unpretentious, compassionate account of a self-reliant, self-respecting, labor-camp prisoner's daily routine astonished the world.

Although desperately poor, Solzhenitsyn's widowed mother belonged to a liberal, intellectual circle in Rostov. Solzhenitsyn came from what, in *The Gulag Archipelago*, he called "an engineering milieu . . . [filled with] unrestrained and inoffensive humor, freedom and breadth of thought . . . well educated and with such good taste. . . . One and all had the stamp of spiritual nobility on their faces." In high school, Solzhenitsyn belonged to a group of four students whose teacher encouraged their writing. All his life, he dreamed of becoming a famous writer; one of his travel letters even reached Maxim Gorky,* whose secretary declared the young man had promise.

In November 1936 Solzhenitsyn planned a "big novel" about the 1917 Revolution and, the following year, a multivolume epic, portions of which, thirty years later, were transferred directly to *August 1914*. But not wishing to leave his consumptive mother, he abandoned hope of studying literature at his father's university, Moscow, and went into mathematics in Rostov. The subject came to him easily, he said; literature would be his spiritual consolation. Meanwhile, he rushed headlong with the spirit of the times; he was as devoted to Marxism-Leninism as he had been to the Orthodox church but at times skeptical, like Gleb Nerzhin, the autobiographical hero of *The First Circle*, who "recoiled from the idea" that Stalin was everything "and was unable to follow the crowd." Restoring Leninist principles, Solzhenitsyn believed, would right all the wrongs in Russia.

At the university Solzhenitsyn met attractive Natalia Reshetovskaya, a chemistry student, proposed to her in 1938, and was married in April 1940.

Solzhenitsyn combined his program in mathematics and physics at Rostov University with the study of literature as an external student at the Moscow Institute of Philosophy, Literature, and History. Three stories he wrote at this time he sent to the novelist Konstantin Fedin and the playwright Boris Lavrenev, but because of the war no reply came. He graduated from the university in June 1941; on June 22, war was declared between Germany and the Soviet Union. Found to be of limited physical fitness, Solzhenitsyn was not accepted into the army until October, when the German advance forced the Russians to mobilize all reserves. First a stableboy in a Cossack battalion and later an artillery officer like his father, Solzhenitsyn described some of his 1942 war experiences and his attitude toward Soviet unpreparedness in a story written twenty years later, "An Incident at Krechetovka Station." During the war itself, he completed several stories and outlined a novel, "The Sixth Year," about a university graduate's year in the army. In correspondence with his three special, high-school friends, Solzhenitsyn imagined, ironically, their postwar success.

His mother's death in January 1944 filled him with grief and guilt; a visit from his wife to the Central Front emphasized their growing differences more than their common joys; letters from his friends became rarer; *Znamya* rejected the stories he had sent Lavrenev; the army plunged forward into Poland, plundering and looting. Solzhenitsyn took copious notes, interviewed soldiers and villagers, and recorded his experiences in a purely autobiographical poem, "The Way," part 9 of which was later published as "Prussian Nights," in the novel *August 1914* and in the documentary *The Gulag Archipelago*. On February 9, 1945, he was arrested for anti-Stalinist statements in letters he had written to his schoolfriend Nikolai on the Ukrainian Front. In *The First Circle*, the description of Innokenti Volodin's treatment on arriving in prison is based on Solzhenitsyn's experience.

In prison, too, there was exile: solitary confinement, interrogation, and torture. As Solzhenitsyn wrote in *The Gulag Archipelago*, "your first cell is a very special one," linking the prisoner with others sharing his fate. Always a serious, dedicated, somewhat humorless man who could tolerate extreme privation, a patriotic Leninist and a stern, even overbearing junior officer, during eight years in prisons and labor camps, Solzhenitsyn changed from an optimistic socialist who planned a great history of the October Revolution to an impassioned religionist determined to document the truth of his time. To that end, he constantly made notes, wrote stories, and composed poetry, committing to memory with the aid of an ingenious rosary-abacus some 12,000 lines of verse. Sometimes his materials were confiscated; sometimes, as in exile after prison, he buried his work in a bottle in his garden; but gradually all of it came together as biography and autobiography presented in thinly disguised fictional form or as personal documentation or, in *The Gulag Archipelago*, as the testimony of 227 witnesses calling their countrymen to account.

The end of World War II did not bring Solzhenitsyn the amnesty granted some prisoners, and he was already in exile "in perpetuity" in Kok Terek when Stalin died in 1953. He had been in prisons such as the Lubyanka and Butyrki, in Krasnaya Presnya, in labor camps near Moscow and in Kazakhstan, and in the special camp, or *sharashka*, at Marfino working with scientists on voice-coding devices. During this period, he established intimate friendships with other prisoners, such as Lev Kopelev* and Dimitri Panin, but his marriage virtually dissolved, partly from political and economic pressure on his wife to disavow association with an enemy of the people and partly from the jolts of life that had driven them apart. The divorce became final in February 1953.

While in the labor camp in Ekibastuz in January 1952, Solzhenitsyn discovered he had a malignant tumor of a lymph node; the tumor was removed and after two weeks' recovery he returned to camp life. Two years later, in January 1954, while working as a math and physics high-school teacher in Kok Terek, he was found to have not only a tumor from metastasis of the malignant lymph node but also an abdominal tumor. Huge doses of radiation at the hospital in Tashkent—coupled with his extraordinary will-power—achieved what had been predicted as only a one-in-three chance of recovery. Solzhenitsyn returned to the faith of his childhood and considered his recovery a divine miracle.

During his last year in prison, Solzhenitsyn worked on "The Way," his 10,000-line, autobiographical "novel in verse," loosely modeled on Tvardovsky's *Vasily Tyorkin*, and *The Feast of the Conquerors*, a play in rhymed iambics about a military banquet at which the characters discuss the consequences of the Russian Revolution and of the conflicts between political loyalty and moral truth. Confiscation of that manuscript and of *The First Circle* by the secret police in 1965 led him to fear terrible recriminations. During the first months of exile, he copied out what he had long kept in his head and wrote a new play, *The Captives*, about his very first imprisonment in Brodnitz before his trial.

Introducing the reader to tsarist colonel Vorotyntsev who figures in *August 1914*, Rubin and Pryanchikov who appear later in *The First Circle*, and Gai, a hero in the labor-camp play *The Love-Girl and the Innocent*, and set in counterespionage police headquarters, *The Captives* portrays what happens to a group of prisoners from first arrival to trial and sentencing, has a large cast synthesizing the world of the camps, and includes scenes of Russian life on both sides of the lines, the author leaning toward the conclusion that the White Russians were right and more "Russian" than the Bolsheviks. Begun a little later in Kok Terek, *The Love-Girl and the Innocent* was the first work undertaken since his arrest that he did not have to memorize and burn piecemeal. It drew heavily on his own experiences of hard labor in several camps and emphasized the thorough corruption of camp life.

The idea for *Cancer Ward* came to him on the day he was released from the Tashkent hospital in midsummer 1954, but the book he began serious work on the following summer was *The First Circle*. By autumn that year, the amnesties that followed Stalin's death touched political prisoners, too: Solzhenitsyn requested the lifting of his exile, and in April 1956 was told that his sentence was annulled and his exile lifted.

He settled down as a math and physics teacher in a provincial village on the Moscow railroad line and took room and board in the peasant hut of Matryona Zakharova. One night, while Matryona, her nephew, and another man were hauling the extra room from her hut across the train tracks to her niece's, a sledge caught on the rails and an unlit engine killed all three. Solzhenitsyn observed the wake and learned all about family resentments and expectations, material he put directly into his celebrated short story, "Matryona's Place," revised and completed in 1960.

In February 1957, he and Natalia Reshetovskaya were remarried; in March, he was rehabilitated; and in June he moved back to Ryazan, the first draft of *The First Circle* in hand. Prison and exile were behind him—he reminded himself of them every year on the anniversary of his arrest by that day eating only the bread and gruel served in the camps—but his sole friends were men he had shared imprisonment with. His writing soon became his mission.

In 1958 a recurrence of cancer was cured by chemotherapy, and the following year he published for the first time an article in the local paper about poor mail service. In May he applied the idea for a sketch called "A Day in a School Teacher's Life" to his experience laying brick in 1952 in the camp at Ekibastuz: "I was helping to carry a hand-barrow full of mortar, and I thought that this was the way to describe the whole world of the camps . . . to describe just one day in the life of an average and in no way remarkable prisoner from morning till night." Narrated in the third person but seen through Ivan Denisovich Shukhov's eyes, the story describes in a colloquial, quick-witted vernacular larded with idioms and imaginative expressions his camp day from reveille to bedtime, from washing down the guardhouse, breakfast, body search, march to the work site and laying brick in freezing temperatures—laying brick so intently he and his gang ignore the final whistle and are almost late for the march to barracks— to small chores, a favor for another prisoner, supper, in turn buying tobacco from another, then small talk among bunkmates and his falling asleep content: "The day was over, a day without a cloud, almost a happy day."

The book's power comes from three sources. First, Ivan Denisovich is clever, self-reliant, and morally good—exactly like the old Russian picaresque folk hero—his wits and skills a match for the terrible camp regime. Second, he is surrounded by a cast of vivid characters, from the Moscow screenwriter Tsezar and the naval captain Buinovsky to Alyoshka the Baptist and the peasant Tyurin— whose continual entrances and exits compose a dramatic portrait of suffering and oppression, indicating that the difference between inside and outside the camps is one of degree—in a sense, the Soviet Union is one huge labor camp— but that those who stoically survive triumph over their oppressors. Third, free of jargon, commercialism, newspeak, or lies, the language is apt, juicy, occasionally obscene, brilliantly imagistic and idiosyncratic, expressing both individual characteristics and auctorial originality—a supple, vigorous Russian that had not been seen in print for more than a generation. Solzhenitsyn wrote the first draft in six weeks in the summer of 1959; he completed his revisions in mid-October.

In May that year, as liberalization continued following Khrushchev's "secret speech" denouncing Stalin, Fedin became secretary-general of the Writers' Union and Tvardovsky was restored to editorship of *Novy Mir*. In October 1961, at the 22nd Communist Party Congress, Tvardovsky supported Khrushchev's call to overthrow the "cult of personality" by insisting on writers' "showing the labors and ordeals of our people in a manner that is totally truthful and faithful to life." In November, Raisa Orlova, Lev Kopelev's wife, took Solzhenitsyn's manuscript to *Novy Mir*; Tvardovsky was enthusiastic; a few weeks later, at an editorial meeting, Solzhenitsyn received a contract and an advance. Soon typed copies were circulating among Moscow's writers and intellectuals, gathering praise. By September 1962, circumventing the censors, Tvardovsky got a copy to Khrushchev, who ordered copies sent to the Central Committee. In October, the Committee formally approved publication. Solzhenitsyn kept meeting Moscow writers; Kopelev took him to meet Anna Akhmatova. And when the November issue of *Novy Mir* appeared with the story, all reviews lauded it, and the magazine sold out overnight. The man who had been sent into exile for crimes against the state was now called "an exemplary citizen and true helper of the Party."

"Matryona's Place" and the freshly written "An Incident at Krechetovka Station" came out in *Novy Mir*'s January issue. Despite a hardening line all through 1963, in July the magazine brought out a Solzhenitsyn story on a contemporary theme—"For the Good of the Cause," about a school principal and idealistic group of students who had to yield a much-needed new building to corrupt local Party bosses and a factory director. In the increasingly restrictive atmosphere, however, the Sovremennik Theater decided to drop consideration of *The Love-Girl and the Innocent*. Elected a member of the Writers' Union and able to live on the income from his work without being called a parasite, Solzhenitsyn gave up teaching.

In May 1964, after *One Day in the Life of Ivan D.* had been prevented by Party interference from winning the Lenin Prize, Tvardovsky read and applauded *The First Circle*. His editorial board offered Solzhenitsyn a contract, but Khrushchev was too deeply involved in trying to hold on against conservative attack to support any more artistic innovation, and the manuscript copies were sequestered in *Novy Mir*'s safe. Solzhenitsyn released some short-short stories for samizdat circulation, whereby they found their way West and were published in the anti-Soviet magazine *Grani*. After Khrushchev's fall in mid-October, Solzhenitsyn secretly sent a microfilm of *The First Circle* to the West for safekeeping. That winter he began working on *The Gulag Archipelago*, which he continued in the summer of 1965 in the countryside of Obninsk in Kaluga Province, but, apprehensive for the security of his manuscripts with *Novy Mir*, he took them in September to his friends' apartment, where he had left other work. The next day the KGB seized them all, three days after arresting *Novy Mir*'s leading critic, Andrei Sinyavsky, for smuggling his work to the West and a day before arresting Yuly Daniel on the same charge. Although sheltered and befriended by such men as the poet and critic Kornei Chukovsky and the physicist Pyotr Kapitsa, Solzhenitsyn indignantly broke with Tvardovsky, who virtually single-handedly had launched his career. Solzhenitsyn's account of these literary events in *The Oak and the Calf*, published in exile in 1979, was attacked as self-serving and biased against former friends.

With the sentencing of Sinyavsky and Daniel to prison, the liberals were set back, and Solzhenitsyn redoubled his solitary efforts to finish *Cancer Ward* and to resist the authorities, often saying he was doing so in the name of the Russian people. "Zakhar, the Pouch," his last work published in the Soviet Union, appeared in *Novy Mir* in January 1966.

Despite increasing repression, the arrests of dissident intellectuals, and rejection of his work by all journals in 1966–67, Solzhenitsyn undertook a series of public readings and lectures in defiance of the KGB. He also tried to make up with Tvardovsky, sending him Part 2 of *Cancer Ward*. Tvardovsky, however, said that there was no chance of bringing it out. Emboldened by the examples of other writers, Solzhenitsyn then arranged for Part 1 to be published in Czechoslovakia and for *The First Circle* to come out in the United States; he meanwhile engaged in a public campaign to get *Cancer Ward* into domestic print. *Novy Mir* did set eight chapters in type, but the Central Committee never approved the work, and the type was broken up. In the summer of 1968 it appeared in Russian in both England and Italy, and *The First Circle* came out in America; translations were soon to follow. Solzhenitsyn had cut himself off from being published in the USSR.

The society of the *Cancer Ward* is isolated. The time is 1955, a year after Solzhenitsyn's treatment; like him, one of the principal characters, Oleg Kostoglotov, a former prisoner now in exile, has abdominal cancer; the other principal is Pavel Rusanov, a high Party official with neck cancer. Much of the novel consists of the conflict between idealism and spiritual values on the one hand, and materialism and expediency on the other. Grouped around the two central figures is a social cross-section of old and young and of the clinic's doctors, led by Lyudmila Dontsova and Vera Gangart, whose humanistic understanding is part of the novel's old-fashioned strength. At the end of Part 1, Kostoglotov's illness is under control, but Rusanov is very ill. In Part 2, new patients appear, more attention is devoted to the doctors, Kostoglotov suffers a severe reaction to radiation, Rusanov is cured—and nearly knocks Kostoglotov down as his car drives away. Critics who supported the novel praised its verisimilitude; opponents said that through Rusanov and his daughter Aviette it ridiculed the Soviet system.

The First Circle also portrayed a closed, isolated society and was closely based on Solzhenitsyn's personal experiences. The plot concerns the efforts by a team of prisoner-scientists, including Lev Rubin, Gleb Nerzhin, and Dimitri Sologdin, to identify the telephone voice of a Soviet diplomat, Innokenti Volodin, who has called the American embassy to warn it of an espionage rendezvous in New York. Around the scientists are a group of men and women, inside and outside the prison, representing the whole society. Volodin is arrested and taken to the Lubyanka, and Nerzhin, who refuses to continue working in the special prison, at the end is shipped off to a labor camp. In their free time, the scientists profoundly debate the rights and wrongs of Soviet society but in their work are connected by skillful novelistic threads to their families, the guards, the administrators, the security forces, the Party, and the highest figures in the government, so that the novel embraces all levels and all attitudes in political life. Again, those who admired the book commended its truthfulness; its critics, however, thought it a libel on Soviet society.

By the end of 1968, Solzhenitsyn's marriage was falling apart again. He not only worked more intensely than ever, launching into *August 1914*, but also began a long controversy with physicist and human rights advocate Andrei Sakharov, a discussion many found reminiscent of the Slavophile-Westernizer debate in the nineteenth century. In November 1969 Solzhenitsyn was expelled from the Writers' Union. In February 1970, Tvardovsky was forced to resign from *Novy Mir*. In October Solzhenitsyn received the Nobel Prize for "the ethical force with which he has pursued the indispensable traditions of Russian literature." In December, Natalia Svetlova, a mathematician who had become his secretary and confidante, bore their son, whom they named Ermolai. In June 1971, YMCA Press in Paris brought out the Russian edition of *August 1914*, the story of General Samsonov's disastrous East Prussian campaign in World War I, and in December, Tvardovsky died. Personal attacks on Solzhenitsyn in the press magnified in 1972. After his "Lenten Letter," with its call to the Orthodox Church to stand up against the Soviet government, and the anti-Western tone of his "Nobel Lecture," liberal dissidents disavowed him, none of whose protests Solzhenitsyn had ever publicly supported.

Natalia Svetlova and Solzhenitsyn had a second son, Ignat, in September 1972. After his birth, Reshetovskaya ceased trying to delay a divorce, which was granted in March 1973. The next month, Natalia Svetlova and Solzhenitsyn married in an Orthodox church outside of Moscow. Late that summer their son Stepan was born.

At the end of December 1973, volume 1 of *The Gulag Archipelago* came out in Paris, and Solzhenitsyn was ready to send off his "Letter to the Leaders." A copy of *Gulag* was found at his typist's, further provoking the KGB, who struck on February 12, 1974, took Solzhenitsyn to Lefortovo Prison and deported him to Germany. After a period of residency in Zurich—where he worked on his historical novel, *Lenin in Zurich* —Solzhenitsyn traveled to Stockholm for his Nobel Prize and then around Europe and America while finishing *October 1916* and *March 1917*, the sequels to *August 1914*. In the summer of 1976 Solzhenitsyn and his family bought a house and settled in Cavendish, Vermont, erecting a high chain-link fence around their place to keep an intrusive society out, but as many of his old friends noted, simultaneously fencing himself in— the eternal exile. His harsh comments on Western society and his equation of Orthodoxy with the spirit of Russia alienated Western intellectuals, but after a dozen years in America, Solzhenitsyn told his biographer he was only a visitor: "It seems to me it is only a matter of a few years before I return to Russia."

Selected Titles: *Stories and Prose Poems* (1971); *Sobranie sochinenii* (Paris, 1978–).

Consult: Michael Scammell, *Solzhenitsyn, a Biography*, with selective bibliography (1984).

F. D. REEVE

In the early summer of 1989 these events were recorded: Solzhenitsyn was readmitted to the Union of Soviet Writers, an official group from which he had been expelled in 1969. The twenty-six-member governing board of the organization declared that his expulsion was contrary to "the principles of socialist democracy" and urged the Soviet government to restore full citizenship to Solzhenitsyn. In addition, it was reported in the Soviet literary journal *Novy Mir* that Solzhenitsyn's works, which have not been permitted publication in the Soviet Union since 1962 (*One Day in the Life of Ivan Denisovich* is the only novel by Solzhenitsyn as yet published in the USSR), would appear in Soviet-sponsored editions. In particular, Solzhenitsyn's acceptance speech for the 1970 Nobel Prize for Literature appeared in the July 1989 issue of *Novy Mir*. Parts of *The Gulag Archipelago*, the autobiographical work in which Solzhenitsyn details the brutalities of labor camps and penal servitude during the long reign of Joseph Stalin, were scheduled to appear in *Novy Mir* in late 1989/early 1990, and the entire volume is later to be published in book form. This is the work that on publication in an English-language edition in Western Europe led to Solzhenitsyn's forced exile.

In July 1989 Solzhenitsyn's historical novel *August 1914* was issued in a revised English-language edition; this edition follows the Russian-language version published in 1983. The revised volume is 854 pages long, almost twice the length of the original English-language version published in 1972. *August 1914* and its successor, *October 1916*, are parts of a tetralogy on the Russian Revolution that bear the overall title *The Red Wheel*. *October 1916* appeared in its original Russian-language version in 1984; it will appear in English in 1991. The third volume, *March 1917*, has been completed and is expected to be issued in the early 1990s (in Russian), while the fourth volume "April 1917" is still in manuscript progress. Solzhenitsyn has been at work on the vast project for the past twenty years.

The English-language edition of *August 1914* and the Russian-language edition of *October 1916* have caused controversy and heated commentary. Debate has ranged from attacks on Solzhenitsyn's biases against non-Russians (he has also been accused of anti-Semitic portraits) to his prejudiced angle of vision on Russian history to an equally impassioned defense of his liberty as a creative artist to shape his material into the huge cast of characters and motivations envisioned in his visionary scheme of things.

*   *   *   *   *

August 26, 1989. Parts of Solzhenitsyn's prison-camp memoir, *The Gulag Archipelago*, appeared for the first time in the Soviet Union. The excerpts were printed in the Soviet journal *Novy Mir* (New Word), which has a large circulation. An earlier and noncontroversial essay, "Live Not by Lies!" (written 1974), had appeared in a monthly Soviet journal (*Twentieth Century and Peace*) not bound by censorship regulation because of its low circulation.

Solzhenitsyn, who has been in exile for fifteen years and most of whose work has not been allowed publication in the USSR, had insisted that publication of *The Gulag Archipelago* precede publication of any of his other banned work in the USSR. His novels, *The First Circle* and *Cancer Ward*, are scheduled for Moscow publication this year. His full Soviet citizenship was restored to him in August, 1990, by direct order from Mikhail Gorbachev.

SONTAG, Susan. Born January 16, 1933, in New York City; she has returned to New York City. Sontag has identified herself with European culture; she has said that she knows European writers "better" than she knows contemporary American literature. Her interests have been the great European literary movements of the twentieth century—Symbolism, Expressionism, Modernism, Deconstructionism, Absurdity and the Theatre of Cruelty. In her own words, she "despises" post-Modernism, a term she finds offensive, and an approach she characterizes as anti-humanistic and academic (Sontag made her comment at a PEN American Center meeting.) She was educated at the University of Chicago and Harvard; she married early to the sociologist Philip Reiff (their child, David Reiff, is now an editor at a New York publishing house), and divorced before returning to New York. She has lived abroad at various periods, the most extensive in the 1960s–1970s when she worked in film and theatre as well as wrote criticism and fiction. In the late 1970s, after her return to the United States, she encountered hostility with the American media and her intellectual colleagues when, during a talk at New York City's Town Hall, she denounced the Soviet Union for its treatment of East European dissidents. She was both cheered and excoriated for her stand, and experienced opprobrium, probably for the first time, from those publications on the Left who had favored her with celebratory attention and previous issues of assenting judgment. Technically, neither an exile nor an expatriate, she typifies the consciousness of the outsider, the alien artist of Modernism whose psychic exile is the rock of his/her being.

Sontag triumphed over an occurrence of cancer, an account of which experience she rendered in *Illness as Metaphor* (1978). This work was also published in 1990 in a single volume containing Sontag's *Aids and Its Metaphors*, previously published in 1989.

Sontag was president of the American Center of PEN from 1987 to 1989; she encouraged attention to world literature and to exiled writers during her tenure in office.

Selected Titles: *The Benefactor* (1963); *Against Interpretation* (1966); *Death Kit* (1967, stories); *Styles of Radical Will* (1969); *Duet for Cannibals* (1970, film script); *Brother Carl* (1974, film script); *On Photography* (1977); *I, etcetera* (1978, essays); *Under the Sign of Saturn* (1980, anthology of Sontag's writings); *A Susan Sontag Reader* (1982).

Consult: Sohnya Sayres, *Susan Sontag: The Elegiac Modernist* (1989).

SORIANO, Osvaldo. Born in 1943 in Argentina; he returned from exile in 1984 after the 1982 Falklands war led to new elections in Argentina. Best known for his sharp satire *No habrá más penas ni olvido* (1980; *A Funny, Dirty Little War* 1982), Soriano left Argentina in protest against military repression in his country. He returned from exile in 1984 and has since played a mediating role in the conflict between those who fled into exile and those who stayed behind. Consistently aware of the writer's responsibility to society, he has admitted he was "intolerant" of writers who chose passive resistance and inner dissent above open protest and rebellion. In a recent interview he called for profound and public soul-searching in order to turn Argentina once again into a "healthy body" of people.

Soriano's novel *Winter Quarters*, published in Spanish in 1982, appeared in the United States in 1989; it is a sequel to *A Funny, Dirty Little War* in that the same locale, the town of Colonia Vela, and the theme of ordinary citizens caught in the sadistic web of the military dictatorship of Argentina during the 1970s is employed. In this novel as in his earlier one, the heroes are fools with the appeal of human aspirations, two has-beens who continue to ply their show-business wares to a weary public. The human comedy of failure is turned into a dark drama of government brutality when it is discovered one of the men had previous associations with the Left and anti-militaristic groups.

Consult: Mitchell Levitas, "Writers and Dictators," *The New York Times Book Review*, August 14, 1989.

SOYINKA, Wole (Akinwande Oluiwole Soyinkya). Born July 13, 1934, in Abeokuta, Western Nigeria; he lives in Abeokuta, Nigeria. Soyinka attempted to negotiate an end to fighting in the civil war in Nigeria in the mid–1960s. A native Yoruba, he talked of compromise between the Hausa-dominated government and the rebelling Ibo leaders of the Biafra secession movement, but was rewarded with suspicion and imprisonment by the central government. Kept in solitary confinement for more than a year, he suffered serious eye disabilities, a condition that threatened at one point to lead to blindness. He wrote of these experiences in his prison memoir, *The Man Died: Prison Notes* (1972). Soyinka served for a time in the Literature Department and as its Chair at the University in Lagos. Political and educational disagreements with government and university factions led to his dismissal (he was at one point accused of trying to seize the university's radio station). He left Nigeria for what he has termed "political exile," for stays in England and the United States; during these periods he worked with the Royal Court Theatre in London and the Yale Repertory Theater in New Haven, Connecticut. When his father died in the 1970s, he was unable to attend the funeral (for fear of punitive detention in Nigeria). Soyinka writes movingly in his most recent work, *Isara: A Voyage Around "Essay"* (1989), of the pain he suffered in this further exile from family and tradition and from paying his final respects to a loved parent. "Essay," the English name he gives to his father, is a metaphorical extension of Soyinka's father's attempt or "essay" to embrace past and present contingencies into a pattern of secure fluidity for his family and tribe; it is also an allusion to John Mortimer's biography of his beloved father, *A Voyage Round My Father*. Soyinka uses English names in *Isara* in a counterpart manner to the Yoruba/African tradition of name-designations for professions and goals; he calls the people who have left the mythic village of Isara "ex-Iles": those who have departed from the island of tradition to a world of modern flux.

From its earliest manifestations, whether in poetry, memoir, prose fiction, drama, or criticism, Soyinka's work has situated itself around the center, and its centrifugal/centripetal spokes, of exile and return. The pattern of a young hero who must decide between Western European modernism and Nigerian tribal customs, of the artist who must consider his responsibility to society—both as inheritor and as revolutionary leader—may be seen in such early works as *The Swamp Dwellers* (Ibadan, 1963), *The Strong Breed* (Ibadan, 1963), *Road* (originally *The Road*, London, 1965); and the popular romantic comedy, *The Lion and the Jewel* (London, 1963). In his poetry Soyinka often pits the memory of an idealized native tradition against the compromising realities of a modernized world; in his novels *The Interpreters* (London, 1965) and *Season of Anomie*, he emphasizes the dislocation and alienation of the educated intellectual in a society that has not yet made peace with the conflicts of its histories and potentialities. In all cases Soyinka shows the tragedy inherent in adherence to any rigidity of codified behavior; what he suggests is an integrated pluralism of differing values and varied customs. In this sense Soyinka differs from Negritude African writers; he has opposed any kind of separatism (even during the 1960s Negritude mania when it was impolitic to stand apart from the black-consciousness movements). His attempt at uniting warring factions during the Nigerian Civil War is another example of his need to encompass rather than to segregate; of his willingness to go beyond assessments of blame for colonialism in a post-colonialist society; of his commitment to preserve or restore pre-colonial customs amid the rush to progressive, and often greedy, mechanization.

Soyinka has published two memoirs—*Ake: The Childhood Years* (1982), an idealization of growing up African, and *Isara*, a complement to *Ake* in its reflection of Soyinka's father's way of life before Soyinka was born. Soyinka often revises biography and historical data for what he sees as deeper and universal truths; his memoir style is similarly liquid, flowing in currents of psychological time and a-logical, symbolist associations. Soyinka received the Nobel Prize for Literature in 1986.

Selected Titles: Plays: *A Dance of the Forests* (London, 1963); *The Lion and the Jewel* (London, 1963); *Three Plays: The Swamp-Dwellers; The Trials of Brother Jero; The Strong Breed* (Mbari/Northwestern University Press, 1963); *Five Plays* [includes all five above-mentioned plays] (London, 1965); *The Road* (Ibadan, 1965); *Kongi's Harvest* (1967); *Madmen and Specialists* (1971); *The Jero Plays: The Trials of Brother Jero and Jero's Metamorphosis* (1973); *The Bacchae: A Communion Rite, from Euripides* (1973); *Collected Plays*, 2 vols. (1973–74); *Death and the King's Horseman* (1975); *A Play of Giants* (London, 1984). Novels: *The Interpreters* (1965); *Season of Anomie* (1973); Poems: *Idanre and Other Poems* (1967); *Poems from Prison* (1969); *A Shuttle in the Crypt* (1972); *Ogun Abibiman* (1977); *Mandela's Earth and Other Poems* (1990). Criticism: *Myth, Literature and the African World* (1976).

Consult: Eldred D. Jones, *The Writing of Wole Soyinka* (3d ed., 1988); Gerald H. Moore, *Soyinka* (rev. ed., 1978); Oyin Ogumba, *The Movement of Transition: A Study of the Plays of Soyinka* (1975).

SPARK, Muriel. Born February 1, 1918, in Edinburgh, Scotland; she lives in Rome, Italy. Muriel Camberg's mother was Presbyterian and her father Jewish. In 1937 she moved to Rhodesia, married, becoming Muriel Spark, and gave birth to a son. In 1944 she left husband and Rhodesia for England, where she lived until 1962; in 1957, she converted to Roman Catholicism and published her first novel, *The Comforters*. She moved to New York in 1962, but has lived in Rome since 1965. She refers to herself as a "constitutional exile" (Karl Miller, *Memories of Modern Scotland* [London, 1970], p. 151). She has lived in four other countries besides her birthplace. The "constitutional exile" feels so at ease with her condition that exile does not loom as of direct thematic significance in her work. She may describe a protagonist trapped in Rhodesia, longing to return to England (not Scotland) in "The Go-away Bird" (collected 1958), or a Scotsman making his way in England in *The Ballad of Peckham Rye* (1960), or various Englishmen in Venice in *Territorial Rights* (1979), but exile is only the situation, not the theme. Instead, the worldview that made Spark a "constitutional exile," that made her describe herself as a "Catholic animal," forms the thematic content of her work (interview with Malcolm Muggeridge, quoted in Ruth Whittaker, *The Faith and Fiction of Muriel Spark* [1982], p. 25).

For Spark, divine will determines events as surely as does the novelist's pen. Therefore, both believer and writer are distanced from the emotional freight of human activity, and geography holds little significance compared to spiritual location. Spark's most clear-headed characters, notably Chairman Colson, Jean Taylor, and Henry Mortimer of *Memento Mori* (1959), remember this truth; for them, death holds little sting. Spark's utter lack of sentimentality; her cool aloofness; her characteristic mixture of frivolity, satire, faith, violence, and the supernatural, are consistent with her worldview—it is God's intention behind events that matters. Thus, reprehensible machinations, as in *The Abbess of Crewe* (1971), may point to some ultimate good even as they satirize earthly institutions. Since with God all things are possible, the events themselves may include capers by the devil (*The Ballad of Peckham Rye*) or phone calls from Death (*Memento Mori*). Seen in this longest view, all earthly concern becomes frivolous.

The "Sparkian distinction" (Whittaker's term) is found also in her other novels, among them, *The Prime of Miss Jean Brodie* (1961), *The Girls of Slender Means* (1963), *The Mandelbaum Gate* (1965), and *Loitering with Intent* (1981), as well as in *The Stories of Muriel Spark* (1985).

Selected Titles: *Mary Shelley: A Biography* (1987, rev. ed. of *Child of Light: A Reassessment of Mary Shelley*, 1951); *A Far Cry from Kensington* (1988).

Consult: Karl Malkoff, *Muriel Spark* (1968); Ruth Whittaker, *The Faith and Fiction of Muriel Spark* (1982).

JOAN GORDON

SPERBER, Manès. Born December 12, 1905, in Zablotow, then Austria-Hungary (now USSR); died February 5, 1984, in Paris, France. Sperber was born in a "little Jewish town in East Galicia" that sustained a richly mystic tradition. During World War I, his family fled from Zablotow four times only to return to it thrice. The fourth move left Sperber and his family in Vienna. In the latter 1920s, Sperber became a student of Alfred Adler. He wrote and lectured on Adler's theory of individual psychology, eventually publishing *Alfred Adler et la psychologie individuelle* (Paris, 1977; *Masks of Loneliness*, 1974). Like most of Sperber's work, it was published first in French, even though it was written in German. From 1927 to 1933, Sperber was on the faculty of the University of Berlin as a professor of psychology. A rift developed between Adler and Sperber because of Sperber's commitment to communism (Sperber had joined the Communist party in 1927; he later resigned) and to his literary interests; as mentor, Adler wanted Sperber, his disciple, to concentrate on the study of psychology. Sperber's late works, particularly the disorganized and musing *Masks of Loneliness*, were his efforts to heal the rift.

When Adolf Hitler came to power, Sperber moved, via Yugoslavia, to France, where he was to remain the rest of his life as literary director for the publishers Calman-Levy. World War I had disrupted Sperber's boyhood; the period *entre deux guerres* had bereft him of illusions. World War II provided further disillusionment for Sperber, and the once-energetic rationalist who had accepted the challenges of society eagerly now tended to withdraw from it. His writing at this point becomes drenched in the fervency of his disillusionment and the potency of his wry personal insight. Yet he also retained his goodwill toward people and the optimism of a secular faith in them.

In Europe Sperber is primarily known as a novelist, for his trilogy *Wie eine Traene im Ozean* (1976; *Like a Tear in the Ocean*, London, 1988), consisting of *Et le buisson devint cendre* (1949; *The Burned Bramble*, 1951), *Plus profound que l'avine* (1952; *The Abyss*, 1952), and *La Baie perdu* (1952; *Journey without End*, 1954). In the United States, 1954 Sperber is also known as an essayist.

Sperber shares in the tragedy of this century in that he, with his gifts and vision, ability and energy, never found a resolution to the problem of humankind's vast inhumanity. Yet in the foreword to *God's Water Carrier* (1987), Elie Wiesel* refers to Sperber as a rationalist who, because of his rebellion against blind faith, remained in the Hebrew religious tradition of parrying with God. Wiesel wrote that the once formally religious and devout Sperber (his father was an Orthodox Jew) broke with family tradition to become a Communist party member and broke with that creed because it was a ''faith'' rather than a rational approach to truth. Werner Rings, in the introduction to *God's Water Carrier*, agrees with Wiesel in calling Sperber a characterological rational rebel, one who must learn to live without faith in the modern world, and to survive such loss of priestly comfort. In the preface to Sperber's *Wolyna*, André Malraux identifies Sperber as an agnostic or secular Jew who never lost his intimacy with the awesome mysteries of existence that his writings invoked as well as evoked.

Selected Titles: *Alfred Adler: Der Mensch und seine Lehre* (1926); *Die Tyrannis und andere Essays* (1987). Autobiography: *All des Vergangere*, a trilogy consisting of *Die Wassertrager Gottes* (1974; *God's Water Carrier*, 1987), *Die vergebliche Warnung* (1975, The Vain Warning), and *Bis man mir Scherben auf die Augen legt* (1977, Until They Lay Potsherds on My Eyes).

Translation: *Man and His Deeds* (1970).

Consult: "Manès Sperber," *Annual Obituary 1984*; Arthur Koestler, *The Trail of the Dinosaur* (1955); W. Kraus, ed., *Schreiben in dieser Zeit: fur Manès Sperber* (1976); Werner Rings, Introduction to *God's Water Carrier* (1987).

JUDITH M. BRUGGER

STEAD, Christina Ellen. Born July 17, 1920, in Australia; died March 31, 1983, in Sydney, Australia. Stead left Australia in 1928 to live in New York, Paris, and London. She wrote all thirteen of her novels while living in Europe. Her first published work was *The Salzburg Tales* in 1934; an earlier-written novel about Sydney homeless people, *Seven Poor Men of Sydney* (1934), was published a few months after *The Salzburg Tales*. Stead's most heralded book is *The Man Who Loved Children* (1940, reprinted 1966), a story of a modern sadomasochistic marriage. She also achieved wide prominence with her later novel, *Cotters' England* (1967).

Consult: Hortense Calisher, in *Encounters*, ed. Kai Erikson (1989); Kate Macomber Stern, *Christina Stead's Heroine: The Changing Sense of Decorum* (1989).

STEIN, Gertrude. Born February 3, 1874, in Allegheny, Pennsylvania; died July 27, 1946, at Neuilly-sur-Seine, France. Stein's family, Americans, moved her between Paris and Vienna for the first five years of her life, after which they settled in California. Neither she nor her siblings were continuously subjected to the standard American system of public education. Her mother died when Stein was fourteen and her father when she was seventeen. Under the influence of her beloved brother Leo, Stein enrolled in Radcliffe College of Harvard University in 1893. It was here that she came under the influence of William James, eventually publishing two papers on automatic and learned motor behaviors. In 1897 she transferred to Johns Hopkins to pursue medicine, but became inconsolably bored with it and unhappy in her private life. In 1901 she broke off her medical studies, and in 1903, at the age of twenty-nine, she moved to Paris to be near her brother Leo, who had already been drawn there by the art scene.

Stein championed the new cubist movement in painting, which Leo rejected, and by 1914 the rift between them was well established. Stein and her lifelong companion, Alice B. Toklas, kept a safe haven in Paris at 5 rue de Fleurus for a large company of the leading bohemians—Pablo Picasso, Ernest Hemingway,* Max Jacob, Guillaume Apollinaire.* Alice would sit with the "wives" while the geniuses entertained and were entertained by Stein. Alice's hashish brownies, served at the gatherings, achieved a lasting fame.

Stein and Toklas stayed in France throughout the European wars, driving a makeshift ambulance named "Aunt Pauline" in World War I. In World War II, they moved to the countryside in the département d'Ain, where they were protected by the locals. The mayor of Bilignin kept their names off the lists of

Jews required by the Germans. Stein was diagnosed with an inoperable cancer in 1946, and died under anesthesia in the hospital.

Although it is perilous to generalize about Stein's opus, her writings can be grouped into three classes: the relatively conventional fictions like *Three Lives* (New York, 1909), *The Autobiography of Alice B. Toklas* (New York, 1933), and *Wars I Have Seen* (New York, 1945); expository prose like *How To Write* (Paris, Plain Ed., 1931) and *Lectures in America* (New York, 1935); and the inimitable works (Stein refused to call her writing "experimental," since "experiments" were something that "scientists" did) *Tender Buttons* (New York: Claire Marie, 1914), *The Making of Americans* (Paris: Contact, 1925), and *Geography & Plays* (Boston, Four Seas, 1922). The more nearly conventional stuff she called "identity" writing, and the innovative works her "entity" writing, which she conceived of as the kind of writing that expressed her being in the same way that "your little dog knows you" as opposed to the way "an audience knows you." Her search for the eternal present, for a new way of signifying, and for her rhythmical innovations were often the butt of criticism in her day, although she was always recognized by other poets as an indomitable, playful, and ever-challenging genius. Most of her works, their manuscripts neatly typed by Alice, were not published during her lifetime, even in Paris. They are now available in the eight-volume *Yale Edition of the Unpublished Writings* (1951–58).

Consult: Richard Bridgman, *Gertrude Stein in Pieces* (1970); Robert Bartlett Haas, *A Primer for the Gradual Understanding of Gertrude Stein* (1971); Bruce Kellner, *A Gertrude Stein Companion: Content with the Example* (1988); Donald Sutherland, *Gertrude Stein, a biography of her work* (1971).

JUDITH M. BRUGGER

STEIN, Sylvester. Born in South Africa; he lives in London. Scion of a distinguished Jewish family in South Africa and nephew of one of South Africa's most celebrated authors, Sarah Gertrude Millin, Stein left South Africa in the late 1950s as a protest against his country's racial edicts and his government's conservative political policies. He wrote two lively accounts of life in South Africa, portraying the daily regimen of prejudice in a humorous manner that brought attention to the stoic patience of the black victims of such sufferings.

STEINER, George Francis. Born April 23, 1929, in Paris, France; he lives in England but is an American citizen. Steiner is a comparatist in his national and group identities as well as in his literary training. His parents were Austrian; he grew up in France; he emigrated to the United States in 1940 and became an American citizen in 1944. He first studied at American universities—he received a B.A. from the University of Chicago in 1948 and briefly attended Harvard University graduate school before receiving a Rhodes scholarship in 1952 for study at Bailliol College, Oxford University; he has also studied at the Sorbonne. He speaks many languages and knows the literature of most European countries.

He has identified with Central Europe as well as Western Europe and has studied Eastern European culture with an avid eye. Steiner is a traditionalist in his plea for preservation of humanism, but also an observer of radical modes of expression, some of which he champions. He has written much on silence as a just mechanism of expression, and on semantics as a means of signifying the history of ideas. Steiner has also written fiction—his novella, *The Portage of San Cristobal of A.H.* (1979) has been dramatized and translated widely.

Steiner has singled out exile writers—among them Vladimir Nabokov* and Samuel Beckett*—as figures who can lead humanity into new spheres of language and insight. By the experience of exile a writer comes to a re-invigoration of perspective through distance and a re-objectification of events. (See Steiner's *Extraterritorial: Papers on Literature and the Language Revolution,* 1971).

Selected Titles: *Tolstoy or Dostoevsky: An Essay in Old Criticism* (1959); *The Death of Tragedy* (1961); *Language and Silence: Essays on Language, Literature and the Inhuman* (1967); *In Bluebeard's Castle: Some Notes toward the Redefinition of Culture* (1971); *After Babel: Aspects of Language and Translation* (1975); *Martin Heidegger* (1978); *Real Presences* (1989).

Consult: Hayden Carruth, "Fallacies of Silence," *Hudson Review* 26 (1973); Alvin H. Rosenfeld, "On Reading George Steiner," *Midstream,* February 1972.

STOW, Randolph. Born November 28, 1935, in Geraldton, West Australia; he lives in Sussex, England. Stow grew up in West Australia and very early began producing novels and poetry tied strongly to that landscape of stark light and distance. His first novel appeared when he was twenty-one; his third, *To the Islands,* won the Miles Franklin Award for 1958. That work, along with the novels, *Tourmaline* (1963) and *The Merry-Go-Round in the Sea* (1965), and the poems of *Outrider* (1963), is considered his finest writing. Of his novels since 1965, only *Visitants* (1979) shows the extraordinary grace of the earlier works: it is a sad possibility that Stow's career may have reached its peak before he was thirty.

Since the mid–1970s, Stow has lived in England; the move was symptomatic. His early works evoke the West Australian landscape and its effects upon individuals in concrete terms; Stow evidenced a strong interest in exploring the aboriginal and white myths that developed there. At the same time, the cause of suffering among Stow's characters lies in their inability to connect the various aspects of their personalities—to commit themselves to their identities, to find wholeness within themselves and within their environment. *To the Islands,* *Merry-Go-Round,* and *Visitants* support such conflicts with the strength and beauty of their authorial vision. But in *Tourmaline,* the characters and the land become representations of Taoist postures. *The Girl Green as a Elderflower* (1979) and *The Suburbs of Hell* (1984) are less than successful in intertwining dark English mythology and gritty modern life. Stow lays claim to a most difficult literary territory: the depiction of characters whose pain is at once highly personal and culturally archetypal, with no loss either of individuality or of general significance. When it lives up to its claim, his writing is harrowingly beautiful. When it does not, the implications of disintegration—perhaps personal—are as dreadful as any of the grim landscapes of the soul that Stow has elsewhere drawn so well.

Had he written nothing since 1965, Stow would still be a major figure in Australian literature. His works are frequently discussed in Australian and Commonwealth journals; he discusses himself in an interview with John B. Beston, *World Literature Written in English* 14 (1975).

Consult: Ray Willbanks, *Randolph Stow* (1978).

JOHN SCHECKTER

STROZ, Daniel. Born April 8, 1943, in Pilsen, Czechoslovakia; he lives in Munich, Germany. Stroz left his country in 1968; he currently heads the exile art magazine *Obrys-Kontur* in Munich. In 1977 he founded the publishing house, Poetry Away from the Home, to publish original Czech work in the West both in Czech and German. He has published his own poems in many journals and in Czech exile magazines in West Germany, Switzerland, and the United States.

Selected Titles: *Dlan plna nadeji* (Munich, 1974; *The Palm Full of Hopes*, 1975); *Zpovednice a moje hvezda* (Munich, 1975, The Confessional and My Star); *Svice do rana* (Munich, 1977, Candle Till the Morning); *Orgie smutku* (Munich, 1978, The Orgy of Sadness).

ANDREJ VLCEK

SU Wei. Born 1953 in China; he lives in exile. During the Cultural Revolution Su was sent to work in the countryside for ten years. In 1978 he was allowed to study at Zhong Shan University in Guandong Province. He studied at the University of California–Los Angeles from 1982 to 1984, where he earned a master's degree in literature. He was a visiting scholar at the Fairbanks Center of Harvard University from 1984 to 1986. From 1987 to June 1989 he served as deputy director of the Department of New Schools of Literary Theory in the Institute for Literary Studies of the Chinese Academy of Social Sciences. He was at this post when the government began its repressive crackdown of the prodemocracy movement. He escaped from China in June 1989.

Consult: PEN American Center Factsheet Program, October 3, 1989.

SU Xiaokang. Born in China; lives in exile in Paris, France. Su is the author of the screenplays for the controversial series "River Elegy," which have come under fire by Chinese officials.

SVIRSKY, Gregory Caesarivich. Born 1921 in Ufa, Bashkiria (foothills of the Ural Mountains, about 600 miles east of Moscow), USSR. In 1922 his family moved to Moscow. He lives in Toronto, Canada. Svirsky completed his studies at the Philological Institute of Moscow University before participating in World War II as an aviation mechanic at a station beyond the Arctic Circle. He took part in the defense of American convoys carrying military cargo into the USSR. For his service, he was awarded military honors.

Svirsky's first-published book, *A Commandment of Friendship* (Moscow, 1947), in which the rigors of military life at a frontline aerodrome are described, was altered by Soviet censors. Censorship of Svirsky's work became more severe when he attempted to publish a scenario in which the protagonist was a Soviet officer thrown into a penal battalion during wartime. In its disfigured state, the scenario *Savage Land* was published in the magazine the *Art of Cinema* (no. 2, 1966).

At the beginning of the 1960s, during the period of the "thaw," Svirsky managed to publish a novel that he personally characterized as a book "about the slavish silence and absence of rights of the working class in the workers' government." According to Svirsky, he succeeded in having it reprinted by affixing an "orthodox" title to it: *Lenin Prospect* ([Lenin Boulevard], Moscow, 1962).

Accepted into the Union of Writers of the USSR, Svirsky twice took advantage of official meetings of the organization to make public denunciations of censorship and of anti-Semitism in the USSR. In a speech in 1968, delivered in the presence of a prominent Party official, he said, "We are so accustomed to lying that we no longer are concerned with even a shade of verisimilitude. We pull into our falsehoods writers who are compelled to speak untruths, to lie in the course of lofty discipline. . . . The writer is belittled, robbed of the most important of his responsibilities, to step forth with his inner thoughts and feelings, and expose them to the public." The text of Svirsky's speech was published in *Le Monde*, the Paris newspaper, on April 28, 1968, and later reprinted in many European and American journals. Svirsky feared arrest, but, instead, became a banned writer expelled from the Communist party, which he had joined during the war. His books were withdrawn from libraries, and he was asked to emigrate or face imprisonment. He left the USSR in 1972 with his wife and son.

Earlier in the 1960s Svirsky had visited several Soviet labor campsites in the northern provinces, which, during the Stalinist era, had achieved notoriety as concentration camps—Oukhta, Vorkuta, Norelsk, Taichet. The experience is reflected in a number of Svirsky's stories, longer fiction, and articles, among them *Polar Tragedy*, published first in the West in the original Russian (West Germany, 1976) and then translated into French and published in Montreal, Canada, in 1978. In this work he showed his skill at recording working-class slang. While under the surveillance of the KGB he wrote, in Moscow, another book, the documentary novel *The Hostages*, which narrated an account of the fate of Russian Jews caught in the 1940s between two oppressors, Hitler and Stalin. The manuscript of the novel was smuggled into Western Europe, and printed first in Paris in the Russian version, then translated into French, English, and Hebrew (Paris, 1974; London and New York, 1976; Tel Aviv, 1978).

The Hostages earned a wide reputation for Svirsky. His following book, *Place of Execution: The Literature of Moral Resistance, 1946–1976*, a survey of modern Soviet literature, also brought attention and praise. The Russian-language newspaper in Paris, *Russian Thought*, paid tribute to his position that while literature is rare in the Soviet Union as a result of the inhibitions of state censorship, it is not impossible. In his study, Svirsky disputed the claims of Aleksandr Solzhenitsyn,* that literature did not exist in the USSR from the 1930s to the 1950s and that writing that does not tell the whole truth is not literature [see *Gulag Archipelago*]. Svirsky posited that a serious body of work came into fruition in the USSR even under the duress of censorship, but at a heavy price for the writer and the reader. Warning of the dangers of a repressive system, in whatever rationalizations of its goals, Svirsky quoted another Soviet writer, Nikolai Berdyaev: "Nationalism always results in tyranny." *Russian Thought* summarized its view of Svirsky's book in this manner: "a compass in the ocean of post-war Soviet literature." (*Place of Execution* was first published in London in the Russian version; an English translation appeared in 1981.)

Svirsky turned to ethnic roots in his later novel, *Breakout* (Tenafly, New Jersey, 1983), in which he renders a fictional account of Soviet Jews who seek refuge in Israel in the 1970s and encounter further problems of identity. A controversial work, the novel has been called a "document-novel" because while the individual characters are the stuff of fiction, they are created out of factual detail and the history of the period and locale. One critic, Y. Rabkin, wrote of it:

Written in Russian and devoted *prima facie* to Soviet Jewry, *Breakout* is in fact a powerful and compassionate picture of contemporary Israel. If translated into Hebrew and English, this book is likely to attract attention in Israel and in the "Anglo-Saxon" diasporas and to become a source of healthy controversy. It is the love of Israel, or in its more generous Hebrew term *Ahavath-Israel*, that makes Svirsky inflict pain on himself and his readers in the hope that the resulting catharsis will be a step forward toward redemption. (*Middle East Focus* [Montreal, Canada] 18, no. 1 [May 1985]) (At present *Breakout* is available in the Russian edition [1983] and in a Hebrew-language edition issued in 1989.)

Svirsky completed another documentary novel, *Parting With Russia*, in 1985. Now a Canadian citizen, he recently managed to retrieve from the Soviet Union a manuscript of a novel he had written there about anti-Semitic activities of Soviet authorities. The novel has been scheduled for publication in the USSR, but censors in 1968 forbade its release. Svirsky is planning to publish in the West this banned work under the title *The Forbidden Novel*.

Selected Title: *Na lobnom meste: Literatura nranstvennogo soprotivleniya 1946–1976* (London, 1979; *A History of Post-War Soviet Writers: The Literature of Moral Opposition*, Ann Arbor, Michigan, 1981).

MARK A. POPOVSKY, translated by Zoric Ward

SZASZ, Bela (pseudonym in English, Vincent Savarius). Born July 9, 1910, in Szombathely, Hungary; he lives in London. While a student of foreign affairs at the Technical University of Budapest and of French and Hungarian languages and literatures at the University of Budapest, Szasz published poems, short stories, and articles in leading Hungarian journals such as *Korunk* (Our Time),

Szabadon (Freely), and *Kortárs* (Contemporary) as well as in the leftist student newspaper *Virradat* (Daybreak). Later he also studied at the Sorbonne in Paris. In Hungary he was one of the initiators of the student communist movement, and in 1932 he was arrested and sentenced to three months in prison. In 1937 he emigrated to Paris and served on the editorial board of the Paris-based Hungarian journal *Üzenet* (Message). In 1939 he traveled to Argentina, where he lived until 1946, working as a correspondent for the *Délamerikai Magyarság* (South American Hungarians). During the war he was editor of the antifascist weekly *Új Világ* (New World) and contributed to several other antifascist papers. Following his 1946 return to Hungary, he became the editor of *Képes Hét* (Pictorial Weekly) and *Jövendö* (Future). In 1948 he became an official at the Ministry of Foreign Affairs and was soon appointed press secretary of the Ministry of Agriculture. In May of 1949, in connection with the show trial of László Rajk, he was arrested and sentenced to ten years of prison as an alleged Western spy. After his release in 1954 he became literary advisor to several publishing houses. During this time he revised Vilmos Göry's nineteenth-century translation of *Don Quixote*, from which he wrote several popular radio plays; translated into Hungarian some of the novels of Benito Pérez Galdós and Theodore Fontane; and edited several short story anthologies for which he wrote introductory studies. Leaving Hungary after the 1956 Revolution, he settled in London, where he still resides. His post–1957 activities include correspondent to the Paris-based *Irodalmi Ujság* (Literary Gazette); editor of the Brussels-based *Szemle* (Review); translator into Hungarian of M. Djilas's *Conversations with Stalin*. In 1963 he published an account of his imprisonment and torture during the Rakosi period entitled *Minden kényszer nélkul* (Without Constraints). In the same year the book appeared in German and French; later it was published in English under the title *Volunteers for the Gallows* (1971). Szasz's work is a significant description of the workings of a police state and of the methods used in show trials. It is more than a personal account of one man's refusal to capitulate to torture; it is a valuable record of some of the broader ramifications of the political trials of the Stalinist period in Hungarian history, especially that of László Rajk.

AGNES HUSZAR VARDY

T ───────────────────────

TABORI, Paul. Born May 8, 1908, in Budapest, Hungary; died in 1974, in London, England, of heart failure. The son of a well-known journalist, Tabori graduated from the Zrinyi *gimnazium* (high school) in 1926, received a diploma in theatrical art from the F. Wilhelm University in Berlin in 1930, and a Juris Doctor degree from the Royal Hungarian University in Budapest in 1932. He was on the staff of the periodicals *Magyarország* (Hungary) and *Szinházi élet* (Theater Life) in Budapest and became a roving correspondent for Central European newspapers from 1926 to 1932. After founding and operating the Mid-European Literary Service from 1932 to 1937, he settled in London in 1937 to work for the British Broadcasting Company; he later became a British citizen. He also worked for several newspapers as film critic and diplomatic correspondent, and was a European correspondent for Reuters. He wrote filmscripts for producer Alexander Korda from 1943 to 1948. He organized and coproduced "A Day of Peace" international film series, in which fourteen nations of various political allegiances participated.

Tabori's major contributions to literature came in organizational work for International PEN, the British Screenwriters Guild, the English PEN Centre, and the Center for Writers in Exile. He was instrumental in founding the International Writers Guild, but is best remembered for his founding work for the PEN Writers in Prison Committee. He wrote, in English, 30 feature films, over 100 documentaries, contributed to 200 newspapers, and wrote and/or edited 100 books, including such titles as *Epitaph for Europe, The Art of Folly, A Century of Assassins, The Companions of the Unseen, Harry Price Ghosthunter, Alexander Korda, Maria Theresa, Doomsday Brain*, and *Song of the Scorpion*. His study of exile, *The Anatomy of Exile* (1972), remains a respected text and a pioneering work. He used pen names like Peter Stafford (his son's name is Peter, and Tabori lived on Stafford Terrace in Kensington in London), Christopher Steven, and Petronius. In 1960 he received the Medal of the City of Paris, and in 1964 the Zita Award of the British Screenwriters Guild. He lectured frequently at American colleges and universities. He was in the midst of preparations for a lecture tour in Africa when he succumbed to a heart attack.

Selected Titles: *Lighter Than Vanity: A Novel of Hollywood* (London, 1953); *Twenty Tremendous Years 1939–1960* (London, 1962); *Dress and Undress: The Sexology of Fashion* (1969); *The Social History of Rape* (London, 1971); *Pioneers of the Unseen* (1972).

DESI K. BOGNÁR

TARN, Adam. Born October 20, 1902, in Lodz, Poland; died June 23, 1975, in Lausanne, Switzerland. Son of a lawyer, Tarn spent his childhood in Switzerland, and after graduating from high school in Zurich, studied in Warsaw and Lille, where he earned his doctorate in economics in 1926. During the following ten years he wrote fiction and journalism. He went to Geneva in 1937, and received his Ph.D. in philosophy there in 1939. At the outbreak of World War II he was in France; there he joined the Polish Army in Exile. In 1940 he fled to the United States, where he resided until 1949, working for, among others, the Secretariat of the United Nations. Upon returning to Poland, he was at first an employee of the Ministry of Foreign Affairs, then literary manager of three Warsaw theaters, and in 1956 became editor-in-chief of the Warsaw drama journal *Dialog*. During the purge of the intellectuals following the student protests of March 1968, Tarn, who refused to sign a resolution condemning his writer-colleagues, was dismissed from his post at *Dialog*. Shortly thereafter he emigrated to Canada and made an unsuccessful attempt to found a drama journal to be published in French and English. In bad health, he moved to Switzerland and died there before finishing a book on Anton Chekhov's drama.

In exile (1969–75), Tarn published several articles on drama, among them "Witkiewicz, Artaud and the Theatre of Cruelty," in *Comparative Drama* (Fall 1969); translations into Polish of Samuel Beckett's *Happy Days* (with his wife, Mary Tarn); and an anthology of American contemporary drama that he had translated into Polish.

His literary works, a prewar novel and several plays written during the 1950s— *Zwykla sprawa* (1950, A Normal Affair), *Ortega* (1952), *Stajnia Augiasza* (1954, Augeas's Stables), *Zmarnowane zycie* (1958, A Wasted Life)— are not of major importance, but he influenced and shaped the course of Polish theater as editor of *Dialog*. The monthly was created in the wake of new cultural institutions at a time of political relaxation in 1956, when a certain amount of experimentation was permitted after the period of total subordination of literature to political goals, 1949–55. Tarn's immediate accomplishment was the introduction to (through translations published in *Dialog*) the works of major contemporary Western dramatists, notably Jean-Paul Sartre, Albert Camus, Friedrich Duerrenmatt, Samuel Beckett,* Eugène Ionesco,* Arthur Adamov, and Harold Pinter.

He should also be credited with making possible the reemergence of Poland's own avant-garde tradition in theater and promoting new writers who discarded naturalistic conventions and the facile optimism of the "factory" and "collective farm" drama prescribed by socialist realism doctrine.

MAREK KEDZIERSKI

TARNAVS'KYJ, Ostap. Born May 3, 1917, in Lviv, Ukraine; he resides in Philadelphia. Tarnavs'kyj began his career as a poet and journalist in 1935. In 1944 he emigrated to Austria, where his first collection of poems, *Slova i mriji* (Words and Dreams), was published in Salzburg in 1948. Laden with a romantic yearning for his lost Ukraine and with an irrepressible *weltschmerz*, Tarnavs'kyj's poetry of that period reflects his exile existence, but it is not without optimism. The collection concludes with these lines: "Somewhere there is joy in this wide world / Somewhere there is happiness pre-ordained for us." Tarnavs'kyj's emigration to the United States in 1949 reinvigorated his literary and journalistic energies. He contributed to numerous émigré journals and newspapers, published several collections of poems and prose studies, and was elected (1975) president of SLOVO, the Ukrainian Writers' Association in Exile. His *Mosty* (Bridges), a collection of poems published in New York in 1956, is a synthesis of his turbulent exile and his past and present life as poet and intellectual. During the course of the last decade his poetry has assumed a more satiric tone, perhaps owing to his collaboration with the Detroit-based Ukrainian humor magazine, *Lys Mykyta* (Mykyta the Fox). He has also translated poems by Shakespeare, Eliot, and Rilke into Ukrainian.

Tarnavs'kyj's most recent collection, *Sotnja sonetiv* (1984, A Hundred Sonnets), is comprised of philosophic verse and individual poems written to old friends, in which the theme of exile plays a secondary role.

Selected Titles: *Zyttija* (1952, Life), sonnet sequence; *Samotnje derevo: poeziji* (1960, The Lonely Tree), poetry; *Kaminni stupeni: novely* i *narysy* (1979, Stone Steps), stories.

Consult: Bohdan Bojčuk and Bohdan T. Rubčak, *Koordynaty* (Munich, 1969, 2: 175–82, a comprehensive and annotated anthology of contemporary Ukrainian poetry written in the West); Frances Carol Locher, ed. *Contemporary Authors* (1978), a bio-bibliographical guide to current writers; George Grabowicz, "New Directions in Ukrainian Poetry in the United States," and Leonid Rudnytzky, "Commentary," in *The Ukrainian Experience in the United States. A Symposium*, ed. Paul R. Magocsi (1979), an analytical survey of Ukrainian émigré poetry since 1945 with a commentary and supplement by L. Rudnytzky; Marta Tarnavs'ka, ed., *Ostap Tarnavs'kyj: Bibliohrafičnyj pokažčyk* (1980), a complete biobibliographical guide to the author's works.

LEONID RUDNYTZKY

TARSIS, Valery. Born 1906 in Russia; he lives in the Federal Republic of Germany. Tarsis left the USSR in 1966, after serving time in a psychiatric hospital for activities against the interests of the state. He recorded this experience in *Palata No. 7* (Frankfurt, 1965; *Ward 7*, 1965). In exile he has continued his chronicle format and realistic style; he has published several novels and an autobiography describing conditions within the Soviet Union.

Selected Title: *Skazanie o siney mukhe* (Frankfurt, 1962; *The Bluebottle*, 1962).

Consult: David Lowe, *Russian Writing Since 1953* (1987).

TAUNS, Linard. Born 1922 in Latvia; died July 30, 1968, in the United States. For their subtle blend of accessibility and deeper meaning, Tauns's published poems, while small in number, have been accorded international stature by critics. He was evacuated from his homeland by the German occupation forces in 1944. After Germany's defeat he remained a displaced person in that country until 1950, when he emigrated to the United States. He died, it has been said, of a broken heart when he was forty-one years old.

TCHICAYA U Tam'si (born Gerald Felix Tchicaya). Born August 25, 1931, in M' Pili, Republic of the Congo; died April 23, 1988, in Paris, France. Tchicaya came to Paris in 1946 with his father, who was a delegate to the French National Assembly, and attended French schools. He began working for UNESCO in Paris in 1960. A major poet, he also wrote several plays of high repute. He was awarded the Grand Prix des Lettres of the Congo Republic in 1978.

Tchicaya's work is demanding, taking its sources from African mythology and European forms, and drawing on concepts from both European and African history. Although an expatriate and a highly literate writer, he returned to African folk legend for source material and invigoration of style. His treatment of such materials was, however, intellectualized and independent of recognized tribal custom. Tchicaya remained in his own view a committed African writer, one who treated issues of his country and of his continent for wider exposure in the Western world and who felt free to expropriate Western spheres of literary influence in his own kingdom of Central African fabulism and realism.

Selected Titles: Poetry: *Le mauvais sang* (1955); *Feu de brousse* (1957); *A triche-coeur* (1960); *Epitome*, with introduction by Léopold Sédar Senghor (1962); *Le Ventre* (1964); *L'arc musical* (1969). Plays: *La veste d'interieur* suivi de *Notes de vielle* (Paris, 1977); *Le Zulu* suivi de *Vivene le fondateur* (Paris, 1977); *Le ventre* suivi *Le Pain ou la cendre; Le destin glorieux du Maréchal Nnikou Nniku Prince qu'on soit: comédie-farce-sinistre en trois plans* (Paris, 1979). Novel: *Les Cancrelats* (Paris, 1980). Translations: *Brush-Fire* (1971), selections from his first five collections; *Selected Poems*, ed. Gerald Moore (London, 1970).

Consult: Gerald Moore, *Twelve African Writers* (1980); Per Wastberg, ed., *The Writer in Modern Africa* (1969).

TEKEYAN, Vahan. Born January 21, 1878, in Constantinople, Turkey (now Istanbul); died April 4, 1945, in Cairo, Egypt. Tekeyan was the youngest of five children of Elizabeth and Calouste Tekeyan. He did not finish secondary school and at age sixteen began working with an insurance firm. The firm transferred him to England two years later on the eve of Turkish Sultan Abdul Hamid's 1896 massacres of the Armenians. He lived in France and Germany before moving to Egypt in 1904, where he began publishing the literary monthly *Shirag*. In 1909 he became editor of *Shirag* in Constantinople, and in 1913–14 he was a principal and a teacher for many Armenian schools in Turkey. It was only by chance that he survived the 1915 genocide committed by the Young Turk government against the Armenians, in which nearly two million lives were lost. As a poet, he would have been among the first to be executed, as were his fellow poets, Siamanto (pseudonym of Adom Yarjanian) and Daniel Varoujan. However, he had been sent to Jerusalem as a representative of the Armenian National Parliamentary Council to settle a church dispute, and at the outbreak of World War I, he left Jerusalem for Cairo, where he followed the reports of the Turkish government's rapidly developing genocide plans.

From 1915 until his death he was a poet without a homeland. He made Cairo his home base, but his important role in Armenian politics, culture, and letters took him to France, Bulgaria, Greece, Syria, and Lebanon during the decades following the genocide. In particular, he played an important role in supervising Armenian refugee homes and orphanages. In 1949 the Committee for the Tekeyan Publication Fund was formed to publish his complete works.

Tekeyan's poems suggest the pain the poet felt for his people and the responsibility of the survivor/escapee of a massacre to provide a record of history before it is forgotten. His poems reflect Armenia's anguish, guilt, torment, and helplessness. Yet his qualities of outrage and anguish are welded to the starkness of his metaphors, the elliptical, meditative quality of his voice, and to his extraordinary ability to speak about a tragic history without surrendering to self-indulgence, sentimentality, or factual one-dimensionality. In this sense he bears a resemblance to poets like Czeslaw Miłosz* and Cesar Abraham Vallejo.*

Tekeyan's poems are filled with the haunting silence that comes from a life of exile. In one of his masterpieces, "On a Sonato of Beethoven's," he brings together an apocalyptic sense of loss, a comprehension of time and space that is both metaphysical and historical, and a dimension of aesthetic experience in which art serves as a ballast in the face of ruin. His music is distinctive and original, his sensibility intricate, and his imagination rooted in the largest moral concerns of our time.

Selected Titles: *Burdens* (1901); *Miraculous Birth* (1914); *From Midnight Until Dawn* (1919); *Love* (1934); *Song of Armenia* (1943); *Odes* (1944); *Vahan Tekeyan: Selected Poems* (1981); *Sacred Wrath: The Selected Poems of Vahan Tekeyan* (1982).

PETER BALAKIAN

THEMBA, Can (Daniel Canadoce Themba). Born 1924 in Marabastad in northern Transvaal, South Africa; died 1968 in Manzini, Swaziland, of complications from alcoholism. After graduating from Fort Hare University College as a scholarship student in 1947, Themba began teaching English. He became a journalist in 1953 when a story he entered in a contest won the prize award, and several other pieces were subsequently published in journals. He worked as an editor for *Drum* and the *Golden City Post*, both in Johannesburg. In 1968 he went into voluntary exile to Swaziland with his family and returned to his first profession, teaching. His works were subsequently banned in South Africa. Lewis Nkosi, a friend and colleague, wrote in an obituary:

Can Themba's actual achievements are . . . disappointing because his learning and reading were . . . substantial and his talent proven; but he chose to confine his brilliance to journalism of an insubstantial kind. It is almost certain that had Can Themba chosen to write a book on South Africa, it would not only have been an interesting . . . book, but it might have revealed a complex and refined talent for verbalizing the African mood. And no doubt, such a book would have been a valuable addition to the literature of South Africa. As it is, we mourn a talent largely misused or neglected; we mourn what might have been. But to have known Themba, to have heard him speak, is to have known a mind both vigorous and informed, shaped by the city as few other minds are in the rest of Africa. (Can Themba, *The Will To Die*, [London, 1972], pp. x–xi).

Themba's only published volume, *The Will To Die* (London, 1972), appeared posthumously, edited by Donald Stuart and Roy Holland.

Consult: Michael Chapman, ''Can Themba, Storyteller and Journalist of the 1950s: The Text in Context,'' *English in Africa* 16, no. 2 (October 1989); Lewis Nkosi, *Home and Exile, and Other Selections* (Essex, England, 1983); Essop Patel, ed., *The World of Can Themba* (1985).

THEROUX, Paul. Born in the United States, he lives half the year in London and half the year in New York. Theroux has been a peripatetic writer since his early days in the Peace Corps. He has been an indefatigable travel writer, sojourning in various lands as he observed foreign customs and collected notes for many books of reportage. He is also a fiction writer whose themes invariably circle round his own and his characters' psychic marginality and their obsession with double, secret living. His recent work, the autobiographical novel *My Secret History* (1989), exemplifies Theroux's sense of exilic identity: his protagonist Andre Parent lives half the year in England, half the year in the United States. He has a mate in each city (in one a wife; in the other, a faithful mistress). Unable to commit himself to one at the expense of surrendering the other, his protagonist refuses a transcendence of the double/doppleganger obsession; instead he insists on the stubborn blinders of his solipsistic perspective of moral behavior. The influence of Catholicism, Joseph Conrad*, Graham Greene,* and the alienation of modernism, stand paramount in his work, and make him, like his literary idols Conrad and Greene, a writer who continues to portray the temptations of a code of morality he continues to resist.

Theroux admits that he, as author, bears a resemblance to the protagonist of *My Secret History* —each was an altar boy, a life guard, a volunteer teacher in Africa—but he claims the resemblance ends in the display of background facts. He asserts that the writer's usage of such facts goes beyond biographic exploitation and/or exposure, and further claims that *My Secret History* was an obsession from which he needed to be released through an immersion into its labyrinthine mazes.

Selected Title: *Riding the Iron Rooster: By Train Through China* (1988); *Sandstorms: Days and Nights in Arabia* (1990); *Chicago Loop* (1990).

TOLLER, Ernst. Born December 1, 1893, in Samotschin, Prussia, Germany (today Szamocin, Poland); committed suicide May 22, 1939, in New York. Toller was both a politically conscious writer, whose major medium of expression was drama, and a social activist, who fought with courage for political objectives. As a member of the Jewish minority in his mostly German, partly Polish, hometown, he developed a strong sense of social justice, and as a volunteer frontline soldier on the western front in World War I, he underwent a lasting conversion from militant patriotism to universal pacifism. After his dismissal from active military duty on the basis of ailing health, he used his oratorical skills in support of striking workers in an ammunitions factory in Munich; he was arrested for his activism. After the revolution of 1918, Toller became a member of Kurt Eisner's separatist socialist government in Bavaria, and, after the latter's assassination, the chairman of the short-lived First Bavarian Räterepublik. Following the overthrow of the Second (communist) Räterepublik by the conservative majority socialist politicians of Bavaria, which was aided by federal German troops, Toller was again arrested and sentenced to five years in prison.

During his prison term from 1919 to 1924, he wrote and published a number of his most successful works, among them the dramas *Die Wandlung* (1920, Transfiguration), depicting the protagonist's development from a German patriot to a pacifist humanist; *Masse-Mensch* (1920, Masses and Man), expressing the conflict between an individualist humanist (a woman) and the nameless representative of the masses (a man) who sets all his faith in the exertion of political power; *Die Manchinenstürmer* (1922, The Machine Wreckers), a Marxist interpretation of the 1915 revolt of the Luddites in England; and *Hinkemann* (1923, Brokenbrow), a chronicle of the unhappy experiences of a cripple emasculated in the war who tries to make a living during the Weimar Republic against the odds of a disloyal wife and widespread unemployment. Toller's dramas show typical stylistic features of the expressionist movement, such as station play, visionary subjectivism, and grotesque exaggeration of nonindividualistic human types. During the years between his release from prison and his final departure from Germany after Adolf Hitler's assumption of power, Toller published several more dramas, including the comedy *Hoppla, wir leben* (1927, Hoppla), written in the style of the new reportorial matter-of-factness, and his autobiography, *Eine Jugend in Deutschland* (1933, I Was a German).

In his exile years when he lived in England but also traveled extensively in other countries, only two books were published under his name. The first is the comedy *Nie wieder Friede*, first published in English as *No More Peace!* (1937). Though the plot in which Napoleon sends St. Francis a declaration of war from heaven was meant as a warning against Hitler, it did not meet with success. Toller's other exile drama is a tragedy, *Pastor Hall* (1939), which depicts the conflicts between a Christian cleric, who adheres to Christ's command of love and peace, and National Socialist authorities in Germany. The quality of these exile dramas falls short of the achievement of his pre-exile works, the first because of its contrived didacticism, and the second because of its insufficient acquaintance with social conditions in Nazi Germany. Perhaps Toller's more significant role in exile was not that of a writer, but of an orator, a skill that he had already developed before exile and that he now extended to foreign audiences. His speech before the PEN Club Congress of Ragusa (today Dubrovnic) caused the Nazi-controlled German Chapter of PEN to leave the Congress in protest and ultimately led to the formation of a separate German PEN Club in Exile chapter in London. A year later, Toller repeated his attack on German intellectuals in Hitler's service at the International PEN Club Congress in Edinburgh, and similarly in 1938 in Paris, and in 1939 in New York. In 1938 he started a one-man mission to help civilians in war-torn Spain. In 1939, after Franco's victory, Toller committed suicide in a moment of both personal and political despair in his New York hotel room. Although the news of his death came as a shock, it served as Toller's legacy of commitment in the fight against totalitarianism.

Consult: Malcolm Pitlock, *Ernst Toller* (1979); John M. Spalek, *Ernst Toller and His Critics* (1968, contains bibliography).

HELMUT F. PFANNER

TORBERG, Friedrich (pseudonym of Friedrich Kantor-Berg). Born September 16, 1908 in Vienna, Austria; died November 10, 1979, in Vienna. Torberg's work is distinguished by his three identities: Austrian, Jew, writer of German literature. His early work is marked by an optimism toward the challenges facing youth. His first novel, *Der Schüler Gerber hat absolviert* (1930; new version *Der Schüler Gerber*, 1954) proved an immediate success, and remains popular today in its many translations. Torberg also published another popular novel concerning youth and the bittersweet triumphs of athletic discipline and sports competition, *Die Mannschaft* (1935). When he fled Austria in 1938 to avoid incarceration in a concentration camp for the crime of Jewishness, he lost some of his buoyant spirit and defense of universalism. His sense of identity as a Jew grew more invidious and remained a part of his consciousness after his return to Austria. Although he grew more genial in his post-World War II period, he was resolute and earnest in Jewish matters and Austria's share of responsibility for the Holocaust. A comparison of his work written during and after his exile experiences—among them *Mein ist die Rache* (Munich/Vienna, 1947; published earlier in English, 1943, *Vengeance Is Mine*); *Hier bich ich, mein Vater* (written 1943–46, published Munich/Vienna, 1948, Here I am, My Father), a novelistic treatment of Jews living in Germany and their varied exploits of courage, cowardice and suffering; and *Golems Wiederkehr* (1968, Munich, Vienna, Return of the Golem), a view of his native Bohemia from both the levels of geography and of artistic spirit—with the apolitical mode of his early fiction is striking.

Torberg found temporary haven in Switzerland in 1938; he moved to France where he volunteered for duty and served in the French army from 1940 to 1941, and reached the United States in 1941 via Spain and Portugal. After a ten-year exile, he returned to Austria, where he founded and edited a cultural journal, *Forum*. The journal, and Torberg's writing during this period, reflects a reborn, if sobered, optimism about the possibility of goodness in human behavior.

Selected Titles: *Die zweite Begegnung* (Munich, 1963); *PPP: Pamphlete, Parodien, Post Scripta* (Munich, 1964 [Briefer Writings]).

Consult: Herbert Ahl, *Literarische Portraits* (1962); Herbert Eisenreich in *Handbook of Austrian Literature*, ed. Frederick Ungar (1973).

TRAN thi Nga. Born August 27, 1927, in Kunming, China; she came to the United States in 1975, and lives in Cos Cob, Connecticut. *Tran* is Madame Nga's family name. *Thi* means *female*. *Nga*, meaning *swan*, is her given name. She is Vietnamese and Buddhist. To the dismay of her traditional family, Tran received a degree in social work from Swansea University (South Wales) in 1966. Twice married and widowed, with four living children, Tran presently works for *Time* magazine. As the only woman working for *Time*'s Vietnam bureau in 1968–75, Tran met poet (and future coauthor) Wendy Wilder Larsen, whom she described in an interview with the writer of this entry as "my boss's wife." In their book, *Shallow Graves* (New York, 1986), Tran re-creates her odyssey in eleven cities from Kunming to Cos Cob. Consisting of more than 200 separate lyrics, the poems in *Shallow Graves* are modeled on the Vietnamese *truyen*, a kind of verse novel. Besides its great beauty and emotional intensity, *Shallow Graves* is important for its emphasis on the lives of women and other noncombat personnel, a side of Vietnam's embattled history with which non-Vietnamese are often unfamiliar. Also important is the collaborative nature of its composition, its polyphonic resonance. *Shallow Graves* was composed over a period of about five years, 1980–85, due as much to Tran's desire to preserve something of her cultural identity for her grandchildren as to heal her own wounds. It received over fifty reviews and became a best-seller.

Consult: Terrence Des Pres, "Sisters to Antigone," *Parnassus* 14, no. 1 (1987): 187–200. There are no full-length studies on Tran.

JUDITH M. BRUGGER

TRAVEN, Bruno (pseudonym of Otto Wienecke, who on his parents' marriage became Otto Feige). Born February 23, 1882, in Schwiebus, Germany (now Poland); died March 26, 1969, in Mexico City, Mexico. As an actor Traven adopted, in 1907, the stage name Ret Marut. For his first attempt at fiction, *An das Fräulein von S.* (1916, To Fraulein von S), he used the pseudonym Richard Maurhut. In 1917, because of his contributions to a radical journal *Der Ziegelbrenner* (The Brickmaker), Traven became suspect as a pacifist agitator. On the establishment of the Räterepublik in Munich in 1919, Marut was made press censor, but Traven fled to Vienna when the Republic of Councils was overthrown.

After years of wandering Marut vanished in Mexico in 1924, to reemerge as the mysterious Traven.

As an exemplar of literature in exile, Traven is unusual in that when, already forty, he was compelled to leave Germany, he had shown little effective promise as a writer. It was the impact of Mexico and its alien civilization that fertilized his genius; yet for an author cut off from the German market, prospects must have seemed dim. The foundation in Berlin, in 1924, of the Büchergilde Gutenberg, a book club closely affiliated with the printers' union, was, however, to provide a timely path of reentry to the German publishing world. In 1926 this body sponsored Traven's first major work, *Das Totenschiff* (*The Death Ship*, 1934). An impressive introduction, separately printed in the guild's journal, signals his intentions. Traven believed that the great "fight for freedom" (World War I) had destroyed individual liberty, permitting the enslavement of mankind by entrenched bureaucrats who, whatever their nationality, abetted one another as members of a universal freemasonry. To escape their clutches, the writer should live in remote anonymity and be content to entertain the reader. The underlying tone is one of disillusionment. Ironically, by seeking isolation, Traven fostered rumors regarding his true identity, thus intensifying interest in his works. By 1960, his gross sales in twenty languages had topped 25 million copies.

Apart from *The Death Ship*, all Traven's novels were now to have Mexican settings. The formula is always the same: robust adventure in a hostile environment of sierra or jungle, yielding a stark message of social deprivation and the need to revolt against "the system." The protagonists, too, share a desolate kinship. They are the "little men," whether poor whites or Indian peons, who find themselves no match either for village entrepreneurs or international big business. In the fruitful years 1926–31, Traven published nine titles, including a volume of short stories and his sole travel book, *Land des Frühlings* (1928, Land of Springtime). Luckily, the advent of Hitler in 1933 failed to stop the German production line, which itself went into exile in Zurich, Vienna, and Prague. Six jungle novels ("The Caoba Cycle"), which in substance constitute the core of his achievement, appeared in rapid succession. Natural products (e.g., oil, cotton), viewed as seducers and adversaries, loom large in these books; above all, mahogany (caoba) becomes an almost personified symbol of the tenacity, recalcitrance, and menace of life itself.

Traven's huge success implies a high degree of readability, based on a talent for narration, suspense, and empathy that chimes well with an American tradition stretching from James Fenimore Cooper to Jack London. Yet Traven was primarily a writer in German. As such, he carved out his literary territory, even if a few liberal spirits like Karl Postl (Charles Sealsfield) and Max Dauthendey had previously explored the Mexican locale. Insofar as his writings have specifically German roots, these are to be found in the individualistic philosophy of Max Stirner. Traven may also be compared with notable British Mexico-fanciers like Malcolm Lowry* and Graham Greene.*

Traven's cult of stoicism in the face of inevitable suffering does little to temper the pervasive gloom of his novels. Whether his deromanticized visions of life in the tropics sprang from innate pessimism, sharpened by the debacle of World War I and its aftermath, and to what extent they may have been intensified by an exile initially forced upon him but later self-imposed, must remain matters for conjecture. In Mexico Traven often simulated a man "on the run," only briefly surfacing as "Hal Croves" to supervise the films for which many of his plots were so well adapted. In exile Traven seems to have indulged in mystification for its own sake; the enigma of his elusive personality remains a challenge.

Selected Titles: *Die Baumwollpflücker* (1929; *The Cotton Pickers*, London, 1956); *Der Schatz der Sierra Madre* (1927; *The Treasure of Sierra Madre*, London, 1934); *Die Brücke im Dschungel* (1927; *The Bridge in the Jungle*, 1938); *Die weisse Rose* (1929; *The White Rose*, London, 1965); *Der Karren* (1931; *The Carreta*, London, 1936); *Regierung* (1931; *Government*, London, 1935); *Der Marsch ins Reich der Caoba* (1933; *March to Caobaland*, London, 1960); *Die Rebellion der Gehenkten* (1936; *The Rebellion of the Hanged*, 1952); *Ein General kommt aus dem Dschungel* (1940; *General from the Jungle*, London, 1954). ·

Consult: M. Baumann, *B. Traven: An Introduction* (1976); W. Wyatt, *The Man Who Was B. Traven* (London, 1980).

CEDRIC HENTSCHEL

TRUMBO, Dalton. Born December 5, 1905, in Montrose, Colorado; died September 10, 1976, in Los Angeles, California. While still in high school, Trumbo began writing stories but was unable to sell anything till 1931. His stories range from brief, even anecdotal studies to traditional realistic works focusing on drifters, orphans, handicapped, and others of life's dispossessed. He wrote (but never published) a full-length novel, "Bleak Street," using flashbacks to describe his life working in a bakery and the neighborhood characters.

Following an essay on film, he began working as an editor on a film magazine and in 1935 published his first novel, *Eclipse*, a small-town satiric work compared by the *Times Literary Supplement* to the work of Sinclair Lewis. A second novel, *Washington Jitters* (1936), is both satiric and explicitly socialistic in its thesis. His successful career as a story-writer changed in 1936 when he started working as a screenwriter for Warner Brothers; between that year and his death, he wrote primarily for the screen, though he still turned out pamphlets, three other novels (including the best-known, *Johnny Got His Gun* [1939]), verse, and a play.

In *Johnny Got His Gun* the protagonist is a quadruple amputee also lacking face, hearing, speech, and unable to communicate with others in any recognized form. Trumbo uses flashback extensively in this work since the character has only memory to draw on; he is a living torso with no life aside from intravenous tubes. He does sense others' touching him, and he can gradually sense time of day and even create a kind of code by his head movements resulting in sexual contact with a nurse. Trumbo's strong pacifistic outlook is explicitly stated in the novel's didactic concluding pages.

Trumbo's screenwriting brought him his greatest notice, however, and eventually he became Hollywood's highest paid screenwriter, commanding up to

$75,000 per script. He churned out numerous scripts for Warner's, beginning with *Love Begins at Twenty* (1936) and including *Road Gang* (1936), a controversial social protest film. He moved to RKO in 1938, where he received shared or sole credit for numerous films, notably *Kitty Foyle* (1940; Academy Award nomination); his ability to dramatize the lives of ordinary folk far surpassed that of most Hollywood writers. *Heaven with a Barbed Wire Fence* (1939) was a notable celebration of typical depression types who find utopia in a town settled by Russian immigrants. *Never to Love* (1940) was the first of several films focusing on father-daughter relationships, and *The Last Sunset* (1961), his best in this mode. Trumbo's antifascism led to greater didacticism, and while *The Remarkable Andrew* (1942, based on his own novel) combines preachiness with fantasy, *Tender Comrade* (1943) celebrates a didactic communal ethic and (for MGM) *A Guy Named Joe* (1943) is a vaguely mystical account of a pilot killed in combat coming back from the dead to inspire a new generation. *The Human Comedy* (1943, based on William Saroyan's novel) offered a sentimental celebration of the family; *Thirty Seconds over Tokyo* (1944) celebrated patriotism during wartime; and *Our Vines Have Tender Grapes* (1945) combines small-town sentimentality with a communal message.

In the fall of 1947 Trumbo was summoned before the House Un-American Activities Committee (HUAC) and six months later was convicted of contempt of Congress, for which he served ten months in federal prison (smuggling out pseudonymously written scripts) and after which (1951–53) he went into exile in Mexico with other blacklisted writers. Using various fronts and pseudonyms, he wrote or collaborated on some thirty screenplays in a black market, including *The Prowler* (1951); *The Brave One* (1956), for which he received (under an alias) an Academy Award and which he wrote while in exile; *Wild Is the Wind* (1957); *The Young Philadelphians* (1959); and *Town without Pity* (1961). He also used an alias for his rewriting of Howard Fast's screenplay for *Spartacus* (1960), but when director Otto Preminger announced Trumbo's role in *Exodus* (1960), Trumbo's involvement with *Spartacus* was acknowledged.

Trumbo's thinking about the Holocaust for *Exodus* led to his starting work in 1960 on his novel *Night of the Aurochs* (published posthumously in 1979), a complex antifascist work combining fantasy and the horrors of the Holocaust. He also dealt with Jewish persecution in his adaptation of Bernard Malamud's *The Fixer* (1968), but aside from *Lonely Are the Brave* (1962), his final scripts such as *The Sandpiper* (1965), *Hawaii* (1966), *Executive Action* (1973), and *Papillon* (1973) are considered somewhat less successful than his earlier ones, as is Trumbo's own heavy-handed adaptation and direction of his *Johnny Got His Gun* (1971).

Trumbo was the best-known of the Hollywood Ten and consequently received greater criticism for his political views and "unfriendly" testimony before the HUAC. Hence his being the first to be recognized publicly in 1960 as no longer blacklisted also enabled others to emerge from anonymity and political scandal. Though not all the scripts he wrote while in exile were of the standard of his preblacklisting work, he proved that he could still produce quality work under onerous circumstances. Indeed, much of his later work—from 1960 till his death in 1976—demonstrably includes some of his worst screenplays, dependent as many are on predictable popular tastes and characterizations. At his best, however, as in his work from the 1930s through the mid–1940s, he deftly combined political conviction with artistic skill.

Selected Titles: *The Remarkable Andrew. Being the Chronicle of a Literal Man* (1939); *Harry Bridges: A Discussion of the Latest Effort to Deport Civil Liberties and the Rights of American Labor* (Hollywood: League of American Writers, 1941); *A Guy Named Joe* (1944); *The Devil in the Book* (Los Angeles: California Emergency Defense Committee, 1956); *Additional Dialogue: The Letters of Dalton Trumbo, 1942–1962*, ed. Helen Manfull (1970); *The Time of the Toad: A Study of the Inquisition in America and Two Related Pamphlets* (1972); *Night of the Aurochs*, ed. Robert Kirsch (1979).

Consult: Larry Ceplair and Steven Englund, *The Inquisition in Hollywood: Politics in the Film Community, 1930–1960* (1980); Bruce Cook, *Dalton Trumbo* (1977); Richard Corliss, *Talking Pictures: Screenwriters in the American Cinema* (1975); Bernard F. Dick, *Radical Innocence: A Critical Study of the Hollywood Ten* (1989); Gordon Kahn, *Hollywood on Trial* (1948); Leonard Kriegel, "Dalton Trumbo's *Johnny Got His Gun*," in *Proletarian Writers of the Thirties*, ed. David Madden (1968); Victor Navasky, *Naming Names* (1980); Nancy Lynn Schwartz, *The Hollywood Writers' War* (1982); Robert Vaughn, *Only Victims: A Study of Show Business Blacklisting* (1972).

PAUL SCHLUETER

TSALOUMAS, Dimitris. Born 1930? on Leros, Greece; he lives in Australia. Tsaloumas's early work was written in Greek and was infused with the contours of Greek life, particularly Patmos when he was growing up under the Italian occupation. He emigrated to Australia after the civil war in the 1950s, a move he considered both a self-exile and a new start in life. Tsaloumas decided to make a full break by learning to write in a new language, English. After his exile he also refused to write any further poems about Greece. However, in the past fourteen years he has published more than seven volumes of poetry that reflect his Greek birthplace and his sense of his own Greek past. Some of his poems concern the Greek Resistance and the daily tragedies and comedies under the occupation. Other poems treat in bold language and modern imagery the serious passions of his Greek forebears. His volume *The Book of Epigrams*, published in a Greek-language version in 1982, appeared in English translation in 1985. Another volume, *The Observation: Selected Poems*, written in English, also appeared in 1985.

TSVETAEVA, Marina. Born September 26, 1892 (Julian calendar) in Moscow, Russia; died August 31, 1941 (Gregorian calendar) in Elabuga, USSR. Between the appearance of her first collection, *Vechernii al'bom* (1910, Evening Album), which she published at her own expense, to her emigration in 1922, Tsvetaeva's literary reputation slowly grew from that of a promising minor poet to one of significant stature. In the year prior to her departure to Berlin in May 1922, she published the collections *Versty I* and *Versty II* (Mileposts I and II; written 1916 and 1917–21 respectively), the verse play *Konets Kazanovy* (The End of Casanova), and the long poem-fairytale *Tsar'-Devitsa* (The Tsar-Maiden; written 1920). Tsvetaeva's flurry of publications obviously achieved its goal: she left her literary legacy for her Russian reading public. The poetry was metrically and stylistically innovative and much more mature than the verse of her first two books. Two other collections from this period remained unpublished in her lifetime: *Junosheskie stixi* (Juvenilia; written 1916), which she must have considered less polished than *Versty I* and *II*, and *Lebedinyi stan* (The Swan's Encampment; written 1920–21). The latter lauds the virtues of the White Army, in which her husband, Sergei Efron, had served since its inception in late 1917. While Efron fought in the south, Tsvetaeva underwent the privations of life in postrevolutionary Moscow. She must have already felt like an internal exile when she defiantly read her poems in praise of the White Army at an Evening of Poetesses reading in 1920. She did not read them out of any political convictions, but rather out of a sense of honor, devotion, and duty, a need to defend the heroism of the downtrodden. It was also part of her nature to be provocative and to go against the grain of accepted practices. Despite a teenage flirtation with radical revolutionary politics, Tsvetaeva remained basically apolitical all her adult life.

After hearing news from her husband in the spring of 1921, she decided to reunite with him in Prague, where a number of émigrés had settled following the civil war. She traveled to Berlin, where she settled into the Bohemian Russian émigré literary circle associated with the famous Prager-Diele Cafe. With over 100,000 Russians in residence, Berlin had become the publishing and cultural center of the emigration. There she renewed friendships with Andrei Bely and Ilya Ehrenburg.* In Berlin she initially familiarized herself with the poetry of Boris Pasternak, to which she reacted with her first critical essay, "Svetovoi liven" (A Cloudburst of Light). She made an important acquaintance with Abram Vishniak, the owner of the Gelikon Publishing House, who published her collections *Razluka* (Separation) and *Remeslo* (Craft) in 1923. Berlin publishers also released her panegyric to Alexandr Blok, *Stikhi k Bloku* (Verses to Blok) in 1922 as well as *Psikheia* (Psyche) in 1923. After a few months, Tsvetaeva settled in Prague with her husband and daughter; they were to live there for the next two-and-a-half years. Tomáš Masaryk's Czech government had established a school for Russian émigrés, and she received a writer's stipend that helped her family survive for a number of years, even after they had moved to Paris in 1926. She found additional income by publishing in the major émigré periodicals in Prague, Berlin, and Paris. Thus emigration served as a major stimulus for Tsvetaeva to publish and to take her place among the leading poets of her time.

The Berlin-Prague period marks the pinnacle of Tsvetaeva's career with the writing of her magnum opus, the collection *Posle Rossii* (1928, After Russia). Like most of her collections, *Posle Rossii* reads like a lyrical diary of the poet's life experiences. It chronicles her heightened elation and a feeling of a new beginning after emigrating, her sense of orphanhood, loss and abandonment, her real and imaginatively hyperbolized love experiences with various personae (including Abram Vishniak, Boris Pasternak, Alexander Bakhrakh, Konstantin Rodzevich), her need to escape the pain of the profane world through death and suicide, and finally, her desire to reconstruct that Russia of her past inside her. The theme of overcoming spatial and temporal barriers between the poet-lover and her beloved dominates the work. Mixed reviews met the collection when it appeared after long delays in 1928. For the most part reviewers simply could not understand its complexities: telegraphic density, ellipticality, paronomastic modality, as well as stylistic and metrical innovations. For the most part a new readership would not come to appreciate her accomplishments until the 1960s and 1970s. Critics now consider Tsvetaeva's last collection one of the finest in Russian literature.

Her verse-fairytale *Mólodets* (The Swain) was published in Prague in 1924. In late 1923 and early 1924, she wrote two additional pathbreaking masterpieces: the long poems "Poèma gory" (Poem of the Mountain) and "Poèma kontsa" (Poem of the End), which document her failed love affair with Konstantin Rodzevich. Her metrical and stylistic innovativeness in these poems puts her at the forefront in the development of the genre of the autobiographical *poema*, a separate geure in the Russian tradition. Tsvetaeva's bisexuality and inability to be satisfied by a single lover had emerged early after her wedding to Efron in 1913, and the liaison with Rodzevich put further strains on her marriage. Perhaps as a result of guilt over the affair, Tsvetaeva became pregnant by her husband and bore a son, Georgy, on February 1, 1925. By this time the situation in Prague had become bleak, and the Czech stipend and honoraria for periodical publications could not support the family, to which her husband contributed little financially. In October 1926 she decided to move to Paris, which had become the new center for Russian emigration. Her husband joined her later.

At first Tsvetaeva enjoyed success among the Paris community following her public reading there in February 1926. Her published diatribe against superficial literary critics, " Poèt o kritike" (1926, The Poet on Criticism), created several enemies for her. Soon after her public praise of the Soviet Russian poet Vladimir Mayakovsky in 1928, émigré periodicals began to publish less of her work; many in the emigration misinterpreted her glowing literary evaluation of Mayakovsky as a political pro-Soviet statement. Paradoxically Tsvetaeva began the path of becoming an exile in exile. Increased isolation, both literary and social, characterized her life in Paris. Some of her major long poems of the Paris period include "Krysolov" (1926, The Pied Piper; begun earlier in Prague), "Popytka komnaty" (1926, Attempt to Reconstruct a Room), "S moria" (1926, From the Sea), and "Novogodnee" (1927, New Year's Greetings), dedicated to the memory of Rainer Maria Rilke.*

Following the mixed reviews that *Posle Rossii* received in 1928, Tsvetaeva's output of lyric poetry atrophied, and she began to write mostly highly impressionistic memoiristic and autobiographical prose, as well as some major critical essays. Besides being uncomfortable with what they perceived as her politics, editors wanted to publish the old, more easily accessible Tsvetaeva, which she was not about to provide for them. Her literary portraits share the same telegraphic, elliptical qualities of her verse: they include memoirs of Maks Voloshin, "Zhivoe o zhivom" (1932, A Living Word about a Living Man); Andrei Bely, "Plennyi dukh" (1934, A Captive Spirit); and Mikhail Kuzmin, "Nezdeshnyi vecher" (1936, An Otherworldly Evening). Among her major critical essays are "Poèt i vremia" (1932, The Poet and Time) and "Iskusstvo pri svete sovesti" (1932, Art in the Light of Conscience).

Tsvetaeva's financial plight worsened, and her husband's health deteriorated as a result of his ongoing bout with tuberculosis. Unhappy in France, her son and daughter with more and more fervor requested that the family return to the Soviet Union. Ariadna returned in 1937 and soon after was imprisoned. Tsvetaeva's husband became involved with the Union for Returnees to the Soviet Union in the 1930s and was implicated as an agent for the NKVD in the assassination of Ignats Reiss. Efron disappeared from sight, and Tsvetaeva was brought in for questioning by the French police. Despite her denial of complicity in the affair, for the most part the émigré community treated her with great disdain. Impoverished, and despite the warnings of her few remaining friends, Tsvetaeva returned to the USSR in 1939.

A reunion with her husband and daughter was short-lived. Both Ariadna and Efron were incarcerated by the secret police; the latter was murdered since he had outlived his usefulness for the NKVD. Tsvetaeva worked for a time as a translator, but, since the Soviets were extremely suspicious of her, the translation work diminished; her old friends for the most part abandoned her. Tsvetaeva was evacuated with her son to Elabuga in the early part of the war. After ten days in this remote town, unable to write or publish her work, unable to bear her hard lot any longer, Tsvetaeva hanged herself on August 31, 1941, in the entranceway of her apartment in Elabuga. Her son, Georgy, left to join the Red Army and died in combat in 1943. Tsvetaeva was buried in the Elabuga cemetery in an unmarked grave, whose exact location to this day has not been discovered.

Tsvetaeva's work has inspired a generation of Russian writers in what amounts to a cult following in the Soviet Union. Her poems were memorized by thousands and circulated in samizdat even before the 1960s when the Soviet government "rehabilitated" her and allowed censored versions for limited distribution.

Selected Title: Collected Works, *Stikhotvoreniia i poèmy v 5-i tomakh* (New York: Russica, 1980–84, [Poetry and Long Poems in 5 volumes] vol. 5 is forthcoming).

Translations: *A Captive Spirit: Selected Prose*, ed. and trans. by J. Marin King (1980); *The Demesne of the Swans*, (1980); *Selected Poems* (1986); *Selected Poems* (1987); *After Russia/Posle Rosii* ed. Michael Naydan (1990), bilingual ed.

Consult: Elaine Feinstein, *A Captive Lion: The Life of Marina Tsvetayeva* (London, 1987); Simon Karlinsky, *Marina Cvetaeva: Her Life and Art* (Berkeley, Calif., 1965;

[*Marina Tsvetaeva: The Woman, Her World, and Her Poetry*, Cambridge, England, 1985]); Ellendea Proffer, ed., *Tsvetaeva: A Pictorial Biography* (1980).

MICHAEL M. NAYDAN

TUCHOLSKY, Kurt. Born January 9, 1890, in Berlin, Germany; died December 21, 1935, in Hindås, Sweden. After qualifying in law in 1914, Tucholsky became a drama critic contributing to the *Schaubühne* (Stage), later *Weltbühne* (World Stage). Military service in World War I strengthened his antimilitarist views. Tucholsky was primarily a journalist and satirist; his witty, uncompromising judgments, sometimes in ballad-form, on life in Germany under the Weimar Republic complement the bitter sketches of Georg Gross. Ever ready to puncture inflated rhetoric and detect false pathos, he grew to dislike communism as well as incipient Nazism. Having settled in Sweden in 1929, he was deprived of German citizenship in 1933. The principal work that Tucholsky wrote in Swedish exile was his best-selling novel *Schloss Gripsholm* (1931; *Castle Gripsholm*, London, 1985). This tale of two German lovers spending a summer holiday in the eponymous Castle, at first a carefree idyll, strikes a harsher note when the visitors confront the sadistic manager of a home for young girls: the evil Frau Adriani symbolizes a canker spreading in European society.

In Sweden Tucholsky found himself increasingly isolated not only from his German roots but from the émigré cliques in France and America. In a letter entitled "Jews and Germans," printed in *Die Neue Weltbühne* (Zurich, 1936, The New World Stage), he countered the polemics of Arnold Zweig* on the same theme and launched a direct attack on his fellow exiles, accusing them of seeking to perpetuate a German culture that had disowned them. This letter was reprinted, without indication of source, in *Das Schwarze Korps*, the organ of Adolf Hitler's Waffen-SS, by which time Tucholsky had already committed suicide. His inflexible honesty of vision had led to literary impotence and disaster.

Selected Title: *Gesammelte Werke*, ed. Mary Gerold-Tucholsky, 4 vols. (Hamburg, 1960–62); Germany? Germany: A Kurt Tucholsky Reader, ed. Harry Zohn (London, 1989).

Consult: Bryan Grenville, *Kurt Tucholsky* (Munich, 1983); Hans Prescher, *Kurt Tucholsky* (Berlin, 1959); Gerhard Zwerenz, *Kurt Tucholsky: Biographie eines guten Deutschen* (Munich, 1979, Biography of a Good German).

CEDRIC HENTSCHEL

TUDORAN, Dorin. Born June 30, 1945, in Timisoava, Romania; he lives in Maryland. Tudoran is a 1968 graduate of the University of Bucharest; he has pursued graduate research at various universities in Europe and the United States. He worked for the BBC (1985–86) and Radio Free Europe (1985–87), and has served as consultant and/or lecturer at the Catholic University of America and the University of Connecticut. Before his exile he was an editor of two literary journals in Romania, *Luceafarul* (1974–80) and *Flacara* (1973–74), and senior editor at Romanian Press Service (1971–73).

Tudoran left Romania with his wife and daughter on July 2, 1985, and reached the United States via Italy in August of that year. He had endured two years of house arrest under twenty-four-hour surveillance, with only his mother and mother-in-law allowed to visit the household. In a final attempt to obtain a visa, he had engaged in a forty-day hunger strike from May through early June 1985, and the attendant publicity aided in the government's delayed approval of his emigration. Tudoran's troubles began when, as a well-established poet in Romania with a wide following, he wrote several essays, published in journals in Western Europe and excerpted for broadcast over Voice of America, Radio Free Europe and the BBC, which criticized the Romanian government structure and administration policies. Tudoran had submitted the articles first to Romanian journals, and when they were refused publication, he sent them out of the country; one of these articles questioned the legitimacy of the current regime and another spoke out against the structure of the socialist state. At that point Tudoran was given a choice of leaving the country or going to jail; he delayed his decision for a year, and when he finally requested the alternative of emigration, he was informed he was "too late," because his case had received unwarranted international attention.

In exile Tudoran works for the Voice of America in Washington, D.C., and edits a literary journal, *Agora, an Alternate Journal of Culture*. He continues to write his poetry in Romanian, claiming a poet cannot change his language. In an interview with the editor of this study, he said that he "dreams in Romanian," and dreams are the vision by which a poet makes contact with meaning. Tudoran's poetry is apolitical, dealing with a sense of spiritual emptiness in the modern world and the few contemporary faiths and values available to transcend such accompaniments of despair; in effect, he says his poetry is a redefinition of the modern self and condition.

Tudoran's experience of exile has made him aware of several paradoxes: in Romania the poet is interested in politics only as a means of survival, whereas in the West, an exiled poet's fortunes depend on his or her playing the game of literary politics. Thus, Tudoran sees the exiled East European poet as a specimen available for exploitation by the media and Western governments. If, however, Tudoran says, the displaced poet is not from a currently fashionable dissident area or does not fit neatly into one of the interstices of current literary politics, he or she is likely to be neglected. Thus, for Tudoran, the quality of literature plays a lesser role in terms of a dissident exiled writer's reputation and fortune, whereas in the East literature may be used as an escape from politics into allegory and ambiguity. Art for art's sake in Tudoran's argument becomes possible in programmed social states, where it thrives periodically on bureaucratic toleration, condescension, and ignorance. In Western capitalistic societies, perversely, such movements stand little chance of survival because they have no viable economic base. For that reason, Tudoran claims, poets have a wide readership and audience in Romania, an audience that understands the poet's coded messages; the tragedy is that the poet's readers can do little with their knowledge.

Freedom in the East for writers, as Tudoran views it, becomes a matter of when to speak out, or whether to keep silent and spread the word through subtler verbal means. In the West all the freedom in the world matters little when and if no audience exists to listen to the writer's words. An audience in the West, Tudoran has concluded, is an amalgam of cultural opinions formed by vague parameters of political bias.

Selected Titles: Poetry: *Short Treatise on Glory* (Bucharest, 1973); *Song in Crossing in the Akheron* (Bucharest, 1975); *A Day in Nature* (Bucharest, 1977); *Sometimes, Floating* (Bucharest, 1977); *Artificial Respiration* (Dacia, Cluj-Napoca, Romania, 1978); *Pedestrian Passage* (Bucharest, 1979); *Distinguishing Characteristics, an Anthology* (Bucharest, 1979). Prose: *Of My Free Will, An Autobiography* (Nord, Aarhus, Denmark, 1986); *Optional Future* (Daphne, Alabama, 1988).

Consult: Dorin Tudoran, "Diary of a Hunger-Striker," *Index on Censorship* (London) 15, no. 4 (April 1986); D. Tudoran, "On the Condition of the Romanian Intellectual," *Europe Media* (Daphne, Alabama, 1988).

TUWIM, Julian. Born September 13, 1894, in Lodz, Poland; died December 27, 1953, in Zakopane, Poland. Tuwim studied law and philosophy at the University of Warsaw. At the start of World War II he escaped from Poland and lived in Brazil and, later, New York. He returned to Warsaw in 1949.

Tuwim's best-known work written in exile is the lyrical epic *Kwaity polskie* (1949, Flowers of Poland), in which he expresses, in almost 9,000 lines, his yearning for his homeland and, conversely, his attack on those Polish exiles who did not return to the land of their birth. The poem mixes a new (for Tuwim) lyricism and nostalgia with an excoriating satire typical of his earlier work. On his return to Poland, Tuwim was greeted with national honors. His later work became mellow and ceremonial.

Selected Titles: *The Dancing Socrates and Other Poems*, ed. Adam Gillon (1968); *Wiersze wybrane* (1973).

Consult: *Julian Tuwim*, Bibliography (Warsaw, 1963).

TZARA, Tristan (pseudonym of Samuel Rosenstock). Born April 16, 1896, in Moinesti, Romania; died December 24, 1963, in Paris. Tzara's pseudonym is a combination of his tribute to Richard Wagner's Tristan (and Isolde) and to the Romanian word for land. His early interest was in symbolism, and with his friend Ion Vinea, he established the literary journal *Simbolul*. In 1915 he moved to Zurich and turned his attention to the movement that would be called Dadaism. He moved to Paris in 1920 and engaged in literary battle there with André Breton* and his Surrealist followers. In 1925 he changed his legal name to the more Dadaist *nom d'identité* Tristan Tzara. He joined the Communist party in the 1930s and served with the Loyalists during the Spanish Civil War. He was a member of the resistance group in southern France during World War II.

Tzara's Dada revolt against traditional form and language has influenced European poetry and drama tremendously, though his own works, with the exception of his Dada manifestos, have commanded little investigative attention. Although

Tzara never considered himself a literal exile, he believed in the role of the artist as outsider and iconoclast. His many journeys, his many disguises (he was famous for games of disguise in Zurich cabarets), and his rejection of rational accessibility of literary culture, provided him with that spirit of the wanderer he so profoundly sought.

U

UHSE, Bodo. Born March 12, 1904, in Rastatt, Germany; died July 2, 1963, in (East) Berlin, German Democratic Republic. Probably because of his upbringing in a Prussian officer's family, Uhse's first political activities were as a member of the Bund Oberland, then, successively, editor of two fascist dailies, and participation at age sixteen in the Kapp-Putsch; later he became friendly with the Strasser brothers, an oppositional wing in the NSDAP. Contact with revolutionary farmers in Schleswig-Holstein effected a change in his attitude, and he started to work with Claus Heim's antifascist farmers' movement. After breaking with fascism, Uhse entered the KPD in 1930 and became the secretary-general of the Antifascist Farmers' Committee in 1932. *Söldner und Soldat* (1935) is a strongly autobiographical novel about this change in his life. In 1933 he emigrated and participated in the International Writers' Congress for the Defense of Culture; in 1936 he joined the International Brigades in Spain as a war commissioner and returned, severely ill, to Paris in 1938. *Die erste Schlacht* (Strassburg, 1938) gives testimony of this experience in Spain.

In 1939 he emigrated to the United States, and a year later to Mexico, where he joined the committee ''Freies Deutschland'' in its political and cultural work and became editor of the literary section of the magazine *Freies Deutschland*; Uhse remained aware of the fact that German literature and culture were now being produced in exile and that not only politics was the issue. In 1944 the German exile publishing house El libro libre in Mexico published his novel *Leutnant Bertram* (English version 1943), centering on a German air force officer who slowly comes to disagree with fascism during his missions over Spain. Uhse's regular sojourns at provincial Cuernavaca and knowledge of Spanish resulted in his various essays (''Mexikanische Geschichten'') in *Freies Deutschland* and *Demokratische Post* between 1944 and 1947. He describes anti-heroic figures caught in material poverty and in conflicting moods of passion, violence, and hopelessness. He does not apply criteria of causality, nor does he judge persons and their actions. "Reise in einem blauen Schwan," "Der Weg zum Rio Grande," and "Der Bruder des Gavillans" are further examples of an exile receiving decisive influence by his host country, producing work entirely different from his European period.

In the summer of 1948, Uhse returned to Berlin via Leningrad because the United States refused to grant him a transit visa. He became chief editor of *Aufbau* from 1949 to 1958, and of *Sinn und Form* in 1962. He was awarded the Medal of National Merit in 1954, became a board member of the East German PEN Club and the German Academy of Art, and became president of the Writers Union of East Germany. Constant travels resulted in various works. He practiced painting in Mexico and had a deep interest in the creative process of painting, manifest in his essay collection *Probleme und Gestalten* (1959); he published several story collections, among them *Die heilige Kunigunde im Schnee* (1949) and *Sonntagsträumerei in der Alameda* (1961). His work *Die Aufgabe* (1958) employs Käthe Kollwitz's diary entries and her sketches (January 25, 1919) of the murdered Karl Liebknecht in the morgue of Berlin in a composite attempt to understand the workings of an artist's creative processes and her views of a political situation. According to his collaborator and biographer Gunter Caspar, Uhse was a sensitive and discreet person affected by specific pressures of literary and artistic trends in the 1950s ("his time was not favorable for him") and by the trials that involved former U.S. emigrants and Spanish Republic partisans in the Civil War. Further trials were Uhse's ill health (he had succumbed to tuberculosis) and family problems: in 1942 he married the former wife of James Agee, they separated, and he married a second time; his son, Stefan, committed suicide in 1973.

Selected Titles: *Wir Söhne* (1948); *Die Brücke* (1952); *Die Patrioten*, vol. 1 (1954); *Tagebuch aus China* (1954); *Im Rhythmus der Conga* (1962). Filmscripts: *Roman einer jungen Ehe* (1952); *China zwischen gestern und morgen* (1957). Editor: *E. E. Kisch, Gesammelte Werke* (1960 ff), in collaboration with Kisch.

Translations: "Bread and Water," in *New Masses* (1946); *They Lived to See It* (Berlin, 1963), stories.

Consult: Bodo Uhse, *Gesammelte Werke in Einzelausgaben*, ed. Günter Caspar (Berlin, 1974ff). See also Günter Caspar, "Erinnerungen an Bodo Uhse," *Neue Deutsche Literatur* (February 1984); Dieter Noll, Preface to the analytical bibliography of *Aufbau* (Berlin, 1978); Fritz Pohle, *Unseren Hass gegen Hitler können wir nicht umwandeln in Sympathie für die Alliierten*; *Exil* (Sonderband, 1987).

                                                    RENATA VON HANFFSTENGEL

UNAMUNO, Miguel de. Born September 29, 1864, in Bilbao, the Basque country, Spain; died of a heart attack in the course of a heated discussion with an academic at Salamanca, regarding mob rule in Italy under Mussolini, on New Year's Eve, 1936. Perhaps the most quixotic expatriation of any man of letters in modern times was Unamuno's celebrated "exile," which lasted six years and boasted a deliberate intention. By the time of his exile—beginning with an edict of banishment in 1924 issued by the government of Primo de Rivera, a dictator he had mercilessly attacked—Unamuno had already authored his major works, including *The Tragic Sense of Life*, a poignant tracing of the conflict between human reason and the irrational longing for purpose and permanence (the latest edition in English, ed. A. Kerrigan, 1972); *Mist* (in *Novela/Nivola*, 1974), in which the main character revolts against his begetter, the author, years before Luigi Pirandello ideated a similar literary uprising; *The Other* (in Unamuno's *Ficciones*, 1976), a play that dramatized the dual persona in everyman, the man-in-history versus the intimate man, a notion that led directly to "The Other" in the pivotal work of Jorge Luis Borges.

Unamuno was deliberately a Don Quixote in public life. He had called on Spaniards (his exhortation put into English in *Our Lord Don Quixote*, 1967) to canonize the don as a national saint of Spain. His "exile" was real enough since he, in full consciousness, confined himself to the impasse of expatriation, and embarked on a quest, full of self-inflicted wounds, for high-minded government and citizenry. In view of what was to overwhelm his country in a short time, his gesture was historically a premature parody, but it was imbued with the highest ideals. It was, too, as with Don Quixote's quest, devoid of any measure of political sense. His polemical fury was wasted and dissipated by the forced march of events.

In September 1923, state power was bloodlessly assumed in Madrid by a military directorate led by General Miguel Primo de Rivera, with the support of King Alfonso XIII. Unamuno had already been relieved of his high post at the University of Salamanca in 1914, and he strove to make himself eligible for another similar reprisal by reacting furiously. He subsequently detailed his opposition to the military directorate in his book *How to Make a Novel* (first published in French, Paris, 1926; in Spanish, Buenos Aires, 1927; in English, Princeton, 1976). The book is a pseudofictive work, whose protagonist is named U. Jugo de la Raza (a compendium of Unamuno's family surnames encompassing the Spanish race, "de la Raza"). It includes passages from the exiled Mazzini's correspondence along with much polemic against stupidity in Spain, and a para-autobiographical memoir of Paris as seen by a disaffected exile.

Unamuno had forced exile upon himself, confining himself in an unenforced (except by himself) expatriation. The drama had begun with a government banishment that was officially revoked soon after it was invoked. Once he "escaped" (no one was stopping him) from his assigned place of banishment in the Canary Islands, embarking on a chartered yacht, he set himself up (after a dismal period in Paris, which he detested almost on sight) at Hendaye on the Spanish-French border. Within sight of the land from which he had exiled himself, he played the role of the exile on a stage before an international audience. He was free to cross the border whenever he chose, but he did not choose to do so. Instead he played the role of aggrieved and beset expatriate, as pure in intention as Don Quixote.

It was an ephemeral *querencia*, a piece of ground that Unamuno seized and favored for his defensive/offensive purpose. It became the arena for the soul's throes (*agonia*) of his immortal self against the death throes (agony) of the body of his material self. He relished, albeit in downcast mood, a deliberate loneliness and isolation, where he could confront the "agony" of outwitting not only the dictator across the frontier but also finite death by means of in-finite thought in prose and, more especially, verse.

Unamuno's exile was thus tripartite:

1. He was ordered out of Spain and left Salamanca accompanied by one policeman and three books. He told the policeman and the small crowd gathered to see him off, "I will come back, not with my freedom but with yours." The three books were Dante and Leopardi in Italian and the New Testament in Greek. He spent barely four months in his assigned place of banishment, at Fuenteventura in the Canary Islands. Albert Einstein in Germany and Gabriele D'Annunzio in Italy wrote him supportive letters.

2. A few days *after* the order of banishment was revoked by the government, he "escaped" in the schooner provided by a wealthy left-of-center publisher in Paris, and proceeded by stages to that capital city. He lodged in a small *pensión*, and consented to be cut off from family, friends, and his university classes in Greek, in order to live in self-imposed "wretchedness." Despite the men of letters who came calling, and the *tertulia* of Spaniards at the Café La Coupole in Montparnasse, he anathematized the capital of France: he detested the superficiality and worldly sophistication of the City of Lights, its grand avenues, and even its famous museums, which he called mausoleums of art; he could not even stand its "History." He exorcised the city, and lasted there a little over a year.

3. He next made his way south and entrenched himself on the Franco-Spanish border on his own "Basque soil"; from there he could both *see* his beloved Spanish earth across the border, and also bombard it with his polemics and denunciations. (He later was also to bombard Basque nationalism.) He refused invitations to lecture and teach in Germany, Switzerland, and both North and South America. He denounced the still relatively harmless dictator as a skirt chaser and a gambler. He wrote voluminously and vitriolically, contributing to the literary pages of the press in Spain, France, and especially the Buenos Aires newspapers. He identified with the great exiles Dante, Fray Luis de León and Quevedo.

In February 1930, a fortnight after Primo de Rivera had diplomatically resigned under pressure from the king, Unamuno walked across the frontier and was acclaimed everywhere.

His exile had been not only a sort of public penance for Spain by a man of deep religious animus, but also, since he had vowed not to return to his country while it accepted the current head of state, it was a drama of purgation by a free man against whom all sanctions had been lifted even before he "fled" to France. It had been, in short, a theatrical performance *en el gran teatro del mundo*, in which he played out on the world stage the role he had assigned himself—and written and directed as well.

He was scarcely back in Spain when he began to have doubts about the Republic he had preached in exile. In the year following his return, the Second Spanish Republic was proclaimed; Unamuno proclaimed it himself in a speech from the Salamanca town hall. Within a year he was writing against it. His disillusion became total. He threatened to go into exile once again (Unamuno in *Ahora*, Madrid, October 3, 1934).

After 1932, all his writings show Unamuno to be a ferocious critic of the Republic he had championed in theory. Unamuno's friend the philosopher Ferrater Mora writes that "even before the proclamation of the Republic, the man who had done the most of any man to bring it about was already taking a stand against it." (quoted in Luis Granjel, *Retrato de Unamuno* [Madrid, 1957], p. 340). In his last epoch, according to Ramón Gómez de la Serna, "he was at war with all sides . . . his instincts foresaw the worst . . . he was like one who feels a hurricane approaching." Unamuno was horrified by the turn of Spanish politics and, at this stage, at the burning of the ancient buildings and churches by Red hordes, "*rojores de sangre*," he said as he envisioned "the tide of red blood rising" and as he told the student body at Salamanca in his last professional lecture on September 30, 1934.

It was only a matter of months before he saw the Republic he had fomented going up in flames as a result of its own torching of the "Eternal Spain" he most prized.

Accounts of his last public appearance are numerous and usually serve in lieu of a clear account of his disconformity with both sides. On that widely heralded occasion he was taken from the platform at the Paraninfo at Salamanca on the arm of Franco's wife, after hearing cries of "Death to the intelligentsia" from General Millán Astray, commander of the Foreign Legion. This event is endlessly cited, but his anathema of the opposing Republican side is not equally cited. Instead, the international media settled on a tendentious and partisan account, by Luis Portillo, as the definitive account; his view was accepted as the authorized account, even as late as 1984 (in vol. 2 of the *Selected Works of Unamuno*, where it was inserted by a rogue editor). The eyewitness report by the economics professor Bartolomé Aragón, who was the only person with Unamuno when he died, was ignored, since Aragón had been, in his student days, a Falangist. Only the writer of this entry (Anthony Kerrigan) with his associates and in the company of Unamuno's eldest son, who had organized his father's flight from the Canary Islands, took the trouble to get Aragón's on-the-spot account. It has never been published.

Unamuno had fled from a petty old-fashioned dictator. When the Civil War broke out, he sided with the Nationalists at first and was removed from his rectorship of the university by those in control of Madrid. Francisco Franco, whom Unamuno initially supported, would make alliances with fascism in a prelude to World War II. Cosmic mass movements would put in perspective the theatricality of Unamuno's voluntary expatriation. He had fled a relatively peaceful, traditional, albeit reactionary, or at least nonprogressive authoritarian regime. What followed made his sacrifice unavailing, the action of a veritable Spanish Don Quixote. He would die, a free man in his mind, but under a species of house arrest.

He was, finally, in José Ortega y Gasset's phrase, *"el morabito máximo,"* "the supreme Marabout," the holy hermit and prophet. In his last years he would often sigh (as repeated to the writer of this entry by his elder son and heir): "If I had only known what was to follow that harmless clown Primo de Rivera, I wouldn't have bothered to 'escape.' What was the point of my exile, after all this?" History, which he had not unseldom mocked, mocked him.

                                                              ANTHONY KERRIGAN

UNDSET, Sigrid. Born May 20, 1882, in East Kalundborg, Denmark; she died June 10, 1949, in Lillehammer, Norway. Undset moved with her family when she was two years old to Christiana (now Oslo), Norway. She grew up in a sophisticated and liberal environment, and early became outspoken in her ideas; she won a travelling scholarship to Italy in 1909, after which she decided to become a full-time writer. Her historical fiction, massive in its detail and compelling in its presentation, earned her the Nobel Prize for Literature in 1928.

During the 1930s, Undset denounced, in various articles and essays, the rise of Nazism and fascism. With her twenty-six-year-old son, she joined the underground forces after Germany's invasion in 1940. When her son was killed in the resistance, she fled to Sweden, then to the United States, where she worked with Norwegian committees in exile on humanitarian and political causes. (She lived for a time in Brooklyn Heights, New York, a few miles from a predominantly Scandinavian neighborhood.) She also continued her writing; two of her books written during this exile period are *Return to the Future* (1942) and *Happy Times in Norway* (1943). It is significant that Undset wrote and published little fiction in exile; the experience of estrangement that characterized her consciousness issued into autobiography and contemporary history. After the liberation of Norway she returned to her home, where she died a few years later.

Undset's great work is her series of novels set in the thirteenth and fourteenth century Norway, and in particular, *The Kristin Lavransdatter* trilogy (1929), which was published earlier in separate volumes: *The Bridal Wreath* (1923); *Mistress of Husaby*, and *The Cross* (1927).

Consult: A. Gustafson, *Six Scandinavian Novelists*.

V ———————————————————————————

VALENZUELA, Luisa. Born November 26, 1938, in Buenos Aires, Argentina; she lives in New York City and returns to Argentina for visits with her family. Valenzuela first came to the United States in 1976 for the publication of the English-language edition of her first book, *Clara: Thirteen Stories and a Novel* (*Hay que sonreir*, Buenos Aires, 1966). During her absence, her home was raided by parapolice and some of her papers and manuscripts confiscated. Although she was fearful, she returned to Argentina and lived there until 1979 when, in an interview with the editor of this study, she said, "People got blindfolded and deaf." She believed in 1979 that if she did not leave Argentina she would not be able to write anymore, not only because of possible harassment by agents of the military dictatorship but also because she no longer knew

what was real anymore. The only way to survive in a country in which people disappear in the middle of the night is to refuse to acknowledge what is happening, but then survival comes at the cost of truth, and such a state of being is impossible for a writer to exist in, such an existence makes it impossible for a writer to write.

Valenzuela was able to secure a visa for the United States because she had been invited to Columbia University as a writer-in-residence.

Valenzuela believes that exile has given her a necessary perspective, the freedom to explore her native land with another "optique," a lens through which she uses her sense of humor and perception of the grotesque as a way of accepting, if not harmonizing, truth and historic reality. Exile has given her "breathing space" in what would otherwise be a desert state; it has allowed her to become a voice telling the story of her land.

Valenzuela believes that distance from language is what may help to preserve it. She holds that Argentinian writers living in exile in Mexico are in greater danger of losing their roots than Argentinian writers living in countries of another language. For Valenzuela, the roots of a writer are in language and not in the identity of a national state; separation from native language and/or country makes the writer more keenly aware of his language and its qualities, while assimilation into a milieu of the mother language blurs linguistic distinction. Valenzuela continues to write in Spanish, though she is fully conversant in English.

Valenzuela now travels regularly to visit her family in Argentina. Her mother, also a well-known novelist (Luisa Mercedes Levinson), lives there, as does Valenzuela's daughter; Valenzuela is divorced from the Frenchman she married when she was seventeen years old. She is working on a novel set in New York in which the main characters are of Argentinian background. She was also reported at work on a play for the Latino Festival in New York.

Valenzuela's work has been variously called metafictional, surreal, and abstract. Characteristic is the presentation of dialogue between characters and their putative creator in the arranging of the narrative content and the rearrangement of already-presented segments of it. Also characteristic is a nonlinear, nonsynchronic line of action that allows for time to work in shifts; the "now" of her material is of psychological currency as well as chronological duration and often of authorial, whimsical dictation. Her work bares its meaning beneath a surface of absurdity in a design that cannot be sequestered by literal reading; thus Valenzuela believes it becomes unavailable for censorship. The literary coding of Valenzuela's work has been analyzed in structuralist terms of Freudian-Lacanian terminology, in Marxist patterns of political dynamisms, and in feminist statements of vision and consciousness. Political discrimination is certainly one of her themes, as are sexual discrimination and sexual tyranny. In her portraits of women often suffering mutilation and/or victimization, Valenzuela draws in deeper strokes. She has said, in her interview with the editor of this study, "Nobody wants to beat or be beaten, but somewhere inside we all want to let ourselves be mauled so as to know, to find ourselves in the last little piece that's left." These may well be the words of an exile trying to find some center after the onslaught of horror, emptiness, and despair from which an exile attempts to begin anew.

Valenzuela is a Guggenheim fellow (1983) and a fellow of the New York Institute for the Humanities. Her books, some of which were first published in Mexico, are now printed in Argentina.

Selected Titles: *Los Heriticos* (1967); *El gato eficaz* (1972; included in *Strange Things Happen Here*, 1979); *Aqui pasan cosas raras* (1975; *Strange Things Happen Here: 19 Stories and a Novel*, 1979); *Libro que nomuerde* (Mexico, 1982); *Cambio de armas* (1982; *Other Weapons*, 1985); *Donde viven las aguilas* (Buenos Aires, 1983); *Cola de lagartija* (Buenos Aires, 1983; *The Lizard's Tail*, 1983); *He Who Searches* (1987); *Open Door* (1988), stories.

Consult: "The Luisa Valenzuela Number," *Review of Contemporary Fiction* 6, no. 3 (Fall 1986).

VALLADARES PEREZ, Armando F. Born May 30, 1937, in Pinar del Rio, Cuba; he lives currently in Spain. Valladares served twenty-two years of a thirty-year prison sentence imposed on him in 1960 on charges of "counterrevolutionary activities." Because he denied the charges and refused to submit to "rehabilitation," he was mistreated severely while in confinement. He describes the horrors of his prison time in his moving poem "Boniato Jail," a version of which appeared in *Confrontation* magazine in 1983 in a translation by Carlos Ripoll.* As a result of his harsh confinement and inadequate medical attention, Valladares suffered partial paralysis. In 1982 he was released from prison after the government of France intervened on his behalf; previously, attempts by humanitarian groups had proven unsuccessful. Valladares moved to France briefly, then came to the United States; he lives now in Spain. He shared, with Angel Cuadra* and Jorge Valls,* the 1982 International Prize of the Hispanic–Puerto Rican Pro-Culture Association, given for artistic achievement in the face of duress.

Valladares's prison writings were smuggled out of the country and published abroad periodically. To date, only one volume of his work has been translated into English.

Selected Titles: *El corazon con que vivo nuevos poemas y relatos "desde mi silla de ruedas"* (Miami, 1980); *Cavernas del silencio* (Madrid, 1983); *Contra toda esperanza* (Barcelona, 1985).

Translation: *Against All Hope: The Prison Memoirs of Armando Valladares* (1986).

Consult: *Prisionero de Castro*, annotated and edited by Pierre Golendorf, with epilogue by Leonid Pliouchtch (Barcelona, 1982).

VALLEJO, César Abraham. Born March 16, 1892, in Santiago de Chuco, Peru; died on Good Friday, April 15, 1938, of unknown causes in Paris. One of the great poets of the Spanish language, Vallejo was a *cholo* whose grandfathers were priests and whose grandmothers were Chimu Indians. The youngest of eleven children, he was raised in a Catholic family strongly unified by his mother and grounded in the traditions of a provincial town. He experienced the loss of this secure world as the first in a series of exiles severing him from his native and Roman Catholic origins and culminating in his life as an expatriate in Europe, where he suffered extreme isolation and poverty until his death during the Spanish Civil War.

As a young man in Peru, Vallejo experimented with fiction and wrote two books that revolutionized Latin American poetry, although few realized what he had done at the time. These books reflect certain crucial early experiences—the social injustice he observed in the mines and on the sugar estates where he worked in 1911–12, the move to Trujillo and then to Lima, along with the volatile love affairs and aesthetic innovation of those years (1913–23), and the death of his brother Miguel in 1915 and the death of his mother in 1918. *Los Heraldos Negros* (1919), at times expressing nostalgia for a lost childhood world and a ruined native culture, critiques *Modernismo* and demystifies the Romantic model of the alienated artist; Vallejo rejects the possibility of a nativist poetry and suspects that the Spanish language itself may be a tool of oppression and self-deception. The poet in *Los Heraldos Negros* is an exile in his own land who recognizes that all human beings are orphans. While this book was favorably received, Vallejo was learning that the demonic artist can expect only ostracism. Under pressure to marry, he ended his involvement with one Otilia in 1919 and was unjustly accused of being the instigator of a riot in his hometown in 1920; he was subsequently arrested and imprisoned for 112 days. *Trilce* (1922), partly the result of Vallejo's feeling of alienation after these events, goes back to birth itself as the first exile; childhood as the second, when consciousness is separated from nature; and adulthood as the third, when the human being is exiled from others by sexual division and time, and from the future by the past. In a thorough critique of the poetic "I," Vallejo finds that the voice is exiled from language, and he pursues the track of the exiled sign through parody, paradox, and the grotesque. Anticipating antipoetry and deconstruction, this virtually untranslatable book had been largely ignored when Vallejo, on June 27, 1923, boarded the *Oroya* for France, never to return.

As an unknown poet in Paris, Vallejo had to adjust to a new language and culture. Eventually he made a tenuous living as a journalist but periodically suffered serious deprivation and illness. In 1929 he met Georgette Phillipart, whom he later married. Although critical of movements, he committed himself to communism and made three trips to Russia. The resulting *Rusia en 1931* (1931) and the novel *Tungsteno* (1931) achieved some success, but Vallejo's political activism led to political estrangement—he was expelled from France, his adopted home, in 1930. Failing as a playwright in Spain, he returned to France in 1932 under orders to keep silent. But when the Spanish Civil War erupted, he resumed his political activism in support of the Republican cause. In 1937 he was offered the opportunity to go back to Peru if he would change his political stance, but he refused. Spain, some have said, was his spiritual home at the end of his life, but he knew that his vision of Spain had been defeated by temporal forces.

Vallejo's greatest work, the posthumous *Poemas Humanos* (1939), consists, according to Juan Larrera, of three books: *Nómina de Huesos*, largely the prose poems and social-realist experiments of the 1920s and early 1930s; *Sermón de la Barbarie*, a dated sequence (September-December 1937); and *España, apárta de mí éste cáliz* (1937). *Sermón de la Barbarie*, in particular, provides a severe critique of Vallejo's hope for history, and undertakes a dialogue between the exiled voice and the silent other, at times the human brother and at times the mute body itself. Ultimately, exile, alienation, and loss seem to have an ontological status in these poems, but it is precisely in these experiences and in the suffering body that Vallejo finds evidence for what Max Scheler calls "the sphere of the Thou" (*The Nature of Sympathy*, 1970, p. 235). Always aware of the oppressive power of script, Vallejo asserts the immediacy of voice as the means of affirming otherness, although the actual achievement remains beyond the reach of art. *España, Apárta de mí éste cáliz* attempts to create the scripture of a revolutionary people, but the suspicion that utopian hopes are illusory and that the horror of war cannot be justified haunts this book and leads straight back to *Sermón de la Barbarie*.

It is a significant irony that Vallejo's poems, so concerned with otherness and with community realized through severance and suffering, should defy translation and suggest that the nature of language exiles even as it discloses the condition of exile.

Translations: *Neruda and Vallejo: Selected Poems*, trans. Robert Bly, John Knoepfle, and James Wright; ed. Robert Bly (1971); *Trilce*, trans. Dave Smith (1973); *The Complete Posthumous Poetry*, trans. Clayton Eshelman and José Rubia Barcia (1980); *The Black Heralds*, trans. Richard Schaaf and Kathleen Ross (1990).

Consult: Jean Franco, *César Vallejo: The Dialectics of Poetry and Silence* (Cambridge, 1976).

MICHAEL MANLEY

VALLS ARANGO, Jorge. Born 1933 in Cuba; he lives in Washington Heights, New York City. Valls wrote stories, poems, and plays, some of them on toilet paper, while serving time in Boniato Prison on a charge of associations with enemies of the Cuban state. Imprisoned in 1964, he was released in 1984, and came to the United States. He shared, with Angel Cuadra* and Armando Valladares,* the 1982 International Prize of the Hispanic–Puerto Rican Pro-Culture Association, given for literary achievement in the face of physical and social duress. In 1983 he received the prestigious International Poetry Prize administered by the De Joost Foundation, based in the Netherlands.

VALTIN, Jan. Born December 17, 1905, in Rhineland, Germany; died January 1, 1951, in Maryland. Valtin is remembered as the author of *Out of the Night*, an autobiography published in 1941 and in which Valtin asserts he was a secret agent of the Comintern. In defecting to the West, Valtin carried with him information about Soviet espionage and policy during the 1930s. Although some critics have questioned Valtin's accuracy, and others his motives, his work proved a sensation of the time, and Valtin became a cult figure of the American Right. He became an American citizen in 1947. Valtin suffered no ill effects of exile; indeed, he became a wealthy author with a farm in Maryland to his credit. He also wrote a series of novels that never achieved the popularity or interest of his autobiography.

Selected Titles: *Children of Yesterday* (1946); *Bend in the River and Other Stories* (1947); *Castle in the Sand* (1947); *Wintertime* (1950).

Consult: Obituary, *New York Times*, January 15, 1951.

VAN DER POST, Laurens. Born December 13, 1906, in Philoppis, South Africa; he lives in London and Suffolk and visits South Africa regularly. While still in his teens, Van der Post joined William Plomer* and Roy Campbell* in writing, editing, and publishing a short-lived but influential South African little magazine, *Voorslag*, in 1926. He and Plomer sailed together to Japan that same year. In England, to which Van der Post emigrated, he wrote several books about South Africa, one of them the popular, nostalgic anthropological study *The Lost World of the Kalahari* (London, 1958). During World War II, he became a highly decorated British officer, and he also spent three years in a Japanese prisoner-of-war camp, a subject on which he has written. After the war Van der Post continued as a world traveler for many years, but his prime writing matter remained South Africa. His three novels set in South Africa—*In a Province* (London, 1934); *The Face beside the Fire* (London, 1953); *Flamingo Feather* (London, 1955)—show the influence of Christian socialism, Jungianism, and a personal mysticism.

Van der Post is an heir to the literary tradition bequeathed by E. M. Forster, but he also reflects the influence of William Plomer and Joseph Conrad.* His first novel, *In a Province*, deals with the relationship of two men of different cultures and races trying and failing to understand each other. Van Bredepoel, the white South African, is a sensitive, lonely man who came to a big city to participate in life. He takes a job as a shipping clerk, hoping to find in humble work the entrance to a vital world. In the boardinghouse in which he lives, he meets a native boy, Kenon, who also has left his farmland for the big city. The novel becomes a record of the love-friendship between van Bredepoel and Kenon, and it ends like E. M. Forster's *A Passage to India* and Plomer's *Turbott Wolfe* in the flickering ideal of a rapprochement between alien groups. This theme of personal and spiritual isolation is found throughout Van der Post's writing. All his heroes are unmade men searching for the vital relationship to connect them to an ocean of community. Van der Post ties this theme of isolation to the color issue in South Africa so that the psychological journey within the individual is completed through identification with his black brother. In *In a Province* the hero comes to maturity through accepting his commitment to the native boy he has befriended; in *The Face beside the Fire* the hero accepts his role in life after a dream in which he identifies with the white-stubbled negroid face of an old man; in *Flamingo Feather* the hero continues his fight for racial harmony after identifying himself in guilt with African vandals and rioters.

Van der Post's later work has not reached the stature of his earlier writing. Although he continues to write nonfiction studies with a broad liberal outlook, the spur of fiction no longer stings him into sparkling expression.

Selected Titles: *Venture to the Interior* (London, 1952); *The Dark Eye in Africa* (London, 1955, 1965); *The Lost World of the Kalahari* (1958); *The Heart of the Hunter* (London, 1961); *A Portrait of All the Russians* (1964, repr. 1967); *African Cooking* (1970); *The Prisoner and The Bomb* (1971); *A Story Like the Wind* (1972); *Jung and the Story of Our Time* (1975);*First Catch Your Eland* (1978, cookbook); *A Walk With a Bushman* (1986).

Consult: Martin Tucker, *Africa in Modern Literature* (1967).

VARGAS LLOSA, Mario. Born March 28, 1936, in Arequipa, Peru; he lives in Lima, Peru. Vargas was a member of an underground cell of the banned Communist party in Peru when he was an undergraduate at the University of San Marcos in Lima. The infatuation with communism lasted a year during which time Vargas and his small cadre of aficionados engaged in "Stalinistic" dialogues of reeducation; the training failed to take hold, as Vargas puts it, because he refused to give up on "decadent" literature and to stop reading James Joyce*, André Gide, and William Faulkner. When Vargas graduated in 1957 he applied for a fellowship for doctoral study in literature at the University of Madrid; he won the fellowship a year later and left for Spain in 1958. He forsook his formal studies after two years at the university and moved on to Barcelona and Paris, where, in the company of other Latin American expatriates, he began to consider himself seriously as a writer.

Vargas returned to Peru in 1975 after sixteen years of what he has characterized as self-imposed literary exile. Since that time he has involved himself in Peruvian and international social matters and served as president of PEN International and in various world human rights organizations. In 1989 he ran for the presidency of Peru on the Libertad party ticket, but lost in a run-off election Vargas's political views have been well observed but proven difficult to define—some call him visionary while others castigate him as well-meaning but conservative in vision. A former celebrator of the Cuban Revolution and Fidel Castro, Vargas turned against that event in history when in its aftermath in 1971 the poet Heberto Padilla* was arrested by the Castro government for his writings. Vargas was also incensed at the brutal treatment of homosexuals forced to work in agricultural communes as a punishment for their gender preference. He is perhaps more accurately to be described as a humanitarian observer, willing to consider new ideas on old issues; he insists on commenting on political matters as part of the totality of the role of the writer in society.

Vargas's first novel, *La ciudad y los perios* (1962; *The Time of the Hero*, 1966), aroused attention in its painting of a military school in Lima. The school became a microcosm of modern Peruvian society, and of the corruption and repression in it. His second novel, *La casa verde* (1966; *The Green House*, 1966), uses two settings, a brothel in a desert town and the surrounding jungle, in which to interweave narratives of personal, religious, and political conflict among missionaries, tribal Indians, Peruvian army officers, foreign investors, and local traders. Both in this and in his earlier novel, written during his expatriate period in Paris and Barcelona, Vargas created a Peru and a Latin America larger than realism, a prototype of the magic realism that claimed many of Vargas's colleagues, among them Gabriel García Márquez* and José Donoso.* Vargas also wrote in his expatriate period *Conversación en La catedral* (1969; *Conversation in the Cathedral*, 1975), a novelistic study of a contemporary Peruvian dictator told from the orientations of different individual and social types. In these three early novels Vargas was experimental and grand in his sweep of site and circumstance; his later work, well-humored and carefully crafted (including the popular *La tia Julia y el escribidor* [1977; *Aunt Julia and the Scriptwriter*, 1982]), is diminished in scope by comparison.

Vargas's break with his former idol Fidel Castro was signaled in his novel *The War of the End of the World*, which he began in 1978 (it was published in 1981 as *La guerra del fin del mundo* and in translation in 1983). Vargas's portrait of nineteenth-century fanatics in the Peruvian countryside who start out with a utopian vision and end in demagoguery and repression of their people has been interpreted as his commentary on Castro and the Cuban revolution. A more sympathetic portrait of a leftist revolutionary, though one tinged with irony and ultimately with Vargas's compassionate rejection, is found in *La via de Alejandra Mayta* (1984; *The Real Life of Alejandra Mayta*, 1986), a novel brilliantly told in several voices and moving in concentric spheres of psychological, chronological, and visionary time.

Vargas wrote two critical studies before his return to Peru: *Gabriel García Márquez: Historia de un deicideo* (1971; Gabriel García Márquez: History of a Deicide) and *La orgia perpetua: Flaubert y "Madame Bovary"* (1975).

In Vargas's most recent novel, *The Storyteller* (1989), the narrator of the "frame" of the novel is a "Peruvian trying to forget Peru" and living an expatriate life in Italy. He recognizes, in a newspaper photograph of an obscure Amazonian tribe, an old college friend, Saul, who had been preparing to become an anthropologist. In unraveling Saul's "story"—that is, how he moved from his Jewish middle-class background into the naturalization processes of the Machiguengas tribe—Vargas, the author, finds one set of clues to the puzzle of Peru, its Indians, its Spanish conquest, its industrialization, and its current divisiveness. The anthropologist's Jewish roots become a motif as well, since, as a Jew, Saul accepts exile as a part of history. Moving from the man Saul to his stories, and told through several different voices, the novel explores the dimensions of the Machiguengas tribe, who "walk away" from "progress" and who remain integral to their beginnings. As a result of listening to these stories, the world-weary narrator comes closer to his grail of self-identity and the understanding of his country, Peru. Vargas uses many surrealistic and hyperbolic techniques to achieve his effects, including a pet parrot named Gregor Samsa, the name of the protagonist in the novella *Metamorphosis* by Franz Kafka,* who metamorphosed into a beetle, one who accepted his transformation both as a culmination of history and a transcendence of it. Vargas Llosa published a collection of stories, *The Cubs*, in 1989, a novel, *In Praise of The Stepmother*, in 1990.

Consult: Gerald Mazorati, "Can a Novelist Save Peru?," *New York Times Magazine*, November 5, 1989; C. Rossman and A. Friedman, eds., *Mario Vargas Llosa: A Collection of Critical Essays* (1978); see also the special Vargas Llosa issue of *Texas Studies in Language and Literature* 19, no. 4 (1977) and of *World Literature Today* 52, no. 1 (1978).

VASSILIKOS, Vassilis. Born November 18, 1934, in Cavala, Greece; he has returned to Greece. Vassilikos left Greece in 1967 as a protest against the military dictatorship of the Colonels Regime which had taken over his country. He lived in self-imposed exile in Western Europe from 1967 to 1974. He is best known for his political thriller Z (1966; Z, 1968), which became a celebrated film by the director Costa-Gavras in 1968. Vassilikos has written several novels that treat the sufferance of exile by individuals unable or unwilling to accept contemporary political conditions in their native countries. Among them are *Kapheneion Emigrek* (1968, Coffeehouse Émigrés) and *Magnetophōno* (1970, Tape Recorder).

Selected Titles: *Trilogie: La Plante* (Paris, 1966, consists of *Le Puit, L'Ange, Le Journal de Z*); *Lunch II* (Paris, 1970); *La Belle du Bosphore* (Paris, 1974); *L'eau de Kos* (Paris, 1978).

Translation: *Fifty, Fifty* (1972).

Consult: Vassilios Christides, entry in *Encyclopedia of World Literature in the 20th Century*, vol. 4, ed. Frederick Ungar and Lina Mainero (1975).

VIDAL, Gore (Eugene Luther Vidal, Jr.; uses pseudonym Edgar Box for mysteries). Born October 3, 1925, in West Point, New York; he lives in Rome, Italy. Vidal has chosen distance from his home country as his response to a feeling of ostracism for his declared homosexuality. Although from an actively political family, he has never felt at home in the United States. He has lived in Europe, Central America, and North Africa.

The City and the Pillar (1948), written in the terse style of Ernest Hemingway,* caused something of a scandal as the first major mainstream novel to present a full realistic picture of homosexuality as a fact of life in America rather than as a dirty secret. *The City and the Pillar Revised* (1968) plays down the melodrama of the original ending in inimitable Vidal fashion by replacing what had been a murder with a homosexual rape.

Dark Green, Bright Red (1950, revised 1968) describes the revolutionary powderkeg Vidal had observed during his stay in Guatemala. The power of the novel is diminished by weak character development. *A Search for the King* (1950) retells the legend of Blondel's quest for King Richard the Lion Heart, whose imprisonment in Austria prevented his return in triumph to his homeland after the Crusades.

Messiah (1954, revised 1965) describes a religious visionary with the horrific plan of seducing the world into committing mass suicide. This novel mirrors Vidal's own feelings as an outcast and shows that he can translate such feelings into literary work of grace as well as force. *Messiah* also marks Vidal's first use of the pseudomemoir, a congenial mode for his witty style.

During the late fifties, most of Vidal's energies were devoted to dramatic writing. *Visit to a Small Planet* (1956) is a television play about a space alien as investigative reporter—the small planet of the exiled creature's study being

Earth. Vidal's major stage work is a serious political drama, *The Best Man* (1960).

In the late sixties, Vidal returned to fiction. *Julian* (1964) is a work about the apostate emperor, a misunderstood alien in a world of changing values. Like *Julian* with its classical setting, the historical novels of Vidal's American roman-fleuve—comprising to date *Washington, D.C.* (1967); *Burr* (1973); *1876* (1976); *Lincoln* (1984); *Empire* (1987); and *Hollywood* (1990)—show his impressive ability to make the names of the past come alive in the present. Another historical novel, *Creation* (1980), although it is his least lively work, gave Vidal a good deal of cultural respectability with its panorama of the birth of civilization seen through the eyes of a grandson of Zoroaster who reports to his master Herodotus the story of a strange odyssey on which he has met Buddha in India and Confucius in China.

Although dismissed by some critics as a popularizer, Vidal presents important social and political commentary in his work. *Kalki* (1978) shows his feeling of ostracism: a disgruntled Vietnam veteran decides to destroy the world—and he succeeds, only to find himself undone by the evil side of his own nature. *Myra Breckinridge* (1968), presenting fiction's first transsexual heroine, uses alternating first-person narrators to expose the superficiality of many contemporary values. *Two Sisters* (1970) is even more radical in its point of view. Built around a comically bad screenplay and combining alternating past and present first-person narrators, this roman à clef about Jacqueline Kennedy, Anaïs Nin,* Norman Mailer, and other jet-setters and culture heroes features Vidal himself as one of the main narrators and shows him finding the artistic and moral freedom in Europe that is denied to him in convention-bound North America.

Among Vidal's controversial nonfiction is *The Second American Revolution* (1982), which includes an insightful study of that "truly subversive" children's writer L. Frank Baum and describes the exile of Dorothy in the Land of Oz. In his recent book, *At Home: Essays 1982–88* (1988), Vidal has to some extent come to grips with life in America. Now when he comments on American culture he can again be witty rather than bitter.

Consult: Robert F. Kiernan, *Gore Vidal* (1982).

CHARLES KOVICH and EDMUND MILLER

VIIRLAID, Arved. Born April 11, 1922, in Padise, Estonia; he lives in Toronto, Canada. Viirlaid studied in Tallinn at the State College of Fine Arts. He was a partisan during the Nazi occupation of his country and escaped to Finland in 1943. He reached Sweden in 1944 and moved to England in 1945. In 1953 he emigrated to Toronto. He has worked as a woodcutter, farmhand, sailor, house painter, photocompositor, and houseman/laborer. He has published nine novels, the settings of which are mainly in Estonia; several of these works are fictional records of the dark period of Soviet and German occupations of his country. Of Viirlaid's work the critic Bernard Kangro has written:

Viirlaid is a realist in prose. His prose works are set in a fixed geographic environment; in a precisely defined period, they attempt to record actual happenings, historical events, and circumstances which can be deduced from reality. His characters, too, are drawn from a familiar, veritable world, though they are at times depicted as symbols. The portraits of his contemporaries are based upon his own experiences, or—as we know—based upon stories he has been told, in an effort to re-create actual case histories. Viirlaid is a herald of truth. His writing might also be called "literature of commitment," if it did not have a contrary streak running through it, which is the antithesis of Viirlaid himself.

Viirlaid has also published six volumes of poetry, a genre in which he is more a romantic celebrator of life than a witness giving testimony on contemporary history. He is presently a free-lance writer living in Toronto. His works have won several prizes and awards; he writes all his work in Estonian.

Selected Titles: Novels: *Tormiaasta I, II* (Lund, Sweden, 1949, A Year of Storms I, II); *Ristideta hauad I, II* (Lund, 1952, Graves Without Crosses I, II); *Seitse kohtupaeva* (Lund, 1957, Seven Days of Judgment); *Vaim ja ahealad* (Lund, 1961, Spit and Fetters); *Kustuvad tuled* (Lund, 1965, The Fading Lights); *Sadu jokke* (Lund, 1965, Rain for the River); *Kes tappis Eerik Hormi?* (Lund, 1974, Who Killed Eric Horm?); Poetry: *Hulkuri evangeelium* (London, 1948, A Vagabond's Smile); *Uks suveohtune naeratus* (London, 1949, A Summer's Night's Smile); *Kasikaes* (Lund, 1978, Hand in Hand); *Igaviku silmapilgutus* (Estonia, 1982, The Wink of Eternity).

Consult: Bernard Kangro, *Poets and Pearlfishers* (Lund, Sweden, 1978, in Estonian).

VOINOVICH, Vladimir. Born September 26, 1932, in Dyushambe, Soviet Central Asia; he lives in Stockdorf, a suburb of Munich, Federal Republic of Germany. Voinovich comes from a Russo-Jewish family. His father was a journalist, his mother a teacher. His father spent five years in a labor camp on a political charge. Of his childhood Voinovich writes: "My life fell together, like that of millions who were of the same age as I. Kindergarten, poems about Lenin, songs about Stalin, first grade, the war, two evacuations, hunger during the war and a half-hungry life after it. My parents simply could not nourish me sufficiently and from the age of eleven I myself began earning my hunk of bread." Of his youth Voinovich writes: "I worked on a *Col-hoz* [collective farm], in construction, in a factory, on the railroad, was an instructor on a district executive committee, and for a short time served as an editor for radio. I served four years as a soldier. I studied little." ("The Soviet Anti-Soviet Union," Ann Arbor, Michigan, Ardis Publishers, 1985).

While a soldier, from 1951 to 1955, Voinovich began writing poems and song lyrics. By the beginning of the 1960s he was the author of approximately fifty songs sung throughout the country. In 1961, the magazine *Novy Mir* (New World) published Voinovich's first prose work, "We Live Here." The protagonists are young city dwellers sent to sparsely settled regions of the country to reclaim land for agriculture. This setting and theme—resettlement of the land for the glory of collective enterprises—were popular at the time and particularly during the decade of the 1950s. Voinovich's tale drew attention by its honesty and by

its freshness of approach. Soviet party critics noted the inclination of the beginning writer to portray the workers' activities as joyless and merely dutiful.
Nevertheless, in 1962 Voinovich was accepted into the Union of Soviet Writers,
a sign of official recognition. His next work, the story "I Want to Be Honest,"
published in *Novy Mir* (no. 12, 1963), resulted in a storm of protest and denunciation of Voinovich by the Soviet press. *Izvestia* (News), *Trud* (Labor), and
Stroitel'naya Gazetta (Builders Gazette) printed fabricated letters by workers
who, as if by their own initiative, protested Voinovich's distortions of the truth
of Soviet life.

For the next seventeen years, until his emigration in 1980, Voinovich managed
to publish only three books in the USSR: *Two Comrades* in *Novy Mir*, no. 1,
1967; a collection of stories and narratives (1972); and a historical novel about
the revolutionary heroine Vera Fousnee, *The Boundaries of Faith* (1972). Voinovich did not succeed in maintaining his position as an official writer, however,
and during the years from 1963 to 1980 he was continually attacked in the party
press and by the KGB. The accusations increased sharply in 1968 when Voinovich signed a letter in defense of his colleagues Yuly Daniel and Andrei
Sinyavsky,* who had been arrested and sentenced to long prison terms in Soviet
labor camps. Voinovich also displeased official Soviet bureaucracy by a series
of public declarations not in conformity with official Soviet policy of social
behavior.

In 1973 Voinovich sent his novel *The Life and the Extraordinary Adventures
of the Soldier Ivan Chonkin* to friends in Western Europe. The novel, which re-
creates the daily life of Soviet society during World War II, is especially critical
of abuses by the Soviet army and on *Col-hozes*. The novel was a tremendous
success in the West; published in Russian in Paris in 1975, it was translated into
English and went through three printings in the United States and three in
England. It has been translated into thirty languages and sold some 500,000
copies. Critics in the United States and Great Britain have praised Voinovich as
a satirist in the tradition of Nikolai Gogol and Vladimir Nabokov*; his novel
has been hailed as the Russian parallel to the Czech comic masterpiece *The Good
Soldier Schweik*, by Yaroslav Gashek. Possibly because of the attention in the
West, Voinovich was expelled from the Union of Soviet Writers in 1974; he
spent the following six years in a limbo of persecution by official silence and
constant harassment. During this time he continued to write and to send his
manuscripts to Western Europe, where they were published to wide acclaim.

In 1977 his novella *The Ivankiada* was issued in English by the American
publishers Farrar, Straus and Giroux. This tale, which went through three printings in the United States and England, tells of an "apartment war" that leads
to an exposure of Soviet bureaucratic corruption. In the tale a high Soviet official
avails himself of the writer Voinovich's apartment, but Voinovich, through his
satirical pen, brings the matter to public attention. The resulting "war" turns
into a grimly truthful piece about contemporary Soviet-style living.

Two more manuscripts by Voinovich reached Western Europe in 1979—a collection of stories, *On the Path of a Reciprocal Correspondence*, and the novel *Pretender to the Throne*. Voinovich also wrote a play, *The Tribunal* (1985), in which he indicts the Soviet system of justice by positing that the average Soviet citizen is humiliated and belittled in Soviet courts by bureaucratic self-interest. The play is filled with humorous incidents, but the tone is far from burlesque, and the implications are tragic in the sense of hopelessness that the satire brings in its wake.

Since his emigration in 1980 Voinovich has lived in a suburb near Munich with his wife and daughter. He is a corresponding member of the Bavarian Academy of Fine Arts, a member of the West German PEN Club, and an honorary member of the Mark Twain Society of America. In 1990 his full Soviet citizenship was restored by a direct order of Mikhail Gorbachev.

MARK A. POPOVSKY, translated by Zoric Ward

Moscow 2042 (published in Russian in West Germany in 1986; in English, 1987) is Voinovich's first novel written in exile. It shows a continuity of his satiric interests—his scoring of bureaucratic pretensions and avarice—and a less controlled focus of tone. The novel is heavily dependent on current events and observations of various dissidents within the Russian exile community in West Germany; it owes much of its bite to parodies of international figures who bear remarkable resemblance to the Ayatollah of Iran and to Aleksandr Solzhenitsyn* in his reputed working-writing habits on his guarded Vermont (U.S.) estate. The protagonist, an exiled Russian writer in Germany who bears a remarkable re-semblance to Voinovich, takes a time trip into the future (Moscow in A.D. 2042) and discovers that the Great Socialist Revolution has become a dictatorship more perverse in its bending of the truth than George Orwell's dystopia of *1984*. The time-traveler witnesses the overthrow of the communist order during the course of his visit; the new leader is a writer who has preached mysticism, Russification, and a necessary submission to a patriarchal figure who will lead the Soviet Union back to the fundamental Russianness of its being. Accepting the title and robes of stardom, the new leader issues decrees mandating proper dress for men and women (nothing shorter than ankle length) and severe punishment for anti–new-social behavior and miscalculations of freedom of expression. Clearly a humanistic, intelligent satire of the dangers of fundamentalism—left and right, secular and religious, parochial and exclusive—it calls for moderation and a balanced compendium of values, but it lacks the passion and brilliance of Voi-novich's earlier, profoundly cutting remarks. Its broad canvas of hyperbolic inanities results in an amusing but pyrrhic victory of self-congratulatory satire.

Selected Titles: *Putem vzaimnoĭ perepiski* (1979, *In Plain Russian*, 1979, stories); *The Fur Hat* (1990).

Consult: Rosalind J. Marsh, *Soviet Fiction Since Stalin* (1985); Robert Porter, *Four Contemporary Russian Writers* (1990).

VYNNYCHENKO, Volodymyr (also spelled Winnitchenko and Wynny-chenko). Born July 26, 1880, in Velykyi Kut, in the Kherson region of Ukraine; died March 6, 1951, in Mougins, France. Vynnychenko became a political activist soon after entering the University of Kiev in 1901. As a member of the Ukrainian Revolutionary party he was arrested several times and ultimately forced to emigrate. During the years of Ukrainian independence he returned to his country and served as secretary-general of the Ukrainian Central Rada in 1917, and then as premier of the directorate, 1918 to 1919. Immediately after the annexation of Ukraine by the Soviets, he emigrated to the West, where he stayed primarily in Prague, and from 1924 in France. He began his literary career at the age of twenty-two, when he published his first stories. Numerous other works followed, including many novels and plays; he wrote political memoirs and sociophilosophical treatises that promoted his ideas of "concordism." He edited several periodicals, both in Ukraine and in Prague, among them *Borot'ba; Robitnycha hazeta; Nova doba;* and *Nova Ukrayina.*

In his literary work Vynnychenko employed realistic portraiture of various classes of Ukrainian society, especially the workers; his case studies were accompanied by psychological analyses. By stressing individual values rooted in good faith, he also exhibited some basic elements of existentialism, especially in his first play, *Disharmony* (1906). In most of his works Vynnychenko dealt with the need for harmony between personal values and civic duties; this approach became popularly known as "honesty with oneself" after the title of his play by that name (1911). In almost two dozen plays (e.g., *The Lie; Sin; The Great Moloch; Bazaar*) he portrayed individual striving for values and the fulfillment of meaningful dreams within existing political and social situations, whether that of Ukrainians, Jews, and/or Russians. Since the individual aspect often was tied to the national or civic, Vynnychenko generally drew in political situations as part of his context. His rather naturalistic plays have been staged in translation in many countries, and translations of his work in other genres have been made in French, German, Polish, Dutch, English, Russian, Norwegian, Spanish, Bulgarian, Italian, and Tartar.

While Vynnychenko's work written in Ukraine included realistic depictions of specific individual concerns and of belief or participation in national causes, the literary works he wrote in exile dealt primarily with universal, and quite often utopian, ideas, settings, and problems. Peace, international cooperation in political-economic spheres, workers' strikes, terrorism, and Eastern religions and their guru leaders are among the subjects of his exile work, for example, *The Sun Machine* (1928) and *The Prophet* (written in 1929, published in 1960). Vynnychenko's choice of these themes and subject matter may be explained in part as the subconscious desire of a former national leader to make known his views on the direction of world events. Vynnychenko also wished to present, or represent, his country to West European eyes and make known its traditions and its new hopes. He followed his science fiction, utopian novel *The Sun Machine* with *The New Commandment,* written in 1932 and first published in French and then in Ukrainian in 1950; its plea for peace is supplemented with his theory of "collectocracy," a philosophic construct that represents joint ownership of industries by employers and employees. Probably because of his government experience and his analyses of international politics, he was able to foresee several historic occurrences: the rise of Hitler, the Hippies' flower-children movement, the Western infatuation with gurus and swamis, and the burgeoning of international terrorism.

Vynnychenko's works were published in the USSR (e.g., a twenty-five volume edition) until the 1930s; he was extremely popular with all classes of readers. During the 1930s he was ignored or severely criticized by official commentators. His name was officially restored in 1988, and his works have begun to reappear in the USSR.

Vynnychenko left several novels and plays unpublished at the time of his death; these are slowly appearing in the United States. His personal diaries and a 700-page bibliography of his work, with over 3,300 entries are being published in Canada.

Translations: *Le Mensogne* (1926, in Italian); *Der weisse Bär und die schwarze Pantherkatze* (1922, in German); *Nouveau Commandement* (1949, in French).

Consult: Kostiuk Hryhoriy, *Volodymyr vynnychenko ta yoho doba* (1980); Larysa M. L. Onyshkevych, "*Prorok*—ostannia drama Vynnychenka," *Slovo* 5 (1973); Vadym Stelmashenko, *VV: An Annotated Bibliography* (1989).

LARISSA M. L. ONYSHKEVYCH

W ———————————————————————

WALCOTT, Derek (Alton). Born January 23, 1930, in Castries, St. Lucia; he lives and teaches in Massachusetts. Walcott's father was a poet who died young, his mother was a gifted amateur actress, and his brother, Roderick, became an established playwright. The encouragement of creative expression was thus something that Walcott experienced in his family milieu, and later at school and from colleagues. He published his first poem when he was fourteen; he published his first book of poems, *Twenty-Five Poems*, in 1948 when he was eighteen (his mother helped pay the expenses). Two years later he had his first play, *Henri Christophe*, produced by the St. Lucia Arts Guild. Walcott left St. Lucia in 1950 on a British government scholarship to University College of the West Indies in Jamaica. After graduation he taught in Jamaica and worked on a newspaper there. In 1959 he moved to Trinidad, where he lived for twenty-two years before moving to the United States to teach and be a writer-in-residence in the Boston area.

Although Walcott early developed a reputation in St. Lucia, Jamaica, and Trinidad, it was not until 1962 that he reached an audience outside the West Indies with *In a Green Night: Poems 1949–1960*. It is in *The Castaway and Other Poems* (1965) that Walcott first takes up the themes of exile and return. His life from this publication forward is migrational and seasonal, moving from the icy North American "white fellowship" to the heat-blackened Caribbean. His poems too move back and forth from shorter lyrics to the longer sequences of *Another Life* (1973), from dramatic narratives to the plays he was producing and directing at the Trinidad Theatre Workshop from 1959 to 1973.

Walcott uses the metaphor of exile loosely, for he has always been able to return home from university teaching in the United States. Yet his success in beginning a Caribbean literary tradition, in writing about that place and culture for the first time, has left him both separated from and connected to his people. As he writes, ''There are homecomings without home.'' Life changes quickly while he is gone; this flux becomes his tropical images of erasure, sea taking away sand, clouds passing. His work in the 1970s focuses on imagined return, and exile comes to mean separation of any kind—divorce, death.

In *The Star-Apple Kingdom* (1979) and *The Fortunate Traveller* (1981), Walcott takes up the historical and political issues of empire. The departure of the British from the West Indies left not only poor, undeveloped former colonies, but also a newborn, sea-born culture that Walcott believes can compete with an aging one. ''These palms are greater than Versailles,'' he writes. His own wanderings give this work a flavor of self-pity and divided allegiance. In these poems, he records the native dialogues of his archipelago. The language of his ancestors' masters mixes with the language of his ancestors. The talk of Walcott's youth was often religious; and private, prayerful metaphors inhabit his work. Raised a Methodist on a Catholic Island, Walcott creates God-fearing people who can question earthly authority. Their symbols and his are those of the church.

Midsummer (1984) is a painterly, mournful collection about the tropics and its opposites. His recent volume, *The Arkansas Testament* (1987), is his most overtly political work. It has Walcott's characteristic tone of public address, rhetoric, and large gesture. Economic injustice and regionalism divide a world of haves and have-nots, and Walcott offers a moral response. His recent poems have a new tightness and pattern, and as always, he celebrates more than he condemns.

In 1990 Walcott published a 325-page poem, *Omeros*, whose narrative spans several centuries of Caribbean history and whose locales range from the Caribbean islands to Europe, Africa and North America. The poem takes its title from the Greek spelling of Homer's name (the poet Homer becomes in Walcott's rendering a figure ostracized from his Greek society) and represents Walcott's grasp at subsuming Caribbean myth, legend and history into one narrative order of being. Moving from age to age—references and allusions go as early as the Trojan War and as late as a modern British pub—the poem achieves its unity through the guidance of mythic calling. History becomes not event but revelation of mystery at its own choice of time. Walcott attempts to infuse into the work his sense of heritage, one that allows physical distance from his native island and at the same time a closeness of indentify with it.

Selected Titles: *The Gulf and Other Poems* (1969); *Another Life* (1973); *Sea Grapes* (1976); *Collected Poems 1948–1984* (1986); *Omeros* (1989).

Consult: Edward Baugh, *Derek Walcott: Memory as Vision: Another Life* (1978); Irma E. Goldstraw, *Derek Walcott: An Annotated Bibliography of His Works* (1984); Robert D. Hamner, *Derek Walcott* (1981).

M. D. STEIN

WALDINGER, Ernst. Born October 16, 1895, in Vienna, Austria; died February 1, 1970, in New York State. Wounded in World War I—he suffered paralysis of the right side of his face and partial paralysis of his right hand—

Waldinger refused the temptations, and limitations, of semi-invalidism. His first novel, *Die Kuppel* (Vienna, 1934, The Cupola), brought him the Julius Reich prize from the University of Vienna. He went into exile when Germany annexed Austria in 1938. In 1947 he became a professor of German literature at Skidmore College; he remained at this post until his retirement in 1965.

Waldinger's writings reflect a *weltschmerz* for his lost Austrian homeland: he was an urban lyricist in a Central European milieu, celebrating Vienna and its Danube wooded shores. His publisher in Vienna, Frederick Ungar, who, like Waldinger, became an exile in New York (and was also his publisher in the United States), wrote that Waldinger believed that "only he who is tormented by longing has a real home, and not he who happens to own property." (Ungar's comments come from Waldinger's poem, *"Nur der hat Heimat, der die Sehnsucht hat."*) Waldinger also believed that poetry was civilization's final defense against barbarism and that through the order of poetry came man's triumph over the bestiality of political aberration. In Waldinger's words, "It is necessary to write poetry in order to hold against that which is most inhuman that which is most humane, a longing for what man should be."

A scholastic man, Waldinger practiced rhetoric: he wrote in many forms— among them ballads, ghazels, tercets, and sonnets—as a discipline. While he was a traditional formalist, he believed, at the same time, in confronting contemporary issues and their historic antecedents. His work is a blend of musical form and social commentary closely allusioned to Austrian history and esthetics; he remains largely untranslated into English.

Selected Titles: *Der Gemmenschneider* (Vienna, 1936, The Gem Cutter); *Die kuehlen Bauernstuber* (1946, The Cool Farmhouse Rooms); *Musik fuer diese Zeit* (1946, Music for These Times); *Glueck und Geduld* (1952, Luck and Patience); *Zwischen Hudson und Donau* (1958, Between the Hudson and the Danube); *Gesxang vor dem Abgrund* (1961, Song Before the Abyss); *Ich kann mit meinem Menschenbruder sprechen* (1965, I Can Talk With My Fellowman).

Translation: *Arabesques: Selected Verse*, with free renderings in English by Rudolph Lindenfeld (Ben Lomond, Calif., 1982).

Consult: Foreword by Frederick Ungar in *Arabesques* (1982).

WAT, Aleksander (also spelled Chwat). Born 1900 in Warsaw, Poland; died by suicide in 1967 in Paris, France. Wat's parents were active members of the Polish-Jewish intelligentsia in Warsaw; his liberal, rationalistic upbringing allowed him open access to many creeds and texts of intellectual experience. Both as poet and theorist, Wat was an active member of the Polish Futurist movement, but in his late twenties his orientation grew increasingly political-determinist. He became the editor of the Polish communist journal, *Literary Monthly*, in 1929 and remained in that office till the journal was shuttered by government decree in 1932. He was arrested by Soviet authorities in 1940 in Lvow, where he fled from the invading German army; he spent several years in Russian prisons during the war. After his release he joined his wife and son in Soviet Central

Asia, and then returned to Warsaw in 1946, acquiring a new following as literary mentor and practicing poet and writer. His increasing disillusionment with the realities of communist policies led him to seek exile in Paris in 1959. In 1964 he visited the University of California at Berkeley for a year as a guest faculty member. In 1967, ailing and with no hope of regaining his health, he committed suicide. His memoir, translated into English in 1988 as *My Century: The Odyssey of a Polish Intellectual*, was published in 1977 in London by an émigré press. The volume, based on a series of interviews Wat gave to his colleague at Berkeley, the poet and writer Czeslaw Miłosz,* expounds on Wat's intellectual affairs with communist ideology and his awakening nightmare of Soviet corruption and tyranny.

Selected Title: *Wiersze* (1957, Poems); *Ciemne swiecidlo* (1968, A Dark Knick-Knack, on existentialism); *Lucifer Unemployed* (1990, stories); *Within the Skin* (1990, poems).

WEIL, Simone. Born February 3, 1909, in Paris, France; died August 24, 1943, in London, England, from tuberculosis. The daughter of agnostic Jewish parents, Simone Weil was a brilliant student of the legendary philosopher Alain at Lycee Henri IV. She earned her *agregation* for a thesis on René Descartes and later became a philosophy teacher herself. Her spiritual odyssey led her to identify with the working classes and the underprivileged, and she gave up teaching to work in a factory. These experiences resulted in the posthumous *La Condition Ouvrière* (1951; The Condition of Work).

During the Civil War in Spain she joined the Republican cause but, through clumsiness, was severely burned and had to return home. Under the initial Nazi occupation she became a farm worker in the south of France; during this time she also experienced a series of spiritual epiphanies that led her to the brink of conversion to Christianity. She began also to read in the Oriental classics, particularly the *Bhagavad Gita*.

From 1939 to 1942 she was enormously productive and wrote numerous essays and kept fascinating notebooks, which were partially published as *La Pesanteur et la grace* (1947, Gravity and Grace) and *Attente de Dieu* (1950, Waiting for God). She also moved further away from her earlier pacifism. As always, the intellectual intensity of her commitments was matched by an emotional intensity.

In May 1942 she was forced to flee with her parents to America, though she desired to join the French underground. While in New York she struggled to find a way to support the resistance and wrote to Charles DeGaulle in London. Finally she landed a position with the Ministry of Interior of the Free French Movement there and wrote her political masterpiece, *L'Enracinement* (1949, The Need for Roots), which outlined the fundamental philosophical principles for a new French constitution. It is one of the most original and persuasive statements of human rights and duties ever formulated. (Like all her works it was published posthumously.) While in England, she refused to eat more than what was available to those living under the occupation, and this fact, combined with her tuberculosis and exhaustion, makes her death in exile a form of martyrdom. To the end of her life she was utterly single-minded.

As a writer Simone Weil was as unusual as she was as a person. Her works fit no easy classifications and cannot be considered ideologically biased. Some of her judgments are extremely harsh, particularly in regard to her views of Judaism and the Roman influence on Christianity. Though inclined toward Karl Marx's social views, she rejects a thoroughly materialistic basis for orthodox communism. Plato was her saint, not Jean-Jacques Rousseau.

Part mystic, part moralist, Simone Weil cannot be understood without allowing for the inevitable contradictions that genius seems to require for expression. She was never baptized a Christian and she seemed to reject her Semitic roots, but she embodied nonetheless a distinctly Christian asceticism with a remarkably Judaic social conscience in a unique manner.

Most of Weil's work has been translated into English.

Selected Titles: *Ouevres Complets*; vol. 1, *Premiers Écrits philosophiques*, ed. Gilbert Kahn and Rolf Kuhn; vol. 2, *Écrits historiques et politiques: L'Engagement syndical*, ed. Geraldi Leroy (Paris, 1989).

Consult: Jacques Caband, *Simone Weil: A Fellowship in Love* (1965); Robert Coles, *Simone Weil* (1987); Gabriela Fiori, *Simone Weil: An Intellectual Biography* (1989); Simone Petrement, *Simone Weil: A Life* (1976).

CHRISTOPHER P. MOONEY

WEISS, Peter (Ulrich). Born November 8, 1916, in Nowawes, Germany; died May 10, 1982, in Stockholm, Sweden. Weiss's father, Eugene, a Czech Jew who converted to Lutheranism, was a successful textile manufacturer; his mother, Frieda Hummel Weiss, a Swiss actress. Weiss's creative impulses were first channeled into photography when his family moved to England in 1934 and he attended the London Polytechnic. When he returned to Europe in 1936, he went to study at the Prague Academy of Art, where he spent two miserable years before returning to his parents' home, which was by then in Sweden. His paintings, done in the surrealist mode, were exhibited in Stockholm (1941), Goteburg (1946), and Berlin (1963). Dissatisfied with the immobility of his painting, Weiss turned first to film and then to the stage. His films were shown at the avant-garde Cinema 16 in New York City: *Hallucinations* (1953), *Faces in Shadow* (1956), and *The Mirage* (1958). The *New York Times*'s Bosley Crowther characterized their "pervasive predilection for solemn and tormenting themes of personal alienation, hallucination, sensory shifts and erotic agitation within abstract emotional voids" (January 29, 1966, p. 13).

Weiss's reputation was established forever with his play *Die Verfolgung und Ermordung Jean Paul Marats, dargestellt durch die Schauspielgruppe des Hospizes zu Charenton unter Anleitung des Herrn de Sade* (1964), translated by Geoffrey Skelton as *The Persecution and Assassination of Marat as Performed by the Inmates of the Asylum of Charenton under the Direction of the Marquis de Sade* (1965). Peter Brooks, who directed the 1967 filming of the piece, said,

"Starting with its title, everything about this play is designed to crack the spectator on the jaw, then douse him with ice-cold water, then force him to assess intelligently everything that has happened to him, then give him a kick in the balls, then bring him back to his senses again" (quoted in Ian Hilton, *Peter Weiss: A Search for Affinities* [London, 1970], p. 40). For Weiss, the juxtaposition of the symbols for ferocious individualism and passionate communalism could terminate only in ambivalence. Although it seems clear that as a man Weiss favored Marat, he worked hard to give the work an open ending, rewriting it at least five times in the first two years of its existence. The theater of ideas that Weiss crafted in *Marat/Sade* found its logical extension in his other major dramatic works. The first of these, entitled *Sangen om Skrapuken* (1967) in its original Swedish, was translated into German by Weiss himself, and thence into English (by Lee Baxandall) as *The Lusitanian Bogey*. This bitter indictment of Portuguese policy in its colonies, which was the first play to be enacted in New York by the Negro Ensemble Company, was hailed by some as a breakthrough in political musicals, condemned by others as discordant, unassimilated, and documentary. When the *Diskurs ueber die Vorgeschichte und den Verlauf des lang andauernden Befreiungskrieges in Viet Nam als Beispiel fur die Notwendigkeit des bewaffneten Kampfes der Unterdrueckten gegen ihre Unterdruecker sowie ueber die Versuche der Vereinigten Staaten von Amerika die Grundlagen der Revolution zu vernichten* appeared in 1968, which was again translated by Geoffrey Skelton (the full English title being *Discourse about the Early History and the Progress of the Prolonged War of Liberation in Vietnam as an Example of the Necessity of Armed Struggle by the Oppressed against Their Oppressors and about the Attempt by the United States of America to Annihilate the Bases of Revolution*), Weiss was again charged by some with straying too far away from the canons of entertainment.

In his two semiautobiographical prose pieces, *Abschied von den Eltern* (Suhrkamp, 1962) and *Fluchtpunkt* (Suhrkamp, 1962), which were later bound together in translation as *Leavetaking and Vanishing Point* (London, 1966), Weiss develops the themes of alienation, self-doubt, and voluntary exile that regularly plagued his existence as a half Jew, a misunderstood child, a noncommunist Marxist, and a German Czech living in Sweden. There was an early, mysterious marriage, which possibly took place while Weiss was in Prague, and which resulted in a child. Although Weiss was never shy with his opinions and has documented his own creative processes fairly copiously, the kind of lacuna that a nameless first wife leaves in his biography blends well with the eerie, suggestive trouble conveyed by his early work. His writings have been said to be in the tradition of the Brothers Grimm, E.T.A. Hoffmann, Hermann Hesse,* Franz Kafka,* and Bertolt Brecht.*

Weiss was married to the artist Gunilla Palmstierna in 1964, and it was she who collaborated with him on the staging and filming of many of his pieces. In his mature works, especially the drama, Weiss escaped the disturbing allegory of the early period and moved toward polemic. He is a major example of the artist who believes in the useful nature of the creative and moral imperatives of art.

Consult: Otto F. Best, *Peter Weiss* (1976); Ian Hilton, *Peter Weiss: A Search for Affinities* (London, 1970); Walter Wager, *The Playwrights Speak* (1967).

JUDITH BRUGGER

WELLEK, René. Born August 22, 1903, in Vienna, Austria; he died 1989 in Westport, Connecticut. Wellek received his doctorate from Charles University in Prague in 1926; he did postgraduate work at Princeton University in 1927–28. Wellek stayed in the United States to teach at several universities, most significantly Yale, where he was a member of the faculty from 1960 until his retirement in 1972. He became an American citizen in 1946.

Wellek's critical works have had an enormous influence on modern theory and literary history. With his colleague Austin Warren he published *Theory of Literature* in 1949, a work that became the source and rationale of New Criticism and its ensuing dominance in literary criticism for two decades. In his last years, Wellek devoted himself to a multivolume *History of Modern Criticism 1750–1950* ; he completed volume 4, *The Later Nineteenth Century*, in 1966.

Selected Titles: *Immanuel Kant in England 1793–1839* (1931); *The Rise of English Literary History* (1941); *The Concept of Realism in Literary Scholarship* (Groningen, 1961); *Confrontations: Studies in the Intellectual and Literary Relations between Germany, England and the U.S. during the Nineteenth Century* (1965). Bibliography: S. G. Nichols, Jr., *Concepts of Criticism* (1963), contains a bibliography of Wellek's writings in English through 1963; Wellek, *Essays on Czech Literature* (The Hague, 1963), contains a bibliography of Wellek's writings in Czechoslovakian through 1963.

Consult: Carolyn Rilar and Phyllis Carmel Mendelson, eds., *Contemporary Literary Criticism* (1977); Joseph Strelka, ed., *Literary Theory and Criticism: Fest-Schrift in Honor of René Wellek*, 2 vols. (Bern, 1984).

WERFEL, Franz. Born September 10, 1890, in Prague, Czechoslovakia; died August 26, 1945, in Beverly Hills, California. Born and raised in the Austro-Hungarian Empire, Werfel never broke his ties with that country's spiritual and cultural traditions. After his early association with the Prague circle of German-language writers, including Max Brod* and Franz Kafka,* Werfel studied in Germany and then became a reader for the Leipzig publishing house of Kurt Wolff, for which he also coedited a series of expressionist books. During World War I he served in the Austrian army, but at the same time he continued his previous career as a writer. The results of his early writing were several volumes of expressionist poems advocating peace and universal brotherhood (e.g., *Wir sind*, "We Are" [Leipzig, 1913] and *Einander*, "Each Other" [Leipzig, 1915]). In 1917, Werfel was stationed in Vienna, where he met Alma Mahler (the former widow of Gustav Mahler), who was then still married to the German architect Walter Gropius. She became Werfel's lifelong companion and later his wife.

The Werfels left Austria together in 1938 and fled via Switzerland, France, Spain, and Portugal to the United States, where they lived for the longest period of their exile in southern California. Already during the 1920s in Austria (with periods of travel and writing in other countries, especially Italy, Egypt, and Palestine), Werfel expanded his writing to other genres, and his works included some very successful dramas (e.g., *Spiegelmensch*, ''Mirror Man''[Munich, 1920] and *Bocksgesang* [Munich, 1921; *Goat Song*, New York, 1926]), novels, short stories, and essays. His literary productivity continued undiminished during the years of his exile. However, there was a shift in the form of his expression from verse to prose and the more psychological approach to the depiction of human character of the pre-exile period (e.g., in the short novel *Nicht der Mörder, der Ermordete ist schuldig* [Munich, 1920; *Not the Murderer*, incl. in *Twilight of a World*, New York, 1937] and in the novel *Der Abituriententag* [Berlin, 1928; *Class Reunion*, New York, 1929]) gradually gave way to a more socially oriented depiction of human undertakings.

An early indication of this development was apparent in the novel *Die vierzig Tage des Musa Dagh* (Berlin, 1933; *The Forty Days of Musa Dagh*, London and New York, 1934), which treats the heroic, albeit hopeless, battle of the suffering Armenians under the onslaught of the Turkish army in the year 1915. Although written before Werfel's escape from the Nazis, the novel shares a number of traits with exile literature, specifically the parallels between the fate of the Armenians as the victims of the Turks and that of the Jews under persecution by the Nazis, and also the fact that the book, when it was completed in 1933, could no longer be published in Germany. Instead, however, its English translation was accepted as one of the Book-of-the-Month Club selections in the United States, and dozens of other translations came out in other countries. On the basis of this and later successes, Werfel became one of the most widely read authors among those having fled the Nazis. Werfel was even able to surpass his own success later when he published the novel *Das Lied von Bernadette* (London, 1941; *The Song of Bernadette*, New York, 1942), which became a best-seller in the United States and in other countries and supplied the Hollywood movie industry with one of its most popular films. In the United States, Werfel also made his influence felt on Broadway: when his biblical play *Der Weg der Verheissung* (Vienna, 1935; *The Eternal Road*, 1936) was staged in New York by the Austro-German exile director Max Reinhardt, Werfel crossed the Atlantic for the first time to attend the rehearsals. Although the author was no longer present in New York when the first public performance occurred on January 7, 1937, and the play, due to bad financial planning, only ran for a few weeks, his name was indelibly connected with this huge spectacle.

In 1944, Werfel's new play *Jacobowsky and the Colonel* (New York, 1944; Germ. ed., *Jacobowsky und der Oberst*, Stockholm, 1944) was performed successfully on Broadway and was subsequently awarded the New York Drama Critics' Award for that year. This play, the plot of which Werfel heard from a fellow exile in a French hotel in the summer of 1940, expresses one of the chief concerns of the author: the reapprochement of the two major Western religions, Christianity and Judaism. The two protagonists mentioned in the title are an anti-Semitic Polish aristocrat and a refugee Polish Jew thrown together by chance on their escape from the Nazis through France. After several adventures in which they repeatedly come close to capture by their persecutors, they find a mutually acceptable modus vivendi and escape on a ship to England, while the woman between them (a symbol of their French host country) vows to keep both their memories alive in Europe. Werfel, a Jew, came himself close to Christianity not only by telling the story of a Roman Catholic saint in *The Story of Bernadette* and choosing other Christian believers for the heroes of his works (e.g., a simple maid in *Der veruntreute Himmel* [Stockholm, 1939; *Embezzled Heaven*, London and New York, 1940]), but also by his close association with Roman Catholic dignitaries in exile and his propagation of traditional Christian values in his essayistic writings (e.g., *Between Heaven and Earth* [New York, 1944; German ed., *Zwischen oben und unten*, Stockholm, 1946]).

In his last work, finished only days before his death and published posthumously, *Der Stern der Ungeborenen: Ein Reiseroman* (Stockholm, 1946; *Star of the Unborn*, New York, 1946), Werfel attempted to give his readers a comprehensive view of his literary and philosophical legacy. The book, which in German is subtitled a "travel novel," is set in the year 101,945, when the characters have only a remote memory of the time in which the book was written. People have conquered most of their former illnesses, and their average life span is over 200 years; their transition from life to death is eased by a gradual shrinking process that leaves them in a flowerlike state. Though social classes still exist— the plot is set in California, from where one can travel with the speed of light to distant stars—only representatives of Judaism and Roman Catholicism, who work and live harmoniously with each other, are left on earth. Since the author himself, as Franz Werfel, is a visitor from the distant past appearing in the novel, he obviously did not want to deny its utopian character. He also carried many elements of his own time into the futuristic framework and juxtaposed humor with serious commentary. While the apparent utopia can be read as a satire on the present age, it also expresses the author's admiration for his American host country. Because of its unclear geographical setting (California has been leveled flat and all dwellings are underground) and its abstract style of narration, the novel also suggests a paradigm of exile. Werfel's last novel did not find as many readers as some of his other works written both prior and during his exile period, though these works too have fallen into relative neglect today. Perhaps the materialistic outlook of many readers is no longer attuned to the spiritually oriented social conservativism of Werfel.

Selected Titles: *Eine blassblaue Frauenschrift* (Buenos Aires, 1941); *Cella oder Die Überwinder* (1942); *Gedichte aus den Jahren 1908–1945* (1946).

Consult: Lore B. Foltin, *Franz Werfel* (Stuttgart, 1972); Lionel B. Steimann, *Franz Werfel: The Faith of an Exile* (Ontario, 1985); Alma Mahler Werfel, in collaboration with E. B. Ashton, *And the Bridge Is Love* (1958).

HELMUT F. PFANNER

WHITE, T. H. (Terrence Hanbury). Born May 29, 1906, in Bombay, India; died January 17, 1964, while traveling in the Mediterranean. At the time of White's birth his parents were resident in Bombay, and after he was brought to

England he retained vivid memories of his childhood in the Asian subcontinent. White's background—he learned Hindustani before English, for example—suggests that, initially at least, he felt somewhat an exile in his parents' homeland; nonetheless, the years spent growing up in the Buckinghamshire home of his maternal grandparents were happy ones. White's parents, however, "loathed each other," White wrote in an autobiographical sketch printed in Sylvia Townsend-Warner's biography, *T. H. White*, p. 27. His father took to drink, and in White's last year at Cheltenham boarding school, his parents went through an unusual (for the times) and embarrassingly public divorce, rendering their adolescent son a social outcast, at least in his eyes. Throughout his youth White "adored passionately" his "strong-willed, imaginative, selfish, beautiful" mother, but as an adult he rejected her just as passionately (she is portrayed as Morgawse in *The Witch in the Wood*). Later White blamed her for making it impossible for him to love a woman, but he condemned the single-sex British public school, with its birching and fagging, for turning him toward homosexuality and sadomasochism. (He diagnosed himself as a sadist, but those who knew him best saw little of this in his nature.)

While attending Queens College, Cambridge, on a scholarship, White developed tuberculosis, and several faculty members who recognized his promise made up a fund to send him to Italy. Here he produced his first extended works— a book of poems and two novels—all of which were ultimately accepted for publication. Returning to take his degree in 1928, White became a schoolteacher, continuing to write in his free time and during vacations. He took up gentlemanly sports—fox-hunting, fishing, fowl-shooting—to which he added such novelties as sports-car driving, airplane-flying, and falconing. He also acquired the only creature he ever loved unreservedly, a red setter named Brownie. Five additional books appeared by 1938; all were well received, but only one, *England Have My Bones* (1936), achieved much popularity.

When World War II broke out, White was staying in Ireland, which remained neutral, and his own strong antiwar feelings induced him to remain there to avoid military service and complete his Arthurian tetralogy, volume 1 of which (*The Sword in the Stone*, 1939) had already appeared. During this philosophic exile White was at his most productive, not only finishing the additional three volumes of *The Once and Future King* (plus a fifth volume, *The Book of Merlyn*, published posthumously [1977]) but also writing *Mistress Masham's Repose* (1946), and translating *The Book of Beasts* (not published until 1954) from medieval Latin—the three works for which he is most likely to be remembered. He also wrote an account of his experiences with falconry (*The Goshawk*, 1951) and a pair of delightful studies of eighteenth-century England, *The Age of Scandal* (1950) and *The Scandalmonger* (1952); two further works arising from his stay in Ireland, *The Godstone and the Blackymor* (1959) and *The Elephant and the Kangaroo* (1947), were less successful.

Despite his conviction that war was "species suicide," White's love for the English countryside and his recognition that Hitlerian Germany represented an evil far greater than that which he believed was embodied in all nations and governments (see the debate in *Merlyn*) led him to return to England and volunteer for military service—only to find himself disqualified by his past tuberculosis and failing vision. After the war, White lived in Norfolk for less than two years before the need to avoid taxes—which would have taken almost all the profits on his books (chiefly from American sales, Book-of-the-Month Club selection of *The Once and Future King* and *Mistress Masham's Repose*, and sale of movie rights for *The Sword in the Stone* to Walt Disney)—drove him into a financial exile in the Channel Islands.

Buying a cottage on Alderney, White continued to seek new experiences (he took up deep-sea diving, and very nearly got married) but wrote little of lasting interest during his final years.

Selected Titles: *Dead Mr. Nixon* (1931); *Darkness at Pemberley* (1932); *Farewell Victoria* (1933); *Earth Stopped* (1934); *Gone to Ground* (1935); *Burke's Steerage* (1938); *The Witch in the Wood* (1939); *The Ill-Made Knight* (1940); *The Master* (1957); *The Once and Future King* (1958).

Consult: John K. Crane, *T. H. White* (1974); François Gallix, ed., *Letters to a Friend: The Correspondence between T. H. White and L. J. Potts* (1982); David Garnett, ed., *The White/Garnett Letters* (1968); Sylvia Townsend Warner, *T. H. White: A Biography* (1967).

RICHARD GRIFFITH

WIESEL, Elie. Born September 30, 1928, in the small town of Sighet in Transylvania, midway between Hungary and Rumania; he lives in New York and commutes to Boston to teach. Wiesel was still a child when he was taken from his home with his family and sent to Auschwitz and Buchenwald, where his father, mother, and younger sister perished. After the war he was brought to Paris where he studied at the Sorbonne. He also spent some time in India and as a reporter travelled throughout Europe, Israel, and North and South America. He has been an American citizen for some years and holds the position of university professor and Andrew Mellon Professor of the Humanities at Boston University. He has been chairman of the Holocaust Memorial Commission in Washington. In 1986 he was awarded the Nobel Peace Prize.

From his first, autobiographical book *La Nuit* (1959; *Night*, 1960), all of Wiesel's works have spoken of exile in the most powerful manner and in the triple sense of exile from home, from one's own humanity, and from one's faith in God and man. "My generation has been robbed of everything, even of our cemeteries," wrote Wiesel in *Le Chant des Morts* (1966) (1968; *Legends of Our Time*, p. 9). "At Auschwitz, not only man died, but also the idea of man" (p. 100). Contemporary literature is dominated by the timeless man of the concentration camp: "dehumanized, naked or in rags, weaned from society and civilization, somebody's victim always, a corpse on reprieve, groping in the dark, drained of hope and dreams" ("On Revolutions in Culture and the Arts" [1973] in *Against Silence: The Voice and Vision of Elie Wiesel*, vol. II, ed. Irving

Abrahamson, p. 71). Although some critics consider all analogies with the Holocaust as demeaning comparisons to the Jewish genocide, the horrible event for Wiesel represents an aberration and culmination point of history from which all today's dehumanization, terror, isolation, and murder of language stem. He ends his book *Paroles d'étranger* (1982) by telling how after the war he entered a period of total disillusionment, silence, asceticism, and isolation: "I felt myself above all a stranger. I had lost my faith, then my sense of belonging and of orientation. My faith in life: covered with cinders. My faith in man: derisory, puerile, sterile, My faith in God: disturbed. Things and words had lost their significance, their axis" (p. 187).

In *Night* Wiesel tells the story of how he was deported from his Hungarian-Jewish village when he was a child of fourteen, how his mother and sister were metamorphosed into the smoke above the crematoriums, how he and his father suffered through Auschwitz, Buchenwald, and forced winter marches until finally, just before liberation, his father died: "Never shall I forget those moments which murdered my God and my soul and turned my dreams to dust" (pp. 43–44).

The pattern of Wiesel's early novels stems out of *Night*. In *L'Aube* (1960; *Dawn*, 1961) Wiesel places what is recognizably the Eliezer of *Night*, now called Elisha, in the position of a Jewish terrorist, killing English soldiers in an effort to secure the independence of the Jewish state in Palestine. In *Le Jour* (1961; *The Accident*, 1961), this same child of *Night*, somewhat older and now an Israeli correspondent at the United Nations, is almost killed by a taxi, and in the course of a long and painful recovery confronts the fact that he had seen the taxi, that he wanted to die, that he did not fight to stay alive even in the hospital. He is one of the "spiritual cripples" who must live apart from men because he tells them something about their common humanity that they cannot bear. Although in *La Ville de la Chance* (1962; *The Town Beyond the Wall*, 1964) Michael wants "to turn his ticket in," like the "Modern Promethean" of the nineteenth century, he avoids madness and brings his unknowable answer into the Dialogue with the Absurd. Both he and Gregor in *Les Pôrtes de la Forèt* (1964; *The Gates of the Forest*, 1966) learn of the exile not only of themselves but of the world. Yet they work their way through the rebellion of the Modern Promethean to the trust and contending of the Job of Auschwitz who meets the living present, including the absurd, with the courage to address and respond. Recalling the era when "all gates were shut tight to us and all eyes full of daggers," in his book of essays and stories *Chants des Morts* Wiesel asserts that it is the Holocaust that may engender that extinction of the human race by nuclear warfare as "the punishment for Auschwitz where, in the ashes, the hope of man was extinguished." "It is as though every country—and not only Germany—had decided to see the Jew as a kind of subhuman species" whose "disappearance did not . . . weigh on the conscience" since "the concept of brotherhood did not apply" to him (*Legends of Our Times*, pp. 180, 188).

In *Le Mendicant de Jérusalem* (1968; *A Beggar in Jerusalem*, 1970), Wiesel went beyond Martin Buber's statement in 1933 that "the Jew is the most exposed person in the world today." Wiesel recognizes that the inhumanity unleashed upon the Jew so threatens the humanity of all men that only in sharing the exposure can any person today become human. In a sense all of Wiesel's other books are preparation for *A Beggar in Jerusalem*, for only here do the living fight *with* the dead and not against them. Even Wiesel's concern in *The Jews of Silence* (1966) with the Jews of the Soviet Union, whose harassment Wiesel was one of the first to make widely known, stands under the sign of the "Modern Job." Out of a situation of exile and constraint the young Jew of Russia made an act of commitment. Toward the end of *Paroles d'étranger* Wiesel gives a magnificent portrayal of the Job of Auschwitz walking the narrow ridge between blind faith and total denial, combining trust and contending in the Dialogue with the Absurd: "Man continues to revolt despite faith, to affirm faith despite revolt" (p. 179).

All of Wiesel's writings express the pathos of the messianism of the unredeemed, the inverted messianism of a cursed century. At the end of his novel *The Gates of the Forest*, the hero Gregor realizes that it does not matter whether or not the Messiah comes or whether he comes too late. The Messiah does not dwell above in glory, David learns in *A Beggar in Jerusalem*, but below in the suffering and exposure of human beings. In 1968 Wiesel suggested that existentially the world has turned Jewish: for two thousand years the Jewish people lived on the edge of extinction; now the whole world lives in the shadow of the atomic bomb. The challenge for everyone is identical with what Wiesel defines as the substance of Judaism—"to remain human in a world that is inhuman." As a child Wiesel dreamed of bringing the Messiah; in 1971 he said he would be satisfied with helping only one person.

Another measure of Wiesel's relation to exile is his retelling the tales and the world of the Hasidim, the popular communal Jewish mystics of eighteenth- and nineteenth-century Eastern Europe. In *Célébrations Hasidique: Portraits et Legends* (1972; *Souls on Fire*, 1972), the first of his Hasidic books, Wiesel asserted that the Hasidim, who knew trust, giving and receiving, sharing and taking part, warmth and generosity could not survive in a society ruled by cold cruelty, a cruelty both impersonal and absurd. In 1972, musing on the fact that the majority of the Jewish victims, more than 3 million, came from Hasidic communities, Wiesel suggested that the Holocaust was a psychological contest between Nazi paganism and Hasidism, between Hitler and the Baal Shem Tov, the founder of Hasidism. The Nazi goal of depriving their victims of all human dignity and turning them into objects could not coexist with the Hasidic goal of glorifying humanity and man's role in Creation.

Wiesel's modern messianism is a continuous call to overcome despair by the unrelenting agency of hope. In *Un Juif Aujourdhui* (1977; *A Jew Today*, 1978) he has written that "we must show our children that in spite of everything, we keep our faith—in ourselves and even in mankind, though mankind may not be worthy of such faith." What such hope against despair means in our contemporary world Wiesel has shown in the way in which he points to the danger of a nuclear holocaust. "Memory may perhaps be our only answer, our only hope to save the world from the ultimate punishment, a nuclear holocaust," said Wiesel in his speech at the Day of Remembrance ceremony in Washington, D.C., on April 24, 1979 (Brown, p. 138).

Wiesel has said that the suffering of anyone (and everyone) involves him and that if he does not speak up—whether for the Palestinian Arab or the Cambodian refugee or the Vietnamese prisoner—he will lose part of his humanity. He has participated in appeals and protests for humanitarian action toward the "boat people" of Southeast Asia and all other victims of injustice. As chairman of the U.S. Presidential Commission on the Holocaust, Wiesel, on behalf of the commission, implored all countries to open their borders and extend rights of refuge and asylum to the boat people. Crueler than the barbarians of antiquity, wrote Wiesel in "The Stranger in the Bible" (in *Paroles d'étranger*), the Nazis tried to dehumanize their victims before killing them: they reduced the stranger to an object. It is possible for human beings to relate to the stranger as a Thou and not an It, Wiesel has written, using the language of Martin Buber.

The Nobel Committee, in conferring its award on Wiesel in September 1986, proclaimed: "His belief that the forces fighting evil in the world can be victorious is a hard-won belief. His message is based on his own personal experience of total humiliation and of the utter contempt for humanity shown in Hitler's death camps. The message is in the form of a testimony, repeated and deepened through the works of a great author. Wiesel's commitment, which originated in the sufferings of the Jewish people, has been widened to embrace all oppressed peoples and races" (*New York Times*, October 15, 1986, pp. 1, 4). Wiesel writes in French. His wife, Marion Wiesel, is his translator.

Selected Titles: *Le Serment de Kolvillàg* (1973; *The Oath*, 1973); *Zalmen, où la Folie de Dieu* (1968; *Zalmen, or the Madness of God*, 1974); *Célébrations bibliques: Portraits et Legends* (1975; *Messengers of God: Biblical Portraits and Legends*, 1976); *Le Testament d'un Poète Juif Assassiné* (1980; *The Testament*, 1981); *Le Cinquième Fils* (1983; *The Fifth Son*, 1985); *Le Crépuscule au loin*, 1987 (*Twilight*, 1988); *L'oublié* (1989); (with John Cardinal O'Connor) *A Journey of Faith* (1990); (with Philippe-Michël de Saint-Cheron) *Evil and Exile* (1990); *From the Kingdom of Memory: Reminiscences* (1990).

Consult: I. Abrahamson, ed., *Against Silence: The Voice and Vision of Elie Wiesel*, 3 vols. (1985); Robert McAfee Brown, *Elie Wiesel: Messenger to All Humanity* (1973); Harry James Cargas, ed., *Responses to Elie Wiesel: Critical Essays by Major Jewish and Christian Scholars* (1978); Ellen S. Fine, *Legacy of Night: The Literary Universe of Elie Wiesel* (1982); Maurice Friedman, *Abraham Joshua Heschel and Elie Wiesel: "You Are My Witnesses"* (1987); Alvin H. Rosenfeld and I. Greenberg, eds. *Confronting the Holocaust: The Impact of Elie Wiesel* (1978). See also Molly Abramowitz, *Elie Wiesel: A Bibliography* (1974).

MAURICE FRIEDMAN

Elie Wiesel returned to Germany in January 1986 for the first time since he was rescued from the Buchenwald concentration camp in 1945. He was in the country as part of a two-day meeting of the German-American Council of the U.S. Holocaust Committee, organized to prevent the world from forgetting the Nazi program of liquidation of 6 million Jews in Europe.

WINCHEVSKY, Morris. Born 1855 in a Lithuanian village near Kovna; died in New York City in 1932. Winchevsky was educated in the Lithuanian capital of Kovna; he worked as a bank clerk in Russia and became active in the revolutionary movement. Writing in Hebrew, he became editor of a socialist newspaper in Königsberg, Prussia, in 1878, an activity that caused his deportation shortly after. In London he began to write in Yiddish as a means of communicating with uneducated Jewish factory workers. He was instrumental in founding the first Yiddish labor daily, *Der Arbeiter Freint* (The Workers Friend) in 1885. He moved to the United States in 1894 and worked as a journalist-editor of socialist organs, and wrote his autobiography. In 1925 his collected works were published by the *Morning Freiheit* (New York) in ten volumes.

WODEHOUSE, P. G. (Pelham Grenville). Born October 15, 1881, in Guildford, England; died February 14, 1975, in Remsenburg, Long Island, New York. Wodehouse went to "public school" (a private preparatory institute) in Dulwich, an "old boys school" he cherished, though with some reservation over its stringent codes. He worked on the (London) *Globe* for several years. His first visit to the United States was for vacation in 1904. On his second American visit in 1909, he brought two stories with him and sold both of them on the day of his arrival; he immediately sent off a cable to the *Globe* announcing his resignation. He became and remained a full-time writer, working several hours each day at his writing until the last day of his life (he died, after a morning's stint at his desk). The United States thus provided him with his first literary success, and with his first, and lasting, wife, Ethel Rowley, whom he met in New York on August 3, 1914, and married on September 30 of that year. The couple rented lodgings in Bellport, Long Island, for $20.00 a month, where Wodehouse could work in quiet surroundings. Years later he would return with his family to another Long Island community, Remsenburg, to gain respite from the one lacerating controversy in his career. That controversy, which was resolved ultimately to Wodehouse's credit, concerns a series of five broadcasts he made over German radio during June and July 1941. As a result of them, he was branded a traitor by the "Cassandra" columnist of the (London) *Mirror*, William Connor, and calls for sanctions against him were made in the British Parliament, the press, and on the BBC, where many of his scripts had been aired. The entire story has been told several times, and the evidence shows that Wodehouse was foolish to have acceded to the request to give the talks and that the German propaganda office was so anxious to have Wodehouse on their "radio" that they allowed him to criticize German (in)efficiency and (dis)order in his characteristically affable but accurate satirical manner. (See Harry Flannery, *Assignment to Berlin*, 1942; Iain Sproat, *Wodehouse at War*, 1981, which contains texts of

Wodehouse's broadcasts and statements made in regard to them by Wodehouse and Ethel Wodehouse.)

Wodehouse and his wife had settled in France in 1932 to live as comfortable expatriates. They purchased a house in Le Touquet, in the Normandy countryside near the Channel. Here Wodehouse worked during the next fifteen years, the most productive and lucrative period of his life; he also received the academic distinction of a D.Litt. degree from Oxford University. He toiled in Hollywood (for high fees) in 1930 (for MGM), in 1936 (for MGM again), and in 1937 (for RKO Pictures). He worked with Guy Bolton and Jerome Kern on several Broadway musicals (he contributed the lyrics for "He's Just My Bill" for the Kern operetta *Showboat*). He returned to his house in Le Touquet in 1937 to work more steadily on his Jeeves books. When the Germans overran France in May 1940, he and his wife were put under supervision; two months later they were sent to Loos prison (Wodehouse was booked under the name Widhouse). He was ordered into a mental institution with some other political detainees in Tost, Silesia (Germany), where he was kept for a year and then allowed to move to a hotel (under supervision) in Berlin. A correspondent for CBS in Berlin, Harry Flannery, asked Wodehouse if he would agree to be interviewed, and Wodehouse accepted the offer. The five "interviews" were broadcast over German radio, instead of CBS as planned and earlier announced to Wodehouse; they concentrated on Wodehouse's comments about his prison treatment by the Germans. Aired in June 1941, and heard in England and the United States as well as in Germany and its conquered lands, the broadcasts caused a furor. Many of Wodehouse's supporters and many in the British government felt betrayed by him; the Germans, though Wodehouse made careful fun of them as inept prison administrators and avoided all mention of their racial/political policies, were pleased with their propaganda coup. It is likely that Wodehouse was innocent of any error but that of political naiveté; it is also possible that he had some fear of the consequences of not acceding to German pressure for the interviews. While Wodehouse remained in German hands, and was treated with some comfort, the British reaction grew in adverse patriotic hostility.

In 1943 the Germans sent Wodehouse and his wife to Paris, again for detention in a comfortable hotel. After the Allied Forces retook Paris, Wodehouse and his wife were arrested by the French police on November 20, 1944, without any specific charges. Ethel Wodehouse was released shortly after, but Wodehouse was ordered confined in a hospital, where he remained until January 20, 1945. Pressure from Britain and the U.S. undoubtedly aided in the campaign to free him from his adopted expatriate country's political machinations: Anthony Eden had spoken (on December 6, 1944) on Wodehouse's behalf to Parliament, declaring that no grounds existed for any charges of treason against Wodehouse.

Between his release from hospital detention and his move to the United States in 1947, Wodehouse and his wife lived in a series of dreary hotels across France. Throughout his ordeal—a black Wodehousian comedy of hearing without listening—Wodehouse remained, according to reports, impeccably polite and observant of his reason. His works, some written in detention (the first was *Money in the Bank*, published in 1946), and those that came after, are not distinguished by bitterness, anguish, unmannerly anger, or lack of mannerly control. They seem as fresh—or as dated—as the work preceding World War II. Yet, Wodehouse was affected enough to change his habitat. Instead of returning to his French house or to England, where anti-Wodehouse feeling persisted, he moved to the United States, where his popularity and esteem had never waned. The Wodehouses lived in a Park Avenue apartment until 1952 when they bought their home on Basket Lane in the east end Long Island community of Remsenburg and began a new, familiar town-and-country life. Three years later, on December 16, 1955, he became a naturalized American citizen.

Britain made amends to Wodehouse in July 1961, when the BBC aired its "Act of Homage and Reparation." Evelyn Waugh was one of the speakers who paid tribute to Wodehouse's behavior during the war, and to Wodehouse's tact and courage while in internment. On January 1, 1975, six weeks before he died, Queen Elizabeth announced Wodehouse's knighthood to the British realm.

Selected Titles: Jeeves Novels and Story Collections: *The Inimitable Jeeves* (1923); *Thank You, Jeeves* (1934); *The Code of the Woosters* (1938); *Ring for Jeeves/The Return of Jeeves* (1953); *Jeeves and the Feudal Spirit/Bertie Wooster Sees It Through* (1954); *How Right You Are, Jeeves* (1960); *Much Obliged, Jeeves* (1971). Blanding Castle books: *Something New* (1915); *Blandings Castle* (1935); *A Pelican at Blandings* (1969); *Sunset at Blanding* (incomplete, London, 1977). Memoir: (with Guy Bolton) *Bring on the Girls!* (1953). Uncle Fred books: *Uncle Fred in the Springtime* (London, 1939). Lyrics for musicals with Guy Bolton (book) and Jerome Kern (music): *Miss Springtime* (1916); *Oh,Boy!* (1916); *Ok, Kay* (1926); *Anything Goes* (1934); *Don't Listen, Ladies* (1948).

Consult: Thelma Cazelet-Keir, ed., *Homage to P. G. Wodehouse* (London, 1973); Joseph Connelly, *P. G. Wodehouse* (London, 1979); Frances Lonsdale Donaldson, *P. G. Wodehouse* (1982); Daniel Garrison, *Who's Who In Wodehouse* (1987); Benny Green, *P. G. Wodehouse: A Literary Biography* (1981); James Heineman and Donald Bensen, eds., *P. G. Wodehouse, a Centenary Celebration 1881–1981* (1981); David Jasen, *P. G. Wodehouse: A Portrait of the "Master"* (rev. ed., 1981 [1974]); David Jasen, *The Theatre of P. G. Wodehouse* (London, 1979); George Orwell, in *Dickens, Dali and Others* (1946); Richard Usbourne, *Wodehouse at Work to the End* (rev. ed., London, 1977).

WOLFSKEHL, Karl. Born September 17, 1869, in Darmstadt, Germany; died June 6, 1948, in Bayswater-Auckland, New Zealand. Wolfskehl saw himself as an inheritor and carrier of high German culture; he traced his roots to a Tuscan-Jewish family that had settled in Mainz during the time of Charlemagne. His first collection of poems appeared in 1903; publication of scholarly and critical articles established his intellectual reputation as well. A disciple and colleague of the abstruse German surrealist poet Stefan George, he joined with George in editing anthologies of surrealist verse and in translating European surrealist poets into German. He issued, in the decades before his exile, dramatic works, epics and lyric poems of rarefied emotion and moral/cultural responsibility. Because he continued to believe in the Germany he knew—a community of philosophy, music, literature, intellect, and sophistication—and because he had faith that such a community of moral and esthetic force would triumph over Nazi barbarity, he did not leave for exile until 1937. In 1938 he reached New Zealand, where he spent the remaining ten years of his life. In New Zealand he proved an indefatigable scholar and enthusiast, continuing in the mold he had set for himself as a German artist. Nearly blind, without friends or his books (he had left behind his fine library) Wolfskehl nevertheless kept pace with new acquaintances, and with reading the work of New Zealand poets and exploring the New Zealand countryside. He recorded these experiences in his last book, *Zehn Jahre Exil: Briefe aus New Seeland* (Letters from New Zealand, 1938–1948), which was published posthumously in 1959.

Selected Title: *Gesammelte Werke* (Hamburg, 1960, Collected Works).

Consult: Michael Hamburger, *A Proliferation of Prophets: Essays on German Writers from Nietzsche to Brecht* (1983).

WOWK, Wira (also spelled Vira Vovk; pseudonym of Vira Selans'ka). Born January 2, 1926, in Boryslav, Western Ukraine; she lives in Rio de Janeiro, Brazil. Wowk began writing poetry at an early age in Ukraine; her first collections were published when she emigrated from Western Europe after World War II to Brazil, where she now resides. A professor of comparative literature, poetics and German literature at the Universities of Rio de Janeiro, St. Ursula's, and Cabo Frio, she has published thirteen books of poetry and prose in Ukrainian. Two have been translated into Portuguese, English, and French. She has also written five studies of leading Ukrainian writers (Skovoroda, Shevchenko, Franko, Stefanyk, and Ukrayinka) and translated them into Portuguese; she has compiled and translated anthologies of Ukrainian literature into both Portuguese and German, and translated into Ukrainian the works of leading European writers. Many of her anthologies are bilingual, with original Ukrainian texts; some are trilingual (e.g., *Meandry/Meandres/Meanders*, in Ukrainian, French, and English).

Wowk's own poems are lyrical, introspective, and abundant in metaphors that stem from Ukrainian folklore or from typical Brazilian Flora. She has written two verse dramas: *Smishnyi svyatyi* (1968, A Funny Saint) and *Tryptykh* (1982, Triptych). *A Funny Saint* discloses her sense of humor and irony as well as elements of mysticism and surrealism; *Triptych* employs Ukrainian laments and pre-Christian ritual songs. In both verse dramas the language varies from the archaic to the contemporary.

Visual as well as aural imagery is essential to Wowk's work. *Triptych* is subtitled "To the Cylindrical Pictures of Yuriy Soloviy" (the artist's work is reproduced in the book). Many of Wowk's volumes include reproductions of art work or her own colored-paper cutouts; her anthologies of Ukrainian literature usually contain work by contemporary Ukrainian artists.

Translation: *Mandala II* (trilingual edition, Ukrainian, Spanish, and English, Rio de Janeiro, Brazil, 1980).

Consult: Larissa M. L. Onyshkevych, "Rizni svity Viry Vovk," *Suchasnist* 9 (1987).

LARISSA M. L. ONYSHKEVYCH

WRIGHT, David (David John Murray). Born 1920 in Johannesburg, South Africa; he lives in England. Wright suffered physical exile as a child through the affliction of deafness. He was sent, when he was fourteen years old, to England to study at the Northampton School for the Deaf; later he attended Oxford University. His poetry often deals with exilic themes, both those of deafness and of separation from home country. He published a record of his conflicting reactions to a return trip home in *A South African Album* (1976). Wright is considered a major translator from the Old English (he published a version of *Beowulf*) and a critic of South African literature; one of his studies is *Roy Campbell* (1961). He was awarded the Guinness Poetry Prize in 1958.

Selected Titles: Poetry: *Poems* (1949); *Moral Stories* (1954); *Monologue of a Deaf Man* (1958). Prose: *Deafness: A Personal Account* (1967).

WRIGHT, Richard. Born September 4, 1908, near Natchez, Mississippi; died November 28, 1960, in Paris, France. Wright was the son of an illiterate share-cropper and a mother who taught school briefly. When Wright's father deserted the family and his mother became ill, Wright was sent to his grandmother, who raised him with strict Seventh Day Adventist discipline. Wright dropped out of high school, ran off to Memphis and then to Chicago, where he worked on a WPA project. In 1932 he joined the Communist party, but over the years grew increasingly disillusioned with Party tactics and discipline. He remained a Marx-ist but wrote of his disaffection and withdrawal from the Party in his essay "I Tried to Be a Communist," published first in 1944 in *Atlantic Monthly* magazine and later reprinted in the collection edited by Richard Crossman, *The God That Failed* (1949).

Wright left for Paris in 1946 at the invitation of Gertrude Stein.* He had suffered harassment in the United States for his outspoken political and social views and was treated as a pariah by government and establishment figures. He was greeted with honor and warmth by the French intelligentsia. Wright was impressed with the European celebration of black achievement and moved his family to Paris in 1947. For the next thirteen years he lived in Paris and became a celebrated figure there. After his trip to Ghana in 1953 he wrote *Black Power*, a call to Pan-Africanism and the benefits of continental African hegemony in contrast to the limits of African national states. Wright's commentary, influenced by his association with the West Indian social analyst George Padmore and W.E.B. Du Bois,* the American writer and social theorist, were not enthusi-astically received by African audiences. Some African writers and intellectuals regarded him as an "outsider" and his comments as naïve. White critics resented Wright's characterization of their African policies as condescending and exploitative: Wright said the psychologically crippled white had created a millstone round Africa's neck by using the continent as a psychosymbolic tool of White redemption. Wright was disappointed by the rejection of his African readers; the disappointment became one of several wounds he experienced as an expatriate who was honored but patronized. Wright's increasing sense of isolation from the mainstream of American events and his figurehead role in African affairs resulted in occasional bitter outbursts. He wrote several novels and works of nonfiction; he wrote for many distinguished black American and African journals, among them *Présence Africaine*, based in Paris; but nothing he wrote in his later, exile years equaled the raging beauty of his early work.

Wright's early novel *Native Son*, considered by some critics the finest book of its kind in its exploration of rage as answer to white condescension, was dramatized into a Broadway success (cowritten with Paul Green) in 1941, and filmed twice, once in the 1950s with Wright playing the lead role of Bigger Thomas, and again in the mid–1980s.

Wright's output during his exile years was prolific, and some of it is still appearing years after his death. Among his late novels are *The Outsider* (1953), *The Long Dream* (1958), and *Lawd Today* (1963). Among his nonfiction studies are *The Color Curtain*, the 1955 report, published first in French, of the 1955 Bandung Asia Conference of Third World Countries; the travel book *Pagan Spain* (1957); and his commentary, *American Hunger* (1977). Wright wrote a still-unpublished novel, ''Island of Hallucination,'' in which he narrates the story of an expatriate writer kept under surveillance by CIA agents because of his Marxist-oriented writings. The novelistic interpretation is a bitter portrayal of Wright's understandable paranoia and very real anger at his harassment by American agents in what he had hoped would be a foreign refuge.

Consult: Michel Fabré, *The Unfinished Quest of Richard Wright* (1977); Addison R. Gayle, *Richard Wright: Ordeal of a Native Son* (1980); Keneth Kinnamon, *The Emergence of Richard Wright: A Study in Literature and Society* (1972); David Ray and R. M. Farnsworth, eds., *Richard Wright: Impressions and Perspectives* (1973). See also *A Richard Wright Bibliography: Fifty Years of Criticism and Commentary, 1933–1982*, compiled by Keneth Kinnamon, with the help of Joseph Benson, Michel Fabré, and Craig Werner (1988).

WYNTER, Sylvia. Born May 11, 1928, to Jamaican parents in Cuba; she lives in the San Francisco area and teaches at Stanford University. Wynter is scholar, teacher, and creative artist. She was taken to Jamaica at two years of age when her parents returned to their native island, and she attended primary and secondary school there. She went to England for her B.A. in modern languages (Spanish, 1949) and her M.A. (1953), both from the University of London. From 1954 to 1959 she traveled in Europe and spent much time in Scandinavia, where she performed as an actress and dancer. In 1958 she met the writer Jan Carew* and later married him (he was her second husband); they moved to British Guiana (now Guyana), the birthplace of Carew. Wynter and Carew collaborated on scripts for the BBC, both in adapting West Indian and other writers to radio and television and in completing her own dramatic work. In 1962 they left British Guiana, then in the midst of riots, and moved to Jamaica, where they planned to set up a professional theater company specializing in original Jamaican scripts, both traditional and modern/experimental.

In 1962 Wynter also published her first novel, *The Hills of Hebron*, loosely arising out of her dramatic play *Under the Sun*, which had been broadcast by the BBC in 1961 and announced for production at the Royal Court Theatre in London. During their two years in Jamaica Wynter wrote several plays and musicals. In 1963 she and Carew separated; he emigrated to Canada and she entered the academic world as a professor at the Mona, Jamaica, campus of the University of the West Indies. In 1967 she started publishing critical articles on Caribbean and African literature. She was invited to teach at the University of California–San Diego campus in 1974, from which institution she went to Stanford University as a professor of Spanish. In resigning from her position at the University of the West Indies in 1975, she effectively signaled her decision to become an expatriate by reason of career.

Consult: Jeannette B. Allis, *West Indian Literature: An Index to Criticism 1930–1975*; Edward Braithwaite, "The Love Axe: Developing a Caribbean Aesthetic, 1962–1974, Part I," *Bim* 16 (July 1977); Part II, *Bim* 17 (December 1977); Victor Chang, in *Fifty Caribbean Writers: A Bio-Bibliographical Critical Sourcebook*, ed. Daryl Cumber Dance (1986); Donald E. Herdeck, ed., *Caribbean Writers: A Bio-Bibliographical-Critical Encyclopedia* (1979).

X ————————————

XU Gang. Born 1945 in Shanghai, China; he lives in exile in the West and prefers that his whereabouts remain unknown. Xu was drafted into the Chinese army in 1962. He began publishing poetry in 1963 and became famous during the Cultural Revolution for his poems in support of the regime. In 1974 he graduated from Beijing University. He worked for the *People's Daily*, China's most important newspaper, for a number of years until 1987, when he was forced to leave that position. He lived in Guangdong between 1987 and the time of the student demonstrations in the spring of 1989. After the military crushing of the prodemocracy movement in June of 1989, Xu went into exile.

Xu's collections of poetry include *The Great River of Full Tide; The Flower of Rain; Dedicated to October; Songs for the Far Away*; and *One Hundred Lyrics*. He has received the National Poetry Prize, the *October Magazine* Award, the Yu Hua Prize, and other awards. His outlook and writing style have changed considerably since his early years as a writer. His poem "Red Azalea on the Cliff" is the title poem of the anthology *The Red Azalea: Chinese Poetry since the Cultural Revolution*, ed. Edward Morin (Honolulu, 1990), which also contains four other translated poems of Xu.

EDWARD MORIN

Y ———————————————————————

YANG Lian. Born 1953 in Berne, Switzerland; he lives in New Zealand. Yang returned with his parents to China when he was one year old. He settled in the country during the Cultural Revolution; he began writing poetry in 1976. Since his early poems were published in *Today* (*Jintian*), the short-lived magazine of the controversial Obscurist poets, he has been associated with that group and has published articles in their defense. Although *Today* was eventually suppressed, its writers received favorable press reaction and relatively mild censure from the government, which eventually loosened controls over its publication. Approved magazines began to publish work by the risk-taking authors of *Today*, none of whom had reputations before the Cultural Revolution (1967–76).

Yang's poems have also appeared in major national magazines, and he has worked for the Central Broadcasting Commission in Beijing. In the early months of 1987, several of his books were banned, yet he has continued to write poetry and a major work of criticism, *The Self-Awareness of Man*. In 1989 he visited Hong Kong, and from there moved with his wife and child to Auckland, New Zealand. Translations of his poems have appeared in several issues of *Renditions: Chinese Literature in Translation* (Hong Kong), in no. 11 of *Frank: An International Journal of Contemporary Writing and Art* (Paris, 1989); and *The Red Azalea: Chinese Poetry Since the Cultural Revolution*, ed. Edward Morin (Honolulu, 1990).

EDWARD MORIN

YANOVSKY, Vasily Semenovych. Born April 14, 1906, in Poltava, Russia; he died July 26, 1989 in Queens, New York City. In 1922 Yanovsky left the USSR illegally with his two sisters and father. Graduating from the medical faculty of the University of Paris in 1937, he received the degree of doctor of medicine. During his university-medical training years he was writing stories and short novels and supported himself by working in an atelier designing and printing scarves. His first novel, *The Wheel* (1928), concerns the youthful impressions of an author living through the famine in Russia during the early post-Revolution years. Warmly received by the emigrant press, it was translated into French. In his novel *The World* (Paris, 1931), Yanovsky drew on his knowledge as a medical doctor to render and to imply comments on the events described; his approach led to charges of imitation of the literary practices of the French writer-doctor, Louis-Ferdinand Céline.* To these charges Yanovsky responded, "Day and night I am looking for a God of love and light, and that you can't find in Céline."

While living in France before World War II, Yanovsky published his novels *Second Love* (Paris, 1935) and *Portable Immortality* (New York), the latter work printed serially in the magazine *Russian Life* before publication in book form. In *Portable Immortality* two groups fighting for a better future for humanity expropriate the same slogan, "Thy kingdom come." Both groups proclaim the goal of earthly paradise, but one tries to achieve its dream on a spiritual plane while the other relies on technological means. The critic Vladimir Varshavsky in his book *The Unnoticed Generation* wrote: "In *Portable Immortality* Yanovsky once more raised a key theme of Russian literature—'The Kingdom of God on Earth.' This is a very difficult theme, and in the twentieth century there are only a few who dare to undertake it." E. Izvolskaya, in commenting on the same book in the American periodical *Triquarterly* (1973), wrote, "Yanovsky is inspired by the idea of humanism, social justice and the transformation of the crude material world by transcendental philosophy and the active participation of the personality in life."

Yanovsky came to the United States in 1942 and became a naturalized American citizen in 1947. His first novel written in the United States was *An American Experience*, published serially in *The New Review* in the late 1940s and in book form by Silver Age Publishing Company in 1982. In the novel a white man in New York City wakes up one morning to discover his skin has turned black. Forced to start a new life as a black person, he finds he must readjust to profound social prejudices of which he is now a focus. The newspaper *Novoe Russkoe Slovo* (The New Russian Word) in its October 24, 1948, issue wrote: "*An American Experience* belongs to that body of work which calls forth lively discussion and at times sharp controversy. This is a good sign. For the most bitter arguments only show that the work has touched to the quick."

Yanovsky also published in Russian two short novels, *The Jaw of the Emigrant* (1957) and *The Hostage* (1957–58), after which work he began writing in English as well. Among his works are *No Man's Time* (1967, with an introduction by W. H. Auden*); *Of Light and Sounding Brass* (1972); *The Dark Fields of Venus: From a Doctor's Logbook* (1973); *The Great Transfer* (1974); and *Medicine, Science and Life* (1978). *No Man's Time* and *Of Light and Sounding Brass* were written in Russian and then translated into English.

Yanovsky's memoir *Elysian Field: A Book of Memory* was published in the original Russian in 1983 by Silver Age Press in New York; the English translation by Yanovsky's wife, Isabella, and himself appeared in 1987. In this book of reminiscences Yanovsky draws on his memories of the bright galaxy of Russian writers and intellectuals in exile in Paris in the 1920s and 1930s. Among his word-portraits are those of Nikolai Berdyaev,* Lev Shestov, Marina Tsvetaeva,* Ivan Bunin,* Dmitry Merezhkovsky,* Ales Adamovich, Boris Poplavsky,* and Vladislav Khodasevich.* The words of Voltaire serve as an epigraph for the book: *"Aux morts on ne doit que la verité."* Richard Howard, in commenting on the book, wrote that "At eighty, Yanovsky has preserved every last drop of the emigre's venom. . . . His account of the Russian literary emigres in France in the twenties and thirties . . . must be read as a concoction *at full strength* of that historically traduced cluster of geniuses and fakes, thrust upon the thorns of life: there is blood on every page." Yanovsky's works have been translated into English, French, and Italian.

MARK A. POPOVSKY, translated by Zoric Ward

YATES, Dornford (pseudonym of Cecil William Mercer). Born August 7, 1885, in Walmer, Kent, England; died March 5, 1960, in Umtali, Rhodesia. A child of a prosperous professional family, cousin of Saki (H. H. Munro), Yates received a traditional upper-class English education at Harrow and University College, Oxford, before studying law and being called to the bar (Inner Temple, 1909). War service in the Levant left him with chronic rheumatism that forced him to leave England for the drier climates of southern France (until World War II) and then Southern Rhodesia (until his death). Reasons for Yates's exile may have been as much social as medical. Living abroad he could better preserve his romantic vision of squirearchal England and insulate himself from the austerities of an increasingly Labour-oriented post-Edwardian England: self-exile from a rapidly changing culture was his means of preserving it for himself and his unabashedly escapist creative work. Many of his novels and stories are elegant, whimsical social comedies featuring Lord Peter Wimsey families, the Pleydells and the Mansels, whose boyish and often genuinely funny hijinks recur in works from *The Brother of Daphne* (1914) to *The Berry Scene* (1947). The other novels are romantic thrillers set in a becastled Ruritania (or Austria), where John Buchan heroes perform "knightly" deeds amid elaborate gothic horrors (dungeons, collapsible floors, quicklime pits, mantraps). Despite the prominence of fast cars, these works are low-tech James Bond adventures, with an emphasis on British codes of gentlemanly behavior. They are marred by occasional Bolshi-bashing, disparagement of lower classes who don't know their place, and unpleasant, genteel anti-Semitism. In 1985 two adventure novels, *Perishable Goods* (1928) and *Blind Corner* (1927), were reprinted.

Consult: A. J. Smithers, *Dornford Yates: A Biography* (1982).

BRUCE R. S. LITTE

YEFIMOV, Igor Markovich (he also writes under the pseudonym Andrei Moscovit). Born August 8, 1937, in Moscow, USSR; he lives and works in Tenafly, New Jersey. Yefimov received an engineering degree from Leningrad

Polytechnical Institute in 1960 and later graduated from the Moscow Literary Institute in 1973. His first book, a collection of novellas and short stories, *High on the Roof*, was published in Leningrad in 1964. Yefimov became a member of the Union of Soviet Writers, and in the next fifteen years published several works of fiction, among them *Look Who's Come* (1965); *The Taurida Garden* (1969); *Plus, Minus, and Timosha* (1971); *A House of Cards under a Storm* (1975); the novella *The Laboratory Girl* (1975); as well as a popular science book about aircraft construction, *The Stronger the Wind, the Faster the Sound* (1976). His books have been translated into Polish, Rumanian, and Slavic. In 1977 Yefimov's documentary-historical novel *Throw Off All the Yokes*, set in seventeenth-century England during the Protestant Revolution, was issued in Moscow. His novel "The Spectacle," however, was consistently rejected by publishers out of fear of official censorship.

Yefimov emigrated with his wife and two children to the United States in 1978. Several works that he was unable to publish in his homeland were subsequently published in the West. Among these are the novels *As One Flesh* (1981) and *The Judgment Day Archives* (1982), both in the original Russian versions. Earlier in 1979, Yefimov published a journalistic account of the Soviet economy, *Without the Bourgeoisie*, and two philosophic works he had written while in the USSR: *Metapolitics* (under the pseudonym Andrei Moscovit) in 1978 and *Practical Metaphysics* (1980), the latter serially printed in the magazine *Grani* in 1973. A large part of the manuscript of *Practical Metaphysics* was smuggled out of the country.

Rich in ideas and varied in form, Yefimov's work has provoked attention and discussion. His *Judgment Day Archives* has been compared both to a detective story and a science fiction fantasy in its unique webbing of form and content. His philosophic speculations are issued in dynamic narration; in the afterword to *Without the Bourgeoisie*, Robert Bowie of the University of Miami wrote:

It is difficult to define the type of book being offered to the reader. Is it a writer's notes on industry and rural economy? But notes are not so carefully documented. Is it a textbook on the economy of socialism? Is it journalistic sketches? But the author, a former engineer, penetrates the technological and organizational peculiarities of contemporary production with more details than are accessible to a journalist.

Yefimov's profoundest speculation is to be found in the two philosophical works issued after his emigration. In *Metapolitics* he poses the problem of politics as a working system: "How on earth to get along with people of different tribes and nationalities, of different languages and colors of skin, of different faiths and traditions, of different professions and capabilities, and can we get along or must we fight with others and overpower our adversaries?" In a review of work in 1979, a critic for *Novoe Russkoe Slovo* (The New Russian Word) writes: "Before me appeared a new book on the world, distinguished principally from all which had been explained to me for fifty years running. . . . The author's . . .

ability to pick out from the different epochs the essential facts, to find the inner unity, greatly stirs the reader's interest."

Metapolitics was issued in an English-language version in 1985.

Yefimov's second philosophical work, *Practical Metaphysics*, has been described by one critic as an "unquestionable contribution to the treasury of philosophical thought" and as an enriching source for the "deepening of classical conceptions of German idealism" (*Grani*, 1978).

In 1987 Yefimov published a documented study of the assassination of President John Kennedy of the United States, *Kennedy, Oswald, Castro, Khruschev* (Tenafly, N.J.: Hermitage Press). After four years of research Yefimov concluded that Fidel Castro had hired the Mafia to kill Kennedy. Castro considered Kennedy a personal enemy who had repeatedly enlisted CIA agents for the killing of the Cuban leader. In 1988 Yefimov's novel *The Judgment Day Archives* was published in English (San Francisco); a long new novel called "The Seventh Wife" was scheduled for 1990.

Yefimov, who has worked at several publishing houses, is now director of the Hermitage Press, which has, since 1981, published more than 100 books by Russian writers in exile.

Translation: *Our Choice and History* (1985).

MARK A. POPOVSKY, translated by Zoric Ward

YOURCENAR, Marguerite. Born June 8, 1903, in Brussels, Belgium; died December 17, 1987, in Mount Desert Island, Northeast Harbor, Maine. The first woman named to the Académie Française (in 1980), Yourcenar was noted as a versatile master of various genres, as a classical scholar, and as a stylist of note in both her own writings and those she translated into French. Her Belgian mother died when Yourcenar was a month old, and most of her education resulted from tutors and her French father. As a child she read French classics, and in her teens she published two volumes of poetry. When she was nineteen she adopted the name "Yourcenar" (a partial anagrammatic nom de plume of her birth-name, "Crayencour") and, independently wealthy, traveled extensively throughout Europe, Asia, and North America. She left Europe in 1939 for the U.S., where she taught French and art history at Sarah Lawrence College from 1940 to 1950, becoming an American citizen in 1947 but later reassuming French citizenship. She and her longtime American companion and collaborator, Grace Frick (who died in 1979), moved to Maine, where she lived until her death. In addition to becoming the first woman inducted into the forty-member Académie Française, she was also a member of the American Academy and Institute of Arts and Letters and the Académie Royale Belge de Langue et de Littérature Françaises.

Yourcenar's writings are noted for their meditative emphasis on mortality, the relevance of myth, and what she called "magic arts," as well as for her wide-ranging ease in drawing on various literatures and languages for allusions and sources. She is also celebrated for her careful psychological analysis of characters who resist established ways of thinking and behaving, particularly in matters of sexual orientation, and her probing into her characters' reflections on the self, human mortality, the ideal of the beautiful, and historical forces.

Though her first published works were volumes of poetry (published in 1921 and 1922), Yourcenar is better known for her fiction, both novels and stories. Her first novel, *Alexis ou le traité du vain combat* (Alexis, or the Treatise of Vain Struggle; *Alexis*, 1984), appeared in 1929 and is an intense first-person account of an aristocratic youth's discovery of and defense of his homosexual feelings, despite illness and an extensive sense of guilt. Her second novel, *La Nouvelle Eurydice* (1931, The New Eurydice), also explores homosexuality but with a triangle (two males and one female) complicating an easy resolution of relationships. In 1934 she published *La Mort conduit l'attelage* (Death Drives the Team), a group of three stories, each in the style of a particular painter, Albrecht Dürer, El Greco, and Rembrandt; these were rewritten and republished in 1981 under the title of *Comme l'eau qui coule* (Like the Water That Flows; *Two Lives and a Dream*, 1987), and one of the stories was expanded as the novel *L'Oeuvre au noir* (1968). In 1934 she published *Denier du reve* (a work issued in revised versions in 1959 and 1971; it was published in English in 1982 as *A Coin in Nine Hands*). This psychologically probing work, set in fascist Rome, concerns a planned assassination of Mussolini, focusing on the characters' inner conflicts and dreams through stream-of-consciousness and flashback techniques. In 1938 she published a collection of stories, *Nouvelles orientales* (*Oriental Tales*, 1985), subsequently expanded in 1962 and 1978; these tales, touching on the fantastic and exotic, reflect the story-within-a-story technique familiar in a number of Yourcenar's later works. And in 1939, she published *Le coup de grâce* (*Coup de Grâce*, 1957; as a film, directed by Volker Schlöndorff, 1978), focusing on a dashing romantic hero, again a homosexual; after this, however, she wrote only a few short works before emigrating to the U.S.

Yourcenar's first major work after emigrating, and her widely acknowledged masterpiece, was *Mémoires d'Hadrien* (1951; *Memoirs of Hadrian*, 1954), a work that consisted of imaginary recollections of the Roman emperor and that received wide praise. Each of the six parts of the work deals with a specific part of Hadrian's life and integrates physical maturing with personality development and complexity.

Her next novel, *L'Oeuvre au noir* (1968; *The Abyss*, 1976), is a three-part historical account of the wanderings of two cousins, one a would-be adventurer wishing to join the king's army, the other one finding greater challenge in literature. In the two men's reflections and activities, Yourcenar is able to raise a number of important philosophical questions, such as the nature of truth and heresy. An omnibus collection of Yourcenar's fiction appeared in 1982 under the title *Oeuvres romanesques*.

In addition to works of fiction, Yourcenar wrote several intriguing autobiographical works. The parabolic *Feux* (1936; *Fires*, 1981) combines verse and prose and is based on some of Yourcenar's diaries, relating such personal accounts to classical and biblical myths. *Les Songes et les sorts* (1938, Dreams and Fates) is a selection of narratives based on Yourcenar's dreams, narratives offering much fuel for psychological interpretation. The two-volume *Le Labyrinthe du Monde* (1974 and 1977, The Labyrinth of the World) stretches the form of the autobiography by exploring, in the first volume, *Souvenirs pieux* (Holy Souvenirs), her mother's personal and family history, and, in the second, *Archives du Nord* (Northern Archives), her father's.

Yourcenar has also written two volumes of plays (*Théatre*, 1971; *Plays*, 1984) noted for conventional, often mythic, forms combined with complex thematic and character analyses. Individual plays worth noting include the following: *Le Dialogue dans le marécage* (1932, Dialogue in the Marshes) is a free rendering of a Noh play. *La Petite Sirène* (1942) is a dramatic retelling of Hans Christian Andersen's "The Little Mermaid." *Electre ou la chute des masques* (1954, Electra, or the Fall of Masques) is an imaginative variation on the legend. *Rendre à César* (1961, Render unto Caesar) is a loose adaptation of Yourcenar's novel, *Denier du rêve*, more realistic than its source but overladen with lengthy speeches. *La Mystère d'Alceste* (1963) is a mystery-play adaptation of another myth. *Qui n'a pas son Minotaure?* (1963, Who Doesn't Have His Minotaur?), what Yourcenar calls a "sacred divertissement," explores the idea that each person has an individual "Minotaur" to overcome.

Yourcenar's poetry includes the two adolescent volumes mentioned above, and a 1956 volume. *Le Jardin des chimères* (1921, The Garden of Chimeras) is an ambitious retelling of the myth of Icarus and Daedalus. *Les Dieux ne sont pas morts* (1922, The Gods Are Not Dead) focuses on the world of Greek antiquity and exotic mythologies such as the story of Scheherazade. *Les Charités d'Alcippe et autres poèmes* (1956; *The Alms of Alcippe and Other Poems*, 1982) also touches on classical mythology as well as on other French writers (e.g., Jean Cocteau).

Yourcenar translated many works into French, including some by James Baldwin,* Constantine Cavafy,* Thomas Mann,* Henry James,* Yukio Mishima, and Virginia Woolf, as well as Greek and Punjabi poetry, and, in *Fleuve profond, sombre rivière* (1966, Deep, Troubled Waters), American Negro spirituals. *La Couronne et la lyre* (1979, The Crown and the Lyre) is a popularized collection of translations from ancient Greek verse. Another work based on American black writing appeared in 1984, *Blues et Gospels*.

Among her miscellaneous nonfiction, *Pindare* (1932), based loosely on the Greek poet, is an unusual mixture of history and fiction. *Sous bénéfice d'inventaire* (1962; *The Dark Brain of Piranesi and Other Essays*, 1984) is a collection of seven essays, all originally written as introductions or for journals. *Mishima ou la vision du Vide* (1980; *Mishima: A Vision of the Void*, 1987) discusses the fiction and suicide of the Japanese novelist. *Les Yeux ouverts: Entretiens avec Matthieu Galey* (1980; *With Open Eyes*, 1984) is a collection of interviews. *Le*

Temps, ce grand sculpteur (1983; Time, the Great Sculptor) includes essays on a wide variety of topics, from Mozart to Zen, from Bede to Greek mythology, from Arnold Böcklin to the decline of Europe.

Yourcenar's longevity and wide range of topics can easily disguise her repeated emphasis on the individual, of any era, who maintains his or her personal integrity regardless of circumstance or catastrophe, who openly acknowledges personal sensuality as well as mortality, and who celebrates the continuity of the past with the present. Her characters are often trapped by their particular time, but their underlying, basic senses of truth and beauty surpass the forces of tyranny or death. Her rigorous celebration of the classical past can easily be seen in her own precise scholarly style; her openness to more recent history and her highly personal tone suggest an unusual degree of concern with honor.

Selected Titles: *En pelerin et en etranger* (Paris, 1990 [posthumous collection of essays]); *Quoi? L'Eternité* (Paris, 1990).

Consult: Jean Blot, *Marguerite Yourcenar* (Paris, 1971; rev. ed., 1980); Mavis Gallant, "Limpid Pessimist," *New York Review of Books*, December 5, 1985; Pierre L. Horn, *Marguerite Yourcenar* (1985); Henri Peyre, "Marguerite Yourcenar: Independent, Imaginative, and 'Immortal'," *World Literature Today* 57 (1983). See also Special Issue *Études littéraires* 12 (1979).

PAUL SCHLUETER

YOURGRAU, Barry. Born 1949 in South Africa; he lives in New York and Los Angeles. Yourgrau left South Africa as a child with his family. He has published two collections of stories, *A Man Jumps Out of an Airplane* (1984) and *Wearing Dad's Head* (Salt Lake City, 1987). He is also a performance poet/writer who has appeared in theaters, clubs, and performance-art spaces as well as radio. Yourgrau says he prefers the "short-short" form, the minimalist approach to literature, because "I've just found I'm most in tune and expressive working small. Brevity and ardor suit me."

Consult: "Afternotes," *Sudden Fiction International*, ed. Robert Shapard and James Thomas (1989).

YU Li-hua. Born November 28, 1931, in Shanghai, China; she lives in Albany, New York, where she teaches at the State University. Yu started her writing career in college by contributing stories to *Literary Magazine* in Taipei, to which she had fled from mainland China in 1949. She came to the United States in 1954 for advanced studies and has lived in different parts of the country since. Yu is a prolific writer whose earlier fiction is dominated by the milieu of the academic community of Chinese intellectuals in the United States. In her short stories, she uses a simple style together with situational irony and satiric wit to present Chinese savants enmeshed in academic intrigues, university politics, and personal tragicomedy. Her characters struggle to cope not only with the inevitable predicaments of confronting an alien culture but with their sense of personal loss and dislocation. Early work includes *Homecoming* (Taipei, 1963), a collection of stories; *Recollections of Ching River* (Taipei, 1963), a novel; and *Again the Palm Trees* (Taipei, 1967), a novel. Like the work of many prolific writers, Yu's writing suffers from occasional carelessness in style and taste; as a reflection of Chinese intellectual life in the 1950s, her books memorialize a certain periodic perspective. Since the mid–1970s she has visited mainland China several times and written a number of essays and stories based on impressions of her visits. Because of her expressed views, Yu's books, which had been popular in Taiwan in the 1950s and 1960s, have become largely unavailable at local markets there.

DOROTHY TSUNGSU WEISSMAN

Z ────────────────────────────────────

ZAGAJEWSKI, Adam. Born 1945 in Lvov, Poland; he lives in Paris. Zagajewski studied philosophy at Cracow University and published his first poems
while a student there; he was active in protesting what he conceived as totalitarian
conditions in his country. His early work is expressed in a satiric tone characteristic of the activist generation of 1968; his poems, reflecting the views of a
large number of university intellectuals, are written, in the words of Czeslaw
Miłosz,* in a "naked speech practically stripped of metaphors." Although Zagajewski has grown more metaphysical in his general consideration of life,
particularly in his relationship to social and political currents, he found the
situation in his country so oppressive that he emigrated in 1981 to France.

The sense of his exile work is largely timeless and stateless in a commitment
to moments of insight in a province of memory rendered as landscape. Spare,
imagistic, direct, the language he employs reveals a sense of yearning for a
resting place from the flux of experience as well as a felt satisfaction in his
phantom soil of learning and growth. Zagajewski has said that writers should
not be policemen of other people's morals. In a PEN International Congress,
held in New York in 1986, he declared:

Freedom of expression is vital, but it may be dangerous for us to become only vigilant
controllers of others' deeds and sins. There is appearing a new race of intellectuals—
controllers of the situation of freedom. I share their interest and anxiety. I am one of
them, and at the same time, I am against them, because I do not always share their vision
of literature.

Yet Zagajewski's poems, shorn of shibboleths and dressed in textured images
of personal illumination, are profoundly moral in their concerns with the individual and his right to dissent; Zagajewski also is intent in his right to silence

as an appropriate measure of behavior.

Zagajewski treats the theme of his Jewish identity in terms of alienation of sensitivity through unexpressed exclusion rather than by overt acts of prejudice. His exilic stance is not only national—a Pole in France—but racial/religious, a Jew searching for meaning in a world whose acceptance of him is forbearance of eccentricity rather than stringless admission of the exotic stranger into the community.

Tremors, Zagajewski's first volume of poems, was published in English in New York in 1985.

ZAMAYATIN, Yevgenii Ivanovich. Born February 1, 1884, in Lebedyan, Tambov province, Russia; died March 10, 1937, in Paris. Zamayatin joined the Bolshevik party in the early 1900s and took part in the 1905 Revolution; he was imprisoned and exiled but returned to Russia illegally to continue his studies. He was again arrested and sent into internal exile, where he wrote *Uezdnoe* (1913; *A Provincial Tale*, 1967). His second novella, *Na Kulichkakh* (1914, In the Provinces), which drew a mocking portrait of a provincial garrison town, resulted in a charge of slander of the Russian military, but he was found innocent of any crime. He spent two years in England during World War I as a designer of icebreakers for the Russian navy.

Zamayatin, who continued to insist on individual creative freedom though he always maintained his profound Bolshevik advocacy, suffered persistent attack by Party-line theoreticians during the 1920s. He was accused of deviationism in his refusal to join the ranks of socialist realism and Stalinist revisionism. The publication of *My* (*We*) in the Russian émigré journal *Volya Rossii* in Prague in 1927 intensified these attacks (*My* was published in a full text in 1952). *We* is a science-fiction tale in which a future national state goes berserk in its regimentation of individual lives—the benevolent tyranny of a profound social experiment becomes a new instance of modern slave conditions in which thinking and moral considerations are forbidden and all judgment is imposed by the state. *We*, which was not published in the USSR, has had a wide influence on Western science fiction and is the model for Aldous Huxley's *Brave New World* and a number of other dystopian fictions.

Depressed and exhausted by the defamatory campaign against him, Zamayatin petitioned Joseph Stalin as head of the Soviet state for permission to leave the country. Through the intercession of Maxim Gorky,* a friend and admirer, Zamayatin was allowed to emigrate in 1931. He spent the remaining years of his life in Paris and wrote very little. Zamayatin, who had battled with czarist bureaucracy before the 1917 Revolution, lost heart in exile. Believing in the communist experiment that his land had undertaken, he did not join Russian émigré circles in Paris, whether they were composed of aristocrats, democrats, and/or anarchists; believing that his country's revolution had spun into a crushing whirlpool of rigid ideology, he knew he stood alienated from fellow communists in the USSR. He hoped for but did not live to see a rehabilitation of his work in his native land.

Zamayatin's work has not been "rehabilitated" in the Soviet Union. The revolutionary writer remains an exile in death, and his works are practically unknown in his native land. It is an ironic tribute to his masterpiece *We* that its author exemplifies victimization by unofficial and official ignorance of his work.

Select Titles: *The Islanders*; *Armored Train 14–69* (Ann Artor, 1978); *The Fisher of Men* (Edinburgh, 1984). See definitive edition, *We* (1975).

Consult: Introductory material by Peter Ruby, Marc Slonim, and Gregory Zilborg, with critical afterword by Vasa D. Mihailovich, in *We* (1975).

ZECH, Paul. Born February 19, 1881, in Briesen, West Prussia, Germany; died September 7, 1946, in Buenos Aires, Argentina. Zech fled Germany in December 1933 after being imprisoned briefly for socialist views expressed in his writings; he left behind his wife and two children. In Argentina he eked out a living writing for exile magazines, among them *Deutsche Blätter* (published in Santiago, Chile) and for the Yiddish periodical *Di Presse*; his brother sent him money for a while but ended his support, leaving Zech in a precarious position. A prolific writer (Zech had written four plays and edited an important journal in one year, 1924), Zech wrote copiously in exile but found few publishers. He alienated the Argentine establishment by propagating his view that the South American native Indian was kept a subject citizen in Argentina by a coalition of German immigrants and Creoles; the coalition, Zech suggested, was a bourgeois power grouping intent on preserving social and economic advantages through racial prejudice. Zech completed his novel, *Deutschland, dein Tänzer ist der Tod* (Germany, You Are Dancing with Death), which he had begun in Germany in 1933; the novel addressed the issue of exile directly, with all its concomitants of rejection and alienation in the refuge land of the émigré.

Selected Titles: *Ich suchte Schmied . . . und fand Malva wieder* (1941, I Was Looking for Schmied . . . and Found Malva Again); *Kinder vom Parama* (1952, Children of Parama); *Die Vögel des Hernn Langfoot* (1954, Mr. Langfoot's Birds); *Die grüne Flöte vom Rio Ben* (1955, The Green Flute of Rio Beni); *Das rote Messer: Begegnungen mit Tieren und seltsamen Menschen* (1955, The Red Knife: Encounters with Animals and Strange Humans); *Menschen der Calle Tuyutí: Erzahlungen aus dem Exil* (1982, People of Tuyuti Street: Tales from Exile [stories]).

Consult: Donald G. Daviau, "Paul Zech as an Interpreter and Mediator of South America," in *Kulturelle Wechselbeziehungen im Exile—Exile Across Cultures*, ed. Helmut F. Pfanner (Bonn, 1986); Ward Lewis, "The Poet and the Tower: A Development in the Images of Paul Zech," in *German Life & Letters*, new series 24 (January 1971).

ZEMDEGA, Aina. Born August 2, 1924, in Talsi, Latvia; she lives in Burlington, Ontario, Canada. Zemdega's father was born of peasant stock, but rose to high bourgeois station in Russia, where he became the owner of a flour mill. When the Revolution broke out in 1917, Zemdega's father returned to his homeland; Zemdega was born there near the Baltic seacoast. She sees herself as a part of several cultures: peasant stock, bourgeois tradition, Russian heritage (her father told her many stories of his "Russian life"), and profound Latvian origins. She was a part of the generation born into the country's first period of independence in many centuries; she was free to taste of many foreign traditions and cultures long denied to her forebears under autocratic czarist rule. That freedom of exposure was shuttered when Soviet troops invaded the country in 1940, followed by the Germans in 1941. Like their neighbors, the Estonians, many Latvians supported Germany as a lesser alternative of evil than the Soviets, who in their one year of occupation had slaughtered tens of thousands of Latvians. When the Soviet forces were returning in triumph to Latvia in 1944, Zemdega and her family left in a fishing boat across the Baltic to Sweden. She lived there for six years, married, and gave birth to her first child. With what she describes as "Soviet pressures" and a fear of the political situation in the cold war period, she and her family emigrated to Canada, where she worked as a bookkeeper. Zemdega divorced and remarried, happily, to a dermatologist, and became a mother again. She published her first book of poetry in 1963, and turned to fiction when, as she puts it, she found she could not say everything in poetry she wanted to say.

Zemdega has distinguished herself both as a musicologist and as a writer. She holds degrees in music from the Royal Conservatory of Toronto and from Trinity College of Music in London (England). Zemdega has written all her work in Latvian (though in an interview with the editor of this study, she ruefully admitted "the Latvian reading public is getting smaller"). None of her work has been published as yet in Latvia. She has chosen exile and separation as her major theme, and described Canada on her return from a visit to Poland a few years ago as a place where she still felt a foreigner, though she has lived in Canada for more than thirty-five years. Identity and the search for roots inform all her work with a special poignancy. In her memoir/novel *Varasava neaizmirst* (written 1983; published in Brooklyn, New York, 1984, In Warsaw They Never Forget), she has her autobiographical heroine attending a musicologists conference in Warsaw and at the same time reliving her past; at the end of the work the heroine is left with a sense of loss and nostalgia rather than any triumph of having moved on. Of her fifth volume of poetry *Viena mūža nepietiek* (Hamilton, Ontario, Canada, 1987, One Life Is Not Enough), the reviewer, Aija Bjornson, in *World Literature Today* (Summer 1988) wrote:

She has written an evocative poetic memoir of her exile experience, perhaps the central experience of all her work. Her poems explore various facets of this theme: the sense of loss and disorientation, the struggle to find and maintain her dignity in a new land, the return to her homeland, and the attempt to find a link both to the past and to the new place that her country has become. These are familiar topics in the work of Latvian emigré poets, but Zemdega treats them with originality. . . . the poems have a muted and meditative tone, as if the poet were carrying on a conversation with herself.

Zemdega expects a book of her prose to be published in Latvia next year, her first publication in her native land.

Selected Titles: Poetry: *Basām kājām* (1963, Barefoot); *Egles istabá* (1968, Spruce Trees in My Room); *Cirsma* (1974, Clearing); *Zem akmena zala zāle* (1980, Under the Rock Green Grass); Prose: *Toreiz Lubes dzirnavās* (1979, Long Ago at Lube Mill); *Lidz vārtien—un tālák?* (1988, As Far as to the Gates—and Then What?).

Consult: Aija Bjornson, *World Literature Today*, Spring 1985 and Summer 1988.

ZHANG Xinxin. Born 1953, in Nanjing, China; she lives in exile in the United States; at present she is a visiting scholar with the Department of Comparative Literature, University of Georgia. Zhang's education was interrupted by the Cultural Revolution, when she was programmed as a farm laborer in the barren north of China. She became a nurse but fell ill with kidney disease; on her recovery she became an administrator in the Communist Youth League. She graduated from the Central Academy of Drama in Beijing in 1984, with a concentration in theater-directing (one of her projects was a theater production of Arthur Miller's *Death of a Salesman*). She later joined the Youth Art Theater and became a well-known performer on Chinese television. Zhang's fiction has also achieved prominence but embroiled her in controversy over the openness of her views and her outspoken criticism of social conditions in China. Her first story, "A Quiet Night," was published in 1979, and was followed by several works of short fiction and essays. Her newest work, written in collaboration with Sang Ye* and published in the United States under the title *Chinese Lives* (New York, 1989), is an oral history of contemporary China.

Consult: Introduction by W.J.F. Jenner and Delia Davin, eds., *Chinese Lives: An Oral History of Contemporary China* (1989).

ZHENG Min. Born in Beijing in 1920. Zheng Min attended the National Southwest Associate University in Kunming during World War II. In 1949 she published a volume of her poems written between 1942 and 1947. Continuing her education in the United States, she received a master's degree in English literature from Brown University in 1951. In the mid–1950s she and her husband, an engineer, returned home to China, where they suffered harassment from government authorities who suspected them of spying for the United States. For many years Zheng Min taught courses in the English language but was not allowed to teach English literature; she also stopped writing poetry until the end of the Cultural Revolution. She has since resumed writing poetry.

After the Cultural Revolution's rigid strictures were lifted, and until her recent retirement, Zheng Min taught English literature at Beijing Normal University.

EDWARD MORIN

ZIEM, Jochen. Born 1932 in Magdeburg, Germany; he lives in West Berlin. Ziem grew up in Germany during the Nazi era and saw his country defeated at the end of World War II. He remained in East Germany, where he studied German literature at the Universities of Halle and Leipzig. In 1955 he moved to West Germany, earning a living there as a construction laborer, a reporter, and later as an editor of a consumer magazine. In 1967 he became a full-time free-lance writer in West Berlin; he achieved success with several of his plays, among them *Nacrichten aus der Provinz* (West Berlin, 1967, News from the Province). He also became well known as a television scriptwriter of high social consciousness. His first book published in the United States was a collection of ten stories, *Uprising in East Germany* (1985), which on the surface details daily lives of bored, frenetic urban creatures but on another level probes contemporary decadence. Like a number of other German writers of his time, Ziem employs savage humor and satire to overscore his points. He fills his tales with a discontent of dying values spreading over both Germanies. In his title story, he narrates an uprising in East Berlin, laudable in its protest against abuses of tyranny but ignoring the reasons for its genesis and sputtering itself out in petty justifications. Ziem's novel *Der Junge* (The Kid) has been scheduled for American publication.

Selected Titles: *Die Einladung* (1967, The Invitation), drama; *Die Versöhnung* (1971, The Reconciliation), drama, sequel to *Die Einladung*.

ZILAHY, Lajos. Born March 27, 1891, in Nagyszalonta, Hungary; died December 1, 1974, in his villa in Yugoslavia. To follow in his father's footsteps, Zilahy studied law and worked briefly in a law office in his hometown, but at an early age he flirted with literature and became a journalist. His first poems were published in 1916. He began writing fiction while recuperating from a wound he received during World War I; his first novel, *Halálos tavasz* (1922, Fatal Spring), a tragic love story, brought him considerable attention. The novel became a theatrical play, and later a film version appeared. *Szépapám szerelme* (1923, The Love of My Great Grandfather) followed, then *Az ezüstszárnyú szélmalom* (1924, The Windmill with Silver Sails), in which an old miller laments the technology taking over his profession. *Két fogoly* (1927, Two Prisoners) is probably based on his experiences on the eastern front during World War I. In *Valamit visz a víz* (1928, Adrift) a fisherman falls in love with the mysterious woman he rescues; the novel was filmed in Hungary, later in Mexico and also as a United States–Czechoslovak coproduction in 1970 (under the title, *Adrift*). Zilahy married Piroska Barczy, the daughter of the mayor of Budapest. His *A lélek kialszik* (1932, The Soul Extinguished) was succeeded by *A fegyverek visszanéznek* (1936, The Guns Look Back), a novel with pacifist views; Zilahy's novel was among several antiwar books published in the period of rising turmoil before World War II. *A szökevény* (1938, The Deserter) and *A földönfutó város* (1939, The Homeless City) appeared soon after.

From 1934 to 1936 Zilahy was editor of *Magyarország* and from 1940 to 1944 of *Híd*, both important journals in which he paid serious attention to the motion picture as an art form. He also founded Pegazus film company and tried his hand at directing. In 1942, after an escape from a bombing raid (in which a housekeeper and her two children were killed), Zilahy gave a fortune of two million Pengős to establish the Zilahy Institute. His charitable/educational gesture was considered "anti-German," and in the spring of 1944, after German troops formally occupied the country, he went into hiding. At the end of World War II, Zilahy became president of the Soviet-Hungarian Cultural Institute; he came to the United States in 1946 to lecture at Columbia University. In September 1947 he brought his family to the United States for permanent residence, a move strongly condemned by the Hungarian Communist party. His books were subsequently banned in his native land for several years. He began writing in English at this point.

Zilahy wrote *The Dukays,* a historical chronicle of a noble family, during World War II. It was published in New York in 1949. In this same year his only son, Mihaly, a Harvard University student, died in an accident. A sequel to *The Dukays, The Angry Angel* was published in 1953, and the third part of what was to become a trilogy, *A Century in Scarlet,* appeared in 1966. Later work includes the sole Hungarian manuscript from this period of his life, *Krisztina es a kiraly* (1954, Christina and the King), as well as his popular book in English, *The Happy Century* (1960).

Zilahy wrote nearly twenty plays and several film adaptations as well as novels, short stories, and essays and articles during his career. Among his plays are *Az ökör és más komédiák* (1920, The Oxen and Other Comedies); *A fehér szarvas* (1927, The White Stag); *Tábornok* (1928, The General); *Tüzmadar* (1932, Firebird); *A tizenkettedik óra* (1933, The Twelfth Hour); *Gyümölcs a fán* (1939, Fruit on the Tree); *Szép anyám* (1943, Dear Mother); and *Fatornyok* (1943, Wooden Towers). His work has been translated into twenty languages; many of his novels and plays have been filmed in Hungary (sometimes directed by him) as well as in the United States and elsewhere.

DESI K. BOGNÁR

ZINIK, Zinovy. Born 1945 in Moscow, USSR; he emigrated in 1975, and lives in London. Zinik studied painting, topology, and dramatic arts; he also was a professional fencer. He emigrated to England in 1975. He writes in English for the *Times Literary Supplement* and has written stories and scripts for the BBC; he also earns his living as a theater/cabaret director. He writes his longer fiction in Russian.

Although five previous novels have been translated and published in several European countries, Zinik has only one novel in English translation, *The Mushroom-Picker* (written 1984, translated 1987; London, 1988; 1989), and this novel is now out of print in both the United Kingdom and the United States. A broad satire of both British and Russian customs, the novel is an oblique but expressionistic comment on the state of displacement. Ostensibly a narrative about an émigré Russian professor and his Sovietophile wife, set both in sophisticated London (amid the appropriate company of liberals, intellectuals, and cosmopolites) and in Moscow, with the appropriate setting of a crowded communal flat in which sexual needs and desires must be accommodated to space limitations, this work of fiction is a series of unasked, unanswered, but nevertheless obtrusive questions. Kostya, the Russian professor who departs from the USSR with his visiting English girlfriend (who loves Soviet communism more than he does, or at least her dreamscape of it) is a food fetishist. Everything meaningful in his life is measured in food imagery, and Kostya justifies his discourse of references on the deprivation of food in his childhood. His new wife grows increasingly alarmed with his obsession but is unable to control the situation. The climax of the novel comes in a scene of mushroom-picking near a nuclear base; Kostya is arrested as a spy, and in the ensuing fracas an addled young companion is impaled on Kostya's food-cutting knife. The final chapter of the novel presents another view of the situation through the eyes of an exile visiting Kostya in prison and trying to bridge the miasma of deceit and self-deceptions endemic to the exile situation. The novel is two-thirds broad comedy, as posturing in style as Lord Byron and Aleksandr Pushkin in their outlandish witty conceits and as exploitive of imagery as hyperbole will allow. The final third is more Conradian in its use of a narrator sifting language in a subtle manner to find some truth beneath the clutter of the surface. In his style Zinik comes by several ways at the meaning of his story, and his work is clearly that of an exile trying on protean shapes for a final fit of illumination, but finding none of the clothes suitable. In attacking all sides—the liberal English friends of the Soviet Union, the rigid communist bureaucrats and their passive party hacks—Zinik is exposing corruption on a macroeconomic scale. More to the point, he is expressing a weariness that may be ascribed to a younger Soviet generation that seems to find all slogans indicative more of style than of substance. Thus he is not denouncing the socialist dream or the regimen necessary to achieve it. The statement of wariness is profound, since it is a stance that declares political passion suspect to those who have heard the banner call of idealism throughout their lives. The new Soviet exile—what may be termed the third generation of the Soviet Revolution—is likely to be a cynic, pure in his ironic disbelief of systemic ordering.

In a recent publication, "Hooks" (*New Yorker*, November 6, 1989), a narrative set in the form of fiction but apparent as a context of his autobiography, Zinik has one of his characters say, "If we get homesick, it's not for our actual home but the home of memory." The declaration is both a statement about the disease and the cure of exile and its inevitable aftermath, nostalgia. That memory of home, which sustains yet also transcends homesickness, becomes for the exile a new condition of disease and despair until it, too, is transcended into a progression of activity within the borders of a new home.

Selected Titles: *Nisha v Panteone* (Paris, 1979; Niche in the Pantheon); *Russkaia Sluzhba* (Paris, 1983; Russian Service); *Peremeshchennoe Litso* (1985; Displaced Person).

ZINOVIEV, Alexander. Born 1922 in the USSR; he lives in West Germany. Zinoviev was a professor of logic and philosophy at Moscow University when his novel *The Yawning Heights* [*Ziyayushcie vysoty*] was published in Switzerland in 1976. Reaction among Soviet bureaucrats proved so adverse that Zinoviev was asked to leave the country, and he emigrated to the Federal Republic of Germany in 1978. Zinoviev's fiction is a steaming pot of philosophical disquisition, angry harangue, and abusive humor. He sees a decline in his country's morality as evidenced in the decadent amorality of Soviet youth no longer politically or socially committed but cynical in their routine acceptance of bureaucratic programming. In his novel *Homo Sovieticus* (West Germany, 1985), he presents his most virulent portrait of this new Soviet man. Using the label *homosos* to describe the phenomenon, Zinoviev also employs the term to describe the third wave of Russian/Soviet exile. This new exile is separated from his country not out of conviction of social ideals but from personal disputes with bureaucracy. He is an exploiter willing to shape his circumstances into rungs up a ladder of exilic opportunity in the West, where he is celebrated as an exotic specimen. Zinoviev slashes out at the exilic communities in Western harbors of refuge in portraits savage with satire of individual vanity and exploitativeness. (His work has origins in both Fyodor Dostoyevsky and Joseph Conrad,* particularly Conrad's *The Secret Agent*.) Other writers describing this phenomenon (though, unlike Zinoviev, not giving it a distinct term of reference)—for example, Zinovy Zinik,* Vladimir Voinovich,* Vassily Aksyonov*—are less vitriolic and less logistical in their presentations. Zinoviev's training in logic as well as his personal and academic exhortatory style, make him an unappealing writer on the surface where good humor counts for readership and possible understanding. However, Zinoviev's vision of Soviet exiles adrift in the babble of their justificatory parochialism is profoundly etched into a frame demanding attention, and, inevitably, controversy before a synthesis of illumination can take shape.

In 1990 full Soviet citizenship was restored to Zinoviev by order of Mikhail Gorbachev.

Translations: *The Radiant Future* (1978); *Logical Physics* (1983); *Reality of Communism* (1984); *The Madhouse* (1986).

Consult: Rosalind J. Marsh, *Soviet Fiction Since Stalin* (1985).

ZOHRAB, Krikor. Born June 26, 1861, in Constantinople, Ottoman Empire (now Istanbul, Turkey); died 1915 on road to Tigranakat, Ottoman Empire. Zohrab left Constantinople in 1905 for Western Europe; he returned in 1908 after Turkish massacres of Armenians had subsided and a Constitutional Reform guaranteeing some freedom of religion was established in 1908. He wrote of these experiences in his book *Etcherougha Etcher ougha Oughevorie Muh Orakru Orakren* (1922, Pages from a Traveller's Diary). He refused to leave Constantinople again in 1915 when arrests and purges of Armenian leaders were taking place. He was assassinated by Turkish fanatics as he was being taken to the court where he was to be tried for "crimes against the state."

Zohrab tended to ignore political realities in his fiction, but, according to Diana der Hovanessian and Marzhed Margossian, he wrote one pamphlet under an assumed name, *La question armeniènne a la lumière des documents* (Paris, 1908), which dealt directly with Armenian history and issues.

Selected Titles: *Kheghjmedankee tysaner* (1900, Voices of Conscience); *Loor tsaver* (1911, Silent Griefs); *Gyankuh inch bes vor ih* (1911, Life As It Is).

Consult: Diana der Hovanessian, entry in *Encyclopedia of World Literature*, gen. ed. L. Klein, Volume 4 (1984); H. Kelikian, "Krikor Zohrab, the Complete Armenian," *Ararat* 17 (1976).

ZSCHORSCH, Gerald K. Born 1951 in East Germany; he lives in West Germany. Zschorsch's major focus has been the issue of the two Germanys and the inevitability of psychic exile for a child of postwar Germany. He moved from East to West in the 1970s. The themes of inner division and the burden of guilt of the fathers passed on to the sons continue to dominate his poetry.

Selected Titles: Poetry: *Glaubt bloss nicht, dass ich traurig bin* (1977, Just Don't Believe I'm Sad; expanded 1981); *Die Drift der anderen Haut* (1981, The Scent of the Other Skin); *Klappmesser* (1983, Switchblade).

ZUCKMAYER, Carl. Born December 23, 1896, in Nachenheim, Germany; died January 18, 1977, in Visp, Switzerland. Zuckmayer moved to Henndorf, near Salzburg, Austria, in 1926. He left for the United States in 1939 after the Anschluss of Austria. Zuckmayer's writings were banned as "degenerate" and "Jewish" by the Nazis (Zuckmayer's grandfather was a Jew). He chose the rural area of Vermont as his state of exile while in the United States. In 1958 he moved back to Europe, this time choosing the mountains of Switzerland as his home.

Zuckmayer's dramatic work was highly praised as well as popular. He integrated regional folklore into his dramas of social concern and daily comedy. His style was generally satiric. He was forced by the banning of any production of his theatrical work to turn to fiction writing: he published several novels in the 1930s that afforded him a living while he remained in Austria. He turned to novel writing again in the 1950s in the United States.

Zuckmayer's play *Des Teufels General* (1946; *The Devil's General*, 1962) brought him back into public notice. In this play Zuckmayer examines the question of moral guilt in the twentieth century in terms of individual behavior to historic events. He also received great acclaim with the publication of his memoir, *Als wär's ein Stück von Mir* (1969; *A Part of Myself*, 1970).

Selected Titles: *Der Hauptmann von Köpenich* (1931; *The Captain of Kopenick*, 1932); *Barbara Blomberg* (1949; Barbara Blomberg); *Der Gesang im Feuerofen* (1950; The Song in the Fiery Furnace); *Engele von Lowen* (1955; Little Angel of Leuven); *Die Fachnachtsbeichte* (1959; *Carnival Confession*, 1961); *Gesammelte Werke*, 4 vols. (1960).

Consult: Thomas Ayck, *Carl Zuckmayer in Selbstzeugnissen und Bilddokumenten* (Reinbech, 1977); Arnold Bauer, *Carl Zuckmayer* (1976); Kurt Opitz, entry in *Encyclopedia of World Literature*, gen. ed. L. Klein, vol. 4 (1984). See also A. J. Jacobius, *Carl Zuckmayer: Eine Bibliographie* (1971).

ZWEIG, Arnold. Born November 10, 1887, in Gross-Glogau, Germany (now Poland); died November 26, 1968, in East Berlin, German Democratic Republic. After studies in Breslau, Munich, and Berlin (1907–14), Zweig served in World

War I (1915–18) before returning from the eastern front to live in Bavaria and later in Berlin. As a Zionist and editor of the *Jüdische Rundschau* he became a conspicuous target in Nazi Germany. In 1933 he emigrated to Palestine, where he edited the antifascist journal *Orient*, but he returned to East Germany in 1948—significantly, the year in which the state of Israel was established. Renouncing chauvinistic aspects of Zionism, Zweig turned to Marxist socialism and in the last two decades of his life upheld the new order in East Germany, becoming the president of the Academy of Arts and of the PEN Center in East Berlin.

Prolific in output, Zweig wrote plays, essays, and short stories, but he was primarily a novelist. The early play *Ritualmord in Ungarn* (1915, Ritual Murder in Hungary), for which he was awarded the Kleist Prize, signaled his preoccupation with the Jewish question. World fame came in 1927 with *Der Streit um den Sergeanten Grischa* (The Case of Sergeant Grischa), a novel based on his previous expressionist play. This story of a wartime judicial execution, allegedly justified for reasons of military necessity, documents Zweig's pacifist stance. He later incorporated the novel in what came to be known as "The Grischa Cycle," to which three further books were added before World War II. The quartet comprises an ambitiously conceived chronicle probing the period 1915–18 and the shortcomings of Wilhelmine society. Zweig's emigration interrupted the flow of the work, but in 1953 he completed an introductory novel dealing with the prelude to World War I. A complementary epilogue exists only in fragments.

Much of what Zweig wrote in exile was directly related to the ongoing struggle and bore only superficial traces of new environments. His *Bilanz der deutschen Judenheit* (1934, Balance-sheet of German Jewry) sought to delineate the role of Jews in German society. The definition of his coreligionists as "proletarians living in comfort" (i.e., in a fool's paradise) gives warning of his later anticapitalist polemics. *Der Typus Hitler* (The Hitler Type), published in Egypt in 1947, castigates the inveterate enemy. Later, in a reminiscent mood, Zweig felt able to channel his experience of exile into a more artistically satisfying mold. Thus in *Traum ist teuer* (1962, The Expensive Dream) he recounts the adventures of an émigré doctor working with the British army in North Africa. It contains hints of the cold war to come.

As a refugee Zweig had played a notable part in the literary war against Hitler, but when the battle was won, he felt drawn back to his roots in a convulsed Europe that he was eager to heal and to reshape. His writings demonstrate that his lengthy stay in Palestine was only an interlude and that the predominant formative influences in his life were his involvement in World War I and his reaction to Wilhelmine society.

Translations: The Grischa Cycle was published in four volumes: *Der Streit um den Sergeanten Grischa* (1927; *The Case of Sergeant Grischa*, 1928); *Junge Frau von 1914* (1931; *Young Woman of 1914*, 1932); *Erziehung vor Verdun* (1935; *Education before Verdun*, 1936); *Einsetzung eines Konigs* (1937; *The Crowning of a King*, 1938).

Other Translations: *Novellen um Claudia* (1912; *Claudia*, 1930); *Insulted and Exiled, the Truth about the German Jews* (London, 1937); *Die Zeit ist reif* (1957; *The Time Is Ripe*, 1962); *The Letters of Sigmund Freud and Arnold Zweig*, The International Psychoanalytical Library, no. 84 (1970).

Consult: H. Baum, *Arnold Zweig, Leben und Werk* (1967).

CEDRIC HENTSCHEL

ZWEIG, Stefan. Born November 28, 1881, in Vienna, Austria; committed suicide February 23, 1942, in Petropolis, Brazil. Zweig traveled in Europe, Asia, Africa, and the Americas throughout his life and early developed a *Weltperspektive* based on direct contacts with famous writers and artists in various cultures. Although he abhorred political conflict, he saw himself as a confirmed European mediator among nations as early as World War I when he was active in the peace movement during his first exile in Switzerland. Zweig conceived of himself as the "good European" who introduces great individuals, even nations, to discerning readers through writing subtle, psychoanalytical portraits of French, Belgian, English, and Russian writers, statesmen, artists, and imaginary figures for his German readers. He also wrote a libretto for Richard Strauss: *Die schweigsame Frau* (1935; The Silent Woman).

In 1934 Zweig set up a second residence in London, but kept his home in Vienna. Faced with anti-Semitic persecution, Zweig left Austria for the last time in 1938. The Nazis confiscated his internationally renowned collection of autographs and bibliophilic rarities, selling and dispersing the collection as a measure of their distaste.

In 1939 Zweig published *Ungeduld des Herzens* (Beware of Pity) and *Worte am Grabe Sigmund Freuds* (Words at the Grave of Sigmund Freud). In 1940 he left England for the United States; in 1941 he moved to Brazil, where he completed *Brasilien: Ein Land der Zukunft* (Brazil: A Land of the Future). He left uncompleted at his death a biography of Honoré de Balzac, on which he had been working for ten years; the manuscript was published in 1946.

Zweig's most important work in exile, *Schachnovelle* (Chess Novella), appeared in 1942 (it was filmed in 1960). In his last complete prose work he attacked fascist brutality as defined by his concept of educated humanism. He juxtaposed one of his protagonists, the primitive and arrogant world-champion chess-player with a famous Austrian lawyer who had been imprisoned and tortured by the Gestapo but who survived the terror of his incarceration by learning to play chess and who extended his liberating obsession to the point of wanting to play against himself, a desire, in Zweig's words, "as paradoxical as jumping across one's shadow." Later, the sensitive refugee defeats the world-champion master in the first round of their match but breaks off the second round because of nervous exhaustion. In Zweig's view, compassionate sensibility and intelligence lose in a battle against rigid perseverance and its accompanying brutality of purpose. The novella has been seen as an autobiographical admission to the inevitable defeat of decadent European middle-class and apolitical humanistic values in a contest with the rabid discipline of totalitarian fanaticism. For such a defeatist attitude about humanism, Zweig was scorned by critics as early as the 1930s, but his last work occasioned the greatest outburst of both pain and anger by his critics.

Zweig considered his growing depression in the 1940s a consequence of the collapse of European ideals that he had cherished. Accordingly, his biography carries a title underlining his sense of loss: *Die Welt von Gestern: Erinnerungen eines Europäers* (1941; *The World of Yesterday: Memories of a European*, 1943).

At the age of sixty, the wealthy, highly respected, and widely read author of works that frequently explored aesthetic labyrinths and the breakdown of a soul in bourgeois society killed himself. His second wife, Lotte, joined him in a suicide pact in their home near Rio de Janeiro—an event that shook the exile community throughout the world. Yet many of Zweig's works foreshadowed an ultimate despair stemming from public and private fears, among them: *Angst* (1920; Fear); *Der Kampf mit dem Dämon* (1925; The Battle with the Demon); *Die Flucht zu Gott* (1927; The Flight to God); *Verwirrung der Gefühle* (1927; Confusion of Feelings); *Triumph and Tragik des Erasmus von Rotterdam* (1934), and the well-known *Sternstunden der Menschheit* (1927, Pivotal Moments of Mankind; *Star*, enlarged to twelve essays in 1936).

Zweig's works in exile and those posthumously published include *Magellan: Der Mann und seine Tat* (1938; Magellan: The Man and His Deed); *Amerigo: Die Geschichte eines historischen Irrtums* (1946; Amerigo: The History of a Historical Misunderstanding); *Briefwechsel mit Richard Strauss* (1957; Correspondence with Richard Strauss); and *Europäisches Erbe: Essays* (1960; European Heritage: Essays).

Consult: Randolph J. Klawitter, *Stefan Zweig: A Bibliography* (1965); E. Allday, *Stefan Zweig: A Critical Biography* (London, 1972); K. Matthias, "Humanismus in der Zerreissprobe: Stefan Zweig im Exil," in M. Durzak, ed., *Die deutsche Exilliteratur 1933–45* (Stuttgart, 1973; includes bibliography). See also Romain Rolland-Stefan Zweig, *Briefivechsel 1910–1940, Band 1: 1910–1923* (Berlin, 1988).

ZWERENZ, Gerhard. Born 1925; he lives in Schmitten, West Germany. An outspoken activist who believes in direct political action, Zwerenz tends to concentrate on social and political issues in his fiction. His 1988 novel *Der Bunker* (The Shelter) concerns the possibilities of an atomic war; his 1973 novel *Die Erde ist unbewohnbar wie der Mond* (The Earth Is Uninhabitable Like the Moon) draws on what Zwerenz sees as capitalistic evil and West German bourgeois mendacity.

Zwerenz left the German Democratic Republic as a young man before he began publishing. His work thus is one not written in exile, but his viewpoint of both Germanys is that of the lonely, embattled artist exiled from his society. He continues to fight his battle to join common citizen and uncommon writer into a web of a working cooperative society. He published his view of life and his program for it in his autobiography, *Der Widerspruch* (1974, The Contradiction).

Selected Titles: *Aufs Rad geflochten* (1959, Broken on the Wheel); *Die Lebe der toten Männer* (1959, The Dead Man's Love); *Casanova oder Der kleine Herr in Krieg und Frieden* (1966; *Little Peter in War and Peace*, 1966); *Kopf und Bauch* (1971, Head and Belly).

ZWI, Rose. Born 1928 in Mexico; she lives in Johannesburg, South Africa. Zwi comes from a Russian, Slavic Jewish family; she has written of her background, and her sense of being an alien in a foreign land, in her three published novels, *Another Year in Africa* (1980); *The Inverted Pyramid* (1981); *Exiles* (1984). She works for a publishing house in Johannesburg.

Of *Another Year in Africa*, a critic wrote: "The exotic placement of Russian Jewish emigrants in South Africa, their memories of pogroms and their ambivalent conflicts in the war against color prejudice make this work fascinating in its potential" (*Confrontation* 39/40).

Appendix A: Waves of Exile in the Twentieth Century

History is of course responsible for exile, and events leave their impress in their aftermath as well as in their duress. The flight of large numbers of citizens from one country to another is due in large measure to those historic events that grow out and continue into civil and political strife, religious fanaticism, economic power struggle, and the desire for cultural and personal expression. Below are listed the major events of this past century that have resulted in exile on a phenomenal scale.

Africa

The suppression of independence in colonial lands in Africa

The repression of human rights for blacks in South Africa from 1948 to 1991

The suppression of dissent in African countries after the colonialist era, particularly Guinea, Kenya, Uganda

Asia

The revolution in China throughout the twentieth century

The Korean divide and war, 1945 (division into North and South); 1950–1953, war and truce; 1973, agreement to seek plans for unification

The Vietnamese wars, 1946 –1973 (from the French Indo-China fighting to the departure of American troops from South Vietnam)

Caribbean and Latin America

The military dictatorships and economic oligarchies in Latin American states

The Cuban repressions, both before and during the Fidel Castro era

The Argentinian nights of terror, 1970–1980

The Chilean repression of civil rights under military rule, 1975–1985

Europe

The Russian Revolution of 1905

The Armenian Genocide

The Russian Revolution of 1917 and the ensuing civil war through the 1920s

The Holocaust, 1933–1945

The German National Socialist (Nazi) program of persecution and annihilation of ethnic minorities

The political terrorism of the Stalinist era in the USSR

The Spanish Civil War, 1936–1939, and the ensuing Francisco Franco rule

The German invasion of Europe, 1938–1944

The Greek Civil War at the end of World War II

The political division of Germany into East and West after World War II

The dissidence movement in the USSR from the 1950s to the 1980s

The Soviet invasion of Hungary, 1956

Military dictatorship in Greece, 1967–1974

Ethnic persecution in Bulgaria, Romania, Turkey, and elsewhere in the Balkans

The coming of socialism to Yugoslavia; the reawakening of nationalist separatism

Middle East/Asia Minor

The search for a Zionist homeland

The struggle for a Palestinian homeland

Repression during the Mohammed Reza Shah Pahlavi era, 1953–1979

Iranian theocracy under the Ayatollah Ruhollah Khomeini

North America

The Black experience with slavery and unequal rights in the U.S.

The Communist witchhunt in the U.S., 1947–1957 via House UnAmerican Activities Committee hearings/investigations (Martin Dies Committee) and Senator Joseph McCarthy's charges and hearings

Across Territorial Boundaries

The women's movement

The gay (homosexual) awakening

Continuing opposition or aversion to the doctrine of communism by those living in communist states

Continuing opposition or aversion to the ethos of capitalism by those living in capitalist states

A psychic sense of alienation from mother Earth and the yearning but inability to express love and recognition for the multitudinous varieties of humankind

Appendix B: Flight and Expulsion: Point of Departure

ANGOLA AND MOZAMBIQUE

Luis Bernardo Honwana, 1967

See also Angolan and Mozambique Writers in Exile

ANTIGUA

Jamaica Kincaid, 1966

ARGENTINA

Miguel Bonasso, late 1970s

Julio Cortázar, 1952 (self-exile)

Andrew Graham-Yooll, 1976

Tomas Eloy Martinez, late 1970s

Alicia Portnoy, 1970s

Manuel Puig, 1957 (self-exile)

Osvaldo Soriano, 1970s

Luisa Valenzuela, 1979 (since 1985, self-exile who returns to Argentina periodically)

ARMENIA

Michael J. Arlen (born in London, Arlen is an exile in absentia because of his ancestors' flight from Armenia)

Michael Arlen (in flight from persecution because of his identity as an Armenian)

Vahan Tekeyan, 1915 (in residence in Turkey)

See also Armenian Writers in Exile

AUSTRALIA

Miles Franklin, 1905–14 (U.S.); 1914–33 (England; she returned to Australia, 1937)

George Johnston, 1955 (returned to Australia, 1965)

Thomas Keneally, 1972

David Malouf, 1970s

Henry Handel Richardson, 1890s

Christina Stead, 1928

Randolph Stow, 1970s

AUSTRIA

Walter Abish, 1938, France 1940

Ingebord Bachmann, 1953

Vicki Baum, 1931

Richard Beer-Hoffmann, 1938

Hermann Broch, 1938

Martin Buber, 1939

Franz Theodor Csokor, 1938

Sigmund Freud, 1938

Arthur Gregor, 1938

Hans Habe, 1938 (born in Hungary)

Peter Handke, 1966 (returned to Austria in 1979)

Stella K. Hershan, 1939

Fritz Hochwalder, 1938

Hermann Kesten, left to work in Germany in his youth. *See* France

Oskar Kokoschka, 1919; 1938

Herbert Kuhner, 1939

Jakov Lind, 1938

Frederic Morton, 1939

Robert Edler Musil, 1938

Robert Neumann, 1934

Joseph Roth, 1933

Lore Segal, 1938

Friedrich Torberg, 1938

Ernst Waldinger, 1938

René Wellek, 1927

Franz Werfel, 1938

Stefan Zweig, 1934 (kept a home in Vienna but lived abroad; left Austria in 1938 as a refugee)

AUSTRO-HUNGARIAN EMPIRE

S. Y. Agnon, 1913–24

Ferdynand Goetel. *See* Poland

Uri Zvi Greenburg, 1924

Moyshe Leyb Halpern, 1908

Rainer Maria Rilke, 1902

BARBADOS

Edward Braithwaite, 1950

Austin Clarke, 1954

George Lamming, 1946

Alfred H. Mendes, 1932

BRAZIL

Jorge Amado, 1948

Fernando Gabiera, 1970

BRITISH WEST INDIES

Jean Rhys, 1906

BULGARIA

Michael Arlen

Elias Canetti (self-exile to Austria and Switzerland as a student; fled Austria in 1938)

Georgi Markov, 1969

Atanas Vasilev Slavov, 1976

CAMEROON

Francis Bébey, 1961–74

Mbella Sonne Dipoko, 1960

Ferdinand Oyono, c. 1955

CANADA

Morley Callaghan, 1928–29 (expatriate)

Mavis Gallant, 1949 (expatriate)

Mordecai Richler, 1951–52; 1954–72 (expatriate)

CHILE

Isabel Allende, 1975

José Donoso, 1949–51; 1958–60, 1967 (returned to Chile in 1980)

Ariel Dorfman, 1973 (teaches at Duke University in U.S. but returns to Chile regularly)

Jorge Edwards, 1973–79 (returned to Chile, 1979)

Pablo Neruda, 1946

Nicanor Parra, 1970s–80s (self-exile)

Antonio Skármeta, 1973

CHINA

Ai Qing, 1929–32

Bei Dao, 1989

Bei Ling, 1989

Bin Xin, 1923

Cai Qi-jiao, 1935–38

Eileen Chang, 1950s

Chao Chi-kang, 1985

Chen Jo-hsi, 1973 (born in Taiwan)

Chen Kaige, 1989

Duo Duo, 1989

Feng Zhi, 1931

Gu Cheng, 1988

Leung Tung, 1975

Li Tuo, 1989

Liu Da-ren, 1949

Liu Zaifu, 1989

Pai Hsin-yung, 1949

Sang Ye, c. 1980

Su Wei, 1989

Su Xiaokang, 1989

Xu Gang, 1989

Yang Lian, 1988

Yu Li-hua, 1949

Zhang Xinxin, 1989

Zheng Min, 1951–54 (educated abroad; returned to China in mid–1950s)

COLOMBIA

Gabriel García Márquez, 1955; 1959

CUBA

Reinaldo Arenas, 1980

Guillermo Cabrera Infante, 1964 (as diplomat in Brussels); 1965

Alejo Carpentier, 1930s

Angel Cuadra Landrove, c.1983

Maria Irene Fornes, 1945

Carlos Franqui, 1955; 1968

Roberto González-Echevarría, 1959

Nicolás Guillén, 1953–58

Pablo Medina, 1961

Heberto Padilla, 1980

Ricardo Pau-Llosa, 1960s

Carlos Ripoll, 1950s

Severo Sarduy, 1960

Armando Valladares, 1982

Jorge Valls, 1984

CZECHOSLOVAKIA

Max Brod, 1939

Hana Demetz, 1949

Jan Drabek, 1968

Jiri Grusa, 1970s

Pavel Kohout, 1979

Oskar Kokoschka, 1938

Milan Kundera, 1979 (teaching in France from 1975)

Arnost Lustig, 1968

Jan Novak, 1969

Josef Skvorecky, 1968

Daniel Stroz, 1968

DENMARK

Isak Dinesen (Baroness Karen Blixen), 1914

Mogen Klitgaard, 1940

EAST GERMANY (German Democratic Republic)

Jurek Becker, 1978

Wolf Biermann, 1976

Martin Gregor-Dellin, 1955

Peter Huchel, 1971

Uwe Johnson, 1959

Heiner Kippardt, 1963

Sarah Kirsch, 1977

Gunter Kunert, 1977

Reiner Kunze, 1977

Monica Maron, 1980s

Jochem Ziem, 1955

Gerald K. Zschorsch, 1970s

Gerhard Zwerenz, 1948

See also Germany; West Germany

EGYPT

Constantine Cavafy, 1882

Edmond Jabès, 1953

EL SALVADOR

Claribel Alegria, 1943 (born in Nicaragua)

Manlio Argueta, 1980

ENGLAND

W.H. Anden, 1939

Anthony Burgess, 1968

Noel Coward, 1945 (tax exile)

Norman Douglas, 1888 (sexual exile)

Lawrence Durrell, 1938 (sojourner)

Graham Greene, 1966 (tax exile)

Christopher Isherwood, 1938 (expatriate via world travels including Iceland, India, Greece, South America, U.S.)

Eric Knight, 1938 (voluntary exile)

D. H. Lawrence, 1919 (expatriate, sojourner)

T. E. Lawrence, 1916

Robert Liddell, 1953 (sojourner)

Malcolm Lowry, 1935

W. Somerset Maugham, 1930s (sojourner)

Frederick Rolfe (Baron Corvo), 1908

Wilfrid Sheed, 1940

T. H. White, 1939; 1947

P. G. Wodehouse, 1932

Expatriates: George Barker, 1933–67; Leonora Carrington, 1937; Arthur C. Clarke, 1970s; William Empson, 1931–34, 1937–39; D. J. Enright, 1948; Ford Madox Ford, 1920s–30; Robert Graves, 1929; Robin Maugham, 1945; Tim Parks, 1980; J. C. Powys, 1920s; Muriel Spark, 1965; Dornford Yates, 1920.

ESTONIA

Ivar Ivask, 1949 (born in Latvia)

Ivar Grunthal, 1944

Aino Kallas, 1944

Bernard Kangro, 1940s

Aleksis Rannit, 1945

Karl Ristikivi, 1943

Arved Viirlaid, 1943

FRANCE

Antonin Artaud, 1946

Georges Bernanos, 1938 (voluntary exile; returned to France in 1945)

André Breton, 1941–45 (returned to France)

Louis-Ferdinand Céline, 1944

Yvan Goll, 1939 (born in Alsace)

Hermann Kesten, 1940 (of Austrian descent, fled from Germany)

Ted Morgan (Sanche de Gramont), 1948

Antoine de Saint-Exupéry, 1940

Saint-John Perse, 1940

Victor Serge, 1917

George Steiner, 1940?

Simone Weil, 1942

Marguerite Yourcenar, 1939 (sojourner, emigrant)

FRENCH GUYANA

Léon-Gontran Damas, 1931 (expatriate to France)

See also Guyana

GERMANY

Theodor Adorno, 1938

Yehuda Amichai, 1936

Erich Arendt, 1933

Hannah Arendt, 1933

Erich Auerbach, 1936

Vicki Baum, 1932

Harold Beaver, 1934

Johannes H. Becher, 1935

Walter Benjamin, 1933

Werner Bergengruen, 1939

Rudolf Borchadt, 1933

Bertolt Brecht, 1933 (returned to East Germany, 1948)

Ferdinand Bruckner, 1933

Alfred Döblin, 1933 (returned to West Germany, 1946–51; 1953)

Hilde Domin, 1931

Lion Feuchtwanger, 1933

Eva Figes, 1930s

Bruno Frank, 1933

Erich Fried, 1938

Yvan Goll, 1939 (born in Alsace)

Oskar Maria Graf, 1933

Günter Grass, 1945

Walter Hasenclever, 1933

Hermann Hesse, 1919

Stefan Heym, 1933

Odon von Horvath, 1934 (born in the Austro-Hungarian Empire in what is now Yugo-slavia; left Yugoslavia for Germany in 1924)

Hans Henny Jahnn, 1915–18; 1934

Ruth Prawer Jhabvala, 1939 (born of Polish parents in Germany)

Hermann Kesten, 1933 (of Austrian descent)

Georg Kaiser, 1938

Annette Kolb, 1914

Else Lasker-Schüler, 1933

Emil Ludwig, 1933

Erika Mann, 1933

Heinrich Mann, 1933

Klaus Mann, 1933

(Paul) Thomas Mann, 1933

Herbert Marcuse, 1933

Theodor Plivier, 1933

Gustav Regler, 1934

Erich Maria Remarque, 1931

Nelly Sachs, 1940

Albrecht Schaefer, 1930s

Anna Seghers, 1933

Manès Sperber, 1933 (born in what is now USSR, grew up in Austria)

Ernst Toller, 1933

Bruno Traven, 1919

Kurt Tucholsky, 1929 (to Sweden, deprived of German citizenship, 1933)

Bodo Uhse, 1933

Peter Weiss, 1934

Karl Wolfskehl, 1937

Paul Zech, 1933

Carl Zuckmayer, 1939

Arnold Zweig, 1933 (returned to East Germany, 1948)

See also Germany; West Germany

GHANA

Ayi Kwei Armah, 1959

Kofi Awoonor, 1967 (returned to Ghana in 1975)

GREECE

Odysseus Elytis, 1967–74 (returned to Greece, 1974)

Nikos Kazantzakis, 1946

Yannis Ritsos, 1948–52 (prison exile on Greek islands)

Dimitris Tsaloumas, 1950s

Vassilis Vassilikos, 1967–74

GUATEMALA

Arturo Arias, 1980s

Miguel Asturias, 1923; 1954

GUINEA, WEST AFRICA

Camara Laye, 1965

GUYANA

Jan Carew, 1945

O. R. Dathorne, 1946

Wilson Harris, 1959

Edgar Mittelholzer, 1947

HAITI

Paulé Barton, 1960s

HUNGARY

Tamas Aczel, 1956

Sándor András, 1956

Martin Esslin, 1944

George Faludy, 1938 (returned to Hungary in 1946; in exile again 1956)

René Fülöp-Miller, 1905 (travelled and worked throughout Europe until 1938)

Clara Gyorgyey, 1956

Hans Habe, 1939 (was working in Germany)

Julius Háy, 1919–33; 1933–34; 1934–46 (returned to Hungary in 1946; in exile again in 1965)

Ephraim Kishon, 1949

Arthur Koestler, 1914 (to Vienna); 1926 (on world travels)

Agota Kristof, 1956

Menyhert Melchior Lengyel, 1931 (returned to Hungary, 1945)

György Lukács, 1919–45; 1956–57

Sándor Márai, 1945

György Mikes, 1938

Ferenc Molnar, 1940

Bela Szasz, 1937; 1956

Paul Tabori, 1937

Elie Wiesel, 1945

Lajos Zilahy, 1947

See also Hungarian Writers in Exile

INDIA

Kamala Markandaya, 1950s (expatriate)

Ved Parkash Mehta, 1940s

Rohinton Mistry, 1975

Dom Moraes, 1953, 1967–84 (expatriate)

Bharati Mukherjee, 1962

Raja Rao, 1929; 1947 (expatriate)

Santha Rama Rau, 1950s (expatriate)

Salman Rushdie, 1961 (expatriate)

Rita Smith, 1953

IRAN

See Iranian Writers in Exile

IRELAND

Samuel Beckett, 1932; 1937; 1940

Brian Coffey, 1928 (expatriate)

Denis Devlin, 1928 (expatriate)

Oliver St. John Gogarty, 1939

Denis Johnston, 1960 (expatriate)

James Joyce, 1904

Thomas MacGreevy, 1928 (expatriate)

Edna O'Brien, 1960 (expatriate)

Sean O'Casey, 1926

Frank O'Connor, late 1954–61 (returned to Ireland)

Liam O'Flaherty (expatriate wanderings, 1917–22; 1935)

See also Northern Ireland

ITALY

Corredo Alvaro, 1920s

Giuseppe Borgese, 1931 (returned to Milan in 1947)

Italo Calvino, 1942–45 (partisan in exile); 1960s–80s (as expatriate in France because of publishing career)

Nicola Chiaramonte, 1934 (France); 1936 (Spain); 1940 (U.S.)

Carlo Levi, 1935–36 (imprisoned in south of Italy)

Primo Levi, 1943–45 (partisan in Val d'Aosta; incarcerated at Auschwitz, 1945)

Alberto Moravia, 1930–35 (expatriate England, France, U.S., Mexico); 1935–36 (expatriate China, Greece); 1943–45 (in flight from Fascist rule to Fondi)

Cesare Pavese, 1935–36 (imprisoned in Calabria)

Ignazio Silone, 1930–45 (returned to Italy 1945)

Mario Soldati, 1929–31

JAMAICA

Claude McKay, 1912

Andrew Salkey, 1952 (born in Panama)

Sylvia Wynter, 1949; 1974 (born in Cuba)

JAPAN

Kazuo Ishiguro, 1960

Hisako Matsubara

JORDAN

Fadia Faqir, 1984

KENYA

Ngugi wa Thiong'o (formerly James Ngugi), 1982

KOREA

Lee Sang, 1936

See also South Korea

LATVIA

Zenta Maurina, 1940

Linard Tauns, 1944

Aina Zemdega, 1944

LEBANON

Kahlil Gibran, 1895–98 (returned to Lebanon, 1898); 1902

Marwan Hassan

Amin Maalouf

LITHUANIA

Jonas Aistis, 1940

Bernardas Brazdžionis, 1944

Chaim Grade, 1939

Marius Katiliškis, 1944

Algirdas Landsbergis, 1949

Algimantus Mackus, 1944

Alfonsas Nyka-Niliūnas, 1944

Henrikas Radauskas, 1944 (born in Poland)

Antanas Škéma, 1944 (born in Poland)

Morris Winchevsky, 1878

MALAWI

Frank Mkalawile Chipasula, 1980

MALAYSIA

Shirley Geok-lim Lin, 1960s

MARTINIQUE

Aimé Césaire, 1920s

Frantz Fanon, 1950

MEXICO

Carlos Fuentes (long periods of self-exile, due to father's career, own diplomatic service, and decision to travel)

Octavio Paz (absence for diplomatic service; travel and lecture tours throughout life)

Rose Zwi, c. 1939 (of east European Jewish descent)

MOZAMBIQUE

Luis Bernardo Honwana, 1967

THE NETHERLANDS

Jan de Hartog, 1947

Hans Koning, 1935

NEW ZEALAND

Katherine Mansfield, 1908

NIGERIA

Buchi Emecheta, 1962 (returned to Nigeria, 1981)

Ben Okri, 1978

Wole Soyinka, 1960s (returned to Nigeria 1970s)

NORTHERN IRELAND

Brian Moore, 1948 (expatriate)

NORWAY

Sigurd Höel, 1940

Sigrid Undset, 1940–46 (returned to Norway at the end of World War II)

PAKISTAN

Talat Abbasi, 1977 (expatriate)

Zulfikar Ghose, 1969

PALESTINE

Mahmoud Darwish, 1970

Edward Said, 1947

PARAGUAY

Augusto Roa Bastos, 1947

PERU

Julio Ortega, 1950s

César Abraham Vallejo, 1923 (self-exile)

Mario Vargas Llosa, 1958

POLAND

S. Y. Agnon, 1907

Sholem Asch, 1909

Stanislaw Baranczak, 1981

Kazimierz Brandys, 1982

Ernst Cassirer, 1933

Joseph Conrad, 1874

Bogdan Czaykowski

Jacob Glatstein, 1914

Janusz Glowacki, 1981

Ferdynand Goetel, 1946

Witold Gombrowicz, 1939

Zbigniew Herbert, 1970s

Marek Hlasko, 1958

Eva Hoffman, 1959

Marek Kedzierski, 1985

Jerzy Kosinski, 1957

Zofia Kossak-Szezucka, 1945

Jan Kott, 1956

Halpern Lewick, 1910 (then part of Russian Empire)

Czeslaw Miłosz, 1951

Sławomir Mrozék, 1963

Zdzislaw Najder, 1981 (after 20 years of intermittent teaching and research scholarship abroad)

Alicia Parizean, 1945

David Pinski, 1892

Henrikas Radauskas (born Cracow, lived in Lithuania; left Lithuania, 1944)

Isaac Bashevis Singer, 1935

I. J. Singer, 1934

Adam Tarn, 1969

Julian Tuwim, 1939–40

Alexander Wat, 1959

Adam Zagajewski, 1982

PORTUGAL

Aquilino Ribeiro, 1910s

REPUBLIC OF THE CONGO

Tchicaya U Tam'si, 1946

RHODESIA

Doris Lessing, 1949 (outlawed from South Africa, 1957)

ROMANIA

Nina Cassian, 1985 (while on teaching exchange program)

Paul Celan, 1947

E. M. Cioran, 1937

Andrei Codrescu, 1965

Mircea Eliade, 1945

Barbu Fundoiani

Eugène Ionesco, 1940

Norman Manea, 1989

Dom Pagis, 1945

Dorin Tudoran, 1988

Tristan Tzara, 1915

RUSSIA

Leonid Andreyev, 1905; 1917

Konstantin D. Balmont, 1905–12; 1920

Ilya Ehrenburg, 1908; 1920

Maxim Gorki, 1906–13; 1921–33

Zinaida Hippius, 1905–13; 1919

Konstantin Korovin, 1917

Dmitry S. Merezhkovsky, 1905–13; 1919

Nathalie Sarraute, 1908

See also Estonia, Latvia, Lithuania, Poland, Ukraine, USSR

SENEGAL

Cheik Hamidou Kane, 1952–59

Sembene Ousmane, late 1940s

Léopold Sédar Senghor, 1928

SOMALI

Nuruddin Farah, 1970s

SOUTH AFRICA

Peter Abrahams, 1939

Perseus Adams, c. 1970

Breyten Breytenbach, 1959

Dennis Brutus, 1965

Roy Campbell, 1927

Jack Cope, 1980s

R. N. Currey, 1925

Anthony Delius, 1956

Ronald Harwood, 1950s

Bessie Head, 1964

Denis Hirson, 1970s

Christopher Hope, 1974

Alfred Hutchinson, 1956

Dan Jacobson, 1961

Keorapetse William Kgositsile, 1962

Daniel Kunene, 1960s

Mazisi Kunene, 1959

Alex La Guma, 1966

Laurence Lerner, 1940s

Rian Malan, 1977–84; 1986

Todd Matshikiza, early 1960s

Bloke Modisane, early 1960s

Rose Moss, 1964

Es'kia Mphahlele, 1957–77 (returned to South Africa in 1977)

M. Oswald Mtshali, 1975

Mbuelelo Vizikhungo Mzamane, 1976

Lewis Nkosi, 1961

Arthur Nortje, 1965

Cosmo Pieterse, 1960s

William Plomer, 1926

F. T. Prince, 1931

Richard Rive, 1965

Sheila Roberts, 1977

Olive Schreiner, 1881

Mongane Wally Serote, 1974

Sylvester Stein, 1950s

Can Themba, 1968

Laurens van der Post, 1926

David Wright, 1934

Barry Yourgrau, 1960s

SOUTH KOREA

Kim Kyung Jae, 1972

Richard E. Kim, 1954 (left North Korea as a child)

SPAIN

Raphael Alberti, 1939

Corredo Alvaro, 1920s

Fernando Arrabal, 1954

Max Aub, 1939 (via France, where he was born)

Francisco Ayala, 1939

Vicente Blasco Ibañez, 1890–91; 1896–97

Alejandro Casona, 1939–62 (returned to Spain in 1962)

Luis Cernuda, 1938

Juan José Domenchina, 1936

Juan Goytisolo, 1957 (self-exile)

Jorge Guillén, 1938

Benjamin Jarnes, 1939

Juan Ramón Jiménez, 1936

Salvador de Madariaga y Rojo, 1939 (returned to Spain in 1976)

José Ortega y Gasset, 1936–49 (returned to Spain, 1949)

Pedro Salinas, 1936

Claudio Sánchez Albornos, 1936

Jorge Semprun, 1938

Ramón Sender, 1938

Miguel de Unamuno, 1924

SRI LANKA

Michael Ondjaate, 1954

SUDAN

Tayeb Salih, 1947

SWEDEN

Vilhelm Ekelund, 1908–21; he returned to Sweden in 1921

SYRIA

Nizar Qabbani, 1971

TANZANIA

Abdubrazak Gurnah, 1970s

TRINIDAD AND ST. LUCIA

Neil Bissoondath, 1973 (emigrant to Canada)

C.L.R. James, 1932; 1965

Alfred H. Mendes, 1932

Shiva Naipaul, 1964

V. S. Naipaul, 1950

Sam Selvon, 1950

Derek Walcott, 1981

TURKEY

Morris Farhi, 1954

Nazim Hikmet, 1951

Krikor Zohrab (Armenian), 1905

See also Turkish Literature of Exile

UGANDA

Taban lo Liyong, 1978

Peter Nazareth, 1973 (of Goan descent)

Okot p'Bitek, 1975

UKRAINE

Emma Andiievska, 1943

Wasyl Barka, 1946

Bohdan Boychuk, 1949

Ihor Kačurovs'kyj, 1946

Jurij Klen, 1931

Eaghor Kostetzky, 1946

Ludmyla Kovalenko, c. 1942

Jevhen Malanjuk, 1944

Oleksander Oles', 1919

Ostap Tarnavs'kyj, 1944

Volodmyr Vynnychenko, 1919

Wira Wowk, 1946

See also Poland, Russia, USSR

UNITED STATES

Bertolt Brecht, 1948

William S. Burroughs, 1951

Charlie Chaplin, 1952

(Leroy) Eldridge Cleaver, 1969 (returned to U.S., 1978)

J. P. Donleavy, 1967

W.E.B. Du Bois, 1961

T.S. Eliot, 1914

Emma Goldman, 1919

Julian Green, 1922

Stefan Heym, 1952

Chester Himes, 1953

Henry James, 1875

Hans Koning, 1975

John Howard Lawson, 1948

Margaret Randall, 1962 (self-exile to Mexico and renunciation of American citizenship; returned to U.S.)

Margaret Schlauch, 1950

Dalton Trumbo, 1951–53

Richard Wright, 1946

Expatriates: Raymond Andrews; James Baldwin, 1948; Djuna Barnes, 1928; Natalie Barney, 1910s; Elizabeth Bishop, 1951; John Peale Bishop, 1918, 1922, 1926; Paul Blackburn, 1950s; Jane Bowles, 1947; Paul Bowles, 1947; Kay Boyle, 1923–41, 1945; Louis Bromfield, 1918, 1925; Bob Brown, 1909; Louise Bryant, 1917; Barbara Chase-Riboud, 1970s; Alfred Chester, 1951; Robert Coates, 1921; Malcolm Cowley, 1917; Robert Creeley; Caresse Crosby, 1922; Harry Crosby, 1917; Countee Cullen, 1928; e.e. cummings, 1917; H. D. (Hilda Doolittle); J. P. Donleavy, 1960s; John Dos Passos, 1917; F. Scott Fitzgerald, 1921; Janet Flanner, 1921; Henry Furst, 1910; Ernest Hemingway, 1917; Russell Hoban, 1969; James Jones, 1958; Langston Hughes, 1920; Anthony Kerrigan, 1951; Penny Lernoux, 1962; Archibald MacLeish; Henry Miller, 1932; Anaïs Nin, 1923; David Plante, 1966; Ezra Pound, 1908; John Reed, 1917; George Santayana; Sam Shepard, 1971–74; Clancy Sigal, 1956; Gertrude Stein, 1903; Susan Sontag; Anne Stevenson; Paul Theroux, c. 1960; Gore Vidal, 1950s; Glenway Westcott, 1920s.

URUGUAY

Mario Benedetti, 1970s

Eduardo Galeano, 1973

Juan Carlos Onetti, 1975

Angel Rama, 1972

Florencio Sanchez, 1898

USSR (Union of Soviet Socialist Republics)

Nizametdin Achmetov, 1987

Gregory V. Adamovich, 1923

Vassily Aksyonov, 1980

Mark Aldanov, 1919

Yuz Aleshkovsky, 1979

Andrei Alekseyvich Almarik, 1976

Leonid Andreyev, 1917

Vadim Andreyev, 1922

Aharaon Appelfeld, 1940 (from Bukovina, now part of USSR)

Natalia Arsiennieva, 1940

Nina Berberova, 1923

Nikolai Berdyaev, 1922

Ghayim Nachman Bialik, 1919

Joseph Brodsky, 1972

Vladimir Bukovsky, 1977

Ivan Bunin, 1920

Paul Celan, 1945 (from area formerly part of Austro-Hungarian Empire; then part of USSR; now part of Romania)

Sergei Dovlatov, 1978

Juri Druzhnikov, 1987

Eugene Dubnov, 1971

Ilya Ehrenburg, 1920

Ivan Elagin, 1950 (earlier in prisoner-of-war camps and displaced persons camps)

Aleksandr Galich, 1974

Gaito Gazdanov, 1920

Maxim Gorky, 1921–33

Michael R. Heifetz, 1980

Zinaida Hippius, 1919

Vyscheslav Ivanovich Ivanov, 1924

Boris Khazahnov, 1982

Vladislav Khodasevich, 1922

Lev Kopelev, 1980

Konstantin Korovin, 1917

Naum Korzhavin, 1974

Anatoli Kuznetsov, 1969

Anotoly E. Levitin–Krasnov, 1974

György Lukács, 1933–45 (after Austria/Germany, 1919–33)

Arkady Lvov, 1976

Vladimir Maximov, 1974

Dmitry S. Merezhkovsky, 1905–12; 1919

Victor Muravin, 1969

Vladimir Nabokov, 1917 (left Germany for France and U.S., 1937)

Victor Nekrasov, 1960s

Michael Peltsman, 1976

Boris Poplavsky, 1921

Mark A. Popovsky, 1977

Irina Ratushinskaia, 1986

Roman Raygorodetsky, 1988

Alexei M. Remizov, 1921

Grigol Robakidse, 1945

Felix Y. Rozimir, 1978

Victor Serge, 1917; 1936

Andrei Sinyavsky (Abram Tertz), 1971

Sacha Sokolov, 1973

Alexandr Solzhenitsyn, 1974

Gregory C. Svirsky, 1972

Valery Tarsis, 1966

Marina Tsvetaeva, 1921

Jan Valtin, 1940

Vladimir Voinovich, 1980

Vasily S. Yanovsky, 1922

Igor M. Yefimov, 1978

Yevgenii Zamayatin, 1931

Zinovy Zinik, 1975

Alexander Zinoviev, 1978

See also Estonia, Latvia, Lithuania, Poland, Russia, Ukraine

VIETNAM

Tran thi Nga, 1975

WEST GERMANY (Federal Republic of Germany)

Wolf Biermann, 1953 (returned to West Germany, 1976)

Hans Magnus Enzenberger, 1957–65

Peter Hacks, 1955

Stephen Hermlin, 1949

Monica Maron, 1950s

See also East Germany; Germany

YUGOSLAVIA

Ivo Andric, 1919–41 (diplomatic service)

Jovan Dučic, 1941

Danilo Kiš, 1979

Mihajlo Mihajlov, 1978

Voranc Prezihov, 1930 (returned in 1939 to fight with Yugoslav partisans)

Bogdan Raditsa, 1946

John Simon, 1939

Appendix C: Refuge and Haven: Points of Arrival

ALGERIA

(Leroy) Eldridge Cleaver, 1970s (via Cuba; later North Korea; North Vietnam; returned to the U.S.)

ARABIA

T. E. Lawrence, 1916 (returned to England)

ARGENTINA

Rafael Alberti, 1941–77 (after France, 1939–41; returned to Spain, 1977)

Miguel Ángel Asturias, 1954–62 (later Western Europe)

Francisco Ayala, 1939–49 (later U.S.; returned to Spain, 1976)

Alejandro Casona, 1939

Eduardo Galeano, 1973

Witold Gombrowicz, 1939–64 (moved to France, 1964)

Ihor Kačurovs'kyj, 1948–69 (after Austria, 1946–48; returned to Europe, 1969)

Pablo Neruda, 1946 (toured Europe later through 1952)

Florencio Sanchez, 1898

Claudio Sánchez Albornos, 1940–76 (after France, 1936; returned to Spain, 1976)

Paul Zech, 1933

AUSTRALIA

Ostap Tarnavs'kyj, 1944

Dimitris Tsaloumas, 1950s

AUSTRIA

Odon von Horvath, 1933–38

Pavel Kohout, 1979

György Lukács, 1918–30 (later Germany, 1930–33; USSR, 1933–45; returned to Hungary, 1945; deported 1956 to Romania; allowed to return to Hungary, 1957)

BOTSWANA

Bessie Head, 1964

BRAZIL

Georges Bernanos, 1938 (via Paraguay; returned to France, 1945)

Julian Tuwim, 1940–46 (also U.S.; returned to Poland, 1946)

Wira Wowk, c. 1946

Stefan Zweig, 1941 (via England, 1938–40; U.S., 1940–41)

CANADA

Neil Bissoondath, 1973

Austin Clarke, 1954–55

Bogdan Czaykowski

Jan Drabek, 1980s (after U.S., 1968)

George Faludy, 1967 (after France and Morocco, 1938; U.S., 1941–46; England, 1956)

Marwan Hassan

Eva Hoffman, 1959 (later U.S.)

Rohinton Mistry, 1975

Brian Moore, 1948–53

Michael Ondaatje, 1962 (via England, 1954)

Alicia Parizean, 1980 (earlier France, 1945–80)

Sam Selvon, 1978 (after England, 1950–78)

Josef Skvorecky, 1968 (via U.S.)

Gregory C. Svirsky, 1972 (via West Germany)

Adam Tarn, 1968

Arved Viirlaid, 1953 (via Sweden, 1944–45; England, 1945–53)

Aina Zemdega, 1950 (after Sweden, 1944–50)

CHILE

Nicolás Guillén, 1953 (later elsewhere in Latin America)

CHINA

Walter Abish, 1940 (later Israel, U.S.)

William Empson, 1937–39; 1947–53

COLOMBIA

Eric Arendt, 1942 (after Switzerland, 1933; Spain, 1938)

Penny Lernoux, 1962 (for professional reporting)

COSTA RICA

Manlio Argueta, 1980s

Paulé Barton, 1960s

CUBA

(Leroy) Eldridge Cleaver, 1970 (later Algeria)

Alex La Guma, 1978 (via England)

CZECHOSLOVAKIA

Oskar Kokoschka, 1919–38 (later England; then Switzerland)

Oleksander Oles', 1920

Volodymyr Vynnychenko, 1919–24 (later France)

DENMARK

Louis-Ferdinand Céline, 1945–51 (returned to France, 1951)

Vilhelm Ekelund, 1912 (via Germany, 1908–12)

DOMINICAN REPUBLIC

Hilde Domin, after 1938 (returned to West Germany)

Lore Segal (later U.S.)

EAST GERMANY (German Democratic Republic)

Wolf Biermann, 1953 (returned to West Germany, 1976)

Alfred Döblin, 1965 (after U.S., 1940–65)

Peter Hacks, 1955

Peter Handke, 1966–73 (later France; returned to Austria, 1979)

Stephen Hermlin, 1949

Stephan Heym, 1953 (after Czechoslovakia, 1933–35; U.S., 1936–52)

Monica Maron, 1950s (returned to West Germany)

Gerald K. Zschorsch, 1970s

Arnold Zweig, 1948 (after Palestine/Israel, 1933–48)

Gerhard Zwerenz, 1948

EGYPT AND NEAR EAST

D. J. Enright, 1948 (later various travels in Far East)

T. E. Lawrence, 1916

Vahan Tekeyan, 1915 (with many travels around the world)

ENGLAND

Peter Abrahams, 1941–57 (later Jamaica, West Indies)

Perseus Adams, 1970

Michael Arlen, 1920s (also United States)

Harold Beaver, 1937 (via Isle of Wight, 1934–37)

Guillermo Cabrera Infante, 1965

Roy Campbell, 1927 (later Spain, Portugal)

Elias Canetti, 1938 (via France)

Luis Cernuda, 1938 (later U.S., 1947; Mexico, 1952)

Joseph Conrad, 1878 (via France, 1874–78); British citizen, 1886

Jack Cope, 1980s

R. N. Currey, 1930s

Bodgan Czaykowski (later Canada)

Anthony Delius, 1956

Eugene Dubnov, 1975 (via Israel, 1971–75)

Duo Duo, 1989

T. S. Eliot, 1915 (via France, Germany, 1914)

Buchi Emecheta, 1962

Martin Esslin, 1944

Fadia Faqir, 1984

Morris Farhi, 1954

Eva Figes, 1930s

Miles Franklin, 1914–33 (after U.S., 1905–14; returned to Australia, 1933)

Erich Fried, 1938

Ferdynand Goetel, 1946

Andrew Graham-Yooll, 1976

Abdulrazak Gurnah, 1970s

Wilson Harris, 1959 (in recent years a world traveler)

Jan de Hartog, 1946 (Isle of Wight and France)

Ronald Harwood, 1950s

Russell Hoban, 1969 (expatriate)

Alfred Hutchinson, 1960 (via Ghana, 1956–60)

Kazuo Ishiguro, 1960

Dan Jacobson, 1961

Henry James, 1876

Ruth Prawer Jhabvala, 1938–51 (later India; U.S.)

Arthur Koestler, 1939 (after many travels: Palestine, 1926; France and Germany, 1927–31; USSR, 1931–33; Spain, 1936–37)

Oskar Kokoschka, 1938 (later Switzerland)

Zofia Kossak-Szezucka, 1945–56 (returned to Poland, 1956)

Alex La Guma, 1966 (later Cuba)

George Lamming, 1950 (after Trinidad, 1946; returned to Barbados, 1980s)

Menyhert Melchior Lengyel, 1937 (later U.S.)

Laurence Lerner, 1940s

Doris Lessing, 1949

Salvador de Madariaga y Rojo, 1939 (with wide travels around the world)

Katherine Mansfield, 1908

Kamala Markandaya, 1950s

Georgi Markov, 1969

Gyorgy Mikes, 1938

Edgar Mittelholzer, 1947–52; 1954–65 (1952, Canada)

Bloke Modisane, 1960s

Dom Moraes, 1953 (returned to India, 1984)

Alberto Moravia, 1930 (later U.S., Mexico, China, Greece, 1935–37)

M. Oswald Mtshali, 1975–79 (returned to South Africa, 1979)

Mbulelo V. Mzamane, 1976 (also U.S.)

Shiva Naipaul, 1964

V. S. Naipaul, 1950

Robert Neumann, 1934

Ngugi wa Thiong'o, 1982

Arthur Nortje, 1954–67; 1970 (Canada, 1967–70)

Edna O'Brien, 1960

Sean O'Casey, 1926

Ben Okri, 1978

Cosmo Pieterse, 1980s (also U.S., 1960s)

David Plante, 1966 (expatriate)

William Plomer, 1929 (via Japan, 1925–29)

Ezra Pound, 1908–21 (later France, 1921–25; Italy, 1925–45; 1958)

F. T. Prince, 1931

Jean Rhys, 1906 (also France)

Henry Handel Richardson, 1890s

Mordecai Richler, 1954–72 (after France, 1951–52, as an expatriate)

Richard Rive, 1970s (earlier U.S.)

Salman Rushdie, 1961–89 (expatriate); 1989 (exile)

Tayeb Salih, 1950s–80 (later Qatar)

Olive Schreiner, 1881–89; 1914–18

Mongane Wally Serote, 1980s (after U.S., Botswana)

Clancy Sigal, 1956

Wole Soyinka, 1970s (also U.S.)

Sylvester Stein, 1950s

Randolph Stow, 1970s

Bela Szasz, 1956 (after France, 1937; Argentina, 1939–46)

Paul Tabori, 1937

Ernst Toller, 1933 (later U.S.)

Laurens van der Post, 1927

Simone Weil, c. 1943

Morris Winchevsky, 1879

David Wright, 1934

Zinovy Zinik, 1975

Stefan Zweig, 1934–38 (self-exile); 1938–40 (later to U.S. and Brazil)

FINLAND

Leonid Andreyev, 1918 (after first exile, 1905, refuge in Germany)

FRANCE

Gregory Adamovich, 1923

Ai Qing, 1929–32

Mark Aldanov, 1919–42 (later U.S., 1942)

Corredo Alvaro, 1920s (mainly France and Germany; also Near East)

Jorge Amado, 1948 (also Czechoslovakia; returned to Brazil)

Andrei Amalrik, 1976 (via The Netherlands and U.S.)

Vadim Andreyev, 1924 (via Turkey, Bulgaria, Germany)

Fernando Arrabal, 1954

Miguel Ángel Asturias, 1923–33; 1966–70 (after 1948–1962, in Argentina; Western Europe, 1962–66)

Konstantin D. Balmont, 1920

Francis Bébey, 1961–74

Samuel Beckett, 1932–37 (wanderings: England, France, Germany; self-exile, France, 1940, mainly Paris)

Walter Benjamin, 1933–40

Nina Berberova, 1923–48 (later U.S.)

Nikolai Berdyaev, 1924–40 (after Germany, 1922–24)

Mongo Beti, 1951

Vicente Blasco Ibañez, 1890–91

Breyten Breytenbach, 1961

Ferdinand Bruckner, 1933–39 (returned to West Germany after 1945)

Louise Bryant, 1923 (expatriate)

Vladimir Bukovsky, 1978

Ivan Bunin, 1920 (via the Balkans)

Morley Callaghan, 1928–29 (expatriate)

Alejo Carpentier, 1930s (also Spain)

Paul Celan, 1948 (via Romania, 1945; Austria, 1947)

Aimé Césaire, 1920s

E. M. Cioran, 1937

Brian Coffey, 1928–32 (expatriate)

Countee Cullen, 1928–30 (expatriate)

Léon-Gontran Damas, 1931

Mahmud Darwish, 1982 (via Lebanon 1970–82)

Denis Devlin, 1928–32 (expatriate)

Mbella Sonne Dipoko, 1960

Alfred Döblin, 1951 (after France and Switzerland, 1933; U.S., 1940–45)

Lawrence Durrell, 1936 (beginnings of travels; Corfu)

Ilya Ehrenburg, 1908–18; 1924–41 (returned to USSR, 1941)

Odysseus Elytis, 1967–74 (returned to Greece, 1974)

Frantz Fanon, 1950

Janet Flanner, 1921 (expatriate)

Barbu Fundoiani

Mavis Gallant, 1949

Alexander Galich, 1974 (via Norway, West Germany)

Gaito Gazdanov, 1920

Ferdynand Goetel, 1946

Julian Green, 1922

Juan Goytisolo, 1957 (later U.S. and Morocco)

Graham Greene, 1966

Walter Hasenclever, 1933–40 (also Yugoslavia, Italy, England)

Peter Handke, 1973–79

Zbigniew Herbert, 1970s

Chester Himes, 1953 (expatriate)

Zinaida Hippius, 1905–13; 1919 (via Poland)

Dennis Hirson, 1970s

Odon von Hórvath, 1938 (after Germany, 1924; Austria, 1933)

Langston Hughes, 1924 (via Spain and North Africa)

Eugène Ionesco, 1940

Edmond Jabès, 1957

James Joyce, 1920–40 (after Italy, 1904–14; Switzerland, 1914–20)

Cheik Hamidou Kane, 1952–59

Nikos Kazantzakis, 1946

Hermann Kesten, 1933–40 (later U.S. and elsewhere)

Vladislav Khodasevich, 1922

Danilo Kiš, 1979

Konstantin Korovin, 1917

Milan Kundera, 1979 (taught in France from 1975)

Anatoli Kuznetsov, 1970s

D. H. Lawrence, 1928–30 (after world travels: U.S., Italy, Germany, Mexico, Ceylon, Australia, and elsewhere)

Carlo Levi, 1938

Amin Maalouf, 1980?

Thomas MacGreevy, 1928–32 (expatriate)

Heinrich Mann, 1933 (later U.S.)

W. Somerset Maugham, 1920s (with frequent world travels)

Vladimir Maximov, 1974

Albert Memmi, 1950s

Dmitry Merezhkovsky, 1905–13, 1919

Henry Miller, 1932–39 (expatriate)

Slawomir Mroźek, 1968

Victor Nekrasov, 1960s

Anaïs Nin, 1923

Sembene Ousmane, late 1940s

Ferdinand Oyono, 1955

Alicia Parizean, 1945–80 (moved to Canada, 1980)

Boris Poplavsky, 1921

Nizar Qabbani, 1987 (via Lebanon, 1971–87)

Raja Rao, 1929–38, 1947–63 (later U.S.)

Alexei M. Remizov, 1924 (via Estonia and Germany)

Aquilino Ribeiro, 1910–20

Augustus Roa Bastos, 1947–89 (after Argentina; returned to Paraguay, 1989)

Joseph Roth, 1933

Severo Sarduy, 1960

Nathalie Sarraute, 1908

Albrecht Schaefer, 1930s

Anna Seghers, 1933 (later Spain, 1937; Mexico, 1940–47; returned to East Germany, 1947)

Jorge Semprun, 1939 (after incarceration in Auschwitz; returned to Spain)

Léopold Sédar Senghor, 1928–35 (returned to Senegal, 1935)

Victor Serge, 1936–40 (later Mexico)

Andrei Sinyavsky, 1971

Susan Sontag (expatriate)

Manès Sperber, 1933 (via Yugoslavia)

Gertrude Stein, 1903 (expatriate)

Tchicaya U Tam'si, 1946

Marina Tsvetaeva, 1926–39 (after Czechoslovakia and Germany, 1921–26; returned to USSR, 1939)

Tristan Tzara, 1920 (after Switzerland, 1915)

Miguel de Unamuno, 1924–30 (also Canary Islands and Basque country)

César Abraham Vallejo, 1923–30; 1932 (Spain, 1930–32)

Mario Vargas Llosa, 1950s–74 (also Spain)

Vassilis Vassilikos, 1967–74 (France and Western Europe)

Volodymyr Vynnychenko, 1924 (via Czechoslovakia, 1919–24)

Alexander Wat, 1960 (also U.S.)

P. G. Wodehouse, 1932–1947 (expatriate, later U.S.)

Richard Wright, 1946

Vasily Yanovsky, 1922–42 (later, U.S., 1942)

Adam Zagajewski, 1982

Yevgenii Zamayatin, 1931

Krikor Zohrab, 1905–8 (returned to Turkey)

GERMANY

S. Y. Agnon, 1913–24

Leonid Andreyev, 1905–7 (returned to Russia, 1907; went into second exile 1918, Finland)

Jurij Klen, 1931

Feng Zhi, 1931

GHANA

Edward Braithwaite, 1955–62

W.E.B. Du Bois, 1961

GREECE

Norman Douglas (travels on islands and mainland and in Capri and Mediterranean from 1904)

George Johnston, 1955–65

Robert Liddell, 1953

HONG KONG

Eileen Chang, 1950s

Leung Tung, 1975 (later U.S.)

INDIA

Ruth Prawer Jhabvala, 1951 (after England, 1939; now resides mainly in New York City)

INDONESIA

Cai Qi-jiao, 1935–38 (returned to China, 1938)

IRELAND

Antonin Artaud, 1946

J. P. Donleavy, 1967

T. H. White, 1939 (later Channel Islands, 1947)

ISRAEL/PALESTINE

S. Y. Agnon, 1907; 1924 (then Palestine)

Yehuda Amichai, 1936

Aharon Appelfeld (via Italy)

Sholem Asch, 1954 (after U.S., 1909–54)

Ghayim Nachman Bialik, 1924 (via Germany)

Max Brod, 1939

Martin Buber, 1938

Eugene Dubnov, 1971–75 (later England)

Uri Zvi Greenburg, 1925 (via Germany)

Michael R. Heifetz, 1980

Ephraim Kishon, 1949 (via Austria)

Else Lasker-Schüler, 1939 (after Switzerland, 1933–39)

Dom Pagis, 1946

Felix Y. Rozimir, 1978

Arnold Zweig, 1933–48 (returned to East Germany, 1948)

ITALY

Ingebord Bachmann (began travels in 1953, mainly Germany, Switzerland, later Italy)

Vicente Blasco Ibañez, 1896

Rudolf Borchadt, 1933

Norman Douglas, 1904 (Capri, also Greece)

Nuruddin Farah, 1970s (after England, now Uganda)

Henry Furst, 1910–30, 1945–67 (expatriate)

Maxim Gorky, 1921–33 (after first exile, 1906)

Vyscheslav Ivanovich Ivanov, 1924

Tim Parks, 1980

Ezra Pound, 1925–45, 1958 (after England, France, 1908–25)

Frederick Rolfe (Baron Corvo), 1908

Florencio Sanchez (via Argentina, 1898)

George Santayana, 1920 (expatriate)

Muriel Spark, 1965, after U.S. (expatriate)

Gore Vidal, 1950s (expatriate)

JAMAICA

Peter Abrahams, 1957 (after England, 1941–57)

Edward Braithwaite, 1983 (after England, 1950–55; Ghana, 1955–62)

Jan Carew, 1962–69 (after wide travels, 1945–62)

JAPAN

Bin Xin, 1946 (after U.S., 1923)

William Empson, 1931–34 (later China, 1937–39)

Lee Sang, 1930s

KENYA

Isak Dinesen (Baroness Karen Blixen), 1914–31

Taban lo Liyong, 1978 (also New Guinea, Sudan)

Okot p'Bitek, 1975

LEBANON

Nizar Qabbani, 1971–87 (later, France, 1987)

MEXICO

Max Aub, 1942 (via France, 1939)

Miguel Bonasso, 1970s

Leonora Carrington, 1942 (via France, 1937–40; Spain, 1940–42)

Luis Cernuda, 1952 (after England, 1938; U.S., 1947)

Juan José Domenchina, 1938

Carlos Franqui, 1955–57 (also U.S.)

Gabriel García Márquez, 1965 (after France/Europe, 1955–57; Venezuela, 1957–59; Cuba, Spain and U.S. in earlier and later travels)

Benjamin Jarnes, 1940

John Howard Lawson, 1948

Pablo Neruda, 1950 (with travels to USSR, France and Latin America)

Margaret Randall, 1962–69 (later Nicaragua)

Gustav Regler, 1939

Anna Seghers, 1940–47 (after France, 1933; Spain, 1937; returned to East Germany, 1947)

Bruno Traven, 1923 (via Austria, 1919)

Dalton Trumbo, 1951–53

MONTE CARLO

Anthony Burgess, 1975 (after Malta, 1968)

MOROCCO

Jane Bowles, 1947 (expatriate)

Paul Bowles, 1947 (expatriate)

Alfred Chester, 1963 (after France, 1950–60) (expatriate)

Juan Goytisolo, 1970s (returned to Spain)

NEW ZEALAND

Gu Cheng, 1938

Karl Wolfskehl, 1938

Yang Lian, 1989 (via Hong Kong)

NICARAGUA

Claribel Alegria, 1979 (after U.S., France, Spain)

Margaret Randall, 1970–84 (after Mexico, 1962–69; returned to U.S., 1984)

NEW GUINEA

Taban lo Liyong, 1978 (later Sudan)

NIGERIA

Mbuelelo Vizikhungo Mzamane

NORWAY

Hans Henny Jahnn, 1915–18 (later Switzerland, 1934)

PUERTO RICO

Carlos Franqui, 1980s (via Italy)

Juan Ramón Jiménez, 1936

Alfonsas Nyka-Nilŭnas, 1949 (via West Germany)

Nicanor Parra, 1970–80s (as itinerant exile-critic)

POLAND

Franz Theodor Csokor, 1938 (also Romania, Yugoslavia)

Margaret Schlauch, 1950

PORTUGAL

Roy Campbell, 1937 (via Spain, after England)

QATAR

Tayeb Salih, 1947 (after long stay in France)

SENEGAL

Ayi Kwei Armah, 1980s

Camara Laye, 1965

SPAIN

Claribel Alegria, 1956–79 (on Majorca, via France, 1952–56; moved to Nicaragua, 1979)

José Donoso, 1967–80 (after Argentina, 1959–60; U.S., 1960–67; returned to Chile, 1980)

Jorge Edwards, 1973–79 (via France)

Eduardo Galeano, 1976–84 (after Argentina, 1973–76)

Robert Graves, 1929 (after Egypt, 1926)

Anthony Kerrigan, 1950s–80s (expatriate)

Robin Maugham, 1950s (on island of Ibiza)

Juan Carlos Onetti, 1975

Victor Serge, 1917

Armando Valladares, 1982 (via France and U.S.)

Mario Vargas Llosa, 1958–75 (France and Spain; returned to Peru in 1978)

SRI LANKA

Arthur C. Clarke, 1979 (expatriate)

SOUTH AFRICA

Rose Zwi, c. 1939

SWAZILAND

Can Themba, 1968

SWEDEN

Bei Dao, 1989

Ivar Grunthal, 1944

Sigurd Höel, 1940

Aino Kallas, 1944

Bernard Kangro, 1940s

Mogen Klitgaard, 1944–50 (later Canada)

Zenta Maurina, 1940 (later Germany)

Karl Ristikivi, 1944 (via Finland)

Nelly Sachs, 1940

Kurt Tucholsky, 1929 (settled in Sweden, deprived of German citizenship, 1933)

Peter Weiss, 1938 (after England, 1934; Czechoslovakia, 1936)

Aina Zemdega, 1944–50 (later Canada)

SWITZERLAND

Werner Bergengruen, 1944

Bryher (Winifred Ellerman), 1920s (via England, France [expatriate])

Charlie Chaplin, 1952

H. D. (Hilda Doolittle), 1920s (via England, France [expatriate])

Julius Háy, 1965 (after first exile, 1919–30, Germany; second exile, 1933–34, Austria; third exile, 1934–46, USSR; returned to Hungary, 1946–65)

Hermann Hesse, 1919

Fritz Hochwalder, 1938

Hans Henny Jahnn, 1934 (after Norway, 1915–18)

Georg Kaiser, 1938 (via Holland)

Hérmann Kesten, 1980s (after U.S.)

Oskar Kokoschka, 1950s (after England)

Agota Kristof, 1956

Else Lasker-Schüler, 1933–39 (later Israel [Palestine])

Anotoly E. Levitin-Krasnov, 1974

Erika Mann, 1933–36 (later U.S.)

Thomas Mann, 1933 (later U.S., 1938–52; returned to Switzerland for second residence period, 1952)

Robert Musil, 1938

Vladimir Nabokov, 1952 (after U.S., 1938–52)

Erich Maria Remarque, 1931; 1950s (lived in U.S., 1937–50s)

Rainer Maria Rilke, 1918 (also France, 1902–11)

Grigol Robakidse, 1945

Ignazio Silone, 1930–45 (returned to Italy, 1945)

Alexandr Solzhenitsyn, 1974–76 (later U.S.)

Adam Tarn, 1969

Friedrich Torberg, 1938 (later France, 1939–41; U.S., 1941 via Spain and Portugal)

Carl Zuckmayer, 1958 (after U.S., 1939–58)

TAIWAN

Chao Chi-kang, 1985

Chen Jo-hsi, 1973

Liu Da-ren, 1949 (later U.S.)

Pai Hsin-yung, 1949–63 (later U.S.)

Yu Li-hua, 1949–54 (later U.S.)

TANZANIA

Ayi Kwei Armah, 1969–70 (after U.S. 1959–66, 1968–69) returned to Ghana, 1966–68; now lives in Senegal)

TUNISIA

Luis Bernardo Honwana, 1967 and after (also Algeria, Switzerland)

TURKEY

Erich Auerbach, 1936–46 (later U.S.)

Constantine Cavafy, 1885

UGANDA

Naruddin Farah (Somalia to England, Italy, now Uganda, 1989)

UNITED STATES

Talat Abassi, 1977 (expatriate)

Walter Abish, 1950s (via Shanghai, Israel)

Tamas Aczel, 1956

Theodor Adorno, 1938 (returned to Germany, 1949)

Jonas Aistis, 1946 (via France, 1940–46)

Vassily Aksyonov, 1980

Mark Aldanov, 1942 (after France, 1919–42)

Claribel Alegria, 1943 (also Mexico, Uruguay, Argentina)

Yuz Aleshkovsky, 1980

Sándor András, 1956 (via England)

Reinaldo Arenas, 1980

Hannah Arendt, 1941 (via France)

Arturo Arias, 1980s

Michael J. Arlen, 1940

Natalia Arsiennieva, 1950 (after Kazakstan, USSR, 1940 and displaced persons camps, 1945–50)

Sholem Asch, 1909 (later Israel, 1954)

Erich Auerbach, 1946 (after Turkey, 1936–46)

Kofi Awoonor, 1969 (via England, 1968; returned to Ghana, 1975)

W. H. Auden, 1939

Francisco Ayala, 1950–76 (returned to Spain, 1976)

Stanislaw Baranczak, 1980

Wasyl Barka, 1946

Vicki Baum, 1931

Richard Beer-Hoffmann, 1939 (via Switzerland, 1938)

Bei Ling, 1989

Nina Berberova, 1948 (via France, 1923–48)

Giuseppe Borgese, 1931 (returned to Italy, 1947)

Bohdan Boychuk, 1949

Kazimierz Brandys, 1982

Bernardas Brazdžionis, 1949

Bertolt Brecht, 1939–52 (after Denmark via Czechoslovakia, 1933; returned to East Germany, 1952)

André Breton, 1940–45 (returned to France, 1945)

Hermann Broch, 1938 (via England)

Joseph Brodsky, 1977

Ferdinand Bruckner, 1939 (via France, 1933–39)

Dennis Brutus, 1965 (via England)

Jan Carew, 1970s

Nina Cassian, 1986

Ernst Cassirer, 1940 (via England, 1933; Sweden, 1935)

Eileen Chang, mid–1950s (after Hong Kong)

Chao Chi-kang, 1985 (also lives in Taiwan)

Chen Jo-hsi, 1960s

Chen Kaige, 1989

Nicola Chiaramonte, 1940 (via France, 1934–36; Spain, 1936–40)

Frank M. Chipasula, 1980

Andrei Codrescu, 1966 (via France and Italy)

Angel Cuadra Landrove, 1983

O. R. Dathorne (via Nigeria, 1959, and England)

Hana Demetz, 1950 (via Germany, 1946)

Alfred Döblin, 1940–65 (via Switzerland, France; returned to East Germany, 1965)

Ariel Dorfman, 1945–54; 1973–83 (also in various European countries; lives in both Chile and U.S.)

Sergei Dovlatov, 1978

Juri Druzhnikov, 1987

Jovan Dučic, 1941

Ivan Elagin, 1950

Mircea Eliade, 1956 (after France, 1945–56)

Lion Feuchtwanger, 1940 (after France, 1933–37; USSR, 1937–38; France, 1938–40)

Ford Madox Ford, 1929

Maria Irene Fornes, 1945

Bruno Frank, 1937 (via Austria, England, France, Switzerland)

René Fülöp-Miller, 1938 (after Western Europe, 1905–38)

Shirley Geok-Lim Lin, 1960s

Zulfikar Ghose, 1969

Kahlil Gibran, 1902

Jacob Glatstein, 1914

Janusz Glowacki, 1982

Oliver St. John Gogarty, 1939

Yvan Goll, 1939

Roberto Gonzáles-Echevarría, 1959

Chaim Grade, 1950 (after USSR, 1939)

Oskar Maria Graf, 1941 (via Austria, Czechoslovakia, USSR, 1933–41)

Arthur Gregor, 1940

Jorge Guillén, 1939 (with many world travels)

Clara Gyorgyey, 1956

Hans Habe, 1940–54 (returned to Germany, 1954, later Switzerland)

Moyshe Leyb Halpern, 1908

Stella K. Hershan, 1939

Stephen Heym, 1936–52 (later East Germany)

Eva Hoffman, 1964 (via Canada, 1959–64)

Christopher Isherwood, 1939

Ivar Ivask, 1949

C.L.R. James, 1965 (U.S. and England) (after U.S., 1938, via England, 1933; lived in U.S. until 1945; returned to England, 1945–50; returned to Trinidad, 1950)

Denis Johnston, 1960

Marius Katiliškis, 1945

Marek Kedzierski, 1986 (also West Germany)

Thomas Keneally, 1972–82 (also England)

Hermann Kesten, 1940

Keorapetse William Kgositsile, late 1950s

Kim Kyung Jae, 1972

Richard E. Kim, 1954 (after South Korea, 1945–54)

Jamaica Kincaid, 1966

Eric Knight, 1938

Annette Kolb, 1941 (after Switzerland, 1918)

Hans Koning, 1947; 1964; 1988 (moved to England, 1939; to Indonesia, 1946; lived in England, 1975–88)

Jerzy Kosinski, 1957

Jan Kott, 1966 (after Europe, 1956–66)

Ludmyla Kovalenko, 1946 (after displaced persons camps, 1944–45)

Daniel Kunene, 1960s

Masizi Kunene, 1959 (via England)

Algirdas Landsbergis, 1949

Menyhert Melchior Lengyel, 1937

Leung Tung, 1975

Halpern Lewick, 1913

Jakov Lind, 1965 (after Israel, 1946; England, 1950; lives in England, U.S. and Mallorca during parts of the year)

Li Tuo, 1989

Liu Da-ren, 1960s

Liu Zaifu, 1989

Malcolm Lowry, 1935 (later Mexico, Canada [expatriate])

Emil Ludwig, 1936 (via Switzerland, 1933)

Arnost Lustig, 1970 (via Yugoslavia and Israel)

Claude McKay, 1912–22; 1933–48 (via England and France, 1920–33)

Algimantus Mackus, 1948

Rian Malan, 1977–84; 1987

Jevhen Malanjuk, 1946

Norman Manea, 1989

Erika Mann, 1936 (via Switzerland, 1933–36)

Heinrich Mann, 1940 (via France, 1933–40)

Klaus Mann (via Switzerland, 1933)

Thomas Mann, 1938 (via Switzerland, 1933; returned to Switzerland, 1952)

Sándor Márai, 1950s (after Italy, 1945–50s)

Herbert Marcuse, 1934 (via Switzerland, 1933)

Hisako Matsubara

Pablo Medina, 1961

Alfred Mendes, 1932–40 (returned to Trinidad)

Ved Parkash Mehta, 1940s

Mihajlo Mihajlov, 1978

Czeslaw Miłosz, 1960 (via France, 1951–60)

Ferenc Molnár, 1940

Brian Moore, 1953 (after Canada, 1948–53)

Ted Morgan, 1945

Frederic Morton, 1939

Rose Moss, 1964

Es'kia Mphahlele, 1957–77 (returned to South Africa, 1977)

Bharati Mukherjee (via Canada, 1962)

Victor Muravin, 1971

Vladimir Nabokov, 1940–61 (via England, 1918–22; Germany, 1922–37; France, 1938–40; returned to Europe in 1961, choosing Montreux, Switzerland as his residence)

Peter Nazareth, 1973

Jan Novak, 1970 (via Austria)

Alfonsas Nyka-Niliŭnas, 1949

Frank O'Connor, 1954–61 (via England)

Liam O'Flaherty, 1917–22, expatriate wanderings, also North and South America, Southern Europe; 1935, expatriate

Julio Ortega, 1970s

Heberto Padilla, 1980

Pai Hsin-yung, 1963 (after Taiwan, 1949–63)

Ricardo Pau-Llosa, 1960s

Michael Peltsman, 1976

Cosmos Pieterse, 1960s (also England, 1970s)

David Pinski, 1892

Mark A. Popovsky, 1977

Alicia Portnoy, 1970s

J. C. Powys (expatriate)

Manuel Puig, 1960 (self-exile via Italy)

Henrikas Radauskas, 1949 (via Germany)

Bogdan Radtitsa, 1946

Angel Rama, 1981 (but denied American citizenship because of the provisions in Walter-McCarran Act barring citizenship to former or present members of the Communist party)

Santha Rama Rau, 1950s

Aleksis Rannit, 1953

Raja Rao, 1963 (after France, 1929–39; France, 1947–63)

Irina Ratushinskaia, 1986

Roman Raygorodetsky, 1988

Erich Maria Remarque, 1937 (later Switzerland)

Carlos Ripoll, 1950

Richard Rive, 1965 (later England)

Sheila Roberts, 1977

Felix Rozimir, 1980 (via Israel)

Edward Said, 1950

Antoine de Saint-Exupéry, 1940

Saint-John Perse, 1940–67 (returned to France, 1967)

Pedro Salinas, 1936

Andrew Salkey, 1970s (via England, 1952)

Sang Ye, after 1980 (via Hong Kong)

Lore Segal, 1951 (via Dominican Republic and England)

Mongane Wally Serote, 1976 (later Botswana and England)

Ramón Sender, 1939 (via France, 1938)

Wilfrid Sheed, 1940

John Simon, 1940

I. B. Singer, 1935

I. J. Singer, 1934

Antonio Skármeta, 1975 (also West Germany)

Antanas Škéma, 1944 (via Germany, 1944–49)

Antanas V. Slavov, 1976

Mark Slonim, 1920s (via Czechoslovakia)

Rita Smith, 1953

Sacha Sokolov, 1973

Mario Soldati, 1929–31 (returned to Italy, 1931)

Alexandr Solzhenitsyn, 1976 (after Switzerland, 1974–76)

Wole Soyinka, 1970s (also England)

George Steiner, 1940?

Su Wei, 1989

Su Xiaokang, 1989

Ostap Tarnavs'kyj, 1949 (via Austria, 1944–49)

Linard Tauns, 1950

Ernst Toller, 1940 (after England, 1933–39)

Friedrich Torberg, 1941–51 (returned to Austria)

Tran thi Nga, 1975

Dorin Tudoran, 1985

Julian Tuwim, 1940–46 (also in Brazil; returned to Poland, 1946)

Bodo Uhse, 1939

Sigrid Undset, 1940 (via Sweden; returned to Norway, 1946)

Luisa Valenzuela, 1979 (returns to Argentina periodically)

Jorge Valls Arango, 1984

Jan Valtin, 1940

Derek Walcott, 1981

Ernst Waldinger, c. 1940

Alexander Wat, 1960s (also France)

Simone Weil, 1942 (later England)

René Wellek, 1927

Franz Werfel, 1940 (via France, Switzerland, England)

Elie Wiesel, 1948 (via France)

P. G. Wodehouse, 1947 (via France, 1932–47)

Sylvia Wynter, 1974 (after England and Scandinavia, 1949; British Guyana, 1958; Jamaica, 1962)

Vasily S. Yanovsky, 1942 (via France, 1922–42)

Igor M. Yefimov, 1978

Marguerite Yourcenar, 1939

Barry Yourgrau, 1960s

Yu Li-hua, 1954 (via Taiwan, 1949–50)

· Zhang Xinxin, 1989

Zheng Min, 1948–54

Lajos Zilahy, 1947

Carl Zuckmazyer, 1939 (moved to Switzerland, 1958)

Stefan Zweig, 1940 (via England, 1938; moved to Brazil, 1941)

USSR

Johannes Becher, 1935

Emma Goldman, 1919

Nazim Hikmet, 1951–63 (also Poland, Bulgaria)

Theodor Plivier, 1933 (emigrated to West Germany, 1945)

John S. Reed, 1917

VENEZUELA

Isabel Allende, 1975

Gabriel García Márquez, 1957 (later Mexico, 1965)

Angel Rama, 1972 (later U.S.)

WEST GERMANY (Federal Republic of Germany)

Nizametdin Achmetov, 1987

Emma Andiievska, 1943

Jurek Becker, 1978

Wolf Biermann, 1976

Martin Gregor-Dellin, 1958

Jiri Grusa, 1970s

Peter Handke, 1966–73

Marek Hlasko, 1958 (also Israel, U.S.)

Peter Huchel, 1971

Uwe Johnson, 1959

Ihor Kačurovs'kyj, 1969 (after Austria, 1946–48; Argentina, 1948–69)

Marek Kedzierski, 1986 (also U.S.)

Boris Khazahnov, 1982

Heinar Kippardt, 1963

Sarah Kirsch, 1977

Lev Kopelev, 1980

Eaghor Kostetzky, 1946

Gunter Kunert, 1977

Reiner Kunze, 1977

Monica Maron, 1980s

Hisako Matsubara

Zdzislaw Najder, 1981

Theodor Plivier, 1945 (after first exile in USSR, 1933–45)

Antonio Skármeta, 1970s (also U.S.)

Daniel Stroz, 1968

Valery Tarsis, 1970s

Vladimir Voinovich, 1980

Jochem Ziem, 1955

Alexander Zinoviev, 1978

Gerald K. Zschorsch, 1970s

Gerhard Zwerenz, 1950s

ZAMBIA

Todd Matshikiza, 1965? (after England, 1960)

Lewis Nkosi, 1970s (after U.S., 1961, England)

NO FIXED PLACE OF ABODE

Ivo Andric (diplomatic service in various capitals of Western Europe)

Octavio Paz (many travels)

Voranc Prezihov, 1930 (Austria, Czechoslovakia, Romania, France)

José Ortega y Gasset, 1936 (from Spain to France, Holland, Argentina, Portugal, U.S., Germany; returned to Spain, 1949)

Appendix D: Exile by Category

EXILE BY ACCIDENT

S. Y. Agnon, from Palestine to Germany, 1913–24

Witold Gombrowicz, from Poland to Argentina, 1939–45; returned to Europe in 1945

EXILE TO AVOID CRIMINAL PROSECUTION

(Leroy) Eldridge Cleaver, U.S. to Europe and Asia

Vilhelm Ekelund, Sweden to Denmark

CULTURAL EXILE

Fernando Arrabal, Spain to France

Sholem Asch, Poland to U.S.

Ingebord Bachman, Austria to Italy

Samuel Beckett, Ireland to France

Elias Canetti, Bulgaria to England

Alejo Carpentier, Cuba to France, Spain

Paul Celan, Romania to France

Aimé Césaire, Martinique to France; returned to Martinique

Eileen Chang, China to Taiwan

Chao Chi-kang, China to Taiwan

Chen Jo-hsi, Taiwan/China to U.S.

E. M. Cioran, Romania to France

Andrei Codrescu, Romania (Transylvania) to U.S.

Joseph Conrad, Poland to England via France

Julio Cortázar, Argentina to France

R. N. Currey, South Africa to England

Léon-Gontran Damas, Guyana to France

Anthony Delius, South Africa to England

J. P. Donleavy, U.S. to Ireland

José Donoso, Chile to Europe

Ariel Dorfman, Chile to U.S.

Lawrence Durrell, England to Greece, Southern Europe, and France

Mircea Eliade, Romania to U.S. via Europe

Feng Zhi, China to Germany

Barbu Fondoiani, Romania to France

Miles Franklin, Australia to U.S. and England

Juan Goytisolo, Spain to France and U.S.

Robert Graves, England to Southern Europe

Zinaida Hippius, Russia to France

Eugène Ionesco, Romania to France

C.L.R. James, Trinidad to U.S. and England

Henry James, U.S. to England

James Joyce, Ireland to Europe

Vladislav Khodasevich, USSR to France

D. H. Lawrence, England to Europe, Sri Lanka, Australia, U.S. and Mexico

Menyhert Melchior Lengyel, Hungary to U.S.

Laurence Lerner, South Africa to England

Robert Liddell, England to Mediterranean and Greece

Amin Maalouf, Lebanon to France

David Malouf, Australia to Europe

Claude McKay, Jamaica to France and U.S.

Albert Memmi, Tunisia to France

Rohinton Mistry, India to Canada

Brian Moore, Northern Ireland to U.S., England, Canada

Dom Moraes, India to England

Mbuelelo V. Mzamane, South Africa to U.S. and England

Shiva Naipaul, Trinidad to England

V. S. Naipaul, Trinidad to England

Edna O'Brien, Ireland to England and U.S.

Sean O'Casey, Ireland to England

Boris Poplavsky, Russia to France

Manuel Puig, Argentina to U.S.

Raja Rao, India to France, U.S.

Henry Handel Richardson, Australia to England

Christina Stead, Australia to England

Paul Tabori, Hungary to England

Tristan Tzara, Romania to Switzerland and France

Mario Vargas Llosa, Peru to Spain and France

Rose Zwi, Mexico (of East European origin) to South Africa

EXILE FOR DIPLOMATIC, EDUCATIONAL, MEDICAL OR CAREER REASONS

Perseus Adams, South Africa to Europe

Ivo Andric, Yugoslavia to Western Europe

Michael Arlen, Bulgaria to England and U.S.

Kofi Awoonor, Ghana to U.S. and England, Brazil and Cuba

Francis Bébey, Cameroon to France

Mongo Beti, Cameroon to France

Bin Xin, China to U.S. and Japan

Neil Bissoondath, Trinidad to Canada

Edward Braithwaite, Barbados to Ghana

Jan Carew, Guyana to U.S.

Aimé Césaire, Martinique to France

Chen Jo-hsi, Taiwan/China to U.S.

Arthur C. Clarke, England to Sri Lanka

R. N. Currey, South Africa to England

Léon-Gontran Damas, Guyana to France

O. R. Dathorne, Guyana to Nigeria, England and U.S.

Jovan Dučic, Yugoslavia to U.S.

Buchi Emecheta, Nigeria to England

William Empson, England to Japan and China

D. J. Enright, England to Egypt and various travels in Far East

Frantz Fanon, Martinique, West Indies, to France

Fadia Faqir, Jordan to England

Feng Xhi, China to Germany

Ford Madox Ford, England to U.S., France

Carlos Fuentes, Mexico to Western Europe, Cuba, U.S. and Latin America

Zulfikar Ghose, Pakistan to U.S.

Jan de Hartog, The Netherlands to Isle of Wight, Great Britain

Aino Kallas, Finland to Estonia, then England, Sweden

Cheik Hamidou Kane, Senegal to U.S.

Penny Lernoux, U.S. to Colombia

Taban lo Liyong, Uganda to U.S.

Ved Parkash Mehta, India to U.S.

Dom Moraes, India to U.S.

M. Oswald Mtshali, South Africa to U.S.

Ben Okri, Nigeria to England

Sembene Ousmane, Senegal to France

Michael Ondaatje, Sri Lanka to Canada via England

Ferdinand Oyono, Senegal to France

Octavio Paz, Mexico to Western Europe, Latin America, India, U.S.

David Pinski, Poland to U.S.

F. T. Prince, South Africa to England

Alexei Remizov, USSR to France

Jean Rhys, West Indies to England

Richard Rive, South Africa to U.S., then England; returned to South Africa

Tayeb Salih, Sudan to England, France and Qatar

Olive Schreiner, South Africa to England

Léopold Sédar Senghor, Senegal to France

Mario Soldati, Italy to U.S.; returned to Italy

Tchicaya U Tam'si, Republic of Congo to France

Derek Walcott, Trinidad to U.S.

René Wellek, Austria/Czechoslovakia to U.S.

David Wright, South Africa to England

Sylvia Wynter, Jamaica to England, Scandinavia, and U.S.

Dornford Yates, England to Rhodesia

Zheng Min, China to U.S.; returned to China

EXPATRIATES

African

Ayi Kwei Armah, Ghana to Tanzania and Senegal

Mbella Sonne Dipoko, Cameroon to France

American

To Brazil: Elizabeth Bishop

To England: H. D. (Hilda Doolittle); T. S. Eliot, Russell Hoban, Henry James, Robert McAlmon, David Plante, Ezra Pound, Clancy Sigal, Sam Shepard, Donald Ogden Stewart (later a political exile), Anne Stevenson, Paul Theroux, Marianne Wiggins

To France: Sherwood Anderson, Raymond Andrews, James Baldwin, John Peale

Bishop, Kay Boyle, Louis Bromfield, Louise Bryant (via USSR), William S. Burroughs (and North Africa), Barbara Chase-Riboud, Alfred Chester (and North Africa), Caresse and Harry Crosby, Countee Cullen, e. e. cummings, John Dos Passos, Max Eastman, F. Scott Fitzgerald, Janet Flanner, Julian Green, Ernest Hemingway, Chester Himes, Langston Hughes, James Jones, Archibald MacLeish, Henry Miller, Anaïs Nin, Ezra Pound, Ned Rorem, Susan Sontag, Gertrude Stein, Virgil Thompson, Carl Van Vechten, Glenway Westcott, Richard Wright

To Italy: Bernard Berenson, Henry Furst, Ezra Pound (after England and France), Gore Vidal

To Spain: Anthony Kerrigan

To Switzerland: H. D. (Hilda Doolittle)

To North Africa: Jane Bowles, Paul Bowles, William S. Burroughs (and Mexico, France), Alfred Chester

Australian

Miles Franklin, to U.S., later England

George Johnston, to Hydra, Greece

Thomas Keneally, to England and U.S.

David Malouf, to Europe and U.S.

Peter Porter, to England

Henry Handel Richardson, to England

Christina Stead, to Europe

Randolph Stow, to England

Canadian

Morley Callaghan, to France

Mavis Gallant, to France

Mordecai Richler, to England, after France

English

W. H. Auden, to U.S.

Bryher (Winifred Ellerman), England to Switzerland

George Barker, to U.S. and Europe

Anthony Burgess, to Malta, Italy, Monte Carlo

Leonora Carrington, England to France to Mexico

Norman Douglas, to Capri and Greece

Lawrence Durrell, to Greece and France

William Empson, to China

D. J. Enright, to Asia and elsewhere

Robert Graves, to southern Europe

Christopher Isherwood, to India and U.S.

D. H. Lawrence, to world travels

Robet Liddell, to Greece

Malcolm Lowry, to U.S., Mexico and Canada

Tim Parks, to Italy

Muriel Spark, to Rhodesia, later U.S.; since 1965, Italy

P. G. Wodehouse, to France, later U.S.

Dornford Yates, to France, later Rhodesia

Irish

Brian Coffey, to France

Denis Devlin, to France

Oliver St. John Gogarty, to U.S.

Denis Johnston, to U.S.

Thomas MacGreevy, to France

Frank O'Connor, to U.S.

Liam O'Flaherty, to world travels

New Zealander

Fleur Adcock, to England

Katherine Mansfield, to England, later France

West Indies and Caribbean

Léon-Gontran Damas, Guyana to France and return

Wilson Harris, Guyana to England, U.S.

C.L.R. James, Trinidad to U.S. and England

Jamaica Kincaid, Antigua to U.S.

George Lamming, Barbados to Trinidad, U.S., England and return

Alfred Mendes, Barbados to U.S. and return

Edgar Mittelholzer, Guyana to England

Shiva Naipaul, Trinidad to England

V. S. Naipaul, Trinidad to England and world travels

Jean Rhys, Dominica island to England

Andrew Salkey, Jamaica to U.S.

Sam Selvon, Trinidad to England, later Canada

Derek Walcott, St. Lucia to U.S.

Sylvia Wynter, Jamaica to England, Scandinavia, later U.S.

South African

William Plomer, to England

Laurens van der Post, to England

Indian

Nirad Chaudhuri, to England

Kamala Markandaya, to England

Dom Moraes, to England

Bharati Mukherjee, to U.S. via Canada

Raja Rao, to France and U.S.

Salman Rushdie, to England

Santha Rama Rau, to U.S.

Pakistani

Talat Abbasi, to U.S.

Zulfikar Ghose, to U.S.

EXILE FROM HISTORIC AND RELIGIOUS ORIGINS

Michael Arlen, Armenia to England

Michael J. Arlen, Armenia to U.S.

Kahlil Gibran, Lebanon to U.S.

Moyshe Leyb Halpern, Austro-Hungarian Empire to U.S.

David Pinski, Poland to U.S.

Vahan Tekeyan, Armenia to Egypt via France and Germany

Morris Winchevsky, Lithuania to U.S.

See also Armenian Writers in Exile; Yiddish Writers

LEGAL EXILE (Tax Reasons and Other)
Anthony Burgess, England to Malta, then Monte Carlo
Noel Coward, England to Bahamas, Bermuda
J. P. Donleavy, U.S. to Ireland
Graham Greene, England to France
Jan de Hartog, The Netherlands to Isle of Wight and France
James Jones, U.S. to France
W. Somerset Maugham, England to France
T. H. White, England to Ireland, later to Channel Islands

PERSONAL/SOCIAL EXILE

Walter Abish, China to Israel, later U.S.

Perseus Adams, South Africa to England

Claribel Alegria, El Salvador to U.S., later France, Spain and Nicaragua

Antonin Artaud, France to Ireland

Ayi Kwei Armah, Ghana to U.S. to Tanzania, later Senegal

Ingebord Bachmann, Austria to Italy

Georges Bernanos, France to Paraguay, Brazil, Tunisia; returned to France

Bin Xin, China to U.S.

Isak Dinesen (Baroness Karen Blixen, Denmark to Kenya; returned to Denmark

Cai Qi-jiao, China to Indonesia to China

Roy Campbell, South Africa to England, Spain, Portugal

Paul Celan, Romania to France

Austin Clarke, Barbados to Canada

Arthur C. Clarke, England to Sri Lanka/Ceylon

Eugene Dubnov, USSR to England

Hans Magnus Enzenberger, West Germany to U.S., Mexico, Norway

Ford Madox Ford, England to U.S., France

Maria Irene Fornes, Cuba to U.S.

Shirley Geok-Lim Lin, Malaysia to U.S.

Günter Grass, Germany/Poland to East Germany

Abdulrazak Gurnah, Tanzania to England

Peter Handke, Austria to France and West Germany

Ronald Harwood, South Africa to England

Zbigniew Herbert, Poland to France

Hermann Hesse, Germany to Switzerland

Kazuo Ishiguro, Japan to England

George Johnston, Australia to Greece

Richard E. Kim, Korea to U.S.

Danilo Kiš, Yugoslavia to France

Eric Knight, England to U.S.

Hans Koning, The Netherlands to U.S. to England, later returned to U.S.

D. H. Lawrence, England to Germany, France, Italy, U.S., Mexico, Australia, Ceylon; died in France

T. E. Lawrence, England to Middle East and Turkey

Kamala Markandaya, India to U.S.

Hisako Matsubara, Japan to West Germany

W. Somerset Maugham, England to France, Italy, and Far East

Ferenc Molnár, Hungary to U.S.

Brian Moore, Northern Ireland to Canada, later U.S.

Ted Morgan, France to U.S.

Es'kia Mphahlele, South Africa to England and U.S.

Sławomir Mrożek, Poland to France

Bharati Mukherjee, India to U.S. via France, Canada

Shiva Naipaul, Trinidad to England

V. S. Naipaul, Trinidad to England

Sean O'Casey, Ireland to England

Liam O'Flaherty, Ireland to U.S., North and South America, Europe

Michael Ondjaate, Sri Lanka to Canada

J. C. Powys, Wales to U.S., returned to Wales

Michael Peltsman, USSR to U.S.

Manuel Puig, Argentina to U.S. and Europe

Richard Rive, South Africa to U.S. and England

Rainer Maria Rilke, Austro-Hungarian Empire to Switzerland

George Santayana, U.S. to Europe

Nathalie Sarraute, Russia to France

Olive Schreiner, South Africa to England; returned to South Africa

Wilfrid Sheed, England to U.S.

Rita Smith, India to U.S.

Dmitris Tsaloumas, Greece to Australia

César Abraham Vallejo, Peru to France

David Wright, South Africa to England

Marguerite Yourcenar, France to U.S.

Zheng Min, China to U.S.

Arnold Zweig, Israel to East Germany

POLITICAL EXILE

Peter Abrahams, South Africa to England and Jamaica, West Indies

Nizametdin Achmetov, USSR to West Germany

Tamas Aczel, Hungary to U.S.

Gregory V. Adamovich, USSR to France

Theodor Adorno, Germany to U.S.; returned to Germany

Jonas Aistis, Lithuania to U.S.

Vassily Aksyonov, USSR to U.S.

Rafael Alberti, Spain to Italy; returned to Spain

Mark Aldanov, USSR to France

Claribel Alegria, El Salvador to Nicaragua

Yuz Aleshkovsky, USSR to U.S.

Isabel Allende, Chile to Venezuela

Corredo Alvaro, Italy to France and Germany

Jorge Amado, Brazil to France; returned to Brazil

Andrei A. Amalrik, USSR to France, also U.S.

Emma Andiievska, Ukraine to West Germany

Sándor András, Hungary to U.S. via England

Leonid Andreyev, Russia to Finland

Vadim Andreyev, USSR to France

Reinaldo Arenas, Cuba to U.S.

Erich Arendt, Germany to Colombia to East Germany

Hannah Arendt, Germany to U.S.

Manlio Argueta, El Salvador to Costa Rica

Arturo Arias, Guatemala to U.S.

Natalia Arsiennieva, Azerbaijan (now USSR) to Poland, later to U.S.

Max Aub, France/Spain to Mexico

Francisco Ayala, Spain to Argentina, later U.S.; returned to Spain

Konstantin D. Balmont, Russia to France

Stanislaw Baranczak, Poland to U.S.

Wasyl Barka, Ukraine to U.S.

Paulé Barton, Haiti to Costa Rica

Johannes R. Becher, Germany to France 1934–35 via Austria, Czechoslovakia, USSR 1935–45; he moved to East Germany

Jurek Becker, East Germany to West Germany

Richard Beer-Hoffmann, Austria to U.S.

Bei Dao, China to Sweden

Bei Ling, China to U.S.

Mario Benedetti, Uruguay to Europe, U.S.

Nina Berberova, USSR to France, later U.S.

Nikolai Berdyaev, USSR to Germany, France

Werner Bergengruen, Germany to Tyrols

Georges Bernanos, France to Brazil and Paraguay

Wolf Biermann, West Germany to East Germany; later back to West Germany

Bin Xin, China (internal)

Vicente Blasco Ibañez, Spain to France

Miguel Bonasso, Argentina to Mexico

Rudolf Borchadt, Germany to Italy

Giuseppe Borgese, Italy to U.S.

Bohdan Boychuk, Ukraine to U.S.

Kazimierz Brandys, Poland to U.S.

Bernardas Brazdžionis, Lithuania to U.S.

Bertolt Brecht, Germany to U.S.; U.S. to East Germany

André Breton, France to U.S.; returned to France

Breyten Breytenbach, South Africa to France

Hermann Broch, Austria to U.S.

Joseph Brodsky, USSR to U.S.

Dennis Brutus, South Africa to U.S.

Vladimir Bukovsky, USSR to France

Ivan Bunin, USSR to France

Guillermo Cabrera Infante, Cuba to U.S. and England

Camara Laye, Guinea, West Africa to Senegal

Italo Calvino (partisan in Piedmont during World War II)

Alejandro Casona, Spain to Argentina

Nina Cassian, Romania to U.S.

Ernst Cassirer, Poland/Germany to U.S. via England and Sweden

Louis-Ferdinand Céline, France to Denmark; returned to France

Luis Cernuda, Spain to Mexico

Eileen Chang, China to U.S., after Hong Kong

Chao Chi-kang, China to U.S.

Chen Jo-hsi, China to Taiwan

Chen Kaige, China to U.S.

Charlie Chaplin, U.S. to Switzerland

Nicola Chiaramonte, Italy to U.S.

Frank Mkalawile Chipasula, Malawi to U.S.

(Leroy) Eldridge Cleaver, U.S. to Asia and Europe

Jack Cope, South Africa to England

Franz Theodor Csokor, Austria to Poland, Romania, Yugoslavia

Angel Cuadra Landrove, Cuba to U.S.

Bogdan Czaykowski, Poland to England, later Canada

Mahmud Darwish, Palestine to France

Anthony Delius, South Africa to England

Alfred Döblin, Germany to U.S. to East Germany

Juan José Domenchina, Spain to Mexico

Ariel Dorfman, Chile to U.S.

Sergei Dovlatov, USSR to U.S.

Juri Druzhnikov, USSR to U.S.

Jan Drabek, Czechoslovakia to Canada via U.S.

W.E.B. Du Bois, U.S. to Ghana

Duo Duo, China to England

Jovan Dučic, Yugoslavia to U.S.

Jorge Edwards, Chile to Spain, via France

Ilya Ehrenburg, Russia and USSR to Western Europe

Ivan Elagin, USSR to U.S.

Odysseus Elytis, Greece to France

Martin Esslin, Hungary to England

George Faludy, Hungary to Canada via France, Morocco and England

Nuruddin Farah, Somali to Italy, now Uganda

Lion Feuchtwanger, Germany to U.S. via France, USSR

Carlos Franqui, Cuba to Puerto Rico, via Italy

Erich Fried, West Germany to England

René Fülöp-Miller, Hungary to Western Europe, then U.S.

Barbu Fundoianu, Romania to France

Fernando Gabiera, Brazil to Algeria, Europe, South America; returned to Brazil

Aleksandr Galich, USSR to France

Eduardo Galeano, Uruguay to Argentina

Gabriel García Márquez, Colombia to Mexico and elsewhere in Latin America via Europe

Gaito Gazdanaov, USSR to Germany

Janusz Glowacki, Poland to U.S.

Ferdynand Goetel, Poland/Austro-Hungarian Empire to England

Emma Goldman, U.S. to USSR

Roberto González-Echevarría, Cuba to U.S.

Maxim Gorky, Russia to Italy; USSR to Western Europe

Oskar Maria Graf, Germany to U.S.

Andrew Graham-Yooll, Argentina to England

Martin Gregor-Dellin, East Germany to West Germany

Ivar Grunthal, Estonia to Sweden

Jiri Grusa, Czechoslovakia to West Germany

Gu Cheng, China to New Zealand

Jorge Guillén, Spain to U.S.

Nicolás Guillén, Cuba to Chile and elsewhere in Latin America

Clara Gyorgyey, Hungary to U.S.

Hans Habe, Germany (born in Hungary) to U.S.; returned to Germany, later Switzerland

Peter Hacks, West Germany to East Germany

Walter Hasenclever, Germany to France

Marwan Hassan, Lebanon to Canada

Julius Háy, Hungary to Germany, Austria, USSR; returned to Hungary

Bessie Head, South Africa to Botswana

Stephen Hermlin, West Germany to East Germany

Stephan Heym, Germany to U.S.; U.S. to East Germany

Nazim Hikmet, Turkey to USSR

Zinaida Hippius, 1905–13, Russia; 1919, USSR, both periods to France

Denis Hirson, South Africa to France

Marek Hłasko, Poland to West Germany (also U.S., Israel)

Sigurd Höel, Norway to Sweden

Eva Hoffman, Poland to U.S. via Canada

Luis Bernardo Honwana, Mozambique to Portugal, Switzerland, Algeria and Tunisia

Christopher Hope, South Africa to England, 1974

Odon von Horvath, Germany (he was born in Yugoslavia) to France

Peter Huchel, East Germany to West Germany

Alfred Hutchinson, South Africa to England via Ghana

Vyscheslav Ivanov, USSR to Italy

Ivar Ivask, Estonia to U.S.

Dan Jacobson, South Africa to England

Hans Henny Jahnn, Germany to Norway, later Switzerland

C.L.R. James, Trinidad to U.S. and England

Benjamin Jarnes, Spain to Mexico

Juan Ramón Jiménez, Spain to Puerto Rico

Uwe Johnson, East Germany to West Germany

Ihor Kačurovs'kyj, Ukraine to Argentina, later Germany

Bernard Kangro, Estonia to Sweden

Marius Katiliškis, Lithuania to U.S.

Nikos Kazantzakis, Greece to France

Marek Kedzierski, Poland to West Germany

Hermann Kesten, Germany to France, later U.S. and Switzerland

Keorapetse William Kgositsile, South Africa to U.S.

Boris Khazahnov, USSR to Germany

Kim Kyung Jae, South Korea to U.S.

Heinar Kippardt, East Germany to West Germany

Sarah Kirsch, East Germany to West Germany

Jurij Klen, Ukraine to Germany

Ephraim Kishon, Hungary to Israel

Mogen Klitgaard, Denmark to Sweden

Arthur Koestler, Hungary to USSR to England

Pavel Kohout, Czechoslovakia to Austria

Oskar Kokoschka, Austria to England, later Switzerland

Annette Kolb, Germany to Switzerland, later Germany to U.S.

Hans Koning, The Netherlands to U.S.

Lev Kopelev, USSR to West Germany

Konstantin Korovin, USSR to France

Naum Korzhavin, USSR to U.S.

Jerzy Kosinski, Poland to U.S.

Zofia Kossak-Szezucka, Poland to England

Eaghor Kostetzky, Ukraine to West Germany

Jan Kott, Poland to U.S.

Ludmyla Kovalenko, Ukraine to U.S.

Agota Kristof, Hungary to Switzerland

Milan Kundera, Czechoslovakia to France

Daniel Kunene, South Africa to U.S.

Mazisi Kunene, South Africa to U.S.

Gunter Kunert, East Germany to West Germany

Reiner Kunze, East Germany to West Germany

Anatoli Kuznetsov, USSR to France

Alex La Guma, South Africa to England and Cuba

Algirdas Landsbergis, Lithuania to U.S.

John Howard Lawson, U.S. to Mexico

Camara Laye, Guinea, West Africa, to Senegal

Lee Sang, Korea to Japan

Doris Lessing, Rhodesia/South Africa to England

Leung Tung, China to U.S.

Carlo Levi, Italy to France

Primo Levi, Italy (partisan in Val d'Aosta, World War II)

Anotoly E. Levitin-Krasnov, USSR to Switzerland

Li Tuo, China to U.S.

Liu Da-ren, China to U.S.

Liu Zaifu, China to U.S.

Taban lo Liyong, Uganda to New Guinea, later Sudan and Kenya

Emil Ludwig, Germany to U.S. via Switzerland

György Lukács, Hungary to Austria/Germany; later USSR; deportation to Romania before return to Hungary

Arnost Lustig, Czechoslovakia to U.S.

Arkady Lvov, USSR to U.S.

Algimantas Mackus, Lithuania to U.S.

Salvador de Madariaga y Rojo, Spain to Western Europe, U.S.

Rian Malan, South Africa to U.S.

Jevhen Malanjuk, Ukraine to U.S.

Osip Mandelstham, penal exile

Norman Manea, Romania to U.S.

Erika Mann, Germany to U.S.

Heinrich Mann, Germany to U.S.

Klaus Mann, Germany to U.S.

Thomas Mann, Germany to U.S., later Switzerland

Sàndor Márai, Hungary to U.S. after Italy

Georgi Markov, Bulgaria to England

Herbert Marcuse, Germany to U.S.

Monika Maron, West Germany to East Germany; returned to West Germany

Tomas Eloy Martinez, Argentina to Western Europe

Todd Matshikiza, South Africa to Zambia

Zenta Maurina, Latvia to Sweden

Vladimir Maximov, USSR to France

Pablo Medina, Cuba to U.S.

Dmitry S. Merezhkovsky, 1905–13, Russia; 1919, USSR; both periods to France

Mihajlo Mihajlov, Yugoslavia to U.S.

Gyorgy Mikes, Hungary to England

Czeslaw Miłosz, Lithuania/Poland to U.S.

Bloke Modisane, South Africa to England

Alberto Moravia, Italy (1943, flight from Fascism to Fondi)

Rose Moss, South Africa to U.S.

Es'kia Mphahlele, South Africa to U.S.

Victor Muravin, USSR to U.S.

Robert Musil, Austria to Switzerland

Mbuelelo Vizikhungo Mzamane, South Africa to Nigeria

Vladimir Nabokov, USSR to Germany to U.S. to Switzerland

Zdzislaw Najder, Poland to West Germany

Peter Nazareth, Uganda (of Goan descent) to U.S.

Viktor Nekrasov, USSR to France

Pablo Neruda, Chile to Argentina; Europe

Robert Neumann, Austria to U.S.

Ngugi wa Thiong'o, Kenya to England

Lewis Nkosi, South Africa to England and Zambia

Arthur Nortje, South Africa to England

Jan Novak, Czechoslovakia to U.S.

Alfonsas Nyka-Niliŭnas, Lithuania to U.S.

Frank O'Connor, Ireland to U.S.

Oleksander Oles', Ukraine to Czechoslovakia

Michael Ondaatje, Sri Lanka to Canada via England

Juan Carlos Onetti, Uruguay to Spain

José Ortega y Gassett, Spain to Latin America and Europe

Julio Ortega, Peru to U.S.

Heberto Padilla, Cuba to U.S.

Pai Hsin-yung, China to Taiwan, later U.S.

Alicia Parizean, Poland to Canada via France

Ricardo Pau-Llosa, Cuba to U.S.

Cesare Pavese, Italy (imprisonment in South Italy)

Okot p'Bitek, Uganda to Kenya

Cosmo Pieterse, South Africa to U.S. and England

Theodor Plivier, Germany to USSR, then West Germany, later Switzerland

Mark A. Popovsky, USSR to U.S.

Alicia Portnoy, Argentina to U.S.

Voranc Prezihov, Yugoslavia to Western Europe

Nizar Qabbani, Syria to Lebanon, later France

Henrikas Radauskas, Lithuania to U.S.

Bogdan Raditsa, Yugoslavia to U.S.

Angel Rama, Uruguay to U.S. and Venezuela

Margaret Randall, U.S. to Mexico and Nicaragua

Aleksis Rannit, Estonia to U.S.

Irina Ratushinskaia, USSR to U.S.

Roman Raygorodetsky, USSR to U.S.

John S. Reed, U.S. to USSR

Gustav Regler, Germany to Mexico

Erich Maria Remarque, Germany to U.S. and Switzerland

Alexei Remizov, USSR to France

Aquilino Ribeiro, Portugal to France

Carlos Ripoll, Cuba to U.S.

Karl Ristikivi, Estonia to Sweden

Yannis Ritsos, Greece (prison exile)

Augusto Roa Bastos, Paraguay to France

Grigol Robakidse, USSR to Switzerland

Sheila Roberts, South Africa to U.S.

Joseph Roth, Austria to France

Edward Said, Palestine to U.S.

Antoine de Saint-Exupéry, France to U.S.

Saint-John Perse, France to U.S.

Pedro Salinas, Spain to U.S.

Claudio Sánchez Albornos, Spain to France, Argentina; returned to Spain

Florencio Sanchez, Uruguay to Argentina

Sang Ye, China to U.S.

Severo Sarduy, Cuba to France

Albrecht Schaefer, Germany to France

Margaret Schlauch, U.S. to Poland

Anna Seghers, Germany to Mexico, later East Germany

Jorge Semprun, Spain to France, returned to Spain

Ramón Sender, Spain to U.S.

Victor Serge, France to USSR, USSR to France, Spain, Mexico

Mongane Wally Serote, South Africa to U.S., later Botswana and England

Ignazio Silone, Italy to Switzerland

Andrei Sinyavsky, USSR to France

Antonio Skármeta, Chile to U.S. and West Germany

Antanas Škéma, Lithuania/Poland to U.S. via Germany

Josef Skvorecky, Czechoslovakia to Canada

Atanas V. Slavov, Bulgaria to U.S.

Mark Slonim, USSR to U.S. via Czechoslovakia

Sacha Sokolov, USSR to U.S.

Aleksandr Solzhenitsyn, USSR to U.S.

Osvaldo Soriano, Argentina to U.S.

Wole Soyinka, Nigeria to England and United States

Sylvester Stein, South Africa to England

George Steiner, France (of Austrian parents) to U.S.; lives in England

Daniel Stroz, Czechoslovakia to West Germany

Su Wei, China to U.S.

Su Xiaokang, China to U.S.

Gregory C. Svirsky, USSR to Canada

Bela Szasz, Hungary to England, via France, Argentina

Paul Tabori, Hungary to England

Adam Tarn, Poland to U.S. and Switzerland

Ostap Tarnavs'kyj, Ukraine to U.S.

Valery Tarsis, USSR to West Germany

Linard Tauns, Latvia to U.S.

Abram Tertz. *See* Andrei Sinyavsky

Can Themba, South Africa to Swaziland

Ernst Toller, Germany to England, U.S.

Friedrich Torberg, Austria to U.S.; returned to Austria

Tran thi Nga, Vietnam to U.S.

Bruno Traven, Germany to Mexico

Dalton Trumbo, U.S. to Mexico

Marina Tsvetaeva, USSR to Czechoslovakia and France

Kurt Tucholsky, Germany to Sweden

Dorin Tudoran, Romania to U.S.

Julian Tuwim, Poland to Brazil and U.S.

Bodo Uhse, Germany to U.S.

Sigrid Undset, Norway to U.S.

Miguel de Unamuno, Spain to France and Canary Islands

Luisa Valenzuela, Argentina to U.S.

Armando Valladares, Cuba to U.S., later Spain

César Abraham Vallejo, Peru to France

Jorge Valls Arango, Cuba to U.S.

Jan Valtin, USSR to U.S.

Vassilis Vassilikos, Greece to Western Europe

Aino Viirlaid, Estonia to Canada

Vladimir Voinovich, USSR to West Germany

Volodmyr Vynnychenko, Ukraine to France

Ernst Waldinger, Austria to U.S.

Aleksandr Wat, Poland to U.S., via USSR

Morris Winchevsky, Lithuania to England

Karl Wolfskehl, Germany to New Zealand

Wira Wowk, Western Ukraine to Brazil

Richard Wright, U.S. to France

Xu Gang, China to Unknown

Yang Lian, China to New Zealand via Hong Kong

Vasily S. Yanovsky, USSR to U.S. via France

Igor M. Yefimov, USSR to U.S.

Barry Yourgrau, South Africa to U.S.

Adam Zagajewski, Poland to France

Yevgenii I. Zamayatin, USSR to France

Paul Zech, Germany to Argentina

Aina Zemdega, Latvia to Canada via Sweden

Zhang Xinxin, China to U.S.

Vasily Yanovsky, USSR to France, later U.S.

Yu Li-hua, China to U.S. via Taiwan

Jochem Ziem, East Germany to West Germany

Lajos Zilahy, Hungary to U.S.

Zinovy Zinik, USSR to England

Alexander Zinoviev, USSR to Switzerland

Gerald K. Zschorsch, East Germany to West Germany

Arnold Zweig, Germany to Israel, later to East Germany

Gerhard Zwerenz, East Germany to West Germany

POLITICAL EMIGRANTS (selective list for representational purposes)

Jonas Aistis, Lithuania to U.S.

Emma Andiievska, Ukraine to West Germany

Bernardas Brazdžionis, Lithuania to U.S.

Jan Drabek, Czechoslovakia to U.S.

Eugene Dubnov, Estonia to Israel, later England

Ivan Elagin, USSR to U.S.

Clara Gyorgyey, Hungary to U.S.

Boris Khazahnov, USSR to West Germany

Algirdas Landsbergis, Lithuania to U.S.

Anotoly E. Levitin-Krasnov, USSR to Switzerland

Mark A. Popovsky, USSR to U.S.

Aleksis Rannit, Estonia to U.S.

Alexei M. Remizov, USSR to France

Felix Y. Rozimir, USSR to Israel

John Simon, Yugoslavia to U.S.

Gregory C. Svirsky, USSR to Canada

Ostap Tarnavs'kyj, Ukraine to U.S.

Wira Wowk, Ukraine to Brazil

Vasily S. Yanovsky, Russia to France, later U.S.

Igor M. Yefimov, USSR to U.S.

PROBLEMATIC EXILE

Salvador Espiru, banned from publishing in his language, Catalan, in Spain

Franz Kafka, exile in his own land

Nicanor Parra, exile in his own land

RELIGIOUS EXILE AND EMIGRATION

Walter Abish, Austria to France to China, later Israel and U.S.

Yehudah Amichai, Germany to Palestine (Israel)

Aharon Appelfeld, USSR to Israel

Hannah Arendt, Germany to U.S.

Sholem Asch, Russia to U.S. and Israel

Erich Auerbach, Germany via Turkey to U.S.

Harold Beaver, Germany to England

Richard Beer-Hoffmann, Austria to U.S.

Walter Benjamin, Germany to France

Ghayim Nachman Bialik, USSR to Israel

Max Brod, Czechoslovakia to Palestine (Israel)

Ferdinand Bruckner, Bulgaria (lived in Germany) to France, U.S.

Martin Buber, Austria to Israel

Hana Demetz, Czechoslovakia to U.S.

Hilde Domin, Germany to Santo Domingo; returned to West Germany

Morris Farhi, Turkey to England

Lion Feuchtwanger, Germany to U.S. via France

Eva Figes, Germany to England

Bruno Frank, Germany to U.S.

Erich Fried, Germany to England

Sigmund Freud, Austria to U.S.

Jacob Glatstein, Russia to U.S.

Yvan Goll, Germany/France [Alsace] to U.S.

Chaim Grade, Lithuania to U.S. via USSR

Uri Zvi Greenburg, Austro-Hungarian Empire to Palestine (Israel) via Germany

Arthur Gregor, Austria to U.S.

Hans Habe, Germany (born in Hungary) to U.S.

Moyshe Leyb Halpern, Byelorussia to U.S.

Walter Hasenclever, Germany to France

Michael R. Heifetz, USSR to Israel

Stella K. Hershan, Austria to U.S.

Fritz Hochwalder, Austria to Switzerland

Odon von Horvath, Germany (born in Yugoslavia) to France

Edmond Jabès, Egypt to France

Ruth Prawer Jhabvala (born of Polish parents in Germany) to England; later to India; she lives in New York

Georg Kaiser, Germany to Switzerland

Aino Kallas, Estonia (born in Finland) to Sweden

Ephraim Kishon, Hungary to Israel

Herbert Kuhner, Austria to U.S.

Else Lasker-Schüler, Germany to Switzerland and Israel

Menyhert Melchior Lengyel, Hungary to U.S.

Halpern Lewick, Poland to U.S.

Jakov Lind, Austria to U.S. and England

Arnost Lustig, Czechoslovakia into hiding in Germany; later U.S.

Ferenc Molnár, Hungary to U.S.

Frederic Morton, Austria to U.S.

Dom Pagis, Romania to Israel

Felix Y. Rozimir, USSR to U.S. via Israel

Salman Rushdie (flight into hiding after sanction of murder by Islamic holy leader, Ayatollah Ruhollah Khomeini)

Nelly Sachs, Germany to Sweden

Lore Segal, Austria to U.S. via Dominican Republic

Isaac Bashevis Singer, Poland to U.S.

I. J. Singer, Poland to U.S.

Antonio Skármeta, Chile to U.S. and West Germany

Manès Sperber, Germany to France

Vahan Tekeyan, Armenia to Egypt

Friedrich Torberg, Austria to U.S. via Switzerland, France, Spain and Portugal

Jan Valtin, USSR to U.S.

Simone Weil, France to England and U.S.

Peter Weiss, Germany to Sweden

Franz Werfel, Austria to U.S.

Elie Wiesel, Hungary to U.S. via France

Krikor Zohrab, Armenian ethnic in Turkey to France, 1905–8

Carl Zuckmayer, Germany/Austria to U.S.

Arnold Zweig, Germany to Israel, later to East Germany

Stefan Zweig, Austria to England, then U.S. and Brazil

SEXUAL EXILE

Reinaldo Arenas, Cuba to U.S.

Constantine P. Cavafy, Egypt

Norman Douglas, Scotland, U. K. to southern Europe

Christopher Isherwood, England to Germany, India, and U.S.

Robin Maugham, England to North Africa and southern Europe

Manuel Puig, Argentina to U.S.

Frederick Rolfe (Baron Corvo), England to Italy

See also Gay and Lesbian Writers in Exile (Harold Acton, Margaret Anderson, John Ashbery, Djuna Barnes, Natalie Barney, Sylvia Beach, Bryher [Winifred Ellerman], John Horne Burns, Truman Capote, Luis Cernuda, Ronald Firbank, Janet Flanner, Charles Henry Ford, E. M. Forster, Robert Friend, Allen Ginsberg, Thom Gunn, Marilyn Hacker, Marsden Hartley, Daryl Hine, Porfirio Barba Jacob, John Lehmann, David Malouf, Erika Mann, Robert McAlmon, Aubrey Menen, James Merrill, H. H. Munro [Saki], Harold Norse, Ned Rorem, Jane Rule, Vita Sackville-West, Tobias Schneebaum, Stephen

Spender, Gertrude Stein, Dunstan Thompson, Carl Van Vechten, Renee Vivien, Glenway Westcott, Patrick White, Oscar Wilde, and Tennessee Williams)

Individual entries are provided on the following writers and literary personalities, while reference to their sexual exile is found in the entry on Gay and Lesbian Writers in Exile.

W. H. Auden, James Baldwin, Jane Auer Bowles, Paul Bowles, William S. Burroughs, Alfred Chester, Countee Cullen, H. D. (Hilda Doolittle), Norman Douglas, Langston Hughes, Christopher Isherwood, T. E. Lawrence, Klaus Mann, Thomas Mann, Robin Maugham, W. Somerset Maugham, David Plante, Manuel Puig, Frederick Rolfe (Baron Corvo), George Santayana, Gore Vidal, Marguerite Yourcenar

General Bibliography

Abramsky, Chimen, Maciej Jachimczyk, and Anthony Polonsky, eds. *The Jews in Poland.* Oxford: Blackwell, 1986.

Adey, David, with Ridley Beeton, Michael Chapman, Ernest Pereira, *Companion to South African English Literature.* Craighall, South Africa: A. D. Donker, 1986.

Alegria, Fernando. *The Chilean Spring.* Translated by Stephen Fredman. Pittsburgh: Latin American Review Press, 1980.

———, ed. *Chilean Writers in English, Eight Short Novels.* Trumansburg, N.Y.: Crossing Press, 1982.

Alexandrova, Vera. *A History of Soviet Literature, 1917–1962: From Gorky to Yevtushenko.* Garden City, N.Y.: Doubleday, 1963.

Anderson, Susan. "Something in Me Died: Autobiographies of South African Writers in Exile," *Books Abroad* [now *World Literature Today*] 44 (1970).

Ash, Timothy Garton. *The Magic Lantern: The Revolution of 1989 Witnessed in Warsaw, Budapest, Berlin and Prague.* New York: Random House, 1990.

Ashcroft, Bill, Gareth Griffiths, and Helen Tiffin, *The Empire Writes Back: Theory and Practice in Post-Colonial Literatures.* New York: Routledge, 1989.

Bach, I. *The German Jew.* Oxford: Oxford University Press, 1985.

Baugh, Edward. *West Indian Poetry.* Kingston, Jamaica: Savacou Publications, 1971/72.

Beier, Ulli, ed. *An Introduction to African Literature: An Anthology of Critical Writings.* 2d ed. Evanston, Ill.: Northwestern University Press, 1979.

Beller, Steven. *Vienna and Jews: 1867–1938: A Cultural History.* Cambridge: Cambridge University Press, 1989.

Benstock, Shari. *Women of the Left Bank: Paris, 1900–1940.* Austin: University of Texas Press, 1986.

Blake, Patricia, ed. *Dissonant Voices in Soviet Literature.* New York: Pantheon, 1962.

Boyce, Carole, and Elaine Savory Fido, eds., *Out of the Kumbla: Womanist Perspectives on Caribbean Literature*. Trenton: Africa World Press, 1988.

Braham, Robert L. *The Hungarian Jewish Catastrophe: A Selected and Annotated Bibliography*. New York: Boulder and Institute for Holocaust Studies of the City of New York, 1984.

Braunech, Manfred. *Autorenlexikon Deutschsprachigen Literatur des 20 Jahrhunderts*. Hamburg: Rowohlt, 1984.

Broe, Mary Lynn, Angela Ingram, eds., *Women's Writing in Exile*. Chapel Hill: University of North Carolina Press, 1989.

Brook, J. M., ed. *Dictionary of Literary Biography Yearbook Annual*. Detroit: Gale Research.

Brown, Deming. *Soviet Russian Literature Since Stalin*. New York: Columbia University Press, 1978.

Brown, Edward J. *Russian Literature Since the Revolution*. Cambridge, Mass.: Harvard University Press, 1982.

Burness, Donald, ed. *Critical Perspectives on Lusophone Literature from Africa*. Washington, D.C.: Three Continents Press, 1981.

Cambridge Guide to Literature in English. Ed. Ian Ousby. Cambridge: Cambridge University Press, 1988.

Cambridge History of Russian Literature. Ed. Charles A. Moser. Cambridge: Cambridge University Press, 1989.

Carpenter, Charles A. *Modern Drama Scholarship and Criticism 1966–1980: An International Bibliography*. Toronto: University of Toronto Press, 1986.

Cartey, Wilfrid. *Whispers from a Continent: The Literature of Contemporary Black Africa*. New York: Random House, 1969.

Chen, Jack. *The Chinese of America*. N.Y.: Harper and Row, 1981.

Chinweiza, and Onwuchekwa Jemie and Ihechukwu Madubuike. *Toward the Decolonization of African Literature*: vol. 1, *African Fiction and Poetry and Their Critics*. Enegu, Nigeria: Fourth Dimension, 1980; Washington, D.C.: Howard University Press, 1983.

Clark, Katerina. *The Soviet Novel: History as Ritual*. Chicago: University of Chicago Press, 1981.

Columbia Dictionary of Modern European Literature. 2d ed. Ed. Jean-Albert Bede and William B. Edgerton. New York: Columbia University Press, 1980.

Contemporary Dramatists. Ed. James Vinson and Daniel Kirkpatrick. New York: St. Martin's Press, 1986.

Contemporary Novelists. 4th ed. Ed. Daniel Kirkpatrick. New York: St. Martin's Press, 1986.

Coser, Lewis A. *Refugee Scholars in America: Their Impact and Their Experience*. New Haven: Yale University Press, 1984.

Crowley, Edward, and Max Hayward, eds. *Soviet Literature in the 1960s*. New York: Praeger, 1964.

Dance, Daryl Cumber, ed. *Fifty Caribbean Writers: A Bio-Bibliographical Critical Source Book*. Westport, Conn.: Greenwood Press, 1986.

Dathorne, O. R. *Dark Ancestor: The Literature of the Black Man in the Caribbean*. Baton Rouge: Louisiana State University Press, 1981.

Demetz, Peter. *After the Fires: Recent Writing in the Germanies, Austria and Switzerland*. San Diego/New York: Harcourt Brace Jovanovich, 1986.

Dictionary of Literary Biography Yearbook Ed. J. M. Brook. Detroit: Gale Research Company Annual.

Domandi, Agnes Korner, ed. *Modern German Literature*. New York: Frederick Ungar Company, 1984.

Duffy, Dennis. *Gardens, Covenants, Exiles: Loyalism in the Literature of Upper Canada*. Toronto: University of Toronto Press, 1982.

Encyclopedia of World Literature. Ed. Leonard Klein. 4 vols. New York: Frederick Ungar Publishing Company, 1981–84.

European Writers: The Twentieth Century, Vol. 9. Ed. George Stade. New York: Charles Scribner's Sons, 1989.

Exil. Ed. Michael Winkler. Frankfurt, 1981– .

"Exile and the Writer," ed. Martin Tucker, *Confrontation: A Literary Journal* (Long Island University, Brookville, N.Y.), nos. 27–28 (1984).

Fanon, Frantz. *Les Damnés de la terre*, 2d ed. Paris, 1968.

———. *Peau noire, masques blancs*. 2d ed., Paris, 1975.

Fermi, Laura. *Illustrious Immigrants: The Intellectual Migration from Europe 1930–1941*. Chicago: University of Chicago Press, 1968.

Ferreira, Manuel, and Gerald Moser, eds., *Bibliography of Portuguese African Literature*. Lisbon: Impr. National-Casa de Moeda, 1983.

Firmat, Gustavo Perez. *The Cuban Condition: Translation and Identity in Modern Cuban Literature*. Cambridge: Cambridge University Press, 1989.

Fleming, Donald, and Bernard Bailyn, eds., *The Intellectual Migration*. Cambridge, Mass.: Harvard University Press, 1969.

Foster, David William, comp. *Handbook of Latin American Literature*. New York: Garland, 1987.

Frank, Joseph. *Through the Russian Prism: Essays on Literature and Culture*. Princeton: Princeton University Press, 1990.

Gazarian Gautier, Marie-Lise. *Interviews with Latin American Writers*. Lisle, Illinois: Dalkey Archive Press, 1990.

González-Echevarría, Roberto. *The Voices of the Masters: Writing and Authority in Modern Latin-American Literature*. Austin: University of Texas Press, 1985.

Goodwin, Kenneth L. *Understanding African Poetry: A Study of Ten Poets*. London and Exeter, N.H.: Heinemann, 1982.

Griffiths, Gareth. *A Double Exile: African and West Indian Writing between Two Cultures*. London: Marion Boyars, 1978.

Guibert, Rita. *Seven Voices: Seven Latin-American Writers Talk to Rita Guibert*. New York: Vintage Books, 1973 [c. 1972]. [Interviews with Pablo Neruda, Jorge Luis Borges, Miguel Ángel Asturias, Octavio Paz, Julio Cortázar, Gabriel García Márquez, Guillermo Cabrera Infante].

Gupta, Brijen K. *India in English Fiction, 1800–1970: An Annotated Bibliography*. Metuchen, N.J.: Scarecrow Press, 1973.

Gurr, Andrew. *Writers in Exile: The Creative Use of Home in Modern Literature*. Studies in Contemporary Literature and Culture. Brighton, Sussex, England: Harvester Press, 1981; Atlantic Highlands, N.J.: Humanities Press, 1981.

Hamburger, Michael. *After the Second Flood: Essays on Post-War German Literature*. New York: St. Martin's Press, 1986.

Havard, Robert G. *From Romanticism to Surrealism: Seven Spanish Poets*. Savage, Md.: Rowan and Littlefield, 1988.

Hayward, Max, and Leopold Labedz, eds. *Literature and Revolution in Soviet Russia 1917–62: A Symposium*. New York: New York University Press, 1963.

Heilbut, Anthony. *Exiled in Paradise: German Refugee Artists and Intellectuals in America from the 1930s to the Present*. New York: Viking Press, 1983.

Herdeck, Donald. *African Authors: A Companion to Black African Writing, 1300–1973*. Washington, D.C.: Three Continents Press, 1973.

———, ed. *Caribbean Writers: A Bio-Bibliographical-Critical Encyclopedia*. Washington, D.C.: Three Continents Press, 1979.

Hertzberg, Arthur. *The Jews in America: Four Centuries of an Uneasy Encounter: A History*. New York: Simon and Schuster, 1989.

Hoffman, Eva. *Lost in Translation: A Life in a New Language*. New York: E. P. Dutton, 1989.

Hosking, Geoffrey. *The Awakening of the Soviet Union*. London: Heinemann, 1990.

———. *Beyond Social Realism*. New York: Holmes and Meier, 1980.

Huggins, Nathan Irvin. *Harlem Renaissance*. New York: Oxford University Press, 1971.

Ivask, Ivar, and J. von Wilpert, eds. *World Literature since 1945*. New York: Frederick Ungar, 1973.

Iyengar, K. P. Srinivasa. *Indian Writing in English*. 2d ed. New York: Asia Publishing House, 1973.

Jackman, Jarrell C., and Carla M. Borden. *The Muses Flee Hitler: Cultural Transfer and Adaptation, 1930–1945*. Washington, D.C.: Smithsonian Institution Press, 1983.

Jahn, Janheinz, comp. and ed. *A Bibliography of Neo-African Literature: From Africa, America, and the Caribbean*. New York: Praeger, 1965.

Jahn, Janheinz, Ulla Schild, and Almut Nordmann, eds. *Who's Who in African Literature: Biographies, Works and Commentaries*. Tubingen: Horst Erdmann Verlag for the German African Society, 1972.

Jonas, Joyce. *Anancy in the Great House: Ways of Reading West Indian Fiction*. Westport: Greenwood Press, 1990.

Journal of Refugee Studies (Oxford University Press), vol. 1– (1988–).

Kamla, Thomas A. *A Confrontation with Exile: Studies in the German Novel*. Bern: Herbert Lang, 1975; Frankfurt: Peter Lang, 1975.

Kanellos, Nicolas. *Biographical Dictionary of Hispanic Literature in the United States: The Literature of Puerto Ricans, Cuban Americans, and Other Hispanic Writers*. Westport, Conn.: Greenwood Press, 1989.

Karlinsky, Simon, and Alfred Appel, Jr. *The Bitter Air of Exile: Russian Writers in the West 1922–1972*. Berkeley: University of California Press, 1977. (Originally published as "Russian Literature and Culture in the West: 1922–1972," *Triquarterly* [Northwestern University] 27–28 [Spring and Fall, 1973]).

Kasack, Wolfgang. *Lexikon der russichen Literatur ab 1917*, Stuttgart, Alfred Kroner Verlag, 1976.

Katz, Jane. *Artists in Exile: American Odyssey*. New York: Stein & Day, 1983.

Khotin, Leonid, ed. *Abstracts of Soviet and East European Emigré Periodical Literature*. Pacific Grove, California, 1981.

Kindlers Neues Literatur Lexikon. Ed. Walter Jens. Work in progress, 20 vols. planned. Munich: Kindler Verlag, 1988, first volume published.

Kingston, Maxine Hong. *The Woman Warrior*. N.Y.: Alfred A. Knopf, 1976.

———. *China Men*. N.Y.: Alfred A. Knopf, 1980.

Klima, Vladimir, and others. *Black Africa: Literature and Language*. Dordrecht, Holland/ Boston: D. Reidel Publishing Company, 1976.

Kontinent 2, Journal of Soviet Writers in exile. Ann Arbor, Mich.: Ardis Publications, 1977.

Kramer, Aaron. *A Century of Yiddish Poetry*. New York: Cornwall Books, 1989.

Kubayanda, Josaphat B. *The Poet's Africa*. Westport: Greenwood Press, 1990.

Kunitz, Stanley J., and Howard Haycraft, eds. *Twentieth Century Authors: A Biographical Dictionary of Modern Literature*. New York: H. W. Wilson, 1942. *First Supplement*, ed. Stanley J. Kunitz. New York: H. W. Wilson, 1955.

Larson, Charles. *The Novel in the Third World*. Washington, D.C.: Inscape, 1976.

Lazarus, Neil. *Resistance in Postcolonial African Fiction*. New Haven: Yale University Press, 1990.

Lewanski, Richard, comp., with assistance of Lucia G. Lewanski and Mayo Deringin. *The Literatures of the World in English Translation: A Bibliography*, vol. 2: *The Slavic Literatures*. New York: New York Public Library/Frederick Ungar Company, 1967.

Lindfors, Bernth. *Black African Literature in English: A Guide to Information Sources*. Detroit: Gale Research, 1979. *Supplement*. New York: Africana Publishing, 1986.

"The Literature of Exile." *Ariel: A Review of International Literature* (University of Calgary, Calgary, Alberta, Canada) 13, no. 4 (October 1982). Special issue.

Locker, Frances C., ed. *Contemporary Authors*. Detroit: Gale Research, annual.

Long, Berel, ed. *Writing and the Holocaust*. New York: Holmes & Meier, 1988.

Longstreet, Stephen. *We All Went to Paris: Americans in the City of Light, 1776–1971*. New York: Macmillan, 1972.

Lowe, David. *Russian Writing Since 1953: A Critical Survey*. New York: Frederick Ungar Company, 1987.

Marotos, Daniel C., and Marnesba D. Hill, eds. *Escritores de la Diaspora, Cubana Manual Bibliografica/Cuban Exile Writers: A Bibliographic Handbook*. Westport, Conn.: Greenwood Press, 1986.

Marsh, Rosalind. *Soviet Fiction Since Stalin: Science, Politics & Literature*. Savage, Md.: Barnes and Noble, 1985.

McCagg, William, Jr. *A History of Habsburg Jews: 1670–1918*. Bloomington: Indiana University Press, 1989.

McMurray, George. *Spanish American Writing Since 1941: A Critical Survey*. New York: Frederick Ungar Company, 1987.

Melber, Henning. *It Is No More a Cry: Namibian Poetry in Exile*. Basel: Baseler Afrika Bibliographien, 1982.

Mihailovich, Vasa D., and Igor Hajek, Zbigniew Folejwski et al., comps. and eds., *Modern Slavic Literatures. II: Bulgarian, Czechoslovak, Polish, Ukrainian and Yugoslav Literatures*. New York: Frederick Ungar Company, 1976.

Moser, Gerald. *A Tentative Portuguese-African Bibliography: Portuguese Literature in Africa and African Literature in the Portuguese Language*. University Park: Pennsylvania State University Libraries, 1970.

Mphahlele, Ezekiel. *The African Image*. rev. ed. New York: Praeger, 1974.

Muchnic, Helen. *From Gorky to Pasternak*. New York: Random House, 1961.

Niven, Alastair, ed. *The Commonwealth Writer Overseas: Themes of Exile and Expatriation*. Brussels: Librarie Marcel Didier, 1976.

Nkosi, Lewis. *Home and Exile*. Longmans Studies in African Literature. New York: Longmans, 1983.

Novak, Arne. *Czech Literature*. William E. Harkins, ed. Ann Arbor: Michigan Slavic Publications (University of Michigan), 1976.

Pachmuss, Temura, ed. *A Russian Cultural Revival: A Critical Anthology of Emigré Literature Before 1939*. Knoxville: University of Tennessee Press, 1981.

Paricsy, Pal, comp. *A New Bibliography of African Literature*. Studies on Developing Countries, no. 24. Budapest: Center for Afro-Asian Research of the Hungarian Academy of Sciences, 1969.

Parker, Kenneth, ed. *The South African Novel in English: Essays in Criticism and Society*. New York: Africana Publishing, 1978.

Petersen, Kirsten Holst, and Anna Rutherford, eds. *Displaced Persons*. Mundelstrup: Dangeroo Press, 1988.

Pfanner, Helmut F. *Exile in New York: German and Austrian Writers after 1933*. Detroit: Wayne State University Press, 1983.

Pfeiler, William K. *German Literature in Exile*. Lincoln: University of Nebraska Press, 1957.

Pike, David. *German Writers in Soviet Exile 1933–1945*. Chapel Hill: University of North Carolina Press, 1982.

Poggioli, Renato. *The Poets of Russia, 1890–1936*. Cambridge, Mass.: Harvard University Press, 1960.

Preminger, Alex, ed. *Princeton Encyclopedia of Poetry and Poetics*. enlarged ed. Princeton: Princeton University Press, 1974.

Priebe, Richard, ed. *Ghanaian Literatures*. Westport, Conn.: Greenwood Press, 1988.

Radcliffe-Umstead, Douglas. *The Exile Into Eternity: A Study of the Narrative Writings of Giorgio Bassani*. Cranbury, N.J.: Fairleigh Dickinson University Press, 1989.

Reeve, F. D. *Twentieth Century Russian Plays: An Anthology*. New York: W. W. Norton, 1973 [c. 1963].

Rilar, Carolyn, and Phyllis Carmel Mendelson, eds. *Contemporary Literary Criticism*. Detroit: Gale Research, annual.

Rosenfeld, Alvin H. *A Double Dying: Reflections on Holocaust Literature*. Bloomington, Indiana University Press, c. 1980.

Rothchild, Sylvia, ed. *Voices from the Holocaust*. N.Y.: New American Library, 1981.

Rovner, Arkady, et al., eds. *Gnosis Anthology of Contemporary American and Russian Literature and Art*, vol. 2. New York: Gnossis Press, 1982.

Sander, Reinhard W. *The Trinidad Awakening: West Indian Literature of the 1930s*. Westport, Conn.: Greenwood Press, 1988.

Schild, Ulla, ed. *Modern East African Literature and Its Audience*. Wiesbaden: B. Heymann, 1978.

Schipper-de-Leeuw, Mineke. *Le blanc et l'occident au miroir du roman negro-Africain de langue francais* (des origines au Festival de Dakar, 1920–1966). Assem, Holland: Van Gorcum, 1973.

Schwartz, Kessel. *A New History of Spanish American Fiction*. 2 vols. Vol. I: *From Colonial Times to the Mexican Revolution and Beyond*; Vol. II: *Social Concerns, Universalism, and The New Novel*. Coral Gables, Florida: University of Miami Press, 1971.

Segel, Harold B. *Twentieth-Century Russian Drama: From Gorky to the Present*. New York: Columbia University Press, 1979.

Seidel, Michael. *Exile and the Narrative Imagination*. New Haven: Yale University Press, 1986.

Seymour-Smith, Martin. *The New Guide to Modern World Literature*. 3d ed. New York: Peter Bedrick Books, 1985; London: Macmillan, 1985.

Shneidman, N. N. *Soviet Literature in the 1970s: Artistic Diversity and Ideological Conformity*. Toronto: University of Toronto Press, 1979.

———. *Soviet Literature in the 1980s: Decade of Transition*. Toronto: University of Toronto Press, 1990.

Singh, R. S. *The Indian Novel in English: A Critical Study*. Atlantic Highlands, N.J.: Humanities Press, 1977.

Slonim, Marc. *Soviet Russian Literature: Writers and Problems, 1917–1977*. 2d rev. ed. New York: Oxford University Press, 1977.

Smith, Gerald Stanton. *Songs to Seven Strings: Russian Guitar Poetry and Soviet ''Mass'' Song*. Bloomington: Indiana University Press, 1984.

Smith, Rowland, ed. *Exile and Tradition: Studies in African and Caribbean Literature*. London: Longmans, 1976.

Spalek, John. *German Expressionism in the Fine Arts: A Bibliography*. Los Angeles: Hennessey & Insalls, 1977.

———, in collaboration with Adrienne Ash and Sandra H. Hawrylchak. *Guide to the Archival Materials of the German-Speaking Emigration to the United States after 1933*. Charlottesville: Bibliographical Society of the University of Virginia, University Press of Virginia, 1978.

———, and Robert F. Bell, eds. *Exile: The Writer's Experience*. University of North Carolina Studies in the German Languages and Literatures, no. 99. Chapel Hill: University of North Carolina Press, 1982.

———, with Joseph Strelka. *Deutsche Exilliteratur seit 1933*. Bern: Francke, 1976.

Spires, Robert C. *Beyond the Metafictional Mode: Directions in the Modern Spanish Novel*. Lexington: University Press of Kentucky, 1984.

Spivak, Gayatri Chakravorty. *The Post-Colonial Critic: Interviews, Strategies, Dialogues*. Ed. Sarah Harasym. New York/London: Routledge, 1990.

Srivestava, Avadhesh K., ed. *Alien Voices: Perspectives on Commonwealth Literature*. Lucknow, India: Print House, 1981.

Stern, Guy, ed. *Exile and Enlightenment: Studies in German and Comparative Literature*. Detroit: Wayne State University Press, 1987.

———. *War, Weimar, and Literature: The History of the Neue Merkur 1914–1925*. University Park: Pennsylvania State University Press, 1971.

Strelka, Joseph, Robert F. Bell, and Eugene Dobson, eds. *Protest, Form, Tradition*. University of Alabama Conference on Exile Literature, March 1975. Birmingham: University of Alabama Press, 1979.

Struve, Gleb. *Russian Literature under Lenin and Stalin, 1917–1953*. Norman: University of Oklahoma Press, 1971.

———. *Soviet Russian Literature*. London: Routledge, 1935.

Svirsky, Gregory. *A History of Post-War Soviet Writing: The Literature of Moral Opposition*. Ann Arbor: Ardis, 1981 [originally published in Russian in London, 1979].

Swanson, Philip, ed. *Landmarks in Modern Latin-American Fiction: An Introduction*. New York: Routledge, 1989.

Tabori, Paul. *The Anatomy of Exile: A Semantic and Historical Study*. London: Harrap, 1972.

———. "Exiles and Refugees," in *Times Literary Supplement*, October 11, 1985. Special issue.

———. *The PEN in Exile, an Anthology* [of exiled writers]. London: International PEN Club Centre for Writers in Exile, 1954.

Taylor, John Russell. *Strangers in Paradise: The Hollywood Emigrés, 1933–1950*. New York: Holt, Rinehart and Winston, 1983.

Terras, Victor, ed. *Handbook of Russian Literature*. New Haven: Yale University Press, 1985.

Thomas, Gareth. *The Novel of the Spanish Civil War (1936–1975)*. Cambridge: Cambridge University Press, 1990.

Twentieth Century Authors: A Biographical Dictionary of Modern Literature. Ed. Stanley J. Kunitz and Howard Haycraft. New York: H. W. Wilson Company, 1942. *First Supplement*, ed. Kunitz. New York: H. W. Wilson Company, 1955.

Twentieth Century Literary Criticism. Ed. Dennis Poupard. Detroit: Gale Research Company. Annual.

Twentieth Century Writers: A Reader's Guide to Contemporary Literature. Ed. Kenneth Richardson. London: Newnes Books, 1969.

Ugarte, Michael. *Shifting Ground: Spanish Civil War Exile Literature*. Durham, N.C.: Duke University Press, 1989.

Voznesenskaya, Julia. ed. *Letters of Love: Women Political Prisoners in Exile and the Camps*. London: Quartet, 1990.

Wagner, Jean. *Black Poets of the United States from Paul Laurence Dunbar to Langston Hughes*. Urbana: University of Illinois Press, 1973.

Wakeman, John, ed. *World Authors 1950–1970*. New York: Oxford University Press, 1973.

Walsh, William. *Commonwealth Literature*. New York: Oxford University Press, 1973.

Ward, A. C., ed. *Longmans Companion to Twentieth Century Literature*. 3d ed. rev. by Maurice Hussey. London: Longmans, 1981.

Wastberg, Per, ed. *The Writer in Modern Africa*. Stockholm: Almqvist and Wiksell, 1968; New York: Africana Publishing, 1969.

Wistrich, Robert S. *The Jews of Vienna in the Age of Franz Joseph*. Oxford: Oxford University Press, 1989.

"The Writer in Exile." Special Issue of *World Literature Today* (1976), ed. Ivar Ivask.

"Writers in Exile: A Conference of Soviet and East European Dissidents." [Conference at Boston University, May 7–8, 1982.] *Partisan Review* 50, no. 4 (1983).

Zell, Hans. *A New Reader's Guide to African Literature*. 2d rev. and expanded ed. New York: Africana Publishing, 1983.

Index

(Numbers in **boldface** indicate biographical dictionary entries)

Contributors

Peter Balakian
Michael J. Arlen; *Vahan Tekeyan*

Philip Balla
Joseph Brodsky

Martin Beller
E. M. Cioran; *Jan Kott*

Jan Blonski
Witold Gombrowicz

Desi K. Bognár
Paul Tabori; *Lajos Zilahy*

Éva Bolgár
Sándor Márai; *Gyorgy Mikes*

Judith M. Brugger
Talat Abassi; *Shiva Naipaul*; *Ezra Pound*; *Manès Sperber*; *Gertrude Stein*; *Tran thi Nga*; *Peter Weiss*

Edward Butscher
Paul Bowles

Joseph Cady
Gay and Lesbian Writers in Exile

Olga Carlisle
Vadim Andreyev (with Richard Davies)

Francesco Cesari
Lawrence Durrell (with Martin Tucker)

Richard Critchfield
Herbert Marcuse

Rae Dalven
  Constantine Cavafy; *Nikos Kazantzakis*; *Yannis Ritsos*

Richard Davies
  Vadim Andreyev (with Olga Carlisle)

Robert DiYanni
  James Baldwin

Manuel Duran
  Pablo Neruda

Timothy E. Dykstra
  T. E. Lawrence

David B. Eakin
  Oliver St. John Gogarty

Henrik Eger
  Stephen Heym; *Hans Henny Jahnn* (with Martin Tucker); *Hermann Kesten* (with Martin Tucker); *Else Lasker-Schüler* (co-entry); *Heinrich Mann*; *Stefan Zweig*

Arlene A. Elder
  Bessie Head

Sharif S. Elmusa
  Mahmud Darwish

W. A. Fahey
  Sean O'Casey

Samuel Fiszman
  Czeslaw Miłosz

Maurice Friedman
  Elie Wiesel

Erica Frouman-Smith
  José Donoso; *Ariel Dorfman*

Andrea Gambino
  Bei Ling

Geoff Gehman
  Eric Knight

Daniela Gioseffi
  Nina Cassian

Joan Gordon
  David Plante; *Jean Rhys*; *Muriel Spark*

Lawrence Graver
  Samuel Beckett (second part)

Richard Griffith
  T. H. White

Clara Gyorgyey
  Hungarian Writers in Exile; *Tamas Aczel*; *George Faludy*; *Julius Háy*; *Ferenc Molnár*

Talat Sait Halman
  Turkish Literature of Exile; *Nazim Hikmet*

Renata von Hanffstengel
  Eric Arendt; Bodo Uhse

Cedric Hentschel
  Britain as a Center for German-Language Writers in Exile; Max Brod; Elias Canetti; Oskar Kokoschka; Else Lasker-Schüler (co-entry); *Zenta Maurina; Theodor Plivier; Gustav Regler; Nelly Sachs; Anna Seghers; Bruno Traven; Kurt Tucholsky; Arnold Zweig*

Stella K. Hershan
  Lion Feuchtwanger

Katherine Hill-Miller
  James Joyce

Douglas Hilt
  Max Aub; Ramon Sender

Milne Holton
  Paul Celan

Diana der Hovanessian
  Armenian Writers in Exile

Marek Kedzierski
  Samuel Beckett (first part) translated; *Witold Gombrowicz; Sławomir Mrożek; Adam Tarn*

Ladd Kelley
  Manuel Puig

Anthony Kerrigan
  Miguel de Unamuno

Veronica Kirtland
  Isabel Allende

George Klawitter
  Anthony Burgess

Charles Kovich
  Ivo Andric; Christopher Isherwood; Malcolm Lowry; Gore Vidal (with Edmund Miller)

Edward Lense
  W. Somerset Maugham

Bernth Lindfors
  Es'kia Mphahlele; Ngugi wa Thiong'o

Bruce R. S. Litte
  Robin Maugham; Dornford Yates

James C. McDonald
  Louise Bryant; John Reed

Michael Manley
  The (Spanish) Generation of 1927; Rafael Alberti; Heberto Padilla; Nicanor Parra; César Abraham Vallejo

Lee Mhatre
  Ved Parkash Mehta; Rita Smith

Jennifer Michaels
  Johannes Becher

Asher Z. Milbauer
  Isaac Bashevis Singer

Edmund Miller
  Frederick Rolfe (Baron Corvo); *Gore Vidal* (with Charles Kovich)

Christopher Mooney
  Hannah Arendt; Walter Benjamin; Simone Weil

David James Moriarty
  Frank O'Connor

Edward A. Morin
  Ai Qing; *Bin Xin*; *Cai Qi-jiao*; *Odysseus Elytis*; *Feng Zhi*; *Gu Cheng*; *Xu Gang*; *Yang Lian*; *Zheng Min*

Eugene Paul Nassar
  Kahlil Gibran

Michael M. Naydan
  Wasyl Barka; *Marina Tsvetaeva*

Estelle Gershgoren Novak
  Israel Joshua Singer (with Maximillian E. Novak)

Maximillian E. Novak
  Israel Joshua Singer (with Estelle Gershgoren Novak)

Larissa M. L. Onyshkevych
  Eaghor Kostetzky; *Ludmyla Kovalenko*; *Oleksandr Oles'*; *Volodymyr Vynnychenko*; *Wira Wowk*

Gregory Orfalea
  Pablo Medina; *Edward Said*

Jasna Peručic
  Janusz Glowacki (with Martin Tucker)

Helmut F. Pfanner
  Alfred Döblin; *Oskar Maria Graf*; *Hans Habe*; *Ernst Toller*; *Franz Werfel*

Mark A. Popovsky
  Juri Druzhnikov; *Ivan Elagin*; *Michael R. Heifetz*; *Boris Khazahnov*; *Anatoly E. Levitin-Krasnov*; *Felix Y. Rozimir*; *Roman Raygorodetsky*; *Gregory C. Svirsky*; *Vladimir Voinovich*; *Vasily S. Yanovsky*; *Igor M. Yefimov*; all entries translated by Zoric Ward

Elizabeth Rajec
  Menyhert Melchior Lengyel

F. D. Reeve
  Aleksandr I. Solzhenitsyn

Arkady Rovner
  Ivan Bunin; *Gaito Gazdanov*; *Dmitry S. Merezhkovsky*; *Vladimir Nabokov* (with Martin Tucker)

Leonid Rudnytzky
  Ihor Kacurovs'kyj; *Jurij Klen*; *Jevhen Malanjuk*; *Ostap Tarnavsk'kyj*

David G. Sarles
Eldridge Cleaver

John Scheckter
Morley Callaghan (with Martin Tucker); *Miles Franklin*; *George Johnston*; *Thomas Keneally*; *Katherine Mansfield*; *Henry Handel Richardson*; *Randolph Stow*

June Schlueter
Peter Handke

Paul Schlueter
Jorge Amado; *Miguel Ángel Asturias*; *John Howard Lawson*; *Robert Liddell*; *Doris Lessing*; *Brian Moore*; *Dalton Trumbo*; *Marguerite Yourcenar*

Susan Schreibman
Irish Modernists (Brian Coffey, Denis Devlin, Thomas MacGreevy); *Claribel Alegria*; *Juan Goytisolo*

Steven Serafin
Andrei Amalrik; *Bertolt Brecht*; *Gabriel García Márquez*

Jacques Servin
Interview with Andrei Codrescu

Donald Shojai
Iranian Writers in Exile

Henry Sikorski
Witold Gombrowicz (additional material); *Zdzislaw Najder*

Stuart Hamilton Smith
(Paul) Thomas Mann

Janice Spleth
Léopold Sédar Senghor

Mirjana Stančić
Danilo Kiš (with Martin Tucker); *Ephraim Kishon*

M. D. Stein
Derek Walcott

Joseph P. Strelka
Hermann Broch; *Joseph Roth* (with Martin Tucker)

Danylo Husar Struck
Emma Andiievska

Victor Terras
Aleksis Rannit

Martin Tucker
All unsigned entries

Agnes Huszar Vardy
Bela Szasz

Tomas Venclova
Jonas Aistis; *Bernardas Brazdžionis*; *Marius Katiliškis*; *Algirdas Landsbergis*; *Algimantas Mackus*; *Alfonsa Myka-Niliŭnas*; *Henrikas Radauskas*; *Antanas Škéma*

Andrej Vlcek
  Jan Drabek; *Pavel Kohout* (with Martin Tucker); *Milan Kundera* (with Martin Tucker);
Josef Skvorecky (with Martin Tucker); *Daniel Stroz*

Rosmarie Waldrop
  Edmond Jabès

Zoric Ward
  Mark A. Popovsky; translated all entries written by Mark A. Popovsky

Donald Gwynn Watson
  G. Cabrera Infante; *Carlos Fuentes*

Dorothy TsungSu Weissman
  Eileen Chang; *Chao Chi-kang*; *Jo-hsi Chen*; *Kim Kyung Jae*; *Leung Tung*; *Liu Da-ren*;
Pai Hsin-yung; *Yu Li-hua*

Alice R. Wexler
  Emma Goldman

R. Darby Williams
  Alfred Chester

Reinhard Zachau
  Yvan Goll

About the Editor

MARTIN TUCKER is Professor of English at the C.W. Post Campus of Long Island University. He is the author of two books, *Africa in Modern Literature* (1967) and *Joseph Conrad* (1976), and more than 15 volumes of literary encyclopedia, among them *The Critical Temper, Moulton's Library of Literary Criticism* (revised and corrected by Tucker), *Modern British Literature*, and *Modern Commonwealth Literature*. He has been the editor of *Confrontation: A Literary Journal* since 1968, and has received two fellowships for editorial distinction. His volume of poems *Homes of Locks and Mysteries* was selected for inclusion in the prestigious English-Speaking Union's Books Across the Seas Program in 1982.